Catholics and Treason

Catholics and Treason

Martyrology, Memory, and Politics in the Post-Reformation

MICHAEL QUESTIER

OXFORD
UNIVERSITY PRESS

Great Clarendon Street, Oxford, OX2 6DP,
United Kingdom

Oxford University Press is a department of the University of Oxford.
It furthers the University's objective of excellence in research, scholarship,
and education by publishing worldwide. Oxford is a registered trade mark of
Oxford University Press in the UK and in certain other countries

© Michael Questier 2022

The moral rights of the author have been asserted

First Edition published in 2022

Impression: 1

All rights reserved. No part of this publication may be reproduced, stored in
a retrieval system, or transmitted, in any form or by any means, without the
prior permission in writing of Oxford University Press, or as expressly permitted
by law, by licence or under terms agreed with the appropriate reprographics
rights organization. Enquiries concerning reproduction outside the scope of the
above should be sent to the Rights Department, Oxford University Press, at the
address above

You must not circulate this work in any other form
and you must impose this same condition on any acquirer

Published in the United States of America by Oxford University Press
198 Madison Avenue, New York, NY 10016, United States of America

British Library Cataloguing in Publication Data
Data available

Library of Congress Control Number: 2021944609

ISBN 978-0-19-284702-7

DOI: 10.1093/oso/9780192847027.001.0001

Printed and bound by
CPI Group (UK) Ltd, Croydon, CR0 4YY

Links to third party websites are provided by Oxford in good faith and
for information only. Oxford disclaims any responsibility for the materials
contained in any third party website referenced in this work.

Acknowledgements

This is a book about narratives, memories, and traditions—mostly Catholic ones—which I have tried, as best I can, to reassemble in some sort of coherent order. It should be said that without the kind assistance of the past and present keepers of Catholic archival collections in this country and abroad, on which so much of what follows is based, I would probably never have pursued this topic. I think that I crossed some kind of Rubicon when I discovered the Westminster Cathedral archives, located near High Street Kensington station. There were days when it seemed to be almost literally a Rubicon because of the constant flooding in and around the search room of what is, perhaps, the most important repository of post-Reformation Catholic letters and papers in the country. In the 1980s it had been moved from the cathedral to what is basically a lean-to garage behind the church of Our Lady of Victories. However, a new custodian, the Reverend Ian Dickie, had been appointed by Cardinal Basil Hume. Those who visited the archive's offices at 16a Abingdon Road were (almost always) made very welcome.

I am grateful also to several other curators of the relevant material for this period—in particular, at Westminster, the Reverend Nicholas Schofield, Susannah Rayner, Peter Kent, and the Reverend William Johnstone; to the librarians at St Mary's College, Oscott, particularly Gerard Boylan and Paul Meller, and at the Birmingham Cathedral archives, the Reverend John Sharp; to Janet Graffius at Stonyhurst; to Geoffrey Scott at Douai Abbey; to Maurice Whitehead and Orietta Filippini at the Venerable English College in Rome; to the Reverend Thomas McCoog SJ at Farm Street, and also, now, to his successors Rebecca Somerset, Mary Allen, and Sally Kent; to Jonathan Bush, who has made accessible the manuscript materials at Ushaw College; and to Jenny Delves at the Southwark Archdiocesan Archives. I have also been obliged to a number of early modern specialists, notably Jennifer Binczewski, Lloyd Bowen, Thomas Cogswell, Jeffrey Collins, Ginevra Crosignani, Jordan Downs, Kenneth Fincham, Andrew Foster, Samuel Fullerton, Eilish Gregory, Matthew Growhoski, Victor Houliston, Peter Jackson, Katherine Lazo, David Magliocco, Kathryn Marshalek, John Marshall, Anthony Milton, Kendra Packham, Mark Rankin, William Sheils, Alexandra Tompkins, Rebecca Warren, Sara Wolfson, and Neil Younger for a stream of extremely useful references which I would never have found myself; to Shanyn Altman, Anne Dillon, Gerard Kilroy, and Lucy Underwood for reading through the whole text; to James Kelly for many conversations about the subject generally; and also to Estelle Paranque for all kinds of discussions about the alleged merits of Tudor government.

vi ACKNOWLEDGEMENTS

I was and remain indebted to Peter Lake. This research venture started with a jointly written piece published in 1994 which had the, at that time, fashionable title 'Agency, Appropriation and Rhetoric under the Gallows...' but which he always referred to simply as 'Bodybits'. Subsequently we tried to revisit the subject of the York martyr Margaret Clitherow, who was pressed to death in March 1586. There are, it has to be admitted, some pretty appalling politically incorrect jokes in the initial chapters of our joint study of the Clitherow case, though it is not clear that anyone really noticed. I will always be grateful to Professor Lake for his insights into the way that martyr narratives were compiled and how one might think about them historically.

I was much assisted in the latter stages of this project by Helen Good and her excellent team of researchers at the Hull University archives, who made available to me their digital images of the Knaresborough papers. In addition to Helen herself, I would like to thank Anne Eastwood, Ashleigh Good, Elizabeth Grove, Margaret Justice, Roger Justice, Paul Mann, and Maureen Noddings, and also Judy Burg of the Hull University archives. I am exceedingly grateful also to the Leverhulme Trust for the award of a research fellowship, one that made it possible to get shot of the mindless tedium of modern university bureaucracy and find enough time to publish what follows.

The Reverend Dickie, as I say, was not a conventional archivist. One imagines his principles for running an archive would probably not nowadays be regarded as compatible with 'best practice'. Of an afternoon, the stacks at Kensington would be wreathed in tobacco smoke from one or other of the collection of his pipes in the search room. Suffice it to say that, after a number of visits on my part, he suggested that I might like the keys to the archive and to drop in whenever I pleased and, while I was at it, to make as much use of the archiepiscopal archival photocopier as I wanted. This I proceeded to do and, in the slightly weird atmosphere of the basement in Kensington among the volumes of stuff collected and guarded, over the years, by the secular clergy of the sixteenth and seventeenth centuries and their successors, I (think that I) gradually learned something of the mentality and attitudes of those who believed that, after the separation of the English Church from Rome, they and their co-religionists had witnessed a period of intense persecution.

I might add that, over the course of time, I have come to have a high opinion of the foundational publications on this subject: for example, the biographical dictionary of the post-Reformation seminarist secular clergy by the Dominican Godfrey Anstruther, and the massive record-series volumes put together by the Jesuits John Morris and Henry Foley; or, again, the oeuvre of Philip Caraman. Sometimes these sources can be slightly unsystematic and, as I have discovered, there are real risks in using them without checking their citations, footnotes, and whatnot. But the fact is that the subject would simply not exist without them. The people who published these, in some ways quaint and probably, even at the time, old-fashioned, books defined the field. My annotated copies of their works are the very last volumes on my shelves that I shall discard. I also have a great respect for the state-of-the-art research and publications of subsequent Catholic scholars, notably Antony Allison and David Rogers. I think Mr Allison was the first person I encountered working among the manuscripts at the Westminster Diocesan Archive. He was as clear and insightful in his late seventies as I imagine he had been when he started his career more than fifty years before, and I will always be indebted to him for his advice and his generosity in sharing his own research. For the purposes of this study I should also mention the work of Patrick Barry in preparing the evidence for the Vatican's processes that led to the 1987 ceremony of beatification of English martyrs. Again and again, I have been astounded by the pinpoint and meticulous accuracy with which the evidence was gathered and laid out by Dr Barry. At one point I had planned to extend this study as far as the later twentieth century, and to take in the way in which the promoters of the Cause, that is to say, the staff of the Office of the Vice-Postulation in London, actually worked and how they contributed to the writing of the history of the post-Reformation period in this country. But that is really another project and, I hope, it will see its way into print elsewhere.

Ian Dickie passed away in late December 2012, having, as he said, experienced his own personal Calvary. Three years before, in December 2009, he had been arrested by officers of the Metropolitan Police in his own church at Buntingford in Hertfordshire after, as it turned out, an entirely false and malicious, though anonymous, allegation had been made that he had sexually assaulted a child. The fabricated accusation was, however, followed up with extraordinary zeal by the authorities. Cut adrift apparently by almost everyone, he contracted cancer of the bladder and, unable to summon up the willpower to seek effective treatment in time, he died in what one might euphemistically call considerable pain. Perhaps this reminds one that even in the twenty-first century, when certain people have banned, as they see it, virtually every form of intolerance and discrimination, questions about persecution and toleration do not seem to have gone away. To the Reverend Ian, this book, though he would probably have disliked a good deal of it, is dedicated.

Preface

Martyrdom has been the subject of increasing scholarly attention in recent years. It is a topic in which politics and religion meet in the most spectacular ways. The narratives of those who suffered excruciating physical punishment, ostensibly in the cause of true religion, are instances of supreme religious exaltation and meaning, an expression—for both the persecuted and the persecutor—of religious belief of the most lofty and extreme sort. While on the part of the (alleged) persecutor the chain of events surrounding arrest, trial, conviction, and execution represented an exercise of awesome annihilating ideological and physical State power, on the part of the persecuted what was at stake was the ultimate religious sacrifice, the clearest affirmation of sanctity available to humanity in a fallen world.

But, of course, a lot of this depends on the tradition from within which those stories are being told and retold. It was a truism, as Sir Robert Bassett noted in his preface to his late sixteenth-century account of the life of Sir Thomas More, that it had been 'an ancient and commendable custom in the Church of God, and no less laudable than profitable always to have had a special care that the lives and deaths of God's saints and martyrs should be with care and fidelity registered and recorded to all faithful posterity'.[1] But these stories comprised acts, or series of actions, the meanings of which were always contestable and contested; one side's martyr was, almost inevitably, the other side's heretic and traitor. The available versions of what happened on these bitter occasions can thus be extremely difficult to reconcile. The mist and confusion arising out of the rumours and gossip which were generated when such people were put on trial for, as they declared, their conscientiously held beliefs and, then, were dragged off to execution often make it difficult to interpret why these events had taken place at all.

Furthermore, these cases in which individuals who claimed to be motivated purely by conscience came into direct conflict with the State have often been front and centre in unashamedly confessional processes of tradition-building. Stories of martyrdom were hardwired into the collective memory of the post-Reformation Catholic community. The process of collecting and collating these narratives of suffering began almost as soon as the events themselves. Contemporaries' recollections of what had happened to those who refused to bend before the will of successive Protestant regimes circulated by word of mouth and in manuscript; and sometimes those recollections found their way into print as well, usually on

---

[1] E. V. Hitchcock and P. E. Hallett with A. W. Reed (eds), *The Lyfe of Syr Thomas More, sometimes Lord Chancellor of England by Ro: Ba:* (Oxford, 1950), preface. For the same point made by John Mush in his account of Margaret Clitherow, see Morris, *TCF*, III (TR), p. 360.

X PREFACE

foreign presses. From time to time, those published narratives were reimported for the edification of the good and the rebuke of those who had been responsible for the sufferings of those who had gone to their deaths for their faith.

In subsequent years, and down through the centuries, these narratives became, if not exactly set in stone, then certainly embedded in the historical traditions of the Catholic community and deeply rooted in its consciousness. Those responsible for that process, titans of the English Catholic tradition such as Bishop Richard Challoner, undoubtedly believed that their retelling of these narratives was entirely objective, supported by first-hand evidence, and in many cases by eyewitness accounts. As they saw it, all of this permitted the writing of a clear and decisive, and thoroughly impartial, historical rendering of the subject. This gathering of records was one of the earliest instances of Catholic historical research. Indeed, some Catholics believed that they could weave these narratives into much broader accounts of the relationship between Church and State following the Reformation of the first half of the sixteenth century.

Many people would, however, see these kinds of narrative as evidence of the most confessional, *parti pris* approach, something that could not be taken seriously by real scholars at all. In fact, even when not phrased in an explicitly confessional register, as a topic, martyrdom, especially when discussed in a Catholic context, has remained highly controversial and, by and large, off limits for genuinely historical discussion. Perhaps, then, it is not surprising that, for some intellectuals, martyrdom represents the point at which religious phenomena cease to be subject to the normal (secular) modes and procedures of historical description, analysis, and still less 'explanation'. For those people, any attempt to subject such events to that sort of explanation must be not only reductionist but an exercise in secularist propaganda. Many of those who consider themselves to be scholars of the Reformation period do indeed find this topic a difficult one to integrate into their view of the early modern world.

In addition, the prevalent mainstream version of the immediate post-Reformation period is one in which the Elizabethan regime is a thoroughly moderate entity, forced to defend itself against Catholic extremists. It is virtually impossible to reconcile this dominant template of a tolerant post-Reformation English Protestant polity with the starkly polarized and confessional accounts of the legal proceedings against separatist Catholics. In those accounts, Catholics are represented as the victims of political witch-hunts which had nothing to do with 'religion' at all.

These difficulties are compounded by the fact that, in the historiography of post-Reformation England, the topic of martyrdom has been dominated by the study of John Foxe, whose *Acts and Monuments* sits at the centre of so many accounts of the period. Foxe was not only a polemicist but also a historian. As is well known, his gathering of material was intended not just to cast the Elizabethan Church and Reformation in a certain mould but also to dredge up what had actually happened in these cases. An enormous amount of scholarly effort has quite justifiably been put into assessing Foxe's use of sources, his rhetorical techniques, and the physical and material processes whereby his writings found their way into multiple forms of print.[2] It is in part because they were printed so many times and in so many formats that Foxe's works have come to dominate the field.

On one level, that is fair enough. But, on another, it represents something of a problem: that is because, by contrast, Catholic martyrdom has tended to be left to Catholic historians of Catholicism. While we now know an enormous amount about Foxe's methods and sources, his models and rhetorical and argumentative techniques, and his political and polemical ends and enemies, the same cannot be said for Catholic martyrologists. Their work never achieved a fraction of Foxe's reputation, not least because, during this period, almost all of it remained in manuscript. In addition, English Catholicism simply lacked its Foxe. The closest that the Catholic community got was the work of Bishop Challoner, and that was only in the mid-eighteenth century when his *magnum opus*, the *Memoirs of Missionary Priests*, was published. Challoner's work is very deliberately designed so as to disguise and/or conceal much of what one would need to know to make historical sense of the events which he describes and of the sources which he used.

All of this has been made worse by the (latent) Protestant triumphalism that remains the ghost in the machine of much post-Reformation historical writing. That triumphalism loads the historical dice against the incorporation of the counterfactuals represented at various points by Catholic issues. It certainly hinders the incorporation of Catholic narratives and perspectives into mainstream accounts of the long Reformation. This matters, but not just because some people think it is a noble task to rescue such suppressed voices from the condescension of posterity. More importantly, if we were to put the Catholic stuff back somewhere near the centre of contemporary politics, which was where it originated, the whole story, both the narrative and the analytic architecture, of the post-Reformation would start to look radically different.

I was, however, faced with something of a choice when I started looking at this material. Or, rather, I had to decide what to miss out. I was becoming increasingly aware that the direction of travel in this corner of the field of early modern studies was firmly towards what one might call the cultural. Many scholars were talking about early modern martyrs in the context of the senses and the emotions. There was also an increasing interest in what people called the material turn, which here essentially meant relics and the physical consequences and remains of martyrdom.[3]

---

[2] The vast majority of the work here, in the last two decades, has been done by Dr Thomas Freeman.
[3] The person, however, who has made the study of English Catholic martyrdom and relics a properly historical one is Dr Janet Graffius; see esp. her doctoral dissertation, '"Bullworks against the Furie of Heresie": Relics, Material Culture and the Spiritual and Cultural Formation of the Sodality of St Omers English Jesuit College 1593–1650' (PhD, Aberdeen, 2018).

xii PREFACE

It was clear that one could not cover everything, certainly not if one wanted a publisher to consider putting it into print. I concluded, in the end, that a relatively *longue durée* study of the memorialization of the relevant individuals was an appropriate one. It had always been in the back of my mind that it would be interesting to try to read the archival material that had been accumulated about Catholic martyrs both in its immediate historical context and with an eye to the way that successive generations of martyrologists and historians, however *parti pris* they had been, might have looked at it.

However, this could not be purely about 'memory', at least not in a methodologically modish way. First and foremost, I wanted to contextualize the well-known cases by reference to political events and networks of contemporary writers and commentators who have almost always been left out of the story. In fact, the more one thought about the published work on this subject, notably by Anne Dillon and Brad Gregory, and, of course, for the oeuvre of John Foxe, by Thomas Freeman, the more it became clear that what are taken by some to be the dominant and fashionable methodological trends in the field at the present time are not sufficient to deal with this material. What one needed here was a sense of narrative, perhaps even something that one might call a 'narrative turn', an approach that focuses squarely on the peculiar circumstances of the English Reformation, the relationship between the English Church and the English State and between political allegiance and religious difference.

Initially I had thought that it would be enough to concentrate just on Challoner's *Memoirs*—his sources, his text, and his assumptions. But, as it became clear how much had gone into his huge book on English martyrdom, it was evident that one would have to look both backward in time, from the point at which Challoner wrote and, to a lesser extent, forward in time as well. This would still primarily be a book about the early modern period, and, for the most part, about the century that started with the crisis-ridden 1570s and 1580s and culminated in the violence of the Popish Plot agitation in 1679. Here, Challoner's work serves as a kind of clearing house for the labours of earlier martyrologists and, in that context, allows us to consider the politics of martyrdom in the later sixteenth and seventeenth centuries in England.

Obviously, this attempt to think historically about the texts solicited and collated by generations of martyrologists and scholars inside the Catholic community, and to situate them back inside the wider contexts that produced them, has to be framed by the knowledge that most of what contemporaries said about these cases was never written down, and much of what was written down was done in a deliberately selective way. Still, the major claim being made here is that it is possible to align the corpus of martyr material that we do have in such a way as to put it back into the contexts out of which it came, and also to make it compatible with some of the more recent movements in the published scholarship on Tudor and Stuart England, from which historiography it has almost always been excluded.

PREFACE xiii

This, I hope, serves as justification both for the approach taken in the chapters in the first Part and also for the fairly extensive narrative Parts which follow. At first glance, there may well appear to be a vast, in fact almost antiquarian, body of evidence there. I toyed with excluding (much of) it, but this would have seriously undercut the claims made above about the book's purposes. My feeling is that an attempt to embrace the devil in the detail allows a reader to answer some of the major questions thrown up by these, at some level, very difficult and distasteful events. Are we witnessing here a persecution in any real contemporary sense of the word? Why did contemporaries get drawn into unwinnable public battles with the savagery of the law and the lust for blood shown by some of the regime's officials? How far did all 'Catholics' see the case alike? Was there a consensus among them that the 'martyrs' had truly suffered for the faith? How far was there a struggle inside the Catholic community to appropriate the memory of the martyrs? And what might all this tell us about a range of related subjects, in particular that constant topic of enquiry among scholars who want to chart the path to modernity, that is to say, the rise of 'toleration'.

I should add, also, that the conventional academic apparatus employed here is not intended to disguise the passion and ferocity of the public politics which gave rise to these events. The texts in question are not treated merely as cultural artefacts or part of a bibliographical jigsaw puzzle. These confrontations were, of course, hardly the norm. Indeed, the whole point about the period is that the full use of the law against Catholics was sporadic. But the events in question were crucial reference points in a series of public debates about the legal status of those who identified as Catholics.

Anyway, the claim here is that, if one could do this, or something like it, one might have an alternative or counterfactual narrative of the period. Many of the more substantial Catholic martyr collections were themselves put together primarily for the purpose of constructing equal and opposite narratives which would challenge writers such as John Foxe, John Rushworth, and Gilbert Burnet. It should be possible to (re)historicize the collections of decontextualized incidents which figure in Challoner's *Memoirs*. By doing this we can recover parts of the politics of the period which many—both contemporaries and, more recently, scholars—have in effect, though for different reasons, tried to ignore. Although the relationship between Foxe and his opposite numbers on the Catholic side will always remain an asymmetrical one, we do have, in Challoner's work and in other places, the records of approximately 180 treason trials of Catholics in the period from the 1570s up until 1681. These trials were generated by some of the more fraught political developments and watersheds of the period, and they mark a series of crucial stand-offs between the post-Reformation State and some of its more ideologically committed Catholic opponents.[4]

---

[4] For the martyrs of the Henrician period and the relationship of their cases to those in and after the Elizabethan era, see pp. 78–9 below.

xiv PREFACE

These sources, therefore, enable us to recover two political histories, or narratives: first, the specific moments in which the trials/executions/martyrdoms themselves occurred; and secondly, the moments in which the compilations in question were produced, since these were intended to enlist the past in order to make polemical points about the present. What I have tried to do here might be described as a double act of contextualization. This is made possible by the hitherto unexploited extent of the manuscript sources, both contemporary ones and, also, later sources which reveal the ways that the gatherers and compilers of this material tended to work. Here one has, if one wants it, a unique resource for the construction of 'memory', but not in the sense of a quasi-accidental accumulation of cultural bric-a-brac, as it were—randomly scattered texts, artefacts, relics, and whatnot, fetching up in various places as the result of arbitrary and haphazard events which were beyond anyone's control. The survival of the materials in question, though undoubtedly affected by random and unpredictable factors, is not simply fortuitous. Rather, the collecting of books and manuscripts on this subject was very often the result of a purposive, politically and polemically conditioned bringing together of certain sorts of material at particular dates in order to make a particular case and/or to reply to specific opponents.

One has here a combination of, first, the immediate reports of specific events and incidents and then a series of stages of subsequent memorialization, as reports of those events and incidents were circulated, both at home and abroad, (sometimes) translated and incorporated into other narratives, and finally anthologized by the likes of Challoner. At virtually no stage was this devoid of ideological context or meanings, even though texts such as Challoner's vigorously represent themselves as essentially detached, and those meanings changed over time and certainly could be enlisted by different people for very different purposes. Since much of this book relies on narrative, the principal focus is on the things said by those who witnessed and/or recalled the relevant events. What they said might take the form of oral or written statements, ones that were intended to speak to and convince other contemporaries who either saw the events in question or were in a position to be recipients of first-hand accounts from those who did. The process of recovery did not stop there, in that the emergence of set narratives was reliant on a later accumulation of such material, and on collation and editing by authors seeking to construct accounts of Catholic martyrdom for their own pietistic, polemical, and indeed political purposes, partly in response also to those who denied the assumptions which Catholics tended to graft onto the relevant events. Strictly speaking, 'memory' here may be the wrong term to use, since the collators and editors did not have personal memories of these events, not even of the first impact and deployment of the accounts that they sought to appropriate for their own purposes. The process of gathering/appropriation, collating, and editing was remarkably varied, and it is the purpose of this book to study that process at crucial moments in the history of the English Catholic community, particularly when the meaning of the martyrological tradition was being contested. Here 'memory' really means the generation of polemically and politically framed versions of the past, where the claim is that the material allows the recovery of a genuinely collective past and an interpretation of an often fraught present. In that these accounts served to frame the collective sense of identity of those who regarded themselves as Catholics and their understanding of their own history, under the cross of persecution, 'memory' here was a product of the personal recollections of individual Catholics who learned or were informed about these shocking stories, and of the way that they internalized them and deployed them. The aim here is to acquire some sense of how these multiple forms of 'memory' or, rather, of remembering, recalling, and, if not forgetting, then certainly of selecting, worked during the post-Reformation period.

My aim, therefore, has been to take the topic out of its conventional hagiographical wrapper, or at least the one that is often assigned to it, and to reroute it via an archive-led process of reconstruction of the origins of the relevant documents in order to put it back into the contexts out of which it came. To do this I have tried to construct a 'who's who' of those who were tracked, watched, arrested, imprisoned, and then, in some cases, prosecuted under the existing law of treason and the new treason statutes; and also, to some extent, a 'who's who' of those who did the tracking, watching, etc. Since the State never sought even to apprehend and restrain, let alone kill, all those against whom a successful prosecution could have been brought under the treason statutes, the historical question of who precisely was killed, when and why, and indeed by whom, becomes crucial.

This, I hope, will also allow us to establish in a rather different way the political structures of what some scholars call the 'Catholic community', and the relationship between the more radicalized or activist versions of contemporary Catholicism and various personifications of the State. Given the salience, throughout the entire post-Reformation period, of various versions and registers of puritanism and anti-popery, and given the intersection between those ideological forces and associated narratives, and indeed critiques of, royal government, the reconstruction (as far as the archives allow) of these martyr incidents will throw light not just on Catholic politics but also on the politics of the State and of English Protestant opinion more widely construed.

Secondly, I wish to recover the textual memorializations of these events as representations, highly structured and doctored instruments of persuasion and propaganda, devised by various Catholic interest groups in order to make these events mean what they undoubtedly believed they meant. That process of textual recovery travels from the emergence of Catholic dissent in Elizabeth's reign and continues through the seventeenth century, up to the Popish Plot agitation of the later 1670s, and then takes in the martyrological writing after the 1688 Revolution, as far as the 1740s. (In the modern era, the heirs of Richard Challoner continued the work of collecting and investigating the relevant archives in order to make the

xvi PREFACE

case at Rome for the unique witness of those in the sixteenth and seventeenth centuries who had been put on trial solely for, as they and their co-religionists saw it, their religious beliefs.)[5]

Here it is worth remarking that although this is, first and foremost, a recovery of the *English* Catholic martyr tradition, and in that respect might seem somewhat narrow when compared with Brad Gregory's account of European martyrs and martyrology,[6] that tradition is itself in part a European one; or, rather, it was one that came out of a Counter-Reformation account of the Reformation in the British Isles. As Challoner himself remarked, it was not just 'English Catholics' who 'looked upon' their co-religionists and proclaimed that they died for their faith as 'martyrs of religion'. 'So has the greatest part of Christians abroad, French, Spaniards, Italians [and] Germans, as appears by the honour showed to' their 'relics'; and 'some of the most celebrated authors abroad have employed their pens in writing their history, as of great and glorious martyrs'. Notable here were Diego de Yepes and Pedro de Ribadeneira.[7] These Europeans observed and commented on what many of them took to be a persecution in England, responding to their co-religionists' claims that they were a Church under the cross.

The final strand of this analysis is, therefore, an attempt to challenge the *trompe l'oeil* assumption that the relatively brief spells of intense 'persecution' were the only moments in the period when Catholicism was a significant political problem. Here one can question also the line that since, by Continental standards, there were relatively few fatal uses of the treason statutes against Catholics, this meant that anti-popery was merely a kind of Protestant fantasy and had little to do with actual Catholics. In fact, the timing of prosecutions of some Catholic separatists, as much as the conscious decision not to proceed against others, has much to tell us about the politico-religious condition of the post-Reformation period. These were, for much of the time, confrontations which no one really wanted—occasions when the conformist compromises which shaped the Reformation settlement irretrievably broke down; but the ensuing fractures tell us quite a lot about the settlement as an attempted experiment in conformity, compromise, and compliance, but always against a background of political uncertainty and ideological conflict.

Centred on the topic of martyrdom and its contemporary narrators, this book is intended to have a precise focus and a clearly delineated, albeit extensive, source base. Its purpose is to speak to central and wider issues in the political, cultural, and religious histories of England and the British Isles after the Reformation, and to address questions of religious diversity, royal authority, political loyalty, secular

---

[5] See M. Questier, *Memory, Sanctity and Religion in England c. 1850–1987* (forthcoming).

[6] B. Gregory, *Salvation at Stake: Christian Martyrdom in Early Modern Europe* (1999).

[7] Richard Challoner, *Memoirs of Missionary Priests*...(2 vols, 1741–2), I, preface, sig. A3^v–4^r.

obedience, and cultural belonging. The aim has been also to put before the general reading public and the scholarly community a little known and hitherto largely unstudied archive which will help to locate the topic of martyrdom in a new setting and to generate elements of an arguably new political narrative of post-Reformation England.

Contents

List of Illustrations	xxi
List of Abbreviations	xxiii
Note on the Text	xxxi

PART I

1. Introduction: Martyrs for the Faith?	3
2. Catholic Martyrdom and the Writing of English Reformation History	23
3. Martyrdom and the Construction of Martyr Narratives	47

PART II

4. 'Sentenced to Die as in Cases of High Treason': The Elizabethan Settlement and the Coming of Intolerance, *c.*1558–1582	77
5. After Campion	119
6. Catholic Martyrs and the Political Crises of the mid-1580s	140
7. The Incestuous Bastard Queen Persecutes the Faithful Servants of Christ	179
8. Catholic Radicalism and the (Re-)Emergence of Catholic Loyalism	229
9. The Coming of Toleration in Late Elizabethan England?	259
10. The Appeal to Rome and the Struggle for the Memory of the Martyrs	288

PART III

11. Tolerance and Intolerance in England after the Accession of James VI	333
12. Mid-Jacobean Confessional Politics and Anti-Popery	376
13. The Protestant Turn Turns Sour	422

xx CONTENTS

14. Towards Toleration? The Change of the Times in Late Jacobean
and Caroline Britain — 449

15. Back to the Future: Catholicism, Persecution, and the Outbreak
of the Civil War — 492

16. The Restoration and the Popish Plot — 538

17. Conclusion: The Afterlife of the Early Modern English Martyr
Tradition — 560

Select Bibliography: Manuscripts — 569
Index — 575

List of Illustrations

1.1.	John Knaresborough's 'Sufferings of the Catholicks'	11
2.1.	Stone marking the site of the Tyburn tree, London	39
4.1.	Reliquaries of the English martyrs, Stonyhurst, Lancashire	115
6.1.	The Execution of Margaret Clitherow	159
6.2.	Portrait of John Clench, justice of queen's bench	165
7.1.	Reliquary provided by John Gerard SJ for relic of Robert Sutton, d.1588	184
9.1.	Reliquary containing the relics of six Catholic clergymen martyred in the sixteenth and seventeenth centuries	271
11.1.	Portrait of Henry Garnet SJ	353
12.1.	Alabaster monument (1617) of Bishop Robert Bennett, in Hereford Cathedral	381
12.2.	Newsletter concerning John Almond's trial and execution, d.1612	416
13.1.	Relic associated with Thomas Maxfield, d.1616	439
14.1.	Portrait of Richard Smith, bishop of Chalcedon	460
14.2.	Portrait of Edmund Arrowsmith SJ, d.1628	472
15.1.	Relic of Ambrose Barlow OSB, d.1641	506
15.2.	Portrait of Francis Bell OFM, d.1643	519
15.3.	The shrine of John Southworth, d.1654, in Westminster Cathedral	536

List of Abbreviations

AAW	Archives of the Archdiocese of Westminster
ABP	Alban Butler's papers, compiled for Bishop Challoner's published lives of missionary priests: Archives of the Archdiocese of Birmingham, R 941 (hierarchical number Z6/11/15)
ABPFC	Alban Butler's further collection of material on the English and Welsh martyrs: Archives of the Archdiocese of Birmingham, R 945 (hierarchical number Z6/11/17)
ABSJ	Archivum Britannicum Societatis Jesu (Farm Street Library and Archive)
Adams, PC	S. Adams, 'The Protestant Cause: Religious Alliance with the West European Calvinist Communities as a Political Issue in England, 1585–1630' (DPhil, Oxford, 1973)
AENB	'An Ancient Editor's Notebook' (St Mary's College, Oscott, Collectanea E [formerly MS 98, now R11781]; printed in Morris, *TCF*, III, pp. 8–59)
Albion, *CI*	G. Albion, *Charles I and the Court of Rome* (1935)
Alfield, *TR*	Thomas Alfield, *A True Reporte of the Death & Martyrdome of M. Campion Iesuite and Prieste*...(n.p. [London], n.d. [1582])
Allen, *BH*	William Allen, *A Briefe Historie of the Glorious Martyrdom of XII. Reverend Priests, Executed within these Twelve Monethes for Confession and Defence of the Catholike Faith* (n.p. [Rheims], 1582)
Allen, *TSMD*	William Allen, *A True, Sincere, and Modest Defence, of English Catholiques...against a False, Seditious and Slaunderous Libel Intituled; The Execution of Iustice in England* ....(n.p. [Rouen], n.d. [1584])
Anstr.	G. Anstruther, *The Seminary Priests* (4 vols, Ware and Great Wakering, 1968–77)
APC	J. R. Dasent et al. (eds), *Acts of the Privy Council of England (1542–1628)*, (32 vols, 1890–1907)
ARCR	A. F. Allison and D. M. Rogers, *The Contemporary Printed Literature of the English Counter-Reformation between 1558 and 1640* (2 vols, Aldershot, 1989–94)
ARSJ	Archivum Romanum Societatis Jesu
ASV	Archivio Segreto Vaticano, Vatican City
AVCAU	Archivum Venerabilis Collegii Anglorum de Urbe (the English College in Rome)
Aveling, *NC*	J. C. H. Aveling, *Northern Catholics: The Catholic Recusants of the North Riding of Yorkshire 1558–1790* (1966)
AWCBC	*Archdiocese of Westminster: Cause of Beatification and Canonization of the Venerable Servants of God George Haydock, Priest and Companions...: Official Presentation of Documents on Martyrdom*...(Sacred Congregation for the Causes of Saints: Historical Section, Rome, 1981)

xxiv   LIST OF ABBREVIATIONS

AWCCBM	Archdiocese of Westminster: Cause of the Canonization of Blessed Martyrs John Houghton, Robert Lawrence, Augustine Webster, Richard Reynolds, John Stone, Cuthbert Mayne, John Paine, Edmund Campion, Alexander Briant, Ralph Sherwin and Luke Kirby, put to Death in England in Defence of the Catholic Faith (1535–1582): Official Presentation of Documents on Martyrdom and Cult (Vatican and Polyglot Press, 1968)
Birch, CTCI	T. Birch (ed.), The Court and Times of Charles the First (2 vols, 1848)
Birch, CTJI	T. Birch (ed.), The Court and Times of James the First (2 vols, 1849)
BL	British Library
Boderie, AMLB	Ambassades de M. de La Boderie en Angleterre sous le Règne de Henri IV…(5 vols, Paris, 1750)
Bodl.	Bodleian Library, Oxford
Bossy, EC	J. Bossy, 'English Catholicism: The Link with France' (PhD, Cambridge, 1961)
Bossy, ECC	J. Bossy, The English Catholic Community 1570–1850 (1975)
Burton, LT	E. H. Burton, The Life and Times of Bishop Challoner (1691–1781) (2 vols, 1909)
Caraman, HG	P. Caraman, Henry Garnet 1555–1606 and the Gunpowder Plot (1964)
Caraman, JG	P. Caraman (ed.), John Gerard: The Autobiography of an Elizabethan (1951)
Caraman, WW	P. Caraman (ed.), William Weston: The Autobiography of an Elizabethan (1955)
CCED	Clergy of the Church of England Database (online, https://theclergy-database.org.uk/)
Challoner, MMP	Richard Challoner, ed. J. H. Pollen, Memoirs of Missionary Priests…(1924)
Clancy, ECB	T. H. Clancy, English Catholic Books 1641–1700: A Bibliography (Chicago, 1974)
Collinson, EPM	P. Collinson, The Elizabethan Puritan Movement (Oxford, 1967)
CP	Cause Papers at ABSJ. The abbreviation CP designates the uncatalogued papers in the archives gathered by the vice-postulators. Those currently retained in box files, labelled with the names of, e.g., individuals or categories associated with the Cause of the English and Welsh martyrs, are likely in the future to be sorted and (re)classified
CRS	Catholic Record Society
CSPD	R. Lemon and M. A. E. Green (eds), Calendar of State Papers, Domestic Series (12 vols [for 1547–1625], 1856–72)
CSPF	J. Stevenson et al. (eds), Calendar of State Papers Foreign, Elizabethan Series, of the Reign of Elizabeth (23 vols in 26, 1863–1950)
CSPI	H. C. Hamilton, E. G. Atkinson, and R. P. Mahaffy (eds), Calendar of State Papers, Ireland (24 vols, 1860–1912)
CSPR	J. M. Rigg (ed.), Calendar of State Papers, relating to English Affairs, preserved principally at Rome (2 vols [for 1558–78], 1916, 1926)
CSPSc	J. Bain et al. (eds), Calendar of State Papers relating to Scotland and Mary, Queen of Scots 1547–1603 (13 vols in 14, Edinburgh, 1898–1969)

CSPSp	M. A. S. Hume (ed.), *Calendar of Letters and State Papers relating to English Affairs, preserved principally in the Archives of Simancas* (4 vols, 1892–9)
CSPV	H. F. Brown and A. B. Hinds (eds), *Calendar of State Papers, Venetian Series* (11 vols [for 1581–1625], 1894–1912)
CUPRP	V. Houliston, G. Crosignani, and T. M. McCoog (eds), *The Correspondence and Unpublished Papers of Robert Persons, SJ*: vol. I: 1574–88 (Pontifical Institute of Mediaeval Studies, 2017)
Cust, *CI*	R. Cust, *Charles I: A Political Life* (2005)
Davidson, RC	A. Davidson, 'Roman Catholicism in Oxfordshire from the Late Elizabethan Period to the Civil War (*c.*1580–*c.*1640)' (PhD, Bristol, 1970)
Devlin, *LRS*	C. Devlin, *The Life of Robert Southwell: Poet and Martyr* (1956)
Dillon, *CM*	A. Dillon, *The Construction of Martyrdom in the English Catholic Community, 1535–1603* (Aldershot, 2002)
Dodd, *CH*	C. Dodd, *The Church History of England*...(3 vols, Brussels [imprint false, printed at Wolverhampton], 1737–42)
Edwards, *EJ*	F. Edwards (ed.), *The Elizabethan Jesuits: Historia Missionis Anglicanae Societatis Jesu (1660) of Henry More* (1981)
EUL	Exeter University Library
FG	Fondo Gesuitico
Foley, *RSJ*	H. Foley (ed.), *Records of the English Province of the Society of Jesus* (7 vols in 8, 1875–83)
GC	ABSJ 46/12/1–2 (transcripts and translations of letters and papers of Henry Garnet SJ)
Ghent MSS	ABSJ 46/24/10 (Penelope Renold: transcripts and photocopies), Ghent State Archives: Ghent Jesuits, archives (K44) and charters (K45), 2 files
Graves, *TN*	M. Graves, *Thomas Norton: The Parliament Man* (Oxford, 1994)
Hartley, *PPE*	T. E. Hartley (ed.), *Proceedings in the Parliaments of Elizabeth I* (3 vols, 1981–95)
HC 1558–1603	P. Hasler (ed.), *The House of Commons 1558–1603* (3 vols, 1981)
HC 1604–29	A. Thrush and J. Ferris (eds), *The House of Commons 1604–1629* (6 vols, 2010)
HHCP	Hatfield House, Cecil Papers
Hibbard, *CI*	C. Hibbard, *Charles I and the Popish Plot* (Chapel Hill, 1983)
Hicks, *Letters*	L. Hicks (ed.), *Letters and Memorials of Fr. Robert Persons, S.J.*, I (CRS 39, 1942)
HJ	*Historical Journal*
HMC	Historical Manuscripts Commission
HMCB	R. E. G. Kirk (ed.), *Report on the Manuscripts of the Duke of Buccleuch and Queensberry*...(3 vols, HMC, 1899–1926)
HMCC	W. D. Fane (ed.), *The Manuscripts of the Earl Cowper*...(3 vols, HMC, Twelfth Report, Appendix, 1888–9)
HMCD	E. K. Purnell et al. (eds), *Report on the Manuscripts of the Marquess of Downshire* (6 vols, HMC, 1924–95)
HMCE	A. W. Montgomerie (ed.), *Reports on the Manuscripts of the Earl of Eglinton*...(HMC, 1885)

xxvi LIST OF ABBREVIATIONS

HMCF	G. D. Burtchaell and J. M. Rigg (eds), *Report on Franciscan Manuscripts preserved at the Convent, Merchants' Quay, Dublin* (HMC, 1906)
HMCL	G. D. Owen (ed.), *Calendar of the Manuscripts of…the Marquess of Bath, preserved at Longleat: Volume V: Talbot, Dudley and Devereux Papers 1533–1659* (HMC, 1980)
HMCM	S. C. Lomas (ed.), *Report on the Manuscripts of Lord Montagu of Beaulieu* (HMC, 1900)
HMCP	F. H. Blackburne Daniell et al. (eds), *The Manuscripts of his Grace the Duke of Portland preserved at Welbeck Abbey* (10 vols, HMC, 1891–1931)
HMCR	H. C. Maxwell-Lyte et al. (eds), *The Manuscripts of…the Duke of Rutland…preserved at Belvoir Castle* (4 vols, HMC, 1888–1905)
HMCS	M. S. Giuseppi et al. (eds), *Calendar of the Manuscripts of the Most Honourable the Marquess of Salisbury* (24 vols, HMC, 1888–1976)
HMCV, III	S. C. Lomas (ed.), *Report on Manuscripts in Various Collections: Manuscripts of T. B. Clarke-Thornhill* (HMC, 1904), III
HR	*Historical Research*
Hughes and Larkin, TRP	P. L. Hughes and J. F. Larkin (eds), *Tudor Royal Proclamations* (3 vols, 1964–9)
IFT	'The Imprisonment of Francis Tregian' ('The Great and Long Sufferings for the Cath[olic] Faith of Mr Francis Tregian…', St Mary's College, Oscott, formerly MS 45, now R03351; printed in Morris, *TCF*, I, pp. 59–140)
JBS	*Journal of British Studies*
Jeaffreson, MCR	J. C. Jeaffreson (ed.), *Middlesex County Records* (4 vols, 1886–92)
JEH	*Journal of Ecclesiastical History*
Kenny, RS	A. Kenny (ed.), *The Responsa Scholarum of the English College, Rome* (2 vols, CRS 54–5, 1962–3)
Kenyon, PP	J. P. Kenyon, *The Popish Plot* (1972)
Kilroy, EC	G. Kilroy, *Edmund Campion: A Scholarly Life* (Farnham, 2015)
Kn. [I–VII]	John Knaresborough, 'Sufferings of the Catholicks', Hull History Centre (Papers of the Constable Maxwell Family): U DDEV/67/1 (5 vols, *c.*1720, relating to the persecution of Catholics 1558–1654); U DDEV/67/2 (a bound collection of materials for U DDEV/67/1); U DDEV/67/3 ('Various Collections and Foul Draughts of the Sufferings of Catholicks': a bound collection of materials for U DDEV/67/1)
Knox, DD	T. F. Knox (ed.), *The First and Second Diaries of the English College, Douay, and an Appendix of Published Documents…* (1878)
Knox, LMCA	T. F. Knox (ed.), *The Letters and Memorials of William Cardinal Allen (1532–1594)* (1882)

LIST OF ABBREVIATIONS   xxvii

L&A	R. B. Wernham (ed.), *List and Analysis of State Papers, Foreign Series, Elizabeth I...* (6 vols, 1964–94)
Lake, *BQB*	P. Lake, *Bad Queen Bess? Libels, Secret Histories, and the Politics of Publicity in the Reign of Queen Elizabeth I* (Oxford, 2016)
Lake and Questier, 'Agency'	P. Lake and M. Questier, 'Agency, Appropriation and Rhetoric under the Gallows: Puritans, Romanists and the State in Early Modern England', *Past and Present* 153 (1996), pp. 64–107
Lake and Questier, *Archpriest*	P. Lake and M. Questier, *All Hail to the Archpriest: Confessional Conflict, Toleration, and the Politics of Publicity in Post-Reformation England* (Oxford, 2019)
Lake and Questier, *Trials*	P. Lake and M. Questier, *The Trials of Margaret Clitherow: Persecution, Martyrdom and the Politics of Sanctity in Elizabethan England* (2nd edition, 2019)
Larkin and Hughes, *SRP*, I	J. F. Larkin and P. L. Hughes (eds), *Stuart Royal Proclamations: Royal Proclamations of King James I 1603–1625* (Oxford, 1973)
Larkin, *SRP*, II	J. F. Larkin (ed.), *Stuart Royal Proclamations: Royal Proclamations of King Charles I 1625–1646* (Oxford, 1983)
Law, *AC*	T. G. Law (ed.), *The Archpriest Controversy....* (2 vols, Camden Society, 2nd series, 56, 58, 1896, 1898)
Loomie, *SJC*	A. J. Loomie (ed.), *Spain and the Jacobean Catholics* (2 vols, CRS, 64, 68, 1973, 1978)
Loomie, *TD*	A. J. Loomie, *Toleration and Diplomacy: The Religious Issue in Anglo-Spanish Relations, 1603–1605* (Philadelphia, 1963)
LPL	Lambeth Palace Library
McClure, *LJC*	N. E. McClure (ed.), *The Letters of John Chamberlain* (2 vols, Philadelphia, 1939)
McCoog, LRS	T. M. McCoog, 'The Letters of Robert Southwell, SJ', in T. M. McCoog, *'And Touching our Society': Fashioning Jesuit Identity in Elizabethan England* (Toronto, 2013), pp. 143–95
McCoog, *SJ*	T. M. McCoog, *The Society of Jesus in Ireland, Scotland, and England 1541–1588: 'Our Way of Proceeding?'* (Leiden, 1996)
McCoog, *SJISE*, I	T. M. McCoog, *The Society of Jesus in Ireland, Scotland and England, 1589–1597: Building the Faith of Saint Peter upon the King of Spain's Monarchy* (2012)
McCoog, *SJISE*, II	T. M. McCoog, *The Society of Jesus in Ireland, Scotland and England, 1598–1606: 'Lest Our Lamp Be Entirely Extinguished'* (Leiden, 2017)
Milward, I	P. Milward, *Religious Controversies of the Elizabethan Age: A Survey of Printed Sources* (1977)
Milward, II	P. Milward, *Religious Controversies of the Jacobean Age: A Survey of Printed Sources* (1978)

xxviii   LIST OF ABBREVIATIONS

Morris, *TCF*	J. Morris (ed.), *The Troubles of our Catholic Forefathers...* (3 vols, 1872–7)
Murphy, *TER*	C. Murphy (ed.), *A True and Exact Relation of the Death of Two Catholicks, who suffered for their Religion at the Summer Assizes, held at Lancaster in the Year 1628. Republished with some Additions...* (1737)
NAGB	M. Questier (ed.), *Newsletters from the Archpresbyterate of George Birkhead* (Camden Society, 5th series, 12, Cambridge, 1998)
NCC	M. Questier (ed.), *Newsletters from the Caroline Court, 1631–1638: Catholicism and the Politics of the Personal Rule* (Camden Society, 5th series, 26, Cambridge, 2005)
n.d.	no date (of publication)
Neale, *EHP*	J. E. Neale, *Elizabeth I and Her Parliaments* (2 vols, 1953, 1957)
NLW	National Library of Wales
n.p.	no place (of publication)
ODNB	*Oxford Dictionary of National Biography*
PC	ABSJ 46/12/3–6 (transcripts and translations of letters and papers of Robert Persons SJ)
Petti, *LDRV*	A. G. Petti (ed.), *The Letters and Despatches of Richard Verstegan (c.1550–1640)* (CRS 52, 1959)
Pollen, *AEM*	J. H. Pollen (ed.), *Acts of English Martyrs hitherto Unpublished* (1891)
Pollen and MacMahon, *VPH*	J. H. Pollen and W. MacMahon (eds), *The Ven. Philip Howard Earl of Arundel 1557–1595* (1919)
Pollen, *UD*	J. H. Pollen (ed.), *Unpublished Documents relating to the English Martyrs* (CRS 5, 1908), I (1584–1603)
PRO	The National Archives, Kew: Public Record Office
Prynne, *PRP*	William Prynne, *The Popish Royall Favourite...* (1643; Wing P 4039)
Questier, *C&C*	M. Questier, *Catholicism and Community in Early Modern England: Politics, Aristocratic Patronage and Religion, c.1550–1640* (Cambridge, 2006)
Questier, *DP*	M. Questier, *Dynastic Politics and the British Reformations 1558–1630* (Oxford, 2019)
RC	Rivers Correspondence (transcripts of newsletters written under the name Anthony Rivers, at ABSJ, 46/9/4/12)
Read, *MSW*	C. Read, *Mr Secretary Walsingham and the Policy of Queen Elizabeth* (3 vols, Cambridge, 1925)
Redworth, *LLC*	G. Redworth with C. J. Henstock (eds), trans. D. McGrath and G. Redworth, *The Letters of Luisa de Carvajal Y Mendoza* (2 vols, 2012)
Renold, *LWA*	P. Renold (ed.), *Letters of William Allen and Richard Barret 1572–1598* (CRS 58, 1967)
Renold, *WS*	P. Renold (ed.), *The Wisbech Stirs (1595–1598)* (CRS 51, 1958)

LIST OF ABBREVIATIONS   xxix

RH	*Recusant History*
RHPN	'Father Richard Holtby on Persecution in the North' (ABSJ, Anglia II, no. 12a, printed in Morris, *TCF*, III, pp. 103–219)
Richardson, RP	W. Richardson, 'The Religious Policy of the Cecils 1588–1598' (DPhil, Oxford, 1993)
RSTC	A. W. Pollard and G. R. Redgrave, *A Short Title Catalogue of Books Printed in England, Scotland and Ireland and of English Books Printed Abroad, 1475–1640*, 2nd edition rev. W. A. Jackson, F. S. Ferguson, and K. F. Pantzer (3 vols, 1976–91)
Sawyer, *WM*	E. Sawyer (ed.), *Memorials of Affairs of State in the Reigns of Q. Elizabeth and K. James I. Collected (chiefly) from the Original Papers of... Sir Ralph Winwood...* (3 vols, 1725) [Winwood Memorials]
SDP	M. Questier (ed.), *Stuart Dynastic Policy and Religious Politics, 1621–1625* (Camden Society, 5th series, 34, Cambridge, 2009)
SJ	Society of Jesus
Smith, *Life*	L. P. Smith (ed.), *The Life and Letters of Sir Henry Wotton* (2 vols, Oxford, 1907)
SR	A. Luders et al. (eds), *The Statutes of the Realm...* (11 vols, 1810–28)
Talbot, *MRR*	C. Talbot (ed.), *Miscellanea: Recusant Records* (CRS 53, 1960)
TD	M. A. Tierney (ed.), *Dodd's Church History of England from the Commencement of the Sixteenth Century to the Revolution in 1688* (5 vols, 1839–43)
Thomas, *WECM*	D. A. Thomas (ed.), *The Welsh Elizabethan Catholic Martyrs: The Trial Documents of Saint Richard Gwyn and of the Venerable William Davies* (Cardiff, 1971)
Tompkins, ECI	A. Tompkins, 'The English Catholic Issue, 1640–1662: Factionalism, Perceptions and Exploitation' (PhD, London, 2010)
TR	John Mush, 'A True Report of the Life and Martyrdom of Mrs. Margaret Clitherow', in Morris, *TCF*, III, pp. 333–440 (Bar Convent Archives, York (MS V, 69))
UCLSC	Ushaw College Library Special Collections
Usher, *REC*	R. G. Usher, *The Reconstruction of the English Church* (2 vols, 1910)
Ward, LT	L. J. Ward, 'The Law of Treason in the Reign of Elizabeth I 1558–1588' (PhD, Cambridge, 1985)
Weinrich, *PREH*	S. J. Weinrich (ed. and trans.), *Pedro de Ribadeneyra's 'Ecclesiastical History of the Schism of the Kingdom of England': A Spanish Jesuit's History of the English Reformation* (Leiden, 2017)
WHN	'Notes by a Prisoner [William Hutton] in Ousebridge Kidcote. From the Original Manuscript at Stonyhurst College' (ABSJ, Anglia VI, no. 19 with extracts from ABSJ, Collectanea M, pp. 170^b–8^a, copied by Christopher Grene from AVCAU, Liber 1422 [Grene, Collectanea F]; printed in Morris, *TCF*, III, pp. 231–330)
YRR	'A Yorkshire Recusant's Relation' (St Mary's College, Oscott, Collectanea E [formerly MS 98, now R11781]; printed in Morris, *TCF*, III, pp. 65–102)

Note on the Text

In the text, dates are given Old Style and, where appropriate in citing Continental sources, Old Style/New Style, but the year is taken to begin on 1 January. The spelling and punctuation of quotations from early modern manuscripts and books have been modernized. Unless otherwise stated, the place of publication of all works cited in this volume is London.

PART I

1

Introduction

Martyrs for the Faith?

The Origins of a Tradition: Richard Challoner's *Memoirs of Missionary Priests* and Catholic Martyrology

This volume deals with the origins and development of the post-Reformation English Catholic martyrological tradition, both in the sense of the events and documents out of which it is fashioned and also of the way that its creators and guardians constructed and preserved it.[1] It is, obviously, not meant to be just a blow-by-blow, or death-by death, account of the travails of contemporary Catholics, nor is it clear what, on its own, such a study would tell one, at least historically. I am interested in what people decided to remember and memorialize and how they went about doing that. But, as I remark in the Preface, I also want to look at that martyrological tradition in a wider historical context and to think about the implications of this branch of Catholic memory for the post-Reformation *longue durée*. I do not wish to privilege Catholic memories over others but I do want to argue that those memories are far more embedded in, and relevant to, what we take to be 'mainstream' accounts of the period than we might otherwise think. At the same time, what 'memory' denotes here is neither some sort of collective popular consciousness nor a kind of cultural residue from the post-Reformation period. Rather, the word is taken to refer to a series of attempts, by contemporaries and by others subsequently, to create a version of the past out of particular testimonies, undertaken with very specific devotional and polemical purposes in mind, all in order to elicit certain responses, emotional and intellectual, from the reader.

So, let us look at and briefly describe the ways in which this kind of memorialization took place. The first major systematic attempt, at least in print, to bring

---

[1] I should point out that, although I have tried to trace as much of the relevant manuscript and printed material as possible, there is no methodical attempt here to set out the relationships between all the relevant texts. That would be another, although very valuable, research project entirely and was carried out, for example, by the researchers based in the Office of the Vice-Postulation in London for the eighty-five martyrs beatified by Rome in 1987; see *AWCBC, passim*. I have tried to keep an eye as far as I can on the provenance of the material that I cite, even though I have not always, in citations of printed primary/manuscript material, given the original source. For a recent exemplary reconstruction of how martyrological sources were written, see E. Patton, 'Four Contemporary Translations of Dorothy Arundell's Lost English Narratives', *Philological Quarterly* 95 (2016), pp. 397–424.

Catholics and Treason: Martyrology, Memory, and Politics in the Post-Reformation. Michael Questier,
Oxford University Press. © Michael Questier 2022. DOI: 10.1093/oso/9780192847027.003.0001

4 CATHOLICS AND TREASON

Catholic memories of persecution together was undertaken by Bishop Richard Challoner. It appeared off the press in the early 1740s as *Memoirs of Missionary Priests*. Here he passed over the Reformation of the 1530s and 1540s and launched more or less straight into his subject with the legal proceedings against the seminary priest Cuthbert Mayne in 1577. Mayne's case is preceded by the briefest of introductions which says merely that the queen, Elizabeth, had at one time 'professed herself a Catholic' but 'now took off the mask and by degrees brought about a total change of the religion of the kingdom'. This was secured by a blatant packing of parliament. The settling of 'the new religion' was 'not only without the concurrence of the clergy but, indeed, in opposition to the whole body of the clergy of the nation'. The true religion would, said Challoner, have died out had it not been for the foresight and spiritual zeal of William Allen and the foundation of the seminaries on the Continent. As Challoner puts it, 'our memoirs of the sufferings of our English Catholics begin with the year 1577...because, from this year, we may properly date the beginning of the great persecution'. 'Little blood' had been 'shed by her before, at least for matters purely religious'. He avers that, 'as to the priests and others who suffered in these persecutions...though we make no question of their religion having been their only crime, yet we have abstained from giving them the title of saints or martyrs, that we might not seem to run before the Church of God, which has not as yet thought proper to declare them such'. He added that, 'for the same reason, we have been very sparing in mentioning miracles, visions or revelations shown in favour of any of these champions of God's truth; for such things, by the decrees of the See Apostolic, ought not to be published till they have been first duly examined and approved by the ordinaries'.[2]

Challoner's preface to the second part of his work makes an even more explicit claim to detachment. His 'intention' was 'not to meddle' in 'any way with religious controversies, or to make apologies for the principles of those whose sufferings we represent, or to discuss the merits of the cause for which they suffered, but barely to give an impartial account of the character of these sufferers, as far as we could learn of them' in 'the most remarkable particulars of their lives and deaths and their behaviour at their execution'. If anyone should 'apprehend that the cruelties here represented may reflect an odium upon the memories of those who were the authors or executors of the sanguinary laws by which so much Christian blood has been shed for more than a whole century, in a nation which of all

---

[2] Richard Challoner, *Memoirs of Missionary Priests...* (2 vols, 1741–2), I, pp. 1–10. For Bishop Challoner's oeuvre, see E. Duffy, 'Richard Challoner, 1691–1781: A Memoir', in E. Duffy (ed.), *Challoner and his Church: A Catholic Bishop in Georgian England* (1981), p. 21, citing Ronald Knox's judgment that Challoner was 'an adapter, an abridger, a continuator'. In his youth, Challoner was placed with the Holman family at Warkworth manor in Northamptonshire. Anastasia, wife of George Holman, was the daughter of William Howard, Viscount Stafford, a victim of the Oates (or Popish) Plot: ibid., pp. 1–2.

others is naturally most averse from shedding of blood, we can only assure him that it was not our design to reflect on the memory of anyone, but barely to represent matters of fact which we hoped might furnish a useful and agreeable scene of history to the English reader'. The bishop also took the opportunity to 'declare how much we are convinced that the more mild proceedings of the present government', that is, in the 1740s, 'with regard to Catholics, are far more agreeable both to reason and religion, more honourable to the nation, and more suitable to that claim of liberty and property which every true Englishman challenges as his birthright'.[3]

Here, then, Challoner's book established itself as a commentary on the nature of tolerance and the desirability of toleration.[4] Was it 'not most agreeable to religion to practise mildness and charity towards our fellow Christians; and, if we suppose them to be in error, to win them over rather by good treatment and good example, and to convince their judgment by proper arguments and evidences of the truth than to compel them by penal laws to play the hypocrites and profess what they do not believe?' Also, 'how much more ought this to be observed if we speak of people who, if they are in the wrong, it is visibly their misfortune and not their fault, having no worldly motives of honour, interest or pleasure to bias their judgment, which is plainly the case of English Catholics?' Protestants were supposed to believe that all Christians should 'steer by the Word of God'. It was surely wrong to 'oblige men to renounce those tenets which they sincerely believe to be conformable to the Word of God, as Catholics do with regard to the doctrine of transubstantiation'. Behind this opening gambit, Challoner lined up all the conventional arguments for toleration which contemporaries had used since the sixteenth century—arguments which he undoubtedly took to be confirmed by the narratives which he then set down.[5]

---

[3] Richard Challoner, ed. T. G. Law, *Memoirs of Missionary Priests...* (Edinburgh, 1878), part II, Challoner's preface, p. 3.

[4] I am very grateful to Shanyn Altman for a discussion about what martyrologists such as Challoner took tolerance/toleration to be. I am grateful also to Alexandra Tompkins for her observation that the preface to the second part of Challoner's work (omitted in Challoner, *MMP*) was more explicit (than the preface to the first part) about the benefits of toleration. See Tompkins, *ECI*, p. 93.

[5] Challoner, ed. Law, *Memoirs*, part II, Challoner's preface, p. 4. Challoner's *Memoirs* comes to an abrupt end, in effect, with the execution of Oliver Plunket on 1 July 1681. Challoner remarks merely that 'I find no more Catholic blood spilt in England for religion during the three remaining years' of Charles II's reign and, 'since the accession of King James II to the throne, though from time to time the Catholics have been exposed to some passing storms, yet by God's mercy the persecution has never raged so far as to come to blood': Challoner, *MMP*, pp. 582, 583. From Challoner's text one would have no idea that the Jacobite movement had ever existed. As Gabriel Glickman says of the Glorious Revolution, 'the seemingly anti-Catholic credentials of the new regime did not take long to establish themselves' and, 'by April 1689, penal legislation was being revived', perhaps unsurprisingly in the context of widespread Catholic refusal to recognize the new order: G. Glickman, *The English Catholic Community, 1688-1745: Politics, Culture and Ideology* (Woodbridge, 2009), p. 22 and *passim*. For the legal penalties inflicted on the Catholic community after the Revolution, see esp. Tompkins, *ECI*, pp. 91–2. For discussions of Challoner's immediate and pastoral purposes in writing the *Memoirs*, see Tompkins, *ECI*, pp. 92–3; Duffy, 'Richard Challoner', p. 21.

6 CATHOLICS AND TREASON

Challoner's bold rhetorical distinctions between politics and religion and his insistence that he was absolutely objective in his historical judgments must have provoked, from some Protestant readers, more than a few sharp intakes of breath, even as many Catholic readers, both then and subsequently, concluded that this saintly missionary bishop was simply telling the truth. At the point that the *Memoirs* appeared, Challoner had a reputation as a vigorous controversialist, in particular for his exchanges with Conyers Middleton. Indeed, in 1737 it was said that the resulting furore had compelled Challoner to leave London and go back to Douai College, although Eamon Duffy shows that 'there is not a single scrap of contemporary evidence that Challoner went to Douai at this time'. (Assuming that his work on the *Memoirs* began at this point, he would therefore have needed the transcripts of Douai manuscripts made by his research assistant, the priest Alban Butler, which were compiled around this time.)[6]

But whichever way one reacts to Challoner's work and, indeed, to the texts in the martyrological tradition on which he drew and to the Catholic narrative of the later Reformation in England which he helped to define, one cannot simply assume that the material which he deployed, and the way in which he set it down, are the product of confessional naïvety. Challoner was, in fact, doing something remarkably similar to (as Peter Lake describes it) what Samuel Clarke did when he wrote his 'Lives' of godly Protestant divines. Challoner and Clarke constructed, with utterly different polemical assumptions but in remarkably similar literary and rhetorical ways, accounts of the kind of religion which they took to be most obviously compatible with the proper operation of the national Church. Of course, Challoner's book was written some considerable time after the events that it commemorated. Clarke's famous work, by contrast, was recording the very

---

[6] Burton, *LT*, I, pp. 99–106, 166–7; Duffy, 'Richard Challoner', pp. 11–12. For Alban Butler's manuscript collections on Catholic martyrdom (containing a number of Challoner's own notes), see Archives of the Archdiocese of Birmingham, R 941, R 945. The Jesuit John Morris's catalogue of the original Douai College file or dossier out of which Butler made his transcripts is retained in ABSJ among the martyrs' Cause papers. It shows the arrangement of the manuscripts before the file was broken up and the material ordered chronologically. For John Pollen's explanation of the relationship between these papers and also what Pollen calls the 'Chalcedon dossier' (a catalogue of which, by John Morris, is also retained at ABSJ), i.e. the papers collected in order to compile Bishop Richard Smith's catalogue of 1628 (AAW, B 28, no. 3) but which, the consensus is, were not used by Challoner, see Challoner, *MMP*, pp. xiii–xiv; ABSJ, CP (P. Barry to L. Whatmore, 6 December 1965); see also AAW, B 31 (unpaginated section: 'list of volumes and bundles: manuscripts from the archives of the cardinal; at the Oratory, Feb. 13, 1876'). *Inter alia*, Butler copied out for Challoner the relevant sections of Anthony Champney's massive manuscript work entitled 'Annales Elizabethae Reginae' (AAW, F 1), which was never published, and in which, as Butler accurately remarks, 'the author shows himself a great enemy' to the Jesuits: ABP, pp. 161–256 (quotation at p. 256). Butler's collection of martyr materials passed, via Charles Butler, to John Kirk and thence to St Mary's College, Oscott, and finally to the Birmingham archdiocesan archives: ABSJ, CP (undated memorandum by Patrick Barry); AAW, Processus Martyrum, 1874, I, p. 98; Burton, *LT*, I, p. 167. For the transcriptions made at Douai for Challoner's use, see Burton, *LT*, I, pp. 166–7; for the publishing history of Challoner's book, see Burton, *LT*, I, pp. 171–2. For the 1924 edition, and the principles on which it was compiled and edited by John Pollen, using and updating the original 1741–2 edition, see Challoner, *MMP*, pp. v–vi, xvi–xvii.

INTRODUCTION   7

recent past. In addition, the clergy at the centre of Challoner's book were not really in any formal sense part of the national Church established by law. At the same time, the way that he narrated their experience of persecution and suffering performs many of the functions that Lake attributes to Clarke's text.[7] Lake suggests that Clarke's book is about the 'formulation and assertion of a certain self-consciously "puritan" style of clericalism in the face of hostile and increasingly distinct versions not only of what puritanism was and why it was a bad thing, but also of what the clergy were for and of how the Christian community should be conceived, created and sustained in and through the ordinances and practices of the visible Church'. Clarke's work in the early 1650s can be seen as the product of a kind of 'write-in campaign', that is, as a version of moderate puritanism and presbyterianism found itself under the gun.[8] That is, arguably, also a very fair description of what Challoner does for a certain sort of Catholicism, though in very different circumstances. As Lake comments, Clarke's lives of the godly 'tended to end with an account of a death scene—of a "good death" which rounded off the story of spiritual achievement and ethical exertion that had preceded it'. This, obviously, is what Challoner does with every one of his martyrs.[9]

Like Clarke, Challoner printed material written by others and he made much of his close adherence to his sources. The 'first and most necessary quality that ought to recommend history is truth'. 'This', he could assure the reader, 'we have been careful to follow to a nicety'. Challoner declared that he had 'given nothing upon hearsays or popular traditions but upon the best authorities; either of grave contemporary writers, informed by such' as were actually there or were 'themselves eyewitnesses of what they write, or of records and manuscript memoirs, penned by such as were eyewitnesses, or otherwise perfectly instructed in the things they deliver; and withal men, as we had reason to be convinced, of the strictest veracity'. Challoner claimed 'not to make panegyrics of any of these brave men but merely to deliver short memoirs of what we found most remarkable in their lives and particularly in their deaths'. He left out a good deal, since 'we had so many to treat of' and 'we have been sometimes forced to be shorter than could have been wished, and to pass many things over' simply in order 'to bring the whole into compass', even though, 'as for some others, we have been obliged to be much shorter than we would, for want of proper lights, having been able to find

---

[7] P. Lake, *Making Memory: Samuel Clarke and the Construction of an English Puritan Tradition* (forthcoming); Samuel Clarke, *The Lives of Sundry Eminent Persons*...(1683); and for Clarke's publications which preceded this volume, see also *ODNB, sub* Clarke, Samuel (article by A. Hughes); P. Lake, 'Reading Clarke's *Lives* in Political and Polemical Context', in K. Sharpe and Z. N. Zwicker (eds), *Writing Lives: Biography and Textuality, Identity and Representation in Early Modern England* (Oxford, 2012), ch. 14.

[8] Lake, *Making Memory*, part II, 'Occasions'; see also A. Hughes, *Gangraena and the Struggle for the English Revolution* (Oxford, 2004).

[9] Lake, *Making Memory*, preface and part I, ch. 1.

8 CATHOLICS AND TREASON

little else of them than that they died at such a time and place and for the cause of their religion'.[10]

Challoner lined up, in one almost entirely undifferentiated row, individuals who, like Clarke's moderate puritans, had often held rather different opinions about key contemporary political and ecclesiological questions. In Lake's words, 'the lives collected by Clarke constructed an ideal of pastoral excellence and effectiveness and of personal godliness, a perfect meld of moderation and zeal, epitomized and lived out by the men memorialized in these works'. Those who were thus memorialized were astonishing in their enthusiasm. In Challoner's book that enthusiasm inexorably had only one (gruesome) outcome while, in Clarke's work, it did not. But the overall scheme and structure in both writers' work are remarkably similar.[11]

Just as Clarke's godly heroes' reputations arguably rested on the acclaim they received from the laity,[12] so it was with Challoner's martyrs—they were vindicated in part by the favourable judgment on their lives and deaths by lay (mostly, but not exclusively, Catholic) observers. Furthermore, Clarke wanted to identify and describe a style of ministry which was based on 'personal and collective piety' and not any specific form of (contentious or otherwise) ecclesiological principles.[13] Challoner likewise excludes any sense that those who figure in his pages were ever at loggerheads, as some of them certainly were, over issues of Church government and/or over the relationship of Church and State. What impliedly and, perhaps, under certain circumstances actually bound them together was their own and others' capacity to visualize Catholicism in England as labouring under the cross of Protestant persecution just as Clarke's godly ministers are encompassed by afflictions laid on them by, on the one hand, bishops and, on the other, sectarian radicals.

This is not to suggest that Challoner's text was simply 'constructed', with some kind of Machiavellian cleverness, by deploying, apparently quite artlessly, the 'rules' for writing godly lives in order, in some manner, to deceive his readers. There is absolutely no evidence that he did not entirely believe in the objective truth of the narratives that he collated and penned; nor, I am sure, did Clarke think that he was manipulating deceitfully the information that he used in order to create his text.

Challoner follows closely those whom he regarded as impeccable authorities— for example, the early clearing-house text of martyr stories, the *Concertatio Ecclesiae Catholicae*.[14] He faithfully transcribes the claims of William Allen (though, as if by magic, transmuted into a moderate and quasi-ecumenical

---

[10] Challoner, *Memoirs of Missionary Priests* (1741–2 edition), I, preface, sig. A2ᵛ; Lake, 'Making Memory', part I, ch. 1.

[11] Ibid., part I, ch. 1.   [12] Ibid., part I, ch. 1.   [13] Ibid., part II, 'Occasions'.

[14] *Concertatio Ecclesiae Catholicae in Anglia Adversus Calvino-papistas et Puritanos…* (Trier, 1588), ed. John Fenn and John Gibbons.

INTRODUCTION 9

register) and those of other polemical texts. He follows the logic of the martyr catalogues compiled in the early seventeenth century, notably the ones drawn up at the direction of Richard Smith, bishop of Chalcedon, which focused on those people, principally clergy, who had suffered for their resistance to the Elizabethan and Jacobean State. These sources hardly ever adverted to the possibility that the martyrs' non-compliance was driven by anything other than, on the one hand, their well-informed consciences in matters purely of religion and, on the other, the tyrannical structure and inflexibility of the Elizabethan penal code. As Challoner put it, 'we have inserted no one's name in our list without being first fully convinced that his religion and conscience' were 'his only treason, which was certainly the case of all who suffered under the penal statutes of Elizabeth 27, viz. either for being made priests by Roman authority, and exercising their functions in England, or for harbouring and relieving such priests'. This was true also of 'those who suffered for denying the spiritual supremacy or for being reconciled to the Catholic Church'. There was 'not a man of them all but might have saved his life if he would but have conformed in matters of religion'. The accusations levelled 'at Father [Edmund] Campion and his companions' concerning 'I know not what conspiracies formed at Rheims and Rome' were nonsense. The 'true cause of their death was the hatred of their religion'.[15]

Challoner had, it seems, thought of beginning his martyrology in the Henrician period but then opted, as we saw, to dive in with the case of Cuthbert Mayne in 1577. He gives no explicit reason for this, but one of the advantages, for him, was that there was no need to discuss the compromises made during the Henrician Reformation, the difficult period of Mary Stuart's early years in England, the Northern Rebellion and the papal bull of excommunication.[16] He thus excluded the likes of Thomas Percy, earl of Northumberland, Thomas Plumtree, John Story, John Felton, and Thomas Woodhouse as well as the Catholic opponents of Henry VIII, for whom, in general, there were fewer available documents anyway. Even if very deftly, the material was forced into a straitjacket which assumed, but really did not explain, a seemingly unrelenting conflict between the Catholic community and the State.[17]

---

[15] Challoner, *Memoirs of Missionary Priests* (1741–2 edition) I, preface, sig. A4^v–7^r, A3^{r-v}; see p. 459 below.

[16] Challoner's own working papers and notes included lists of the Henrician martyrs; see AAW, B 28, no. 12, pp. 353–78, written in Challoner's hand, starting with John Houghton in 1535. Thomas Graves Law noted to William Walker on 19 March 1878 that 'we turned up the other day a neatly little written MS book of a dozen pages or so, drawn up by Challoner in his own handwriting while vice-president of Douai. It is a catalogue with a few notes of all the martyrs, including [those under] Henry VIII, as if he at the time intended to write of these earlier ones in his memoirs': UCLSC, UC/P9/2/11. The 1836 edition of Challoner's work is prefaced with the addition of material on the Catholic victims of the Henrician State: *Modern British Martyrology; commencing with 'The Reformation', A.D. 1535...* (1836). I am grateful to Peter Lake for discussions of this point.

[17] Contemporary issues which would disrupt the martyrological form and thrust of the book were usually omitted. Thus in the case of William Bishop, who returned to England as the newly created

10   CATHOLICS AND TREASON

Collecting Evidence about Catholic Martyrs in Reformation England

Actually, the formal efforts to recover the evidence of martyrdom long predated Challoner. Indeed, the first direct instruction from Rome to gather such evidence came in 1626 with the congregation of Propaganda's orders to Bishop Richard Smith to proceed with this exercise. Smith's agents began to consult the appropriate historical and legal documents. This included, for instance, assize records which have not survived. In mid-1643 a commission was set up to proceed with the so-called Ordinary process (that is, led by local episcopal authority) in this respect, but its work was suspended when the relevant documentation fell, late in that year, into the hands of the parliament. However, during the civil wars and in the Popish Plot agitation of 1679–81, Catholic commentators and writers continued to collect and publish accounts of those whom they regarded as Catholic martyrs.[18]

The work of reconstructing the Catholic martyr tradition resumed properly in the early eighteenth century with the work of the northern priest John Knaresborough, who served for years as the chaplain of the gentleman Charles Towneley. Knaresborough's volumes of material, which came to rest in the papers of Cuthbert Constable of Burton Constable, Holderness, show that he was actively soliciting both orally transmitted memories as well as manuscripts and printed books.[19] (See Figure 1.1.) It has been suggested by Rebecca Warren that, since Knaresborough started his collections around 1705, he must have been, if not exactly replying to, then certainly responding to, the massively publicized and controversial efforts of Edmund Calamy to fashion a kind of civil-war martyrology of ejected and persecuted ministers. He must also have been shadowing John Walker's response to Calamy, though Knaresborough did not limit himself to the period of the civil war and the Interregnum.[20]

---

bishop of Chalcedon in 1623, declaring his readiness to suffer for the faith, there is absolutely no sense of Bishop's former record as a distinctly left-of-centre appellant agitator, with quasi-Gallican, loyalist, and violently anti-Jesuit tendencies; see Challoner, *MMP*, pp. 360–1; cf. Anstr., I, pp. 36–8.

[18] See Chapters 13, 14, and 15 below.

[19] On 11 December 1720 Cuthbert Constable wrote to Knaresborough that 'I was always well pleased with your commendable design of searching out all the sufferers for justice's sake and of letting the world one day know those true heroes: this will be a work both curious, instructive and profitable to all good people and will encourage others to follow their example': Kn., VII, p. 553.

[20] Edmund Calamy, *An Abridgment of Mr Baxter's History of his Life and Times. With an Account of Many Others of those Worthy Ministers who were Ejected* (1702), ch. 9; Edmund Calamy, *An Account of the Ministers, Lecturers, Masters, and Fellows of Colleges and Schoolmasters: Who Were Ejected or Silenced after the Restoration in 1660, By or Before, the Act of Uniformity; Design'd for the Preserving to Posterity the Memory of Their Names, Characters, Writings, and Sufferings* (2nd edition, 1713); A. G. Matthews (ed.), *Walker Revised: Being a Revision of John Walker's Sufferings of the Clergy during the Grand Rebellion 1642–60* (Oxford, 1948). I am very grateful to Dr Warren for this suggestion and for discussion of this topic. Dr Samuel Fullerton has pointed out to me that records survive for John Walker's method of information-gathering (Calamy himself printed some of Walker's list of questions: Edmund Calamy, *Church and Dissenters Compar'd*...(1719), pp. 4–11), in particular the

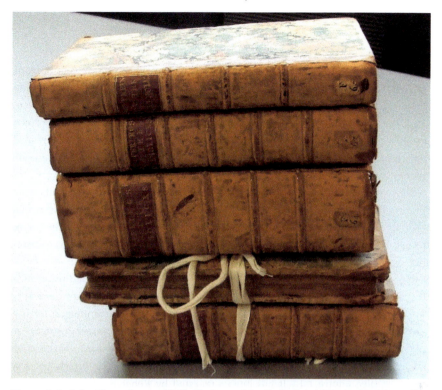

Figure 1.1 John Knaresborough's 'Sufferings of the Catholicks' (Constable Maxwell family papers, reproduced with acknowledgement to the trustees of the Herries Chattels Trust).

It would have been good if more of Knaresborough's working papers had survived. But, just by way of example, on the subject of the priest and popish-plot martyr John Kemble, Knaresborough received information, including Kemble's gallows speech, via letters of 19 December 1706 and 28 October 1707 from the priest Edward Coyney, whose father had fought for Charles I at Naseby. Robert Jefferson sent Knaresborough a 'picture', an engraved portrait of Thomas Pickering OSB, and promised anything else that he could supply, 'if it can furnish you with any particulars in your commendable enquiry'. About the martyr Thomas Thwing who had helped bring Mary Ward's institute to York, Knaresborough had 'Mrs Lassells's note of 24 December 1711'.[21] Some of Knaresborough's knowledge of

---

correspondence over whether to use the material in John White, *The First Century of Scandalous, Malignant Priests...*(1643); see esp. Bodl., MS J. Walker, c. 1, fo. 95^r (John Prince to John Walker, 20 December 1703); Bodl., MS J. Walker, c. 2, fo. 123^v (John Chichester to Walker, 12 June (?) 1705). I am extremely grateful to Dr Fullerton for these references.

[21] Kn., VI, unpaginated section; Anstr., III, p. 225; Thwing was Mrs Lassells's brother. Thwing's execution speech is endorsed by Knaresborough to the effect that it was 'received' by Sir Miles Stapleton 'from Mr Thwing's own hand the morning he went to execution'. The speech had been

12 CATHOLICS AND TREASON

Nicholas Postgate's case came via a letter of 5 October 1705 from one Mrs Fairfax, who had seen Postgate in prison. She gave Knaresborough 'a piece of cloth dipped in Mr Postgate's blood' by one Garlick, a servant of Mr Tunstall of Wycliffe. Concerning Postgate, Knaresborough also had a letter of 17 February 1708 from the priest John Danby.[22] One of Knaresborough's copies of John Southworth's execution speech came to him from the Worthington family of Blainscow.[23] A Jesuit, one 'F.P.', wrote to Knaresborough on 31 July 1706 that he was 'glad of the opportunity of serving you...in a matter of so pious a concern as that [which] you are engaged in'. The Jesuit offered his orders' 'annals' since the year 1612 concerning eleven English Catholic martyrs.[24]

The Lancashire priest Brian Orrell mentioned that Knaresborough had twice written to him for information. Orrell had resolved 'to enquire after the sufferings of' Ambrose Barlow, Edward Bamber, Thomas Whitaker, and William Thompson, though of 'the two last I cannot learn...[even though] I have asked several persons'. Some of Orrell's evidence was obtained from 'Mr Barlow'. This was in all likelihood the priest Edward Booth, who was a godson of Ambrose Barlow. Booth himself had it 'by tradition from several hands'. In the case of Barlow's martyrdom, Knaresborough could get the facts 'more authentically and fuller from the originals usually kept at Barlow [Hall], now in Mr Thomas Towneley's hands, or at least a transcript as I am informed' by the priest John Blackburn, which he 'obtained...when last in Lancashire'. Orrell had also made enquiries, though unsuccessfully, after a number of 'books or records' which Knaresborough had asked for.[25] A letter from Christopher Tootell, uncle of the historian Charles Dodd (*vere* Hugh Tootell), dated 21 June 1707, said that he (Christopher Tootell) had passed on Knaresborough's 'letter by Mr Barlow [Booth] to Mr Blackburn', asking for information about Ambrose Barlow.[26]

---

accompanied by the letter from Thwing's sister, i.e. 'the widow Lascelles' (24 December 1711); she could not remember the month of his birth because 'the book which had all our ages in it was lost in the ill times': Kn., VII, p. 273, citing the letter in Kn., VI, unpaginated section. Knaresborough noted also that there was an inscription recording Thwing's fate engraved on the 'copper plate dug up out of the grave, and now...in the keeping of Mr [Ralph] Thoresby of Leeds': Kn., VII, p. 273.

[22] Kn., VI, unpaginated section (*AWCBC*, pp. 2436, 2437-9); Anstr., III, p. 46; Challoner, *MMP*, pp. 548-9.

[23] Kn., VI, unpaginated section.   [24] Kn., VI, unpaginated section.

[25] Kn., VI, unpaginated section (letter of John Martin *vere* Brian Orrell to John Knaresborough, 1 July 1707: *AWCBC*, pp. 2380-3); Challoner, *MMP*, pp. 483-4; ABSJ, CP (Edward Bamber): J. E. Bamber, 'The Venerable Edward Bamber: Some New Facts', *Downside Review* 56:1 (1938), pp. 31-45. Booth was chaplain to the Houghton family at Park Hall, where the Jesuit Edmund Campion had been entertained and where he finished his *Rationes Decem*: Anstr., III, p. 19; Kilroy, *EC*, p. 196.

[26] Kn., VI, unpaginated section. Edward Booth was named as a source for the events at John Thulis's execution: UCLSC, UC/P1/B2, p. 1 (*AWCBC*, pp. 1983, 1984), an account of Lancashire martyrdoms written by Christopher Tootell; see pp. 13-14 below. For Tootell, a friend of John Gother—who was in effect Challoner's mentor at Warkworth manor in Northamptonshire, the home of the Holman family, see Burton, *LT*, I, p. 7; Duffy, 'Richard Challoner', p. 3; Anstr., III, pp. 228-30. In this list of Lancashire martyrdoms it is recorded that, of one story concerning Thomas Whitaker's attempt to escape, 'this passage good old Mr Edward Blackburn', perhaps the father of John Blackburn, 'told to Mr [Thomas] Roydon, and Mr Roydon to me, the last time I saw him': UCLSC, UC/P1/B2, p. 14. For Roydon, see

INTRODUCTION   13

A manuscript notebook written by the same Christopher Tootell was at one time in the possession of the priest Joseph Bamber, who was heavily involved in the mid-twentieth-century efforts to secure Rome's formal recognition of English and Welsh martyrs of the Reformation.[27] The notebook contained material about Lancashire martyrdoms and was compiled, in *c.*1720, very probably in connection with Knaresborough's own project for gathering martyr material. It was certainly prepared in response to a request for information, since at one point Tootell says (though he then crosses this out) that 'of Mr John Penketh' and other martyrs 'you shall have a true account as soon as I can procure it'.[28] It was remembered by several witnesses that, as the martyr 'Mr [Edward] Bamber went up the ladder, he sent by a young woman (who stayed to see him executed) two of King Edward's sixpences to Richard and Grace Ridley... who lived at a house of Mr Bamber in Brindle'. The priest who was about to die also 'took a handful of money and threw it towards the poor, with a smiling countenance'. The narrator had his 'account... from several persons worthy of credit, viz. 1ˢᵗ Mr Kitching... who served at [the] Ridleys' aforesaid and had lately one of the sixpences... which he gave as a present to Mr Bamber's nephew'. The second source was 'Mr Robert Swarbrick, who had his information of John Hodgson aged ninety-six years and yet of perfect memory'; and his third was 'George Hilton who was... husband to Grace Ridley above mentioned and lives at Mr Bamber's house commonly called Ridlup; he is a serious good Catholic and has heard his wife Grace tell it many a time'. One 'James Fathect, a Protestant living in Little Dale, was present at the execution of the last priest that suffered at Lancaster, who threw some of King Edward's shillings among the crowd of poor people'. He kept two of them and still had them 'the last time' that one 'James Murnnen saw him, which was about seven years ago and said he would keep them whilst he lived and would charge his children after to keep them for a memorandum'. When 'the aforesaid priest was executed, after his head was cut off and his bowels taken out, the executioner took the heart in his hand and said "Behold the heart of a traitor"', whereat 'the head spoke and said, "No, 'tis the heart of a true subject in a traitor's hand" '. Fathect had told this to Murnnen (an 'honest pious Irish man... a great sufferer') and to 'several other neighbours'. Murnnen gave this account to the narrator.[29] As

---

J. R. Baterden (ed.), 'The Catholic Registers of Kendal...', *Miscellanea* (CRS 32, 1932), p. 50; Anstr., III, pp. 191–2.

[27] UCLSC, UC/P1/B2; for identification of Tootell as the author, see Kn. VI, unpaginated section (Christopher Tootell to John Knaresborough, 21 June 1707); Lancashire Record Office: RCFE/2/1/(v) (Christopher Tootell to Mr and Mrs Walton, 9 June 1723).

[28] UCLSC, UC/P1/B2, pp. 1–2, 23; *AWCBC*, p. 1982; the Jesuit John Penketh in fact survived the Popish Plot: Challoner, *MMP*, p. 564. For John Knaresborough's use of Christopher Tootell's information, see Kn., II, p. 229. For Joseph Bamber's announcement of the discovery of the notebook to the meeting in April 1963 at Farm Street of the diocesan representatives for the martyrs' Cause promotion, see ABSJ, CP (Minutes of Meetings of Diocesan Representatives of the Office of the Vice-Postulation, 24 April 1963, 31 Farm Street, London, p. 9).

[29] UCLSC, UC/P1/B2, pp. 3–5 (*AWCBC*, pp. 2363, 2365).

14 CATHOLICS AND TREASON

for the fate of the Franciscan, John Woodcock, executed on the same occasion, the information came from 'Seth Woodcock, nephew of the martyr and son of the high constable', brother of the martyr. He had 'heard it from his father many times'.[30]

The priest John Yaxley had, as he wrote to Knaresborough on 17 July 1707, despite 'all my searching and enquiring', not found 'any records or registers'. But the rest of Yaxley's letter was a treasure trove of oral tradition. When the priests 'Mr [Richard] Holiday, Mr [John] Hogg and Mr [Richard] Hill' and Edmund Duke were hanged at Durham on 27 May 1590, 'a brook near the common gallows, at the time of their execution, ceased to flow, and has remained so ever since, and is…called Dryburn to this day' (actually, it already had that name). Yaxley, who was resident at that point at Coxhoe in Durham, had been taken to see the hollow 'from whence it issued and the marks of its former channel'. This was a 'constant tradition here'. Yaxley also relates the story of the conversion of Robert Maire and his wife when they were present at the execution of Hogg and the others. Mrs Maire was disinherited by her puritan father. His will, which deprived her of her inheritance, could still be seen 'in the archives of Durham'. The spiteful father gave his 'remaining substance to the public uses and pretended charities for that city, unless his graceless daughter Grace, as he calls her in his will, should conform', with an offer that she should get £100 every Sunday she went to church. She stuck to her principles and never did comply. The same letter contains the story of the prominent northern Catholic Roger Widdrington renouncing his conformist past when he watched the execution of John Boste.[31] Yaxley himself reckoned to have come from a martyr family. As he explained in November 1722, his grandfather's elder brother had lost his estates in the civil war, while his grandfather, a captain of a troop of horse, himself suffered a long imprisonment. His uncle, Edward Yaxley, was a soldier in the garrison during the famous siege of Basing House in Hampshire and 'was slain there in cold blood with…many others'. The priest Yaxley had 'heard my father', Richard Yaxley, 'say that before' his brother Edward 'was slain, being questioned, he declared he was a Roman Catholic and, upon that, he was immediately killed, it may well be supposed *in odium fidei* as well as for loyalty' to the king. Richard Yaxley was 'with Colonel [Henry] Gage in Oxford' when it was besieged. He escaped both the plague there and the enemy, although he suffered much hardship.[32] From the recently ordained priest John Phillips (alias Elston), Knaresborough obtained a

---

[30] UCLSC, UC/P1/B2, pp. 5–8 (*AWCBC*, p. 2364).

[31] Kn., VI, unpaginated section (*AWCBC*, pp. 926, 927); Challoner, *MMP*, p. 600; Anstr., III, p. 257; see esp. p. 202 below.

[32] Kn., VI, unpaginated section: John Yaxley to Thomas Roydon, 23 November 1722 (this letter was written just after Knaresborough's death). Yaxley added that he did not know whether he was related to the Elizabethan martyr priest Richard Yaxley.

INTRODUCTION 15

speech made by the Oates Plot victim Lawrence Hill and several of the pamphlets generated by the trials.[33]

Knaresborough had, therefore, established where some of the relevant material might be found. We have in his draft writings the shadowy outline of a kind of Catholic republic of letters and an information network which prefigure the nineteenth- and twentieth-century networks which built up, gradually, the case that was eventually made successfully to Rome for the beatification and canonization of those whom Catholics in England and Wales had traditionally regarded as martyrs. Here we can also see a kind of post-Restoration association and affinity between various shades of Jacobitism, Catholicism, and antiquarianism which allowed for the construction of a version of the Reformation past which was subsequently compatible with some nineteenth-century Church of England reactions to the perceived historical triumphalism of evangelical Protestantism.

One Thomas Metcalfe, a bookseller in Drury Lane, wrote to Knaresborough on 4 March 1707 mentioning Charles Eyston of East Hendred in Berkshire and his library of works on religious topics. Eyston was reputed to have 'the greatest collection of memoirs both in manuscript and print on that subject', that is, Knaresborough's project, 'of any man in England'. It was to be hoped that he 'might lend them for a time or...give us some account of what he has of that nature'. Metcalfe offered to liaise with Eyston through the priest Henry Preston.[34] On 9 March 1707, Eyston wrote to Preston that he was very glad that there was 'so pious and useful [a] design in hand as to perpetuate the memory of our English martyrs'. He had 'often lamented the want of such a work'. This was because 'the example of those glorious champions would animate us to bear with patience' the 'afflictions' which Catholics still suffered because of their religion. He thought someone definitely ought to do it, though it would not be him, despite the fact that he was bored witless by the prospect of pursuing 'husbandry' and 'country sports' in rural Berkshire.[35]

---

[33] Kn., VI, unpaginated section; Challoner, *MMP*, p. 524 (a short extract of the full speech contained in Knaresborough's papers); Anstr., III, p. 168.

[34] Kn., VI, unpaginated section; for Charles Eyston, see Glickman, *The English Catholic Community*, p. 214; G. Glickman, 'Gothic History and Catholic Enlightenment in the Works of Charles Dodd', *HJ* 54 (2011), pp. 347–69, at pp. 351–2; *ODNB, sub* Eyston, Charles (article by T. Harmsen); Anstr., III, pp. 175–6. Martyrological texts had been left as a legacy to Eyston by the convert to Rome Joshua Basset (d.25 June 1715), who had in January 1687 been appointed by James II as master of Sidney Sussex College, for whom, see *ODNB, sub* Basset, Joshua (article by N. Rogers). The copies of the books sent to Eyston by Bassett are still at Hendred House, East Hendred: Edward Courtney, *R.P. Petri Writi, Sacerdotis Anglie Societ. Iesu*...(Antwerp, 1651); Joannes Rubeus, *Narratio Mortis in Odium Fidei Londini in Anglia Illatae R. A. P. Mauro Scotto*...(Rome, 1657); Maurice Chauncy, ed. Arnold Havens, *Commentariolus de Vitae Ratione et Martyrio Octodecim Cartusianorum*...(Ghent, 1608; for the complex publication history of which see ARCR, I, nos 238–9).

[35] Kn., VI, unpaginated section; see also Kn., VII, p. 241. One of the texts which Charles Eyston could have loaned to Knaresborough was Nicholas Harpsfield's 'A Treatise of Marriage...', which had been transcribed in 1706 by Charles's brother William; see N. Pocock (ed.), *A Treatise on the Pretended Divorce between Henry VIII and Catharine of Aragon*...(Camden Society, new series, 21, 1878), preface; E. V. Hitchcock and E. W. Chambers (eds), *The Life and Death of Sr Thomas Moore, knight,*

16   CATHOLICS AND TREASON

Eyston was, however, soon engaged in reading similar sources to the ones used by Knaresborough in order to construct his own work on the pre-Reformation Church and the religious orders, and their fate at the hands of Henry VIII and his mercenary butchers. The first part of Eyston's work, entitled 'A Poor Little Monument to all the Old Pious Dissolved Foundations of England', focused on the pre-Reformation Church's monastic institutions. It incorporated a searing attack on the venality of the Henrician State, and it lambasted Bishop Gilbert Burnet's version of the sixteenth-century Reformation. Partly via its references to the works of High Churchmen and Nonjurors as sources, Eyston's account of the cynicism of the secular power's assaults on the religious in the period up to Henry VIII's desecrations of the Church and executions of non-compliant clergy serves as a kind of analogue to the attacks on Erastianism in his own time. (Eyston also made use of the earl of Castlemaine's *Catholique Apology*.)[36] Likewise, Gabriel Glickman judges that Jeremy Collier's description of the treatment of St Anselm by King William II was a 'thinly veiled parallel' of the ill usage of the Church in the 1690s. This was a narrative which was followed closely by Charles Dodd, the publication of whose *Church History* coincided with the release of Challoner's *Memoirs*.[37]

Knaresborough's papers brought together information on the case of Lady Margaret Constable. Lord Dunbar ('who has a very good memory', said Mr Tunstall, Knaresborough's informant) remembered in June 1718 that she had been arrested, with 'two other ladies'—'Lady St John' and, according to the family servant and retainer Mrs Rains, 'Lady Eure'—at Upsall Castle for 'harbouring two priests'. The latter two women conformed and were reprieved. Lady Constable

sometimes Lord High Chancellor of England...by Nicholas Harpsfield (Oxford, 1932), pp. cciv–ccv. Eyston used Harpsfield in his own 'A Poor Little Monument to all the Old Pious Dissolved Foundations of England: A Short History of Abby's, All Sorts of Monastery's, Colleges...', unpaginated manuscript at Hendred House, p. 253. In 1719 Eyston sent to Thomas Hearne a copy of part of Harpsfield's manuscript; see T. H. B. M. Harmsen, *Antiquarianism in the Augustan Age: Thomas Hearne 1678–1735* (Oxford, 2000), p. 269; Bodl., Rawlinson (letters) 5, no. 40, H 27b, no. 279. In a letter of 2 April 1707 Preston mentioned that Brian Orrell had made 'a collection out of [John] Stow' and that he (Preston) himself had made 'some notes of my own out of Sir Richard Baker's chronicle': Kn., VI, unpaginated section; for Baker (who wrote against William Prynne's *Histrio-Mastix*), see *ODNB*, sub Baker, Richard (article by G. H. Martin). Baker was one of the sources heavily relied upon by Eyston and was also a source for Knaresborough: Eyston, 'A Poor Little Monument', in the section on Gilbert Burnet in the 'Alphabetical Catalogue of Writers...'. Eyston was at this date collecting very considerable numbers of Catholic books; for the visit in 1717 by Thomas Hearne and Thomas Rawlinson to view Eyston's collection, see Harmsen, *Antiquarianism*, p. 270; Bodl., Rawlinson (letters) 5, no. 12. For Eyston's later correspondence with Thomas Hearne, soliciting texts on *inter alia* English martyrs of the Reformation, see Bodl., Rawlinson (letters) 5, nos 13, 15, 26, 27, 29. In 1716 Hearne had published a Latin edition of William Roper's life of Sir Thomas More; see E. V. Hitchcock (ed.), *The Lyfe of Syr Thomas Moore...* (1935), p. xvi.

[36] Eyston, 'A Poor Little Monument', esp. the preface (dated 4 September 1719), pp. 158–9, ch. 25, and *passim*, as well as the section on Burnet in the 'Alphabetical Catalogue of Writers...'); for Castlemaine, see pp. 507, 540–1, 540 n.15, 556–7 n.82 below.

[37] Glickman, *The English Catholic Community*, p. 215. For a forensic account of the way that Dodd's *Church History* is constructed, see Glickman, 'Gothic History'.

INTRODUCTION   17

was condemned to death but was herself reprieved via the good graces of Thomas Sackville, Lord Buckhurst, though only after a transfer of half the manor of Hackness to the earl of Huntingdon did not immediately secure the required result. The two priests, it was claimed, were called Ingleby and Mush. This last piece of information about the priests was very unlikely to be true, as Mr Tunstall was aware.[38] But it demonstrates that there was a long memory in some of these families associated with resistance to the Elizabethan Reformation.

Knaresborough's martyrology was really an attempt to write a history of the English Reformation since the accession of Elizabeth. It relied on what one might call the usual-suspect texts—the historical writers who had, to a greater or lesser degree, queried aspects of some of the godlier Protestant accounts of the coming of the Reformation—among others William Camden, John Stow, Edmund Howes, Sir Richard Baker, Peter Heylyn, and Jeremy Collier. Collier was a leading nonjuring foe and critic of Burnet.[39] These were more or less exactly the same works as the books to which scholars and historians such as Charles Eyston had already turned.[40] Eyston's own contacts were with Nonjurors and Jacobites such as Thomas Hearne.[41] For Eyston, John Stow could be believed when he 'protested...that he never was swayed by favour or fear in any of his writings but that he had impartially to the best of his knowledge delivered the truth'. The 'collector hereof' (meaning Eyston himself, presumably) had 'heard Sir Roger L'Estrange, a very good judge in History, say that it was a reproach to the nobility and gentry of this kingdom that the best and most impartial historiographer England had had since the Reformation was John Stow the tailor'.[42]

[38] Kn., VI, unpaginated section: C. Tunstall to John Knaresborough, 19 June 1718, writing from Burton Constable (the letter says that 'one [priest], being a young man, made his escape'); HC 1604–29, III, p. 634. It is more than possible that there is a confusion here with the incident when Lord Sheffield arrested two priests 'in one house' belonging to Sir Henry Constable, and a third absconded: HMCS, XVIII, p. 247; see p. 365 below. Mrs Rains was 'a servant' to Mr Tunstall's 'aunt [Mrs] Constable': Kn., VI, unpaginated section: C. Tunstall to John Knaresborough, 19 June 1718. Mrs Rains believed that John Mush had been executed, which, as Mr Tunstall knew, he had not been, whereas Francis Ingleby definitely was put to death.

[39] A. Starkie, 'Contested Histories of the English Church: Gilbert Burnet and Jeremy Collier', Huntingdon Library Quarterly 68 (2005), pp. 335–51; ODNB, sub Howes, Edmund (article by C. DeCoursey); Baker, Richard (article by G.H. Martin); Collier, Jeremy (article by E. Salmon); W. Nicolson, The English, Scotch and Irish Historical Libraries...(3rd edition, 1736), pp. 117–18. Collier was a crucial source for demonstrating that the dissolution of the monasteries had been driven by mercenary considerations: Eyston, 'A Poor Little Monument', p. 153. For Challoner's deployment of some of the same sources (i.e. as were used by Knaresborough and Eyston) in order to write his account of Oliver Plunket, see Challoner, MMP, pp. 574–6.

[40] See, e.g., Eyston, 'A Poor Little Monument', ch. 24.

[41] See pp. 15–16 n.35 above. Eyston had been suspected of and imprisoned for Jacobite political activism: ODNB, sub Eyston, Charles (article by T. Harmsen); Harmsen, Antiquarianism, pp. 256–7. For the connection between Jacobitism and antiquarianism, see P. Monod, Jacobitism and the English People, 1688–1788 (Cambridge, 1989), p. 287; Glickman, The English Catholic Community, pp. 209 f.

[42] Eyston, 'A Poor Little Monument', in the section on Stow in the 'Alphabetical Catalogue of Writers...'.

18   CATHOLICS AND TREASON

As is well known, Burnet's providence-laden version of the Reformation described the way in which godly reform took hold in spite of the questionable religious opinions of Henry VIII and the disaster of the accession of Mary. This line was simply reversed by Knaresborough. Having related the failure of the Marian religious settlement, Knaresborough comments that 'we may observe that the judgments of God are never more fearful than when he punishes the sins of a people with the loss of their religion'. 'Had not Almighty God been highly provoked, it would not have been in the power of a small number of men, however confederated, to have effected such a total suppression of the ancient and established religion of this kingdom' and to have done this 'so suddenly'.[43]

Knaresborough died in late 1722. He never had sufficient time, it seems, to get his drafts into publishable form. Knaresborough's intellectual successor was Charles Dodd, and indeed Knaresborough had followed Dodd's early works.[44] Dodd's massive three-volume history of the English Church does something not dissimilar to Knaresborough's project. It is not primarily a martyrology, but it incorporates material about those who were regarded as martyrs by their co-religionists.[45]

Bishop Challoner, writing and publishing at around the same time as Dodd, concentrated, by contrast, on producing a historical martyrology. Challoner's was a work of huge proportions. At one level, Challoner's book was about the sharpest of the political conflicts of the period up to 1681. But from it, as we have already remarked above, many of the relevant political clues and signposts were methodically extracted so that it could pass as in some sense a pastoral work, entirely compatible with Challoner's exercise of his ministry in mid-eighteenth-century London. Challoner himself, writing to Lord Teynham in July 1742, shortly after publication, said merely that his lordship would find in it 'many rare examples of Christian piety and fortitude' which would encourage him to 'follow with a constancy worthy of a Christian nobleman the happy and glorious path of virtue and religion in spite of all opposition of the world, the flesh and the Devil'. In other words, the book would serve a similar function to that of Challoner's more obviously devotional volumes.[46] It is a pastoral encouragement to the reader to contemplate the virtues of the martyrs. As we have seen, in that there is an argument in it, it is that these people died for their 'religion' alone. This was not, of course, exactly a conceptual novelty—it was the line taken in almost all sixteenth- and seventeenth-century martyrology. But his work is fundamentally different from

---

[43]   Kn., I, pp. 58–9; cf. Starkie, 'Contested Histories', pp. 345–6.

[44]   Pages of Dodd's *Flores Cleri Anglo-Catholici. Or an Account of All the Eminent Clergymen, who, by their Virtue, Learning and Deaths, have Supported the Cause of the Church of Rome, in England since 1500* (np, nd [*c.* 1720]) are among Knaresborough's working papers: Kn., VI, unpaginated section.

[45]   Dodd, *CH*.

[46]   R. Luckett, 'Bishop Challoner: The Devotional Writer', in Duffy, *Challoner and his Church*, pp. 71–89, at p. 79, citing Burton, *LT*, I, p. 197.

some of the earlier sources on which he could equally well have drawn, for example Nicholas Sander and the work of the Jesuit Pedro de Ribadeneira, on whom, of course, he did draw. Challoner virtually excludes any kind of historical narrative wrapper, such as the one that Knaresborough deployed, although Challoner trusted that his work 'would not be disagreeable to the lovers of history, of what persuasion soever they might be in matters of religion'. In fact, he wrote that 'the following sheets are presented to the reader as a supplement to English history, which appeared to the publisher' to be 'so much the more wanting' in the context of 'how much the less the trials and executions of Catholics...have been taken notice of by the generality of English historians'. For 'if men of all persuasions read with pleasure the history of the lives and deaths, even of the most notorious malefactors', not because they were 'delighted with their crimes but because they there' encountered 'an agreeable scene of stories unknown before' and often came across 'a surprising boldness and bravery in their enterprises, how much more may it be expected that every generous English soul should be pleased to find in the following memoirs so much fortitude and courage, joined with so much meekness, modesty and humility, in the lives and deaths of so many of his countrymen who have died for no other crime than their conscience'.[47]

On the other hand, the polemical overtones of the *Memoirs* could hardly be ignored by contemporaries.[48] John Lingard 'used to declare', or so said his friend T. E. Gibson, that Challoner's work constituted 'the best state papers he had ever examined and that the time would come when they would supersede [John] Foxe's lying stories even' in the opinion of 'many of the most prejudiced' sort of people.[49]

This sense of the capacity of Challoner's text to set the record straight and, potentially, to rewrite English history remained very much alive in the nineteenth century. The campaigner and MP William Cobbett, though not himself a Catholic, supported Catholic emancipation. In the mid-1820s, relying heavily in places on John Lingard's massive multivolume *History of England* (which itself did refer to Challoner), Cobbett wrote and published an account of the Reformation which was entirely compatible in places with Challoner's book.[50] Thomas Law's preface to the 1878 edition declared how surprising it was that, 'until the last few years, the fearful story which' Challoner related 'with such remarkable accuracy and moderation should have failed to obtain a hearing'. It was in many ways bizarre that 'Foxe's "Book of Martyrs", notwithstanding the repeated exposure of its

---

[47] Challoner, *Memoirs of Missionary Priests* (1741–2 edition), vol. I, sig. A2^{r-v}.
[48] S. Gilley, 'Challoner as Controversialist', in Duffy, *Challoner and his Church*, pp. 90–111, at p. 105.
[49] Burton, *LT*, I, pp. 172–3.
[50] William Cobbett, *A History of the Protestant Reformation in England and Ireland* (1896), esp. chs 9–11; see also J. Drabble, 'Mary's Protestant Martyrs and Elizabeth's Catholic Traitors in the Age of Catholic Emancipation', *Church History* 51 (1982), pp. 172–85.

20   CATHOLICS AND TREASON

exaggerations and absurdities', had 'never ceased to be a popular work with all classes in this country', so much so that 'every child' knew 'something of the executions for heresy in the reign of Mary Tudor'. However, 'many an English gentleman' had grown up 'in total ignorance of the fact that, under the government of Elizabeth, with the active co-operation of the Anglican bishops, there were put to a most barbarous and shameful death for conscience's sake at least one hundred and twenty-four Catholic priests and as many as fifty-seven laymen and women'. Many more were completely ignorant of 'how long and how fiercely this persecution raged' and that, 'in the subsequent reigns, the penal laws increased rather than diminished in number and severity'. For the 'blood of Catholics, lay as well as clerical, continued to flow on the scaffold up to the year 1681, when the total number of English martyrs (excluding those of Henry VIII) was reckoned at about two hundred and sixty'. Moreover, 'the same sanguinary laws remained in full force during the greater part of the eighteenth century, subjecting the Catholic priest at all times to constant molestation by prosecutions, fines or even imprisonment for life, for the sole crime of saying Mass'. Law believed that 'within the last few years... the real facts of the case have become more generally known', and the 'importance of their bearing on the history of the Reformation in this country' was 'better understood', while the 'true character and heroism of this noble army of Catholic martyrs' was 'more justly appreciated'.[51]

These assumptions and perceptions were what lay behind the later nineteenth- and twentieth-century investigations of Reformation history in order to satisfy the questions asked by the relevant curial officials in Rome, who were asked to declare that those who had the reputation in the Catholic community as martyrs for the faith should be formally recognized as such. That, however, is not what the rest of this volume is about. Rather, we work back from Challoner and his sources in the eighteenth century into the Reformation period in order to ask some of those difficult questions about the issue of persecution and toleration, and how contemporaries, Catholics and others, remembered and recorded the events which eventually became, in some sense, set in stone in Challoner's book on the subject. The contemporary accounts of the relationship between different kinds of Catholic and the State have been routinely excluded from so-called 'mainstream' narratives of post-Reformation politics. Even where contemporary memorialization of the topic of persecution and martyrdom has made it into modern-day scholarship, the tendency has been to deprive the events in question of the contexts which help us make sense of them politically.[52] This volume asks whether it

[51] Challoner, ed. Law, *Memoirs*, part I, T. G. Law's preface, pp. ix–x. For the problems of the 1878 edition, see Burton, *LT*, I, p. 172. Law had recently published *A Calendar of the English Martyrs of the Sixteenth and Seventeenth Centuries* (1876).

[52] See, e.g., A. Walsham, 'Beads, Books and Bare Ruined Choirs: Transmutations of Catholic Ritual Life in Protestant England', in B. Kaplan, B. Moore, H. van Nierop, and J. Pollmann (eds), *Catholic Communities in Protestant States: Britain and the Netherlands c. 1570–1720* (Manchester, 2009), pp. 103–22, at p. 116.

INTRODUCTION 21

is possible to put them back into the contexts out of which they came, and what that might tell us about the period as a whole.

Of course, the tendency is still in some quarters to regard 'Catholic history' as (at best) marginal. To be fair, there have been times when confessionally Catholic historians have given other scholars every reason to regard Catholic scholarship as essentially conservative (and not in a good way), hidebound, introspective, and obsessive.[53] In 2005 Ethan Shagan commented on a conference on the topic of English Catholicism in the Reformation, held in the late 1990s. The purpose of the conference had been to 'break free of the constraints' with which it had traditionally been encumbered, that is to say, 'its largely conservative framework' and 'the hagiographic tone of traditional scholarship'. Unfortunately, as Professor Shagan remarked all too accurately on the day's proceedings, 'despite the best intentions of both the organizers and the speakers', it 'was as if an invisible force field was preventing English Catholic history from reaching out to the wider world'.[54]

But if at various points in the period itself Catholicism (and particularly Catholic separatism) seemed to be anything but conservative and certainly not marginal, equally there has been more than a hint of English exceptionalism in the supposedly 'mainstream' scholarly responses to Catholic historiography of the post-Reformation period. Here we have an un- or barely stated assumption that the emergence of whatever it is that people take to be a consensus in the Church of England about its doctrine and its history (though there is little agreement among modern historians, let alone theologians, about how such a consensus might be defined) was crucial to the formation of the English national character and had nothing to do with most of contemporary Europe. Anything in the post-Reformation English Church which seemed to look towards the principal European States of the period and their national Churches, and of course the papacy, could therefore be discounted.

The records of Catholic separatism were not generated out of the ether but came out of a fairly precise set of political events and circumstances and polemical opinions and responses. They can be reintegrated into a narrative of the period which is arguably a mainstream one, that is to say, centred on a range of events and sources which are still to be found in many published accounts of the period. In fact, one can make a case that, from the later nineteenth century onwards, and particularly after the last war, Catholic attempts to describe and construe historically, this way and that, what they took to be an aberration in their national Church hundreds of years before, and to narrate the resulting

---

[53] Alison Shell points to the assumption that 'Catholic' history almost inevitably has to have 'conservative roots': A. Shell, *Catholicism, Controversy and the English Literary Imagination, 1558–1660* (Cambridge, 1999), pp. 6, 9.

[54] E. Shagan (ed.), *Catholics and the 'Protestant Nation': Religious Politics and Identity in Early Modern England* (Manchester, 2005), preface, p. vi.

oppression, as they saw it, of their co-religionists during that period, captured some of the principal uncertainties and ambiguities in the ways that religious identities were defined in England and Britain during the sixteenth and seventeenth centuries. I think it is even fair to say that it remains impossible to narrate the principal ideological collisions of post-Reformation England without the material that was central to the work of, among others, Bishop Challoner. This, at least, is the implication of Parts II and III of this volume.

In the next chapter, however, we briefly look at the way in which contemporary martyrologies were written (and rewritten) by Catholics; in other words, at how the contemporary case was made that Catholic Christians were suffering what could empirically be demonstrated to be a persecution, and why that might be significant. We look also at how successive Tudor and Stuart regimes replied to that claim; and then at the ways in which successive generations of historians have tried to deal with that corpus of material.

2

Catholic Martyrdom and the Writing of English Reformation History

The Appropriation of Tradition

Chapter 1 claimed that there ought to be a connection between, on the one hand, the way that modern scholars write about the Reformation in the British Isles and, on the other, the compiling of martyrological materials both in the period itself and subsequently. But because of the way in which those materials were brought together, particularly during the later nineteenth and earlier twentieth centuries by Catholic scholars, other scholars, to put it mildly, did not take them seriously.[1] Notoriously, in the 1950s Hugh Trevor-Roper expressed a withering contempt for the English Jesuit literary-historical tradition. Elizabethan Catholics who met death for the sake of religion ('bores') had, Trevor-Roper thought, been 'martyred again... not by Protestants but' by writers such as Philip Caraman and Christopher Devlin, who tried to make out that they were as pure as the driven snow when, actually, they were not.[2] Quite what Trevor-Roper would have thought of the noted Dryden scholar Professor Anne Barbeau Gardiner's review of Anne Dillon's volume on sixteenth-century martyrology, published in 2002, is anyone's guess. Professor Gardiner makes the claim that the book in effect endorsed the Elizabethan State's decision to prosecute certain Catholics as traitors. For Gardiner, Dillon's account of Clitherow is a case of 'blaming the victim'.[3] Another review, again by Professor Gardiner, has seen the formulation of the term CINO ('Catholic in Name Only') to describe those 'intellectuals' who want to 'deconstruct the English martyrs'. The preliminary blurb which prefaces the review warns the leading Catholic historical society in the United Kingdom that

---

[1] See M. Questier, *Memory, Sanctity and Religion in England c. 1850–1987* (forthcoming).
[2] H. Trevor-Roper, *Historical Essays* (1957), p. 113, cited in McCoog, *SJ*, p. 6. There were, in fact, post-war Catholic scholars who dissociated themselves from what they regarded as a too one-sided Catholic version of the past. See, e.g., A. F. Allison and D. M. Rogers, review of L. Hicks, *An Elizabethan Problem: Some Aspects of the Careers of Two Exile-Adventurers* (1964), in *RH* 8 (1965–6), pp. 285–7; cf. L. Hicks, 'Elizabeth's Early Persecution of Catholics', *Month* 147 (1926), pp. 289–304.
[3] A. B. Gardiner, 'Open Season on Catholic History in the UK?', http://www.newoxfordreview.org/reviews.jsp?did=0104-gardiner. See also S. Caldwell, review of Lake and Questier, *Trials*, reviews page, *Catholic Herald* (19 August 2011), claiming that the text in question was 'sneering' at the memory of the martyrs. One former colleague of mine, on reading this chapter in typescript, opined, not unreasonably, that direct involvement in the Catholic historiography of the Reformation in England could be likened to 'living in a box of frogs'.

Catholics and Treason: Martyrology, Memory, and Politics in the Post-Reformation. Michael Questier, Oxford University Press. © Michael Questier 2022. DOI: 10.1093/oso/9780192847027.003.0002

24 CATHOLICS AND TREASON

its members are 'blind to the enemy within' and 'oblivious to the damage it is doing to the Faith of the English martyrs whose lives they have long championed'.[4]

On this basis, serious scholars might conclude that it is best to leave well alone. But, in fact, as Thomas Freeman points out, it is not just Catholicism which has had its difficulties here: 'if martyrdom is at the heart of early modern English religion and religious culture, for the past few decades' in its entirety 'it has been consigned to the margins of scholarship'.[5] Recent writing, principally by Dr Freeman himself, has started to drag it into the mainstream. In addition, one can cite here the work of Brad Gregory on comparative martyrology, Peter Marshall on the politics of the Henrician treason laws, John Knott and Susannah Monta on the literary and dramatic potential of martyrology, and Anne Dillon on the visual depiction of martyrdom.[6] But, as Freeman rightly says, above all there remains the problem of the 'distaste which scholars feel for martyrs and the religious "fanaticism" which they epitomize'.[7] There has also been a seemingly inexorable divide between those who work on Protestant martyrs and those who work on Catholic ones, just as there is a more generally unequal and asymmetrical relationship between the Protestant and Catholic historical and historiographical traditions.[8] While the Protestant martyrs of the English Reformation have almost always been located near the centre of the narrative of that Reformation, and are associated with the emergence, in some sense, of Western liberal modernity and tolerance, this is simply not the case with the Catholic victims of the early modern English and British State. That side of the topic has much less often attracted scholarly attention, certainly not for the period after 1558. In turn, those who know most about Catholic martyrology have been the least prepared to discuss it or allow that someone else might know about it, or be able to discuss it, at all.

Beyond these difficulties, there is a more general problem caused by the records of Catholic martyrdom. At least until quite recent times, most of the surviving

---

[4] A. B. Gardiner, 'Blaming the Victim', published in *Christian Order* (2011), http://www.christian-order.com/features_2011/features_junejuly11_bonus.html, including preliminary comment. The blurb preceding the review incorporates its own virtual fatwa: 'until such time as Anne Dillon and Michael Questier are prepared to renounce their injurious views, all faithful Catholics are obliged to spurn them and their works [3 [sic for 2] Thess. [3:] 6, 14]'.

[5] T. S. Freeman, 'Introduction: Over their Dead Bodies: Concepts of Martyrdom in late Medieval and early Modern England', in T. S. Freeman and T. F. Mayer (eds), *Martyrs and Martyrdom in England c. 1400–1700* (Woodbridge, 2007), p. 4.

[6] B. Gregory, *Salvation at Stake: Christian Martyrdom in Early Modern Europe* (1999); P. Marshall, 'Papist as Heretic: The Burning of John Forest, 1538', *HJ* 41 (1998), pp. 351–74; J. R. Knott, *Discourses of Martyrdom in English Literature, 1563–1694* (Cambridge, 1993); S. Monta, *Martyrdom and Literature in Early Modern England* (Cambridge, 2005); Dillon, *CM*; A. Dillon, *Michelangelo and the English Martyrs* (Farnham, 2012); see also A. G. Dickens and J. Tonkin with K. Powell, *The Reformation in Historical Thought* (Oxford, 1985), ch. 2; J. T. Rhodes, 'English Books of Martyrs and Saints of the Late Sixteenth and Early Seventeenth Centuries', *RH* 22 (1994), pp. 7–25.

[7] Freeman, 'Introduction', p. 5, citing C. Marsh, *Popular Religion in Sixteenth-Century England* (Basingstoke, 1998), p. 7.

[8] Freeman, 'Introduction', p. 6; see also, e.g., Knott, *Discourses*, p. 10. The obvious exceptions here are Professors Gregory and Monta.

THE WRITING OF ENGLISH REFORMATION HISTORY   25

material was retained in inadequately catalogued manuscript volumes and little-read printed texts. The manuscripts have traditionally been kept in relatively little-used repositories that were off the radar of most scholars; and, one suspects, the survival of the relevant material has itself often been merely fortuitous.[9] If, for example, we did not have John Mush's famous life of Margaret Clitherow, as we easily might not, we would know next to nothing about her circumstances and why the York authorities proceeded against her in the way that they did. In addition, Catholic martyrological writers deliberately did not gather, and even excluded, quite a lot of what the historian might nowadays want to know. As Dr Freeman has convincingly shown, the danger of accusations of pseudo-martyrdom made it necessary to identify the victim as closely as possible with universally accepted martyrological models, mostly from the early Church, and hence to 'prune away' ephemeral details which detracted from that outcome.[10] Also, for those Catholics who wanted to publish accounts of martyrs at or shortly after the time of their deaths, there were risks in being too specific. As William Allen wrote in August 1583, concerning his *Briefe Historie of the Glorious Martyrdom of Twelve Reverend Priests*, 'we have a difficulty in publishing all that we have written. Grave dangers ensue to the Catholics from any detailed description of their persons or affairs. Their names, rank and holy deeds should indeed be published, and might be read both with pleasure and profit. But the Catholics will not allow it, lest they be betrayed by these indications and hurried off to prison or even to death.'[11]

[9] The suppression of the Society of Jesus in the eighteenth century was, archivally speaking, a catastrophe. As James Connell narrated it to Charles Plowden, 'after the abolition [of the Society], orders were given to examine and clear the archives [and] whole baskets of papers were then thrown out by persons who little knew the value of many of these papers': Edwards, *EJ*, p. 370. Many manuscripts of the English College at Douai were destroyed during the French Revolution. Even as the vice-postulators were struggling in the 1960s to map out the documentary trail left by English Catholic martyrs, Joseph Bamber reported on 29 November 1961 that, at Chingle Hall at Goosnargh in the Lancaster diocese, there was, apparently, a contemporary place of concealment for Catholic clergymen and that a quantity of manuscript material had been found there but it had been incinerated (because the owners 'could not read the Old English'): AAW, Go. 2/147 (Minutes of Meetings of Diocesan Representatives of the Office of the Vice-Postulation, 29 November 1961, 31 Farm Street, London).

[10] T. S. Freeman, '"Great Searching out of Bookes and Autors": John Foxe as an Ecclesiastical Historian' (PhD, Rutgers, 1995), p. 104. For an analysis of the martyrologist's construction of constancy and patience, see ibid., pp. 115, 116, 137 (arguing that 'the *apatheia* Foxe described in his martyrs was modelled on the *apatheia* Eusebius described in the martyrs of the early Church'). Cf. P. Collinson, 'Truth and Legend: The Veracity of John Foxe's Book of Martyrs', in A. C. Duke and C. A. Tamse (eds), *Clio's Mirror: Historiography in Britain and the Netherlands* (Leyden, 1985), pp. 31–54, at p. 48. For this aspect of Foxe's oeuvre, see also J. N. King, 'Fiction and Fact in Foxe's Book of Martyrs', in D. Loades (ed.), *John Foxe and the English Reformation* (Aldershot, 1997), pp. 12–35; T. S. Freeman, 'Fate, Faction and Fiction in Foxe's *Book of Martyrs*', *HJ* 43 (2000), pp. 601–23; T. S. Freeman, 'The Importance of Dying Earnestly: The Metamorphosis of the Account of James Bainham in Foxe's Book of Martyrs', in R. N. Swanson (ed.), *The Church Retrospective* (Studies in Church History, 33, Suffolk, 1997), pp. 267–88; S. Covington, *The Trail of Martyrdom: Persecution and Resistance in Sixteenth-Century England* (Notre Dame, Ind., 2003), p. 20.

[11] Knox, *LMCA*, p. 203, trans. in William Allen, ed. J. H. Pollen, *A Briefe Historie of the Glorious Martyrdom of Twelve Reverend Priests...* (1908), p. x.

26 CATHOLICS AND TREASON

Whether confidentiality was an issue or not, there was still an understandable tendency on the part of Catholics to exclude what did not seem to fit with the martyrological archetypes which governed such narratives. The description in Alban Butler's papers of the sufferings of Anthony Middleton and Edward Jones remarked at one point that the trial proceedings at the Old Bailey on 4 May 1590 turned into an argument about the words of the indictment—that, against the statute of 1585 which made treasonable the return to the country of seminary clergy, they came 'contemptuously...into this realm of England'. At this point, 'the two chief justices alleged many reasons to prove it contempt' and 'many other vain speeches and invectives were spoken against' Jones 'by the lord mayor and others, which are not worth the rehearsing'.[12] The Jesuit Christopher Grene's later seventeenth-century martyrological collections omitted huge amounts of material which would have been really useful for us to have; as, for example, when he jotted, in an entry dealing with a letter of 6 May 1607 sent from Richard Blount SJ, '2½ foliis chartae scribit multa de persecutione de Eduardo Coco [Sir Edward Coke]', but Grene did not elaborate as to what Blount had written.[13]

There remains, even now, a real question as to how the historian should approach the topic of martyrdom. 'Martyrs' are not an obvious 'class' of people (for the purposes of systematic archive-based research) in the same way as MPs or civil lawyers. Attempts made in the past to recover all knowable biographical details about these people had something of a distorting effect. The bulk of what the promoters of the 'Cause' of the English and Welsh martyrs gathered from archival sources was essentially quotidian (evidence of birth, early life, locality, genealogy, education, and so on). The claim, even if only implicit, is that their origins, upbringing, and, in the case of clergy, vocation and career were so self-evidently unexceptional, except for the fervour of their spiritual zeal, that the eventual legal proceedings against them could not but be understood as simply

---

[12] Pollen, *UD*, p. 183 (ABPFC, fo. 6ʳ).

[13] ABSJ, Collectanea M, p. 100ᵇ. Grene probably thought it unnecessary to copy out many of his sources in full. He could not have known that so much of the material from which he was copying was going to be destroyed, i.e. at the time of the Society's suppression in the eighteenth century. John Morris remarked he had 'done more than any other man to save the records' of the martyrs' 'sufferings from perishing and to transmit to us materials for the history of the times of persecution in England': Morris, *TCF*, I, p. 3. For an excellent account of the content and extent of Grene's work, see *AWCBC*, pp. 2514–16. For the location of, and relationship between, Grene's 'Collectanea' volumes, see Morris, *TCF*, III, pp. 3–7; *AWCBC*, p. xlvi; Pollen, *UD*, p. 191 (for the martyrological volume which was once at the English College in Rome, labelled 'A', and which was subsequently, as it appears, broken up). In AAW, A IV, material from item no. 35 onwards was formerly the entire Collectanea B volume; it is now located at ABSJ. There is another volume of Grene's martyrological writings (based principally on a series of printed sources, but using Grene's Collectanea M) located at Stonyhurst: Stonyhurst MS A V, no. 21. Collectanea F is kept at the English College in Rome (AVCAU, Liber 1422); it includes items secured by Henry Garnet (such as, for example, John Fletcher's narrative of his imprisonment) and sent by Garnet to Robert Persons: Morris, *TCF*, III (IFT), p. 326; Foley, *RSJ*, III, pp. 215–20; *AWCBC*, p. 588 (Patrick Barry's analysis of Collectanea F, item 1). For Grene, see A. Czaja, 'Catholic History and Memory in Christopher Grene's Collectanea' (MPhil, Cambridge, 2013).

malicious, that is, as the State decided to pervert the machinery of justice in order to arrest, convict, and execute them. In turn this contributed to the Catholic tyrannophobe account of the period. This was because so much of what one could recover of the everyday existence of separatist Catholics apparently gave one absolutely no clue as to why some of them should have been targeted for destruction, except for the tiny minority of those involved in actual conspiracies, and they, by implication, were untypical and were, of course, excluded from Rome's processes for establishing heroic sanctity.

So, if we try to do as Brad Gregory recommends, that is, 'confront [the] fundamental religious sensibilities, convictions and practices of committed Christians' who died for their faith and 'reconstruct' rather than 'deconstruct their [the martyrs'] commitments and experiences as far as the evidence permits',[14] how do we go about that task? Some scholars, especially from literature departments, are suspicious of Gregory's approach. Alice Dailey, for example, detects here 'the limitations of historicist readings of martyrology that elide the centrality of discursive form to both the performance and narration of martyrdom'. Furthermore, 'inattention to the literary structures that order the reproduction of martyrdom' disregards 'the constitutive pressure that form asserts over historical events'.[15]

Stories of martyrdom do not, therefore, simply tell you what the martyr actually thought, and that may well be right. On the other hand, there is a limit to what analysis of discursive structures can tell you at all in this respect. For what it is worth, I suppose I am inclined to a 'what-he-said' response to Gregory's explanation of his own methodology.[16] I am also disposed to sympathize with Alison Shell's doubts about, as she puts it, the 'recent fashion for body scholarship' in martyr studies. Seeing 'the corpse on the scaffold more as an opportunity to dissect an inert body with the scalpel of theory' than to tell one anything about the actual person to whom the body belonged raises as many problems as it solves.[17] Anyone who doubts the good sense of Professor Shell's words about the poverty of theory needs only to go to, for example, Ingatestone Hall (a shrine to Catholic Jacobitism) and see the glass case containing the blood-stained suit of clothes

---

[14] Gregory, *Salvation*, pp. 1–2, 8, 10, 11, 15; cf. S. Ditchfield, 'Martyrs are Good to Think With', *Catholic Historical Review* 87 (2001), pp. 470–3.

[15] A. Dailey, *The English Martyr from Reformation to Revolution* (Notre Dame, Ind., 2012), pp. 4–5; see also A. Dailey, 'Making Edmund Campion: Treason, Martyrdom, and the Structure of Transcendence', *Religion and Literature* 38 (2006), pp. 65–83, esp. at p. 66; D. Anderson, *Martyrs and Players in Early Modern England: Tragedy, Religion and Violence on Stage* (Farnham, 2014), p. 14; T. D. Kemp, 'Translating (Anne) Askew: The Textual Remains of a Sixteenth-Century Heretic and Saint', *Renaissance Quarterly* 52 (1999), pp. 1021–45.

[16] See also Anderson, *Martyrs and Players*, p. 14, sensibly stating that the 'two impulses' (theoretical and empirical) do not have to be 'mutually exclusive'.

[17] Alison Shell, review of Dillon, *CM*, at www.history.ac.uk/reviews/review/342. By the same token, as Lisa Clughen once noted, it is all very well, as one academic chose to do, to refer to the Spanish civil war as a 'text', until someone in the audience reminds those listening that 'my father died in that text': M. Reisz, 'Reality Checks', *Times Higher Education* (23 December 2010), p. 40.

28 CATHOLICS AND TREASON

worn by the third earl of Derwentwater at his execution in 1716 after the failed rebellion in favour of the Old Pretender, James III;[18] or, for that matter, to Wardley Hall and view the skull preserved there, by tradition that of the Benedictine Ambrose Barlow, and realize that, whoever it belonged to, at some point, medical evidence suggests, it was impaled on a pike.[19] Joseph Bamber's dramatic medico-historical reconstruction of the execution of Miles Gerard is all too stomach-churningly credible.[20]

Of course, the impression given, quite deliberately, by Challoner's *magnum opus* is that everything one would need to know about the subject is both know-able and known. But, as we have seen, in so many cases the exact circumstances of what happened are simply not possible to recover. About some clergy's arrests, prosecutions, and executions we know virtually nothing. Thus in the case of Richard Horner, who was executed on 4 September 1598 in York, that crucible of contemporary religious politics, we still have little enough idea even about who he was (other than that he came from Bolton Bridge and was ordained in 1595), let alone the chain of events which led up to the trial. All Challoner could say was that 'he was arraigned and condemned merely as a Catholic priest'.[21]

But we also need to think about how we do know the things that we know. We should try to ascertain what was recorded by whom, and what was not, and what that might mean historically. This was a topic which was first seriously addressed by Anne Dillon back in the 1990s.[22] While only a tiny fraction of what happened in many martyrs' cases was documented, almost everything we have on the

---

[18] A. Hamilton, *The Chronicle of the English Augustinian Canonesses Regular of the Lateran, at St Monica's in Louvain* (2 vols, 1906), II, pp. 201–2, 208–10 ('a most beautiful glory appeared over the hearse' following the execution, and his heart 'remained incorrupt' and 'miracles were wrought at his tomb' (p. 209)); for the testimony given by Gilbert Dolan OSB on 10 December 1888 to the Westminster process about the reverence accorded by the Petre family to Derwentwater's physical remains which had been removed from Dilston to Thorndon Hall in October 1874, see AAW, B 57, session. 37, pp. 3, 5.

[19] For Ambrose Barlow's skull, see J. E. Bamber, 'The Skull of Wardley Hall', *RH* 16 (1982), pp. 61–77; see Figure 15.1. As the medical report obtained for the vice-postulators put it, 'an instrument of some kind' had been 'driven into the skull base, immediately behind the palate, with such force as to break the hard basisphenoid and to shatter or crack the walls of the nasal fossae and of the orbits. The blow must have been delivered in a downward direction, upon the upturned base of the skull'. The likelihood was that, while the person's head was 'newly severed from the trunk', it 'was impaled on a pike or similar implement': AAW, Go. 2/147 (Office of the Vice-Postulation, Farm Street, London, bulletin no. 49, 12 September 1961: report read by…the bishop of Salford [George Beck] on the occasion of the authentication of the relic of Blessed Ambrose Barlow); Bamber, 'The Skull', pp. 75–6. For the similar condition of Cuthbert Mayne's skull, see *AWCCBM*, p. 112; and for the state of Christopher Wharton's skull preserved as a relic at Downside Abbey, see *AWCBC*, p. 1322. The archaeological evidence provided by the exhumation in March 1954 of the remains in a grave at the Lady Chapel at Mount Grace, Osmotherley, suggested that one person buried there (possibly Margaret Clitherow) had indeed suffered the penalty of pressing to death (*peine forte et dure*): AAW, Go. 2/147 (papers for 1961: report by James Walsh on Lady Chapel, Mount Grace; Walsh to Cardinal Godfrey, 1 September 1961).

[20] J. E. Bamber, 'The Secret Treasure of Chaigley', *RH* 17 (1985), pp. 307–29.

[21] Challoner, *MMP*, p. 236.

[22] Dillon, *CM*; A. Dillon, 'The Construction of Martyrdom in the English Catholic Community to 1603' (PhD, Cambridge, 1999).

THE WRITING OF ENGLISH REFORMATION HISTORY   29

Catholic martyrs of the post-Reformation period was assembled for a specific purpose by someone or other; nothing like as systematically as John Foxe did for the Marian martyrs, but nevertheless with a very clear set of priorities.

Those priorities were inevitably controversial. The formulation of a martyrological record and roll of honour meant including some people and excluding others.[23] The battles of the sixteenth and seventeenth centuries were still being fought in the eighteenth and the nineteenth centuries by writers such as Charles Dodd and Mark Tierney and, indeed, Charles Butler and John Milner. This does not mean that martyrology is always simply a code for something else—a deployment of the language of suffering and sacrifice for purely Machiavellian political ends, even though some contemporaries certainly accused others of using martyr stories in precisely that way. But the circumstances and events which produced these occasions of public bloodletting and the hinterland of lower-level legal penalties and harassment were inherently politically structured, just as much as were the attempts in subsequent years to produce narratives of them which seemed to leave the 'politics' out.

We need to think also about what I believe are called 'known unknowns'—a phrase/concept which is nothing like as stupid as it is often taken to be. Even those texts, such as Challoner's, which artfully conceal as much as they reveal, leave a trail of clues, scattered here and there, as to the context and circumstances of the events which they record—clues which, moreover, tell us about the political conflicts of the period in a way that virtually no other source can. Sometimes those unknowns are impenetrable. This is one reason for not looking in detail at the Henrician Reformation. Although the life and tribulations of Sir Thomas More at one time seemed to constitute an entire subfield, and there were, on some counts, approximately fifty Catholic martyrs in the period 1535–44, for many of these earlier instances of martyrdom there is not always a great deal of historical evidence available.[24] It is also probably true to say that there was a qualitative difference between, on the one hand, the kinds of confrontation which occurred over religion in the first half of the sixteenth century and, on the other, the violence inflicted on Catholics after 1558, although, of course, virtually all martyr stories have a number of common features.[25]

---

[23] For the first systematic martyrological fact-finding exercise inside the English Catholic community, led by Bishop Richard Smith (during his struggle in the mid- and later 1620s to impose his authority on members of the religious orders), see pp. 459–65 below. See also T. S. Freeman, '"Imitatio Christi with a Vengeance": The Politicisation of Martyrdom in Early-Modern England', in Freeman and Mayer, *Martyrs and Martyrdom*, pp. 35–69.

[24] G. F. Nuttall, 'The English Martyrs 1535–1680: A Statistical Review', *JEH* 22 (1971), pp. 191–7, at pp. 192, 195; ABSJ, CP (Thomas Ashby): memorandum by Patrick Barry, 14 July 1965. See also the comments on Henrician martyrdom in Chapter 4 below.

[25] See, e.g., A. Marotti, *Religious Ideology and Cultural Fantasy: Catholic and Anti-Catholic Discourses in Early Modern England* (Notre Dame, Ind., 2005), pp. 77–89; for similar features in what one might call secular martyrology, see M. Kishlansky, 'Martyrs' Tales', *JBS* 53 (2014), pp. 334–55; M. Zook,

30 CATHOLICS AND TREASON

The majority of this volume will, however, follow the accumulation of texts about post-Reformation martyrdom starting in the later 1570s and dealing with cases from the middle of Elizabeth's reign onwards. Most historians have accepted that, for a number of years after 1558, the relatively modest legal structures of conformity and compliance left the majority of the conservative- and Catholic-minded in relative peace. It is the breaking of that uneasy status quo out of which the principal post-Reformation Catholic martyrological tradition comes. This is the assumption rooted in, among other texts, Bishop Challoner's *Memoirs of Missionary Priests*, following the line of thought in, for example, William Allen's *Briefe Historie* and other publications which damned the mid-Elizabethan regime as a tyranny.[26]

With the end of Elizabeth's reign, one might have expected Catholic discussions of persecution to have faded into the background. The accession of James Stuart saw a peace with Spain which radically changed the relationship between England/Britain and continental Europe. But the topic remained a live one—not least because some Catholics were determined to make sure that it was not forgotten;[27] and, also, because during the seventeenth century, there were periodic lurches backwards and forwards between de facto tolerance and bouts of what Catholics could convincingly claim were persecutory bigotry and violence—notably during the civil wars and again, if briefly, in the Popish Plot agitation of 1679–81.[28]

Persecution and the Catholic Community in (Post-) Reformation England and Britain

Was there a harsh and unrelenting persecution of Catholics in post-Reformation England? Many Protestants of the time tended to say that, if they had witnessed

---

'Violence, Martyrdom, and Radical Politics: Rethinking the Glorious Revolution', in H. Nenner (ed.), *Politics and the Political Imagination in later Stuart Britain: Essays Presented to Lois Green Schwoerer* (Woodbridge, 1997), pp. 75–95, esp. at pp. 82–8; A. Lacey, ' "Charles the First, and Christ the Second": The Creation of a Political Martyr', in Freeman and Mayer, *Martyrs and Martyrdom*, pp. 203–20; J. Coffey, 'The Martyrdom of Sir Henry Vane the Younger: from Apocalyptic Witness to Heroic Whig', in Freeman and Mayer, *Martyrs and Martyrdom*, pp. 221–39; A. Milton, *Laudian and Royalist Polemic in Seventeenth-Century England: The Career and Writings of Peter Heylyn* (Manchester, 2007), p. 128.

[26] ARCR, I, nos 8–11, pp. 972–1011; for Pedro de Ribadeneira's *Historia Ecclesiastica*'s following of Sander, see Weinreich, *PREH*.

[27] For the efforts after 1603 to construct comprehensive and accurate martyr catalogues, see Chapter 11, esp. at p. 371 n.165 below. For the best introduction to the successive catalogues, from 1585 to *c.*1730, of English martyrs, see AWCBC, pp. 2505–13; AWCBC, pp. xlviii–li; see also C. A. Newdigate, 'Quelques Notes sur Les Catalogues des Martyrs Anglais dits de Chalcédoine et de Paris', *Analecta Bollandiana* 66 (1938), pp. 308–33, comparing and analysing the Chalcedon catalogue and the Paris catalogue (AAW, B 28, nos 3 and 10). For other catalogues (including those by John Mush and John Bavant) which are now lost, see AWCBC, pp. 317, 319, citing AAW, B 28, no. 10, p. 302.

[28] See Chapters 12–15 below.

THE WRITING OF ENGLISH REFORMATION HISTORY   31

real persecution in their days, it was during the uniquely frightful, though mercifully brief, reign of Mary Tudor. That, after all, was the lesson of John Foxe's work. Alexander Nowell, dean of St Paul's, allegedly remarked in August 1581 to the pain-wracked Jesuit Edmund Campion, who had been severely tortured in the Tower of London, that for every Catholic who might conceivably have been 'hardly handled' there were 'whole hundreds of Protestants burnt by Catholics'.[29] In any case, some claimed, Campion had not really been badly treated at all.[30] One early seventeenth-century pamphlet, Francis Burton's *The Fierie Tryall of Gods Saints*, declared that 'if the number of persons suffering, and the number of years of both sorts wherein they suffered be compared, and the cause of all their sufferings admitted to be alike, just or unjust (of which there is no comparison) yet did the cruelty of Queen Mary and her popish clergy outstrip Queen Elizabeth and King James conjoined, more than ten for one'. Furthermore, said Burton, 'if I should nominate all those persons who in less than six years', during the reign of Mary Tudor, 'were famished...imprisoned, died in prison, forced to fly, whipped, tortured and tormented only for matter of religion, and some of these by the very hands of bloody Bishop [Edmund] Bonner himself, they would far exceed the number of all such priests and Jesuits as the papists can produce to have endured in England any kind of torture or corporal punishment whatsoever for religion (as they falsely pretend) or otherwise for these fifty and odd years since'.[31] Similarly, Bishop William Barlow in 1609 asked rhetorically whether imposing fines on husbands for their wives' recusancy could be legitimately described as a persecution, at least when compared with the cruelty of the burning of Perotine Massey, who was 'great with child', as recorded in John Foxe's catalogue of martyrs.[32]

This might seem like hyperbole but, at Richard White's execution at Wrexham in October 1584, when the crowd urged the officials to 'take compassion upon the poor prisoner and to let him die', the officials were unwilling to oblige. The hangman himself 'wanted still to do this execution answerable to the bloody wills of the magistrates by reason of which he put the martyr to double pains and

---

[29] Kilroy, *EC*, p. 277, citing Paolo Bombino, *Vita et Martyrium Edmundi Campiani...* (Mantua, 1620), p. 225 (English translation, Bodl., Tanner MS 329, fo. 94ʳ). For Catholic apologias for the Marian treatment of Protestants, see, e.g., Thomas Harding, *A Reioindre to M. Iewels Replie against the Sacrifice of the Masse* (Louvain, 1567), fos 178ʳ, 178ᵛ, 179ʳ, 180ʳ, 181ʳ; Robert Persons, *An Epistle of the Persecution of Catholickes in Englande. Translated out of Frenche into Englishe...* (Douai [imprint false; printed at Rouen], n.d. [1582]), pp. 5–7 ('To the Honourable Lords of her Majesty's Privy Council', written by 'G.T', possibly Gabriel Thimbleby); ARCR, II, no. 627.

[30] Robert Persons said that when the news of Campion's torments became public, i.e. when he 'did utter it in an open audience and in the hearing of our adversaries', they retorted that 'it was a merry pastime', for he 'was cramped or pulled a little, not in earnest but in jest': Persons, *An Epistle*, p. 88; see also *A Declaration of the Favourable Dealing of her Maiesties Commissioners Appointed for the Examination of Certaine Traitours...* (1583), sig. A2ᵛ, Aa3ʳ, A4ʳ⁻ᵛ, cited by Kilroy, *EC*, p. 369.

[31] Francis Burton, *The Fierie Tryall of Gods Saints...As a Counter-poyze to I.W. Priest his English Martyrologe...* (1612), p. 5; ibid., 'A Post-Script to the Well Affected Reader', pp. 4–5.

[32] William Barlow, *An Answer to a Catholicke English-man...* (1609), p. 140.

32 CATHOLICS AND TREASON

exceeded in cruelty the bloody sentence pronounced against him'. For, 'having made a little hole in' White's 'belly', the hangman 'pulled out of the same his guts by piecemeal'. This 'device' did not really work, so he 'mangled' White's 'breast with a butcher's axe to the very chin most pitifully'. Then he tore out 'his entrails' and 'threw them into the fire before his face'. During all of this, White tried to conduct some sort of conversation with the executioner. He 'lifted up his head and shoulders over the hurdle and beholding so cruel a slaughter he said', in Welsh, 'O good God, what is this?', only to be told by the 'jailor' that 'it is an execution for the queen's Majesty'.[33]

But many contemporary Catholics were in absolutely no doubt that they were the victims of a horrendous and tyrannical abuse of the law. In the wake of the trials and executions of Edmund Campion and his friends, Robert Persons wrote that those who were for other crimes condemned to the dreadful penalties specified by the law 'find such favour as either they are...fully dead before they be cut down from the gallows' or at least they 'are suffered to hang till they be half dead...to dull the sense and feeling' of pain 'in the torments following'. But Catholic traitors were 'no sooner hanged than the hangman' cuts 'the halter in sunder and, while they are yet alive...and...of perfect sense and feeling, he brings them to the other torments' and he does this in such a way, 'with such dexterity', that 'they speak also distinctly and plainly after their bowels be dug up...and while the butcher's fingers are scratching at their very hearts and entrails'.[34]

Richard Barret wrote an account of the execution of George Haydock and four others on 12 February 1584. Haydock had expired before being cut down, but the others were conscious when they were disembowelled. To 'increase the violent anguish of the pain they followed a new and untried method, cutting open the breast and dividing it gradually, to reach the heart by stages. No other way, they thought, could more increase and prolong the anguish'—so much so that even 'a certain heretic exclaimed that they were too savage in their thirst for human blood'.[35] Thomas Pilchard was in 1587 'most cruelly mangled, for, being cut down alive and laid on his back, the executioner being a cook and unskilful or careless, first cut him over thwart the belly' and then 'all over the hand'. The 'people' yelled 'out upon' the executioner, at which point 'he began to slit' Pilchard 'up the belly and to pull out his bowels'. The priest 'raised himself and, putting out his hands, cast forward his own bowels, crying out *Miserere mei*'.[36] In 1588, John Hewett, 'either by the malice or negligence of the executioner', 'endured a long and painful

---

[33] Thomas, *WECM*, pp. 120–1.   [34] Persons, *An Epistle*, pp. 96–7.
[35] Renold, *LWA*, p. 91.
[36] Pollen, *UD*, p. 288 (ABSJ, Anglia VII, no. 26, notes made by John Gerard in his draft catalogue of martyrs since 1587, starting with Mary Stuart); for William Warford's version of the same events, see Pollen, *AEM*, p. 263 (ABSJ, Collectanea M, p. 138ª).

death: in so much that the blood burst out at his mouth, nose, ears and eyes'.[37] As for the layman William Pikes in 1591, wrote the Jesuit priest John Gerard, when 'he was cut down alive', the 'officers standing by stretched out his hands and, with their halberds, thrust them through and fastened them to the ground'.[38] Joseph Lambton's execution in 1592 was botched. The hangman was a convicted felon. He lost his nerve halfway through the process, leaving Lambton cut open. The officials then had to persuade a 'Frenchman' to finish Lambton off.[39] In the case of John Rigby, executed in 1600, 'when he felt them pulling out his heart, he was yet so strong, that he thrust the men from him, who held his arms'. Only after all this did 'they cut off his head and quarter...him' and 'disposed of his head and quarters in several places in and about Southwark'.[40]

In the case of Hugh Green at Dorchester, on 19 August 1642, the combination of a bungled execution and a grisly aftermath, even at this distance of time, almost beggars belief. While the priest 'was calling on Jesus, the butcher did pull a piece of his liver out, instead of his heart, and tumbling his guts out, every way', tried to 'see if his heart were not amongst them'. 'Then, with his knife, he raked in the body of this most blessed martyr, who even then called on Jesus'; and this went on 'for more than half an hour', during which time, said the eyewitness narrator Elizabeth Willoughby, 'methought my heart was pulled out of my body, to see him in such cruel pains, lifting up his eyes to heaven, and not yet dead'. Only then did one of the Catholic spectators prevail upon the sheriff to decapitate him. Willoughby recorded in some detail the local population of Dorchester's hatred for Catholics. When she and another gentlewoman asked the sheriff for Green's body, he assented but, 'if we should have offered to carry' away Green's remains, the 'blinded Dorcestrians' would 'have thrown the body and us into the fire'. The 'ungodly multitude...from ten o'clock in the morning, till four in the afternoon, stayed on the hill and sported themselves at football with his head, and put sticks in his eyes, ears, nose and mouth, and then they buried it near to the body, for they durst not set it upon their gate'. This was, apparently, because when the priest John Cornelius had been executed there in 1594, 'they set up his head upon their town gate, and presently there ensued a plague, which cost most of them their lives'.[41]

---

[37] Pollen, *UD*, p. 290 (ABSJ, Anglia VII, no. 26).

[38] Pollen, *UD*, p. 292; Challoner, *MMP*, p. 169.

[39] Anstr., I, p. 205; D. Woodward, '"Here Comes a Chopper to Chop off his Head": The Execution of Three Priests at Newcastle and Gateshead, 1592–1594', *RH* 22 (1994), pp. 1–6, esp. at pp. 1, 3; see pp. 223–4 below.

[40] Challoner, *MMP*, p. 245.

[41] Challoner, *MMP*, pp. 426–7; Kn., IV, pp. 28–31; the versions of Willoughby's memoir from which John Knaresborough worked may be AAW, OB III/ii, nos 179–80; for another narrative of Green's execution, which appears to be derived from Willoughby's but has significant differences, see AVCAU, Liber 1422 [Grene, Collectanea F], section 11; see also p. 515 nn.125–126 below. For the circulation of the substance of Willoughby's account, see, e.g., Jean Chifflet, *Palmae Cleri Anglicani*...(Brussels, 1645), pp. 45–63; Challoner, *MMP*, p. 428. For Knaresborough's copy of Green's gallows oration, see

34 CATHOLICS AND TREASON

These were, as it were, the headline cases. But Catholics regularly claimed that there was also a good deal of suffering in the, by virtually any measure, fairly appalling prison accommodation of the day.[42] This was, they said, a kind of living martyrdom. A number of imprisoned Catholics died in these dreadful places.[43] Roger Wakeman in Newgate was incarcerated near to 'where the quarters of all such as suffer are boiled' and where other prisoners emptied 'their tubs'. The 'filthiness of the air and horrible stink' eventually killed him in November 1582.[44] There were long-term detainees in the Yorkshire gaol system, particularly in the Hull blockhouses where prisoners lived in conditions of, it was said, unbelievable squalor.[45] One narrative in Christopher Grene's manuscripts relates the case of one Mr Horsley who was imprisoned in Hull in c.1580 after speaking disdainfully of the Prince of Orange. Horsley was 'condemned to have his ears cut off' and then he starved to death in gaol, and 'he lay dead so long (how long none knows) that the rats had eaten his face and other places'.[46] As John Knaresborough recorded it, in 1591 'when there was a pestilential fever' raging in York Castle, the Catholic prisoners petitioned to 'have their confinement exchanged into a more wholesome climate during the time of the pestilence'. But 'their...request was rejected unless they would go to church'. When they refused, they were 'left to the mercy of the...distemper'. With 'the infected air and want of proper helps in their sickness and hunger and cold, together with the intolerable stench of the prison, there perished miserably Mr Christopher Watson, a gentleman of great worth and piety and, with him, in a very short time, about twenty more of his companions and...fellow prisoners'.[47]

The question remains, though, how far and in what sense does all of this constitute 'persecution'? The slightly awkward truth for Catholic martyrologists of the period was that there were relatively few martyrs in Reformation and post-Reformation England. This was the case made by, among others, Geoffrey Elton

---

Kn., VI, unpaginated, 'The Speech of Mr Hugh Green...', with the note that it was 'brought from the place of execution by Mrs Martin of Salisbury...who, with divers other Catholics', was present; and she 'delivered it to one Mrs Coffin who is still living and of a great age'.

[42] See, e.g., Persons, *An Epistle*, pp. 79–81, 90–2.

[43] See, e.g., Morris, *TCF*, III (AENB), pp. 26–30, 35–7; Challoner, *MMP*, pp. 104–5 (Thomas Cotesmore, Robert Holmes, Roger Wakeman, James Lomax, Mr Ailworth), 108–9 (Thomas Crowther, Edward Pole, Lawrence Vaux, John Jetter, John Feckenham), 120 (John Harrison), 129 (Martin Sherson, Gabriel Thimbleby). For Christopher Grene's catalogues of 'martyrs and confessors' at York, 1582–1590, i.e. those who died in prison as well as those who were put to death, see Pollen, *UD*, pp. 191–4 (citing ABSJ, Collectanea M, pp. 190^b–1^a; St Mary's College, Oscott, Collectanea E [formerly MS 98, now R11781]); for Grene's more elaborate but, as he was aware, not entirely accurate listing of those who might be reckoned to have died in prison, see Stonyhurst MS A V, no. 21, pp. 44f (and, for the York cases, see pp. 94f).

[44] Anstr., I, p. 369; Challoner, *MMP*, p. 104; ABSJ, Collectanea M, p. 169$^{a–b}$.

[45] Morris, *TCF*, III (WHN), *passim*.

[46] Foley, *RSJ*, III, p. 769 (AVCAU, Liber 1422 [Grene, Collectanea F], section 4, p. 88^b).

[47] Kn., VI, p. 289. By contrast, in October 1611 it was reported that when a priest in the Clink prison died of the plague, permission was given to other Catholic clergy there to leave, as long as they agreed to 'discharge the house': AAW, A X, no. 135, p. 387.

in his, in effect, apologia for Thomas Cromwell.[48] Even by contemporary Catholics' calculations, there were (only) a few hundred people who suffered death by execution for what could be claimed to be their religion. That might still sound like prima facie evidence of cruelty and persecution. But still, there was no equivalent in England of, say, the Council of Troubles in Flanders, or the carnage that occurred during the wars of religion in France; nothing, that is, like the St Bartholomew's Day Massacre, even if that sort of bloodshed was on many occasions the result of popular violence as much as of regime-directed repression.[49]

The use of secular power to regulate religious dissent was not necessarily irrational—in the sense that one might think it would be if it involved punishing people only for their conscientiously held theological beliefs. 'Religion', even in a narrow sense of the word, was (and is) almost never about matters purely spiritual. Everyone knows this, but it is probably worth reiterating the point. To cite the commonplace remarks of just one contemporary disquisition on these topics (a discourse on the Low Countries, written in c.July 1578), even 'the very atheists' conceded that 'there is no foundation on which commonwealths may be more firmly established...than religion'. Indeed, it was the 'chief basis of the power of monarchs and the execution of the laws, the obedience of the subjects, the worshipfulness of magistrates, the terror of evil-doers, and mutual friendship among men'. For this reason, as the law had always recognized, 'one only inviolable religion ought to be tolerated'. Otherwise the 'commonwealth must fall'. Thus, 'no sedition is more dangerous either for the State or for religion or for laws and customs than when the subjects are divided between two opinions'.[50]

Most tolerationist argument of this period tends to concede that coercion in matters of religion is not inevitably wrong of itself, and may even in certain circumstances be positively necessary; but, the claim is that, in some specific cases, those doing the coercing have chosen to coerce the wrong people and that their actions are malicious and cruel.[51] The 'modern' mind, by contrast, tends to regard all 'persecution' simply as a monumental folly.[52] It assumes that toleration, when it came, must have resulted from a rational rejection of religious fanaticism and from the State's decision to step in and prevent religion-based discrimination and

[48] G. R. Elton, *Policy and Police: The Enforcement of the Reformation in the Age of Thomas Cromwell* (Cambridge, 1972), ch. 9.

[49] For the making of this case by contemporary Protestants, see, e.g., Gryffith Williams, *The Best Religion...* (1636), pp. 119–20. I owe this reference to Peter Lake. See also B. Diefendorf, *Beneath the Cross: Catholics and Huguenots in Sixteenth-Century Paris* (Oxford, 1991); Covington, *Trail*, pp. 158–9, 162–3, citing W. Monter, 'Heresy Executions in Reformation Europe 1520–1625', in O. P. Grell and R. Scribner (eds), *Tolerance and Intolerance in the European Reformation* (Cambridge, 1996), pp. 48–64; Graves, *TN*, p. 244; A. Tulchin, 'Massacres during the French Wars of Religion', *Past and Present* (2012), supplement 7, esp. at pp.100–26.

[50] *CSPF 1578–9*, p. 109.

[51] There were some writers in this period who argued for something like toleration on principle, e.g., Sebastian Castellio: Anderson, *Martyrs and Players*, pp. 47–53.

[52] Gregory, *Salvation*, p. 345.

36 CATHOLICS AND TREASON

violence. But, for many an early modern mind, toleration was likely to prevent the proper and right regulation of the Church and commonwealth. It would actually interrupt the appropriate and godly practice of the Christian faith. At one fairly obvious level this was because heterodox members of society would be able to spread their errors. As Brad Gregory puts it, 'the prospect of doctrinal pluralism horrified and disgusted people such as John Calvin and William Allen' alike.[53] Furthermore, many people saw toleration as the correlative of tyranny or, at least, of the tyrant's tendency to permit damage to be done to the true Church and true religion for the sake of temporal political advantage. This was precisely the charge made against those whom some contemporaries pejoratively described as 'politiques'. A toleration beyond what was godly allowed a bad ruler to accept and promote those who were bad Christians. This was the point of the royal supremacy—religion was too important to be left to the whim of individual rulers; hence the duties imposed by the supremacy on those who exercised royal authority.[54]

The (for some) unpalatable truth was that, in England, a case could be made that the Elizabethan regime, even in its most allegedly repressive phases, could show remarkable restraint.[55] There is evidence enough that, in Tudor and Stuart England, if those who were convicted of capital offences relating to the royal supremacy wanted to pull back, they only had to signify that they would gesture at some sort of conformity and the whole thing would stop. Even in martyro-logical accounts constructed around an allegedly unrelenting hostility on the part of the authorities to those who were non-compliant, there is often an element of dialogue and negotiation between those who were stubbornly defiant and those who were prepared, in principle and, often, in practice, to pursue them to their deaths. Sir Thomas More, who had a reputation as a hardliner, said (as Professor Gregory notes) that 'little rigour and much mercy [should be] showed where simpleness appeared and not high heart or malice'.[56] Apparently this had been the case even in Mary's reign, at least out in the provinces. Ralph Houlbrooke's fascin-ating study of Marian Norwich emphasizes how much effort was made to seek compromises with those who might be prepared to offer a modicum of conform-ity; or, rather, it describes both a savage repression there, from time to time, but also a series of sometimes very successful efforts to use more moderate forms of persuasion to secure public displays of compliance.[57] The authorities could do

---

[53] Ibid., p. 346.

[54] See J. Rose, *Godly Kingship in Restoration England: The Politics of the Royal Supremacy, 1660–1688* (Cambridge, 2011), esp. ch. 1.

[55] See also, for a European context, Gregory, *Salvation*, p. 6.   [56] Ibid., p. 76.

[57] R. Houlbrooke, 'The Clergy, the Church Courts and the Marian Restoration in Norwich', in E. Duffy and D. Loades (eds), *The Church of Mary Tudor* (2006), pp. 124–46. Patrick Collinson sug-gests that John Foxe hid the extent to which the Marian regime achieved a thoroughgoing conformity, arguably much more effectively (though in very different circumstances and over a different chrono-logical span) than was managed by Elizabeth's government; see P. Collinson, 'The Persecution in Kent', in Duffy and Loades, *The Church of Mary Tudor*, pp. 309–33.

THE WRITING OF ENGLISH REFORMATION HISTORY   37

this not least because (and one can pick this up if one reads between the lines of many contemporary martyrologies) those who were ideological dissenters did not actually court martyrdom most of the time. Even Sir Thomas More, when he was under the gun, declined to explain exactly why he refused to swear the oath of succession. He hoped, it seems, to shield himself via his silence.[58] The body count as a result of State violence was a fraction, in England, of what it was in Ireland. Even at this distance of time, reading through the Irish calendars of state papers in the later Elizabethan period is a sickening task. The recurrent blood-baths there in the later sixteenth century, and particularly in the 1590s, are, to modern eyes, astonishing, although the regime was dealing there with a quasi-colonial revolt (or, rather, a series of them) and, for the most part, the Irish perception of English oppression is not written up in terms of the experience of martyrdom.[59]

We should probably also keep in mind that our, essentially Western, perceptions of what constitutes unjustifiable cruelty are themselves a problematic category. Our readings of these martyr narratives are coloured by modern sensibilities about the inflicting of pain, particularly in the context of beliefs that the death penalty does not serve the cause of justice; and also by our fear of the kind of mob which appears to take a perverted pleasure in witnessing the infliction of cruelty. Our perspectives are, inevitably, influenced by the gradual move, in Britain at least, in the nineteenth and twentieth centuries towards abolition of the death penalty altogether—so well documented by, for example, V. A. C. Gatrell's very scholarly, but intentionally nauseating, history-of-the-emotions-led *The Hanging Tree*.[60] But, in the early modern period, people tended not to be particularly squeamish about pain and the inflicting of pain. As David Nicholls remarks, it is 'a cliché to say that people in the sixteenth century were inured to the spectacle of

---

[58] Gregory, *Salvation*, p. 263.

[59] See, e.g., J. S. Brewer and W. Bullen (eds), *Calendar of the Carew Manuscripts preserved in the Archiepiscopal Library at Lambeth, 1515–1624* (6 vols, 1867–73), III, pp. 220–60, *passim*. For reflections on the Irish experience of martyrdom in the same period, see P. J. Corish, 'The Irish Martyrs and Irish History', *Archivum Hibernicum* 47 (1993), pp. 89–93. The identification in the later nineteenth century of those regarded as having suffered for the faith in Ireland initially followed a similar path to that taken in England. More than 260 people had their causes considered in and after the 1890s, but in 1975, on Rome's advice, the number was radically reduced and, in September 1992, 17 Irish martyrs were beatified by John Paul II: Corish, 'The Irish Martyrs', p. 89. As Corish remarked in 1989, still the only canonized Irish martyr was Oliver Plunket; the 'very complexity of the structures of persecution' in England left a plethora of records about which people had suffered for their consciences, whereas 'the Irish martyrs inhabited a world that kept fewer records': P. Corish, *The Irish Martyrs* (Dublin, 1989), pp. 3, 4. For the contemporary works which claimed to identify those who had, primarily in the Elizabethan period, suffered in Ireland for the Catholic faith, see ibid., pp. 90–1.

[60] V. A. C. Gatrell, *The Hanging Tree: Execution and the English People 1770–1868* (Oxford, 1994). For a version of Gatrell's case made by reference to the early modern period, see F. Barker, *The Culture of Violence: Tragedy and History* (Manchester, 1993), esp. at pp. 190–1. I would suspect that even a brief and matter-of-fact survey of the work of those who were on the Home Office's official list of public executioners during the nineteenth century and down to the 1960s would be fairly horrific, not to say nauseating, to the average modern-day reader.

38 CATHOLICS AND TREASON

violence' and 'encountered physical cruelty far more casually than we do in the twentieth'.[61] As Sarah Covington sensibly says, 'executions in general were...a deeply ingrained, even quotidian, reality for sixteenth-century English people', as much as they were on the Continent, though one suspects also that there would be people in many of the English counties who did not regularly, if ever, witness these things, and had no desire to, whereas in London and York it was, if not exactly unavoidable, then far more regularly visible.[62] We tend to read the contemporary martyrologies' intense dwelling on what the martyrologists undoubtedly took to be cruelty, often of an appalling kind, as if it were a 'modern' rejection of the use of torture and capital punishment altogether. In the case of high crimes, principally political assassinations, it was not in fact thought inappropriate to torture the condemned to death. Thus George Gilpin reported in an entirely matter-of-fact way in July 1584 that Balthazar Gérard, who had purged the world of William of Orange, had his 'right hand pressed and burnt off with a hot iron engine...[and] afterwards the flesh [was] pulled from his legs, arms and other parts with fired pincers and [only] then [was] his body cut open and quartered alive, during which torments he continued resolute'.[63]

Sympathy for those convicted as heretics was in similarly short supply. When the Jesuit Robert Southwell witnessed three Judaizers being burnt in February 1583, 'two alive and one dead', in Rome in the Campo dei Fiori, very close to the English College, he made the conventional comment that only (dying for) the truth made someone a martyr: 'even to this day do the Jews die in defence of the fables of their Talmud...wherein notwithstanding besides, the denial of the coming of Christ, there are very many ridiculous things'.[64] Southwell certainly showed no compassion for the Arian Francis Kett, who was burned very much alive at Norwich in 1589. Kett 'held that neither Christ nor the Holy Spirit was God; that Christ was not born of the Virgin Mary; that no one should take an oath for any reason whatever'; that 'there should be no magistrates in a Christian republic'; and that children 'ought not to be baptized'. Kett, said Southwell, was 'condemned to death by persons almost like himself' and 'was shortly afterward burned', though he put on 'the perverse appearance of piety'. In a carbon copy of so many executions of Catholics, there were relic hunters there, and 'neither the

---

[61] D. Nicholls, 'The Theatre of Martyrdom in the French Reformation', *Past and Present* 121 (1988), pp. 49–73, at p. 59.

[62] See Covington, *Trail*, pp. 158 (citing P. Jenkins, 'From Gallows to Prison: the Execution Rate in Early Modern England', *Criminal Justice History* 7 (1986), pp. 51–71, at pp. 52–3), 162–3; D. Hay et al. (eds), *Albion's Fatal Tree: Crime and Society in Eighteenth-Century England* (1975).

[63] *CSPF 1583–4*, p. 596. Gérard was regarded, by some, as a martyr, and made show of a martyr-like patience and constancy at his death: *CSPF 1583–4*, p. 627; *CSPF 1584–5*, p. 68.

[64] See Devlin, *LRS*, p. 84; Robert Southwell, *An Epistle of Comfort*...(Paris [imprint false, printed secretly at Arundel House, London], n.d. [1587–8]), fos 184ᵛ–5ʳ.

fellow's bones nor his very ashes could be found, so eagerly did' certain people 'try to get these dregs'.[65]

Nor did people who condemned the State's cruelty, as they saw it, towards their co-religionists necessarily empathize with those condemned for more mundane criminality.[66] Among those who helped to define the English Catholic martyrological tradition was the remarkable Luisa de Carvajal, a high-born Spanish visitor to London in the early seventeenth century. She admired the passion and the zeal of those Catholics, principally clergy, who were still going to the scaffold in James's reign. But her maximum response, outside Newgate, on a July morning in 1607, when confronted with the sight of 'thirteen or more criminals [who] were' being 'brought down and strapped into the carts', was that it was only a 'sad spectacle to see them going off to die' at Tyburn because they had 'no enlightenment or comfort' and were 'so close to eternal damnation'. (See Figure 2.1.) The

Figure 2.1 Stone marking the site of the Tyburn tree on the traffic island at the junction of Edgware Road, Bayswater Road, and Oxford Street, London.

---

[65] McCoog, LRS, p. 156 (Robert Southwell to Claudio Acquaviva, 7 September 1588).
[66] Cf. Dillon, *Michelangelo and the English Martyrs*, pp. 233–5.

40 CATHOLICS AND TREASON

other Catholics watching with her had, like her, thought that they were going to see the execution of a priest. On being told that the priest in question had been reprieved, they simply lost interest and started to drift away, and were bothered neither one way nor the other about the condemned criminals who were about to be hanged.[67]

The priest Benjamin Norton chuckled in October 1613, even if grimly, at the dismal sight of convicted felons in Newgate being carted off to Tyburn. At the end of a long letter mainly about the impending marriage of Viscount Rochester and Frances Howard, Norton, who was undoubtedly a good and holy priest and, indeed, was one of the principal gatherers during the later 1620s of English Catholic martyrological material, noted that 'of late, a friend of mine, having some business at Newgate, was put in a fright that he should have been stayed there by reason of a great throng of people that came about the place. But the matter was this—some four or five prisoners were to suffer that day and, before they were to die, a man and a woman which were two of that company, would needs be married before they went, and so they were.' They 'came into the cart with rosemary in their hands but they needed no ribbons for hempen halters did serve their turn well enough.'[68]

In addition, contrary of course to all the martyrological literature which said that Catholics were treated with excessive and reprehensible cruelty, we have to take seriously the claims made by the regime's officers and pamphleteers that those Catholics who were indicted under the treason statutes were being dealt with for sedition and not for their religion (even though regime spokesmen consistently also made the link between popery and treason). This was the line pumped out in Lord Burghley's *Execution of Justice in England* of 1583, the royal proclamation of 18 October 1591 (also penned by Burghley), and numerous other statements of the regime's case, including what was said at treason trials themselves.

Many Catholics responded with real scepticism to this claim, and we have to take that seriously as well. But the whole point about Burghley's 1583 pamphlet was that it was meant in part to appeal to a conformist/partially conformist and conditionally loyalist Catholic constituency. It has always been difficult to define exactly who might have been in that constituency. Loyalist Catholics did not have a party card, as it were. But all through the period there were Catholic voices

---

[67] Redworth, *LLC*, I, p. 260. Carvajal did, however, remark in her letters from London not just on what she took to be the persecution of Catholics and on the appalling conditions in the rudimentary prison system in London but also on the savagery of the English penal law more generally, and commented that 'they cleanse society through indiscriminately hanging for this crime' of theft, 'even children of eleven or ten. Every month in London twenty people are hanged, twenty-four perhaps or even twenty-six and very rarely' fewer: Redworth, *LLC*, II, p. 149 (Carvajal to the marchioness of Caracena, 6/16 April 1611).

[68] AAW, A XII, no. 178, p. 394; for Benjamin Norton's gathering of martyr material, see pp. 462–4 below.

THE WRITING OF ENGLISH REFORMATION HISTORY   41

which said that an all-out war with the forces of the State did no one any good. Some of those killed by the State for their priesthood might well have been martyrs; but, some Catholics said, after the plots and conspiracies which Catholic clergymen, particularly Jesuits, had allegedly fomented, these martyrs had come close to dying in a bad cause. This was not what Catholic religion in England, indeed anywhere, should be about. In the later 1590s there was a visible moving-closer-together of, on the one hand, those Catholics who were starting to reject the political radicalism of, for example, the French Catholic Holy League (which itself stood as a sponsor to some of the more committed Catholic interventions in Elizabethan politics) and, on the other, the regime's members who were prepared to exploit what appeared to be the new green shoots of Catholic loyalism as a weapon against what they took to be puritan radicalism. This was especially evident during the so-called Archpriest Dispute in and after 1598.[69]

At the same time one might not want to over-sanitize the actions of, in particular, the Elizabethan State in its enforcement of the law. Some contemporaries evidently thought that, from time to time, it was genuinely tyrannical.[70] The problem, in short, is this. If those Catholics who were indicted and hanged were conspirators and traitors in the way that the State described, why did the majority of them not actually do something obviously and actively conspiratorial and treasonous? Why did priests insist on saying Mass in situations where they were likely to be reported, arrested, arraigned, and, in a number of cases, executed? If, on the other hand, these Catholic victims of the State were telling the literal truth when they said that all they wanted to do was dispense the sacraments of the Church in the manner regarded as normative by the majority of the Christian Church in the West, why should the queen's government in England be so keen to hunt them down?

Faced with these kinds of confusion, there has been an attempt on the part of some scholars of the period, notably John Bossy, to avoid what they regard as the asphyxiating and historically misleading effects of martyr obsession altogether. Bossy says at the start of his groundbreaking *English Catholic Community 1570–1850* that his aim is to escape from the account of post-Reformation Catholicism based on martyrdom and victimhood. Up to the point that he published this book in 1975, the quotidian existence of the 'missionary priest' had 'not been a matter of much interest to historians' and was 'normally thought worth recording, as in Challoner's *Memoirs of Missionary Priests*, only if it had

---

[69] See Chapters 9 and 10 below.

[70] See Ethan Shagan's well-judged remarks about what, in the period, one might take to have been 'moderate': the term 'moderate' can cause confusion because the 'usage tends to carry...normative moral content': E. Shagan, *The Rule of Moderation: Violence, Religion and the Politics of Restraint in Early Modern England* (Cambridge, 2011), pp. 19–20. See also M. Graves's account of Thomas Norton as essentially moderate, which was not how many contemporary Catholics saw him: Graves, *TN*, pp. 271, 273, 274.

42 CATHOLICS AND TREASON

ended on the scaffold'. Bossy suggested that 'a hasty reader of Challoner would hardly suppose that the priests of whom he wrote did very much of note between the day they arrived in England and the day they were arrested'. So, said Bossy, one should try to get away from all that and not concern oneself with what he called the 'martyrological perspective'. Rather, one should deal with 'the priest in so far as he survived to get on with his ministry'.[71]

As is quite well known, much of Bossy's oeuvre relied on, as he himself acknowledged, the publications of John Aveling. Aveling was undoubtedly the greatest local historian of his generation, despite the extremely difficult conditions in which he carried out his research.[72] Aveling had an essentially liberal ideological and historical agenda. His textbook on the period, entitled *The Handle and the Axe*, provoked, so he told me, some irate telephone calls from members of the Catholic Record Society. In Aveling's early modern Yorkshire, for which he reassembled and worked out the relationships between thousands of separatist and semi-separatist Catholics, the blood-and-guts version of post-Reformation Catholic history was, if not an irrelevance, then something of a distraction—a ripple in the day-to-day existence of provincial Catholics as they tried to negotiate the sporadic interference, by the central and local authorities, in their own lives and practice of their faith. Aveling's influence can be detected in so much of Bossy's thought about the period. Even though their world views were rather different, taken together they were Patrick Collinson's and Diarmaid MacCulloch's worst nightmare, the complete antithesis of the 'howling-success' story of the English Reformation.[73]

Bossy's sociological perspective on post-Reformation Catholicism generated a masterpiece. But it was produced in part by deliberately, as he himself stressed, excluding the question of the relationship between Catholics and the State. Historical discussions of martyrdom are about precisely that relationship. Indeed, martyrdom tells us more about that relationship than almost any other topic, despite (or, perhaps, because of) its atypicality.

In addition, Bossy's work was often read with insufficient care. As a result, it was enlisted for other, and incompatible, historiographical purposes, and particularly in an attempt to show that Catholicism retreated into a kind of enclave where it was in effect invisible. There was a kind of compatibility between, on the one hand, what Bossy was thought to have said and, on the other, the so-called 'revisionist' account of the English Reformation/s which tended to play down the

---

[71] Bossy, *ECC*, p. 250; see also J. Bossy, 'Afterword', in J. E. Kelly and S. Royal (eds), *Early Modern English Catholicism: Identity, Memory and Counter-Reformation* (Leiden, 2017), pp. 246–54, at p. 246.

[72] ABSJ, CP (John Pibush), letter to David Day, 13 February 1967, concerning Aveling's scholarship. By this stage, Aveling had already left Ampleforth Abbey. The refusal to let him have enough research time was not unconnected with this; see letter from J. C. H. Aveling to M. Questier, 5 December 1991 (in author's possession).

[73] See, e.g., D. MacCulloch, 'The Impact of the English Reformation', *HJ* 38 (1995), pp. 151–3, at p. 152.

extent of ideological conflict generated by the period's State-led changes of religion and which argued that, in any case, seminary clergy were unwilling to evangelize 'the people'. Christopher Haigh picked up on Bossy's own claim made in his *English Catholic Community* that 'the cult of martyrdom which characterized the early phase of the mission looks almost like a necessary aid in the transition from the high clerical condition of the pre-Reformation Church to the situation of the missionary priest'; in other words, that cult was essentially an invention. Most priests were not martyred, and their lives were relatively mundane.[74] So, 'although heavy fines and horrific deaths were inflicted upon some lay Catholics', the vast majority of them were never seriously threatened. 'Persistent persecution', Haigh suggests, was employed against only a 'handful of notorious malcontents'. The 'Elizabethan regime did not have the administrative capacity for a sustained campaign of persecution and, in many counties, conservative and crypto-Catholic magistrates were able to moderate pressures from the centre'.[75] This is not, in itself, wholly inaccurate and, indeed, is consistent with the oeuvre of, for example, Aveling. But to follow Geoffrey Nuttall's lead and start calculating, as Haigh does, the 'casualty rate' among seminarists via percentages threatens to become misleading.[76] At the same time, the fact that in and after the later sixteenth century the numbers of those executed under the Elizabethan treason statutes dropped markedly itself is historically of some considerable significance.

Ironically, a way of thinking historically about the problem of martyrdom and 'persecution' has long been in plain sight in the work of John Bossy himself, in spite of his protestations that he was not really interested in or concerned with it. Bossy's doctoral thesis, which predated by over ten years his *English Catholic Community*, rejected the claims of what he called the 'liberal Actonians'—Richard Simpson, Arnold Oskar Meyer, and, 'with modifications', the Jesuit John Pollen, at least to the extent that they located the centre of gravity in the Catholic community among those who understood the difference between spiritual allegiances and temporal ones. They 'attempted to reconcile Catholicism with acceptance of the established order' and could be regarded 'as forerunners of toleration and the free Church in the free State'.[77] But, as Bossy saw it, Meyer and the others were

---

[74] Bossy, *ECC*, p. 250; C. Haigh, 'From Monopoly to Minority: Catholicism in Early Modern England', *Transactions of the Royal Historical Society*, 5th series, 31 (1981), pp. 129–47, at p. 135. See also C. Haigh, 'The Church of England, the Catholics and the People', in C. Haigh (ed.), *The Reign of Elizabeth I* (1984), pp. 195–219; C. Haigh, 'The Continuity of Catholicism in the English Reformation', *Past and Present* 93 (1981), pp. 37–69.

[75] C. Haigh, 'Revisionism, the Reformation and the History of English Catholicism', *JEH* 36 (1985), pp. 394–406, at p. 401.

[76] Ibid., pp. 401–2; Nuttall, 'The English Martyrs'. One function of Nuttall's impeccably researched article is to remind us that the statistics of martyrdom need careful interpretation, although, as Eamon Duffy points out, a calculation of how many Catholic seminarist clergymen, as a proportion of those returning from the seminaries, were executed in Elizabeth's reign is fairly shocking: *ODNB, sub* Allen, William (article by E. Duffy).

[77] Bossy, *EC*, pp. 4–5.

44 CATHOLICS AND TREASON

looking for the kind of statements about loyalty and separation between politics and religion which some English Catholics and, indeed, Christians all over Europe, from time to time, made in the sixteenth and seventeenth centuries, but not necessarily for the reasons that the liberal Actonians would have liked.

Bossy's PhD thesis took a different tack. It focused on the English Catholic diaspora and on the presence of English Catholics in the religiously and politically chaotic and succession-crisis-ridden kingdom of France. Bossy's early work was really about the rise and subsequent fall of a revolutionary impulse among English Catholics. One driver or instigator of that impulse was a sense of fury and outrage at what Bossy, among other historians, chose to call the 'triumph of the laity'. The 'English Reformation was to an important degree a victory of lay society over the Church'. The 'clerk [cleric] had either to accept' that the world had changed, or 'to be quiet, or to get out'. But in the interim there was a fair opportunity for rage, not just at the heretical infection of Protestantism but also at the State-led asset stripping of the material wealth of the Church and the destruction of the religious orders. This 'provided the frame of a radical criticism of Elizabethan society', nothing less than a 'revolt of the clerks'—the famous phrase for ever associated with Bossy's doctoral dissertation. This is something which is more usually associated with puritanism. But here it is part of the 'formation of Elizabethan Catholicism', and particularly among those Catholics who left or were forced out of the universities.[78]

The mindset and hope of those faced in 1559 with the Elizabethan settlement and its immediate aftermath were, Bossy argues, that normal modes of doing things—'legal, military, political [and] diplomatic—would suffice to create the opportunity for nature to reassert itself'.[79] This is completely congruent with mainstream accounts of the first decade of the queen's reign. In those years, she was faced by a serious threat from France and Scotland and was reliant on Philip of Spain, and, clearly, she was much more comfortable with that than having to deal with the recurring toxic surges of puritan demands for reform of the national Church and intervention abroad on the side of European Protestants. But those Catholics who went into exile subsequently developed a different view of the world: 'they knew the Elizabethan order as a fact of daily life, they had felt its weight and had no reason to suppose that it would disappear overnight, nor to trust in the return of an old order of which they had very little experience. They saw the Elizabethan settlement not as unnatural but as intolerable. The spiritual impetus they had generated in refusing it moved them to work, in the present and the concrete, to change it in the name of a newer and purer form of religion.'[80]

---

[78] Bossy, EC, pp. 12–14. For an explicit statement to this effect, from the scaffold in July 1600, by Thomas Benstead, see *AWCBC*, p. 1388 (citing from Richard Verstegan, *Brief et Veritable Discours, de la Mort d'aucuns Vaillants et Glorieux Martyrs*...(Antwerp, 1601), sigs Cii^v–Diii^r).

[79] Bossy, EC, p. 20.   [80] Bossy, EC, p.20.

THE WRITING OF ENGLISH REFORMATION HISTORY   45

Some Catholics eventually found themselves prepared to go to and finally beyond the wire in the face of what some contemporaries saw as a rupture of the proper balance between spiritual and temporal. Bossy goes on (even more significantly, in some ways, because he himself was essentially out of sympathy with what he was describing here): 'they knew that unless every man did all he was capable of, gave himself entirely, [and] accepted death as a possible or even the probable' outcome, 'the new Jerusalem would not appear. It would not, as [John] Milton expressed it, descend from above: it had to be built.' Potentially, this implied building through blood. 'If they believed—in the words of Campion—that the enterprise was God's and, being God's, could not be withstood, they knew that God's enterprise was nothing if not embodied in the enterprise of every man.'[81]

Here, then, the well-known, if not actually banal, commonplace—that the blood of the martyrs is the seed of the Church—really meant something. So did the polemics about who possessed the spirit of martyrdom, and about the belief that the martyr's spirit and witness were the essential glue for the continuity of the true Church. They were of frighteningly immediate relevance for anyone who accepted the starkly enunciated case made by some Englishmen that the national Church was a filthy and frightful, corrupt and obscene deformity ruled over by a bastard tyrant queen-bitch and her gang of puritan ne'er-do-wells, involved in no end of foreign schemes to destabilize Catholic regimes abroad for their own nefarious purposes and benefit, all of which had to be opposed not just through 'missionary action' but also 'political action', which implied, 'and would be likely to involve, violence'.[82]

The accession of James VI in England in 1603 allowed a number of Catholics to argue that his rule should, by rights, be more tolerant than that of his predecessor.[83] According to them, the problem and challenge which had allegedly been constituted by the rise of separatist Catholicism should have gone away at this point. Some Protestants retorted that the Elizabethan statutes against recusancy and against the Roman Catholic clergy were still necessary in order to prevent the spread of popery. This was a situation which persisted for most of the seventeenth century. It is one which did not really fit inside Bossy's research agenda, and he did not pay it much attention.

So, what follows is an attempt at a form of cultural history with the political violence put back. There was always a risk, as Peter Lake, to whom I showed a version of this piece, commented, that it would turn out to be just 'one bloody martyr after another'. But, at the absolute minimum, a tour of the contemporary sites of execution is at least one way of getting into the dual question of why Catholicism was such a crucial component of post-Reformation politics and why that sort of politics involved, from time to time, what some contemporaries

[81] Bossy, EC, pp. 20, 21.   [82] Bossy, EC., p. 24.   [83] Questier, DP, pp. 272–6.

46 CATHOLICS AND TREASON

referred to as popery. These State-led displays of violence are a means of opening up the otherwise opaque structures of a settlement of religion which was based on conformity, that is, people doing what they were told and, if they were not fully in sympathy with whatever the status quo was, not actually saying what they thought. If you line up all these cases, end to end as it were—more or less as Bishop Challoner himself did—they tell you something about the incursion of aspects of the Counter-Reformation into English and British politics which you cannot easily get from any other source. Traditional Catholic accounts of successive Reformation and post-Reformation regimes insist that the martyrs are the outstanding representatives of post-Reformation Catholicism. As is clear even from those traditional accounts, most Catholics were never close to becoming martyrs themselves. One can see how a superficial acquaintance with those martyr narratives might seem to suggest that contemporary Catholicism was largely restricted to and defined by a zealot core which had little connection with and relevance to anything else. But the issues which informed the prosecutions of those who did end up dying for their 'religion' were of concern to many more people than those whom the mainstream historiography of the period has tended to regard as zealots. We have to read those martyr narratives in context in order to work out what the violent confrontations between a minority of undoubtedly zealous Catholics and the regime of the day tell us about the wider Catholic community and the political processes associated with the reform of 'religion' in sixteenth- and seventeenth-century England. In Chapter 3 we will look at the way that martyr narratives were constructed; then we move, via the two decades or so of sporadic hostility between the queen's government and the Catholic fraction of the national Church, into what might be termed the martyrological crucible of the period, that is to say, the 1580s, which witnessed a sustained and violent confrontation between separatist Catholicism and the State.

3

Martyrdom and the Construction of Martyr Narratives

Before launching, in the next chapter, into the political chronology of persecution and in/tolerance, we look here at some of the recurring characteristics of the narratives that tended to circulate immediately after arrest, trial, sentence, and execution. There is, of course, a case for a systematic study of such stories with an eye to the templates and texts that they employ from the martyrologies of previous centuries; but that is really a different kind of enterprise. Clearly, in the construction of contemporary martyrology there was recourse to literary forms from earlier times, and particularly from the early Christian Church.[1] Here, however, I want briefly to point to other facets of the manuscript and printed accounts of treason trials and executions of Catholics, that is to say, attributes that are more immediately linked to the particular circumstances which had brought this or that individual to his doom—the processes deployed by the authorities in order to extract maximum value from the decision to prosecute and, of course, the ways in which those who were put on trial tried to disrupt those proceedings and the assumptions of those who were doing the prosecuting; the composition and reactions, this way and that, of the audiences in court rooms and of the crowds that gathered to witness the execution of sentence; the range of rhetorical tropes available to those who, at the gallows, had no recourse other than the court of public opinion—which included, in the case of clergymen, the exercise of their preaching skills and, very often, ministration to other convicted felons; the circulation of (often contradictory) reports about what had happened and who had won the public-relations battle; and, in the various political contexts that framed such events, speculation—framed inside stories of providential occurrences—about what had happened afterwards to those who had been responsible for the persecution of good Catholics.

---

[1] See B. Gregory, *Salvation at Stake: Christian Martyrdom in Early Modern Europe* (1999), p. 280.

Catholics and Treason: Martyrology, Memory, and Politics in the Post-Reformation. Michael Questier,
Oxford University Press. © Michael Questier 2022. DOI: 10.1093/oso/9780192847027.003.0003

48 CATHOLICS AND TREASON

Killing a Priest in Reformation England

On Wednesday, 4 March 1590, a seminary priest, one Christopher Bales, was executed in Fleet Street. He had been sentenced to death under the Elizabethan treason statute of 1585 only a few days before. Now, said an eyewitness of his death, 'according to his judgment before passed, and the quality of his offence, he was laid upon a hurdle, and from thence drawn into Holborn and so through Fetter Lane conveyed into Fleet Street'. At the place of death, a 'new gibbet' had been erected for the purpose of dispatching him, 'and people in great abundance resorted to see the prisoner executed'. The privy council had postponed the execution of sentence, following the formal court verdict, in order to 'give some order for the manner thereof'.[2]

This eyewitness, a largely hostile one, noted with painstaking accuracy the events of that day. The 'priest came thither apparelled in the habit of a gentleman, in a doublet of black satin, cut with great cuts and drawn out with white silk', and with 'a pair of small round pane hose and, on every pane, a fair gold lace; his nether stocks were of purple silk, and a pair of boots over them, gentleman-like, turned down at the knee and faced with velvet'. He had 'a black felt hat on his head, and his hair was very long, so that he could hardly be known from an ordinary gentleman'. After a short delay, because the 'gibbet was not full ready', the authorities started to dismantle the dashing image of wealth, good looks, and gentility which he had constructed for himself, just as they were about to deconstruct him physically through the penalty of drawing and quartering, the distinguishing feature of the sentence for high treason: 'his boots were pulled off and his nether stocks also, whereby his feet and legs were naked, his other clothes hung loose about him, and so went he up the ladder'.

Just before the hangman turned him off, Bales 'began to speak unto the people, showing them that he was a priest'. He 'went about to defend the popish religion colourably and seemed to justify himself, by saying he had not offended her Majesty'.[3] At this point, a royal official declared that Bales was definitely a traitor. He was 'a seminary priest' and 'thereby a sworn enemy to this land'. He had 'lived out of the land among her Majesty's enemies' and he 'was again lately returned only to persuade her Majesty's subjects from their due obedience'. His 'confession' was read out to the crowd, evidently an examination before trial. In this it was

---

[2] *A True Recitall touching the Cause of the Death of Thomas Bales, a Seminarie Priest, who was Hanged and Quartered in Fleet-Street on Ashwednesdaie last past. 1590. Whereunto is Adioyned the True Cause of the Death of Annis Bankyn, who upon the Next Day following was Burned in Saint Georges fields about Sixe of the Clocke at Night* (1590), sig. A2^r; the first part of this pamphlet is reprinted in *Miscellanea* (CRS 32, 1932), pp. 429–31; see also Challoner, *MMP*, pp. 160–1; *APC 1589–90*, p. 378; *APC 1590*, p. 131. For Bales's arrest, see Anstr., I, p. 19; see also pp. 202, 203–4, 210–11 below. For the execution of Annis Bankin, see AVCAU, Scr. 36/8/1, which mentions that she had been convicted of poisoning her aunt.

[3] *A True Recitall*, sig. A2^{r-v}.

MARTYRDOM AND THE CONSTRUCTION OF MARTYR NARRATIVES 49

alleged that he had defended the papal deposing power, 'whereby', says our narrator, he denied the royal supremacy 'which is high treason of itself'. The official harangued the people further, stressing that, in this context, the treason statute of 1585 which condemned Romish clergy ordained abroad merely for their return to England was just, and so 'our holy Judith…sways the sword of justice with great wisdom and mercy'. God would watch over her.[4]

The regime had now made its public case for the proceedings against Bales; and 'this popish priest…after a few popish prayers mumbled to himself, was turned' off 'the ladder and permitted to hang until he was dead'. This was another sign of the queen's extraordinary mercy. He was then quartered 'in several pieces, to be set up in several places, to the example of all others hereafter'. Just in case anyone had failed to understand the significance of these proceedings, 'over the gibbet was written in great letters the cause of his death in these words, viz. For Treason and Favouring of Foreign Invasion'.[5]

In the afternoon of the same day, two others, Nicholas Horner and Alexander Blake, were hanged, respectively in Smithfield and Gray's Inn Lane. They had been found guilty of harbouring Bales; theirs was a felony offence under the 1585 statute which made treasonable the fact of his ordination and return into the country. Their executions seem to have been much less elaborate affairs, though Horner also had 'a title set over his head'. The basic point about the queen's justice had already been made. Our narrator noted that 'the one [Horner] died a very obstinate papist' but 'the other [Blake]' was 'a very penitent person' and was 'sorry that he had transgressed her Majesty's laws in that case: which thing he only did for worldly benefit'.[6]

Other reports of these executions added to and substantially changed the 'official' account. At Bales's trial, as one Catholic witness remembered, he had challenged the judges to say whether St Augustine of Canterbury, sent into England by Pope Gregory, was a traitor and, if not, why he, Bales, should be one, since he came for no other purpose than Augustine had done.[7] The Jesuit Henry Walpole said that at the gallows Bales very stoutly denied the charge of treason.[8] Another rehearsal of Bales's words at execution has him say 'that, if he were again free in France and at liberty to remain there', or to return, 'knowing that he should die', he would come back 'if he might gain but one soul unto God'.[9] Robert Southwell SJ's account of the priest's martyrdom, written on 8 March 1590, conceded that Bales had affirmed the use of the papal deposing power for just causes and had indeed made the statement about St Augustine and Pope Gregory. But he added

---

[4] Ibid., sig. A2ᵛ–3ʳ.   [5] Ibid., sig. A3ᵛ.   [6] Ibid.

[7] Challoner, *MMP*, p. 160; Weinreich, *PREH*, pp. 575–6; ARCR, I, no. 1004; ABSJ, Collectanea M, p. 56ᵃ⁻ᵇ (extracted and translated from *Relatione del Presente Stato d'Inghilterra. Cavata de une Lettera de li 25. di Maggio scritta di Londra*…(Rome, 1590; ARCR, I, no. 312), and printed in Pollen, *UD*, p. 179).

[8] Pollen, *AEM*, pp. 307–8 (ABSJ, Collectanea M, p. 189ᵇ).   [9] ABSJ, Collectanea M, p. 53ᵃ.

50 CATHOLICS AND TREASON

that Bales's scaffold performance included the singing of psalms. Southwell also described the 'hangman, with hands all bloody with this butchery and quartering' having to rush to Smithfield to 'execute...a man of probity', namely Horner. Southwell did not mention, however, the alleged pusillanimity of Blake.[10] (Bishop Challoner's account was taken from a variety of sources—the Spaniards Diego de Yepes, bishop of Tarazona, and the Jesuit Pedro de Ribadeneira, as well as John Stow and the English priest Anthony Champney.)[11] Southwell's letter, retained in the State paper series, is annotated: 'this relation was translated [into] Spanish and presented to all the grandees of Spain to make them conceive that the number and persecution of Catholics in England was great'.[12] Peter Penkevell claimed that Horner had been arrested merely because he had 'made a jerkin for a priest'.[13] Another account said that Horner had visions in prison both diabolical and angelic.[14]

The Ideological Significance of Inflicting Punishment: Theory and Practice

The narratives concerning the victims of 4 March 1590 incorporate many of the attributes that one might expect in such stories, just as virtually all accounts of martyrdom and indeed the inflicting of capital punishment in this period share certain similarities or, rather, were shaped by certain contemporary assumptions and expectations.[15] But these ideologically charged instances of the execution of justice inevitably generated a number of different versions of what had happened on the occasions when the law of treason was used against Catholics such as these.

[10] Foley, *RSJ*, I, pp. 325–6. Southwell's letter, translated by Henry Foley, is assigned in error in *CSPD* to 28 February 1590: *CSPD 1581–90*, p. 650; PRO, SP 12/230/104, fo. 165[r–v]. Peter Penkevell remembered that Bales was 'cruelly tortured in Bridewell by [Richard] Topcliffe': Pollen, *AEM*, p. 289 (ABSJ, Collectanea B, pp. 1–5). Penkevell himself had briefly served the Catholic gentleman Richard Shelley while he was imprisoned in the Marshalsea: Pollen, *AEM*, p. 283. His brother, Mark Penkevell, moved into the circle of Catholics who looked to Richard Bancroft for patronage and eventually accepted a Church of England benefice (West Tarring in Sussex), to which he was instituted on 18 December 1605: Anstr., I, p. 271; *HMCS*, XII, p. 312; West Sussex Record Office, typescript (W. D. Peckham, Chichester Institutions).

[11] Challoner, *MMP*, p. 160; Weinreich, *PREH*, pp. 575–6. Yepes's martyrology (*Historia Particular de la Persecucion de Inglaterra...* (Madrid, 1599)) was, it appears, compiled in large part out of existing printed texts by the Jesuit Joseph Creswell: A. J. Loomie, *The Spanish Elizabethans: The English Exiles at the Court of Philip II* (1963), pp. 206–7 (citing AAW, E II, fo. 132[r]); ARCR, I, no. 284; D. M. Rogers, introduction to the Scolar facsimile reprint in 1971 of Yepes's *Historia Particular*.

[12] PRO, SP 12/230/104, fo. 165[v]. One of Grene's manuscripts (apparently citing, as his source, an account by Nathaniel Bacon, alias Southwell SJ) records that Bales was 'put to death in his gloves which caused some suspicion that he had been tormented in the hands': AVCAU, Scr. 36/8/1.

[13] Pollen, *AEM*, p. 290.

[14] Pollen, *AEM*, pp. 310–11 (ABSJ, Collectanea M, p. 191[b]; *AWCBC*, pp. 900–1).

[15] See esp. P. Lake, 'Deeds against Nature: Cheap Print, Protestantism and Murder in Early Seventeenth-century England', in K. Sharpe and P. Lake (eds.), *Culture and Politics in Early Stuart England* (1994), pp. 257–83.

MARTYRDOM AND THE CONSTRUCTION OF MARTYR NARRATIVES 51

Interested parties wanted to fix these events with their own interpretation of them. Royal officials attended the deaths of convicted Catholic traitors and, sometimes, harangued those who were watching. Regime pamphleteers pumped out cheap print versions of Catholic traitors' alleged treasons. Notoriously, in Mary's reign, Miles Huggard had pointed to the inappropriate demeanour, for allegedly good Christians, of the Protestants who were brought to book for heresy.[16] Under Elizabeth, from the late 1570s onwards, Protestant writers performed a similar manoeuvre. Anthony Munday in particular took great delight in mocking the alleged cowardice of clergy such as Ralph Sherwin, Edmund Campion, Luke Kirby, John Shert, and Thomas Cottam.[17] In 1607, the Protestant narrator of the execution of Robert Drury noted that, at the moment of being hanged, Drury 'caught fast hold with his left hand on the halter about his head and very hardly was enforced to let it go'.[18]

Catholics became adept at writing and circulating their narratives of such events. As we saw with Robert Southwell's brief account of Bales, they could be put into words on the day itself, or shortly after. They could then be sent abroad, where they could be put into print and, sometimes, they were reimported.[19] By the later years of Elizabeth's reign, one finds these accounts of Catholic martyrs becoming contested among Catholics as much as between Catholics and Protestants. The serious rifts that developed within the Catholic community at that time meant that some Catholics tried to deprive their co-religionist opponents of the kudos conferred by appropriation of, and association with, martyrdom; or, rather, martyr stories started to incorporate those rifts and antagonisms.[20]

How, then, was the State's deployment of the harshest kinds of legal penalty supposed to protect the queen and her government against sedition and treason, other than merely by killing those who were supposedly seditious? And how were the spectators supposed to read the messages written into the State's performance of the administration of justice? As is well known, James Sharpe's seminal article on the topic of 'last dying speeches' depicted, following Michel Foucault, the gallows as a theatre of punishment. Here the power of the State was inscribed on the body of the felon (or traitor) who, before being physically killed and sometimes actually dismembered, made a public admission of guilt. He also declared his repentance and thus proclaimed the justice of the proceedings which had brought

---

[16] Miles Huggard, *The Displaying of the Protestants...* (1556), fos 46ᵛ–50ᵛ.

[17] Lake and Questier, 'Agency', p. 76, citing Anthony Munday, *The English Romayne Life...* (1582), p. 47.

[18] *A True Report of the Araignment...of a Popish Priest, named Robert Drewrie...* (1607), sig. D4ʳ.

[19] For the definitive account of this process, as also for the rhetorical and polemical strategies deployed in the writing of English Catholic martyr accounts of the Elizabethan period, see Dillon, *CM*, chs 2, 3.

[20] See Chapters 9 and 10 below.

52   CATHOLICS AND TREASON

him to his end.[21] This determination of the authorities to achieve closure via the execution of justice was obviously not exclusively an English one, nor indeed was it limited to the early modern period. In France, concludes David Nicholls, 'the ideologically constructed community's vengeance on the disturber of its order', via 'the painful and thoroughly deserved total extirpation of the outsider', was supposed to see the spectators go away 'content that this order had been restored' and fully convinced that the 'threat had been contained by the ritual of degradation, expulsion and destruction'.[22]

Another line of interpretation, associated principally with Thomas Laqueur, has been that these graphic scenes of cruelty and degradation frequently included a carnivalesque inversion of the purposes and agenda of the State, in which the voyeuristic behaviour of the crowd detracted from the supposed majesty of royal justice.[23] Equally, from time to time, the State could take over and exploit those carnivalesque elements of the performance of justice. There is ample evidence of this in continental European States, for example in France when heretics were taken to execution, drawn in carts in such a way, suggests Nicholls, as to recall 'both carnival parades and the similar processions preceding the performance of mystery plays'. Thus, in the case of Anne Audebert at Orléans in 1549 and Adrien Daussi at Paris in 1559, they rode 'to execution in dung-carts', which device itself was a reference to 'the processions of the Feast of Fools in which minor clergy in the role of fools rode in dung-carts throwing excrement at the crowds'.[24] As Nicholls comments, on some occasions the carnivalesque elements of all this could be 'integrated into a spectacular display of civic political and religious solidarity, expressing expiation for communal sins and intercession for divine intervention to put an end to social or natural evils and in which all "respectable" social groups and corporations were expected to participate'.[25]

There seems to have been rather less of the civic ceremonial in the English equivalents of these occasions, although, as so many stories in Foxe and Challoner indicate, even the less developed rituals of public execution in England could be choreographed for didactic purposes. Despite the absence of elaborate civic ceremonies, the separate elements of executions for treason, even in England, were not only, as we saw in the previous chapter, physically unspeakable but also highly symbolic. They were nowhere described more graphically than by the Jesuit

---

[21] J. Sharpe, '"Last Dying Speeches": Religion, Ideology and Public Execution in Seventeenth-Century England', *Past and Present* 107 (1985), pp. 144–67; M. Foucault, trans. A. Sheridan, *Discipline and Punish* (New York, 1977), p. 66.

[22] D. Nicholls, 'The Theatre of Martyrdom in the French Reformation', *Past and Present* 121 (1988), pp. 49–73, at pp. 64–5.

[23] T. Laqueur, 'Crowds, Carnival and the State in English Executions, 1604–1868', in A. Beier, D. Cannadine, and J. Rosenheim (eds), *The First Modern Society: Essays in English History in Honour of Lawrence Stone* (Cambridge, 1989), pp. 305–55; cf. Lake, 'Deeds'.

[24] Nicholls, 'Theatre', p. 62.

[25] Ibid., p. 60.

MARTYRDOM AND THE CONSTRUCTION OF MARTYR NARRATIVES   53

Robert Persons in his *Epistle of the Persecution*. 'First...the person condemned' was 'drawn...to the place of execution' and was 'for his greater torment...half strangled with a halter'. Then 'is he to be let down' and, 'while he is coming to himself, his privy members may be cut off and burnt in the fire before his face'. Then 'his belly is to be ripped up with a knife, his guts hauled out and, while he lies...panting and struggling, his heart, lungs, liver and all his bowels and entrails must be plucked forth by the butcher and thrown into the fire there at hand'. Finally, 'his body is boiled, cut in pieces and hanged by quarters at divers gates of the city', while his 'goods and possessions...are all forfeited and no part thereof must descend to his wife, children or kindred...and they also for this one man's sake are to be blotted with ignominy and the whole posterity of this dead creature utterly attainted...in blood forever'.[26] However clumsily carried out, the abattoir-ish act of hanging, drawing, and quartering was a brutal physical demonstration of the implications of treason. Thus the significance of the cutting off of the trai-tor's 'privy members' was that 'his issue' was 'disinherited with the corruption of blood'.[27]

The authorities often went to considerable lengths to maximize the propaganda effect of these executions. The scripting of the penalties for treason started with the trials of the accused and continued through to the scaffold, with the kind of verbal and other sorts of harassment narrated in such detail by a range of Catholic martyrologists. Once the bloodletting was over, the remains of the victims were displayed in positions and locations where the consequences of the crime would be viewed and understood by a wider public than watched the execution. After the putting to death of the prior of the London Charterhouse, John Houghton, in May 1535, one of his arms was brought back from Tyburn and was nailed to the door of the Charterhouse.[28] The seminary priest Cuthbert Mayne was hanged in late 1577 on an unusually high gallows at Launceston. His remains were, at the direction of the privy council, dispersed throughout the region. His head was impaled on a pole and set up in the centre of Launceston. One of the quarters of his dismembered body was fixed to the castle walls there. The other three quarters were set up prominently in other places, including Barnstaple.[29] In the case of the layman Richard White, executed at Wrexham in October 1584, 'the head and one quarter were sent to Denbigh castle', which, said the Catholic account, 'is the seat' of Robert Dudley, earl of Leicester, 'the sponsor of legal butchery', while 'another

---

[26] Robert Persons, *An Epistle of the Persecution of Catholickes in Englande. Translated out of Frenche into Englishe*...(Douai [imprint false; printed at Rouen], n.d. [1582]), pp. 67–8.

[27] C. Gittings, *Death, Burial and the Individual in Early Modern England* (1984), p. 70; see also Ward, LT, pp. 194–5.

[28] *ODNB, sub* Houghton, John (article by J. Hogg).

[29] Lake and Questier, 'Agency', p. 70. In the official retribution after the Walsingham conspiracy of 1537, the executions took place at Norwich, Great Yarmouth, and King's Lynn as well as Walsingham itself: G. R. Elton, *Policy and Police: The Enforcement of the Reformation in the Age of Thomas Cromwell* (Cambridge, 1972), p. 148.

54 CATHOLICS AND TREASON

quarter was shown at Ruthin where he was first hurled into chains'; another was set up at Holt, and 'another on the gallows' itself at Wrexham, 'which was suspended to strike terror into passers-by for more than two months'.[30] When the danger from the Armada ships had passed in August 1588, the queen's government staged executions of selected Catholic clergy all over London.[31] In 1616, John Thulis's body parts were 'hung up at four of the chief towns of the county'—Lancaster, Preston, Wigan, and Warrington.[32]

But even when scripted by authority, the executions of felons, traitors, and heretics were open to subversion of various kinds. On some occasions those who were supposed to comply with the judicial process signally failed to do so. This could, as Nicholls says, involve everything from preaching to singing psalms or merely 'body language'. (Sometimes the authorities permitted this, or did not think to stop it; at other times there were attempts to impose literal gagging orders, in one case involving the use of a tennis ball.)[33] The condemned might also subvert the proceedings by refusing to communicate at all. In the case of Thomas Pilchard at Dorchester in March 1587, it was 'thought he had stopped his ears with wool at his death, for he never answered [a] word to anything they said, but attended [to God] only'.[34] At other times, circumstances could almost conspire to allow those who had been condemned to address their audience but not necessarily in the way that royal officials deemed appropriate. In the case of Nicholas Garlick in July 1588 at Derby, 'when he came to the place' of execution, 'he was commanded to go up the ladder, which he embraced and kissed'. But 'the fire' kindled to burn his bowels, once they had been ripped out, 'was not ready', and so 'he spoke much unto the people to this effect, to have care to save their souls. The officers did often interrupt him but still he spoke until they put him off the ladder'.[35] Garlick was executed with Robert Ludlam and Richard Simpson. Their remains were stolen away after their deaths—another form of subversion which happened frequently after the executions of those whom Catholics reckoned had been unjustly condemned.[36]

The performance of royal power could thus be impeded or, more subtly, be taken over by a number of different agencies and interest groups. This is, in large part, what the bulk of the martyrologies of Reformation and post-Reformation England (as much as elsewhere in Europe) record. The majority of martyr narratives describe struggles for control both of the proceedings against those who had

---

[30] Thomas, *WECM*, p. 251. [31] See pp. 187–90 below.
[32] Challoner, *MMP*, p. 344. [33] Nicholls, 'Theatre', p. 63.
[34] Pollen, *UD*, p. 289 (ABSJ, Anglia VII, no. 26).
[35] Foley, *RSJ*, III, p. 226 (AVCAU, Liber 1422 [Grene, Collectanea F], section 1, p. 2ᵃ); ABSJ, Collectanea N/ii, p. 45ᵃ⁻ᵇ; *AWCBC*, pp. 589–90. Henry Garnet contributed the story that these priests effected the conversion of a Protestant woman convicted of murder: *AWCBC*, p. 586 (ARSJ, FG 651/624: Garnet to Claudio Acquaviva, 29 October 1588).
[36] See, e.g., AAW, A IV, no. 1, p. 8 (*AWCBC*, pp. 602–3), cited in Challoner, *MMP*, p. 132.

MARTYRDOM AND THE CONSTRUCTION OF MARTYR NARRATIVES   55

been arraigned and sentenced and were then executed and, then, of the way in which those events were narrated and interpreted.

Although we often have very little record of what transpired in the court rooms where the trials of Catholics were conducted, claims were made by a range of Catholic writers that the proceedings were disrupted there by a refusal on the part of the accused to comply with established rules of court procedure. This might take the form either of singing *Te Deums* at various points in the proceedings, or of refusing to accept trial by a jury.[37] Perhaps the best known instance of this kind of uncooperativeness occurred in the case of Margaret Clitherow, the York butcher's wife. Her refusal to plead to the indictment drawn up against her left the council in the North and the queen's judges there with little choice in law other than to have her pressed to death (*peine forte et dure*), which was the penalty for refusal to comply at the arraignment stage of legal proceedings in a felony case. The results were viewed in Europe in an engraving made by Richard Verstegan.[38]

Trials and executions could be subverted also by formerly hostile or indifferent observers declaring in favour of the condemned. Henry Walpole claimed to have been converted to Rome by the physical spilling onto him of Edmund Campion's blood.[39] John Gennings said that he had been converted by his brother Edmund Gennings's witness, suffering, and death, even though he, John, had formerly been a 'perverse puritan'.[40] The Northumberland gentleman Roger Widdrington witnessed John Boste's execution and, hearing a voice from the crowd denying Boste's treason, at the very moment that Boste's heart was pulled out, he 'was so struck that he was thereupon reconciled'.[41]

One of the most frequently reported subversions of the usual processes of justice against convicted Catholic clergy was the priest's persuasion of condemned felons in the prisons and even at Tyburn and other sites of execution to profess the Catholic faith. This was an obvious disruption of royal authority because it forestalled the attempts of Church of England ministers to attend to the spiritual needs of the condemned.[42] (That kind of evangelization was something that, of course, began in the gaols. There are so many reports of the practice of a rigorist evangelical Catholicism in the prisons by those clergy being kept there that one could probably write an entire book just about that.[43]) So thoroughly convinced

---

[37] Lake and Questier, 'Agency', pp. 77–8.   [38] Lake and Questier, *Trials*, ch. 5.

[39] Pollen, *AEM*, p. 40 (AAW, A II, no. 38, pp. 185–8).

[40] *The Life and Death of Mr Edmund Geninges Priest, crowned with Martyrdome at London, the 10. Day of November [i.e. December], in the Yeare M.D.XCI* (St Omer, 1614), pp. 103–10; ARCR, II, no. 338 and p. 250; Questier, *C&C*, pp. 267–8.

[41] Challoner, *MMP*, p. 600; Kn., VI, unpaginated section; letter of John Yaxley to John Knaresborough, 17 July 1707; see pp. 60–1 below.

[42] Lake and Questier, 'Agency', p. 86.

[43] Leslie Ward's excellent PhD thesis shows how the practical administrative problems of implementing the 1585 statute against Catholic clergy led to the incarceration of comparatively large numbers of clergy in the prisons: Ward, LT, pp. 281, 283. For the London prison system, see *Miscellanea I*

56 CATHOLICS AND TREASON

were the felons hanged with the priest James Thompson in November 1582, when they witnessed him refusing to enter into debate with the attendant Protestant minister at the scaffold, that they also refused to have anything to do with him.[44] When Robert Dalby and John Amias were tried in early 1589, a felon named Bramley witnessed a globe of light hanging from the roof of the court. It was enough to convert him to Rome. At execution, he 'refused to pray with the ministers, saying he had been too long of their synagogue'.[45] William Pattenson, locked in a cell in Newgate with seven others in January 1592, converted a number of them and, 'when they came to the gallows, they...confessed their fault'.[46]

The Jesuit Edward Oldcorne, sentenced to death for his alleged involvement in the Gunpowder conspiracy, encountered a Calvinist felon in prison in 1606 and converted him before they were hanged together. Oldcorne 'made good proof in this one patient how great dexterity and skill he had in the curing of diseased souls'.[47] In 1607 Robert Drury pronounced absolution over a condemned (Catholic) murderer in the courtroom where he was himself sentenced for treason.[48] In 1610 the Benedictine John Roberts's 'last dying speech' turned into a godly sermon.[49] Edmund Arrowsmith converted a felon in prison before execution in 1628. One narrative of these events stated that the felon was offered a reprieve if he would renounce Rome. But he refused and thus Arrowsmith turned a horse-thief into a martyr.[50] George Fisher, under sentence of death in March 1629, converted nine of the ten criminals who kept him company.[51] At Tyburn in early 1642 Alban Roe converted two felons, who were 'observed to make signs of sorrow and repentance; and, when they were asked by the Calvinist minister to sing a psalm after the puritan manner, they turned away their faces'.[52] Hugh Green's example may have converted two of the 'three poor women' who were hanged before the execution of his own sentence at Dorchester in August 1642; the two 'had sent him word the night before that they would die in his faith'. He was not allowed to 'see and to speak with them', but they sent word to 'desire him that, when they had made a confession of their sinful life at the gallows and should give him a sign...he then should absolve them'.[53]

We have a detailed narrative of the prison ministry conducted, in the shadow of death and in the face of the authorities' attempts to suppress it, by the priest

---

(CRS 1, 1905), pp. 47–8, and the prison lists printed on pp. 48 f., and in *Miscellanea II* (CRS 2, 1906), pp. 219–88.

[44] Challoner, *MMP*, p. 72.   [45] Morris, *TCF*, III (AENB), p. 51.

[46] Pollen, *AEM*, p. 117 (James Younger's information, February 1595: ABSJ, Anglia VI, no. 23); Pollen, *UD*, p. 292 (ABSJ, Anglia VII, no. 26).

[47] J. Morris (ed.), *The Condition of Catholics under James I: Father Gerard's Narrative of the Gunpowder Plot* (1871), pp. 271–4.

[48] See pp. 355–61 below.   [49] Lake and Questier, 'Agency', pp. 86–7; see p. 398 below.

[50] Murphy, *TER*, pp. 30–1.   [51] Anstr., II, p. 109.

[52] Pollen, *AEM*, p. 342 (Nymphenburg papers).   [53] Challoner, *MMP*, p. 423.

MARTYRDOM AND THE CONSTRUCTION OF MARTYR NARRATIVES   57

William Davies. He was finally executed at Beaumaris on 27 July 1593.[54] His prison-based evangelism combined spiritual ministrations with theological dispute. He had been approached in prison by a suffering demoniac, an 'officer' who was 'oppressed' in his body 'with burdens and pains' and who was 'scared' with the repeated 'clatter of chains' and by 'horrible visions'. In fact, Davies 'was visited by many people coming from places as distant as eight, ten and twenty miles away, some weighed down with sin, others tormented with spiritual troubles, still others in quest of advice and spiritual comfort'. Davies 'found a remedy for all kinds of troubles, discharging those affected' and leaving them 'consoled and comforted'. Those who were unable to call on him in person 'wrote him letters and sent messages relating their troubles'. The 'written communications' which he received 'were rewarded', for 'the ignorant were taught, the weak were strengthened' and the 'disconsolate were consoled'. The results were 'remarkable, for in that ignorant county where there had been originally but one declared Catholic, in a short time there came into being a great number of them'. This was all of a piece with the disputations which Davies conducted with the 'many heretical ministers' who 'visited the prison', including 'one by the name of [Hugh] Burgess', a canon of Bangor Cathedral, who was in the habit of turning up with bagloads of books.[55]

The disruptive implications of Davies's evangelizing can be read off from the authorities' attempts to force him into a public show of conformity. Following Davies's conviction for treason at his first trial in mid-1592, he was moved to Ludlow gaol where the sheriff Richard Corbet tried to make him attend a Protestant service. When Davies showed himself unwilling to comply, 'four men... got hold of him and forced a book of prayers... into his hands' and seated 'him in the same row as the vicar' in order that Davies should 'read vespers'. He then hurled 'the book into the middle of the church'. The sheriff ordered the vicar to read the service. Davies found himself restrained from leaving the church, and he started at the top of his voice to recite vespers 'according to the Roman breviary'. Not surprisingly, 'all was noise and confusion'. When some sort of order was restored, he declared his hatred for the 'hypocrisy with which they pretended to serve God without faith or religion', leaving the sheriff to tell him that 'he could thank his own stupidity since his case was now lost'.[56] Eventually he was transferred back to Beaumaris, where he and the four Catholic students who had been arrested with him in March 1592 lived in what resembled a religious community. He was put on trial (again) on 18 July 1593.[57] After his execution nine days later,

---

[54] *AWCBC*, pp. 1113–14; for the proceedings against Davies, see pp. 237, 237 n.44 below.
[55] Thomas, *WECM*, pp. 269, 271. For Davies's spiritual activism and asceticism in prison, see Thomas, *WECM.*, pp. 279, 281, 283.
[56] Thomas, *WECM.*, pp. 275, 277; *AWCBC*, p. 1114. For Richard Corbet, see *HC 1558–1603*, I, pp. 655–6.
[57] *AWCBC*, p. 1114.

58   CATHOLICS AND TREASON

recorded Bishop Yepes's martyrology, Davies's cassock and other apparel were taken back by the executioner to the prison. They were placed, 'still flowing with blood', on the table on which Davies had celebrated the Mass. These garments were divided up amongst Catholics. The 'whole cassock, stained with blood', was kept in a 'certain part of the realm' so that priests might with 'great devotion' wear it 'under their sacerdotal vestments' when they recited Mass.[58]

Faced with these kinds of subversion of the rites associated with the penalties for treason, the State and its officials could, as we might expect, retaliate. They could simply try to silence the condemned. In 1679, David Lewis prepared a long gallows speech but wrote at the end of the manuscript that he was 'prohibited in public to utter' it.[59] Of course, if there was a really hostile crowd, those officials did not need to do much to impose silence on convicted Catholics. Catholic narratives sometimes say that the condemned were confronted by baying anti-popish mobs. In June 1573, at Tyburn, Thomas Woodhouse declared that, rather than he owing the queen an apology, she should sue to the pope for forgiveness. This provoked cries from the crowd of 'Hang him, hang him, this man is worse than Story', that is, the recently hanged and disembowelled Dr John Story. John Nelson's Latin prayers and professions of his Catholic faith in early 1578 were interrupted by catcalls of 'away with you and your Catholic Romish faith'.[60]

John Mush provided one of the most detailed descriptions of the one-sided confrontations at the scaffold during the early and mid-1580s. Describing the string of recent victims at York, he claimed that 'at the place of execution' the 'ministers' were deliberately stationed so as to 'molest and trouble us with their ignorant, railing, slanderous, blasphemous and frivolous questions, disputations, accusations and lies'. With the 'gross puritans and fantastical merchants and craftsmen', they shouted out that 'we be traitors, papists, seducers and [the] queen's enemies, in great despite mocking and slandering us, belying and blaspheming the Catholic faith'. By this 'damnable means they also intend to murder our souls, that the moving [of] us to impatience and disquiet of mind in our last agony may send us to their master, Satan, and so destroy not only our bodies but also our souls'. Something like this had allegedly happened in the case of the unfortunate priest Alexander Crow, who physically tumbled from the gallows in late 1586 in what looked to some like a bungled attempt at suicide. Perhaps more than one such victim, faced with the reality of what was about to happen, tried to end it before the unspeakable horrors of the full penalties for treason were inflicted on them. As Mush put it, the persecutors 'raised slanders of divers, that standing upon the ladder, ready to be cast from it, they hanged themselves, when

---

[58]   Thomas, *WECM*, p. 291.   [59]   ABSJ, Anglia VII, no. 27; AAW, A XXXIV, no. 138.
[60]   Lake and Questier, 'Agency', pp. 97–8; *ODNB*, *sub* Woodhouse, Thomas (article by T. M. McCoog); Challoner, *MMP*, p. 10.

MARTYRDOM AND THE CONSTRUCTION OF MARTYR NARRATIVES   59

either by faintness, sickness, slip of foot, or sudden stirring of the ladder', they fell from it.[61]

The narratives of the 1588 purge of Catholic clergy in London suggest that they were allowed to say nothing or, if they tried, their voices were drowned out by angry crowds.[62] John Thomas, hanged in Hampshire in August 1593, called for 'all good Catholics to say one Pater Noster with' him. But the hangman, Bull, 'punched him two or three [times] in the breast with his fist' and told him to pray in English, though the martyr-to-be resolutely refused.[63]

But, in many of the cases in which Catholics were convicted and executed for treason, the victims were allowed to address the watching crowd, even if some people were scandalized by this. When in December 1610 the Benedictine John Roberts was hanged, it appears that the sheriff was happy to let him speak, despite the protests of another royal official.[64] The newsletter writer John Chamberlain reported that two priests, William Scot and Richard Newport, who were hanged at Tyburn on 30 May 1612, were 'suffered to talk their fill, but whose fault it was I know not'.[65]

What are we to make of this? Why allow condemned traitors to lecture all and sundry from under the gallows? Why permit them to appropriate and twist the conventions of the 'last dying speech' when they, in speaking at all, were supposed merely to affirm the legitimacy of the proceedings against them? To this there is no simple answer. But, in the first place, considerable attention was paid to the last words of the condemned.[66] Simply to silence them might indeed look like tyranny. The regime's case against those (relatively few) people who were dealt with under the treason legislation against Catholics was that the sovereign was merciful and that they were not condemned for their 'religion' but only for sedition. This case was likely to be undermined by literally or metaphorically gagging them.

It may well be also that there were limits to the controls that the State could impose, particularly when the watching crowd was not uniformly hostile to the condemned. Crowds were frequently diversely constituted, containing undoubtedly some very angry and unfriendly elements, often urged on by the likes of royal officials such as Sir Francis Knollys and Richard Topcliffe. But, if the Catholic narratives are anything to go by, the State's victims frequently had sympathetic hearers as well. This could certainly be the case in regions which were

---

[61] Morris, *TCF*, III (YRR), pp. 97, 98; Challoner, *MMP*, pp. 128–9. As Diego de Yepes's text narrated it, Crow claimed to have been tempted in prison by a monstrous vision which had told him that he was already condemned to Hell and urged him to suicide: Yepes, *Historia Particular*, pp. 128–32; Challoner, *MMP*, pp. 126–8; see p. 169 n.127 below.

[62] See pp. 187–9 below.

[63] ABSJ, Anglia VII, no. 25 (Pollen, *AEM*, p. 233). This man is not incorporated in contemporary Catholic martyr catalogues: Pollen, *UD*, p. 232.

[64] See p. 398 below.   [65] McClure, *LJC*, I, p. 355.   [66] Lake, 'Deeds'.

60 CATHOLICS AND TREASON

conservative in religion. Thus the execution of William Davies, hanged, as we saw, at Beaumaris, was, according to the surviving Catholic narratives, not popular in the locality.[67] Perhaps William Allen, though hardly an impartial narrator, was speaking something like the truth when, even in the crisis years of the early 1580s, he wrote, principally of executions in London, that 'a few of the people set on by the ministers that use to follow the gallows' encouraged the 'rest that stood further off to cry "away with them, away with them"'; but 'thousands went home after the sight of so notorious a spectacle, as the constancy of the martyrs yielded that time, sighing, weeping and lamenting' what had happened.[68] John Gennings noted that the crowd at his brother's execution was composed of 'Protestants who came rather to behold the spectacle' and of Catholics who looked on in order to 'confirm their faith' and even to 'participate although not in act, yet at least in desire with him in his martyrdom'.[69]

The execution of John Boste at Durham in 1594 was a major political event. The authorities by all accounts had been seeking for years to bring him to justice. The spectators were kept away from the cart and not allowed to speak to him, 'and the justices were appointed to note the manner of execution and observe the people's behaviours'. Boste was not permitted to deliver the speech which he had planned to make.[70] But, despite all this effort to exert control over the proceedings, it seems that public opinion in the North-East could not be so easily controlled. One account sent to Robert Persons by the priest John Cecil noted that, 'when they took off the good father', Boste, 'to the place of execution, more than 300 ladies and women of good position...all with black hoods, which with us is a sign of gentlewomen...set out to follow him'.[71] The future martyr Christopher Robinson was there and said that he thought he would never again 'see such resort of people' as were at Boste's execution, 'but especially of gentlemen and gentlewomen'. Robinson wrote that 'one Banister, the [lord] president's man, said, confirming it with an oath...that the Devil is amongst the people here...which flock together thus to see a traitor die. I wish to God, said he, that all the rest of them were hanged up like dogs with him.' Also, 'a minister, seeing country gentlewomen at the execution, whereof there were not a few', demanded why they were there. They said that they wanted to hear Boste speak.[72] John Yaxley recorded much later, in July 1707, that when 'Mr Boste suffered, the hangman pulling out his [heart] and showing it to the crowd with a "Behold the heart of a traitor", a voice was heard to this effect, "no, the heart of a servant of God"'. Minutes before Boste was hanged, said Robinson, a Protestant clergyman had accused the martyr of sedition. A 'gentleman', whom Robinson took to be Edward Musgrave of

---

[67] Pollen, *AEM*, p. 139 (ABSJ, Collectanea M, p. 107[b]).   [68] Allen, *BH*, sig. cii [r].

[69] *The Life and Death of Mr Edmund Geninges Priest*, pp. 90–1.

[70] Morris, *TCF*, III (RHPN), p. 209.   [71] Pollen, *UD*, p. 286 (ABSJ, Collectanea M, p. 160[a]).

[72] Kn., VII, p. 509.

MARTYRDOM AND THE CONSTRUCTION OF MARTYR NARRATIVES   61

Allston Moor, declared that Boste 'had behaved himself very well'; in fact he had 'behaved himself marvellously well'.[73]

The hanging of the Douai priest Thomas Maxfield in 1616 appears to have been intended to teach the London Catholic community a number of uncomfortable lessons. But our accounts of it suggest that it provoked a kind of Catholic political demonstration around the Tyburn gallows, one which we can locate reasonably precisely inside the politics of the mid-Jacobean period.[74]

On many occasions, therefore, the carrying out of executions of convicted traitors generated comment and dispute which simply could not be controlled by official demands for silence. The extent to which the executions of Catholics fomented debate can be gleaned from the unusually well-documented instance of the martyrdom of Henry Heath at Tyburn on 17 April 1643. One narrative that we have of it was written by 'a layman, no scholar' who nevertheless set down a detailed description of a to-and-fro discussion at the gallows—in some ways utterly bizarre, in the light of what was about to happen. Heath prayed for the conversion of England as well as to 'take away all...hardness of heart from all Protestants and heretics'. Then a 'young minister' interjected that it would be more appropriate if Heath were to renounce Rome. (It transpired that they were both from Northamptonshire.) This led to a theological debate between them about 'the imputed righteousness of Christ' with citations from St Thomas Aquinas and the prophet Daniel. Then another Church of England clergyman approached and disputed with Heath but seemed more sympathetic and, having finished, 'pulled his hat over his eyes, seeming to pray for him'; at which point one 'of the redcoat soldiers...asked if the father died in the faith of Christ to whom the [first] minister answered, yes, but not for the faith of Christ, to whom a woman standing by asked the minister his reason, who answered [that] he died for opinions [only], to whom a young man replied that he could not die for opinions seeing that he makes public confession of believing [as] the Church had in all ages, and does now believe'. This caused the minister to riposte that 'the name of the Church cozened all the young'. But 'the young man replied that, using his own expression, it cozened us no more than it did St Augustine...to which the minister answered that St Augustine spoke not of the Roman Church'. The young man quoted another place in which St Augustine answered his enemies by citing the succession of 'the priests or bishops of Rome in the seat of St Peter'. For good measure the young man alluded to St Jerome to the effect that it was 'impossible for error to have access to the Roman Church'. To this the minister said that at this time there was 'more need of prayer than disputation'. At this point the minister

---

[73] Challoner, *MMP*, pp. 600, 598; Kn., VI, unpaginated section; letter of John Yaxley to John Knaresborough, 17 July 1707. When Boste had 'stood at the bar', and there 'came a minister' who rudely 'said "you are not worthy to tread upon the earth"', Musgrave 'took him a sound knock upon the breast' (this is a passage which Challoner excludes): *Miscellanea I*, p. 91.

[74] See pp. 433–40 below.

62   CATHOLICS AND TREASON

worked out that the condemned priest was Henry Heath and realized that they had known each other at Cambridge, though they had been at different colleges. The minister returned to the attack by claiming that Catholics gave too much emphasis to personal merits as opposed to those of Christ. This provoked the unnamed young man to refer to 'the place so much abused by the Protestants [out] of [Cardinal] Bellarmine'. The argument was still going on when the execution of sentence finally happened and the life was choked out of the victim.[75]

Now, of course, this is not to say that every such occasion witnessed these kinds of arguments. But from accounts such as these one has a sense of the diversity of opinions and sympathies among those who watched these scenes. Indeed, it seems, from both Catholic and Protestant narratives, that there might be, in addition to the overtly hostile and the openly sympathetic watchers, another constituency, a kind of third force, which might, though not on confessional grounds, be potentially well disposed towards the condemned, particularly if they behaved appropriately and with courage.[76]

This is a reading which is confirmed by scraps of information and evidence recoverable from the margins and interstices of both Catholic and Protestant accounts of the executions of Catholics. One gets a sense of this floating but potentially sympathetic constituency from those occasions when it appeared that the condemned had been or might be treated with unnecessary cruelty. At Chelmsford in 1582 some of the onlookers intervened, apparently with the licence of the officials present, to make sure that John Paine was dead before he was drawn and quartered. The sight of Thomas Pilchard's messy death caused 'the people' to murmur 'much at it'. In February 1595, members of the crowd hastened the death of Robert Southwell, who had been left dangling by an 'unskilful hangman'. They also prevented the hangman from cutting him down prematurely, although they may well have been responding to the lead given on this occasion by noble spectators, notably Lord Mountjoy.[77] One strongly Protestant sheriff, Paul Tracy of Stanway, made sure at Gloucester in August 1586 that the priest John Sandys was 'bloodily butchered' by an amateur with an 'old rusty knife full of teeth like a sickle'. Sandys thought he had a deal with Tracy 'to suffer him to hang until he died' and then found out, too late, that he did not.[78] Stephen Rowsham, however, was early in the following year saved from the grotesque treatment that had been meted out to Sandys at the gallows. The 'very common

---

[75] ABSJ, Anglia V, no. 14 (*AWCBC*, pp. 2166–9); cf. Challoner, *MMP*, pp. 439–47; Kn., IV, pp. 117, 163–6. For a longer narrative in Latin, see AVCAU, Liber 1577 (Anstruther Martyrs File): ABSJ, A IV, no. 12.

[76] This was primarily Peter Lake's perception, incorporated into Lake and Questier, 'Agency', pp. 95–107; see also D. Anderson, *Martyrs and Players in Early Modern England: Tragedy, Religion and Violence on Stage* (Farnham, 2014), pp. 66–7.

[77] Challoner, *MMP*, pp. 43, 212; Pollen, *AEM*, p. 321; Pollen, *UD*, p. 288 (ABSJ, Anglia VII, no. 26); Devlin, *LRS*, p. 324.

[78] Pollen, *AEM*, pp. 336–7 (ABSJ, Collectanea M, pp. 145^b–6^a); see also pp. 164–5 n.109 below.

MARTYRDOM AND THE CONSTRUCTION OF MARTYR NARRATIVES 63

sort of people' in Gloucester 'cried out upon the officers' and even some preachers 'sued that Mr Rowsham should not be so handled'. Another source says that Rowsham had been pelted with ordure by 'a graceless company of apprentices and youths', set on by 'the persecutors'. But the dean of Gloucester, Anthony Rudd, and the 'preachers there... exclaimed against that inhumane dealing', that is, the savagery that had been used against Sandys; and so Rowsham was allowed 'to hang until he were dead'.[79] A newsletter written by Edward Coffin in late May 1611 insisted that the large crowd which had watched the execution of John Roberts and Thomas Somers in London in December 1610 had evinced real sympathy for these two clergymen.[80]

God's Revenge on the Persecutors

In the wake of subversive popular responses to these brutal demonstrations of royal justice came stories of the misfortunes allegedly experienced by the oppressors of good Catholics—stories with which contemporary martyrologies are littered. Here contemporaries could see God Himself handing down judgment and inflicting punishment on those who had hounded the faithful and who, in such short order after their victims had perished, met untimely and miserable fates in a way that could not be mere coincidence. This was a common theme in European martyrology. David Nicholls argues that Jean Crespin created a ' "Golden Legend" of Protestantism, in which persecutors invariably died horrible deaths', something 'which at times came perilously close to traditional miracle-tales'.[81] Thomas Freeman has demonstrated how central the narratives of providential punishment are in Foxe.[82] They are certainly prominent in English Catholic martyrology; and the alleged events can usually be shown to have some foundation in fact even if the cause-and-effect aspect of them is not really capable of historical proof.[83]

So, for all the passivity of the godly martyr-elect in the face of judgment and death, God from time to time was believed to have stepped in with His own version of the execution of justice on some of the truly guilty, the petty tyrants whose

---

[79] Pollen, *AEM*, pp. 333, 332 (ABSJ, Collectanea M, pp. 143ᵇ–4ᵃ); ABSJ, Collectanea M, p. 27ᵃ (Rowsham's 'persecutors had provided many boys and placed them upon a dunghill to annoy the blessed martyr by throwing filth on him'); Morris, *TCF*, III (AENB), p. 42; Lake and Questier, 'Agency', pp. 101–2; *AWCBC*, pp. 322, 334, 483, 500.

[80] ABSJ, Anglia III, no. 103 (Edward Coffin to [Robert Persons?], 18/28 May 1611; translation in ABSJ, CP (George Napper). Coffin said also that the crowd prevented Roberts and Somers from being butchered alive, as the watching crowd in Oxford had done in the case of George Napper in November 1610: ABSJ, Anglia III, no. 103.

[81] Nicholls, 'Theatre', p. 66.

[82] T. S. Freeman, 'Fate, Faction, and Fiction in Foxe's Book of Martyrs', *HJ* 43 (2000), pp. 601–23; see also S. Monta, *Martyrdom and Literature in Early Modern England* (Cambridge, 2005), ch. 3.

[83] See Dillon, *CM*, pp. 102–3.

64 CATHOLICS AND TREASON

spite and malice were so self-evident. The devastating outbreak of disease at the Oxford assizes in July 1577 was interpreted by Catholics as a result of the unjust sentence on the Catholic bookbinder Rowland Jenks. As soon as he was condemned, as one narrative recalled, 'there arose suddenly and forthwith such a mist and damp in the hall, as so perfumed all our heads (says the writer) that we almost were all smothered: very few escaped untaken at that instant: such as were stricken, very shortly died. The jurors died presently. Justice Bell chief baron, Sir William Babington, Mr Wainman and many others sickened there but died not in the hall. It would be tedious to tell all their names that died of this sickness; for within the town there died above 300 and abroad in other places above 200 more', but only men, not women and children, 'bleeding to death at all the vents and issues of their bodies'.[84] As for the 'hangman who imbrued his hands in...[Cuthbert Mayne's] innocent blood' later in the same year, 1577, 'in less than a month's time' he 'became mad and soon after miserably expired'.[85] One of Campion's judges found his hands covered in blood after the condemnation and died almost at once.[86] Campion's betrayer, George Eliot, allegedly was 'eaten up with lice' and 'died cursing the hour that he had ever served the queen'.[87] The children of Richard Houghton of Park Hall, Campion's patron, who had slandered the priest Lawrence Johnson by falsely accusing him of sleeping with their stepmother, showed themselves in their true colours when 'one of the daughters begot a bastard with her father's horse-keeper and after lived so loosely that she' was subsequently compelled to 'beg from door to door'. The 'second daughter was no better than the first in preservation of her chastity' and 'after some time passed in satisfying of her filthy pleasure of carnality' was forced to 'cloak the matter' by marrying a 'base peasant' and had to leave for Ireland 'where she lived in extraordinary misery and no less disgrace'. The son and heir was similarly lustful, became a 'vagabond', went overseas, and may have committed suicide.[88]

According to Richard Barret, writing in Rheims on 6/16 April 1584, a priest who had arrived from England recited 'some extraordinary examples of God's avenging justice on those who behaved most harshly in accusing and harassing Catholics'. One of the officials in the Marshalsea, who had been responsible for the taking of the priest Everard Hanse, lost his job and became demented. He

---

[84] See AAW, A II, no. 14, p. 43 (manuscript transcript of a printed pamphlet); *APC 1577–8*, pp. 25–6; Nicholas Sander, trans. and ed. D. Lewis, *Rise and Growth of the Anglican Schism...*(1877), pp. 307–8; John Stow, *The Summarie of the Chronicles of England...unto...1579* (1579), p. 442. For the deaths of Lord Chief Baron Sir Robert Bell, Sergeant Nicholas Barham, and the juror Sir Robert Doyley, see *HC 1558–1603*, I, pp. 424, 392, II, p. 53.

[85] Challoner, *MMP*, p. 6.

[86] Robert Southwell, *An Epistle of Comfort...*(Paris [imprint false; printed secretly at Arundel House, London], n.d. [1587–8]), fo. 202^r.

[87] ABSJ, Collectanea N/i, no. 6, pp. 108, 170.

[88] AAW, A III, no. 27, pp. 105–6. The writer of this note added that 'here is nothing...contained which I did not hear of one of sufficient credit who knew all the parties': AAW, A III, no. 27, p. 106.

MARTYRDOM AND THE CONSTRUCTION OF MARTYR NARRATIVES   65

uttered 'dreadful and impious blasphemies' and, after 'lying...in misery for some days, the lower region of his body burst asunder, forcing his entrails to protrude and causing his immediate death'. This, presumably, was God's ironic imitation of the evisceration aspect of the sentence for treason recently inflicted on Hanse. The rack-master Thomas Norton's wife 'was affected with a furious insanity of the worst kind' and 'his father and uncle became paralysed'. Norton himself, who 'in the Tower had afflicted so many with the tortures of the rack, came to die and to endure the tortures of Hell' (he had expired on 10 March 1584).[89]

It was claimed in the case of the martyr Richard White (d. October 1584) that virtually everyone who crossed him regretted it. Even being slightly critical of him constituted a serious health-and-safety risk. One of the judges in the case died soon after White was condemned. The 'greatest part of the jury dropped away miserably and never lived to see the next assize following'. One of White's enemies contracted the plague and expired, 'often naming the martyr and cursing the hour he took him'; and 'no man from the beginning of his sickness might well approach near him alive nor dead for the horrible stink of his body'. By this 'terrible example', said the narrator, 'the persecutors' should 'learn to take heed how they anger the servants of God'.[90]

A minister named Frost had attended the execution of Francis Ingleby on 3 June 1586, having also witnessed the crushing of Margaret Clitherow on 25 March. He had tried unsuccessfully to persuade Ingleby to recant and, after the execution, Frost 'returned into the city' of York and stormed into the nearest church. He 'stayed a while to assemble his audience' and, 'full of malice, anger and hatred, went up into the pulpit' and poured out his detestation of Ingleby and declared that he hoped 'all Catholics might come to the same end'. After half an hour of this performance 'he suddenly fell down in the pulpit...speechless'. He never recovered.[91]

---

[89] Renold, *LWA*, p. 96; Graves, *TN*, pp. 15, 393–4, 402–3, 404; *ODNB*, *sub* Norton, Thomas (article by M. Axton).

[90] Thomas, *WECM*, pp. 128–9.

[91] ARSJ, Anglia 37, fo. 204^r (*AWCBC*, p. 298); Anstr., I, p. 181; Morris, *TCF*, III (TR), p. 430. The narrative written by the Jesuit Thomas Stanney on 2 November 1609 said that he had copied material of Henry Garnet concerning 'schismatics and heretics' into a 'book relating to the minister who, preaching against Mr Ingleby, martyr, fell down dead in the pulpit': ABSJ, Collectanea P/ii, p. 582^a (*AWCBC*, pp. 297–8). Christopher Grene's list of persecutors who had providentially bitten the dust included Sir Francis Walsingham, the earl of Leicester, and Sir John Fettiplace (who fell off his horse during a search for priests and broke his neck): ABSJ, Collectanea M, p. 50^b; ABSJ, Collectanea N/i, no. 6, p. 107. For John Gerard's account of Richard Young's miserable death, see Caraman, *JG*, p. 92. In c.1936, the parish priest of Hathersage told Edward Ellis that an aged lady 'of the district had said to him that it was commonly held in those parts that the plague which devastated the village of Eyam in Derbyshire' in the mid-1660s 'was God's punishment on the villagers who had mocked...the two priests [Nicholas Garlick and Robert Ludlam] when they were being taken...through the village to their trial and death at Derby': ABSJ, 45/2/3/4 (Edward Ellis, bishop of Nottingham to Philip Caraman, 13 November 1962); P. Slack, *The Impact of Plague in Tudor and Stuart England* (Oxford, 1985), pp. 268–9.

66 CATHOLICS AND TREASON

Robert Southwell's *Epistle of Comfort* of 1587 had an entire chapter entitled 'A Warning to the Persecutors'. It swept up many of these circulating stories about the fate of the oppressors. While Southwell concentrated principally on the increase of the faithful under the lash of persecution, he also reminded his readers that 'never does the impiety of the wicked rage against us but', immediately, 'God's heavy revenge does accompany their wickedness'. Having rehearsed the bad ends of harassers of the early Church, Southwell turned to these more recent ones: 'one Young, an apostate…pursuing a Catholic at Lambeth fell down on the sudden… and, foaming at the mouth, presently died'. 'Justice Bromley', who condemned Richard White, had gone senile ('bethered and childish') and 'never sat in judgment since', while most of the trial jurors perished. 'Rack-master' Norton's fate was very instructive. 'Upon his deathbed in desperate manner [he] cried out that he was racked more cruelly than ever he racked any'. George Blythe, 'a man of special authority in the council of York', spoke 'in derision' of a priest and, within a few hours' fell down a staircase in the king's manor, the lord president's residence in York. He 'lived not many days after[wards]'. Southwell repeated the circulating stories about Henry Cheke and Ralph Hurlestone. Southwell said that, when Hurlestone croaked, the smell was so bad that 'the very ground where he lay, as it is credibly reported, retained the stench' and 'they were fain to draw him away with long ropes at a boat's tail in the river, not being able to endure him in the boat' because of the appalling smell.[92]

Sir Walter Aston, of Tixall in Staffordshire, 'a great persecutor, especially of Mr [Robert] Sutton the martyr', executed on 27 July 1588, 'twice at his examination' struck Sutton. Afterwards, Aston was 'the principal means or agent' in Sutton's 'martyrdom' and 'was buried on May day next after'. There was 'a priest' who, 'being within some three miles of the house [on] the same day, saw with many others such terrible' flashes of lightning, 'besides many monstrous thunderclaps, as had seldom been seen before, but only', and surely significantly, on 'that day' when the earl of Leicester 'was buried'. Those same lightning flashes 'seemed to ascend upwards from round about the house of Tixall into the air, and not contrariwise like other lightning; much like squibs for the fleeting upward violently, but incomparably with greater light and terror'.[93] The Jesuit Christopher Grene's

---

[92] Southwell, *An Epistle of Comfort*, fos 196ʳ, 200ʳ, 201ʳ-2ʳ; ABSJ, CP (Francis Ingleby; drafts for beatification process, 1987); Morris, *TCF*, III (AENB), p. 59. Christopher Grene says, presumably in error, that it was Cheke who had the accident on the stairs: Pollen, *AEM*, p. 322 (ABSJ, Collectanea M, p. 50ᵇ); *AWCBC*, p. 290. Ingleby was executed on 3 June 1586, presumably very shortly after trial. Cheke, who was a nephew of Lord Burghley, died on 23 June: *HC 1558–1603*, I, pp. 596–7. For Sir George Bromley, chief justice of Chester, see *HC 1558–1603*, I, p. 490.

[93] Morris, *TCF*, III (AENB), pp. 57–8 (*AWCBC*, p. 630); see pp. 182–3 below. This source, the so-called 'ancient editor's notebook', was compiled as a kind of preparatory list of providential stories. It has an entire section on God's judgments on the wicked, though not just on those who persecuted the martyrs—for example, it includes Richard Barnes, bishop of Durham, who allegedly had a drink problem, and Robert Aston, 'parson' of Mucklestone in Staffordshire, who was 'the first married priest that ever was in that diocese' and was 'one of Foxe's confessors in his Book of Monuments'—he 'lost his

MARTYRDOM AND THE CONSTRUCTION OF MARTYR NARRATIVES   67

volume labelled 'Collectanea F' noted that Aston, who had knocked Sutton 'with his staff... to the ground' during Sutton's examination, also 'protested openly that if the evidence he gave took not place, he would never sit on the bench again; nor no more he did, for shortly after he fell sick, to whom the Devil appeared'.[94]

It was not exactly unpredictable that the earl of Leicester's death should have been hailed by Catholics as a work of God. Robert Southwell on 7 September 1588 saw God balancing out the 'most unjust and most glorious' executions of the 'fourteen martyrs' in London at the end of August via the 'singular punishment' of this loathsome man; for, 'on the same day of the week following as that on which the martyrs suffered the previous week, and at the same time of day when they were executed, namely towards noon', the wretched Leicester 'who was the chief author of this great cruelty... passed away merely by relapse into' a fever. He was 'a compendium of iniquity, a monster of crimes who, while he lived, left nothing with respect to wickedness undone'. Leicester was cursed by the multitude as much as by Catholics—'his soul and his very corpse alike they tear to pieces with a thousand curses'.[95]

God, in other words, moved in relatively unmysterious ways. Challoner's own verdict on all this was that, even if Leicester had been carried off by 'divine justice', the persecution went on, as indeed it did. The late summer of 1588 saw a further spate of executions.[96] But God was not going to tolerate this for long! Sir Francis Walsingham, so said some Catholic narrators (notably, again, Southwell in his *Humble Supplication*), made a bad end. As Challoner summarized it, he expired blaspheming and with his urine gushing forth at his nose: he 'died miserably on the 6th of April 1590 of an ulcer and impostume in his bowels, which reduced him to that wretched condition, that whilst he was yet alive he yielded so insupportable a stench that scarce anyone could bear to come near him'.[97] Edmund Duke's betrayer in 1590, 'a pretended Catholic', perished 'miserably'.[98] In William Davies's case in 1593, the 'hangman, not long after, for some crime falling into the hands of justice, declared at the gallows' that 'God had justly, on that account, brought him to suffer a shameful death'. Equally, the 'constable... that apprehended Mr Davies was seized immediately' with an inflammatory disease which in the end 'corrupted' his 'whole body, so as to yield a most loathsome stench, insupportable

---

wits': Morris, *TCF*, III (AENB), pp. 57–9. For the alleged (but ineffectual) repentance of Richard Topcliffe's associate Nicholas Thorne (or Thornes) for his cruelty to Catholics, see Foley, *RSJ*, III, p. 227 (AVCAU, Liber 1422 [Grene, Collectanea F], section 1, pp. 2ᵃ, 3ᵃ); ABSJ, Collectanea M, p. 179ᵇ; see also C. Jamison (ed.), revised by E. G. W. Bill, *A Calendar of the Shrewsbury and Talbot Papers in Lambeth Palace Library and the College of Arms: volume I* (1966), p. 79.

[94] Foley, *RSJ*, III, p. 232 (AVCAU, Liber 1422 [Grene, Collectanea F], section 1, p. 6ᵃ; *AWCBC*, p. 631). Aston died on 2 April 1589; he had, in 1586, lodged Mary Stuart at Tixall while Sir Amias Paulet went through her personal papers at Chartley in order to assist the legal case against her: S. T. Bindoff (ed.), *The House of Commons 1509–1558* (3 vols, 1982), I, p. 347.

[95] McCoog, *LRS*, p. 183 (Robert Southwell to Claudio Acquaviva, 7 September 1588).

[96] Challoner, *MMP*, p. 134.   [97] Challoner, *MMP*, p. 164.

[98] ABSJ, A V, no. 8 (unfoliated).

68 CATHOLICS AND TREASON

to himself and to all that came near him; and in this manner he miserably expired'.[99]

A year after John Cornelius's execution at Dorchester in July 1594 a plague afflicted the town and 'the living were not sufficient to bury the dead'. In 1587 Thomas Pilchard had been executed there and the town was repeatedly struck by lightning and thunderbolts until Pilchard's quarters were taken down from the town walls. Henry Walpole's execution, it was said, drove Henry Hastings, earl of Huntingdon, to an early grave, in anguish of mind, calling for his Catholic brother Walter.[100] John Glanville, the judge who sentenced the martyrs Thomas Sprott and Thomas Benstead in mid-1600, had, said the Jesuit Henry Garnet, 'most maliciously against law made them [to] be found guilty'. On 27 July 1600 the judge fell awkwardly from his horse and broke his neck. Although his servant was initially accused of murdering him, a view of the corpse showed, it was claimed, 'his brains strangely coming forth both at his nose and mouth' and other injuries (gashing and scorching) which seemed not to have been inflicted by human agency.[101]

In contrast to the physical stench given off by the persecutors, the martyr's own saintliness might give off a sweet perfume, alerting the faithful to his spiritual qualities and to the fact that his flesh did not immediately suffer mortal corruption, as was the case with the martyr Richard White: God 'infused such grace into these quarters of his body, which faithless men deemed only worthy of being hanged at that awful spot of the gallows...that they gave off from afar a most sweet smell'.[102] In 1651, London Catholics acquired the remains of the Jesuit Peter Wright. Those 'who visited the sacred deposit before it was embalmed' bore 'witness to having inhaled divers heavenly odours such as they had never before experienced'.[103] On the other hand, to the enemies of God, the martyr's scent might be poison. After Thomas Pilchard's horrific execution, as John Gerard recorded, 'the officers returning home, many of them died presently crying out they were poisoned with the smell of his bowels'.[104]

---

[99] Challoner, *MMP*, p. 196; see also Thomas, *WECM*, p. 289.

[100] Challoner, *MMP*, pp. 201, 221; Pollen, *AEM*, p. 266 (ABSJ, Collectanea M, p. 139ª).

[101] Challoner, *MMP*, p. 247; *AWCBC*, pp. 1372–4, 1377–9 (Bodl., MS Eng. th. b. 2, pp. 422–3), 1389–90; Thomas Worthington, *A Relation of Sixtene Martyrs: Glorified in England in Twelve Monethes. With a Declaration. That English Catholiques Suffer for the Catholique religion. And that the Seminarie Priests agree with the Iesuites* (Douai, 1601), sig. F5ʳ⁻ᵛ; Thomas Fitzherbert, *A Defence of the Catholyke Cause*...(Antwerp, 1602), fo. 13ʳ; *HC 1558–1603*, II, p. 193. Garnet's letter to Robert Persons on 16 August 1600 admitted that Glanville 'made a feast at his house and went to bring his guests on the way and had a horse led by on which he, getting up to ease himself, his man by chance picked him over instead of helping': ABSJ, Collectanea P/ii, p. 552ᵇ. For Glanville's fate ('that famous miracle'), see also ABSJ, Anglia III, no. 99 (John Price to Robert Persons, 19 February/1 March 1610; the relevant passage is omitted in the transcript printed in TD, II, pp. ccclxxvi–ccclxxviii).

[102] Thomas, *WECM*, p. 251.

[103] Foley, *RSJ*, II, p. 549.

[104] Pollen, *UD*, pp. 288–9 (ABSJ, Anglia VII, no. 26); cf. Pollen, *AEM*, p. 321 (ABSJ, Collectanea M, p. 196ᵇ). For the bringing together of the stories about Pilchard, see Dillon, *CM*, pp. 104–5.

MARTYRDOM AND THE CONSTRUCTION OF MARTYR NARRATIVES   69

In and after the Jacobean period, as the number of treason trials of Catholics went down, inevitably there are fewer of these revenge narratives. But, for example, in April 1611 the Jesuit missioner Richard Holtby in Yorkshire still had things to say about the Catholic community's enemies. Sir Hugh Bethel 'of late died, a pernicious fellow, at whose death there was such rumbling and jumbling as if all the devils in Hell had…come for him'. In addition, in the case of the 'two Askews, father and son, both vile persecutors', Askew Snr was struck 'lame all of one side; and the son, going to see his father sick, by the way fell suddenly dead from his horse'.[105] In 1612, there were claims that, immediately after the executions of the priests Richard Newport and William Scot, the sea off Plymouth turned red as blood and gave off an unbearable stench.[106] Of the last English martyr before the civil war, the Jesuit Edmund Arrowsmith, there was a tradition that an informer, a farmer named Crook, appropriated the Jesuit's cloak which was made into a suit for the farmer's son, who was promptly thrown from his horse and killed while the rest of the Crook family's progeny, as *The Lancashire Daily Post* put it in October 1924, were 'deformed or dwarfs'.[107]

After the Popish Plot trials of the later 1670s and early 1680s, a document entitled 'a true relation of some judgments of God against those who accused the priests and other Catholics after the pretended plot in England' described the ghastly ends of those who had conspired against the faithful. One of David Lewis's accusers, himself a dwarf, one Mr Trot, 'a little after' Lewis's 'execution, fell down dead in the public street, covered with vermin'. In August 1680, William Bedloe died, blaspheming and cursing those who had suborned him to accuse the innocent; and his tongue 'came out of his mouth so long, black and swollen that it was impossible to draw it back again'. Despite strenuous efforts to keep the news from the public, 'this frightful case was spread through all the city of Bristol'. In 1681 'Dr [Israel] Tonge died in the house' of the rogue Stephen College, 'of starvation and eaten up with vermin', so it was said. College, who had 'encouraged the mob to insult' the virtuous Elizabeth Cellier 'on the pillory', was 'himself hung and quartered'. Others who had denounced Cellier came to bad ends as well—two of them went mad.[108] Richard Morrice was one of the accusers of the virtuous and aged priest Nicholas Postgate. While he lived, testified the priest John Danby,

---

[105] ARSJ, Anglia 37, fo. 124ᵛ. A nineteenth-century history of Leominster recorded the tradition that the carpenter who made the gallows for Roger Cadwallader's execution was hanged on it himself: G. F. Townsend, *The Town and Borough of Leominster*…(Leominster, 1863), pp. 86–7; AWCBC, pp. 1824, 1826 (Townsend cites manuscript notes by [Thomas] Blount, the Herefordshire antiquarian).
[106] See p. 411 below.   [107] *The Lancashire Daily Post* (13 October 1924).
[108] Foley, *RSJ*, V, pp. 74–5, 867, 929 (translation of extracts of ABSJ, Anglia V, no. 100, a document cited by Henry Foley in AAW, Processus Martyrum, 1874, I, p. 259); Kenyon, *PP*, pp. 276–7. John Plessington remarked in his execution speech that one of his accusers, Robert Wood, was 'suddenly killed': *The Speech of…Mr William Plessington, who was executed at Chester*…(1679); see also Challoner, *MMP*, p. 541.

70 CATHOLICS AND TREASON

Morrice was 'abused by everyone with the odious name of Hang-Priest'.[109] Here the Tory reaction in and after 1680 becomes part of the process whereby God punished those who brought false witness against the faithful.

Treason and Conscience, Religion and (Popular) Politics

At some very basic level, all of these events and stories can be assimilated into a broader early modern European crime-and-punishment culture. But they tell us also about the considerable ideological complexities surrounding these executions. When the State confronted its Catholic subjects and critics around and on the scaffold, there were presented to public view ambiguities and ambivalences that, as we have seen, are not easily contained within Sharpe's, Foucault's, and even Laqueur's accounts of how this sort of judicial transaction and these discursive structures were supposed, by some, to work. In fact, as is evident from many of the martyrological narratives themselves, the kind of State power being constituted by these performances was a product of a series of complex interactions between different ideological fractions and forces, each of which attempted to appropriate the forms and genres made available by these events for its own purposes.

At certain points in the period before 1603, the drift of events meant that a particular kind of Protestant, that is to say (moderate) puritan, might get the chance to constitute the State. Or, rather, there were times when the English queen was forced to turn to a puritan constituency, particularly when Catholic voices seemed to be turning against her. But there was an element here of a deal with the Devil since the price of this support was the kind of concession to moderate puritan opinion to which Elizabeth was temperamentally opposed. In the course of proffering what they claimed was true loyalty to the queen, godly Protestants were able to enlist for their own purposes the workings of the treason law. They did this in order to define, by their own lights, how Church and State should be governed under the monarchy, but a monarchy which was properly and appropriately counselled. Something like this certainly happened in the proceedings against the Jesuit Edmund Campion, during which a roll call of mid-Elizabethan moderate puritans lined up in order to discredit him.[110]

But of course the early and mid-1580s legislation against Catholic clergy and indeed Catholic separatism more generally was the product of a series of rather specific political crises, generated in part by the divisions and dysfunctions of the

---

[109] Kn., VI, unpaginated section (John Danby to John Knaresborough, 17 February 1708). The excise man, John Reeves, who arrested Postgate came to a bad end for, as he was 'the chief instrument, so the judgments of God were' harder 'on him than on the rest' (he probably committed suicide): Kn., VI, unpaginated section (Danby to Knaresborough, 17 February 1708).
[110] See pp. 111–14, 111 n.170 below.

MARTYRDOM AND THE CONSTRUCTION OF MARTYR NARRATIVES 71

queen's government but far more by the threat from Mary Stuart and, eventually, by the decision to intervene in the Netherlands and in effect to declare war against the Spanish monarchy.[111] Inevitably, some Catholics denounced the raft of new laws as a puritan conspiracy both against them and, ultimately, against Elizabeth herself. As they saw it, the persecutors were attacking, intimidating, attempting to silence, and ultimately to destroy those who were, in reality, loyal subjects who, as it happened, also knew better than anyone the dangers inherent in contemporary puritanism. In the later 1590s and then, especially, after 1603 that Catholic critique fed into the conformist pushback against aspects of puritanism that was part and parcel of the politics of James VI's accession in England. In turn, that made the continued use of the penal law against Catholics, if anything, more controversial than before.[112]

Thus, every time a Catholic priest was executed for treason (and, after the passing of the 1585 statute, this was almost always on the basis of proof of the mere fact of his ordination) or his patron was hanged merely for harbouring him (a penalty stipulated by the 1585 statute), the issue of where legitimate exercise of royal authority ended and where tyranny and persecution began was up for public discussion. Here the boundaries between the State and the Church, religion and treason, private conscience and public non/compliance were made available for inspection and renegotiation. The processes of prosecution exposed all kinds of fault lines not just between Catholics and Protestants but among Catholics themselves. This comes out clearly in the saga of Margaret Clitherow in York. Even at the point in the mid-1580s when many Catholics would probably have agreed that they were experiencing something like persecution, the fact was that a number of Clitherow's co-religionists were far from sure that her out-and-out opposition to the local State in York was the right approach to take. Some of them may have thought that she brought her terrible fate on herself.[113] One should say also that there were other Catholics, in York and elsewhere, who must have thought that she was absolutely right and that, faced with the State's tyranny, not even minimal conformity was acceptable, even if the consequences were so potentially appalling.

Under the often dreadful pressure thus loaded onto those of a Catholic persuasion, the fractures and fissures caused by doubts about how far it was licit to reject royal authority might map onto other fault lines inside the Catholic community. Historians are familiar, even if sometimes only superficially, with the quarrels between Catholics during the 1590s and early 1600s—sometimes called the 'appellant' or 'Archpriest' controversy. The protagonists are frequently, for shorthand purposes, referred to as 'Jesuits' and 'seculars', although, as with so many divisions of opinion in the period, it is never quite as simple and clear-cut as

---

[111] See Chapters 5 and 6 below. [112] See Chapters 11–13 below.
[113] Lake and Questier, *Trials*.

72   CATHOLICS AND TREASON

convenient terminology of this sort suggests.[114] The matters in dispute between the two sides often enough took the form of incredibly pernickety disagreements about Church government and regulation of the clergy. But they were also phrased by reference to the relationship of the Catholic community to the State and to what might happen in the future. These frictions worked themselves out publicly in, among other places, the trials and executions of Catholics. There seems, for example, to have been a more positive investment, by some Jesuit clergy and their friends, in the evangelism of the prison conversion and the overt emotionalism of the last dying speech, embedded as they were in the martyrologies of the period.[115] But other clergy were not likely to surrender the evangelical and moral high ground in this respect. Indeed, in the gaols where priests themselves were held, the public polemical and personal stakes might potentially be very high. While some clergy spent years in prison doing, one assumes, not very much, technically the gaols were holding these people (after the passing of the 1585 statute) as de facto traitors on some early modern equivalent of death row; they could, in theory, almost at any point be dragged off to execution. Something like this certainly did happen in August–October 1588.[116] What these potential martyrs said and did was crucial for the definition of what Catholicism in Protestant England actually meant.

The gaols were the subject, therefore, of a good deal of public interest and attention.[117] They could be taken to be a visible sign of the Church under the cross and there were Catholic attempts to make the prisons where priests were held by the regime—for example, Wisbech in East Anglia—into showcases of clerical talent and spiritual example.[118] The priest William Clarke, a bitter enemy of the Jesuits, saw the dissensions at Wisbech in the 1590s as part of a Jesuitical conspiracy to achieve dominion over other clergy: 'could there be a better means devised' for those people than to 'begin in that place', that is, the prison in Wisbech Castle, 'where the gravest and best deserving priests of our country were in durance for Gods cause, by the presence of whom the very house was a Sion unto our country and a lantern unto all Catholics abroad'. Once the Society had established its influence there, 'without check or control, what priest durst to have gainsaid their dominion abroad but', immediately, 'he should have his mouth stopped with the voluntary submission of those grave priests and designed

---

[114] See Chapters 9 and 10 below for the dispute itself, triggered by the appointment of George Blackwell as archpriest with authority over the English secular clergy.

[115] Lake and Questier, 'Agency', esp. at pp. 87–95.   [116] Ward, LT, pp. 286–91.

[117] P. Lake with M. Questier, *The Antichrist's Lewd Hat: Protestants, Papists and Players in Post-Reformation England* (2002), ch. 6.

[118] Lake with Questier, *The Antichrist's Lewd Hat*, p. 294; Caraman, *HG*, pp. 169–70; Robert Persons, *A Briefe Apologie, or Defence of the Catholike Ecclesiastical Hierarchie, & Subordination in England...* (n.p. [Antwerp], n.d. [late 1601]), fos 64ᵛ–5ʳ. Leslie Ward estimates that, in January–March 1588, at least eighteen priests were sent from the London prisons to Wisbech: Ward, LT, p. 283.

MARTYRDOM AND THE CONSTRUCTION OF MARTYR NARRATIVES 73

martyrs'?[119] Martyr discourses were not the preserve of any one interest group, clerical tendency, or section of the community. All through the period, for a variety of reasons, different sorts of Catholics tried to appropriate them.

Some appellant writers in fact went so far as to allege that the State could not be blamed for seeking to prevent Catholic sedition against the queen. In their view, even someone such as Edmund Campion might be regarded as having provoked the regime into the action it took against him and his associates. Others, obviously, did not agree. But there was no denying that, particularly in the later sixteenth century, the ministry of certain Catholic clergymen could be regarded as confrontational.[120] Christopher Devlin's excellent account of Robert Southwell's ministry, although focused primarily on Southwell's spiritual qualities and Jesuit charism, suggests also how incendiary such clergy might be in London in the later 1580s and early 1590s, although Devlin regarded the Elizabethan State as a persecutory one. The 'centre of resistance' in London, says Devlin, 'was the Ward of Farringdon...a square subtended from the old west wall of the city, with diagonals from Blackfriars to Holborn Bars and from Temple Bar to Greyfriars, or Christ-Church Hospital'. It was inside this area that eighteen priests and lay Catholics were, in a two-year period, arrested and, 'within this square, they were executed'. The regime's purpose was to strike 'terror into the surrounding inhabitants' who presumably were aware of the concentration of these clergy in their midst and of the challenge that they represented.[121]

Southwell had powerful, indeed aristocratic, patrons who were prepared to receive him into their London houses. In Southwell's case, for some of the time his safe haven was Sackville House on the Strand. It was for people such as Lady Margaret Sackville (the sister of Philip Howard) that Southwell produced some of his well-known literary work.[122] From Arundel House, he was able to issue his inflammatory *Epistle of Comfort*, which accused the regime of a vicious persecution of good Catholics.[123] Right next to Sackville House was the Bridewell precinct and also the gaol where a number of Catholic prisoners were tortured.[124] Near Holborn Bars there was Southampton House, where Mary Wriothesley, countess of Southampton, harboured seminary clergy.[125] Close to Southampton House was the residence of Swithin Wells, whose own links were with the Wriothesley family in Hampshire and whose circle was the target of Topcliffe's

---

[119] William Clarke, *A Replie unto a Certaine Libell, latelie set foorth by Fa: Parsons...intituled, a Manifestation of the great Folly...*(n.p. [London], 1603), fo. 4ᵛ, cited in Lake with Questier, *Antichrist's Lewd Hat*, p. 293.

[120] See Chapters 5 and 6 below.   [121] Devlin, *LRS*, p. 215.

[122] Devlin, *LRS*, pp. 215–16, 230–1.   [123] ARCR, II, no. 714.   [124] Devlin, *LRS*, p. 216.

[125] Devlin, *LRS*, p. 218. For John Hambley's account of the extensive Catholic networks in this area of London in the early and mid-1580s, see PRO, SP 12/192/46. i.

74 CATHOLICS AND TREASON

campaign against London Catholics in late 1591, though only after Wells had provoked the authorities for years and years.[126]

Most of the signposts and indicators which would tell us why, under certain circumstances, Catholic separatists came into conflict with the State and its agents were, of course, edited out of Challoner's apotheosis of Catholic martyrdom, or, at the very most, they remain in the shadows of Challoner's and other martyrologists' texts. But the only partially chamfered edges of the conventional format of the martyr stories, of the kind referred to during this chapter, tell us things about post-Reformation politics that are not just worth knowing but, indeed, cannot easily be recovered from elsewhere. In other words, those occasions on which Catholics were done to death by the State were ones in which a good deal of contemporary and entirely mainstream conflict about the connection between religion and politics was present. The claim made in the rest of this volume is that, by reconstructing, where possible, the narratives of arrests, trials, and executions in the contexts in which those events occurred, keeping in mind the potential for political message-sending inherent in the operations of public justice, we can restore some historical coherence to this material without simply deconstructing Catholic martyrdom out of existence.

[126] Devlin, *LRS*, p. 218; Questier, *C&C*, pp. 64–5, 267.

PART II

4

'Sentenced to Die as in Cases of High Treason'

The Elizabethan Settlement and the Coming of Intolerance, *c.*1558–1582

The claim in the preceding chapters has been that there is no automatic or obvious disconnect between the English Catholic martyrological tradition and the ways in which we look at the political history of the early modern period. Indeed, the two should be read against each other. So where, then, do we start?[1] In some ways, the obvious place to have begun would have been with the Catholic victims of the juggernaut habitually referred to, by scholars, as the Henrician (or sometimes 'the king's') Reformation, even though the casualties of Henrician repression were not just Catholic ones. The high-profile Catholic targets of the king, Sir Thomas More, and Bishop John Fisher, have been the subject of intense scholarly interest over the years.[2] Nicholas Sander's history of the Reformation recognized More as a leading opponent of the royal supremacy asserted by Henry VIII.[3] With Fisher and other Henrician Catholic martyrs, More figured in the *Ecclesiae Anglicanae Trophaea* of 1584 and in Richard Verstegan's *Theatrum Crudelitatum Haereticorum Nostri Temporis* of 1587. In 1588 Thomas Stapleton's *Tres Thomae*, incorporating a biography of More, was published at Douai. Other biographies of him circulated widely in manuscript, notably his son-in-law William Roper's. Four English and two Latin lives had been written before 1600.[4]

---

[1] This chapter in places relies on P. Lake and M. Questier, 'Puritans, Papists and the "Public Sphere" in Early Modern England: The Edmund Campion Affair in Context', *Journal of Modern History* 72 (2000), pp. 587–627.

[2] The bibliography for just this aspect of the Henrician Reformation is very large, but see esp. H. A. Kelly, L. W. Karlin, and B. G. Wegemer, *Thomas More's Trial by Jury: A Procedural and Legal Review, with a Collection of Documents* (Woodbridge, 2011); B. Gregory, *Salvation at Stake: Christian Martyrdom in Early Modern Europe* (1999), ch. 7; P. Marshall, 'Papist as Heretic: The Burning of John Forest, 1538', *HJ* 41 (1998), pp. 351–74; G. Bernard, *The King's Reformation: Henry VIII and the Remaking of the English Church* (2005); and the review by Ethan Shagan in *JBS* 45 (2006), pp. 389–91; W. Sheils, '1535 in 1935: Catholic Saints and English Identity: The Canonization of Thomas More and John Fisher', in D. J. Crankshaw and G. W. C. Gross (eds), *Reformation Reputations: The Power of the Individual in English Reformation History* (2020), pp. 159–88.

[3] Nicholas Sander, ed. D. Lewis, *Rise and Growth of the Anglican Schism...* (1877), pp. 120–6.

[4] D. Shanahan, 'The Family of St. Thomas More in Essex 1581-1640', *Essex Recusant* 1 (1959), pp. 62–74, at p. 62; Giovanni Battista de Cavalleriis, *Ecclesiae Anglicanae Trophaea...* (Rome, 1584), engraving 27; Gregory, *Salvation*, p. 273; ARCR, I, nos 944–6.

Catholics and Treason: Martyrology, Memory, and Politics in the Post-Reformation. Michael Questier, Oxford University Press. © Michael Questier 2022. DOI: 10.1093/oso/9780192847027.003.0004

78   CATHOLICS AND TREASON

Recently, Anne Dillon has shown, in a work of quite staggering erudition, how the martyrdom of the English Carthusians in the mid-1530s was repackaged in the 1550s.[5] In the early seventeenth century, two martyrologists who went into print, John Wilson and Thomas Worthington, explicitly stated that there was a continuity between the first of the Henrician martyrs and those who had recently come to grief in the early years of James I.[6]

But, as suggested above, there are some important distinctions to be made between what happened before 1558 and after that date. There is a sense that the king's victims in the 1530s were not really recalled in the same way by Catholics as those who suffered under Elizabeth. Stanley Morison judges that the cult of More is essentially a modern creation.[7] More's struggle with the regime was, as much as anything, about the jurisdictional connection between the English Church and the see of Rome, and about the nature of oaths and what could be sworn in conscience and what could not. In the later sixteenth century, by contrast, the change in the scope of the treason law made it possible for Catholics to allege that it was the profession of the true faith itself which was being steadily criminalized. As Brad Gregory says, 'the Henrician martyrs had not died as part of a movement; rather, they had stood still while the world around them moved'.[8] This is not to say that some contemporaries—notably Cardinal Reginald Pole—did not take those martyrdoms intensely seriously at the time they occurred;[9] and, of course, the Henrician martyrs were heavily represented among those whom Pope Leo XIII beatified in December 1886 and May 1895. But, as Professor Gregory points out, 'Pole's dramatic exaltation of the new martyrs and extensive defence of papal authority were not part of a sustained celebration or veneration', and, 'in the mid-1530s, the conditions were not right for widespread, popular recognition of the Henrician martyrs'.[10] In Mary's reign a number of people, notably

---

[5] A. Dillon, *Michelangelo and the English Martyrs* (2012); see also Dillon, *CM*, pp. 52–62; Maurice Chauncy, *Historia Aliquot Nostri Saeculi Martyrum...*(Mainz, 1550).

[6] John Wilson, *The English Martyrologe conteyning a Summary of the Liues of the...Saintes of the Three Kingdoms, England, Scotland, and Ireland....Whereunto is Annexed in the End a Catalogue of Those, who have Suffered Death in England for Defence of the Catholicke Cause, since King Henry the 8. his Breach with the Sea Apostolicke, unto this Day....*(n.p. [St Omer], 1608); Thomas Worthington, *A Catalogue of Martyrs in England: for Profession of the Catholique Faith, since the Yeare of our Lord, 1535...unto this Yeare 1608* (np [Douai], n.d. [1608]).

[7] S. Morison, *The Portraiture of Thomas More by Hans Holbein and After* (1957), p. 40. See also M. Anderegg, 'The Tradition of Early More Biography', in R. S. Sylvester and G. P. Marc'hadour (eds), *Essential Articles for the Study of Thomas More* (Hamden, Conn., 1977), pp. 1–25, at p. 20; M. Robson, 'Posthumous Representations of Thomas More: Critical Readings' (PhD, Leeds, 1996), p. 140; Gregory, *Salvation*, pp. 254–5.

[8] Ibid., pp. 260, 268.

[9] Ibid., pp. 265–8. Prominent here was none other than Margaret Pole, countess of Salisbury; cf. ABSJ, CP (Margaret Pole): J. E. Paul to Philip Caraman, 4 and 13 November 1962; Caraman to Paul, 6 and 14 November 1962.

[10] Gregory, *Salvation*, pp. 267, 268.

'SENTENCED TO DIE AS IN CASES OF HIGH TREASON' 79

Bishop Stephen Gardiner, who were associated with the reaction against the Protestant reform measures of Edward VI's time, absolutely did not want to be reminded of the way that, some years before, they had either condemned or simply failed to stand with their fellow Catholics.[11]

The sense of Professor Elton's round-up of the cases of those who fell foul of the new treason statutes in the 1530s is that very many of these people were speaking against the reform of religion but were never, as far as we know, considered to be Catholic martyrs.[12] The claims of the group around Elizabeth Barton (the so-called 'nun of Kent') collapsed, in the public eye at least, in the face of the decision of other Catholics, including Sir Thomas More, to distance themselves from her.[13] Jonathan Gray suggests that, even at its most hard line, the Henrician State in the 1530s and 1540s proceeded by way of negotiation, as often as not by offering various kinds of oath, in order to elicit assent to its most recent courses, although one imagines that most of the king's and Thomas Cromwell's victims would not have seen it thus.[14]

Geoffrey Elton's student Leslie Ward makes much the same case for the Elizabethan State, even in the war years of the 1580s.[15] But it is still arguable that those who were arraigned as traitors on grounds of religion after 1558 (in fact, in and after the 1570s), compared with the martyrs of the 1530s and 1540s, stood in a different relationship to the authority which prosecuted and killed them, that is, compared with what happened under Henry VIII. Bishop Challoner and others were able to construct catalogues of those, mainly clergy, who had been condemned to death for what could, however controversially, be argued, and was certainly declared by their co-religionists, to be an issue exclusively of 'religion'.[16] Although the legal and physical consequences of treason were fairly similar all through the period, the politics of repression, if that is how one sees it, shifted significantly during the later sixteenth century; and, partly as a result, the relevant archives are much fuller.

---

[11] T. S. Freeman, 'Introduction: Over their Dead Bodies: Concepts of Martyrdom in late Medieval and early Modern England', in T. S. Freeman and T. F. Mayer (eds), *Martyrs and Martyrdom in England c. 1400–1700* (Woodbridge, 2007), pp. 1–34, at pp. 11–12.

[12] G. R. Elton, *Policy and Police: The Enforcement of the Reformation in the Age of Thomas Cromwell* (Cambridge, 1972), chs 6, 7, esp. pp. 301 f. For the Henrician enhancement of the existing treason law, see esp. D. Alan Orr, *Treason and the State: Law, Politics, and Ideology in the English Civil War* (Cambridge, 2002), pp. 16–20.

[13] E. Shagan, *Popular Politics and the English Reformation* (Cambridge, 2003), pp. 65 f., 72 f., esp. pp. 86 f.

[14] J. Gray, *Oaths and the English Reformation* (Cambridge, 2013), esp. chs 3, 4.   [15] Ward, LT.

[16] See Challoner, *MMP*.

80 CATHOLICS AND TREASON

The Elizabethan Settlement and the Culture of Conformity in Post-Reformation Politics

Of course, what the Elizabethan settlement of 1559 was designed to do, in the first instance, was to prevent public conscience-based conflict, that is, once the non-compliant higher clergy of the Marian Church had gone abroad or had been locked up. The new regime, for entirely prudential political reasons, not least of which was the unsettled path of the succession in line to the recently crowned Elizabeth, was obliged and determined to create a kind of internal ideological unity in the British Isles which would serve to discourage the French from interfering in Scotland; and for that reason the settlement of religion had to look like a Protestant one. There was an English military incursion across the Scots border in order to uproot the French regent, Mary of Guise, and to remodel the Scots polity. When the regent's daughter, Mary Stuart, returned, she was forced to acculturate herself and her own Catholic tendencies in such a way as to rule in the context of a firmly Anglo-Scottish amity, constructed on the basis of allegedly shared Protestant religious values.[17]

In other respects, however, the Elizabethan reform of the English Church was channelled into a relatively low-grade conformist arrangement which, though it brought about the rapid extirpation of the Marian Counter-Reformation, was never going, on its own, to produce a Continental-style Protestant Reformation.[18] With France experiencing its own turmoil at that moment, there was nothing to be gained, as far as Elizabeth was concerned, from alienating the Spanish court. Nor, for her, was there any point in estranging Mary Stuart's supporters in England or, indeed, the mass of what may, in some regions, have been a religiously conservative majority of the population. Hence Elizabeth's frequent distancing of herself from some of her godlier Protestant courtiers and churchmen. Any kind of purely Protestant-centred account of good government and true religion remained, as far as the queen was concerned, off limits, although there were quite a few Protestants who, given half a chance, would have taken their revenge on their Catholic enemies and would have done so as a way of committing the queen to a more hard-line version of the Protestant Reformation.[19] In October 1559, Christopher Goodman, who was still in Edinburgh, simply could not believe that, as he saw it, the evil Catholic persecutors were going to get away with what they had done in Mary's reign.[20] On 26 September 1562, one newsletter from Louvain

---

[17] Questier, *DP*, ch. 1, esp. at pp. 33–4.

[18] For a major revision and statistical analysis of the number of clergymen deprived in the wake of the settlement of 1559, see P. Marshall and J. Morgan, 'Clerical Conformity and the Elizabethan Settlement Revisited', HJ 59 (2016), pp. 1–22.

[19] R. Harkins, '"Persecutors under the Cloak of Policy": Anti-Catholic Vengeance and the Marian Hierarchy in Elizabethan England', *Sixteenth Century Journal* 48 (2017), pp. 357–84, at p. 362.

[20] *CSPSc 1547–63*, p. 257; Harkins, '"Persecutors under the Cloak of Policy"', pp. 362–3.

'SENTENCED TO DIE AS IN CASES OF HIGH TREASON' 81

reported that 'the Catholic bishops are kept in close confinement and the new bishops are not ashamed to preach publicly that they ought to be put to death, lest they should live to put them to death' instead.[21] But this was something that did not happen.

This did not prevent some Catholic observers from concluding that they were witnessing a new persecution. Nicholas Sander wrote a long memorandum in circa mid-1561 for the papacy. He described, as he viewed it, the evils of what Elizabeth had done and what appeared to be the impending martyrdoms of the suffering servants of Christ in the English Church.[22] But political circumstances made real repression unlikely. Although there were rumours in early 1563 that Elizabeth herself had said that she would put prominent Catholics to death, the turn of events in France, notably the defeat of the prince of Condé at Dreux, meant that, even if she had been inclined to go in that direction, she had to draw back.[23] The fact was that, faced by the apparently unstoppable rise of Mary Stuart in Scotland, Elizabeth certainly now dared not alienate her own Catholic constituency in England. The attempt by Archbishop Matthew Parker and Bishops Robert Horne and Edmund Grindal, and also Sir William Cecil and Lord Robert Dudley, to use the 1563 treason legislation against Edmund Bonner failed. Elizabeth had no intention of seeing martyrs being made by resorting to this statute. Hence Elizabeth's well-known instruction to Archbishop Parker that her bishops should not tender the oath of supremacy for a second time, since a second refusal would trigger a treason prosecution under the act.[24]

Traditionally, historians of the period have tended to see a systemic shift in the relationship between the regime and the Catholic community somewhere towards the end of the 1560s. Mary Stuart's deposition in Scotland, after the collapse of her marriage to Henry, Lord Darnley and his murder, and then her flight across the border into the North of England, radicalized the already problematic English succession question. Matters were made worse when Mary, in yet another black-widow union and despite her existing marriage to James Hepburn, earl of Bothwell, sought to woo Thomas Howard, duke of Norfolk. When this new dynastic project started to spin out of control, Norfolk's brother-in-law Charles Neville, earl of Westmorland, and his fellow malcontent Thomas Percy, earl of Northumberland, were bumped into a rebellion, one which reprised some of the language and the imagery, particularly the Five Wounds banners, of the Pilgrimage of Grace in 1536. This was a revolt which, despite its numerous

---

[21] *CSPR 1558–71*, p. 105. See also S. Gratwick and C. Whittick, 'The Loseley List of "Sussex Martyrs": A Commission of Enquiry into the Fate of their Assets and the Development of the Sussex Protestant Martyrology', *Sussex Archaeological Collections* 133 (1995), pp. 225–40.

[22] *Miscellanea I* (CRS 1, 1905), pp. 34 f.   [23] Questier, *DP*, pp. 40–1.

[24] *CSPSp 1558–67*, p. 392; for the 1563 statute and the problems of its enforcement, see Ward, LT, pp. 46 f. and ch. 4, p. 200 f. (esp. at p. 208); L. J. Ward, 'The Treason Act of 1563: A Study of the Enforcement of Anti-Catholic Legislation', *Parliamentary History* 8 (1989), pp. 289–308, esp. at pp. 292–8.

82 CATHOLICS AND TREASON

overlapping causes, lapsed very rapidly into the language of religion and the struggle against heresy. The rebels secured, though late in the day, the excommunication of Elizabeth via the papal bull *Regnans in Excelsis*. It declared her deposed and her subjects absolved of their allegiance to her.[25] Some of the earls' adherents, such as William Smith of Esh, cited papal authority to justify the act of rebellion.[26] The rebel clergy, notably William Holmes, used sacramental power to absolve from schism as a means of grafting the rebel laity more firmly onto the cause.[27] Nicholas Sander in 1571 looked back, in print, on the Northern Rising and concluded that those who had been executed for their part in it were true martyrs.[28]

But it was far from clear that there was majority support among Catholics/conservatives for this act of civil disobedience, though it had also been, at a practical level, simply the wrong time of the year to start a revolt.[29] Several hundred people were hanged under, in effect, martial law as a warning to others. But there was no final consensus among Catholics at this moment, if ever, that all the rebels who perished were martyrs, even though the earl of Northumberland immediately after his execution in 1572 was revered, by some northerners, including for example Margaret Clitherow's friend Oswald Tesimond, as precisely that, and he was beatified in the nineteenth century.[30]

Shortly after the 1569 rising failed, John Felton obtained a copy of the papal bull of excommunication, to which Pius V had affixed his signature on 25 February 1570, from the Florentine banker Roberto Ridolfi via the Spanish ambassador Guerau de Spes's chaplain. Felton posted it up on the gate of the bishop of London, in St Paul's churchyard.[31] Felton had also given a copy to a

---

[25] Several English Catholics had given evidence at the curia in Rome in the process leading to the issue of the decree: J. H. Pollen, *English Catholics in the Reign of Queen Elizabeth* (1920), pp. 148–51. For a discussion of the purposes of the bull, see P. Hughes, *The Reformation in England* (3 vols, 1954), III, pp. 272–6. For the earl of Northumberland's alleged reluctance to go into rebellion, see *CSPF 1581–2*, p. 16. For the place of religion in the rebellion, see K. Kesselring, '"A Cold Pye for Papistes": Constructing and Containing the Northern Rising of 1569', *JBS* 43 (2004), pp. 417–43.

[26] S. Taylor, 'The Crown and the North of England 1559–70: A Study of the Rebellion of the Northern Earls, 1569–70, and its Causes' (PhD, Manchester, 1981), p. 180.

[27] Ibid., p. 231.

[28] P. Holmes, *Resistance and Compromise: The Political Thought of the Elizabethan Catholics* (Cambridge, 1982), p. 27, citing Nicholas Sander, *De Visibili Monarchia Ecclesiae, Libri Octo* (Louvain, 1571), book VIII, pp. 686–738. Book VII, as Gerard Kilroy notes, concludes with the fate of Dr John Story: Kilroy, *EC*, p. 83. For Christopher Grene's opinion that those who were detected and executed for the conspiracy in Norfolk in 1570 died for their religion, see Stonyhurst MS A V, no. 21, p. 153.

[29] J. T. Cliffe, *The Yorkshire Gentry from the Reformation to the Civil War* (1969), pp. 168–71.

[30] Lake and Questier, *Trials*, p. 217.

[31] N. Williams, *Thomas Howard, Fourth Duke of Norfolk* (1964), pp. 195, 196; TD, III, appendix II; R. B. Wernham, *Before the Armada: The Growth of English Foreign Policy 1485–1588* (1966), p. 307; Hughes and Larkin, *TRP*, II, no. 577; *CSPSp 1568–79*, p. 266; *Concertatio Ecclesiae Catholicae in Anglia Adversus Calvino-papistas et Puritanos...* (Trier, 1588), ed. John Fenn and John Gibbons, sig. L^v–3^r. The indictment of 4 August 1570 stated that Felton and an Irishman named Cornelius had performed this act at 'about eleven o'clock at night' on 24 May; a second indictment named Felton alone: *Fourth Report of the Deputy Keeper of the Public Records* (1843), p. 265. Hughes and Larkin suggest that the

'SENTENCED TO DIE AS IN CASES OF HIGH TREASON' 83

gentleman of Lincoln's Inn, a known Catholic whose premises were searched and, as a result, the bull was found. Felton was arrested the next day—by a troop of over 500 men led by the lord mayor, the lord chief justice, and the two sheriffs. This looks like a major public-relations exercise on the regime's part.[32] Since the bull was nailed to the bishop of London's gate, one assumes it was aimed at least in part at Edmund Grindal. Antonio de Guarás wrote that the 'day and the hour of' Felton's 'execution were unusual ones, for fear of the people'.[33]

For Ridolfi, the spirit of martyrdom was alive and well among the English Catholics under the lash of the 'new Jezebel', even though there were some who yielded 'to sheer force and fear'.[34] However, the series of turning points that did not turn (for Mary Stuart) in 1569–72 does not seem to have radicalized the Catholic fraction of the English national Church. There were some, such as Felton, who indicated their hostility to aspects of the queen's government. But not many did so. There was, of course, the former MP John Story, extradited from Flanders;[35] and there was Thomas Woodhouse—the first of the Catholic clergy executed in the 1570s who was not taken in open rebellion. Imprisoned as early as May 1561, Woodhouse seems to have deliberately provoked the regime. He refused to denounce the 1570 bull of excommunication. He was said to have thrown written papers out of his prison window to stir up public opinion against the queen. He urged Sir William Cecil to tell Elizabeth to submit to the papacy. At execution on 19 June 1573 he said that Elizabeth should beg forgiveness both from God and the pope.[36]

---

bull was publicly displayed on 2 June 1570: Hughes and Larkin, *TRP*, II, p. 341. Felton's daughter said it was on 25 May and that Felton had been aided and abetted by Laurence Webb: Pollen, *AEM*, p. 209 (AAW, A II, no. 2, p. 3).

[32] Pollen, *AEM*, pp. 209–11. Felton's wife had been a maid of honour to Mary Tudor. Felton's daughter claimed that he sent his ring from the scaffold itself on 8 August in St Paul's churchyard to Thomas Radcliffe, earl of Sussex, to be given to the queen. Felton's wife had, by Mary Tudor, been 'recommended to Queen Elizabeth, whose playfellow she was in her childhood for which cause...Elizabeth always bare a good affection unto her' and subsequently granted her 'liberty under her letters patent to keep a priest'; see Pollen, *AEM*, pp. 211–12; see also ABSJ, Collectanea M, p. 88[b]; John Partridge, *The End and Confession of John Felton, the Rank Traitor...* (1570).

[33] *CSPSp 1568–79*, p. 267.   [34] *CSPR 1558–71*, pp. 416–17.

[35] John Story, MP and Regius professor of civil law at Oxford, had enthusiastically hunted Marian Protestants and had gone abroad to serve King Philip in Flanders. He was forcibly repatriated in 1570 and indicted and executed in 1571 (technically for having supported the Northern Rising and for encouraging the duke of Alba to invade, and also for his association with other suspected persons): *CSPF 1569–71*, pp. 220 (Story's distribution of funds to the scholar-exiles at Douai and Louvain), 330; *ODNB*, *sub* Story, John (article by J. Lock); *A Declaration of the Lyfe and Death of Iohn Story...* (1571); *HC 1558–1603*, III, pp. 451–2; Ward, *LT*, pp. 139–40; Kilroy, *EC*, pp. 24–5. Richard Topcliffe remembered watching Story's execution, evidently with considerable satisfaction; see EUL copy (classmark Rowse/Pol) of Girolamo Pollini, *Historia Ecclesiastica della Rivoluzion d'Inghilterra...* (Rome, 1594), p. 496 (Topcliffe's annotation). Leslie Ward demonstrates that two sections of the 1571 treason statute (13 Eliz., c. 1) 'were a direct result of a judicial ruling on the crown's case against' Story, technically an extension of the principles enshrined in the Edwardian treason act (passed in Hilary term 1351; 25 Edward III, c. 5): Ward, *LT*, p. 18.

[36] For Woodhouse, see *ODNB*, *sub* Woodhouse, Thomas (article by T. M. McCoog); Ward, *LT*, p. 133. For an account of Woodhouse's imprisonment and trial, sent to Rome by Henry Garnet in

84 CATHOLICS AND TREASON

But that was about it. At this point, whatever doubts some Catholics harboured about Elizabeth, she still had no incentive to stoke their sense of discontent. During the parliamentary sessions of 1571, 1572, and 1576 she refused to assent to proposals to force Catholics to receive the Protestant communion, even though the 1571 parliament had seen a tightening up of the treason law following the Northern Rebellion.[37] For the queen's more vigorously Protestant servants, this tense stand-off was just about acceptable as long as their version of what constituted good government of the Church was implemented. Outspoken members of the Catholic community could simply be isolated. In York, the recently promoted Archbishop Grindal and the lord president, Henry Hastings, earl of Huntingdon, had thought it a good idea to shut the outspoken Yorkshire physician Dr Thomas Vavasour up in solitary confinement at Hull, where he would be able to 'talk' only to the 'walls'.[38]

Catholics, Puritans, and Persecution in the Mid- and Later 1570s

Still, if there was some kind of uneasy status quo in the early 1570s, it did not last. It is possible that, for whatever reason, Catholic dissent was on the increase during the mid- and later 1570s.[39] It is highly likely that it was encouraged by the queen's suspicions about what she took to be puritan agitation and which famously came to a head with the royal order to Grindal, now archbishop of Canterbury, to suppress the religious exercises known as prophesyings. For Grindal and his friends, the prophesyings were a kind of extra tier of clerical training, a thoroughly evangelical mode of furthering the purposes of the Reformation and also of beating down popery and hence of teaching the proper understanding of obedience to Christian princes.[40] The evidence that papists

mid-1600, see ABSJ, Collectanea M, pp. 161ᵇ–6ᵃ; see also ABSJ, Collectanea P/ii, p. 552ᵇ; AAW, B 28, no. 12, p. 359. Leslie Ward notes that Woodhouse was 'the first to be tried under the 1571 act (13 Eliz., c. 1) for saying that Elizabeth was not "queen of England, France and Ireland" but "a heretic and usurper of the crown"': Ward, LT, p. 20. Richard Topcliffe described Woodhouse as 'a viperous traitor': EUL copy (classmark Rowse/Pol) of Pollini, *Historia Ecclesiastica*, p. 497.

[37] P. Collinson, *Archbishop Grindal: The Struggle for a Reformed Church* (1979), pp. 213, 225. For the statute of 1571, creating five new treasons, see Ward, LT, pp. 50–3.

[38] C. Cross, *The Puritan Earl: The Life of Henry Hastings third Earl of Huntingdon 1536–1595* (1966), p. 230; for Dr Vavasour and his wife, Dorothy, see Foley, *RSJ*, III, pp. 233–9 (AVCAU, Liber 1422 [Grene, Collectanea F], section 4, fos 43ʳ–52ʳ).

[39] The privy council act books in and after 1575 suggest that there was a vigorous campaign in various parts of the realm, e.g. in Staffordshire in the wake of a royal progress there during late July and August 1575 (M. H. Cole, *The Portable Queen: Elizabeth I and the Politics of Ceremony* (Amherst, 1999), p. 188), to compel more overt forms of conformity from visibly recalcitrant Catholics. One of those targeted in Staffordshire was the father of the Jacobean priest-martyr Thomas Maxfield: W. R. Trimble, *The Catholic Laity in Elizabethan England* (Cambridge, Mass., 1964), pp. 76–80; APC 1575–7, p. 93 and *passim*.

[40] Collinson, *EPM*, pp. 168–76, 191–2; R. Houlbrooke, 'The Protestant Episcopate 1547–1603: The Pastoral Contribution', in F. Heal and R. O'Day (eds), *Church and Society in England: Henry VIII to*

'SENTENCED TO DIE AS IN CASES OF HIGH TREASON' 85

resented the prophesyings was itself proof that those who sponsored them were politically reliable and that their mode of Protestantism was a guarantee of the royal supremacy over the Church. Bishop Thomas Bentham said that the papists' 'fretting and fuming' had made him 'the rather to like and allow' of the prophesyings, 'for in my simple judgment no exercise does more set down all papistry and superstition than this'.[41]

For the queen, though, the prophesyings were an expression of popular (in the worst sense of the word) political activity.[42] In December 1576, Grindal simply refused to obey her when she commanded their suppression. He even went so far as to reprimand her—'remember, madam, that you are a mortal creature'.[43] In the months preceding his now inevitable suspension from office (he was sequestered in May 1577 and royal orders then went out to the bishops to suppress the prophesyings), he obstructed all attempts, notably by Robert Dudley, earl of Leicester, to secure a compromise. This virtually forced the queen to sack him.[44]

Admittedly, there is not much explicit evidence of a coherent and organized Catholic reaction to the queen's crushing of Grindal. For the time being, anyway, the pressure was on moderate puritans. The future martyr Montford Scott was arrested in December 1576 along with Dominic Vaughan, a Marian priest. The privy council was told that both of them were 'practising to seduce her Majesty's people by their lewd persuasions from the doctrine of the Gospel'. The council on 23 December instructed Grindal to discover 'such as are and have been factors of…their lewd enterprises'. But apparently this did not serve even to keep them under lock and key. Scott simply returned to Douai in May 1577, after which he was ordained at Brussels and came back to England in June 1577.[45] John Paine, a future victim of the Jesuit Edmund Campion's nemesis George Eliot, was arrested in late April/early May 1576 but was released before March 1577.[46]

Even if Catholics were not actively and publicly exploiting Grindal's catastrophe, one imagines that a number of (in the main, conformist) Catholics were able

---

James I (1977), pp. 78–98, at pp. 89–90; Graves, *TN*, p. 329; P. Lake, 'A Tale of Two Episcopal Surveys: The Strange Fates of Edmund Grindal and Cuthbert Mayne Revisited', *Transactions of the Royal Historical Society*, 6th series, 18 (2008), pp. 129–63, esp. at pp. 130–6; S. E. Lehmberg, 'Archbishop Grindal and the Prophesyings', *Historical Magazine of the Protestant Episcopal Church* 34 (1965), pp. 87–145.

[41] Ibid., p. 92, cited in Lake, 'A Tale', pp. 138–9.

[42] Ibid., p. 132. This controversy was, as Peter Lake notes, a practical expression of the debates between Thomas Cartwright and John Whitgift during the Admonition Controversy: P. Lake, '"The Monarchical Republic of Queen Elizabeth I" (and the Fall of Archbishop Grindal) Revisited', in J. McDiarmid (ed.), *The Monarchical Republic of Early Modern England: Essays in Response to Patrick Collinson* (Aldershot, 2007) pp. 129–47, esp. at pp. 136–7.

[43] Lehmberg, 'Archbishop Grindal', pp. 128–41 (quotation at p. 140); Lake, 'A Tale', p. 135.

[44] Collinson, *Archbishop Grindal*, pp. 237–49; Lehmberg, 'Archbishop Grindal', pp. 92–3. For Elizabeth's letter of 7 May 1577 to the bishops for the suppression of prophesyings (an instruction which, however, applied only to the southern province), see Collinson, *EPM*, pp. 196, 210.

[45] Anstr., I, p. 303; *APC 1575–7*, pp. 255, 256; Knox, *DD*, p. 121; *AWCBC*, p. 966.

[46] Anstr., I, p. 266.

86 CATHOLICS AND TREASON

to mimic and produce what Professor Lake calls the '"royalist" or monarchical construal of the polity and an excoriating account of a whole range of political modes and methods as subversively popular and puritan'.[47] How far this was the case can be picked up from the attempts of Grindal's friends to defend him against his angry royal mistress. Grindal's supporters resorted to a national anti-popery campaign and, notably, they commissioned the survey of recusancy taken in October 1577.[48] The survey has been taken as evidence simply 'of how little impact the government's policies had made since 1559'.[49] But, at the point that it was carried out, it served as a means to defend the beleaguered archbishop, that is, by showing the queen where the real danger came from. On the survey returns are listed some of the names of hardliners, such as the future York martyr Margaret Clitherow and the future Chelmsford martyr Paine.[50] The survey also demonstrated how many partially conformist Catholics there were. Thus Bishop Thomas Cooper cited one Mr Brooksby who, for 'a long time, has not come to his parish church, nor received the sacrament, but of late being convened he is contented to have service in his house and to resort to the same himself', though not necessarily in a 'reverend manner'. Robert Dymock, a JP, 'of late...has yielded to come to the church' but 'so slackly and seldom...as it cannot be any great token of his amendment'.[51]

These, as it happened, were precisely the people whom the queen did not want to see pushed into outright opposition to the 1559 settlement of religion. Those churchmen who were not in sympathy with Grindal, even though they were hardly in favour of crypto- or any kind of Catholicism, were well aware of what the queen did not want to see. Bishop John Whitgift's certificate from Worcester said that, while there were some in his diocese 'of whom there goes a doubtful fame', he refrained for the time being from certifying them to the council.[52] Bishop Richard Cheyney of Gloucester reported known Catholics and others who, for reasons such as sickness or fear of arrest for debt, had avoided their parish churches, but he also cited those who were 'commonly called puritans' and who 'wilfully refuse to come to church, as not liking the surplice, ceremonies and other service'.[53] Edmund Freke in his diocese of Norwich emphasized that his returns comprised 'partly...the papists' and 'partly...the peevish precise sort'.[54] In Cambridge, the vice-chancellor Richard Howland, a one-time supporter of Thomas Cartwright but subsequently a bitter anti-puritan, a client of Whitgift

---

[47] Lake, '"The Monarchical Republic"', pp. 139, 145.

[48] Lake, 'A Tale', pp. 137–8, 140–1. The results of the enquiry are archived in the State Papers Domestic series. Over 1500 names were returned by the end of the year: P. Ryan, 'Diocesan Returns of Recusants for England and Wales. 1577', *Miscellanea XII* (CRS 22, 1921), p. 9; Trimble, *Catholic Laity*, pp. 81–8.

[49] Ward, LT, pp. 55, 92.   [50] Ryan, 'Diocesan Returns', pp. 20, 49, and *passim*.

[51] Ibid., pp. 52–3.   [52] PRO, SP 12/118/11, fo. 21ᵛ.

[53] Ryan, 'Diocesan Returns', pp. 3, 81–3 (PRO, SP 12/117/12, fo. 26ʳ).

[54] PRO, SP 12/117/27, fo. 64ʳ.

'SENTENCED TO DIE AS IN CASES OF HIGH TREASON'   87

and an eventual butt of Marprelatian satire, insisted that there was no recusancy in the city or university of Cambridge at all.[55]

At the same time, it is possible that the fracturing of what may briefly have been a kind of Grindalian status quo in the Elizabethan Church helped to generate a sharper-edged expression of Catholicism inside that Church, that is, of exactly the sort that moderate puritans could point to as subversive. The recruitment of ordinands into the new Catholic seminary system on the Continent may have been encouraged by these observable fissures in the national Church. The future martyr William Dean, a Church of England curate who went abroad to seek ordination, had been at Caius College where, notoriously, it was claimed that 'the whole company of scholars...seemed to be divided into Protestants and papists'. One of the fellows, Richard Swale, was a prominent anti-puritan. John Aveling points to Dean as a leading light in Swale's 'faction'.[56] Another of Swale's favourites and clients was Edward Osborn who, after being refused a degree, went to the new seminary at Rome and then to the college at Rheims.[57] Another Caius member, Robert Sayer, admitted to the college in July 1576, was subsequently impeded in his efforts to take his degree because he had 'by secret conference...laboured to pervert divers scholars' and 'had used divers allegations against divers points' of Bishop John Jewel's *Apologia Ecclesiae Anglicanae*. He had also been associated with the future martyr John Fingley and had sent 'papistical books...into the country'.[58]

The future martyr John Bodey was ejected from New College, Oxford, where he was a fellow and had recently taken his MA in February 1576, which suggests that he had been more or less fully conformist up to that point.[59] Richard White, executed on 17 October 1584, had, he said, conformed until 1576 and, 'since [that time], he came not' to church.[60] Another future martyr, John Boste, who, as a fellow of The Queen's College, must have conformed, seems also to have gone into

---

[55] PRO, SP 12/118/35, fo. 88[r]; P. Lake, *Moderate Puritans and the Elizabethan Church* (Cambridge, 1982), pp. 170–1.

[56] BL, Lansdowne MS 33, no. 46, fos 92[r], 91[v]; *HC 1558–1603*, III, p. 466; J. C. H. Aveling, *The Catholic Recusants of the West Riding of Yorkshire 1558–1790* (Proceedings of the Leeds Philosophical and Literary Society, Literary and Historical Section, X, pt 6, Leeds, 1963), p. 209; C. Law, 'Religious Change in the University of Cambridge, c.1547–84' (PhD, Cambridge, 2013), esp. at p. 232.

[57] Anstr., I, pp. 261–2; BL, Lansdowne MS 33, no. 46, fo. 91[v]. Among the other clergy who had been at Caius was the future Jesuit Richard Holtby, who arrived at Douai in August 1577: Anstr., I, p. 175; Law, 'Religious Change', p. 232.

[58] Law, 'Religious Change', pp. 232–3, citing BL, Lansdowne MS 33, no. 46, fo. 92[r]; Anstr., I, pp. 302–3; D. Lunn, *The English Benedictines 1540–1688: From Reformation to Revolution* (1981), pp. 16–17. Fingley matriculated at Caius in 1573. He had a reputation as 'an arrant papist' and was believed to be already ordained: *AWCBC*, pp. 304–5; BL, Lansdowne MS 33, no. 47, fo. 93[r], no. 46, fo. 91[r], 91[v]. He arrived at Rheims in February 1580: Anstr., I, p. 117.

[59] Pollen, *AEM*, pp. 49–50.

[60] NLW, Denbighshire Gaol Files, Great Sessions 4/5/4/8. I am very grateful to Lloyd Bowen for this reference.

88 CATHOLICS AND TREASON

separation in 1576, that is, around the time that the Grindal business was kicking off.[61]

The first stages, therefore, of what one might call a mid-Elizabethan Catholic martyr-centred narrative and which, in Challoner's *Memoirs* and indeed in most recent historical renderings of the period, seems to come essentially out of nowhere, can be linked to the fall of Grindal in the mid-1570s, though one crucial precondition was the recent establishment of the seminary college at Douai in Flanders. On Peter Lake's highly convincing account, it was no accident that the attempt within government to protect Grindal and to persuade the queen to change her mind coincided with the arrest and prosecution of the seminary priest Cuthbert Mayne down in Cornwall.[62]

While Bishop William Bradbridge of Exeter had been on visitation in his diocese, the Cornish authorities had attempted to strike against known Catholics. In connection with an entirely different matter—the reported transgressions of Anthony Bourne—on 8 June 1577, the high sheriff of the county, Sir Richard Grenville, had searched the residence of Francis Tregian. Tregian was a nephew of the leading West Country Catholic, Sir John Arundell. Grenville had then arrested Mayne, who was Tregian's chaplain, and a number of other Catholics as well. In the house there was found a papal bull (actually, an out-of-date printed jubilee) and some Catholic books.[63] One early Jacobean account narrated that, at that time, 'the sea being much infested with English pirates and piracies, upon complaint thereof made by the subjects of sundry princes', there had been 'a very ample commission from the lord admiral, directed unto' Sir John Arundell, Francis Tregian, and Ambrose Digby 'to examine, punish and redress the said abuses'. Once the commission started its work, Sir Richard Grenville, 'the sheriff of the county with sundry other persons of note and account were presented and accused as offenders in that behalf'. The 'commissioners thereupon were so mightily maligned by those that were culpable as the offenders sought by all means their overthrow and total ruin, the which they rather effected for that the foresaid commissioners were all known Catholics'. Even as this commission was

---

[61] Pollen, *UD*, p. 222 (PRO, SP 12/245/131); *ODNB*, *sub* Boste, John (article by J. A. Lowe); see also *CSPF 1581–2*, p. 622.

[62] Lake, 'A Tale', pp. 139 f. Mayne was ordained at Douai in 1575: Anstr., I, p. 224. William Allen stated that Mayne had been unsympathetic to reformed religion while at St John's, Oxford, and had left in a hurry for Douai after letters which had lobbied him to renounce his function there came to the notice of Grindal (Mayne was warned to abscond by his 'countryman and friend', the future martyr Thomas Ford): Allen, *BH*, sig. Diiii^{r-v}.

[63] *APC 1575–7*, pp. 338, 375, 390; *APC 1577–8*, pp. 6–7; A. L. Rowse, *Tudor Cornwall: Portrait of a Society* (1941), pp. 345–7 (describing pre-existing enmities among the Cornish gentry which were in part pursued by reference to religious division); *CSPF 1577–8*, p. 175; Morris, *TCF*, I (IFT), p. 65; Lake, 'A Tale', p. 139; Ward, *LT*, pp. 221, 222; Dodd, *CH*, II, pp. 171–2. Bishop Bradbridge's survey of recusancy taken at Exeter on 28 October 1577 included the local Catholic gentry whom he had already identified in late June 1577: Ryan, 'Diocesan Returns', pp. 75–7. Anthony Bourne was the son of Sir John Bourne, principal secretary to Mary Tudor; see PRO, SP 15/26/3; PRO, SP 12/152/67.

'SENTENCED TO DIE AS IN CASES OF HIGH TREASON' 89

at work, 'there came likewise a commission from the council unto the said sheriff and others for the apprehending of a gentleman called Mr Anthony Bourne upon some egregious fact that he had committed'. 'Hereupon the said sheriff with nine or ten justices of peace associated unto him...took occasion to enter and search the house' of Francis Tregian.[64]

If this Jacobean narrative is accurate, and there was an entrenched division of opinion in the county about the wisdom of attacking Spanish vessels, it certainly might explain why Tregian became the victim of Grenville and his associates.[65] In other parts of the country at this time there were signs that proceedings against Catholics were becoming harsher. At Oxford, during the so-called Black Assizes of 4–6 July 1577, the Catholic bookbinder Rowland Jenks was sentenced to have his ears cropped. The assize judges had been directed by the council to proceed against Jenks 'for certain seditious speeches by him uttered very maliciously', for which he had already 'been detected before the vice-chancellor' of the university and interrogated by the attorney-general and solicitor-general.[66] After conviction, as the Jesuit Robert Persons related it, Jenks was 'first made to stand openly in the market place to his reproach and infamy, then were his ears nailed hard and fast to a poste and a knife was put into his own hand, there withal to cut his own ears in sunder and so to deliver himself'. This was 'a severe sentence above measure'— at least that was what God seems to have thought and this explained the 'wonderful judgment' subsequently when 'the two judges and wellnigh all the jury' and 'many of the justices and freeholders...died all of a strange kind of disease', though the ill-informed 'imputed' it 'to magic and sorcery, as practised by Catholics'.[67]

Other Catholics seem to have been expressing themselves at least as volubly as Jenks. Ann Foster of York was, it appears, one of a group of women in York, including Margaret Clitherow, who flaunted their Catholicism in the face of the authorities; they were both cited in the October 1577 survey of Catholics. They ended up in gaol and, eventually, Mrs Foster died there.[68] It was ordered that her

---

[64] BL, Additional MS 21203, fo. 18^r; Rowse, *Tudor Cornwall*, p. 347.

[65] A list, dated 26 September 1577, of commissioners to deal with piracy did not include Tregian, and the name of Sir John Arundell was struck out: PRO, SP 12/115/32, fo. 95^v. Two of those named on this list, Sir John Killigrew and Francis Godolphin, who were cousins, were no friends of local Catholics. Killigrew had fought a duel with Ambrose Digby and had targeted Spanish shipping: *HC 1558–1603*, II, pp. 198, 395–6.

[66] *APC 1575–7*, pp. 368–9.

[67] Robert Persons, *An Epistle of the Persecution of Catholickes in Englande. Translated out of Frenche into Englishe*...(Douai [imprint false; printed at Rouen], n.d. [1582]), p. 150 (a translation of Robert Persons, *De Persecutione Anglicana, Epistola*...(Rouen, 1581)); see also pp. 63–4 above.

[68] 'An Account of the Travels, Dangers and Wonderful Deliverances of the English Nuns of the Famous Monastery of Sion. From their first leaving England to their Settlement at Lisbon in the Kingdom of Portugal', EUL (Syon Abbey Archive), MS 389, box 3, item 116, ch. 3, unpaginated; Ryan, 'Diocesan Returns', pp. 15, 20; see also *Relacion que Embiaron las Religiosas del Monasterio de Sion de Inglaterra ....Traduzida de Ingles en Castellano, por Carlos Dractan*...(Madrid, 1594); ARCR, I, no. 741. For the origins of the Syon Abbey MS, see AAW, B 57, session 33, pp. 1–2.

90 CATHOLICS AND TREASON

lifeless body should 'be brought out of prison and laid openly on the [Ouse] bridge in the common street for all the world to gaze and wonder at'. Her husband denied responsibility for her actions but arranged for her to be buried with the remains of the earl of Northumberland, to whom she had a great devotion. Mr Foster opened the earl's grave and, 'without any hindrance, laid her with the blessed martyr's relics'.[69]

In September 1577, Francis Tregian was summoned before the privy council. It was the earl of Sussex (the principal conciliar advocate, as it turned out, of the queen's plan to wed the duke of Anjou) who made the most strenuous, though ultimately unsuccessful, efforts to persuade the openly recusant Tregian to conform.[70] Mayne, Tregian, and others were then arraigned on 16 September 1577 at the assizes at Launceston.[71] Dr Ward notes that the proceedings against Mayne and the others were pushed through by the assize judges, or at least by the senior judge Roger Manwood and by the bishop of Exeter, not in the first instance by the council as such.[72] Mayne and sixteen others were charged under the acts of 1563 and 1571. But only eight of those indicted with Mayne were from that region. The remaining seven were tried in their absence. One of them was William Wiggs, the future priest and associate of the eventual martyr Thomas Alfield.[73] Another was the Londoner Simon Lowe, whose son John was ordained at Rome and was executed at Tyburn on 8 October 1586.[74] As Ward notes, Tregian and the fifteen other laymen charged under the 1563 and 1571 acts were 'accused of aiding Mayne after

---

[69] 'An Account of the Travels'; A. Hamilton, *The Chronicle of the English Augustinian Canonesses Regular of the Lateran, at St Monica's in Louvain* (2 vols, 1906), I, pp. 167–73. The exact date of Mrs Foster's death is not known; but the 'Account' says that the priest John Marsh was one of her confessors. He was not ordained until April 1579 and left for England only in May 1580: Anstr., I, p. 219. Mrs Foster's son, Seth, was at Rome in 1579 and, after ordination in late 1581, left Rome in early 1582; he was at Rome when he heard the news of Mrs Foster's fate: Anstr., I, p. 123; 'An Account of the Travels', ch. 2. I am very grateful to James Kelly for advice on this point (see also J. E. Kelly, *English Convents in Catholic Europe, c. 1600–1800* (Cambridge, 2020), pp. 137–8). Seth Foster was in sympathy with the Holy League in France in the mid-1580s; for the Rouen convent of the Bridgettines (which Seth joined as chaplain in March 1584) and the League, see Bossy, *EC*, pp. 84f; Anstr., I, p. 123. Seth Foster's sister-in-law was Isabel Langley, daughter of the martyr Richard Langley; she died in gaol in York on 3 December 1587: Aveling, *NC*, p. 187; Morris, *TCF*, III (WHN), pp. 325–6. For the reprinting in Yepes's *Historia Particular de la Persecucion de Inglaterra...* (Madrid, 1599) of the preface (fos 1ʳ–13ʳ), written by Persons out of material supplied by Seth Foster, which is in the *Relacion que Embiaron las Religiosas del Monasterio de Sion de Inglaterra*, see ARCR, I, nos 741, 284; EUL (Syon Abbey Archive), MS 389, box 3, item 116, ch. 1.

[70] Rowse, *Tudor Cornwall*, p. 348; Morris, *TCF*, I (IFT), pp. 69–70. For Sussex's advice to the queen in late August 1578 as to how the match might serve to stabilize the Netherlands and prevent either French or Spanish hegemony there, see *HMCS*, II, p. 195.

[71] For the proceedings against Mayne and the other indicted Catholics, see L. J. Ward, 'The Treason Act of 1563: A Study of the Enforcement of Anti-Catholic Legislation', *Parliamentary History* 8 (1989), pp. 289–308, at p. 301; Ward, LT, pp. 53, 223–31; Rowse, *Tudor Cornwall*, p. 348; Lake, 'A Tale', p. 140; Morris, *TCF*, I (IFT), pp. 70–119; Anstr., I, p. 225; Allen, *BH*, sig. Diiiʳ; AAW, A II, no. 15, pp. 49–64, reproduced in *AWCCBM*, pp. 120–39. Ward shows that the account in Morris, *TCF*, I (IFT), is not completely accurate.

[72] Ward, LT, p. 223; *AWCCBM*, p. 134.   [73] Ward, LT, p. 224; Kilroy, *EC*, p. 47.

[74] Ward, LT, p. 230; Anstr., I, pp. 214–15; see p. 165 below.

'SENTENCED TO DIE AS IN CASES OF HIGH TREASON'   91

he had committed' his offence, so they could not be successfully prosecuted unless he was convicted. This was the first time that these two statutes had been used in this way.[75]

Mayne faced, in fact, six charges, four of them under the 1571 legislation.[76] He was, in controversial circumstances, found guilty of bringing the aforementioned papal printed jubilee into the realm.[77] The 1571 act (13 Eliz., c. 2) had really been drafted with the 1570 bull of excommunication in mind, though it was in effect a strict liability offence under the 1571 statute to possess any papal document of that kind. The privy council eventually insisted on Mayne's execution, although one of the assize judges, Sir John Jeffrey, had been uncertain of the case against him.[78] Despite the technical fact of Mayne's guilt, it was crucial for the State to prove, as his interrogators to their own satisfaction did on the day before his execution, that he endorsed papal political authority as it might be applied against a temporal ruler whose realm had allegedly fallen into heresy, and the reform and correction of which might be achieved by the use of force.[79] In addition, the council claimed that Mayne and those others arrested at the same point were known to be notoriously hostile to the queen's government. Mayne had not just the papal jubilee in his possession but also, presumably in manuscript form, a 'special treatise against the book of common prayers'.[80] The council had already, on 12 November, issued its warrant for the execution. Mayne was hanged on 30 November 1577 at Launceston on an unusually high gallows and, specifically, on a market day. This was designed to be as public an event as possible.[81]

---

[75] Ward, LT, pp. 226–7, 230. For the legal chaos in prosecuting Mayne's alleged aiders and abetters, and for the complexities of the outcomes in these cases, see Ward, LT, pp. 227–30.

[76] Ward, LT, pp. 224–5; AWCCBM, pp. 127–8, 140–3.

[77] AWCCBM, pp. 110–11. Mayne argued that the force of the bull/jubilee was already terminated since the jubilee year which it announced had come to an end at Christmas 1575, so he could not have promulgated it, as charged, after that date: AWCCBM, p. 110.

[78] Ward, LT, pp. 224 f.; Morris, TCF, I (IFT), pp. 75 f. (Sir John Popham's delivery of the crown's case against Mayne), 91 (Sir John Jeffrey's doubts), 97–8; Persons, An Epistle, p. 133. For the issue of what was in the papal bull for which Mayne was prosecuted, see Ward, LT, p. 225. The council's decision to have Mayne's case reviewed by the entire judicial bench before ordering sentence to be carried out itself indicates how controversial the business was: Ward, LT, p. 231.

[79] Lake, 'A Tale', p. 144.

[80] APC 1575-7, pp. 6, 7, 85, 375, 390. On 29 November 1577 Mayne was quizzed about the 'words found in a book of his, signifying that though the Catholics did now serve, swear and obey, yet if occasion were offered they should be ready to help the execution': PRO, SP 12/118/46, fo. 105ᵛ (AWCCBM, p. 150).

[81] Lake, 'A Tale', pp. 135–6, 137, 140–1; Read, MSW, II, pp. 280–3; APC 1577-8, p. 85; Morris, TCF, I (IFT), pp. 98–100; Allen, BH, sig. Diiiʳ. For the subsequent additional legal proceedings against Tregian, see BL, Additional MS 21203, fo. 18ʳ⁻ᵛ; Rowse, Tudor Cornwall, pp. 351–4. For the link between this strike against English Catholics and the search at midnight on 19/20 October 1577 of the house of the Spanish agent Antonio de Guarás and the interrogation of him concerning his correspondence, see Lake, 'A Tale', pp. 145–6. There was an attempt to deal with Grindal's case in the star chamber in late November 1577, though illness prevented the archbishop from appearing there. As Lake points out, this coincided more or less exactly with Mayne's execution down in the West Country: Lake, 'A Tale', pp. 142, 146.

92   CATHOLICS AND TREASON

Soon after Mayne's death, the priest John Nelson and one Thomas Sherwood were accused of treason, condemned, and executed in London. There was no mystery as to why Sherwood was arrested. He was a nephew of Francis Tregian. As it was related right at the end of William Allen's *Briefe Historie*, he was about 'to go over to the seminary'. Sherwood was persuaded to offer to 'retract his words in respect he affirmed her Majesty to be a heretic and usurper'; but he refused to answer other questions. The council then ordered that he should be racked, principally in order to 'discover other persons as evil affected...as himself'.[82] His indictment under the 1571 act (13 Eliz., c 1) in queen's bench declared that on 20 November, after his arrest and under interrogation by the recorder of London, William Fleetwood, he had said that 'the pope has power and authority to depose any Christian prince or king' and, if the pope had deposed Elizabeth, which he had, then 'she is deposed and...a usurper'.[83] Nelson had been arrested on 17 November while he was saying Mass. He allegedly, and under pressure, eventually blurted out that the queen was a schismatic and a heretic.[84] The executions took place in the first week of February 1578. Henry Killigrew in delight reported on 22 February to William Davison in Flanders that 'one Sherwood, brought before the bishop of London', John Aylmer, had 'behaved so stubbornly that the bishop' would now 'show the more favour to those miscalled puritans'.[85]

Faced with what appeared to be a distinctly hostile turn in the conduct of the queen's government, publicly advertised in the executions of three Catholics and the imprisonment of others, it was not surprising that some Catholics had themselves started to become more openly belligerent. Not long after, Calvinist hostility forced the senior members of the English college at Douai to move, as they did in March 1578, to Rheims and into the patronage orbit of the noble house of Guise (Mary Stuart's relatives) and the Holy League. The League had been formed initially in 1576 in response to the deal, known as the *Paix Monsieur*, done with the duke of Anjou and his supporters. The Guise clan had every incentive to fund a madrasa-style institution such as the Rheims seminary.[86] Shortly before the seminary members' move, and in the same letter which reported Sherwood's interrogation by Aylmer, Killigrew noted that there had recently been a debate at the Sorbonne in which one disputant, 'urged by the house of Guise', 'would fain have the crown [of France] brought to election, lest the king and his brother dying without issue, it should fall to the king of Navarre and that house, which neither the pope nor the papists can abide'. The topics were as follows: first, that 'kings

---

[82] *APC 1577–8*, p. 111; Allen, *BH*, sig. Dviii^v; Ward, LT, p. 231.

[83] Ward, LT, pp. 20, 231–3; Persons, *An Epistle*, pp. 92–6; Thomas Fitzherbert, *A Defence of the Catholyke Cause...* (Antwerp, 1602) (2nd part, with separate title page, entitled *An Apology of T. F.*), fo. 4^v; Pollen, *AEM*, p. 5 (ABSJ, Collectanea M, p. 158^a); *CSPF 1579–80*, p. 389.

[84] Allen, *BH*, sig. Dv^v; Allen, *TSMD*, pp. 74–5; Ward, LT, pp. 232, 233.

[85] *CSPD Addenda 1566–79*, p. 532 (PRO, SP 15/25/74).   [86] Questier, *DP*, p. 110.

'SENTENCED TO DIE AS IN CASES OF HIGH TREASON'   93

chosen by the people govern with more benefit to the commonwealth than those by succession'; 'secondly, that it is lawful to depose and kill a king that oppresses his people and the laws of his realm; and, thirdly, that', while it was 'not lawful for any private man to attempt anything against the person of a wicked prince or tyrant', it was licit 'for the states and magistrates' to do this.[87] In late 1578 the Rheims seminary professor Gregory Martin's *Treatise of Schisme* was published. It posited the need for absolute separation from heretics. It said in fairly uncompromising terms that those in schism, in other words conformist Catholics, were making possible the spread of full-blown heresy. It also had a rather threatening scriptural reference to the tyrant-slayer Judith and her tyrant-victim Holofernes.[88]

The public and popular political impact of the three treason trials in late 1577 and early 1578 and the resulting butchery can perhaps be gauged from a short broadside which appeared in print subsequently. It reproduced both a circulating Catholic manuscript libel which had allegedly been posted up in St Paul's in London (and must have been referring to the three recent executions—of Mayne, Sherwood, and Nelson) and a Protestant reply to it. The Catholic libel's versification was crude yet direct:

> Turn over the chain, good Jack-an-ape
> But keep well cut behind you,
> Lest Smithfield fire do burn your arse,
> If heretic it find you.
> God grant her highness, long to reign,
> Not only here but evermore.
> Yet must we not forsake our faith,
> Though we be martyred therefore.
> And as for all your conjuring knacks,
> the times will try who loves her best.
> But puritan if she will not be,
> If long she live, I think her blest.

The writer, who evidently did not aspire to laureate status, carried on to the effect that 'we thirst for that which you do threaten', but the persecutors could be sure that, when they had shed 'guiltless blood', the 'curse of God' would 'root' them out and bring them 'all to [a] shameless end'.

---

[87] *CSPD Addenda 1566–79*, p. 533 (PRO, SP 15/25/74).

[88] Gregory Martin, *A Treatise of Schisme. Shewing that al Catholikes Ought in any Wise to Abstaine altogether from Heretical Conuenticles, to witt, their Prayers, Sermons, &c* (Douai [imprint false; printed in London], 1578), sig. Dii[r–v]; ARCR, II, no. 524.

94 CATHOLICS AND TREASON

The Protestant reply which followed immediately after, coming from a self-styled 'true Christian and therefore a faithful subject', simply used a mirror image set of verses:

> Turn from your pope you Jack-an-ape,
> and keep well your neck I [ad]vise you,
> Lest halter, axe, and hell you take,
> if traitor they do find you,

and so on, arguing that Elizabeth did not seek to make martyrs, which, in any case, these Catholic sedition-mongers were not and never could be. She wanted only her subjects' loyalty.[89]

At this point, as is clear from a glance at Challoner, the attack dogs had to stop or, rather, draw back from using the full scope of the law. Robert Morton, nephew of the 1569 rebel Thomas Norton and also of Nicholas Morton, who was one of those who had procured the bull of excommunication against Elizabeth in 1570 (and with whom he spent three years in Rome), was arrested in mid-1578. With the relevant questions written out by William Cecil, Lord Burghley, he was interrogated in early August by Bishop Aylmer, William Fleetwood, and Sir Owen Hopton. But he was then released via the good offices of influential friends at court.[90] The cleric Thomas Metham was detained in October 1578, but he was indicted under the 1563, not the 1571, statute; and he merely ended up in the gaol at Wisbech in summer 1580.[91]

This did not mean that Catholic observers thought they were witnessing a move into anything like de facto tolerance. At Douai, it was recorded that on 15 February 1579, 'or thereabouts, were sent from Paris and England two letters declaring the tyrannical dealing of the peevish preachers in England towards the godly Catholics'. The 'Suffolk and Norfolk gentlemen' who had been imprisoned 'for their conscience' in 1578 during the queen's progress into East Anglia were still in prison. At the insistence of Aylmer and Fleetwood, a Douai seminarian called Tippet had recently been arrested in London and had been 'whipped at a cart's tail' and was then 'bored through the ear with a hot iron'. This torment he endured 'with a wonderful patience, not letting to make protestation of his faith

---

[89] *A Reply with the Occasion thereof, to a Late Rayling, Lying, Reprochful and Blasphemous Libel, of the Papists, set upon Postes, and also in Paules Church in London* .... (1579?), sig. A3ʳ, A4ʳ, A4ᵛ. The printer appears to be Hugh Singleton, who was prosecuted for involvement in the publication of John Stubbs's *Discoverie of a Gaping Gulf*; *ODNB, sub* Singleton, Hugh (article by N. Mears).

[90] Anstr., I, pp. 238–9; PRO, SP 12/125/31; *HMCS*, II, pp. 191–2. Ward notes that at the summer assizes at New Salisbury on 28 August 1578 three people were charged under the 1563 act with resorting to the Catholic rites of baptism for their children. Ward speculates that this was the assize judges' attempt to follow up on the convictions secured at the recent trials in Cornwall, but the court of queen's bench dismissed the cases: Ward, LT, pp. 218–19.

[91] Ward, LT, pp. 213, 233; Anstr., I, pp. 228–9.

'SENTENCED TO DIE AS IN CASES OF HIGH TREASON' 95

all the way of his martyrdom'.[92] The future martyr Richard White was first hauled in and interrogated over his nonconformity in October 1579, that is, at more or less exactly the point that the queen's apparent determination to press ahead with her project for an Anglo-French marriage treaty caused a crisis in the privy council and triggered a surge of popular opposition.[93]

Nevertheless, the prospect of a dynastic match with François, duke of Anjou, made it undesirable, for the queen, to allow the kind of savagery which had recently been used against Mayne, Nelson, and Sherwood, though, equally, the queen absolutely did not want a reputation as a witless crypto-Catholic. This was more or less what John Stubbs tried to pin on her in autumn 1579 with his inflammatory pamphlet against the match entitled *The Discoverie of a Gaping Gulf*. Stubbs and his associates notoriously suffered the consequences. In turn, Stubbs's polemic opened up spaces for conformist Catholics such as Henry Howard to pose as supporters of the queen and enemies of, as Howard called them, 'peevish puritans'.[94] Leicester wrote to Burghley from Kenilworth on 20 October 1579 that the 'papists were never in that jollity [that] they are at this present in this country'.[95]

Probably chewing the metaphorical carpet, the queen's principal secretary, Sir Francis Walsingham, who had coordinated the recent recusancy survey, had to write letters to provincial officials in late 1579/early 1580 telling them to hold off for the time being. The queen's wish was that, by and large, Catholic separatists were to be left alone.[96] In late April 1580 there were prominent Catholics who had been 'convened before the commissioners for causes ecclesiastical' but who now remained 'abroad upon bonds'. Among them were five priests including Montford Scott and also, astonishingly, the gentleman James Leyburn whose expressions of hatred for Elizabeth proved to be so violent that some Catholics were unsure whether to set down his subsequent execution as a true martyrdom.[97]

According to the Spanish ambassador in the previous month, the queen was still unwilling to allow direct action against Catholic nonconformity, although the power to insist on the Anjou marriage had in effect passed from her.[98] A case in point here was the Catholic William Carter. He had been an apprentice in the 1560s to John Cawood the elder, a royal printer. He had also been a client and

---

[92] Knox, *DD*, pp. 148–9, recording the contents of the two letters (written by the Marian clergymen Francis Ryd[ell] and Alban Dolman) from England; ABP, pp. 68–9; Questier, *DP*, p. 114.

[93] NLW, Denbighshire Gaol Files, Great Sessions 4/5/4/7–8. The investigations which led to his interrogation took place in mid-September 1579: NLW, Denbighshire Gaol Files, Great Sessions 4/5/4/9–10.

[94] L. E. Berry (ed.), *John Stubbs's Gaping Gulf with Letters and other Relevant Documents* (Charlottesville, 1968), appendix II, p. 179.

[95] BL, Harleian MS 6992, no. 56, fo. 112ʳ.

[96] Read, *MSW*, II, pp. 283–5, citing PRO, SP 12/45/27.

[97] BL, Harleian MS 360, no. 30, fos 49ʳ, 50ʳ; *AWCBC*, pp. 966–7 (Scott had been arrested in Cambridge in 1578); see p. 130 below.

[98] *CSPSp 1580–6*, p. 22; Pollen, *English Catholics*, p. 356.

96 CATHOLICS AND TREASON

secretary of Nicholas Harpsfield, the author of *Dialogi Sex*, a substantial reply to, among others, John Foxe.[99] Carter was, as Bishop Aylmer noted on 30 December 1579, arrested at this point—for a second time. In his house was found a pamphlet in French entitled 'the innocence of the Scottish queen'. It was 'a very dangerous book', in which the author called Mary Stuart 'the heir apparent of this crown' and raged against the execution of the duke of Norfolk in 1572, defended the rebellion of 1569, and attacked Burghley and the former lord keeper, Sir Nicholas Bacon.[100] But nothing was done permanently to silence Carter at this time.[101]

True Lies: Edmund Campion and his Alleged Treasons

The Anjou match was a public-relations disaster for Elizabeth. She had pegged her political credibility to the expression of a personal wish that the marriage should go ahead. She had, however, been blocked in the privy council as some of her councillors refused to commit themselves to the project, which then lingered on through later 1579 and 1580. Although it is difficult to establish an exact archival paper trail for this, there may have been a connection with perhaps the single most significant Catholic intervention of the mid-Elizabethan period—namely the mission of or, as some would have considered it to be, the agitation by, the Jesuits Edmund Campion and Robert Persons and their associates in 1580–1. Traditionally, at least in Catholic accounts of the period, this was a watershed moment when the queen's government showed itself in its true persecutory colours. Campion's story is well known, though it is also the subject of a recent groundbreaking book by Gerard Kilroy, a volume which has completely changed, in several respects, our view of the mid-Elizabethan period.[102]

---

[99] *ODNB, sub* Carter, William (article by I. Gadd); Graves, *TN*, p. 247; T. Birrell, 'William Carter (ca. 1549–84): Recusant Printer, Publisher, Binder, Stationer, Scribe—and Martyr', *RH* 28 (2006), pp. 22–42.

[100] BL, Lansdowne MS 28, no. 81, fo. 177^r; *ODNB, sub* Carter, William (article by I. Gadd); Birrell, 'William Carter', pp. 23–4, noting that the book in question was John Leslie, *L'Innocence de la Tres Illustre, Tres-Chaste, et Debonnaire Princesse, Madame Marie Royne d'Escosse* (Rheims, 1572), which incorporated a translation of a section of the pamphlet entitled *A Treatise of Treasons against Q. Elizabeth, and the Croune of England* (Louvain, 1572); ARCR, I, no. 726. Thomas Norton claimed that Nicholas Harpsfield, Carter's former employer, had made the final version of Leslie's *A Treatise concerning the Defence of the Honour*...(Liège and Louvain, 1571, in three parts; ARCR, II, no. 501) much more explicitly hostile to Elizabeth: BL, Additional MS 48029, fo. 58^r; *AWCBC*, pp. 29–30, 36; see also K. Coles, '"Printed at London Anonymous": Was there ever an Attempt to Publish the First Edition of the *Defence* of Mary Queen of Scots in England?', *Review of English Studies*, NS, 49 (1998), pp. 273–81.

[101] Birrell, 'William Carter', p. 24. Carter was released in mid-June 1581, though a recusancy indictment followed soon after: *AWCBC*, p. 2. Professor Birrell suggests that Carter enjoyed the patronage of the prominent Catholic George Gilbert and the printer Stephen Brinkley and, through them, Thomas, Lord Paget: Birrell, 'William Carter', p. 23. For Carter's publications list, see ibid., pp. 31–7; E. Duffy, 'Praying the Counter-Reformation', in J. E. Kelly and S. Royal (eds), *Early Modern English Catholicism: Identity, Memory and Counter-Reformation* (Leiden, 2017), pp. 206–25, at pp. 214–16.

[102] Kilroy, *EC*. Campion is one of the Forty Martyrs of England and Wales and one of the few who could be said to be a 'name' outside the immediate confines of the modern Catholic community—he

'SENTENCED TO DIE AS IN CASES OF HIGH TREASON' 97

Campion's courage, resilience under torture, and the highly controversial nature of his trial and execution have been taken virtually to define what Catholic martyrdom in the period meant. For Professor Kilroy and indeed for those who memorialized Campion after his death, the sufferings of this scholar-priest demonstrated that 'this was an age far from golden for those of the population who were living in nightly fear of arrest and imprisonment'. The circulation of 'their manuscripts...in secret...offer us torch-lit glimpses of the dark underside of early modern England'.[103] Campion was a former Oxford man, an exile, and a university teacher in Prague for many years. He had no recent political record as such, though during the 1560s he had looked to the earl of Leicester and Sir Henry Sidney as patrons. It is not clear how far he knew what sort of bear pit he was entering.

To many scholars of the period, however, Campion's trial and execution appear to be, if not an irrelevance, then the product of bizarre contemporary confusions about where to locate the dividing line between religion and politics. As Professor Wallace MacCaffrey has it, the arrests, trials, convictions, and executions of Catholics were the outcome of a dreadful misunderstanding. The Catholic seminary clergy thought that what they were doing was merely 'religious' and, apparently, did not realize that they could be blamed and held to account for the 'political' ambitions of their controllers, who remained safely abroad while sending their clerical associates into the crucible of Elizabethan conflict over such things.[104] Yet even the most cursory glance at the politics of the Anjou match, and at the surviving snippets of Catholic speculation and comment about it, tells us why Campion could not be ignored. In fact, that slew of conjecture and gossip and the regime's eventual retaliation ought logically to be central to almost any account of the later 1570s and early 1580s.

In July 1580, that is, at precisely the point that the regime decided to crack down on Catholic separatism, and Campion and his confrère Persons arrived and started to crank up the rhetoric of non-compliance (particularly via their call for out-and-out recusancy), Anjou and his agents were still pushing for a marriage treaty, principally to underwrite his determination and capacity to intervene in Flanders on the side of the rebels against the king of Spain, Philip II.[105] The basis

was the subject of a celebrated biography by Evelyn Waugh: E. Waugh, *Edmund Campion: Scholar, Priest, Hero and Martyr* (3rd edition, 1961).

[103] G. Kilroy, *Edmund Campion: Memory and Transcription* (Aldershot, 2005), pp. 8–9.

[104] W. T. MacCaffrey, *Queen Elizabeth and the Making of Policy, 1572–1588* (Princeton, N.J., 1981), pp. 146–9.

[105] Questier, *DP,* ch. 2, esp. at pp. 126–31. William Allen, who at this time was the rector of the Rheims seminary, had arrived in Rome in October 1579 and, supported by Persons (and also by Oliver Manaerts SJ and Claudio Acquaviva SJ), had persuaded the Society's general, Everard Mercurian, to allow a Jesuit mission to be despatched to England. Mercurian had previously been unwilling to authorize such a thing. Thomas McCoog argues that Persons was responding to advice from England that the time was ripe to intervene, even though 'no extant account of the consultation'

98 CATHOLICS AND TREASON

for a confessionally mixed dynastic union of this kind was that it would not release or generate any kind of Catholic political reaction or activism. To those Protestants who had viewed the match with distaste, the Campion mission appeared to be evidence of exactly that kind of activism—proof that everything they had said about the risks of the Anjou venture was true. Once the polemical temperature started to rise, as it did very soon after their arrival, Campion and Persons proved to be vocal critics of the queen's government of the Church, which they took to have been corrupted by, among other things, the errors of puritanism. For some Catholics, that is, those who did not think that Anjou was a champion of true religion, the Campion–Persons agitation was, one must assume, a way of exposing the falsehoods and half-truths which, they suspected, would be used to usher in a politique Anglo-French alliance.

Worse still, Ireland was in rebellion (again)—and this revolt had papal backing. It did not take much imagination to link the civil strife there with the changes in Scotland, where the young James Stuart was in the process of casting off the influence of the Anglophile Protestant regent, the earl of Morton. Taking into account the emergence of what looked like a Catholic popular agitation in England, a contemporary Protestant observer could be forgiven for thinking that there was currently in train a carefully constructed Catholic conspiracy, coordinated right across the British Isles. For his part, Persons said he was 'heartily sorry' that he and his friends' coming to England should have coincided with the regrettable recent events in Ireland. But that, undoubtedly, was not enough to convince the privy council.[106]

We get a sense of how the regime might have perceived all this from the informer Charles Slade's description of the disloyal banter which he said had been going round in Rome even before Campion and his friends set off on their journey.[107] To some scholars, this is simply evidence of the Elizabethan regime's

---

concerning the mission specifically 'mentioned the French match': T. M. McCoog, 'The English Jesuit Mission and the French Match, 1579–1581', *Catholic Historical Review* 87 (2001), pp. 185–213, at pp. 195–6; McCoog, *SJ*, pp. 126–8, 129–33, 136–9.

[106] Hicks, *Letters*, pp. xiii–xiv. Morton had briefly lost power in February/March 1578, recovered it, and then was overthrown in late 1580: *CSPSc 1574–81*, pp. 275–8, 279–82, 296, 301, 569; Questier, *DP*, p. 130. For the Irish revolt, see Kilroy, *EC*, chs 5, 6.

[107] As William Allen related it, Slade, 'that notorious varlet, and infamous Judas…came from Rome in the company of divers English men whose names and marks he took very diligently'; and, 'being arrived at Paris, there he presented the lord ambassador [Sir Henry Cobham] with the names and marks he had taken, who sent them over to the queen's council, and from them they were sent to the searchers of the ports': Allen, *BH*, sigs Bviii^v–C^r. Slade said that he had contacted Cobham on 6 April 1580, though there is no trace of it in the surviving papers of Cobham's embassy: Talbot, *MRR*, p. 241. However, on 8 April Cobham wrote back to England that 'the papists write from Rome to their associates resident in these parts that they should be of good comfort', partly because of recent events in Portugal but also because 'the heretics of England will not be suffered to continue long in their mischievous proceedings, but a way shall be devised to cut them off' before long, and that included 'the usurper of authority, the puddle of lasciviousness, the very Antichrist', Elizabeth herself, and 'her wicked counsellors and minions': *CSPF 1579–80*, pp. 218–19; see also *CSPF 1579–80*, pp. 165, 159, 171. One assumes there must be some connection between Slade and an informer, going under the

'SENTENCED TO DIE AS IN CASES OF HIGH TREASON' 99

intelligence service doing due diligence, as it were, on those who had been detected as risks to national security.[108] The manuscript record of Slade's information is, admittedly, problematic.[109] There is no corroborating evidence that those on whom Slade informed actually said the things which he attributed to them, or even that they did so in the sneering tone that he claimed they used. Still, it is not impossible that some of the exiles in Rome associated with the coming Jesuit mission were, to put it mildly, contemptuous of the mid-Elizabethan regime and of the queen herself. According to Slade, John Pascall spoke openly about the queen's alleged promiscuity, illegitimate progeny, and heresy. Many of these people were caught up in the regime's subsequent and violent response to the Campion–Persons mission. The ones who were arrested and executed for their alleged treasons became the collective core of the Elizabethan Catholic martyr tradition.[110] On 27 August 1579, there was (again, this is known only from Slade's evidence) a meeting of English Catholics at Solomon Aldred's house in Rome.[111] The talk was not just of the apparently impending marriage of the queen to Anjou but also of the 'safe landing in Ireland' of 'the pope's legate' Nicholas Sander, James Fitzmaurice Fitzgerald, who was 'the pope's general', and with them the king of Spain's general... with 500 Spaniards'. Their intention was 'to deliver to the king of Spain the quiet possession of... all Ireland'. On 8 October, at the English College, William Allen 'made an oration to all the company' in praise of the recent invasion. Crucially, Allen 'showed them that it was the pope's pleasure to send some priests into England... to let the people understand what his Holiness was minded to do' in the near future.[112]

On 26 November 1579 Henry Orton and Robert Johnson arrived in Rome and brought with them a copy of the recent proclamation against John Stubbs's *Discoverie of a Gaping Gulf.*[113] By mid-December 1579, Pascall was saying that the pope had renewed the excommunication of Elizabeth ('Mistress Bess'), that

---

name 'Rowland Russell', whose testimony Cobham mentioned on 15 April, all in the context of the fact that 'there are certain priests come from Rome and now going over': *CSPF 1579–80*, p. 235. For Slade, see also L. Hicks, *An Elizabethan Problem: Some Aspects of the Careers of Two Exile-Adventurers* (1964), pp. 108–9. Once he had got back to London, Slade tried to track down and arrest Campion and his friends: Hicks, *Letters*, pp. xxi, 68–9, 88, 132 [*CUPRP*, pp. 168, 185, 281–2]; Allen, *BH*, sig. b^{v}.

[108] S. Alford, *The Watchers: A Secret History of the Reign of Elizabeth I* (2012), ch. 4.

[109] Kilroy, *EC*, p. 134. For the two manuscripts of Slade's evidence (BL, Additional MS 48029, fos 121^{r}–42^{v}; and, with significant variations and omissions, his second 'book', BL, Additional MS 48023, fos 94^{r}–109^{v}), see Kilroy, *EC*, p. 134, n. 15.

[110] Talbot, *MRR*, p. 220; McCoog, *SJ*, p. 136. Pascall, with Persons and Luke Kirby, also believed that Sir Christopher Hatton 'was the only favourer of Catholics which are in England': Talbot, *MRR*, p. 220. Pascall was arrested in late 1580 and recanted: *APC 1580–1*, p. 294.

[111] Talbot, *MRR*, p. 221. For Aldred, who supplied intelligence to the Elizabethan regime but may also have been a kind of ultra-loyalist Catholic, see Read, *MSW*, II, pp. 425–6; L. Hicks, 'An Elizabethan Propagandist: The Career of Solomon Aldred', *Month* 181 (1945), pp. 181–90; *CSPSp 1580–6*, p. 532.

[112] Talbot, *MRR*, pp. 221, 224; Kilroy, *EC*, pp. 127–8, 134. See also Talbot, *MRR*, pp. 225–6, for the dinner at Dr Nicholas Morton's house on 24 November 1579, at which similar sentiments were expressed.

[113] Talbot, *MRR*, p. 226; Kilroy, *EC*, p. 134.

100 CATHOLICS AND TREASON

the Spanish conquest of Ireland was complete, and that the subjection of England must follow. Pascall and Luke Kirby had 'received letters lately out of England' which related that Philip intended to secure a marriage between young King James in Scotland and one of Philip II's daughters. Either Philip would 'steal the king of Scots into Spain' or he would 'have a dispensation from the pope and marry them by pictures and so make them king and queen of England, which kingdom he would give in dowry with his daughter and the rather because the queen of Scots is the right heir to the crown'.[114] On 29 December, claimed Slade, the leading Englishmen in Rome met together and compared notes over the progress of the marriage proposed for Elizabeth with the duke of Anjou. They noted that there was a 'great murmuring...in the city of London' against the duke. Kirby had received news of the banishing from the court of the earls of Leicester and Bedford and of Sir Francis Walsingham, and, apparently, also of Sir Christopher Hatton. It was thought that they would lose their places on the council. This would free up spaces for others who would support the queen's preferred foreign policy aims. Rumours received by the French diplomatic service in England about the queen's threatened cabinet reshuffle (so as to get her own way over the match) had filtered out as well. 'It was written' that in their places there would be substituted Henry Percy, earl of Northumberland, 'Lord Montague, Sir Thomas Cornwallis and [Sir William] Cordell, master of the rolls', that is to say, conformist but, nevertheless, known Catholics.[115]

James Fitzmaurice Fitzgerald had not survived long in Ireland.[116] The news of his death was greatly lamented by these English Catholic exiles in Rome, but it was resolved that 'it was requisite and needful to send more priests into England'. William Allen was already assembling those to be dispatched. Catholic notables were also being picked out as contacts, including Lord Henry Howard. The same Englishmen in Rome were allegedly also sharing out prospective ecclesiastical dignities among themselves. Allen was nominated to the see of Canterbury.[117]

Slade reported in late January 1580 that the bull of excommunication of 1570 'was newly imprinted again and commonly sold' in Rome. There was more news about the execution of sentence against John Stubbs. It was said 'that two judges were put from the bench for saying it was very hard justice'.[118] Slade had travelled

---

[114] Talbot, *MRR*, p. 228; for an equally damning account of a conversation between Thomas Goldwell, Nicholas Morton, and Allen on 13 December 1579, see Kilroy, *EC*, pp. 134–5, citing BL, Additional MS 48023, fos 114ʳ–15ʳ.

[115] Talbot, *MRR*, pp. 229–32. The ambassador Michel de Castelnau, seigneur de Mauvissière, reported a version of this rumour on 29 October 1579: Pollen, *English Catholics*, p. 317. The claim about the 'great murmuring...in the city of London' is omitted from the version of Slade's statement in BL, Additional MS 48023, fo. 102ʳ. For Cornwallis's tendency towards occasional conformity, see PRO, SP 12/43/9, 10, 10. i.

[116] Kilroy, *EC*, p. 128.

[117] Talbot, *MRR*, pp. 229–32. For the subsequent phases of the revolt in Ireland, see Kilroy, *EC*, chs 5, 6; Questier, *DP*, pp. 128–9.

[118] Talbot, *MRR*, pp. 232–3.

'SENTENCED TO DIE AS IN CASES OF HIGH TREASON' 101

from Rome with Robert Johnson, who, the informer said, had told the cardinal of Bologna that the priests' function in England was to 'reclaim and reconcile the queen's Majesty and her people to the Catholic faith again'. But, since she was not cooperating, the supreme pontiff's will and pleasure was that those priests should 'call all the Catholics together and so to make a sudden resistance and rebellion against the queen's Majesty which has governed the same realm of England and Ireland worse than ever did Jezebel, for the space of twenty-two years'. As Slade, Johnson, and Thomas Cottam approached Troyes, the latter two 'talked' of 'a great suit and contention in law' between 'the earl of Leicester and Mr Lodowick Greville', who they said was 'as faithful a Catholic as any was in England'. They also said that the earl was 'a whoremonger', for Elizabeth 'had a child by the earl, although it was kept...secret'.[119] Then, in mid-April 1580, once Slade had arrived at Rheims, he allegedly witnessed John Hart preaching a fire-and-brimstone sermon about heresy in England. Hart pointed the finger of blame at Elizabeth. She had 'behaved herself worse than ever Jezebel did' and, 'with her counsel', one day would want 'to recant', but by then it would be 'too late'.[120]

There is, as I say, absolutely no way of telling how far any of this really represented the true mind of Campion's friends. Nowhere else are these people on record as mouthing off (and in public, too) in the way that Slade claimed they did. On the other hand, it is not impossible that while their formal utterances about the queen were couched in the conventional language of respect for monarchical authority, their private conversations were not, though it would still have been unwise to say such things out in the open. Gerard Kilroy's line is that, while we cannot know whether Slade set down an iota of truth here, Campion had been first and foremost a university lecturer in Prague and had no investment in Allen's and Sander's harder-edged version of the Counter-Reformation, even if he was well aware of it. Professor Kilroy argues that Campion was exactly as he described himself—a man of God and of prayer, leading a Jesuit mission in obedience to his superiors and seeking to confront and repel error, and, if necessary, tyranny. That exercise was made almost impossible by the radicalism of Nicholas Sander and, behind him, William Allen. It was the Irish revolt in 1579 that provoked the Elizabethan regime's violent reaction to Campion rather than anything which the Jesuit himself said or did. This seems right. At the same time, Campion had been

---

[119] Talbot, *MRR*, pp. 238, 240–1. Lodowick Greville was one of those named in the infamous pamphlet 'Leicester's Commonwealth' as one of Leicester's intended victims: D. C. Peck (ed.), *Leicester's Commonwealth: The Copy of a Letter Written by a Master of Art of Cambridge (1584) and Related Documents* (Athens, Ohio, 1985), pp. 122, 210.

[120] Talbot, *MRR*, pp. 242–3. The second manuscript version of Slade's allegations omits the claims about John Hart's sermon: BL, Additional MS 48023, fo. 109[r]. An abstract of Hart's confessions asserted that it was Gregory Martin who had 'appointed Hart to make the seditious sermon' in which he praised the recent martyrs Cuthbert Mayne and John Nelson (though, if it is the same sermon as that cited by Slade, that particular detail is not mentioned there): BL, Additional MS 48035, fo. 179[r]. I am very grateful to Mordechai Feingold for discussion of John Hart.

102 CATHOLICS AND TREASON

a man of the world or, at least, of the university, and he must have been aware of the implications of what he was doing.

The instigators of the Campion venture could not but have recognized that there was a horribly convincing logic to Slade's, and presumably others', characterization of the Jesuit mission and its purposes. Some of the English exiles in France had already accepted Guise patronage. The principal author of the mission was the director of the seminary now located in the Guise heartland of Rheims. The published work of the seminary staff member Gregory Martin strongly implied that the seminarist view of heresy was that it was exactly as 'abominable' as Slade related that Campion's associates said it was. Even Campion's progress across Europe was deliberately designed to garner public attention. He and his travelling companions went so far as to confront Theodore Beza as they passed through Geneva and to challenge him to a disputation.[121]

All this makes the line that the Campion enterprise was some kind of Counter-Reformation-lite exercise virtually untenable. For Christopher Haigh, clergy such as Campion came merely 'to preach the gospel and provide sacraments'.[122] But Leslie Ward argues convincingly that, 'when looked at closely as a chain of events', what Campion and Persons did seems 'to represent a concerted...assault on the government', if we take 'government' to mean the expressed wishes of the queen and her counsellors.[123] Persons's account of the mission, though written with a good deal of hindsight, makes clear that he and Campion were already well aware of the privy council's displeasure at their determination to enter the country and that they had strategies to deal with it—strategies that were high-risk but politically logical.[124] The inclusion of the former bishop of St Asaph, Thomas Goldwell, among Campion's travelling companions was highly controversial. Allen admitted that Goldwell's approach (he never in fact crossed the Channel) 'put marvellous conceits into the council's heads that there was some great and new attempt or invasion' imminent.[125]

This is not the place for an in-depth analysis of the politics of the Anjou match. But whichever way it worked out (and whether Anjou was seen as a cat's paw for a heretical regime in England and its friends on the Continent or, by contrast, as John Stubbs saw him, as the agent of a European Catholic conspiracy), it is not hard to discern how these Jesuit clergymen's programme for, as they saw it, revitalizing the faith in their native country would have political consequences.

---

[121] Robert Persons, trans. and ed. J. H. Pollen, 'Of the Life and Martyrdom of Father Edmond Campion', *Letters and Notices* 11 (1876-7), pp. 219–42, 308–39, and vol. 12 (1878), pp. 1–68, at vol. 12, pp. 4–5, 6–8. For the journey from Rome of Campion's travelling party, see Kilroy, *EC*, pp. 146–63.

[122] C. Haigh, 'The Continuity of Catholicism in the English Reformation', *Past and Present* 93 (1981), pp. 37–69, at pp. 55–6.

[123] Ward, LT, p. 238; Persons, 'Of the Life', vol. 12, pp. 15 f.   [124] Ibid.

[125] Allen, *BH*, sigs eviii^v-f^r. Goldwell had been involved in securing the excommunication of Elizabeth: Kilroy, *EC*, p. 148. Goldwell (allegedly because of illness) and Nicholas Morton dropped out of the mission before it crossed the Channel: Kilroy, *EC*, p. 159.

'SENTENCED TO DIE AS IN CASES OF HIGH TREASON' 103

Persons himself claimed that he and Campion were actively in contact with 'some principal persons of the court', though he did not name them.[126] It was clear enough that, if large parts of the conformist Catholic community were persuaded to go into separation, that would make what the queen personally wanted more or less impossible. This would be the case even if, for example, Campion's declarations about what might be taken to be theologically orthodox technically avoided topics which might be categorized as overtly 'political', that is, in a purely secular sense. There were, of course, regime members who, observing the current course of events in Scotland, and particularly the disintegration of the Anglophile earl of Morton's authority, did not need Campion and Persons or anyone else to encourage them into a harsher enforcement of conformity.[127]

Persons, Campion, and their friends must have been aware that, once they started to question the assumptions on which the queen's government was conducting its public business, this would open up spaces for debate which could not easily be closed down except by overwhelming force on the regime's part. Campion's first major sermon after his arrival was preached in a large private house on 29 June near Smithfield. Its subject matter, papal primacy, was frankly provocative.[128] Persons made sniffy remarks about the disquiet expressed by some of the Catholics who attended the so-called synod of Southwark, held somewhere on the south bank of the Thames shortly after his and Campion's arrival; these Catholics were worried by the implications of Persons's and Campion's programme.[129] The risks run by Catholics who associated in broad daylight with each other in this way were made clear when Slade secured the arrest of Henry Orton in Holborn as he was on his way to the synod meeting. At the same point, Slade also detained the priest Robert Johnson.[130] But, after the Southwark gathering, the two Jesuits went on a series of carefully organized shire-by-shire preaching tours. They wrote out statements which would be made public if they were arrested. Campion's was leaked by the Hampshire Catholic separatist Thomas Pounde—the notorious challenge (or 'brag').[131]

[126] Persons, 'Of the Life', vol. 12, p. 22; Lake and Questier, 'Puritans', p. 617; Kilroy, *EC*, p. 43. On 28 July 1580, reported Roger Manners, the 'French cause' was still going 'forward', i.e. while parliament was not in session: *HMCR*, I, p. 120.

[127] In early May 1580, even before Campion and his friends disembarked, the council ordered a crackdown on northern Catholicism, and this was presumably the origin of the extensive purge at York and across the North conducted by the earl of Huntingdon in July/August, soon after the Jesuit-led travelling party arrived in June: Aveling, *NC*, pp. 98–9; Hughes, *The Reformation in England*, III, pp. 427–40; PRO, SP 12/141/28.

[128] Ward, LT, p. 237; Kilroy, *EC*, pp. 167–8.

[129] McCoog, 'The English Jesuit Mission', pp. 196–9; Kilroy, *EC*, pp. 169–70.

[130] Kilroy, *EC*, pp. 170–1; Edwards, *EJ*, p. 84.

[131] Lake and Questier, 'Puritans', pp. 601–7; McCoog, *SJ*, pp. 146–8; Ward, LT, pp. 237–9. For the circulation of Campion's 'brag', see, e.g., PRO, SP 12/147/74, fo. 129ʳ; *APC 1580–1*, pp. 270, 285; Ward, LT, p. 239; Kilroy, *EC*, pp. 172–3.

104 CATHOLICS AND TREASON

Catholics' concerns about the regime's likely reaction to all this did not prevent Persons from putting into print, on a clandestine press, his *Brief Discours* about church attendance and recusancy. This pamphlet was published in circa November 1580, and it attacked conforming Catholics as schismatics. It called for all good Catholics to separate from the national Church.[132] It also told the queen some home truths about puritanism in the Church of England. It declared how much freedom troublemakers, such as John Field, were given compared with Catholics who were being harassed for their beliefs. The *Brief Discours*'s crucial manoeuvre was to cast the question of dis/obedience to the act of uniformity as a matter exclusively of religion, considerably shrinking, therefore, the extent of royal authority over the Church. It is difficult to be certain how many of a Catholic temperament did now go into separation. But Allen and Persons declared that it was many thousands.[133]

Campion's letter written to the Jesuit superior general in November 1580 more or less explained why, even without his and Persons's pamphleteering, the authorities might have become determined to silence him: 'I ride about some piece of the country every day' and 'the harvest is wonderful great'. Crowds of 'young gentlemen', that is, the socially influential and wealthy, flocked to him daily, along with an increasingly ideologically mobilized clergy ('priests whom we find in every place').[134] The whole project was framed in Campion's mind in terms of a contest with the ageing John Foxe. As Campion saw it, 'of their martyrs they brag no more now' since, 'for a few apostates and cobblers of theirs' who had been burned, 'we have bishops, lords, knights, the old nobility, patterns of learning, piety and prudence, the flower of the youth, noble matrons and, of the inferior sort, innumerable, either martyred at once or, by consuming imprisonment, dying daily'. For Campion, 'at the very writing hereof, the persecution rages most cruelly'.[135] Of course, at that point, there was no contest between, on the one hand, the number of victims recorded by Foxe and, on the other, the Catholic body count racked up by the Elizabethan regime in England. But that was something which might soon change.

On 10 January 1581 the regime issued a proclamation explicitly against Catholic seminarist clergy. By this point, leading crypto-Catholic courtiers had already been detained and Elizabeth's government was faced by potential

---

[132] The pamphlet was produced on a press in Greenstreet House at East Ham, a property owned by Edward and Eleanor Brooksby; she was the daughter of William, Lord Vaux, whose family and friends supplied so many of Campion's and Persons's contacts: Robert Persons, *A Brief Discours contayning Certayne Reasons why Catholiques Refuse to Goe to Church....* (Douai [imprint false; printed secretly at Greenstreet House, East Ham], 1580); ARCR, II, no. 613; Kilroy, *EC*, pp. 189–90.

[133] Knox, *LMCA*, p. 55; Hicks, *Letters*, p. 58 [*CUPRP*, p. 132].

[134] Allen, *BH*, sig. evᵛ–viʳ; *CSPD Addenda 1580–1625*, pp. 24–5; for the letter, see also McCoog, *SJ*, p. 148.

[135] Allen, *BH*, sig. eviiʳ.

'SENTENCED TO DIE AS IN CASES OF HIGH TREASON' 105

catastrophe in Scotland following the arrest of the earl of Morton.[136] The new English parliament assembled on 16 January.[137] It heard calls by government spokesmen, notably Sir Walter Mildmay, for a toughening of the law; and the session saw, after a lot of back-and-forth drafts in Lords and Commons, the first new anti-Catholic legislation for ten years.[138] The bill, introduced into the Commons by Sir Francis Knollys, was heavily revised. In its watered-down format, it passed into law on 10 March. John Neale suggests that the queen must have 'intervened to scale down' the bill's 'severities'.[139] But the act did create three new treasons. Since allegiance was being withdrawn from the queen by means other than papal bulls, it was now made an offence to claim to have the power to absolve/reconcile and withdraw the subject from obedience, actually to do this, or, oneself, to withdraw one's allegiance in that fashion.[140] In this session also there was introduced a bill which became 23 Eliz., c. 2—'An Act against seditious words and rumours uttered against the Queen's most excellent Majesty'. This statute (no prizes for guessing against whom it was directed) allowed a felony conviction against those who should 'devise and write, print or set forth', or procure the publication of, 'any manner of book, rhyme, ballad, letter or writing, containing any false seditious and slanderous matter to the defamation of the queen's Majesty that now is, or to the encouraging, stirring or moving of any insurrection or rebellion', if such an offence was not already treasonable under the existing law.[141]

The regime's nets now started to close. At around the time that Persons's printing press at Stonor Park was churning out hundreds of copies of Campion's *Rationes Decem*, the premises used by Persons in Bridewell were betrayed. A midnight search, conducted by Thomas Norton, netted Alexander Briant in a nearby property. The regime on 3 May ordered Briant to be tortured (again), if necessary, to get information out of him.[142]

After Campion's book was printed, William Hartley, formerly at St John's College, Oxford, and recently ordained (at Châlons in February 1580), took 400

---

[136] Hicks, *Letters*, p. xxvii; Ward, LT, pp. 56–7, 241.

[137] Ward, LT, p. 56.

[138] Ward, LT, pp. 57–61; Neale, *EHP*, I, pp. 386–92; F. X. Walker, 'The Implementation of the Elizabethan Statutes against Recusants 1581–1603' (PhD, London, 1961), pp. 119–34; H. Bowler (ed.), *Recusant Roll No. 2 (1593–1594)* (CRS 57, 1965), pp. xii–xiv.

[139] Neale, *EHP*, I, pp. 387–8; Ward, LT, pp. 58–9.

[140] Ward, LT, pp. 59–60. Neale points out that the arguably crucial qualifying clause ('for that intent') concerning the reconciling of the queen's subjects to Rome and the withdrawal of their obedience was not present in the earlier versions of the bill: Neale, *EHP*, I, pp. 388–9.

[141] *SR*, IV, p. 659; Ward, LT, pp. 39–40. For the application of the statute, see, e.g., *APC 1581–2*, pp. 180–1; Ward, LT, p. 39, n. 105. Neale contends that amendments in the Commons to the draft of this bill were the product of MPs' fears that it might stretch to puritans as well as Catholics (as indeed in later years it did): Neale, *EHP*, I, pp. 393–7.

[142] Hicks, *Letters*, pp. xxvi, xxxvii, 81, 88 [*CUPRP*, p. 186]; Allen, *BH*, sig. fiiiᵛ; Lake and Questier, 'Puritans', p. 607; Kilroy, *EC*, pp. 196, 197, 210, 213–14; *APC 1581–2*, pp. 37–8. Professor Kilroy shows that the conflicting dates in the sources for so many of these events make it impossible to be certain in what exact order these events actually occurred: Kilroy, *EC*, pp. 206, 210–11; *Miscellanea II* (CRS 2, 1906), p. 182; see also Ward, LT, p. 242.

106 CATHOLICS AND TREASON

copies of it to Oxford in order to have it bound and to distribute it there. As Professor Kilroy notes, after the sheets had been bound, Hartley gave them to specific individuals and, during the night before the university act (the three-day occasion involving speeches and prize-giving), he left a number of copies in St Mary's Church so that, when that self-congratulatory event kicked off on 27 June 1581, those attending had Campion's words in front of them.[143]

The royal marriage discussions with the French were still just about alive, but the negotiating teams of the English and French courts were moving towards a non-dynastic agreement, one which would not secure any measure of tolerance for the queen's Catholic subjects.[144] The Spanish ambassador Bernardino de Mendoza's correspondence shows that certain English Catholics were turning to Spain.[145] Campion was arrested at Lyford Grange in July 1581 by the informer George Eliot.[146]

The regime was determined now, more than ever, to destroy Campion's credibility and reputation. It did this in the first instance by spreading rumours about him, notably that he had betrayed other Catholics.[147] The privy council went after Campion's patrons. It needed to know how far Campion's evangelizing was creating a gentry-led separatist and propagandizing core inside the English Catholic community.[148] For example, the Lancashire authorities were instructed on 2 August 1581 'to repair unto the dwelling-houses of certain persons' who had been 'harbourers of Edmund Campion' and particularly 'the house of Richard Houghton, where it is said' that 'Campion left his books'. Sir Henry Neville and Ralph Warcop were told to go to 'Lady [Cecily] Stonor's house' in Oxfordshire and to 'make diligent search and enquire for certain Latin books dispersed abroad in Oxford at the last commencement...and also for such other English books as of late have been published for the maintenance of popery, printed also there as it is thought

[143] McCoog, *SJ*, p. 153; Ward, *LT*, pp. 242–3. Kilroy's reconstruction of this event is exemplary and makes clear how much of a challenge to the establishment Campion was mounting, despite his loyalist address to the queen herself: Kilroy, *EC*, pp. 202–4.

[144] For the continuation of the talks over an Anglo-French alliance in later 1581, see Read, *MSW*, II, pp. 57 f.

[145] *CSPSp 1580–6*, p. 97.

[146] Kilroy, *EC*, pp. 220–37. Allen recorded that Eliot averred to Campion himself, after his trial, that he would not have done as he did if he had known that 'any further harm or trouble than imprisonment should have happened' to the Jesuit: Allen, *BH*, sig. bv^v; Edwards, *EJ*, p. 126.

[147] R. Simpson, *Edmund Campion* (1896), pp. 339–40, 348–9; Kilroy, *EC*, chs 8, 9. For the instructions issued to those (including Thomas Norton) ordered to interrogate Campion and others who had been arrested, in particular as to how far they endorsed Nicholas Sander's *De Monarchia Ecclesia* and Richard Bristow's 'Motives' (i.e. Bristow's *A Briefe Treatise*...(Antwerp, 1574)), see *APC 1581–2*, pp. 144–5. Undoubtedly the regime also wanted to see if it could turn Campion. Hence the examination of him on 26 July 1581 in front of the earl of Leicester, his former patron; and, subsequently, an interview with the queen herself; the claim was that he was offered high ecclesiastical preferment in return for compliance; see Knox, *LMCA*, p. 102; Kilroy, *EC*, pp. 268–9; M. Colthorpe, 'Edmund Campion's Alleged Interview with Queen Elizabeth I in 1581', *RH* 17 (1985), pp. 197–200, at p. 198. A similar offer may have been made to Ralph Sherwin: Challoner, *MMP*, p. 31; AAW, A IV, no. 22, p. 119.

[148] Ward, *LT*, pp. 244–5. For the gentry houses which had received Campion, see Kilroy's excellent reconstruction of Campion's itinerary: Kilroy, *EC*, ch. 6, esp. pp. 191–7.

'SENTENCED TO DIE AS IN CASES OF HIGH TREASON' 107

by one Persons, a Jesuit, and others' and to find the 'press and other instruments of printing'.[149]

The extraordinary range of people whom Campion and his associates had visited on their tour of the shires, revealed in letter after letter from the council to local authorities with orders to arrest and interrogate them and search their houses, gives us an indication of how far Campion had penetrated into gentry networks, both separatist and partially conformist, in a number of counties. One council letter of 5 September 1581 noted that Gervase Pierrepoint, one of Campion's conductors on his rural rides, had been committed to a form of house arrest 'upon hope that he might be reduced to conformity, for that he is shortly to take upon him the exercise of [the] office of sheriff'.[150] Indeed, the range of gentry families which welcomed Campion and Persons, taken together with the privy council's stream of orders to diocesan bishops to try to extort some measure of conformity from those who had gone into separation, shows how serious were the claims being made by Persons that the English Catholic community in its entirety either had rejected, or was in principle prepared to reject, the kind of conformist compromises inside the national Church which, up to that point, had more or less held together.[151]

Some regime insiders pushed hard for the coming retaliation against Campion to be staged in such a way as to roll back the tide of public speculation which the Jesuits and their friends had unleashed. On 11 August 1581, Lord Hunsdon had written, from faraway Berwick, that it would be 'a most happy turn to her Majesty' if the queen should deal with Campion and 'his receivers and comforters as they deserve'. But he remarked to Burghley that, if the queen neglected her own security 'by dealing mildly with them that seek her destruction, as she has hitherto done, it were better' that Campion 'had not been taken' in the first place. The queen 'and all her good subjects' would repent if leniency were showed here, for 'the papists wax proud and arrogant, both men and women, especially in these north parts'.[152]

Unfortunately, it was not as simple as this. Exactly how problematical it might prove had just been demonstrated by the rather disastrous public-relations consequences of the recent treason proceedings against the priest and former minister Everard Hanse in late July 1581, shortly after Campion's own arrest. Hanse had

---

[149] *APC 1581–2*, pp. 148–9, 154. For similar letters to the earl of Huntingdon and other regional governors, see, e.g., *APC 1581–2*, pp. 152–4. For the subsequent sequestration of the press and the arrest 'of the printers at Stonor's Lodge', see *APC 1581–2*, pp. 186, 264. For Richard Houghton of Park Hall, see Kilroy, *EC*, p. 196.

[150] *APC 1581–2*, p. 194; see also Kilroy, *EC*, pp. 259–60.

[151] For, e.g., the attempts in Winchester diocese to bring recusants to conformity, see *APC 1581–2*, p. 203. For the occasional report of recusants who had actually, or apparently, recanted, see e.g. *APC 1581–2*, pp. 223–4, 236.

[152] J. Bain (ed.), *Calendar of Letters and Papers relating to the Affairs of the Borders of England and Scotland* (2 vols, Edinburgh, 1894–6), I, p. 71.

108 CATHOLICS AND TREASON

been detained in the Marshalsea prison 'when he desired to speak with some prisoners (because he had alms to deliver to them)', as Persons said. Hanse had been arraigned on 28 July and was executed a mere three days later.[153] Under interrogation by William Fleetwood, Hanse had conceded that he was in some sense 'subject to the pope', even in England. The pope had 'as much authority and right in spiritual government in this realm as ever he had, and as much as he has, in any other country, or in Rome itself'. Upon these words, as Allen later described it, 'the heretics (as their fashion is to falsify all things and by contrived slanders to make odious the servants of God) gave out afterwards in print' that Hanse 'should say "that princes had not any supremacy or sovereignty in their own realms but the pope only": which was far from his and every Catholic man's mind'. His subsequent statement that he would 'have all men to believe the Catholic faith as I do' brought a treason indictment 'upon the new statute made in the last parliament, which was out of hand done', or so said Allen, though Leslie Ward points to evidence that Hanse was indicted under the 1571 treason statute for uttering traitorous words. Hanse in effect acknowledged what he was charged with, and he was sentenced accordingly, after which he was badgered by Robert Crowley and other ministers. They claimed that 'he should affirm to them in talk, "that treason to the queen was no sin before God". Which slander they were not ashamed to put out in print.'[154]

One pamphlet about Hanse came out on the day of the execution at Tyburn, that is, on 31 July when Hanse was disembowelled while he was still very much alive.[155] Four days later, a licence was issued for another pamphlet, apparently by Crowley.[156] The reason was that the hack journalist Anthony Munday had produced his own distinctly sadistic account of the trial and execution, and admitted that Everard had been completely sentient when his stomach was cut open.[157]

[153] Anstr., I, p. 146; Persons, *An Epistle*, p. 158.

[154] Allen, *BH*, sigs Cvii^v–D^v; Allen, *TSMD*, pp. 3–4; [Robert Crowley], *A True Report of the Araignement & Execution of the late Popishe Traitour, E. Haunce, Executed at Tyborne, with Reformation of the Errors of the Former Untrue Booke Published concerning the Same* (1581), repr. in *Miscellanea* (CRS 32, 1932), pp. 394, 396–7; Persons, *An Epistle*, p. 113; ABSJ, Collectanea M, p. 89^b; Dillon, *CM*, p. 76; Ward, *LT*, pp. 299–300, citing *HMCL*, p. 35 (Burghley to the earl of Shrewsbury, 6 August 1581: Hanse was 'charged with traitorous words...maintaining the pope's action to be lawful in publishing against her Majesty an excommunication and a sentence that she was not a lawful queen nor her subjects bound to obey her, for which fault he was condemned and suffered as a traitor'. Burghley stressed that 'these actions are not matters of religion but merely of State'); AAW, B 28, no. 10, p. 285. Robert Crowley and Henry Tripp had confronted Thomas Pounde in prison, generating an extended dispute between them, on the basis of a manuscript challenge issued by Pounde: Robert Crowley, *An Aunswer to Sixe Reasons...* (1581); Persons, *An Epistle*, pp. 114–17.

[155] Dillon, *CM*, p. 76, citing *The Most Trayterous Protestation of Henrie Everit alias Everit Duckette* (1581).

[156] i.e. Crowley, *A True Report*; Dillon, *CM*, p. 76.

[157] Anthony Munday, *The Araignement, and Execution of a Wilfull and Obstinate Traitour, named Eueralde Ducket, alias Hauns: Condemned at the Sessions House, for High Treason, on Friday, beeing the 28. of Iuly, and Executed at Tiborne on Monday after, being the 31. day of the same Moneth. 1581. Gathered by M. S.* (1581). Godfrey Anstruther argued that Crowley produced his pamphlet because Munday admitted the regime's sadism; but one could argue also that Munday's work set down too

'SENTENCED TO DIE AS IN CASES OF HIGH TREASON' 109

Crowley averred that 'most' of Munday's 'book is untrue and many parts thereof do lay open the honour of justice to slander and the cause of religion to some disadvantage of cavilling speeches'.[158] Crowley added that it had been 'thought good by some' that Hanse should be dispatched immediately after he was convicted. This was because otherwise 'some papist might...get access unto him and advise him...to keep back such matter as otherwise he would more freely have uttered to the confutation of Doctor Allen's Apology', that is, William Allen's published defence of the seminary colleges, 'which bears the world falsely in hand that papists be true subjects'. This 'matter was not feared in vain, as afterwards fell out in his qualifying of his speech touching treason against the queen to be no sin'. But, still, a delay there was. At Tyburn, Hanse did indeed qualify 'his former words', said Crowley. Hanse declared 'that he meant it only of the treasons of denying the supremacy', when, raged Crowley, everyone knew this was not true, 'for he spoke it generally of all treasons against the queen...so giving to understand that (as he said at his arraignment) he took the queen for a prince lawfully deprived by the pope's authority'.[159]

Anyway, for all Crowley's efforts at damage control, the news was out—the regime had, as it were, misspoken.[160] All of this was an easy target for the acid pen of Robert Persons. His *Copie of a Double Letter* concerning the 'manner of the death of one Richard Atkins, executed by FIRE in Rome, the second of August 1581' referred to 'the two printed papers of Master Everard Hanse's execution, both which, though penned by his adversaries, and in some points not agreeing together', were sufficient, thought Persons, to tell the reader what had really happened. In reply, Persons printed a narrative of what the alleged lunatic heretic Atkins had done in Rome in order to demonstrate 'the great difference between the constant patience of true confessors and the perverse obstinacy of heretics in all ages by Satan's subordination falsely imitating the same'.[161] Persons claimed that Atkins had, in England, 'been whipped openly' and had been 'either thrust into Bridewell or Bedlam in London for certain lewd speeches against the queen' and would have 'suffered death, as is thought, had he not been deemed a madman'.

---

much of what Hanse actually said: G. Anstruther, 'A Missing Martyr Pamphlet', *London Recusant* 5 (1975), pp. 67–71. For Munday, see esp. D. Hamilton, *Anthony Munday and the Catholics, 1560–1633* (Aldershot, 2005), esp. pp. xvii–xviii, 31–1, 39, 47–9, 66, 87; cf. Kilroy, *EC*, p. 315; and see also A. Hadfield, *Lying in Early Modern English Culture: From the Oath of Supremacy to the Oath of Allegiance* (Oxford, 2017), pp. 5–11.

[158] Crowley, *True Report*, repr. in *Miscellanea*, p. 391.

[159] Ibid., pp. 397–8; William Allen, *An Apologie and True Declaration of the Institution and Endevours of the two English Colleges...* (Mounts in Henault [imprint false; printed at Rheims], 1581); see also Persons, *An Epistle*, pp. 74–5.

[160] *HMCL*, V, p. 35; Anstr., I, pp. 146–7; Anstruther, 'A Missing Martyr Pamphlet'. For Burghley's and Norton's justification of the regime's treatment of Hanse, see Graves, *TN*, pp. 251, 258.

[161] Robert Persons, *The Copie of a Double Letter sent by an Englishe Gentilman from beyond the Seas...* (n.p. [Rheims], n.d. [1581]), pp. 3, 5. Persons got his information via William Good in Rome: ARCR, II, no. 623.5. Persons's *Copie of a Double Letter* was sent via Paris by Allen across the Channel, as Sir Henry Cobham reported on 22 January 1582; see *CSPF 1581–2*, p. 460.

110   CATHOLICS AND TREASON

This was all so different from the true martyr-priest Hanse. For Persons, Atkins was a classic combination of heresy, sin, and 'frenzy'. The madman was condemned after he grabbed 'the holy chalice' and hurled it 'among the people' at a Mass in 'the chief church of Rome'. He was also 'convicted of a number of heretical articles' in addition to 'all the heresies of the new English Church, as that the pope was a devil, there' were 'no sacraments', and so on.[162] Persons wrote to his fictive recipient that, 'if you communicate the case to M. Foxe, perhaps he can make something of it', as he did for the 'martyr in Portugal' William Gardiner and 'other [just] as stinking stuff as this'.[163] In his *Epistle of the Persecution*, Persons similarly played up what he took to be the regime's hypocrisy when, 'afraid lest some perchance would be moved with the martyrdom of that innocent [man]', Hanse, 'they gave out in two contrary books, the one impugning the other, certain monstrous errors and paradoxes'.[164]

Persons rounded off his own deeply disturbing account of the heretic Atkins with the note that, 'being ready to close up, fresh advices are come by this last post of Paris, of the betraying and apprehension of Master Campion and others through the filthy treason of one Eliot'.[165] Following this public news management disaster in the case of Everard Hanse, it was likely that the regime's destruction of Campion would be far more sophisticated. Campion's arrest itself turned into a major publicity exercise. As Persons narrated it, they had lately led 'through the city of London twelve Catholics, whereof five were priests and the rest were of good estate and calling'. These were the people who had been 'found praying and at Mass all in one house with Master Edmund Campion'. He was 'slandered as a seditious person and, to that end and effect, a large paper was most spitefully written with great letters which they forced him to bear upon his head in this triumph'.[166]

The ripping out of Campion's fingernails appears to have forced him to reveal the names of his harbourers who, as we saw, were then hounded and harassed.[167] There was a barrage of strategically placed stories designed to discredit the Jesuit mission. It was put about that Campion had 'confessed whatsoever they had demanded of him, especially at whose houses and in what places he had been'. It was 'further bruited abroad that he had promised a recantation of', said Persons, 'I know not what'. It all seemed highly unlikely; but people were unsure what to think when 'many gentlemen and some of the nobility were called up to London... and charged with a supposed confession of Master Campion'. Furthermore, the

---

[162] Persons, *Copie*, pp. 7–13.

[163] Ibid., p. 23; T. S. Freeman and M. Borges, '"A Grave and Heinous Incident against our holy Catholic Faith": Two Accounts of William Gardiner's Desecration of the Portuguese Royal Chapel in 1552', *HR* 69 (1996), pp. 1–17.

[164] Persons, *An Epistle*, p. 74.   [165] Persons, *Copie*, p. 21.   [166] Persons, *An Epistle*, p. 82.

[167] G. Anstruther, *Vaux of Harrowden: A Recusant Family* (Newport, 1953), pp. 115–16; *CSPSp 1580–6*, p. 153; Persons, *An Epistle*, p. 83; Kilroy, *EC*, p. 343; see pp. 106–7 above. At execution, the spectators could see that 'all his nails had been dragged out in the torture': *CSPSp 1580–6*, p. 231.

'SENTENCED TO DIE AS IN CASES OF HIGH TREASON'   111

lieutenant of the Tower 'affirmed openly at a common session that there were no Catholics under his ward which refused to go to the church'. This implied that those detained had caved in and conformed.[168]

Further damage to Campion's reputation was attempted via a series of disputations (four of them) staged in the Tower between 31 August and 27 September 1581, although it was presumably still hoped that he might make concessions. Here, the regime turned, whether the queen liked it or not, to a variety of puritan divines, who might well have regarded themselves as on the outside track after the Anjou debacle, in order to face down Campion.[169] The debates were convened and conducted before audiences holding diverse opinions in religion. Campion was confronted with several opponents, including the presbyterian William Charke, who had already printed a reply to the 'brag', and the moderate puritans William Fulke, Roger Goad, William Day, Alexander Nowell, and John Walker. John Field and William Whitaker were among those who served as notaries.[170] They attacked Campion for, *inter alia*, defaming John Calvin, perhaps aware that Jerome Bolsec's infamous *Life of Calvin* had been read openly in the refectory at Douai.[171] It has been suggested that the changing format of the disputations

[168] Persons, *An Epistle*, pp. 88–9; Kilroy, *EC*, p. 256.

[169] Lake and Questier, 'Puritans', pp. 620–1; Ward, LT, p. 246 (for the convincing argument that it was the queen who may have urged the disputations, since 'most of the council, as well as the bishop of London, were clearly against such a move'); J. V. Holleran, *A Jesuit Challenge: Edmund Campion's Debates at the Tower of London in 1581* (New York, 1999); Hicks, *Letters*, pp. 95, 107 [*CUPRP*, p. 217]. For the most recent and fullest account of the disputations (the first was well attended, the rest were essentially private affairs), see Kilroy, *EC*, ch. 9. For Bishop Aylmer's opposition to the disputations, see T. M. McCoog, '"Playing the Champion": The Role of Disputation in the Jesuit Mission', in T. M. McCoog (ed.), *The Reckoned Expense: Edmund Campion and the Early English Jesuits* (Woodbridge, 1996), pp. 119–39, at p. 136. A fifth disputation was cancelled when Aylmer warned against it: Kilroy, *EC*, p. 293.

[170] Lake and Questier, 'Puritans', pp. 620–1; McCoog, *SJ*, pp. 149, 154–5; Alexander Nowell and William Day, *A True Report of the Disputation or rather Private Conference had in the Tower of London, with Ed. Campion Iesuite, the last of August. 1581* (1583); this tract incorporated a second work, by John Field, *The Three last Dayes Conferences had in the Tower with Edmund Campion Iesuite, the 18: 23: and 27. of September. 1581*. For Charke's publications, see William Charke, *An Answere to a Seditious Pamphlet lately Cast abroad by a Iesuite, with a Discoverie of that Blasphemous Sect* (1580); idem, *A Replie to a Censure Written against the Two Answers to a Iesuites Seditious Pamphlet* (1581). John Foxe apparently considered writing against what Campion had said in the Tower debates, using texts supplied to him (Foxe) by Thomas Norton; see E. Evenden and T. S. Freeman, *Religion and the Book in Early Modern England: the Making of Foxe's 'Book of Martyrs'* (Cambridge, 2011), pp. 281–2. William Whitaker cleared the text of his *Responsionis ad Decem illas Rationes, quibus Fretus Edmundus Campianus Certamen Ecclesiae Anglicanae Ministris Obtulit in Causa Fidei...*(1583) with Burghley: PRO, SP 12/162/6. As the regime tried to sign up those Protestants who had been alienated by the enforcement of ceremonial conformity, Thomas Cartwright was commissioned in early July 1582 by Sir Francis Walsingham to work on a riposte to the Rheims New Testament, even though the project was then reassigned to Thomas Bilson: PRO, SP 12/154/48; Milward, I, pp. 48–9, 50; Thomas Bilson, *The True Difference betweene Christian Subiection and Unchristian Rebellion...*(1585); Thomas Cartwright, *A Confutation of the Rhemists Translations, Glosses and Annotations on the New Testament...*(1618); Collinson, *EPM*, p. 235. Walsingham was also in contact with John Rainolds concerning a reply to the Rheims New Testament: PRO, SP 12/154/16, fo. 28[r–v]. Nowell's and Day's publication of the Protestant accounts of the disputations did not appear in print until January 1583: Kilroy, *EC*, p. 273.

[171] Holleran, *A Jesuit Challenge*, pp. 95, 96, 144, 145, 146, 147; P. Marshall, 'John Calvin and the English Catholics, c. 1565–1640', *HJ* 53 (2010), pp. 849–70, at pp. 855–6; Knox, *DD*, p. 145. Persons's

112 CATHOLICS AND TREASON

indicates that, at the first of them, Campion, though at an appalling disadvantage, came off best. As Kilroy argues, the sight of the tormented and physically wrecked Jesuit, badgered by puritan divines who were all too obviously hand in glove with those who had actually tortured him, made the queen's government look like a tyranny.[172] Leslie Ward plausibly suggests that it was the disputations, which enhanced rather than damaged Campion's reputation, that spurred the council to put the Jesuit and some of his associates on trial.[173]

Probably by this stage nothing could have saved Campion other than his complete capitulation. But so calculated had been his and his friends' pitch to the public, and so considerable the support which they had generated within the Catholic community, that convicting him of treason was going to be fraught with risk. Instructions were issued on 29 October 1581 to rack Campion again, and other prisoners in the Tower also, 'upon certain matters'. Further warrants went out for searches of the houses of some of his former patrons.[174]

The politically amorous duke of Anjou had arrived back in the country. The possibility of some sort of diplomatic deal was now on. To allow any hint of sympathy for the rigorist Catholic expressions of faith associated with Campion would, for the regime, have been unthinkable. Anjou's attendants were prepared to attend divine service as prescribed for the English national Church, even in the chapel royal itself. The sight of it must inevitably have influenced some Catholics to throw in the towel. Mendoza claimed on 7 November 1581 that the determination to wipe out Campion and his friends was intended not only to show how much of a bond there was between England and Scotland but also to persuade English Catholics that Anjou was not going to do anything for them.[175] In these circumstances, the string of conformities at the end of the year on the part of Campion's harbourers, noted here and there in the council's letters, was not really surprising.[176]

Campion and seven others were arraigned in queen's bench on 14 November.[177] The indictments were drawn under the 1351 treason statute rather than the regime's recent treason act, though Ward has identified a draft indictment against

---

Briefe Censure (written in reply to William Charke and Meredith Hanmer, who had attacked Campion's 'brag') referred to Bolsec's work: Marshall, 'John Calvin', p. 856, citing Robert Persons, *A Defence of the Censure...* (Rouen, 1582), pp. 77–86.

[172] Kilroy, *EC*, p. 272.

[173] Ward, *LT*, p. 247. The security arrangements during the disputations were lax. Some of those who attended were able to talk to other imprisoned clergy in the Tower, who were thus able to get their words out into the public domain. This included Alexander Briant's own account of how he had been tortured: Persons, *An Epistle*, 'The Copie of a Letter...', unpaginated.

[174] *APC 1581–2*, pp. 249–50; Kilroy, *EC*, p. 313.

[175] *CSPSp 1580–6*, pp. 210–11; Questier, *DP*, pp. 134–5.

[176] *APC 1581–2*, pp. 261, 268, 290.

[177] Kilroy, *EC*, p. 300. The seven others were: Ralph Sherwin, Luke Kirby, Thomas Cottam, Robert Johnson, Edward Rishton, James Bosgrave, and Henry Orton. For the significance of trial in queen's bench, i.e. rather than by special commission, see Ward, *LT*, p. 105.

'SENTENCED TO DIE AS IN CASES OF HIGH TREASON' 113

Campion alone, charging him, it seems, under the 1581 statute with having withdrawn the queen's subjects from their allegiance. The decision not to proceed on this basis suggests that the regime, although it had the explicit backing of the judges that an indictment of Campion under the 1581 act was possible, did not have the confidence to use its new statutory weapon and preferred therefore to resort to a charge under the 1351 act which was almost certainly spurious.[178] These eight Catholics were brought into court again on 16 November, on which day seven others were similarly arraigned.[179] Lord Vaux, Sir Thomas Tresham, Sir William Catesby, and others were dealt with in star chamber on 15 November for receiving the Jesuit and for hearing Mass.[180]

But even after all the preparing of the ground, the prosecution of Campion and his co-accused perhaps did not produce quite the desired result.[181] Allen, in the following year, ridiculed the proceedings on 20 and 21 November, on which two days Campion and those indicted with him were tried. Relying in part on the testimony of Thomas Fitzherbert, Allen wrote that 'they charged them with one crime of conspiracy; divers of them never seeing one another before they came to that bar in their lives, nor never writing one to one another, nor proved by any testimony or presumption that ever any two of them together, or any one alone, had any such talk or intention of conspiracy'. The queen's counsel 'charged them with no other thing, all that day long, but with other men's faults, not being able to prove that they all, or any of them, ever consented unto them; yes, and with divers things, whereof they could none of them possibly be partakers'; as 'the insurrection of the North, the commotion in Ireland, the pope's excommunication of the queen, D. [Nicholas] Sander's writings, D. [Richard] Bristow's "Motives", D. Allen's approving the book, letters intercepted of I cannot tell whom, of what, or to whom; with ciphers and characters that could not be read, but yet must needs mean some persons, places and preparations for invasion'. Allen went on to give chapter and verse as to how court procedure had been perverted. Evidence had been admitted from Munday, Slade, and Eliot which was obviously perjured, so as to secure guilty verdicts which should never have been delivered.[182] Thomas Fitzherbert said that 'a gentleman of good account, a lawyer, and an

---

[178] Ward, LT, pp. 13, 168–9, 235–6, 247; Kilroy, EC, pp. 299–300; AWCCBM, pp. 292 f. As Ward points out, there were procedural advantages for the crown in using the 1351 act, as opposed to its own more recent treason legislation: Ward, LT, p. 166.

[179] Kilroy, EC, p. 301. Those arraigned on this day (16 November) were John Colleton, Lawrence Johnson (alias Richardson), John Hart, Thomas Ford, William Filby, Alexander Briant, and John Shert.

[180] A. G. Petti (ed.), Recusant Documents from the Ellesmere Manuscripts (CRS 60, 1968), pp. 5–13; Anstruther, Vaux, pp. 120–35.

[181] For the fullest account of the trial, see Kilroy, EC, ch. 10.

[182] Allen, BH, sig. av^v–vi^r, et seq.; Pollen, AEM, pp. 38–9 (AAW, A II, no. 38, pp. 185–8); Kilroy, EC, p. 301. The allegations of vice which had been deployed against such people as Thomas Cottam (see p. 122n.17 below) were turned by Allen back on the government witnesses, or 'the offal of the world' as Allen described them, 'known to be of no religion, of every religion, cozeners, dissemblers, spies... and some of them to be charged with adultery, murder and such like crimes': Allen, BH, sig. avii^v–viii^r.

114   CATHOLICS AND TREASON

earnest Protestant, yet a friend of mine' believed that Campion was going to be acquitted. Lord Chief Justice Wray admitted privately that the convictions were for reason of State.[183]

This is the line, by and large, of Campion's most recent and definitive biographer, Gerard Kilroy.[184] It has to be said, if the transcripts of the Popish Plot trials of 1679–81 almost exactly one hundred years later are anything to go by, this kind of shocking irregularity in legal process does not exactly come as a surprise. On the other hand, a non-*parti pris* observer might have wondered at the evidence offered by Eliot about Campion's sermon at Lyford in Berkshire on 16 July, which Campion himself admitted dealt with the topic of 'that wherein it should please God to make a restitution of faith and religion' in England.[185]

The trial was, indeed, less about the alleged conspiracy (which undoubtedly never took place in the way that several witnesses described) and more about the recent Catholic polemicizing and propagandizing which undoubtedly were a threat to the queen's authority. All this perhaps explains the different fate of one of the accused, John Colleton. He had been arrested at Lyford with Campion on 17 July 1581 but was acquitted. He was able to call a witness, the lawyer John Lancaster, who was from Milverton in Somerset, as was Colleton himself. Lancaster testified that he had been with Colleton in Gray's Inn on the day that he was supposed to have been plotting treason at Rheims, where he had never in fact been at all.[186] Colleton was deported, eventually, in January 1585. But, early in James I's reign, it was claimed, at the hearing in star chamber which dealt with Thomas Pounde's alleged offences, that Colleton had been spared back in 1581 ostensibly because it was known that he was of a loyalist temperament.[187]

---

[183] Pollen, *AEM*, pp. 38–9 (AAW, A II, no. 38, pp. 185–8); see also Kilroy, *EC*, pp. 327–30. Perhaps Fitzherbert's friend is the same as Henry Walpole's acquaintance the lawyer Mr Strickland, who came to the same conclusion: Pollen, *AEM*, p. 43. For Wray, see *HC 1558–1603*, III, p. 653; Ward, LT, pp. 97–8.

[184] As Gerard Kilroy has emphasized, Campion at trial was not prepared publicly to endorse the papal deposing power, or, rather, he rehearsed the doubtfulness and uncertainty among Catholic theorists as to whether the pope could excommunicate princes, and personally he refused to commit himself completely either way: Kilroy, *EC*, pp. 314–15, citing BL, Harleian MS 6265, fos 18ᵛ–19ʳ.

[185] Kilroy, *EC*, pp. 228, 316–17.

[186] Anstr., I, p. 83; Ward, LT, pp. 169–70, 243; J. B. Wainewright, 'Ven. James Fenn (?1540–1584)', ABSJ, CP (James Fenn), p. 10; Kn., VI, pp. 20–1. A plea similar to Colleton's was made by the priest Thomas Ford. One 'Nicholson', i.e., as Wainewright surmises, the priest Richard Norris (already under suspicion over the circulation of Campion's 'brag'), offered to give evidence on Ford's behalf, but, as a result, one assumes, Norris was imprisoned in the Marshalsea on 17 December 1581, while Ford was subsequently convicted and executed. Norris was also from Milverton in Somerset. He was arraigned on 5 February 1584, along with James Fenn; see Wainewright, 'Ven. James Fenn', pp. 10–11; Anstr., I, p. 255; Kn., VI, p. 21.

[187] *HMCV*, III, p. 144. John Hart, who had been sent to England on 5 June 1580 and had been arrested almost at once (Anstr., I, pp. 153–4), was tried and sentenced with Campion; but on 1 December 1581, the day of Campion's execution, he promised Walsingham that in return for a royal pardon he would act as an informer against William Allen and his associates. He was reprieved (again) on 27/28 May 1582: Anstr., I, pp. 153–4; PRO, SP 12/150/80; Kilroy, *EC*, p. 350.

Figure 4.1 Reliquaries of the English martyrs, Stonyhurst, Lancashire. The rope with which the Jesuit Edmund Campion was bound to the hurdle on which he was taken to execution at Tyburn on 1 December 1581, and a corporal used in the Tower of London by several Catholic clergymen to say Mass (reproduced with the permission of the British province of the Society of Jesus).

The regime was now confronted with a difficult choice, that is, of whether or not to kill Campion.[188] One person who had no sympathy for Campion was the duke of Anjou. He would not do anything to save the Jesuit and his co-condemned Ralph Sherwin and Alexander Briant. They were dragged to Tyburn on 1 December 1581.[189] (See Figure 4.1.) Famously, the Valois prince was petitioned on that morning, during a game of tennis, to save Campion's life, but he refused.[190]

---

[188] Kilroy, *EC*, p. 331. John Foxe is supposed to have petitioned the council for Campion to be reprieved. To the same end, a number of Catholics approached the French and the Spanish ambassadors: Kilroy, *EC*, pp. 331–3.

[189] Sherwin had been taken in the 'chamber' of Nicholas Roscarrock, who was made to listen to Sherwin being tortured: Allen, *BH*, sig. f^v, fii^r; Anstr., I, p. 312.

[190] McCoog, 'The English Jesuit Mission', pp. 204–5; J. Bossy, 'English Catholics and the French Marriage, 1577–81', *RH* 5 (1959–60), pp. 2–16, at p. 10; Kilroy, *EC*, p. 333. Persons, who had already gone into exile, used the priest Edward Grately to approach Anjou: Hicks, *Letters*, p. xli; ARSJ, Anglia 30/i, fo. 200^v (for which reference I am grateful to Ginevra Crosignani).

116 CATHOLICS AND TREASON

The event was attended by thousands of spectators, including 'divers of her Majesty's honourable council'. No one was to be in any doubt that this was the will of the queen.[191] Richard Topcliffe was there.[192] Campion's famous 'We are made a spectacle to the world' speech was interrupted by the 'great heretic' Sir Francis Knollys and the sheriffs, who badgered him to admit that he was guilty of treason. Campion retaliated by declaring that he had confessed under torture and also that the regime had wrongly convicted Lawrence Johnson (alias Richardson), mistaking him for another man, who had carried the manuscript of Campion's major polemical statement *Rationes Decem* to Persons.[193] Then 'one [Thomas] Hearne, a schoolmaster', read out 'the new advertisement', that is, the *Advertisement and Defence for Truth against her Backbiters*, a short explanatory pamphlet about the regime's proceedings and Campion's alleged crimes, 'openly with loud voice unto the people'.[194] As Professor Kilroy says, Campion, despite the heckling, managed to declare himself loyal to the queen. Henry Walpole said that he had been converted by the sight of the execution and, specifically, when he was splashed with Campion's blood as his quarters were thrown into the cauldron provided for boiling them.[195] Campion's performance at Tyburn is said to have won over many of the spectators. Persons recorded that Lord Charles Howard used his sword in order to prevent Campion being cut down and disembowelled before he was dead.[196] Knollys interrupted also when Sherwin, who was hanged immediately after Campion, tried to justify himself to the crowd on the topic of what constituted treason. But neither Campion nor Sherwin would answer questions about the 1570 bull of excommunication.[197]

Central to the hostile critique of what the regime had done was the priest Thomas Alfield's *True Reporte*. According to Alfield, the execution of Briant was made worse 'by [the] negligence of the hangman'.[198] But, Alfield said, some spectators had 'prevented the bloody purposes of' the 'cruel tormenters' and he hoped that God would 'reward that gentleman who, after M. Sherwin was put from the cart, turned back and said, "This man was a wise man. God, I say, reward him, God increase his honour"'.[199] Catholics in London had seen what had happened to Everard Hanse earlier in the year. They were, said Alfield, determined not to let

[191] *CSPSp 1580–6*, pp. 231–2; Challoner, *MMP*, pp. 28, 34; Allen, *BH*, sig. d^r.
[192] EUL copy (classmark Rowse/Pol) of Pollini, *Historia Ecclesiastica*, p. 572. For Topcliffe, see *HC 1558–1603*, III, pp. 513–15; F. W. Brownlow, 'Richard Topcliffe: Elizabeth's Enforcer and the Representation of Power in King Lear', in R. Dutton, A. Findlay, and R. Wilson (eds), *Theatre and Religion: Lancastrian Shakespeare* (Manchester, 2003), pp. 161–78.
[193] Allen, *BH*, sig. d^{r-v}; *CSPSp 1580–6*, p. 231; Kilroy, *EC*, pp. 337–8; see also Allen, *BH*, sig. avi^v; Anstr., I, p. 190; Kilroy, *EC*, pp. 195–6.
[194] Allen, *BH*, sig. d^v; Alfield, *TR*, sigs C^v–2^r; *An Advertisement and Defence for Trueth against her Backbiters, and specially against the Whispring Favourers, and Colourers of Campions, and the Rest of his Confederats Treasons* (1581); Kilroy, *EC*, pp. 338–9.
[195] Pollen, *AEM*, p. 40 (AAW, A II, no. 38, pp. 185–8); Kilroy, *EC*, p. 344; see p. 55 above.
[196] Kilroy, *EC*, p. 341.   [197] Alfield, *TR*, sig. C2^r, C3^v–4^r; Kilroy, *EC*, pp. 341–2.
[198] Alfield, *TR*, sig. D2^v; Kilroy, *EC*, p. 342.   [199] Alfield, *TR*, sig. D3^r.

'SENTENCED TO DIE AS IN CASES OF HIGH TREASON' 117

the regime's hacks tell the same lies about Campion and the others. As a result, 'many good Catholic gentlemen' made sure that they were present in order to witness what took place.[200]

Alfield's *True Reporte* was penned primarily as an antidote to the *Advertisement and Defence for Trueth against her Backbiters*.[201] But he noticed also that Thomas Norton had fallen from grace. As Alfield said, it was Norton, 'now prisoner', who, 'for the better face of his own disloyalty and treason, procured these her Majesty's true and most loyal subjects to be accused, condemned and executed for treason'.[202] Roger Manners confirmed on 5 December 1581, only four days after Campion and his two friends were hanged and disembowelled, that it was Norton's meddling in the Anjou business which had seen him incarcerated in the Bloody Tower. He was imprisoned 'for his over-much and undutiful speaking touching' the duke of Anjou's 'cause'. It was this, rather than Norton's stroppiness and outspokenness in the parliament in early 1581, which had led to his disgrace.[203] For his part, Norton, who was never short on self-pity, wrote from the Tower, 'methinks I hear her Majesty's evil subjects say: "Lo, the hand of God and his vengeance...upon this wretch that so served against the Catholics"'.[204] That very probably was what they did say. It was easy to see how Norton's (temporary) disgrace would fit, as it did, into a discourse of providential punishment of the persecutors of God's faithful servants. It reminds us also that here what has often been regarded as (the most traditional version of) 'Catholic history' maps onto the narratives of Elizabethan high politics. Whether or not the queen's government

[200] Alfield, *TR*, sig. A3^v–4^r; Dillon, *CM*, pp. 76–7.

[201] Alfield, *TR*, sig. A4^v. For the *True Reporte*'s composition (Alfield was accompanied to Tyburn by one of the Dolman family, whose father had been a client of the countess of Lennox) and its printing, in Smithfield, see PRO, SP 12/153/78, fo. 153^r; ARCR, II, no. 4; Dillon, *CM*, pp. 79–80, 90 (it was published by Richard Verstegan). For the distribution in Paris of another version of Campion's execution (*L'Histoire de la Mort*...), which Henry III tried to suppress, and for its subsequent translation into Latin and Italian and its incorporation into the *Concertatio Ecclesiae Catholicae*...(Trier, 1588), see *CSPF 1581–2*, pp. 441, 444, 454, 465; ARCR, I, nos 196–204; Kilroy, *EC*, p. 351; for the compilation of the *Concertatio*, see D. M. Rogers's introduction to the Scolar facsimile reprint (1970) of the 1588 edition; Dillon, *CM*, pp. 81–2; Thomas, *WECM*, pp. 140–1; *AWCBC*, p. 53 (the book used 'material received from English sources' which the editors 'translated as necessary and arranged for publication', though the first-hand sources are, understandably, generally not identified). For the ambassador Bernardino de Mendoza's circulation of his secretary Pedro Serrano's narratives of what had happened to Campion, Sherwin, and Briant, see *AWCCBM*, pp. 320–3 (J. Morris, 'A New Witness about B. Edmund Campion', *Month* 78 (1893), pp. 457–65: translation of BL, Egerton MS 2769, fo. 9$^{r–v}$); Kilroy, *EC*, p. 343. Anthony Munday replied to Alfield and to the French pamphlet defending Campion with *A Breefe Aunswer Made unto Two Seditious Pamphlets*...(1582); for the pamphlet campaign against Campion, see also Milward, I, pp. 61–9. The official account of the proceedings against Campion and other clergy was entitled *A Particular Declaration or Testimony, of the Undutifull and Traiterous Affection Borne against her Maiestie by Edmond Campion Iesuite*...(1582); ARCR, I, no. 196; see also PRO, SP 12/152/91, fos 158^r–9^r.

[202] Alfield, *TR*, sig. B2^r. Alfield attacked Munday's *A Discoverie of Edmund Campion* as a pamphlet which had 'been perused by no worse man than by M. Norton, a supposed traitor in the Tower': Alfield, *TR*, sigs D4^v–E^v.

[203] Graves, *TN*, pp. 390–3; *HMCR*, I, p. 130.

[204] Graves, *TN*, p. 395.

118 CATHOLICS AND TREASON

miscalculated in its dealings with Campion, particularly in allowing him a public platform in the Tower disputations, and then by resorting to a dubious set of legal proceedings against him and his associates, the fact was that a kind of emergent Catholic pressure group had been able to raise the polemical and political stakes in its dealings with the regime. Not unreasonably, the queen and council saw themselves under attack from a Catholic rhetoric of toleration which was intensified by the regime's own increasingly harsh response to that Catholic critique. Notable here was the hard-hitting sequence of pamphlets written by William Allen during the 1580s, pamphlets which condemned the queen's government as verging on tyranny. In the face of this assault it was perhaps inevitable that the regime would retaliate by extending the law of treason and, as it had with Campion, by enlisting moderate puritan opinion in the face of a sizeable Catholic move into separatism.

5

After Campion

Discipline and Punish

If the queen's ministers had thought that the prime-time hanging and eviscer-ation of Edmund Campion and his friends would be the end of the matter, they soon found that they were wrong. There was a surge of publicity across continen-tal Europe about the Jesuit's martyrdom, and there was a predictably hostile reac-tion within some sections of the English Catholic community.[1] At the end of February 1582, Richard Verstegan's clandestine press (which had been used to print Alfield's *True Reporte*) was seized by Recorder Fleetwood.[2] Verstegan fled abroad and very soon turned out his *Praesentis Ecclesiae Anglicanae Typus*. This was a broadsheet of six woodcuts which depicted the treatment of Campion, Everard Hanse, and others.[3] Stephen Vallenger had, apparently, prepared accounts of the Tower disputations for the press, and he was charged by Sir Walter Mildmay with having written Alfield's *True Reporte*. He was tried in star chamber on 16 May 1582 and had his ears sliced off. He died in prison in November 1591.[4] In circa June 1582, John Hamerton of Hellifield in Yorkshire, formerly a servant of Bishop Edmund Bonner, came to the authorities' attention for having said that Campion and his friends had, like John Felton and John Story, been 'wrongfully condemned' and had 'died like apostles and martyrs'. Hamerton also said that he had, back in the day, 'helped to set fire and faggot to the most [of them] that were burned in Smithfield, for the which he yet rejoices to think how they fried in the flame and what good service he had done God in furthering their deaths'.[5]

---

[1] See also G. Kilroy, 'A Tangled Chronicle: The Struggle over the Memory of Edmund Campion', in A. Gordon and T. Rist (eds), *The Arts of Remembrance in Early Modern England: Memorial Cultures of the Post Reformation* (2nd edition, Abingdon, 2016), pp. 141–60.

[2] A. G. Petti, 'Richard Verstegan and Catholic Martyrologies of the later Elizabethan Period', *RH* 5 (1959–60), pp. 64–90, at pp. 67–9; Kilroy, *EC*, p. 360. Verstegan may have been assisted in the publish-ing of Alfield's *True Reporte* by the printer William Carter; see T. Birrell, 'William Carter (ca. 1549–84): Recusant Printer, Publisher, Binder, Stationer, Scribe—and Martyr', *RH* 28 (2006), pp. 22–42, at p. 37.

[3] Kilroy, *EC*, p. 360; Richard Verstegan, *Praesentis Ecclesiae Anglicanae Typus* (n.p. [Rheims], 1582); ARCR, I, no. 1293.

[4] Questier, *C&C*, p. 160; A. G. Petti, 'Stephen Vallenger (1541–1591)', *RH* 6 (1962), pp. 248–64; A. G. Petti, *Recusant Documents from the Ellesmere Manuscripts*, pp. 13–18; Kilroy, *EC*, pp. 283–4; J. V. Holleran, *A Jesuit Challenge: Edmund Campion's Debates at the Tower of London in 1581* (New York, 1999), p. 226.

[5] PRO, SP 15/27/93, fo. 141ʳ (*CSPD Addenda 1580–1625*, p. 63).

Catholics and Treason: Martyrology, Memory, and Politics in the Post-Reformation. Michael Questier,
Oxford University Press. © Michael Questier 2022. DOI: 10.1093/oso/9780192847027.003.0005

120   CATHOLICS AND TREASON

The attempted purge of the separatist tendencies among Catholics certainly did not come to an end with Campion's death. Eleven Catholic clergymen were executed in 1582, eight of them during April and May, the majority of them for their supposed involvement with Campion's alleged conspiracy.[6] Perhaps the highest-profile case at this point was that of John Paine, though he was dealt with separately from the other clergy associated with Campion. He had gone to Douai and had been ordained at Cambrai in 1576. As we saw, back in England he had been imprisoned and was set at liberty in March 1577. He was then arrested in early July 1581.[7] This was very shortly before Campion was taken in Berkshire. Paine was racked more than once between August and October 1581. He was not put on trial with Campion but was detained in the Tower.[8] George Eliot claimed that Paine was part of an assassination conspiracy (in favour of Mary Stuart) against Elizabeth and leading privy councillors. As the queen's sergeant, John Puckering, related later in the 1580s, at the trial of Philip Howard, earl of Arundel, if the conspiracy had succeeded and 'her Majesty was slain', it was intended in London to drag 'her through the streets by the hair of her head'.[9] On Paine's view, said Eliot, 'it should be no greater an offence to kill the queen than to dispatch a brute beast'. The formal grounds of the indictment were that on 7 January 1579 and at other times Paine had conspired to murder Elizabeth and had incited Eliot to the same purpose. Paine naturally enough denied this. In retaliation, he brought up Eliot's distinctly sleazy reputation; but Paine was convicted anyway.[10] We have no idea whether there was a scintilla of truth in what Eliot said. It is possible that

[6] Challoner, *MMP*, pp. 39–72; see also Yale University Library, Beinecke Rare Book and Manuscript Library, Osborn a18. It was annotated by Richard Topcliffe thus: 'A consolatory letter to a traitor near the gallows, found at Bellamy's at Uxendon', and 'A very traitorous work pretended to be the answers of Piers Plowman to the printed interrogatories of allegiance, but in truth a way to instruct papists how to answer traitorously and defends [*sic*] the traitors for martyrs that died at Tyburn in Anno 1582'. The manuscript is dated 27 and 28 May 1582; see M. Rankin, 'Richard Topcliffe and the Book Culture of the Elizabethan Catholic Underground', *Renaissance Quarterly* 72 (2019), pp. 492–536, at p. 514.
[7] Anstr., I, p. 266; see p. 85 above.
[8] B. Foley, 'Bl. John Payne, Seminary Priest and Martyr—1582', *Essex Recusant* 2 (1960), pp. 48–75, at pp. 54, 55.
[9] Foley, 'Bl. John Payne', pp. 59–60; Foley, *RSJ*, II, pp. 586–8 (BL, Lansdowne MS 33, no. 60, fos 145ʳ–9ʳ); Pollen and MacMahon, *VPH*, pp. 276, 291.
[10] Allen, *BH*, sig. Ciiiʳ–viᵛ (quotation at sig. Ciiiᵛ); Foley, 'Bl. John Payne', pp. 59–60; Kilroy, *EC*, p. 321; J. S. Cockburn (ed.), *Calendar of Assize Records: Essex Indictments: Elizabeth I* (1978), p. 222. Eliot served in the Petre household at Ingatestone in Essex. He may have previously been at Cowdray in Sussex where, at one time, there was a servant-from-hell of the same name whom the first Viscount Montague found intensely annoying: Questier, *C&C*, p. 196. Several of the households which Eliot denounced in the early 1580s were on the Sussex/Hampshire border: Questier, *C&C*, p. 196; BL, Lansdowne MS 33, no. 60, fos 145ʳ–9ʳ. (I have recently noticed that a list of the servants in the household of the second Viscount Montague in *c.*1594 includes one 'George Eliot'. It is possible, therefore, that there is no connection between Campion's nemesis and the George Eliot who was at Cowdray: BL, Harleian MS 6998, fo. 149ᵛ. But, equally, there is no reason why someone who had infuriated the first viscount should have been retained in the family's service down to the 1590s.) For Paine's refutation and denunciation of Eliot, see Allen, *BH*, sig. Ciiiʳ. For the bargain by which Eliot negotiated immunity from the criminal charges pending against him, see Kilroy, *EC*, pp. 223–5, 242.

AFTER CAMPION   121

Ingatestone (where Paine's patrons, the Petre family, resided) was a hotbed of regicidal radicalism, but, on the whole, it seems unlikely.[11]

Paine was sent on 20 March 1582 from the Tower to the assizes at Chelmsford. He was condemned, sentenced, and then executed on 2 April 1582, the day after the date of another royal proclamation against seminary clergy.[12] In prison on the day before execution, Paine was badgered by 'Dr Withers' and 'Dr Sone'. One assumes that 'Sone' was Robert Some who had in the early 1570s been a supporter of Thomas Cartwright and was now a chaplain to the earl of Leicester. George Withers, whose roots were in radical London Protestantism, had been suspended temporarily by Archbishop Parker in 1565 and was eventually appointed, by Bishop Edwin Sandys, as archdeacon of Colchester. Though he put his former presbyterianism to one side, he was a hard-line if technically conformist puritan. He apparently turned a blind eye to the Dedham classis and objected to Archbishop Whitgift's subscription campaign in 1584.[13]

Bull, the hangman of Newgate, had been sent down to Essex to dispatch Paine.[14] It seems probable that Paine's fate was a relatively uncoded warning to those in the Ingatestone area that his wealthy and conformist gentry patron, Sir John Petre, could no longer protect his clients as he had once done. William Allen simply said that 'there were...raised new bruits and muttering of uneven dealing in the sending away of M. Paine so far off to be arraigned and executed'.[15]

At this time, according to a news report sent out to the duke of Anjou in Flanders, there was open enmity between the earl of Leicester and the earl of Sussex. (Sussex functioned as a patron to the Petre family.) The queen had had 'long conference' with Sussex in the week ending 30 April 1582 and then had an almighty bust-up with Leicester. She allegedly reproached 'him rudely of many disloyalties' and said that he had 'broken the match' with Anjou, which would otherwise have been 'to the comfort of her people and assurance of posterity'. Whether or not Elizabeth actually said this, or something like it, the narrator added that 'the earl of Sussex likewise had joined with the principal nobility of the realm in nature of a league against the said earl of Leicester to ruin him and his house and had the Catholics on his side' as well as others. In the following week, it

---

[11] However, Mary Cleere of Ingatestone had been sentenced by Justices Southcot and Gawdy on 6 March 1577 to be burned for declaring that Elizabeth 'was base born' and that 'another lady', i.e. Mary Stuart, 'was the right inheritor thereunto': Ward, LT, p. 190.

[12] For the proceedings against Paine, see Allen, BH, sig. Ciii[r]–vii[r]; Challoner, MMP, pp. 40–3; CSPSp 1580–6, p. 336. One of Allen's sources was, it seems, John Paine's brother, Jerome (CSPF 1581–2, p. 493), for whom see Anstr., I, p. 266; Miscellanea II (1906), pp. 259, 262, 265, 281; Miscellanea III (CRS 3, 1906), pp. 25, 26, 27, 28, 29; Ward, LT, p. 298; PRO, SP 12/210/30, fo. 57[v] (CSPD 1581–90, p. 484).

[13] ODNB, sub Some, Robert (article by S. Wright), and Withers [Wither], George (article by B. Usher and J. Craig); ODNB, sub Penry, John (article by C. Cross), for John Penry's later pamphlet attack on Some.

[14] Allen, BH, sig. Cvi[r–v].   [15] Allen, BH, sig. bviii[v].

122 CATHOLICS AND TREASON

was claimed, there had been 'a great quarrel between' them and there was a real risk of their retinues attacking each other.[16]

If this is close to the truth, it might help to explain the rush of executions of Catholic clergy which followed shortly after, in late May 1582. In other words, if the earl of Sussex had known (conformist) Catholics in his entourage and, despite the public-relations difficulties of the Anjou business, was seen as a political alternative to the ambitions of Leicester and his friends, then it would have been logical for some people to proceed now against those who had been put on trial with Campion and were associated by the public with his supposed treasons. Allen recounted the hanging of Thomas Ford, John Shert, and Robert Johnson on 28 May 1582, and of William Filby, Luke Kirby, Lawrence Johnson, and Thomas Cottam two days later.[17] The regime broadcast in print the answers made by these Catholics when tendered the, as they were commonly called, 'bloody questions'.[18]

There are signs that, up to the bitter end, the privy council would have been satisfied with recantations rather than the violent public dumbshow of the penalties for treason. Rather than dispatch them all at once, these executions took place one by one. John Shert was forced to watch Thomas Ford hang and then to see 'his fellow bowelled and beheaded'.[19] The hanging and dismembering of one was followed by an offer to the next of a chance to swear loyalty to the queen, abjure fealty to the papacy, and secure a reprieve.[20]

However, even as the administrators of the Rheims seminary were gearing up for a no-holds-barred struggle with the queen's ministers, and while Robert

---

[16] *CSPF Jan.–June 1583* [Addenda section for 1582], pp. 595–6, 597.

[17] Allen, *BH*, sigs Aiiii^v–Bviii^v; *APC 1581–2*, pp. 144–5, 147, 171–2, 249, 428. Richard Topcliffe and William Charke were prominent at Tyburn on 30 May: Allen, *BH*, sigs B^v; *Concertatio Ecclesiae Catholicae in Anglia Adversus Calvino-papistas et Puritanos...* (Trier, 1588), ed. John Fenn and John Gibbons, sig. Z2^v. Lawrence Johnson had been resident with the Houghton family at Park Hall, where Campion had stayed, finished his *Rationes Decem*, and left his books: AAW, A III, no. 27, pp. 105–8; Kilroy, *EC*, p. 196; see p. 116 above. For the circumstances of Cottam's arrest, incarceration, and interrogation (Charles Slade had travelled from Lyons with Cottam), see Anstr., I, pp. 90–1; PRO, SP 12/140/43, fo. 90^r; Kilroy, *EC*, p. 160; Talbot, *MRR*, pp. 240–1. William Allen wrote that, at Tyburn, a 'minister, amongst other things, willed' Cottam 'to confess his wicked and lewd behaviour which he had committed in Fish Street about four years since', which Cottam denied: Allen, *BH*, sig. Bvi^v; *Concertatio*, sig. Aa2^r; see also Weinreich, *PREH*, pp. 480–1.

[18] *A Particular Declaration or Testimony, of the Undutifull and Traiterous Affection Borne against her Maiestie by Edmond Campion Iesuite...* (1582), sigs Cii^r–Diii^r; Allen, *BH*, sig. A^r–iii^r; see also *Concertatio*, sigs X4^v–Y2^v. For the 'bloody questions', see Renold, *LWA*, p. 80, citing TD, III, pp. iv–v (the questions used originally in the proceedings against Campion). The *Particular Declaration* emphasized the difference between the answers of clergy such as Thomas Ford, who affirmed the papal deposing power 'upon certain occasions', and the answers of others, such as James Bosgrave and Henry Orton, who were potentially loyalist: *A Particular Declaration*, sigs Ciii^r, Dii^r–iii^r. Bosgrave was reprieved on 1 December 1581. A Catholic manuscript, left in the porch of St Giles-without-Cripplegate (Robert Crowley's church) in July 1582, said that the regime was lying about Bosgrave and Orton: Kilroy, *EC*, pp. 334–5, citing Foley, *RSJ*, III, pp. 292–4 (PRO, SP 12/254/53. ii).

[19] Allen, *BH*, sig. Av^v–vi^r.

[20] Allen, *BH*, sig. Bvii^r–^{v}. Cottam was similarly urged to 'call for mercy': Allen, *BH*, sig. Bviii^r; Edwards, *EJ*, p. 166.

AFTER CAMPION   123

Persons was releasing his persecution narrative in multiple translations,[21] it appears that the regime (or sections of it) looked for an accommodation with Mary Stuart. This took the form of the so-called association scheme, which would, in principle, have seen her repatriated to Scotland to share, in some manner, in the sovereignty of her son James VI. Though the regime in London in the end regarded this as undesirable, the pressure on Elizabeth from the political coupling of James and Mary then slackened off temporarily with the so-called Raid of Ruthven, which led to the ejection from Scotland of James's new favourite, the Francophile and conformist-Catholic duke of Lennox.[22]

For whatever reason, after this spate of bloodletting in late May 1582, the regime's urge to kill seems to have abated somewhat. For example, five days after John Paine's execution, the pamphleteer-priest Thomas Alfield was arrested—on 7 April 1582, allegedly turned in by his own father.[23] The council issued a warrant to interrogate him under torture. A decision was made to send him to the North with the cleric William Dean, to be 'proceeded with according to law'. But he was released in or before September 1582. Topcliffe had a good deal of evidence against Dean as well, but he had been ready to comply, even to the extent of appearing as a prosecution witness against an indicted Catholic. Dean was deported in January 1585.[24] The pamphlet published about Alfield in 1585 said that he had been let go 'upon his hypocritical submission'. Allen had admitted as much in September 1582, though, in print in 1583, he said that Alfield had, faced with torture, agreed 'only to go to their church once, and that with many qualifications', and he had subsequently repented. So it looks as if even Alfield was temporarily able to come to some sort of accommodation with the authorities.[25] The London printer William Carter was arrested yet again after a search of his rooms in Hart Street in July 1582. During this search, Topcliffe found a number of

---

[21] CSPF 1581–2, pp. 465, 471, 486, 511, 552, 571, 584–5, 586, 587; V. Houliston, Catholic Resistance in Elizabethan England: Robert Persons's Jesuit Polemic, 1580–1610 (Aldershot, 2007), p. 34; ARCR, I, nos 874–84; ARCR, II, no. 627; Ward, LT, p. 251; Kilroy, EC, pp. 362–3.

[22] Questier, DP, p. 143.   [23] Anstr., I, p. 3.

[24] APC 1581–2, pp. 400–1, 432; Knox, LMCA, p. 163. Topcliffe declared that Dean, formerly a curate at Monk Fryston, counselled the queen's subjects 'not to come to the church nor to receive the communion', and persuaded 'the queen's subjects that the pope of Rome was supreme head and governor of the Church of England and not her Majesty'. Also, 'he did wish the queen's Majesty's death traitorously': Pollen, UD, p. 26 (PRO, SP 12/152/54); see also Petti, 'Richard Verstegan', p. 69. Dean had 'said six or seven Masses since his coming over in London. The most of them' were 'at one Mistress Alford's house within Salisbury Court where he lodged most', i.e. the wife of Francis Alford, cousin of Lord Buckhurst, and a one-time supporter of Mary Stuart. Walsingham intervened to stop the prosecution of Mrs Alford (on the promise of her conformity): Pollen, UD, pp. 26, 29; HC 1558–1603, I, pp. 335–8. Dean gave evidence against one Mrs Rogers for attending Mass at Mrs Alford's; this meant that Walsingham regarded him in a favourable light (and so his indictment in 1583 did not proceed): Ward, LT, pp. 261–2; Pollen, UD, p. 29 (BL, Lansdowne MS 35, no. 26).

[25] Anstr., I, pp. 3, 100; Knox, LMCA, p. 163; The Life and End of Thomas Awfeeld a S. P. and Thomas Webley a Dyers Servant in London...Executed at Tyburn 6 July 1585 (1585), sig. Aiiii[v]; William Allen, A True Report of the Late Apprehension and Imprisonnement of Iohn Nicols...(Rheims, 1583), sig. F[r]. Dean had been arrested on 21 February 1582.

124   CATHOLICS AND TREASON

manuscripts—principally Nicholas Harpsfield's and the ones written out by Vallenger, which recorded the Campion disputations. Carter was shoved into the Tower. Thomas Norton penned a damning account of the manuscripts discovered in Carter's premises. Carter was 'thought to have kept his master's [Harpsfield's] purpose to publish' these manuscripts 'as their cause might have cause of advantage and, in the meantime, to spread them by written copies'. All of Carter's 'books tend expressly to prove her Majesty unlawfully born and some of them by the way to deface and dishonour both her own royal person and the persons of her highness's father, mother, grandmother' and others and also 'the laws of the parliament made for limitation of the crown to her Majesty'. 'Among Carter's papers, which he says were Harpsfield's', lay a 'form of covert answering' to questions about whether Catholics had to be loyal 'in the meantime till another do in fact possess her place'.[26] But the use of the rack on Carter was not reported until November 1582, and he was not put on trial until 1584.[27]

Some Catholics were undoubtedly drawing back at this point and, indeed, there are reports of widespread conformity among those who had temporarily gone into separation in 1580-1. But for others, that is, for those who thought that compromise was as sinful as the tyranny that seemed to license it, there was now no going back. As one letter (perhaps by Persons) had put it, just before Campion's execution, 'there be men in the world which drink blood as easily as beasts do water', but 'because the earth does not open and presently swallow them down they think all is well'. But all that might change: 'juxta est dies perdicionis et adesse festinant tempora'.[28] Allen's take on the trials of 1581 and 1582 laid into what he took to be the Machiavellian and politique (in the worst sense of the

---

[26] BL, Additional MS 48029, fos 58ᵛ-9ᵛ (*AWCBC*, pp. 31-2, 34); EUL copy (classmark Rowse/Pol) of Girolamo Pollini, *Historia Ecclesiastica della Rivoluzion d'Inghilterra...* (Rome, 1594), p. 575; Birrell, 'William Carter', pp. 24-5, 39 (the papers recording the Tower disputations passed from Topcliffe to John Foxe and are now in BL, Harleian MS 422; Holleran, *A Jesuit Challenge*, pp. 225-7; Kilroy, *EC*, p. 284); for the books in question, see *AWCBC*, pp. 36-7, two of which dealt with Henry VIII's divorce proceedings—the 'Vita Henrici VIII' (see C. Bémont (ed.), *Le Premier Divorce de Henri VIII et le Schisme Angleterre: Fragment d'une Chronique Anonyme en Latin* (Paris, 1917), p. 5) and 'A Treatise of Marriage...' (see N. Pocock (ed.), *A Treatise on the Pretended Divorce between Henry VIII and Catharine of Aragon...* (Camden Society, NS, 21, 1878)). Topcliffe referred to 'the rabble of traitors', Nicholas Harpsfield, Sir Thomas Fitzherbert, Bishop Bonner, and Nicholas Sander, 'who did all compile together the English history which' Topcliffe now had in his possession, 'extant written by Doctor Harpsfield when they...were prisoners in the Fleet and in the Marshalsea' in 'Aᵒ 1 & 2 Eliz.'; see Topcliffe's annotation of the EUL copy (classmark Rowse/Pol) of Pollini, *Historia Ecclesiastica*, author's preface, and see also pp. 12, 666 (for Topcliffe's seizure of the 'written chronicle or history...under Harpsfield's and Carter's own hands'), sig. Dddʳ (for Topcliffe's claim that Carter 'sold written copies' of 'Harpsfield's book' for '20ˡⁱ a copy'). In Greenstreet on 13 April 1582, Topcliffe had seized a manuscript of Nicholas Harpsfield's life of Sir Thomas More (the manuscript belonged to Sir Thomas's grandson, Thomas More of Barnburgh): E. V. Hitchcock and E. W. Chambers (eds), *The Life and Death of Sʳ Thomas Moore, knight, sometimes Lord High Chancellor of England... by Nicholas Harpsfield* (Oxford, 1932), pp. xiii, xxxi, 294-6.

[27] *Miscellanea IV* (CRS 4, 1907), pp. 74, 75; Kilroy, *EC*, p. 361.

[28] Hicks, *Letters*, p. 120 (PRO, SP 12/150/67, dated 26 November 1581) [*CUPRP*, p. 245]. I am grateful to Victor Houliston for advice on this document.

word) purposes and practices of the regime. As Allen phrased it, 'religion to worldly men, especially to many atheists nowadays whom men call…politiques, seems not material any further than as it pertains to the preservation or destruction of the civil State'. But the politique prescription for civil peace, Allen warned, was not necessarily going to work since, 'daily, more and more are zealous favourers in England' of 'Catholic religion'. The Machiavels therefore sought 'to make a division between the two sorts' of Catholics, 'weaker and stronger', 'for the easier overthrow of them both, indeed hating and fearing no less the close dissembler than [the] open professor'.[29] But, if Allen could help it, this was not going to happen. What Allen really wanted was a version of what actually occurred, later, in France; that is to say, a Catholic league, a drawing together of all those who might want to see a Catholic union (of hearts, minds, and weaponry) based on an understanding of how the State and true religion intersected and could be preserved from the meddling self-interest of heretics and politiques: 'if we should hold our peace, heaven and earth would condemn us and we should be partakers of the vengeance that the cry of this innocent and sacred blood calls for at God's hand against their persecutors'.[30]

Here the recent visible evidence of the trials and executions/martyrdoms of good Catholics was crucial. It was proof that the queen's government had warped and corroded what political obedience and loyalty actually meant. It was an 'ungodly practice' to put men to death 'in the people's sight for causes whereof they were never directly indicted and arraigned and which' are 'by law no treason at all'. This suggested that, 'of the former offences whereof they were accused and condemned, they were not at all guilty'. Moreover, the regime had used its brutal interrogators and thoroughly nasty bully boys 'to draw out of them by six articles or interrogatories not what treasons or trespasses they had committed (which was none) but what they had in their cogitations, what were to be done, what they would do if such a thing or such a thing should fall'; and, 'if they had been in Ireland when the rebellion was there, what would they have done'.[31]

In other words, said Allen, the regime had redefined treason and pushed the boundaries of political obedience into novel and dangerous areas. The new thought police were playing vicious mind games which were completely out of kilter with anything resembling justice: 'now confessing the prince to be our liege and sovereign, doing all duties of subjection to her that the laws of God, nature or the realm and all nations require, only not making her our God, yet we must be further demanded by authority, oath or torment what we will do in such and such cases to come, or perchance never to come'.[32]

By contrast, puritanism was demonstrably disloyal. If 'the law might proceed upon such supposals and intentions of things to come, what hearts should you

---

[29] Allen, *BH*, sig. aiii[v]–iiii[r].   [30] Allen, *BH*, sig. av[r].   [31] Allen, *BH*, sigs bviii[v]–c[r].
[32] Allen, *BH*, sig. ciii[r].

126 CATHOLICS AND TREASON

find in the puritans, think you, upon this only supposition, if the queen should but go back to be a papist; if they were upon their oath demanded what they would do, or wish in their hearts to be done'? Referring to John Stubbs, Allen pointed out the limits of godly Protestant loyalty: 'they that could not but utter in most traitorous words and books their cankered stomachs only for a little conference that her Majesty had of marriage with a Catholic prince, what affection would they bear to her if she reduced herself and [her] realm to the Catholic faith which they so much hate?' But it was these puritans who were deputed 'to sound our hearts in this kind'. They were precisely the ones who, 'by oaths, interrogatories and other undue means, purposely drive simple plain-meaning men that never offended their laws in word, deed nor thought into the compass of their treasons'.[33]

Could anyone be in any doubt who the queen's real political opponents and critics were? Thomas Norton was now 'justly put into the Tower for seditious words and plain treason'. Allen sarcastically suggested that the rack should be used to get Norton to explain some of the private comments he had recently been making about the way he had been treated. Norton's wife, said Allen, 'can tell also where her husband did lay up Stubbs's book', the *Discoverie of a Gaping Gulf,* 'against her Majesty for a secret treasure, which gear well sifted would betray worse affection and intention too than they shall ever find in Catholics while they live'. 'This Stubbs, being the queen's deadly enemy and then' locked up 'in the Tower for his traitorous book, was of M. Lieutenants [Sir Owen Hopton's] counsel in all things'. William Charke, who had written against Campion and was 'once put to silence for puritanism, or a worse matter, if worse can be, sent his book against F. Campion to be perused' by Hopton.[34] Those who had infuriated the queen, said Allen, had saved their political hides by erecting a myth, as Allen saw it, of a Catholic conspiracy.

Dr Allen was precisely not one of those who thought that Norton's discomfiture was the basis for a return to the sort of compromise arrangement that had characterized the regime's dealings with Catholics during much of the 1570s. Many who read Allen's defence of Campion and his friends would merely have snorted with derision; but he was onto something here. Even those who did not usually think in terms of conspiracy theory might buy into the claim that there had been a coup inside the regime itself. In the context of all the modern historical interest in the republicanism of the so-called monarchical republic of Elizabeth Tudor, they might not necessarily have been all that far off the mark. Through much of the early and mid-1580s, some people were contemplating schemes for an interregnum in the event of Elizabeth's death and in the face of the

---

[33] Allen, *BH*, sig. ciiii[r–v]. Allen referred here particularly to the cases of John Nelson in 1578 and Everard Hanse in mid-1581: Allen, *BH*, sig. ciiii[v].

[34] Allen, *BH*, sig. cv[v]–vi[r].

AFTER CAMPION   127

still looming threat from Mary Stuart—schemes which were absolutely intolerable to Elizabeth herself.[35]

In this way, Allen deftly extended the range of the existing Catholic evil-counsellor rhetoric which had been set out in, for example, the *Treatise of Treasons* of the early 1570s. He believed that he could detect the coils of a puritan conspiracy one tier lower down, as it were, that is, among the rogue agents and the malicious hangers-on of the queen's counsellors, on whom judgment was still technically out. Allen pointed to these malevolent busybodies who were, as he saw it, perverting the normal courses of the law: 'we suffer not so much at her Majesty's hands or her gravest counsellors as by these sinful, irreligious persons, their ill informers'. There is a closish match between, on the one hand, Allen's description of those people and, on the other, the men of business who are at the centre of Michael Graves's account of the mid-Elizabethan period. Allen reminded his readers that Thomas Norton had been personally responsible for the arrest, during a midnight raid, of Alexander Briant in April 1581.[36]

Allen's words must have packed extra punch, because it would have been obvious that he had inside information. What he printed about the conduct of Catholic internees in the Tower of London and what the officials there said about them presumably came from the lieutenant Sir Owen Hopton's daughter Cicely, who was a known Catholic sympathizer. This applied particularly to the comments about the difference in demeanour between Campion and Norton: 'this blessed F. Campion amongst the rest passed his time with such godly spiritual exercises, with such patience and sweet speeches to his keeper and others that had to deal with him who afterward, having the custody of Norton, comparing their conditions together, said plainly he had, before, a saint in his keeping and now a devil'.[37] From the same source, perhaps, came the story that Sherwin would 'never be forgotten in the Tower, for some words which he spoke when he was ready to go to execution'. William Charke could 'best report them, who stood hard by him. Some of Charke's fellow ministers said those words could not come from a guilty conscience'. The same may be true of the tale that, during the torture of Alexander Briant, Dr John Hammond, who, with Norton, 'caused needles to be thrust under'

---

[35] For the most recent (and best) study of this topic, see Lake, *BQB*.

[36] Allen, *BH*, sigs cvi[v], fiii[v]; see p. 105 above. For the closeness of Norton and Fleetwood to their conciliar patrons, primarily Burghley and Sir Nicholas Bacon, see Graves, *TN*, pp. 27, 48, 82. For Norton's working relationship with Fleetwood and the lawyer John Hammond, see Graves, *TN*, pp. 52, 74. Hammond, a civil lawyer and nephew of Alexander Nowell, became chancellor of the diocese of London in 1575: *ODNB*, *sub* Hammond, John (article by P. White). Norton worked with Hammond on a variety of tasks (e.g., in addition to torturing Catholic detainees, the government of Guernsey: Graves, *TN*, pp. 81, 142–4) and, though Graves does not dwell on it, with Richard Topcliffe as well.

[37] Allen, *BH*, sig. c[v]–cii[r]; for Cicely Hopton, see *HC 1558–1603*, II, p. 336. Subsequently it transpired that she was the means by which Catholic prisoners (principally Throckmorton Plot suspects) received and passed information: Ward, LT, p. 148.

128 CATHOLICS AND TREASON

Briant's 'nails', 'stamped and stared, as a man half beside himself' when Briant would not say where Campion was.[38]

Within the Catholic martyrological wrapper which has traditionally encased these narratives there is a crucial historical and historiographical issue. The current orthodoxy, implicit in so much of the work on the Elizabethan 'monarchical republic', is that people such as Thomas Norton were not oppositional puritan lunatics but, rather, were essential to the stability of the Elizabethan polity.[39] In Graves's work, Norton's activism, his pamphleteering, his part in the erection of a rudimentary police state, and his use of torture, when the council would let him, are the day-to-day activities of a good civil servant who might just as easily be dealing with the legal and civic concerns of the city of London, which indeed was what he also did. Graves's line about Norton is compatible with Patrick Collinson's own normalization, as it were, of the puritan impulse in mid-Elizabethan politics. Collinson's response, faced with the contemporary Catholic portrayal of puritanism as a lethal entropic threat to the integrity of the commonwealth, was simply that 'extremist Catholics' produced a 'strange chronicle' of Elizabeth's reign. For Collinson, characters such as Persons were, thankfully, not the 'mainstream', so one did not have to worry about them too much.[40] However, in the early 1580s, with Norton locked up in the Tower and Grindal still in disgrace, there must, for some contemporaries, have been a question as to what the mainstream now was. One has to say that, on Graves's own account, Norton comes across as obsequious, sycophantic, and self-pitying beyond belief—a Damian McBride for his times, but without the wit, frankness, and charm.[41] 'Norton', says Graves, 'was dedicated to his own trinity of God, queen and council' and, 'if his boldness in speech occasionally embarrassed the council' and 'if he was too single-purposed for Elizabeth's liking', 'his devotion, energy and talents were never questioned'.[42] Probably not by those within his own immediate circle, but they definitely were by others.

Indeed, in these Catholic martyr texts of the early 1580s we have a series of claims that the regime was now in crisis, hijacked by puritan insiders. Those insiders' aims were far from obviously endorsed by the regime's own chief

[38] Allen, *BH*, sig. fii^v, fv^r; Graves, *TN*, pp. 250–1; *APC 1581–2*, pp. 37–8.

[39] Graves, *TN*, p. viii.

[40] P. Collinson, *This England: Essays on the English Nation and Commonwealth in the Sixteenth Century* (2011), pp. 150–1.

[41] As a modern-day man of business, McBride fabricated lurid rumours about opposition MPs for release via the internet, presumably in the belief that his employer, the then prime minister, would endorse this mode of political activism. The relevant emails were then released by a blogger, the early twenty-first-century equivalent of Thomas Alfield, forcing the prime minister to cut McBride adrift (though he did not end up in the Bloody Tower but, rather, at a Catholic school in Hampstead and then in employment with the charity CAFOD). At Peterhouse, McBride 'wrote a final-year dissertation in praise of inciting violence and rumour-mongering in politics': http://en.wikipedia.org/wiki/Damian_McBride.

[42] Graves, *TN*, p. 76.

executive—Elizabeth Tudor. The carefully positioned Catholic critique of the lines of policy with which the queen was known to be out of sympathy provoked that puritan insider clique into public acts of revenge—after ramming through new legislative definitions of Catholicism/popery which were, misleadingly, phrased by reference to the queen's safety.

This in turn produced the manoeuvre described so well in John Bossy's sparkling essay on the 'heart' of Robert Persons, namely the move by some Catholics into a much sharper enmity towards the queen herself and a tendency, eventually, to identify the crimes committed by her ministers with her directly.[43] This is something which at least some of the prosecutions of Catholics for treason during the rest of the 1580s and during the early 1590s reveal with startling clarity.

This, however, was the calm before the storm, that is, before the queen's military intervention in the Netherlands. And, while the executions in the South temporarily stopped, three Catholic clergymen were executed in York between August and November 1582. Crucially, at least two of them were prosecuted under the new treason legislation. The priest William Lacey was arrested on 22 July 1582 in York Castle gaol, where he had said Mass for the Catholic prisoners there.[44] In August 1582, two more clerics, Richard Kirkman and James Thompson, were apprehended by a local justice of the peace. Lacey, Kirkman, and Thompson were then arraigned at the York assizes on 11 August.[45] Henry Cheke reported to Henry Hastings, earl of Huntingdon, that at the assizes there was a 'great assembly, especially of papists, so as the court was in great disorder by reason of the press of people'. The judges were 'forced to make room themselves like ushers'. But those judges were evidently determined not to flinch in the use of the new law. The attorney-general, Sir John Popham, had, it appears, been sent to conduct the prosecution.[46] The privy council was content to issue execution warrants, and Lacey and Kirkman were hanged at York on 22 August 1582. Thompson was killed shortly after, on 28 November.[47]

---

[43] J. Bossy, 'The Heart of Robert Persons', in T. M. McCoog (ed.), *The Reckoned Expense: Edmund Campion and the Early English Jesuits* (Woodbridge, 1996), pp. 141–58.

[44] The subsequently infamous Thomas Bell was also present on that occasion but, with two other Catholic clergymen, evaded arrest. The first was the soon-to-be-notorious Anthony Tyrrell. The second, William Hart, remained free only until December; see Ward, LT, pp. 252–4; *Concertatio*, sig. Bb2[r–v]; Lake and Questier, *Trials*, p. 32.

[45] Ward, LT, pp. 254–5; Allen, *TSMD*, p. 4; cf. Anstr., I, p. 199 citing LPL, MS 3198 (formerly Talbot MS G), fo. 216[r] (G. R. Batho (ed.), *A Calendar of the Shrewsbury and Talbot Papers in Lambeth Palace Library and the College of Arms*, vol. II (HMC, 1971), p. 126): Martin Birkhead claimed to the earl of Shrewsbury, 11 August 1582, that Lacey had been indicted not under the 1581 act but under the statute of 1571 (13 Eliz., c. 2) 'for obtaining of a bull and popish orders' from Pope Gregory XIII and that he had with him 'many other indulgences, writings, instruments, relics, beads, broaches, laces and trifles brought from Rome'. Kirkman was indicted under the 1581 act for reconciling; he had been arrested with a 'Mass book, chalice, wafer-cakes, wine and all things ready to say Mass': LPL, MS 3198 (formerly Talbot MS G), fo. 216[v]; Allen, *TSMD*, p. 4. For Thompson, see *Concertatio*, sig. Cc[v]–3[r]; Anstr., I, pp. 350–1.

[46] Ward, LT, p. 254.   [47] Ward, LT, pp. 254–5; Anstr., I, p. 351; Challoner, *MMP*, p. 72.

130   CATHOLICS AND TREASON

It is possible that what was going on in the North was a didactic demonstration that the activities of recently arrived seminarists were not compatible with the prevailing culture of largely conformist Catholicism in the region. Hence the use in York of indictments under the 1581 statute even while, at this time, in the South, William Dean and William Carter, as we saw, were respited. The priest and former minister John Chapman, arrested on 7 August 1582, who had held benefices in the national Church down in Dorset, was also spared, although he remained stubbornly silent when asked whether Elizabeth was 'supreme head and governess'. There was ample evidence that he was part of a quite widespread network in the South-West for distributing Catholic propaganda; but he was left alive and, after going into exile, he did not come back.[48]

In the North, William Hart had been arrested on 25 December 1582, and on 11 January 1583 he was charged under the 1581 statute, at the quarter sessions in York, with having reconciled two people to Rome.[49] Hart had allegedly acquired the title of 'apostle of Yorkshire' on account of his ministry and preaching and, in prison, 'by his assiduity' in 'disputing, encouraging and confirming many'.[50] He was convicted at the assizes and was executed on 15 March 1583. Hart was one of the circle of clergy around Margaret Clitherow. He may have offered minimal concessions over the issue of churchgoing. It seems that leading moderate puritan divines, including Matthew Hutton and Edmund Bunny, had forced him into debate about this question and 'were pleased to publish that they did not doubt but that he would easily be brought over to their side'. But in the end he could not be persuaded to comply.[51] Bunny read out the papal bull of excommunication at the Knavesmire gallows in York seconds before Hart was pushed off the ladder.[52] Hart's letters from prison got into John Gibbons's and John Fenn's *Concertatio Ecclesiae Catholicae*.[53] Seven days later, James Leyburn was hanged at Lancaster for denying Elizabeth's supremacy. He had no time for the queen. In his opinion, she was 'a usurper, and unlawful, a lascivious and very wicked person'. Some Catholics, for example the future archpriest George Birkhead, were unsure that Leyburn was a martyr in the true sense of the word.[54] Another priest in Yorkshire,

---

[48] Anstr., I, pp. 72–3; Pollen, *UD*, pp. 31–4 (PRO, SP 12/155/8, 8. i). Chapman had gone abroad to Rheims with John Adams, the former vicar of Winterborne St Martin: Pollen, *UD*, p. 32.

[49] Ward, LT, p. 255; Challoner, *MMP*, p. 74.   [50] ABSJ, A V, no. 8 (unfoliated).

[51] Challoner, *MMP*, p. 74; Ward, LT, p. 255. When Lancelot Boste was arrested on 6 February 1584, there was 'found with' him 'an exhortation to papistry written by' William Hart: Pollen, *UD*, p. 63 (PRO, SP 15/28/58. i, iv).

[52] Challoner, *MMP*, pp. 75–6.

[53] Challoner, *MMP*, pp. 76–9 (ABP, pp. 321–4); *Concertatio*, sigs Ee2ᵛ–Ff4ʳ. John Thorpe recorded that Hart's godfather, the Jesuit William Good, 'kept many of his spiritual letters that he wrote in prison': ABSJ, A V, no. 8 (unfoliated).

[54] AAW, A III, no. 61, pp. 243–4; Pollen, *UD*, p. 66 (PRO, SP 15/28/59. i); Pollen, *AEM*, pp. 212, 217–21; AAW, A III, no. 70, p. 273 (printed in Knox, *DD*, pp. 352–3); cf. *Concertatio*, sig. Cc3ᵛ; Nicholas Sander, ed. and trans. D. Lewis, *Rise and Growth of the Anglican Schism*...(1877), p. 317. See also A. Wright, 'The Layburnes and their World circa 1620–1720, the English Catholic Community and the House of Stuart' (PhD, St Andrews, 2002), pp. 12–13, 60–1.

AFTER CAMPION 131

Richard Thirkeld, was arrested a week after Hart's execution and was charged at York under the 1581 statute. He was hanged on 29 May 1583.[55]

There was, in fact, a fatal prosecution in the South at this point—in Hampshire, where John Slade and John Bodey were executed after conviction on the basis of an arraignment under the 1563 treason statute.[56] As Leslie Ward explains, they had been 'indicted for extolling the papal supremacy' and were convicted at Southampton in autumn 1581 at the summer assizes, that is, at the same time as the regime was trying to bring the Campion agitation under control. At this point they were sentenced to a term of two years of imprisonment, though it is not clear that they were incarcerated for all of that time.[57] As George Birkhead reported on 24 April 1583, they were put on trial again. They were then proceeded against, once more, on 19 August at the assizes. This was five days, as it happened, after John Whitgift's nomination to Canterbury. Slade was hanged on 30 October at Winchester and Bodey at Andover on 2 November.[58] When they were 'indicted under the "second branch"' of the 1563 statute, the judges disagreed as to whether they had committed the actual offence set down in the statute.[59] In the end, Sir Roger Manwood's reading of the procedural provisions of the 1563 act took precedence over the views of those who had not wanted to convict.[60]

It is just possible that Bodey's and Slade's final trial was staged as a response to the events in Scotland in late June 1583 when the young king, James VI, freed himself from the clutches of the Anglophile Protestant party at court which had been responsible for the Ruthven Raid in the previous year.[61] But, if this was the case, no one explicitly mentioned it. What we may have here, instead, is a

---

[55] Ward, LT, pp. 255–6; J. C. H. Aveling, *Catholic Recusancy in York 1558–1791* (1970), p. 71.

[56] Ward, LT, p. 258. These were, as Dr Ward points out, 'the first and only trials for high treason' under that act: Ward, LT, p. 258. William Hart was aware of the proceedings in progress against John Bodey down in Hampshire: Challoner, *MMP*, p. 78.

[57] Ward, LT, p. 258. A search of the prison at Winchester on 11 January 1583, conducted by *inter alia* Sir Richard Norton and Thomas Fleming, turned up a number of Catholic printed texts: Pollen, *AEM*, pp. 50–1; PRO, SP 12/158/9, fo. 16^r. Fleming, who sat as MP for Winchester in 1584, had been recorder there since 1582, and was a client of Secretary Walsingham: *HC 1558–1603*, II, p. 139.

[58] Allen, *TSMD*, p. 5 (Bodey and Slade 'were condemned to death...at two divers sessions, and that...twice (a rare case in our country), the latter sentence being to reform the former (as we may guess in such strange proceedings) which they perceived to be erroneous and insufficient in their own laws'); Ward, LT, p. 260; see also Pollen, *AEM*, pp. 50–3; Knox, *DD*, p. 353. For the legal complexity of the prosecutions of Slade and Bodey, see L. J. Ward, 'The Treason Act of 1563: A study of the Enforcement of Anti-Catholic Legislation', *Parliamentary History* 8 (1989), pp. 289–308, at pp. 303–4.

[59] Ward, LT, pp. 258–60, citing *Les Reports de Sir John Savile...* (1675), pp. 46–7.

[60] For Sir Roger Manwood (knighted in 1578), see Ward, LT, pp. 98–100. One of the judges to whom the case was referred in Easter term 1583, William Ayloff, believed that the prosecution was flawed. At the Hereford winter assizes in 1584, Ayloff was the presiding judge when Edward Jones was tried but acquitted on a charge of speaking in favour of papal supremacy: Ward, LT, p. 261.

[61] Questier, *DP*, p. 146. In early June 1583, three puritan separatists—Thomas Gibson, Elias Thacker, and John Copping—had been put on trial, and the latter two were hanged, respectively on 4 and 6 June, for denying Elizabeth's supremacy over the Church; a number of separatist texts (by Robert Browne) were publicly burnt. Catholics such as Persons made much of this, pointing also to works such as Browne's *Treatise of Reformation without Tarrying for Anie...* (1582) as an encouragement to rebellion: Hicks, *Letters*, pp. 176, 180–1 [*CUPRP*, pp. 366–7]; Collinson, *EPM*, pp. 204, 212.

132 CATHOLICS AND TREASON

provincial demonstration, facilitated by a hardliner in the judiciary, of puritan opinion at a time when, as we have mentioned, there was a serious push from some within the regime to do a deal with Mary Stuart, the so-called association scheme which would have seen her repatriated to Scotland. How much chance of success this project ever had is not clear; but, following the counter-coup by James against the Ruthvenites in the middle of the year, Mary had started to raise the stakes in her negotiations with Elizabeth. To some English Protestants it must have looked as if the supposed Anglo-Scottish Protestant ideological consensus and associated political amity between the two realms were coming apart at the seams.[62]

The proceedings against Bodey and Slade certainly had starkly puritan overtones. Laurence Humphrey (one of those deputed previously to deal with Campion's *Decem Rationes*) was wheeled out to destroy the pair's reputations by disputation. Humphrey, who had been dean of Winchester since 1580, barracked them, at their trial, on the topic of royal/temporal power over the Church.[63] The godly Sir William Kingsmill was present at the executions of both men. 'Mr Kingsmill', as Challoner calls him, harangued Bodey under the gallows about the royal supremacy.[64] Kingsmill had also lectured Slade on the supremacy.[65] The future bishop of Hereford, Robert Bennett, who at this stage was a chaplain to Lord Burghley and master of the St Cross Hospital in Winchester, was at Slade's execution and told him not to 'abuse the people'.[66] On 3 November, the day after Bodey had been killed, Bennett wrote to Burghley warning him of the 'backwardness of this county in religion'. The justices had required Bennett to debate with the condemned men 'for the better satisfying of the people' as to the 'causes of their death', and he found them to be completely obstinate over the issue of papal authority. Bennett noted 'in the people a favour and liking of them'. 'Great numbers' were 'carried away with them into stubborn recusancy'. The 'wisest' sort had concluded that the 'long delay of their execution' had 'wrought the country's great

---

[62] Read, *MSW*, II, pp. 391–3, 396–7; Lake, *BQB*, p. 97; Questier, *DP*, ch. 3 *passim*.

[63] Pollen, *UD*, pp. 39–44 (PRO, SP 12/162/8). Laurence Humphrey, president of Magdalen, was changing his position on ceremonial conformity at this point, a shift which was probably made easier by these public victories over Catholic dissidents. See *ODNB, sub* Humphrey, Laurence (article by T. S. Freeman).

[64] Challoner, *MMP*, p. 84. The Kingsmills were a leading puritan family in Hampshire with connections beyond it, e.g. with Bishop Pilkington of Durham; four of Sir William's brothers were MPs. Henry Kingsmill had been a Marian exile. Richard Kingsmill MP of Highclere had been prominent in the 1566 succession debates and, says Alan Harding, his 'election for Hampshire to the parliaments of 1584 and 1586 was...a victory for the puritan faction' there: *HC 1558–1603*, II, p. 400. John Kingsmill had been chancellor to Bishop Horne of Winchester who, said William Warford, was responsible for ejecting both Slade and Bodey from New College, Oxford: *HC 1558–1603*, II, p. 399; ABSJ, Collectanea M, p. 132ª.

[65] AAW, A III, no. 89, pp. 341–2 ('The Severall Executions and Confessions...') (Pollen, *AEM*, pp. 56–65). One copy was sent to Richard Barret; see Renold, *LWA*, pp. 98, 99. For the published version, see *The Severall Executions & Confessions, of Iohn Slade & Iohn Bodye: Traitours...*(1583).

[66] Pollen, *AEM*, pp. 60–1, 62.

AFTER CAMPION   133

harm'. This was evident from 'the multitudes of their late revolts and the general contempt of the preaching of the Word', particularly in Winchester. The underlying problem was the non-residence of those who 'possessed...the livings of the country' and the consequent lack of preaching. The likely outcome was the 'advantage of wicked attempts'. Bennett's warning was contextualized by the exposure of the Throckmorton Plot.[67] Shortly after, there were raids on the houses of known Catholics in Winchester.[68]

The fate of Bodey and Slade did excite popular comment. One John Hardy was hauled up for claiming, at a dinner table in Farnham, that Bodey had won the argument against his antagonists. A local godly Protestant preacher, Peter German, took Hardy to task over his view that Bodey and Slade had been in the right.[69] The published account entitled *The Several Executions and Confessions*, which purported to have been written by a Protestant but may well have been penned by a Catholic masquerading as a Protestant, was said by William Allen to have been suppressed because it was too candid.[70] One of the judges, William Peryam, who ironically had a reputation as a puritan, had serious doubts as to the guilt of the accused.[71]

Leslie Ward suggests that the policy of the authorities in the South remained (merely) the imprisonment of seminarist clergy. At least twenty priests, by early 1584, were incarcerated in London gaols. Even William Hartley, the distributor of Campion's *Rationes Decem*, gaoled in 1581, was not prosecuted until 1584, although he was detected on 24 August 1582 saying Mass in the Marshalsea.[72] Elsewhere, puritans may well have felt that they were facing an uphill struggle against Catholic sedition. In mid-January 1584, the Warwick JP Job Throckmorton recited how he had arrested one William Skinner. Skinner was alleged to have

---

[67] BL, Lansdowne MS 39, no. 46, fo. 183^r.

[68] For the search of Lady West's house on 6 December 1583, see PRO, SP 12/164/14, fo. 24^{r-v}. In February 1584, an informer, Thomas Dodwell, alerted the authorities that she was harbouring priests (including Robert Nutter, Thomas Pilchard, Roger Dickenson, and Robert Holmes): PRO, SP 12/168/34, fo. 81^v. For Dodwell, see *AWCBC*, p. 225.

[69] The matter was reported on 10 January 1584, with affidavits from those involved, by the leading Surrey Protestants William More, George More, and Laurence Stoughton to Sir Francis Walsingham: Pollen, *AEM*, pp. 52–3; Pollen, *UD*, pp. 48–50 (PRO, SP 12/167/15, 15. i, ii). It appears that the vicar of Farnham at that point, Daniel Craft, was subsequently the target of puritan attacks, and specifically of claims that Peter German should have taken the vicarage instead, and that he had said that some of the local inhabitants 'did follow the preacher as dogs do a...bitch': BL, Additional MS 48064, fo. 74^{r-v}; CCED, ID 106462, ID 69585.

[70] Allen, *TSMD*, pp. 5, 6; *The Severall Executions & Confessions*.

[71] Ward, LT, pp. 258–9; *HC 1558–1603*, III, pp. 208–9.

[72] Ward, LT, p. 261; *Miscellanea II*, p. 221; Anstr., I, p. 156. Ward argues that this policy indicated a 'considerable lack of initiative on the part of the government': Ward, LT, p. 262. Bishop Aylmer wrote to Burghley on 5 December 1583 in order to denounce the laxity of the Marshalsea. He mentioned Hartley by name. The 'wretched priests, which by her Majesty's lenity live there as it were in a college of caitiffs, do commonly say Mass within the prison and entice the youth of London unto them, to my great grief, and as far as I can learn do daily reconcile them', i.e. incurring the penalties of the 1581 statute: Pollen, *UD*, p. 47 (BL, Lansdowne MS 38, no. 87, fo. 212^r). Among the other clergy detected for saying Mass in the Marshalsea was Richard Norris: Anstr., I, p. 255; *Miscellanea II*, p. 221.

134   CATHOLICS AND TREASON

said some uncompromising things about Elizabeth and 'the evil of Queen Anne her mother' and 'the unlawfulness of the marriage betwixt King Henry and her', and to have spoken also in favour of the title of Mary Stuart. But, complained Throckmorton, 'men that promised mountains beforehand have, when it came to the pinch, performed but molehills'—all as a result of local Catholics' 'secret labouring underhand and threatening' of the relevant witnesses. When Skinner was put on trial at the Warwick assizes, he was acquitted.[73]

On the other hand, faced with the turn of events in Scotland, particularly after the royal counter-coup against the Ruthvenite faction there, the queen's councillors in England had carried the war to the enemy by, instead, unearthing the, as it turned out, real enough conspiracy in autumn 1583 which we know as the Throckmorton Plot.[74] This inevitably had consequences for those who would not make their peace with the Elizabethan court. The rehabilitated Thomas Norton, who in 1584 published his *Discoverie of Treasons* about the conspirator Francis Throckmorton, had also composed in late 1583 a kind of work-in-progress memorandum for the privy council, his 'Chain of Treasons'. It argued that there were similarities between the duke of Norfolk's and Throckmorton's treacheries, and it has a prominent section on the texts which were discovered in the printer William Carter's premises when they were raided.[75] Norton said that there was, 'found among Carters papers', 'a form of covert answering' to questions which might be put to a Catholic about his allegiance.[76]

All of this, stated Norton, was a new phase of the 1569 treason and rebellion in the North. There was, he claimed, a constituency in England which still wanted to see an Englishman on the throne in place of Elizabeth. That man would marry Mary Stuart who would take up her Scottish crown again. The finger of suspicion pointed at Lord Henry Howard ('he must be a bachelor or a man unmarried', as Howard was). Norton said that those who were appointed to interrogate the priest John Hart 'did most earnestly press and urge him to tell who was the noble person that should be elected'. Hart would not answer but, when he was asked to whom 'the favours and wishes of the seminarians did most incline, or whom they would

---

[73] Ward, LT, pp. 185–6; PRO, SP 12/167/21 (fos 54^r–5^r), 21. iii (fo. 58^r); *CSPD 1581–90*, p. 152; for this case in its local context, see P. Marshall, 'Choosing Sides and Talking Religion in Shakespeare's England', in D. Loewenstein and M. Witmore (eds), *Shakespeare and Early Modern Religion* (Cambridge, 2015), pp. 40–56. Among other such cases at this time, on 20 February 1584 at Rochester, Samuel Alkyngton of Canterbury was tried (though he was acquitted) for speaking in favour of papal authority: Ward, LT, p. 220.

[74] See J. Bossy, *Giordano Bruno and the Embassy Affair* (1991); J. Bossy, *Under the Molehill: An Elizabethan Spy Story* (2001).

[75] BL, Additional MS 48029, fos 60^r, 61^v; *ODNB*, *sub* Norton, Thomas (article by M. Axton). As Graves describes it, the 'Chain of Treasons' was 'yet one more white paper designed for councillors' eyes only and certainly not intended for publication' and went further than the regime's own standalone publication on the Throckmorton business, i.e. *A Discoverie of Treasons*...(1584), though much of that pamphlet came from Norton's 'Chain': Graves, TN, pp. 269–70.

[76] BL, Additional MS 48029, fo. 59$^{r–v}$.

AFTER CAMPION 135

be most glad to have so advanced or whom they best liked', Hart 'gave commendation to the Lord Henry Howard, brother to the late duke'. Norton remembered that Gregory Martin, whose patron and employer had once been the late duke and who was the author of the *Treatise of Schisme*, had said at Rheims that Lord Henry would do well to get out of the country and come to Rheims. Norton also said that a text by the bishop of Ross in favour of Mary, 'this book of his purgation', was 'sent from himself [Martin] to the same Lord Henry'.[77]

On 10 January 1584 William Carter was put on trial. Norton himself delivered the main prosecution speech. Topcliffe's annotations on one of the surviving copies of the *Treatise of Schisme* have been construed as evidence of Topcliffe's involvement in preparing the prosecution case against Carter. Bishop Aylmer added his opinion—that Carter had been dealt with leniently up until that point, and pointed to his employment by Cawood and Harpsfield. The unfortunate printer was convicted of publishing Martin's *Treatise of Schisme*, which urged recusancy and cited as a role model the scriptural figure of Judith, who cut off the head of the tyrant Holofernes. Carter denied that the figure of Holofernes in Martin's text referred to the queen; but Carter was hanged, drawn, and quartered the very next day at Tyburn.[78]

At this time, Elizabeth's new ambassador in Paris, Sir Edward Stafford, was trying to secure the suppression of Richard Verstegan's depictions of Elizabeth's cruelty. Verstegan had arrived back in Paris from Rome in autumn 1583 and was putting together his martyrological texts, which appeared under the title *Descriptiones* and *Briefue Description*. Stafford had an agent who kept him informed of the printers' progress. On 8 January 1584, Stafford reported that he had secured the arrest of the printers and had made an official protest at the French court. Stafford understood that these Catholics intended to give presentation copies to the French king, Henry III, 'as if he would take pleasure in seeing things so prejudicial to the reputation of his good sister and neighbour'. This,

[77] BL, Additional MS 48029, fos 60^{r-v}, 61^v.

[78] Challoner, *MMP*, p. 100; *ODNB*, *sub* Carter, William (article by I. Gadd); Birrell, 'William Carter', pp. 28–31; Graves, *TN*, p. 248; Allen, *TSMD*, p. 10; *Concertatio*, sigs Ii3^r–Ll^r. Carter had printed 1250 copies of Martin's *Treatise of Schisme*. He had the manuscript text with Allen's approbation on it: BL, Additional MS 48029, fo. 59^v; EUL copy (classmark Rowse/Pol) of Girolamo Pollini, *Historia Ecclesiastica della Rivoluzion d'Inghilterra*...(Rome, 1594), pp. 575, 667. For the copy of Martin's *Treatise* annotated by Topcliffe, now in the Bodleian Library (press mark: 8. C. 95 Th.), see *AWCBC*, pp. 11, 12, 14–15; ARCR, II, no. 524; Kilroy, *EC*, p. 361; Eyston MSS, Hendred House, East Hendred (Thomas Hearne to Charles Eyston, 15 February 1719). William Herle noted on 22 July 1584 that the assassin of William of Orange, Balthazar Gérard, 'avowed his deed to be lawful, first for that the king of Spain had invited all men to kill a rebel...and secondly by the example of Judith, a holy and chaste person, who yet feigned herself to be a harlot, that she might kill the irreligious tyrant Holofernes'. Herle declared that among the Jesuits it was a 'maxim' that 'they be all Judiths that kill princes...as may appear by the book Carter printed...and worthily suffered for it...at Tyburn'. It was in this context that one should read the founding 'of their seminaries...one even at Dieppe...upon the brim of England by your [Elizabeth's] adversary, the Guise': *CSPF July 1583–July 1584*, pp. 627–8; P. Guilday, *The English Catholic Refugees on the Continent 1558–1795* (1914), p. 129.

136 CATHOLICS AND TREASON

however, provoked a furious reaction from the exiles, as Stafford noted on 18 January. Dr Allen had come to Paris from Rouen and, at the exiles' instigation, the papal nuncio, Girolamo Ragazzoni, went to court to lodge his own protest. Henry, who was in the middle of one of his bouts of public Catholic zeal, made a diplomatic answer but admitted that he was unwilling for his princely 'neighbours' actions to be set out at every man's pleasure'. Stafford followed up with another audience, asking for exemplary punishment. But Henry subsequently sent a message telling Stafford not to get things out of perspective: 'it was but an execution set out in print, a common thing both in France and all places'. Stafford begged to differ and told the messenger, Bernabé Brisson, to 'look at the titles' of the 'two papers' in question, 'the one being the title of cruelty showed in her realm, a thing abhorred in all princes, the other disdaining to name her queen of England'. The publication was not in fact suppressed. Verstegan was detained in January 1584 but then was swiftly released at the insistence of the nuncio.[79]

---

[79] *CSPF July 1583–July 1584*, pp. 231, 299–300, 305–6, 315–17, 319, 321–3, 332, 342, 416–17; Kilroy, *EC*, p. 365; Richard Verstegan, *Descriptiones quaedam illius Inhumanae et Multiplicis Persecutionis, quam in Anglia propter Fidem Sustinent Catholicè Christiani* (n.p. [Paris], n.d. [1583–4]); see also the Rome edition of 1584 (ARCR, I, no. 1284) in which the engravings are the ones by Giovanni Battista de Cavalleriis; and, for the French edition, see *Briefue Description des Diuerses Cruautez que les Catholiques endurent en Angleterre pour la Foy* (np [Paris], n.d. [1583–4]); Dillon, *CM*, p. 231. As Gerard Kilroy observes (Kilroy, *EC*, p. 363), the second illustration in this publication (Rome edition) is probably a visual version of a passage in Robert Persons, *An Epistle of the Persecution of Catholickes in Englande. Translated out of Frenche into Englishe…* (Douai [imprint false; printed at Rouen], n.d. [1582]), pp. 127–8. For Verstegan's printed oeuvre and for the mural depictions of martyrdom (by Nicolò Circignani) in Rome, see Dillon, *CM*, chs 3–5; Kilroy, *EC*, pp. 365–6; C. Highley, 'Richard Verstegan's Book of Martyrs', in C. Highley and J. King (eds), *John Foxe and his World* (Aldershot, 2002), pp. 183–97. Richard Barret remarked in November 1584 to the rector of the English College in Rome, Alfonso Agazzari, that 'in those beautiful pictures', sent from Rome to Rheims at this time, 'I seem to see the greatest religious splendour and glory of your Church and of all England'. Barret rejoiced that 'it was a most opportune and suitable time for the pictures to be sent and brought to Dr Allen' because at 'the same hour' the cardinal of Guise and the dukes of Guise, Mayenne, and Nevers 'vouchsafed to the greatest consolation of all ours' to visit the college at Rheims; and 'nothing…could have been presented' which was 'more acceptable to them': Renold, *LWA*, p. 114; see also Dillon, *CM*, pp. 235, 237; A. Dillon, *Michelangelo and the English Martyrs* (Farnham, 2013), pp. 302–3; Bossy, EC, pp. 58, 60, 62. One of the editions of Robert Persons's *De Persecutione Anglicana, Epistola…* (Rouen, 1581; ARCR, I, no. 874), produced in Rome by Georgio Ferrari in 1582 (ARCR, I, no. 876), had six copperplate engravings of martyrdom (derived from Verstegan's *Praesentis Ecclesiae Anglicanae Typus*; see p. 119 above; ARCR, I, no. 1293). As A. G. Petti says, 'these engravings seem to have been used' by Circignani for the mural paintings on the walls of the church in the English College in Rome in 1583. These murals were then reproduced by Giovanni Battista de Cavalleriis in his *Ecclesiae Anglicanae Trophaea…* (Rome, 1584); ARCR, I, no. 944; Petti, 'Richard Verstegan', p. 65; Kilroy, *EC*, pp. 364–5. See also M. Whitehead, '"Established and Putt in Good Order": The Venerable English College, Rome, under Jesuit Administration, 1579–1685', in J. E. Kelly and H. Thomas (eds), *Jesuit Intellectual and Physical Exchange between England and Mainland Europe, c. 1580–1789* (Leiden, 2018), pp. 315–36, at p. 323; C. M. Richardson, 'Durante Alberti, the *Martyrs' Picture* and the Venerable English College, Rome', *Papers of the British School at Rome* 73 (2005), pp. 223–63. For the complexities of the loyalties of Sir Edward Stafford, see D. C. Peck (ed.), *Leicester's Commonwealth: The Copy of a Letter written by a Master of Art of Cambridge (1584) and related Documents* (Athens, Ohio, 1985), pp. 24–5.

The Execution of Justice

Faced with the threat from the Scottish queen, the inclination of Elizabeth's principal spin doctor, Lord Burghley, was still to try to work his way into the minds of Catholic loyalists or, rather, of those of a Catholic inclination who could be persuaded not to support the more radical ideas and schemes of some of their coreligionists. Burghley's *Execution of Justice in England*, printed in late 1583, argued that the queen's law was enforced against Catholics not for their religion but for sedition and treason. Catholics who were not guilty were left alone or at least were not badly treated.[80] Burghley's pamphlet drew a biting reply from William Allen, under the title *A True, Sincere, and Modest Defence*, published in 1584.[81]

The release of Burghley's pamphlet occurred shortly before a new batch of trials of seminary clergy under the 1351 statute, that is, rather than under the more recent treason legislation. This was also timed so as to anticipate further legislation which would be laid before the forthcoming parliament.[82] About four weeks after William Carter was hanged, there was a slew of arraignments of Catholic clergy, all of course in the context of the subscription campaign against nonconformity waged by the new archbishop of Canterbury, John Whitgift. Indictments were laid against fifteen clergymen on 5 February 1584. On 6 February, six of them were arraigned at Westminster; five (James Fenn, George Haydock, John Munden, John Nutter, and Thomas Hemerford) were brought back the next day and convicted. The sixth, the Jesuit Jasper Heywood, demonstrated some degree of compliance. The lord chief justice, Sir Christopher Wray, noted that 'Heywood...reforms himself in some things and is likely to have favour'.[83] Edward Bacon wrote pessimistically to his brother Nathaniel from London on

---

[80] Sir William Cecil, *The Execution of Justice in England*...(1583); D. Anderson, *Martyrs and Players in Early Modern England: Tragedy, Religion and Violence on Stage* (Farnham, 2014), pp. 3–5; Ward, LT, pp. 263–4. For the distribution on the Continent of the *Execution of Justice, inter alia* by William Herle, see *CSPF July 1583–July 1584*, p. 628. For the regime's vindication (probably penned by Thomas Norton) of the queen against the rumours concerning the use of torture, see *A Declaration of the Favourable Dealing of her Maiesties Commissioners appointed for the Examination of Certaine Traitours*...(1583); this can be read as a precursor of the *Execution of Justice*: Milward, I, pp. 68–9; Kilroy, *EC*, pp. 368–9, 370.

[81] For the publication and dissemination of Allen's work via a press in Rouen, see *CSPF July 1583–July 1584*, p. 522 (Sir Edward Stafford's warning on 30 May 1584 that attempts to hinder or suppress such pamphlets make 'some think that it is truth and therefore we are afraid of its coming abroad'); *CSPF 1584–5*, pp. 33, 126, 207; for William Rainold's Latin translation of Allen's tract, see ARCR, I, no. 18. A version of Burghley's general argument had been sent in April 1582 in the form of instructions to Sir Henry Cobham in Paris to explain Elizabeth's mind: *CSPF 1581–2*, pp. 659–60.

[82] For the charges against the accused, see Ward, LT, pp. 263–4. Ward notes Burghley's memorandum of December 1583, which sets out the regime's future strategy here (treason trials, deportation, and 'prisons specially provided'): Ward, LT, p. 263, citing PRO, SP 12/164/2, fo. 4^r (*CSPD 1581–90*, p. 134).

[83] Ward, LT, pp. 264–5; HMCR, I, p. 161; Pollen, *UD*, pp. 51–7; Anstr., I, pp. 159, 240. For the indictment of three more clergymen (Robert Nutter, Thomas Stevenson, and William Smith) in Easter term 1584, see Ward, LT, p. 266.

138 CATHOLICS AND TREASON

6 February 1584. Not all was as the puritan godly would have it. Admittedly, the former Marian privy councillor in exile Sir Francis Englefield had been 'indicted' at 'Westminster of high treason, and divers others, Jesuits, are likewise indicted'. But the secretary of the earl of Northumberland, William Wicliffe (who had been caught up in the Throckmorton conspiracy) had been released from the Tower, and the chances were that only 'some poor knave or other shall die for the rest at the end of the term' merely in order 'to send news into the country, and I think that is all the good that shall come to the Church of God of all the rumours and fears lately talked of'.[84]

The five priests convicted on 7 February were, however, executed on 12 February at Tyburn. The reason for trying these clergy was, suggests Dr Ward, 'unknown but seemingly arbitrary'.[85] As Ward notes, Chief Justice Wray recorded that 'some of them very loudly' had 'said the pope might deprive princes for heresy', although, at Tyburn, Haydock had said that he acknowledged Elizabeth as his 'lawful queen'.[86] This was something that the regime's spokesmen on the day did not accept. The sheriff, John Spencer, who was 'much incensed' against Haydock and the others, proclaimed that 'there is, since your arraignment, worse matter found against you' by none other than Anthony Munday; and Spencer summoned him out of the crowd towards the gallows to testify that, in Rome, Haydock had actively wished for the death of the queen.[87] Haydock had certainly declared at his first interrogation that in France it was being said that Campion had died for religion and that 'all men did cry out' against 'the queen's tyranny all France over'. The 'king of France did make his martyrdom to be printed at Paris and to be cried about the streets'.[88] On Haydock's own account as it was reported by Robert

[84] A. Hassell Smith and G. M. Baker (eds), *The Papers of Nathaniel Bacon of Stiffkey*, II (Norfolk Record Society, 49, 1982–3), p. 282; Bacon added that it was rumoured that 'certain obscure Jesuits shall be arraigned tomorrow', whereas 'for the preachers, those of Suffolk and divers others of other countries [i.e. counties] have made a supplication to the council' and on 'Sunday next, they are to have answer', in other words, all as a result of Archbishop Whitgift's subscription campaign: ibid.; *ODNB*, *sub* Whitgift, John (article by W. Sheils); Collinson, *EPM*, pp. 250f., esp. at p. 255.

[85] Ward, LT, p. 265; Thomas Fitzherbert, *A Defence of the Catholyke Cause*... (Antwerp, 1602), (2nd part, with separate title page, entitled *An Apology of T. F.* ...), ch. 13. Among those who were convicted (but escaped the full consequences) was Richard Norris, who was known by the privy council to have been involved in the distribution of Campion's 'brag': Anstr., I, p. 255.

[86] Ward, LT, p. 265; *HMCR*, I, p. 161; Pollen, UD, p. 60 (Grene's transcript of the document which was translated into Latin for publication, in part, in the *Concertatio*; ARSJ, Anglia 37, fos 5ᵛ–8ᵛ [new foliation], formerly Collectanea M, part ii; *Concertatio*, sig. Ll3ʳ). For John Nutter, see also Anstr., I, pp. 258–9, 86; Pollen, *UD*, pp. 37–8 (PRO, SP 12/158/17). For John Munden, see Challoner, *MMP*, pp. 98, 99; Anstr., I, p. 240. For the informer Thomas Dodwell's report of the views of James Fenn (and Andrew Fowler, Samuel Conyers, and William Hartley), in particular that they 'rejoice generally when any news comes...that King Philip comes hither with his army', see Foley, *RSJ*, VI, p. 726 (PRO, SP 12/168/35, fo. 84ᵛ). Fenn's brother, Robert, was arrested on 12 February 1584, i.e. the day of James Fenn's execution, but he was merely deported on 19 September 1585: Anstr., I. pp. 114–15; Renold, *LWA*, p. 92.

[87] *AWCBC*, p. 81; Pollen, *UD*, pp. 60–1.

[88] Pollen, *UD*, p. 59. Haydock had contacted Catholics in the London prisons and had been arrested by, among others, Charles Slade, who gave evidence against him and the others convicted on 7 February: J. Gillow (ed.), *The Haydock Papers*... (1888), pp. 26–7; Pollen, *UD*, p. 58; Ward, LT, p. 265; AAW, B 28, no. 10, p. 295.

AFTER CAMPION 139

Persons in August 1583, in response to a challenge from an unnamed minister, he (Haydock) had written over the door of his cell that the pope was the head of the English and of the universal Church and 'to him, Queen Elizabeth as well as the rest of the world must be subject, if they would be saved'.[89] Haydock also affirmed on 18 January 1584 to the recorder of London, William Fleetwood, his belief that the queen was a heretic, a statement which he repeated at Tyburn, despite his claim that he meant her no harm.[90] Norton had demanded that Haydock should be pumped for information about the recent Throckmorton conspiracy and be made to admit that 'a catalogue of names of men and havens' which he had seen at Rome was the same as the one taken from Francis Throckmorton.[91]

It looks, therefore, as if the arrest, interrogation, and trial of Haydock and the others may have been meant to show the public how far the Throckmorton business might be taken to have extended. Thomas Hemerford allegedly said, even at Tyburn, that he would take the part of an invading military, papally sponsored force if its purpose was to root out heresy. Perhaps this was what led to particular brutality in his case: 'when the tormentor did cut off his members', he screamed in agony, and one narrator wrote that 'I heard it myself, standing under the gibbet'.[92]

Here we have evidence for, as Elizabeth Tudor might have seen it, the disintegration of the conformist assumptions and accommodations which had previously underwritten her relationship with her Catholic-minded subjects. The political language that defined that relationship appeared to be changing radically, and not necessarily in a way that suited the queen. There were Catholic clergy who were now openly saying the formerly unsayable. Despite the evidence of actual (Catholic) sedition, detected and exposed during the investigation of the Throckmorton affair, there was a chorus of disapproval both at home and abroad which called all this a persecution. Although this allowed a certain sort of puritan to pose even more enthusiastically as the epitome of the moderation that was supposed to define the settlement of religion, that pose could be construed by others as itself a kind of sedition, just as some had said during the unfortunate business with Edmund Campion. This situation worsened when the enforcement of the law against Catholic separatism started to fuse in 1584 and after with the question of the bond of association and with other republican schemes for dealing with the unsettled succession.

---

[89] Hicks, *Letters*, p. 181 [*CUPRP*, p. 368]; *AWCBC*, pp. 93–4; cf. *Concertatio*, sig. Mm2ʳ.

[90] Challoner, *MMP*, p. 86; Pollen, *UD*, p. 61. For Fleetwood, see P. R. Harris, 'William Fleetwood, Recorder of the City, and Catholicism in Elizabethan London', *RH* 7 (1963–4), pp. 106–22.

[91] BL, Additional MS 48029, fo. 62ʳ.

[92] Pollen, *UD*, p. 62. For Hemerford's indictment, see Ward, LT, p. 264. There was a confrontation between the sheriffs John Spencer and William Masham over the conduct of the execution: Pollen, *UD*, p. 62. For the barbarous treatment of Haydock, see also Anstr., I, p. 159; Renold, *LWA*, pp. 88–91; Pollen, *UD*, p. 61; for the differences between the extant versions of Haydock's execution, see *AWCBC*, p. 120.

6

Catholic Martyrs and the Political Crises of the mid-1580s

Catholic Denunciations of Tyranny

For all Lord Burghley's best efforts in print, some people were now claiming that the English were witnessing a massive escalation of oppression. As Richard Barret wrote to Alfonso Agazzari on 21 February 1584, 'in England the persecution daily increases in an extraordinary manner' and, 'in almost every port, watchers are stationed, with authority to examine everyone'. Although the queen feared that 'the hearts of her subjects' would be 'alienated' from her, large numbers of Catholics were nevertheless being hauled off to prison.[1] In Paris on 18 March 1584, Francis Nedham observed that Elizabeth was 'most slanderously reviled by the English papists' and by the French too 'for the cruelties and tyranny, as they term it, used against those who are but suspected to be or even to favour papists'. With 'open exclamations' it was declared 'how many are daily put to death with sundry kinds of torments only for professing their consciences, insomuch that they are daily prayed for here in the pulpits'. The bishop of Paris, Pierre de Gondi, ordered 'the people to give devotions and exhibitions unto the Englishmen of Rheims, which are in extreme misery, being deprived of their goods and country, which they are forced to leave by the tyranny of the queen'.[2]

Politically, this was an issue of some moment, that is, if Catholic opinion, rather than being cowed and crushed by the recent trials and executions, could be enlisted against Elizabeth and in favour of the rehabilitation of Mary Stuart. That was obviously the view of some of the regime's enforcers. In mid-1584, Topcliffe set down, as he saw it, the case for the regime and its enforcers to go in even harder than before. On his account, even in the wake of the Throckmorton Plot's discovery, there was still no appropriate surveillance of those who were a danger to the queen. He claimed that there had 'assembled' in the city of London 'lately from all' over England 'a great number of' leading Catholic seminary clergy, and others too, including 'some captains or soldiers' who had served the rebel earl of

---

[1] Renold, *LWA*, p. 68. For those who died in prison in 1584 and 1585, see, e.g., Challoner, *MMP*, pp. 104–5, 108–9; Anstr., I, pp. 174, 212, 368–9; PRO, SP 12/172/111, fo. 165ʳ; Pollen, *UD*, p. 192 (ABSJ, Collectanea M, p. 191ᵃ).

[2] *CSPF July 1583–July 1584*, p. 420.

Catholics and Treason: Martyrology, Memory, and Politics in the Post-Reformation. Michael Questier,
Oxford University Press. © Michael Questier 2022. DOI: 10.1093/oso/9780192847027.003.0006

CATHOLIC MARTYRS AND THE POLITICAL CRISES OF THE MID-1580S   141

Westmorland. The priests themselves 'walk as audaciously disguised in the streets at London as any soldier . . . and their wonted fear . . . is turned into such mirth and solace amongst themselves as though the day of their expectation was passed or, at the furthest, was coming tomorrow'. Now 'my poor instruments', said Topcliffe, referring to his agents, 'have rather with tears betrayed their fear' than dare to 'speak all they dread'. But in spite of this there was 'small regard taken in London, or about the city, of these men'.[3]

The regime's repressive measures, if that is what they were, continued to be fairly precisely targeted. Raids took place on houses in London on 27 August 1584. Coordinated by Topcliffe himself and by Richard Young, they were described by the newly arrived Jesuit William Weston, and they are fully documented in the State papers.[4] Among those arrested by the sheriff John Spencer (one of those who had officiated at the executions on 12 February 1584) were those residing in known Catholics' dwellings, such as Gilbert Wells's in Holborn and those of the cartographer John Speed and the Catholic printer Gabriel Cawood, whose father, John, had been William Carter's patron.[5] This may have been, as much as anything, an attack on the capacity of the Catholic community in London to produce and distribute printed works. Among those whom Alderman Cuthbert Buckle detained in St Mary Overies, near to Montague House, was Edward Hartley, servant to Cecily Stonor who had harboured Campion's press.[6]

Anyway, this was the situation on which William Allen's *A True, Sincere, and Modest Defence* commented and capitalized.[7] It made a maximum case for papal authority and is, I suppose, the single most important statement of the period, from the exile Catholic community, on the linked topics of persecution, martyrdom, and tyranny. Allen declared that he had no intention 'purposely to

---

[3] BL, Lansdowne MS 72, no. 40, fo. 115ᵛ. This manuscript is endorsed '1592' but, via internal dating and especially the reference to the arrest by Topcliffe at Islington of the priest Thomas Worthington (and his imprisonment in the Tower on 19 June 1584), it must have been written soon after that date: Anstr., I, p. 387. Here Topcliffe said that Worthington, a priest called Thomas Brown (using the alias of Revel) and one Humphrey Maxfield were among those who commended the recently executed James Leyburn and said that he died for 'avowing the Scottish queen was queen of England and our sovereign [was] but Elizabeth Boleyn' and that 'a miracle was seen upon [James] Leyburn's quarters at Preston'; and furthermore that Edward Arden had behaved well at his arraignment and John Somerville had been murdered to shut him up, and that there 'would never be [a] merry world' until Mary Stuart reigned in England and her son ruled in Scotland: BL, Lansdowne MS 72, no. 40, fo. 116ʳ; for the Arden-Somerville case, see *ODNB*, *sub* Arden, Edward (article by W. Wizeman).

[4] Caraman, *WW*, pp. 31, 39; PRO, SP 12/172/102–15.

[5] PRO, SP 12/172/102, fo. 149ʳ; PRO, SP 12/172/111, fo. 165ʳ; Anstr., I, p. 174; PRO, SP 12/172/112, fo. 168ʳ. Gilbert Wells himself was arrested at Southampton House. See also D. Flynn, *John Donne and the Ancient Catholic Nobility* (Bloomington, Ind., 1995), p. 127.

[6] PRO, SP 12/172/104, fo. 155ʳ. Presumably Edward Hartley was a relative of William Hartley, the priest (and future martyr) who was convicted in February 1584 but was deported in January 1585, and was also a client of Lady Stonor: Anstr., I, pp. 155–6; see pp. 105–6 above.

[7] For Allen's *True, Sincere, and Modest Defence*, see esp. Lake, *BQB*, pp. 136–9; and for its publication, see Knox, *LMCA*, pp. 239–40.

142 CATHOLICS AND TREASON

dishonour our prince and country', even though the present 'disorder' came from the 'partiality of a few powerful persons abusing her Majesty's clemency and credulity'. But 'we set forth the truth of all these actions for the honour of our nation', and also 'for the memory and honour of such notable martyrs as have testified the truth of the Catholic faith by their precious death[s]', as well as 'to communicate our calamities with our brethren in faith' and with 'the Churches of other provinces standing free from this misery'. Finally, said Allen, it was necessary to defend 'the doings of the said holy confessors and their fellows in faith against the manifold slanders and calumniations of certain heretics or politiques, unjustly charging them with treason'. Allen insisted that those who had been tried and executed had been 'persecuted...for mere matter of religion' and 'upon the transgression of new statutes only, without any relation to the old treasons, so made and set down by parliament in Edward III's time', even though, of course, it was precisely under that legislation that Campion and others had been convicted.[8]

Allen said that he had resorted to print only in the face of a massive, organized, and malign regime-led cascade of pamphleteering against good Catholics: 'princes and communities in disorder have a thousand pretences, excuses and colours of their unjust actions: they have the name of authority, the shadow of laws, the pens and tongues of infinite at their commandment' and 'they may print or publish what they like' and 'suppress what they list'. King Richard III had done no less—'what solemn libels, proclamations' and 'orations were put forth to justify his abominable iniquity?'—and the duke of Northumberland and the prince of Orange had been just as bad.[9]

Then Allen went through the relevant cases, starting with Cuthbert Mayne, convicted under the statute 13 Eliz. c. 1. For Allen, the *Execution of Justice*'s claim that 'none is asked, by torture, "what he believes of the Mass or transubstantiation or such like"' was quite ridiculous. It presupposed that there was 'no question pertaining to faith and religion but touching our inward belief. Whereas...it concerns religion no less to demand and press us by torture, where, in whose houses, what days and times we say or hear Mass, how many we have reconciled, what we have heard in confession; who resorts to our preachings, who harbours Catholics and priests; who sustains, aids or comforts them' and also 'where Catholic books are printed, and by whom, and to whom they be uttered in England'. Allen extended as far as he could the range of things which could be considered to fall within the category of religion. Since the interrogators asked their questions with 'evil intent', Catholics were entitled, indeed required, to refuse to disclose what the interrogators demanded. In the case of the printer William Carter, Allen regarded it as evidence of tyranny that it had been demanded of him, under torture, 'upon what gentlemen or Catholic ladies he had bestowed or intended to bestow certain

---

[8] Allen, *TSMD*, sig. *3ʳ⁻ᵛ, pp. 1–2.   [9] Allen, *TSMD*, sig. *4ʳ.

CATHOLIC MARTYRS AND THE POLITICAL CRISES OF THE MID-1580S 143

books of prayers and spiritual exercises and meditations'. This was as bad as racking Campion 'about the Irish commotion'. Allen wrote that John Hart, though not martyred, was 'tormented' by 'famine and filthy dungeons' only because he 'would not yield to' the puritan John Rainolds, 'with whom you appointed him to confer'.[10]

In a separate chapter Allen dealt with the proceedings against Campion and his co-defendants. The 'forgery and false accusation' against them were 'now... clearly discovered to all Englishmen'. The prosecutions rested on the perjured evidence of low-life criminal scum.[11] Marian Protestants, by contrast, had not been persecuted. They were not martyrs. By the same token, those same heretics had been genuinely guilty of rebellion 'against the See Apostolic and all lawful spiritual regiment proceeding from the same'. They had got what they deserved—so no need for sympathy there. Burghley had compiled 'a glorious muster of archbishops' but 'indeed there was but one', Thomas Cranmer, 'and he [was] a notorious perjured and often relapsed apostate, recanting, swearing and forswearing at every turn, and at the very day and hour of his death, sacrilegiously joined in pretended marriage to a woman, notwithstanding his vow and order'. Foxe's other martyrs were base and contemptible, 'in so much that the very saint-woman [Perotine Massey], whose child (as he [Burghley] says upon lying Foxe's credit) burst out of her belly into the fire, was nought of her body; and therefore, to cover her incontinence, [she] would not utter to the officer her case'. Allen explained that there was a crucial 'difference between our martyrdom and the due and worthy punishment of heretics who, shedding their blood obstinately in testimony of falsehood against the truth of Christ and his holy spouse and out of the unity of the same, are known malefactors and can be no martyrs, but damnable murderers of themselves'. The Protestant contention was that 'the martyrs of their sect in Queen Mary's time denied not their lawful queen'. Really? Cranmer was 'convicted and condemned openly of high treason'. 'Was not your... martyr... [Nicholas] Ridley a high traitor, publicly preaching and proclaiming at Paul's Cross in London, both Queen Mary and this queen [Elizabeth] to be bastards and to have no right title to the crown?' And 'were not all the pack of your Protestants confederated or acquainted with Wyatt's conspiracy and open rebellion against their prince and country?' Catholics, by contrast, were not traitors since they knew how to distinguish between different kinds of obedience, and particularly between the kind of obedience owed to earthly rulers and the sort that should be given to spiritual authority. In any case, the difficult decisions about whether to obey temporal rulers could be decided by the papacy.[12] As for Burghley's claim

---

[10] Allen, *TSMD*, pp. 2 f., 10, 11, 13, 14.   [11] Allen, *TSMD*, pp. 18–19, 25–6, ch. 2 *passim*.

[12] Allen, *TSMD*, pp. 40–1, 45, 56–7, and chs 3–7 *passim*. This point about Foxe's pregnant martyr Perotine Massey, in Guernsey, had been made by Thomas Harding in his *A Reioindre to M. Iewels Replie against the Sacrifice of the Masse* (Louvain, 1567), fos 184ᵛ–5ʳ. Allen's account of the just and unjust use of force in matters of religion and belief is virtually identical to the one made by Harding in

144 CATHOLICS AND TREASON

that lay Catholics were largely left alone, even if they did not affirm the royal supremacy, Francis Tregian was the proof that the regime was telling lies. The cases of Bodey and Slade showed the same. There were 'many' who had 'fled for religion' and were 'wholly sacked and spoiled of all they possessed'.[13]

Allen concluded that, if it walked like and talked like a persecution, it was exactly that. 'If our fellows in the Catholic faith through Christendom could...see all the prisons, dungeons, fetters, stocks [and] racks that are through the realm occupied and filled with Catholics', and watch them being hauled into court with 'the vilest sort' of criminals and, then, rotting in gaol as well as dying on the scaffold, those observers could no longer be in any doubt.[14] Allen was certain that these were not just the here-and-there outbreaks of irrational injustice but the inevitable outworking of the godless policy of the Elizabethan State. The 'revolt from the See Apostolic' and the 'spoil of churches and clergy...by which they made their entry into this new blessedness' were part and parcel of the determination to 'make the subjects of Scotland, first, then of France and last of all of Flanders and divers other States to rebel against their lawful princes', with all the predictable miseries that would follow.[15] God, of course, would teach them a lesson in the end. Even now God had 'defeated all their drifts in Scotland'. It was the madness of heresy to 'attribute their troubles or apprehended fears to the excommunication' levied in 1570 'and to the godly endeavours of Catholic priests, instructing the people, peaceably to their salvation'.[16]

Crucially, towards the end of the pamphlet Allen made a direct reference to what he took to be the dynastic underpinnings of all the present troubles. It was 'but a small comfort and remedy for these our public distresses' that Burghley's *Execution of Justice* 'by shameful flattery' reminded Elizabeth that she was 'a maiden queen'. Would that 'God, instead of her Majesty's virginity', had provided that 'we might...have had, for the realm's safety, issue of her body in honourable wedlock'. But that had not happened and, now that the 'noble line and issue' of 'King Henry' had in effect failed, 'they will not suffer us to go to the next of the same royal blood descending from the renowned prince, Henry the seventh'. The real traitors had done this by 'most shameful packing of certain puritans and ambitious persons' so as to promote the rival claim of an unnamed 'emulous house'. And they did this 'both by forsaking God and the Catholic religion on the one side' and, on the other, 'by refusing and...shamefully abusing the only next, true and lawful heir' to the throne. It was a tragedy that 'the conjunction and uniting' of 'the two noble realms of England and Scotland into one monarchy'

---

his *Reioindre*, pp. 178–89; see P. Holmes, *Resistance and Compromise: The Political Thought of the Elizabethan Catholics* (Cambridge, 1982), p. 49.

[13] Allen, *TSMD*, p. 54.   [14] Allen, *TSMD*, pp. 173–4.   [15] Allen, *TSMD*, p. 177.

[16] Allen, *TSMD*, pp. 179, 180.

CATHOLIC MARTYRS AND THE POLITICAL CRISES OF THE MID-1580S 145

was being prevented by the corrupt practices of the evil men who were the sworn enemies of the House of Stuart.[17]

Here, said Allen, was the significance of the recent instances of true martyrdom. He asserted, in reply to Burghley, that 'it is neither pope nor priest...that desires' the 'destruction' of the queen and her realm. This could be shown by the pope's 'solicitude' for her and, also, by the 'voluntary death' of Catholics and 'the shedding of their own blood, seeking their brethren's salvation and the reconcilement of their country to Christ and his vicar'. Elizabeth's real enemies were those who had advised her to 'forsake the Church and [the] See Apostolic'. The martyrs of the last few years were no different from Sir Thomas More and Bishop John Fisher, 'who resisted upon great love and duty to their sovereign, dissuading both his divorce from the Church and from his wife'.[18]

Allen took particular care to refute the allegations recently made against clergymen in the North and to say that they were charged only with 'hearing confessions' and 'absolving and reconciling sinners'. Allen's target here was the 1581 statute's assumption that, as he put it, 'all parties so reconciled' were freed from 'their obedience to the queen'. As Leslie Ward points out, Burghley's *Execution of Justice* carefully avoided mentioning the trials recently staged in York where the accused were charged under the 1581 statute.[19]

Allen was now pointing the finger of blame directly at the queen. He accused her of the kind of barbarism which in his 1582 martyrology, *A Briefe Historie*, he had attributed to others. Thus on 6 March 1584, from Rheims, Allen wrote to the Jesuit Alfonso Agazzari that Elizabeth herself had gone on the record as saying that she wanted slaughter, and lots of it: 'we shall steep not only our hands but our arms' in the blood of the 'papists'.[20]

Out in the provinces there were, here and there, public expressions of the same kind of anger as Allen evinced in his printed work. The Lancashire recusant John Finch was arrested by the earl of Derby. Taken with him was a priest, George Ostcliff.[21] Finch had expressed his admiration for James Leyburn as well as for

---

[17] Allen, *TSMD*, pp. 190–2. This, of course, was the case which had, in part, been made in *A Treatise of Treasons against Q. Elizabeth, and the Croune of England* (Louvain, 1572), and which Mary Stuart continued to make; see, e.g., *CSPSc 1585–6*, pp. 163–5.

[18] Allen, *TSMD*, p. 193.   [19] Ward, LT, pp. 256–7, citing Allen, *TSMD*, p. 4.

[20] Renold, *LWA*, p. 75. Richard Barret repeated in a letter of 26 February/7 March 1584 the words allegedly spoken by the queen: Renold, *LWA*, p. 84.

[21] Ostcliff was one of those who had been put on trial with Campion, though Ostcliff never went to execution and was deported in June 1586. See Pollen, *UD*, p. 80 (ABSJ, Anglia I, no. 19); Kilroy, *EC*, p. 299; Anstr., I, p. 262; AAW, A III, no. 94, pp. 355–63 (concerning John Finch and James Bell), an incomplete version of ABSJ, Anglia I, no. 19. For the origins of, and relationship between, these texts, see Pollen, *UD*, p. 74. Another incomplete version is in Alban Butler's papers, the same basic text as AAW, A III, no. 94, pp. 355–63 (which is followed, at pp. 364–6, by an, again, incomplete account of James Bell), but with various verbal differences which suggest they were both taken from a third text, i.e. ABP, pp. 329–38 (annotated on p. 338: 'is not this the original account translated into Latin by the *Concertatio*?', i.e. *Concertatio Ecclesiae Catholicae in Anglia Adversus Calvino-papistas et Puritanos*...(Trier, 1588), ed. John Fenn and John Gibbons, sigs Rr4ᵛ–Ss3ᵛ).

146 CATHOLICS AND TREASON

Edmund Campion.[22] According to one Gilbert Marshall, Finch had also said, 'if we had the upper hand of them, as they have of us, they should die, every one of them'.[23] Catholics said that the authorities tried to destroy Finch's reputation—via stories that he, like Campion, had shopped his friends—and specifically that Finch had 'betrayed a priest' and 'many other Catholics'. Even though 'very few Catholics and not many Protestants did believe this malicious lie...yet it was so faced out for a month or two that few durst control it'.[24] When Finch remained obstinate, he was sent to the Fleet prison in Manchester. He and others, including Thurstan Arrowsmith, the grandfather of the Caroline martyr Edmund Arrowsmith, were so intransigent that the overseers of the gaol suggested to the privy council that these prisoners should be forced to listen to godly Protestant sermons. 'At dinner time a minister' was directed 'to come in and read and expound a chapter of their Genevan bible'. Finch made it clear that he had absolutely no time for this.[25]

Then, as Challoner narrates, the authorities 'spared neither threats nor promises to induce him to go to church; which, when they could not persuade him thus, they dragged him thither by downright violence through the streets', banging his head 'all the way upon the stones' and 'then they thrust him into a dark stinking dungeon'. The authorities even spread the rumour that he had become desperate. On 28 November 1583, the bishop of Chester, William Chaderton, reported that Finch had, the day before, sat through the recital of 'morning prayer' at Manchester and had then tried to commit suicide by drowning himself.[26] One contemporary Catholic account said that, being brought out of his 'dungeon', he had thrown himself into the nearby river, but 'to what end God knows—the 'heretics say that he would have destroyed himself', whereas 'others think that he did it only for penance for his former suspected offence, for that he went', as this source said, 'so quietly...with them to the church'.[27]

Finch was finally indicted under the 1581 statute (with three Marian priests—Thomas Williamson, Richard Hatton, and James Bell) for affirming that 'the pope and bishop of Rome' had 'authority and jurisdiction in England' and was the 'head of the Catholic Church and that a part of that Church is in England'.[28] One Catholic report of the subsequent execution of Finch and Bell said that 'the judges had commandment given them by counsel (as it is known since) to execute but two at the most' at that assizes. This was why only Finch and Bell were hanged at

---

[22] Pollen, *UD*, pp. 44, 84.   [23] Pollen, *UD*, p. 45 (PRO, SP 12/163/2. i, fo. 5ʳ).
[24] Pollen, *UD*, pp. 80–1.
[25] Pollen, *UD*, pp. 23–5 (PRO, SP 12/152/48; PRO, SP 12/153/6, 45), 82; Challoner, *MMP*, p. 362; *Concertatio*, sig. Tt3ʳ.
[26] Challoner, *MMP*, p. 102; *Concertatio*, sig. Tt3ᵛ; Pollen, *UD*, pp. 46 (PRO, SP 12/163/84), 82, 84.
[27] Pollen, *UD*, pp. 83–4; *Concertatio*, sig. Tt4ᵛ.
[28] Pollen, *UD*, p. 86; Ward, LT, p. 257.

CATHOLIC MARTYRS AND THE POLITICAL CRISES OF THE MID-1580S   147

Lancaster on 20 April 1584.[29] Exactly what the public thought of these proceedings is uncertain. But Francis Throckmorton, who was executed on 10 July, perhaps as a kind of tit-for-tat response to the assassination of William of Orange, allegedly proclaimed from the gallows that 'he would not ask pardon of the queen... but said that she ought to ask pardon of God and the State for her heresy and misgovernment in allowing innocent men to be killed every day unjustly', a reference in part, presumably, to these recent executions at Lancaster.[30]

The same kind of provincial test of strength occurred in the case of Richard White. Our narratives of his resistance of the State's imposition of conformity are some of the fullest of this period. They are, therefore, worth reviewing in some detail. 'Being... placed in Orton [Overton] among his wife's friends', the bishop of Chester, William Downham, 'and his officers began to molest him for refusing to receive at their communion table. In the end, after some troubles, he yielded to their desires', much against his own conscience but at the persuasion of one Roger Puleston. The result for White was a providential Hitchcockian attack by 'a fearful company of crows and kites' as soon as he had 'come out of the church'. It was this which had persuaded him to 'become a Catholic' in what he must now have regarded as the true sense of the word.[31] The long contemporary descriptions of him, one of which was published in the *Concertatio Ecclesiae Catholicae*, in effect allow that White more or less pushed the authorities into taking action against him, even though his public performance of separatism meant that he was already fairly unpopular with local puritans. At the same time, local conformists/crypto-Catholics failed to stand by him. John Salusbury of Rug, for example, tried to buff up his credit in front of Gabriel Goodman, dean of Westminster, by telling White (in prison at Ruthin) to his face that he 'was an unprofitable member of the

---

[29] Pollen, *UD*, p. 78 (ABSJ, Anglia I, no. 20). For Bell's ordination in March 1547, see W. M. Fergusson Irvine (ed.), *The Earliest Ordination Book of the Diocese of Chester 1542-7 & 1555-8* (Lancashire and Cheshire Record Society, 1895), printed in *Miscellanies relating to Lancashire and Cheshire*, IV (Lancashire and Cheshire Record Society, 43, 1902), pp. 69, 70.

[30] Hicks, *Letters*, pp. 226-7 [*CUPRP*, pp. 486-7]; J. Bossy, *Under the Molehill: An Elizabethan Spy Story* (2001), pp. 123-4. Ireland saw an analogue of these executions of English Catholics—Dermot O'Hurley, archbishop of Cashel, was hanged in June 1584: Hicks, *Letters*, p. 238 [*CUPRP*, p. 508]; *ODNB*, sub O'Hurley, Dermot (article by D. Edwards); P. Corish, *The Irish Martyrs* (Dublin, 1989), pp. 11–13. For this and for the construction in the 1580s of an Irish Counter-Reformation martyrology, in particular in Richard Stanihurst, *De Vita S. Patricii, Hiberniae Apostoli Libri Duo*... (Antwerp, 1587), but also in the work of John Howlin, Peter Lombard, Conor O'Devany, and David Rothe, see C. Lennon, 'Taking Sides: The Emergence of Irish Catholic Ideology', in V. Carey and U. Lotz-Heumann (eds), *Taking Sides? Colonial and Confessional Mentalités in Early Modern Ireland: Essays in Honour of Karl S. Bottigheimer* (Dublin, 2003), pp. 78–93, at pp. 84 f.

[31] Thomas, *WECM*, pp. 49, 87; for Roger Puleston, see *HC 1558–1603*, III, pp. 260–1. The printed narrative in the *Concertatio* omits the story about the crows and kites and says that White became a recusant when he was advised by seminary clergy to withdraw from 'the impious meetings of schismatic men': Thomas, *WECM*, pp. 87, 142, 147. White was arrested on a number of occasions, one of them being, significantly enough, in July 1580, shortly after Edmund Campion's arrival in England: Thomas, *WECM*, p. 51. For the answers to questions put to him in September 1579, see NLW, Denbighshire Gaol Files, Great Sessions 4/5/4/7–10. I am very grateful to Lloyd Bowen for this reference.

148 CATHOLICS AND TREASON

commonwealth', though Salusbury did this 'plainly against his own conscience'. God taught him a lesson because he soon sickened and died.[32]

As with Finch, there were concerted efforts to trash White's reputation with other Catholics. In May 1581, just before Campion's arrival from the Continent, White's enemies decided to damage his credit by making it appear that he had attended a sermon delivered by a Protestant preacher. Persuasion failed, however, to cajole him into anything like satisfactory compliance. Eventually, six of the sheriff's officers carried him to the local church. In fact they 'took the servant of God upon their shoulders with his heels upward and so bare him in procession-wise round about the font (a very strange spectacle to the beholders)' and lodged him 'under the pulpit'.[33]

This may have been a kind of conformist version of the shaming rituals of contemporary popular culture.[34] But in White's case it did not work because he rattled his chains so loudly that the preacher's words were drowned out. A subsequent attempt by his enemies to 'make him away' failed. Even a nobbled local jury refused to convict on a capital charge and simply fined him for disturbing divine service. After this he was indicted under the 1581 recusancy statute.[35] He did nothing to help himself by mocking the judge, Sir George Bromley, over the issue of recusancy fines. White offered the judge six pence in part payment for his now massive accumulating debt to the queen's exchequer.[36]

At an assize hearing at Wrexham in May 1582 there was a further attempt to preach Protestant doctrine to the assembled prisoners. White was there and, again, he and others complained to the judges that 'they came not thither to hear sermons but to receive law and justice'. They also heckled the preacher, allegedly in three different languages. Local puritans now attacked the sheriff, Edward Hughes, for his leniency towards Catholic separatists. But according to this Catholic account these people—'hot puritans' (who were 'certain peddlers and tinkers who then bore some sway' in Wrexham)—demanded the appointment of four 'overseers' whose job would be to make the lives of imprisoned Catholics even more wretched than they currently were. D. Aneurin Thomas suggests that these 'puritans' may have been the same people as those who were agitating for

---

[32] Thomas, *WECM*, pp. 88–9. For Gabriel Goodman, and his interests in Wales (at Ruthin), see Thomas, *WECM*, p. 133; *ODNB, sub* Goodman, Gabriel (article by C. Knighton).

[33] Thomas, *WECM*, p. 90.

[34] See M. J. Ingram, 'Ridings, Rough Music and Mocking Rhymes in Early Modern England', in B. Reay (ed.), *Popular Culture in Seventeenth-Century England* (1985), pp. 166–97. At White's arraignment in October 1584, 'at the bar' he 'blessed himself whereat a young gentleman there present made no little pastime, often crossing his body in derision and casting withal mocks and moves with his head and mouth' towards White: Thomas, *WECM*, p. 104. White's fellow sufferer, the priest John Bennett, was subjected in prison to the attentions of a crowd of 'wanton youths', of 'high birth' but with 'depraved morals and degenerate habits', who brought a 'jester' with them and 'showed the priest of God so much barbarism and filth with obscene acts' that he could barely bring himself to tell his friends all the disgusting details: Thomas, *WECM*, p. 215.

[35] Thomas, *WECM*, pp. 91–2.   [36] Thomas, *WECM*, p. 92.

CATHOLIC MARTYRS AND THE POLITICAL CRISES OF THE MID-1580S 149

the nomination of moderators who would regulate the process of puritan reform which was subsequently instigated in Wrexham. Integral to this was the ministry of Christopher Goodman, who had, after being deprived of his Bedfordshire benefice in 1571, come back to this region. This was a classic instance of the unwritten Elizabethan rule that, as it were, puritanism on tour ought to stay on tour. Goodman organized the kind of puritan exercises in Chester that the queen had demanded should be banned. He also took 'special order that the poor Catholics in the castle' at Chester should 'reap no benefit by the poor man's box and other relief which is in the city gathered for prisoners'. One of the 'overseers' who was appointed, David Edwards, was violently hostile to White and was responsible at one point for arresting him. The *Concertatio*'s narrative of White's difficulties concedes that, when Edwards effected White's arrest in July 1580, White responded by beating him unconscious, though the narrative adds that White felt extremely penitent for his display of intemperance.[37]

A treason indictment followed shortly after, instigated by Edwards and his associates. This was based on the legal weaponry supplied by the new statute law. The charge was that White and others had persuaded a man 'to abstain from the church and to acknowledge the pope's authority'; but the prosecution failed.[38] All during 1583, and particularly at the assizes in May, White was badgered and questioned (eventually with the use of manacles) about his attitude to the royal supremacy and to papal authority, and about whether he had been reconciled to Rome contrary to statute.[39]

White had provided his enemies with a lot of ammunition. His poems contain not only a versified rendering of Robert Persons's *Brief Discours* but also some stanzas in praise of William the Silent's assassin, which must have been written at some point shortly before the final legal proceedings against White in autumn 1584. Hilariously, the English Jesuit John Pollen judged that the verses in question were 'plainly wanting both in forbearance and in good feeling', although 'the other records of the martyr show that under other circumstances he could be and was both calm and patient'.[40] But, by virtually any standards, White's versifying is quite direct: 'Thou Orange, fat (and) tedious / Everyone is glad that thou art are enclosed in the grave. / Thou drivedst yonder to sadden us; / Do thyself now be silent.' White sang two *Te Deums* to himself when he heard the news that William

---

[37] Thomas, *WECM*, pp. 92–4, 50, 94, 149, 151. The Holywell manuscript omits to mention White's violent response to Edwards: Thomas, *WECM*, p. 88. In 1584 Goodman refused to subscribe to Archbishop Whitgift's articles. See Collinson, *EPM*, p. 118; *ODNB*, *sub* Goodman, Christopher (article by J. Dawson), stressing that Goodman was a client of the earl of Leicester; see also A. Peel (ed.), *The Notebook of John Penry 1593* (Camden Society, 3rd series, 67, 1944), p. 42.

[38] Thomas, *WECM*, pp. 95–6.

[39] Thomas, *WECM*, pp. 98f, 173f. White's principal adversary here was Thomas Atkins, who was the procurator-general of Wales and deputy attorney to the council in the marches: *HC 1558–1603*, I, p. 361.

[40] Pollen, *UD*, pp. 90–1, 93–5, 98–9.

150   CATHOLICS AND TREASON

had been shot. 'A man with a gun (very good [was] his understanding) / Slew him (well done to him!).' The rest of the poem rejoices in the number of famous Protestants who must already, or would shortly, be in Hell.[41]

It was hardly surprising (one assumes that White's poetic jottings became public knowledge) that another treason indictment was brought against him—on 9 October 1584. There were witnesses who were prepared to swear that White and others had said that the pope was 'supreme head of the Church'. Also, one witness had 'heard White rehearse certain rhymes of his own making against married priests and ministers' and 'secondly that he called the Bible a bubble', though White and the others who stood indicted for affirming the papal supremacy argued that the witnesses against them had been suborned.[42] The deputy justice for the Chester circuit, Simon Thelwall (a known supporter of the earl of Leicester), recited the substance of Burghley's recently published *Execution of Justice in England*. He 'roved over the insurrection in the North, the excommunication of Pius V, [John] Story and [John] Felton, Dr [Nicholas] Sanders's coming into Ireland, [Edmund] Campion and his fellows, [Edward] Arden and [John] Somerville, Francis Throckmorton, aggravating the prisoners to be [of] one religion with the persons before named'.[43] The *Concertatio*'s account of the trial attributed the death of White indirectly to Leicester by gesturing at White's antagonist, the judge Sir George Bromley, as a client of the earl. Evan Lloyd, who was present as a commissioner for hearing cases brought against Catholics, was similarly denounced. Lloyd enlisted under Leicester in the expedition to the Netherlands in 1586.[44]

White was executed at Wrexham on 17 October 1584 with, if one takes literally the principal narrative of his death, shocking cruelty and/or incompetence.[45] Just before death, White referred to the fact that he had been 'a jesting fellow' and that he might conceivably have 'offended...that way, or by my songs'.[46] The extent to which the authorities wanted the execution to demonstrate the risks of public jesting was indicated by the sheriff's determination that White should not expire swiftly. Fearing that White 'should die too soon', the sheriff ordered that he should be 'cut...down', something which provoked a hostile reaction from the crowd.

[41] Pollen, *UD*, p. 98. Another of White's poems celebrates the Black Assizes in Oxford in 1577 when, as we saw, Rowland Jenks was arraigned and when so many of the queen's officials perished from gaol fever: Pollen, *UD*, p. 97; see p. 89 above.

[42] Thomas, *WECM*, pp. 104–8. It appears that White was indicted (again?) under the 1581 statute: Ward, *LT*, p. 297; AAW, B 28, no. 10, p. 298.

[43] Thomas, *WECM*, p. 109.

[44] Thomas, *WECM*, pp. 229, 235; cf. *HC 1558–1603*, I, p. 490, identifying Lord Burghley as Bromley's principal patron. For Simon Thelwall, see *HC 1558–1603*, III, p. 483, and for Evan Lloyd, see *HC 1558–1603*, II, pp. 482–3.

[45] Thomas, *WECM*, pp. 115–21; pp. 31–2 above. For the discrepancy over the date of the execution, see Thomas, *WECM*, pp. 115, 135: the *Concertatio* assigns it to 17 October, while the Holywell MS puts it on 15 October.

[46] Thomas, *WECM*, p. 120.

CATHOLIC MARTYRS AND THE POLITICAL CRISES OF THE MID-1580S 151

After a certain amount of delay, 'the rope was cut' and White revived. This led to his being disembowelled alive.[47]

A few days before White's execution, a royal proclamation was printed which demanded the 'suppression of books defacing true religion, slandering [the] administration of justice' and 'endangering' the queen's 'title'. This was aimed fairly and squarely at William Allen's *True, Sincere, and Modest Defence*. The 'libels...dispersed through this realm by divers seditious and traitorous persons' not only undermined 'true religion' but also slandered 'the present...government with cruelty'.[48]

People quite as outspoken as Richard White were evidently not the norm, although he was probably giving vent to opinions about recusancy that were widely shared in some regions of the country. But the regime's problem was that White's frankness and Allen's published work were not simply the rantings of marginalized radicals. Allen's *True, Sincere, and Modest Defence* incorporated a forceful expression of one particular contemporary reading, even if it verged on spiritual absolutism, of the Church's power to counsel and, if necessary, correct secular rulers. Allen's polemics expressed very clearly the claim that the Church had the capacity to police the boundaries between, on the one hand, certain aspects of the power of the State and, on the other, the practice of the faith. By 1584, Allen and his associates were moving towards the expression of the same kind of political theory which was adopted in France by the Holy League.

Mass Deportations, the Bond of Association, the Approach of War, and the 1585 Statute against Catholic Clergy

Even now, there was still no settled determination, it seems, inside the regime to implement widely the sharpest of the new statutory weapons available to it in its war with its Catholic critics. Burghley had, almost a year before, proposed mass deportations instead.[49] This policy was subsequently expedited at the direct insistence of the queen.[50] The first large-scale chucking-out exercise took place on 21 January 1585, after the parliament had adjourned. Twenty-one Catholics (all except one of them were clergymen) were sent to France. In September, more clergy, from London and the North, were sent away.[51]

---

[47] Thomas, *WECM*, pp. 120–1.   [48] Hughes and Larkin, *TRP*, II, no. 672; Ward, LT, p. 266.
[49] Ward, LT, p. 263.
[50] Pollen, *UD*, pp. 102–3 (PRO, SP 12/175/38: Thomas Wilkes to Walsingham, 20 December 1584, noting the queen's order to get on with it); PRO, SP 12/176/9, fo. 17ʳ.
[51] Challoner, *MMP*, pp. 109, 110; Pollen, *UD*, p. 103; Knox, *DD*, pp. 12–13; Renold, *LWA*, pp. 135–42; Ward, LT, pp. 266–9. For the September deportations, see Renold, *LWA*, p. 183. For those who chose not to return, and for those who did, see Ward, LT, p. 269; Renold, *LWA*, p. 134.

152 CATHOLICS AND TREASON

These deportations were almost certainly an attempt to avoid treason trials which the regime, or at least the queen, did not want. Some of the deportees were known to be loyalists.[52] William Allen declared that this enforced exile was a terrible injustice (the clergy in question said that 'they were conscious of no treason towards their prince' and 'many among them had never been arraigned on this count'). He made this complaint to the cardinal of Como, papal secretary of state, presumably in order to counter the rumours that large numbers of recently ordained English clergy were simply giving up the struggle and, admitting defeat, were returning to the Continent.[53]

The regime's attempt to rid itself, as it thought, of this aspect of the Catholic problem was part and parcel of the emergence of quasi-republican fail-safe devices in late 1584 and early 1585—the bond of association and the planning for a possible interregnum.[54] These expedients traded off the exposure of the Parry Plot. Part of this general project was the passing of a new measure against Catholic seminary clergy and their harbourers, that is, 27 Eliz., c. 2, 'An Act against Jesuits, seminary priests and such other like disobedient persons'. Peter Lake has argued that the decision to use the treason law against William Parry—who had been brave (or mad) enough to speak out in parliament on 17 December 1584 against the draft bill—provided a vehicle for those councillors who wanted a way to reply to recent Catholic tracts, such as William Allen's and John Leslie's, and also finally to cut off and repudiate the offers of accommodation coming via Mary Stuart's secretary Claude Nau.[55] Dr Ward comments that the new statute was an extrapolation of the royal proclamation of 1 April 1582. The draft of the statute was probably 'worked on by the same committee' which was 'appointed for the bill for the queen's safety'. The principal provision of the new act made it high treason for a subject of the queen who had been ordained abroad to enter her English realm, while those abroad who had enrolled in the seminaries were held similarly guilty

---

[52] Some deportees were later prominent on the loyalist wing of the community, e.g. William Bishop, who had been arrested at Rye in early 1582 and, in 1583, was convicted of plotting the death of the queen at Rheims and Rome (Anstr., I, p. 37; Renold, *LWA*, pp. 69, 70), John Colleton (who had been arraigned with Campion but had been acquitted), William Warmington, and the eventual renegade William Tedder. Also deported were those, e.g. James Bosgrave and Henry Orton, who had already distanced themselves from those Catholics who had been executed for treason: Renold, *LWA*, p. 140. But among the deportees there were also those who were (or later showed themselves to be) otherwise inclined, e.g. William Hartley, Robert Nutter, and William Dean. For Robert Nutter, see G. Anstruther, *A Hundred Homeless Years: English Dominicans 1558–1658* (1958), ch. 3; see also pp. 292–5 below.

[53] Renold, *LWA*, pp. 132–3.

[54] Peter Lake has argued that the tendency to study and expound the Collinson-generated concept of 'monarchical republicanism' by concentrating on theoretical approaches to law and constitutional theory rather misses the point, in the sense that the urgency driving the arguments of those who were trying to provide for an interregnum came almost exclusively from, as they saw it, the queen's refusal to cooperate with their own legitimate concern for the political future. See Lake, *BQB*, pp. 165–7 and chs 7, 9 *passim*. I am grateful to Professor Lake for several discussions of this topic.

[55] Lake, *BQB*, pp. 179–93; Neale, *EHP*, II, pp. 33–47; Read, *MSW*, II, pp. 401–6.

CATHOLIC MARTYRS AND THE POLITICAL CRISES OF THE MID-1580S   153

if they failed to return in a set time. It was, *inter alia*, declared a felony offence, downgraded from treason by the Lords, to harbour seminary clergy.[56]

The implications of the draft statute provoked the formulation of a toleration petition to the queen which was presented personally to her at Greenwich by Richard Shelley in March 1585. The signatories specifically condemned the 'late devilish attempt of Parry, that execrable wretch', even though, as far as papal authority was concerned, they would say only that they denied the pope had authority 'to license any man to consent to sin, or to commit any act against the divine law'; and 'much less can this disloyal, wicked and unnatural design or attempt by any means be made lawful, that a subject may seek the destruction of his lawful sovereign'. This raised questions about sovereigns who might be regarded as not 'lawful'. But the petition insisted that, as for the clergy whom the petitioners had personally encountered, they all took the queen to be their 'true and lawful queen, *tam de jure quam de facto*'. The problem was caused primarily by the 'foul slanders heaped upon' the Catholic clergy 'daily... from the pulpits and other malicious libellers from the press'. The petitioners reiterated that it was 'heresy' for any subject to 'lift up his hand against God's Anointed'.[57]

Shelley rapidly found himself in prison, though the petitioners may have been trying to mobilize the queen's unease about the ratcheting up of pressure on Catholics.[58] Much later, in 1621, Richard Broughton claimed that the recusant Robert Price of Washingley had reported the words of Henry Grey, earl of Kent, to the effect that Elizabeth 'did not confirm that statute [of 1585]... which disabled it to be a law'; and a servant of the lord chancellor, Sir Thomas Bromley, witnessed 'that this bill was not passed by the queen's consent'.[59]

None of this, however, could prevent a final retaliation against those Catholics who had been associated with the queen's strategy in the late 1570s for an Anglo-French dynastic treaty. In late May 1585, Philip Howard, earl of Arundel, had been dragged off a ship on which he had intended to get to France. He had been

---

[56] Ward, *LT*, pp. 62–7 (quotation at p. 63), 272; *SR*, IV, pp. 706–7. For the passage of the bill and for the new treasons that it created, see Ward, *LT*, pp. 63, 64–5. Ward notes that, even though the crown did use witnesses, they 'were not required by law in the cases of those tried for treason under the anti-Catholic acts of 1571, 1581 and 1585': Ward, *LT*, p. 67. The royal proclamation of 1 April 1582 had stated that 'all the Jesuits, seminary men and priests' coming into the queen's dominions 'in such secret manner [should] be... held, esteemed and taken for traitors to her Majesty', and 'all... such as... receive, harbour, aid, comfort, relieve and maintain any such Jesuit, seminary man, or priest as is aforesaid' would be dealt with as abettors of traitors. All those currently at the seminaries who did not return in three months would also be reputed traitors: Hughes and Larkin, *TRP*, II, p. 491; Ward, *LT*, pp. 61–2; J. Bellamy, *The Tudor Law of Treason: An Introduction* (1979), pp. 72–3.

[57] R. B. Manning, 'Richard Shelley of Warminghurst and the English Catholic Petition for Toleration of 1585', *RH* 6 (1961–2), pp. 265–74; AAW, A IV, no. 4, pp. 33–8; Kn., I, pp. 114–23 (quotations at pp. 115, 116, 117, 118); D. Flynn, '"Out of Step": Six Supplementary Notes on Jasper Heywood', in T. M. McCoog (ed.), *The Reckoned Expense: Edmund Campion and the Early English Jesuits* (Woodbridge, 1996), pp. 179–92, at p. 189.

[58] Questier, *C&C*, p. 97.

[59] Richard Broughton, *English Protestants Plea, and Petition, for English Preists and Papists, to the present Court of Parlament*... (n.p. [St Omer], 1621), pp. 45–6.

154 CATHOLICS AND TREASON

betrayed by an ultra-loyalist Catholic inside the Howard affinity, the priest Edward Grately, who served as a kind of point man for those of his co-religionists who felt that the Catholic community was now taking an ideological wrong turn.[60] This led to the incarceration of members of Arundel's circle and to a spate of rumours that they would surreptitiously be done away with by poison and other means. Among them was the earl of Northumberland. Though he was not exactly a martyr, Northumberland, who was Arundel's friend, was found in his prison cell in the Tower on 21 June 1585 with three bullets in him. The official, if not necessarily convincing, line (the ambassador Bernardino de Mendoza said it was frankly 'hard to believe') was that he had decided to shoot himself because he had already been ruined by the confessions of his client William Shelley. The regime's spokesmen had to work quite vigorously to refute those 'that report maliciously of the proceedings against the earl of Northumberland'. Robert Southwell said later, in December 1588, that the earl of Arundel was imprisoned in the Tower in the same place as Northumberland 'was slain, not as the story goes, by his own hand but by the criminal act of a hangman concealed there, who entered by a secret passageway'.[61]

But, as the regime finally geared up for all-out war in Flanders, that is, after the assassination of William of Orange in mid-1584, the sense is that, in order to create something like national unity, the bloodletting at home had to stop; or at least it was potentially unwise to give the impression that the queen's government was engaging in anything like a full-scale persecution. This would explain, first, the deportations and then the passing of an *in terrorem* statute which might dissuade the deported priests from coming back.

The extent to which the queen's and/or council's strategy was working can be gauged from Allen's sounding off in a letter to his friend Alfonso Agazzari of 2/12 June 1585 that no one (abroad) was taking the English persecution seriously. Even the pope 'was not well informed about English affairs'. What more could be done even after 'so many books written about the persecution, the martyrs, the institution of the colleges and the sending of priests' and after 'so much blood shed before the whole world, from so many and such cruel writings and public laws published against our and your efforts'?[62] Allen enclosed a copy of the recent statute against Catholic seminary clergy and urged Agazzari: 'I hope that you will see to the transcribing of this cruel statute in an Italian hand' and show it 'to our

---

[60] *CSPSp 1580–6*, p. 537; Renold, *LWA*, p. 161; Pollen and MacMahon, *VPH*, pp. 99–113, esp. at p. 109.

[61] *CSPSp 1580–6*, p. 542; L. Hicks, *An Elizabethan Problem: Some Aspects of the Careers of Two Exile-Adventurers* (1964), pp. 26–7; *HMCS*, XIII, pp. 270–81; McCoog, *LRS*, pp. 191–2. For Charles Paget's denial in mid-July 1585 of the regime's case against Northumberland, see *CSPSc 1585–6*, pp. 28–9. William Shelley was himself put on trial in February 1586: Hicks, *An Elizabethan Problem*, pp. 46f; BL, Lansdowne MS 45, no. 75, fos 164^r–75^r. Arundel refused to conform despite the persuasions of Lord Henry Howard and others that he should do so: Pollen and MacMahon, *VPH*, pp. 150–1.

[62] Renold, *LWA*, p. 153.

CATHOLIC MARTYRS AND THE POLITICAL CRISES OF THE MID-1580S   155

patrons', especially to the Jesuit superior general Claudio Acquaviva.[63] One of Walsingham's informants wrote from Paris on 4/14 June that there had recently been 'printed the book of the popish rebellious martyrs of England', produced in the residence of Michel de Monchy, an associate of the bishop of Ross and also of Robert Persons. Paris itself now echoed to the thundering noise of sermons against Elizabeth.[64] Nevertheless, Dr Allen, for one, evidently did not think that the noise was loud enough. On 23 June/3 July 1585, Allen wrote again in fury to Agazzari in order to deny the 'rumours about the lessening of the persecution in England, which I understand are current there [in Rome]'.[65]

The first cleric to be arraigned after the passage of the new law was none other than Thomas Alfield, although he was in fact charged under 23 Eliz., c. 2, that is, the act against 'seditious words and rumours uttered against the queen's most excellent majesty'. The informer Thomas Dodwell had volunteered evidence against him, as against other clergy and their patrons. On Dodwell's account, Alfield, like several others, deserved to be 'apprehended with as much speed as may be', for such people withdrew 'more subjects from their obedience towards her Majesty than any in England of equal number'.[66] Alfield had been arrested (again) in September 1584. His indictment stated that he had distributed between 500 and 600 copies of Allen's *True, Sincere, and Modest Defence* in the parish of All Saints, Bread Street.[67] He was arraigned and convicted in the first week of July 1585, along with Thomas Webley and William Crab.[68] But it was not just the formal content of Allen's book which was at issue. On 30 March 1585 Alfield had been extensively grilled about the duke of Guise's 'taking of arms...against the French king'. He was asked whether he had heard that Guise, 'after he has got his purpose in France, shall be employed either in Scotland or England'. His

---

[63] Renold, *LWA*, pp. 154, 155.

[64] *CSPF 1584–5*, pp. 524–5 (the identity of the book in question is uncertain—Gerard Kilroy has suggested to me that it could be Verstegan's *Descriptiones*). For Michel de Monchy, who was archdeacon of Rouen, see J. Bossy, 'The Heart of Robert Persons', in T. M. McCoog (ed.), *The Reckoned Expense: Edmund Campion and the Early English Jesuits* (Woodbridge, 1996), pp. 141–58, at p. 144; Bossy, *EC*, pp. 82–4, 90; V. Houliston, 'Why Robert Persons would not be Pacified: Edmund Bunny's Theft of *The Book of Resolution*', in McCoog, *The Reckoned Expense*, pp. 159–78, at p. 162; for de Monchy's role in the formulation of the 1582 Guisite project to launch an invasion of the British Isles, see S. Carroll, *Noble Power during the French Wars of Religion: The Guise Affinity and the Catholic Cause in Normandy* (Cambridge, 1998), p. 189.

[65] Renold, *LWA*, p. 161. A correspondent of Mary Stuart, writing from France, claimed on 14/24 October 1585 that 'many English[men] with certain intelligence which they have at Rome and in England spread abroad the bruit that' Elizabeth was, 'for the present, very benign and clement, and that she no longer prosecutes anyone for the Catholic religion': *CSPSc 1585–6*, pp. 146, 147.

[66] Foley, *RSJ*, VI, p. 726 (PRO, SP 12/168/35, fo. 84ᵛ).

[67] Kilroy, *EC*, p. 372; Pollen, *UD*, pp. 112, 114. Ralph Emerson was arrested in Bishopsgate on the day that Alfield was indicted; Emerson was in charge of a consignment of copies of 'Leicester's Commonwealth' which he had brought in from Norwich: Kilroy, *EC*, p. 372; Caraman, *WW*, pp. 1–3, 7–8.

[68] Anstr., I, p. 3; E. H. Burton and J. H. Pollen (eds), *Lives of the English Martyrs*, 2nd series (1914), I, pp. 151–63; *The Life and End of Thomas Awfeeld a S. P. and Thomas Webley a Dyers Servant in London...Executed at Tyburn 6 July 1585 (1585)*, sig. Aiiiiᵛ, Avʳ.

156 CATHOLICS AND TREASON

interrogators also wanted to know whether he had a commission 'from the English Catholics in France to put the Catholics in England in hope of deliverance by the duke of Guise with the assistance of the pope and the king of Spain', and whether he knew of 'a plot laid for the depriving of the king of Navarre of his succession'. Did Henry III have 'secret intelligence with the duke of Guise'? Also, what was being done to get the Scottish queen out of her prison? And what 'plot' was there for the 'changing of religion in Scotland' and what did he believe about King James VI's 'religion'? And what was the Jesuit William Holt doing in Scotland? Exactly how Alfield was supposed to know about all these issues was not clear. But it looks as if the idea was to connect his pamphleteering firmly with the rise of the Holy League in France and the new phase of the French succession crisis and its implications for the British Isles.[69]

Alfield, in his own defence, admitted that he had imported Allen's book. But he asserted that it was 'a loyal book, a lawful book, a good and a true book' and that it had been printed in Paris 'under the king's privilege'. It was regarded as 'a good and a lawful book throughout all the universities in Christendom beyond the seas'. Moreover, 'it touched nothing but matters of religion'.[70] The Latin indictment was read out in the court (twice, in fact) and cited long passages of Allen's pamphlet. The jury was asked to peruse the indictment and the book itself.[71] The formal task of replying to Allen's work was allotted to Thomas Bilson and his answer came out in the following year.[72]

The significance of the Alfield case can be gauged also from the regime pamphlet published against him. It said that he had stirred up the populace in London to sedition. This pamphlet had been put into print in order to refute those who said that Alfield's death 'was only for conscience's sake'. Alfield and his associates had imported and dispersed seditious books, and indeed he was guilty under the 1585 statute and 'deserved a sharper punishment' as in 'cases of high treason'. Thomas Webley and William Crab had been favourers of 'the Gospel' until they were turned by Alfield. Furthermore, Alfield dealt so far with Webley and Crab, whom he perverted, that 'he brought them acquainted at Throckmorton's house with one of his servants...to which place they often did repair'.[73] At the gallows, Alfield

---

[69] For the interrogation of Alfield, see Pollen, *UD*, pp. 106–8 (PRO, SP 12/169/42); see also PRO, SP 12/179/61, fo. 123^{r-v}. Edmund Rainolds, the brother of the Catholic exile William Rainolds and of the Oxford puritan divine John Rainolds, was detained and questioned in Oxford because he had received books from Alfield (Allen's reply to Burghley and William Rainolds's own reply to Whitaker): Pollen, *UD*, pp. 108–9 (PRO, SP 12/178/36, fo. 83^{r-v}).

[70] Pollen, *UD*, p. 118 (BL, Lansdowne MS 45, no. 74).

[71] Pollen, *UD*, pp. 112–17 (BL, Lansdowne MS 33, no. 58), 118–19 (BL, Lansdowne MS 45, no. 74); Ward, *LT*, p. 187. Ward comments that indictments had 'propaganda value' and often incorporated 'highly elaborate preambles': Ward, *LT*, p. 170.

[72] Thomas Bilson, *The True Difference betweene Christian Subiection and Unchristian Rebellion...* (1585); Lake, *BQB*, pp. 219–25.

[73] *The Life and End*, sig. Aiii^r, Aiiii^r, Aiiii^v, Av^v–vi^r. William Crab appears to have offered to conform: Pollen, *UD*, p. 105; but, for his arrest at Chichester with Henry Webley in April 1586 as they

CATHOLIC MARTYRS AND THE POLITICAL CRISES OF THE MID-1580S   157

and Webley rejected the prayers of any except Catholics. Again, Alfield offered to 'justify' Allen's text, but he claimed to be a loyal subject of the queen.[74]

At exactly this moment, Elizabeth was being dragged, metaphorically kicking and screaming, into a military confrontation with Spain. Anjou's failure in Flanders had already convinced some Protestants that a politique axis for opposing Philip II in the Netherlands (William of Orange had done his best to preserve a cross-confessional alliance against Philip II) was inadequate. What was required was a full-scale league based on shared Protestant values.[75] It is easy to see how an already potentially separatist Catholicism in England might be radicalized by this drift inside the regime away from the queen's own previous inclinations. A combination of the coming of war, the reaction in France to the possible succession of a Protestant, and, in England, the moves, including the bond of association, to divert the succession away from Mary Stuart inevitably provoked Catholic opinion. For all William Allen's complaints that no one really gave a damn about the sufferings of his co-religionists in England, the rise in France of a radical Catholic critique of the exercise of monarchical power now created a sympathetic audience for the sufferings of English Catholics.

While Thomas Alfield was the only Catholic cleric to suffer in the metropolis in 1585 (and not even under the most recent legislation), in York the authorities availed themselves almost immediately of the new statutory powers against Catholic seminary clergy and their patrons.[76] The first victims of the 1585 statute were Marmaduke Bowes and the priest Hugh Taylor. Taylor was, wrote John Mush, arrested by Lord Eure 'when he searched a Catholic man's house'. At the same time, said Mush, 'they murdered a secular gentleman', Bowes, 'for harbouring the same priest long before he was apprehended in another man's house'. Bowes was detained and released on bail before appearing at York on the charge of harbouring. Bowes and Taylor were both put to death—Taylor on 26 November 1585 and, as Mush recorded, Bowes on the following day.[77] Taylor was, said Mush, executed on the Friday in order to forestall open public dissent. The 'time wherein they intend to murder us is kept as secret and unknown as may be...ever

---

with others were trying to get to France, see *Miscellanea II* (1906), pp. 242, 244, 251, 254; *AWCBC*, pp. 663–5.

[74] *The Life and End*, sig. Avii^r–viii^r.

[75] Adams, PC, pp. 40f; *CSPF 1584–5, passim*.

[76] Ward notes that the council in the North was granted 'discretionary power to oversee the legal proceedings' against seminary clergy under the 1585 statute: Ward, LT, p. 89.

[77] Anstr., I, p. 345; Challoner, *MMP*, p. 107; *AWCBC*, pp. 173, 175–6; Morris, *TCF*, III (YRR), p. 84; Morris, *TCF*, III (TR), p. 367; Ward, LT, p. 274 (noting that they may have been condemned by the council in the North rather than by the assize judges). For the construction of and sources for Challoner's account, see *AWCBC*, p. 202. For the contemporary and subsequent accounts of the charges against Taylor and Bowes (it seems that the indictments were both under the 1585 statute, but other offences, i.e. denying the royal supremacy and, in Taylor's case, having faculties to absolve, were mentioned by way of addition during the trial proceedings), see *AWCBC*, pp. 174, 205, 207; for the statement by Thomas Worthington that Bowes had spoken against the royal supremacy, see AAW, B 28, no. 10, p. 299.

158   CATHOLICS AND TREASON

choosing such times as the people will least suspect any such thing'; and thus 'they condemned Mr Hugh Taylor one Friday with the felons and, within two or three hours after, murdered him, and reserved the other condemned prisoners until Saturday'.[78] The dumbshow of official violence and retribution was intensified by the speed with which the State's Catholic victims were almost literally rushed from their trials to the gallows.

Challoner recycles the story that Bowes had been determined, if he could, to free Taylor.[79] Bowes's bluff Yorkshire outspokenness rebounded on him when he rode to the York assizes and demanded the release of the cleric.[80] It was known that Bowes was a conformist, that is, a so-called church papist. Much later, Lady Grace Babthorpe remembered that Bowes was 'a good schismatic'.[81] As Thomas Dodwell had put it in early 1584, 'the schismatics who come to church and yet in heart are papists' were the ones who did 'most mischief, having dispensation to entertain priests when many recusants do not for fear of the penal statutes'.[82] It looks as if Mr Bowes was used as a kind of test case by the northern authorities in order to demonstrate that cosy semi-conformist patron-priest arrangements should not stand in the face of the new laws against Catholics. Mush said that the northern council members' 'malice was so great against' Bowes, 'and they so vehemently thirsted for his blood', that the inadequacy of the evidence offered against him (by Martin Harrison, a tutor in his household) made no difference. The council judged 'it to be convenient and necessary for the politic maintaining' of 'their tyrannical State that now and then they murder some, though unjustly, for the terrifying of the country'. Despite this, Mush believed that 'this cruel fact was loathsome and horrible to the country'. It may well be that the authorities had expected Bowes to conform again in some way. But he did no such thing: 'before his death he was made a member of the Catholic Church, the which he boldly confessed with great alacrity of mind, lamenting that he had lived in schism so long, and without fear of death desired not to live any longer, but that his death might be some part of satisfaction for his schismatic dissembling past'.[83]

Mush evidently saw in Bowes's case a foreshadowing of the suffering and death of Mush's own patron and friend, the separatist Margaret Clitherow.[84]

---

[78] Morris, TCF, III (YRR), p. 96.

[79] Challoner, MMP, pp. 106–7; AAW, A IV, no. 22, p. 127 (AWCBC, p. 220).

[80] AAW, A IV, no. 22, p. 127.

[81] AWCBC, p. 217, printing the relevant section of AAW, A VI, no. 100, p. 368; the transcript in Morris, TCF, I, p. 244, has 'a poor schismatic'.

[82] Foley, RSJ, VI, p. 726 (PRO, SP 12/168/35, fo. 84ᵛ).

[83] Challoner, MMP, pp. 106–7; Morris, TCF, III (YRR), pp. 84–5; Morris, TCF, III (TR), p. 367.

[84] Lake and Questier, Trials, pp. 87–8, citing Morris, TCF, III (YRR), pp. 84–5, (TR) 365–7; for Mush's authorship of the relevant passages in the so-called 'Yorkshire Recusant's Relation' (Morris, TCF, III (YRR), pp. 65–102), see AWCBC, pp. 193–4; Dodd, CH, II, p. 115. Mush asserted, in fact, that the Clitherow case was brought by the council in the North in response to criticisms of its own handling of the Bowes case. Allegedly, the assize judge Francis Rhodes 'reprehended the council for that unjust part against Mr Bowes, saying that by law they did great wrong, and ought not to have condemned him

CATHOLIC MARTYRS AND THE POLITICAL CRISES OF THE MID-1580S 159

Figure 6.1 The Execution of Margaret Clitherow (reproduced from Richard Challoner, *Martyrs of the Catholic Faith* (1878)).

(See Figure 6.1.) Mush's narrative of her life can be read simply as a record of social and religious dysfunction in the city of York. But there are echoes here also of a sense that harsh punishment of separatist Catholics was one of the devices via which the Protestant opponents of Mary Stuart were looking to ensure that the succession, in the event of Elizabeth's death, went to a stop-Mary-Stuart candidate, namely the earl of Huntingdon. Huntingdon, who was lord president of the council in the North, was the brother-in-law of the earl of Leicester. As is well known, this perception was given vent by the publication of the companion piece to Allen's *True, Sincere, and Modest Defence*, that is, the pamphlet popularly known as 'Leicester's Commonwealth', which had been put out in summer 1584.[85]

---

upon the evidence of an infamous person'. They 'turned the matter' upon the assize judges by 'earnestly labouring them to execute more shameful judgment' on Clitherow on the strength of one arguably inadequate witness 'than they themselves had done before against Mr Bowes', though it appears that Rhodes needed little encouragement to see Mrs Clitherow convicted: Morris, *TCF*, III (TR), pp. 438–9; *AWCBC*, p. 186; cf. K. Longley, 'The "Trial" of Margaret Clitherow', *Ampleforth Journal* 75 (1970), pp. 334–64, at p. 345. In the first edition of Lake and Questier, *Trials*, I have in error referred to Francis Rhodes as John Rhodes.

[85] *The Copie of a Leter, Wryten by a Master of Arte of Cambridge*...(n.p. [Paris?], 1584); D. C. Peck (ed.), *Leicester's Commonwealth: The Copy of a Letter Written by a Master of Art of Cambridge* (1984)

160   CATHOLICS AND TREASON

It was rooted in the sense of disillusion among the exiles in France after the failure of the queen's dynastic policy in the later 1570s. The informer Richard Lacey, in the course of a detailed report of March 1584 on the words of the priest and future martyr Montford Scott, said that 'the papists' were saying that, among others, Leicester and John Stubbs were 'most cruel tyrants against all Catholics'. The 'papists' cursed them and hoped for the day when 'the Protestants' should get what was coming to them and 'especially...these arch-heretics' who would 'then go to the pot'.[86] It was remembered that the priest Francis Ingleby, who also served as a chaplain to Mrs Clitherow, had a low opinion of the earl of Leicester.[87]

Technically the recently released 'Leicester's Commonwealth' was a loyalist pamphlet. It protested that anyone with a real concern for Elizabeth's safety would want to stop the puritan coup against her, which would start almost inevitably if Mary Stuart were to be assassinated. But this Catholic analysis of the sins of the earl of Leicester could just as easily be taken as a bitterly hostile critique of Elizabeth herself because she had signally failed to correct the vices and evils of her corrupt court.[88]

The reworked text of Nicholas Sander's excoriating *De Origine ac Progressu Schismatis Anglicani* was published in 1585, and then it appeared again, after more rewriting, in 1586, and subsequently in further editions.[89] The most recent and authoritative account of its ideological structure comes from Peter Lake. He shows that it represents a systemic shift in Catholic political thought away from blaming evil counsellors and into a direct attack on the queen herself. Sander had died in Ireland in 1581, in the aftermath of the failed rebellion there. But the continuation of his book now extended his censure of Henry VIII into an assault on Elizabeth. It denounces the recent persecution and especially the statute passed in the 1585 parliament.[90] The 1586 version expanded on the 1585 edition's description of Elizabeth's cruelties. It is as if Sander's text has simply been merged with material from Allen's own recent *Briefe Historie* and from other publications, for

---

and Related Documents (Athens, Ohio, 1985), pp. 5, 25 f. (a discussion of the authorship of the piece); S. Adams, 'Favourites and Factions at the Elizabethan Court', in S. Adams, *Leicester and the Court: Essays on Elizabethan Politics* (Manchester, 2002), pp. 46–67, at pp. 49–50.

[86] Pollen, *UD*, pp. 72–3 (PRO, SP 12/169/19, fos 30ᵛ–1ʳ); Anstr., I, p. 303. Richard Lacey, brother of the future martyr Brian Lacey, claimed that he was put out of Sir Edward Suliard's service because he regarded Roman Catholicism as a 'bloody religion': Pollen, *UD*, p. 73; Anstr., I, p. 303. For the search for Scott, ordered by the privy council in January/February 1584, see *CSPD Addenda 1580–1625*, pp. 104–5 (PRO, SP 15/28/57, 58, fo. 126ʳ).

[87] Lake and Questier, *Trials*, p. 85.

[88] For 'Leicester's Commonwealth', see Lake, *BQB*, pp. 116–32, and *passim*.

[89] See C. Reutcke, 'The Popish Invasion: Reception and Uses of Nicholas Sander's *Schismatis Anglicani* during the Long Reformation (1585–1688)' (MLitt, St Andrews, 2014).

[90] Lake, *BQB*, ch. 11; Nicholas Sander, *Doctissimi Viri Nicolai Sanderi, de Origine ac Progressu Schismatis Anglicani, Liber*...(Cologne [imprint false, printed at Rheims], 1585); Nicholas Sander, *Nicolai Sanderi de Origine ac Progressu Schismatis Anglicani Libri Tres*...(Rome, 1586); ARCR, I, nos 972–1011. For the role of the deported priest Edward Rishton in seeing the book into print, see Ward, *LT*, p. 270.

CATHOLIC MARTYRS AND THE POLITICAL CRISES OF THE MID-1580S   161

example, the *Concertatio Ecclesiae Catholicae*.[91] The martyrological record is brought up to date with the deaths of Marmaduke Bowes and Hugh Taylor and also of Edward Stransham and Nicholas Woodfen (see below).[92] There was a continuum now, stretching forward to the present time from the sacrifice made in the mid-1530s by Sir Thomas More and Bishop John Fisher. All of this, Professor Lake notes, is combined with a 'point-by-point refutation of the official justification for the intervention in the Low Countries'. Sander's book incorporates an attack on Leicester for, among other things, his role in the Netherlands project. Since it was written in Latin and then was translated into French, it was clearly designed for a Continental/French audience as much as, and perhaps more than, for an English one. It was a dire warning about the potentially disastrous future for the French nation if the heretic Henry of Navarre was allowed to take the French crown.[93]

It was probably no coincidence that the number of clergy and their patrons who came under the gun now started to increase. In early 1586 the priest Nicholas Woodfen was put on trial. He had worked at one time for the separatist Swithin Wells.[94] According to the informer Dodwell, Woodfen had been an associate of Thomas Alfield and, with Alfield, he had actively persuaded the queen's subjects to withdraw their obedience.[95] Woodfen was hanged, with Edward Stransham, at Tyburn on 21 January 1586. Woodfen had, however, also served the Browne family at Cowdray, the head of which, the first Viscount Montague, was regarded as a loyalist. The first viscount's brother, Francis Browne, had helped to guarantee Woodfen a living of sorts.[96] It may be that the authorities were now trying to send explicit messages to Catholic patrons, even the loyalists, that they should absolutely not have anything to do with such clergy.[97]

---

[91] See, e.g., Sander, *De Origine* (1586), p. 470. Both the 1585 and 1586 editions incorporated a justification of Allen's *True, Sincere, and Modest Defence*; see Nicholas Sander, ed. and trans. D. Lewis, *Rise and Growth of the Anglican Schism*...(1877), pp. 334 f.

[92] Sander, *De Origine* (1586), pp. 498 f. (*AWCBC*, p. 199). The additional material is directly attributable to Robert Persons and William Allen: ARCR, I, no. 973; Lake, *BQB*, p. 257.

[93] Lake, *BQB*, p. 277; Sander, *De Origine* (1586), p. 491. Henry III was during this period virtually forced into an alliance with Navarre and this made aspects of the English Catholic martyr tradition even less welcome at the French court. In July 1586 the ambassador Sir Edward Stafford easily persuaded Henry III to imprison the distributors of 'a book which is again printed and published here of the execution of Campion and other priests and the queen's cruelty': *CSPF June 1586–June 1588*, p. 48.

[94] Anstr., I, p. 385; Pollen, *UD*, p. 129 (BL, Harleian MS 360, fo. 35^r); Challoner, *MMP*, pp. 112, 591.

[95] Foley, *RSJ*, VI, p. 726 (PRO, SP 12/168/35, fo. 84^v).

[96] Challoner, *MMP*, p. 112; AAW, A III, no. 59, pp. 239–40; ABP, pp. 325–6; Questier, *C&C*, p. 315. Richard Davies (stationed with Lady Tresham in Tothill Street) had obtained an abode for Woodfen (they were both from Leominster) in Fleet Street when he first arrived in London: Challoner, *MMP*, p. 112; *AWCBC*, pp. 221–2, 224, 235–6. Davies had been an associate of Campion and Persons: *Miscellanea II*, p. 274. For Davies's narratives of martyrs compiled during Bishop Richard Smith's fact-finding mission of the mid-1620s, see, e.g., AAW, A IV, no. 1, p. 1 (concerning Richard Dibdale and others); pp. 461–2 n.46 below.

[97] Stransham may have been betrayed by Walsingham's most successful mole Thomas Rogers (alias Nicholas Berden), with whom Stransham came back to England in July 1585: Anstr., I, p. 337; Pollen, *UD*, p. 122; *CSPF 1584–5*, p. 716 (part printed, from the version in the additional State Papers series,

162 CATHOLICS AND TREASON

Richard Sergeant was hanged at Tyburn on 20 April 1586, along with William Thompson.[98] Thompson appears to have been among those involved with the Jesuit William Weston in the notorious exorcisms of 1585–6 when Weston tried to cast out evil spirits from the bodies of various demoniacs. Thompson had been a chaplain to the future martyr Anne Line.[99] Robert Anderton and William Marsden were executed on 25 April 1586, five days after Sergeant and Thompson. They were both from Lancashire but were arrested on the Isle of Wight, where their ship had been driven to dock because of a storm. They had a case under the extant law that the number of days they had been within the queen's dominions was not enough to permit them to be charged with treason under the 1585 statute. But they were obvious enough targets in other respects. Marsden may have assisted the polemicist William Rainolds with his published works, notably against William Whitaker. Anderton was a noted orator. He had been Allen's choice to deliver an address to the French notables who, in April 1583, visited the seminary college in Rheims.[100]

William Warford's narrative of the trial of Marsden and Anderton stresses that the local bishop, Thomas Cooper of Winchester, subjected them at the assizes to a tirade about papal authority. Cooper even cited the scandalous alleged reign of the so-called Pope Joan. This led the two priests to ask whether he had a problem with Elizabeth Tudor being 'head' of the Church in England. 'Surely whether we call her Pope Joan or Pope Elizabeth matters little.' Despite this, and despite the jury finding the two clerics guilty, the lord chief justice refused to proceed to sentence and said that he would have to refer himself to London. The fact was that they had indeed not been in the country for a sufficient time before arrest in order to allow a prosecution under the 1585 treason statute. They had also adopted an explicitly loyalist front towards their interrogators. They were transferred to London on 10 March. The privy council register entry of 16 March 1584 records

PRO, SP 15/29/39, fo. 54r; Pollen and MacMahon, *VPH*, p. 78). Although Stransham had been associated in England with Robert Persons's enemy Jasper Heywood (who himself had been deported in 1585), Stransham's name came up also in connection with the conveying of communications to Francis Throckmorton in the Tower: Pollen, *AEM*, p. 254; Pollen, *UD*, pp. 121, 124 (PRO, SP 12/180/32, fo. 74v). Stransham was also the carrier of the formal opinion of the future Cardinal Toledo concerning the unlawfulness of attending Protestant churches: Pollen, *UD*, pp. 121–2. For Rogers's capacity to insinuate himself into Catholics' confidence, see, e.g., *Miscellanea II*, p. 275.

[98] Anstr., I, p. 305; Ward, LT, p. 275. Sergeant and Thompson were tried on 18 April: *AWCBC*, p. 244. Thompson was arrested at the residence of Robert Bellamy (at Harrow), who was, however, not tried for harbouring but instead under the 1581 statute for the offence of hearing Mass. Bellamy subsequently absconded from gaol and 'fled into Scotland and so into Germany': Ward, LT, p. 275; *AWCBC*, pp. 244, 248, 265.

[99] Anstr., I, p. 351; F. W. Brownlow, *Shakespeare, Harsnett and the Devils of Denham* (1993), p. 170; Caraman, *JG*, p. 83; *AWCBC*, pp. 244, 260; Challoner, *MMP*, p. 258.

[100] Pollen, *AEM*, pp. 67, 68 (ABSJ, Collectanea M, p. 134a–b); Anstr., I, pp. 8–9, 218; AAW, A III, no. 64, pp. 253–5 ('Ad Praecipuos Prelatos...'); Ward, LT, pp. 276–8; William Rainolds, *A Refutation of sundry Reprehensions...by which M. Whitaker Laboureth to Deface the late English Translation...of the New Testament* (Paris, 1583). Rainolds later wrote a work of leaguer political theory, his *De Iusta Reipub. Christianae in rrges* [*sic*] *Impios...* (Paris, 1590).

CATHOLIC MARTYRS AND THE POLITICAL CRISES OF THE MID-1580S   163

the order for their interrogation 'concerning their obedience and subject-like duty to her Majesty and the State' to see if they remained 'constant in the faithful protestations' which they had made 'before the justices at the assizes at the time of their arraignment'.[101] In principle the council was prepared to take them at their word, that is, if they would subscribe those 'faithful protestations'. The problem was that the people deputed to determine this issue were the far-from-sympathetic Robert Bennett and the civil lawyer John Hammond. By April there had been extracted sufficient treasonable matter to finish the two priests off. They were taken back down to the coast and across to the Isle of Wight, where they were hanged on 25 April.[102] The council used a royal proclamation to advertise and explain the trial and execution of these clergymen. They had been indicted under the new statute.[103] The council sent to Sir George Carey a declaration (presumably the proclamation itself) to be 'publicly read and published', so 'that the people may understand the cause and reasons of their reprieve and what has moved her Majesty to suffer the judgment of the law to be executed upon them, to which end direction is given to the sheriff to cause divers copies thereof to be set up and fixed in public places to the view of the people'.[104] The proclamation intimates that Anderton had got close to some form of compliance, but neither priest would agree not to meddle with the queen's subjects 'in matters of religion', which, the proclamation said, showed their bad intent despite their outwardly loyalist statements.[105]

As we have seen, the council in the North was already running its own discipline-and-punish programme against leading Catholic clergy and their friends in and around York. One notorious outcome of this was the intended

[101] Pollen, *AEM*, pp. 70–3; *APC 1586–7*, p. 33. For William Warford's martyrology (the original is AAW, A IV, no. 12, pp. 65–84, and Grene's copy is ABSJ, Collectanea M, pp. 131ᵇ–43ᵃ), see Pollen, *AEM*, pp. 249–78; *AWCBC*, p. 294. Anderton had taught Warford the Hebrew language: Pollen, *AEM*, p. 69. Later, in 1599, Warford tried to persuade the priest John Cecil (who, ironically, had informed on him back in 1591) not to reply to a published defence of James VI written by William Creighton. Warford urged Cecil that he should write rather against Calvin, Luther, Rainolds, or Whitaker than 'against a poor Jesuit'. Warford asked whether there were not 'in England, Topleys [i.e. Topcliffes], tyrants and termagants, against whom you may write whole philippics, and fill all printers' shops with invectives': Sawyer, *WM*, I, p. 110; Anstr., I, p. 370. Warford's manuscript account of the English martyrs (up to William Spenser in 1589) may have been elicited from him (by Persons) as a way of trying to suppress divisions among the Catholic clergy, though in other respects Persons was happy enough to exacerbate them and, also, to reprove Creighton for his support for James VI.

[102] Anstr., I, p. 8. Hammond had prepared, for Burghley, prior to the publication of his *Execution of Justice*, two discourses on the question of excommunication of princes. Hammond was predictably an enemy of Whitgift's subscription campaign: Collinson, *EPM*, pp. 202, 257–8; see also *HMCS*, II, pp. 367–70; *ODNB, sub* Hammond, John (article by P. White).

[103] Ward points out that the proclamation was 'the first official announcement of the passage of the 1585 statute': Ward, LT, p. 277.

[104] *APC 1586–7*, pp. 57–8, 91–2; Hughes and Larkin, *TRP*, II, no. 680.

[105] Pollen, *AEM*, pp. 77–80; Hughes and Larkin, *TRP*, II, no. 680. Ward notes that, in the twelve months following the passing of the 1585 statute, ten seminary priests were executed but, since a further thirty-five had been arrested and gaoled, this left the authorities wondering, in June 1586, what to do about them: Ward, LT, pp. 278–9.

164 CATHOLICS AND TREASON

show trial, though in the end not a trial at all, of Margaret Clitherow. She had refused to plead to the new statutory charge of harbouring a seminary priest, that is, the felony offence defined by the 1585 statute. Her chaplain, Francis Ingleby, was arrested and was subsequently hanged at York on 3 June 1586. This was not long after Clitherow's own execution on 25 March 1586.[106] Had she agreed to comply with court procedure, she would have been charged with harbouring him and also John Mush. So controversial was the decision to take action against her that the judge on circuit, John Clench, would not consent to the carrying out of sentence on her, that is, the *peine forte et dure* for her refusal to plead. (See Figure 6.2.) Mush not only wrote the story of her life but also penned a damning prose indictment of what he saw as Huntingdon's violent and corrupt perversion of the queen's authority in the North. This was in fact a death-by-death local martyrology—a text which also described a kind of war against the people, waged through the new anti-Catholic statutes and all for the purpose of achieving something rather close to the political objectives of the earl of Leicester and his crew. Mush's text could easily have been entitled 'Huntingdon's Commonwealth'. The burden of the piece was that there was a puritan rebellion in the making and that, in the North, it was common knowledge that Huntingdon himself had been on the verge of revolt over the queen's project to marry the duke of Anjou.[107]

Once a deal had been done between Elizabeth and the Scottish king, namely the treaty signed at Berwick in July 1586, the regime in London had the green light to proceed against Mary Stuart, which it did by flushing out the conspiracy allegedly led by Anthony Babington.[108] The conspirators were executed in two batches, on 20 and 21 September 1586.[109] Several of those caught up in the plot had been assistants to the Jesuit William Weston when collectively they

[106] For Ingleby's arrest, allegedly more or less by chance, and for the differing narratives of it, see Pollen, *AEM*, p. 258; *AWCBC*, p. 271. Ingleby's brother David was the subject of intelligence reports on his links with Scottish Marians; see, e.g., *CSPSc 1586–8*, p. 196.

[107] Lake and Questier, *Trials*, p. 117 and ch. 6 *passim*; Morris, *TCF*, III (YRR), pp. 100–1; the Paris catalogue names only Ingleby as having been harboured by Clitherow: AAW, B 28, no. 10, p. 301.

[108] For the arrests made in connection with the conspiracy, see *Miscellanea II*, pp. 257–61. For the most recent rewriting of the regime's use of the Babington conspiracy as a vehicle to coerce Elizabeth into destroying Mary Stuart, see Lake, *BQB*, ch. 12.

[109] *CSPSc 1586–8*, pp. 25–9, 33–9. In the interim, on 11 August 1586, John Sandys had been butchered with appalling savagery at Gloucester. Paul Tracy, the Protestant sheriff, as we saw above, made absolutely sure that Sandys died in indescribable agony: Pollen, *AEM*, pp. 336–7 (ABSJ, Collectanea M, pp. 145ᵇ–6ª); pp. 62–3 above; *AWCBC*, pp. 323, 334–5, 339 (for martyr catalogues wrongly locating Sandys's execution in 1587). Sandys's arrest may have been the product primarily of local antagonism. A manuscript in the archive of the English College in Rome claims that Sandys had been tutor to the family of the admiral Sir William Winter before going abroad to be ordained. Sandys returned to the area and made contact with a local clergyman identified (in our source) as the 'dean of Lydney (a rural dean in that diocese)', whose enemies then secured Sandys's arrest. When Sandys was sentenced by the judge, Manwood, they protested that 'they never meant him harm but only to be revenged on the dean': *AWCBC*, pp. 321, 328–9, citing AVCAU, Scr. 21/2/2; *ODNB*, *sub* Winter, William (article by D. Loades). According to John Thorpe's notes, the Protestant clergy who were present 'exclaimed against' the 'inhuman dealing' used on Sandys: ABSJ, A V, no. 8 (unfoliated). The 'dean' of Lydney could be the vicar of Lydney, Thomas Turner, who had been cited in 1576 for his allegedly popish tendencies

Figure 6.2 Portrait of John Clench, justice of queen's bench (reproduced from an engraving by Wenceslaus Hollar, in Sir William Dugdale, *Origines Juridiciales* (1680)).

conducted the exorcisms in Buckinghamshire and the London area in 1585 and 1586.[110] John Ballard, who was condemned for Babington's conspiracy, had been associated with Weston as, of course, had Babington himself. Richard Dibdale, John Lowe, and John Adams, who were tried at the Old Bailey on a charge under the 1585 statute, probably on 7 October 1586, and were hanged together at Tyburn the next day, were named, after the event, as part of Weston's team of exorcists.[111]

---

and for immoral practices: N. Herbert (ed.), *A History of the County of Gloucester*... V (Oxford, 1996), p. 79. I am grateful to Kenneth Fincham for this suggestion.

[110] For a chronology of the exorcisms of 1585–6, see F. W. Brownlow, 'An Edition of Samuel Harsnet's *A Declaration of Egregious Popish Impostures*' (PhD, Birmingham, 1963), appendix I.

[111] Ward comments that 'little evidence survives to explain' why, of all the clergy imprisoned in London, these three should have been proceeded against, but she notices Dibdale's reputation as an exorcist: Ward, LT, p. 280. Thomas Dodwell had denounced Adams as one of those who persuaded the queen's subjects away from their obedience: Foley, *RSJ*, VI, p. 726 (PRO, SP 12/168/35, fo. 84^v). For doubts about whether Lowe and Adams actually took part in the exorcisms, see *AWCBC*, pp. 367, 370, 375, 376. After ordination, Dibdale had returned to England with Richard Sherwood, whose brother John was also one of the exorcists at Denham. Richard and John may have been relatives of the seminarist and martyr Thomas Sherwood (see pp. 92–3 above): *AWCBC*, p. 371. Dibdale was arrested on 24 July 1586 with two other priests, at Walsingham's direction, in Tothill Street in London, where Richard

166 CATHOLICS AND TREASON

Weston himself, after his arrest, had been a horrified witness to the violent popular response to the breaking of the alleged plot—'I heard the bells pealing all over the city', and the guard set to watch him told him it was a celebration of the 'capture of certain papists' who had plotted to kill Elizabeth and set up Mary Stuart in her place and, in addition, to make Weston himself bishop of London. From his window, Weston could see the celebratory bonfires in the street. Looking out towards the Thames, he could also see Catholic gentlemen, 'tied hand and foot', being ferried 'along the river, up and down between the Tower of London' and the law courts where they were put on trial. It was 'easy to notice when these men were taken along the river in boats, for you could pick them out by the uniforms and weapons of the soldiers'. He knew that they were being sentenced to death, and he believed that he himself would be tortured for information and subjected to the same eventual fate.[112]

Anthony Tyrrell, who had assisted at the public demon expulsion ceremonies conducted by Weston, accused Weston's clerical friends and fellow exorcists, along with others, of Babington's treason. Although Tyrrell claimed that the charge against Dibdale was conjuration, this was not treason as such. Other contemporary sources say that Dibdale, like the others, was indicted under the new statute.[113] Dibdale had been on government watch lists since the early 1580s at least. Though not yet ordained, he had already been arrested back in June–July 1580, presumably in the series of sweeps which were triggered by the knowledge that Campion and his friends were arriving in the country.[114] He was a chaplain in the house of the Lancashire gentleman Richard Bold. Bold had been sheriff of his county as late as 1576 but had fallen out with his patron, the earl of Leicester. Bold's household at Harleyford (Harlesford) in Buckinghamshire had welcomed the two Jesuits, Robert Southwell and Henry Garnet, in July 1586.[115] Bold had signed the bond of association in 1584, but he was, allegedly through Leicester's malice, imprisoned after the exposure of the Babington Plot. Bold played down

---

Davies was resident at a house belonging to the Tresham family; they were with the wife of Edmund Peckham, who had hosted the exorcisms: Morris, *TCF*, II, pp. 165–6; Anstr., I, p. 101; *AWCBC*, pp. 422–4. A hostile ballad against the three (Dibdale, Adams, and Lowe) was entered at the Stationers but has apparently not survived: *AWCBC*, p. 373. For Richard Davies's account of Dibdale, see Challoner, *MMP*, p. 117; AAW, A IV, no. 1, p. 1 (ABP, p. 341). Davies claimed that one of the demoniac maids exorcized by Dibdale became 'concubine to Bancroft, called archbishop of Canterbury, and had a child by him': AAW, A IV, no. 1, p. 1 (ABP, p. 341).

[112] Caraman, *WW*, pp. 81–4.

[113] Caraman, *WW*, p. 98, citing Morris, *TCF*, II, pp. 411–12. For Dibdale's indictment, see ABSJ, Collectanea M, p. 91ᵃ; Ward, *LT*, p. 298; *AWCBC*, pp. 372–3 (indictments of Lowe and Adams). For Tyrrell's accusations against Lowe and Adams, see *AWCBC*, pp. 368, 386–92; see also *CSPSc 1586–8*, pp. 31–3 (Tyrrell's confession of 21 September 1586). Dibdale 'at his death [was] charged by Topcliffe of conjuration, and that he did those things by delusion of the devil', which Dibdale vehemently denied: Pollen, *AEM*, p. 285 (Peter Penkevell's narrative: ABSJ, Collectanea B, pp. 1–5).

[114] Anstr., I, p. 101. Dibdale had been let out of the Gatehouse prison on 10 September 1582 and simply returned to Rheims: Anstr., I, p. 101.

[115] Caraman, *WW*, pp. 69–70, 76; McCoog, *SJ*, p. 173; M. Hodgetts, *Secret Hiding-Places* (Dublin, 1989), p. 5.

CATHOLIC MARTYRS AND THE POLITICAL CRISES OF THE MID-1580S   167

the antagonism between himself and the earl, but he was released only after Leicester's death.[116] Weston said that, after his own arrest, he was accused of having 'persuaded a certain gentleman', presumably Bold, 'to withdraw the military assistance he was giving to the earl of Leicester in the unjust war he was waging with the heretics of Flanders against the king of Spain'. The gentleman in question had provided a retinue of 'horses and men furnished at his own expense', and 'I had argued with him, so they said, and spoken at great length to demonstrate the injustice of that war'. Those in charge of the interrogation were well informed. They knew that Weston had preached in Bold's house 'before a group of gentlemen' and were aware of 'the text of Scripture on which' he 'had preached' and of 'sections and odd sentences from the sermon'. Weston conceded, though not to the interrogator, that 'a great part of what he said was true', even if it was mixed with untruth.[117] The clergy who were rounded up at this point, even if not directly involved in the madness of the Babington business, may have been associated with a kind of stop-the-war rhetoric which, in association with the cause of the Scottish queen, triggered the arrests and prosecutions which subsequently occurred.[118]

Some Catholics evidently had doubts about whether it was right or necessary to follow the same route to the bitter end. The priest John Hambley had been arrested at Chard in Somerset at Easter 1586 and was arraigned and sentenced under the 1585 statute at the Taunton assizes. He made a gesture at conformity and then absconded from prison.[119] He had then been retaken on 14 August 1586, that is, as the news of the Babington conspiracy was breaking. Hambley had on his own account been reconciled to Rome by the Babington plotter John Ballard. Four days later he signed a statement giving evidence against other clergy. He also, said John Piers, bishop of Salisbury on 20 August, was 'not so obstinate ... but he can be contented (so he may obtain mercy of her Majesty, and pardon for his life) to forsake the pope, come to the church and willingly follow her Majesty's proceedings, as he bears us in hand'. Hambley said that among those to whom he resorted in London was the ultra-loyalist priest William Tedder in the Marshalsea prison (Tedder recanted in 1588), who, even in early 1583, was already being suspiciously well treated, as William Allen thought. Another priest

---

[116] Caraman, WW, pp. 70–1, 76; for Bold's interrogation on 6 September 1586, see CSPSc 1585–6, pp. 698–701. One Mr Bold, identified by Simon Adams as Richard Bold, was part of Leicester's funeral procession from Kenilworth to Warwick on 10 October 1588: S. Adams (ed.), Household Accounts and Disbursement Books of Robert Dudley, Earl of Leicester, 1558–1561, 1584–1586 (Camden Society, 5th series, 6, Cambridge, 1995), p. 449.
[117] Caraman, WW, pp. 88–9, 95; CSPSc 1585–6, pp. 654, 699–700. Richard Bold was a cousin of Sir George Peckham, whose house hosted some of Weston's exorcisms: Caraman, WW, p. 76; McCoog, SJ, p. 174. In one prison list, of September 1586, Weston's name is annotated thus: 'promised to have been made a bishop', presumably if the alleged conspiracy had succeeded: Miscellanea II, p. 257.
[118] For William Weston's account of what the Babington conspiracy was, see Caraman, WW, ch. 12.
[119] Anstr., I, p. 144. Hambley said he had been persuaded to separate from the national Church by reading Robert Persons's Brief Discours: PRO, SP 12/192/46. i, fo. 71ʳ; AWCBC, pp. 516, 524–5.

168 CATHOLICS AND TREASON

whom Hambley visited in the same prison was Richard Norris, who, as we saw, had been involved in the spreading of Campion's 'brag' but who in February 1584 was one of the arraigned and convicted clergy who escaped death and, with known loyalists, was deported in January 1585. Hambley also attended a Mass where William Warmington was present—in the early seventeenth century Warmington came out publicly in favour of the controversial 1606 oath of allegiance.[120] Hambley had, of course, decided to train for ordination at Rheims. In the end, he withdrew his gesture of compliance; he was brutally dealt with at the next assizes at Salisbury.[121]

The Babington business was soon concluded, and Mary Stuart was now a dead queen walking. At this point, the hangings, even if not the quotidian harassment, of Catholic clergy in London temporarily stopped.[122] Back in the North, however, the authorities continued to use maximum force against the Catholic separatist core in and around the city of York. John Fingley was executed at the Knavesmire on 8 August 1586. He had probably conducted his ministry in the circle around Margaret Clitherow. Fingley's mother watched him being killed.[123] Other victims of the regime in York at that point were part of the same nexus of separatist Catholicism, for example Robert Bickerdike and Richard Langley.[124] Langley served as a patron to Margaret Clitherow's chaplain, John Mush.

---

[120] Anstr., I, pp. 144, 255, 347, 370–1; PRO, SP 12/192/46, 46. i, fos 70^r–5^r; AWCBC, pp. 518–34; William Warmington, A Moderate Defence of the Oath of Allegiance...(n.p. [London], 1612).

[121] Hambley was executed at Salisbury, probably in March 1587: AWCBC, p. 2578; see pp. 167–8 below.

[122] For those Catholics who were convicted of treason in 1585–6, see Ward, LT, pp. 297–8. Ward suggests that at this point the hardliners on the council were being blocked and simply kept deferring what to do with imprisoned clergy: Ward, LT, pp. 280–1. The draconian recommendations, made by e.g. Thomas Rogers, were not followed: Miscellanea II, pp. 272–6.

[123] Anstr., I, p. 117; AWCBC, pp. 306, 313–14 (AAW, F 1, p. 835). Fingley was indicted under the provisions of the 1585 statute, but the Paris catalogue entry added that he had said the queen was a heretic and that he had reconciled one Frances Webster: AAW, B 28, no. 10, p. 302; AWCBC, p. 306; AWCBC, pp. 2489, 2491; for the imprisonment and death in York Castle of Webster on 29 June 1585, see Morris, TCF, III (WHN), pp. 324–5.

[124] The date of Bickerdike's execution is said in some sources to have been 23 July 1586, but it may have been in early August 1586: AWCBC, pp. 363–4, 365. For the arrest and execution of Richard Langley (of Rathorpe Hall), see Pollen, AEM, pp. 225–7, 305–6; see also Lake and Questier, Trials, pp. 115–16. Bickerdike was suspected of aiding the priest John Boste: J. C. H. Aveling, Catholic Recusancy in York 1558–1791 (1970), p. 204; AWCBC, pp. 346–7; Lake and Questier, Trials, p. 231. In the later 1620s it was recorded that, in Bickerdike's case, the 'causa mortis' was that 'reconciliatus fuerit ecclesiae Catholicae, et haereticorum conventicula adire noluit', but 'damnatus ob verba (nimirum ex zelo religionis Catholicae prolata)', and, as the assize records (many of which, for the North, no longer exist) revealed, 'passus sit se a religione Protestantium abduci, et obedientiam pontifici Romano promisisset': AAW, B 28, no. 10, pp. 302, 363–4; AWCBC, p. 343. Mush had claimed that Bickerdike's eventual conviction, after, it seems, two acquittals, was procured by coercion of the jury. William Hutton said that it was based on a malicious accusation (that he had defended Francis Ingleby from the jibes of an unnamed minister's wife at the time of Ingleby's execution): AWCBC, pp. 292, 340–3, 349–54, 357–8, 361–2; Morris, TCF, III (YRR), pp. 90–2, (WHN) 310–11; for an analysis of these and other charges against him (aiding John Boste and speaking treasonable words), see AWCBC, pp. 340–2. After the conviction, 'some gentlemen, being in company with' the judge Francis Rhodes 'before he departed from Yorkshire', queried whether Bickerdike's words were really 'treason by any statute and law': Morris, TCF, III (YRR), p. 92. Bickerdike's sister was Bridget Maskew, who was subsequently a

CATHOLIC MARTYRS AND THE POLITICAL CRISES OF THE MID-1580S   169

Langley was hanged, for harbouring, on 1 December 1586. Catholic sources claimed that he had 'built a very well hidden house underground, which was a great place of refuge for priests during the persecution'.[125] This would explain the descent on Langley's residences on 27 October 1586. The raid led also to the arrest of John Mush and another priest. According to Mush the jury at Langley's trial had to be switched to prevent its members, who included Langley's 'honest neighbours', from acquitting him. The absconding of Mush and two other priests may have hastened Langley's execution.[126] Briefly in court Langley encountered the priest Alexander Crow and asked for his blessing. Crow had recently been arrested in the East Riding. He was tried by the council in the North and was hanged on 30 November 1586, one day before Langley.[127]

Robert Southwell had recently arrived from the Continent. On 21 December 1586, he wrote to Claudio Acquaviva and declared that, after the recent executions, the 'sacred blood is still warm, those wounds still open, and those bruises may still be seen, with which God redeemed the souls that we are tending'.[128] For Southwell, however, the onslaught of the enemy gave Catholicism in England a coherence which it had not had before. Or, rather, as he saw it, a sizeable section of contemporary society was now looking for a voice which he and his friends believed they could supply, even potentially at a terrible cost to themselves. 'You have "fishes" there' in Rome, he wrote to Alfonso Agazzari on 22 December 1586, which, in England, '"when disembowelled, are good for anointing to the eyes and [to] drive the devils away", while, if they live, "they are necessary for useful medicines" [Tobit 6:5–9]'.[129]

This identification of the blood of the martyrs as a source of spiritual healing found its way into contemporary martyrdom narratives. Diego de Yepes's text on English martyrs singled out a case in Hampshire of a man into whom a demon entered because he had been to church on just one occasion. But he was 'delivered by a Catholic priest, a prisoner for his faith who, having reconciled him by confession, and given him the holy communion, sent him home perfectly cured, giving him withal, as a defence against the devil, the cassock of another priest who

---

long-term prisoner in York Castle: *AWCBC*, pp. 354–5 (citing St Mary's College, Oscott, Collectanea E [formerly MS 98, now R11781], p. 259).

[125] Pollen, *AEM*, pp. 305–6.

[126] Morris, *TCF*, III (YRR), pp. 93–4; Pollen, *UD*, p. 314; *AWCBC*, pp. 381, 432, 436. Langley's daughter (Isabel Foster) was arrested and died in prison in December 1587: Morris, *TCF*, III (WHN), p. 326; Foley, *RSJ*, III, p. 735. The priest arrested with Mush may have been Cuthbert Johnson: *AWCBC*, p. 381. The two who absconded with Mush were, it seems, Johnson and Bernard Pattenson: Pollen, *AEM*, p. 306.

[127] For Crow's arrest at South Duffield, and his trial, see *AWCBC*, pp. 425–6, 431, 436, 448; cf. Lake and Questier, *Trials* (1st edition, 2011), p. 115. For Protestant claims that Crow had on the scaffold, in effect, attempted suicide, see Challoner, *MMP*, pp. 128–9; pp. 58–9, 59 n.61 above. (A number of authorities fix the date of Crow's death as November 1587, but northern sources unambiguously assign it to 30 November 1586, as does the Paris catalogue: AAW, B 28, no. 10, p. 303.)

[128] Pollen, *UD*, p. 313 (ABSJ, Collectanea P/ii, p. 510).

[129] Pollen, *UD*, p. 318 (ABSJ, Collectanea P/ii, p. 518).

170   CATHOLICS AND TREASON

had suffered martyrdom a little before'. This process could also work in reverse. Another individual, an Oxford student, was similarly freed from demons but, when he returned to the university, back the demons came. So 'that he might not lose his place which he enjoyed before in his college, he concealed his being a Catholic, and went to the Protestant service'. 'Shortly after' this, 'he hanged himself in despair'. This was a dreadful parody of true martyrdom. It came out of the diametric opposite of the peace of mind experienced by those who avoided the taint of heresy through imitating the example and following the counsel of God's priests.[130]

Southwell's argument was not necessarily accepted in its entirety by all other Catholics. A case in point is Anthony Tyrrell. Tyrrell had in the early 1580s been an associate of Thomas Bell, the northern missionary priest who fell out rather badly with Mush and his friends because Bell had argued that there was no point goading the queen's officials into harsh retaliation against Catholics over the issue of separation.[131] When Tyrrell was caught up in the Babington business, he betrayed almost every Catholic he knew. In prison, he vacillated over his faith.[132] While, for contemporary Catholics, renegades such as Tyrrell were the rats that joined the sinking ship of the national Church in England, they had ideological soulmates in seminarist clergymen such as Christopher Bagshaw, a critic of the hard-line Personsian justification of aggressive separatism and political resistance theory.[133] The regime must have sensed that, as the war against Spain escalated, some Catholics were finally going to be forced to choose one side or the other.[134] Among those who were involved in bringing down Mary Stuart were, of course, Catholics such as Gilbert Gifford and his friends, notably Edward Grately. Grately

[130] Challoner, MMP, pp. 118–19. For the use of the physical remains of Robert Sutton (d.27 July 1588) to cure a demoniac, see pp. 182–3 n.17 below.

[131] Lake and Questier, Trials, ch. 7 and passim.

[132] Anstr., I, p. 362. For the extant versions of Tyrrell's (Catholic) account of his wavering in religion, see AWCBC, pp. 382–4.

[133] Anstr., I, pp. 14–15; for Walsingham's 'good opinion' of Bagshaw, noted by another loyalist, Solomon Aldred, in April 1586, see CSPD Addenda 1580–1625, p. 175. For Bagshaw's enmity towards Persons at Balliol College in the 1570s, see A. Kenny, 'Reform and Reaction in Elizabethan Balliol, 1559–1588', in J. Prest (ed.), Balliol Studies (1982), pp. 17–51, esp. at pp. 28–32. There were ugly rumours in circulation about Bagshaw's release from gaol in London at some point after 20 July 1587. His arrest had occurred in connection with the search for Thomas Alfield. But Walsingham had intervened to free him: Anstr., I, pp. 14–15; PRO, SP 12/179/61; PRO, SP 12/182/3, 4; Renold, WS, pp. 325, 329; ABSJ, Collectanea M, p. 201ᵃ.

[134] In a letter of 27 May/6 June 1588, William Gifford expostulated to Humphrey Ely that Viscount Montague had spoken 'most cruelly against the queen of Scotland in the parliament before her death to have her executed': Pollen, UD, p. 143; BL, Lansdowne MS 96, no. 23, fo. 69ʳ; cf. Questier, C&C, p. 145. There is no other evidence that Montague did this (or even that he was present in the 1586 parliament); but Gifford, who erred in thinking that Montague had recently died, may have been referring to something that Montague had said while the trial commission was sitting on Mary's case at Fotheringhay; see also HMCL, V, p. 74.

CATHOLIC MARTYRS AND THE POLITICAL CRISES OF THE MID-1580S 171

and Gifford were reported in April 1586 to be ready to compose a pamphlet vindicating Elizabeth's proceedings against Catholics.[135]

Royal Martyrdom

The long campaign in England to exclude Mary Stuart from the succession ended with her being permanently barred in February 1587 by something that also looked very like a coup against Elizabeth herself, who, for so long, had tried to prevent precisely this.[136] The 1586–7 parliament's proceedings left Elizabeth little room for manoeuvre. From the provinces there had been a lobbying campaign to keep up the relentless pressure on the English queen. The earl of Huntingdon had reported from Newcastle on 18 November 1586 that 'this country was never in so bad terms since I did know it, as it is at this day'. While some Catholics, including even some of those who harboured seminary clergy, were conforming—to the extent that they came 'to the communion'—the leading northern seminarist John Boste had allegedly been saying that 'the day of triumph' would be 'on their side shortly' and, if that was the case, no one could doubt what he meant.[137]

The sentence of the trial commission was published on 3 December 1586. Elizabeth could not hold out. The result was the combination of farce and tragedy which put an end to the life of the queen of Scots at Fotheringhay on 8 February 1587. The French court had done almost nothing to intervene. The court in Edinburgh was determined to do very little either, apart from some ineffectual blustering after the event in order to gloss over the fact that King James VI had moved one step closer to the English crown.[138] As one memorandum put it in early 1587, there was a justified suspicion that James had cut Mary adrift even while making 'a show of entreating and working for her, but in truth for his reputation only, being glad his mother is out of the way, whom he greatly feared'.[139]

Challoner summarizes the weight of Catholic opinion since the time of the execution: 'as her constancy in the Catholic religion was the chief cause of her death, whatever might otherwise be pretended, so is she usually reckoned

---

[135] Read, MSW, II, p. 432; HMCS, III, p. 139; W. Murdin (ed.), A Collection of State Papers relating to Affairs in the Reign of Queen Elizabeth…from 1571 to 1596 (1759), pp. 510–12. For Gilbert Gifford's eventual delivery on his promise, by writing a reply to Allen's pamphlet defending Sir William Stanley's surrender of Deventer, see p. 177 n.166 below; see also CSPSc 1586–8, p. 202.

[136] Mary was proceeded against under 27 Eliz., c. 1; see Ward, LT, pp. 35–6.

[137] PRO, SP 15/29/157, fos 238ᵛ–9ʳ. For Boste, and his connections with Scotland, see CSPD Addenda 1580–1625, p. 163 (PRO, SP 15/29/62); Pollen, UD, p. 216 (BL, Lansdowne MS 75, no. 22); J. Bain (ed.), Calendar of Letters and Papers relating to the Affairs of the Borders of England and Scotland (2 vols, Edinburgh, 1894–6), I, p. 258; see pp. 239–40 below.

[138] Read, MSW, III, pp. 56–7.

[139] CSPSc 1586–8, p. 244. For James's admonition to Elizabeth of 26 January 1587 against killing Mary, see CSPSc 1586–8, pp. 247–8.

172 CATHOLICS AND TREASON

amongst those who suffered for religion'.[140] This was the case made by Robert Southwell in his poem 'Decease, release'—'Alive a queen, now dead I am a saint / Once Mary called, my name now martyr is'.[141]

In London there was wild rejoicing at Mary's demise. Thomas Pounde recalled how, while he was in the White Lion prison in Southwark, 'out of my window, I saw the bonfires and banquets in the streets' for Mary's death. A scornful 'justice' said to Pounde 'in derision, at [the] sight of her picture in my chamber, that he was sorry for the loss to all papists of so great a friend'.[142] In York, the recently arrested Ralph Cowling was 'much abused; some cast filth on him, others would have drawn him, and another taken with him, through the fires which then were made in the streets for triumph concerning the queen of Scots'.[143]

By contrast, in Paris Mary was publicly acclaimed as a martyr, not least because this was one very good way to needle Henry III, who had failed to save her, just as he was rather conspicuously failing to safeguard the French crown and Church from a Huguenot successor, Henry of Navarre. Illustrations of Mary's fate, derived from Richard Verstegan's work, were posted up in the French capital, and they were viewed by substantial crowds. As Sir Edward Stafford reported it in June, five thousand people each day were trooping along in order to view the pictures and to be lectured by some 'English knave priests' on the topic of persecution, while others, stationed there 'purposely for the matter', explained 'how likely Catholics' were 'to grow to that point in France if they' were to be afflicted with a heretical king. Stafford claimed that he had not, since he arrived in France, seen anything done in such a furious manner.[144] A representation of Mary's death figured in Verstegan's *Theatrum Crudelitatum Haereticorum Nostris Temporis* as one of a string of outrageous heretical atrocities which included, with an equally striking visual depiction, the death of Margaret Clitherow.[145] Perhaps the most evocative contemporary account of Mary as a suffering servant of Christ came in Pedro de Ribadeneira's extensive chapter on her imprisonment, trial, and execution, the bulk of which was published in 1588.[146]

---

[140] Challoner, *MMP*, p. 121.   [141] Devlin, *LRS*, p. 147.

[142] Foley, *RSJ*, III, p. 615 (PRO, SP 14/21/48, fo. 122ᵛ); *CSPV 1581–91*, pp. 256, 258; *CSPSp 1587–1603*, pp. 27, 35; *CSPSc 1586–8*, p. 441; D. Cressy, *Bonfires and Bells: National Memory and the Protestant Calendar in Elizabethan and Stuart England* (1989), p. 76.

[143] Anstr., I, pp. 91–2; Morris, *TCF*, III (WHN), pp. 280, 323–4. Cowling was a convert of the martyr William Hart: Aveling, *Catholic Recusancy in York*, p. 71.

[144] Dillon, *CM*, pp. 163–9; *CSPF 1586–8*, p. 316; A. G. Petti, 'Richard Verstegan and Catholic Martyrologies of the later Elizabethan Period', *RH* 5 (1959–60), pp. 64–90, at pp. 70–7; *CSPSp 1587–1603*, pp. 32, 45; M. Greengrass, 'Mary, Dowager Queen of France', in M. Lynch (ed.), *Mary Stewart: Queen in Three Kingdoms* (Oxford, 1988), pp. 171–94, at pp. 182–3, 184–5, 187–8; Bossy, *EC*, pp. 111–12.

[145] Lake and Questier, *Trials*, p. 126; Richard Verstegan, *Theatrum Crudelitatum Haereticorum Nostri Temporis* (Antwerp, 1587), pp. 85, 77. For the visual strategies employed in the *Theatrum*, see C. Highley, 'Richard Verstegan's Book of Martyrs', in C. Highley and J. King (eds), *John Foxe and his World* (Aldershot, 2002), pp. 183–97, at pp. 184 f.

[146] Weinreich, *PREH*, pp. 510–36.

CATHOLIC MARTYRS AND THE POLITICAL CRISES OF THE MID-1580S 173

Thus, while some Catholics tried to find ways to play down their differences with the Tudor regime, others made the case that the queen's government was exactly the evil despotism that they had always said it was. Some of those who might previously have offered a modicum of compliance now would or could not. Thomas Pilchard was executed at Fordington Green, just outside Dorchester, on 21 March 1587, though it proved difficult to find anyone to kill him and the execution was bungled because of the hesitancy of the fellow who had been hired as, or coerced into the role of, hangman.[147] But, before Pilchard died, it appears that he managed to persuade the hesitating priest, John Hambley, to withdraw the kind of compliance that he had been offering up to this point. 'Inveighing much against his former fault', Hambley was executed at Salisbury at the Lent assizes in 1587.[148] Another York martyr who may have been at one time on the cusp of non/compliance was Edmund Sykes. Sykes was one of those northerners who had been deported in September 1585. He returned and was arrested—betrayed by his own brother.[149] The date of his execution is not in fact certain—either 23 March 1587 or, more likely, 23 March 1588.[150] The narrative in Christopher Grene's manuscripts notes that Sykes had, under arrest at York, briefly conformed ('through feebleness and infirmity he went to church') before he was sent abroad.[151] When Sykes was put on trial, the judge reminded him of 'his former actions' and Sykes replied that it was merely 'the infirmity of weakness' which had caused him to 'go to your service' and 'not for any liking I had of it, the which I have repented and now detest to do it; neither did I wholly that which was required, or like of your doing, wherefore I was kept in prison, and so banished'. In prison Sykes practised a rigorous asceticism—a rebuke to anyone who thought that he was in two minds about his past conformity and his impending fate.[152] Challoner recorded, out of the Yorkshire priest Anthony Champney's long manuscript history of the period, that the 'prince of darkness' himself had attacked Sykes before the trial. 'Other Catholics who were kept prisoners in the same gaol, though not in the same room, heard in his room a noise as it were of one that was

---

[147] Challoner, *MMP*, p. 121; Anstr., I, p. 276; Pollen, *AEM*, p. 263 (ABSJ, Collectanea M, p. 138ᵃ); *AWCBC*, pp. 456, 457, 460; see p. 32 above. At Gloucester, Stephen Rowsham, who had been deported in September 1585, was killed at about this point but with less overt cruelty than had been used against John Sandys in the previous year; see pp. 62–3 above.

[148] Challoner, *MMP*, p. 125; Pollen, *UD*, p. 289 (ABSJ, Anglia VII, no. 26); Pollen, *AEM*, pp. 268–70 (ABSJ, Collectanea M, pp. 139ᵇ–40ᵇ); *AWCBC*, pp. 519, 521, 554.

[149] Challoner, *MMP*, pp. 121–2; Pollen, *AEM*, p. 328; Morris, *TCF*, III (WHN), pp. 272, 312.

[150] *AWCBC*, pp. 562, 565, 569; Alban Butler's notes had Sykes's execution in 1588, but Challoner opted for 1587, relying on Anthony Champney's 'Annales Elizabethae Reginae': ABP, p. 108; Challoner, *MMP*, p. 122. The modern research into Sykes for the purposes of beatification locates the martyrdom in March 1588 (*AWCBC*, pp. 559, 562, 575), as did Christopher Grene: Stonyhurst MS A V, no. 21, p. 129 (which, however, gives the date as 3 March; cf. Pollen, *UD*, p. 192).

[151] Foley, *RSJ*, III, p. 736 (AVCAU, Liber 1422 [Grene, Collectanea F], section 4, p. 69ᵃ); *AWCBC*, pp. 557–8, 568–9. Sykes had been betrayed to the authorities in 1585: *AWCBC*, pp. 567, 568.

[152] *AWCBC*, p. 569; G. Bradley and A. Lonsdale, 'The Venerable Edmund Sykes of Leeds, Priest and Martyr', *Thoresby Society Publications* 53 (1972), pp. 167–70, at p. 170.

174   CATHOLICS AND TREASON

disputing and contending with him, whom he rebuked and rejected with contempt; and when afterwards they asked him what was the matter, he told them "that the devil [or, as the Latin has it, *a malo daemone*] had been there to trouble and molest him, and to tempt and urge him to renounce his religion".[153]

The Scottish queen's demise triggered a furious reaction from her supporters in Scotland. This was a wave of feeling that the young king, James, exploited (even though he did not intend to give way to popular demands there for revenge against Elizabeth).[154] This meant that Scotland would continue to be a focus for English Catholic aspirations. On 11/21 May 1587 the priest Thomas Bayly at Rheims reported a visitor's news from England that 'there is great persecution' and that 'they begin to persecute...the schismatics' as well. However, the Scottish courtier Colonel William Stuart had been at Rheims and had said that King James was 'something bent towards the Catholic religion'.[155] The future martyr Christopher Buxton wrote from Paris to the Jesuit William Holt on 9 June 1587, as he contemplated how to get back to England, that 'for our direction over the seas what way we shall take, we are not yet certain'. But 'every man thinks' that 'to go in by Scotland is the best [way], because of great liberty which is [given unto] the Catholics there of late time'.[156]

Actually, one of the great ironies of the public destruction of the Scottish queen was that it seems to have released a surge of anti-puritanism in England. In early 1587, the parliament saw the passing of the new recusancy statute as well as debates over the puritan 'bill and book', but Sir Christopher Hatton on 4 March 1587 sounded off in the Commons against puritan dissent.[157] There may have been a connection between the emergence of this regime-led anti-puritan reaction and the reluctance of the authorities in London to use the new statute law against imprisoned Catholic clergy.

While Catholics did not exactly notice anything approaching tolerance for themselves, they did comment on what looked like hostility to puritans. Thus Robert Southwell reported on 26 August 1587 on the travails of Giles Wigginton, evidently with some glee, that is, when Bishop Aylmer, initially rather

---

[153] Challoner, *MMP*, p. 122; *AWCBC*, p. 572 (AAW, F 1, pp. 844–5).

[154] Questier, *DP*, p. 174. It is possible that a Scottish priest called George Douglas was arrested because he had spoken out against Elizabeth's treatment of Mary; he appears to have been tried at the Lent assizes at York in 1587 and was executed in the following September: *AWCBC*, pp. 2538–44, 2563–9.

[155] BL, Lansdowne MS 96, no. 25, fo. 71ʳ (Pollen, *UD*, p. 140).

[156] Pollen, *UD*, p. 146 (ABSJ, Anglia I, no. 32). Buxton, however, landed in Kent, was arrested in November 1587, and was executed in October 1588; see pp. 192–3 below.

[157] Hartley, *PPE*, II, p. 338. The new recusancy measure ('for the more speedy and due execution of certain branches of a statute made in the 23rd year of the Queen's Majesty's reign') was brought into the House of Lords on 11 March 1587. It received the royal assent within a fortnight; see H. Bowler (ed.), *Recusancy Roll No. 2 (1593–1594)* (CRS 57, 1965), pp. xxii–iii. For the 'bill and book', see Collinson, *EPM*, pp. 303–29.

CATHOLIC MARTYRS AND THE POLITICAL CRISES OF THE MID-1580S   175

unsuccessfully, tried to prevent Wigginton from preaching against episcopacy.[158] This might just explain the behaviour of the martyr manqué Anthony Tyrrell in early 1588. His government handlers had decided it was time for him to preach a really edifying recantation sermon at Paul's Cross. Tyrrell turned up at the cross in order to declaim but, unknown to his handlers, he had changed his mind again. From this public pulpit he launched into a denunciation of the queen's government. He declared that he had 'come to this great throng with the purpose, as is believed, of abjuring the ancient faith' but, instead, he embraced 'wholeheartedly the Roman Catholic Church and religion', from which he had 'fallen, as by the instigation of the Devil'. Not only that but, said Tyrrell, 'the spirit of God raises me up and I return to the same. I am ready, relying upon God's help, to die in its defence', that is, to become a martyr, and thus to 'wash away the heavy weight of my earlier offences'. It did not take long for the master of ceremonies, the very puritan John Rainolds, and other officials to realize that something was going horribly wrong here. Tyrrell was pulled out of the pulpit, but he had anticipated this and so had just enough time to tear up the officially prepared and approved recantation and to scatter copies of what he wanted to say into the crowd. One of those copies was picked up by the future martyr Richard Leigh and was taken off to be copied out and further distributed.[159] Tyrrell, it might be argued, though he had no real intention of becoming a martyr, had been reading the political tea leaves and had concluded that things had changed—at least sufficiently to pull a stunt like this.

The Rise of Catholic Resistance Theory

Even if the use of the law against Catholics slackened off, the death of the Scottish queen and the diversion of the succession to the Calvinist James VI meant that, for the Catholic hardliners, nothing had changed—at least not for the better. William Allen left no doubt of this in his *Copie of a Letter Written by M. Doctor Allen*. It was allegedly a response to Roger Ashton's letter of enquiry to Allen of 20 March 1587. Ashton was one of Sir William Stanley's captains in Flanders and claimed to be concerned with the moral justification for the recent surrender of the town of Deventer to the Spaniards. Allen replied on 13/23 April.[160] Allen's

---

[158] McCoog, *LRS*, pp. 156–7. For Wigginton, see Lake and Questier, *Trials*, pp. 92, 95, 98, 99–100, 102, 211, 228.

[159] McCoog, *LRS*, p. 163 (Southwell to Acquaviva, 22 January 1588); Lake and Questier, *Trials*, pp. 151–2. Thomas Rogers reported in June 1586 to Walsingham that the recently arrived Richard Leigh had said Mass 'in Newgate to the papists' there: *CSPF June 1586–June 1588*, p. 35. For the claim that the priest Lewis Barlow, arrested and gaoled in December 1587, had turned Tyrrell, see *Miscellanea II*, p. 280 (PRO, SP 12/206/76); Morris, *TCF*, II, p. 385 (PRO, SP 12/199/91).

[160] ARCR, II, no. 8; William Allen, *The Copie of a Letter Written by M. Doctor Allen...*(Antwerp, 1587). There were Latin, French, and Italian translations: ARCR, I, nos 13–17. Ashton was brought to

176 CATHOLICS AND TREASON

basic point was that Elizabeth was waging an unjust war and therefore Stanley and his associates had done nothing wrong in rendering the town to Spanish troops—indeed, they were obliged by conscience to do as they did.[161]

But Allen was starting to push into the realm of practical resistance theory and made a number of crucial statements here about the connection between the war in Flanders and the persecution of Catholics in England. In the past, 'English wars' were 'renowned for justice' but no longer, at least not when the likes of the earl of Leicester were in charge of them. English military activity was now 'infamous' and was undertaken for the benefit 'of rebellious and seditious persons'. If truth be told, Elizabeth had a long track record of participation in such ventures, not just in Flanders but also in Scotland and France.[162]

The pamphlet pursued the theme that a soldier's sacrifice in battle could itself be a martyrdom. It could be the moral equivalent of the sacrifice which had been made by clergy who were arrested and executed by Elizabeth's wicked regime. Allen explicitly said that he was not 'so restrained to students' matters' that he gave no thought to 'men of' Stanley's 'vocation…knowing that state of life to be necessary for the commonwealth, godly, honourable and especially appointed by God for defence of justice and religion'. A marginal comment on the first page read: 'many soldiers [are] great saints and martyrs'.[163] The analogies followed thick and fast. Injustice abroad was matched by persecution at home. 'In their civil government', the queen's officials 'cause the Catholic judge to give sentence of death against the priests whose innocence they know and whose religion in heart they believe to be true. They make one Catholic neighbour to accuse another and one nobleman to condemn another.' Likewise, 'in their wars, they serve themselves of Catholics' as they had done with Sir William Stanley, 'and by English Catholics they destroy Catholics abroad' so 'that, foreign Catholics being overthrown, they may more easily overthrow their own at home'.[164] Allen would not allow that Catholics could serve the queen with a good conscience. The war was unjust not only because the Netherlands belonged to Philip II but also because Elizabeth had been excommunicated. Allen wheeled out the usual scriptural

book and finally executed on 23 June 1592—as Challoner alleged, following the Paris catalogue, for previously 'procuring a dispensation from Rome to marry his second cousin', but the prosecution was evidently driven by the issue of Deventer's surrender, despite the doubtful aspects of the prosecution case: Challoner, *MMP*, p. 186; AAW, B 28, no. 10, p. 314; Petti, *LDRV*, pp. 55, 56, 57; see also *APC 1590–1*, pp. 356–7; *APC 1591*, pp. 127–8; *APC 1591–2*, pp. 440, 524; *Miscellanea II*, pp. 280, 281.

[161] Richard Topcliffe claimed that it had been a gross error to send the priest Thomas Worthington into exile in January 1585, since he had, alleged Topcliffe, persuaded Stanley to give up Deventer and had been instrumental in the publication of Allen's pamphlet in favour of Stanley: PRO, SP 12/235/8, fo. 15ʳ; Anstr., I, p. 387.

[162] Allen, *The Copie of a Letter*, sig. A5ᵛ–6ʳ. Sir Edward Stafford commented, having seen a copy of the pamphlet, that 'I think shortly they will make killing of one's father, if he be a heretic, lawful': *CSPF June 1586–June 1588*, p. 368.

[163] Allen, *The Copie of a Letter*, sig. A3ʳ.

[164] Ibid., sig. A7ᵛ–8ʳ.

CATHOLIC MARTYRS AND THE POLITICAL CRISES OF THE MID-1580S   177

instances to prove his point: 'it was no crime…for Jehoiada the high priest to revolt from the usurping Queen Athalia, nor for others to do the same against wicked King Ahab', with King John, Richard III, and Lady Jane Grey not far behind. Whether a 'revolt' was 'lawful' and 'honourable' depended on the 'justice or injustice of the cause'.[165]

All through Allen's pamphlet, there is an equivalence drawn between the function of the soldier and the function of the priest. 'Of all men in the world, the soldier should most especially attend to his conscience', for, if he fights against God and in 'defence of heretics', he is 'doubtless to be damned forever'. But 'to die in lawful wars, for defence of justice', and 'for defence of true religion and God's honour', this is 'in most cases plain martyrdom'. 'For redressing the evils' which had befallen the realm of England 'it is as lawful, godly and glorious for you to fight as for us priests to suffer and to die. Either the one way, or the other, for defence of our fathers' faith, is always in the sight of God, a most precious death and martyrdom.' On the basis of the unimpeachable authority of St Augustine, who had said something rather similar, Allen could conclude that 'so goodly a thing it is for the priest and soldier to concur in the service of God and their country together'.[166]

In the preceding, somewhat episodic, narratives of regime-directed action against Catholic separatism, glossed by Allen as the makings of tyranny, we have the outline of a fundamental change in Elizabethan politics. As the Elizabethan State availed itself of new statutory penalties against Catholic separatists, even more of the constraints on what Catholics could say were being removed. Here they both anticipated and followed some of their co-religionists in France, faced as they were with the possible accession of a Huguenot. Catholic accounts of the regime had morphed from regret at the limits on the queen's sovereign authority and freedom of choice imposed by her bad counsellors into claims that the

---

[165] Ibid., sig. B^r–2^r, B3^{r-v}.

[166] Ibid., sigs A8^r, B7^{r-v}. There was a reply written to Allen's pamphlet by Mary Stuart's betrayer, Gilbert Gifford, though it purported to be penned by a Jesuit: L. Hicks, 'Allen and Deventer (1587)', Month 163 (1934), pp. 505–17, at pp. 515–17; Devlin, LRS, pp. 154–5; Knox, LMCA, pp. 299–301 (ABSJ, Collectanea P/i, p. 329^a); Holmes, Resistance and Compromise, pp. 251–2. In late 1587, the council had written to the newly appointed lords lieutenant to direct them to publicize a work (presumably Gifford's) penned in reply to Allen's defence of Sir William Stanley: PRO, SP 12/205/70, fo. 132^{r-v}. The pamphlet in question (which Robert Southwell apparently saw but which is no longer extant) had the title The Answere of Diverse Catholick English Gentlemen to a Certain Seditious Book Veiled with the Name of D. Allen. This pamphlet claimed that, at a location in London, strongly implied to be Montague House, an unnamed Jesuit (whom the reader might just about deduce was Southwell himself) declared that majority English Catholic opinion would not believe that Allen had written the defence of Stanley. Those Catholics who confronted the Jesuit concluded that it was lawful to serve against the Spaniards: Devlin, LRS, pp. 154–5. The future convert to Rome, Henry Constable, also composed a draft (but never published) reply to Allen: ODNB, sub Constable, Henry (article by C. Sullivan), citing National Library of Ireland, Marsh MS, Z3.5.21, item 8 ('A short view of a large examination of Cardinal Allen, his traitorous justification of Sir W. Stanley and Yorke, written by Mr. H. Cons[table], and this gathered out of his own draft'). I am very grateful to Eilish Gregory for providing me with a copy of this manuscript.

servants of God, faced with intolerable injustice and a lethal threat to the faith, were entitled to contemplate the removal of a monarch who had offended God so heinously. The principal contemporary Catholic martyrological texts of this period cannot therefore be taken entirely on their own terms, at least not superficially, nor undoubtedly would their compilers have expected them to be read in that way. Just as much as at other points in the period, they are located in contemporary arguments about where the line of division lay between 'politics' and 'religion', where the power of the State to intervene in and to regulate such matters could be taken to terminate, and where popular political forces might be thought legitimately to be able to displace sovereign authority. The rough edges of these martyr narratives (in particular the doubts and tergiversations of those who were faced with the consequences of non-compliance) allow us to read off aspects of these debates that are otherwise usually hidden from us.

7

The Incestuous Bastard Queen Persecutes the Faithful Servants of Christ

The Spanish Armada

Following Mary Stuart's execution, some English Catholics proclaimed their support for the use of Spanish military power against Elizabeth. William Allen's pamphlet written to accompany and justify the Spanish Armada famously described Elizabeth as 'an incestuous bastard, begotten and born in sin of an infamous courtesan', Anne Boleyn, who herself had been executed for adultery, treason, heresy, and incest. And in case anyone could not remember exactly what Anne B. had done with Lord Rochford, Allen reminded them. For her part, Boleyn's daughter Elizabeth was also an 'infamous, deprived, accursed, excommunicate heretic', the very shame of her sex and princely name; the chief spectacle of sin and abomination in this our age; and the only poison, calamity and destruction of our noble Church and country'.[1]

Allen then went on to recite in precise detail a list of Elizabeth's sins, which was pretty much all of them—everything from desecrating the churches to murdering the Queen of Scots. Allen's work now directly associated Elizabeth, a tyrant, with the crimes of the earl of Leicester: 'with the foresaid person and divers others', declared Allen, 'she has abused her body'. The outcome was a tyranny for which the queen was primarily responsible; and it was one linked to the dynastic moral dysfunction inherent in the history of the Tudors since the time of the incestuous Henry VIII. Corruption of blood led to the heretical, and every other moral, infection of the commonwealth. Elizabeth's lust was what prompted her to assist the Dutch against their lawful sovereign, Philip II.[2] Elizabeth's failure to deal with the issue of the succession was, alleged Allen, the result of her refusal to abstain from her itch for her paramour Leicester.[3] Unsurprisingly, a proclamation, dated 1 July, was issued which declared martial law against possessors of papal 'bulls,

---

[1] William Allen, *An Admonition to the Nobility and People of England and Ireland...* (Antwerp, 1588), *passim* (quotations at pp. 11, 54); William Allen, *A Declaration of the Sentence and Deposition of Elizabeth, the Usurper and Pretensed Queene of Englande* (n.p.[Antwerp?],n.d. [1588]); see also G. Parker, *The Grand Strategy of Philip II* (1998), pp. 201–2; *CSPF Jan.–June 1588*, p. 489.

[2] Allen, *Admonition*, p. 19; see also Lake, *BQB*, pp. 302–11. [3] Allen, *Admonition*, p. 20.

Catholics and Treason: Martyrology, Memory, and Politics in the Post-Reformation. Michael Questier, Oxford University Press. © Michael Questier 2022. DOI: 10.1093/oso/9780192847027.003.0007

180   CATHOLICS AND TREASON

transcripts, copies, libels, books and pamphlets'. It singled out the already printed broadside summary of Allen's pamphlet.[4]

Robert Southwell wrote on 10 July 1588 that 'the asps' eggs have burst and the poison has begun to pour forth and to spread far and wide with the most certain destruction of many'. There was licence for anyone who felt like it to harass Catholics.[5] But in fact there were no Catholics executed under the new statute law in London between the deaths of John Lowe, John Adams, and Richard Dibdale on 8 October 1586 and the hangings of 28 August 1588, and probably none at all in 1588 until the Derby executions in July of that year.[6] Among the prison lists from this period, there is one drawn up in late 1586 and annotated by Thomas Phelippes and by the spy Thomas Rogers. It is peppered with comments about Catholic detainees. Most of them are recommended for deportation but it is also what one might call a death-wish list. Noting that Lowe and Adams had been executed already, it suggests that James Taylor ought to 'be hanged [since] he was taken with [Edward] Abington' and was himself implicated in the Babington Plot. Ralph Ithell, arrested on suspicion of complicity in Babington's conspiracy, should be executed as well. Jonas Meredith was also 'worthy to be hanged', 'being once banished before and sent over by' Mary's agents Thomas Morgan and Charles Paget. William Weston should be 'well kept, if not hanged', and hanging was what was good for William Wiggs, Isaac Higgens, Thomas Smith and Thomas Simpson.[7] But none of them actually were.[8]

It appears, therefore, that after Mary Stuart had been terminated, despite the anti-popish bonfires, bell-ringing and what not, there was a willingness on the part of the regime, which was now experiencing a legitimist turn in favour of James VI, not to push the Catholic issue to its furthest and most ideologically charged points, at least not for the time being. Still, as almost everyone knew by summer 1588, the Armada was coming. It looks as if the London Catholic community was well aware what might now happen. The correspondence of the Jesuits Henry Garnet and Robert Southwell suggests that, with Catholic lawyers in attendance, meetings were held between Easter and July at which it was discussed whether a loyalist compromise could be hammered out, one which was

---

[4] Hughes and Larkin, TRP, III, no. 699, quotation at p. 17; CSPSp 1587–1603, p. 355; PRO, SP 12/211/56, 56. i.

[5] McCoog, LRS, pp. 170–1 (Southwell to Acquaviva, 10 July 1588).

[6] It is possible, as we remarked above, that Edmund Sykes was executed on 23 March 1588 rather than 1587; see ABP, pp. 108; pp. 173–4, 173 n.150 above. But cf. the claim made by a memorandum retained in Burghley's papers, dated December 1586, that the execution of seminary priests was not having the desired effect—'as experience shows in respect of their constancy or, rather, obstinacy', their deaths moved 'men to compassion' and drew 'some to affect their religion upon conceit that such an extraordinary contempt of death' could not 'but proceed from above': BL, Lansdowne 97, no. 14, fo. 157ʳ.

[7] Miscellanea II (1906), pp. 272–3.

[8] Anstr., I, pp. 11, 166–7, 185–6, 227, 317–18, 323, 345, 380.

THE INCESTUOUS BASTARD QUEEN 181

sufficient to satisfy government interrogators.[9] How far would Catholics be able to preserve their ideological independence in the face of insistent demands for explicit displays of obedience? As we have already seen, the priest John Hambley had found this an impossible circle to square. It seems that something similar happened at Derby in July 1588, that is, when the priests Nicholas Garlick, Robert Ludlam, and Richard Simpson were executed there. The earl of Shrewsbury had personally led the search party which sought to detain John Fitzherbert at Padley Hall in Derbyshire and which had secured the arrest of Garlick and Ludlam and others. The three priests were hanged together on 24 July 1588, very shortly before the Armada ships appeared in the Channel.[10] Simpson may have been suspected by the authorities of persuading people away from their allegiance to the queen.[11] But, rather like John Hambley, Simpson had initially made an offer of compliance. Following his arrest, he was 'arraigned and condemned', said Garnet, but, 'yielding then to some conference and to hear a sermon', he 'was reprieved'. Nevertheless, when push came to shove, as Hambley himself had done, Simpson changed his mind. He 'repented this fact and did recant his doing openly so that then he was most hardly used till the [next] assizes'. He died along with the other two who in fact had persuaded him to go back on his offer of compliance. When Simpson 'was in quartering, the people cried, "a devil, a devil", because he had on him a shirt of hair, but the wiser sort said he wore it because he had fallen'.[12] Simpson's lapse and recovery were celebrated in verse form.[13] His heroism was mentioned

[9] Devlin, *LRS*, pp. 168–9.

[10] Challoner, *MMP*, pp. 129–31; Anstr., I, p. 215; AAW, A XXI, no. 47, p. 170 (Richard Smith's notes); Caraman, *HG*, p. 73; *AWCBC*, p. 577. John Fitzherbert was reprieved. Arrested at the same time was the Yorkshire attorney Nicholas Elvish, whose wife was sister of the priest Thomas Metham: Foley, *RSJ*, III, pp. 751–2 (AVCAU, Liber 1422 [Grene, Collectanea F], section 4, p. 78ᵃ); *AWCBC*, p. 591. Simpson, who may formerly have held a benefice in the Church of England, had been taken earlier: *AWCBC*, pp. 604, 605. On 16 September 1586, a spy had written to Walsingham that 'one Hughes of Winchester' had seen Garlick, the 'demonite' (implying, perhaps, that he was one of the exorcists associated with William Weston), a few days before and that he 'labours with great diligence in Hampshire and Dorsetshire'. He should be 'intercepted, for these hellish priests are the poisoners and infectors of all the wicked ones in England': *CSPSc 1586–8*, p. 21; Anstr., I, p. 127. A confession extracted in October 1584 out of a Tideswell man, Ralph Miller, who was Garlick's cousin, had admitted that Garlick 'hoped, ere it be long, to have all things in the old order, for the whole country about them were Catholics...and very desirous of priests': Anstr., I, pp. 126–7; PRO, SP 12/173/64, fo. 101ʳ.

[11] One Henry Slater had volunteered the information that a priest called Simpson (presumably Richard Simpson) had 'dealt with him to go beyond the seas into some Catholic country where he might be instructed in the truth'. Slater went first to Bergen-op-Zoom and 'thence to Sir William Stanley', presumably just after the point that Stanley had handed over Deventer to the Spaniards: PRO, SP 12/185/70, fo. 173ʳ (this document is undated and it is unclear when the events narrated in it occurred).

[12] Anstr., I, pp. 126–7, 215–16, 316–17; Challoner, *MMP*, pp. 130, 132; AVCAU, Liber 1422 [Grene, Collectanea F], section 1, pp. 3ᵇ–4ᵃ; *AWCBC*, p. 590. Challoner used, *inter alia*, the narrative compiled for Richard Smith in 1626 by Richard Broughton and the one by the priest Robert Bagshaw (described as Garlick's 'scholar'), who was a cousin of the notorious Christopher Bagshaw; see AAW, A IV, no. 1, pp. 6–10 (for the transcript supplied by Butler, see ABP, pp. 347–9); Anstr., I, pp. 17–18.

[13] One poem was, apparently, written by an eyewitness and it was reproduced in part by Bishop Challoner: Challoner, *MMP*, pp. 132–3; AAW, A IV, no. 1, pp. 9–10; *AWCBC*, p. 590. For the publication in 1604 of this verse, with others, see pp. 335 n.8 below. The Vincent Eyre collection at Ushaw (Vincent

182   CATHOLICS AND TREASON

by Garnet to Claudio Acquaviva. Garnet himself was shortly to be in the forefront of the campaign against the conformist ideologue Thomas Bell.[14]

Here, then, we have a section of the Catholic community still poised right on the edge between compliance and resistance. The regime, however, seems to have decided to cut through all the waffle about partial obedience.[15] A privy council letter was sent out to Recorder Fleetwood and Sir Thomas Egerton instructing them to work out what was to be done about the Catholic clergy who were in prison. Fleetwood and Egerton replied on 20 July 1588, the day that the Armada was sighted off the Lizard, with a list of 'articles to be offered to the papists and recusants of this time, to discern those that carry traitorous and malicious minds against her Majesty and the State from them whose simplicity is misled by ignorant and blind zeal'. They advised that something should be done about those that 'do either obstinately refuse to make any answer at all, or subtly ([as] many in like cases have heretofore done) excuse themselves that they are unlearned and ignorant and so not able to answer herein, or that they ought not' to 'be examined of things future, or to like effect'. It was high time to 'repress their malice'. This was, in so many words, to recommend using the so-called 'bloody questions', although those who were known to be seminary clergy could simply be dealt with under the provisions of the 1585 statute.[16]

The approach of the Spaniards' ships may explain the treatment of the priest Robert Sutton in Staffordshire. He had been apprehended in the company of, among others, Erasmus Wolseley and William Maxfield. Sutton was sent to London and then was dispatched back to Stafford for trial and execution on 27 July 1588. According to Thomas Worswick, 'the priest was a very reverend learned man and at his arraignment disputed very stoutly and learnedly'. Another account said that at the gallows Sutton preached a sermon on 'the candle we receive in baptism and in the hour of death'. His execution was, said Worswick, 'done in a most villainous butcherly manner by one Moseley, who with his axe cut off his head (while he had yet sense, and was ready to stand up) through his mouth'.[17]

Eyre was the brother of the Reverend Thomas Eyre, first president in 1808 of Ushaw College) has a transcript of another poem on the same martyrs, principally commemorating Simpson's change of heart; the paper is dated 1703 but the date of composition is uncertain: ABSJ, CP (Nicholas Garlick, draft papers for 1987 beatification); UCLSC, UC/P28/2/100; *AWCBC*, p. 580. This poem was presumably kept by the Eyre family because it records also that John Fitzherbert, arrested at the same time as the priests, was reprieved—this was because 'Thomas Eyre of Holme Hall near Chesterfield that married' John Fitzherbert's daughter, Jane, 'sold his manor of Whittington near Holme Hall' to secure Fitzherbert's pardon, though Fitzherbert died in prison in 1590: UCLSC, UC/P28/2/100; cf. Stonyhurst MS A V, no. 21, pp. 79–80.

[14] Caraman, *HG*, p. 74; ABSJ, GC (Garnet to Acquaviva, 29 October 1588).

[15] Ward, LT, p. 284.   [16] Pollen, *UD*, p. 151 (PRO, SP 12/212/70).

[17] *AWCBC*, pp. 619, 646 (citing William Salt Library, Stafford, Salt MSS, no. 369, pp. 136–7), 631 (Foley, *RSJ*, III, p. 232 (AVCAU, Liber 1422 [Grene, Collectanea F], section 1, pp. 5ᵇ–6ᵃ)); Ward, LT, p. 285; D. M. Rogers, 'Ven. Robert Sutton of Stafford: A Note on his Family and Early Life', *Biographical Studies* 2 (1953–4), pp. 150–66. Sutton had served as a minister in the national Church at Lutterworth in Leicestershire and was converted by his younger brother William (John Gerard's Greek language

THE INCESTUOUS BASTARD QUEEN   183

This case threatened to reveal the kind of cosy cross-confessional relationships and accommodations within the county community which were normally supposed to be invisible to the queen's government. Sir Thomas Fitzherbert's nephew (also Thomas), who entered into a feud with the JP William Bassett, alleged that when 'Robert Sutton, the Lord Paget's traitorous priest' was 'condemned for treason', Bassett, who was also a nephew of Sir Thomas Fitzherbert and was, despite being an office-holder, heavily implicated in the local Catholic community, 'dealt secretly with him'. (See Figure 7.1.) Sutton begged 'that he might live' if only 'to reveal matter of great importance and treason'. At that point, Bassett was sheriff of Staffordshire. He could quite easily have delayed the execution but he refused because, allegedly, he wanted to prevent Sutton revealing 'more matter' than he (Bassett) deemed appropriate. On this account, which was, of course, a hostile one, Bassett had, therefore, not suddenly discovered his inner loyalist but was defending his version of the local status quo, even if that required the death of a seminary priest.[18] That local closeness of connection may have been indicated also by the reprieves and pardons issued to those, arrested with Sutton, who were 'well beloved in the town'.[19]

---

tutor). He had, 'before his going over', in *c*.February 1577 'first told all his parish out of the pulpit that he had taught them false doctrine'. He now 'willed them to embrace the Catholic faith, which [he] then himself meant to follow': Pollen, *UD*, p. 291 (ABSJ, Anglia VII, no. 26); Anstr., I, pp. 343–4; Pollen, *AEM*, pp. 323–4 (ABSJ, Collectanea M, pp. 47ᵇ–8ᵃ; *AWCBC*, pp. 636–7); Morris, *TCF*, III (AENB), p. 8; C. W. Foster (ed.), *Lincoln Episcopal Records*...(Lincoln Record Society, 2, Lincoln, 1912), pp. 317, 319. Robert Sutton's physical remains were later said by William Maxfield's son, the priest-martyr Thomas Maxfield, to have cured a demoniac—Maxfield witnessed the exorcism of a 'person possessed by a furious devil', conducted by the controversial seminarist Edward Hands (alias Johnson), who was also from Lutterworth; this event was recounted by Challoner (who had Maxfield's letter of *c*.August/September 1615 narrating the event): Challoner, *MMP*, p. 123; J. H. Pollen (ed.), 'The Life and Martyrdom of Mr. Maxfield, 1616', *Miscellanea III* (CRS 3, 1906), pp. 30–58, at pp. 52–3 (AAW, St Edmund's College, Ware MSS, 16/9, no. 8; ABP, p. 339; *AWCBC*, pp. 640–2); Anstr., II, p. 143; pp. 435–6 below. For Sutton's thumb, 'deposited' by John Gerard (it was given to him by Abraham Sutton, the martyr's brother) 'in a silver and glass reliquary', see Caraman, *JG*, pp. 49–50, 227; Pollen, *AEM*, p. 326 (ABSJ, Collectanea M, p. 48ᵃ⁻ᵇ; *AWCBC*, pp. 636–7); Dillon, *CM*, pp. 108–9. For the reliquary, see PRO, SP 14/19/72, fo. 136ʳ; Pollen, *AEM*, p. 326; *AWCBC*, pp. 638–9; and see Figure 7.1.

[18] BL, Harleian MS 7042, fo. 226ʳ (for the original text, in Topcliffe's hand, see BL, Harleian MS 6998, fos 249ʳ–50ᵛ). Thomas Fitzherbert alleged that, 'about the time when letters were sent down to the old earl of Shrewsbury to apprehend Richard Fitzherbert and Martin Audley' as well as unnamed seminary priests at the residence of Sir Thomas Fitzherbert at Norbury, Bassett sent Randall Swinnerton to 'Norbury to give warning to Richard Fitzherbert' and the others 'to fly away': BL, Harleian MS 7042, fo. 226ʳ. For Bassett's dealings with other Catholics, see BL, Harleian MS 7042, fos 225ᵛ–6ʳ; *HC 1558–1603*, I, p. 404, II, pp. 125–6; *CSPD 1591–4*, pp. 372, 379–81 (PRO, SP 12/245/98, 138); Questier, *C&C*, pp. 185, 200–1; Neale, *EHP*, II, pp. 313–18. For the council's directions of 30 May 1590 for the arrest of Richard Fitzherbert, see LPL, MS 3200, fo. 71ʳ (*APC 1590*, pp. 141–2, dated 20 May); and for the arrest itself, see *APC 1590*, pp. 368, 370, 451. For Thomas Fitzherbert's further accusations of Bassett, see BL, Harleian MS 7042, fos 226ʳ–7ʳ. For the context for the Bassett/Sutton case, see esp. the investigation of Nicholas Blackwall, who provided limited protection for recusants and was removed from office (as clerk of the peace) in 1588, see A. G. Petti (ed.), *Roman Catholicism in Elizabethan and Jacobean Staffordshire: Documents from the Bagot Papers* (Staffordshire Record Society, 1979), pp. xiv, 30, 33–5, 43.

[19] Foley, *RSJ*, III, p. 232 (AVCAU, Liber 1422 [Grene, Collectanea F], section 1, p. 6ᵃ). For Wolseley's pardon, see *AWCBC*, p. 626, citing PRO, C 66/1330, mm. 19–20 (8 August 1589). For the recovery, by the wife of Erasmus Wolseley, of other relics of Sutton, see *AWCBC*, pp. 648–51.

Figure 7.1 Reliquary provided by John Gerard SJ for relic of Robert Sutton, d.1588 (reproduced with the permission of the British province of the Society of Jesus, and with acknowledgement to Agnes Spragg).

Continued dissent may well have been perceived by many Catholics as a luxury which they could not now afford. The earl of Shrewsbury reported on 9 August 1588 to the queen that he had, on the previous Sunday, gone to 'those parts of Derbyshire where I lately took John Fitzherbert' and the seminary clergy in his house, 'of purpose only to reduce unto some good order the multitude of ignorant people heretofore by them seduced'. At 'one sermon [preached] before me', there 'came above two hundred persons, whereof many had not come to church twenty years before, and as many not since the beginning' of the queen's reign.[20]

A privy council warrant directed to, among others, Richard Topcliffe, dated 14 August 1588, started the ball rolling in order to sort out the clergy who were clogging up the London prisons. They should be 'proceeded with according to the law and as the quality of their offences shall have deserved'. They should also be confronted with 'such questions as were heretofore made to others, and are in a printed book wherewith some of them are acquainted, and such other questions

[20] PRO, SP 12/214/51, fo. 113r.

THE INCESTUOUS BASTARD QUEEN   185

as they shall think meet touching their allegiance to her Majesty and their country'.[21] The end product of a week's interrogations can, it seems, be found in the queen's sergeant John Puckering's papers.[22] Here there seems to have been an attempt to detect and separate out those Catholics who could be confidently reckoned to be really dangerous from those who were perceived as, if not exactly friends to the present government, then at least at one remove from the zealots. Prominent here, among the names of potential loyalists, was Jonas Meredith. He had been part of the so-called Welsh faction in the English College in Rome in the late 1570s. Having come back to England, he was arrested and released more than once. He was in fact one of those taken with Philip Howard, earl of Arundel, in April 1585. He went off again to Rome in late 1585/early 1586 on behalf of Charles Paget and Thomas Morgan. Mary Stuart was said to be paying Meredith's travel expenses.[23] William Clargenet was similarly on Puckering's not-so-little list but he was not proceeded against either. He ended up, briefly, at Wisbech and was at one time an enemy there of the Jesuit William Weston. So it is quite possible that he too made the right kind of loyalist noises at this point.[24] It was the same story with the future appellant priest John Bolton, who had been arrested back in 1585, and also with James Taylor, who had been taken at the house of Edward Abington of Hindlip and had been accused of complicity in the Babington business. He had, like Bolton, been removed to Wisbech, where he eventually signed the appeal against the archpriest George Blackwell on 17 November 1600 and then, as did Bolton, put his name to the appellant petition at Paris on 3 May 1603, after they had both been deported.[25]

Some of those who were known harbourers of clergy must have done some sort of deal, because they were not prosecuted to the full extent of the law. For instance, Henry Foxwell, noted in 1588 as a 'receiver of priests', was said to have been 'by the humble suit of his wife reprieved'. A prison list of 30 November 1586 had recorded that, although Foxwell was 'a special companion and of familiarity with' the Babington plotter Henry Donne, 'lately executed, by whom he was

[21] *APC 1588*, pp. 235–6; Pollen, *UD*, pp. 151–2; Ward, LT, p. 286.

[22] Pollen, *UD*, pp. 152–7 (BL, Harleian MS 6998, fo. 232^r); for the difficulties in interpreting this document, see *AWCBC*, pp. 667–70.

[23] Anstr., I, p. 227; *CSPD Addenda 1580–1625*, p. 167; see also *CSPF Sept. 1585–May 1586*, p. 276. Once Meredith was imprisoned in Wisbech, he consistently sided against the Jesuit interest group there: Anstr., I, p. 227. Thomas Morgan wrote, in April 1604, that Meredith was related to the Cecil family and Meredith attributed the 'prolongation of his life' to the deceased Lord Burghley: PRO, SP 78/51, fo. 150^r.

[24] Pollen, *UD*, p. 155. Although he was Weston's enemy, Clargenet did in September 1598 acknowledge the allegedly Jesuited archpriest George Blackwell's authority: Anstr., I, p. 75; Renold, *WS*, pp. 114, 116.

[25] Pollen, *UD*, p. 155; Anstr., I, pp. 43, 345. For the Appellant (or Archpriest) Dispute, see Chapter 10 below. For a loyalist declaration made at this time by the future seminarist and martyr George Napper, see PRO, SP 12/224/109, fo. 166^r. It was being noted in July 1589 that Catholics were being released from incarceration if they took a 'solemn oath' to the queen that they would resist incursions by enemy princes, principally Philip II: PRO, SP 12/225/51, fo. 82^r.

186 CATHOLICS AND TREASON

persuaded to be a Catholic', he nevertheless 'offers hope of conformity so he may be conferred withal by one Mr Hancock, a preacher of Dorsetshire'. Perhaps this saved him in 1588.[26] Similarly, one John Valentine, convicted under the 1581 statute, one assumes, of being reconciled to Rome, secured a reprieve. The annotation against his name reads 'recante et relente'.[27] Several other clergy could easily have come to grief but did not—for example, David Kemp, John Vivian, and John Marsh—though actually the unusual circumstances of their arrests (at sea) meant that they technically were outside the compass of the new treason law.[28]

Among those who were convicted of being reconciled to Rome—for example, Thomas Felton, Henry Webley, and Hugh More—some are listed by Puckering as having refused a pardon, presumably when some sort of offer was made to them. Others, for instance Thomas Hall and Robert Bellamy, have scribbled against their names the words 'take the queen's part'; that is to say, they gave a satisfactory reply to the killer question about foreign invasion. By contrast, the layman Richard Lloyd (condemned for harbouring a priest called William Horner) had the words 'take the queen's part' entered against his name, but those words were crossed out and he was hanged on 30 August.[29] James Claxton also had those words marked against his name and then scored through. He too was hanged.[30]

Something similar may have happened with John Hewett (alias Weldon). He served the gentleman John Gardener of Grove Place, and he was one of those who

[26] Morris, *TCF*, III (AENB), pp. 34–5; Pollen, *UD*, pp. 154, 158; *Miscellanea II*, pp. 262, 266, 267, 268; for Foxwell's indictment in 1587 under the treason statute 25 Edward III and under the statute 23 Eliz., c. 1 in 1588, see Ward, LT, p. 298; cf. Pollen, *AEM*, p. 286 (ABSJ, Collectanea B, p. 2; *AWCBC*, p. 682). The 'preacher' in question may have been John Hancock (CCED, ID 57185), who, however, was beneficed in Somerset. Foxwell was noted by Puckering to have been reconciled to Rome by the priest John Baldwin: Pollen, *UD*, p. 158.
[27] Pollen, *UD*, pp. 153, 154; *A Briefe Treatise Discovering in Substance the Offences and Ungodly Practices of the Late 14 Traitors Condemned the 26 of August 1588. With the Manner of the Execution of Eight of Them...*(1588), sig. A6ʳ (*AWCBC*, p. 673); cf., for the recantations of John Valentine and one William Pere, L. E. Whatmore, *Blessed Margaret Ward* (OVP, n.d.), pp. 16–18.
[28] Pollen, *UD*, p. 155; Anstr., I, pp. 194–5, 219, 367. John Vivian had served as chaplain to Roger Martin of Long Melford who, though a stubborn separatist, may have been regarded as a loyalist: *CSPF 1579–80*, p. 389; Anstr., I, p. 367; Z. Dovey, *An Elizabethan Progress: The Queen's Journey into East Anglia, 1578* (Stroud, Gloucestershire, 1996), pp. 89, 107. John Marsh may have been a chaplain to the stubborn recusant Ann Foster in York; see p. 90 n.69 above. For the Bridgettine narrative of how Vivian and Marsh were taken (detained at La Rochelle and brought back to England) and subsequently released, on the petition of the French king, see 'An Account of the Travels, Dangers and Wonderful Deliverances of the English Nuns of the Famous Monastery of Sion. From their first leaving England to their Settlement at Lisbon in the Kingdom of Portugal', EUL (Syon Abbey Archive) MS 389, box 3, item 116, ch. 3 unpaginated, ch. 9.
[29] Pollen, *UD*, p. 154; Challoner, *MMP*, pp. 133, 135–6, 138 (relying on AAW, A IV, no. 1, pp. 3–6; ABP, pp. 344–7); *AWCBC*, p. 701. For Lloyd (whom Challoner names as Richard Flower), brother of the priest Owen Lloyd, see also Pollen, *UD*, pp. 194–8; Challoner, *MMP*, p. 141; *AWCBC*, pp. 696–9. Henry Webley may have been a relative of Thomas Webley, executed in 1585, but there is no direct evidence for this, although he (Henry) was arrested at Chichester in 1586 with William Crab, who had been an associate of Thomas Alfield and Thomas Webley: *AWCBC*, pp. 658, 663–5; see pp. 156–7 n.73 above.
[30] Pollen, *UD*, p. 154; Challoner, *MMP*, pp. 134, 140.

THE INCESTUOUS BASTARD QUEEN   187

had been involved in William Weston's exorcisms in 1585–6.[31] Hewett had promised conformity at the Middlesex sessions, where a treason charge was brought against him on 17 March 1587.[32] He was released in July and returned to the Continent. He was then taken at Sluys on 5 October 1587, while he was making his way towards the prince of Parma. Hewett was carrying with him the relics of recent English Catholic martyrs as well as 'maps of the seacoast and all the havens northward'. He was forcibly brought back to England from Flanders and thus had a good case that he was not guilty under the 1585 treason law. He also said that he would fight for the queen against an invading army, but he was eventually hanged at Mile End in London on 5 October 1588.[33] In Puckering's notes, 'take the queen's part' was written against his name, as also the words 'deserves to go over'. But, whatever he said, it did not save him. Hewett was known to the regime as a one-time associate of the notorious northern priest John Boste.[34] The regime's pamphlet account of his trial recited that, although he insisted he had been brought back from the Continent against his will, it was believed that he had gone to Flanders 'meaning... to kill the earl of Leicester', who, 'being advertised of [this fact], caused' Hewett 'to be apprehended and sent over into England'.[35]

The Armada campaign had allowed this process to be taken to its maximum extent. Some people's protestations of loyalty were no longer enough, even though it appears that a number of Catholic peers and gentry had offered to serve against the approaching Spanish forces.[36] Eight Catholics were hanged on 28 August. The executions were not concentrated at Tyburn but were distributed around London.[37] At the same time, the full penalty for treason was not used. Grene noted sarcastically in his manuscript volume in which were narrated these martyrdoms that 'you will see a little piece of paper (pasted together with little notes) in the top of the page concerning a pamphlet printed at London of the unheard-of clemency... of the queen towards' these martyrs 'condemned on... 28 [26]

---

[31] Anstr., I, p. 162; PRO, SP 12/199/4, fo. 11ʳ; F. W. Brownlow, *Shakespeare, Harsnett, and the Devils of Denham* (1993), pp. 169, 202, 211.

[32] Anstr., I, p. 163; Jeaffreson, *MCR*, II, pp. 192–3.

[33] Anstr., I, pp. 163–4, citing *CSPF April–Dec. 1587*, pp. 349, 405–6.

[34] Pollen, *UD*, pp. 63, 156.

[35] *A True Report of the Inditement, Arraignment, Conviction, Condemnation, and Execution of John Weldon, William Hartley and Robert Sutton*... (1588), sigs Bᵛ, C3ᵛ and *passim*.

[36] Questier, *C&C*, pp. 167–8; Kn., I, pp. 127–8, citing 'The Lay Catholic Petition... to King James 1604, ch. 5th', which mentions the offer made in 1588 to Lord North by the imprisoned gentry at Ely that they should 'share in the common danger' and 'venture their lives in the defence of their queen and country', and says that 'the like offer was made by the Lord Vaux and others of the chief Catholics in many parts of the kingdom'; see also *APC 1588*, pp. 167, 313. For Sir Thomas Cornwallis's note to Burghley on 29 October 1588 that Vaux and other recusants had been 'convened' before privy councillors and had 'subscribed certain articles' and were 'with favour dismissed': BL, Harleian MS 6994, no. 81, fo. 152ʳ.

[37] Anstr., I, p. 78; cf. Ward, *LT*, p. 287. For the regime's pamphlet, entered at the Stationers on 28 August, justifying the executions of the eight victims who were hanged on that day, and saying that they had intended to raise rebellion, see *A Briefe Treatise Discovering in Substance the Offences and Ungodly Practices of the Late 14 Traitors*; *AWCBC*, pp. 671, 676.

188 CATHOLICS AND TREASON

August 1588'.[38] William Gunter was hanged on that day, outside the theatre at Holywell Lane, Shoreditch.[39] Thomas Holford was hanged on the 28th as well. He was a client of the Scudamore family at Holme Lacy but had also been at the Bellamy household in November 1584 with Richard Davies, who was an avid collector of martyr stories. It appears that Holford had behaved provocatively by celebrating a Mass in Chester Castle in August 1585. He had avoided arrest on several occasions in the 1580s but was taken as he left the Holborn residence of Swithin Wells.[40] William Dean was executed at Mile End, also on 28 August 1588.[41] On Robert Southwell's account, Dean (hanged along with Henry Webley, his harbourer) was desperate to speak to the crowd 'while on the way to execution'. But this was prevented. A 'shout was suddenly raised' so that 'not a word could be caught by the bystanders'. When 'under the gibbet', he tried again; but he was 'gagged... with a cloth thereby not only stopping his speech but very nearly suffocating him', that is, before he was turned off.[42] Likewise, John Gerard noted that 'Mr Dean, for exhorting the people as he sat in the cart was sore hurt by an officer with a bill upon the head' and 'his mouth was also stopped and muffled with a handkerchief'.[43] On 28 August also had died Robert Morton—in Lincoln's Inn Fields. He was a nephew of the man who had procured the papal excommunication of Elizabeth in 1570.[44] Another of those who perished on that day was Thomas Felton—hanged with James Claxton, probably at Isleworth in Middlesex. Felton was the son of the notorious John Felton who had in 1570 fixed the bull of excommunication to the bishop of London's gates. He was not actually ordained but, noted Challoner, he had received the tonsure from the cardinal of Guise in 1583. Both Claxton and Felton had been released earlier in the 1580s and had been allowed to go abroad but had returned.[45] Felton had been dragged, or rather carried, bound to a chair, to Protestant service in the chapel in Bridewell. He, 'having his hands at first at liberty, stopped his ears with his fingers [so] that he might

---

[38] ABSJ, Collectanea N/i, no. 6, p. 65 (a reference, apparently, to Grene's no longer extant Collectanea A); see also ABSJ, A V, no. 8 (unfoliated), information relating to 'Richard Leigh'.

[39] Anstr., I, p. 140; Challoner, *MMP*, p. 135.

[40] Anstr., I, pp. 171, 172; Challoner, *MMP*, pp. 136–8 (based on AAW, A IV, no. 1, pp. 1–3; ABP, pp. 342–3); Pollen, *UD*, pp. 109–11 (PRO, SP 12/178/67).

[41] Anstr., I, p. 100; for the interception, at Walsingham's direction, of the letters of Edward Shelley and William Dean at Colchester, see HHCP 176/109 (*HMCS*, IX, pp. 86–7); see also Essex Record Office, reference code T/A 391/6 (D/Y, 2/6), pp. 121, 125–6, 127.

[42] Pollen, *UD*, p. 327 (ABSJ, Collectanea P/ii, p. 527).

[43] Pollen, *UD*, p. 289 (ABSJ, Anglia VII, no. 26).

[44] Anstr., I, pp. 238–9 (Morton's harbourer Richard Martin was hanged on 30 August 1588: *AWCBC*, pp. 715, 716). Morton was hanged along with the gentleman Hugh More: Challoner, *MMP*, p. 136. More was noted by Puckering to have been 'reconciled to the see of Rome by one Thomas Stevenson, a Jesuit', i.e. the priest who is thought to have harboured radical political views and may have counselled the Gunpowder plotter Robert Catesby: Pollen, *UD*, p. 158; Questier, *C&C*, p. 311; AAW, B 28, no. 10, p. 305ᵇ. See also E. Unsworth, 'Hugh More of Grantham and the More Family', *The Lincolnshire Historian* 2 (1965), pp. 43–5. Much later, in June 1595, Topcliffe claimed to Sir Robert Cecil that Morton, before arriving at the English College in Rome in April 1586, had been part of a conspiracy to release Mary Stuart: *HMCS*, V, pp. 238–9 (HHCP 32/94).

[45] Challoner, *MMP*, pp. 138–9; Pollen, *UD*, pp. 289–90; *CSPSc 1586–8*, p. 245.

THE INCESTUOUS BASTARD QUEEN   189

not hear what the minister said'. The officials responded by binding his 'hands also to the chair'. He responded by stamping his feet and by 'shouting and...crying oft times "Jesus, Jesus"' so as to drown out the voice of the preacher. At trial at the Newgate sessions, Felton denied the royal supremacy though he said he would not have joined the Spaniards, had they got ashore.[46]

Of those executed at Tyburn on 30 August, one observer 'saw them being taken in a cart' to be hanged, 'followed by an enormous crowd of people' shouting and cheering.[47] Among them was Edward Shelley, convicted of harbouring William Dean, though, significantly, Henry Walpole claimed that Shelley was 'condemned for the keeping of the book called "my lord of Leicester's Commonwealth"'. Edward was the brother of Richard Shelley, who had forced his way through the security cordon to present the 1585 toleration petition to the queen.[48] The priest Richard Leigh was hanged with Edward Shelley and others, including Margaret Ward and John Roche, who had both helped William Watson to abscond from prison. Leigh was, as we saw, one of those who had helped to make a public non-sense of the intended showcase recantation of Anthony Tyrrell at Paul's Cross—the one which had made Tyrrell's puritan handlers look like idiots. That would probably not have endeared Leigh to the London authorities.[49] Southwell reported that Ward 'was flogged and hung up by the wrists, the tips of her toes only touch-ing the ground, for so long a time that she was crippled and paralysed'.[50] Watson had, under intense pressure, recently attended a Protestant service in Bridewell and had been released. Watson had returned to Bridewell and had denounced his former fault, and had then been rearrested, following which he made his escape, leaving Ward and Roche to suffer for assisting him.[51]

---

[46] Challoner, *MMP*, pp. 139–40; AAW, A IV, no. 1, pp. 5–6. Felton's 'causa mortis' was that 'ecclesiae Catholicae reconciliatus fuisset': AAW, B 28, no. 10, p. 305[b]. Peter Penkevell mentioned that 'also in company with these' who were executed immediately after the Armada was one 'Mistress Lowe, arraigned and condemned for harbouring of priests'. She was reprieved 'by her husband's means' but soon after died in prison: Pollen, *AEM*, p. 287; Morris, *TCF*, III (AENB), p. 36. Another source set down that she had been betrayed by the renegade priest William Tedder: ABSJ, Collectanea M, p. 194[a].

[47] *CSPSp 1587–1603*, p. 420.

[48] Pollen, *UD*, p. 158; Pollen, *AEM*, p. 307 (ABSJ, Collectanea M, p. 189[b]).

[49] See p. 175 above. Henry Foxwell, scheduled for execution at this time, was reprieved: AWCBC, p. 703; see pp. 185–6 above. Southwell recorded a courtroom dispute between Leigh and Bishop Aylmer: Pollen, *UD*, p. 326. For Leigh, see also *CSPF 1586–8*, p. 35. Topcliffe was present when he was executed: ABSJ, A V, no. 8 (unfoliated).

[50] Pollen, *UD*, p. 327; Caraman, *HG*, p. 78 (for the claim that Recorder Fleetwood was not in favour of the process against Margaret Ward). For Ward's offence, which had been made a felony by 14 Eliz., c. 2, see Ward, *LT*, pp. 28–9. The account in Yepes is reproduced more or less without alteration in Challoner, *MMP*, pp. 142–5; Diego de Yepes, *Historia Particular de la Persecucion de Inglaterra*...(Madrid, 1599), pp. 614–18; for the differences between Yepes and Christopher Grene's notes derived from George Stoker's narrative (Pollen, *AEM*, pp. 311–13), see Whatmore, *Blessed Margaret Ward*, pp. 8–13.

[51] Challoner, *MMP*, pp. 142–4. Much later, in 1599, Watson said that his Catholic enemies were citing the misfortunes of Ward and her accomplice, the waterman John Roche, in rescuing Watson ('executed by Topcliffe's cruelty') in order to 'terrify' his patrons 'for receiving of' him: Law, *AC*, I, p. 216. By the

190 CATHOLICS AND TREASON

For Catholic commentators such as the Jesuit Robert Southwell it was essential to show precisely that the regime was not being rational and selective in its harshness but was waging a war indiscriminately against the people. Southwell had been physically present on 28 August to watch Gunter's execution and that of Richard Leigh and the others on 30 August. The very next day he wrote that, 'after the peril of the Armada had passed and the army which they had enrolled on land had been disbanded', the queen's government vented 'with inhuman ferocity the hatred they had conceived against the Spaniards' on Catholics. The trials were so rigged that, claimed Southwell, even the judges were doubtful about the evidence offered by the crown. Southwell declared that those who publicly showed any sympathy for the State's victims were arrested.[52]

Exactly how intense a public-relations battle was going on here can be picked up from the production by the regime's disinformation and dirty tricks department (in fact, by Lord Burghley) of a pamphlet entitled *A Copie of a Letter*, the text of which was attributed to the recently executed priest Richard Leigh.[53] Burghley had already advised Sir Francis Walsingham on 12 June 1588 not just that Cardinal Allen's lately published work should be suppressed as overtly treasonable but also that it should be answered in the name of English Catholics.[54]

The claim in Burghley's ventriloquization of a recognizably Catholic loyalist case, through (the conveniently dead) Leigh, was that the majority of English Catholics had absolutely no desire to meet or have anything to do with their alleged friends and saviours, the Spanish Armada ships and the contingents of troops from the army of Flanders, other than to repel them from their beloved sovereign Elizabeth's shores. The alleged author, Leigh, says that he had moved silently among the troops gathered at Tilbury and realized, to his horror, how popular Elizabeth was. Elizabeth is supposed to have delivered her famous speech there on 9 August 1588, and Leigh was already in the Tower on 4 July 1588. Obviously this did not bother Burghley. As Peter Lake explains, the *Copie of a Letter* rehearses the central arguments of the *Execution of Justice* and argues that no one really suffered under Elizabeth Tudor for the sake of religion.[55]

time Yepes's book appeared in print, it could only be read as blaming him for the executions of Ward and Roche.

[52] Pollen, *UD*, pp. 325–7; Devlin, *LRS*, pp. 172–4. Pedro de Ribadeneira's version of these events relied on Robert Persons, *Relacion de Algunos Martyrios, que de Nuevo han Hecho los Hereges en Inglaterra, y de Otras Cosas Tocantes a Nuestra Santa y Catolica Religion. Traduzida de Ingles en Castellano, por el Padre Roberto Personio* (Madrid, 1590; ARCR, I, no. 894); see Weinreich, *PREH*, p. 559.

[53] Sir William Cecil, *A Copie of a Letter...* (1588).

[54] Pollen and MacMahon, *VPH*, p. 169 (PRO, SP 12/211/15, fo. 24^r).

[55] Cecil, *Copie of a Letter*, pp. 21–2; Lake, *BQB*, pp. 312–21; S. Frye, 'The Myth of Elizabeth at Tilbury', *Sixteenth Century Journal* 23 (1992), pp. 95–114. For the many editions of the *Copie of a Letter*, see Lake, *BQB*, p. 320. For the reply to Burghley written by Richard Verstegan and others, see *The Copy of a Letter, lately Written by a Spanishe Gentleman...* (n.p. [Antwerp], 1589), esp. at pp. 6, 37–8.

THE INCESTUOUS BASTARD QUEEN   191

In other words, in the crucible of the Armada campaign and its immediate aftermath, the regime may have been trying to sustain that trademark Burghleian separation between politics and religion, even though Catholics who were being prosecuted under the new statute law would have distinguished between religion and politics in a different way.[56] Even in the instances where the full horror of the law was inflicted on Catholic clergymen, the State's agents, or some of them, did not want to admit that there was any kind of legal novelty in the proceedings. In the case of the trials at Chichester on 30 September 1588 of Edward James, Ralph Crockett, John Owen, and Francis Edwards,[57] the lawyer who conducted the prosecution, Thomas Bowyer, argued that the new statute was not a legal innovation but simply a facilitator of existing treason legislation. The 1585 statute was made, he said, 'for the ease and satisfaction' of the jury 'at trial to prove the overt fact'. How so? Because the pope was 'the queen's capital enemy'. He had 'by sentence deprived her of her estate and absolved her subjects of their allegiance'. In consequence, 'any subject adhering to the pope' was a traitor 'even by the common law'. This included 'those taking priesthood under' the pope's authority 'and returning to win the queen's subjects to their faction'. One of the accused had allegedly said that 'it was a cruel law to make their religion and the taking of priesthood to be treason'. Bowyer, as he saw it, set the record straight. The defendants were not 'in question for any matter of religion but their offence was apparent treason to go about to draw the queen's subjects from their obedience... with adhering also to the pope known to be the queen's mortal enemy'. So the accused 'had no cause to find fault with the law or to allege any cruelty therein'. Bowyer also cited the extant examinations of these people by a variety of government interrogators as sufficient proof of their guilt. The Sussex four are all listed in Puckering's notes dealing with the indictment of clergy at this time.[58]

The pressure on the defendants in this case was such that John Owen recanted. The bishop of Chichester, Thomas Bickley, set out how they were 'deceived and

---

[56] At this point, the council proposed to send the priest James Harrison and his harbourer Thomas Heath up to Stafford for trial and execution there, but they never went: *AWCBC*, pp. 705–7 (PRO, SP 12/216/21, 22. i; Pollen, *UD*, pp. 163–5); Petti, *Roman Catholicism*, pp. xi, 43–4; it was alleged that, at the time of the arrest at Comberford Hall in Staffordshire on 8 April 1588, 'they so cruelly used Mrs Heath...tossing and tumbling her that she, thereby frightened, died the Friday following': Morris, *TCF*, III (AENB), p. 16; Anstr., I, p. 151. Harrison remained in the Tower until 1590 and must, after being moved to the Marshalsea, have been released; he was executed, much later, in March 1602: Anstr., I, p. 151; see pp. 320, 320 n.124 below. Likewise, the council's intention to send the priest Alexander Gerard and his brother Thomas back to Lancaster for the same purpose was not carried into effect: *AWCBC*, pp. 707; PRO, SP 12/216/20, 22. ii.

[57] Crockett and James had been held in gaol in London for over two years: Ward, *LT*, p. 288; Anstr., I, pp. 48, 189; *Miscellanea II*, p. 243; for Crockett's arrest, see PRO, SP 15/29/101, fos 152^r–3^r; PRO, SP 12/188/46, fos 163^r–4^v. That this was meant to be a show trial is indicated by Lord Buckhurst's suggestion, after the grand jury had returned its decision on the evening of 30 September, that the rest of the proceedings should be postponed until the next morning so that 'greater resort from the further parts of the shire [Sussex] might be present': Ward, *LT*, p. 289.

[58] Ward, *LT*, pp. 289–90; Anstr., I, p. 94; PRO, SP 12/217/1, fos 1^r–4^v (quotations at fos 2^v, 3^r); Pollen, *UD*, pp. 155, 157.

192 CATHOLICS AND TREASON

abused in such points' of their religion, which itself 'was made but a cloak to cover their treasons'.[59] The chances are that Owen, known to Bickley during his time in Oxford, was already on a knife-edge between the more aggressive separatist positions available to Catholics and the conformist options which were, we know, being pushed at this moment by other Catholic clergy. In the articles that Owen was made to swear publicly the words used to describe papal authority— 'Antichristian and traitorous'—were 'by one of the justices' amended to merely 'traitorous'.[60]

On 1 October, the others were dragged to Broyle Heath outside Chichester to be butchered. According to Bowyer, the crowd watching the execution was largely hostile or, rather, became hostile when Crockett and James prayed in Latin. The authorities may have believed that Edward James was potentially conformable. He had, with Anthony Tyrrell, been allowed to witness the conference and disputation on controverted religious topics between William Weston and the young Lancelot Andrewes, that is, after Weston was arrested in 1586.[61] In fact James did not waver; but, at the last moment, the sight of Crockett and James being hanged persuaded Francis Edwards to change his mind and he was reprieved.[62]

At Canterbury, also on 1 October 1588, three priests were executed— Christopher Buxton, Gerard Edwards, and Robert Wilcox. Buxton was direct enough about his political loyalties. He explicitly said that he would 'not take her Majesty's part against [an] army, nor do anything to hinder his religion'.[63] Gerard Edwards, whose alias was, rather provocatively, 'Campion', had gone on the record, as Puckering noted, to say that he wished 'he were no worse traitor than Campion that was executed for treason'. Edwards would not 'directly say if' he would 'take the queen's part against the king of Spain's army', but he would 'pray that the Catholic Romish Church' might 'prevail', even 'if an army' should come 'by the apostolic authority to deprive her Majesty and to restore Romish religion'.[64] Wilcox was amazingly defiant if indeed he said, as it was reported, that he would

---

[59] Anstr., I, p. 263; Ward, LT, p. 291; PRO, SP 12/217/1, fo. 2ᵛ.

[60] E. H. Burton and J. H. Pollen (eds), *Lives of the English Martyrs*, 2nd series (1914), I, p. 486.

[61] Caraman, WW, pp. 130–1, 135–6 (Caraman identifies the unnamed priest cited by Weston as Edward James); see also N. Tyacke, 'Lancelot Andrewes and the Myth of Anglicanism', in P. Lake and M. Questier (eds), *Conformity and Orthodoxy in the English Church, 1560–1660* (2000), pp. 5–33, esp. at p. 9. Edward James was known to have been involved in the turning of Anthony Tyrrell in late 1586/ early 1587, i.e. when Tyrrell (temporarily) rejected his new-found loyalty to the queen: PRO, SP 12/199/41, fo. 74ʳ.

[62] Burton and Pollen, *Lives*, I, pp. 487–8.

[63] Pollen, UD, p. 161. Buxton had been a pupil of Nicholas Garlick at Tideswell: AWCBC, pp. 576, 603. Another of those who was hanged on this occasion, a gentleman called Robert Widmerpole, was, said Challoner, 'for some time tutor to the sons of Henry Percy, earl of Northumberland'. The cause of his indictment was that he had 'introduced a priest into the house of the countess of Northumberland': Challoner, MMP, p. 147. On the same day, 1 October, John Robinson was hanged at Ipswich: Anstr., I, p. 294. 'Mr Robinson's head [was] fetched from Ipswich with apparent danger out of the midst of the town': Morris, TCF, III (AENB), p. 52.

[64] Pollen, UD, p. 160.

THE INCESTUOUS BASTARD QUEEN   193

'pray for the army that shall come hither to supplant religion.'[65] At least one person had to be prosecuted for speaking out in favour of the Canterbury martyrs. John Gardener was charged with saying in November 1588 that Buxton and the two priests who were executed with him, whom Gardener referred to as Jesuits, were 'better than the Protestants and died better than they would do'. Gardener also expressed his wish that the Armada should triumph. He refused to believe that the Spanish expeditionary force had entirely failed in its purposes.[66]

The regime's own caveats about puritanism were now, if only temporarily, much less in evidence. One week before the Canterbury executions, the priest William Way was executed at Kingston upon Thames. After conviction (at the Newgate sessions rather than in front of the Surrey commissioners), he was transported by river to be hanged in Surrey. He was executed there on 23 September 1588. Katharine Longley plausibly suggests that Kingston was selected as the place for Way's execution because of the strength of puritan feeling there, even though John Udall, who had a lectureship at Kingston parish church and had been working with the puritan printer Robert Waldegrave, had been deprived only two months before—in July 1588.[67]

Indeed, one of the printers of the pamphlet which described the proceedings against John Hewett was, it is suggested, none other than Waldegrave. The pamphlet narrated Hewett's execution and those of William Hartley and the layman Robert Sutton.[68] This Robert Sutton, a layman from Kegworth in Leicestershire, up to the last moment affirmed that he would take the queen's side 'against what pope or potentate soever'. But he baulked when he was told that he must affirm the royal supremacy.[69] Or, rather, he was said to have confessed 'her

[65] Pollen, *UD*, p. 161.

[66] Questier, *C&C*, p. 40 (Gardener was indicted in February 1589). Cf. P. Marshall, 'Choosing Sides and Talking Religion in Shakespeare's England', in D. Loewenstein and M. Witmore (eds), *Shakespeare and Early Modern Religion* (Cambridge, 2015), pp. 40–56, at p. 48–9.

[67] Ward, LT, p. 287; K. Longley, 'He was Especiall…': Blessed William Way, Martyred at Kingston-upon-Thames, 23 September, 1588', *Southwark Record* (July 1952), pp. 141–6, at p. 144; *ODNB, sub* Udall, John (article by C. Cross); Kingston History Centre, Kingston-upon-Thames Chamberlains' Accounts, KD5/1/1 (formerly D. IV, b. 1), p. 122; Canterbury Cathedral Archives, Literary MS, C. 2, no. 84, fo. 1ʳ (letter of 12 September 1588 of the privy council to the commissioners of oyer and terminer for Surrey to secure, if possible, the services of the moderate puritan lawyer James Dalton to assist in the prosecution of those to be indicted); Pollen, *AEM*, p. 307 (ABSJ, Collectanea M, p. 189ᵇ); ABSJ, CP (William Way); *HC 1558–1603*, II, pp. 8–9. Waldegrave had at this point relocated to East Molesey, close to Udall's parish: *ODNB, sub* Waldegrave, Robert (article by A. J. Mann); Collinson, *EPM*, pp. 391f, 497.

[68] Anstr., I, pp. 163–4; for Waldegrave's involvement in the printing of the pamphlet, see Early English Books Online database; for the date of the pamphlet (24 October 1588), see C. A. Newdigate (ed.), 'Some Hostile "True Reports" of the Martyrs', pt 3: 'Fourteen Martyrs of the Armada Year', in *Miscellanea* (CRS 32, 1932), p. 411. Waldegrave appears to have taken part in the printing of this pamphlet at the point that he was working with John Penry. This was also the period in which he turned out the first of the Marprelate pamphlets: *ODNB, sub* Waldegrave, Robert (article by A. J. Mann); A. Peel (ed.), *The Notebook of John Penry 1593* (Camden Society, 3rd series, 67, 1944), pp. xiii, xviii.

[69] Anstr., I, p. 164; *A True Report of…John Weldon*, sig. Ciiiᵛ–ivʳ; Challoner, *MMP*, p. 151.

194 CATHOLICS AND TREASON

Majesty [to be] supreme governor within her Highness's dominions over all persons but not over all causes'.[70] Hartley, convicted at the Middlesex sessions on 18 September 1588 with Sutton and Hewett, was executed at Shoreditch outside the theatre. He had in the early 1580s escaped the regime's vengeance against Campion.[71] At trial, however—so the hostile regime pamphlet account said—'it was testified to his face, by the oath of one Walton then present, that a letter was sent this last summer by the said Hartley out of England to Paris, to certain seminary priests there'. The letter expressed 'the full resolution of the said Hartley, and some other [of] his confederates (immediately upon the landing of the Spaniards) to have suppressed her Majesty's Tower of London and to have fired the city'. Hartley denied this, of course, but there was read out 'a part of his own examination' in which he allegedly said that if, after Rome had excommunicated the queen, a papal army came into the country he would pray for its success and that it 'might prevail in that cause of Catholic religion'. Moreover, 'in that faith he would spend (if he had them) ten thousand millions of lives'.[72] As for Hewett, the pamphlet at some considerable length rehearsed the haranguing of him by an unnamed Protestant minister who delivered in effect a puritan sermon, history lecture, and bizarre prayer session at the gallows and, in the course of all this, insisted that 'not the pope but the prince has had, and ought to have, the supreme authority in all causes within their own dominions, yes, even over the bishops themselves'.[73]

The ripple of retaliatory violence continued outward into the provinces. Edward Burden was executed at York in late November 1588. Robert Dalby was hanged subsequently with John Amias [Anne] in the same place in mid-March 1589.[74] One of the Catholic spectators at the double execution was the future

---

[70] A True Report of... John Weldon, sig. B[r]. Among Alban Butler's papers there is 'an extract from a letter dated Gand [Ghent] 1 September 1630', from one William Nayler, who remembered that 'in the year 1590 or 1591 [in fact, 1588] I saw one Mr Sutton a layman and a schoolmaster put to death at Clerkenwell in London; to whom the sheriff promised to procure his pardon if he would but pronounce absolutely the word "all" for he would that he should acknowledge the queen to be supreme head in all causes without any restriction but he would acknowledge her to be supreme head [only] in all causes temporal': ABP, p. 547. For William Nayler, see HMCS, XVI, p. 261, XXI, p. 228; ABP, pp. 547–9. By contrast, John Gerard claimed that Sutton was 'executed only for that he had been shriven' by 'one Mr Blythe, an old priest in Newgate': Pollen, UD, p. 291 (ABSJ, Anglia VII, no. 26); see also AAW, B 28, no. 10, p. 307.

[71] Anstr., I, p. 156; Jeaffreson, MCR, I, p. 180, II, pp. 193–4; Devlin, LRS, p. 174 (for the mooted link with Shakespeare's The Comedy of Errors); R. A. Foakes (ed.), The Comedy of Errors (1991), pp. xvii–xviii.

[72] A True Report of... John Weldon, sigs A4[v]–B[r]. I assume that Walton was the same man who had been at Rheims and testified against the earl of Arundel: Pollen and MacMahon, VPH, pp. 244, 262, 272, 277, 286, 288.

[73] A True Report of... John Weldon, sig. B3[r]. As Charles Newdigate noted, the unnamed Protestant minister at Mile End must have been the author of the pamphlet: Newdigate (ed.), 'Some Hostile "True Reports"', p. 411.

[74] Challoner, MMP, pp. 151, 152–3; G. Anstruther, 'Corrections to C. A. Newdigate's "Our Martyrs"', Biographical Studies 1 (1953–4), pp. 112–16, at p. 113; Pollen, AEM, pp. 328–30; Foley, RSJ, III, pp. 737–8, 739–40 (AVCAU, Liber 1422 [Grene, Collectanea F], section 4, pp. 69[b]–70[a], 70[b]–1[a]); cf.

THE INCESTUOUS BASTARD QUEEN   195

appellant priest Anthony Champney. He included the event in his unpublished 'Annales', and he remembered that an unnamed gentlewoman forced her way through to the gibbet and 'declared an extraordinary motion and affection of soul' before being bundled away.[75] Although the regime was still plugging away with its claims that it did not punish people for religion, Champney was obviously not convinced. In later years he was an implacable foe of the Society of Jesus and a vocal loyalist Catholic priest. But since he, soon after witnessing this execution in York, presented himself at Rheims, it is possible that the sight of it may have helped, in effect, to radicalize him.

To some Catholics, it seemed that a horrific and total purge was beginning. Peter Penkevell, who from inside his London prison watched so many of his friends being dragged off to execution, believed that 'all the priests in Wisbech and very many other Catholics' would be 'arraigned'. It was only the earl of Leicester's death on 4 September which, Penkevell thought, temporarily stopped these killings.[76] By 20 December 1588 Southwell could write that 'now the fierce cruelty has let up' and, 'although it has not ceased to be cruelty, yet there is in the cruelty a certain degree' of shame. Some Catholic gentry were being released from their prisons; and 'for some time now no one has been led to the scaffold' even though 'many expect it, among them the illustrious earl of Arundel'.[77]

Inevitably this string of cases, which bulks quite large in Challoner's *Memoirs* and other martyrologies (although comparatively little is known about many of the martyrs of the late 1580s), looks like, if not exactly a massacre, then a step change in the Elizabethan State's relationship with Catholicism—a surge of cruelty, spurred on by the war, which can be directly linked with the increasingly oppositional tenor of the seminaries and their leading spokesmen—ideologues such as Robert Persons. As at other points in this volume, the claim is that this is something which can be conveyed only through a narrative rather than, say,

---

Pollen, *UD*, p. 192. For problems identifying John Amias (perhaps *vere* William Anne of Frickley, near Wakefield), see Anstr., I, p. 7; ABSJ, CP (John Amias [Anne]): Ernestine Anne to Charles Newdigate, Corpus Christi, 1928. Dalby had allegedly attempted suicide out of despair while he was a minister in the Church of England; he had arrived at Rheims on 30 September 1586: Pollen, *AEM*, p. 330; Anstr., I, p. 96. At about this point, in Gloucester, a glover, one William Lampley, was executed, on one account 'for persuading some of his kin to the Catholic religion', even though the judge, Manwood, 'seemed unwilling that he should die, and therefore made him that offer that, if he would but say he would go to church, he should have his pardon', but to no avail: AWCBC, pp. 744, 748–9, 752; Morris, *TCF*, III (AENB), p. 43.

[75] Challoner, *MMP*, pp. 152–3; E. M. Charlton, *Burghwallis and the Anne Family* (privately printed, n.d.), pp. 13–14.

[76] Pollen, *AEM*, pp. 287–8; for Penkevell's imprisonment, see AWCBC, p. 882; *Miscellanea II*, p. 283. Ribadeneira wrote that Elizabeth insisted on the deaths of those who had been condemned before the earl of Leicester died: Weinreich, *PREH*, p. 559.

[77] McCoog, *LRS*, p. 187 (Southwell to Acquaviva, 20 December 1588). James Clayton, who had come to England with John Hambley, was arrested at Christmas 1588 as he tried to make contact with the Catholics in prison at Derby. He was believed to have been 'conversant with [Thomas] Alfield'. He was sentenced at the next assizes but died in prison on 22 July 1589: Anstr., I, p. 79; PRO, SP 12/153/78, fo. 153ᵛ; AVCAU, Liber 1422 [Grene, Collectanea F], section 1, p. 4ᵇ.

196 CATHOLICS AND TREASON

through a purely statistical analysis. It is only the archival sources that allow us to glimpse or guess at what might have been at stake in such cases, individually and collectively, and how contemporaries might have interpreted them. The question was, then, what would happen when, even as the war continued, other political issues—and, first and foremost, the subject of the succession, in both England/ Britain and France—started to be resolved in ways that were quite beyond the control of Persons and his friends?

Anti-Popery and Anti-Puritanism

Lord Chancellor Hatton's opening and closing speeches in the 1589 parliament were, for all his lengthy comments about the threat from Spain and from Catholic traitors, scathing about the danger from puritans—'men of a very intemperate humour', as he called them on 4 February. Richard Bancroft preached his anti-puritan Paul's Cross sermon on 9 February 1589. This helped to stoke up even further the Marprelate agitation.[78] This did not mean, of course, that the regime had any collective intention of publicly presenting a kinder face to Catholic separatists. In April 1589 it was decided to put the earl of Arundel on trial for, as the former Spanish ambassador to London Bernardino de Mendoza put it, 'having had an understanding' with the Armada. Arundel had, it was alleged, 'joined the Holy League' and had procured a priest to say a Mass for the success of the Spanish king's forces.[79]

There is no evidence that those Church of England clerics whom scholars now tend to call avant-garde conformists harboured much sympathy towards Catholic separatists—why would they? But the emergence of a Bancroftian platform against puritan sectaries may have begun to problematize the continuation of the legal assault against Catholic priests and their patrons. At the same time, this meant that insistence on the use of the treason law against Catholic separatist clergy and their harbourers was one of the diminishing number of positions which remained available to those who looked with horror at the bedding in of a conformist anti-puritanism. The obvious example here was Sir Francis Knollys.

---

[78] Questier, *DP*, p. 186; Hartley, *PPE*, II, p. 419; Collinson, *EPM*, pp. 396–400.

[79] *CSPSp 1587–1603*, pp. 515–16, 530–1, 536; A. G. Petti (ed.), *Recusant Documents from the Ellesmere Manuscripts* (CRS 60, 1968), pp. 32–3; PRO, SP 12/223/77–8, 85–6; Pollen and MacMahon, *VPH*, pp. 185–289, esp. at pp. 211–13; *HMCL*, V, pp. 99, 100. Henry Garnet recorded on 1 May 1589 that Arundel's condemnation was both unexpected and deeply unpopular; and when the 'crowd saw the earl coming out' of Westminster Hall 'with the axe edge turned in towards him...suddenly there was a great uproar that was carried miles along the river bank'. Faced with some peers' refusal to convict, Burghley had personally urged Arundel's condemnation only, swearing that sentence would not be carried out: ABSJ, GC, pp. 32–3, 41–2 (ARSJ, FG 651/624); Caraman, *WW*, p. 20; Devlin, *LRS*, pp. 191–5; Caraman, *HG*, pp. 92–3. Mendoza in Paris reported the rumour that other Catholic prisoners would also be condemned and face death: *CSPSp 1587–1603*, p. 536.

THE INCESTUOUS BASTARD QUEEN 197

On 20 March 1589, Knollys sounded off to Secretary Walsingham that Archbishop John Whitgift and his colleagues were subverting the royal supremacy. The bishops' assertions were the 'highway to popery'.[80] On 24 May, he lectured Burghley on 'the dangerous consequences that may ensue to her Majesty's safety by the loose bridle given to the ambitions and covetousness of our bishops'. He took the opportunity to enclose a copy of a letter which he had just sent to Dr John Hammond, someone who, as we have seen, could also be relied on to hound and prosecute popish clergy with thoroughness and who also despised the new *jure divino* episcopal claims to superiority.[81]

Significantly, Knollys was heavily involved in the prosecution of four Catholics in Oxford in mid-1589 within days of the judicial condemnation of the earl of Arundel, in the proceedings against whom Knollys had been so active. It seems highly likely that this episode in Oxford was intended to serve as a commentary on the recent trial of this now utterly disgraced Catholic peer. On 18 May, the clergymen Richard Yaxley and George Nichols and the gentleman Thomas Belson and a servant, Humphrey ap Richard, had been arrested at the Catherine Wheel in Oxford.[82] Belson had briefly been at the Rheims seminary and had been detained in the summer of 1585. This was almost certainly because he had been involved in carrying messages between Arundel and William Allen at Rheims and had been betrayed by the earl's chaplain (but also Walsingham's client) Edward Grately. After the Babington business, Belson had been deported but then had returned from the Continent.[83] For his part Yaxley had, on arrival in England, made contact with Richard Dibdale and was caught up in William

[80] PRO, SP 12/223/23, fo. 36ʳ.

[81] *HMCS*, III, pp. 412–13, 367; W. D. J. Cargill Thompson, 'Sir Francis Knollys's Campaign against the *Jure Divino* Theory of Episcopacy', in W. D. J. Cargill Thompson, *Studies in the Reformation: Luther to Hooker* (1980), pp. 94–130, at pp. 113–14, 125–6; Richardson, *RP*, pp. 22f; *ODNB*, sub Knollys, Francis (article by W. T. MacCaffrey); see pp. 127–8, 163 n.102 above. For the other letters that Knollys sent to Burghley and to Walsingham on this issue, see, e.g., BL, Lansdowne MS 59, no. 8, fo. 15ʳ; SP 12/223/62, fo. 110ʳ; BL, Lansdowne MS 61, nos 54, 57, 66 (fos 151ʳ, 157ʳ, 174ʳ); BL, Lansdowne MS 64, nos 32, 69 (fos 86ʳ, 162ʳ); BL, Lansdowne MS 65, no. 60, fo. 170ʳ; BL, Lansdowne MS 68, no. 84, fo. 190ʳ; for Whitgift's response to Knollys in autumn 1589, see BL, Additional MS 48064, nos 12, 35 (fos 94ʳ, 226ʳ–34ʳ).

[82] Whereas Challoner says that these Catholics were detained by university officials, the arrests were in fact made by agents sent down from London, i.e. Richard Elsworth and John Bradford, on the privy council's own warrant: Challoner, *MMP*, p. 154; Davidson, *RC*, pp. 453, 454; Anstr., I, pp. 250–1, citing PRO, E 351/542, mem. 128ᵛ. For Belson, see Kilroy, *EC*, p. 51 (Belson had been taught by the Oxford Catholic Hebrew scholar George Etheridge); C. Kelly, *Blessed Thomas Belson: His Life and Times 1563–1589* (Gerrards Cross, 1987), esp. ch. 10. For Knollys's role in prosecuting Arundel, see Pollen and MacMahon, *VPH*, pp. 232, 235, 249, 264, 265.

[83] Kelly, *Blessed Thomas Belson*, pp. 74f; *Miscellanea II*, pp. 261, 264; *Miscellanea III* (CRS 3, 1906), pp. 21, 22, 23, 24; Pollen and MacMahon, *VPH*, p. 132. Christine Kelly suggests that there may have been a family relationship between Belson and Grately: Kelly, *Blessed Thomas Belson*, p. 77. Belson had come back to England in the company of the soon-to-be arrested and executed Francis Ingleby, who served as a chaplain to Margaret Clitherow: Knox, *DD*, p. 201; see p. 164 above. The authorities already had the confession of one William Forrest, an admirer of Campion, who testified that Belson and his brother had urged him to avoid the church, for it was 'rather a hell than heaven to come to church': PRO, SP 12/173/29, i, fo. 48ʳ.

198　CATHOLICS AND TREASON

Weston's exorcisms. In late 1586/early 1587 he attempted to secure the release of one of the alleged demoniacs, Sara Williams, when, soon after Dibdale's execution, she was imprisoned at Oxford for recusancy.[84]

Belson's interrogation in Oxford was led by university senior management—the vice-chancellor, Martin Heton, and the president of St John's, Francis Willis, who had close connections with the London godly. Knollys supervised the transfer of the prisoners back to Oxford after a violent cross-examination of the priests in London.[85] Knollys was, says Challoner, 'appointed to be present at their trial to overawe the jury'. First the harbourer, the owner of the Catherine Wheel inn, was condemned in praemunire; then the others were sentenced and were executed on 5 July 1589.[86] A letter sent to Sir Francis Englefield in Spain described how news of the trial and execution had come to Antwerp—particularly of how Yaxley and Nichols had been horrendously tortured in Bridewell. It was claimed that two renegade clergymen, Anthony Tyrrell and one other, had been 'brought in to confront them, especially Mr Yaxley, who[m] they testified to be a seminary priest'. Tyrrell was fresh from his second attempt at a recantation sermon at Paul's Cross, in late 1588. He had finally been persuaded, presumably by the sight of the Armada and by the recent executions of Catholics, to do this in the way that the authorities demanded. Yaxley had been sent to the Tower and threatened with further torture. All the accused had gone back to Oxford. There, at an 'open assize', they had been 'condemned by the verdict of a puritan quest picked out of purpose and, after, executed'. The letter writer added that 'it were too long to recite all' these martyrs' 'disputes with the puritans and other their godly sayings and examples'.[87]

On this occasion, the condemned were stopped from speaking on the scaffold, or at least from addressing the crowd. The 'standers-by seemed to have more than an ordinary compassion' for Yaxley because of his 'youth, beauty and sweet behaviour'; but after the sentence was carried out and 'their heads were set on the old walls of the castle...some false zealots disfigured their faces, cutting...them with their knives, because of the extraordinary beauty that was observed in them'.[88]

[84] *AWCBC*, pp. 756–7; Samuel Harsnett, *A Declaration of Egregious Popish Impostures*...(1603), pp. 191–2, 203–5, 208.

[85] For the interrogation in London, see Davidson, RC, p. 458; see also *ODNB*, *sub* Heton, Martin (article by B. Usher). Edmund Lilly, master of Balliol, was named as one of the interrogators: *AWCBC*, p. 780.

[86] Challoner, *MMP*, p. 157. Nichols had reconciled a convicted felon (a 'noted highwayman', one Harcourt Taverner, the son of Richard Taverner, sheriff of Oxfordshire in 1569, and himself the great-uncle of the antiquarian Anthony Wood) in October 1587, i.e. while Nichols was at liberty and working in Oxford: Davidson, RC, pp. 460–2; Weinreich, *PREH*, pp. 572–3.

[87] Pollen, *UD*, pp. 168–9; Davidson, RC, p. 458; Anstr., I, p. 251; *AWCBC*, pp. 766–9; Caraman, *HG*, pp. 82–3.

[88] Challoner, *MMP*, pp. 157–8. Ribadeneira, relying on Persons, retailed the story (which appears in Challoner) that, when the quarters of the martyrs had been hung from the city walls, Nichols's right hand rose up of its own accord in a threatening posture: Weinreich, *PREH*, p. 571.

THE INCESTUOUS BASTARD QUEEN   199

Within hours of George Nichols and Richard Yaxley being hacked to bits in Oxford, Knollys put pen to paper in order to write to Burghley. With Pavlovian predictability, he tied in the recent trials to the rise in the national Church of a new Whitgiftian clericalism. Knollys observed that he had, in Oxford, also found 'two sorts of subjects', both clerical and lay. The one sought to maintain the queen's 'jurisdiction touching her supreme government', but the other kind tried to 'maintain the jurisdiction of my lord archbishop', that is, Whitgift. On the plus side, though, the man who had taken the Catholic prisoners down to Oxford to be proceeded against 'by the order of Mr Topcliffe and of Mr Attorney' could tell Burghley how their treatment had daunted the papists 'that before this proceeding here did proudly advance themselves as though they ought to be taken for good subjects'. Knollys enclosed Whitgift's 'archdeacons' articles of inquisition lately set out to be answered by the inquiry of churchwardens...of every...parish'. With dripping and mordant sarcasm, Knollys added that, if Burghley would persuade Whitgift to get the bishops to acknowledge the queen's royal supremacy and to admit publicly that they had 'no superiority over their inferior brethren' except as they derived it from the queen, this would guarantee the queen's safety. It would also 'overthrow the traitorous' practices 'of all Jesuits and seminaries'— such as the very people that Knollys had, only a few hours before, watched being strangled and dismembered before the mob sliced their heads into pieces.[89]

On 30 August 1589, seven weeks or so after the execution of Nichols and the others, Knollys wrote from Ewelme to Burghley and to Walsingham about a warrant which had been issued earlier in the year and had been sent down into the county in order to arrest popish clergy. The two bearers of the warrant (one of whom, Richard Elsworth, had brought down Nichols and the others to London) had searched 'the house of one Mr [John] English, dwelling...near to Watlington and there' they 'found a recusant, naming himself Randall'. Mr Randall was Mr English's brother-in-law. The kicker was that Mr English was a servant of Lord Chancellor Hatton. Randall allegedly confessed that he was a priest, although he retracted that confession in front of Knollys. To justify himself, Randall had claimed that he was of 'Lord Montague's sect and as ready a man to fight against the Spaniards as my Lord Montague was'. Randall's appeal to the loyalist CV of Anthony Browne, first Viscount Montague, would probably not have impressed Knollys. The fact that the lord chancellor's circle harboured Catholic separatists even while Hatton presumed to lecture parliament on the evils of puritan separatism was evidently too egregious for Knollys to ignore. In his letter Knollys also lamented to Burghley that he felt 'discouraged to serve her Majesty faithfully against these popish traitors and traitorous recusants because I do not find myself

[89] BL, Lansdowne MS 61, no. 47, fo. 138^{r-v}; see also H. Bowler and T. McCann (eds), *Recusants in the Exchequer Pipe Rolls 1581–1592* (CRS 71, 1986), p. 20; *AWCBC*, p. 764.

200 CATHOLICS AND TREASON

well backed nor countenanced in my standing in defence of her Majesty's right in her supreme government against the foul claimed superiority of bishops'. He said also that he was not surprised there were so many Martinists, 'since our bishops do encroach upon her Majesty's supreme government'.[90]

The Oxford martyrs' cases were written up and sent abroad.[91] The narrative then appeared in multiple pamphlet translations—in Italian, French, and Spanish. The one in French was for the attention principally of leaguer Catholics, just in case they were unaware what horrors the rule of a heretic inflicted on the faithful.[92]

There are other martyrs in 1589 about whom, by contrast, we know relatively little. William Spenser was executed at York on 24 September 1589. He was approached on the morning after the trial by John King, future bishop of London, who at this time was a domestic chaplain to the recently arrived Archbishop John Piers and had known Spenser in Oxford, where Spenser had been a fellow of Trinity. King allegedly offered, for the sake of 'old acquaintance', that 'if you confer I will get you stayed and then after [I will get] your pardon'. But Spenser would have none of it, nor would he when King approached him again at the gallows.[93] Hanged with Spenser was one Robert Hardesty, perhaps a relative of the priest William Hardesty who was from Hampsthwaite in the West Riding.[94] William

---

[90] BL, Harleian MS 6994, no. 106, fo. 197^{r-v}; Davidson, RC, pp. 260–1; Questier, C&C, p. 125; Cargill Thompson, 'Sir Francis Knollys's Campaign', pp. 117, 239.

[91] AWCBC, pp. 762 f.

[92] ARCR, I, nos 894–8; Davidson, RC, pp. 452–4. Davidson identifies, as the 'prime source', the pamphlet Breve Relatione del Martirio di doi Reverendi Sacerdoti et doi Laici, seguito l'anno MDLXXXIX. in Oxonio, Citta di Studio in Inghilterra, 1590 (Rome, 1590), but cf. ARCR, I, no. 894 (below); and for the French translations, see Discours Veritable du Martyre de deux Prestres et Deux Laycz...(Paris, 1590; ARCR, I, no. 895; this translation was arranged by Robert Bellarmine, to whom a copy of Persons's work had been sent from Rome by Joseph Creswell; AWCBC, pp. 762, 777, 791); Sommaire Discours du Notable Martyre...(Lyon, 1590; ARCR, I, no. 896), the full title of which described Elizabeth as a second Jezebel: Davidson, RC, p. 454. Bellarmine wrote to Joseph Creswell on 9/19 February 1590 acknowledging that he had received a report of the martyrdoms from Creswell and that, 'in order to encourage our own French Catholics, the account will soon be translated into French and published', because France was in danger of going the same way as England. Bellarmine was at that point in Paris, serving as a counsellor to Cardinal Enrico Caietani: Davidson, RC, p. 453, citing J. Brodrick, The Life and Work of Blessed Robert Francis Cardinal Bellarmine, S. J. 1542–1621 (2 vols, 1928), I, p. 204; AWCBC, p. 791. Christine Kelly suggests that the French translation, Sommaire Discours, might have been written by Robert Tempest, Thomas Belson's relative by marriage: Kelly, Blessed Thomas Belson, p. 85. Persons's Relacion de Algunos Martyrios incorporates Relacion de Quatro Martyrios; the latter work was, according to Allison and Rogers, either written by Robert Persons or translated by him from a now lost original in England: ARCR, I, no. 894. Persons's work, or the text on which it was based, was incorporated into Ribadeneira's text, and, predictably, it appeared in Yepes's Historia Particular: AWCBC, pp. 762, 792, 808, 822.

[93] AWCBC, p. 847; Anstr., I, p. 329; ODND, sub King, John (article by P. McCullough).

[94] Foley, RSJ, III, pp. 740–2 (AVCAU, Liber 1422 [Grene, Collectanea F], section 4, pp. 71^a–2^b); AWCBC, pp. 834–5, 846, 853 (indicating that Hardesty was not charged with aiding Spenser but with assisting Catholics, including clergy, in York Castle gaol); AVCAU, Scr. 21/2/2 (account of Spenser and Hardesty); ABSJ, Collectanea M, p. 53^b.

THE INCESTUOUS BASTARD QUEEN 201

Hardesty was almost certainly already an associate of the loyalist Thomas Bell and, like him, would soon cross the line and renounce Rome.[95]

The immediate post-Armada period arguably witnessed the peak of the fortunes of the Holy League in France following the immolation of Henry III and the attempt to exclude Henry of Navarre from the succession to the French crown. With the further radicalization of French politics and the appeal to papal authority in order to direct the succession away from the line of direct hereditary right, there was inevitably a sense for some Catholics that what was good for France was, despite the failure of the Armada, definitely still good for England. Nicholas Fuller and James Dalton reported to the council on 12 December 1589 that the recently taken priest Francis Dickenson was 'very arrogant...and desperate'.[96] Dickenson had allegedly claimed that, 'if any bull of Pius Quintus, Gregory the thirteenth or Sextus Quintus to deprive her Majesty of her crown be published and not revoked by the pope, the same ought [to] be obeyed by the subjects of England'. Equally the queen should not 'be obeyed as a lawful queen by her subjects in England or Ireland for the pope...has power to deprive the queen and to discharge her subjects of their allegiance towards her'. Dickenson's opinion was that 'if the pope should set out such a bull and send an army to deprive the queen and to set up the Catholic Romish religion he would take part in that case with that army, and persuade as many Catholics as he could to do the like'. When the queen was 'put down', the crown should go to the man that was 'next of blood, being a Catholic'. This was an articulation, of course, of the case being made by the League in France now that Henry III was dead.[97]

Miles Gerard, who had been arrested with Dickenson, was adjudged by Fuller and Dalton to be 'a simple fellow misled by evil persuasion'. But, simple or not, Gerard allegedly said much the same—that the pope had 'supreme authority above all kings and princes whatsoever in causes ecclesiastical and, for that cause in such cases, he has authority over and above the queen in this realm'. Furthermore, he declared that the 'pope has authority to deprive all kings and queens, if it seems necessary and expedient for the Catholic Romish religion of the Catholic Roman Church'. These, at any rate, were the words that the interrogators wrote down. It was not completely clear whether Gerard would himself instruct Catholics to fight for an invading force.[98]

---

[95] Anstr., I, p. 148; Lake and Questier, *Trials*, pp. 139–40, 166, 167, 238, 245; Morris, *TCF*, III (RHPN), p. 193.

[96] Pollen, *UD*, p. 171 (PRO, SP 12/229/27, fo. 44^r). Dickenson, with Miles Gerard, had been betrayed before they embarked at Calais on their cross-Channel journey; they were arrested on board ship at Dover on 24 November 1589: Pollen, *AEM*, p. 314; Anstr., I, pp. 101–2, 130. In Bridewell, Topcliffe used torture in order to obtain a confession from Dickenson: Anstr., I, p. 102; Thomas Fitzherbert, *A Defence of the Catholyke Cause...* (Antwerp, 1602), (2nd part, with separate title page, entitled *An Apology of T. F. ...* (1602)), sig. C2^{r-v}.

[97] Pollen, *UD*, p. 172 (PRO, SP 12/229/27. i, fo. 45^{r-v}).

[98] Pollen, *UD*, pp. 171 (PRO, SP 12/229/27, fo. 44^r), 173 (PRO, SP 12/229/27. ii, fo. 47^r).

202 CATHOLICS AND TREASON

Both Dickenson and Gerard were hanged on 13 April 1590.[99] As Anstruther remarks, 'the guilty were normally executed in the county town where the treason was first committed'. But this was not what happened on this occasion.[100] The execution took place in Rochester. There is no contemporary explanation for this. But there was perhaps a link with Rochester's position close to the coast. The Jesuit John Curry said that they were charged with having been 'commissioned to draw off sailors from England for the service of the Catholic king'.[101] If they had had the opportunity to do this, they would have been following the line taken by William Allen in his recently published defence of Sir William Stanley.[102]

There was a posthumous attempt to destroy Dickenson's reputation for godliness. Topcliffe claimed that the priest had been 'naughty with women'. This was exactly the same accusation that Topcliffe made to the priest Christopher Bales's face 'in the sessions house'.[103] Bales had been hanged in Fleet Street on 4 March 1590 on 'a pair of gallows erected over against Fetter Lane'.[104]

Other fatal prosecutions followed. All in all, they suggested that the room for negotiation between the authorities and those who might be marked for death had shrunk to almost nothing. Thus Matthew Hutton, generally regarded as a moderate in his dealings with separatist Catholics, was responsible, it appears, for the arrest on 11 April of Edmund Duke, Richard Hill, John Hogg, and Richard Holiday on evidence supplied by an informer. These four clerics were very swiftly arraigned and on 27 May 1590 they were hanged at Durham, in fact at nearby Dryburn, in front of an allegedly sceptical crowd—'scarce any said "God save the queen" at their death'.[105]

---

[99] Anstr., I, pp. 102, 130; Challoner, *MMP*, p. 162. Miles Gerard knew the seminarist George Hethershall, who had been arrested on 12 February 1584 at Great Sankey, near Warrington: Pollen, *UD*, p. 170 (PRO, SP 12/229/5, fo. 15^r); Anstr., I, pp. 175–7.

[100] Anstr., I, p. 102.   [101] Pollen, *AEM*, p. 315.   [102] Allen, *The Copie of a Letter.*

[103] Pollen, *AEM*, p. 322; AVCAU, Scr. 36/8/1; William Watson, *A Decacordon of Ten Quodlibeticall Questions concerning Religion and State* (n.p. [London], 1602), p. 266; Thomas Fitzherbert, *A Defence of the Catholyke Cause...* (2nd part, *An Apology of T. F. ...*), sig. C2$^{r–v}$.

[104] Challoner, *MMP*, p. 160; see p. 49 above for the hanging on the same day of Alexander Blake and Nicholas Horner. For Horner, see *AWCBC*, pp. 889–91. Horner's case was cited in Robert Persons's attack on the October 1591 proclamation, his *Elizabethae Angliae Reginae Haeresim Calvinianam Propugnantis...per D. Andream Philopatrum* (Antwerp, 1592), pp. 198–9; *AWCBC*, pp. 896–7. Bales's harbourer, Henry Thirkell, turned renegade: Anstr., I, p. 19; *CSPD* 1591–4, p. 496.

[105] Challoner, *MMP*, p. 164; *APC 1590*, pp. 70–1; Anstr., I, p. 107; ABSJ, GC, p. 58 (ARSJ, FG 651/624: Garnet to [Acquaviva], 13 September 1590); Morris, *TCF*, III (AENB), pp. 40–1. Duke had come out on the side of the Jesuit administrators of the English College in Rome in mid-1585 (M. J. Cashman, 'The Gateshead Martyr', *RH* 11 (1971), pp. 121–32, at p. 122; ABSJ, Collectanea N/i, p. 35) and had in late December 1589 expressed the desire to make the spiritual exercises: ABSJ, Collectanea M, pp. 101^b–3^b. One of Challoner's sources was the Durham priest and future appellant Cuthbert Trollop, who relayed the story of miraculous occurrences (the well, from which water was taken to boil the martyrs' remains, dried up, and 'little glistering things...upon the bushes' nearby were observed by Mrs Dorothy Hodgson) at the time of the execution: AAW, A IV, no. 22, p. 123 (partly reproduced in Challoner, *MMP*, p. 164, relying on ABP, p. 412); see also Knaresborough's letter from John Yaxley of 17 July 1707: pp. 14–15 above. One of Duke's arms ended up at St Omer: ABSJ, Collectanea N/i, p. 35; *AWCBC*, pp. 922–4 (ABSJ, Anglia V, no. 72). See also A. M. C. Forster, 'The Maire Family of County Durham', *RH* 10 (1969–70), pp. 332–46.

THE INCESTUOUS BASTARD QUEEN   203

The same kind of no-compromise message may have been worked into the executions, three weeks earlier, on 6 May 1590 of Edward Jones (arrested in Fleet Street) and of Anthony Middleton (taken by Topcliffe in Clerkenwell). Middleton and Jones were hanged in the places where they were arrested. Topcliffe, who had tortured Jones, was very much in evidence.[106] Jones was strung up 'near the Conduit', that is, at the end of Shoe Lane and near St Bride's Church. Christopher Devlin plausibly suggests that, taking into account that George Beseley and Montford Scott were also hanged there in the following year, the authorities wanted to intimidate the residents of Sackville House, which was opposite, principally because of Robert Southwell's association with members of the Sackville family.[107]

Jones himself had been remarkably uncompromising at trial on 4 May 1590. He had declared that the statute law did not apply to him because he came not 'contemptuously' into the realm, that is, as the wording of the indictment ran. After sentence was passed, he warned the recorder: 'Take heed what you do...for *quis extendet manum suam in Christum domini et innocens erit?*'. Moreover, he said, Mary Tudor's burning of heretics was justified. But, under Elizabeth, 'so many priests and Catholics' were 'butchered' without justice. It is slightly difficult to believe that Jones was able to say this out loud in open court. The narrator says that 'they shouted against him...as the Jews did against St Stephen'.[108] Peter Penkevell's view was that Jones was allowed to say all this because the judges hoped 'the conclusion would make for their purpose'—in other words, that Jones would appear to be so extreme that the execution of the queen's justice on him would appear to be entirely justified.[109] Our principal account of the trial notes that among those who 'scoffed' at Jones's admonition to the recorder was Francis Flower, who was the uncle of the puritan separatist Robert Browne, though he was also a client of the lord chancellor, Sir Christopher Hatton.[110]

On 5 May, Middleton and Jones 'were brought into the church of S. Sepulchre', which was located relatively close to Newgate, where they were being held. There, the two priests 'disputed with great learning, as I have heard, with the doctors'. This disputation may have been staged precisely because of the challenge which Jones had in effect issued at trial and which the authorities evidently could not let pass.[111]

'Upon the gallows on which they were hanged', noted Challoner from Ribadeneira's work, 'the executioners had caused to be written in great letters, FOR TREASON AND FOREIGN INVASION, to make their cause more odious

---

[106] Anstr., I, pp. 192–3, 229; Pollen, *UD*, pp. 182–5 (ABPFC, fos 6ʳ–8ᵛ).
[107] Devlin, *LRS*, pp. 230–2; Challoner, *MMP*, p. 163.   [108] Pollen, *UD*, pp. 183–5.
[109] Pollen, *AEM*, pp. 290–1.
[110] Pollen, *UD*, pp. 184–5; *HC 1558–1603*, II, pp. 141–2. I am very grateful to Neil Younger for bringing this to my attention.
[111] Pollen, *UD*, p. 185.

204   CATHOLICS AND TREASON

to the people', that is, more or less the same as had been done in the case of Christopher Bales in March 1590.[112] According to John Curry, writing six days after the execution, once Jones saw the placard he 'cried out that that it was utterly false'. He 'was allowed to speak a few words'. He said that he was 'being put to death because he had tried to help his hapless country'. This was not what the officials wanted to hear, and so 'the heretics ordered him to be thrown from the ladder and... while yet alive, his belly was ripped open and his bowels pulled out and flung into a fire'. In order to 'terrify' Middleton, he was deliberately 'placed... so near' the butchering of Jones that Jones's blood splashed all over him; after which Middleton was hurried off to a gallows in Clerkenwell. However, the narratives used by Challoner said that the watching crowd, or some of it, did not believe what they were being told by their masters. This 'artifice did not take, and the spectators, instead of applauding their proceedings, departed highly displeased with these tyrannical measures'. Middleton was barely allowed to address the crowd and could just about get out that he died for the Catholic faith. This provoked an unnamed 'gentleman' to exclaim, 'Sir, you have spoken very well'. If the Catholic narratives reflect anything like accurately what happened on that day, this suggests that, even in London, the regime had a problem controlling public opinion, although it was not two years since the Armada ships had gone by the south coast.[113]

If things were this tough for the regime and its agents in London, one can imagine how much more difficult it might be out in the provinces.[114] We get some sense of this from the refusal of the judges at the Lancaster assizes to follow the privy council's extremely detailed instructions in July 1590 to hang Richard Blundell of Little Crosby and his priest Robert Woodruff.[115] Within two weeks the privy council was almost screaming for the assize justices in Lancaster to do something about the apparent cascade of the population there into recusant separation. The council evidently thought that a trial of Blundell and his priest would concentrate the minds of Lancashire Catholics.[116] But this is not what

---

[112] Challoner, MMP, p. 163; Weinreich, PREH, p. 574; Pollen, AEM, p. 316; Relatione del Presente Stato d'Inghilterra. Cavata de une Lettera de li 25. di Maggio scritta di Londra...(Rome, 1590), p. 4; p. 49 above; Morris, TCF, III (AENB), pp. 45–6.

[113] Pollen, AEM, pp. 316–17; ABSJ, A V, no. 8 (unfoliated); Challoner, MMP, p. 163.

[114] Topcliffe complained to the earl of Shrewsbury on 30 June 1590 that he (Topcliffe) was currently, 'among such malefactors, reputed a bug or like a scarecrow when I come into an unwonted place, country, or unto a man of your honour's estate': C. Jamison (ed.), revised by E. G. W. Bill, A Calendar of the Shrewsbury and Talbot Papers in Lambeth Palace Library and the College of Arms: volume I (1966), p. 79.

[115] The council noted that 'there were certain books found' in Blundell's house, including Richard Bristow's 'Motives' (A Briefe Treatise...(Antwerp, 1574)) and, apparently, a defence (Alfield's) of Campion. Woodruff ended up not on the gallows at Lancaster but in Wisbech Castle in 1594, though admittedly Blundell died in Lancaster gaol: Anstr., I, p. 385; APC 1590, pp. 267, 310–12; ODNB, sub Blundell, William (article by D. Woolf); A. Goss and T. Gibson (eds), Crosby Records: A Chapter of Lancashire Recusancy (Manchester, 1887), p. 21; BL, Harleian MS 7021, no. 12, fo. 142ʳ.

[116] APC 1590, pp. 335–41.

THE INCESTUOUS BASTARD QUEEN   205

happened—perhaps because the known anti-puritan judge Thomas Walmesley was there.[117]

The period of what looks like indiscriminate use of the treason penalties against Catholic clergy and their patrons lasted for a relatively short time. Those proceedings certainly did not come to an end. In the years after the Armada there were more high-profile treason trials of Catholics, mainly of clergy. The Catholic community continued to recognize such people as martyrs, and to insist that the queen's government was guilty of persecution. But the legal processes that ensnared separatist Catholics look, once again, like part of a series of political negotiations and manoeuvres and intersected with and glossed other political questions and concerns.

The Catholic Rejection of Compromise: Henry Garnet, Robert Southwell, Richard Holtby, and the 1591 Proclamation

Despite the constraints preventing the likes of Knollys and Topcliffe from inflicting what they considered appropriate punishment on more of the separated Catholic community, the evidence of further repression was deployed by the Catholic critics of compromise in order to condemn those of their co-religionists who advised even partial compliance. Henry Garnet's long missive of 25 May 1590 to his superior general, Claudio Acquaviva, about Middleton and Jones (rejoicing that there were 'in England so many who rinse their stoles in the blood of the Lamb, who love Christ during life, and imitate Him in death') also insisted on the need for absolute separation from the heretical national Church. Here Garnet faced down the arguments of the likes of Thomas Bell in favour of a modicum of obedience to royal authority. Garnet's letter of 25 May set out the basic argument which he later elaborated in his excoriating printed attacks on Bell, that is, in 1593—an argument which had found its fullest expression in John Mush's manuscript assault on Bell back in 1588. A crucial part of that case was the claim that the best intentioned of the new clergy, particularly those who looked to the Society of Jesus for leadership and example, were setting the agenda, over and against the shabby little compromises which had been so common up to this point. Perhaps there were constant confessors before the seminaries started sending their priests back home. But they were as nothing compared to the zeal of the new clergy now: 'how many of the older priests of the pontifical priesthood' had these new priests 'roused out of the older schisms, or of the languid or

---

[117] Walmesley was known to be less hostile to Catholic separatists than other judges: *APC 1590*, p. 195; Collinson, *EPM*, pp. 406–7; *HC 1558–1603*, III, p. 569; *HMCS*, XVIII, p. 36. Back on 6 June 1580, Thomas Norton had warned Burghley about the proposed promotion of Walmesley to be a serjeant-at-law. Norton repeated the rumours that Walmesley was at best a crypto-Catholic and that his family was worse: Graves, *TN*, p. 222.

206   CATHOLICS AND TREASON

unenergetic have they inspired to strive energetically, or of the unlearned and inexperienced have they cultivated with advice and instruction?' Their willingness to suffer and to die rejuvenated the faith among the faithful. 'How much was perpetrated before their arrival without any awareness of crime!' What vile 'superstition, deception' and 'filthy oaths against the Roman pontiff and the religion of Christ were tolerated!' Apart from 'those few whose constancy in these dark times was as admirable as it was rare, there were unnumbered ones, Catholic in name, but in fact betrayers of their holy religion and apostates who themselves frequented the churches of the heretics and led their sons and whole families thereto'. Almost all Catholics had complied, even to the extent of receiving 'the sacrilegious last supper' as they tried to serve 'both Baal and Christ'. But all this had changed after the arrival of the seminary clergy.[118]

After the repulse of the Armada and into the early 1590s, the continuing evidence of the martyr's spirit was given an arguably even more aggressive twist by Garnet and his friends. The extraordinary zeal of those who stood out against the fetid heretical stench of the corrupted national Church could be seen at its purest in the self-sacrifice of those who went to execution and refused to reject Christ or the authority of his vicar on earth. Their business was 'prayer and devotions', a completely separate matter from whatever it was that Philip II might, or might not, be planning to do. Good Catholics were hunted from pillar to post and all because they would not swear to take the queen's part in 'a war, however unjust' and deny the pope's authority 'to excommunicate or depose the queen'.[119]

Of course, the vast majority of Catholics were never faced directly with the either/or choice which Garnet posed. But, for example, in May 1591 an arrest of the Catholics at the house of Thomas Watkinson at Menthorpe in the East Riding led to the 'fall' (that is, conformity) of all those detained, except for the priest Robert Thorpe and Watkinson himself; and they were executed at York on 31 May.[120] Thorpe said he would support an invading papal army, though 'by his beads' only. When asked whether, 'if he had authority from the pope to kill the queen...he would exercise it...he answered that he would not'. But, urged to 'be a good subject and go to the church, and hear a sermon, and use what religion you will', he predictably refused. He preached an aggressive Catholic sermon from the gallows and 'exhorted men to become Catholic, and to beware...tyrants' such

---

[118] ABSJ, GC, pp. 52–7 (ARSJ, FG 651/624: Garnet to Acquaviva, 25 May 1590 (translation supplied by Thomas McCoog)); Lake and Questier, *Trials*, chs 7, 8.

[119] ABSJ, GC, pp. 52–7.

[120] Anstr., I, pp. 353–4; Challoner, *MMP*, p. 165; Dodd, *CH*, II, p. 128; Foley, *RSJ*, III, pp. 747, 748–50 (AVCAU, Liber 1422 [Grene, Collectanea F], section 4, pp. 75ᵃ, 76ᵃ–7ᵃ). The source for Challoner here was once again Anthony Champney (Thorpe served as Champney's confessor) and also Lady Grace Babthorpe (her narrative, AAW, A VI, no. 100, pp. 367–70, was transcribed for Challoner by Butler, ABP, pp. 399–408). The JP who made the arrest was John Gates of Howden: Challoner, *MMP*, p. 166. For the Jesuit Richard Holtby's narrative of the trial, see Morris, *TCF*, III (RHPN), pp. 179–83.

THE INCESTUOUS BASTARD QUEEN   207

as Topcliffe. Topcliffe berated the executioner and demanded that he should get on with it 'or else he himself would come and do it' himself. Like Thorpe, Watkinson refused conformity even though, back in 1581, he had, badgered by the high commission, offered compliance.[121]

The layman Lawrence Humphreys (executed at some point in 1591, though the precise date is uncertain) went further and allegedly said that the queen was a whore and a heretic.[122] In the case of George Beseley, executed on 1 July 1591, John Cecil remembered that to make him 'the more odious... they proposed this most barbarous and bloody question, what he would do in case the pope should command him to kill the queen' and he 'answered that he thought it a meritorious act, being so commanded'.[123] He was executed with Montford Scott in Fleet Street.[124] There was at this point also a provincial show trial at Winchester. The

[121] Morris, *TCF*, III (RHPN), pp. 180–1, 182; *AWCBC*, pp. 936–7, 941 (Borthwick Institute, York, HCAB 10, fo. 80ʳ), 946–51, 952–6.

[122] Foley, *RSJ*, III, pp. 296–7; Challoner, *MMP*, pp. 592–4; Pollen, *AEM*, pp. 235–8; see also Pollen, *UD*, p. 394 (AAW, B 24, no. 101); L. Underwood, *Childhood, Youth and Religious Dissent in Post-Reformation England* (Basingstoke, 2014), pp. 45–6, 139–41. According to one manuscript, the judge summoned Humphreys's employer, one 'William Danstin', who confirmed that his employee had called the queen a heretic: ABSJ, Anglia VII, no. 25. Thomas Stanney's account, retained in the Brussels State archives, indicates that Humphreys's words were spoken, in Danstin's house, in the presence of soldiers who were to embark for France: ABSJ, CP (Lawrence Humphreys); cf. ABP, pp. 377–88; Challoner, *MMP*, pp. 591–6.

[123] Pollen, *UD*, p. 200; Challoner, *MMP*, p. 167; *AWCBC*, pp. 984, 987. For the order for Beseley's interrogation, directed to (among others) Richard Topcliffe, see *APC 1590–1*, p. 204.

[124] Anstr., I, p. 28; Challoner, *MMP*, p. 167 (dating the execution to 2 July). For the rumours that were spread about George Beseley and Montford Scott, repeated *inter alia* by the earl of Derby to the earl of Shrewsbury, see *AWCBC*, pp. 981–2, citing College of Arms (London), Talbot Papers, H, p. 333. For the trial at the Newgate sessions, see *APC 1591*, p. 247; ABSJ, Collectanea M, p. 187ᵃ. For the alleged (and highly unlikely) Beseley plot, see *CSPD 1591–4*, p. 162 (and *passim*). For Robert Humberson (Humberstone), Beseley's 'familiar companion and confederate', who was interrogated with him, see *APC 1590–1*, p. 204; Pollen and MacMahon, *VPH*, p. 346; Knox, *DD*, pp. 217, 220; *Miscellanea II*, pp. 257, 267, 276–7; Caraman, *WW*, pp. 206, 211–12 (the death of Robert Humberstone in the Tower in 1599). Challoner wrote also that 'some say the servant of the inn where he [Beseley] was apprehended was executed at the same time for aiding and assisting him': Challoner, *MMP*, pp. 167–8; *AWCBC*, pp. 994–7. For the trial of Beseley's alleged harbourers in the North (Mr and Mrs Dalton and John Wells), see Foley, *RSJ*, III, p. 756 (AVCAU, Liber 1422 [Grene, Collectanea F], section 4, p. 81ᵃ). For the celebration of the recent martyrdoms of Beseley and others at the visit of Philip II to the seminary at Valladolid on 24 July/3 August 1592, see PRO, SP 94/4, fos 81ʳ–2ʳ; *L&A 1591–2*, p. 427; M. E. Williams, *St Alban's College Valladolid* (1986), p. 11. Scott had, said Peter Penkevell, been marked down for banishment, but Topcliffe secured his execution on the grounds that 'it was good policy to put him to death' for his 'austere life was a means to draw the people unto him' and Scott was 'accounted for a saint': Pollen, *AEM*, p. 291 (ABSJ, Collectanea B, p. 5; *AWCBC*, p. 990). John Copley testified in 1599 to the college authorities in Rome that his sister, Margaret Gage, had been 'condemned to death with her husband [John] after two years of imprisonment because a priest, later martyred [i.e. George Beseley, cited by name in the relevant assize documents] had said Mass in their house'; they had been 'reprieved on their way to the scaffold' but she 'lost her husband's estates and revenues to Lord Howard of Effingham', who took a twenty-one-year lease of the estates, renewed in 1612. Howard was presumably the unnamed peer who intervened again in 1601, in order to protect his interest in the estate, to prevent Mrs Gage from suffering the consequences of her being arrested with Anne Line: A. Kenny (ed.), *The Responsa Scholarum of the English College, Rome* (2 vols, CRS 54–5, 1962–3), I, p. 21; P. Revill and F. W. Steer, 'George Gage I and George Gage II', *Bulletin of the Institute of Historical Research* 31 (1956), pp. 141–58, at p. 149; Challoner, *MMP*, p. 258; *AWCBC*, pp. 969, 1008–11 (PRO, Assizes 35/34/6, nos 2,

208 CATHOLICS AND TREASON

priest Roger Dickenson and a lay associate, Ralph Miller, who had a long track record of dissident behaviour, were executed six days after Beseley, on 7 July 1591.[125] From the narrative which Robert Persons received in Spain, it looks as if this was meant to be a replication of the arrest, trial, and execution of Thorpe and Watkinson about five weeks before. On that occasion, as we saw, those detained at the same time as the priest were, with the exception of Watkinson, forced into abject conformity. One narrative of Dickenson and Miller says that, 'together with these two men, eight or nine young maidens were condemned to death for the same reasons, for having confessed to priests and [having] heard Masses'. The 'judges thought...that they would condemn one' and thereby 'terrify and upset the rest'. Apparently the maidens in question did not buckle; and the judges baulked at doing anything other than sending them back to gaol.[126]

Within a month the queen was down in West Sussex on a progress into Hampshire. On her itinerary was a visit to the palace of Cowdray, the home of the loyalist Catholic peer Lord Montague. Through the vehicle of elaborately staged entertainments, there was, it appears, a good deal of comment from the viscount's entourage about the current situation in religion and politics. It may have been contextualized by the recent use of the treason statutes in Hampshire.[127] It is possible also that, by August 1591, it was known that there would soon be a draconian royal proclamation designed to drill down into the recusant Catholic core and into its occasional conformist penumbra. If so, the performances at Cowdray in front of the queen may have been an attempt to pre-empt the proclamation, of 18 October 1591, which would appear shortly.[128]

In late November/early December 1591, Robert Southwell provided, in a long screed sent to Richard Verstegan, perhaps the most explicit commentary on and most developed account of what some Catholics now regarded as the onset of an

---

3, 61); cf. Weinreich, *PREH*, pp. 600–1. Robert Gage, Margaret's brother-in-law, had been one of the Babington conspirators: *CSPSc 1586–8*, p. 38.

[125] The material cause of the execution was alleged to be that 'Dickenson returned into the realm after banishment': ABSJ, Anglia VII, no. 25. Dickenson prayed for the queen and even conceded that the pope was 'a man subject to all calamities...as we all are, and can do nothing without Christ': Pollen, *AEM*, pp. 92–5 (ABSJ, Collectanea M, pp. 146^b–7^b), 96 (ABSJ, Collectanea M, p. 196^a). Miller was also offered a reprieve (in return for conforming), but he refused it: ABSJ, Collectanea M, p. 196^a. Dickenson was 'condemned of treason for reconciling of malefactors unto the Catholic Church', while Miller was 'condemned of felony [*sic*] upon the statute of persuasion': Pollen, *AEM*, p. 96 (ABSJ, Collectanea M, p. 196^a). For the execution at Dorchester, during 1591, of William Pikes (or Pike), who had been converted to Catholicism by Thomas Pilchard, see AAW, B 28, no. 10, p. 313; AAW, A IV, no. 22, p. 117; ABP, p. 409; AAW, A XXVI, no. 156, p. 441; Pollen, *UD*, p. 289; Pollen, *AEM*, p. 267; *AWCBC*, pp. 456, 1012–24.

[126] Pollen, *UD*, p. 203 ('Avisos de Inglaterra...', ABSJ, Collectanea B, pp. 31–4); *APC 1590–1*, pp. 234–5.

[127] E. Heale, 'Contesting Terms: Loyal Catholicism and Lord Montague's Entertainment at Cowdray, 1591', in J. Archer, E. Goldring, and S. Knight (eds), *The Progresses, Pageants, and Entertainments of Queen Elizabeth I* (Oxford, 2007), pp. 189–206, esp. at pp. 195 f.

[128] Questier, *C&C*, p. 172.

THE INCESTUOUS BASTARD QUEEN   209

even more intense phase of persecution than they had previously experienced.[129] 'They, of every priest', wrote Southwell, 'lightly give it out after his death, and before, in his absence, that he would have killed the queen and that he came to prepare people for an invasion', even though 'no such word or saying' appeared 'in his indictment' or could be 'proved with any colourable argument' nor was ever imagined 'by the priests themselves'. This was what had happened in the case of 'the last two martyrs, Mr Beseley and Mr Scott, most impudently and falsely, without any likelihood or show'. This led Southwell to say that on such fantasies a police state had been erected. On the basis of deliberately leaked rumours that 'there were certain priests and papists come out of Spain to kill the queen', they 'caused...thereupon watches in the inns and great ado—no such imagination being in any man's head but their own, nor any priests being then come over'. Thinking back, said Southwell, the Babington conspiracy was 'wholly of their plotting and forging, of purpose to make Catholics odious and to cut off the queen of Scots'. It was atheists and spies who had manufactured these lies in order to create the illusion of treason and threat.[130]

While the queen's government provided merely the impression of balance, for example by executing the puritan pseudo-martyr William Hacket, this was proof of how far the puritan infection had got into the national Church. Hacket, 'a most blasphemous man calling himself greater than God', had been hanged on 28 July 1591. He was 'commonly known to have been a puritan and highly esteemed by that sect'. When the puritans saw that 'his blasphemies [were] so great', they 'were ashamed of his death'; but such hypocrites were they that 'they...gave it out that he was a papist, which many of the vulgar sort did verily believe and say'.[131]

The recent prosecutions of good Catholics were just one aspect of the concerted campaign of disinformation and harassment: 'if anyone wants work or money', as long as 'he can rail against Catholics or print anything to their disgrace', then 'it is current and goes presently abroad *cum privilegio*. And many poor printers and needy libellers make the best part of their living by our slanders. No pamphlet [is] written ordinarily but the railing against Catholics is one part of the book', just as 'no sermon' is 'lightly made but papists are ever part of the theme and a principal commonplace or common supply for want of other matter'. 'Stages' were 'beholden to papists for many of their interludes'.[132]

---

[129] For the dating of this manuscript, see Petti, *LDRV*, p. 17.

[130] Petti, *LDRV*, pp. 2–3. As Lucy Underwood has pointed out to me, Southwell had, perhaps, partially changed his mind since his letter of 21 December 1586 in which he referred to the alleged plot as 'that wicked and ill-fated conspiracy': Pollen, *UD*, p. 314.

[131] Petti, *LDRV*, p. 2. For the demonstration in July 1591 by Hacket and his 'confused' puritan friends Edmund Copinger and Henry Arthington, see Collinson, *EPM*, p. 424. Hacket figured in, e.g., Ribadeneira's work as an instance of false martyrdom: Weinreich, *PREH*, pp. 592–5.

[132] Petti, *LDRV*, pp. 4–5. See also Robert Southwell, *An Humble Supplication to her Maiestie* (n.p. [printed secretly in England], 1595 [1600–1]; ARCR, II, no. 717), pp. 76–8, 77–8.

210 CATHOLICS AND TREASON

As the gears of the penal law against Catholics had cranked higher and higher, the assertion in regime pronouncements that it was nothing to do with religion was, thought Southwell, at last being tested to destruction: 'they falsely give out in proclamations, books and pamphlets, as well at home as abroad, that none are here troubled for their conscience but only for other crimes, except by a little pecuniary sum (as they call it)'.[133] Southwell glanced here at the proclamation of 18 October 1591, in which the recusancy statutes were indeed glossed as a tolerant measure. They were, said the proclamation, proof that 'none do suffer death for matter of religion'. Catholics were 'known not to be impeached for the same either in their lives, lands, or goods or in their liberties but only by payment of a pecuniary sum as a penalty for the time that they do refuse to come to church'. The regime was very moderate, the proclamation insisted, considering that the controllers of the seminaries had assured Philip II that, although the 1588 Armada had failed, 'many thousands...of able people' would rise up 'to assist such power as he shall set on land'.[134]

But Southwell was not having any of this. At 'every arraignment or execution, Catholics are commonly offered' their 'lives and liberties if they will but go to church; which doubtless can be no satisfaction for any temporal treason but only for matters of religion'.[135] Moreover, 'when any Catholic or priest is arraigned, they' stuffed 'the indictment with many odious lies; of conspiracy for killing the queen, stirring the subjects to rebellion from their obedience...and yet, when they come to proofs, they can prove nothing in the world but that he is a priest, or relieved priests; and yet, nothing else being witnessed—yes, that not known but by the priest's confession—the jury cries "*billa vera*" to all the indictment'. Then 'the whole indictment is enrolled as if the party had been convicted of all that it contained. And upon this they brag that none has been arraigned but for treason, as (say they) their indictments show in the records.'[136]

To his sarcastic rendition of the proclamation's claims about the function of the statutes against seminary clergy, Southwell joined the enormities committed by Richard Topcliffe and his friends, who simply enjoyed their work too much. They 'torture those that be taken, with manacles, in which some hang nine hours together, all their body being borne upon their hands, so that oftentimes they swoon upon the torture, and are hardly recovered and yet oftentimes hanged up again: thus Mr Bales, Mr Jones...and almost all the priests that have been taken

---

[133] Petti, *LDRV*, p. 5.

[134] Hughes and Larkin, *TRP*, III, pp. 87–9; Petti, *LDRV*, p. 23; McCoog, *SJISE*, I, pp. 22–4. For the way in which the proclamation was put into effect, see Richardson, *RP*, pp. 151–2. The impact of the proclamation was presumably heightened by the execution at Tyburn on *c*.3 November 1591 of the Irishman Sir Brian O'Rourke: *ODNB, sub* Rourke, Sir Brian (article by E. Schoales); *CSPI 1588–92*, pp. 386, 387–8; J. McCavitt, *Sir Arthur Chichester: Lord Deputy of Ireland 1605–1616* (Belfast, 1998), p. 139; *CSPSc 1589–93*, pp. 470–2, 478, 480–1, 482–3, 484, 485, 487–9, 492–6, 505, 589.

[135] Petti, *LDRV*, p. 5.   [136] Petti, *LDRV*, p. 10.

any time' in the last five years. They 'whip priests naked, as they did Mr Beseley and Mr Jones, in such cruel sort that the persecutors themselves said that they had charms to endure so patiently such tortures'. Topcliffe used the sleep deprivation techniques associated with modern intelligence services. According to Southwell, those interrogated became 'almost past their senses and half besides themselves, and then' Topcliffe 'begins to examine them afresh in that impotent mode'. Topcliffe would probably nowadays euphemistically describe some of his techniques as the use of stress positions, although some commentators have suggested that what Topcliffe did with manacles and suspension actually mimicked the pain of crucifixion. As for Edward Jones, Topcliffe allegedly dragged him by his 'privy parts' down the stairs, 'so filthy and shameless is their cruelty'.[137] After Southwell's own arrest in July 1592, Verstegan commented that, 'because the often exercise of the rack in the Tower was so odious and so much spoken of the people', Topcliffe had 'authority to torment priests in his own house, in such sort as he shall think good'.[138]

A crucial plank of Southwell's case was that Catholics were harassed because they were the ones who were prepared to speak out against the more general abuses inflicted on all of the queen's subjects, irrespective of their confessional status, not least because of the horrendous financial and social burdens of the illegal war that the queen was currently waging. As Southwell put it, 'it is strange to see how God makes the whole realm to taste of the same scourges that Catholics are wronged with'.[139] The injustices inflicted on Catholics were part and parcel of the ills with which the commonwealth was generally shot through and of the deprivation and harassment which came with war: 'as they spoil us, so was England before this time never acquainted with so common beggary, the people never so needy, oppressed, on the one side, with raising of rents, paying fines, and infinite devices of gentlemen to undo their tenants; on the other side, never so many subsidies exacted in three kings' times as in this only queen's: so many taxes and fifteenths, one ever overtaking another' and, 'if there be no money, they take cattle, selling them at half the price; and leaving many poor folks and their children ready to famish to serve the queen, or rather to maintain the king of Navarre, or to help' the Portuguese pretender 'Don Antonio, or to send men to Flanders, to the consumption of English treasure and disturbance of Christian princes'.[140]

The Catholic discourse of in/tolerance was, therefore, about far more than the sufferings and grievances of individual Catholics. As R. B. Wernham points out, taxes raised directly, that is, through parliament, covered only half of the total cost of the war from 1585 to 1603. The crown resorted to 'desperate and

---

[137] Petti, *LDRV*, p. 9; Devlin, *LRS*, pp. 285–7; Southwell, *Humble Supplication*, pp. 63–4. For the torture of Francis Dickenson, see p. 201 n.96 above; and of Christopher Bales in Bridewell, see Pollen, *UD*, pp. 178–9. Grene notes that, amongst other torments, Bales was hung by the 'privy members': ABSJ, Collectanea M, p. 64b.
[138] Petti, *LDRV*, p. 58.   [139] Petti, *LDRV*, p. 11.   [140] Petti, *LDRV*, p. 12.

212 CATHOLICS AND TREASON

burdensome expedients'—not just monopolies and patents but also sales of crown lands and expropriation of Church revenues and property. These were things that Southwell castigated as well: 'one begs that none may sell cards but sealed with his seal, and thus come in thousands; another that none may sell starch but warranted by him; the like of wines and almost all kind of ware', and so on.[141] On one reading, the stream of privy council letters and warrants in the early 1590s threatening sharp legal reprisals and punishments for virtually everything, from refusal to contribute to the war effort all the way to desertion, could be taken as quite consistent with what Southwell identifies as tyranny.[142]

The queen's willingness to listen to evil counsel had meant that the 'liberties of the subjects' were 'in many things impaired—a thing to English ears unheard of before the tyranny of this time'. It was impossible even to 'go over sea without licence'. Wealth-creating commerce had been irreparably damaged: 'the merchants have lost their best places of traffic and have no farther scope on the sea than to ports of least profit'.[143] War, said Southwell, was what allowed these bastards to use what were in effect emergency powers to govern, and that included the new treason statutes of the 1580s against lay Catholics and their patrons. Simultaneously the war permitted Burghley and his cronies to amass a fortune out of the profits of the conflict. Private greed merged seamlessly with public injustice and fuelled the squalid stream of propaganda against Catholics and also the work of the intelligence services and their grubby little *agents provocateurs* which spawned the ludicrous claims about Catholic sedition.

Southwell's condemnation of the persecuting tendencies of the regime was, therefore, one component of a much larger attack on an allegedly corrupt, sick, and dying society. The aristocracy was thoroughly 'servile', as were the officials in each shire, the 'lieutenants and justices', which explained, incidentally, how the hateful 'promoters' and 'pursuivants', whose rampages parasitized and impoverished so many, were able to get away with it. The prisons were never 'so full of debtors, thieves, murderers and all kinds of wicked persons'. But who could be surprised when 'all vice' was 'so rife that many sins' were 'esteemed no faults, and the very greatest reckoned but slight matters, so that all their penalties cannot be sufficient to keep their prisons empty'? Never could anyone remember 'so many hanged and executed for vice' and 'never in England so much bloodshed without [civil] war'. Some golden age, then![144]

The social effects at home of the war abroad were terrible. Troops were 'sent forth against their wills into France, Flanders, Portugal, and neither maintained in the field with victuals nor paid their salary, nor used with courtesy, but put to

---

[141] R. B. Wernham, *The Making of Elizabethan Foreign Policy 1558–1603* (1980), pp. 88–9; Petti, *LDRV*, p. 12. For the forced loan of 1589, see *HMCL*, V, p. 98.

[142] See, e.g., *APC 1591*, pp. 201–2; *APC 1592*, pp. 213–15, 235, 252, 277.

[143] Petti, *LDRV*, p. 13.   [144] Petti, *LDRV*, p. 13.

all adventures till famine or' injuries made 'them impotent'. Then they were sent home 'to pester the country with beggars, the highways with thieves, and all places with idle and most vicious vagabonds'. 'Widows and fatherless children' were left 'in extreme misery' by this madness. The result was the 'overthrow' of the country 'against which, by these means', the queen's government had 'stirred all Christendom and made it the most hateful nation under heaven or, at least, in Europe'.[145]

Like so many tyrannies, this odious crew had used the alleged threat from abroad which, if it existed, their own folly had created, to intimidate or rather to 'cozen the people'. Those responsible made no attempt to secure peace, 'nor means of composition'. They intended, rather, 'to see the people destroyed in an almost impossible resistance', after which, like the spineless cowards they were, the guilty men would 'fly' or 'make their party good by selling the realm'.[146]

Corruption and tyranny had met and embraced in the ambition of the loathsome Lord Burghley, the 'most malicious and cruel counsellor of her Majesty', whose 'feigned surmises and odious fictions' had 'robbed the commons, dispeopled the country of the best soldiers, kept the nobility in thraldom and the gentlemen in the basest servility that England ever knew: a man that consumes his prince of more than twenty thousand pounds by the year, of which he at the least picks twelve out of the court of wards, which was never more full of wards and suits, yet never so little beneficial to the prince—to omit his fleecing her of the subsidy money, of recusants' lands and goods, of infinite exchequer gains, unseen and unknown but to himself and his accomplices'.[147] The sequestration of good Catholics' estates was nothing therefore to do with religion, or even the perverted form of Christianity practised in England. It was, however, part and parcel of the web of corruption spun by the vile lord treasurer.

The deranged self-interest or, rather, rampant insatiability of those who had spent their whole lives battening off the queen's sovereign power had left the central question of the succession entirely open. Southwell pointed to the 'exceeding miseries and dangers' that threatened 'all men...in regard that, if her Majesty should die, there' was 'none known whom to follow or to accept as their prince', not least because there were 'so many and so different styles and competitors to the crown'. There would in short, as a result of the bad stewardship of those entrusted with office under the queen, soon be a civil war. The 'divisions of sects, each now condemning [the] other, will be as ready to be each other's ruins'. At that point, 'every one fearing [the] other as either different in religion, or not agreeing in one competitor', they would immediately 'seek each other's overthrow'. 'Private quarrels of noblemen and gentlemen' would, 'by parts taking, grow to open uproars'. There would be chaos, with 'country against city' and 'one against

---

[145] Petti, *LDRV*, pp. 13–14. See also Wernham, *Making*, pp. 91–2.   [146] Petti, *LDRV*, p. 14.
[147] Petti, *LDRV*, p. 14.

214 CATHOLICS AND TREASON

another, like a company of mad men, all fearing, none obeying, none ruling but by sword and fire'. The rule of law would, in effect, be abrogated. Then, 'if any foreign power be ready to assault us (as they pretend the king of Spain to be), what better opportunity can be taken than to come to a people dismembered among themselves'?[148] In the end, England would be just like France—a polity in ruins—though, naturally, Southwell would not blame good French Catholics for that but, rather, the determination of a combination of heretics and politiques to force a heretic king on a Catholic people.

Perhaps the climax of Southwell's polemic, at least in the harder-edged private manuscript version which he sent to Richard Verstegan, was the fate of the persecutors—a staple, as we have seen, of so many Catholic martyrologies. The earl of Leicester, 'in revenge of his cruelty against Catholics', got what he deserved. For, on 'the same day sevennight that he had caused divers priests and other Catholics [that is, the post-Armada victims] to be cruelly murdered in London in divers places of the city', he 'sickened', perhaps through poison administered by a forewarned quarry. He was as ugly 'a corpse as he was filthy in manners'. The bad deaths of persecutors such as Leicester were the diametric opposite of the witness of the martyrs. Leicester 'died without any signs of a Christian, more like a dog than a man. His stomach was with the poison eaten, and great holes made therein'; and everyone hated him. As for Walsingham, at the last 'his urine came forth at his mouth and nose, with so odious a stench that none could endure to come near him'. Both died in beggary. But, said the saintly Southwell, this was no more than 'the just judgment of God'.[149]

The proclamation of 18 October 1591, which Southwell attacked, was arguably incompatible with the anti-puritanism of Lord Chancellor Hatton and Archbishop Whitgift. It was claimed by Richard Verstegan on 12 December 1591 that the proclamation came out only after Hatton's death on 20 November. The proclamation had been 'printed two or three times before its publication, partly because' of the arrival of the news 'of the death of Pope Gregory XIV, of whom there had been particular mention in the first impression' but also because Hatton 'had been averse to the publication of this edict, as it is thought'.[150] Francis Holyoake committed to paper his absolute delight at the passing of Hatton: 'great comfort is to the Church by the death of the lord chancellor, and appearance of deliverance

---

[148] Petti, LDRV, pp. 14–15.

[149] Petti, LDRV, p. 16; Southwell's report of Leicester's death appeared in Richard Verstegan, A Declaration of the True Causes of the Great Troubles, Presupposed to be Intended against the Realme of England (n.p. [Antwerp], 1592), p. 53; Petti, LDRV, p. 32; see also, for Southwell's An Epistle of Comfort, p. 73 above.

[150] Petti, LDRV, pp. 35, 37; Richard Verstegan, An Advertisement written to a Secretarie of my L. Treasurers of Ingland...(n.p. [Antwerp?], 1592), sig. A7ᵛ (for which reference I am grateful to Neil Younger); Weinreich, PREH, p. 599. For the speculation about the deceased Hatton's religion, see, e.g., Verstegan, An Advertisement, sig. A7ʳ; Lake, BQB, p. 342; see also Dr Younger's forthcoming biography of Hatton.

THE INCESTUOUS BASTARD QUEEN 215

to the ministers'. Holyoake commented also on a 'great assembly' of papists 'near to Holborn, convened at an open Mass', where many were 'apprehended and condemned'.[151] Notoriously, at this time, Richard Topcliffe and Richard Young barged in on the Catholics who were attending a Mass privately celebrated by Edmund Gennings at the Holborn residence of the Hampshire separatist Swithin Wells. Topcliffe was 'thrown down the stairs by Mr Brian Lacey's man', Sydney Hodgson, 'at the chapel door'.[152] As Challoner quaintly puts it, 'arising from their devotions', they 'thought proper to oppose force to force, so to prevent the profanation of the sacred mysteries'.[153]

The arraignment of those detained in Wells's house, with others, appears to have taken place on 4 December. All of this was very shortly after, as it seems, the proclamation was made public. (Southwell's *Humble Supplication* was almost finished by 10 December, the day of the executions.)[154] Among the State's victims here was Swithin Wells himself. Even though he had not been present at the Mass, he was a known recusant.[155] The privy council warrant which ordered the interrogation of Brian Lacey, who was not at the Mass either, described him as 'a disperser and distributer of letters to papists and evil-affected subjects'.[156]

It seems likely that these Catholics had either staged a kind of demonstration against the proclamation or, perhaps, they were targeted by the London authorities in order to prove that the proclamation meant what it said. After the arraignment, the trial followed on 6 December. The outcome was not really in any doubt,

---

[151] LPL, MS 2004, fo. 7ʳ (dated, however, to 21 November 1592). Among those who appear to have been arrested in connection with this incident was 'Edward Knight, my lord [of] Canterbury's launderer': Pollen, *UD*, p. 207 (PRO, SP 12/240/109). Holyoake commented that 'a launderer of the archbishop was one, and not the least. I pray God, all the rest of his men that are papists may be likewise taken': LPL, MS 2004, fo. 7ʳ.

[152] Challoner, *MMP*, pp. 174–5; Richardson, *RP*, pp. 60–1; Questier, *C&C*, p. 267; *APC 1591–2*, p. 92 (here the date of the arrest of Gennings and his friends is assigned to 28 November 1591; Challoner, following *The Life and Death of Mr Edmund Geninges Priest, crowned with Martyrdome at London, the 10. Day of November [i.e. December], in the Yeare M.D.XCI* (St Omer, 1614), p. 64, locates it on 8 November); Pollen, *AEM*, pp. 100–1 (ABSJ, Anglia VI, no. 23, James Younger's account, also assigning the arrest of Gennings to 28 November); Pollen, *UD*, p. 206. Gennings had come back to England with Alexander Rawlins (who was executed at York in 1595) and one Hugo Sewel. Gennings was harboured initially at 'a gentleman's house within two or three miles of Whitby'. This suggests a residence of the Cholmley family, who were notorious as patrons of the seminarist clergy in that area: Challoner, *MMP*, p. 172; *HC 1558–1603*, I, p. 604.

[153] Challoner, *MMP*, p. 175.

[154] Devlin, *LRS*, p. 239; V. Houliston, 'The Lord Treasurer and the Jesuit: Robert Persons's Satirical *Responsio* to the 1591 Proclamation', *Sixteenth Century Journal* 32 (2001), pp. 383–401, at p. 385. Southwell's pamphlet referred to the 'three priests' arraigned at Westminster 'even since the proclamation', i.e. Gennings, Eustace White, and Polydore Plasden: Southwell, *A Humble Supplication*, pp. 58–9.

[155] In August 1586, Wells admitted to knowing Anthony Babington (though, he said, not well): Pollen, *UD*, p. 132 (PRO, SP 12/292/18).

[156] *APC 1591–2*, pp. 15, 39–40. Lacey was executed 'as a reliever of priests' because when Montford Scott 'had warrant for banishment, in the time that he should have had for taking leave of his friends, he [Lacey] accompanied him as his man' and, 'after [being] apprehended with him', would not 'tell at whose houses they had been': ABSJ, Collectanea M, p. 54ᵇ. For the denunciation of Brian Lacey by his brother, Richard, back in March 1584, see Pollen, *UD*, p. 72.

216 CATHOLICS AND TREASON

but the thing was a major public occasion. Topcliffe's antics in court were related by the priest James Younger, who claims to have been an eyewitness. Among those on the bench of judges were Lord Chief Justice Wray and John Aylmer, bishop of London. Recorder Fleetwood made witty asides at the priest Polydore Plasden's expense, and Sir John Popham and Sir Edmund Anderson expatiated at some length on how the recent statutes should keep the queen's subjects in true obedience. Anderson boasted that he had in his 'time adjudged above sixty...papistical traitors to the gallows'. Topcliffe pitched in to say that all seminary priests must be traitors because they held with Nicholas Sander, Richard Bristow, and William Allen. He cited a passage from Allen's *Apologie* to the effect that Allen 'did maintain it lawful for the servant in case of heresy to forsake his master'. Topcliffe announced that he would reveal 'what another of them executed of late did hold' and drew out 'a little note-book, sometime Mr Beseley's the martyr', which allegedly said that 'it was lawful for the subject to disobey, yes, to kill his sovereign in case he be a heretic'. 'And this all priests do hold', Topcliffe intoned, 'although peradventure they dare not utter their mind[s] plainly'.[157]

The priests Eustace White (who had been taken at Blandford on 1 September) and Edmund Gennings, along with Plasden and the laymen Wells, Brian Lacey, John Mason, and Sydney Hodgson, were all, on 10 December, hanged and, in the case of the priests, thoroughly butchered. James Younger was among those who witnessed the events of that morning and wrote them down for Robert Persons.[158] White had been interrogated under torture on 25 October 1591. Topcliffe had hung him up by the hands for eight hours—and he drove Topcliffe berserk by promising to pray for him at the gallows, since Topcliffe had 'great need of prayers'.[159]

Gennings was hanged with Wells in Gray's Inn Fields, while Plasden, White, and the three others convicted with them were hanged at Tyburn. There was an altercation between Topcliffe and Wells in which Topcliffe said in so many words

---

[157] Pollen, *AEM*, pp. 102–3; cf. Challoner, *MMP*, p. 175. For Fleetwood's removal from office soon after the trial, allegedly in connection with his warning a Catholic of impending proceedings against his family, see Petti, *LDRV*, pp. 40, 44; P. R. Harris, 'William Fleetwood, Recorder of the City, and Catholicism in Elizabethan London', *RH* 7 (1963–4), pp. 106–22, at p. 118.

[158] Pollen, *AEM*, pp. 100f. For the report written by Stephen Barnes for Francis Barber concerning Eustace White, see Challoner, *MMP*, p. 182 (provided for Challoner by Butler: ABP, pp. 417–18; see also ABPFC, fo. 4ᵛ); for Barnes, see *AWCBC*, p. 473; Anstr., I, p. 24. Barnes claimed that White became involved in a dispute with the minister at Blandford, one Dr Howell, and that 'some, that were very hot Protestants before, became very calm' (whatever that means) and that some of the people at Blandford considered putting up a petition to the queen in White's favour: Challoner, *MMP*, pp. 183–4. At trial, the serving man Hodgson had appeared to offer a measure of compliance and was briefly respited, though his refusal to conform then brought a conviction: Pollen, *AEM*, pp. 106–7. The executions of Gennings and the others were recorded in considerable detail (allegedly by his brother) and ended up in pamphlet form in 1602 and 1603, in effect a kind of toleration tract, before being reprinted in 1614: Questier, *C&C*, p. 267; *The Life and Death of Mr Edmund Geninges*; ARCR, II, no. 338 and p. 250 (for doubts about the traditional attribution of the pamphlet to John Gennings).

[159] Anstr., I, pp. 377–8; Challoner, *MMP*, p. 184. For White's own graphic account (sent in a letter to Henry Garnet) of his being tortured, see Pollen, *AEM*, pp. 123–6 (ABSJ, Anglia I, no. 66).

THE INCESTUOUS BASTARD QUEEN   217

that Catholics were the product of sexual intercourse with cattle ('dogbolt papists!...you follow the pope and his bulls...I think some bulls begot you all'), and Wells said that, 'if we have bulls to our fathers', then Topcliffe had emerged from a cow's vagina. Topcliffe, presumably on the orders of the council, shouted to Gennings, 'confess your fault, your popish treason' and 'the queen by submission no doubt will grant you pardon'. Gennings refused and launched into a public declaration about the duty to obey God and not man. Topcliffe, seeing the moment slipping away, ordered the functionaries to 'turn the ladder' and the 'rope to be cut immediately'. Gennings then had to be tripped in order to execute the rest of the sentence. Since he was 'little or nothing stunned', it was not surprising that he screamed in agony ('oh, it smarts', in the sanitized version compiled by Challoner). But Gennings still managed to pray even while he was being eviscerated. Catholic bystanders tried and apparently succeeded in taking parts of the dismembered body. This may not have looked like the majesty of royal justice.[160] Sir Walter Raleigh had turned up at Tyburn, where the others were executed on the same day. He believed that Plasden satisfied the test of loyalty because Plasden acknowledged Elizabeth as his lawful queen and, to Topcliffe, said that he (Plasden) 'would counsel all men to maintain the right of their prince'. This declaration was enough for Raleigh. He was all for sending off for a reprieve. Only with difficulty was he forestalled by Topcliffe.[161]

In the proceedings against Gennings, Wells, and the others there was no explicit mention of the recent proclamation and its impending implementation. But Verstegan, for one, may have regarded them in the same light. On 24 February/ 5 March 1592, in the same letter in which he narrated the recent executions, he commented that 'by the new Cecilian inquisition there are certain commissioners ordained in every shire to take the examinations of Catholics'. These busybodies appointed other, inferior busybodies who 'once a week (or every day in the week if they please) go from house to house and examine those they find, of what religion they are, and whether they do go to the church; and, as they find them doubtful in their answers, they do present them to the further examination of the commissioners'. But what was arguably worse was that they broke the unspoken compact between servant and master—for the 'servants of recusants they do either persuade by flattery or compel by torture, in hanging them up by the hands, to betray their masters' by 'discovering what priests' their employer 'does relieve, what persons do frequent the house, and the like'.[162]

---

[160] Pollen, *AEM*, p. 108; Lake and Questier, 'Agency', p. 81; Challoner, *MMP*, pp. 176–8. For Charles Newdigate's identification of the incompatibility in places between the accounts by James Younger (Pollen, *AEM*, pp. 100f.; ABSJ, Anglia VI, no. 23) and the one formerly attributed to John Gennings (*The Life and Death*), see ABSJ, CP (Polydore Plasden), typescript: 'Blessed Edmund Genings [*sic*] and Polydore Plasden...', pp. 20–4.

[161] Pollen, *AEM*, pp. 111–14.

[162] Petti, *LDRV*, p. 39. Verstegan believed at this point that Nicholas Fox had been 'executed at Norwich', though in fact he died subsequently in the Tower; his patron, Robert Grey of Marton, was also gaoled: Petti, *LDRV*, pp. 39, 42–3; cf. Weinreich, *PREH*, p. 600.

218   CATHOLICS AND TREASON

This was not necessarily the experience of every recusant who was confronted with the commissioners in his shire. As William Richardson points out, the instructions to the commissioners were that they should not 'press any person to answer to any questions of their conscience for matters of religion' but only whether they attended church.[163] But, for Verstegan and his friends, all of this was linked with greater issues. Following Hatton's death, Burghley 'means to make himself *dictator in perpetuum*' since he was 'descended of princes'. This was a sly dig at Burghley's attempts to upgrade his ancestry's social standing, roundly mocked in, among other places, Verstegan's own *Advertisement Written to a Secretarie of my L. Treasurer's of Ingland*.[164] During this period, so Verstegan later said, he had contemplated writing a piece called either 'The Second Confusion of Babilon' or 'The Confusion of Albion', in which he would demonstrate that Albion was the real Babylon of Revelation and 'that the woman sat upon a rose-coloured beast, and the rose is the arms or banner of England' and 'moreover that the woman was drunk with the blood of saints'. Here, Elizabeth was the whore of Babylon in Revelation 17, and the saints were the English Catholics who gave their lives for the faith.[165]

Verstegan could point to other victims of the invasiveness of the regime's new policy. Back on 22 January 1592 the priest William Pattenson had been hanged at Tyburn. His harbourer in Clerkenwell, Lawrence Mompesson, had fled. He eventually ended up in Brussels. But Mompesson, it seems, was not fully recusant. According to James Younger, who was in the house when the officers arrived, Mompesson was in the habit of standing 'behind the door' while Pattenson was saying Mass so as 'to hear and not to be seen by the servants'. Pattenson was serving as a chaplain in a household headed by someone who had not wanted to risk the penalties of full separation. This was precisely the sort of household that was targeted by the 1591 proclamation and by the commissions which were set up in order to find out which Catholic clergymen were being retained and sheltered behind a wall of relative or occasional conformity.[166] Verstegan said that Pattenson, 'the night before he suffered', was 'in a dungeon in Newgate with seven prisoners that were condemned for felony'. He 'converted and reconciled six of them, to whom also he ministered the sacrament, which the seventh, remaining a

---

[163] Richardson, RP, p. 151.
[164] Petti, *LDRV*, pp. 39–40; Verstegan, *An Advertisement*, pp. 37–9; Richardson, RP, pp. 150–2.
[165] Petti, *LDRV*, pp. 142, 143.
[166] Petti, *LDRV*, p. 43; *CSPD 1591–4*, p. 262 (PRO, SP 12/242/122, fo. 220ʳ); Pollen, *AEM*, pp. 115–16; BL, Lansdowne MS 96, no. 62, fo. 152ᵛ; BL, Harleian MS 6848, fo. 88ʳ [new foliation]; Anstr., I, p. 271; Morris, *TCF*, III (AENB), p. 49; Pollen, *UD*, p. 292 (ABSJ, Anglia VII, no. 26); BL, Harleian MS 6998, fo. 226ʳ; Morris, *TCF*, II, p. 385. An informer, Malivery Catelyn, had written to Walsingham on 31 October 1586 that he had been at Mompesson's Clerkenwell residence with Anthony Fortescue and that he met a chaplain of Mompesson's wife (he said the chaplain's name was Mr Green) and noted that 'their speeches tended to the wrongs [that] the Scottish queen daily endures': *CSPSc 1586–8*, pp. 110, see also pp. 151–2.

THE INCESTUOUS BASTARD QUEEN   219

heretic', revealed 'in the morning'. Six of these felons 'died Catholic' and this 'made the officers to be the more fierce and cruel unto the priest, who was cut down and bowelled being perfectly alive', that is, in revenge for his mounting a public and explicitly Catholic challenge through the voices of the others.[167]

Professions of loyalty on their own were still not enough. The priest Thomas Pormort was executed in February 1592.[168] He had been attached to the household of Owen Lewis, bishop of Cassano, who was a fairly consistent enemy of Robert Persons; and Persons made unflattering remarks about Pormort's time in the English College in Rome. Pormort himself had been named by John Cecil in late May 1591 as one of those Catholic clergy, including Christopher Bagshaw and John Fixer, who were unsympathetic towards the Spaniards. But none of this did Pormort any good and he was hanged.[169] Richard Topcliffe would have had no time for Pormort's supposed loyalism—not after what Pormort had said about him. Pormort had managed to record and circulate damaging rumours about Topcliffe's nauseating familiarity with the ageing Tudor queen. Allegedly, Topcliffe had said that 'he was so great and familiar with her Majesty that he' had groped her sacred Majesty on many occasions, by putting his hands 'between her breasts and paps and in her neck', and that 'he has felt her belly, and said unto her Majesty that she had the softest belly of any womankind'. Furthermore, 'he is so familiar with her that, when he pleases to speak with her, he may take her away from any company' and 'he did not care for the council, for that he had his authority from her Majesty'.[170] Pormort was hanged in St Paul's churchyard on 20 February 1592.

---

[167] Challoner, *MMP*, pp. 185–6; Petti, *LDRV*, pp. 39–40.

[168] Pormort was arraigned on 18 February 1592 on two counts: one of being a seminary priest and the other of reconciling one John Barwise. See ABSJ, Collectanea N/i, no. 6, p. 73; Pollen, *UD*, p. 292 (ABSJ, Anglia VII, no. 26); Pollen, *AEM*, pp. 118–20 (ABSJ, Anglia VI, no. 23); Petti, *LDRV*, pp. 97–8 (ABSJ, Anglia I, no. 68); *AWCBC*, pp. 1030, 1032, 1040–2 (PRO, C 66/1379, mems 5–6), 1046–50.

[169] G. Anstruther, 'The Sega Report', *Venerabile* 20 (1960–1), pp. 208–23, at pp. 219–20; AWCBC, pp. 1029, 1053–4, 1055. Despite sending out signals that he was a loyalist, Pormort had tried to mend fences with the Society of Jesus and, once he was in London, specifically with Robert Southwell: PRO, SP 12/238/181, fo. 278[r–v]. The statements about Pormort made subsequently by James Standish countered the rumour that Pormort was arrested because of 'the destitution to which he was reduced by the injuries done him by the' Jesuits: Pollen, *UD*, p. 189; Devlin, *LRS*, pp. 220–1. Soon after Pormort's death, a Marian priest called Richard Williams was executed; he had 'relieved with money and clothes one [Francis] Shaw, a relapsed priest' who, presumably, betrayed him: Pollen, *AEM*, pp. 120–1; Pollen, *UD*, pp. 230–1; McCoog, *SJISE*, I, p. 61; Anstr., I, p. 306; Petti, *LDRV*, pp. 49, 52, 54.

[170] Petti, *LDRV*, p. 97 ('a copy of certain notes written by Mr Pormort, priest and martyr, of certain speeches used by Topcliffe unto him while he was prisoner in the house and custody of... Topcliffe', 'the which notes were since delivered to [William] Waad, one of the clerks of the council' and were shown to the council in November [1591]; Pollen, *UD*, pp. 209–11; ABSJ, Anglia I, no. 68); see also Pollen, *AEM*, pp. 119–20; C. Levin, *'The Heart and Stomach of a King': Elizabeth I and the Politics of Sex and Power* (Philadelphia, 1994), pp. 141–2. For the dating of these allegations, see *AWCBC*, p. 1039. As Frank Brownlow has commented, Topcliffe was a long-standing royal servant, a kind of private avenger, with whose services Elizabeth never fully dispensed: F. W. Brownlow, 'Richard Topcliffe: Elizabeth's Enforcer and the Representation of Power in King Lear', in R. Dutton, A. Findlay, and R. Wilson (eds), *Theatre and Religion: Lancastrian Shakespeare* (Manchester, 2003), pp. 161–78. Pormort also threw doubt on the truth of the recently exposed Hesketh conspiracy by retailing Topcliffe's slanderous comments about the Stanley family: Petti, *LDRV*, p. 97; McCoog, *SJISE*, I, p. 149.

220 CATHOLICS AND TREASON

Topcliffe made him 'stand in his shirt almost two hours upon the ladder in Lent time, upon a very cold day', and 'urged him to deny' his allegations, 'but he would not'.[171] Nevertheless, this was a pointer to, as some saw it, the link between avant-garde conformist notions and the leaving of the door ajar for expressions of Catholic loyalism.

The proclamation, coming as it did after the demise of Hatton, may in fact have acted as a green light for those provincial governors and administrators who thought that the queen's government was insufficiently hard-line towards Catholics. Just over a month after Pormort's execution, a young man named James Bird was hanged in Winchester. Although Bird had, as Benjamin Norton subsequently testified, been at the Rheims seminary and had contravened the 1581 statute's provisions concerning reconciliation to Rome, the judge Sir Edmund Anderson (who was happy to hang almost anyone, from recusants to witches, but who was known to be hostile also to puritan separatism) harangued the jury to the effect that recusancy alone implied reconciliation to Rome and on this ground therefore the separatist Bird must die.[172] Henry Garnet reported a follow-up case from Winchester. One John Thomas, a Catholic, though formerly 'a reader in the Calvinist ministry' (apparently he was a curate at Thruxton in Winchester diocese), had been indicted on the same charge as had been brought against James Bird. Thomas offered conformity after sentence was passed against him at the same Lent assizes which saw Bird hanged. Thomas was granted a reprieve but then changed his mind and was executed some months later.[173]

---

[171] Pollen, *AEM*, p. 120. Topcliffe also compelled Barwise to appear at the execution and to repeat his words of recantation: *AWCBC*, p. 1031.

[172] See AAW, B 28, no. 10, p. 314 (citing the evidence of Thomas Manger); see also L. Underwood, 'Persuading the Queen's Majesty's Subjects from their Allegiance: Treason, Reconciliation and Confessional Identity in Elizabethan England', *Historical Research* 89 (2016), pp. 246–67, at p. 255. The priest Benjamin Norton recorded that the Hampshire authorities had been searching for him (Norton) when Bird was arrested. Norton remembered also that 'one Mr Cook, then a well-willer to Catholics, but afterwards a good Catholic, talking with' the future lord chief justice, Sir Thomas Fleming, 'about these proceedings', said to him that, 'by this reason, your lordship may hang whom you list of the younger sort of such as had been Protestants and were become Catholics', and Fleming actually agreed. There was a story in circulation (set down by Anthony Champney) that Bird's severed head had bowed to his father, a conformist Winchester office-holder, which proved that Bird Jnr knew what true obedience was: Pollen, *UD*, pp. 231–2 (ABSJ, Anglia I, no. 73), 394–5 (AAW, B 24, no. 101); Challoner, *MMP*, p. 188. It is possible that Bird Snr was one of the officials involved in the search of Lady West's house on 6 December 1583: PRO, SP 12/164/14, fo. 24[r–v] (a report of the search, sent to Walsingham, and bearing the signatures of Richard and Anthony Bird, as well as of Thomas Fleming); p. 133 n.68 above. One James Bird (presumably the same as the martyr), 'son of Mr Anthony Bird, mayor [of Winchester]' of the parish of St Lawrence in Winchester, is listed as a recusant there in 1583: PRO, SP 12/160/26, fo. 56[v]. Richard Bird, mayor of Winchester (1571–2, 1577–8, 1584–5), had been MP for Winchester in 1571, and was presented as a recusant in 1582: *HC 1558–1603*, III, pp. 437–8. For the date of James Bird's execution (25 March 1592), see Anstruther, 'Corrections', p. 113; ABSJ, Anglia VII, no. 25, fo. 51[v]; cf. Challoner, *MMP*, p. 188.

[173] Pollen, *UD*, p. 232; CCED, ID 108316; McCoog, *SJISE*, I, p. 61; see also, for this case, ABSJ, Anglia VII, no. 25, which says that John Thomas was 'hanged and quartered for the like offence as James Bird was'.

THE INCESTUOUS BASTARD QUEEN   221

The high point of the onslaught against Catholic separatism was probably the arrest of the Jesuit Robert Southwell. He had run a virtually one-man campaign in circulating manuscripts and in print against the regime's cruelties and was associated with a casuistical justification of, as it was termed, equivocation, that is, a determination to defeat the purposes of the regime's investigators and interrogators. In summer 1592, Topcliffe hunted down Southwell and took him at Uxendon, the home of the Bellamy family. (The Bellamys had been badly mauled over the Babington business. One of Mrs Bellamy's sons had been executed, and two others died in prison as, indeed, did Mrs Bellamy.[174]) Anne Bellamy, daughter of Mrs Bellamy's son, Richard, was persuaded to turn informer. Allegedly she had been raped by Topcliffe and, as part of the subsequent cover-up, she was married off to Topcliffe's equally repulsive associate, Nicholas Jones.[175] Southwell was arrested on 25 June 1592.[176] Verstegan related that, after Southwell had been taken, Topcliffe sent his mole, Thomas Fitzherbert, 'to the court to tell what good service he had done, and so fell to searching of the house, finding there much massing stuff, papistical books and pictures', which he boxed up and sent off to 'his lodging at' Westminster.[177]

It appears that Topcliffe had had to wait until Southwell was outside central London in order to arrest him. According to Robert Barnes, who, with Richard Blount, was nearly taken on the same day as Southwell, Anne Bellamy had tried but failed to trap the Jesuit in Holborn.[178] Christopher Devlin speculates that, at this stage, it was Southampton House which was providing the Jesuit with security.[179] Also, if John Klause is right about the very pronounced verbal echoes in Shakespeare's *Titus Andronicus* of Southwell's language in his *Humble Supplication* and his *Epistle of Comfort*, then Southwell must have been projecting his voice, with a degree of powerful social and even aristocratic protection, into a public

---

[174] Petti, *LDRV*, p. 53.

[175] Petti, *LDRV*, p. 54; Questier, *C&C*, pp. 245, 249; Devlin, *LRS*, pp. 275, 276, 278, 279. Anne Bellamy gave evidence against Southwell at his trial to the effect that he had propounded to her the allegedly subversive style of equivocation which the prosecutors then used to attack the Society of Jesus as a whole: Devlin, *LRS*, p. 311. One Nicholas Jones (perhaps Topcliffe's, by all accounts, vile companion) was described in June 1596 as a 'yeoman of her Majesty's chamber' and was ordered to arrest the Catholic (and future cleric) Anthony Fletcher, a servant at River Park in Sussex of Mrs Browne, the first Viscount Montague's daughter-in-law: *APC 1595–6*, pp. 481–2; Anstr., II, p. 113.

[176] Petti, *LDRV*, pp. 52, 53, 57 (ABSJ, Collectanea B, pp. 49, 53); Devlin, *LRS*, pp. 279–82; McCoog, *SJISE*, I, pp. 48–9. For the bills found, on 26 June 1592, against Catherine Bellamy for harbouring Southwell and the priest Richard Davies, see Jeaffreson, *MCR*, II, pp. 196–8.

[177] Petti, *LDRV*, pp. 68 (ABSJ, Collectanea B, p. 49), 70.   [178] Devlin, *LRS*, pp. 276–8.

[179] Devlin, *LRS*, p. 277. For Southwell's frequenting of aristocratic houses in London, see McCoog, *LRS*, p. 191 (Southwell to Acquaviva, 28 December 1588). For Devlin's discussion of Southwell's influence on the London literary scene, see Devlin, *LRS*, pp. 262f. John Klause, like Devlin, surmises that among Southwell's at-arm's-length noble patrons and protectors was the earl of Southampton; see Devlin, *LRS*, p. 277; J. Klause, *Shakespeare, the Earl and the Jesuit* (Fairleigh Dickinson Press, 2008), pp. 19–21 and *passim*. See also N. Pollard Brown, 'Paperchase: The Dissemination of Catholic Texts in Elizabethan England', in P. Beal and J. Griffiths (eds), *English Manuscript Studies*, I (Oxford, 1989), pp. 120–43, at pp. 132–3.

222 CATHOLICS AND TREASON

discussion of the question of persecution and toleration.[180] Verstegan recounted on 22 July/1 August 1592 how Topcliffe tortured Southwell 'on four separate occasions by hanging him up by the hands, and in other ways, demanding of him whether he was a Jesuit or not, and what his name was' and, perhaps, in order to see what he knew of the so-called Hesketh conspiracy.[181]

The priests Joseph Lambton and Edward Waterson were picked up almost as soon as they landed in Northumberland in the middle of 1592.[182] Lambton came from Rome accompanied by Francis Montford and had intended to go to Scotland. Montford, who had been ordained in the Lateran on 13/23 June 1591, subsequently became a political agent for the earl of Tyrone. Waterson joined them but contrary winds forced them into Northumberland, not far from Newcastle. They were betrayed by the 'shipmen', and they were taken into custody by Edward Lewen, who was the mayor of Newcastle, and by Henry Sanderson. Lewen was a client of the earl of Huntingdon and Sanderson was an associate of Tobias Matthew, dean of Durham. Lewen was particularly esteemed by the 'precise sort'.[183]

Waterson was interrogated in the first instance by Tobias Matthew.[184] According to the Jesuit Richard Holtby, 'some of the jury' were unhappy and they 'required the statute book, that they might proceed the more assuredly'. This was

[180] Klause, Shakespeare, the Earl and the Jesuit, pp. 21–2, 131–43, and passim; J. Klause, 'Politics, Heresy, and Martyrdom in Shakespeare's Sonnet 124 and Titus Andronicus', in J. Schiffer (ed.), Shakespeare's Sonnets: Critical Essays (1999), pp. 219–40; Devlin, LRS, pp. 272–3; Robert Southwell, An Epistle of Comfort...(Paris, [imprint false: printed secretly at Arundel House, London], n.d. [1587–8]).

[181] Petti, LDRV, p. 52; Devlin, LRS, pp. 285–8.

[182] Anstr., I, pp. 204–5, 371. The recently ordained John Thulis was arrested at about the same time in Northumberland. Verstegan believed on 20/30 October 1592 that Thulis had been executed, although in fact he survived until 1616, when he was hanged, along with a layman, Roger Warren: Petti, LDRV, p. 92; see pp. 432–3 below.

[183] AAW, A XI, no. 255, pp. 755–7 (Richard Broughton's narrative, derived here from Robert Musgrave); Anstr., I, pp. 232, 204–5; Morris, TCF, III, p. 222 (ABSJ, Anglia I, no. 74: here, in Richard Holtby's account, it is Christopher Lewen, the town clerk of Newcastle, who is involved in the arrest, rather than Edward Lewen, the mayor). A privy-council letter to Matthew Hutton on 6 April 1591 noted that Sanderson was 'greatly maliced and threatened for...his good offices by the kindred and friends of...ill-disposed persons': APC 1591, p. 40. Lambton had been abandoned by several of his relatives (including Lord Eure, though this was hardly surprising—Eure sat in judgment on him at the trial). Musgrave, who subsequently married 'one who was' Lambton's 'cousin german', was one of the few who had tried to intervene on his behalf. Details of the execution came to the narrator (Broughton) also from two eyewitnesses, Jane and Dorothy Hodgson: AAW, A XI, no. 255, p. 756; Pollen, UD, p. 231. A notice of Waterson's death found its way into the 'Annales Elizabethae Reginae' (AAW, F1, p. 902) compiled by Anthony Champney; Waterson had been reconciled to the Catholic faith in Rome by Richard Smith, the future bishop of Chalcedon. Lambton was the son of one of the servants of the Browne family at Cowdray where Smith was chaplain at one time, as was the future archpriest George Birkhead, Lambton's uncle: Challoner, MMP, p. 187; Questier, C&C, passim; Anstr., I, pp. 371–2. For the compiling of the records of Waterson's case, see Dillon, CM, pp. 107–8. For Holtby, see esp. Aveling, NC, pp. 165, 166; J. C. H. Aveling, The Catholic Recusants of the West Riding of Yorkshire 1558–1790 (Proceedings of the Leeds Philosophical and Literary Society, Literary and Historical Section, X, pt 6, Leeds, 1963), p. 218.

[184] ABSJ, Collectanea M, p. 151a.

THE INCESTUOUS BASTARD QUEEN   223

probably because of the circumstances in which the accused were arrested—they had not been in the country long enough in order to be indicted under the 1585 statute. But one of the judges said that 'the law was clear enough, and therefore they needed not the statute book'. After conviction, 'the dean used some speeches unto the priests...as that he demanded first of Waterson the cause of his going over', that is, before he enrolled at the seminary. Waterson allegedly said that he was impressed into service on one of the queen's ships and implied that Elizabeth was guilty of piracy.[185]

Lambton was executed on 31 July 1592 with what seemed like more than usual cruelty and incompetence. There was the obligatory 'kettle of water that was in heating and...the butcher's board whereupon he was to be cut'. But the felon paid to do the deed panicked and, as the accounts of the chamberlains of Newcastle upon Tyne confirm, a Frenchman (a surgeon) had to be paid to assist in finishing Lambton off.[186] For his part, Waterson had shown signs of potential compliance, perhaps when he saw the body parts of the dismembered Lambton when they were dumped in front of him in the prison, though Holtby denied this.[187] Waterson had, said the earl of Huntingdon on the day of Lambton's death, made 'suit...to the judges and me to have conference with some learned' men. He had then been 'stayed' from execution. He was also made to go 'to hear sermons at three several times'. A minister called Holdsworth 'brought him a heretical book to read, affirming that it would abide all touches, and left it with him'. Waterson tested it by putting it in the fire, with predictable results. He then absconded but was retaken. He was finally executed, also at Newcastle, on 8 January 1593, though, according to Cuthbert Trollop, the hurdle 'stood still' and nothing the officials could do would make the horses move. Garnet recited the same claims in his long letter to Acquaviva of 17 March 1593.[188] On the way to the gallows, a minister called James Bamford, who was a preacher in Newcastle, preached an anti-popery exhortation to Waterson to come out of Babylon, but to no effect.

---

[185] Morris, *TCF*, III, pp. 223–4 (ABSJ, Anglia I, no. 74; ABSJ, Collectanea M, pp. 151ᵇ–5ᵃ).
[186] Morris, *TCF*, III, pp. 225–7; cf. Pollen, *UD*, p. 231; D. Woodward, '"Here Comes a Chopper to Chop off his Head": The Execution of Three Priests at Newcastle and Gateshead, 1592–1594', *RH* 22 (1994), pp. 1–6, at pp. 1, 3–4; *AWCBC*, pp. 1064–6, 1069–70; cf. Challoner, *MMP*, p. 190. For the date of Lambton's death, see *AWCBC*, p. 1064. Subsequently, in February 1598, Henry Sanderson denounced the conformist (and future MP) William Jenison, who had been sheriff in 1593–4: 'we have pregnant presumptions that when he was sheriff, by his means, and [by the] help of Thomas Carr, the hand of Lambton, the seminary priest, was cut off from the quarter that was set up, and carried away': *CSPD 1598–1601*, p. 24 (PRO, SP 12/266/60); *CSPD Addenda, 1580–1625*, p. 345 (PRO, SP 15/32/62. i); *HMCS*, VIII, pp. 384, 386; *HC 1558–1603*, II, p. 376; M. Questier, 'Practical Anti-Papistry during the Reign of Elizabeth I', *JBS* 36 (1997), pp. 371–96, at p. 389.
[187] Morris, *TCF*, III, p. 227.
[188] Pollen, *UD*, pp. 212 (BL, Harleian MS 6995, no. 76), 231; Morris, *TCF*, III, pp. 227–29; Challoner, *MMP*, pp. 187–8 (relying in part on the transcript of AAW, A IV, no. 22, pp. 121–2, in Butler, *ABP*, pp. 410–11). Tobias Matthew wrote to the earl of Huntingdon on 23 November 1592 to say that Waterson had done 'much harm' in Newcastle by saying Mass in the prison and the town, i.e. in the period during which Waterson was reprieved; a copy of this letter is in ABSJ, CP (Edward Waterson).

224 CATHOLICS AND TREASON

Any conformist inclinations he might have had were now gone or were not enough for the Protestant hardliners in the North.[189]

If we want to know how one section of the Catholic community reacted to the multipronged attempt in the early 1590s to rip the lid off that community and to peer inside the spaces which, some Catholics alleged, were private and should not be violated in this way, we can scan Holtby's long narrative about what he took to be the rise of a new and menacing surveillance state. 'If they seek to know us, we are betrayed and described unto them; if they search, they find us; if they find, they commit us; but, whether they find or no, they ransack, rob and spoil us'. To stay 'at home, if it be espied, we dare not; and to fly far we are forbidden by statute'. Under the recusancy statute of 1593, 'five miles are our compass', that is, of travel without first getting some sort of licence. If 'we converse openly, if we buy or sell, if we traffic in our necessary affairs, or take care of our own commodities; if we laugh, recreate ourselves or carry any indifferent countenance, then are we either too wealthy, or else too well, to live'. Furthermore, 'if we live in secret, and delight ourselves to be solitary, if we cut off all access of our neighbours, or refuse to keep company with such as love us not, then do we busy our heads in their conceit, to devise against them secret conspiracies; and our leisure is a sufficient argument, with them, that we occupy ourselves about no other matter save only to stir and contrive seditious factions'.[190]

In any case, what possibility was there of any kind of Catholic conspiracy when there was this level of surveillance, infiltration, and coercion?[191] Holtby argued that this kind of constant harassment was starting to break apart the social structures which held the Catholic community together. He lamented that 'so odious a thing it is amongst all, to be suspected or accounted a Catholic' because 'even those who in their hearts love our religion do, notwithstanding, hate our profession of the same'. This destroyed the natural economy of Catholic religion and meant that conformist Catholics and potential sympathizers did not dare 'to speak for us...lest it breed their discredit'. Even 'our parents and kinsfolk refuse to show us that friendship which both the law admits and nature exacts, lest they should seem so to affect our faith, by favouring our persons'.[192]

In some respects, these evils were not new. The text compiled by the so-called 'ancient editor' in early 1592 could point to similar cases that in fact preceded the enforcement of the 1591 proclamation. He noted the 'husbands accused by their wives' and the 'fathers by their children, et e converso'. Here was a proto-Orwellian world of mutual denunciation, a kind of family-based terror: 'one Mr Francis Rolson was apprehended and condemned to die by the procurement and

[189] Morris, TCF, III, pp. 229–30; James Bamford, Carpenters Chippes...(1607), pp. 55–65.
[190] Morris, TCF, III (RHPN), pp. 120–1; see also TD, III, pp. 130 f. For Holtby's account of the 1591 proclamation, see Morris, TCF, III (RHPN), pp. 152–3.
[191] Morris, TCF, III (RHPN), pp. 121–2.   [192] Morris, TCF, III (RHPN), pp. 123–4.

THE INCESTUOUS BASTARD QUEEN   225

evidence of his own son', though 'the precedent' was 'so bad' that 'he had his pardon'. Then there was the infamous case of 'Mr John Fitzherbert', who 'in like manner' was 'molested and troubled by his own son, imprisoned, and there dead'. This vile little individual, Thomas Fitzherbert, aided and abetted by the equally repellent Topcliffe, had 'sought by all means to take away the life of old Sir Thomas Fitzherbert, who made' Fitzherbert Jnr 'his heir and brought him up from a child'. He had 'caused him to be suspected of statute treason and to be committed to the Tower', where, in the end, he perished. The nauseating nephew had 'procured also divers of his uncle's tenants to be imprisoned in Stafford, and there some of them are dead'. Also there was 'my Lady Englefield against Sir Francis, the old countess of Derby against her husband, my Lady Paget against my lord, Mrs [Jane] Shelley against her husband remaining condemned in the Gatehouse, the countess of Shrewsbury', presumably Bess of Hardwick, 'against Father Abraham', whoever he was. Also 'a father in London caused his son to be whipped and burnt through the ear for being a Catholic'.[193]

But was the new tyranny really worse than what had gone before? Holtby said that, without a shadow of a doubt, it was. The 'laws, as by tract of time they have never remitted anything of their former rigour, but by new additions thereunto from year to year marvellously increased the same, so they manifestly declare the progress of their authors in hatred and malice'. 'Continually the latter parliaments do excel the former in cruelty, whereby we may easily conjecture what we daily suffer in these later years and what more we may expect at their hands in time to come.' Even more now than in the past, the claim that conformity was about secular obedience was patently false.[194]

Holtby then launched into an attack on Lord President Huntingdon. This decrepit old tyrant was as bad as ever. Nothing had diminished 'his bloody and cruel mind against Catholic men and their religion'. Even after all this time, he still had 'no deep reach in matters of weight or judgment'. He worked through his spies, his 'informers, his executioners', his 'picked companions, so ready to run, to seek, to take, to spoil and to execute whatsoever he bids them'. But, despite his own 'weak constitution of body, yet it...[was] incredible what pains he' personally took 'both day and night, in watching, in writing, in travelling, without respect of frost' and 'snow'. His own personal 'religion', puritanism, was framed to suit his dynastic prospects—for he was still 'a competitor to the crown'. Huntingdon was 'a prince of puritans, wherein he shows great zeal and forwardness externally, and all are welcome to him that are accounted friends of that faction'.[195]

The sins of Huntingdon's enforcers were legion. Some of their names crop up regularly in contemporary Catholic martyrologies and denunciations of the late

---

[193] Morris, *TCF*, III (AENB), pp. 25–6.   [194] Morris, *TCF*, III (RHPN), pp. 129, 130–2.
[195] Morris, *TCF*, III (RHPN), pp. 132–3.

226 CATHOLICS AND TREASON

Elizabethan persecution. First and foremost there was Henry Sanderson, 'a bankrupt merchant and base companion' who 'for his pretended zeal in puritanism and Machiavellian subtlety' was 'a special instrument' to the lord president.[196] The persecution was intensified when such people by-passed the often ramshackle but formal machinery of local government. Significantly, Sanderson had absolutely no respect for the sheriff of Newcastle.[197] 'Others', wrote Holtby, were 'placed in public office and authority, to countenance, aid [and] assist these other catchpolls, that no resistance be made nor any attempt be frustrated'. If any public official appeared to be 'negligent, calm, of mild disposition, loath to be a persecutor or disturber of his neighbours' or did anything 'to favour the afflicted, then means' were 'devised, either to sharpen and prick them forward by checks, threats, or flatteries, or else utterly to discountenance or displace them, and thrust into their rooms others of less honesty and more cruelty'. Huntingdon sought to control the choice of such people, 'in such offices as go by election of voices, or are at the disposition of some other superior officers'. He demanded of those 'chosen into the office of sheriff' that he should have 'the nomination of their undersheriff'. In 'corporate towns', the same was the case with 'the mayors and other officers at his disposition'. Thus it was that 'sheriffs and other superior officers', though 'of their own nature otherwise modest and reasonable', were 'forced to use much cruelty, lest they be accused of slackness by their own substitutes, being factors for the lord president'. Their 'substitutes' used 'their office at their pleasure and discretion' to do whatever they liked. Their superiors dared not 'correct or find fault with them' because they were afraid of Huntingdon.[198]

By name, Holtby listed those who had shopped Catholics to the authorities: John Spence; Francis Eglisfield, who was the frontman in the sting operation which resulted in the arrest of the priest John Boste on 10 September 1593; 'one Thomson' who arrested 'Sir Henry Stapper', a Marian priest, and so on. These people were assisted by a rabble of criminals who did the day-to-day mulcting of Catholics, notably Luke Hutton, 'nephew unto the false bishop of Durham that now is'.[199]

If one wanted proof of the way in which the police state was now functioning, Holtby cited the coordinated searches across Yorkshire, Durham, and Northumberland on Candlemas, 2 February 1593. Although 'the chief commissions for searching were directed to the justices', it was others ('who ordinarily' were 'joined in commission to oversee the justices' actions [so] that no favour be showed') who really ran the show. Holtby then proceeded to recite a litany of the petty and not so petty tyrannies inflicted on good Catholics, everything from the harassment of

---

[196] Morris, *TCF*, III (RHPN), p. 134.   [197] Morris, *TCF*, III (RHPN), pp. 134–5.
[198] Morris, *TCF*, III (RHPN), pp. 136–7.
[199] Morris, *TCF*, III (RHPN), pp. 145, 147–51. For a similar case made by the 'ancient editor', see Morris, *TCF*, III (AENB), pp. 14–18 (listing those who were corruptly exploiting the recusancy statutes).

THE INCESTUOUS BASTARD QUEEN   227

a woman in labour to the arrest of the priest Anthony Page. He also described the purge of conformist gentry who had recusant wives—for example, Ralph Gray, William Fenwick, and Francis Radcliffe. Huntingdon had personally sat in commission at Durham and Newcastle. The commissioners met in the latter place in Sanderson's own house.[200]

Even if one assumes that Verstegan, Holtby, and other commentators were using a fair amount of hyperbole in their descriptions of all this, the fact remains that all through 1592 and early 1593 Lord Burghley was actively soliciting and receiving statements from the provinces concerning the way in which the 1591 proclamation was being enforced.[201] In Warwickshire, for which there survive very full records of the commissioners' work, we can see how the Catholic community there was investigated in order to demonstrate how far surface conformity hid exactly the evils which the proclamation condemned.[202] The Warwickshire commissioners reported that Lady Philippa Gifford, having been denounced and indicted as a recusant, wrote to the commissioners to say that she had 'reformed herself' and went to 'the church (as she said) in Buckinghamshire'. But that was no longer good enough—'nobody gave testimony of her conformity but herself'. She had to do it all again in front of some of the 'commissioners of that county', though she still had not complied by the time the report was written.[203] John Arrowsmith had made 'some show of conformity and' went to church; but 'when the preacher' processed 'up to the pulpit to preach', Arrowsmith went 'presently out of the church, and' said 'he must needs go out of the church when a knave begins to preach'.[204] Burghley must have used these reports in order to drive forward the proposed draft legislation against Catholic recusants which was prepared for the parliament in early 1593.[205]

Holtby's words are a running Catholic commentary, though one which is generally excluded from conventional accounts of the period, on post-Armada Elizabethan politics. One can see how his (and Garnet's and Southwell's) claims

---

[200] Morris, *TCF*, III (RHPN), pp. 137–43, 154–9; Anstr., I, p. 264.

[201] Richardson, RP, p.146. For the lists sent in from Durham by Matthew Hutton on 13 January 1593, see PRO, SP 12/244/8, 8. i. For Burghley, these reports would expose the unacceptable levels of accommodation between popery and the local authorities whose legal duty it was to suppress it. For the use of the renegade seminary priest Thomas Bell's information (containing hundreds of names of recusants in the North, mainly in Lancashire) by Burghley to reinforce the work of the recusancy commission, see F. X. Walker, 'The Implementation of the Elizabethan Statutes against Recusants 1581–1603' (PhD, London, 1961), pp. 319–20; Lake and Questier, *Trials*, pp. 133–7; Goss and Gibson, *Crosby Records*, p. 22; cf. *CSPD 1591–4*, pp. 158–9 (PRO, SP 12/240/138).

[202] For the reports of the commission in Warwickshire, see PRO, SP 12/243/76, 76. i. For the operation of the commission in London, see Petti, *LDRV*, p. 50 (ABSJ, Collectanea M, p. 127ᵃ); and in Norfolk, see A. Hassell Smith and G. M. Baker (eds), *The Papers of Nathaniel Bacon of Stiffkey*, III (Norfolk Record Society, 53, 1987–8), pp. 127–31, 132–3, 135–7, 141, 146–8.

[203] PRO, SP 12/243/76, fo. 204ᵛ.

[204] PRO, SP 12/243/76, fo. 215ʳ. Verstegan noted that in one Warwickshire parish there had been 'found seven score recusants': Petti, *LDRV*, p. 72.

[205] Lake and Questier, *Trials*, p. 136; *CSPD Addenda 1580–1625*, pp. 339, 342–3, 344–5 (PRO, SP 15/31/50, 59, 59. i, 59. ii, 62, 62. i); see pp. 232–6 below for the 1593 parliament.

228 CATHOLICS AND TREASON

about persecution became tied in with the intra-Catholic disputes about occasional conformity, that is, the ones associated with the priest Thomas Bell. Even
though Bell may well have spoken for a large section of the Catholic community
which indeed did not want recusancy to be pushed to the point where it could be
identified with sedition, Bell's critics were able to destroy him with the claim that
all good Catholics had, in spirit at least, to adhere to a unity based on rejection of
a false faith enforced by a tyranny. This was not a new argument. The same case
had been made earlier in the 1580s, for example in York by those associated with
Margaret Clitherow. But the political circumstances of the later 1580s and early
1590s gave it an extra edge. The stand-out case here must be the reported comments alleged to have been made by the lawyers Anderson and Fleming, even if in
the context of one specific instance, to the effect that proof of recusancy was as
good as proof of treason. If this was really the line taken by the queen's government, rammed through with the most appalling cruelty against those who were
merely good Christians, it could be argued that the compromises suggested by
Bell were really just capitulation.[206]

Yet even in the stand-off between these sharply articulated and bitterly divided
positions on this aspect of the exercise of royal authority, there were ambiguities.
If someone such as Polydore Plasden could persuade Sir Walter Raleigh that he
was a loyalist, then it was not certain how easily or for how long the queen's officials could proceed against all Catholic separatists indiscriminately.[207] As we have
also seen, this was the moment which saw the rise of an arguably new strain of
anti-puritanism in the national Church. There had long been enemies of puritan
reform embedded in the higher reaches of the Elizabethan Church and State. But
contemporaries must have been aware of the potential compatibility of, on the
one hand, discourses of the kind pumped out by Holtby and Verstegan and, on
the other, the public and violent denunciations of puritanism coming from the
pen of Richard Bancroft. It was, as we shall see in the next chapter, against this
background that the numerically fewer but sometimes very high-profile prosecutions of Catholic clergy, such as the leading northern priest John Boste and the
Jesuits Robert Southwell and Henry Walpole, took place.[208]

---

[206] For the sending out of the country, by Henry Garnet and his friends, of persecution narratives,
principally from York, which could be taken as vindications of the uncompromising position on recusant separation taken by Garnet and others, against the likes of Thomas Bell, see Lake and Questier,
Trials, pp. 175–82; ABSJ, CP (Margaret Clitherow): Patrick Barry to Katharine Longley, 24 January
1969; Longley to Barry, 26 January and 2 February 1969.
[207] See pp. 216–17 above.   [208] See Chapter 8 below.

8

Catholic Radicalism and the (Re-)Emergence of Catholic Loyalism

The savagery of the later 1580s and early 1590s made it extremely difficult for Catholic casuists such as Thomas Bell to argue for a principled compromise over recusant separation. But this did not mean that others would not continue to say, as they had always done, that it was possible to be a good Catholic and yet not think that only Spain could save the world. The seminarist and future Catholic pamphleteer Anthony Copley had rehearsed to William Waad in December 1590 how he had voluntarily returned to his native land as a true subject of the queen. He gave as much information as he could about Englishmen in Flanders, Spain, Rome, and elsewhere.[1] A month later he claimed that, because of Spain's contempt for the English, 'English gentlemen beyond [the] sea begin more to look homeward, and wish the preservation of the realm against...invasion'.[2] In summer 1591, not long before the release of the royal proclamation of 18 October, we find the priest John Cecil, himself the source of some of the Catholic martyrological material of the period and an architect of the appellant agitation in the later 1590s, intervening with Sir Robert Cecil to seek some sort of official countenance for a Catholic loyalist agenda.[3] This priest wrote to his namesake Sir Robert on 4 June 1591 to convey his gratitude for Burghley's 'warrants of protection'. Cecil (the priest) and an unnamed 'companion', presumably the similarly minded clergyman John Fixer, were 'required to detect all such as they shall find approving the Spanish practices, and to confirm the well-affected in their allegiance'. In return John Cecil asked 'whether such Catholics as are good subjects' would 'incur the penalties of the laws by receiving them', even though this would still technically be an offence under the 1585 statute.[4] Eight days later, he wrote again to say that the leading Catholic laymen Lord Vaux and Sir Thomas Tresham

---

[1] BL, Lansdowne MS 64, no. 9, fos 25^r–36^v.

[2] BL, Lansdowne MS 66, no. 25, fo. 74^r. In c.early January 1591, Waad urged Lord Burghley to allow Copley to confer with Lancelot Andrewes about religion, in anticipation that he might actually renounce Rome: BL, Lansdowne MS 66, no. 26, fo. 76^r; see also BL, Lansdowne MS 66, no. 66, fo. 117^r.

[3] For the Appellant (or Archpriest) Dispute, see J. H. Pollen, *The Institution of the Archpriest Blackwell: A Study of the Transition from Paternal to Constitutional and Local Church Government among the English Catholics, 1595 to 1602* (1916); Chapter 10 below. For John Cecil's intelligence work for Sir Robert Cecil, see Anstr., I, p. 64; *CSPD 1591–4, passim.* Cecil apparently handed over the correspondence of Sir Francis Englefield and Robert Persons which is calendared in *CSPD Addenda 1580–1625*, pp. 296–8, 311–14 (PRO, SP 15/31/100–6, 160–1, 163–6).

[4] *CSPD 1591–4*, p. 52; Anstr., I, pp. 64, 118.

Catholics and Treason: Martyrology, Memory, and Politics in the Post-Reformation. Michael Questier,
Oxford University Press. © Michael Questier 2022. DOI: 10.1093/oso/9780192847027.003.0008

230   CATHOLICS AND TREASON

were 'accounted very good subjects and great adversaries of the Spanish practices'. It was 'said amongst them that, if an occasion be offered', they would 'requite the relaxation now afforded them' by Sir Robert's 'moderation'.[5]

Toleration was, John Cecil said, the way to build up a loyalist core who would wrest control of the English Catholic community away from the likes of Allen and Persons. He had even proposed to Lord Burghley that certain unnamed English Catholics should 'form a corporation to gain authority, and then dissolve the seminaries, and discharge' Cardinal Allen 'from the management of English affairs'.[6] John Cecil told Burghley not to persecute Catholics—neither to force them to 'apostatize' nor, on the other hand, to put 'them to death'. He insisted that 'in place of one put to death, ten come in from the seminaries, and twenty go over to the seminaries; their martyrdom is the greatest service to opponents abroad, for accounts are printed, painted and published, and princes are moved to compassion'.[7] On 3 July 1591 John Cecil wrote to Sir Robert that Persons's 'drift, in his book of the new martyrs of England' and the whole purpose of the 'seminary of Valladolid' were, taken together, 'to persuade people that' Philip II had 'the hearts of more than a third part of the realm, and that they are ready to assist him, and have no hope but in Spain'.[8] John Cecil said that he found 'all things in England contrary to the relations made in other countries'. In those other places it was said 'in their books and pulpits that a most rigorous persecution' was 'practised here upon Catholics, and that the number of them in durance is such that the old prisons will not hold them' and that 'the torments they suffer are infinite and the manner of their deaths intolerable'. He claimed that he found all this to be utterly untrue. The reality was that in England there was 'great peace, tolerance, tranquillity and moderation, with wonderful clemency and almost a general liberty...of all'. Also, what was said by the Catholic hawks on the Continent about the proliferation of their co-religionists in England was deeply misleading: 'they publish the number of Catholics to be infinite and the receipt and entertainment of priests secure', whereas the true number was 'less by many thousands and the entertainments harder by many hundred than they make it'. He said that he could 'devise a means how they may be informed in Spain of those false suggestions and of the true state of things here'.[9]

Anti-League pamphleteers in France were already arguing that Jesuit clergy came merely to stir up sedition. As one pamphlet put it, 'what faith did ever permit us to attempt against the lives of our princes, or what murderers of princes

---

[5] *CSPD 1591–4*, p. 56.

[6] *CSPD 1591–4*, p. 43. Cardinal Allen was appointed prefect of the English mission by Gregory XIV in September 1591: McCoog, *SJISE*, I, p. 112; Knox, *LMCA*, pp. 335–7.

[7] *CSPD 1591–4*, p. 42.   [8] *CSPD 1591–4*, p. 67.

[9] *CSPD 1591–4*, p. 60; see also *CSPD 1591–4*, pp. 70–1 (John Cecil to Sir Robert Cecil, 7 July 1591, referring to 'that part of Robert Persons's book on the Valladolid seminary stating that there are 30,000 Catholics in prison in England, when there are not 200, and that three fifths of the people are Catholic when the contrary is the truth').

CATHOLIC RADICALISM   231

were there ever (except among them) canonized for martyrs?' Nor were 'the bones and quarters' set up 'upon the Tower or gates of London' to be revered as 'relics'; for indeed they were 'tokens of rebellion, murders, assaults and treasons'.[10] The enemies of the Catholic League argued for toleration. As Peter Lake explains it, this 'produced an account of the relations between Church and State, between the spiritual powers of the clergy and those of the Christian prince', which 'more or less perfectly replicated those adduced by defenders of the English Church and the royal supremacy against the Catholics'. Some English Catholics were now buying into precisely those arguments.[11]

The League found that in the end it could not defeat Henry IV in battle even if his sieges of their urban strongholds almost invariably failed. The resulting impasse brought, as John Bossy says, the League's 'internal contradictions...out into the open'. The radical political theory which underpinned the revolt against the crown became untenable, as did the position of English exiles within the structures of the League. For them, 'the economy of the emigration was entirely upset' since 'there was neither security for institutions, nor facility of communication for movement and transport, and without these it was impossible to pursue the objects for which the emigration existed'. Eventually there would have to be an accommodation with Henry IV. When that happened, the émigré Catholics associated with the League would have to face reality—and that meant either taking themselves to the Spanish Netherlands or Spain, or ditching resistance theory altogether. This 'political readjustment' would involve 'a series of social, intellectual and emotional readjustments' and eventually 'a total conversion of outlook which would', as Bossy interpreted it, 'liquidate the ideology' of the seminarist 'enterprise once and for all'.[12]

There was another, if rather obvious, reason for this prospective shift of a section of the community into loyalism. The simple fact was that the decapitation of the Scottish queen in 1587 had, although it promoted her Calvinist son in the line of succession, made it likely that many, if not most, English Catholics would insist that they now recognized James VI as truly the son of the martyr Mary Stuart and that he deserved their support and allegiance. Legitimist Catholics could not unreasonably think that their position on the succession was now in keeping with that of Elizabeth herself. She may not have openly identified James as her heir, but there was no sign that the Tudor court seriously had anyone else in mind.

Faced with the prospect of James VI's eventual accession, however, some leading Catholic exiles (and particularly the author or authors of the *Conference about the Next Succession to the Crowne of Ingland*) cranked up the quasi-republican rhetoric of elective monarchy in order to argue against entirely automatic

[10] *A Letter, Written by a French Catholicke Gentleman...*(1589), p. 22, cited in Lake, *BQB*, p. 256.
[11] Lake, *BQB*, p. 256.   [12] Bossy, EC, pp. 149, 200–1.

232 CATHOLICS AND TREASON

hereditary blood-right succession and, in effect, against James's right to succeed Elizabeth solely on that basis. They probably did not speak for the majority of their co-religionists. But that did not mean that those in the forefront of the recent measures against Catholic separatism were going to drop their guard. For those such as Burghley, popery remained the real threat. For that reason, as he saw it, the attack on the puritan classis movement by Sir Christopher Hatton, John Whitgift, and Richard Bancroft was a wrong turn.[13] Thomas Pormort, executed in February 1592, had not only said some fairly direct things about Topcliffe's familiarity with Elizabeth but also reported Topcliffe's words about Archbishop Whitgift. As Christopher Grene recorded it, Topcliffe offered Pormort 'his liberty if he would say that he was a bastard of the archbishop of Canterbury, and that the archbishop had maintained him beyond the seas'. (Pormort was, it seems, a godson of Whitgift. He certainly used the name Whitgift as an alias.) On Pormort's account, Topcliffe had said that Whitgift 'was a fitter counsellor in a kitchen among wenches than in a prince's court'. Topcliffe had declared to the JP Richard Young that 'he would hang the archbishop and 500 more if they were in his hands'. Pormort repeated much of this at trial, 'openly at the bar'. Whitgift obviously had no incentive to protect Pormort as such. But Persons's informant, James Younger, said that, following sentence, the priest 'would have admitted conference'. Although 'the judge replied that it was too late', Whitgift 'sent his chaplains' to Pormort and ordered the sheriff to defer the carrying out of sentence. It was this which provoked Topcliffe to sue directly to Burghley for 'a mandamus to the sheriff to execute the priest that self-same day'.[14]

The Meeting of the 1593 Parliament

The previous year, 1592, had seen a series of triumphs for the regime's enforcers against Catholic clergy and those associated with them. But the parliament which assembled in 1593 saw a significant reverse for those who hoped that new legislation would reinforce the effects of the October 1591 proclamation. The gathering witnessed a new legislative push against Catholics but also something of an anti-puritan reaction. The draconian draft legislation against recusants, in the form initially of two bills, bifurcated into one watered-down anti-Catholic bill and one anti-puritan/sectary bill.[15]

---

[13] Lake, *BQB*, *passim* and esp. pp. 330–3; see also *CSPD Addenda 1580–1625*, p. 320 (PRO, SP 15/32/7). For Burghley's increasing isolation over the issue of puritan nonconformity, see Collinson, *EPM*, p. 411.

[14] Petti, *LDRV*, pp. 97–8; Pollen, *AEM*, p. 119. For James Younger's arrest and confessions later in 1592, see Anstr., I, p. 392; PRO, SP 12/242/121, 122, 125.

[15] Neale, *EHP*, II, pp. 280f, esp. at 294–6; Richardson, *RP*, pp. 79–115, esp. at pp. 95–7.

CATHOLIC RADICALISM   233

Just before parliament opened, the authorities had been provoked by a demonstration in Cheapside by the parishioners of the puritan separatist Roger Rippon, who had recently died in Newgate.[16] Richard Verstegan believed erroneously that Rippon, 'a Brownist', had been 'hanged for his seditious tongue', but he later noted, accurately enough, that, after Rippon died in prison, 'his body was begged by some of his consorts, who did put it in a coffin and covered it over with black cloth and brought it before the door where the judge was lodged that had condemned him', that is, Richard Young, who could be harsh towards puritans even if not as much as towards separatist Catholics: 'on the four corners of the coffin were fixed railing libels against the judge, affirming that this was the sixteenth martyr that they had martyred for the profession of the true gospel of Christ'.[17]

The altercation in parliament over the new conformity legislation marked something of a watershed moment. On 28 February 1593, two days after James Morice's stinging attack on high commission procedure and his attempt to bring in a measure against it, the puritan Henry Finch said 'he liked very well of the matter of the bill'; that is, he liked the initial version of the measure against recusancy which had been laid before the house and now received its second reading. But he 'desired a kind of explanation to be inserted in it', in other words that it should not 'touch... such honest godly men' as went sermon-gadding because of a non-resident, unlearned, or negligent minister in their own parish. Nathaniel Bacon used the moment also to attack episcopal justice.[18]

By 12 March 1593 the relevant bill, presented again in the Commons, had been revised so as to be restricted to Catholics, though some of its penalties had been scaled down. On the following day there was a furious debate as to who ought really to be caught by it.[19] The measure went no further than the reading on 17 March of amendments made in committee.[20] The attempt to turn the screw against Catholic separatists and their clergy was being disrupted by events. Not only had there been the unfortunate incident involving Roger Rippon, but the ecclesiastical commissioners had also made a mass arrest of Protestant separatists

---

[16] Richardson, RP, p. 94.

[17] Petti, LDRV, pp. 114 (ABSJ, Collectanea B, p. 83), 116–17; A. Peel (ed.), The Notebook of John Penry 1593 (Camden Society, 3rd series, 67, 1944), pp. vii, xx, 39, 46, 48, 49–52, 55, 68.

[18] Hartley, PPE, III, pp. 50–1; T. E. Hartley, Elizabeth's Parliaments: Queen, Lords and Commons, 1559–1601 (Manchester, 1992), pp. 98–9; Neale, EHP, II, pp. 268–70, 274, 282–3; Richardson, RP, p. 93. As Richardson points out, Richard Bancroft's two principal anti-puritan texts (Survay of the Pretended Holy Discipline... (1593) and Daungerous Positions and Proceedings, Published and Practiced within this Iland of Brytaine, under Pretence of Reformation, and for the Presbiteriall Discipline... (1593)) were in preparation before parliament met: Richardson, RP, p. 93. Bancroft's Survay was entered at the Stationers on 5 March 1593: Petti, LDRV, p. 120.

[19] Neale, EHP, II, pp. 284–5.

[20] Richardson, RP, pp. 97, 99; Neale, EHP, II, pp. 285–6. On this day also, 17 March 1593, Topcliffe attempted to make his charges of popery stick against the crypto-Catholic William Bassett (for whom, see p. 183 above) when, together, they appeared at the bar of the House of Commons, but the speaker, Edward Coke, cut him off: Neale, EHP, II, p. 316.

234 CATHOLICS AND TREASON

in Islington Woods. John Penry was detained there, though he absconded.[21] Verstegan wrote on 1 April 1593 that 'there were eighty puritans lately taken at a sermon in Finsbury Field [i.e. Islington] and with them...Mr Martin Marprelate is thought to be taken.'[22]

This brought protests from some godly MPs. Puritan obstructionism in parliament appears to have provoked a brutal retaliation against leading Protestant sectaries. As Professor Neale points out, when the original recusancy bill stuck in the Commons, it led to the introduction of a new anti-sectary bill in the Lords.[23] It began there on 27 March, was passed, and came down to the Commons by 31 March.[24] Neale judges that the way in which the bill was written was sufficiently loose as to be capable of snaring 'puritans as well as separatists.'[25] Although 'Burghley sponsored the measure', he was, concluded Neale, at this point 'outcountenanced in court and council' by Archbishop Whitgift.[26]

Henry Barrow, John Greenwood, and three other puritan separatists had already been proceeded against at law. They were tried under the 1581 act against seditious words—a statute which had been designed for the punishment of Catholic subversion. They were convicted. Verstegan set down in detail the charges against them; and the things they were accused of saying were fairly extreme. The regime's line was that these puritan separatists 'and the papists were [both] pioneers for the king of Spain, the one beginning at the one end, and the other at the other end; and so at the last they would meet at the heart of the middle'.[27] In the Commons on 13 March, Miles Sandys had spoken 'to the bill of recusancy'—to the effect that it should not 'be restrained to popish recusants only' but should take in 'the Brownists and Barrowists' also. The lawyer James Dalton had made a similar demand.[28] Barrow, Greenwood, and the others were

---

[21] Richardson, RP, p. 97; ABSJ, Collectanea B, p. 80.

[22] Petti, LDRV, pp. 114, 116–17; ABSJ, GC, pp. 154–5 (ARSJ, FG 651/624: Garnet to Acquaviva, 10 June 1593). Verstegan noted that Matthew Sutcliffe had published his Matthaei Sutlivii de Catholica, Orthodoxa, et Vera Christi Ecclesia, Libri Duo...(1592) and had dedicated it to the earl of Essex. Sutcliffe attacked Verstegan, not least for his Theatrum Crudelitatum Haereticorum Nostri Temporis, another edition of which had appeared in 1592. As Verstegan put it, Sutcliffe 'says that for my making those martyrs which are no better than traitors I do deserve a very terrible death, the which he describes': Petti, LDRV, pp. 114–15. At this point, however, Sutcliffe had also published an anti-puritan pamphlet, An Answere to a Certaine Libel Supplicatorie, or rather Diffamatory, and also to certaine Calumnious Articles, and Interrogatories...(1592), and, Verstegan noted, it was intended to be presented to the 1593 parliament: Petti, LDRV, pp. 119 (ABSJ, Collectanea B, p. 78), 120.

[23] For the origins of this new bill ('An Act for Explanation of a Branch of a Statute...'), see Richardson, RP, pp. 104 f; Neale, EHP, II, p. 287. Richardson suggests that Whitgift was not the originator of it, but it is not clear, then, who was.

[24] Richardson, RP, p. 105; Neale, EHP, II, pp. 286–7.   [25] Neale, EHP, II, p. 287.

[26] Neale, EHP, II, p. 288; for a narrative of this episode which makes Burghley seem less isolated, see T. Rabb, Jacobean Gentleman: Sir Edwin Sandys, 1561–1629 (Princeton, 1998), pp. 16–17; for Richardson's brilliant account of Burghley's involvement in the formulation of the new anti-sectary legislation, see Richardson, RP, pp. 105–9.

[27] Petti, LDRV, pp. 132, 144–7.

[28] Richardson, RP, p. 97; HC 1558–1603, III, p. 342, II, p. 9; Hartley, PPE, III, p. 124.

CATHOLIC RADICALISM 235

tried on 21–23 March and were sentenced to hang for felony, that is, for 'devising' and publishing seditious books.[29]

But there was a real uncertainty as to what the regime would now do with or to them. Sir Thomas Egerton and Sir John Puckering exchanged frantic notes to see whether the execution could be postponed. Would it be possible to obtain some gesture of compliance?[30] On 26 March, Barrow asked for a 'Christian and peaceable conference' and then, on 27 March, for a disputation, a move which was unwelcome, predictably, to Whitgift, but it did secure a temporary reprieve.[31] There was a conference of sorts on 30 March between Barrow and various clergy, but he posed uncompromisingly as a martyr. It was exactly at this moment, that is, on five consecutive days (27–31 March 1593), that Burghley tried to get his preferred piece of anti-sectary legislation through the Lords. It was not limited to Catholics and this may have been why Whitgift and his friends did not oppose it.[32]

On 31 March, Barrow and Greenwood were hauled off to Tyburn, but Burghley intervened to stop the execution.[33] Although Burghley had, technically, been working with Whitgift up to this point, he was now doing his best to thwart the archbishop.[34] According to Thomas Phelippes, Burghley had been petitioned that 'in a land where no papist was put to death for religion, theirs', that is, Barrow's and Greenwood's, 'should not be the first blood shed who concurred about faith with what was professed in the country'.[35] In the few days that remained to them they were able to write an account of their misfortunes which mimicked aspects of Catholic martyrdom narratives. Briefly, they were respited again from the gallows. This provoked the 'exceeding rejoicing and applause of all the people, both at the place of execution, and in the ways, streets and houses as we returned'.[36] As Verstegan subsequently reported these events, the condemned were 'carried unto the place of execution' and the 'halters' were 'put about their necks and tied fast unto the gallows', but then 'they were presently untied and carried back again alive'. Verstegan thought that the 'officers durst not execute them by reason of the great multitude of puritans there present' and also 'flocking together in the city of London'. These puritans 'began openly to murmur and to give out threatening speeches, insomuch that a present commotion was feared'.[37]

The murmurs of discontent at the onslaught against puritan separatists in London were the context for the introduction into the Commons of the new measure against sectaries; the first reading of that bill was on 2 April 1593.[38] The Commons' puritan voices ripped into it when it was presented, for a second

[29] Richardson, RP, pp. 101–2. [30] Richardson, RP, p. 102.
[31] Richardson, RP, pp. 103–4. [32] Richardson, RP, pp. 104–5, 107.
[33] Richardson, RP, pp. 107–8; Petti, LDRV, pp. 131, 133; Peel, The Notebook, p. xxii. There had already been one reprieve on 24 March: Petti, LDRV, p. 132.
[34] Richardson, RP, pp. 108–9. [35] Petti, LDRV, p. 133 (CSPD 1591–4, p. 341).
[36] Petti, LDRV, p. 133, citing An Apologie or Defence of such true Christians as are commonly called Brownists...(Amsterdam, 1604), pp. 92–3.
[37] Petti, LDRV, p. 131. [38] Richardson, RP, p. 109.

236 CATHOLICS AND TREASON

reading, on 4 April 1593. Henry Finch insisted that the 1581 measure, to which the sectary bill referred, was intended exclusively against Romanists. In committee the new bill was altered out of recognition, principally by limiting it to puritan sectaries. An instruction was given in fact to draw a new bill altogether.[39]

The interest group in the Lords which was rebuked by the Commons committee for altering the original bill then took its revenge. On 6 April 1593 Barrow and Greenwood were executed at Tyburn. Burghley tried again to save them but without success. John Penry had returned from Scotland, and had been arrested at Stepney on 22 March. He was put on trial in the fourth week of May, and sentenced under the 1581 statute against seditious words. The execution warrant was signed by Sir John Puckering and Sir John Popham. Penry was hanged at Southwark on 29 May. The day before, he had appealed to Burghley to seek a pardon from the queen, but Burghley was unable to prevent his death.[40]

Penry had allegedly said that Elizabeth's rule was so malign that 'you', the queen, 'have suffered the gospel to reach no further than the end of your sceptre'. The true exponents of the gospel were regarded as 'seditious' merely for pointing out the truth—'you are not so much an adversary unto us poor men as to Christ Jesus' and 'thus much we must say that in all likelihood, if the days of your sister, Queen Mary, and her persecution had continued unto this day…the Church of God in England had been far more flourishing in England than at this day it is'.[41] Verstegan recorded how the 'followers' of Barrow and Greenwood, 'canonizing them for more than martyrs, do inveigh privately against the bishops as the principal procurers thereof'.[42]

These events, as much as the committee-based strife in parliament over the appropriate legal balance to be struck in the punishment of separatists of various kinds, were, one assumes, truly extraordinary for an Elizabethan public which had, quite recently, witnessed the promulgation of the proclamation of 18 October 1591 and, over the previous few years, had seen a parade of Catholic traitors being strung up and disembowelled in plain sight.[43] Even while the war with Spain was in full swing and the queen's servants were facing down the existential threat from

[39] Neale, *EHP*, II, pp. 288–90; cf. Richardson, *RP*, pp. 109–11. According to Richardson, those who spoke in favour of the bill were 'working to a brief from Burghley': Richardson, *RP*, p. 109.

[40] S. Babbage, *Puritanism and Richard Bancroft* (1962), p. 38; *CSPD 1591–4*, pp. 341–2; Collinson, *EPM*, pp. 388–9, 428; Richardson, *RP*, pp. 111–12, 115, 117, 118–20, 122; Neale, *EHP*, II, p. 291; Peel, *The Notebook*, pp. vii, xxi, xxii; *ODNB, sub* Penry, John (article by C. Cross). For Verstegan's account of Penry's indictment, see Petti, *LDRV*, pp. 168–70. Udall died in prison in 1593, although he had been pardoned: Richardson, *RP*, p. 78. For the martyrological tradition around Penry, see Peel, *The Notebook*, pp. vii–viii.

[41] Petti, *LDRV*, p. 170.

[42] Petti, *LDRV*, p. 151.

[43] For the final version of the 1593 anti-separatist legislation, see Neale, *EHP*, II, pp. 296–7. Richardson suggests that Burghley eventually got his way over the final form of the legislation and 'secured a significant tactical victory over Whitgift': Richardson, *RP*, pp. 112–14.

CATHOLIC RADICALISM   237

popery, those who by their own lights were good Protestants were being hounded and accused of sedition.

Not surprisingly there were Catholics who thought all this was pure gain, even though, for example, Anthony Page was executed at York on 20 April 1593 and William Davies was hanged at Beaumaris in July 1593.[44] Verstegan opined to Robert Persons on 20/30 April 1593 that, as for the 'late book against the puritans', that is, Bancroft's *Survay of the Pretended Holy Discipline* which had been 'set forth by the authority of the bishops', 'there was never [a] book set forth by our English heretics nor any other, more advantageous for us'. This was because John Calvin and Theodore Beza were there 'deciphered to be no better than seditious and rebellious spirits'. Their 'practices, drifts and sinister getting to credit and government in Geneva' stood 'displayed and proved by their acts, consultations and private letters to their fellow ministers—yes, Beza's seditious letters to the puritans in England'.[45]

It was, however, unthinkable that Persons and his friends could simply buy into a Whitgiftian and Bancroftian future—certainly not in the way that some of their own Catholic critics clearly now began to imagine might one day be

---

[44] For Page, see Challoner, *MMP*, p. 189; J. C. H. Aveling, *Catholic Recusancy in York 1558–1791* (1970), p. 71. Page was from Harrow-on-the-Hill and was almost certainly connected with the Bellamy family: Anstr., I, pp. 264, 265. He was arrested at the house of one William Thwing ('a schismatic' and relative of the future martyr Edward Thwing), who was acquitted of harbouring on the evidence of his sister, who testified 'that she alone had brought' Page 'into the house': ABSJ, Collectanea M, p. 151ᵃ; Morris, *TCF*, III (RHPN), p. 139; http://www.stirnet.com/genie/data/british/tt/thweng2.php; see pp. 292–4 Chapter 10 below. For Davies, see Petti, *LDRV*, p. 164; pp. 56–8, 60 above. Davies had been arrested in March 1592. For the date of the execution (27 July 1593), as stated by Challoner, *MMP*, p. 196, supported by at least one contemporary source (Robert Parry's diary), see NLW, Plas Nantglyn MSS, 1: *Archaeologia Cambrensis*, 6th series, 15 (1915), p. 119 (*AWCBC*, p. 1133). A. G. Petti suggested from Richard Verstegan's correspondence that it was in early May 1593, though Verstegan must here have been in error; see ABSJ, Collectanea B, p. 113 ('Mr Baines's advices', 1 June 1593). For Davies's own description of his arrest, interrogations, and trial, see Pollen, *AEM*, pp. 128–36 (a holograph letter (ABSJ, Anglia VII, no. 9), so it appears, which came into the hands of Henry Garnet). John Bennett recorded that Davies's plea for banishment, on the basis that he was 'never acquainted' with the statute under which he was condemned, was dismissed because he was 'stubborn', i.e. because he refused to 'reveal' anything 'to her Majesty's commodity': ABSJ, Collectanea M, p. 107ᵃ (Pollen, *AEM*, pp. 137–8; *AWCBC*, pp. 1136–9); see also *HMCS*, XII, p. 212; Thomas, *WECM*, pp. 34, 55, 62, 64, 65, 66, 261–95, 297, 313. Davies had been involved in the operation of a clandestine printing press in Wales (at Little Orme's Head); the printer was a Welshman called Thackwell, who was attacked in 1588 by the writer who went under the name of Martin Marprelate: Thomas, *WECM*, pp. 58–60; D. M. Rogers, '"Popishe Thackwell" and Early Printing in Wales', *Biographical Studies* 2 (1953), pp. 37–54; PRO, SP 12/200/31; Martin Marprelate, *Oh Read Over D. John Bridges/for it is a Worthy Worke...* (1588; RSTC 17453), p. 23.

[45] Petti, *LDRV*, pp. 134–5; Babbage, *Puritanism*, pp. 33–4; see also BL, Additional MS 29546, no. 28, fos 119ʳ–20ʳ (the reply of 'a papist to Barrow...some of his questions'). For Bancroft's output at this time, see P. Lake, 'The "Anglican Moment"? Richard Hooker and the Ideological Watershed of the 1590s', in S. Platten (ed.), *Anglicanism and the Western Christian Tradition* (Norwich, 2003), pp. 90–121, esp. at pp. 93–4, 96. Bancroft's *Dangerous Positions* explicitly compared 'the devilish and traitorous practices of the seminary priests and Jesuits' with the 'lewd and obstinate course held by our pretended reformers, the consistorian puritans' because both tried to 'steal away the people's hearts from their governors, to bring them to a dislike of the present state of our Church': Bancroft, *Dangerous Positions*, pp. 2–3; *ODNB*, *sub* Bancroft, Richard (article by N. Cranfield).

238 CATHOLICS AND TREASON

possible. As far as Persons, and indeed Richard Verstegan, Henry Garnet, and Richard Holtby were concerned, the State was still sponsoring the same savage tyranny, even if, for whatever reason, it was now posing as an equal-opportunity persecutor. In early December 1593 Verstegan declared that 'the queen' remained 'at open defiance with all Catholics, and detests priests', and so the 'persecution' was 'like to be great'.[46] While the 1593 parliament was sitting, Garnet had recited the material which his confrère Holtby had sent down to London about the brutality being used against their co-religionists in the North. Holtby had drawn up a long list of the houses which had been raided and of the people who had been arrested. One unlucky young woman had taken refuge out in the open and awoke to find a snake sliding down her throat. Perhaps this is some kind of metaphor for the violation of Catholic innocence by Protestant cruelty and corruption, in the form of a serpent, but, all in all, these events were proof enough of a systematic hounding of Catholics, sufficient to refute claims that temporal obedience was all that the regime required. In this long screed Garnet denounced the now openly renegade Thomas Bell as a persecutor, though his fall from godliness had 'brought great profit to our cause'. The utter hypocrisy of his teaching on conformity was plain for all to see. Southwell, from his prison cell in the Tower of London, gave his opinion that Bell was 'excessively addicted to faction'.[47]

The Perceived Dangers of Catholic Legitimism: John Boste, John Ingram, and Henry Walpole

Whether or not there was, at this point, the kind of widespread repression of good Catholics that Henry Garnet and Richard Holtby still claimed, the regime was deeply suspicious of Catholics who were trying to cultivate the good graces of the Scottish king. At opportune moments during the 1590s James talked the language of tolerance in order to make sure that he did not lose his Catholic constituency in either Scotland or, for that matter, England. A number of Catholics started to look at James in the way that moderate leaguers had viewed, before his conversion, the Calvinist Henry of Navarre.

Some Protestants, including those who figure regularly in Catholic martyrological stories of the time, harboured intense suspicions of the king of Scotland. Tobias Matthew, dean of Durham, regarded the young James as 'a deeper dissembler...than is thought possible for his years'. In the early 1590s, as James deployed the language of politique centrism in his dealings with an increasingly tetchy

---

[46] Petti, *LDRV*, p. 193.
[47] ABSJ, GC, pp. 92f, 99, 103–4 (ABSJ, Anglia I, no. 73, part printed and translated in Pollen, *UD*, pp. 227–33). In Rome, in Cardinal Allen's circle, it was understood that Bell had betrayed 'above 700 [Catholics]': *L&A 1592–3*, p. 374. For Bell's information against Lancashire Catholics, see AAW, A IV, no. 38.

CATHOLIC RADICALISM 239

Presbyterian Kirk and a violent but potentially conformist Catholic spectrum in Scots politics, Matthew started to channel financial support to James's personal and political foe, the frequently rebellious Francis Stuart, earl of Bothwell.[48] Here, some of the more aggressively anti-popish voices in the English Church were starting to line up as critics of James's preferred strategy for securing the English crown, a strategy which incorporated Catholics on both sides of the border.[49]

Indeed, it is possible that what Garnet and Holtby represented as relatively indiscriminate purges of good Catholics may have been more carefully targeted; for example, in the case of the intelligence-led operation which resulted in the arrest of the priest John Boste on 10 September 1593 at Waterhouses near Durham. An informer, Francis Eglisfield, stayed outside the house but made sure that Boste did not escape. The sting was masterminded by the ubiquitous Hull customs official Anthony Atkinson, who specialized in tracking certain sorts of Catholic clerics and their patrons all over the North of England.[50] According to Cuthbert Trollop, Eglisfield 'confessed and communicated like a Judas' and then 'went presently forth and met Sir William Bowes and divers others to apprehend Mr Boste'. They rampaged through the house but did not find Boste and 'thought they had been deluded'. Still, 'the traitor bade them pull down the house or burn it, for he was sure the priest was in it' and 'they thereupon, violently breaking, found him'.[51] Boste was the chaplain of the rebel earl of Westmorland's daughter, Lady Margaret Neville. She was arrested at the same time and faced a felon's death for harbouring him. Atkinson said that these people were involved in sending intelligence information out of the country. He said that he had conferred with Boste, only one day before the arrest was effected, and asked him 'whether he was the one that wrote and sent letters of intelligence overseas of the state of England or no' and Boste more or less admitted it, though he said the 'chief intelligence givers of matters of State are about the court'.[52] Boste himself confessed on 11 September 1593, the day after his arrest, that he had gone 'divers times into

[48] Richardson, RP, p. 203. Matthew was sending financial support to Bothwell by April 1594: Richardson, RP, pp. 203, 214.

[49] For Verstegan, King James was 'a man irresolute in anything, mutable in his favours, of no religion but for advantage': Petti, LDRV, p. 164.

[50] Challoner, MMP, p. 203; Morris, TCF, III (RHPN), pp. 194–5; M. Questier, 'The Politics of Religious Conformity and the Accession of James I', HR 71 (1998), pp. 14–30; Pollen, UD, pp. 215–27. Among those involved in hunting down Boste was Atkinson's associate, the Durham cleric Henry Ewbank. Ewbank had been 'chamber fellow' to Boste at The Queen's College, Oxford, and indeed they had been at the same school in Westmorland: Pollen, UD, p. 220. Charles Thursby remembered that Tobias Matthew also 'had known' Boste 'in the university': AAW, A IV, no. 1, p. 13. The Waterhouses property where Boste was arrested was kept by William Claxton, the son of a 1569 rebel: Pollen, UD, p. 220 (PRO, SP 12/245/131); see also J. B. Wainewright's notes (p. 13) in ABSJ, CP (John Boste).

[51] AAW, A IV, no. 1, pp. 11–12 (for the material in Alban Butler's papers, see ABP, pp. 419–20; ABPFC, fo. 4ᵛ, used in Challoner, MMP, pp. 202–3).

[52] Pollen, UD, pp. 222–3 (PRO, SP 12/245/131). Back in late December 1585 the intelligence agent Thomas Rogers had noted that the letters of Scots Jesuits were sent to Paris by Boste via the Newcastle-to-Dieppe route: CSPD Addenda 1580–1625, p. 163 (PRO, SP 15/29/62).

240   CATHOLICS AND TREASON

Scotland, in which realm he was some time at Edinburgh, some time at the Lord Seton's, some time at Ferniehurst and at other places', though, he said, not since 1588.[53] Atkinson was told by a Catholic that, at Douai, Boste was spoken of as if he were a bishop, 'and God be thanked of his long reign for he had done much good' and 'his taking was greatly lamented'.[54]

What with Boste's known range of contacts it was perhaps not entirely convincing when he protested that he was 'but a plain priest to say Mass and matins' and that he was 'no meddler in matters of State'. Via a carefully placed informer, one Henry Duffield, the regime, which had not got anything out of Boste by force, learned a good deal.[55] Boste claimed to have seen the young King James 'pull forth his left pap' in the presence of 'two or three Jesuits and show them a lion that he has growing there under it' and brag that 'I must have the Tower of London ere it be long for all this'. Now, believed Boste, the Scots king 'waits only for fit opportunity'.[56] Boste was deceived by Duffield into recommending him to Joseph Constable, brother to Sir Henry Constable, and he would 'acquaint you with as many as you will'.[57] The lieutenant of the Tower, Sir Michael Blount, alleged that Boste had friends who served the young Viscount Montague, and who planned to 'set him out of prison'.[58] Among those named by Atkinson in connection with Boste was the shadowy dissident David Ingleby, the brother of Margaret Clitherow's martyr-chaplain Francis and son-in-law of the rebel earl of Westmorland. David Ingleby's name had come up in the investigation of the Babington Plot back in 1586, as had Boste's.[59] Boste had also had dealings with the exile Francis Dacre.[60]

Here was credible evidence that clergy of this kind were creating a cross-border Catholic consensus which might rupture crucial aspects of the current and supposedly solidly Protestant Anglo-Scots amity. Boste had had access to the so-called 'Cecil's commonwealth' tracts, though he was deliberately vague about exactly what he had seen and where. Boste remarked of one book that it told 'the

---

[53] Pollen, *UD*, p. 216 (BL, Lansdowne MS 75, no. 22, fo. 44[r]); see also *CSPSc 1589–93*, pp. 265, 855.

[54] HHCP 203/152 (*HMCS*, XIII, p. 497).

[55] HHCP 203/150 (*HMCS*, XIII, pp. 494–7); for Henry Duffield, see PRO, SP 77/8, fo. 112[v]. Boste was allegedly 'fifteen times before the councillors and torturers examined': Foley, *RSJ*, III, p. 765 (AVCAU, Liber 1422 [Grene, Collectanea F], section 4, p. 86[a]). Boste expected in November 1593 merely to be sent to Wisbech (via the good offices of John Thornborough, bishop of Bristol): *HMCS*, XIII, p. 494.

[56] HHCP 203/150 (*HMCS*, XIII, p. 495); *HMCS*, IV, pp. 411, 416, 420; C. R. Markham (ed.), *A Tract on the Succession to the Crown (A.D. 1602) by Sir John Harington* (1880), p. 121; see also Adams, PC, pp. 154, 174; *HMCB*, III, p. 84; *CSPSp 1587–1603*, p. 85 (Mendoza's report of 10/20 May 1587 that James's birthmark was 'caused by his mother's alarm when she was pregnant' and saw David Rizzio 'stabbed to death before her eyes').

[57] HHCP 203/150 (*HMCS*, XIII, p. 495).   [58] HHCP 170/21 (*HMCS*, IV, p. 432).

[59] Pollen, *UD*, p. 222; *CSPSc 1586–8*, p. 31.

[60] Pollen, *UD*, p. 223. Back in April 1590, Robert Bowes had notified Burghley and Walsingham that Boste was in Northumberland with 'one Rockwood [Thomas Rookwood?]' who was 'sometimes towards the earl of Arundel': *CSPSc 1589–93*, p. 265; Pollen and MacMahon, *VPH*, p. 377.

old fellow [Lord Burghley] how many houses of honour he has pulled down and made away with to set himself and his sons up withal'. Duffield added that he would not 'commit to paper the blasphemy that' Boste 'has told me concerning the book'. But Boste allegedly said that 'if we live…till the next spring we shall have wars…for, said he, there was an epistle delivered to the queen in Latin' which told her that if she allowed her subjects liberty of conscience, her Catholic neighbour princes would be her friends but, if not, they would be her enemies. Piously, Boste averred that he would willingly 'be pulled in pieces tomorrow upon the rack on…condition' that the queen and Richard Topcliffe were 'good Catholics'.[61]

Of Boste's arrest, Huntingdon was said to have bragged that they had taken one of the 'greatest stags in the forest'.[62] Presumably on the strength of Atkinson's information about the postmaster John Carr of Newcastle and his links with Boste (specifically that Carr had harboured Boste in July 1592), Carr was arrested on Huntingdon's warrant, as Holtby narrated. Carr was put on trial and was 'condemned at this Lammas assize last past', in 1593. Carr confessed in return for a reprieve.[63]

Topcliffe was soon in on the act. Along with Sir Robert Cecil and Sir John Wolley, he interrogated Boste. Perhaps Boste had concluded that he now had nothing left to lose. Topcliffe said that he had 'never heard a more resolute traitor'. Boste was 'sorry' that there were 'not twenty priests for every one popish priest in England' and that he had 'not won to the Church Catholic, twenty for every one'. He would 'take' the queen's 'part, if the pope of himself' should 'send an army against her Majesty, but if the pope by his Catholic authority do proceed against her to deprive her as a heretic, then he cannot err, nor the Church' and 'Catholics must obey the Church'.[64] Boste was confronted, presumably in York, with the renegade cleric Anthony Major. Boste was made to look at Major's list of places in the North where, the renegade said, they had both been. Boste was tortured while his former co-religionist Major stood and watched.[65]

On 31 January 1594 a gaol delivery started at Durham. The dean, Tobias Matthew, preached a long sermon, largely in praise of Huntingdon. The charge to the jury was made by Humphrey Purfrey and incorporated a 'bitter invective against the pope'. The following day, Candlemas Eve, Lady Margaret Neville was

---

[61] HHCP 203/151 (*HMCS*, XIII, p. 496).

[62] Morris, *TCF*, III (RHPN), p. 195. When Boste was dragged in front of Huntingdon immediately after his arrest, wrote Charles Thursby, the lord president 'made a prolix speech concerning the long search that had been made for' Boste, who had used 'cunning shifts' which had 'deluded the diligence of his officers' as they searched for 'so notorious a traitor': AAW, A IV, no. 1, p. 13.

[63] Pollen, *UD*, p. 221; Morris, *TCF*, III (RHPN), p. 178; Foley, *RSJ*, III, p. 765 (AVCAU, Liber 1422 [Grene, Collectanea F], section 4, p. 86ᵃ).

[64] Pollen, *UD*, p. 218 (PRO, SP 12/245/124).

[65] Morris, *TCF*, III (RHPN), p. 196. Atkinson had advised that Major should be pumped for information about Boste since he 'did much use Boste's company': Pollen, *UD*, p. 222.

242 CATHOLICS AND TREASON

arraigned along with Grace Claxton (who had been arrested with Lady Neville), John Speed, and Thomas Trollop. Lady Neville was persuaded to plead guilty. Mrs Claxton was confronted with the example of two renegade priests who had once been her chaplains but who, said Huntingdon, 'now…detest the Mass'.[66] John Speed was arraigned for 'aiding and assisting…priests, whom he used to serve' by 'guiding and conducting' them 'from one Catholic house to another'.[67] Then Thomas Trollop was similarly dealt with for harbouring the priest Bernard Pattenson. Trollop had 'for the same matter…been' arraigned 'four or five years past' and had had 'the benefit of a pardon granted in the parliament anno 29°'. He was told that the pardon would take no effect unless he conformed and went to church, but he refused.[68] Sentence was passed on all of them. The bishop of Durham, Matthew Hutton, used 'flattering words' and, by 'fair promises and deceitful persuasions', persuaded Lady Neville to capitulate 'into the participation of heresies'.[69]

Huntingdon then went to Newcastle, leaving orders 'with the sheriff to execute them with the rest' of the felons 'that had judgment of death'. But, the 'next day, being Sunday', a petition turned up in Newcastle in which Mrs Claxton 'alleged herself to be with child'. Huntingdon's answer was, basically, tough luck. She was out of time—the petition had not been entered 'before judgment'. But she was stayed from the gallows. On returning to Durham, Huntingdon concluded that, as usual, he had been right all along—'my first answer was agreeable to law'—and she should hang. Unfortunately, one could not ignore the clack, clack, clack of critical tongues; so, irritably, he wrote to Burghley on 11 February 1594. In this letter, however, he was able to take solace from the fact that John Speed had, the week before, indeed been strung up. Still, Margaret Neville had, for the time being, been let off and, worse, Huntingdon could not easily avoid reprieving the allegedly pregnant Mrs Claxton. This was simply ridiculous, said the godly lord president. Yet 'to stop the mouths of those that incline always falsely to slander the mercy and justice of this happy and gracious government', he 'willed the sheriff to make choice of some eight or more grave women to go to her' to determine whether 'she was with child', which infuriatingly it turned out she was.[70]

---

[66] Morris, *TCF*, III (RHPN), pp. 184–7. Holtby speculated that Huntingdon was referring to William Hardesty and Anthony Major or perhaps to Thomas Bell himself: Morris, *TCF*, III (RHPN), p. 187.

[67] Challoner, *MMP*, p. 197; Morris, *TCF*, III (RHPN), p. 188; Foley, *RSJ*, III, p. 760 (AVCAU, Liber 1422 [Grene, Collectanea F], section 4, p. 83ᵃ).

[68] Morris, *TCF*, III (RHPN), pp. 188–9.   [69] Morris, *TCF*, III (RHPN), pp. 189–90.

[70] Pollen, *UD*, pp. 238–9 (BL, Harleian MS 6996, no. 34, fo. 66ʳ); C. Cross, *The Puritan Earl: The Life of Henry Hastings third Earl of Huntingdon 1536–1595* (1966), p. 245. Verstegan reported to Roger Baynes on 6/16 April 1594 that 'many women have been hanged (particularly in the North) for having given priests assistance and lodging': Petti, *LDRV*, p. 210. According to Holtby, the informer Francis Eglisfield was prepared to make 'suit' for Claxton to obtain the reprieve: Morris, *TCF*, III (RHPN), p. 191. Mrs Claxton's pardon request appears to have been subscribed by Bishop Hutton: PRO, SO 3/1, fo. 476ʳ. Holtby says that she renounced both 'her heavenly Father and [her] everlasting crown' (i.e., like

CATHOLIC RADICALISM 243

Tobias Matthew seconded Huntingdon's demands for the smack of firm government. He wrote to Burghley on 16 October 1593, shortly after the taking of Boste. Matthew referred, evidently with some approval, to the customs official Atkinson's harsh comments about Bishop Hutton's 'slackness or slowness in his proceedings'. Burghley had been kind enough to congratulate Matthew for his 'readiness against seminary priests and such like'. But Matthew warned (no great surprise, this) that the North was swarming with Catholic nonconformists. He hoped that the recent 'commission of enquiry against the wives and servants of recusants, when it shall be returned' to Burghley in London 'may not be suppressed or, by respect of persons, unevenly handled'. Matthew cited, as proof that the law was not being properly enforced, the case of Thomas Trollop. He had, as we saw, been arraigned for harbouring Bernard Pattenson. Trollop stood 'indicted upon that felony' and 'remains still in the gaol of Durham unexecuted, I see not how', commented Matthew—by rights he ought to have been hanged already.[71]

It was not hard to see what the likes of Matthew were worried about. At the point that Boste was arrested, the signs from Scotland were that James VI was, even in the wake of the so-called Blanks conspiracy, uncovered in late December 1592, constructing exactly the sort of cross-confessional alliances that many English Protestants regarded with such suspicion.[72] The Scots king appeared determined to mend fences with those Scottish Catholics who had allegedly been at the centre of the Blanks Plot. At Fala in October 1593, James consented, or so it seemed, to meet the leading Scottish Catholic peers, that is, George Gordon, earl of Huntly, and his friends. Richard Verstegan noted that James's 'private conference with the Catholic lords and his seeming to incline unto them has greatly incensed the ministers against him' and James was now 'for his own security' being driven to look to a Catholic constituency for support. Indeed, he was 'willing to accept of any party and will be indifferent to any religion, seeing that among the ministers he can expect no security, having had so much experience of their mutinous humours and their insolent demeanours towards him, having given him so great aversion from them'.[73]

Of course, it was exactly this politique tendency of the young king that had steam copiously issuing from Robert Persons's ears—and, if King James did not already have an 'aversion' to Persons, the Jesuit was making sure that he soon would, that is, as he secured the publication of the *Conference about the Next*

Margaret Neville, Mrs Claxton conformed): Morris, *TCF*, III (RHPN), p. 191. It is possible that John Speed, executed on 4 February 1594, may have already been in dispute over other matters with the authorities in Durham; see *APC 1590*, p. 195.

[71] Pollen, *UD*, pp. 218–20 (PRO, SP 15/32/89); Anstr., I, p. 270. Pattenson and Trollop had been taken by the Durham prebendary Henry Ewbank, and Pattenson had absconded: Pollen, *UD*, pp. 219–20. For Thomas Trollop's reprieve, in effect, on a legal technicality, see Morris, *TCF*, III (RHPN), p. 190. Subsequently Pattenson was reported to be with Lady Katherine Gray: Anstr., I, p. 270.

[72] For the Blanks conspiracy, see Questier, *DP*, pp. 198–200.   [73] Petti, *LDRV*, p. 195.

244   CATHOLICS AND TREASON

Succession about the Crowne of Ingland.[74] But some Scots presbyterians and some English puritans were vocal critics of the Scots king. Verstegan noted that the English ambassador in Scotland, Lord Burgh (who was a relative of Richard Topcliffe), was a 'perfect puritan' and was in cahoots with the Kirk's presbyterian ministers who 'do most band against the king.'[75] All of this opened up an arena for the expression of a kind of Catholic loyalism which, to some Protestants, concerned as they were about what the Scottish king would eventually do, was no great comfort.

The extent to which English Protestant officials worried about English Catholic infiltration into Scotland can be picked up from the case of the Jesuit Henry Walpole. Walpole, who was a chaplain to the English regiment in Flanders, was arrested in December 1593 shortly after entering the country near Flamborough Head. He had been sent to take the place of Robert Southwell as Henry Garnet's assistant in the English Jesuit mission. The suspicion must have been that he was trying to make for Scotland. Walpole was kept in York until late February 1594.[76] At this point, the queen's physician, Rodrigo Lopez, was being interrogated for his alleged conspiracy against Elizabeth.

In the interim, Topcliffe made sure that he was a prominent spectator at William Harrington's execution on 18 February 1594.[77] At Tyburn on that day there were ten men and thirteen women hanged for felony before Harrington met his doom. In the short interim between their deaths and his, Harrington disputed with a minister *inter alia* about 'St Peter's primacy'. Then there occurred a furious exchange with Topcliffe, who demanded that Harrington should acknowledge his treason and confess that he had called the queen a tyrant. Harrington riposted that Topcliffe was the real 'tyrant and...bloodsucker'. But his tyranny would not

---

[74] R. Doleman [pseud.], *A Conference about the Next Succession about the Crowne of Ingland...* (n.p. [Antwerp], 1594). It is likely that a number of authors contributed to the text; see ARCR, II, no. 167; P. Holmes, 'The Authorship and Early Reception of *A Conference about the Next Succession to the Crown of England*', *HJ* 23 (1980), pp. 415–29; V. Houliston, *Catholic Resistance in Elizabethan England: Robert Persons's Jesuit Polemic, 1580–1610* (Aldershot, 2007), pp. 72–92.

[75] Petti, *LDRV*, p. 195; Questier, *DP*, p. 201. Topcliffe recalled that, in the 1530s his grandfather Thomas, Lord Burgh, had defended Anne Boleyn (he was her lord chamberlain) from the accusations levelled against her: Girolamo Pollini, *Historia Ecclesiastica della Rivoluzion d'Inghilterra...* (Rome, 1594), EUL copy (classmark Rowse/Pol), Topcliffe's annotation on the author's preface.

[76] ABSJ, GC, pp. 180, 182 (ARSJ, FG 651/624: Garnet to Acquaviva, 3 January and 10 March 1594). For the circumstances of Walpole's arrest, see McCoog, *SJISE*, I, p. 153; Caraman, *HG*, p. 178. Walpole's companions who were arrested with him (that is, his brother Thomas and Edward Lingen) had been in military service under Sir William Stanley when he surrendered Deventer: Ward, *LT*, pp. 175–6.

[77] Harrington was arrested at the inns of court in the chamber of Henry Donne (John Donne's brother), who died subsequently in prison: Anstr., I, p. 149; R. C. Bald, *John Donne: A Life* (1970), p. 58; for his indictment in late June 1593, and postponement of trial, see ABSJ, Anglia I, no. 77 (printed in J. Morris, 'The Martyrdom of William Harrington', *Month* 20 (1874), pp. 411–23); ABSJ, Collectanea B, p. 123 ('Advices from England', 20 July 1593); PRO, SP 12/245/66, fo. 99^r (dated speculatively to July 1593 in *CSPD 1591–4*). Samuel Harsnett later circulated the rumour that Harrington had been married to one of the demoniacs of Denham, Friswood Williams: F. Brownlow (ed.), *Shakespeare, Harsnett, and the Devils of Denham* (1993), pp. 78, 376; *APC 1592*, pp. 355–7, 360; Morris, *TCF*, II, pp. 103–7.

prevent the growth of the faith: 'we were 300 in England; you have put to death 100', but '200 are left' and, 'when they are gone, 200 more are ready to come in their places'.[78] John Stow noted that Harrington was cut down so quickly that he was still fully conscious and physically struggled with the executioner—though Challoner's account insists that this did not detract from Harrington's pious and zealous witness.[79]

On 25 February 1594 (the same day on which confessions were being dragged out of the alleged plotters Dr Lopez, Manuel Luis Tinoco, and Esteban Ferreira da Gama), Walpole was hauled off to London in order to let Topcliffe do to him what he did best. Walpole's own principal confessions were made between 27 April and 17 June.[80] The priest John Ingram was caught up in the proceedings against Walpole and against Boste. He had been taken when he briefly came over the border from Scotland; he was on a boat near Norham, trying to cross back again, when he was arrested on 25 November 1593. For a time he posed as a Scot.[81] But Huntingdon knew on 12 February 1594 not only that 'with Scotland' Ingram was 'greatly acquainted' but also that he was an associate of, 'amongst others', 'the earl of Huntly, with whom (as to me it is very constantly affirmed) he has been for the most part of one year and a half, and so great is the reputation of him with the arch-papists of Scotland and some others that' those people would, had they known in time, have tried to stop him being sent from Berwick. Huntingdon wanted to escort Ingram down to London himself because he was determined to 'say somewhat' to Elizabeth herself which he would not put in writing. Huntingdon had views about what was going on in Scotland, views which were so controversial that he would not commit them to paper.[82]

Ingram had served as a chaplain for the previous eighteen months to Sir Walter Lindsay of Balgavies Castle. Lindsay was a son of the ninth earl of Crawford and a man of business in Flanders and Spain for the earl of Huntly. Ingram was, as Huntingdon conjectured on 23 February 1594, 'freighted...with many shrewd practices against her Majesty by them that sent him into Scotland, whither it seems he was directed'.[83] Ingram had been in Scotland during the Spanish Blanks episode and had watched Balgavies Castle being demolished in retaliation for the alleged plot. He said at his trial that 'he was pursued in Scotland' and was

---

[78] ABSJ, Anglia I, no. 77.   [79] Challoner, *MMP*, p. 197 (reporting Stow's words).

[80] McCoog, *SJISE*, I, pp. 153–4; Caraman, *HG*, pp. 178–84; Pollen, *UD*, pp. 239, 241, 244–68. Walpole was named in John Daniell's confession 'of certain practices invented beyond the seas against her Majesty', made on 25 February: *CSPD 1591–4*, pp. 442–3 (PRO, SP 12/247/91).

[81] Anstr., I. p. 183; J. Bain (ed.), *Calendar of Letters and Papers relating to the Affairs of the Borders of England and Scotland* (2 vols, Edinburgh, 1894–6), I, p. 513; ABSJ, A V, no. 8 (unfoliated).

[82] Pollen, *UD*, pp. 239–40 (BL, Harleian MS 6996, no. 35, fo. 68ʳ).

[83] Pollen, *UD*, p. 241 (BL, Harleian MS 6996, no. 37, fo. 72ʳ). Ingram was a relative of the Englefield family, and Sir Francis Englefield maintained him financially during his seminary training: M. J. Cashman, 'The Gateshead Martyr', *RH* 11 (1971), pp. 121–32, at p. 121; ABSJ, A V, no. 8 (unfoliated). Thomas Walpole heard Robert Bruce tell William Holt SJ at Brussels that he had written letters of introduction to Scotland on Ingram's behalf: Pollen, *UD*, p. 243 (PRO, SP 12/248/24).

246 CATHOLICS AND TREASON

'constrained to avoid the same for fear of his life. He came into England and stayed but ten hours and, returning to Scotland, was taken upon the waters of [the] Tweed.'[84] On 8 March 1594 Huntingdon, whom Ingram called, in the twentieth of the series of epigrams that he composed while in prison, 'the bloody monster of the North', certified that he had finally worked out who Ingram was, and insisted that Ingram should be sent to London from York Castle gaol.[85]

Lindsay's narrative of Scots Catholicism, written after the confrontation at Glenlivet in 1594 between, on the one hand, Huntly and his associates and, on the other, a royal army led by the earl of Argyll, alleged that English clergy had been driven into Scotland by the rigours inflicted on them as a result of the 1591 proclamation. There they found a polity in which the insolent ministers of the Kirk threatened excommunication equally against the king and their social betters. It was the Jesuit priests sent by Pope Gregory XIII who persuaded those Catholics who had gone so far as to subscribe 'certain heretical articles' (merely in order 'to please the king and gratify the ministers') that this was gravely sinful. It was into this debate that John Ingram was parachuted. When good Scottish Catholics had learned how reprehensible conformist compliance really was, David Graham, the 'laird of Fentry' and Lindsay himself 'were the first to recant and oppose the ministers'. Fentry had been 'beheaded in Edinburgh by command of the king', and he had died as 'a glorious martyr'. Lindsay 'withstood the ministers for a long time with the help of an English priest', Ingram, 'who lived in his house as [a] chaplain, said Mass, and preached sermons, which' Lindsay 'invited heretics and others to attend, not without signal benefit, for many became converted to our holy faith'. This, in turn, drove the heretic ministers wild with fury. They obtained a royal warrant to arrest Lindsay. But clan loyalties meant that Lindsay, the son of the earl of Crawford, could use the threat of retaliation by his kinsmen to keep his enemies at bay. It was Lindsay's example that had provoked Huntly, and the earls of Errol, and Angus into open declarations of Catholicism. In turn 'the ministers' of the Kirk 'had recourse to the queen of England'; and, for their part, the Catholic nobles 'appealed to the pope and to the king of Spain', and they had been outed for the so-called Blanks conspiracy. But they had only been doing their duty, to their faith and to their king.[86]

The process which in England was described by royal proclamations as treasonable was therefore, in Scotland, being represented as a defence of the true

---

[84] Morris, *TCF*, III (RHPN), p. 201.

[85] Pollen, *UD*, pp. 241–2 (BL, Harleian MS 6996, no. 40, fo. 78ʳ), 281 (ABSJ, Anglia VII, no. 8). Ingram's identity was established by Thomas Walpole: Pollen, *UD*, p. 243 (PRO, SP 12/248/24). In a letter of July 1594 Ingram referred to 'those which out of Scotland made' an 'offer of a thousand crowns (as my lord chamberlain in my presence imparted)' for his release: Pollen, *UD*, p. 284 (AAW, A IX, no. 65, pp. 213–19; ABP, p. 430; ABSJ, Collectanea M, pp. 43ᵃ–4ᵃ (partial copy)).

[86] W. Forbes-Leith (ed.), *Narratives of Scottish Catholics under Mary Stuart and James VI* (1889), pp. 352–5; Sir Walter Lindsay, *Relacion del Estado del Reyno de Escocia...* (n.p. [printed in Spain], n.d. [1594]); *CSPSp 1587–1603*, pp. 588–9 (misdated to 1591).

religion, social order, and monarchical authority by good Catholics. Ingram wrote of his admiration for (the right sort of) Scots in his epigrams.[87] His fourth epigram salutes the 'glorious band, born of a soil / that scorns to bear the yoke of any foreign tyrant!'[88] Presumably, Ingram was not referring to the Spaniards when he used the term 'foreign tyrant', so he must have meant Elizabeth Tudor.

Boste and Ingram were tried in Durham.[89] Among the pieces of evidence available against Ingram was, predictably, the fact that he was an associate of the Scottish Jesuits James Gordon and William Creighton; and also that he knew Edmund Yorke, who was a nephew of Rowland Yorke, the man who had sensationally betrayed the sconce of Zutphen to the Spaniards in 1587, at which time Sir William Stanley let the Spaniards into Deventer.[90] Ingram's defence was that, as we saw, he had come across the border only for a short time, had no intention of remaining in England, and therefore could not be liable under the 1585 statute, but to no avail.[91] After judgment was given, related Richard Holtby, Huntingdon himself challenged Boste to admit that he had been at a marriage ceremony at Arthington in Nidderdale, where the Babington plotter John Ballard was present and told Boste of an imminent Spanish assault. This, said Huntingdon, Boste had 'traitorously concealed'. Boste claimed that he had counselled Ballard to avoid any kind of involvement in such matters: 'it is our function to invade souls and not to meddle with these temporal invasions'.[92] Christopher Robinson's account says that he heard it reported that the lord president accused Boste of 'marrying a gentleman who wished upon the day of the marriage the death of the prince'.[93]

---

[87] Pollen, *UD*, p. 272. The epigrams are in ABSJ, Anglia VII, no. 8. See A. Shell, 'The Writing on the Wall? John Ingram's Verse and the Dissemination of Catholic Prison Writing', *British Catholic History* 33 (2016), pp. 58–70.

[88] Pollen, *UD*, p. 278.

[89] Anstr., I, p. 183. Matthew Hutton was on hand at the Durham assizes on 22 July 1594 in order to deliver a 'bloody' (i.e. anti-popery) sermon; he urged the judges to inflict the full penalties of the law on the accused: Morris, *TCF*, III (RHPN), pp. 198–9. Knaresborough transcribed Christopher Robinson's narrative of the trial (the original of which is lost). It was sent to the priest Richard Dudley, who appears to have been involved in the Blanks conspiracy in Scotland: Kn., VII, pp. 501–9 (*Miscellanea I* (CRS 1, 1905), pp. 85–91); *CSPSc 1593–5*, pp. 23f; *AWCBC*, p. 1242. Boste had confessed the indictment, and so no jury was required, but Robinson reported that he saw the jury giving their verdict against Boste as well as Ingram and George Swallowell: Kn., VII, p. 501; Morris, *TCF*, III (RHPN), p. 200. Ingram had been tortured in London by Topcliffe. William Hutton (Margaret Clitherow's friend) may have seen Ingram (at York) after he was brought back in mid-July 1594 from London to the North to stand trial. Hutton said that Ingram had 'hung by the joints of his fingers and arms in extreme pain so long that the feeling of his senses' was 'clean taken from him': Morris, *TCF*, III (WHN), p. 314. For Ingram's own description of his confrontation with Topcliffe ('my bloody Saul'), see ABSJ, Collectanea N/i, p. 46. The account in Christopher Grene's Collectanea F says of Boste, back in Durham, having been tortured in London, that 'when he sat on his knees…he was all in a heap, as if he had been all in pieces': Foley, *RSJ*, III, p. 766 (AVCAU, Liber 1422 [Grene, Collectanea F], section 4, p. 86ᵇ).

[90] Pollen, *UD*, pp. 242–3 (PRO, SP 12/248/24); Petti, *LDRV*, p. 240; McCoog, *SJISE*, I, p. 149; *ODNB*, sub York [sic], Rowland (article by S. Clayton).

[91] Morris, *TCF*, III (RHPN), p. 201.   [92] Morris, *TCF*, III (RHPN), p. 205.

[93] Kn., VII, p. 508. Topcliffe had written to Puckering on 10 October 1593 that he had 'charged' Boste 'with accompanying…Ballard a little before he was taken, and he could not deny it': Pollen, *UD*,

248 CATHOLICS AND TREASON

Boste was executed on 24 July 1594—the same day that the trial proceedings concluded.[94] Considerable cruelty was used in killing him. He was 'scarce turned off the ladder but the rope was presently cut' and 'the bloody hangman began presently to rip up his belly and pull forth his bowels', while, 'at the taking out of his heart, the martyr spoke aloud thrice "Jesus, Jesus, Jesus forgive you"'.[95] Robinson's narrative stresses how much the authorities were determined to exercise a measure of crowd control and yet the crowd, or sections of it, were sympathetic to Boste.[96]

A man called George Swallowell was convicted on the same day as Boste and Ingram.[97] While Ingram was executed at Gateshead, Swallowell was taken to Darlington and hanged there. Swallowell had initially denied the charge against him (that he had persuaded 'one John Willie from the religion established unto the Romish religion') and had attributed the accusation to the malice of one Dr Robert Bellamy.[98] Swallowell had been a 'reader and...schoolmaster' at Houghton-le-Spring in Durham and had allegedly been persuaded by an imprisoned gentleman recusant that, on scriptural grounds, Elizabeth Tudor could not be head of the Church. 'Not long after', Swallowell 'publicly professed' the same 'from the pulpit'. He was arrested and imprisoned.[99] At trial, and as sentence was handed down, Swallowell again accused Bellamy of seeking his 'blood for some advantage to himself by making profit of my place in Sherburn House', where, alleged Swallowell, he was 'brought up...under' the puritans and former Marian exiles 'Mr Thomas Lever and Mr Ralph Lever, and by them preferred'. The Lever brothers had indeed both held the mastership of Sherburn Hospital. Ralph

p. 218 (PRO, SP 12/245/124). For Christopher Robinson, see J. E. Bamber, 'The Venerable Christopher Robinson, martyred at Carlisle in 1597: The Evidence concerning his Place of Birth and the Place and Date of his Execution', *RH* 4 (1957–8), pp. 18–37.

[94] Challoner, *MMP*, p. 204; Morris, *TCF*, III (RHPN), pp. 204–9; cf. Cashman, 'The Gateshead Martyr', pp. 129–30.

[95] AAW, A IV, no. 1, p. 12; Challoner, *MMP*, p. 204.

[96] See pp. 60–1 above; Cashman, 'The Gateshead Martyr', p. 130. The sight of Boste's heart being ripped out and the voice of Edward Musgrave raised in commendation of Boste apparently convinced the, at that point, conformist gentleman Roger Widdrington that he should renounce his conformity to the Church of England: Challoner, *MMP*, pp. 598, 600; Kn., VI, unpaginated section; letter of John Yaxley to John Knaresborough, 17 July 1707; p. 55 above. There were several circulating accounts of Boste's execution. One narrative, sent to Robert Persons, came from John Cecil, who was politically associated with the Scots Catholic nobility. Cecil was named by Boste, in his conversations with Duffield, as someone whom, 'if they had him, they would hang him': Pollen, *UD*, pp. 285–6 (ABSJ, Collectanea M, p. 160ª); Cashman, 'The Gateshead Martyr', p. 130; *HMCS*, XIII, p. 494; another narrative seems to have been compiled by the Jesuit Charles Thursby: AAW, A IV, no. 1, p. 13.

[97] Morris, *TCF*, III (RHPN), pp. 193, 203 f.; A. M. C. Forster, 'Blessed George Swallowell', *Ushaw Magazine* 80 (1970), pp. 81–9.

[98] Morris, *TCF*, III (RHPN), p. 203.

[99] Challoner, *MMP*, pp. 206–7. Challoner's material came in part from a narrative (AAW, A IV, no. 22, pp. 13–15) by the Yorkshire priest John Jackson, which was supplied to Challoner by Butler: ABP, pp. 420–3.

CATHOLIC RADICALISM 249

Lever, who had died back in 1585, had quarrelled with Bellamy, who was the vice-dean of Durham.[100]

At this point, challenged by Lord President Huntingdon to 'defy the pope and his laws and all seminary priests and Jesuits', and to agree to fight 'in her Majesty's behalf against the pope, the king of Spain and all papists, her enemies', and to take the oath of supremacy, Swallowell did just that. Weirdly, though, when Swallowell saw that Boste and Ingram would not budge, he changed his mind. Boste had kneeled down and, 'stretching forth his hands, thanked God that [He] had given him grace to confess His Name before them all', while Ingram recited a *Te Deum*. Faced with this, Swallowell announced that he would perish with them: 'I will be a Catholic and die as they do'. This provoked the court 'into a laughter against him upon his sudden change'. They 'commanded the two priests from the bar' and tried to get Swallowell to change his mind back again. As the source available to Richard Smith in the 1620s (and to Challoner in the eighteenth century) recited, Boste said ' "Hold yourself there...and my soul for yours", and with these words he laid his hand upon his head', which provoked Lord President Huntingdon to bark out, 'away with Boste, for he is reconciling him'.[101]

We cannot be certain what lies behind this series of twists and turns or why a, at one time, presumably convinced Protestant minor cleric should have done this. But Swallowell's outburst in the pulpit at Houghton-le-Spring, where Bellamy had been rector up till 1589, may reflect some sort of response to the 1593 parliament and the equating of puritan and Catholic separatism and to the fatal prosecution, during the parliament, of Protestant separatists as well as Catholic ones. According to Holtby's narrative, Swallowell's little revolt at Houghton-le-Spring and, then, imprisonment must have been in about mid-1593, that is, just after the parliament, although it was alleged against him that he had commented on the executions of Edmund Duke and the others, back in 1590, that those 'priests were martyrs before God'.[102] Whenever it was that Swallowell began to veer towards the Catholic faith, the northern authorities had every incentive, even up to the end, to get him to recant. In order to 'terrify him the more, they led him by two great fires, the one made for burning his bowels, the other for boiling his quarters; and withal four ministers attended him to strive to bring him over to their way of thinking', but without success.[103] Holtby's caustic description of the persecution in the North actually concludes with Swallowell's sacrifice. His 'soul' received 'a whole hire, though he came not to the vineyard before the eleventh hour'.[104]

---

[100] Morris, *TCF*, III (RHPN), p. 206; *ODNB*, *sub* Lever, Thomas (article by B. Lowe), and Lever, Ralph (article by D. Marcombe).

[101] Morris, *TCF*, III (RHPN), pp. 206–8; AAW, A IV, no. 1, p. 14; Challoner, *MMP*, p. 207.

[102] Morris, *TCF*, III (RHPN), pp. 203–4.

[103] Challoner, *MMP*, p. 207; Morris, *TCF*, III (RHPN), p. 212. Unlike Holtby, Challoner says that Swallowell was still alive when he was disembowelled.

[104] Morris, *TCF*, III (RHPN), p. 213.

250 CATHOLICS AND TREASON

Other parts of the country had recently seen equally dramatic action against Catholics. On 15 March 1594, Topcliffe had led a series of raids on Catholic houses across London. Among the targets, apparently, were the Jesuits Henry Garnet and John Gerard. Gerard was in fact arrested in Holborn soon after Easter.[105] Garnet wrote that there was 'such a hurly burly in London as was never seen in man's memory, no, not when [Sir Thomas] Wyatt was at the gates'.[106] The secular priest John Cornelius was apprehended, with other Catholics, at Chideock Castle in the West Country on the night of 13/14 April.[107] Then, wrote Garnet, there 'followed the arraignment' of Patrick Cullen, 'who was innocently condemned for intending the queen's death' and in his 'arraignment...Jesuits were maliciously slandered'. Rodrigo Lopez was executed with his alleged accomplices Tinoco and da Gama on 7 June 1594 at Tyburn. On Garnet's account, Lopez 'showed himself, at his death, of the queen's religion'. This was 'to the discredit of Catholics, although most unjustly'. By contrast, the others 'showed great religion in their death'.[108]

[105] ABSJ, GC, p. 195 (ABSJ, Anglia I, no. 81); Foley, *RSJ*, IV, p. 46; McCoog, *SJISE*, I, p. 163; Caraman, *HG*, pp. 185–8; Caraman, *JG*, pp. 65, 229. Topcliffe had been using an informer, one John Frank—a servant in the Wiseman household, who betrayed Gerard: Caraman, *JG*, pp. 64–5, 68; McCoog, *SJISE*, I, pp. 164–5; *HMCS*, V, p. 25.

[106] ABSJ, GC, pp. 195 (ABSJ, Anglia I, no. 81).

[107] ABSJ, GC, pp. 195 (ABSJ, Anglia I, no. 81); McCoog, *SJISE*, I, p. 167. Cornelius had been involved in the Denham exorcisms in 1585–6: Brownlow, *Shakespeare*, pp. 24, 88–9, 166, 167, 169; *CSPSc 1586–8*, p. 33 (Tyrrell's confession of 21 September 1586 concerning Cornelius's preaching); Questier, *C&C*, p. 189. He was executed at Dorchester on 3 (or 4) July 1594: Anstr., I, p. 88; McCoog, *SJISE*, I, p. 78; *HMCS*, IV, p. 510; Foley, *RSJ*, III, pp. 435–74. Cornelius and Lady Arundell (the widow of Charles, eighth Baron Stourton, and, latterly, of Sir John Arundell of Lanherne) with the priest John Sherwood (d. Lent 1593) had got out of London just before Christmas in 1591, i.e. just after the release of the 1591 proclamation: ABSJ, CP (John Cornelius); Anstr., I, p. 313. Evidently they expected to be left undisturbed in the West Country. But a household servant (or, as Verstegan has it, 'an unknowing idiot') informed on them to the high sheriff of Dorset, Sir George Morton. The eventually successful search at Chideock Castle, Dorset, the house of Lady Arundell, was, said Verstegan, made by Sir Walter Raleigh and Sir Ralph Horsey: Petti, *LDRV*, pp. 212, 213; see also Caraman, *WW*, pp. 125–6; Foley, *RSJ*, III, pp. 451, 453, 462. Cornelius was charged also with possessing a copy of *Philopater* (i.e. Robert Persons, *Elizabethae Angliae Reginae Haeresim Calviniam Propugnantis...per D. Andream Philopatrum* (Antwerp, 1592)): ABSJ, CP (John Cornelius); *HMCS*, IV, p. 510. He made his profession as a Jesuit just before death: Anstr., I, p. 88. For the execution, shortly before which he pronounced, in front of witnesses in London, the three vows of the Society, see Petti, *LDRV*, pp. 247, 248; McCoog, *SJISE*, I, pp. 78, 167; Foley, *RSJ*, III, pp. 471–2; see also D. Underdown, *Fire from Heaven: Life in an English Town in the Seventeenth Century* (1992), pp. 17–18. Thomas Manger is the source for much of Challoner's account of Cornelius: ABP, pp. 424–6. Executed with Cornelius were two Irish servants of the family (John Carey and Patrick Salmon) and also a nephew of Sir John Arundell (d. Nov. 1590), one Thomas Bosgrave, the son of his (Arundell's) sister Johanna's second marriage (to Leonard Bosgrave): Challoner, *MMP*, p. 199; ARSJ, Anglia 37, fo. 27ʳ. According to Henry More SJ, the judge Thomas Walmesley tried to postpone the execution of sentence as long as possible: Edwards, *EJ*, p. 226. For narratives of Cornelius's martyrdom, see E. Patton, 'Four Contemporary Translations of Dorothy Arundell's Lost English Narratives', *Philological Quarterly* 95 (2016), pp. 397–424; E. Patton, '"God is Wonderful in His Saints": Dorothy Arundell Contemplates Martyrdom and Pilgrimage on both Sides of the Channel' (forthcoming).

[108] ABSJ, GC, p. 195 (ABSJ, Anglia I, no. 81); P. Hammer, *The Polarisation of Elizabethan Politics: The Political Career of Robert Devereux, 2nd Earl of Essex, 1585–1597* (Cambridge, 1999), pp. 158–9.

Among these arrests and trials, the case of Henry Walpole tells us a good deal about the dynamics of contemporary politics and of the collisions between different versions of loyalty and conformity. One might have expected the Jesuit Walpole, Garnet's confrère, to have been an equally hard-line member of the, as it were, no-turning-back group in the Catholic community. But Walpole's confessions in mid-1594 (the authenticity of which, it has to be said, has been disputed) suggest something slightly different.[109] Walpole appeared to speak, if they are his words, to an explicitly loyalist agenda. He distanced himself from other Catholics such as Sir William Stanley and, particularly, Sir Francis Englefield. Walpole declared on 13 June 1594, admittedly whilst he was in the Tower, that Englefield had said in his hearing that the 'Catholics in England were much to be blamed'. They 'desired the restoring of their religion, yet they would not allow of the' necessary 'means', that is, 'by admitting the Spaniards'. Walpole said that he could not go along with this. Indeed, he believed that the Spaniards' 'insolence and vice' were 'most odious to God, and that their coming...by force would not only be the woeful ruin of the commonwealth and my dearest country, but also their example, especially of soldiers, make such as are of their religion to stagger, because for peace, moral virtue and good government of the commonwealth, I, in my poor judgment do not know any comparable unto England, not considering religion at all'.[110]

Here, then, Walpole was getting very close to the language of the enemies of the Holy League in France and indeed of a range of English Catholics, all the way from Anthony Copley and John Cecil to Lewis Lewkenor, who were making exactly these noises about what they took to be the intolerable ambition, cruelty, hypocrisy, and malice of the Spaniards and the essential disconnect between true religion and Habsburg global ambition.[111] Walpole said also, in his statement of 14 June 1594, that Robert Persons had sent him to England to 'win men...to the popish religion', as well as to recruit candidates for the seminaries.[112] But presumably Walpole interpreted this in a purely spiritual sense and believed that he could

---

[109] Pollen, *UD*, pp. 244–68 (PRO, SP 248/78, 91, 112; PRO, SP 12/249/4, 12, 13, 14, 16, 44, 45); McCoog, *SJISE*, I, pp. 153–62.

[110] Pollen, *UD*, p. 256.

[111] For the complexities of Anthony Copley's take on Catholic martyrdom, expressed in his allegorical poem *A Fig for Fortune* of 1596, see S. Monta, *Martyrdom and Literature in Early Modern England* (Cambridge, 2005), pp. 100 f. Lewis Lewkenor had gone on the record, after giving up his career as a mercenary in Spanish service, to say that, in the trials of Catholic clergy, 'her Majesty has always proceeded therein in so gracious and merciful a sort that she has witnessed sufficiently to the world how loath she is to come unto blood': Lewis Lewkenor, 'The Estate of English Fugitives under the King of Spaine and his Ministers', in A. Clifford (ed.), *The State Papers and Letters of Sir Ralph Sadler*...(2 vols, Edinburgh, 1809), II, p. 272. For the successive published editions of Lewkenor's work, see W. J. Tighe, 'Five Elizabethan Courtiers, their Catholic Connections, and their Careers', *British Catholic History* 33 (2016), pp. 211–27, at p. 222.

[112] Pollen, *UD*, p. 260.

252 CATHOLICS AND TREASON

obey his superior in this way without breaking the queen's law, at least not in a material sense.

One possibility is that the confessions which Walpole made in London were purely the result of the torture used on him by Topcliffe.[113] It has been suggested also that those confessions are partly forgeries. W. F. Rea argued, from the evidence that Walpole gave about the recent crop of Catholic pamphlets, especially Persons's *Philopater*, that these statements were, at least in part, concocted by his interrogators and were meant to tempt Walpole's imprisoned confrère Robert Southwell into recanting. When that did not happen, they were discarded (until Walpole's trial); but there is no direct evidence for this.[114]

Yet another possibility is that Walpole was, by a show of ultra-loyalism, trying to outflank those Catholics, including some clergy, who were arguing, and had done so for some time, that a degree of compliance on the part of Catholics was necessary in order to placate the queen's government.[115] While he was in York Castle, Walpole was made to dispute on a range of theological issues with Protestant ministers. Among those disputants were the renegades (or, as they themselves saw it, good subjects of the queen and good Christians) William Hardesty and, crucially, Thomas Bell. Bell had gone over to the established Church when he had lost the argument with other Catholics, notably Henry Garnet and John Mush, over the rights and wrongs of occasional conformity. If Walpole was trying to upstage Bell and Hardesty and indeed those Catholics who had at one time looked to them for ideological leadership, then it was entirely logical for Walpole to do as he did. He clearly wanted his words to be publicized. He had written up for Huntingdon a version of the disputations, and also a harangue in which he 'warned all to guard themselves from false prophets'; and he demanded that future debates should be properly witnessed. Walpole said that Huntingdon behaved courteously towards him. The earl provided his Jesuit prisoner with paper and books.[116] Huntingdon may have thought he had a major public-relations coup in the offing, though actually Walpole was not intending to make the kinds of concession which ultimately the regime would have required.

---

[113] McCoog, *SJISE*, I, p. 157.

[114] McCoog, *SJISE*, I, pp. 159–61; W. F. Rea, 'The Authorship of "News from Spayne and Holland" and its bearing on the Genuineness of the Confessions of the Blessed Henry Walpole, S. J', *Biographical Studies* 1 (1951–2), pp. 220–30; Pollen, *UD*, pp. 265–6. For John Gerard's claim that Richard Young told him (while he—Gerard—was in prison in the first half of 1594) that Southwell had offered 'to treat with a view to accepting our religion', see Caraman, *JG*, p. 75.

[115] The confession/statement, written in the first person and dated 13 June 1594, is, like three of the others, in Walpole's own hand, though different from the handwriting of the signature: Pollen, *UD*, photographs facing pp. 190, 259; McCoog, *SJISE*, I, p. 157. On the other hand, that of 14 June 1594 (which speaks of the 'popish religion') is written in the third person and is merely signed by him: Pollen, *UD*, p. 260.

[116] Challoner, *MMP*, p. 222; McCoog, *SJISE*, I, p. 154; PRO, SP 12/248/51 (H. Foley (ed.), 'Two Conferences in the Prison at York with Father Walpole, S. J., An. Dom. 1594. Related by Himself', *Letters and Notices* 9 (1873), pp. 46–63, esp. at p. 46). Among the other Protestant clergy involved were John Favour, John Bennett, and William Goodwin: McCoog, *SJISE*, I, p. 154.

CATHOLIC RADICALISM   253

In London, Walpole was, as we saw, interrogated under torture. Under torture, most people will say anything. Still, he declared on 13 June 1594 that he had told the notorious mercenary soldier Jacomo Francesco that it would be wrong to seek the death of the queen; he claimed also that the self-declared Catholic loyalist Charles Paget 'told me, seeing I loved peace, [that] he would tell me of a peace which he laboured to make for the good of all our nation'. Walpole declared that Robert Persons's line was that 'Catholics, and chiefly we religious men, ought to suffer violence but offer none, chiefly to princes'; and, said Walpole, Persons 'added that our means were by persuasion and prayer'. A marginal note in this confession recorded that the renegade Anthony Major said that this account of Persons's views was all hogwash—a conclusion with which Paget and his friends would, as it happened, have heartily concurred.[117]

Anyway, this was the script to which Walpole committed himself. Walpole's long statement of 17 June 1594 explicitly said that he 'never allowed of the ambition of the popes or any of their unjust usurpation over princes and their kingdoms' and that he thought that 'hostility or invasion of the Spaniard would prejudice both the commonwealth and the Catholic religion'. Even more startlingly, Walpole declared that he would conform himself 'to the laws of the realm, whether I live or die, God willing, not doubting but my sincere intention will appear and redound to the honour of God, the service of my prince and country, without prejudice of the Catholic faith'. As for that faith, he would 'ever profess' it and would not refuse 'to go to the church, and if' he 'were worthy as others be (I being very mean in learning) there preach only such doctrine as my conscience does tell me and the spirit of God to be manifestly deduced out of the word of God, attributing to her Majesty as much honour, power and jurisdiction in temporal and spiritual persons and causes as I can perceive the learned of both the universities do agree upon'. Walpole said he hoped that he would 'reduce many to this conformity by private conference'. He said also that, 'having conferred with divers learned Protestants of the clergy at York', he 'did find much less difference' than he had previously thought. He said that he was 'persuaded that, if there were a free assembly and consultation of learned men of all sorts of opinions in religion within the realm, they might concur in some general conformity and unity to the great comfort of them all and render thereby' to 'her Majesty's royal person and the state of the realm' some 'service against all foreign dangers and attempts'.[118]

Technically almost everything Walpole says about political loyalty is compatible with the Catholic position on that topic expressed principally by the appellant clergy later in the 1590s, though they strove not to make any concession on the issue of churchgoing. In some respects, Walpole's position is not a million

---

[117] Pollen, *UD*, pp. 252, 253.   [118] Pollen, *UD*, pp. 266–7.

254 CATHOLICS AND TREASON

miles from that of, say, the Scottish Jesuit William Creighton.[119] The implication is that Walpole, like other Catholics who had adopted a loyalist persona, could see a future in which confessional difference, extending even to separatism/recusancy, could be regarded as compatible with political loyalty. But, assuming his confessions represent what he actually thought, this carefully constructed loyalist pitch still was not acceptable, and did not save him.

Southwell's Revenge—the Discrediting of Richard Topcliffe

Walpole's fellow Jesuit Robert Southwell perished at Tyburn in late February 1595.[120] Despite the headlines created by the recent Chastel assassination attempt in France, there were signs that public opinion was not uniformly happy with the annihilation of this influential Catholic cleric.[121] In January 1595, Topcliffe had already lamented to Sir Robert Cecil that 'it was a particular grief, and mine especially', that he and his friends were 'often taken to be cruel'.[122]

The reasons for the decision to proceed against Southwell, after he had been in prison for so long, have never been entirely clear.[123] Possibly his teaching on equivocation was the last straw. It was certainly a central issue at his trial.[124] But

---

[119] Just as Walpole and Ingram were rounded on by renegade Catholic clergy, so Edward Osbaldeston was identified by the renegade Thomas Clarke, who betrayed him (and Francis Sayer) at Tollerton on the night of 30 September 1594. Osbaldeston was executed on 16 November 1594 at York: Challoner, *MMP*, pp. 208–10 (relying on a copy of a letter by Osbaldeston written to another prisoner in York Castle, archived by Alban Butler, ABP, pp. 431–4, presumably taken from AAW, A IX, no. 65, pp. 219–22; there is another copy, by Richard Holtby, in ABSJ, Anglia II, no. 12 (Foley, *RSJ*, III, pp. 9–11; ABSJ, CP: Penelope Renold to Patrick Barry, 21 March 1969), which is endorsed with a note that Osbaldeston had a 'desire and vow' to enter the Society: *AWCBC*, pp. 1180); see also ABSJ, Collectanea N/i, p. 56ᵇ; *AWCBC*, p. 1184 (citing Grene's own copy, ARSJ, Anglia 37, fos 27ᵛ–9ᵛ). Thomas Clarke had been a client and chaplain of the Constable family: Anstr., I, p. 76; Morris, *TCF*, III (RHPN), pp. 113, 122, 175; Foley, *RSJ*, III, p. 765. Sir Henry Constable's wife, Margaret (Dormer), was indicted for harbouring Osbaldeston: Anstr., I, p. 76; *HMCS*, V, p. 77; M. Questier, 'Sermons, Separatists and Succession Politics in Late Elizabethan England', *JBS* 52 (2013), pp. 290–316, at pp. 303, 307. Clarke had preached recantation sermons on 15 April and 1 July 1593 (on this latter occasion, Clarke followed one Mr Buckeridge, presumably John Buckeridge, at Paul's Cross); Thomas Clarke, *The Recantation…* (1594).

[120] On 19 November 1594, Garnet had observed, in a letter to Persons, that 'Sir Thomas Wilkes goes into Flanders, as it is thought, for peace: whereupon the arraignment of the three Jesuits, Southwell, Walpole and Gerard, is stayed': ABSJ, GC, p. 201 (ABSJ, Anglia I, no. 82; Foley, *RSJ*, IV, p. 49).

[121] For Jean Chastel and the exploitation of his crime in order to attack the Society of Jesus in France, see R. Descimon, 'Chastel's Attempted Regicide (27 December 1594) and its Subsequent Transformation into an "Affair"', in A. Forrestal and E. Nelson (eds), *Politics and Religion in Early Bourbon France* (Basingstoke, 2009), pp. 86–104.

[122] *HMCS*, V, p. 91.

[123] For a nuanced discussion of why the regime decided to kill Southwell and Walpole (and not, e.g., William Weston), see McCoog, *SJISE*, I, pp. 185–90.

[124] McCoog, *SJISE*, I, pp. 186–9. Garnet's letter to Acquaviva of 22 February 1595 claimed that the date of Southwell's trial was kept confidential 'and, in order to divert the crowd from the court at Westminster, they ordered that a notorious highwayman be hung at Tyburn at the very time': Petti, *LDRV*, p. 225 (ABSJ, GC, pp. 220–1; ABSJ, Anglia II, no.1; Foley, *RSJ*, I, p. 377).

even so, at least if we believe the Catholic reports of the trial in February 1595, something like the moral victory went to the Jesuit. Topcliffe allegedly responded entirely inappropriately when Southwell accused him of torture ('I had rather have endured ten executions', said Southwell); and, when Topcliffe said that the Jesuit could point to no physical signs of torment, Southwell retorted: 'ask a woman to show her throes'.[125]

The Catholic accounts of Southwell's passion and death are a celebration of his Jesuit identity, but they claim that his demeanour at execution, and his prayer for the queen and realm, led to his being 'hanged till he was dead through the cry of the people, who would not suffer him sooner to be cut down'.[126] A narrative entitled 'A brief discourse of the condemnation...' said that Lord Mountjoy stopped the disembowelling from taking place until Southwell had expired.[127] When Southwell's lifeless corpse was decapitated, allegedly no one shouted 'Traitor, traitor'.[128] Verstegan noted that a 'Protestant lord' (presumably Mountjoy) 'wished that, when he died, his soul might go with his'.[129]

Perhaps unsurprisingly in view of the exchanges at the trial, Topcliffe was not visible on the morning of the execution. Then, shortly after, when his taking of money in the recent Fitzherbert case became public, he found himself in prison, even though, as Verstegan remarked with regret, it was only for a very short time and so 'Barrabas is freed and Christ delivered to be crucified'. Still, Verstegan judged, this was as much for Topcliffe's cruelty towards Southwell as for peculation and for his related libelling of the lord keeper. Here we get a sense that, even with the war against Spain showing no sign of stopping, some of the ideological certainties of former times were now open to question. According to Topcliffe himself, as he had written directly to the queen on Good Friday (or, as Topcliffe called it, 'evil Friday') 18 April 1595, 'since I was committed [to prison], wine in Westminster has been given for joy at that news, and in all prisons rejoicings'. In a nightmare of his own creation, he imagined the 'fresh dead bones' of Southwell and Walpole rising from the ground and dancing 'for joy' at his disgrace. Topcliffe found himself, therefore, in exactly the same situation experienced by Thomas Norton in late 1581 and early 1582, seething with resentment at his enemies' pleasure at his recent reversal of fortune. 'Now at Easter, instead of a communion,

---

[125] Pollen, *UD*, p. 335 (from the narrative written by the secular priest Thomas Leak: ABSJ, Anglia VI, no. 24); Caraman, *HG*, p. 196; Devlin, *LRS*, pp. 288, 309–10; Edwards, *EJ*, p. 243. Persons wrote in July 1584 that 'truly to be hanged is child's play in comparison with being tortured': Hicks, *Letters*, p. 223 [*CUPRP*, p. 479].

[126] Petti, *LDRV*, p. 223.

[127] Petti, *LDRV*, p. 225, citing 'A brief discourse of the condemnation and execution of Mr Robert Southwell, priest of the Society of Jesus', ABSJ, Anglia II, no. 1 (printed in Foley, *RSJ*, I, pp. 364f); Devlin, *LRS*, p. 324; see also A. Marotti, 'Southwell's Remains: Catholicism and Anti-Catholicism in Early Modern England', in C. C. Browne and A. Marotti (eds), *Texts and Cultural Change in Early Modern England* (1997), pp. 37–65, at p. 51.

[128] Foley, *RSJ*, I, p. 375.   [129] Petti, *LDRV*, p. 243.

256 CATHOLICS AND TREASON

many an *Alleluia* will be sung of priests and traitors in prisons and in ladies' closets for Topcliffe's fall, and in further kingdoms also.'[130] As John Gerard recounted it, 'Catholics like myself who were in prison for the faith began to hold up our heads when we saw our arch-enemy Aman about to be hanged on his own gibbet'. More people started to attend 'the sacraments and the ceremonies of the Church' in the prison where Gerard was.[131]

Henry Walpole's trial at the Lent assizes in York had in fact been somewhat less controversial than Southwell's in London. Huntingdon demanded that a special commission should be issued for Walpole to be tried in York, and that is eventually what happened on 3 April 1595. Neither at trial nor in the face of execution did Walpole now make any further concessions.[132] In the course of the prosecution case against him, wrote Garnet later (on 20 June 1595), there were read out 'five or six' of Walpole's confessions, 'putting an evil interpretation on them all'.[133]

Of Walpole's death on 7 April, executed with the secular priest Alexander Rawlins, Verstegan said that he spoke 'so courageously...that he moved 2,000 persons to shed tears'.[134] Henry More recorded that there were efforts at the last

[130] *HC 1558–1603*, III, p. 514; Petti, *LDRV*, pp. 232, 234, 238; BL, Harleian MS 6998, fos 184^r–5^v. John Gerard said that Topcliffe 'had in some way insulted members of the council while (if I am not mistaken) he was pleading before them in a most brazen way on behalf of his son', Charles, who had 'struck a man dead' in Westminster Hall, and this is what led to Topcliffe Snr being gaoled: Caraman, *JG*, pp. 99, 236.

[131] Caraman, *JG*, pp. 99–100.

[132] Ward, *LT*, pp. 175–6 (citing BL, Harleian MS 6996, fos 54^r, 56^r, 72^r); McCoog, *SJISE*, I, pp. 183–5. At trial, Walpole argued with the judge Francis Beaumont about whether the evidence of his (Walpole's) dealings abroad was sufficient to justify an indictment under the 1585 statute. Walpole could also claim that he was taken before the time limit, set in the act, to declare himself to a justice of the peace. But Beaumont, who had sat at Boste's and Ingram's trial, said that ultimately it was a matter of whether he had consorted with known traitors and had intended to draw the queen's subjects away from their allegiance: Challoner, *MMP*, pp. 225–6; McCoog, *SJISE*, I, pp. 183–6; Kn., VII, pp. 502–3. For Walpole's trial, see the narrative in Henry Garnet's letter of 20 June 1595: ABSJ, GC, pp. 300–6 (ARSJ, Anglia 31/i, fos 93^r–106^v); Edwards, *EJ*, pp. 267–70. Garnet noted that Beaumont was reckoned to have been a crypto-Catholic; his mother was one of Garnet's spiritual clients and was the aunt of Anne Vaux; Garnet had said her requiem Mass: Caraman, *HG*, pp. 200–2. See also Joseph Creswell, *Historia de la Vida y Martyrio que Padecio en Inglaterra...P. Henrique Valpolo...* (Madrid, 1596); Joseph Creswell, *Histoire de la Vie et Ferme Constance du Pere Henry Valpole...* (Arras, 1597).

[133] ABSJ, GC, p. 303 (ARSJ, Anglia 31/i, fos 93^r–106^v).

[134] Petti, *LDRV*, p. 242; see also Caraman, *HG*, pp. 199–200; AVCAU, 21/2/1–2 (autograph letters and eyewitness accounts of the martyrdoms of Rawlins and Walpole, and of Rawlins's interrogation and trial; it appears that these were sent to Richard Holtby, who dispatched them to Rome, including a letter from Rawlins to Holtby written on 'St Thomas's day'). Rawlins may have been involved in the Denham exorcisms in 1586. He had been arrested at that point and he had been deported and had then returned to England with Edmund Gennings in April 1590: Brownlow, *Shakespeare*, p. 362; *Miscellanea II*, pp. 261, 264, 267. Rawlins had been taken again, on Christmas Day 1594, in the house of Thomas Warcop, by a thirty-strong search party brought down from London by the Hull customs official Anthony Atkinson, who had arrested John Boste. Taken with Rawlins was the sister of the renegade priest William Hardesty. (While interrogating Rawlins, Huntingdon had urged him to 'be as conformable as Major, Bell and Hardesty', who had once been 'obstinate' and now were 'obedient'; and he asked him whether he had been at Peter Knaresborough's house 'with John Mush'.) Hardesty blenched at the prospect of his sister getting, as it were, the full treatment—he suggested that she might be put under house arrest so that he could 'persuade her' to conform, but she refused: Foley, *RSJ*, III, pp. 767–8 (AVCAU, Liber 1422 [Grene, Collectanea F], section 4, p. 87$^{a–b}$); ARSJ, Anglia 37, fo. 72^v; Anstr., I,

CATHOLIC RADICALISM   257

minute to secure a reprieve for Walpole, evidently because of his loyal demeanour. One Mr King (presumably John King, who was still in York at this time) argued with him, and asked him whether he would 'accept of the prince's laws', for then he might 'have favour', though to no avail. But Walpole, like Rawlins, was allowed to expire before being disembowelled and quartered.[135]

It was now that Garnet penned some of his bitterest comments about the queen. In his letter of 20 June 1595, in which he narrated Walpole's trial, Garnet wrote that Topcliffe had 'so impressed the mind of the queen with the danger which they say overhangs her by reason of the Catholic priests, that she herself is often wont to ask, when will there be another execution, saying that it is now long since there has been one'. Garnet could not refrain from pointing to the 'judgment and justice of God' shown forth in Topcliffe's recent disgrace.[136] Verstegan, writing on the same day in Antwerp, was sure that, although Topcliffe was now 'released out of prison', 'his commission' was 'taken from him'. Those around the queen were desperately trying 'to persuade the world that these hard courses were against the queen's mind', although this was the result of 'fear and cowardice— they may perhaps think to profit more by this than by rigour'.[137] Verstegan may have been reflecting on the authorities' unwillingness to put to death, for example, the harbourers of John Boste. Matthew Hutton, for one, had been lobbying Lord Burghley in late 1594 and the early months of 1595 to secure Lady Margaret Neville's reprieve. She was, after all, apparently conformable.[138] Sir Robert Cecil wrote to Hutton on 16 April 1595 that he had reminded the queen of 'the pardon for the Lady Neville, by whose example' others might 'be induced to show the like conformity'. The queen's leniency would 'stop the lying tongues of them that would insinuate by libels and railings that her Majesty's mercy is too seldom showed'. He omitted to mention that this mercy had not been shown to Walpole

---

p. 285; AVCAU, Scr. 21/2/1–2. Warcop was detained with Rawlins but absconded; he was retaken and was hanged in 1597: Anstr., I, pp. 285–6; Challoner, *MMP*, p. 232; see p. 270 below. Warcop had acted as a host to the priest Alexander Markland at a place called Thornton Woods and had evaded the authorities when Markland was arrested. Some of Rawlins's final letters were written to Warcop and testify to the intense spiritual relationship between priest and patron: Aveling, *NC*, pp. 162–3; AVCAU, Scr. 21/2/1–2. Both John Mush and Rawlins had been at Grosmont at the property tenanted by John Hodgson. The renegade Thomas Clarke said he had seen them and other priests there. The extensive 'list of certain priests that are in the north country' (PRO, SP 12/245/24, fo. 38ʳ; Foley, *RSJ*, III, p. 6) may be Clarke's information, or based on it, although Aveling suggests that Clarke was inventing some of his claims so as to ingratiate himself with the regime: Aveling, *NC*, p. 160.

[135] Edwards, *EJ*, pp. 272–3; AVCAU, Scr. 21/2/1 (eyewitness report of executions of Rawlins and Walpole); Foley, *RSJ*, III, p. 14; *ODNB*, *sub* King, John (article by P. McCullough).

[136] ABSJ, GC, p. 298 (ARSJ, Anglia 31, fo. 84ʳ *et seq*).

[137] Petti, *LDRV*, p. 242 (Verstegan to Baynes 20/30 June 1595).

[138] J. Raine (ed.), *The Correspondence of Dr Matthew Hutton*...(Surtees Society 17, 1843), pp. 92, 6–8. Lord Henry Howard, on 20 February 1595, wrote to Hutton on behalf of his 'poor niece' (Lady Neville) and said that he knew Hutton's 'disposition' was not 'to break any twig that will be bent'. She was one such—not a potential martyr at all, for 'her disposition is mild, her actions honourable, her mind harmless': ibid., pp. 98–9. On 10 April 1595, Hutton was with the queen, again 'making petition for the poor distressed lady...shewing her pitiful estate' and how genuinely she had changed: ibid., p. 100.

258 CATHOLICS AND TREASON

nine days before, despite all the Jesuit's compliant utterances in front of his interrogators, though Walpole had not in fact conformed, while Lady Neville had. But, said Cecil, presumably echoing the mind of the queen, 'God be thanked, no kingdom has under any of God's ministers ever tasted so many good fruits' as England did of the queen's grace; and so he had got the queen's signature in favour of Lady Neville.[139]

Of course, ultimately the queen's government had not really experienced any kind of crisis of conscience over its dealings with Catholics. Topcliffe gradually got back to his role of roving law enforcer.[140] On the other hand, Verstegan's letter, just cited, remarked to Roger Baynes that 'you will marvel with me at the news which I now shall send you: there is now very great hope given that the queen will proceed so mildly that none shall be troubled for their conscience so they give not otherwise just cause of offence. This is given out by some in principal authority.'[141]

On the surface, that might be regarded as an extraordinary statement, coming as it did so soon after the one point in the period when there was, so it seemed to some people, still a State-sponsored terror against separatist Catholics and even against some of those who merely sympathized with them. Yet even in the starkest Catholic narratives of martyrdom in the later 1590s there are asides to the effect that not all the queen's officials regarded all Catholics as the kind of seditious actors that anti-popery rhetoric indicated. That sense of a divergence of views inside the regime fractured the English Catholic community. So much of the 'Catholic' narrative of the years immediately preceding the accession of James VI in 1603 is generated by the disputes that set one Catholic against another as they speculated about what might happen next.[142] But the resulting fissures allowed some sections of the community to move into a different relationship with the late Tudor regime, one predicated on expectations that a more tolerant future was in the offing.

---

[139] Ibid., p. 101. For Hutton's grateful note to Cecil on 17 April 1595, saying that the pardon did 'plainly declare a divine and heroic clemency in so mighty a prince', see *HMCS*, V, p. 176.

[140] In August 1597 Topcliffe was required to lead an investigation into the play 'The Isle of Dogs': *ODNB*, *sub* Topcliffe, Richard (article by W. Richardson); *HC 1558–1603*, III, p. 515. In late 1597 he was still being employed, with other government officials, to investigate more quotidian forms of crime by the use of torture: *APC 1597–8*, pp. 165, 187; see also *APC 1598–9*, p. 428.

[141] Petti, *LDRV*, p. 242.

[142] Lake and Questier, *Archpriest*; see Chapters 9 and 10 below.

9

The Coming of Toleration in Late Elizabethan England?

The Approach of a European Peace, the Conversion of Henry IV, and the Impending Accession of James VI

The 1590s is sometimes referred to by historians of the period as the 'nasty nineties', though more often because of the anti-puritan reaction sponsored by Richard Bancroft and his friends rather than because of any concern at the, here and there, still brutal assault on the separated Catholic community.[1] A range of contemporary Catholics evidently had views about the nasty nineties just as much as about the fairly unpleasant eighties. But, nasty or not, some facts of political life were getting difficult to deny. One was that the war with Spain was not going to last forever. Eventually there would have to be a European peace of some sort, certainly between France and Spain. After that, it would be very difficult for the English to keep on fighting. During the later 1590s what appeared to be, at times, the one-man earl-of-Essex show, and the earl's agitation for continuing the war, started to look increasingly out of step with political reality. The second was that the carnage in war-torn Ireland could not carry on indefinitely. Thirdly, the moment when the queen's government was dissolved might not now be that far away.

If anyone doubted that the new monarchy, almost certainly a Stuart one, was likely to be substantially different from what went before, they needed to look only at the recent turn in Scots politics, that is, after 1595 when those Catholics who had challenged the crown and had lost on points now seemed to be making their way back into the inner circles around the king. The rebel peers George Gordon, earl of Huntly, and Francis Hay, earl of Errol, had to go into exile for a time; but when they returned they made a show of conformity and for the rest of the 1590s James made it his business to appoint conformist Catholics to senior posts in his administration.[2]

---

[1] P. Collinson, 'Ecclesiastical Vitriol: Religious Satire in the 1590s and the Invention of Puritanism', in J. Guy (ed.), *The Reign of Elizabeth* (Cambridge, 1993), pp. 150–70, at p. 154; J. Wormald, 'Ecclesiastical Vitriol: the Kirk, the Puritans and the Future King of England', in Guy, *The Reign of Elizabeth*, pp. 171–91, at p. 171.
[2] Questier, *DP*, pp. 215–16, 230–40 *passim*.

Catholics and Treason: Martyrology, Memory, and Politics in the Post-Reformation. Michael Questier, Oxford University Press. © Michael Questier 2022. DOI: 10.1093/oso/9780192847027.003.0009

260 CATHOLICS AND TREASON

In this same period, the conversion of Henry of Navarre had already had transformative effects on French politics and also on the political attitudes of the English Catholic exiles who resisted aspects of Elizabeth's government of the Church.[3] Of course, despite the stream of conjecture of some Catholics, no one really believed that James VI was going to imitate his French opposite number and announce his desire to be reconciled to Rome. It was virtually certain, however, that, when he took Elizabeth's crown, there would be substantial changes in his new kingdom's relationship with continental Europe.

Obviously, there is not room here to give even the briefest outline of the twists and turns of the long-running succession campaign which brought James VI to England in 1603. But the process of speculating about the accession generated a set of debates between the Catholic community and the Elizabethan authorities about persecution and toleration and also, among Catholics themselves, about the question of how far Catholics should accommodate themselves to the reasonable political demands of the Tudor queen and the State and then, with more enthusiasm, to those of her successor. What one saw here was the emergence of a Catholic loyalist stance which replicated a good deal of the hostile politique and Hispanophobe response to the programme of the Holy League in France during the late 1580s and early 1590s. All of this was central to much of the public politics of the Stuart accession.[4]

There were many English Catholics who were still never going to enthuse about King James. The *Conference about the Next Succession* made that clear enough. Its probable principal author, the Jesuit Robert Persons, would not trust James VI round the side of a glass wall. In any case, said Persons, James's own personal religion was 'puritanism'; and not just in the sense of adherence to erroneous doctrine but also in his 'extreme ingrate and unnatural dealing towards his mother', who was a true Catholic martyr. This would make 'every man of good nature, of what religion soever he be, to have aversion to be under his government'. What could others expect 'at his hands who, to her that bore him and made him a king, was so unkind?' He made 'small demonstration...since of his grief' at what had happened to her. His creepy diplomatic agent, the master of Gray, 'betrayed her in England'. That this was on James's instructions was 'the more easily believed for that the very day when the news of his mother's slaughter came into Scotland...he shut himself up into a chamber (as those that were present of his own nation do report) together with his chancellor, the greatest enemy his mother had in all Scotland, and there passed the day' in guffaws of 'such laughter' that even the chancellor and his friends were forced to tell James to tone it down and 'somewhat better to dissemble the matter'.[5]

---

[3] Bossy, EC, ch. 3 and conclusion.   [4] See Questier, *DP*, ch. 4 *passim*.
[5] ABSJ, PC, pp. 387–8 (Persons to Sir Anthony Standen, 29 August/8 September 1595, ABSJ, Collectanea P/i, fo. 310ʳ); McCoog, *SJISE*, I, pp. 258–9.

THE COMING OF TOLERATION IN LATE ELIZABETHAN ENGLAND? 261

But not every Catholic saw matters thus and not necessarily those who had at one time stood out against any kind of compromise with the Tudor State. Perhaps the single most striking case here was John Mush, formerly the associate of Henry Garnet and the biographer of Margaret Clitherow. By the later 1590s Mush had broken with his Jesuit friends. He was chosen in 1601 as one of the proctors for the new appeal to Rome against the recently instituted archpresbyterate, that is, the system of government created by Rome for the secular clergy of the English mission.[6]

To explain very briefly, the appellant business began with the attempt in 1598 by English Catholic priests to lobby Rome to think again about the way it had decided to govern the Catholic community in England, that is, in the absence of a system of direct episcopal regulation. Rome had at one time considered the appointment of bishops but opted instead to set up an archpresbyterate in England and nominated, as archpriest, George Blackwell. This provoked a good deal of opposition because Blackwell was regarded, by some, as a cat's paw of the Society of Jesus. However, the agitation against him in the first instance failed because it did not have the kind of diplomatic backing in Rome which would have given the appellant priests' representatives any chance of success there.[7]

By the end of the 1590s, there were two (equal and opposite) Catholic discourses of toleration doing the rounds. The first was generated by the appellant clergy. Their case, briefly stated, was that the weeding out of bad/Jesuit influences in the Catholic community would allow for a peace with the queen's government and whatever came after it. The second came from Persons and his friends. They thought that mere toleration was not worth having. Indeed, it was their own refusal to compromise which had forced the Elizabethan State to draw back, to some extent, from its insane cruelty; and this had happened, as much as anything, because the *Conference about the Next Succession* had blown the gaff on the attempt to push the succession through by stealth, that is, without anyone being allowed to discuss the big issues involved, particularly that of religion. On 13/23 November 1596 Richard Verstegan wrote to Roger Baynes that 'the persecution has not been great since the publication of the book on the succession'.[8] Persons insisted to the bemused Scottish Jesuit, William Creighton, in the same month that, 'after the publication' of the *Conference*, Catholics in England and in Scotland 'were treated much more mildly'. Before the *Conference* appeared, 'the king of Scotland had' David Graham, laird of Fentry, 'beheaded on account of his

---

[6] Anstr., I, p. 241; see p. 308 below.
[7] J. H. Pollen, *The Institution of the Archpriest Blackwell: A Study of the Transition from Paternal to Constitutional and Local Church Government among the English Catholics, 1595 to 1602* (1916).
[8] Petti, *LDRV*, p. 249.

262   CATHOLICS AND TREASON

Catholic faith', that is, after the Blanks Plot, 'but no one, as far as I know, after the book was published'.[9]

The Discontents of Anti-Popery in the Mid- and Later 1590s and the Limits of Intolerance

The Case of William Freeman

One of the sources for tracking this shift in late Elizabethan politics is, as we might expect, the continuing attempt by some of the crown's servants to prosecute Catholic clergy. One extremely well-documented case was that of the secular priest William Freeman, who was indicted, convicted, and hanged at Warwick on 13 August 1595, perhaps as a result of the accusations made against the prominent local Catholic gentleman Ralph Sheldon.[10] The arrest and trial took place out in the provinces, and it predated by some three years the formal stages of the Archpriest Dispute. But the fact that the long and detailed narrative of his martyrdom rests in the archives of the Society of Jesus (in the papers of Christopher Grene SJ) suggests that Jesuit clergy and their friends may have seen it as significant for more than the mere bravery displayed by Freeman in the face of the authorities.[11]

The Revd Freeman had a reputation for practising a particularly muscular form of Christianity. In January 1589, on the way up the Thames, the crew of the ship he was on decided either to apprehend or if necessary to slay him and his friends. But Freeman with four other clergymen 'drew out their rapiers' to force the ship to land at Gravesend. The 'mariners' were told to keep under 'the hatches' or they themselves would be killed. The implication of the extant narrative of Freeman's case is that his apostolate in Warwickshire and Worcestershire was quite confrontational: 'great and daily were the labours he bestowed for some years, travelling ordinarily on foot to comfort the meaner sort in weariness of body and sundry perils, from which notwithstanding he was marvellously delivered', and, on one occasion, 'out of the hands of pursuivants by whom he was

---

[9] Knox, *LMCA*, p. 385 (transcript and translation at ABSJ, PC, p. 519). For Persons's justification of the book in his letter to Don Juan de Idiaquez, 21 April/1 May 1597, see ABSJ, PC, pp. 596–8 (AAW, A VI, no. 32); V. Houliston, 'The Hare and the Drum: Robert Persons's Writings on the English Succession, 1593–6', *Renaissance Studies* 14 (2000), pp. 235–50. For the view, by the mid-1590s, that Scotland was a tolerant environment for English Catholics, see e.g. *CSPSc 1595–7*, p. 108.

[10] Pollen, *UD*, pp. 345–60 ('Of the Apprehension of Mr William Freeman...': AVCAU, Liber 1422 [Grene, Collectanea F], section 5, pp. 90^b–100^b); Dillon, *CM*, pp. 109–10.

[11] The route via which this narrative got into Grene's papers is unclear. John Pollen thought that the secular priest Anthony Champney, when compiling his 'Annales', 'had some information derived from this paper, though [Richard] Challoner', who quoted Champney, 'never saw it': Pollen, *UD*, p. 345.

THE COMING OF TOLERATION IN LATE ELIZABETHAN ENGLAND?   263

arrested'. The same narrative describes his battles with one local clergyman who tried but failed to secure his detention.[12]

Now, of course, we have only this one manuscript account to rely on. But the implication of it is that Freeman was, despite the constraints of the law, exercising a quasi-public ministry in a kind of safe haven constituted by local gentry families. He was 'placed with' Dorothy Heath and received protection also from 'Mr [William] Combe, allied by marriage...unto Mistress Sheldon', that is, Jane Sheldon, 'with whom Mr Freeman now conversed'.[13] Moreover, Combe 'came to be a favourite of some in authority, as namely' of 'Doctor Whitgift, superintendent first of Worcester and now of Canterbury', as well as of Lord Burghley and the lord keeper, 'by which means he grew to be of some countenance and account in the country'. This led him to advance his fortunes by securing grants of land from the Sheldon and Heath families, not least because Mrs Heath was a recusant and periodically was imprisoned for the same. Combe's greed facilitated a series of deals which protected some of those who were in question locally for their separatism.[14] This, one takes it, also served to protect a fairly stroppy evangelical separatist clergyman, that is to say, Freeman himself, although this was precisely the situation which the proclamation of 18 October 1591 and its attached commissions were supposed to have sorted out; and, as we have seen, there had been a particularly concerted effort in Warwickshire, as much as in other places, in the wake of the proclamation, to grub up and expose separatist Catholicism.[15]

Anyway, says our anonymous narrator, this 'fair weather was but a gleam to prepare a greater storm for...a special commission was procured and directed' from Archbishop Whitgift and others, 'the effect whereof...was to search the house of Dorothy Heath'. The commissioners appointed were Combe himself and Andrew Boardman, who was 'parson of Alvechurch, and vicar of the high church, Warwick'. Combe seemed unwilling to have anything to do with the resulting search. When it took place on 5 January 1595 it appeared that he was very glad that 'they found nothing saving a prayer book or two'. But soon afterwards, and apparently almost by accident, Freeman was arrested.[16]

The clergyman at hand to deal with the priest was none other than Andrew Boardman. But he was not the usual (in Catholic accounts) sarcastic embodiment of Protestant anti-popish malice. As the holder of the benefice at Alvechurch, he had become vicar of St Mary's Warwick on 11 January 1591 in place of Leonard

[12] Pollen, *UD*, pp. 346–7.

[13] Pollen, *UD*, p. 348. Dorothy Heath was the widow of William Heath (the brother of Nicholas Heath, the former archbishop of York) and the daughter of Sir Thomas Blount of Sodington, Worcestershire: AVCAU, Scr. 21/2/2. Combe had been MP for Warwick in 1593 and was a JP. Combe's elder brother had been a 'misliker' (of Protestantism) in the 1564 survey of JPs: *HC 1558–1603*, I, p. 635. The Sheldons possessed salt pans at Droitwich. Combe had been returned as MP to the 1589 parliament for this borough: *HC 1558–1603*, I, pp. 634–5.

[14] Pollen, *UD*, p. 348.   [15] PRO, SP 12/243/76, 76. i; see pp. 227, 227 n.202 above.

[16] Pollen, *UD*, pp. 348–9, 350; Challoner, *MMP*, p. 228.

264 CATHOLICS AND TREASON

Fetherston. While he was at Warwick he had clashed with the leading Elizabethan puritan Thomas Cartwright, who was, at that point, master of the earl of Leicester's hospital there.[17]

Freeman's 'friends' sent a petition to London; it was 'preferred at the council table and proceeded with good success and favour' until 'it came to the view' of Whitgift, 'who, having perused the same, wrote underneath as follows, "Sue no further, for he is a seminary priest", and withal threw back the petition'.[18] This was, as it happened, not long before the theological fireworks of the William Barrett affair in Cambridge in and after April 1595.[19] This put Whitgift on his guard when faced with an overtly Calvinist retaliation against an apparent heterodoxy which questioned Calvinist doctrines of grace. For all his anti-puritanism, Whitgift himself refused to tolerate the kind of full-scale reaction against Calvinist theology which had emerged in the inflammatory sermons preached in March and October 1594 in London by Lancelot Andrewes and Samuel Harsnett. On Professor Lake's account, when the leading puritan divine William Whitaker 'broached the subject of predestination in Cambridge in an oration at Great St Mary's' in February 1595 in front of a high-profile audience, including the earl of Essex, 'he was not opening hostilities but, rather, rallying university and court opinion against' an 'anti-Calvinist sally' in the previous year. One imagines that, in this context, it would have been quite impossible for Whitgift to have been seen as soft either on popery or the causes of popery.[20]

Combe apparently intimated to Freeman and Mrs Heath that they might be released 'by his means'. Freeman refused to abscond for fear of 'scandal'. 'During the time of his imprisonment, Mr Boardman and some other ministers came to dispute with' Freeman, but to little effect.[21] Freeman was not indicted at the Lent assizes, even though Lord Chief Justice Popham was in town and took the time to interrogate him. There was as yet no proof that he was a priest; he would not admit it.[22]

Our narrative says that there was then, in effect, a local conspiracy against Freeman, facilitated by the malice of the judge Sir Edmund Anderson. The 'night before the assizes', Anderson 'conferred' with Freeman's 'principal adversaries,

---

[17] See ODNB, sub Boardman, Andrew (article by A. H. Grant, rev. S. Wright); Pollen, UD, p. 350.

[18] Pollen, UD, p. 351.

[19] For William Barrett, who, it seems, followed the opinions of Peter Baro, Lady Margaret professor of divinity in Cambridge, when he (Barrett) preached a sermon on 29 April 1595 which refuted the doctrines advanced by William Whitaker concerning (universal) grace, see ODNB, sub Barrett, William (article by E. Allen).

[20] P. Lake, 'The "Anglican Moment"? Richard Hooker and the Ideological Watershed of the 1590s', in S. Platten (ed.), Anglicanism and the Western Christian Tradition (Norwich, 2003), pp. 90–121, at p. 109.

[21] Pollen, UD, p. 351. Combe tried to blackmail Mrs Heath 'to resign up into his hands the lease of her park at Alvechurch'. If she agreed, he said he would try to procure her liberty and Freeman's as well: Pollen, UD, p. 351.

[22] Pollen, UD, pp. 351–2, 350.

THE COMING OF TOLERATION IN LATE ELIZABETHAN ENGLAND?   265

and still in all their packing the conclusion was that he should die'. What they needed was a witness. It emerged that when Freeman was indicted at the assizes held on '11 or 12 August' 1595 there was a felon in the gaol who would testify against him (that Freeman had absolved him), which the felon duly did.[23] Anderson declared, 'what seditious fellows priests were, of their attempt in Ireland, of the Spaniards' matters, etc.' Freeman gave as good as he got. He had said that, 'if more of the Protestants in Queen Mary's days had been cut off, the rest would have been more quiet now'. Anderson retorted that Freeman was a 'prattler and a seducer of the queen's people'.[24]

Mr Justice Clench was there as well—the judge who had been very reluctant to kowtow to the hawks on the council in the North who had insisted in March 1586 that Margaret Clitherow should be crushed to death. Clench conceded that Freeman was guilty under the law but had very little else to say about it. The Catholic narrator, who claimed to have been an eyewitness, said also that 'never a one of the justices', that is, the JPs, 'spoke anything against' Freeman 'that I heard'. Or, rather, only one did—the puritan and Dudley client Sir Thomas Lucy of Charlecote, who had been tutored by John Foxe and who had a record of hostility to Catholics in the region.[25]

To some, therefore, this must have looked like a local puritan strike against a long-serving Catholic clergyman. There was disagreement and confusion also among the jury as to whether and on what grounds they should convict. According to our narrator, 'on the next morrow, one of them', the foreman apparently, 'being asked wherefore they found Freeman guilty', declared that he 'denied the queen to be supreme head of the Church'; but another exclaimed, 'no … he did not so but refused to answer, which is not to deny'. Also, 'what witness had you against him' besides the felon? The foreman riposted that 'Harry, the gaoler, heard him speak' the relevant treasonable words; and allegedly Freeman also admitted that he was a priest. No, he did not, said the other—Harry 'did but depose he heard Gregory say so'. So what, said the foreman, 'it were no matter if all such as he were hanged'.[26]

The decision was taken, however, to execute Freeman. This caused yet more local controversy. Boardman and another minister went to talk to him in the prison. A 'schismatical gentleman' (that is, a conformist Catholic) tried to persuade Freeman that he should 'reconcile himself—meaning to Calvin's company', but Freeman refused.[27] At the gallows, Freeman carried on disputing with Boardman over religion. Still, it was embarrassingly apparent how much basic Christian theology they more or less shared. Freeman also made a fairly striking

---

[23] Pollen, *UD*, p. 352.   [24] Pollen, *UD*, pp. 353–4, 355.
[25] Pollen, *UD*, p. 355; *HC 1558–1603*, II, p. 355. For Sir Thomas Lucy, see C. Enis, 'The Warwickshire Gentry and the Dudley Ascendancy 1547 to 1590' (PhD, Reading, 2011), *passim*.
[26] Pollen, *UD*, p. 356.   [27] Pollen, *UD*, p. 357.

266   CATHOLICS AND TREASON

declaration of loyalty to the queen. Instead of haranguing the trussed-up victim as Richard Topcliffe would have done, Boardman 'made protestation that he bore him no malice', 'and that which I have done', said he, 'I did it, put in commission in that behalf of my prince and country, and therefore I hope that you will forgive me and not think any ill in me?' Freeman replied that Boardman had not 'offended' him and that 'I find no fault with you', for 'you have used me like a worshipful gentleman'. The priest expressed the same sentiment to the sheriff's officers.[28]

If Boardman's was the local voice of Whitgiftian and, perhaps, even anti-puritan opinion (he had been ordained by the deeply anti-puritan Bishop Freke[29]), then this may tell us something about the dynamics of the confrontations which had led to the death of this priest. We are told that after Freeman had prayed and committed himself to God he was turned off the ladder. 'Presently cut down he was not, but hanged some time', though 'whether he was fully dead or not (according to the judge's sentence) it may be doubted, for that his heart trembled in the executioner's hand and, as some reported that saw it, the same leaped thrice out of the fire: and, [when] his head [was] chopped off, his mouth gasped twice'. But 'never a one of the standers-by made any clamour, or spoke any word against him'. Indeed, 'some there were that reviled the executioner and said it was no matter if he went in the other's case'. Others 'noted much the hardness of his knees and said "surely he was a good man and used much prayer"'. Mr Boardman made no effort to conceal the fact that he took absolutely no pleasure in what had happened: 'the night after, supping with some gentlemen', he 'was demanded by one of them what he thought of the man. He answered that he thought his soul was in heaven'. The day after Freeman's 'quarters were set up' Boardman came 'down the street' and, 'looking toward them, shook his head, pulled his hat' down over his eyes 'and presently returned into his own house'; and 'another minister, also present at his death, reported afterward that he never saw [a] man die more confidently'.[30]

The branch of the Catholic community that tended to express an interest in the emergence of novel forms of anti-puritanism in the national Church was the one associated with the critics of the Jesuits. But there is no evidence that, although Freeman was regarded as a martyr by his secular clergy confrères, he was aligned with those who were shortly to lead the first appeal against the new archpriest, George Blackwell, and his Jesuit friends. If he had been, it is unlikely that this narrative would have been retained by Jesuit clergy. It may have been thought that Freeman's witness testified to the need to refuse compromise in the face of puritan aggression and, in the end, the persecution would cease, a lesson compatible with the claims made at this time by Robert Persons and his associates.

[28] Pollen, *UD*, pp. 358–9.   [29] CCED, ID 67793.   [30] Pollen, *UD*, pp. 359–60.

THE COMING OF TOLERATION IN LATE ELIZABETHAN ENGLAND? 267

The Troubles of Northern Catholics and the Difficulties of Matthew Hutton

There had never been complete unanimity among the authorities about how to discipline Catholic separatism. But the resulting uncertainties were, if anything, more visible at this point in the North when the queen's representatives there decided, towards the end of 1596, to hang three lay Catholics. The executions took place on 29 November in York. The victims had been snared by a kind of sting operation against Catholic separatists in York Castle gaol. A bigamist Protestant minister named William Lowther had been committed to the gaol by the recently appointed Archbishop Hutton and the high commission. Lowther was then lobbied by the recusant George Errington and others—as the ecclesiastical commissioner Edward Stanhope described it—'not to say service amongst the prisoners'.[31] Lowther betrayed them to the York authorities, claiming that they had urged him to break his oath of obedience to the queen for 'the pope had...authority in ecclesiastical causes' and that they had used 'many other vile speeches as that, if the pope sent an army, they were to take with him rather than with her Majesty's forces'; and, furthermore, 'if he were troubled in conscience in these points, they would (after his bailment) send him to a priest that should reconcile him, give him penance, and dispense with him for the same'.[32] Lowther then persuaded these Catholics to make available to him the services of a seminary priest. William Knight wrote to Henry Abbot of Howden to contact the priest in question, Thomas Atkinson. Lowther met Abbot, who 'laid open his mind unto him with very hard words of her Majesty and the State, and rode with him' to Richard Stapleton's house, though it appears that no meeting between Atkinson and Lowther actually took place. Stapleton's wife was Elizabeth Pierrepoint, granddaughter of Bess of Hardwick and formerly a servant of Mary Stuart.[33] Abbot was, said Lowther, about to go overseas and 'told where himself was reconciled, [and] Richard Stapleton and others' also, by 'that priest, about Corpus Christi day last'.[34]

The inevitable arrests followed. Among those taken was Edward Fulthrop. He confessed that he had been reconciled in Flanders when he 'served as a chief clerk under the treasurer of her Majesty's forces there'. All were arraigned and convicted

---

[31] K. Longley, 'Blessed George Errington and Companions: Fresh Evidence', RH 19 (1988), pp. 39–46, at p. 41, citing and printing BL, Additional MS 30262, E. 2.

[32] Longley, 'Blessed George Errington', pp. 41–2.

[33] Ibid., p. 42. Lady Grace Babthorpe later provided her own memories of this incident and also of the circumstances (a family quarrel) which had led to the imprisonment of William Knight: AAW, A VI, no. 100, pp. 368, 369 [Morris, TCF, I, pp. 243–5]. Knight had been charged on 11 May 1591 by the high commission with recusancy; he was gaoled in York Castle in October 1593 and was sent to Hull in January 1594; see Borthwick Institute, York, HCAB 11, fo. 346^r, HCAB 12, fo. 153^v; AWCBC, pp. 1218–19, 1221.

[34] Longley, 'Blessed George Errington', p. 42.

268   CATHOLICS AND TREASON

of treason. As Stanhope, who also had a reputation as an enemy of puritans, casually wrote, 'with as good exhortations as I could, I gave judgment of them; the men to be hanged, drawn and quartered, the women to be burned, which I told them was not for heresy but their due judgment for high treason'. Fulthrop showed signs of compliance and so was, with the two women, reprieved and, said Stanhope, Abbot as well, 'we not [being] willing to make the execution too bloody at one time'.[35] Stanhope dutifully reported, however, that on 29 November 'we executed George Errington', a man called William Gibson, 'and William Knight, who died most traitorously'. They could not 'be persuaded to pray for her Majesty by any means'. When they tried to 'publish that they died for their conscience, the whole people cried "Traitors! Traitors!" '[36]

But not everyone in York was equally sanguine about the supposedly good effects of all this. Or, rather, there were now some people, notably Matthew Hutton, who were getting sour glances for their apparent softness towards Catholics. A circulated copy of a letter by Roger, Lord North, in early 1597 claimed that recusancy had increased in the North of England because of the 'remissness' of Hutton, 'so that, many being presented, none are punished', which the 'justices and others generally well affected do openly complain of'. Catholics were now calling Protestants heretics even to their faces; and there were 'a great number of church papists whose wives, being recusants, the people are made [to] believe they have a toleration for them from her Majesty'. North said that Mr Goodwin, one of the high commissioners, had previously, on 25 November 1596, openly in York Minster 'preached' in front of Archbishop Hutton 'and others' at the gaol delivery 'before the late arraignment', that is, of, among others, Lowther's Catholic victims. Goodwin had said that, 'since the death of the late earl of Huntingdon' and of Archbishop John Piers, 'papists' had 'increased' and 'many indifferent Protestants' had been added to their number. Moreover, some justices had 'grown key cold'.[37] Since Errington, Gibson, and Knight were hanged only four days later, one might have thought this would have been enough for the likes of Lord North; but evidently it was not; or, rather, he and his friends knew, or

[35] Ibid., p. 43. For Stanhope, see *HC 1558–1603*, III, pp. 437–9. Anthony Atkinson claimed that, at Waterhouses, in the house where Boste was arrested, George Errington, with others, had been present 'at the Mass' on 12 and 13 July 1593: Pollen, *UD*, p. 220 (PRO, SP 12/245/131). Stanhope noted that Errington had, in late 1593, been 'detected' by the informer Francis Eglisfield and others 'to be a notable conveyor of' John Boste and other seminary priests. Errington 'had served the king of Spain' and was, says Christopher Grene, arrested in November 1593 (and was sent to Durham in mid-July 1594, apparently for trial): Longley, 'Blessed George Errington', p. 41; *AWCBC*, pp. 1221, 1222.
[36] Challoner, *MMP*, pp. 229–30 (relying in part on AAW, A IV, no. 22, p. 132: evidence given in 1626 by Elizabeth Ellison); Petti, *LDRV*, p. 250; Longley, 'Blessed George Errington', p. 43. Challoner, following Anthony Champney, includes the (briefly) reprieved Abbot among the martyrs of 29 November 1596: Challoner, *MMP*, p. 230; *AWCBC*, p. 1214.
[37] BL, Lansdowne MS 84, no. 104, fo. 236ʳ. For complaints during 1596 that northern separatists were escaping the full financial consequences of their recusancy, see, e.g., J. C. H. Aveling, 'The Recusancy Papers of the Meynell Family of North Kilvington...', *Miscellanea* (CRS 56, 1964), pp. 47–8.

THE COMING OF TOLERATION IN LATE ELIZABETHAN ENGLAND? 269

thought they knew, that this was not Hutton's preferred mode of dealing with such people.

There was, of course, no toleration imminent in the North—as the priest Christopher Robinson also found out when he was arrested on 4 March 1597.[38] Garnet explained to Persons in April 1597 that the priest Robinson had 'in a purchased gaol delivery' been 'hanged at Carlisle' in late March. The 'rope broke twice and, the third time, he rebuked the sheriff of cruelty'. In the end they used 'two ropes' and then, 'says he, by this means I shall be longer a-dying'. Robinson, as we saw, had written an account of the trial and execution of John Boste. It may be that this spurred on the proceedings against him, though he had also been associated with the loyalist Catholic Robert Fisher, who was actively agitating against the Society of Jesus at this time.[39] John May, the serving bishop of Carlisle, reported that the execution had 'terrified a great sort of our obstinate recusants'. But he also said that there were 'notable seminaries or Jesuits' who made their way across his 'diocese without controlment, such' was 'the careless or partial dealing of some' of the 'justices'. One of those priests was Richard Dudley, to whom Robinson had sent his report of Boste's martyrdom and who, May said, was 'termed, by the aforesaid Robinson and other his associates, the angel of that profession'. But there was a stubborn refusal to arrest Dudley: it was 'known to many of our gentlemen that the said angelical Jesuit or seminary' was 'harboured in these parts, yet none of them' would, even though they saw him, 'lay hands on him'.[40]

On 5 May 1597 the council in London dealt with Archbishop Hutton's question about the Catholics who were awaiting execution—'Edward Fulthrop and one Henry Abbot, as also two women by name Anne Tesh and Bridget Maskew'.[41] The

---

[38] Anstr., I, p. 293. Leonard Musgrave of Johnby Hall, near Penrith, was charged with sheltering Christopher Robinson: *AWCBC*, pp. 1239, 1250–1 (PRO, C 66/1496, mm. 5–6). At some point, either before or after Robinson's trial and conviction under the 1585 statute, Henry Robinson, the provost of The Queen's College, Oxford, who in 1598 became bishop of Carlisle, is said to have visited him in an attempt to turn him: *AWCBC*, pp. 1239, 1240, 1253 (AAW, F 1, p. 969), 1254.

[39] ABSJ, GC, p. 421 (ABSJ, Collectanea P/ii, p. 548); Anstr., I, p. 293; *Miscellanea I* (CRS 1, 1905), pp. 85–91; for Robert Fisher, see *AWCBC*, pp. 1245, 1247. Challoner, following Anthony Champney's 'Annales' and Richard Smith's catalogue of 1628, located the execution in August 1598: Challoner, *MMP*, p. 235. For the actual date of the execution, see *AWCBC*, pp. 1239, 1240, 1242.

[40] HHCP 53/28 (*HMCS*, VII, p. 298); *AWCBC*, pp. 1248–9; see p. 247 n.89 above.

[41] *APC 1597*, pp. 91–2. Edward Fulthrop appears to have been the Newcastle merchant against whom the informer Samuel Wharton testified on 13 May 1595 that he (Fulthrop) was a client of Lord Lumley. Wharton said that Fulthrop had been 'in Bergen-op-Zoom in Brabant' ten or twelve years previously and that, 'being a merchant', Fulthrop frequented 'the English house at Middleburgh where, under colour of merchants' letters', he sent communications 'to Newcastle and other places in Northumberland, to divers papists in the North' and particularly to his relative by marriage Ursula Taylor at '[South] Shields near Newcastle': *HMCS*, V, pp. 203–4. For Wharton's other confessions (he was arrested on suspicion of spying for the Spaniards), see : *HMCS*, V, pp. 184, 220, 488, 489; *CSPD 1595–7*, pp. 141, 143 (PRO, SP 12/255/11, 19); see also AAW, A V, no. 44, p. 137; W. Kelly (ed.), *Liber Ruber Venerabilis Collegii Anglorum de Urbe: Annales Collegii Pars Prima: Nomina Alumnorum I. A.D. 1579–1630* (2 vols, CRS 37, 40, 1940–3), pp. 88–9. For Ursula Taylor and her connection with George Errington, see A. M. C. Forster, 'The Venerable George Errington', *Biographical Studies* 3 (1955), pp. 322–33, at

270 CATHOLICS AND TREASON

council's answer was that the two women (Tesh had been a friend of Margaret Clitherow) were to be reprieved temporarily and, as for Fulthrop and Abbot, it was up to the northern council to decide what to do with them, 'as also with Joseph Constable', the friend of the recently executed John Boste.[42]

Hutton wrote to Burghley on 6 July 1597 that, two days before, Fulthrop, who had obviously not been compliant enough, had finally been hanged as well. So had Abbot. There 'was likewise now executed' William Anlaby, 'a priest made at Douai and one [Thomas] Warcop that received him'. (See Figure 9.1.) Hutton noted that Warcop had 'formerly received one Neale', that is, the priest Alexander Rawlins, who had been hanged with Henry Walpole on 7 April 1595. As we saw, Rawlins had been arrested in Warcop's house by Anthony Atkinson, though Warcop had then absconded. At execution Warcop, like the others, refused to pray satisfactorily for the queen.[43] Atkinson recorded for Sir Robert Cecil's benefit that Warcop was 'of Babington's conspiracy and was of counsel with' David Ingleby 'in all matters'.[44]

These Catholics had been entirely obstinate. But Ingleby's associate Joseph Constable had not. Constable 'did openly at the bar before the justices of assize confess his errors in religion and his offence against her Majesty and her laws and, making his submission in very humble manner', he 'discovered what seminaries...had resort unto him'. He had 'taken the oath of her Majesty's supremacy before this council most willingly' and he promised 'to receive the sacrament and bring in his son'. To the ever optimistic Hutton's way of thinking it looked as if

pp. 325, 326. For Fulthrop, see Aveling, NC, p. 160. Ann Forster speculates that the travel route which Errington ran through Newcastle was betrayed to the authorities by the, at times, close-to-renegade priest Edward Grately (who betrayed the earl of Arundel as he tried to leave the country in 1585). Errington was in the Tower for more than a year from mid-1585. For Errington's interrogation in August 1585, after he was taken, going from Newcastle to France, see Pollen, UD, pp. 125–6; see also Miscellanea II, p. 261. Henry Sanderson had arrested Errington in February 1591, 'being their chieftain and guide'. Roger Ashton was taken at this time at South Shields. Ursula Taylor was arrested soon after, i.e. for harbouring them. Taken with Ashton was Robert Musgrave: Forster, 'The Venerable George Errington', esp. at pp. 325–7, citing HMCS, X, pp. 202–5; Foley, RSJ, III, p. 745, 751, 754; Miscellanea III (CRS 3, 1906), pp. 21, 22, 23, 24. Errington was examined by the northern council (with Richard Topcliffe in attendance) on 22 May and 24 May 1591. However, he and the seminary priest George Williams absconded on 4 December 1591: Forster, 'The Venerable George Errington', pp. 326–7. Errington was arrested (again) shortly after John Boste was taken, in or around November 1593: ibid., pp. 327–8. Though Errington was sent back to Durham with Boste on 16 July 1594, he was not hanged with him: ibid., pp. 328–9; Foley, RSJ, III, p. 765.

[42] APC 1597, pp. 91–2. Edward Stanhope described Tesh and Maskew as 'very perilous women, not only for their recusancy but [also] for speaking boldly against the State, persuading others and dealing abroad with women in their childbirth, popish christening of children and suchlike': Longley, 'Blessed George Errington', p. 41.

[43] BL, Lansdowne MS 84, no. 79, fo. 176ʳ; Challoner, MMP, pp. 231–2; HMCS, VII, p. 230; see pp. 256–7 n.134 above. Champney said that, 'whereas many Catholics were kept prisoners for their conscience in Hull Castle', Anlaby found ways to minister to them, along with the priest Thomas Atkinson (who, as we saw, had been approached by Henry Abbot): Challoner, MMP, p. 232. Anlaby's severed head was probably recovered by local Catholics; his skull ended up at the English convent at Bruges: E. M. Charlton, Burghwallis and the Anne Family (privately printed, n.d.), p. 15.

[44] HMCS, VII, p. 300.

Figure 9.1 Reliquary containing the relics of six Catholic clergymen martyred in the sixteenth and seventeenth centuries—William Anlaby, Thomas Somers, Montford Scott, John Lockwood, Ambrose Barlow OSB, and Oliver Plunket (reproduced with the permission of the trustees of Ushaw Historic House, Chapels and Gardens).

Constable had been 'fully reclaimed from popery'.[45] The squire Richard Stapleton, to whose house Henry Abbot had taken the renegade Lowther, was similarly under threat. But, like Constable, Stapleton concluded that conformity was the

---

[45] BL, Lansdowne MS 84, no. 79, fo. 176ʳ; Aveling, *NC*, pp. 141–2; M. Questier, 'The Politics of Religious Conformity and the Accession of James I', *HR* 71 (1998), pp. 14–30, at p. 17.

272   CATHOLICS AND TREASON

better part of valour. At Hutton's direction he also offered a measure of compliance which was sufficient to save himself from the gallows.[46]

Evidently Hutton was not particularly squeamish. He had reported obediently enough on the killing of Fulthrop and the others, though perhaps he was badgered into participation in these executions in part by the sarcastic comments of Lord North. Hutton had no particular problem with witnessing Catholic separatists swinging from the gallows if they had been convicted under the law. But his modus operandi, as it had been with Margaret Neville, was to tend towards clemency, that is, in return for conformity. Hutton complained to Burghley on 27 May 1597 that he had had 'ill success in a suit for a pardon for' one 'Miles Dawson, seminary priest, whom I converted wholly the last summer from popery'. 'Upon his coming to the church, receiving the holy communion and taking the oath of supremacy, I and the council', the previous Michaelmas, had 'joined in petition' to the queen for a royal pardon and commended it to one of the masters of requests and Sir Robert Cecil himself. But nothing had been done in Michaelmas term, or even in Hilary. Hutton had been compelled to send a financial gratuity. 'Some say that Mr Topcliffe did hinder the pardon', though Topcliffe had denied it. What was the point of all this charitable argument with Catholic separatists if nothing seemed to come of it? Hutton urged Burghley just to get on with it and reminded him that, 'since the conversion of Richard Stapleton and his wife, who received the holy communion publicly in the minster of York on Whitsunday last', he (Hutton) 'had been dealing with Joseph Constable and his wife' and had 'brought him to hear divine service'. Mrs Constable had promised to do the same. Hutton urged that Constable should be immediately freed on bail. The rest of the council in the North were 'precise in that matter' because Constable had already been indicted for harbouring a seminary priest; but, Hutton reminded Burghley, legal advice sent down on 19 March 1597 had demonstrated that the 'indictment was erroneous in two or three points'.[47] Hutton had in fact been congratulated in early May 1597 by Whitgift and by the privy council for getting Catholic separatists to reform themselves, even though, as Hutton said, the harder-line Tobias Matthew had 'scarcely dealt' in a 'brotherly' manner 'with me in some letters lately written concerning' the recusant wife of the Durham gentleman Nicholas Tempest.[48]

---

[46] Challoner, *MMP*, pp. 229, 230. Stapleton was a first cousin of the rebel sixth earl of Westmorland: H. E. Chetwynd-Stapylton, *The Stapeltons of Yorkshire* (1897), p. 159; for Stapleton's conformity, see PRO, E 368/532, mem. 244[a–b].

[47] BL, Lansdowne MS 84, no. 78, fo. 174[r]; J. Raine (ed.), *The Correspondence of Dr Matthew Hutton*... (Surtees Society 17, 1843), pp. 111, 115. For Dawson's confessions, conformity, and pardon, see Anstr., I, pp. 99–100; *HMCS*, VI, pp. 430–2.

[48] P. Lake, 'Matthew Hutton—a Puritan Bishop?', *History* 64 (1979), 182–204, at p. 188; Raine, *Correspondence*, pp. 117–18, 303. On 16 March 1597, Hutton had written to Whitgift on behalf of Nicholas Tempest, whose wife, to Tempest's 'great grief', was a recusant but, 'for anything' that Hutton could tell, 'neither a persuader nor any way dangerous or hurtful to her children or any other' (also, her uncle was the third Lord Eure): *CSPD 1595–7*, pp. 370–1 (PRO, SP 12/262/69). Back in 1585

THE COMING OF TOLERATION IN LATE ELIZABETHAN ENGLAND? 273

Within a few months, Hutton could even think that he was presiding over a small tsunami of conformity and compliance. Not only had Dawson, finally 'pardoned by the queen at my request', brought 'two women recusants to the Church', and preached 'very well' but the recusant William Vavasour, 'after much and long conference with me', had 'yielded to hear divine service and sermons, whose example, I trust, will do much good'.[49]

On one level, one might argue, this was business as usual—the occasional intimidatory deployment of the 1580s statutes inside a wrapper of relative moderation. At another, though, this could be taken as a gesture towards, or prediction of, a potentially new environment for Catholic dissent. Hutton himself appeared at this point to be on the up. Stanhope wrote on 2 June 1597 that the archbishop 'rides abroad and looks not better or fresher this seven years'.[50] But many crown officials were not so sanguine. Some of the letters which wended their way down to regime members in London from the small band of really aggressive attack dogs and enforcers in the North insisted that, as far as they were concerned, things were worryingly not as they had been, and that former certainties about inflicting harsh punishment on popish traitors were being undermined. Even Stanhope, who was no enemy of Hutton, remarked of Joseph Constable's conformity that, 'whether [it was] of conscience or for fear of present death, standing outlawed upon felony, I refer to further proof'.[51] It was difficult not to speculate that the slackening of the law might have something to do with Catholic anticipation that things would go better for them when James VI took Elizabeth's crown. It was public knowledge that Hutton was a supporter of King James's right to be acknowledged as Elizabeth's successor.[52]

This is not to say that the expressions of Protestant dismay at the extent of popery were anything particularly novel—nothing that Sir Francis Knollys could not have said in the late 1580s.[53] But the frustrations experienced by godly Protestants faced with a wall of what they took to be fake loyalty and time-serving obedience were effectively summarized by Sir Francis Hastings's allegation, made in 1598 in his *Watch-Word*, that 'their whole Catholic government and religion,

---

Hutton had not denied the accusation made against him by Archbishop Sandys that he (Hutton) used moderation in trying to persuade recusants to attend Church: Aveling, *NC*, p. 114.

[49] *HMCS*, VII, p. 404 (Hutton to Sir Robert Cecil, 28 September 1597). The conforming recusant was not *Sir* William Vavasour, as indicated in *HMCS*, but William Vavasour of Hazlewood who married Anne, daughter of Sir Thomas Manners, son of Thomas Manners, earl of Rutland. Their second son, Henry Vavasour, made no reference to this event when he sued to enter the English College in Rome: HHCP 55/78; Anstr., II, p. 327; Kenny, *RS*, I, p. 286.

[50] *HMCS*, VII, p. 230.   [51] *HMCS*, VII, p. 230.

[52] Sir John Harington, *A Briefe View of the State of the Church of England...* (1653), pp. 186–90. Claire Cross convincingly suggests that the date of Hutton's sermon in which he spoke on this topic, much to Elizabeth's annoyance, must be early 1596: *ODNB*, *sub* Hutton, Matthew (article by C. Cross).

[53] For the rhetoric of anxiety in post-Reformation anti-popery, see, e.g., C. Z. Wiener, 'The Beleaguered Isle: A Study of Elizabethan and Early Jacobean Anti-Catholicism', *Past and Present* 51 (1971), pp. 27–62.

274 CATHOLICS AND TREASON

I am sure, they', the Catholics, 'long for'. And 'yet, to pronounce these men to carry hollow hearts to Queen Elizabeth, is thought to be an uncharitable sentence'.[54] In August 1596 Topcliffe had claimed to know that the priest George Hethershall, who was himself supposed to be securely locked up, was resorting to 'other traitors' in the London prisons. Among his associates were Edward Hughes and one Thirkell. From them Hethershall had received a copy of the *Conference about the Next Succession* and 'the pedigree', that is, the genealogical chart incorporated in the same publication. From that book Hethershall and his friends 'drew note...tending all to the advancement of the infanta of Spain and against the queen's Majesty'. They also had 'a traitorous written book' which condemned the queen's proceedings 'against papists by laws' and 'against the Scottish queen'. Hethershall 'used to say Mass and to reconcile as if he had been in Rome'. According to Topcliffe, it was intended in Michaelmas term that Hethershall should be arraigned on a variety of counts. Topcliffe added that 'he shows mischief by his look'—although this was still not, technically, the basis for a capital indictment.[55] But, whatever kind of looks Hethershall had been giving Topcliffe, he was not hanged. He was still working in Lancashire in 1616, by which time no worse fate had befallen him than to have become a Benedictine.[56]

Despite the executions, during the first half of the 1590s, of prominent northern Catholics such as Boste, we find the customs official Anthony Atkinson lecturing the earl of Essex in September 1596. In the course of a diatribe about fraud in the customs, Atkinson told the earl that he knew exactly where some of the North's most seditious Catholics were. Yet nothing was done about them. As a result, seminary priests arrived and were 'more harboured and accounted of than ever they were'. Their number increased and they had grown 'headstrong since my lord of Huntingdon died'. They expected 'a day for their purpose'. Atkinson believed that, without protection, he himself would not 'escape the wolves'. Actually Essex was at this time offering his own patronage to loyalist Catholics, such as the former Jesuit Thomas Wright. So it is not clear what the earl was likely to do for the likes of Atkinson.[57]

The Arraignment of Robert Barnes and his Friends

To see how far things had arguably changed from the high point of, as some saw it, Elizabethan savagery against Catholic separatism, one can look at the notorious case in 1598 in which Topcliffe managed to create a public-relations disaster.

---

[54] Francis Hastings, *A Watch-Word to all Religious and True Hearted English-Men* (1598), p. 78.
[55] *HMCS*, VI, pp. 312–13.   [56] Anstr., I, pp. 176–7.
[57] *HMCS*, VI, p. 378. For Thomas Wright, see McCoog, *SJISE*, I, pp. 277–8; M. Questier, 'Sermons, Separatists and Succession Politics in Late Elizabethan England', *JBS* 52 (2013), pp. 290–316, at pp. 300–1, 310.

THE COMING OF TOLERATION IN LATE ELIZABETHAN ENGLAND?   275

We know that he was scoping around imprisoned Catholic clergy early in that year, trying to score polemical points against them in front of high-profile audiences. Thus in February 1598, in the company of the queen's doctor George Baker, he confronted Thomas Wright himself. Wright was being held in the dean of Westminster's house, where he (Wright) had been more closely confined since the scandal caused by his proselytizing of the poet William Alabaster. Topcliffe summoned the puritan Stephen Egerton to argue with Wright. As Egerton and Wright traded syllogisms with each other, Topcliffe chipped in and 'drew forth certain letters written' by Thomas Pormort and George Beseley 'to declare what naughty men they were'.[58]

Topcliffe then sought to bring the imprisoned Franciscan John Jones to the gallows. Topcliffe had already tried to trap Jones in summer 1596; and Jones was indeed arraigned and convicted in July 1598. But Topcliffe's clumsy attempts simultaneously to prosecute the recusant Robert Barnes for harbouring Jones turned distinctly sour since it left the regime open to accusations of persecution, tyranny, and torture, which the judges either could not or would not fully either endorse or suppress.[59] Barnes was a gentleman-servant of the second Viscount Montague, who, at this time, was hovering on the outside of the patronage circle of the earl of Essex.[60] His own account of the speeches he made during the trial, if his narrative represented what actually transpired in the courtroom, is astonishing—and is worth reciting at some length.

Barnes described how, 'at my first apprehension by Mr Topcliffe, he accused me of fourteen articles of treasons and felonies'. By 1598 Barnes had already been 'now four years in continual durance'.[61] However, it was Barnes's tirade, allegedly without interruption, following his own arraignment in queen's bench, with Jane Wiseman on Friday, 30 June 1598, and his reappearance in court on the following Monday, which must have been electrifying.[62] Mr Justice Fenner was presiding. The charges involved the 'hearing [of] sundry Masses' and the 'relieving and harbouring' of the priest George Hethershall (who, as we saw, had allegedly possessed a copy of the notorious *Conference about the Next Succession*) and of the Franciscan Jones. Barnes and Wiseman 'were demanded by the clerk of the court whether' they 'were guilty of those felonies or not'. There was a delay caused by Barnes's initial refusal to be tried by a jury, 'for my adversary, Topcliffe, had often threatened me to pick out a jury that should condemn me'. Barnes counter-offered a hearing to be settled by the 'judgment of my lord chief justice, Mr

---

[58] McCoog, *SJISE*, I, pp. 316–17; ABSJ, A VII, no. 49, fo. 29ᵛ *et seq.*, esp. at fo. 34ʳ; *ODNB*, *sub* Baker, George (article by G. Ungerer).
[59] Questier, *C&C*, pp. 244–50; Challoner, *MMP*, p. 234; Petti, *LDRV*, p. 252. Jones was well disposed towards the Society of Jesus: Caraman, *HG*, pp. 252–3; Caraman, *JG*, p. 86.
[60] Questier, *C&C*, p. 239.   [61] *HMCS*, VIII, pp. 273–4; TD, III, p. ccvii.
[62] See 'The Arraignment and Speech of Robert Barnes', 8 July 1598: TD, III, Appendix 37 (ABSJ, Anglia II, no. 41); Pollen, *UD*, pp. 364–70.

276 CATHOLICS AND TREASON

Attorney-General, Mr Solicitor, Mr Bacon and Mr Recorder of London'. Barnes's 'cause' had, he claimed, already 'been often discussed' in front of them; and they had 'cleared' him 'many times of all Mr Topcliffe's inventions'. For procedural reasons, said Edward Fenner, this was simply impossible. English law did not work like that. The long and the short of the business was that one Nicholas Blackwell, a servant of Jane Wiseman, swore that Barnes consorted with and maintained Jones in a way which was sufficient to trigger the penalties of the 1585 statute. But what was extraordinary was the defence which Barnes said that he was allowed to mount on his own behalf. Jones was also present and simply denied what Blackwell said. A written statement from one Stannardine Passy, who was inexplicably absent, was produced by Topcliffe. A slew of arguments ensued over whether Passy had written it at all. The signature differed from the rest of the document. The burden of it was that Passy had seen Jones say Mass in front of various Catholics, including three of the surviving members of the ill-fated Bellamy family. The clerical attire which he used (supplied by the Wiseman family) was produced by Topcliffe. The claim was that Barnes had assisted at the Mass.

There was by now considerable confusion, at least according to Barnes's narra-tive of the trial. In fact, the proliferation of details of who said what about what to whom must have left most of the court pretty confused. A key witness had not turned up and a principal witness statement was arguably a forgery. Barnes said that Passy had now withdrawn his statement, which in any case had been given under duress. In the face of Barnes's denial of all the accusations, Topcliffe splut-tered that Hethershall had had a copy of the *Conference*, 'wherein he would have had the puppet of Spain to have had right unto her Majesty's crown'. Topcliffe brought 'forth the book and asked' Barnes if he knew 'the same'. Barnes said he had never seen the thing in his life.

Then, allegedly with the leave of the court, Barnes recited his defence. The 'first original of all my troubles', declared Barnes, 'proceeded' from that fornicating bitch, Anne Bellamy, the one who had betrayed the Jesuit priest Robert Southwell. Having got herself in the family way (with Topcliffe of all people), Topcliffe and his equally loathsome sidekick Nicholas Jones had 'practised' with her for the arrest of the saintly Jesuit. She was the one who had sent the fatal letter telling Topcliffe how to identify Southwell and where he would be concealed at Uxendon manor. After this, Anne B. had married Jones in effect to cover up Topcliffe's fling with her—and there had been some urgency since she was, at that point, begin-ning to resemble a beached whale.

Topcliffe had then demanded a property settlement from the family in order to keep Jones in funds; and, when the Bellamys refused, Topcliffe had caused Anne B. to accuse various others, 'promising and assuring...to obtain their liv-ings' via a royal grant once the accused were convicted. So she had denounced

THE COMING OF TOLERATION IN LATE ELIZABETHAN ENGLAND? 277

Barnes, saying that he harboured the priest George Birkhead. In other words, the process against himself, so Barnes asserted, was a shameful spin-off from the equally shameful proceedings against the Jesuit priest and martyr Southwell.

The crucial point, however, was not so much the details of how he had been arrested (Barnes had certainly provided maintenance for, and had been an associate of, George Birkhead and other clergy) as what Barnes was now allowed to say about Topcliffe's methods of suborning and threatening witnesses. Topcliffe was such a phenomenal hypocrite that, in trying to extort incriminating information, he had threatened Mrs Bellamy that, 'unless she would condescend to that which her daughter accused her of, he would pick out a jury out of Middlesex that should condemn her'. Then 'he would hang her'. He had called her an 'old witch' and claimed that she had had intercourse with twenty seminary priests. This coerced her into giving evidence against Barnes, which she later retracted.

Having eventually failed with Mrs Bellamy, Topcliffe and Nicholas Jones then started to intimidate one James Atkinson into testifying against Barnes. Atkinson remembered that, when he initially proved non-compliant, Jones 'swore that...he would dash out' his 'brains with his sword' and 'Mr Topcliffe swore' that, if Atkinson would not accuse Barnes, 'he would chop off his legs with his sword that lay there; he would break his thighs, send him to a place where the plague should devour him, being, at that time, in the city of London, or else where the rats should eat the flesh from his bones'. Initially Atkinson decided to give in—he was trembling so violently that Jones asked him 'if he were troubled with a quaking ague'. Barnes had been arrested on 5 June 1594 and was initially shoved into the king's bench gaol. Then, on the basis of suborned and intimidated witness statements, he had been removed to the Gatehouse prison, where he had languished ever since in conditions of filth, misery, and airless 'stench'. When Atkinson withdrew his confession, Topcliffe said he would suborn the jury empanelled for Barnes's case; he would also torture Barnes and, 'going with him from Mr Attorney's unto' the house of Lord Burgh (the puritan who had recently served as ambassador to Scotland and who was a relative of Topcliffe by marriage), Topcliffe had 'threatened to hang' Barnes 'as high as the trees growing there' and would 'make' Barnes's 'head and feet to meet together' and 'enforce' him finally to confess that with which he was charged.

Only after the verbal equivalent of pages and pages of denunciation of the late Elizabethan State, or at least its under-officers, as a corrupt tyranny, did the presiding officials say that Barnes 'urged matters too much against Mr Topcliffe, being such a member for the State; and that it made' Barnes's 'matter to have the less favour'. He was told to 'go forward to the matter of' his 'indictment'. Fenner went so far as to describe Topcliffe as a 'good statesman'. But Barnes was still able to protest that Topcliffe had entrapped him and held him prisoner unjustly. Barnes declared that he had often sued 'unto the lords of the council for my

278   CATHOLICS AND TREASON

deliverance' and 'my lord treasurer said it was a shame unto the whole State to detain men in prison so long, without trial or deliverance; and Sir Robert Cecil, looking upon my petition, said [that] they could not in honour deny it, being so reasonable'.[63] Actually this did not, in the short term, do Barnes much good. On 3 July 1598 a jury found him guilty and he was sentenced to hang.[64] Mrs Wiseman refused to plead and was sentenced to the *peine forte et dure*, the same penalty as had been inflicted on Margaret Clitherow.[65]

As for the Franciscan priest John Jones, one of the judges, the supposedly independent and fair-minded John Clench, told him that he might well not have been actively involved in conspiracy but he was guilty under the 1585 statute. Sentence was carried out on 12 July 1598 at the execution site of St Thomas-a-Watering in Southwark.[66] Topcliffe was present at the gallows, trying to get the condemned man to admit that he would, given the chance, have taken part with an invading army, though the Franciscan priest ignored him. To damn the condemned man in the opinion of the spectators on that day, Topcliffe then recalled the 1585–6 exorcisms conducted by the Jesuit William Weston, a narrative of which had been copied out by Robert Barnes himself.[67] During the trial Topcliffe had produced 'the book of exorcisms' and had declared that Barnes had written it, which Barnes admitted, 'out of a copy of Mr Bartholomew Bellamy'.[68] At the execution, wrote Henry Garnet, the crowd was on Jones's side and, when the officials moved to draw the cart away, three or four men temporarily interposed in order to let Jones carry on speaking.[69]

---

[63] TD, III, pp. cxci–ccx. For allegations of Topcliffe's malfeasance in the case of both Barnes and a former servant, one John Harrison, whom Topcliffe accused of being a seminary priest, see also *APC 1595-6*, pp. 237, 241. The consensus is that Atkinson died as a result of Topcliffe's further use of torture: TD, III, p. cciv; Pollen, *UD*, p. 287.

[64] Pollen, *UD*, pp. 364–5. John Pollen identified one Henry Lok as an agent in the proceedings against Barnes and remarked on the 'very inferior puritan hymns which he wrote in later life, after he had failed in the dishonourable trade of spying'. Lok claimed that he was Mrs Wiseman's nephew. He appears to have been the puritan MP of the same name: Pollen, *UD*, pp. 364, 370, 374–5; *HC 1558-1603*, II, pp. 484–5; M. Rankin, 'Richard Topcliffe and the Book Culture of the Elizabethan Catholic Underground', *Renaissance Quarterly* 72 (2019), pp. 492–536, at p. 509.

[65] Caraman, *JG*, pp. 52–3; Pollen, *UD*, pp. 366–7.   [66] Challoner, *MMP*, pp. 234–5.

[67] Pollen, *UD*, p. 373 (ABSJ, Anglia II, no. 40); ABSJ, GC p. 498 (translation); *HMCS*, VIII, pp. 273–4; Challoner, *MMP*, pp. 234–5, citing Anthony Champney's 'Annales' and Garnet's account which had found its way into Bishop Yepes's *Historia Particular de la Persecucion de Inglaterra...* (Madrid, 1599). The 'book of exorcisms', it appears, was passed by Sir Robert Cecil to Richard Bancroft and Samuel Harsnett, and was used in Harsnett's *A Declaration of Egregious Popish Impostures...* (1603). Barnes denied that he had personally been at the exorcisms and he insisted that, 'touching my allegiance to my queen and country, I showed manifest signs thereof in 1588, well known to many captains and gentlemen in the country' (*HMCS*, VIII, p. 274), a claim which he made also in an undated letter to Lord Keeper Puckering when he refuted Topcliffe's allegation that he (Barnes) had procured a Mass to be said for the success of the Armada: BL, Harleian MS 6998, fo. 24[r]. This suggests that he may have stood alongside the first Viscount Montague in summer 1588 when he offered his services against the Spaniards: Questier, *C&C*, pp. 124, 167–8.

[68] ABSJ, Anglia II, no. 41, fo. 137[r–v] (material omitted from transcript in TD, III).

[69] Pollen, *UD*, p. 374 (ABSJ, Anglia II, no. 40); ABSJ, GC p. 500 (translation). According to Garnet, writing on 21 October 1598, 'one Christopher Blackall of the Temple', who was 'unknown to be a

THE COMING OF TOLERATION IN LATE ELIZABETHAN ENGLAND? 279

We might still think that, because the proceedings ended with the death of the godly Franciscan priest and the sentencing of Mr Barnes and Mrs Wiseman, the public was not witnessing some sort of turn towards tolerance. Nor was there much clemency on view in York at this time. There were four Catholics hanged there between April and September 1598. One of these people, John Bretton, was aggressively separatist.[70] He was said to have spoken against the queen. He was executed on 1 April 1598 for felony under the 1581 statute against seditious words (23 Eliz., *c.* 2). He was the only post-Reformation Catholic to be executed under this piece of legislation.[71] Peter Snow, executed at York on 15 June 1598 with his harbourer Ralph Grimston, a gentleman resident at Nidd, was one of those clergy who had been spotted at Grosmont priory.[72] Challoner, following the evidence collected for Richard Smith in the 1620s, concedes that Grimston, who had aided and assisted him, had, 'as it is said', raised 'his weapon to defend him at the time of his apprehension'.[73] About the fourth victim, the priest Richard Horner, however, we know virtually nothing.[74]

In the case of the Franciscan priest, Jones, probably nothing could have saved him, but neither Robert Barnes nor Mrs Wiseman became martyrs. Despite

---

Catholic' (and whose father was a 'hot heretic'), on a moonlit 'night this last month went with his man and took down a quarter' of the executed priest 'about Lambeth fields' and was arrested: ABSJ, GC, p. 507 (ABSJ, Collectanea P/ii, p. 546).

[70] *AWCBC*, pp. 1258–62, 1273–7, 1286 (suggesting that Bretton must, at death, have been aged about 70).

[71] Challoner, *MMP*, p. 233; *AWCBC*, pp. 1263, 1268; *AWCBC*, p. 2493. Hugh Bowler argues that Anthony Champney 'must have been personally acquainted' with Bretton because 'their strongly recusant families lived in neighbouring villages': H. Bowler, 'Further Notes on the Venerable John Bretton', *RH* 15 (1979), pp. 1–10; *AWCBC*, p. 1287. Bretton had been detected as a separatist back in 1577: P. Ryan, 'Diocesan Returns of Recusants for England and Wales. 1577', *Miscellanea XII* (CRS 22, 1921), p. 32. For his sons who were ordained as clergy, see Anstr., I, p. 53, II, p. 36. The formal charges against him, extracted in the 1620s from the York assizes records by Bishop Richard Smith's agents, ended up in the so-called Paris catalogue. Bretton had allegedly hoped 'to see the death of the queen'. Unspecified individual witnesses said that he trusted 'to see the crown on the head of a Catholic'. By contrast, Thomas Worthington's martyr catalogue of 1614 stated simply that Bretton was 'reconciled to the Roman Catholic Church and urged others to embrace the same religion'. He 'denied the spiritual primacy of the queen': Bowler, 'Further Notes', pp. 6–7; AAW, B 28, no. 10, p. 318; *AWCBC*, p. 1291; see also H. Bowler, 'Exchequer Dossiers, 2: The Recusancy of Venerable John Bretton, Gentleman, and of Frances his Wife', *Biographical Studies* 2 (1953–4), pp. 111–34. Frances Bretton subsequently conformed (on 1 June 1601) in front of Archbishop Hutton: PRO, E 368/504, mem. 137ᵃ.

[72] Foley, *RSJ*, III, p. 6 (PRO, SP 12/245/24). For Grimston's arrest in November 1593, and for his indictment at the Lent assizes in 1594, see Foley, *RSJ*, III, p. 760; Morris, *TCF*, III (RHPN), p. 193; *AWCBC*, pp. 1294, 1297, 1301. For the information received from Ralph Fisher in 1626 about Grimston and Snow (Fisher had been arrested in Grimston's house in November 1593), see AAW, A IV, no. 22, p. 130; *AWCBC*, p. 1300.

[73] Challoner, *MMP*, p. 233; AAW, A IV, no. 22, p. 130. For the Grimston family and its Catholic associations, see R. Hughey and P. Hereford (eds), *Elizabeth Grymeston and her Miscellanea* (1934), esp. at pp. 76 f.

[74] Anstr., I, p. 175. In the case of another individual, Matthew Harrison, cited by Anthony Champney as having suffered martyrdom at York in 1599, we cannot be sure that he was executed there, or in fact anywhere else: Anstr., I, p. 152; Challoner, *MMP*, p. 236. Two other Catholics, John Lion and James Dowdall, are reckoned to have been martyred respectively in July and August 1599: Challoner, *MMP*, p. 236; M. S. Kristich, 'James Dowdall of Drogheda: An Irish Martyr', *Journal of the Armagh Diocesan Historical Society* 20 (2004), pp. 43–66; AAW, B 28, no. 10, p. 319.

280 CATHOLICS AND TREASON

Jones's impending execution, Barnes's friend George Birkhead had thought on 20 June 1598 that 'all sorts of people grow, as it were, weary of their fury against us, save only such as are our mortal enemies and incense her highness's indignation against us'. The 'pursuivants indeed are not so frequent nor wander up and down so often in such outrageous manner as they were wont to do', although there were more commissions being issued for the tracking down of the goods and estates of convicted recusants. Poor Catholics were still harried from pillar to post. Yet 'some rumours are cast abroad of peace, of toleration in religion' and 'of I cannot tell what'.[75]

Moreover, Barnes, who was the gentleman-servant of a leading Catholic peer, had, as we saw, been permitted in a formal court hearing to denounce the enforcement of the statutes against Catholic separatism and to allege, more or less without interruption, that the knavery of Topcliffe and his friends was contrary to the will of the queen's leading privy councillors. It would have been almost unthinkable in the early 1590s, for example, for a defendant such as Barnes to have been allowed to say what he said. Moreover, as virtually everyone must have known, Barnes had actually been doing most of the things that Topcliffe alleged. In addition, even if hardliners in the North were dispatching the likes of outspoken Catholics such as John Bretton, there was still a chasm between those who thought that real and harsh coercion was the best way to deal with Catholic separatism and those who did not. Archbishop Hutton himself was unwilling even to accept that separatist Catholics should be compelled to listen to Protestant preachers, as he more or less said out loud in 1600 when Catholic prisoners in York Castle were forced to attend sermons. This exercise was instituted and presided over by Sir Robert Cecil's brother, Thomas, Lord Burghley, and it lasted for the best part of a year between late 1599 and late 1600.[76] Burghley did not share Hutton's opinions on this score. On 22 February 1600, in the sight of the prisoners, a visibly shaken seminary priest, James Bolland, 'with a sorrowful countenance and a quivering voice' read 'a recantation of his religion and priesthood'. Burghley boasted to his brother on 1 March 1600 that the 'country' was in 'good order' and, he believed, 'soon eighteen out of every twenty recusants will come to the church'. Even 'in the worst parts of this shire...500 have come in this three weeks so that a notable papist complained that the common people are declining

---

[75] ABSJ, Collectanea P/ii, p. 444ᵃ.

[76] Questier, 'Sermons', pp. 302–3. For the sermons, see William Richmond, 'A Trewe Storie of the Catholicke Prisoners in Yorke Castle...', ABSJ, A V, no. 6 (referred to in error in Questier, 'Sermons' as Anglia A II); Kn., VI, p. 260 (Knaresborough used the version of William Richmond's manuscript in the 'library of Richard Towneley Esq.'); Talbot, *MRR*, pp. 276–7; *AWCBC*, p. 1210; there is an extract of a separate narrative, covering the same events, in AVCAU, Scr. 21/2/2. Alban Butler provided Challoner with the narrative written by Lady Babthorpe (AAW, A VI, no. 100, pp. 367–70; ABP, pp. 399–408) which described, in passing, the sermon series; but Challoner relied on Knaresborough's transcripts from Richmond's account: Richard Challoner, *Memoirs of Missionary Priests...* (2 vols, Philadelphia, 1839), I, pp. 251–61 [excluded from Challoner, *MMP*]; ABP, pp. 401–3.

THE COMING OF TOLERATION IN LATE ELIZABETHAN ENGLAND? 281

from them'. But obviously they needed more encouragement. One of the prisoners, an ageing priest called Christopher Wharton, was hanged, drawn, and quartered on 28 March 1600. There was a sense that, among the internees in York Castle, there was a measure of support for the earl of Essex, who, in some quarters, had acquired a reputation as a favourer of tolerance. According to the castle gaol-keeper, Robert Redhead, the prisoners actively followed the fortunes of the earl. They cheered when it seemed that he was on the up, and they were overcome with dismay when he was not.[77]

Statistically it might appear that, in the later 1590s, not dissimilar numbers of Catholics were still being treated with the same brutal harshness as in previous years. But the persecution narratives that have survived point to the political uncertainties of the moment, and suggest that Catholics were increasingly able to ask whether the regime meant what it said about the supposed link between conformity and loyalty.

The Case of John Rigby

In London in 1600 there may have been a kind of test case over precisely that issue of Catholic non/conformity and alleged disloyalty and sedition. It took place right in the middle of the arguments between Catholics during the Archpriest Controversy about what constituted political obedience. A Lancashire gentleman, John Rigby, was, almost by accident it seems, indicted in the capital under the statute law against persuasion and reconciliation to Rome. The claim of Thomas Worthington's printed narrative of the case was that Rigby was in the service of Sir Edmund Hudlestone. Hudlestone's daughter, Mrs Fortescue, was 'summoned to the sessions house in the Old Bailey for causes of religion'. Because she was too ill to appear, Rigby went 'to testify ... for her in that court'.[78] Rigby ended up being indicted for treason. The point was that Rigby had been at one time a partial or occasional conformist. His 'circumstances, being narrow', said Bishop Challoner,

---

[77] Questier, 'Sermons', pp. 305, 306, 309–12; Richmond, 'A Trewe Storie', fo. 29ʳ; ARSJ, Anglia 37, fo. 60ᵛ. For Wharton's arrest by Sir Stephen Procter 'within the park of Sir William Ingleby', see Anstr., I, p. 377; PRO, STAC 8/18/1, fos 51ʳ, 118ʳ; PRO, STAC 8/19/10, pt I, fo. 22ʳ; C. Howard, *Sir John Yorke of Nidderdale 1565–1634* (1939), p. 14.

[78] Thomas Worthington, *A Relation of Sixtene Martyrs: Glorified in England in twelve Monethes. With a Declaration. That English Catholiques suffer for the Catholique religion. And that the Seminarie Priests agree with the Iesuites* (Douai, 1601), sig. A4ʳ⁻ᵛ; Challoner, *MMP*, p. 239; Caraman, *JG*, pp. 80–1, 232–3. Henry Hudlestone, the son and heir of the family, was a patron of John Gerard SJ: Caraman, *JG*, p. 33; see also Caraman, *HG*, p. 271. A raid on the Marshalsea prison on 26 February 1600 led to the arrest of forty-eight men and women who were listening to a sermon delivered there by a Scots Capuchin called John Chrysostom Campbell: *CSPD 1598–1601*, p. 398 (PRO, SP 12/274/50, fo. 71ʳ⁻ᵛ); *HMCS*, IX, p. 287 (Campbell's arrest, reported by Lord Cobham on 11 August 1599). One of those detained at the sermon was one 'Ralph Rigby, a late servant to Sir Edmund Hurlestone [*sic*]', who was then imprisoned in the Clink: PRO, SP 12/274/50, fo. 71ʳ—it is not clear if this is, in fact, John Rigby.

282   CATHOLICS AND TREASON

'obliged him to take to service, where, through human frailty (though he was always a Catholic in his heart) he sometimes went to the Protestant church, for which he afterwards heartily repented'.[79] Having repented, it was alleged, Rigby made his confession to the imprisoned Franciscan John Jones, that is, at some point before Jones ended up on the gallows in summer 1598. Rigby 'was by him reconciled to God' and, from 'that time', he 'lived a very exemplary life and was the instrument of the reconciliation of divers others'. In fact, it was John Gerard who gave Rigby absolution.[80]

Rigby appears to have been targeted by the prominent anti-papist Sir Richard Martin. Worthington's 1601 narrative said that Rigby, in the course of his 'service' to Sir Edmund Hudlestone, 'was sent by his master to Sir Richard Martin, alderman of London, about certain business'. What it was, Worthington left unstated; but Rigby's demeanour did not endear him to Martin, who harboured thoughts of revenge and got his chance when Rigby turned up to represent Mrs Fortescue.[81] Sir Richard was a prominent goldsmith and a former lord mayor of London. He and his wife, Dorcas Ecclestone, had been supporters of Thomas Cartwright against John Whitgift in the Admonition Controversy, so it was fairly clear where their political and religious sympathies lay.[82] Sir Richard had been one of London's sheriffs in 1581 and had supervised some of the executions of Catholic clergy at that time. Anthony Munday's *A Breefe and True Reporte of the Execution of Certaine Traytors* (1582) had been dedicated to him.[83]

As Worthington described it, Rigby behaved entirely appropriately in court in February 1600, 'but the commissioners' were 'much discontented to be thus frustrated of the gentlewoman's appearance'. Alderman Martin, perceiving Rigby 'to be the same man that had heretofore been with him and had offended him, suddenly and with choler began to examine him of his own faith and religion before he was otherwise apprehended or accused or had any cogitation of answering for himself'. Rigby responded with 'admirable resolution and courage to the

---

[79] Challoner, *MMP*, p. 238; Worthington, *A Relation*, sig. A3ᵛ–4ʳ; Dillon, *CM*, pp. 111–12. The Rigby narrative forms the first and major section of Worthington's *Relation*. Rigby was a cousin of Worthington (Rigby's grandmother Alice Rigby was a daughter of Edward Worthington of Blainscow): ABSJ, CP (John Rigby), citing F. R. Raines (ed.), *The Visitation of the County Palatine of Lancaster...1613* (Chetham Society, 82, Manchester, 1871), p. 24 (though the martyr John Rigby is not shown there).

[80] Challoner, *MMP*, pp. 238–9; Worthington, *A Relation*, sig. A3ᵛ–4ʳ; Caraman, *JG*, p. 80.

[81] Worthington, *A Relation*, sig. A4ʳ⁻ᵛ.

[82] *ODNB*, sub Martin, Richard (article by C. E. Challis); Collinson, *EPM*, p. 140; M. White, 'Power Couples and Women Writers in Elizabethan England: the Public Voices of Dorcas and Richard Martin and Anne and Hugh Dowriche', in D. Wolfthal and R. Voaden (eds), *Framing the Family: Representation and Narrative in the Medieval and Early Modern Periods* (Medieval and Renaissance Texts and Studies, 2005), pp. 119–38; M. White, 'A Biographical Sketch of Dorcas Martin: Elizabethan Translator, Stationer, and godly Matron', *Sixteenth Century Journal* 30 (1999), pp. 775–92.

[83] In a dedication written on 6 November 1591, Samuel Cottesford had addressed Martin (among others) and urged him to root papistry out of the city of London; see Samuel Cottesford, *A Treatise against Traitors...*(1591), sigs *ʳ⁻****ᵛ.

THE COMING OF TOLERATION IN LATE ELIZABETHAN ENGLAND? 283

astonishment of his adversaries'. This landed him in gaol. What Worthington then reproduces in his text is said to have been 'written by' Rigby 'himself, word by word'. Worthington's pamphlet, as is obvious from its extended title, was a pointed contribution to the Archpriest Dispute. It served as a riposte to the claims by some of the secular clergy that the Jesuits in England were harming the Catholic community. Worthington was trying to refute the assertions made by some of the appellant clergy that the Tudor regime would grant toleration to the right sort of Catholic, that is, if they guaranteed their loyalty to the queen and expelled the Jesuit firebrands from within their midst. There followed in Worthington's text 'a copy' of Rigby's examination on 14 February 1600 before Alderman Martin, Justice Dale, and others. Martin was evidently determined to make an issue of it and asked, 'what are you that will swear' (as the 'oath' was tendered)—'a papist?' Rigby was evasive, though he probably did not help matters by laughing at Martin's words—to which Martin responded, 'are you a papist, a Protestant, a puritan or what religion are you of?' Faced with a long session of, as it were, religious taxonomy for dummies, Rigby would not give a direct reply, but he also point-blank refused to 'go to church'. After a further to-and-fro exchange about exactly what kind of Catholic Rigby was, it emerged that he had been a conformist of some sort, though he had, he said, never received the Protestant communion and had ceased conforming once he was taken into service by the Hudlestones and the Fortescues. Rigby obfuscated about how far he had altered his religion and said he would take the queen's part in a military confrontation with the papacy. But he clammed up when asked what he would do if the pope 'should come to settle the Catholic religion'. Unsurprisingly, Rigby refused to take the oath of supremacy. On 17 February, Rigby appeared before Lord Chief Justice Popham and was asked the same sort of questions. He said that Sir Edmund Hudlestone was a conformist and volunteered the, as we saw, false information that he, Rigby, had been reconciled by the recently executed John Jones.[84]

Rigby was, on 3 March 1600, 'brought to...[his] trial', but 'nothing was said' to him. On the evening of that day he was summoned before the judges, Gawdy and Dale. Francis Gawdy said that he had been told by one of Archbishop Whitgift's servants that Rigby now believed that he 'had answered...ignorantly'. He was 'sorry for that' which he had 'done' and was 'willing to become a good subject and go to church'. If he did this, his admission of a treasonable offence would be overlooked.[85] Gawdy had been a client of the Howard family and had a connection via

---

[84] Worthington, *A Relation*, sig. A5^r–8^r. Another anti-appellant, Thomas Fitzherbert, incorporated a description of Rigby's sufferings in his pamphlet of 1602: Thomas Fitzherbert, *A Defence of the Catholyke Cause...*(Antwerp, 1602), fo. 10^r; see also Richard Verstegan, *Brief et Veritable Discours, de la Mort d'aucuns Vaillants et Glorieux Martyrs...*(Antwerp, 1601); R. Verstegan, *Corte ende Waerachtich Verhael...*(Antwerp, 1601); A. G. Petti, 'Richard Verstegan and Catholic Martyrologies of the Later Elizabethan Period', *RH* 5 (1959–60), pp. 64–90, at pp. 82–5.

[85] Worthington, *A Relation*, sigs A8^v–B^r.

284 CATHOLICS AND TREASON

marriage with the former lord chancellor, Hatton, to whom he may have owed his nomination as a justice of the queen's bench.[86] Rigby absolutely denied that he had been 'sorry' for anything but still claimed to be a good subject of the queen. It is possible that his remarks were informed by the knowledge that the queen's agents, led by Sir Robert Cecil, were about to go to Boulogne for the, in the end, abortive peace negotiations there. Justice Dale was, by contrast, openly hostile: 'you are a cogging cozening fellow and get your living, no man knows how, by cogging and lying'. Rigby reminded Dale that 'the ancestors of the house... whence I came were gentlemen five hundred years before your grandfather was [a] justice'.[87]

On the following day, proceedings began against Rigby at the 'sessions at St Margaret's Hill' in Southwark. The case, although hardly very prominent in the great scheme of late Elizabethan politics, incorporated a real sense of the contingencies created by the archpriest business. In the face of a treason indictment, Rigby launched a direct attack on the State's interpretation of the law against reconciling to Rome. He said that he had indeed been reconciled, as he 'lawfully might be' for 'it is also allowed in your book of common prayer, in the visitation of the sick that, if any man find himself burdened in conscience, he should make his confession to the minister'. Secondly, he was, he said, 'never reconciled from any obedience to my prince, for I obey her still'. Although he 'sometimes went to church against' his will, he was 'never of any other religion than the Catholic' one. 'Thirdly', although Rigby 'went to church' in the past, this was 'for fear of temporal punishment'. He was 'never minded to fall from the old religion'. He 'needed no reconciliation'. Fourthly, the judges should explain 'the meaning of the statute to the jury'. Was it 'treason for a man fallen into the displeasure of God, through his sins, to be reconciled to God again by him to whom God has committed the authority of reconciliation', that is, a priest? The judges said it was a 'Romish priest' and therefore treason. But Rigby said 'it was by a Catholic priest who had the liberty of the prison'. Any man could 'come unto him'. By 'the statute', this was 'no treason'.[88]

Via a quadruple lock, Rigby thus questioned most of the assumptions behind the 1580s legislation which, if his assertions were true, was now redundant. This is not to say that Rigby's arguments were of themselves particularly novel. But in the context of the debates during the Archpriest Controversy it was certain that what happened to Rigby would be taken by the archpriest George Blackwell's supporters as good evidence that what they said about the queen's malign and

---

[86] *HC 1558–1603*, II, p. 178.
[87] Worthington, *A Relation*, sig. B[r–v]. For Dale's committing to prison those Catholics who were arrested at the Clink prison on Low Sunday 1602, see RC, p. 55 (AAW, A VII, no. 39); p. 324 n.139 below.
[88] Worthington, *A Relation*, sig. B2[r–v].

THE COMING OF TOLERATION IN LATE ELIZABETHAN ENGLAND? 285

persecutory regime was true. Appellant pamphleteers, by contrast, did not celebrate the likes of Rigby.

Justice Gawdy was perplexed and urged Rigby not to throw his life away needlessly: 'her Majesty and her laws are merciful. If you will yet conform yourself and say here, before the jury goes forth, that you will go to church and submit your self, we will proceed no further'; but Rigby said that he would then 'fall into the bottomless pit of Hell'. So that was that. Even after sentence was passed, Gawdy (as Clench had done with Margaret Clitherow) asked again whether the accused would not relent, or just offer something by way of compliance and accommodation; but Rigby would not budge. Gawdy was hardly gratified when Rigby announced that he forgave the court and 'all other persecutors' whatsoever. But the judge was still unwilling that sentence should be carried out. Rigby carried on under a reprieve until the next assizes, on 19 June.[89]

After sentencing was deferred, Rigby wrote out an account of his travails and 'sent it to a dear friend who keeps safe the original'.[90] But evidently copies were circulated and sent out of the country. From Brussels one Catholic commentator reflected on the verdict in Rigby's case—the letter was dated 16/26 April 1600, that is, after conviction but while Rigby was still reprieved. This writer thought that, whatever happened to Rigby, the persecution of Catholics in their 'lands and goods' was 'worse than ever'. The ubiquitous parasite Thomas Felton had a private commission to throw convicted recusants off their lands and take their goods and chattels, in the performance of which function he was 'borne out' by Lord Chief Justice Popham, 'and [by] some others in authority, in what injustice soever' that 'he commits'.[91] It was hardly encouraging that 'this manner of rigorous proceeding' should be used 'in the very time of parley of peace' at Boulogne, where there were negotiations in progress to try to end the war against Spain. It gave 'us small hope of any ease or toleration to ensue thereby unto Catholics as many expected that there would' be. On the other hand, says this writer, the queen's government was ill-advised to provoke Catholics when, 'in all reason and policy', it would have been better for the safety of the realm and the security of the queen, by 'clemency' and 'some merciful toleration', to 'regain their hearts' and not to drive them to desperation by these 'violent rigorous courses'.[92] More to the point, no one could ignore the widely circulating and ever more insistent rumours in Flanders and across the Continent that, when James Stuart took the English crown, he would make changes to the government of the national Church. 'With years' he 'grows

---

[89] Ibid., sig. B2^v–4^r.   [90] Ibid., sig. B4^r.

[91] PRO, SP 77/6, fo. 157^r (*CSPD 1598–1601*, p. 421). This letter was probably obtained and sent back to England by the intelligencer John Petit. For Thomas Felton, see T. Cogswell, 'Destroyed for doing my Duty: Thomas Felton and the Penal Laws under Elizabeth and James I', in K. Fincham and P. Lake (eds), *Religious Politics in Post-Reformation England: Essays in Honour of Nicholas Tyacke* (Woodbridge, 2006), pp. 177–92; T. Cogswell, 'John Felton, Popular Political Culture, and the Assassination of the Duke of Buckingham', *HJ* 49 (2006), pp. 357–85.

[92] PRO, SP 77/6, fo. 157^r (*CSPD 1598–1601*, p. 421).

286 CATHOLICS AND TREASON

wise in this point, beginning...to comply with Catholic princes' and 'promising further that he will be a Catholic when he has obtained the crown of England and tolerate Catholic religion in his country the meanwhile'. A report had come from Rome that William Creighton and one Dr Drummond were assuring the pope and curia in Rome that James's queen, Anne of Denmark, was a 'zealous Catholic' and that she was 'reconciled and confessed often'. This made a nonsense of the treatment of people such as Rigby who had been condemned merely for being reconciled to Rome. Moreover, said these rumours, James had been influenced 'by reason of a miracle happened to him by an Agnus Dei' given to him by Anne. It had saved him at sea from the storm called up by the North Berwick witches, with whom James's mortal enemy the earl of Bothwell was supposed to have been in league. The writer of this letter was far from convinced that the Scots court would honour its promises, but, even so, the persecution of Catholics in England might serve as the 'very highway and the best means' for James to take Elizabeth's crown.[93]

This did not prevent Rigby's eventual fate. Indeed, it may have contributed to it. On Thursday, 19 June 1600, in Southwark the notoriously hard-line judge, George Kingsmill, was the one who sat 'upon criminal matters'. 'Justice Gawdy [sat] upon civil [matters] only.' Rigby 'was produced again to the bar and [was] asked' by Kingsmill 'whether he would yet go to the church, or no'. He made it clear that he would not and was told that his time was up. We cannot, as with so many of these accounts, verify exactly what happened here. But Worthington's narrative insisted that it was 'well known...that the judges put his name twice in the calendar of those that were to die' on the following Saturday, 'and twice out again the same day, before he was executed'. Justice Gawdy tried 'to reprieve him longer'. Justice Kingsmill, however, 'would needs have him to die'. In the end, Justice Gawdy, 'seeing his intention crossed by Kingsmill, who the third time put his name in that calendar again, and so delivered it up amongst those which should die, turned himself from the company and was, by some, seen to weep'.[94]

When, on 21 June 1600, Rigby was finally executed at St Thomas-a-Watering, so Worthington's narrative claimed, Roger Manners, earl of Rutland, and Captain Edmund Whitelock, who were both in the circle of the earl of Essex, publicly declared their sympathy for Rigby. Whitelock asked for his prayers.[95] It may be that here the conformist Catholic wing of Essex's entourage was signalling a kind

---

[93] PRO, SP 77/6, fo. 157^{r-v} (*CSPD 1598–1601*, p. 421).

[94] Worthington, *A Relation*, sig. B4^r–5^v; Challoner, *MMP*, pp. 242–3.

[95] Worthington, *A Relation*, sig. B7^v; Challoner, *MMP*, pp. 243–4. The earl of Rutland's family was one of those that may have offered patronage to John Gerard: Caraman, *JG*, pp. 180, 250. For Whitelock, see *ODNB*, *sub* Whitelock, Edmund (article by R. Spalding); J. P. Sorlien (ed.), *The Diary of John Manningham*...(Hanover, N.H., 1976), pp. 130, 344.

THE COMING OF TOLERATION IN LATE ELIZABETHAN ENGLAND?   287

of protest against what they took to be religious persecution, though Rigby's outspokenness caused the officials to butcher him with gratuitous cruelty.[96]

Of course, most extant Catholic execution narratives of this period tend to avoid mentioning the fractures inside the contemporary Catholic community. The whole purpose of such narratives was to make Catholic Christianity in England appear to be one and indivisible and to persuade the public that it represented a united front against those who, for whatever reason, seemed to hate true religion. But this account of Rigby was, as we saw, embedded in an aggressively pro-Jesuit and anti-appellant pamphlet. Virtually no contemporary who read it could have failed to understand the implications of the way that Rigby's trial and execution were set out. As the reign neared its end, the prosecutions of Catholics were increasingly bound up with the political manoeuvring associated with the coming accession of James VI of Scotland and the fissures among Catholics that this imminent event caused.

---

[96] Worthington, *A Relation*, sigs B8ᵛ–Cʳ; Challoner, *MMP*, pp. 243–5. The barbarity of the execution was reported to Robert Persons via a letter of 1 August 1600 written by James Standish: ABSJ, Collectanea N/i, p. 56ᵇ.

10

The Appeal to Rome and the Struggle for the Memory of the Martyrs

The *Fin de Siècle* Disputes among Catholic Clergy and the Question of Persecution

As we saw, by the stage that John Rigby was put to death, the so-called Archpriest Dispute was already raging inside the Catholic community. It served as a running commentary on some of the major questions generated by the increasingly imminent change of dynasty.[1] As John Bossy remarked, it also had a 'comic side'. If one wanted to know what it was like, at least as far as the quarrels among clergy in the prisons were concerned, one needed only to summon up a 'mental picture of the younger members of an Oxbridge combination room interned for the duration' but, at the same time, 'trying to turn it into an evangelical community and a light to the Gentiles'.[2] The often visceral dislikes that some clergy harboured for others came out into the open as the dispute became increasingly public, and those dislikes were themselves exacerbated as different interest groups tried to calculate who might be included in, or excluded from, royal favour when the new regime was inaugurated.

Those antagonisms which were generated by the archpriest business from time to time became caught up in the State's officials' attempts to enforce the treason law against Catholic clergy. Thus, when Thomas Benstead and Thomas Sprott were arrested, and were executed at Lincoln on 1 July 1600, the case sparked rumours that this had happened because of the factional divisions among Catholics.[3] Sprott was a known supporter of the recently appointed archpriest,

---

[1] See J. H. Pollen, *The Institution of the Archpriest Blackwell: A Study of the Transition from Paternal to Constitutional and Local Church Government among the English Catholics, 1595 to 1602* (1916); Lake and Questier, *Archpriest*.

[2] Bossy, *ECC*, pp. 44–5. For the troubles in the English College in Rome during this period, see A. Kenny, 'The Inglorious Revolution 1594–1597', *Venerabile* XVI (1957), pp. 240–58, XVII (1958), pp. 7–25, 77–94, 136–55.

[3] *AWCBC*, pp. 1352–3. For the circulation and publication on the Continent of narratives concerning Sprott and Benstead, see *AWCBC*, pp. 1365–76; *Relacion del Martirio de los dos Sacerdotes...* (Seville, 1600); ARCR, I, no. 91 (suggesting that this pamphlet is taken from the same source as the material which appears in Thomas Worthington, *A Relation of Sixtene Martyrs: Glorified in England in twelve Monethes. With a Declaration. That English Catholiques suffer for the Catholique religion. And that the Seminarie Priests agree with the Iesuites* (Douai, 1601)); Richard Verstegan, *Brief et Veritable Discours, de la Mort d'aucuns Vaillants et Glorieux Martyrs...* (Antwerp, 1601), sigs Cii^v–Diii^r.

Catholics and Treason: Martyrology, Memory, and Politics in the Post-Reformation. Michael Questier, Oxford University Press. © Michael Questier 2022. DOI: 10.1093/oso/9780192847027.003.0010

THE APPEAL TO ROME 289

George Blackwell.[4] Some of the archpriest's friends concluded that their appellant opponents had informed against Benstead. Benstead had escaped from Wisbech on 10 March 1600 and had then been sent by Henry Garnet to work in Lincolnshire, where he was apprehended again.[5]

Faced with the news of the arrest, some people concluded that the archpriest's enemies were enlisting the powers of the State in their own war with their Catholic opponents. Such people were behaving exactly like the renegades who in the early 1590s had betrayed Catholics to the authorities. It was no secret that Benstead hated the leading appellant Christopher Bagshaw, who, indeed, did not endear himself to people and seems to have had something like a clerical version of Tourette's syndrome. In Rome in 1601, Persons put together a large volume, under the title A Briefe Apologie, for publication in Antwerp and circulation back in England. In it he copied out the text of a letter written by Benstead on 28 April 1600 to Garnet, in which the martyr condemned the proceedings of the appellants and said how reprehensible the behaviour of their faction in Wisbech, led by Bagshaw, had been. Bagshaw had said that he credited the claims made about Jesuit involvement in the recent Squire Plot, an alleged attempt to assassinate the queen. Benstead averred that the accusations were utterly false. He and Bagshaw went at it hammer and tongs over the veracity of the plot allegations. Bagshaw declared that the Jesuits 'used nothing but dissembling and equivocations'. Benstead mounted a qualified defence of equivocation (the shade of Southwell was clearly not very far away) and Bagshaw snapped back with an unqualified denunciation of it. Persons declared that Benstead's and Sprott's arrest, soon afterwards, near the Tower of London, was not an accident, as one of Benstead's letters implied.[6] Putting two and two together, it looked as if Bagshaw must have gone straight to the authorities and told them not only where Benstead was but also that he was the wrong sort of Catholic.

This was, in fact, one of those occasions when two and two did not equal four. Or, rather, the increasingly toxic relationships between some Catholics made it inevitable that people would jump to conclusions. The prosaic truth was that the arrest had been just sheer bad luck. In his pamphlet entitled An Appendix to the

---

[4] AWCBC, p. 1351; ABSJ, Collectanea P/ii, pp. 570^b–1^b; ARSJ, Anglia 37, fo. 72^v.

[5] AWCBC, p. 1362; Anstr., I, p. 33. In mid-August 1600, Garnet affirmed that he had assisted Benstead both before and after he broke prison at Wisbech 'and sent him into Lincolnshire about the beginning of May, to be placed there': ABSJ, GC (ABSJ, Collectanea P/ii, pp. 552^b–3^a). Sprott had also been assisted by Garnet: Anstr., I, p. 329.

[6] Robert Persons, A Briefe Apologie, or Defence of the Catholike Ecclesiastical Hierarchie, & Subordination in England…(n.p. [Antwerp], n.d. [late 1601]), sig. Cc2^v–5^r; ABSJ, Anglia II, no. 57; ARSJ, Anglia 37, fos 79^v–80^r. See also Martin Aray, The Discoverie and Confutation of a Tragical Fiction, Devysed and Played by Edward Squyer…(Antwerp, 1599). By contrast, the leading appellant Thomas Bluet was happy to affirm in March 1602 the reality of the plot (in representations made to Cardinals Borghese and Arrigoni, the adjudicators of the 1602 appeal to Rome): CSPD 1601–3, p. 170. For the Squire Plot, see F. Edwards, 'Sir Robert Cecil, Edward Squier and the Poisoned Pommel', RH 25 (2001), pp. 377–414.

290   CATHOLICS AND TREASON

Apologie, Persons was forced to admit this. What had happened was that one of Benstead's letters had been mistaken for another, and this was how the confusion had occurred.[7] Garnet had had to tell Persons that unfortunately Benstead's death could not be blamed on Bagshaw and therefore, in Persons's pamphlet, 'those ten lines' which made the allegation 'should be blotted out'.[8] Dutifully, Persons instructed his readers that 'in the *Apologie*, pag. 20, the reader is to omit the nine lines immediately following these words: "Thus far wrote that good priest".[9] The appellant priest Robert Charnock subsequently vented his fury in print that many of Persons's books had been circulated 'uncorrected' so as to make it appear that Benstead had in effect been murdered by his co-religionists.[10]

In the context of the Archpriest Dispute's central questions, this might look like a peripheral matter. But one of the central issues in the dispute between different Catholic factions and interests was whether, on the one hand, Catholic (Jesuitical) sedition provoked the State's retaliation against all Catholics indiscriminately or whether, on the other, bad and quasi-schismatic Catholics (who were united only by their own self-interest and hatred of good Catholics) were selling out to a heretical regime, if necessary by betraying their friends and by allowing that regime to tyrannize over a divided Catholic body.

All this came out in Thomas Worthington's biting little martyrological pamphlet entitled *A Relation of Sixtene Martyrs*, the one which, as we saw in the last chapter, related in such detail what had happened to the unfortunate John Rigby. Worthington referred back to the case of the priest Christopher Wharton, who had come to grief in York in March 1600. It had been 'opprobriously objected' to Wharton, 'as also to some others, to the offence of many' and the 'scandal of the weak', that 'the seminary priests were' at enmity with 'the Jesuits'. Worthington's pamphlet was altered and augmented 'to explicate more fully' Wharton's 'answer to that false and absurd slander' as well as to add in new cases of persecution since the appearance of the first version of the pamphlet.[11]

Worthington then launched into a pamphlet-within-a-pamphlet account of why the appellant case could not be credited. It is probably the single clearest statement of the assumptions and world view of the supporters of the beleaguered archpriest Blackwell. The entire piece is phrased by reference to recent

---

[7] Robert Persons, *An Appendix to the Apologie...* (Antwerp, n.d. [late 1601 or early 1602]), fo. 25ʳ; Caraman, *HG*, p. 289. Sprott and Benstead were arrested at the Saracen's Head in Lincoln during the search for 'certain malefactors who had committed a robbery': Challoner, *MMP*, p. 245. Thomas Fitzherbert dwelt on the lack of proof for the charges against them: Thomas Fitzherbert, *A Defence of the Catholyke Cause...* (Antwerp, 1602), fos 12ᵛ–13ʳ, 13ᵛ.

[8] ABSJ, GC (ABSJ, Collectanea P/ii, p. 554ᵃ; 16 December 1601); Caraman, *HG*, p. 289.

[9] Persons, *An Appendix*, fo. 25ʳ.

[10] Robert Charnock, *A Reply to a Notorious Libell intituled a Briefe Apologie or Defence of the Ecclesiastical Hierarchie...* (n.p. [London], 1603), pp. 16–17.

[11] Worthington, *A Relation*, C7ᵛ *et seq.*, and 'An Advertisement to the Reader touching the contents, order and title of this book'.

THE APPEAL TO ROME   291

prosecutions of Catholic clergy and their patrons. These cases, said Worthington, demonstrated that Catholics in England were now a perfect representation of the Church under the cross of persecution. Worthington looked back to 1558 and to the coercion used in 'the last general revolt from the Catholic religion in our country'. The hierarchy was wiped out. The former prelates 'still kept their titles and right, as well of their dignities as of their holy functions'; but the 'ecclesiastical hierarchy of the Church of England, for lack of succession of ordinary spiritual pastors, did wholly decay and cease'. However, 'continually there remained some few constant Catholics, and some few Catholic priests, which ministered the holy sacraments'. The little flock survived and 'this good seed of Catholic religion, conserved by God's goodness, was...prospered much by sundry good books, written by diverse learned and zealous men, in defence of the Catholic faith'. The great William Allen saw the need for a 'succession of priests' and founded the Douai seminary and other colleges.[12] Worthington's point was that, after the new clergy started coming back into the country, 'then the seminaries and the Society, with other priests remaining of the old store', that is, Marian clergy ordained before November 1558, 'laboured jointly and merrily together for the conversion of our country *unamines* [*sic*] *in dono Dei*'.[13] The new priests flooded in 'and especially...Jesuits...whom the heretics little expected and less wished'. This produced a severe persecution. But 'no malice' was 'able to overthrow the work of God'. For 'Catholics increased in number, and in courage, and more were willing to suffer and to die for their faith than before'. 'More and more were incensed with [a] desire to go to the seminaries, and some immediately to the holy Society, that so they might enter into the same work and be participant of the same glorious reward', but all in order 'to convert their countrymen from schism and heresy'.[14]

The response was predictable enough. Malicious individuals shouted and screamed about 'treason, sedition' and 'conspiracy against the queen and the realm'. Of course, people with sense knew that this was rubbish and that these accusations were made 'for policy's sake'. The queen's cruelty was a vain attempt to crush the seminarists' 'zeal'. Who could be surprised at this? Christ himself said that he came to bring not peace but a sword. But it was noteworthy that 'some of the queen's council' concluded that it was 'vain to kill priests in England, so long as more come after them, from the seminaries and from a religious Society that dies not'. Recorder Fleetwood heard of the arrival of 'Lawrence Johnson...afterwards a martyr' and declared that 'we strive in vain', for 'this new brood will never be rooted out'. 'Doctor Humphrey of Oxford' regretted 'the putting to death of Father Campion'. This certainly showed that the appellants were talking bilge when they attacked the Society of Jesus and its friends, and demanded that 'all the

---

[12] Ibid., sig. D^r *et seq.*   [13] Ibid., sig. D3^{r-v}.   [14] Ibid., sig. D3^v–4^r.

292 CATHOLICS AND TREASON

Jesuits and many others' should be 'removed from this work both within and without the realm'. 'Whence then came this ill seed, this dislike, this dissension, this debate?' Well, obviously, from Satan. But if one wanted it explained in terms comprehensible to a historian of the emotions, it was jealousy. The Devil had 'so bewitched some by ambition, vain liking of themselves, and desire to be esteemed and preferred before others', that when those people saw 'other men do more good, have more credit and be more esteemed than themselves' they 'began to repine' and 'could not abide to hear others more commended than themselves'. As night followed day, 'hastiness of nature' and 'proneness to anger, with little mortification of inordinate passions...made some priests less desired of other Catholics'. Inevitably the 'diligence of heretics took hold of the occasions to nourish and egg forward these humorous fantasies'. This was how the shameful appeals to Rome against George Blackwell had started.[15]

But those who were not bewitched by Satan also had the spirit of self-sacrifice. Here the case of Christopher Wharton was particularly significant. He had 'always agreed with the reverend fathers of the Society of Jesus' and was not jealous of them; and he was 'as ancient, as grave and as learned a graduate of the university of Oxford' as any of the trouble-making appellants. Actually, he had been at Trinity College with the archpriest George Blackwell. Wharton was 'now exalted to a glorious crown of martyrdom'.[16]

Needless to say, this analysis of the outcome of these quarrels was hotly rejected by Worthington's enemies. As they saw it, it was the calculating and cynical interference in politics by the Society of Jesus and its friends that provoked the State to lash out by using the law against Catholic clergymen indiscriminately, some of whom might have been reckoned to be seditious, but others of whom were clearly innocent of what they were suspected to have done.

Accession Politics and the Contestation of Catholic Martyrdom

Not every case involving prosecutions of Catholic clergymen in the late Elizabethan period referred to the Archpriest Controversy. The indictments might just as easily be driven by local circumstances. In mid-July 1600 at Lancaster there were proceedings which resulted in the execution of the priests Edward Thwing and Robert Nutter. Nutter was one of five clergymen, including Thomas Benstead, who had broken out of Wisbech Castle on 10 March 1600.[17] As a prisoner in the castle, Nutter had been very firmly on the side of the Jesuit

---

[15] Ibid., sig. D4^v–6^v et seq. [16] Ibid., sig. F^r.
[17] Anstr., I, p. 260. While in Wisbech, Nutter already had a reputation as 'a very perilous man': PRO, SP 12/199/91, fo. 172^v. For his hostility to Christopher Bagshaw, see Inner Temple, Petyt MS 538/38, fo. 399^r (AWCBC, p. 1464); G. Anstruther, *A Hundred Homeless Years: English Dominicans 1558–1658* (1958), pp. 66–7.

THE APPEAL TO ROME   293

William Weston and he was, predictably, a supporter of the archpriest Blackwell, as was Thwing.[18] But the context for the prosecutions of these two priests seems to have been the authorities' perception of cascading lawlessness in Lancashire and, more immediately, the notorious incident of rioting reported there in May 1600, the same month as Thwing and Nutter were arrested. The instigator of the violence, alleged Bishop Richard Vaughan of Chester, was another Catholic priest, Thurstan Hunt. William Brettergh had been appointed high constable of West Derby hundred and had tried to make arrests of Catholic recusants in the parishes of Huyton and Childwall in May 1600. The result was a series of retaliatory physical attacks on Brettergh's farm animals.[19]

After absconding from Wisbech, Nutter must have gone straight back to Lancashire and into the middle of the local civil war between Brettergh and his enemies. On 21 May 1600, Bishop Vaughan had written to Sir Robert Cecil that he had been informed by the JP Thomas Hesketh of the recent 'apprehension of certain seminary priests'. One of them was under guard, while the other, 'Father Robert without a surname'—that is, Nutter—had absconded.[20] It appears that both Nutter and Thwing were taken after they had visited their friend the Jesuit Richard Cowling. Nutter was dragged away from his captors, probably while he was being taken to Lancaster Castle gaol. But he was then retaken. Vaughan took the opportunity to complain to Cecil that it was very difficult to arrest 'any priest in these parts because of their many favourers of the best sort'. Nutter had temporarily escaped from his keepers' clutches even when he was 'so well attended and watched'.[21]

Nutter was back in custody by 4 July. John Knaresborough recorded in the early eighteenth century that he had 'seen a manuscript account...now in the custody of Mr [Christopher] Tootell of Ladyewell near Preston in Lancashire' (Ladyewell Chapel at Fernyhalgh), that is, the uncle of Charles Dodd. The manuscript mentioned 'a dispute had in Lancaster Castle between these two martyrs on

---

[18] *AWCBC*, pp. 1413, 1415; ABSJ, Collectanea P/ii, pp. 570b–1b.

[19] See *ODNB*, *sub* Brettergh [née Bruen], Katherine (article by S. Hindle); B. W. Quintrell, 'Government in Perspective: Lancashire and the Privy Council, 1570-1640', *Transactions of the Historic Society of Lancashire and Cheshire* 131 (1982), pp. 35–62, at p. 48; R. G. Dottie, 'The Recusant Riots at Childwall in May 1600: a Reappraisal', in J. I. Kermode and C. B. Phillips (eds), *Seventeenth-Century Lancashire: Essays presented to J. J. Bagley* (Transactions of the Historic Society of Lancashire and Cheshire 132, Liverpool, 1983), pp. 1–28, esp. at pp. 15–16, doubting Hunt's involvement in the reported outbreaks of violence. For the identification of significant numbers of recusants in Childwall during the 1590s, see ibid., p. 5.

[20] *HMCS*, X, pp. 153–4. Vaughan's letter of 21 May must have crossed with that from the privy council of 25 May 1600, which noted Nutter's and Thwing's arrest: Anstruther, *A Hundred Homeless Years*, p. 71; *APC 1599–1600*, p. 348.

[21] *HMCS*, X, p. 154; Anstruther, *A Hundred Homeless Years*, pp. 71–2. For Richard Cowling's description of the Catholic community in his part of Lancashire, see Anstruther, *A Hundred Homeless Years*, pp. 70–1, citing ARSJ, FG 651/614; Anstruther, 'The Venerable Robert Nutter OP...', *Archivum Fratrum Praedicatorum* 27 (1957), pp. 359–402, at pp. 377, 396–7. Cowling's father had died as a prisoner in York Castle on 1 August 1587: Anstr., I, p. 91; see also p. 172 above.

294 CATHOLICS AND TREASON

the one part and two Protestant ministers'. The encounter had been sufficiently formal to have a title: 'A censure upon the disputation had within the castle of Lancaster the 4th day of July anno domini 1600 between the two reverend priests Mr Nutter and Mr Edward Thwing on the one side and Mr [Ralph] Tirer, vicar of Kendal' and 'Mr [Henry] Porter, vicar of Lancaster' on the other, 'in the presence of Mr Anderton, Mr Preston, etc.' Porter had a local reputation as a puritan. This all took place approximately three weeks before the trial, which occurred prob-ably on Monday 24 July, followed by the swift execution of sentence on 26 July.[22] Knaresborough noted that the copy he had seen 'was called the Catholic copy— by this I found there was another in the Protestants' hand and in many things differing from this'.[23]

At execution, Nutter refused to pray for Elizabeth or to acknowledge the law-fulness of her title. Thwing defended equivocation, the doctrine which had caused Robert Southwell so much trouble. Thwing argued, or was driven to defend the notion, that the pope could depose sovereign princes because 'he could...for any offence take away the freehold or inheritance of a private person being not his subject'. He had also said that the 'law made for the banishment of Jesuits and seminaries was wicked and unjust'. This gave Thomas Hesketh the opportunity at the arraignment to 'set forth unto all the hearers many just causes for which the law was made, and that that law was more merciful and mild than any of the ancient laws of this nation or any other nation against such like offendings'. At the gallows, Thwing was challenged by Hesketh to pray for Elizabeth and to say whether she was lawfully queen—he conceded that she was 'his lawful queen' and even said that he would pray for her—but he refused to deny that the pope's excommunication might have deprived the queen of her title. Hesketh claimed that 'many that were favourers of popery and were present at the arraignment and at the execution...did say that they would not have thought the papists had held such gross opinions, either against her Majesty or in religion', not least because Bishop Vaughan 'at the arraignment, touching divers points of religion, did so fully by disputation and argument with the priests discover their weakness that, I hope, many hearers that were before staggering are confirmed'. Hesketh did not 'doubt that much good' would 'come by this little severity, as well to terrify the priests from these parts, as for the satisfaction of the people'. For there was 'never any seminary priest executed in that country before'. That kind of 'toleration' had 'made them overbold'. If their harbourers were 'sharply dealt with', then 'the country would be reformed'.[24]

---

[22] *AWCBC*, pp. 1415, 1416; Anstruther, *A Hundred Homeless Years*, pp. 46, 72–5; Anstr., I, p. 260; Kn., VII, p. 216; Anstr., III, p. 230. Nutter's brother had been hanged in 1584; see p. 138 above. For Henry Porter, see *VCH Lancashire*, VIII, pp. 22–33 (under 'advowson').

[23] Kn., VII, p. 216.

[24] *HMCS*, X, pp. 284–5 (Thomas Hesketh to Sir Robert Cecil, 17 August 1600); Anstr., I, pp. 259–60, 356–7; Anstruther, *A Hundred Homeless Years*, pp. 72–4. At execution, Nutter declared that

THE APPEAL TO ROME   295

However, not everyone in the locality was convinced by Vaughan's rhetoric. According to Richard Cowling, some of the watching crowd swarmed over the scaffold on 26 July 1600 while the ritual horror of the execution was unfolding. They seized the body parts of the dismembered clergy—their 'garments, fingers, hair and anything they could lay their hands on'. Officials tried to stop the disorder, but the women who were present 'snatched the hearts of the martyrs from the blazing fire and made off with them'. Subsequently, the 'heads and quarters' were taken as well and ended up in Catholics' houses.[25]

A not dissimilar case was unfolding at Durham at the same point—a case in which a known loyalist was targeted for destruction by the hard men of the local State who evidently did not believe Catholics' professions of loyalty. On Midsummer Day, 24 June 1600, Bishop Tobias Matthew's factotum, the gentleman Henry Sanderson, had hunted down the priest Thomas Palaser in Durham. Palaser had been arrested and imprisoned in London back in March 1597, at which point he had represented himself to the clerk of the council, William Waad, as a loyal subject of the queen and had delivered a detailed report of the Spanish troop movements and naval strength which he had witnessed in Galicia and Portugal.[26] Palaser then, on 29 May 1597, absconded from the Gatehouse prison in London with the loyalist priests Francis Tilletson and Robert Hawkesworth. He had, as he explained to Waad, believed that Topcliffe had been on the verge of securing his arraignment, something which did not generally end well. Palaser said that he regarded Elizabeth as 'his sovereign and prince, and no other'. He said also that, if the regime wanted to stop foreigners invading, this could be 'easily performed... by granting liberty to Catholics'.[27] An informer in October 1597 had identified Palaser as 'a deadly enemy of the Jesuits' and stated that, presumably in addition to all the information that he had given about Spanish naval strength, he 'had concerted a plot to be presented' to Sir Robert Cecil 'for the removing of the Jesuits out of England'. Palaser had had to be dissuaded by Tilletson and Hawkesworth, for whom, apparently, this would have been taking loyalism a step too far.[28]

---

he had been professed into the Dominican order while he was in Wisbech: *HMCS*, X, p. 283; AAW, A XV, no. 109, p. 293. For Hesketh, see *HC 1558–1603*, II, p. 305; *HC 1604–29*, IV, pp. 666–7; Quintrell, 'Government in Perspective', p. 43.

[25] Anstruther, *A Hundred Homeless Years*, p. 75; *AWCBC*, pp. 1425–6 (ARSJ, FG 651/614). For the well-known attack on the vicar's house at Garstang on 20 August, not long after the executions of Nutter and Thwing, see *HMCS*, X, p. 311; *CSPD 1598–1601*, pp. 466–7 (PRO, SP 12/275/64); M. H. Curtis, 'The Trials of a Puritan in Jacobean Lancashire', in C. R. Cole and M. E. Moody (eds), *The Dissenting Tradition: Essays for Leland H. Carlson* (Athens, Ohio, 1975), pp. 78–99, at p. 86.

[26] *HMCS*, VI, pp. 124–5; *AWCBC*, pp. 1475–6, 1518–22 (citing a memorandum sent to the duke of Sessa, 1597, which claimed that Palaser had been dispatched back to England to counsel Catholics not to lose heart after the failure of the recent Armada and had caved in after his arrest: Vatican Library, Cod. Lat. 6227, fos 16^r–17^r).

[27] Anstr., I, pp. 267–8; *HMCS*, XIV, pp. 289–90; see also *HMCS*, VII, p. 223.

[28] *CSPI 1601–3*, p. 603 (PRO, SP 63/213, fo. 39^v).

296   CATHOLICS AND TREASON

Palaser's performance of loyalty was close enough to the general thrust of appellant claims about their duty to the queen. This was something which would often guarantee a Catholic cleric a measure of protection, even though, in late 1598, Palaser did in fact come out in support of the newly appointed archpriest, George Blackwell.[29] But, with Richard Sayer and John Talbot, Palaser was arrested, by Sanderson and others, in the house of John Norton at Lamesley in County Durham. Loyalists or not, they did not go quietly. As Tobias Matthew narrated it on 27 June 1600, Norton 'followed Mr Sanderson up and down the house with a fowling piece charged with hail shot'. He levelled his weapon at him and fired but, at that moment, one of Matthew's servants stabbed Norton with his rapier under the arm, and Norton missed his mark.[30]

Palaser, Norton, and Talbot were all sentenced on 6 August but not executed until 8 September 1600.[31] In the light of Palaser's one-time closeness to the appellant position, this may have been part of a public-relations exercise—that is, to show that posing as a loyalist did not cut it as far as Bishop Matthew and his friends were concerned and, equally, to demonstrate what they thought of the line being taken by some privy councillors, notably Bishop Bancroft, who offered a limited measure of patronage to appellant leaders.

Then, back in Lancashire, came the arrests of the priests Robert Middleton and Thurstan Hunt. The subsequent prosecution was driven in the first instance by local concerns. Hunt, as we saw, may have been involved in teaching William Brettergh a lesson about religious plurality in Lancashire by slashing his farm animals. The privy council was already demanding an investigation into the Brettergh affair. A council letter of 24 September 1600 had arrived in the county and had instructed Vaughan that the facts should be established as to what exactly had happened when hostile Catholic gangs had attacked the property of Brettergh and of another gentleman, John Wrightington.[32]

Hunt was arrested on 1 October 1600 when he and three others, fully tooled up, attacked the convoy taking Robert Middleton to Lancaster. Middleton had

[29] *AWCBC*, p. 1476. With, among others, Robert Nutter and Edward Thwing, Palaser signed a letter of 8 November 1598 in favour of Blackwell: ABSJ, Collectanea P/ii, pp. 570^b–1^b.

[30] *HMCS*, X, pp. 204–5; Anstr., I, p. 268. These events did not make it into Cuthbert Trollop's affidavit in 1626 about the arrest, though Leonard Brakenbury's account mentioned that Talbot drew his sword: AAW, A IV, no. 22, pp. 125, 126 (ABP, pp. 413–14); *AWCBC*, p. 1478. Trollop stated that he had heard from Eleanor Forcer (via a maid who used to work in Durham gaol) that there had been an attempt to poison Palaser and the others in prison, though why, considering they were shortly to be hanged, is far from clear: Challoner, *MMP*, pp. 250–1; AAW, A IV, no. 22, p. 125 (ABP, p. 413). For the proceedings in and after 1588 against Talbot for his recusancy, see *AWCBC*, pp. 1523–9. For the problem of John Norton's identity, see A. M. C. Forster, 'Who was John Norton, the Martyr?', *RH* 6 (1961–2), pp. 56–67.

[31] Challoner, *MMP*, pp. 250–1; *APC 1599–1600*, p. 543; for the date of execution, see *AWCBC*, pp. 1479. Sayer escaped death only by conforming: *AWCBC*, pp. 1490, 1491, 1493 (AAW, F 1, p. 994). Margaret Norton obtained a pardon for harbouring Palaser: *AWCBC*, pp. 1501–2 (PRO, C 66/1591, mm. 26–7).

[32] *CSPD 1598–1601*, p. 482 (PRO, SP 12/275/102).

been detained the day before by Sir Richard Houghton.[33] On 2 October 1600, Henry Breres of Preston testified that the previous day, as he and other officials were moving Middleton to Lancaster gaol, they were, five miles from Preston, passed on the road by a party of riders who demanded to know whether Middleton was a priest. Shortly after, as Breres and the others, with their prisoner, skirted past Garstang parish, they were confronted again by the 'same four horsemen' who demanded that Middleton should go with them. There was a violent struggle. One of the riders was none other than Hunt himself. He tried to shoot one of the officials, James Dike, but his pistol failed to fire. Hunt was unhorsed by Dike and fled the scene but was pursued. He was eventually apprehended about a mile away although, by this stage, his pistol was working and he fired it at, and wounded, one Gervase Traves. Hunt was taken to Preston and interrogated there. He claimed that he was acting in self-defence. In justification of the attempt to free Middleton, Hunt merely said that he had heard of his confrère's arrest and knew him to be an 'honest man' and that 'his cause was good'. He also thought that Catholics were not 'traitors'; he and his co-religionists were entitled to use force to defend themselves.[34]

---

[33] Pollen, *UD*, pp. 384, 386–7; Dottie, 'The Recusant Riots', pp. 12–13. For Middleton's arrest, see Pollen, *UD*, pp. 388–9 (ARSJ, Anglia 37, fos 58ᵛ–60ʳ; *AWCBC*, pp. 1644–7). Vaughan reported on 3 November 1600 concerning his enquiry into the 'riots committed on the person and the cattle' of William Bretiergh, who himself was given the letter to take to Cecil in London. The 'chief authors', said Vaughan, 'had conveyed themselves out of the way', but 'the principal seducer of the people in that part to such barbarous practices was Thurstan Hunt, a desperate seminary priest'; he was 'a treacherous practiser and barbarous butcher' and had 'plotted and performed all the outrages in these parts' and was also 'the first man that assaulted the messengers' who were guarding Middleton: *HMCS*, X, p. 373; see also *APC 1599–1600*, pp. 757–8. Robert Middleton may have been the nephew of Margaret Clitherow, though this is uncertain: Anstr., I, pp. 230–1; J. C. H. Aveling, *Catholic Recusancy in York 1558–1791* (1970), p. 73. Middleton was one of the seventy-nine priests who had signed a letter on 8 November 1598 in support of the new archpresbyterate: Anstr., I, pp. 230–1; Pollen, *UD*, p. 384 (ABSJ, Collectanea P/ii, pp. 570ᵇ–1ᵇ). He had first been arrested, by Lord Burghley, with the priest Martin Nelson (the brother of John Nelson, who was executed at Tyburn on 3 February 1578) at Ripon at Christmas 1599 but was not detained for long: Anstr., I, pp. 231, 246; *CSPD 1598–1601*, p. 378 (PRO, SP 12/274/10: Thomas Cecil, Lord Burghley to Sir Robert Cecil, 8 January 1600). Martin Nelson, who served as a chaplain to Lady Scrope at Whitby in *c.*1591 (PRO SP 12/244/5, fo. 6ᵛ), had been arrested in summer 1594. He had recanted in January 1595 but, subsequently, he reneged on whatever promises he had made to the authorities. Middleton may conceivably have gone free after his first arrest because the deal was that Nelson would recant (again) and indeed Nelson obtained a second royal pardon in January/February 1601. In April 1610, Nelson was still working as a priest in South Wales: Anstr., I, p. 246; *CSPD 1598–1601*, pp. 378–9 (PRO, SP 12/274/10), 542; cf. *AWCBC*, p. 1574; see p. 391 below.

[34] Pollen, *UD*, pp. 386–7; *HMCS*, X, p. 336 (HHCP 81/84); Worthington, *A Relation*, sig. F7ᵛ. Henry Hodgkinson, mayor of Preston, Thomas Hesketh, and Ralph Ashton also described the attempted rescue. Hodgkinson had dispatched the travelling party which was to take Middleton to Lancaster. They confirmed that '[Gervase] Traves, a stranger that passed by and took their part', was 'sore wounded with the shot of a pistol'. Hodgkinson and the others interrogated Hunt back in Preston: HHCP 81/90 (*HMCS*, X, pp. 335–6). 'After about the year 1601', related William Blundell, Mr Traves, 'by reason' of the 'hurt he had in furthering the taking of Mr Hunt the priest, got a new grant of two parts' of Blundell's estates and 'laboured very busily to get possession or composition, but...got neither': A. Goss and T. Gibson (eds), *Crosby Records: A Chapter of Lancashire Recusancy* (Manchester, 1887), p. 32.

298 CATHOLICS AND TREASON

At the same time, this arrest, and the subsequent interrogations and trial, revealed how the Catholic community in Lancashire was actively engaged in the politics of the regime's dying days. Hunt was carrying an inflammatory anti-puritan petition. Crucially, this document alleged that the earl of Essex was a frontman for a puritan conspiracy against the queen. One of the branches of the supposed conspiracy was located in Lancashire, and it was led by Sir Richard Molyneux and Bishop Vaughan.[35] The petition was addressed directly to the queen and protested that, 'if the conspiring puritans had impeached but the liberties, goods, possessions and lives of Catholics', the writer and other Catholics would nobly have suffered in silence. But the truth was that the puritans 'wickedly and traitorously' intended to procure the 'death or deposition' of the queen, the 'alteration of the State', and the 'utter ruin of this realm'. The writer felt bound to alert the queen. He was motivated only by 'the innocence of our case, the uprightness of our carriage and' by 'loyal love to the sacred unction of your Majesty'. The guilty parties, in order 'more covertly' to 'effect their wicked treasons and avert your Majesty's law', had availed themselves of 'the sword of persecution in a scabbard of liberty'. They had deceived the queen by claiming that Catholics were rebellious. But these puritans were persecutors of the worst sort—'they search, they rob, they spoil, they forswear, they impanel juries, they indict without law, against all truth' and they sought thus to turn the queen against her good Catholic subjects so as better to put into effect their conspiracy against her.[36]

Hunt was writing in the Leicester's Commonwealth tradition of the censure of puritan sedition, except that now the threat allegedly came from the earl of Essex. This was not the potentially amenable politique Essex who seems to have been the focus of Catholic aspirations on the appellant wing of the community. This was, rather, the heir of Leicester, enlisting the worst humours of an already disordered commonwealth in order to seize the crown. Hunt's petition stated that Molyneux had conspired the recruitment of 10,000 soldiers. Bishop Vaughan had promised to commit himself to the insurrection. John Nutter, the dean of Chester, was the linkman 'between the bishop and Sir Richard'. The rebellion would have been launched 'if the earl of Essex in Ireland had prospered and returned with power appointed'. Furthermore, the knight marshal, Sir Thomas Gerard, had written to his brother-in-law Molyneux 'the last year' when it 'was said that your Majesty was dead, that he should not stir until he heard more from him again; at what time it was said "there will be rising", "there will be rising"'.[37]

[35] *CSPD 1598–1601*, pp. 485–7 (PRO, SP 12/275/115, 115. i, ii (Pollen, *UD*, pp. 381–4), iii); *HMCS*, X, p. 336; *APC 1599–1600*, pp. 757–8. For the suggestion that the petition was written in 1599 while Essex was in Ireland, see *AWCBC*, p. 1611.

[36] Pollen, *UD*, pp. 382–3 (PRO, SP 12/275/115. ii).

[37] Pollen, *UD*, pp. 383–4 (PRO, SP 12/275/115. ii). For John Nutter, dean of Chester and rector of Sephton, see CCED, ID 32188; R. V. H. Burne, *Chester Cathedral: From its Founding by Henry VIII to the Accession of Queen Victoria* (1958), pp. 65–6; Goss and Gibson, *Crosby Records*, pp. 22 (Nutter's

THE APPEAL TO ROME 299

On the day that Hunt was taken and interrogated, he admitted not only that the draft toleration petition to the queen was in his handwriting but also 'that he purposed to have made many copies thereof and to have fixed them in divers public places, to the end' that 'notice thereof might come to her Majesty'. He would not say 'what reasons moved him to affirm the contents of the letter' but he was 'ready to declare the same to the council if he were called thereunto'. More than that he was not prepared to say, although he recognized 'her Majesty to be lawful queen'.[38] He was also carrying two other documents. The first was a letter of the archpriest George Blackwell declaring that one of his appellant critics (Robert Charnock) was suspended from his clerical functions; the second was a statement of the case against the appellants, written by Blackwell himself.[39] Although that was not the primary focus of the investigation which followed the attempted rescue of Middleton, there was a direct connection between this aggressive expression of Lancashire Catholicism and the struggle inside the wider Catholic community over its future prospects.

The privy council, naturally, did not credit Hunt's loyal protestations. On 15 October it issued a warrant for Middleton and Hunt to be sent to London. The council demanded to know 'who were the rest of the confederates in so great an insolence which we find needs special redress and reformation in those parts, being grown to so intolerable a boldness and head as it is amongst that infected sort of people'. Hunt and Middleton were imprisoned in the Gatehouse. Here Middleton was admitted into the Society of Jesus.[40] Hunt continued to insist that he and his co-religionists were the last and best defence of the queen against puritan conspiracy, and that Essex had been on the verge of a *coup d'état* just before he was recalled from Ireland and disgraced. Essex had surveyed the mouth of the Mersey as the appropriate place for a fleet to lie at anchor. The earl's partner in crime, Bishop Vaughan, 'did preach that this war was great but the greatest was to come'. Furthermore, it was known that Essex had 'sent letters' to Vaughan, Peter Warburton (vice-chamberlain of Chester), Sir Richard Molyneux, Sir Richard Houghton, and others to make themselves ready. It appeared that the rebellion was imminent. The letter which Sir Thomas Gerard wrote to Molyneux also stoked up local Catholics' 'suspicion'. Houghton had been stockpiling weapons. Taking all this into account, what were good Catholics supposed to think about Essex and his ambitions? Surely there was going to be a military coup? The trouble lay in proving it. The people who had discussed these things with the likes of Hunt would rather perjure themselves than confirm what he had testified. But the

---

arrest of William Blundell in November 1593 during 'the time of [Thomas] Bell's persecution'), 23 (Nutter's and Molyneux's detaining of Blundell's wife, 27 May 1598).

[38] *HMCS*, X, pp. 335–6.   [39] *AWCBC*, p. 1575; PRO, SP 12/275/115. iv, v.

[40] Anstr., I, p. 231; *APC 1599–1600*, pp. 720, 721. After Middleton's imprisonment in London, Garnet authorized his reception into the Society, which Middleton had been requesting for some time: Anstr., I, p. 231; *AWCBC*, p. 1631; Foley, *RSJ*, IV, p. 584.

300 CATHOLICS AND TREASON

point was that William Brettergh 'or his disciples' had 'said that, if her Majesty should grant any toleration unto the papists', then 'she was not worthy to be queen and, before that should be', there would be real trouble. It had also been said that, in that case, 'the earl of Essex was the worthiest to be king and that, whereas the papists look for a change, there would be change by Michaelmas day, as near as it was, but little to their good'.[41]

This collision of ideologically informed local interests and antagonisms ended in the, for that part of the country, still very unusual sight of a treason trial of Catholic clergy. There had, locally, been trouble in getting Lancashire recusants to contribute to the cost of the wars in Ireland.[42] Nor had some people welcomed the stationing of crown-sponsored godly preachers in the county.[43] There is scattered evidence also that clergy of Nutter's and Middleton's persuasion had been conducting exorcisms in the region; and, indeed, it was Sir Richard Molyneux and Bishop Vaughan who, a few years back, had tried to stamp them out. These Catholic exorcisms were, almost certainly, a kind of riposte to the triumphs claimed by the puritan exorcist John Darrell in Lancashire.[44]

On 9 November 1600 the council instructed the queen's law officers that they should deal with the written examinations taken by Vaughan of those suspected of the attacks on Brettergh's farm animals. In addition, the council said, there should be 'exemplary proceeding' against Hunt and Middleton. It was clearly intended that the two issues should progress in tandem and that the one should gloss the other.[45] Jesuit clergy pointed to all this as proof that, as Richard Blount reported to Rome shortly after the Hunt–Middleton arrests, things were worse than ever for good Catholics; perhaps because a certain kind of Catholic was really under the gun and also because the Jesuit Blount and his friends absolutely would not concede the increasingly insistent appellant claim that there was, or might be, anything like tolerance for the 'right' (for Blount, of course, the 'wrong') sort of Catholic. As Blount had averred on 22 October 1600, while he narrated the Hunt–Middleton episode, the 'persecution was never more hot than at this instant for, albeit for policy sake, they are not so bloody altogether as in time past, yet do

---

[41] PRO, SP 15/34/20, fos 37^r, 38^r; *CSPD Addenda 1580–1625*, pp. 399–400 (misdated to November 1599). For, ironically, the reputations of Sir Richard Houghton and Sir Richard Molyneux as crypto-papists, see AAW, A IV, no. 38, pp. 448, 445; *HC 1558–1603*, II, p. 344, III, pp. 62–3; *HC 1604–29*, IV, pp. 802–4, V, pp. 345–7; Lake and Questier, *Trials*, pp. 134, 141–2.

[42] *CSPD 1598–1601*, pp. 7–8 (PRO, SP 12/266/18, 18. i–iii).

[43] For the institution in Lancashire of preachers with royal stipends, see *CSPD 1598–1601*, p. 153 (PRO, SP 12/270/20); *HMCS*, IX, pp. 91–2 (Vaughan to Cecil, 6 March 1599); Dottie, 'The Recusant Riots', p. 6.

[44] *HMCS*, VIII, pp. 213 (HHCP 61/82), 293 (HHCP 63/22); F. Brownlow (ed.), *Shakespeare, Harsnett, and the Devils of Denham* (1993), pp. 55, 250; George More, *A True Discourse concerning the Certaine Possession and Dispossession of 7 Persons in One Familie in Lancashire . . .* (1600), p. 5.

[45] *CSPD 1598–1601*, p. 485 (PRO, SP 12/275/115). The council's letter enclosed the information gleaned from Henry Breres and the documents taken when Hunt was arrested: *CSPD 1598–1601*, pp. 485–9 (PRO, SP 12/275/115. i–v).

THE APPEAL TO ROME   301

they otherwise more grievously by many degrees afflict the Catholic part than by death itself', in other words by financial and other penalties.[46]

Hunt was not the only one who had pointed to the earl of Essex as a magnet for puritan clients.[47] William Sterrell, the earl of Worcester's secretary, wrote to Robert Persons on 13 January 1601 that Essex's 'house' at Temple Bar was 'open to all comers…wherein he discovered himself to affect popularity'. He had 'many chaplains and…many exercises or puritan sermons or rather conventicles'. He 'drew multitudes' to him as well as leading malcontent peers, in short, 'the whole pack of puritans'.[48]

Some Catholics of Hunt's persuasion must have regarded it as no accident that the earl now behaved according to type and went into rebellion, on 8 February 1601—so much for the ridiculous recent accusations made against Catholics![49] Essex was beheaded in the Tower on 25 February, declaring that he was neither papist nor atheist. The regime, however, had absolutely no interest in Essex being seen as the leader of a puritan coup. Perhaps this was why Middleton and Hunt had already been brought down to London, as they were in November 1600, that is, in order to put a stop to the circulating rumours that Essex could draw on the support of a godly Protestant constituency. The two priests desperately tried, on the last day of February 1601, to get word out in a letter (marked 'read and burn it') to a priest friend in another prison that Essex's recent attempt had genuinely been a puritan plot.[50]

---

[46] ABSJ, Collectanea M, p. 96ᵃ (Morris, *TCF*, I, p. 193) 'It would grieve your heart', Blount told Persons, 'to hear the hourly general complaints of all that sort of the most inhuman and conscience-less dealing towards them' with 'whole families daily ruined, of all such as are not able to pay' the £20 monthly fine levied on those who were recusants 'or did omit to pay it at their first conviction, not being afterwards admitted to pay if they would, but two parts of all their lands to be forfeited to the queen and all their goods and all arrears of the' £20 fine 'monthly, to be levied upon them notwithstanding'. This was 'prosecuted in every shire with great violence' by Lord Chief Justice Popham 'principally' so that 'no former conveyances of lands will take place, no law will be allowed in that behalf, nor no lawyer can be hired to plead their case'. 'Often' their 'household stuff' was 'sold before their faces'. 'This kind of dealing' was 'executed upon one and the self-same person, so long and so often as anything' was 'to be found to seize upon for the queen': ABSJ, Collectanea M, p. 96ᵃ⁻ᵇ (Morris, *TCF*, I, pp. 193–4). See also Blount's letter of 18 November 1600: ABSJ, Collectanea M, pp. 96ᵇ⁻7ᵃ.

[47] There were a number of prominent puritans, for example John Burgess and Sir Francis Hastings, who had approached Essex with spiritual and political counsel, or were otherwise close to him: *HMCS*, X, pp. 185, 372; *HMCS*, XI, p. 212; see also Collinson, *EPM*, pp. 444–6.

[48] RC, pp. 6–7 (AAW, A VII, no. 1). On 29 May 1601 Archbishop Hutton recalled that he had sent Essex a message that the 'common voice' in the North was that he (Essex) made 'too much of preachers inclining to puritanism' and heard 'their sermons commonly twice a day': *HMCS*, XI, p. 209. Sterrell was formerly employed by Essex: *HMCS*, V, p. 105. Thomas Phelippes identified Sterrell to Essex as a Catholic intelligencer: *HMCS*, VI, pp. 511–12; see also P. Hammer, *The Polarisation of Elizabethan Politics: The Political Career of Robert Devereux, 2nd Earl of Essex, 1585–1597* (Cambridge, 1999), pp. 154–5; R. B. Wernham, *After the Armada: Elizabethan England and the Struggle for Western Europe 1588–1595* (Oxford, 1984), p. 449. Sterrell was named to Cecil by Ralph Winwood in April 1602 as a Catholic newsgatherer: Sawyer, *WM*, I, p. 404.

[49] For the Essex revolt, see P. Hammer, 'Shakespeare's *Richard II*, the Play of 7 February 1601, and the Essex Rising', *Shakespeare Quarterly* 59 (2008), pp. 1–35.

[50] HHCP 77/29 (*HMCS*, XI, p. 109). The letter was intercepted and sent by Richard Bancroft to Sir Robert Cecil, who, he supposed, would make 'some use of it': *HMCS*, XI, p. 109.

302 CATHOLICS AND TREASON

The regime predictably sought to exploit Essex's revolt by characterizing it as a Catholic/popish conspiracy. Henry Garnet, noting that 'Our Lord has heard at last the cry of innocent blood spilt and of the many outrages, robberies and sacrileges' perpetrated at Cadiz, observed that those whom he called 'the puritans' were 'anxious by every means to impute these tumults...to the Catholics'. To 'this end', they 'caused the ministers in their sermons to tell the people that the pope and the king of Spain had conspired with the earl'. There were, admitted Garnet, some Catholics involved in the rebellion. But 'they were very few and were young men and they had not the approbation of any priest or people of wisdom'. They had vainly believed that, if the earl 'were successful in his purposes, he would repeal all the statutes against Catholics'. Such people were now furiously trying to distance themselves from Essex's public catastrophe and were insisting that he had been duped by puritans. More fool them, said Garnet—they should have listened to the likes of the now doomed Thurstan Hunt and to the friends of Spain, the Society of Jesus, and all good European Catholics. The truth was that you could not subscribe to an allegedly patriotic war against the House of Austria and pretend that there would be no bad domestic political consequences.[51]

The queen's government could not ignore this groundswell of Catholic popular and public opinion. The need for damage limitation may have been the motivation for the trial of the priest John Pibush. Pibush's uttering of allegedly treasonable words in prison led to a former sentence on him being carried out at St Thomas-a-Watering, Southwark, on 18 February 1601.[52] Garnet had picked up rumours that Pibush might be reprieved, for 'it was thought, on account of the tumults caused by the earl of Essex, the holy martyr would not have to die'. But, so the word went, the queen expressly ordered Popham to 'proceed with the utmost rigour of the laws against the Catholics' and so Pibush went to the gallows. Garnet alleged that immediately after Pibush was hanged, a 'proclamation was made' which ordered the crowd to disperse and which provoked muttering from the spectators who had been unimpressed by Essex's fate and 'went away murmuring..."see now, they have butchered a poor sick priest"'.[53]

---

[51] ABSJ, GC (11 March 1601: ARSJ, Anglia 31/i, fos 172^r–83^v; also, in part, translated and printed in Foley, *RSJ*, VII/2, pp. 1345–67). For those Catholics who had thought favourably of Essex, see, e.g., Anthony Copley, *An Answere to a Letter of a Iesuited Gentleman, by his Cosin, Maister A. C. Concerning the Appeale; State, Iesuits* (n.p. [London], 1601), p. 69; Inner Temple, Petyt MS 538/54, no. 51, fo. 214^r (Humphrey Ely to Sir Robert Cecil, 20/30 August 1602).

[52] For the circumstances of Pibush's original arrest in Gloucestershire in mid-1593 and the subsequent legal proceedings against him, see Pollen, *AEM*, pp. 335–6 (ABSJ, Collectanea M, p. 145$^{a–b}$; this report was written in *c.* later 1594/early 1595); Anstr., I, p. 274; *HMCS*, VI, p. 313; Pollen, *UD*, pp. 337–40; Foley, *RSJ*, VII/2, pp. 1347–53 (ABSJ, GC (11 March 1601; ARSJ, Anglia 31/ii, fos 172^r–83^v)); McCoog, *SJISE*, II, pp. 234–5; Caraman, *HG*, pp. 268f, 274f. Pibush's name was allegedly on the list of those who were sent off to Wisbech in January 1601, but Sir John Popham had crossed it out, 'no one knew why': Challoner, *MMP*, pp. 252–3 (relying on AAW, F 1, p. 1008); for the circumstances which allegedly led to the carrying out of the death sentence on Pibush, see ABSJ, GC (11 March 1601); Foley, *RSJ*, VII/2, pp. 1348–9.

[53] ABSJ, GC (11 March 1601); Foley, *RSJ*, VII/2, pp. 1353–5. On 17 July 1601, Garnet recorded that 'of these last searches...none of the council knew thereof but only Popham and the queen, to whom

THE APPEAL TO ROME   303

Nine days after Pibush's execution, Anne Line, Roger Filcock, and Mark Barkworth were hanged. Some contemporaries linked their trials and executions with the Essex rising. A correspondent of Thomas Phelippes noted from Brussels on 3/13 April 1601 that the news was that Essex's 'plot' was 'laid by the puritans'. Essex had 'showed it at his arraignment, in his life and death'. But what was fairly shocking was that 'some in authority, whose throats had been cut long ere this by those furious spirits if they had prevailed', were 'not ashamed to seem to clear those that are known to be guilty and to impose the crime upon the innocent Catholics'. This was the reason that, 'in the midst of those tragic actions', they had 'executed three or four poor priests (the one [presumably Pibush] condemned four or five years ago) and a Catholic gentlewoman Mrs Anne Line for harbour-ing of priests only'.[54] The writer admitted that Essex's co-conspirator and father-in-law, Sir Christopher Blount, had 'died a Catholic', but so what?—he lived 'in schism all his lifetime'. This commentator took the opportunity to compare all this with what looked like relative tolerance in Ireland, where 'Mass' was 'openly said in Waterford, and the friars there [were] set up'. The friars in question went 'begging up and down…as freely and safely as in times past'.[55]

Anne Line was an obvious target. She ran a virtually open house for Catholic clergy in London. It made her in effect a London equivalent of Margaret Clitherow of York. The raid on her residence on 2 February 1601 had been intended to net not just her but her clergy as well. One of them, Francis Page, absconded but was then retaken.[56]

The priest Roger Filcock's arraignment on 23 February turned into an oppor-tunity to air in public some of the arguments raging at that point within the Catholic community over the archpriest. Bishop Richard Bancroft was present in the court. He declared that he had seen a copy of a letter from Robert Persons to Henry Garnet which said that the students in the English College in Rome who opposed the Society of Jesus did not have the spirit of true martyrs—they grew 'to such insolence that all their actions proceeded of passion'. They came 'into

---

Popham is said to have promised the taking of twenty Jesuits and the archpriest and his twelve assis-tants', i.e. in order to wipe out the Catholics opposed to the appellants: ABSJ, GC (17 July 1601; ABSJ, Collectanea P/ii, p. 539).

[54] PRO, SP 77/6, fo. 258^{r-v} (CSPD 1601–3, p. 25 [calendared in error to 3/13 April]).

[55] PRO, SP 77/6, fo. 258^v (CSPD 1601–3, p. 25). For Blount's capacity to combine Catholicism with his place in the entourage around the earl of Leicester (Blount was one of the agents used in 1585 to infiltrate the circle around Mary Stuart) and then around the earl of Essex, see ODNB, sub Blount, Sir Christopher (article by P. Hammer).

[56] Caraman, JG, pp. 82–6; M. Dodwell, Anne Line: Shakespeare's Tragic Muse (Brighton, 2013); for the sentencing and reprieve of an apprentice, one Ralph Slyvell, who had helped Page to abscond, see Dodwell, Anne Line, p. 98; ARSJ, Anglia 37, fo. 18^v. Thomas Jollett's account says that Popham was the driving force behind the proceedings against Line: G. Kilroy, Edmund Campion: Memory and Transcription (Aldershot, 2005), p. 21. Challoner (relying on Anthony Champney's 'Annales' [AAW, F 1], pp. 1009–13) said that Margaret Copley, wife of John Gage of Haling, was arrested in Line's house as well, though she was 'by the interest of a certain nobleman', i.e. Lord Admiral Howard, 'after some time set at liberty': Challoner, MMP, p. 258; Foley, RSJ, VII/2, p. 1357. Margaret Copley-Gage had escaped death once already, i.e. for harbouring George Beseley; see pp. 207–8 n.124 above.

304   CATHOLICS AND TREASON

England upon spleen without any spark of religion or devotion'. Filcock denied the sense that Bancroft read into the letter and said that it was 'a slander raised upon the Catholics by malicious people to disgrace the cause'. Filcock challenged Bancroft to produce it, which Bancroft either could or would not.[57]

Filcock was executed with Mark Barkworth on a freezing cold winter's day (27 February 1601). In fact, said Garnet, the execution took place in the middle of a snowstorm.[58] Sentence was carried out at Tyburn after Anne Line, with others, had been hanged. Filcock was taunted that there 'were many papists that were associate[d] with the earl of Essex'. He 'answered that there was not any of account'. He said, furthermore, that one such Catholic, Francis Tresham, had been mad to combine with 'such a damnable crew of heretics and atheists'.[59] Barkworth was jeered at by the crowd in the streets after his trial. Some of them shouted that he had been 'one of the ringleaders of the revolt'.[60]

At the gallows, said Thomas Jollett, when Filcock was accused by a 'busy officious fellow' of religious error, Barkworth retorted: 'we see...that the earl of Essex...was but a worldly man, yet many bore him such an affection that they were content to follow him even to the death, yes, and that in a bad cause; and should I then be afraid to lay down my life for my God? No, sir, if I had a thousand lives'. His antagonist retorted: 'you lay lurking to watch your opportunity, that if any tumult should have been, you and such as you' would have been 'as ready as the rest; and if the earl of Essex had gotten the day, you' would have made 'account to have your Church exalted'. To this Barkworth responded that 'I did that day pray as heartily for her Majesty and the state of our country as ever I did in my life'. This, however, did not stop Barkworth from taunting his antagonist by

---

[57] Foley, *RSJ*, VII/2, p. 1360; Bodl., MS Eng. th. b. 2, pp. 112–15 (Filcock's own account of his trial, followed by a narrative of the execution: *AWCBC*, pp. 1538–47, for the authorship of which piece, see *AWCBC*, p. 1546), at p. 113. Filcock also lectured the lord chief justice on the judicial subversion of due process and the coercion of juries: *AWCBC*, p. 1546. For the identity of the compiler of Bodl., MS Eng. th. b. 2 (Thomas Jollett), see Kilroy, *Edmund Campion: Memory and Transcription*, esp. pp. 13–14 and ch. 1 *passim*; M. Sena, 'The Underground Catholic Church in England 1580–1625' (PhD, Princeton, 2017), appendix I. Dr McCoog argues that the letter cited by Bancroft is that from Persons to Garnet of 2/12 July 1598, i.e. as it appears in ABSJ, Collectanea P/ii, pp. 438ᵇ–42ᵇ (ABSJ, PC, pp. 568 f); see McCoog, *SJISE*, II, p. 236; for another copy, presumably the one that Bancroft possessed, see Inner Temple, Petyt MS 538/38, fos 416ʳ–21ᵛ, as printed in Law, *AC*, I, pp. 21–38.

[58] Challoner, *MMP*, p. 257; Anstr., I, p. 21; Foley, *RSJ*, VII/2, p. 1363; Kilroy, *Edmund Campion: Memory and Transcription*, pp. 18–20. As Martin Dodwell notes (M. Dodwell, 'Revisiting Anne Line: Who was She and where did She come from?', *RH* 31 (2013), pp. 375–89, at p. 387), there are four surviving contemporary accounts of the execution of Line and the others: Henry Garnet's letter of 11 March 1601; a narrative in *HMCR*, I, pp. 369–70; Champney's 'Annales', pp. 1009–13; and Thomas Jollett's narrative, Bodl., MS Eng. th. b. 2, pp. 117–18 (transcribed in D. Shanahan, 'Petticoats on the Gallows', *Essex Recusant* 10 (1968), pp. 107–10). I am very grateful to Mr Dodwell for discussions of Line's case. For the renegade seminarists who volunteered evidence against Filcock and Barkworth, see A. J. Loomie, 'Spain and the English Catholic Exiles 1580–1604' (PhD, London, 1957), pp. 316–21; Kilroy, *Edmund Campion: Memory and Transcription*, p. 19; Bodl., MS Eng. th. b. 2, pp. 104, 108, 111.

[59] Anstr., I, p. 116; *HMCR*, I, p, 370; *AWCBC*, p. 1543.

[60] Challoner, *MMP*, p. 255, relying on Henry More SJ; see Edwards, *EJ*, p. 323; Bodl., MS Eng. th. b. 2, p. 112.

THE APPEAL TO ROME 305

pointing out that Essex had once been 'generally beloved' among the people, and at death professed himself a Protestant, but 'many did openly divulge that he and many of his principal followers were reconciled papists'.[61] Barkworth, who was dragged to Tyburn in the habit of a Benedictine, and declared himself, just before death, to be 'a priest and a monk', said he would endure any kind of death, and any kind of pain, rather than 'die in that religion' that 'the earl of Essex died in'.[62] On Garnet's account, Barkworth, who had had a difficult time with the Jesuit administrators at Valladolid, had sent strands of his own hair and particles of clothing to both Garnet and George Blackwell.[63] The butchery of Barkworth was much worse even than that used on Filcock. Barkworth was disembowelled alive. The authorities were more 'exasperated against him'.[64] Garnet's agent was at the execution. In all likelihood this was the Jesuit priest Richard Blount. He cut away part of the sleeve of Anne Line's gown and drew it through the blood of Filcock and Barkworth. Later the remains were dug up by London Catholics. According to Blount, when 'certain resolute Catholics intended to take up' Anne Line's 'body in the night time out of the place where it was dishonourably buried in the same grave and under the bodies of divers malefactors', it was the saintly countess of Arundel who 'sent her coach with them, and therein brought the body to her own house where it was kept with reverence till it could be conveniently disposed of by those who had more interest therein'.[65]

Four days later, on 3 March 1601, directions were given by the council that the two priests, Hunt and Middleton, were to be taken back to Lancaster and tried there. The council issued an open warrant to ensure that royal officials along the route to the North intervened, if necessary, to stop violent attempts to free them.[66] On the very last day of March, a further interrogation of the two priests prompted Hunt to accuse one of Sir Richard Molyneux's servants of having boasted that the earl of Essex could have had the English crown. Molyneux told Cecil that these accusations were the result of Molyneux's zeal in suppressing popish disorder in that region. Hunt himself, said Molyneux, had maintained 'at the bar with great

---

[61] AWCBC, p. 1544 (Bodl., MS Eng. th. b. 2, pp. 114–15).

[62] AWCBC, p. 1545 (Bodl., MS Eng. th. b. 2, p. 115).

[63] Foley, RSJ, VII/2, p. 1362; McCoog, SJISE, II, p. 237.

[64] Foley, RSJ, VII/2, pp. 1365–6; Edwards, EJ, p. 324. For public sympathy for Barkworth, see ABP, p. 438. It was declared by Thomas Achym, that Barkworth had said to an unnamed English gentleman that he expected 'an alteration of estate' for the queen could not 'live long' and, moreover, 'whosoever did kill her Majesty could not choose but be canonized a saint, for the deed was meritorious': HMCS, XI, pp. 269–70. This, of course, is only a third-hand narrative of what Barkworth may or may not have said. But Barkworth's own account of his responses to interrogation (which requires a separate study on its own) suggests that he was doing nothing to make the authorities think that he was well disposed towards the late Tudor regime: Bodl., MS Eng. th. b. 2, pp. 103–9.

[65] AWCBC, p. 1533; Foley, RSJ, VII/2, p. 1366. Richard Blount was the author of the manuscript lives of Philip Howard, earl of Arundel, and his wife, Anne Dacre (ex. inf. Elizabeth Patton). Blount says that he was present at Anne Line's execution; see H. Fitzalan-Howard (ed.), The Lives of Philip Howard, Earl of Arundel, and of Anne Dacres, his Wife (1857), p. 293.

[66] APC 1600–1, pp. 194–5, 198.

306 CATHOLICS AND TREASON

vehemence', and had similarly declared 'in his sermons to the papists when he was at liberty', that 'it was no offence before God to kill any Protestant who should seek to apprehend any seminary priest'.[67]

The execution took place probably on 3 April—very swiftly, only a few hours after sentence.[68] Perhaps this was a sign of the local political pressures engendered by the trial. Middleton's sister tried unsuccessfully to obtain a reprieve. A Catholic account said that, on the day of their deaths, Middleton and Hunt 'reconciled two or three felons, who professed their faith and refused before their death to pray with the minister'. As the felons were hanged one by one, the priests shouted and called on them 'to die Catholic'. It seems that the locality may have been unwilling to assist with the execution. In 'all Lancaster there could not be found any that would either lend horse or cart or hurdle or any suchlike thing for their death; so the sheriff was fain to take one of his own horses to draw the sledge. The fire was [so] little, that the entrails of the first put out their fire; so that Catholics, who were by, took what they would'. Both clergymen were executed 'in their cassocks'. The officials may have in deference to local sentiment tried to avoid disembowelling them alive. 'Hunt was already dead' by that stage, but Middleton was cut down 'alive by error, as some think'. The sheriff who supervised the proceedings was Sir Cuthbert Halsall. He had been knighted in Dublin in 1599 by the earl of Essex but he was, early in James's reign, removed from the JPs' bench for his suspected popery. Halsall intervened to decapitate Middleton swiftly as he began to revive. Our Catholic narrator here said that 'everyone lamented their death, for all the world perceived their innocence; and not only Catholics but schismatics and...all sorts strove to have something of theirs for relics'.[69]

There was probably also some interplay between these Lancashire trials and the furore concerning the demise of William Brettergh's unfortunate wife. There was an acrimonious pamphlet exchange about her notorious crisis of faith in her final illness, that is, before she died on 31 May 1601. Her admirers produced a puritan quasi-martyr narrative which described how she resisted the forces of Satan that tempted her even at the very end. She was the subject of two funeral sermons—one delivered by the stipendiary royal preacher William Harrison and

---

[67] HHCP 181/135, 137, 138 (*HMCS*, XI, pp. 165–7); Dottie, 'The Recusant Riots', p. 14; Anstr., I, p. 180; HHCP 85/143 (*HMCS*, XI, p. 160).

[68] *AWCBC*, pp. 1577, 1655–6.

[69] Pollen, *UD*, pp. 389–90; ARSJ, Anglia 37, fos 59^v-60^r; *AWCBC*, pp. 1577–8; *HC 1604–29*, IV, p. 521. For Halsall's family relationship to Thomas Hesketh and Sir Richard Molyneux, see http://www.stirnet. com/genie/data/british/hh4aa/haslsall1.php. The Lancashire martyrdoms of the late Elizabethan period were memorialized in a thirty-three stanza ballad entitled 'A Song of Four Priests that Suffered Death at Lancaster': Pollen, *UD*, p. 385: BL, Additional MS 15225, fos 31^r-3^r (this manuscript collection of ballads was copied in 1616 or after: *AWCBC*, p. 1433); see H. E. Rollins (ed.), *Old English Ballads 1553-1625* (Cambridge, 1920), pp. xxiii, 70–8, citing as, in all probability, a reply to this Catholic ballad, a work, no longer extant, licensed on 7 July 1601 under the title *A Short Poeme Conteyning an Answere to Certen Godles and Seditious Balledes Spred Abroad in Lancashire*.

THE APPEAL TO ROME 307

the other by William Leigh, who was beneficed at Standish. The paean of her by these representatives of the local godly explicitly compared what she had endured with the sufferings of, among others, 'the Lord Cobham...Richard Hunne...Thomas Bilney and...Perotine Massey, holy martyrs'. The cruelty of the papists could be detected in 'murdering the martyrs, in persecuting the Protestants and now of late in these parts in beating and wounding the bodies [and] in killing and spoiling the cattle of those which withstand them by public authority'. The *Brief Discourse of the Christian Life* of Mrs Brettergh said that it was her custom to 'read some godly writer, or expositor of Scripture', or Foxe's 'book of martyrs'. She 'was seen to weep most bitterly when either she had read of that which touched her affections...or of the cruel martyrdom which the dear children of God were put unto by the cruel and wicked tyrants of former days'. Local Catholics were poking fun at her. Harrison's efforts were intended 'to clear her from the slanderous reports of her popish neighbours' though, as Steve Hindle points out, the Catholic side of these exchanges does not survive.[70] But out of these confrontations in the provinces, as much as in the more rigidly choreographed executions in London of Anne Line and her companions, contemporaries would have deduced that the politics of the forthcoming accession would be phrased in part through the legal processes which were supposed to penalize Catholic separatism.[71]

The Archpriest Controversy and the Late Elizabethan State

Catholic commentators who were watching these blood-soaked clashes, and were recording and circulating accounts of them, were certainly construing them as part of a broader struggle over the political future. Let us return to Henry Garnet's narrative of 11 March 1601, which dealt with the recent martyrdoms of Catholics. Here the issues generated by the Archpriest Dispute were thrown into sharp relief. 'We find by experience', wrote Garnet, 'that all those who go to martyrdom come from those who love us...and are obedient to the most reverend archpriest, who is a very holy, learned person and revered by all good Catholics'. Those who suffered the ultimate penalty for the sake of their consciences were 'all of them ours'.

---

[70] William Harrison and William Leigh, *Deaths Advantage little Regarded, and The Soules Solace against Sorrow. Preached in Two Funerall Sermons at Childwal in Lancashire at the Buriall of Mistris Katherin Brettergh the third of Iune 1601. The One by William Harrison, one of the Preachers Appointed by her Maiestie for the Countie Palatine of Lancaster, the other William Leygh ....Whereunto is Annexed, the Christian Life and Godly Death of the said Gentlewoman* (1602), esp. at sigs A3^v–4^r, M5^r–P7^v; this publication went through many editions; see also *ODNB, sub* Brettergh [née Bruen], Katherine (article by S. Hindle), citing PRO, STAC 5/A8/31; PRO, SP 12/275/102, 115; Dottie, 'The Recusant riots', pp. 6–7, 22; Quintrell, 'Government in Perspective', p. 48.

[71] Cf. the execution in Scotland of James Wood, laird of Boniton, on 27 April 1601. Some Scots Catholics said it was for religion, but others, notably William Creighton SJ, denied it; see McCoog, *SJISE*, II, pp. 308–10.

308   CATHOLICS AND TREASON

But 'from those who' were 'unwilling to have peace with us, martyrdom surely and evidently holds aloof'. Indeed, the appellants and their misguided sympathizers 'every day... continue to be arrested, imprisoned and discovered—more than we are—but either they flee, or escape, or turn renegade'. Garnet's thoughts immediately turned to John Rigby's martyrdom. Rigby had shown 'a great desire to join the Society as a coadjutor' and how could this not have been connected with his readiness to die for the faith? As for Thomas Benstead and Thomas Sprott, executed at Lincoln in July 1600, Sprott certainly had wanted to be received into the Society. Equally, the recent martyr John Pibush was 'devoted' to Garnet.[72] What Garnet would not allow was that the appellant project was anything other than the result of cowardice and cynicism. The claim of its proponents was that they could secure a *modus vivendi* with the late Tudor State and a toleration for good Catholics who were politically loyal. But, for this case to be convincing, the State would have to rein in the use of the statute law against Catholic separatists, and that was something that was not currently happening.[73]

In late 1601, another secular-clergy appeal against the archpriest George Blackwell wended its way to Rome. The appellants' proctors (Thomas Bluet, John Mush, Christopher Bagshaw, and Francis Barnaby) were allowed by the privy council in September/October 1601 to leave the country. They travelled via Paris in order to secure the goodwill of the French court.[74] The places of Bagshaw and Barnaby were then in effect taken by Anthony Champney and John Cecil. The new appeal was underwritten in Rome by Henry IV's ambassador, Philippe de Béthune, even though Henry, who was seeking to reintegrate and restore the Society of Jesus in France, could not publicly support the appellant programme.[75]

Soon after the appellants' representatives set out, the English political nation was treated to the extraordinary sight of rancorous exchanges in the parliament of late 1601 as to whether it was appropriate to impose harsher legal penalties on Catholic separatists. The Commons witnessed back-and-forth exchanges between leading puritans such as Sir Francis Hastings and Sir William Knollys and their critics about whether the racking up of punishment for nonconformity was likely to spread true religion and/or guarantee the queen's safety. The end result was the, to some, astonishing sight of the voting down of a bill which tried to levy more effectively the recusancy fines imposed by the 1559 act of uniformity. Some

---

[72]   ABSJ, GC (11 March 1601; ARSJ, Anglia 31/i, fo. 172[r] *et seq.*).

[73]   Two more Catholics were arraigned and executed, at Tyburn, on 24 August 1601—Nicholas Tichborne and Thomas Hackshot. Seeing his brother, the priest Thomas Tichborne, taken along a London street in early 1601, Nicholas Tichborne and Hackshot had dragged him away from the official in charge of him; and this had led to their arrests and trials: Anstr., I, p. 358.

[74]   Pollen, *The Institution of the Archpriest Blackwell*, p. 66; *APC 1601*, pp. 205, 299–300; J. Bossy, 'Henri IV, the Appellants and the Jesuits', *RH* 8 (1965), pp. 80–112.

[75]   McCoog, *SJISE*, II, pp. 282f.; Lake and Questier, *Archpriest*, part I, ch. 5.

people wondered whether this was the result of a kind of popish conspiracy inside the regime, of which the appellant agitation was merely one tentacle.[76]

The new appeal generated a widespread and organized lobbying campaign in England before the appellants' agents set out.[77] They arrived in Rome on 4/14 February 1602. They stayed there for most of the year. The battle with their critics (Robert Persons and his friends) gave the appellant clergy the opportunity to make a range of loyalist statements. 'Infinite lies … [are] spread here to dishonour her Majesty', reported Thomas Bluet, not least the claim that Bancroft, Cecil, and the queen herself did 'most tyrannically persecute [Catholics] again.'[78] With the support of the French, the appeal was heard by curial officials. The final result was something of a draw. Blackwell was not dismissed, but he and his supporters were forced to make concessions to their opponents.[79]

The Archpriest Controversy pamphlets from the time of the new appeal dealt primarily with the intricacies of the jurisdictional issues generated by the appointment of Blackwell. But some of them dwelt also on the twin topics of persecution and tolerance. Appellant writers wanted to cleanse Catholic martyrology of its radical associations and to point the way to a more pluralist society and State. There were, the appellants said, appropriate contemporary models of religious coexistence. 'In Germany', wrote the peerless anti-Jesuit pamphleteer William Watson, there was never going to be confessional unity. But 'in civil conversation, one with another, and for life, government and order, the emperor, though a Catholic, finds as great service and concord amongst his subjects, and they again use and enjoy all their immunities, freedoms and liberties with as great content and quiet living in one province, in one city, in one town, in one street, yes, and in one house … as if they were all of one mind, faith and religion'. The lesson was clear—one should be more like the Germans. And if that was not an entirely convincing argument, what about the French? In France, observed Watson, 'we see what liberty of conscience wrought. Did it not as well animate the Huguenots to join with King Henry of the house of Valois, then a Catholic in show, howsoever the Jesuits censure of his heart, as it did of like sort the Catholics to join with the now most Christian and Catholic king Henry IV, then a Protestant?' Those Catholics stuck 'as sure and fast to his Christian Majesty as if he had been of their own Catholic religion and profession'. They did so 'with great alacrity of mind, in

---

[76] P. Lake and M. Questier, 'Thomas Digges, Robert Parsons, Sir Francis Hastings, and the Politics of Regime Change in Elizabethan England', *HJ* 61 (2018), pp. 1–27, at pp. 4–9.

[77] Persons, *Briefe Apologie*, sig. +7ʳ⁻ᵛ.   [78] *HMCS*, XII, p. 154.

[79] The Holy Office's judgment, made on 10/20 July 1602, delivered in August/September 1602 and approved by Clement VIII, reprimanded Blackwell as well as his opponents. The formal expression of the papacy's decision came in the shape of a breve of 25 September/5 October 1602: Pollen, *Institution*, pp. 90–4; TD, III, pp. clxxxi–iii; AAW, A VII, nos 63, 64, 66; Lake and Questier, *Archpriest*, p. 121.

310 CATHOLICS AND TREASON

regard of his present right to that crown, and their future hopes of his conversion to their Church and faith, as afterwards it happened, God so sweetly disposing'.[80]

In fact, said Watson, in several other countries—Poland, Sweden, and Flanders—'Catholics' mixed freely 'with those of other professions'. The only places where this was not possible were the regions where the 'consistorian Calvinian Cartwrightian puritans' ruled 'the roost, and...a company of ministers or exorbitant superintendents' overtopped 'prince, prelate and all, as in Scotland and Geneva'.[81] From this one could easily deduce that a form of absolute monarchy, free from all that nonsense about popular choice, was the way to guarantee civil peace—hence, of course, the need for good Catholics and indeed good Christians everywhere to render obedience to their princes. This was why 'all kings and princes of this age have judged it in policy the fittest, wisest, safest and most honourable and princely course they would have taken: to grant liberty of conscience to their subjects'.[82]

Now, Elizabeth Tudor had not chosen to do this, and yet she was the equal in 'wisdom' of any other monarch. The fault lay partly with those Catholics, Jesuits, and others who behaved very like the worst sort of puritans, seeking through popular agitation to subvert her monarchy. This was why more 'severity' had been 'used against Catholics' than 'any Catholic king or prince of other professions, either Christian or heathen' deployed 'against either subjects or foreigners of contrary religions unto the said princes throughout the world [at] this day'. It was far from clear that Elizabeth Tudor was personally a more savage persecutor than any other crowned head in Europe or anywhere else. But even if this was the case, the fact was that, 'as the affliction of Catholics in England' had been 'extraordinary...and many an innocent man' had 'lost his life, so also' had 'the cause been extraordinary', in other words that some Catholics (the 'Spanish faction') had pursued 'treacherous courses' and had provoked the queen beyond measure.[83]

Here, then, it was possible for Catholics such as Watson to face down those of their co-religionists whom they took to have been seditious. Watson looked at the archpresbyterate, cooked up by the 'bastardly vicar of Hell' (Robert Persons); and Watson concluded that the treasons of the Jesuits were all but identical to those of the presbyterians in the Scottish Kirk. Both were determined to secure a form of elective monarchy and, as a result, to plunge the commonwealth into the chaos which came from 'popularity'. This, said Watson, was what the pernicious archpresbyterate was all about. The clue was in the 'presbyter' bit of the term 'archpresbyterate'. It was a shadow or figure of what all temporal government and authority would be like if the Jesuits were to get their way.[84] But, by contrast,

[80] William Watson, *A Decacordon of Ten Quodlibeticall Questions concerning Religion and State* (n.p. [London], 1602), p. 275.
[81] Ibid., pp. 275–6.   [82] Ibid., p. 276.   [83] Ibid., pp. 276–7.
[84] Ibid., pp. 157–8.

THE APPEAL TO ROME   311

Watson insisted that the queen and State would never have a reason for thinking that good and loyal Catholics would seek 'any alteration and change of the ancient laws and customs which both puritans and Jesuits do greedily gape after and labour for'.[85]

Appellant writers could thus claim to be not simply an embattled fraction of the English Catholic community but representatives of a much wider European movement (incorporating, for example, prominent Gallican theorists in France)—a crusade at the heart of which was a reaction against the ills caused by the misguided beliefs of republican and monarchomach theorists on both sides of the confessional divide.[86] In France, following Jean Chastel's attempted assassination of the king, Gallicans had secured the ejection of the Society, at least from those regions of the country under the jurisdiction of the *parlement* of Paris.[87]

Like many of the other appellant writers, John Mush subscribed to a version of the regime's policy and self-image which was quite compatible with, say, Lord Burghley's *Execution of Justice*. (Mush seems temporarily to have forgotten all about the martyred saint and his own patroness, Mrs Margaret Clitherow, or perhaps he had persuaded himself that times had now changed.) Burghley had protested, as we saw, that at no point had loyal Catholics—those who correctly distinguished between conscience and temporal obedience—had any cause to fear the law of treason. The proof was, said Mush, that this had been observable even in the case of some Jesuits. Jasper Heywood SJ, who just happened to be one of Robert Persons's many enemies, had enjoyed 'such extraordinary favour of the lord of Leicester, that' when Heywood was imprisoned 'in the Tower, he...had there more liberty and found more friendly usage than all the priests in the other prisons throughout England', even 'when many Catholic priests were closely shut up, rigorously used and cruelly executed'. Mush said also that Heywood had had 'many conferences with Sir Christopher Hatton and received favours of him before he [Heywood] was apprehended'.[88] One appellant document pointedly remembered that 'Heywood the Jesuit called a synod in Norfolk', ironically 'by Persons's direction'. Heywood used it to 'abrogate the Saturday fasts and also the

---

[85] Thomas Bluet, *Important Considerations, which Ought to Move all True and Sound-Catholikes, who are not wholly Iesuited, to Acknowledge without all Equivocations, Ambiguities, or Shiftings, that the Proceedings of her Maiesty, and of the State with Them, since the Beginning of her Highnesse Raigne, have Bene both Mild and Mercifull* (n.p. [London], 1601), sig. ***5ᵛ–6ʳ. (In his *Decacordon*, p. 334, Watson admitted that he was the author of the *Important Considerations* or at least of its 'Epistle' to the reader.)

[86] For an exemplary account of what Gallicanism meant in the context of the French wars of religion, see E. Nelson, *The Jesuits and the Monarchy: Catholic Reform and Political Authority in France (1590–1615)* (Aldershot, 2005), pp. 13–15 and *passim*.

[87] For the expulsion of the Jesuits from the regions of France which were subject to the jurisdiction of the *parlement* of Paris, see Anthony Copley, *Another Letter of Mr A. C. to his Dis-Iesuited Kinseman, concerning the Appeale, State, Iesuites....* (n.p. [London], 1602), p. 24; L. Parmelee, *Good Newes from Fraunce: French Anti-League Propaganda in Late Elizabethan England* (Woodbridge, 1996), p. 148.

[88] John Mush, *A Dialogue betwixt a Secular Priest, and a Lay Gentleman* (Rheims [false imprint, printed at London], 1601), pp. 40–1.

312 CATHOLICS AND TREASON

fasts upon diverse vigils of Our Lady's feasts' and to 'forbid priests to preach'; but crucially he also 'inhibited the promulgation of a treatise allowed by Cardinal Allen containing the Acts of Twelve Martyrs', that is, William Allen's own inflammatory pamphlet, *A Briefe Historie of the Glorious Martyrdom of XII. Reverend Priests*.[89]

It was certainly possible, the appellants argued, for Catholics to demonstrate loyalty to the queen and to have dealings with her ministers without in any way compromising the purity of the Catholic faith. In the case of those priests who were known to have associated with Richard Bancroft, namely Thomas Bluet and William Clarke, Mush said merely that their record as good Catholic priests, and indeed as prisoners, spoke for itself. It was ridiculous, said Mush, to view them in the same light as those who, in the late 1580s and early 1590s, had apostatized— priests such as the notorious Thomas Bell.[90] Any kind of favour or tolerance received from the State was proof that 'our priests simply...deal in matters of religion only and no whit...intermeddle in State affairs'. They did not 'concur with Father Persons and his associates in their plotting about titles, successors, invasions and disposing of the crown and realm either in her Majesty's time or after her decease'.[91]

By contrast, the default position on these topics of writers such as Robert Persons was the one set out, as we saw, by Thomas Worthington in his *Relation of Sixtene Martyrs*.[92] The self-evident martyr-status of virtually all those who had suffered death at the hands of the queen's government proved beyond doubt that they had been killed for their religion alone and not for anything which might be described as 'politics'. Persons and his friends averred, moreover, that the martyrs, like the vast majority of Catholics, had been in sympathy with the aims and ideals of the Society of Jesus. It was the Society which had valiantly held out against the regime and resisted the kind of shady deals and compromises which otherwise would have undermined and corrupted the pure expression of the faith of the separated Catholic community. The appellants, however, had been ready to give up the struggle, to cut and run, and to do a deal with the State in order to ease the burden of persecution, though only for themselves and their fautors—not for

---

[89] LPL, Fairhurst MS 2006, fo. 264ᵛ; T. M. McCoog, 'Construing Martyrdom in the English Catholic Community, 1582–1602', in E. Shagan (ed.), *Catholics and the 'Protestant nation': Religious Politics and Identity in Early Modern England* (Manchester, 2005), pp. 95–127, at pp. 102, 103. Persons retorted simply that this appellant assertion about Heywood was 'most false': Robert Persons, *A Manifestation of the great Folly and Bad Spirit of Certayne in England calling themselves Secular Priestes....* (n.p. [Antwerp], 1602), sig. K2ʳ⁻ᵛ. Heywood's differences with Persons and Allen had become irreconcilable by 1585 when Heywood himself (arrested in December 1583) was sent into exile: D. Flynn, *John Donne and the Ancient Catholic Nobility* (Bloomington, Ind., 1995), pp. 115–16, 123, 137. For the synod in question, convened in East Anglia in spring 1583 (though, as Dr McCoog notes, the 'precise date and location are unknown'), see McCoog, *SJ*, pp. 167–8; Knox, *DD*, pp. 353–5; Christopher Bagshaw, *A Sparing Discoverie of our English Iesuits...* (n.p. [London],1601), pp. 47–8.

[90] Mush, *Dialogue*, pp. 45–7, 49–50; see also Copley, *Another Letter*, p. 8.

[91] Mush, *Dialogue*, p. 54.   [92] See pp. 290–2 above.

anyone else. Their stubborn selfishness and quarrelsomeness also sullied the witness of good Catholics who had suffered for the sins of others.[93]

The appellants were, of course, determined to deny Jesuit assertions that the Society had first claim to the tradition and spirit of martyrdom. The poet and former seminarian Anthony Copley insisted, 'show you me from Father Ignatius's time, their founder, to this day (which is now well-nigh a hundred years since) half so many martyrs throughout the whole world, in all that time, of the Society as have been of our seminaries within these thirty years here in our country'. Moreover, 'to this day, there is not so much as one canonized saint of the order, confessor, or martyr; no, not their founder [Ignatius] himself'. Just possibly, admitted Copley, there might have been 'some two or three' who were well regarded by holy Church, though they had not done much good for their own country. Perhaps Copley's own cousin, Robert Southwell SJ, had been a martyr. But Robert Persons himself 'ran away most cowardly from the like honour' of martyrdom, 'and is at this day an arrant traitor to his prince and country'. Jasper Heywood was not much of a hero. He had procured his own banishment. As John Heywood had said, when he learned that his son had joined the Society, 'Jesus, Jasper, who made you a Jesuit?' And then there was Thomas Lister—he was 'a libeller and rank schismatic' who had attacked the appellants as schismatics simply because they would not obey the archpriest.[94]

Watson commented on the 'falsehood, impiety and arrogance' in the Jesuits' 'records... of the memorable acts done by their Society, forsooth, here in England. viz. how that they only were persecuted, and not the seminary priests; how such and such, and in general, all that opposed themselves against their proceedings had suffered disgrace and shame, and came to miserable ends, notwithstanding... that there be a whole brown dozen twice over-told of glorious martyrs, all seminary priests, all defamed by them'.[95] The truth was, therefore, that there had been good priests who had suffered martyrdom. Some of them had been the Jesuits' vehement critics. According to Watson, the Jesuits' Catholic opponents took 'a right apostolic course'. Though they did not positively seek a violent death, and laboured 'to stop all occasions of shedding any man's blood', nevertheless, 'if some must be shed', they rather exposed 'themselves with patience to all hazards

---

[93] Persons had written to Garnet in July 1598 that Cardinal Baronius 'often told me that our youths', that is, those in the English College who opposed the Jesuits, 'bragged much of martyrdom but they were *refractarii* (that was his word) and had no part of' a 'martyr's spirit, which was in humility and obedience': Law, *AC*, I, p. 29; for William Watson's fury at the sight of this letter of Persons, see Watson, *Decacordon*, p. 128.

[94] Copley, *An Answere*, pp. 15, 106–8. See also Copley, *Another Letter*, p. 26, pointing to the 'pau-city' of English Jesuit martyrs. For Lister, see McCoog, *SJISE*, II, p. 100. Henry More SJ argued later that there were (relatively) few Jesuit martyrs not just because of the 'paucity' of their overall numbers but also because the persecutors feared that 'those Catholics [who were] considered to be leaders of the rest might, by their constancy in dying', animate their co-religionists: Edwards, *EJ*, p. 244.

[95] Watson, *Decacordon*, p. 5.

314 CATHOLICS AND TREASON

in suffering of their own blood to be shed for preaching, teaching and exercising of all other priestly functions'. They did not seek 'to shed [blood] or to have any others to be shed, either by invasions, rebellions, or other treasons or conspiracies whatsoever, as the Jesuits do'.[96] Watson claimed that the Jesuits' opponents who had died on the scaffold had suffered simply and merely for their faith. John Mush—who himself had once come close to trial and execution—wrote similarly that 'many priests' whom the Jesuits and their allies 'have sought vehemently to discredit by this report of being their adversaries, and therefore have disgraced them in what they could...are now glorious martyrs in heaven; which, being rejected and persecuted by them, yet laboured in Gods vineyard here' in England 'as painfully and fruitfully...as any Jesuit in the realm'. Indeed, 'when it came to the trial of their virtue, their resolution and their constant charity...the Jesuits' adversaries were always found no less patient in torments and prisons and no less courageous in shedding their blood for defence of Christ's cause than any of the Jesuits'. If anyone wanted proof, it was 'manifest (to let all the rest of the martyrs and confessors pass) in the blessed priests M. John Ingram, M. Thomas Pormort and M. Lanton [Joseph Lambton], glorious martyrs'. They had been among 'the number of the Jesuits' adversaries' and had been 'not a little afflicted and disgraced by them for the same'.[97] By contrast, the appellant John Bennett suggested that, even if it could be shown that the Jesuit priests and their sympathizers 'were more persecuted' than other Catholics, 'perchance this reason might be given thereof', that the privy council had 'found by the Jesuits' letters, which they have often intercepted, as also by some books of theirs, that they came not so much into England to set forward religion, as they would be thought to do, and as the other priests only attend to, but to further a State faction'.[98]

---

[96] Ibid., p. 186.

[97] Mush, *Dialogue*, pp. 77–8; for Pormort's alleged difficulties with the Society, see AAW, A V, no. 36, p. 121. William Clarke claimed that, as for Persons's 'vaunting of martyrs that favoured his faction and proceedings, where one has liked them, of such as have died of late, I think three have disliked and disclaimed them', namely John Jones, John Pibush, Mark Barkworth, 'and divers others': William Clarke, *A Replie unto a Certaine Libell, latelie set foorth by Fa: Parsons...intituled, a Manifestation of the great Folly*...(n.p. [London], 1603), fo. 58[r]. The martyr William Harrington 'was so oppressed with such calumnies that, having honest means for his liberty offered him, he rejected it, saying...that he must be hanged to prove himself honest'. Clarke said that while Pibush was in Gloucester prison he was 'calumniated...as inconstant in his faith'. Polydore Plasden 'was so wronged by...John Gerard's dealing...that he could not be received among his old acquaintance in London'. This had led to him being arrested and executed: ibid., fo. 17[r–v]; see also AAW, A V, no. 36, p. 121. Protestant pamphleteers picked up what they took to be the double-dealing in this appellant gloss on martyrdom. The author of *An Antiquodlibet* argued that in Watson's *Decacordon*, 'howsoever' the author 'seems elsewhere to admire her Majesty's clemency and equity in her proceedings, being rapt into a wonder that...any Romanist should be left alive', he 'does notwithstanding exceedingly deprave the honourable justice of the State, calling it an unjust vexation, and vaunting that numbers of their faction have died of late years amongst us in the glorious condition of martyrs': *An Antiquodlibet*...(1602), pp. 105–6, 107, referring to Watson, *Decacordon*, p. 277.

[98] *Copies of Certaine Discourses*...(Rouen [imprint false, printed at London], 1601), pp. 110–11.

THE APPEAL TO ROME 315

While the Jesuits and their friends declared that the persecution was an attempt to destroy the faith of godly and religious Catholics (opposed within their own community only by an emulous and contentious minority), the appellants continued to insist that the aversion of the Jesuit clergy and their friends from any kind of accommodation with the queen's government had more sinister motives. Only by continuing to provoke the regime into violence against Catholics more or less indiscriminately was it possible for Jesuit meddlers to create the kind of fissures and dissension within the English polity which could incite rebellion and facilitate a foreign invasion. They themselves profited from the divisions and quarrels that they fomented.[99] It was a frequent refrain of some of the secular clergy, as one memorandum sent in 1597 to Rome put it, even before the appointment of the archpriest, that it was commonly said in England that, had it not been for the 'pride and ambition' of the Jesuits, there would already have been some sort of toleration.[100] William Clarke declared that a toleration would be fatal to the Society because one condition of a lasting peace between Catholics and the State would be that the Jesuits would be forced to leave the realm.[101]

Christopher Bagshaw argued that in some sense the harm caused to English Catholics by the Society of Jesus was worse than the damage done by Protestants and 'it is come to this pass now that the Catholics stand in more fear of the Jesuits than of the heretics'. Furthermore, 'the Jesuits have so persecuted some priests that are now martyrs as that their death has been imputed partly to the heretics and partly to the Jesuits'.[102] No mention here, of course, of the ruthless and sadistic agents of the State who figured in the Catholic pamphlets which had dealt with martyrdom. Watson declared that 'a greater persecution is and must ensue by Blackwell's archpresbytery than ever came to Catholics by the Protestant civil magistrates'. This was because the archpresbyterate 'opened the way to all rebellion, freeing everyone to speak or do what they list or can against any except Jesuits and all under pretence of zeal in taking...the pope's part by defending' Blackwell's 'authority and calling and esteeming of us all that resist it to be schismatic or worse'. Also, 'whereas, before, some few were' made infamous by privately 'opposing' themselves 'against the Jesuits, now all that obey not Blackwell are so persecuted' by the Jesuits' and their friends' 'railing and slanderous tongues as none can live free'.[103] As John Bennett put it, if the secular clergy did engage, which by and large they did not, in Persons's conspiracies 'for the foreign invasion [of], or civil wars in, our own country', then they were 'subject to' the 'most

[99] Watson, *Decacordon*, p. 151.   [100] Inner Temple, Petyt MS 538/38, fo. 343^r.
[101] Clarke, *Replie*, fo. 80^{r-v}.
[102] This was one of a number of charges contained in an appellant memorandum (Law, *AC*, I, pp. 7–16, retained in Richard Bancroft's papers) which was printed in Christopher Bagshaw, *A True Relation of the Faction begun at Wisbich, by Fa. Edmonds, alias Weston, a Iesuite*...(n.p. [London],1601), sigs K2^r, L^r–3^v; see also AAW, A V, nos 64, 78, 79; AAW, A VI, no. 57; Inner Temple, Petyt MS 538/38, fos 337^r–9^v, 355^r–7^r; Persons, *Briefe Apologie*, fo. 22^v.
[103] Law, *AC*, I, p. 93.

316 CATHOLICS AND TREASON

grievous death', the one reserved for traitors. But, if they did not, they were made ignominious to the rest of the world by the malice of their Catholic enemies.[104] Bennett thought it was bizarre that, on Persons's account, 'all that do not like his proceedings or his treatises of matters of State, do meddle more in matters of State than he or any other'.[105]

The line taken in several of the appellant pamphlets was, as the regime itself claimed, that the queen had not used force against Catholics until she was compelled to do this by the overwhelming evidence of their sedition. After the northern rising of 1569, said the pamphlet entitled *Important Considerations*, who could be surprised that the queen had been 'moved with great displeasure' and that, in the 1571 parliament, 'a law was made containing many branches' against Catholics? The statute went too far, but the queen had been provoked excessively. In any case, 'the execution' of the new penal code 'was not so tragic as many since have written and reported of it'. Catholics had continued to goad the regime quite needlessly. Nicholas Sander's *De Visibili Monarchia* had defended the 1569 rebels. Those among them who had been put to death, declared the *Important Considerations*, were really not Catholic martyrs. They had been 'arraigned, condemned and executed by the ancient laws of our country for high treason'.[106] Furthermore, 'from the time of the said rebellion and parliament, there were' hardly 'above twelve that in ten years' were 'executed for their consciences (as we hold, although our adversaries say, for treason) and, of those twelve, some perhaps can hardly be drawn within our account, having been tainted with matters of rebellion'.[107]

Many of those who had subsequently suffered under the law of treason were, the *Important Considerations* argued, 'far from those seditious humours, being men that intended nothing else but simply the good of our country and the conversion of souls'. But 'how could either her Majesty or the State know so much? They had great cause...to suspect the worst.' Things had once been different. The queen herself had, in 1576, vetoed the draconian draft legislation in parliament. In fact, 'the estates of the whole realm assembled in parliament anno 1576 were pleased to pass over us', and 'the ancient prisoners that had been restrained more narrowly in the year 1570 were...again restored to their former liberty'.[108]

It was the Jesuit-led madness of 1580 which had brought new legislation onto the statute book as the State was goaded by the outrageous defiance of clergy such

---

[104] *Copies of Certaine Discourses*, p. 111. See also Clarke, *Replie*, fos 57ᵛ–8ᵛ. For the Jesuits and their friends, it was the other way round. Garnet commented, back in 1596, that 'as though a persecutor at home were not enough...we must be most unjustly tormented abroad' by the accusations of the Jesuits' enemies. He believed that the conflict among English Catholics in Rome originated in 'the workshop of Cecil and Topcliffe': ABSJ, GC, p. 383 (Garnet to Claudio Acquaviva, 16 April 1596; ARSJ, Anglia 38/ii, fo. 177ᵛ); Caraman, *HG*, p. 220.

[105] *Copies of Certaine Discourses*, p. 111.   [106] Bluet, *Important Considerations*, pp. 11–13.

[107] Ibid., pp. 16–17.   [108] Ibid., p. 17.

THE APPEAL TO ROME   317

as Robert Persons and Edmund Campion. The State had been justified in regarding Campion and Persons with suspicion, for their 'mission' seemed to coincide with the 'mission' of the soldier-adventurer Thomas Stukely and the warrior-priest Nicholas Sander in Ireland. The Jesuit firebrands were the real cause of the sufferings of Catholics 'upon these occasions'.[109]

The Jesuits ignored the good advice that they received from their co-religionists. Conspiracies followed thick and fast as Catholics, some more guilty than others, were crushed by the State for their presumption: Francis Throckmorton, Edward Arden and John Somerville, William Parry, Henry Percy, eighth earl of Northumberland, and Anthony Babington. Babington's attempt was 'so apparent, as we were greatly abashed at the shameless boldness of a young Jesuit', that is, Robert Southwell 'who, to excuse the said traitors and qualify their offences, presumed in a kind of supplication to her Majesty', his *Humble Supplication*, 'to ascribe the plotting of all that mischief to Master Secretary Walsingham'.[110] The appellants put Southwell's manuscript into print with a false date on it to make it seem that it had been printed while he was still alive.[111] The *Important Considerations* published what the Jesuit Richard Blount alleged that Bluet and others were verbally spreading around London. In the Clink prison, wrote Blount on 9 April 1601, Bluet railed 'most impudently' against Persons and all Jesuits, and so did 'all the rest of that crew', 'calling us all traitors to the State'.[112] Moreover, alleged Bluet and his associates, Persons had turned the seminaries into recruiting grounds for traitors.[113]

The blanket response of Persons and his friends was that, if there were plots and sedition, this had nothing to do with the Society of Jesus. Thomas Fitzherbert asked: 'what matter of State was so much as objected to M. Palaser, the priest, or to M. Talbot and to M. John Norton, condemned and executed the same year at Durham, the first only for being a priest and the other two for having been acquainted with him, and not detecting him?' What about the 'virtuous widow' who was condemned 'the last year at York for harbouring a priest called M. Christopher Wharton who was executed also with her'? (In fact Eleanor Hunt, Wharton's patron, was reprieved.) Fitzherbert cited also 'Mrs Line', who was killed merely for receiving priests 'against whom no matter of State, but only their religion and priesthood was proved, which was also most evident in M. John Pibush, M. Mark Barkworth, at London the last year, and M. Robert Nutter, M. Edward

---

[109] Ibid., p. 14.   [110] Ibid., pp. 22–3.

[111] ARCR, II, no. 717. The appellants in Rome in mid-1602 cited Southwell's book as 'heinous matter': ABSJ, PC, p. 1288 (TD, III, p. clxxix; ABSJ, Anglia III, no. 22). To the pope, Persons excused Southwell's *Humble Supplication* despite its controversial subject matter, saying that if it might be found to 'include any incautious statement on matters of faith...it is something entirely spurious and supposititious which had been added to it' by the person who procured it to be printed: ABSJ, PC, pp. 1196–7 (ABSJ, Collectanea P/ii, p. 466ᵇ).

[112] ABSJ, Collectanea M, p. 95ᵃ.   [113] Bluet, *Important Considerations*, pp. 30–1.

318 CATHOLICS AND TREASON

Thwing, M. Thurstan Hunt and M. Middleton at Lancaster, as also in the case of M. Filcock...all of them martyred only for being Catholic priests'.[114]

The intra-Catholic arguments at this point about martyrdom were part of a wider debate between the appellants and their critics about what it meant to evangelize in the Catholic tradition. For Bluet, the way to bring the faith to the English nation was not through 'Jesuitical plots' and 'treasons and invasions'. Instead, the 'ancient manner of planting the Catholic faith has been, by preaching, prayers, private instructions, confessions' and 'absolutions', and by 'the exercising of other priestly functions, given *ad aedificationem* not *ad destructionem*, to teach obedience, not rebellion'.[115]

John Bennett insisted that the to-and-fro contentions over the archpresbyterate had dispatched hundreds of souls to Hell. The Catholic cause was, as a result, so badly damaged that 'the labours of all the priests of England, yes, I say more, all their blood', that is, if they were all to be martyred, would 'never recover what hereby' had 'been lost'.[116] The potentially good example set by Catholic martyrdoms was being corrupted by exactly the kind of tainted motives which the regime claimed to detect among those Catholics whom it put to death. By contrast, the appellants protested that they themselves evangelized in the manner that Christ 'left...to all his apostles to imitate'.[117] With his customary savage wit, Bagshaw mocked Persons as the fount of counterfeit martyrdom and said in effect that he would make a good (false) martyr himself. Persons had militated against toleration for English Catholics, said Bagshaw, because 'a toleration would make the Catholics of England dull and without spirit'. This made Bagshaw reflect that 'it is indeed quickness that this father desires, but such a quickness as deserves a quick dispatch at the gallows' and 'we trust he shall never draw our Catholics here to any such quickness but that, after our dull manner, we shall forever continue her Majesty's most faithful subjects' and, therefore, not fall into the danger of the law.[118]

This was where the question of episcopal government in the English Church, which was so central to the archpriest affair and for which a number of secular clergy lobbied and agitated, was crucial. In a narrow legal sense, the institution of a Catholic episcopate in the queen's dominions was completely irreconcilable with several of the principal Reformation statutes. Almost inevitably, said the appellants' enemies, the State would retaliate. If Rome were to institute Catholic jurisdictional authority of that kind within the English realm, there would in short order be an even more intense persecution raised against Catholics than the one that they were currently suffering. But the appellants' claim was that episcopal authority, understood rightly, was a guarantee of good order among Catholics

---

[114] Fitzherbert, *A Defence*, fo. 10[r-v]; for Wharton and Hunt, see Challoner, *MMP*, pp. 237, 238.
[115] Bluet, *Important Considerations*, pp. 1–2.   [116] LPL, Fairhurst MS 2014, fo. 121[v].
[117] Watson, *Decacordon*, pp. 184, 231–3.   [118] Bagshaw, *A Sparing Discoverie*, p. 69.

THE APPEAL TO ROME 319

and would serve as a firewall against precisely the sort of sedition practised by those who misused and distorted contemporary theory about the political powers inherent in the papacy and in the 'people'. The appellants, *sotto voce* at first but increasingly stridently later on, demanded that Rome grant full episcopal jurisdiction to an English Catholic clergyman, in other words to one of their own number, who would exercise that power appropriately and for the good of the Church and in no way in opposition to the will, or at least the real and best interests, of the State and certainly not in the manner that the archpresbyterate's authority had been allegedly hijacked and used by a narrow, factional, foreign-controlled, and Jesuitical interest.[119] As Watson saw it, had it not been for the archpresbyterate, there would already have been a form of Catholic episcopate, though one which would have functioned 'privately, as it was in the apostles' time and primitive Church' and would not have antagonized the queen.[120]

Episcopal government was not just about the mechanics of clerical administration. The appellant writers argued that the special characteristics of episcopacy (crucially, the sacrament of confirmation as conferred by a bishop, particularly in a time of persecution) were essential to the spiritual health of the Church.[121] The reinforcement in this way of the usual structures of the Church would sustain it and prevent Catholics falling away from the faith. The obvious point of comparison here was Ireland. It was 'an island subject to her Majesty' and with 'like diversity of religion as England' had. But it was 'never in all this while destitute of one, two or more' bishops, 'made successively by the favour and appointment of the see apostolic'.[122] Robert Persons, unsurprisingly, could not accept this. It implied that the papacy had erred in 'suffering England to be so long without bishops'.[123]

The appellants' demands were, however, equally intolerable to some within the regime who regarded their programme as a Trojan horse, designed to secure tolerance by stealth. If, to prevent this, it was necessary to resort again to the use of the treason statutes, so be it. That was exactly what happened as Elizabeth's reign drew to a close. Richard Blount, writing on 5 May 1602 and looking back on the last couple of months, remarked with bitter irony that John Mush had proved 'a true prophet' when he 'wrote in a letter about a year since (as I remember) that

---

[119] For the first appeal's request for 'subordination', see John Bennett, *The Hope of Peace*.... (Frankfurt [imprint false; printed in London], 1601), p. 28; see also Persons, *Briefe Apologie*, sigs R6^v–S2^v. For petitions formulated by leading appellants in May 1598 for a grant of episcopal authority, see ABSJ, Anglia II, no. 47.

[120] Watson, *Decacordon*, pp. 151–2.

[121] For John Colleton's extensive comments on the necessity of an episcopate for the provision of the sacrament of confirmation, see John Colleton, *A Iust Defence of the Slandered Priestes*...(n.p. [London], 1602), pp. 16–18. See also Charnock, *A Reply to a Notorious Libell*, pp. 137–41. For contemporary debate about the necessity of episcopal government over the Church, see A. F. Allison, 'A Question of Jurisdiction: Richard Smith, Bishop of Chalcedon and the Catholic Laity, 1625–1631', *RH* 16 (1982), pp. 111–45.

[122] Colleton, *Iust Defence*, p. 16.

[123] Persons, *Briefe Apologie*, fo. 169^v.

320   CATHOLICS AND TREASON

these broils', that is to say, the battles between the appellants and their enemies, 'would not be ended without blood and that, whosoever should happen to have the victory, it should cost them the best blood in their veins'. For the fact, as Blount bitterly observed, was that 'now have we had six executed together, two in the North and four in London'. The two martyrs in the North were James Harrison and Anthony Bates, hanged in York on 22 March 1602. Bates's wife was condemned as well, but she was reprieved on the grounds of her pregnancy.[124]

Those Catholics who had suffered at Tyburn on 20 April 1602, recorded Blount, were the priests Francis Page, Robert Watkinson, Thomas Tichborne and the layman James Duckett, as well as, said William Sterrell, 'one [Peter] Bullock, a stationer', though, wrote Sterrell, the latter two were hanged on the previous day, with Duckett exhorting Bullock, who had denounced Duckett, to die as a Catholic. Duckett was a godson of James Leyburn, who had been executed in 1583.[125] He had come to the authorities' notice for a number of illicit publications and particularly of devotional works.[126] But he was executed for 'divulging' Robert Southwell's 'answer to the proclamation', that is, his *Humble Supplication*, 'which the malcontents printed' but which the archpriest George Blackwell had 'prohibited as a thing out of season'.[127] Watkinson had been picked out by a spy, one John Fawther, who had been at the English college at Douai.[128]

For commentators who were aligned with the archpriest, there was a grim satisfaction to be had here that the self-styled loyalist enemies of the Society were finding out at first hand what persecution was really like. Duckett denied the

---

[124]   AAW, A VII, no. 41, p. 232; RC, p. 64 (AAW, A VII, no. 39); Anstr., I, pp. 150–1; ABSJ, GC (Garnet to Persons, 14 April 1602; ABSJ, Collectanea P/ii, p. 554ᵃ). James Harrison had been harboured by Thomas Heath of Comberford Hall, Staffordshire, and had been lodged in the Tower on 11 May 1588, while Heath had been dispatched to Newgate. In March 1602 Harrison was arrested again (by Sir Stephen Procter) and was hanged, with Anthony Bates: Pollen, *UD*, pp. 154, 162–3; Anstr., I, p. 151; PRO, KB 9/675, pt II, no. 206; see p. 191 n.56 above. According to Procter, Bates had been a servant to Sir John Yorke of Nidderdale: ABSJ, CP (James Harrison); PRO, STAC 8/19/10, pt I, fo. 22ʳ; C. Howard, *Sir John Yorke of Nidderdale 1565–1634* (1939), p. 14.

[125]   AAW, A VII, no. 41, p. 232; RC, pp. 57–9 (AAW, A VII, no. 39); Jeaffreson, *MCR*, II, pp. 199–200; Lake and Questier, *Archpriest*, p. 113. For Challoner's narrative of James Duckett, derived from an account by Duckett's son, the Carthusian John Duckett, see Challoner, *MMP*, pp. 261–4, based on the version in Alban Butler's papers (ABP, pp. 623–31); AAW, A VII, no. 74, pp. 339–42 (transcript in Pollen, *AEM*, pp. 238–48). The Carthusian's narrative strongly implied that Duckett had, before his conversion, been of a puritan disposition.

[126]   Pollen, *AEM*, pp. 241–5. William Sterrell recounted on 28 April 1602 how Duckett had initially 'pleaded effectually for himself' (he had been 'promised pardon if he would accuse others'). The 'jury...delivered their verdict [of] not guilty, yet the chief justice made them go together again and, at their second return, they were of another mind': RC, p. 58 (AAW, A VII, no. 39).

[127]   AAW, A VII, no. 41, p. 232 (for Grene's summary of this letter, see ABSJ, Collectanea M, p. 98ᵇ); RC, p. 58 (AAW, A VII, no. 39); Lake and Questier, *Archpriest*, p. 113. Tichborne's harbourers, George and Mary Bailey, had secured pardons after being prosecuted in March 1601: Jeaffreson, *MCR*, I, p. 269, II, pp. 198–9.

[128]   RC, p. 57 (AAW, A VII, no. 39); AAW, A VII, no. 37, pp. 215–16 (John Fawther's report of 10 April 1602); Anstr., I, p. 372; HMCS, XIV, p. 123. (It appears that PRO, SP 12/283/86. ii (*CSPD 1601–3*, pp. 180–2) may be another information by Fawther, delivered to Richard Bancroft and passed on by him to Sir Robert Cecil on 27 April 1602.) See also Lake and Questier, *Archpriest*, pp. 113–14.

THE APPEAL TO ROME   321

charges against him, particularly that he had had, in his possession, copies of Southwell's pamphlet. But he admitted that he had been involved in the binding and distribution of a work by Richard Bristow, his *Briefe Treatise*.[129]

It was equally satisfying that some of those who had been opposed to the Jesuits were now, under the lash of adversity, changing their minds. Thomas Tichborne had, it seems, once been reckoned an enemy of the Society of Jesus.[130] But it was said that a search of his chamber in the Clink prison revealed letters from Blackwell and from Garnet himself. In fact, Tichborne had recently written in the most effusive terms to Blackwell. Back in late March 1598, according to Garnet, William Waad had, after Tichborne was first arrested, 'charged him with being one of the malcontents in the college at Rome'. Tichborne repudiated the accusation, though Waad urged,'never deny it...you shall fare the better for it'.[131] The informer John Bird noted that Tichborne had been betrayed by the renegade priest William Atkinson, presumably when Atkinson detected that Tichborne was no longer the loyalist that Atkinson may have once thought that he was.[132] Christopher Grene's notes made in Rome in the later 1670s relate that Atkinson 'afterwards confessed, as...appears by several of his letters written and yet extant, that' William Watson's excoriating attack on the Jesuits, entitled *A Decacordon of Ten Quodlibeticall Questions*, 'did first persuade him to betray' Tichborne, and that Watson had approved what he (Atkinson) did.[133]

As Blount and Sterrell saw it, however, none of this would have happened had the appellants not provoked the malice of those hard-line Protestants who disapproved of these secular priests' approaches to and collaboration with the regime. These recent executions had been staged to 'satisfy in some sort the puritans' who had begun to suspect that the privy council was leaning towards tolerance for

---

[129] Pollen, *AEM*, pp. 245–7.

[130] On 2 May 1599 Garnet had written to Persons that Tichborne had broken 'out of prison' and declared his 'obedience' and, Garnet hoped, would 'do well, though in the Clink all the malcontents did resort unto him': ABSJ, GC (2 May 1599; ABSJ, Collectanea P/ii, p. 552b).

[131] ABSJ, Collectanea P/ii, pp. 545–6; ABSJ, GC, p. 471 (ABSJ, Collectanea P/ii, p. 551); ABSJ, A V, no. 8 (unfoliated); AAW, A VII, no. 28, p. 193 (Bartholomew Audley [i.e. Thomas Tichborne] to George Blackwell, 7 [or 9] February [1602]).

[132] *HMCS*, XII, p. 265; Fitzherbert, *A Defence*, fo. 13r; Anstr., I, p. 13.

[133] ABSJ, CP (Thomas Tichborne; Christopher Grene, 'De Thoma Tichburno...', c.1678, transcribed from AVCAU, Scr. 36/8/3). Blount evidently had not entirely forgiven Tichborne for his previous opposition to the Society. Blount claimed that Tichborne had 'said nothing, neither at his arraignment nor at his death by reason of his weakness (as I take it) and not being well able to hear what was said unto him. He was suspected before of favouring the discontented and at his arraignment was charged by the chief justice [Popham] of dissolute life and thereby to have gotten the French disease whereunto, he replying nothing, many condemned him in their own conceits and much speech is of it of all sorts but, howsoever it be, he has now made amends for all': AAW, A VII, no. 41, p. 232. Garnet still harboured doubts about Tichborne and said that not only had he been declared by Popham to have had the 'French disease', which was 'scandalous to Catholics, being very probable', but also that (even if he had 'died a martyr') he was 'too neutral in his life': ABSJ, GC (Garnet to Persons, 5 May 1602; ABSJ, Collectanea N/i, p. 38; ABSJ, Collectanea P/ii, p. 547).

322   CATHOLICS AND TREASON

some Catholic clergy, that is, those who were useful politically.[134] Garnet wrote to
Persons on 5 May 1602 not only that the appellant lobby had brought all this
down on themselves and others but also that the outcome had shown how morally bankrupt the appellants were. Robert Southwell had penned 'a very good
answer to the proclamation but it could never be set forth'. When one Mr Boswell
(possibly the secular priest John Bosvile) 'either for lucre or malice meant to print
it, your friend Henry', that is, Garnet himself, 'seeing that now matters were
quieted, and many other answers divulged, and that it might breed new troubles,
requested' the archpriest Blackwell 'to forbid it'. But the wretched appellants
refused to take any notice and now look what had happened—though perhaps
this was a kind of justice since the appellants had been trying to exploit the saintly
Southwell's work for their own thoroughly nasty and venal purposes. The 'malcontents' had tried to save Duckett and Bullock 'and had, for that effect, Sir John
Stanhope's letters'. The fact that Blackwell had tried to prevent Southwell's work
being printed at all showed that he was more in touch with what the late
Elizabethan regime wanted than were the appellants.[135]

Francis Page had been the true hero. He had pronounced the necessary vows in
order to be admitted into the Society of Jesus on the morning of the execution. At
Tyburn he declared himself to be a Jesuit. He 'died [a member] of the Society with
much alacrity and spiritual joy'. Page's action may well have been interpreted by
observers as itself an intervention in the Archpriest Dispute.[136] Robert Watkinson
also perished 'very resolutely and with much edification'. Since Watkinson had
been denounced by John Fawther, it was possible to see him as a victim of the
kind of double-dealing which, the Jesuits and their friends thought, characterized
the whole of the appellant agitation.[137]

---

[134] AAW, A VII, no. 41, p. 234; RC, pp. 60–1 (AAW, A VII, no. 39), cited in Lake and Questier,
Archpriest, p. 114. Sterrell said, however, that the queen was entirely behind the cruelty used against
these Catholics and had personally ordered Popham to 'proceed': RC, p. 61; P. Martin and J. Finnis,
'"The Secret Sharers": "Anthony Rivers" and the Appellant Controversy, 1601–2', *Huntingdon Library
Quarterly* 69 (2006), pp. 195–238, at p. 230.
[135] ABSJ, GC (5 May 1602; ABSJ, Collectanea P/ii, p. 547); RC, p. 58 (AAW, A VII, no. 39); Martin
and Finnis, '"The Secret Sharers"', p. 227. Despite his having worked for the appellants, Duckett had,
said Garnet, 'died well and asked forgiveness' of Blackwell and the Jesuits 'for adhering to the malcontents': ABSJ, GC (5 May 1602); Caraman, *HG*, p. 295. Blount also thought that Duckett 'died exceedingly well, disclaimed the malcontents... and spoke to his wife to burn all such books of theirs as were
in his house': AAW, A VII, no. 41, p. 232. Mark Barkworth claimed that Sir John Stanhope (Edward
Stanhope's brother) had, on four occasions, 'written and spoken for me': Bodl., MS Eng. th. b. 2, p. 106
(for which reference I am grateful to Lucy Underwood).
[136] ABSJ, GC (5 May 1602; ABSJ, Collectanea P/ii, p. 547); ABSJ, Collectanea P/ii, p. 554ᵃ; ARSJ,
Anglia 31/i, p. 233; McCoog, *SJISE*, II, p. 300. Page's words at execution were 'interrupted... by a clam-
orous minister that had more drink in his head than wit': RC, p. 59 (AAW, A VII, no. 39). Anthony
Champney's 'Annales' mentioned Page's membership of the Society but, predictably, not the circumstances: AAW, F 1, p. 1023.
[137] AAW, A VII, no. 41, p. 233. For the stories which arrived back at Douai and were incorporated
in the college diary, from which they found their way into Challoner's text, see E. H. Burton and
T. L. Williams (eds), *The Douay College Diaries...* (CRS 10, 1911), pp. 40, 334–5; AAW, B 28, no. 12,
p. 374. The minister who had harangued Page at the gallows also urged Watkinson ('calling him

THE APPEAL TO ROME   323

The horrors inflicted on these Catholics had, however, not been enough to assuage the concerns of the regime's hardliners. A letter written by a Catholic in London on 18 May 1602 reported the dissent rumoured to have been expressed in the privy council, apparently in late April 1602, about the way that Catholics were being dealt with. Sir William Knollys 'made a long and biting speech to incite the rest of her Majesty's...council against us'. He condemned 'the liberty of late granted unto Catholics'. Therefore, 'to prevent rebellion which was justly feared' from Catholics, 'some rigour of force must be showed'. He was seconded by 'the lord chief justice', Sir John Popham. 'Both affirmed...that great danger would ensue, seeing' that 'priests had more favour than many ministers; yes, idolatry (as they termed it) was practised freely about the realm'. 'Papists' were 'grown so bold that they durst publicly speak of toleration in religion'. Exactly 'how contrary it would be to the safety of this realm, and to the noble mind of her Majesty, whose safety was so long continued by' the 'defence of the gospel, all men might judge'. Popham and Knollys insisted that priests must die 'according to the law'. In addition, 'all recusants should be imprisoned and all armour and horses taken from them'. Other council members were unhappy with this. They thought that it might 'provoke so many gentlemen of worth who either paid monthly for their conscience according to the statute or else yielded two parts of their lands and livings'. Besides this, 'it would much stain her Majesty's credit abroad to prosecute men so violently for their conscience only', especially since she proclaimed that she 'prosecuted none for conscience but for practices' against the State.[138]

But, as this writer observed, in spite of these doubts voiced among his conciliar colleagues, Popham had been given a privy-council warrant to proceed against priests who 'came before him' as long as he used 'his discretion'. As a result, he 'directed a search' of 'the Clink where only such priests are imprisoned as the State had favoured, whose lives he chiefly desired because he might so have ample liberty to hang all at his pleasure'. He wanted to 'overthrow' the 'credit' of those 'whom he knew were most protected'. During the search, there were 'taken above thirty Catholics with Mr Watson...who were all committed to several prisons; and Watson, pleading his protection, his letters were twice or thrice rejected'

Robin, swearing that he knew his parents, and him from his infancy') to 'submit himself to her Majesty who had mercy yet in store': RC, p. 59 (AAW, A VII, no. 39).

[138] LPL, MS 3472, fo. 24ʳ; Lake and Questier, Archpriest, pp. 111–12. William Sterrell had, in mid-January 1601, observed Popham's liaising with Thomas Felton in the enforcement of the recusancy statutes: RC, pp. 9–10 (AAW, A VII, no. 1). Sterrell had also noted in early March 1602 how 'the lord keeper and chief justice do much mislike that, by the favour of the bishop of London, the discontented [i.e. the appellant clergy] have such liberty': RC, p. 35 (AAW, A VII, no. 29). In mid-1602, Sir Thomas Cecil, Lord Burghley, the lord president of the council in the North, himself was perplexed by what he took to be the privy council's leniency and favour shown to the appellant Cuthbert Trollop, to whom Bancroft had actively extended his patronage: CSPD 1601–3, pp. 211–12 (PRO, SP 12/284/52); HMCS, XII, pp. 194, 232–3, 238, 243; Anstr., I, pp. 363–4; M. Questier, 'Sermons, Separatists and Succession Politics in Late Elizabethan England', JBS 52 (2013), pp. 290–316, at pp. 313–14; Lake and Questier, Archpriest, pp. 124–5.

324 CATHOLICS AND TREASON

because Popham 'had verily purposed to begin with him'. William Clarke and Francis Barnaby 'had their chambers spoiled and all books, pictures and the like taken from them'.[139] Popham and his friends were evidently trying very hard to disrupt the appellants' semi-public performance of loyalist Catholicism, currently being sponsored by Richard Bancroft and his associates. Sterrell reported that, on the day after the search, Archbishop Whitgift sent for Watson out of the king's bench prison. Bancroft was present as well. They told Watson's keeper to get lost and then gave Watson 'a warrant under both their' and Sir Robert Cecil's 'hands'; and they offered that 'if any fees were due...they would see the same discharged'. Via Bancroft's intervention, 'most of the rest of the company', that is, those in the prison, 'that stood anything affected to the faction [the appellants] or had any money to give, are since discharged'.[140]

This partial rebuff for the lord chief justice was taken by the appellants as a sign that they were still likely to benefit by their policy of accommodation with the regime.[141] But as the forensic investigations of the appellant business by Patrick Martin and John Finnis have conclusively shown, the appellants' representations on this score at Rome were repackaged and broadcast by their enemies there so as to alienate the queen's government in London.[142] One newsletter retained in Sir Robert Cecil's papers, written on 4/14 June 1602 and sent from Venice but reporting events in Rome, alleged that the appellants, once they had arrived in the holy city, had 'presented to his Holiness' a document in which Elizabeth asked 'that all the censures published against her by former popes' might 'be removed'. In return for this act of grace, she was prepared to guarantee 'that all the Catholics in her realm' should 'have security for the public exercise of their religion'. She also 'greatly' commended 'the goodness and sanctity of the pope, calling him the true vicar of Christ and teacher of the people'. Henry IV was said to 'be the author and mediator' of all this.[143] As John Bossy comments, the thing 'rebounded unfortunately when news arrived that Elizabeth had just executed' a number of Catholics. When the appellant priest John Cecil had an audience with the pope and trotted

[139] LPL, MS 3472, fo. 24^r. On 28 April 1602, Sterrell wrote for Persons's benefit a report on (it would appear) the same search. Popham's men raided the Clink 'on Low Sunday', i.e. 11 April, on the basis either of the 'treachery' of the renegade William Atkinson 'as most think...or by falsehood in fellowship amongst the discontented themselves (as the manner of proceeding with Watson ministered suspicion)': RC, p. 55 (AAW, A VII, no. 39); Lake and Questier, *Archpriest*, pp. 112–13. Following the executions of Page and the others, people thought William Clarke would be proceeded against, but Bancroft prevented this: RC, p. 60 (AAW, A VII, no. 39). According to Sterrell on 26 May 1602, Atkinson had been thrown into Newgate because he now refused to cooperate with Popham and even said that he would not have done what he did 'if he had thought [that] they would have put them to death': RC, p. 77 (AAW, A VII, no. 44).

[140] RC, p. 56 (AAW, A VII, no. 39).   [141] LPL, MS 3472, fo. 24^r.

[142] Martin and Finnis, '"The Secret Sharers"', pp. 229–31 and *passim*.

[143] HMCS, XIV, p. 217. For a newsletter to similar effect from Rome, dated 29 May/8 June 1602, see HMCS, XII, p. 253. John Bossy notes the appearance at this point of a story in the Roman Gazette that Elizabeth wanted to make her peace with the papacy and would concede toleration. Bossy attributed the appearance of the story to the French ambassador, Philippe de Béthune: Bossy, EC, pp. 264–5.

THE APPEAL TO ROME   325

out his spiel about toleration, the pope said that, regrettably, he (John Cecil) had got it all wrong.[144] A note of 5/15 June, passed to Sir Robert Cecil by Thomas Phelippes, declared that the rumour of toleration, 'being boldly avouched by many...was partly believed until the relation of the last English martyrs arrived' which 'much helped the archpriest's cause'.[145]

This was certainly ammunition for those who wanted to argue that the attempted cohabitation of the appellants with the regime simply made matters worse than they already were.[146] But Anthony Copley replied that it was puritans who wanted 'to drive' Catholics 'to despair'. It was those puritans who were the real threat to the queen's safety. In any case, good Catholics (though not Jesuits, of course) would remain loyal. It should be remembered 'how little Queen Mary profited this realm in Catholic religion by her severity against Protestants'.[147] Catholics who provoked the State into persecution and suffered as a result would not be martyrs. A number of 'Jesuited Catholics' were 'surly' in the face of authority. Instead, thought Copley, 'our obedience and service ought...to be discreet and as much as may be to edification'. For 'the Protestants that suffered in Queen Mary's time for their errors in religion were in this point many of them to be commended, they fashioning their terms very reverently to the civil magistrate; and shall we then that are Catholics be to learn of them'? Good Catholics should therefore 'hope that, seeing blood will have blood, the Protestants' hand, that we are now under, will one day be satisfied for the Protestant blood, in my opinion, too profusely shed, and other their vexations in the aforesaid good queen's days'.[148]

Endgame: Proclamations and Protestations

If some who, by their own lights, were loyalist Catholics thought that their launching of themselves into a public debate about the problems posed by puritanism, as Copley and his friends had done, would persuade the regime to allow a public and formal measure of tolerance to them, they were not rewarded in the way that they hoped, although the French ambassador, Christophe de Harlay, count of Beaumont, was given vague assurances about some sort of future and informal restriction of the law as it applied to Catholic separatism.[149] In the dying days of the queen's government, a royal proclamation of 5 November 1602 denounced all Catholic clergy alike. It made virtually no distinction between the Jesuits and their Catholic clerical opponents and it absolutely denied that there would or could be 'toleration of two religions'. The Catholics' hopes for a

---

[144] Bossy, EC, p. 265.
[145] PRO, SP 12/284/88. i (CSPD 1601–3, p. 227); Martin and Finnis, ' "The Secret Sharers" ', p. 230; see also CSPD 1601–3, p. 228 (PRO, SP 12/284/89. i); Martin and Finnis, ' "The Secret Sharers" ', p. 230.
[146] RC, p. 67 (AAW, A VII, no. 42).   [147] Copley, Another Letter, pp. 17–18.
[148] Ibid., p. 19.   [149] Bossy, EC, pp. 283, 283^{b-c}.

326   CATHOLICS AND TREASON

toleration were accompanied 'with very great liberty and intolerable presumption'.[150] On 23 October/2 November 1602, Beaumont attributed the imminent proclamation to the puritans.[151] Professor Bossy interprets the release of the proclamation as a shattering blow for the appellant cause. The returning appellant agents, in Paris, tried to persuade Henry IV to intervene to get the proclamation modified, but they were unsuccessful.[152] The proclamation, however, left just a scintilla of doubt about whether all Catholics were equally tarred with the same taint of treason. Some appellants thought that it implied they were potentially acceptable to the queen.[153] An angry letter to Sir John Popham, written on 1 December 1602, said that the Catholics 'interpret the proclamation rather to be a reproof of the busy Protestants called pamphleteers than a denunciation of justice against their treacheries'. The writer hoped that Popham would teach such people a lesson.[154]

In one sense, what the regime was trying to do here was, simply as one might expect, to hold the ring in expectation of King James's arrival in London. This was an event that could not be that far off.[155] On 15 December 1602, Sterrell believed that the proclamation had not yet been put into effect. Beaumont concluded on 28 December/7 January 1603 that the queen herself was satisfied enough with the courses taken by the appellants in Rome.[156]

The appellants' last gambit came when a group of thirteen priests signed and submitted a protestation of allegiance. Four of them took it to Bancroft on the night of 31 January 1603. The protestation repudiated the use of papal authority against the queen.[157] It was a response to the proclamation's wafer-thin offer to lift the sentence of exile on the 'secular priests that are at liberty and, in some things, opposite unto the Jesuits' if they should, before the first day of January, present themselves to one of a named set of officials (privy councillors, bishops, etc.) and acknowledge 'sincerely their duty and allegiance unto us'.[158] But the protestation

[150] Hughes and Larkin, *TRP*, III, no. 817 (quotation at p. 253); RC, pp. 122, 127 (AAW, A VII, nos 60, 61); McClure, *LJC*, I, p. 171; Lake and Questier, *Archpriest*, pp. 122–4. For the purpose of the proclamation, see Martin and Finnis, 'The Secret Sharers', pp. 233–5.

[151] Bodl., Carte MS 82, no. 179, fo. 145ʳ⁻ᵛ. On 25 November/5 December, however, Beaumont believed that Sir Robert Cecil intended to use the proclamation to rebut puritan attacks on himself: Bodl., Carte MS 82, no. 187, fo. 146ʳ; Lake and Questier, *Archpriest*, p. 122.

[152] Bossy, 'Henri IV', p. 88.   [153] Law, *AC*, II, p. 221.

[154] *HMCS*, XII, pp. 499–500. The origin and even the date of this letter are obscure. It is calendared, speculatively, to 1602, and this would make sense in the context of the November 1602 proclamation.

[155] There was, especially during and after mid-1602, a clear split on the privy council (with Popham and Egerton opposed to Bancroft) about how to deal with the appellants; see Martin and Finnis, 'The Secret Sharers', p. 216.

[156] RC, p. 135 (AAW, A VII, no. 68); Bodl., Carte MS 82, nos 192, 193; Lake and Questier, *Archpriest*, p. 123.

[157] Bossy, *ECC*, p. 35; Bossy, 'Henri IV', pp. 89–90; *CSPD 1601–3*, pp. 285–6 (PRO, SP 12/287/14); Lake and Questier, *Archpriest*, pp. 126–7. For Bossy's explanation of how limited in scope the protestation was, see Bossy, *ECC*, p. 39; and for its sponsors' explanation of why it had to be so (for otherwise their credit with other Catholics would be dashed), see *HMCS*, XII, pp. 631–2.

[158] Hughes and Larkin, *TRP*, III, no. 817 (quotation at p. 254), cited in Lake and Questier, *Archpriest*, p. 127.

THE APPEAL TO ROME   327

was rejected by the privy council. Those Catholic clergymen who had presented it were imprisoned.[159]

The priest William Richardson was, as the newsletter writer John Chamberlain noted, 'taken in Clements Inn' and was 'executed at Tyburn' on, as it seems, 17 February, five days after his arrest. He was known not to be sympathetic to the appellants—very much not, said Garnet.[160] Sterrell commented that Richardson was a victim of Lord Chief Justice Popham's malice. Popham had barged into the courtroom on 16 February, 'interrupting other trials' in progress, and had demanded that Richardson should be arraigned at once. According to Sterrell, Popham was in effect the only witness against him. At Tyburn, the priest spoke 'against the chief justice's cruelty, on whom alone he laid the guilt of his blood', while 'all the rest of the council seem to plead ignorance of the fact'. But Richardson 'was less favoured for not favouring the faction', that is, the appellants. At his arraignment he had explicitly praised the Jesuits as 'good and religious men'. This undoubtedly did not help his cause.[161] Sterrell claimed also that Popham, 'in his circuit…intended to have put four more to death at Bury', that is, from among the Catholics who were imprisoned at Framlingham. One of those would almost certainly have been Cuthbert Trollop, whom Bancroft had just saved from the wrath of Lord President Burghley. But 'the council signified her Majesty's pleasure to the contrary'.[162]

It seems that those in the regime who did not want to see all Catholics treated equally harshly may have got their retaliation in when, at the same time as the proceedings against Richardson, a 'youth of Merton College' named Thomas Darling was 'censured' in star chamber. As John Chamberlain recounted, Darling 'pretended heretofore to be dispossessed of a devil' by John Darrell. The star chamber judges ordered that he should 'be whipped and lose his ears for libelling' the Oxford vice-chancellor, John Howson, whose recent preaching had excited puritan anger, though in fact Darling had said a good deal else and had 'taxed' Lord Buckhurst and Sir Robert Cecil 'of papistry, as also' Sir John Fortescue, Archbishop Whitgift, and Bishop Bancroft.[163] Sterrell recorded that, on 18 February 1603,

---

[159] Bossy, ECC, pp. 40–1.

[160] McClure, LJC, I, p. 186 (cited in Lake and Questier, Archpriest, p. 127); CSPV 1592–1603, p. 561; RC, p. 142 (PRO, SP 12/287/50); ABSJ, GC (16 March 1603; ABSJ, Collectanea P/ii, p. 554b). Some sources (e.g. Bodl., Carte MS 82, no. 207, fo. 148r; McClure, LJC, I, p. 186) date his execution to 16 February.

[161] RC, pp. 142–3 (PRO, SP 12/287/50), 152–3 (PRO, SP 12/287/51); Anstr., I, pp. 288–9; Lake and Questier, Archpriest, p. 127. Beaumont reported on 26 February 1603 that the lord chief justice had a list of 'permitted' priests and that one, i.e. Richardson, who was not on the list was arrested while celebrating Mass and had been executed: Bodl., Carte MS 82, no. 207, fo. 148r.

[162] RC, p. 160 (PRO, SP 12/287/52); HMCS, XII, p. 243.

[163] McClure, LJC, I, pp. 186, 185 (Howson's recent sermon in Oxford, which Chamberlain sent to Carleton with his letter of 11 February 1603); Lake and Questier, Archpriest, p. 128; ABSJ, Anglia III, no. 9 (Richard Blount to Robert Persons, 17 February 1603 (misdated to 14 February 1602 and partially mistranscribed in Foley, RSJ, I, pp. 18–19, and followed uncritically in Questier, C&C, pp. 262–3)); for Howson's preaching in 1597 and 1598 at Paul's Cross, see K. Fincham and N. Tyacke,

328 CATHOLICS AND TREASON

Darling was taken into Cheapside and 'there set on the pillory' and 'had one of his ears cut off'. But, owing to the intervention of the countess of Warwick, the full penalty was not inflicted.[164]

For its part, the privy council was trying hard to spin the imminent accession of James Stuart as an essentially seamless and Protestant continuation of Tudor rule. It was also trying to protect itself from accusations, which were far from inaccurate, that it had enlisted one influential strand of contemporary Catholic opinion in order to prevent the accession from being dominated by puritan agitation for further reform. The problem was that the appellant agitation had created an echo chamber of speculation about how the settlement of religion might change with the arrival in London of a new monarch.

The scattering of treason arraignments in the run-up to the accession, reviewed in this chapter, alerts us to the significance of the Catholic contribution to the debates over *fin de siècle* succession politics. While the English State inflicted the treason statutes' penalties on some Catholic separatists, it granted others a voice in the discussion of the political future. Conventionally, scholars have tended to see the Catholic 'issue' as virtually irrelevant in England by the end of the sixteenth century. Despite the temporary popularity of so-called 'revisionist' accounts of the English Reformation, in which European Protestant notions are reckoned to have been much less prevalent in England than formerly thought, the majority historical position is—believe me—still largely that of William Trimble, articulated back in the 1960s. For Trimble, by the end of the Tudor period, the 'Catholics of England...constituted a disenfranchised, leaderless, amorphous group dependent for their welfare upon the will and the whim of the governing authorities'.[165]

In the context of all the research published since the 1960s on what John Bossy called the 'Catholic community', that might seem to be an obsolete perspective; but it is the one that by and large persists in the 'mainstream' literature. One can see how Trimble arrived at some of his conclusions. After all, there was never a Catholic equivalent, in parliament, the established Church, in the court, and in regional power centres of what scholars have termed the 'puritan movement' of Elizabeth's reign. But one of the claims made in this (and indeed the previous) chapter is that the deployment of the law against Catholic separatists was becoming, if anything, more controversial during the 1590s.

Of course, as Lucy Underwood has rightly pointed out to me, there was hardly an execution of a separatist Catholic in this whole period which was not highly

---

Altars Restored: The Changing Face of English Religious Worship, 1547–c. 1700 (Oxford, 2007), pp. 86–7. For Darrell's exorcisms, see T. S. Freeman, 'Demons, Deviance and Defiance: John Darrell and the Politics of Exorcism in late Elizabethan England', in P. Lake and M. Questier (eds), *Conformity and Orthodoxy in the English Church, c.1560–1660* (2000), pp. 34–63, esp. at pp. 36, 39, 46, 48.

[164] RC, pp. 144 (PRO, SP 12/287/50), 160 (PRO, SP 12/287/52); Lake and Questier, *Archpriest*, p. 128.

[165] W. R. Trimble, *The Catholic Laity in Elizabethan England* (Cambridge, Mass., 1964), p. 266.

controversial. But the martyr narratives just before 1603 alert us to the shifting context for those prosecutions. They certainly serve as a guide to the significance, particularly in, for example, the maelstrom of metropolitan politics, of a Catholic voice, or rather, Catholic voices at the centre of contemporary debate about what the future held.[166] By the end of the 1590s, it seemed inevitable that the relationship between the British Isles and continental Europe was, for the first time in a generation, going to be defined by peace rather than by war. Sooner rather than later there would be a new dynasty and, perhaps, a revision of the never-particularly-settled religious settlement. Here the often discordant Catholic voices that commented on the divisions inside the outgoing regime would continue to be all too audible.

[166] Lake and Questier, *Archpriest*, esp. part II.

PART III

11

Tolerance and Intolerance in England after the Accession of James VI

On 24 March 1603, Elizabeth expired at about four o'clock in the morning—'easily, like a ripe apple from the tree', as the diarist John Manningham famously phrased it—though a fair number of Catholics may have been in no doubt that this particular apple was going straight down to Hell. As the martyrologist John Knaresborough narrated in the early eighteenth century, the last of the Tudors was 'summoned to give an account of her stewardship before a tribunal where, without respect to persons, the greatest monarchs as well as their subjects are sentenced according to their works'—so, yes, she was almost certainly destined for the underworld.[1] A Spanish translation of the proclamation issued by the English privy council on 24 March included speculation as to why the queen had fallen into her fatal decline—perhaps it was melancholy caused either by the execution of her court favourite, the earl of Essex, or by remorse for the deaths of so many Catholic clergymen, the last of whom, William Richardson, had been put to death only weeks before she died.[2]

For those who watched both the dying light of the regime and the apparently petty vindictiveness of its final days, the question was: what would actually happen when Elizabeth's place was taken by James Stuart? As all contemporaries were fully aware, James's reconstruction of royal authority in Scotland had, in the face of much of the Kirk's hostility, been floated on the basis of confessional inclusivity. After the spate of Catholic rebelliousness there in the first half of the 1590s, even former rebels such as Lord Huntly, if they showed themselves to some degree conformable to the Kirk, were welcomed back into the fold. High office was conferred now on some people who had a (crypto-)Catholic background and political identity, notably Lord Henry Howard.[3]

---

[1] R. P. Sorlien (ed.), *The Diary of John Manningham of the Middle Temple, 1602–1603* (Hanover, N.H., 1976), p. 208; Kn., I, p. 148. Robert Persons similarly had no doubt about where Elizabeth's black soul was going: ABSJ, Anglia III, no. 39 ('the speech in my book about the queen's death').

[2] A. F. Allison, 'Lawrence Anderton, S. J.: A Postscript', *RH* 16 (1983), pp. 316–18, at p. 316, citing *La Declaracion que Hizo el Conseio de Estado*…(Seville, 1603); ARCR, II, no. 1064.

[3] Questier, *DP*, ch. 4 *passim*.

Catholics and Treason: Martyrology, Memory, and Politics in the Post-Reformation. Michael Questier,
Oxford University Press. © Michael Questier 2022. DOI: 10.1093/oso/9780192847027.003.0011

334 CATHOLICS AND TREASON

Temporary Royal Forbearance and its Swift Withdrawal

Of course, James's idea of tolerance was not necessarily going to be the same as that of the English lobbyists (both Catholic and puritan) who approached him in the period before the accession and, indeed, after it as well. As soon as he took Elizabeth's crown, he was faced by a series of organized and widespread petitioning campaigns. The puritan one is well known, the Catholic one less so.[4] There was certainly a surge of Catholic agitation even as James started his journey southwards. The priest Anthony Champney wrote to his confrère John Cecil on 21 April/1 May 1603 that they should encourage the pope and 'all such Catholic princes as have sent their ambassadors' to the new king 'to solicit him for a freedom of religion'. 'Besides many Catholic gentlemen who have been with him', the appellant priest William Watson had been admitted into the royal presence, 'as he himself reports', and he 'was very well entreated'.[5] Not surprisingly, the 'lord chief justice and some others' were trying to 'have the oath of supremacy still continued'. The king was not yet in London, but Elizabeth was now entombed, as of 28 April. 'No priests' had been 'executed, nor any Catholics restrained'. Furthermore, Champney had heard of a letter which had come 'from the king to inhibit all process against Catholics till his coming'. In Scotland, James had promised the appellant priest Cuthbert Trollop that 'he would not molest any Catholics in their life or livelihood for their conscience and bade them not fear he would...fulfil his word'. Another clergyman, Thomas Hill, had given the king a petition and talked with James 'before he came to York'. Regrettably, the renegade William Atkinson had 'espied' Hill, and John Thornborough had caused Hill to be 'apprehended'. However, it was more likely that 'the puritans' would be the ones to 'discontent the king'.[6]

The greatest martyr of them all, Mary Stuart, was available as a reference point for Catholics to phrase their loyalist appeals to her son. On 28 March 1603, the Jesuit Henry Garnet had petitioned the new king. He denied that Jesuits had ever really subscribed to resistance doctrines and affirmed that they had always offered up prayers for the Queen of Scots.[7] The author (probably Sir Thomas Tresham) of a pamphlet entitled *A Petition Apologeticall* declared to the king that 'we may,

---

[4] Questier, *DP*, ch. 5.

[5] LPL, MS 2006, fo. 177ʳ (the letter is signed 'Francis Foster' but is in the hand of Anthony Champney; the names of both are on the appeal of 23 April/3 May 1603, drawn up at Paris (Anstr., I, pp. 71, 122), but this letter was written from England).

[6] LPL, MS 2006, fo. 177ʳ⁻ᵛ. The publication in 1602 and again in 1603 of a pamphlet describing the sufferings of the martyr-priest Edmund Gennings back in 1591 may have been a contribution to the arguments for toleration of Catholics: Questier, *C&C*, pp. 267–8; ARCR, II, no. 338 and p. 250.

[7] ABSJ, Anglia III, no. 41 (printed in T. M. McCoog, 'Harmony Disrupted: Robert Parsons, S. J., William Crichton, S. J. and the Question of Queen Elizabeth's Successor, 1581–1603', *Archivum Historicum Societatis Iesu* 73 (2004), pp. 149–220, at pp. 217–19).

TOLERANCE AND INTOLERANCE IN ENGLAND

without offence to any, confidently affirm that they were not Catholics that caused your mother's untimely death'.[8]

Searches for, and arrests and convictions of, clergy were still taking place in mid-1603.[9] At that point the so-called Bye and Main conspiracies came to light. The Bye Plot was the outcome of the disillusionment of appellant clergy and their associates at the king's failure to follow through on what they took to be his promises of tolerance. The priests William Watson and William Clarke were tried and executed later in the year, with considerable brutality, at Winchester.[10] Jesuit clergy and their friends could hardly not point out that Watson and others had pontificated about the virtues of loyalty but, when push came to shove, they had turned out to be traitors. Four years later Philip Woodward wrote that Watson had been 'content to have it blown out in print, that so many blessed martyrs, as constantly shed their blood for the profession of Christ, suffered for treason against the queen and State'. Yet he was 'executed for treason against his royal Majesty that now is'. Had Watson's cause 'been like theirs whom he condemned, no question but his death had been less blameless in the eyes of the world and far more precious in the sight of God'.[11] Watson's and Clarke's cases were almost an anti-martyrdom, though, in his last dying speech from the scaffold, Clarke did pose as a martyr. Even after all the evidence that he, with others, had volunteered that they had conspired to seize the court and hold the king as a prisoner in the Tower of London, Clarke declared that he believed that he had got 'hard measure' and 'imputed it to his function', that is, because he was a priest, 'and therefore he thought his death meritorious, as a kind of martyrdom'.[12]

---

[8] John Lacey, *A Petition Apologeticall, presented to the Kinges Most Excellent Maiesty, by the Lay Catholikes of England, in Iuly last* (Douai, 1604), p. 29. In 1604 there was published a martyrological anthology (the first of the verse compositions in it, on Mary Stuart, had been written by the Jesuit Robert Southwell): *Epitaphs, the First, upon the Death of...Marie, late Queene of Scots. The Other, upon the Death of Three Most Blessed Marters...with Certaine Letters, Sent from One Friend to Another being in Prison* (Rouen [false imprint, printed secretly in England], 1604); A. Smith (ed.), *The Last Years of Mary, Queen of Scots: Documents from the Cecil Papers at Hatfield House* (1990), pp. 88–94. The second epitaph commemorates Nicholas Garlick, Robert Ludlam, and Richard Simpson, executed in July 1588; an excerpt was incorporated in the evidence gathered by Bishop Richard Smith in the 1620s: *Epitaphs*, pp. 6–10; *AWCBC*, pp. 595–9, 601, 604; Challoner, *MMP*, p. 133.

[9] John Sugar in Warwickshire was arrested with his harbourer Robert Grissold in July 1603: Anstr., I, p. 341; see pp. 337–40 below; Challoner, *MMP*, pp. 275–6; *AWCBC*, p. 1659. In the same month, Lord Vaux's house was searched for the Jesuits John Gerard and John Percy. The searchers had a privy-council warrant (with Lord Henry Howard's signature on it) and 'the pretence was that' Gerard and Percy 'had resolved to kill the king': ABSJ, Collectanea M, p. 97^b.

[10] Lake and Questier, *Archpriest*, epilogue, part ii; M. Nicholls, 'Treason's Reward: The Punishment of Conspirators in the Bye Plot of 1603', *HJ* 38 (1995), pp. 821–42.

[11] Philip Woodward, *The Dolefull Knell, of Thomas Bell....* (Rouen [imprint false; printed at Douai], 1607), pp. 36–7.

[12] M. Lee (ed.), *Dudley Carleton to John Chamberlain, 1603-1624: Jacobean Letters* (New Brunswick, 1972), p. 47. For George Blackwell's account of the execution of Watson and Clarke, see ASV, Borghese MS II, 448, a–b, fo. 333^{r-v}. For Copley's more sympathetic narrative, which averred that Watson had prepared for death in an exemplary way, see Biblioteca Apostolica Vaticana, Vatican City, Barb. Lat. 2190, fos 145^v–6^r (transcript and translation at ABSJ, 100/967/4, pp. 2269–70, 2286–7); see also Lake and Questier, *Archpriest*, pp. 272–4.

336 CATHOLICS AND TREASON

Some Catholics concluded that James's attitude towards them had never been benign at all. Richard Blount insisted on 31 July 1603 that the king had 'inveighed very bitterly' against those Irishmen who had recently petitioned for royal tolerance. Sir Robert Cecil had added that the 'papists were the fuel to nourish all treasons in a commonwealth, so that', remarked Blount, 'the hopes of poor Catholics be all dashed and they expect now a worse world than in the queen's time'.[13] By November, in England, the suspension of aspects of the statutory penalties for recusancy, which temporarily had taken effect in mid-1603, was itself rescinded. In February 1604 a royal proclamation announced to the world how far Catholics had got it wrong if they thought they had liberty to do as they pleased. The king's speech of 19 March to the 1604 parliament dwelt at some length on the topic—this was the one in which he acknowledged the Church of Rome as 'our mother Church' but said also that Catholic clergy were 'no way sufferable to remain in this kingdom'. James did not hold back in listing their 'errors and wrong opinions'; and the parliament was swiftly presented with a new recusancy bill.[14]

Looking back, a few years later, Robert Persons reckoned that James's 'sweet and mild aspect towards Catholics, at his first entrance, was soon, by art of their enemies, averted long before' the Gunpowder conspiracy 'fell out'. The fact was that 'all the most cruel statutes and penal laws made by Queen Elizabeth were renewed and confirmed...with addition of others, tending to no less rigour and acerbity', that is, in the parliament of 1604. As a result, those penalties were exacted 'with great severity'. The 'payment of the twenty pounds a month or two parts of their goods and lands for recusants (once remitted by his Majesty...) were not only recalled again but the arrearages thereof in like manner exacted; and, for levying whereof, throughout sundry shires of the realm, especially in the North, there was such ransacking of men's houses, such driving away of their cattle from their grounds, such straining of their rents, such vexing of their tenants, not known perhaps to his Majesty, as if the whole country had been given over to spoil and desolation'.[15]

But, in truth, some of the Catholic petitioning campaign during 1603 and early 1604 had really been pushing the tolerance envelope. Professor Loomie notes that Thomas Hill's petition to King James had a 'tone and argument...certain to arouse the worst suspicions' of the king, what with its comparison between the Catholics of England and the Israelites under King Jeroboam who became so

---

[13] ABSJ, Collectanea M, p. 97^b.

[14] Questier, C&C, pp. 271–2; James I, The Kings Maiesties Speech...the 19. Day of March 1603 (1604), sigs B4^r–C3^v.

[15] Robert Persons, The Iudgment of a Catholicke English-man Living in Banishment for his Religion...(n.p. [St Omer], 1608), p. 42. For Bishop Barlow's reply to Persons, see William Barlow, An Answer to a Catholicke English-man...(1609), esp. at pp. 136–43, poking fun for example at Persons's claim that it was a persecution that 'men should be bound to pay for their wives' recusancy'.

TOLERANCE AND INTOLERANCE IN ENGLAND   337

exhausted by his tyrannies as to take 'a just occasion to leave their due obedience'. Hill found himself hauled into star chamber in April 1604.[16] He was one of the sources whom William Udall cited as evidence that there had been a French proposal to seize the English crown before James was fully able to assert his claim to it.[17] In his own mind, Hill was undoubtedly as loyal as the next man but, on 30 April 1604, he was sentenced to death and, from Newgate prison, he wrote an exhortatory letter to another self-styled Catholic loyalist, Sir Thomas Tresham, a letter which Tresham annotated to the effect that Hill was expecting 'to have been the next day executed at Tyburn'. Hill would have been the first such casualty of the reign, but he was reprieved.[18]

Others were not so fortunate. The priest John Sugar had been detained in mid-1603, as Richard Blount reported, 'in Warwickshire with some four or five other country farmers', one of whom was Robert Grissold of Rowington. He and they were immediately arraigned at the summer assizes at Warwick in front of the hanging judges Kingsmill and Anderson. Three of the accused succumbed to the pressure. But Sugar refused to call the pope a 'knave', as Anderson urged him to do, and he was convicted under the 1585 statute. Grissold, who was equally determined not to yield, was convicted of harbouring the priest. Sentencing was deferred. Sugar and Grissold availed themselves of the general pardon issued at the beginning of the reign (they obtained it on 19 November 1603), though it was no defence against a treason charge. Their case was then reviewed at the Lenten assizes in 1604, by which time things were getting less easy for Catholic separatists. They were remanded back to prison. At the summer assizes in 1604, on 13 and 14 July, they were brought back before the court at Warwick. They were arraigned again, so it seems, and were hanged almost immediately, on 16 July. Massive pressure to get them to conform had been applied but without success.[19] Grissold protested strongly that he had not harboured the priest since he 'never saw' him 'before the time' that he was 'taken with him' and 'was but in his com-

---

[16] Loomie, *TD*, p. 14. According to William Sterrell, once again at William Atkinson's instigation, Thomas Hill was arrested (in London) in late March 1604: RC, p. 167 (AAW, A VII, no. 84); *HMCS*, XV, p. 232; Loomie, *TD*, p. 14. When Guy Fawkes went to Spain in pursuance of the so-called 'Spanish treason', he carried with him a translation into Spanish of Thomas Hill's petition which had been given to James at York: A. J. Loomie, *Guy Fawkes in Spain: The 'Spanish Treason' in Spanish Documents* (*Bulletin of the Institute of Historical Research*, Special Supplement no. 9, 1971), pp. 22–3.

[17] *HMCS*, XVI, p. 9.

[18] *HMCV*, III, pp. 114–15; Anstr., I, p. 167; G. Anstruther, *Vaux of Harrowden: A Recusant Family* (Newport, 1953), p. 278; cf. Persons, *Iudgment*, p. 44.

[19] Challoner, *MMP*, pp. 275–80 (relying in part on 'an old manuscript relation...sent me [Challoner] from Warwickshire', which appears to be ABP, pp. 439–43, as well as ABP, p. 444, a passage based on one of Thomas Worthington's catalogues and also on Arnauld Raisse, *Catalogus Christi Sacerdotum, qui ex Nobili Anglicano Duacenae Ciuitatis Collegio Proseminati, Praeclarum fidei Catholicae Testimonium in Britannia Praebuerunt* (Douai, 1630), on whom Knaresborough also relied, though Challoner did not, apparently, refer to Knaresborough here: Kn., II, pp. 9–13); Anstr., I, pp. 341–2; ABSJ, Collectanea M, p. 97[b]; Anstruther, *Vaux*, p. 384; *AWCBC*, pp. 1659–60, 1666, 1680–2; *HMCS*, XVI, pp. 189–90; PRO, C 67/70, mem. 21. John Grissold, of Rowington, was a retainer of the Vaux family and was a servant of Henry Garnet: Caraman, *HG*, p. 384; PRO, SP 14/216/70, 188.

338   CATHOLICS AND TREASON

pany at the instant of his apprehension' and he 'never gave him anything' and 'never received him into' his 'house'.[20] The judge had no answer to this other than to say that conformity alone would generate a reprieve. Kingsmill seems to have been working with puritans in the county, or at least with those who objected to what they saw as unwarranted tolerance of Catholics but who thought that the new parliamentary legislation was the green light to set the world to rights.[21]

Was this what King James really wanted? The Venetian ambassador Nicolò Molino believed, on 25 July/4 August, that the 'execution' had been 'delayed until news' came 'that the king had confirmed the old laws against Catholics'. But Molino thought that it was the puritan 'magistrates' who were really to blame. The king himself had declared that he wanted 'neither' the 'life nor goods of any man on account of his religion' and was 'annoyed at this event' but had 'taken no steps as yet to prevent its recurrence'.[22] Others, however, said that James had been adamant in this case. According to the usually well informed William Sterrell, 'the king seems displeased with the judge [Kingsmill] for this manner of proceeding and yet the same judge... said openly that he had special direction from the king so to do; yes, more, that his Majesty secretly commanded him to proceed' even 'though prohibition or reprieve should come from himself or any of his council'.[23] Michael Walpole recounted that, at Sugar's 'condemnation, the judge' had openly 'protested the rigorous execution of the law hereafter'. It had been 'commanded by parliament and again, in particular, by the king so straightly as that he would not have his own letters to have credit to the contrary and much less' those of 'any other councillors'.[24]

---

[20] ARSJ, Anglia 37, fo. 104ᵛ.

[21] Anstr., I, pp. 341–2. For Kingsmill's explanation of the proceedings to the privy council, see HMCS, XVI, pp. 189–90 (with an emphasis on how much opportunity had been given to Sugar and Grissold to conform, a report confirmed independently by Blount on 1 August 1604: ARSJ, Anglia 37, fo. 103ʳ⁻ᵛ).

[22] CSPV 1603–7, p. 172. A rumour was still current among Catholics almost twenty years later that James, 'when hearing of a priest [i.e. John Sugar, whom Richard Broughton called Freeman and may have been confusing with William Freeman, who had been executed at Warwick back in 1595] put to death for his priesthood, by the judges of Warwick, soon after his Majesty's coming hither, with sign of sorrow' asked why he could not have purchased a pardon: Richard Broughton, English Protestants Plea, and Petition, for English Preists and Papists, to the present Court of Parlament... (n.p. [St Omer], 1621), sig. D3ᵛ; Kn., II, p. 4; Challoner, MMP, pp. 273–4; AAW, B 28, no. 12, p. 374.

[23] ARSJ, Anglia 37, fo. 115ʳ. In 1609, William Barlow cited the executions of Sugar and Grissold as evidence of James's clemency, i.e. when so many others could have been dealt with in the same way: Barlow, An Answer, p. 137.

[24] ABSJ, Collectanea M, p. 49ᵇ (Pollen, AEM, pp. 321–2: Christopher Walpole to Robert Persons, 9/19 September 1604, recording the details of Michael Walpole's letter from Bruges of 7/17 August). The duke of Lorraine's envoys in autumn 1604 claimed that James had not only said to them that he recognized 'the Roman Church as the Mother Church, and the pope as the universal vicar of the whole Church', but also that he was unhappy that, during the recent parliament, there had been a statutory confirmation of the penalties against them. But James said that he would ensure that no Catholic would suffer on religious grounds: W. B. Patterson, 'King James I's Call for an Ecumenical Council', in G. J. Cuming and D. Baker (eds), Councils and Assemblies (Studies in Church History, 7, Cambridge, 1971), pp. 267–75, at p. 273 (citing PRO, PRO 31/9/88, pp. 121–2); PRO, SP 14/9A/25, fo. 59ʳ.

TOLERANCE AND INTOLERANCE IN ENGLAND   339

Sugar was hanged first and butchered according to sentence, and then, in a bizarre ritual, said Richard Blount, the 'rope' being drawn 'through the bowels and blood of the poor priest, they put it about Grissold's neck, calling him fool that would die such an opprobrious death when he might save his life by going only to church'.[25] The source followed by Bishop Challoner said that Grissold 'was by nature so timorous and weak that he once swooned at the sight of his thumb being only pricked with an awl, yet at the gallows he was, by the grace of the Holy Ghost, so much strengthened', that he went through with it, even when faced with 'the sight of Mr Sugar's bleeding body'. According to Challoner's text—now lost (the 'old manuscript relation' dispatched to him from Warwickshire)—it was Grissold who took the halter and 'dipped it in Mr Sugar's blood'.[26] Sterrell claimed that there had been 300 Catholics present at the execution; and he said also that 'a young gentleman, a knight of good worth' there, 'was so moved as he publicly protested he would never more go to church'.[27] An account in the Borghese manuscripts in Rome says that there were forty guards stationed around the scaffold so as to avert disorder, but they still could not prevent, in effect, a popular demonstration in which 200 people soaked their handkerchiefs in the blood of the priest.[28]

This kind of violence against Catholic separatism was hardly being replicated everywhere.[29] It is tempting to think, though none of the documents explicitly says so, that this was connected with the negotiations currently in train with the representatives of the king of Spain and the archducal regime in Flanders which led to the signing of the treaty of London on 18/28 August 1604. It is possible that, in Warwickshire, local forces and sympathetic members of the judiciary were using the trial to gloss those negotiations and possible also that the king was tacitly allowing them to do this.

The killing of Sugar and Grissold in Warwickshire was followed quite swiftly by another trial and execution—of Laurence Baily at Lancaster in August 1604. He was indicted for taking part with others, including one Rawson who was similarly condemned, and using force to release a priest from arrest, namely James Gardiner, who had been taken on the previous 15 July, the day before Sugar and

---

[25] ARSJ, Anglia 37, fo. 103ᵛ. This report notes that Sugar had once been in a benefice in Warwickshire. For a possible explanation of how Sugar refused the oath of supremacy at Oxford but then took a Church of England benefice before entering the college at Douai in 1599, i.e. that he had perhaps leaned the other way in religion and had refused the supremacy oath for that reason, see AWCBC, pp. 1657–8; see also Kn., II, pp. 10–11; Raisse, *Catalogus Christi Sacerdotum*, pp. 68–70 (AWCBC, pp. 1692–3; one of Raisse's sources of information was Henry Heath OFM).
[26] Challoner, *MMP*, p. 279; AWCBC, p. 1683.   [27] ARSJ, Anglia 37, fo. 115ʳ.
[28] Anstr., I, p. 342; ASV, Borghese MS III, 124, g. 1, fo. 35ᵛ; AWCBC, pp. 1673–4; for the arrest of demonstrators at the execution, see ARSJ, Anglia 37, fo. 104ʳ.
[29] Thomas Montford, the brother of the appellant priest Francis Montford, was reprieved at the summer assizes in summer 1604, apparently in the West Country: Anstr., I, p. 233; PRO, SP 14/9A/12, fo. 27ʳ (a letter from Arthur Harris at the 'Mount', presumably St Michael's Mount); HMCS, XVII, pp. 434, 435–6.

340   CATHOLICS AND TREASON

Grissold were put to death.[30] This daring intervention was a reprise of the exploit of Thurstan Hunt and his friends back in autumn 1600 in challenging the local officials who were taking the priest Robert Middleton to Lancaster.[31] Sterrell's letter of 29 August 1604 said that the priest, Gardiner, had been snatched 'away by the Catholics who had laid above fifty horses in diverse places in ambuscades to deliver' him 'or lose their lives'. Those 'that had the custody of him fled upon the first encounter'.[32]

Whatever the motivation for these provincial shows of judicial force, the central regime was evidently determined to follow up on the recent negotiations with the Spaniards and to show that the new understanding with the House of Austria was not going to usher in an unwarranted leniency to Catholic separatism in England. When Thomas Pounde was dragged into star chamber in late November 1604, the proceedings turned into a show trial designed to justify the recent crackdown on Catholic dissent. He had condemned the execution of Baily and also the persecuting of 'one Atkinson, an ancient priest in the time of Queen Mary'.[33] According to William Sterrell on 12 December 1604, Pounde's petition to the king on this topic was 'partly in prose and partly in verse'.[34] Atkinson had allegedly 'published at the assizes that he had authority upon a man's penitence to forgive any sin, albeit it were the deposing or killing the king', and this had caused 'many hundreds... to relapse and fall to error'.[35]

Sir Thomas Tresham's account of the proceedings against Pounde insisted that it was ridiculous to pretend that the ageing cleric Atkinson was some kind of lunatic regicide. He had been lured into making the statement that he did. (Actually, it seems that Atkinson had been condemned at the York assizes over the royal supremacy.)[36] But the attorney-general, Sir Edward Coke, also used the

---

[30]   Anstr., I, p. 126; AAW, B 28, no. 10, pp. 323–4 ('causa mortis, ob praetextum... quod operam suam praestitisset [?] ne sacerdos a litoribus caperetur'). The attorney-general, Sir Edward Coke, protested that 'Baily... was no papist but a Protestant, and he' came 'with eighty more to rescue a notorious priest'. Gardiner had allegedly 'said he could raise 4,000 strong and would by such a day surprise such a castle': W. P. Baildon (ed.), *Les Reportes del Cases in Camera Stellata 1593 to 1609 from the Original MS. of John Hawarde* (privately printed, 1894), pp. 184–5. For Sterrell's account of Rawson's conviction for giving money to a priest, and for the carrying out of sentence despite Rawson's offer to conform, see ARSJ, Anglia 37, fo. 115ᵛ.

[31]   See pp. 296–7 above.

[32]   ARSJ, Anglia 37, fo. 115ʳ. James Gardiner was one of the clergy named in Thomas Bell's extensive denunciation of Lancashire conformist and separatist Catholicism in the early 1590s: AAW, A IV, no. 38, pp. 438, 439, 452. For the pardons issued on 18 May 1605 to, *inter alia*, Thomas and Henry Clifton over their involvement in the liberation of Gardiner, see *CSPD 1603–10*, p. 217. Richard Kirkham and James Smith were, on 9 May 1608, also pardoned for their part in this incident: Anstr., I, p. 126.

[33]   Baildon, *Les Reportes*, pp. 182–3, 184–5 (where the trial date is given as 29 October 1604); Questier, *C&C*, p. 278; ARSJ, Anglia 37, fo. 116ʳ.

[34]   ARSJ, Anglia 37, fo. 116ʳ.   [35]   Baildon, *Les Reportes*, p. 185.

[36]   *HMCV*, III, pp. 146–7. Sterrell noted on 29 August 1604 that at York Sir Edward Phelips, 'late speaker of the parliament', had instilled terror into the northern Catholic community by condemning 'old Atkinson, a Queen Mary priest, of praemunire for refusing to answer or swear to the supremacy'. Phelips had been substituted in place of the judge Sir Thomas Walmesley (who was believed by some to be a crypto-Catholic): ARSJ, Anglia 37, fo. 115ʳ; pp. 204–5 above. For Phelips, see *HC*

occasion to declare, in Burghleian fashion, that 'there was not anyone in all Queen Elizabeth's time that suffered death for religion or conscience but' only 'for treason to the person of the prince or State or withdrawing or seducing the people from their obedience'.[37]

The attorney-general's speech, said Sterrell, 'was more than an hour long'.[38] It was a point-by-point justification of the Elizabethan law on conformity. Tresham said that Coke described 'how profitable to these realms it would be to have the same laws put in speedy, due and exact execution' and also 'how inconvenient' it would be 'to have any toleration of religion or connivance of permitting favour to the Catholics in matter of religion'. Coke 'seriously protested that there were above 1,500 recusants' who had 'converted and become communicants' after Baily and Rawson were executed (who, themselves, 'died Protestants'). Tresham observed with bitter irony that, 'in the course of his whole narration and charge', Coke 'severed Mr Pounde's proceeding from matter or nature of religion, yet afterwards, in sounding the day's victory, he gloried in [a] triumphant' manner, 'saying that this day the Protestant religion had gained the greatest victory against the Catholic that at any time erst they had'.[39] Equally bitterly, Tresham remarked that, when Pounde tried to protest 'in what strange wise the queen of Scots was here deprived of her life', he was 'interrupted and not permitted to persevere therein'.[40]

The star chamber judges suggested a range of punishments for Pounde. The news of the trial's outcome circulated widely. On 2 December 1604, John More related to the diplomat Ralph Winwood in the United Provinces not only that the recent Royston puritans' petition had angered the king but also that Pounde had been sentenced to 'lose one of his ears here in London and the other in the country where he dwells', to pay a £1,000 fine and suffer perpetual imprisonment 'if he impeach not those that advised him to commence his suit', though some of the sentence was remitted.[41] Cecil proposed that Pounde should 'have papers set on him to notify the cause of his punishment, saying that he else of himself would not acknowledge it'.[42] Henry Garnet wrote later, on 10 April 1605, that 'Mr Pounde stood publicly in Westminster Hall on a form with a paper on his head'.[43] He was then dragged up to the North and, in York, was compelled 'to make acknowledgment of his fault'. Apparently he refused, 'otherwise than' to say 'that, if he had offended, he was sorry for it'; but in Lancaster 'he confessed his fault and

---

1558–1603, III, pp. 216–17. In January 1606, Lord Sheffield warned the earl of Salisbury against allowing Walmesley 'to come to this circuit again; which if he should do, things standing as they do, it could not but overthrow all, for the papists have ever borne themselves much upon his favour': *HMCS*, XVIII, p. 36; *HC 1558–1603*, III, p. 569.

[37] Baildon, *Les Reportes*, pp. 183–4; see also ASV, Segretario di Stato, Inghilterra, 19, fo. 8ʳ⁻ᵛ.

[38] ARSJ, Anglia 37, fo. 116ʳ.

[39] *HMCV*, III, pp. 139–47 *passim*, quotations at pp. 141, 144 (cited in part in Questier, *C&C*, p. 279); G. Kilroy, *Edmund Campion: Memory and Transcription* (Aldershot, 2005), pp. 16–17.

[40] *HMCV*, III, p. 144.   [41] Sawyer, *WM*, II, p. 36.   [42] *HMCV*, III, p. 141.

[43] ABSJ, GC (10 April 1605; ABSJ, Collectanea P/ii, p. 608ᵃ).

342 CATHOLICS AND TREASON

with humility submitted himself'.[44] Presumably this is what secured remission from the full extent of the star chamber penalty.[45]

What looks like, on one level, the pointlessly sadistic harassment of an unfortunate old man could also be construed as a sophisticated public-relations exercise. Something like this may have been repeated in other places. The Venetian ambassador Molino reported on 20/30 March 1605 that 'the persecution of Catholics' was proceeding apace with brutal searches of Catholics' houses, while priests that were arrested were 'threatened with execution' and 'recently at Oxford...a priest was actually taken up to the gallows to terrify him and the others'.[46]

This visible harshness towards recalcitrant Catholics undoubtedly made it easier for the regime to punish puritan nonconformity. The privy council had sent orders to the bishops in December 1604 to deprive nonconformists at the end of the period of grace allowed to register conformity after the canons formulated and promulgated earlier in the year.[47] Archbishop Richard Bancroft urged the bishops to detect and excommunicate obstinate recusants so as to dispel circulating rumours of a toleration while, at the same time, the bishops should allow deprived ministers a few months more to see if they would comply.[48]

This, naturally, did not satisfy everyone. The new lord president of the council in the North, Edmund, Lord Sheffield, complained on 27 March 1605 that he resented having to keep London informed if he planned to hang Catholics who had been convicted on capital charges. Two servants of Mr Thomas Darcy of Hornby (namely Thomas Welbourne and William Browne) were, said Sheffield, 'committed to York Castle...for seducing of the king's subjects from their obedience and many other undutiful pranks'. They had 'been tried this assize and condemned of high treason'. It was now up to the king to decide what should happen to them. But James ought to keep in mind that, 'being asked whether, if the pope should invade any of his Majesty's kingdoms, they would fight against him, they refused...to answer'.[49] These two unfortunates were indeed in the end executed—

---

[44] HMCS, XVII, pp. 143, 144 ('A true declaration of the proceedings at the last assizes in the counties of York and Lancaster', sent as an enclosure by Sir Edward Phelips to Viscount Cranborne); PRO, SP 14/5/73 (misdated in calendar [CSPD 1603–10, p. 63] and now apparently lost).

[45] Bishop Barlow took the remission by the king of the 'corporal' penalty and the fact that 'no penny is yet demanded of the fine by sentence imposed' on Pounde as a sign of the regime's incredible leniency: Barlow, An Answer, p. 139.

[46] CSPV 1603–7, p. 232. The priest may have been Adam Green: TD, IV, pp. xcv–vi.

[47] PRO, SP 14/10/61; S. Babbage, Puritanism and Richard Bancroft (1962), chs 6, 7, esp. at p. 150. John Chamberlain claimed on 26 January 1605 that the number of the non-compliant was greater than anticipated: McClure, LJC, I, p. 201.

[48] PRO, SP 14/13/25, fos 64^r–5^v.

[49] HMCS, XVI, p. 44 [misdated to 1604]; AAW, B 28, no. 10, p. 324; see also HMCS, XVII, pp. 110, 143–4; for Lord Sheffield, see Adams, PC, pp. 433–7; for the Darcy family, see Aveling, NC, p. 176. Persons noted that Welbourne was proceeded against 'only for that he had used some words of persuasion to a certain woman to be a Catholic, notwithstanding the prohibition of her husband, who followed so hotly the matter against him, as he caused him to be put to death': Persons, Iudgment, p. 45. Sheffield had also pilloried one Thomas Robinson 'for beating a minister in the church'. Robinson had uttered 'very seditious speeches against the king, being a notable recusant', to the effect that he had

TOLERANCE AND INTOLERANCE IN ENGLAND   343

there was no mercy for them, and Sheffield got his way.[50] By contrast, though, when the priest Thomas Briscow was, at Lancaster, 'condemned of high treason', the 'execution of him' was 'stayed until his Majesty's pleasure' was 'known'. This was principally because he 'seemed to be of mild disposition, free from practice, and much condemning all persuaders or stirrers to faction or rebellion'. He was sent into exile.[51]

Cecil reminded Sheffield, in a note of 1 April 1605, that the king's own recent letter should serve as proof 'how barbarous an untruth it is in any man to suspect any change of his Majesty's religious profession and purpose to banish superstition'. This was demonstrated no less by the king's determination to root out pluralism and non-residence than by his willingness, in principle, to confirm Sheffield's proceedings against Romish agitators. For his part, on 24 April 1605 Sheffield could claim to be delighted that 'the justice done upon Pounde and others' at 'this last assizes' had 'done great good in these parts, for now the papists have left their brags, of which before they were very prodigal'. He was also pleased that 'the king's letter' recently dispatched to Archbishop Matthew Hutton and to himself had 'likewise cleared many foolish doubts, which vain people had conceived, of greater favour intended to the priests than I know was ever meant'.[52]

Whitsun Riot

Whatever the king's government intended at this point, some provincial Catholics were not showing much in the way of compliance. Summer 1605 saw what some interpreted as the stirrings of Catholic rebellion, notably in the Allensmore riots in Herefordshire. The disturbances in question were pumped for their very considerable polemical potential by the vehemently anti-popish bishop of Hereford, Robert Bennett (the churchman who had been so prominent back in late 1583 when John Bodey and John Slade had been executed in Hampshire). What had started out as a local dispute over the clandestine burial of a deceased excommunicate Catholic recusant in Whitsun week 1605 became, so it was claimed, a

---

expected a violent change of religion: *HMCS*, XVI, pp. 44–5; *HMCS*, XVII, pp. 124, 144; see also (misdated in) Foley, *RSJ*, III, p. 136 (PRO, SP 14/13/52B).

[50] Challoner, *MMP*, pp. 280–1. The consensus seems to be that another alleged victim at this time, one Fulthering, was in fact the same man as Browne: ABSJ, CP (William Browne); ABP, p. 134; G. Anstruther, 'Corrections to C. A. Newdigate's "Our Martyrs"', *Biographical Studies* 1 (1953–4), pp. 112–16, at p. 115; cf. the erroneous rendering, following Challoner and Foley, in Questier, *C&C*, p. 279.

[51] *HMCS*, XVII, p. 144; TD, IV, p. xcv. Briscow was deported in November 1605: Anstr., I, p. 51. For Persons's somewhat garbled version of the proceedings against Briscow, as well as against 'M. Green, Tichborne and Smith', see Persons, *Iudgment*, p. 44; for Barlow's riposte to Persons on this point, see Barlow, *An Answer*, pp. 138–9.

[52] *HMCS*, XVII, pp. 157, 124 (draft letter speculatively dated to March 1605 or later, but actually written on 1 April).

344 CATHOLICS AND TREASON

dangerous tumult when the bishop's officers tried to take the Catholic burial party into custody.[53]

It was far from clear that the privy council collectively wanted to endorse Bishop Bennett's determination to pursue the matter. Molino concluded that it had been decided to blame 'the magistrates', presumably Bennett and his friends, for the Allensmore business, and to proceed warily rather than risk encouraging 'the other Catholics in the country to join the rebels'.[54]

But Bennett himself provided for the regime in London a terrifying prospectus of what a tolerated popular Catholicism might look like, that is, one where the statutes drafted by Elizabethan legislators no longer applied. He also summarized the likely implications of the recent Catholic toleration campaign. He had, he wrote on 1 June 1605, during the previous year 'surprised almost sixty persons going to Mass'. He had 'certified, and was commanded to give notice to, the judges of assize'. The miscreant Mass-goers 'were indicted of an unlawful assembly. They brought a *certiorari* to remove the matter to king's bench, whence it never yet returned, nor [was] anything done there; and hereat they glory, and say I received rebuke, both at the council table and otherwise.' Those same people sought Bennett's 'disgrace by libels and contumelies of all kinds'. He said also that a recent recusancy commission had been subverted; for 'they impanelled a jury like themselves'. Of itself, a lot of this was hardly new. Complaints about the slackness of justice in this respect were ten a penny across much of the period. The issue, though, was that the region's Catholic separatists had 'a lewd conceit that the king favours their course' and 'sundry of the justices' were 'unworthy of their places'. This was what had made the rioting possible in the first instance.[55] It was the antithesis of the control that Sheffield claimed to have imposed in the North.

On 13 June 1605 Bennett certified the arrests of the ringleaders of the supposed rebellion, principally of a man called William Morgan.[56] Morgan was questioned five days later. One of the topics raised was the involvement in these disturbances of the priest, appellant sympathizer, signatory of the 1603 protestation of allegiance, and, also, future martyr, namely Roger Cadwallader, and what he knew about the preparations being made by various recusants to 'solicit...for the Catholics'. Morgan seems to have alleged that he had himself a family connection with the new archbishop of Canterbury, Richard Bancroft.[57]

---

[53] Questier, *DP*, pp. 298–9; R. Mathias, *Whitsun Riot: An Account of a Commotion amongst Catholics in Herefordshire and Monmouthshire in 1605* (1963). For a definitive study of the disturbances which occurred in the wake of the clandestine burial of Alice Wellington on 21 May 1605, see W. Brogden, 'Catholicism, Community and Identity in Late Tudor and Early Stuart Welsh Borderlands' (PhD, Birmingham, 2018), ch. 1.

[54] *CSPV 1603–7*, p. 252.   [55] *HMCS*, XVII, p. 235.

[56] *HMCS*, XVII, pp. 258–9. For William Morgan of Treville, see Brogden, 'Catholicism, Community and Identity', ch. 1, esp. at p. 30.

[57] PRO, SP 14/14/45, fo. 104[r-v]; *AWCBC*, pp. 1819–20. Morgan said also that he 'would deal with one Griffith', Bancroft's client (i.e. the priest George Williams) in order to limit the damage caused by

TOLERANCE AND INTOLERANCE IN ENGLAND 345

Bennett argued that tolerance had brought not peace but rebellion against lawful authority.[58] An informant's testimony from the Welsh borders in *c.* June 1605 warned similarly that, 'except good order be taken in time, the recusants, by the Jesuits' persuasions, will take up arms against the king'. Three of these Jesuits— Robert Jones, Thomas Lister, and Edward Oldcorne—were the 'chief that labour with the people in those parts to that effect'. They and their clerical colleagues had 'nothing in their mouths but the sword, the sword and wars'. They said, allegedly, that 'there is now no further hope for Catholics, being leapt out of the frying pan into the fire'. There was no 'other course to be taken for them but only by force to free themselves. And the rather to move the people, they brag much that they shall have assistance from the king of France and the king of Spain.' The informer said that, in fact, this had alarmed many Catholics in Wales who wished that 'the Jesuits with all their adherents' were 'out of the land'.[59]

King James told the judges on 9 June 1605 at Greenwich that it was high time that the laws be properly enforced against Catholics. Two days later, a correspondent of Sir Everard Digby reported the king's words (apparently James droned on for three whole hours) and, in particular, that, 'for the rebellious behaviour used in Herefordshire, he thinks it needless any longer to spare their blood who, contemning his Majesty's clemency used towards all men of their profession, have broken forth into so manifest a demonstration of their disloyalties against his laws and justices' and 'his officers'.[60]

Did this, however, mean that there was going to be a new procession of hanged and disembowelled Catholic martyrs? James had an extraordinary ability to say one thing and mean something slightly different. Sir Henry Neville was less sanguine about the likely outcome of the king's directions. The king had given to the judges a 'very straight charge to be diligent and severe in their circuits against recusants... yet it is generally feared that there will be none of the priests executed without which I doubt all the other provision will be fruitless, for they are the

---

the recent incident. Williams used the alias of Rice Griffith: Anstr., I, pp. 381–2, 408. Benjamin Norton in late 1610 said that the authorities had a 'spleen' against Cadwallader 'for his burying the dead in Wales at the first coming of the king': *NAGB*, p. 90 (AAW, A IX, no. 94, p. 315; *AWCBC*, p. 1876). Dr Brogden notes that it was unlikely that Cadwallader, or any seminary priest, was present at the funeral itself; but he celebrated a Mass subsequently, and twelve of those who attended it had been present at the burial: Brogden, 'Catholicism', p. 275, citing PRO, SP 14/14/53, fo. 120^r.

[58] See e.g. *HMCS*, XVII, pp. 258–9; Talbot, *MMR*, pp. 135–42.

[59] PRO, SP 14/14/40, fo. 95^r. According to the Venetian ambassador Molino on 15/25 June 1605, the council also thought for a time that it was facing something like an actual rebellion: *CSPV 1603–7*, p. 248. By mid-August, Sir Henry Wotton was reporting to the earl of Salisbury that news of the 'late tumultuous insolence committed by the papists about the edge of Wales' had reached Venice from 'divers places': Smith, *Life*, I, p. 330.

[60] *HMCS*, XVII, p. 254. Edward Turner, vicar of Edlington in Lincolnshire, alleged on 27 November 1606 that on or about 20 June 1605 one William Smith in that parish 'did justify and commend the death and cause of two traitorous priests (lately executed at Lincoln)', i.e. Thomas Sprott and Thomas Benstead, in July 1600: C. W. Foster (ed.), *The State of the Church in the Reigns of Elizabeth and James I as Illustrated by Documents Relating to the Diocese of Lincoln*, I, (Lincoln, 1926), p. xciii.

346 CATHOLICS AND TREASON

root and fountain of all the mischief'. Such people would 'never be satisfied, nor made sure to the State, unless they may have their whole desire', that is, complete toleration. 'Impunity' would not be enough. If they obtained it, whatever 'impunity' meant, 'assuredly they will not rest there' until 'they have obtained a further liberty'.[61]

Nevertheless, taking his cue from what the king might be thought to have meant, Bishop Bennett claimed on 9 August 1605 that, like the good magistrate that he was, he had been 'repressing the riots and furies of popish recusants', sparing 'neither pains nor charge', and the 'effect has been such as no good man can malign' it, though presumably quite a lot of other men could malign it quite easily. But the fact was that 'above 200' had 'submitted and conformed'.[62]

Exactly what was at stake here politically was revealed by a pamphlet written by one Thomas Hammond which described the Allensmore incident. The pamphlet sought to refute Catholics who tried 'to persuade any of his Majesty's subjects that the times' were 'like to alter, and that a toleration should be granted, thereby wronging his Majesty exceedingly, who is so fully settled in the truth'. Hammond's pamphlet, the substance of which is in the form of a newsletter written from London, recited the burden of a speech by the lord chancellor, Sir Thomas Egerton, on 20 June 1605 in star chamber to the judges. James had been informed, said Egerton, that 'the number of papists in England was mightily increased' since March 1603. The king demanded the establishment of a 'perfect unity in religion', with which task the judges were entrusted.[63]

But the interpretation of whatever it was that had happened at Allensmore as incipient rebellion did not suit some highly placed members of the regime, not least of whom was Archbishop Bancroft. After all the political capital he had risked on the appellant business, he was predictably averse to evidence that tolerance, however limited, for loyalist Catholics was likely to provoke disobedience and actual revolt. Indeed, it appears that Bishop Bennett and his officials were deliberately targeting those Catholics in the region who had been involved in the appellant agitation, probably with the intended knock-on effect that Bancroft's credit would be damaged.[64] Bennett complained to Robert Cecil, recently promoted as earl of Salisbury on 9 August 1605, about the supposedly loyalist priest

---

[61] Sawyer, WM, II, pp. 77–8.

[62] HMCS, XVII, p. 360. An informer who had tried but failed to arrest Roger Cadwallader told the earl of Salisbury in October 1605 that Bennett's pursuit of the priest George Williams and his 'forwardness against recusants' had been 'the occasion of the reformation of many in these parts': HMCS, XVII, p. 455.

[63] Thomas Hammond, The Late Commotion of Certaine Papists in Herefordshire. Occasioned by the Death of one Alice Wellington, a Recusant, who was Buried after the Popish Maner, in the Towne of Allens-Moore, neere Hereford, upon Tuesday in Whitsun Weeke last past. 1605. With other Excellent Matter thereby Occasioned. Truely Set forth (1605), sigs A3^v–4^r, B^{r-v}, B2^r, B2^v–3^v. For Sir Thomas Egerton's star chamber speech, of 20 June, see also D. Newton, The Making of the Jacobean Regime: James VI and I and the Government of England, 1603–1605 (Woodbridge, 2005), p. 111.

[64] Questier, DP, p. 299.

TOLERANCE AND INTOLERANCE IN ENGLAND 347

George Williams. This priest 'gave out' that Bancroft 'had persuaded the king that all those tumults were nothing but a broken head or two', and had repeated this to the 'seditious recusants who had made riots about Hereford'.[65] Williams had also conducted the appellant pamphleteer William Watson 'about this country to rec-usants' houses, immediately before his apprehension' as a suspect in the Bye Plot. Williams had been associated with Cadwallader, who had appellant sympathies, and also with the priest John Scudamore, who had renounced Rome and had become a client of Bancroft.[66] According to Bishop Bennett, Bancroft had actually recommended Williams to him 'as a priest who had submitted, taken the oath [of supremacy], abjured his priesthood and promised special service'. But, since that time, Williams had made no more than a 'semblance of service'. He had been 'say-ing Mass, seducing the people, reconciling, confessing, marrying, assuring the priests and recusants of a toleration, disclosing my [Bennett's] purposes, hinder-ing service, bringing more priests into these parts, and such like'. Bennett had arrested him but, at the assizes, letters from Bancroft had been produced. Williams was 'dismissed upon bond to appear in the' court of king's bench 'next term, to the great applause of papists and great appalling of well-affected men'.[67]

For Bennett, there was evidently the threat of a community of interest building up between, on the one hand, a certain kind of Bancroftian conformist agenda and, on the other, a style of entrenched Catholic loyalism. This was proof of exactly the danger against which moderate puritans had been frantically warning for years. For Bennett and his friends, that danger must have become more pro-nounced when the local magnate, crypto-Catholic and certainly anti-puritan Edward Somerset, earl of Worcester, was sent down to deal with the Allensmore incident.[68] Once the earl arrived, he tried to downplay it all. On 5 July he wrote to Salisbury that he hoped the king would be 'better pleased with a brief assurance of the quiet state of the country than to stay long for a more exact account of par-ticular men's disloyal actions', even though he would deal with offenders appro-priately. Worcester said he had arrived on 29 June and had laid down the law to everyone, including the presumably rather irritated Bishop Bennett. Worcester told them that the king would definitely not tolerate popish superstition and then, himself, had done in essence not very much. He discovered one priest,

---

[65] *HMCS*, XVII, pp. 360–1, 456.   [66] *HMCS*, XVII, p. 456.

[67] *HMCS*, XVII, p. 361. On 24 August, Bennett sent in the depositions against Williams 'for evi-dence when he shall appear at the king's bench', which, significantly, Bennett said he had 'collected the more carefully' because 'I am informed' that Bancroft 'takes it offensively at my hands, as well that I certified the late riots to the council and not to him, as that I presumed to apprehend' Williams: *HMCS*, XVII, p. 389.

[68] *CSPV 1603–10*, pp. 254, 259. As Diana Newton points out, in sending Worcester to deal with the problem, James was bypassing the godly Edward, Lord Zouch, who was lord president of Wales: Newton, *Making*, pp. 111–13. According to Molino on 3/13 July, the news of Worcester's approach triggered a deputation to London of local Catholics to plead their loyalty. But the deputation's three members were 'clapped into prison' in London and were 'condemned to death' (on what grounds it was left unclear), though sentence was then respited: *CSPV 1603–7*, p. 259.

348 CATHOLICS AND TREASON

probably George Williams, but the man 'pleaded my lord's grace of Canterbury's protection'.[69]

Appended to Hammond's narrative was a 'Copy of a second letter from Hereford', which described how Lord Worcester was dispatched from London in order to set all in order. Worcester had imprisoned the ringleaders and the obstinate but then took a milder course with the others, 'seeking to win them unto the truth', and had converted a number of 'stiff recusants'.[70] It may be that Hammond's pamphlet was intended to make the anti-puritan earl seem favourable to the cause of the Gospel. But Bishop Bennett had noted in his letter of 9 August that scandalous 'reports were raised that the earl of Worcester had given' him 'and all the justices a check for sending up...untrue suggestions' about the local Catholics.[71] The Venetian diplomat Molino reported back on 31 July/10 August that Worcester had returned to London and was saying that the whole thing had been blown out of proportion. He had merely imprisoned 'a few fellows of the baser sort...more to show that he had done something than because they deserved punishment'.[72]

For all the claims by Catholics that they were as loyal as they said they were, there were other Catholic, or apparently Catholic, voices which were sharper-edged. One manuscript separate which circulated at around this time declared in a rather threatening vein that James would have done well to remember the Catholics, those who had 'loved the mother', the martyr Mary Stuart, and had 'run the same fortune with her in her adversity, and therefore would with all gladness have embraced the son with like true affection in his better fortunes'. But he should understand that Catholics were not a 'people to be trampled upon'. James had also failed to 'remove such as had abused their credit with the late queen, to the oppression of the people'. This would have been a 'compendious...way...of taking revenge' on 'the procurers of his mother's death; through neglect of which point of duty and honour, not only Europe but the whole world rings his reproach and infamy'. Equally James should have 'stayed his hand a while from taxing the people with any payments'. He ought to have relieved them of the 'Egyptian impositions wherewith for so many years they were oppressed'. But what did he do? The moment that he was king he 'denounced war against the Catholics and picked them out for the men whom he would expose to all manner of persecution'. The statutes against them were confirmed and the king himself ordered the judges 'to proceed against them with as much extremity and rigour as law would permit'. 'Everywhere' the king had 'made his discourse what a pestilent race they are...what scorpions in a State, and how dangerous to prince and commonwealth'. The writer

---

[69] HMCS, XVII, pp. 304–6. [70] Hammond, The Late Commotion, sig. E3^r.
[71] HMCS, XVII, p. 360. [72] CSPV 1603–7, p. 266.

TOLERANCE AND INTOLERANCE IN ENGLAND 349

commented with bitterness not just on James's broken promises but also on what the writer took to be a diminution of James's authority. He had talked the politique talk before he took the crown, but now his worthless assurances meant that he had 'made himself weak and others strong'. Those others—evil counsellors—would appropriate his power. His subjects had longed 'to see justice done upon some...that had formerly abused both prince and people', but the king, 'even upon his first entrance', conferred 'new titles of honour upon them, setting them in rank with the foremost of the ancient nobility of this realm'. Out of this promotion of evil counsellors came a host of iniquities—the persecution of Catholics again, of course, and also royal extravagance. The imposition of financial burdens came in spite of the peace dividend that the king was now enjoying following the end of the war.[73]

There was, therefore, a visible connection between, on the one hand, Catholic protests against alleged persecution and, on the other, the publicization of critiques of royal government which themselves are part and parcel of so many of the mainstream political narratives of the early Jacobean period. Catholic toleration discourse could and did veer alarmingly between the immediate post-accession welcome for the heir of Mary Stuart and, by contrast, much more aggressive claims that James had abandoned substantial planks of the platform on which he had pitched his case for the English crown. As Molino reported, in late August 1605, the king spoke at university disputations during his Oxford progress and, in the presence of both the Venetian and the French ambassadors, warned the audience to fly 'the perfidious and cursed superstition of Rome'.[74] In early October 1605, Molino said that imprisoned priests in London were being taken off to internal exile. This was technically in line with James's declaration that he would 'touch neither goods nor blood of any for religious opinion'. But, as Molino saw it, recusancy penalties were being enforced as harshly as in Elizabeth's time, in addition to the executions in York during the summer.[75] On the ambassador's account, the 'poor Catholics' were being cut adrift by the new papacy of Paul V, who had been elected on 6/16 May 1605. The pope instructed George Blackwell and other clergy that he

---

[73] A. G. Petti (ed.), *Recusant Documents from the Ellesmere Manuscripts* (CRS 60, 1968), pp. 148–50. Petti convincingly dates this manuscript to *c*.1604–5. I am inclined to think it may be later rather than earlier within the period of those two years. Since we cannot exactly identify the author, it is just possible that it is a piece of Protestant-generated disinformation; on the other hand, it certainly reflected the opinions of some Catholics. See also *CSPV 1603–7*, pp. 165, 176. Conrad Russell's account of the combined effect of 'recalcitrant taxpayers', an 'obstinate House of Commons', a 'nervous and extravagant king', and the need for continued military spending even in peacetime (for example on the cautionary towns in the Netherlands) makes it easy to see how expectations of the new king might soon be disappointed: C. Russell, eds R. Cust and A. Thrush, *King James VI and I and his English Parliaments* (Oxford, 2011), p. 18.

[74] *CSPV 1603–7*, p. 270; for the disputations, see PRO, SP 14/15/37–40; ARSJ, Anglia 31/ii, fo. 723[r–v].

[75] *CSPV 1603–7*, p. 270.

350   CATHOLICS AND TREASON

could not approve 'the Welsh rising'. They were to 'warn all Catholics to live quietly and without sedition or tumult'.[76] John Gerard recalled the point at which it had all gone wrong in 1604 when the persecution, as he saw it, was resumed. The new tyranny had 'set those gentlemen', the Gunpowder plotters, 'upon that furious and fiery course which they afterwards fell into'.[77]

Shortly before the Gunpowder Plot broke, a letter—the bulk of which was written on 4 October 1605—was addressed to Robert Persons by Henry Garnet, who was staying with Sir Everard Digby after returning from a Catholic pilgrimage to Holywell. It summarized what it took to be a general sense of betrayal among Catholics. 'The courses taken are more severe than in Bess's time', remarked Garnet. 'Every six weeks' there was 'a general court'. Juries identified and assessed 'the goods of Catholics' which were then sequestrated 'contra ordinem juris'. The 'commissioners in all counties' were 'the most earnest and base puritans who otherwise the king discountenances'.[78] The 'judges...openly' protested 'that the king' would 'have blood'; and he had 'taken blood in Yorkshire'. The king had hitherto been lenient to 'papists', but no longer. 'The execution of two in the North' was 'certain', namely of the unfortunate Welbourne and Browne. It was 'done upon cold blood, that is, with so great stay after their condemnation'. It indicated 'a deliberate resolution of what we may expect' in the future. What could Pope Paul V do? Nothing. People might talk in Rome of the 'easy proceedings' with Catholics in England, but it was all lies. Garnet said that he believed 'the best sort of Catholics' would be stoical in the face of adversity, 'but how these tyrannical proceedings of such base officers may drive particular men to desperate attempts, that I cannot answer for'. A postscript of 21 October added that news had come from Ireland of 'a very severe proclamation against all ecclesiastical persons', that is, the proclamation of July 1605, reissued in October, and 'a general command for going to the churches, with a solemn protestation that the king never promised nor meant to give toleration'.[79]

[76] *CSPV 1603–7*, pp. 279–80. Blackwell's admonitory letter to this effect (that Catholics should not attempt to secure toleration via unlawful means), 'especially to such as are in or about those parts in which such unlawful matters are suspected to have been contrived or devised', was issued on 22 July 1605: *CSPV 1603–7*, p. 259; PRO, SP 14/15/13, fo. 27ʳ.

[77] J. Morris (ed.), *The Condition of Catholics under James I: Father Gerard's Narrative of the Gunpowder Plot* (1871), pp. 29–30.

[78] TD, IV, p. ciii (for the original letter, see AAW, A VII, no. 106; and for Grene's transcript, see ABSJ, Collectanea P/ii, pp. 563ᵇ–4ᵃ); Caraman, *HG*, pp. 325–8. For Sir Henry Wotton's allegation in May 1605 that Robert Persons, at Naples, was cursing James as a heretic and likely 'by little and little, to be worse than the late queen against the papists', see Smith, *Life*, I, p. 328.

[79] TD, IV, pp. civ, cvi. Canon Tierney cited this letter as evidence that Garnet knew, or came to know, of the Gunpowder Plot before it was attempted: TD, IV, pp. cii–iii; see also UCLSC, UC/P25/7/812, 814, 816, 821 (John Lingard to Mark Tierney, 16 April 1839, May 1839, 17 June 1839, 12 November 1840); cf. for John Morris's refutation of this claim, Morris, *The Condition of Catholics*, pp. ccxxv–xxx.

Gunpowder Plot, Henry Garnet, and the Oath of Allegiance

Then, indeed, in early November 1605 came the part conspiracy and part media event of the Gunpowder Plot. Catholic terrorists allegedly tried to explode a bomb under the parliament at Westminster. There is an extensive literature on the plot and its origins. Some of it, it has to be said, is extremely complex. Much of that literature is driven by the ultimately impossible-to-resolve debate about whether the plot was as the regime described it or whether the narrative of the conspiracy released to the public was the product of incredibly devious black-ops media manipulation.

I have to confess that the arguments this way and that are largely beyond the range of my understanding. The majority view of the gunpowder episode is the one set out by Mark Nicholls—which, in brief, says that the claims over the years that the thing was a Machiavellian scheme concocted inside the regime do not hold water. But, whatever it was, it is historically of some considerable significance. While one might have expected the regime to have unleashed the undoubtedly pent-up forces of anti-popery against the wider Catholic community with a slew of trials and executions that would have dwarfed the previous use of the treason law against Catholics, this was precisely what did not happen. The king had no intention of allowing any such thing.[80]

The legislation introduced into the parliament in early 1606 to counter the threat from Catholic insurgency contained, among other measures, a new oath of allegiance. Some Catholics immediately condemned it as a disguised version of the oath of the royal supremacy and said that it was an upping of the persecutory stakes. But other Catholics saw it differently—that is, as a subtle reworking and restatement of what some loyalist Catholics thought privately, even if they did not always express it publicly.[81]

The regime's public exploitation of the gunpowder business generated an intense debate not just about true political loyalty and obedience but also about what suffering, persecution, and martyrdom were. One gets an immediate sense of this from the media furore over the 'martyrdom' of Henry Garnet, the Jesuit superior in England. As is well known, after he was tracked down and arrested in late January 1606 at Hindlip Hall, he virtually admitted concealing what he had known of the intended treason (though, indirectly, through and under the seal of the confessional) and suffered as a result, both physically and reputationally. On the scaffold he was taunted by hostile spectators. On the other hand, the regime was taking a real risk by prosecuting him. As an intelligencer (Thomas Barnes, it

---

[80] M. Nicholls, *Investigating Gunpowder Plot* (Manchester, 1991). For the conformities in response to news of the plot, see M. Questier, *Conversion, Politics and Religion in England, 1580–1625* (Cambridge, 1996), pp. 117, 137.

[81] For the procedural rules governing the tendering of the oath, see H. Bowler (ed.), *London Sessions Records 1605–1685* (CRS 34, 1934), p. xli.

352 CATHOLICS AND TREASON

seems—writing from St Omer) warned on 26 April/6 May, if Garnet were to be executed for things that had been said under the seal of confession, he would be 'the first' person 'in this world that ever suffered for any such matter'. His Jesuit confrères saw his case as an opportunity to insist that, in England, Catholics died for religion, not for treason.[82] Some Catholics regarded the plot as an opportunity to revisit the central issues of the Archpriest Controversy. The former appellant proctors John Cecil and Anthony Champney arrived in Rome in May 1606 and petitioned the papacy to appoint a bishop or bishops directly over the English Catholic community. Episcopal governance would, it was claimed, prevent such conspiracies in the future.[83]

Notoriously, a miracle from heaven seemed to testify to Garnet's innocence. (See Figure 11.1.) It was described in considerable detail in John Gerard's narrative of the plot.[84] From London on 8 November 1606, Richard Blount wrote that 'a Catholic person' in the city had 'kept, since the execution of Mr Garnet, a straw that was imbrued in his blood'. In 'these days past, being viewed again by the party and others, they' glimpsed 'in the ear of the straw a perfect face of a man dead, his eyes, nose, beard and neck so lively representing Mr Garnet as not only in my eyes but in the eyes of others which knew him it' did 'lively represent him'. Furthermore, this had 'been seen by Catholics and Protestants of the best sort and diverse others who much admire it'. Blount said that 'this you may boldly report for, besides ourselves, a thousand others are witnesses of it'.[85] Bancroft was among

---

[82] PRO, SP 77/8/i, fo. 98^r; Caraman, *HG*, pp. 321–2, 436–7; for the basis of Garnet's indictment, see D. Alan Orr, *Treason and the State: Law, Politics, and Ideology in the English Civil War* (Cambridge, 2002), p. 53. For news from Flanders of preparations to print an apologia for Garnet, see, e.g., PRO, SP 77/8/i, fo. 191^r. On 24 September 1606, Sir Thomas Edmondes noted that the long-term prisoner of conscience Francis Tregian (arrested back in 1577 over his association with the martyr Cuthbert Mayne) had been persuaded by 'our English Jesuits' to take himself to Spain because it was believed that the sight of him would 'amplify the report of the persecutions of England': PRO, SP 77/8/i, fo. 169^v.

[83] PRO, SP 77/8/i, fo. 122^r; Anstr., I, p. 71; TD, V, pp. 10, clv; AAW, A VIII, no. 19, p. 63 ('Copia di una informatione...'), no. 20, pp. 67–75 ('Brevis informatio de duobus presbyteris Anglis ex numero appellantium qui nuper Romam venerunt, et de negotiis eorum'), for a copy of which see ABSJ, Anglia VII, no. 75; see also Sawyer, *WM*, II, p. 282; TD, V, pp. xiii–xiv (Robert Persons's memorandum against Anthony Champney and John Cecil, 16/26 May 1606) and pp. xiv–xx (a separate position paper against them, of presumably similar date).

[84] Morris, *The Condition of Catholics*, pp. 301–5.

[85] ABSJ, Collectanea M, p. 100^a. For the other miracles which allegedly occurred after the deaths of Henry Garnet and Edward Oldcorne (including the story that a crow which 'feasted upon one of the quarters upon the gates' at Worcester, where Oldcorne was put to death, though whether it was Oldcorne's body or not was uncertain, 'presently fell down stark dead'), see ABSJ, Anglia VI, no. 65; see also Caraman, *JG*, pp. 202–3; Morris, *The Condition of Catholics*, pp. 305–6. Challoner's account of Garnet and Oldcorne was confined to an appendix (Richard Challoner, *Memoirs of Missionary Priests*...(2 vols, 1741–2)), II, pp. 15–16, 476–85; Pollen's edition of Challoner moves the appendix into the main text: Challoner, *MMP*, pp. 282–91. For the reluctance of the witnesses whom Bancroft hauled in for questioning to endorse the miracle of the wheat-straw, see, e.g., AAW, A VIII, no. 13, p. 41; see also Usher, *REC*, II, pp. 180–1; *HMCD*, II, p. 454; Caraman, *JG*, pp. 201–2. For Sir Charles Cornwallis's protests in Spain concerning Garnet in mid-1607, see Sawyer, *WM*, II, p. 300; PRO, SP 94/14, fos 95^v, 107^r. One of those interrogated was Robert Barnes of Harleton, co. Cambridge. He said he had been imprisoned for ten years. Just possibly he was the Robert Barnes who was arraigned back in 1598 and had been allowed to denounce Topcliffe; see pp. 275–80 above. If Topcliffe's antagonist had been

Figure 11.1 Portrait of Henry Garnet SJ (reproduced by permission of the governors of Stonyhurst College, Lancashire).

those who were determined to expose and ridicule the burgeoning cult.[86] The word was also that the members of the Society were planning an apocalyptic revenge for what had happened to Garnet against all those whom they regarded as their enemies.[87]

---

released at around the start of James's reign, he would indeed have been in prison for about ten years. Robert Gray in 1593 said that one Robert Barnes, whom I take to have been the same person, had lands in Cambridgeshire: PRO, SP 12/245/138, fo. 222^r.

[86] Bancroft recorded that he had given a warrant to his client, the renegade priest John Scudamore, 'for the apprehension of one Barret, who went up and down with a miracle of Garnet's head supposed to be upon a straw'. Allegedly Barret 'drew his rapier' and had 'hurt' Scudamore: AAW, A VIII, no. 13, p. 41. For Bancroft's further interrogations of Catholics about Garnet's straw, revealing the way that it had circulated around the Catholic community: see AAW, A VIII, no. 15, pp. 47–8, no. 16, p. 51 (for another copy, see AAW, OB III/ii, no. 174, printed in Foley, *RSJ*, IV, pp. 127–8), no. 17, pp. 55–6, no. 18, p. 59.

[87] PRO, SP 77/8/i, fos 114^v, 122^r, 126^v, 155^r, 162^v, 176^{r-v}. The priest Humphrey Sicklemore (who wrote in *c.* May 1606 that Garnet's fate was directly attributable to the malice of the earl of Salisbury: Anstr., I, p. 316; *HMCS*, XVIII, p. 138; *CSPD 1603–10*, pp. 286, 289 (PRO, SP 14/18/66, 91), 307 (PRO, SP 14/19/102), 313 (PRO, SP 14/20/46)) was denounced in April 1606 by one John Healey for, *inter alia*, having tried to persuade him to murder the earl of Salisbury and, when Healey interjected, what 'if I should be thereupon taken and executed?', Sicklemore allegedly replied, 'then...you should die a

354 CATHOLICS AND TREASON

On 10 December 1606 the English ambassador in Brussels, Sir Thomas Edmondes, said that the Brussels pulpits had been echoing with reports of Garnet's straw. The Spanish ambassador had offered 600 crowns for it.[88] Eight days later he reported that 'the miracle of the straw' had been 'confirmed by letters written' to Brussels by the high-born Spanish visitor to London, Luisa de Carvajal y Mendoza. This came with a 'relation also of God's judgment otherwise strangely showed upon some Catholic gentlemen who for the avoiding of the penalty of the statute did of late conform' and went 'to the church'. Sir William Roper had gone mad and Richard Cotton had broken his leg.[89] English women coming to Brussels to enter religion, said Edmondes on 4 February 1607, brought the news that they had seen the straw 'fourteen times'. It grew 'in show more angelical, as they say, by the lively brightness thereof, together with an appearance of wings'.[90] By 18 February, Edmondes was sending a specimen drawing of the straw (the 'forged miracle') back to Cecil. Representations of this kind were being distributed everywhere. Edmondes had made a formal complaint to the archduke about the acclamation of Garnet as a martyr and the printing of these images. Apparently, the archduke did his best to suppress these drawings, though the Jesuits in Brussels appealed against his decision.[91]

The Spaniards, like the archduke, wanted to avoid a falling out with the British king. In late 1606, news had reached London that the common executioner in Madrid had already incinerated an allegedly inaccurate Jesuit-sponsored printed translation of the recusancy statutes passed in the English parliament. A copy of the offending piece had been dispatched, along with a Spanish account of Garnet's

martyr and be assured of immediate salvation': PRO, SP 14/20/46, fo. 102[r]; see also PRO, SP 14/86/96, fo. 159[r]. Sir Thomas Edmondes reported, on 16 June 1606, a poison plot against Salisbury: PRO, SP 77/8/i, fo. 121[r] (*HMCS*, XVIII, p. 169).

[88] PRO, SP 77/8/i, fo. 194[r].

[89] PRO, SP 77/8/i, fo. 199[r-v]. For Luisa de Carvajal's newsletters about Garnet, see G. Redworth, *The She-Apostle: The Extraordinary Life and Death of Luisa de Carvajal* (2008), pp. 121–4; G. Redworth, *LLC*, I, pp. 117f.

[90] PRO, SP 77/8/ii, fo. 32[v].

[91] PRO, SP 77/8/ii, fos 38[r-v], 41[r]; L. Duerloo, *Dynasty and Piety: Archduke Albert (1598–1621) and Habsburg Political Culture in an Age of Religious Wars* (2009), pp. 182–3. On 3 March 1607, the English ambassador in Paris, Sir George Carew, reported that he had shown the Flemish ambassador in Paris 'the picture of the straw (which Sir Thomas Edmondes sent me [from Brussels]) with Garnet's head in it, cut in brass, *cum privilegio*': PRO, SP 78/53, fo. 247[r]. James's ambassador in Spain, Sir Charles Cornwallis, noted on 9 April 1607 that the Jesuits in Flanders had printed 'this feigned and ridiculous miracle' and, though the archducal government there had suppressed this, in Spain 'a painter had been procured to make divers pictures' of Garnet, 'setting it forth in the worst manner to draw his Majesty' King James 'into opinion of cruelty' and had 'under it... written... "Henrico Garnett Ingles, martore-sado en Londres"'. Cornwallis protested that Garnet could be regarded as 'a martyr...only by those' who saw James I as a 'tyrant': Sawyer, *WM*, II, pp. 300–1. Just over a year later, on 24 August 1608, Carew sent Salisbury the 'portraits of certain Jesuitical martyrs of whom one may say', as Cardinal Basilios Bessarion 'is reported to have said, of one canonized in his time, *isti novi sancti, cogunt me dubitare de veteribus*. Some bookbinders do tell me that in those copies sent into Spain the picture of Jacques Clément [*sic* for Jean Chastel] is inserted, who attempted to murder this king [i.e. Henry IV]. But it is omitted in those which are designed for this country': PRO, SP 78/54, fo. 145[v].

TOLERANCE AND INTOLERANCE IN ENGLAND   355

execution, by Sir Charles Cornwallis to Salisbury in a letter of 26 November 1606. The publication led to a rebuke for the Spanish ambassador in London, Pedro de Zúñiga.[92] Cornwallis claimed on 14 January 1607 that he had virtually succeeded in getting the translation suppressed. Up to that point, 'every religious house' in Madrid had had a copy, and 'their preachers usually helped out their sermons with declarations against the cruelties of England, some of them affirming that much easier it was for the Christians in the days of Diocletian'. But 'now there is hardly one of those translations to be found'. The 'most part of the ambassadors in this court' had 'copies of my letters and annotations' and had sent them back to their masters.[93]

Robert Drury, George Gervase, Matthew Flathers, and Thomas Garnet

Some Catholics may have thought that the Jacobean State could now be persuaded to show a tolerant face to those who were not regicidal maniacs. But the signs were not all good. On 26 February 1607, the priest Robert Drury was hanged, drawn, and quartered at Tyburn. He had been arrested, about two weeks before, with another priest, William Davies.[94] Blount recorded the course of the trial on 20 February and the convictions of, and public sympathy for, the two priests.[95] Blount insisted that Drury was now a friend to the Society, although

[92] Sawyer, WM, II, pp. 269, 271, 280; Bodl., Carte MS 85, no. 71, fos 337^v–40^v (Antoine le Fèvre de la Boderie to Nicolas de Neufville, seigneur de Villeroy, 11/21 February 1607); Boderie, AMLB, II, pp. 76–7, 131; CSPV 1603–7, p. 449; Loomie, SJC, I, p. 174; A. J. Loomie (ed.), English Polemics at the Spanish Court: Joseph Creswell's Letter to the Ambassador from England: The English and Spanish Texts of 1606 (New York, 1993), introduction, pp. 15–21 (for the translation of the statutes made by the former embassy chaplain James Wadsworth); James Wadsworth Snr, Las Leyes nuevamente hechas en el Parlamēto de Inglaterra esto Año de M.DC.VI. contra los Catolicos Ingleses que llaman Recusantes traduzidas de su original impresso en Ingles (n.p. [Madrid?], n.d. [1606]); ARCR, I, no. 1342.2. There were accusations also that the Spanish embassy in London was responsible for, or certainly had not prevented, the importing and distribution of printed works in defence of Garnet: Bodl., Carte MS 85, no. 72, fos 340^v–1^r; see also CSPV 1603–7, p. 486.

[93] Sawyer, WM, II, pp. 281–2. Cornwallis took real satisfaction on 19 April 1607 from the fact that the Spanish court had suppressed the circulating pictures of the Jesuit. Joseph Creswell SJ had disclaimed all knowledge of them: Sawyer, WM, II, pp. 303–4, 307.

[94] Drury had, said one account, been arrested on 10 February with Davies at the house of John Stansby in the Whitefriars in London. Drury was interrogated the next day in front of Richard Vaughan, bishop of London (d. 30 March) by Sir Edward Stanhope and Sir John Bennett, and subsequently was disputed with by Thomas Morton, Vaughan's chaplain: Anstr., I, p. 105; AWCBC, pp. 1698, 1714, 1740; ABSJ, Collectanea M, p. 99^b; for the indictments of Drury and Davies, see Bowler, London Sessions Records 1605–1685, pp. 24–6, 381. The puritan Richard Rogers in 1606 had noted that 'since the discovery of the powder treason' Vaughan had 'restored... suspended ministers': M. M. Knappen (ed.), Two Elizabethan Puritan Diaries. By R. Rogers and Samuel Ward (Chicago, 1933), p. 32.

[95] ABSJ, Collectanea M, p. 99^b.

356   CATHOLICS AND TREASON

Drury had signed the appeal of 17 November 1600 and, with other appellant clergy, had put his name to the protestation of allegiance of early 1603.[96]

The pamphlet which described the proceedings against him said that 'divers traitorous and dangerous papers were shown, which had been taken in his custody'. They were incriminating enough. 'One of them seemed to be' Robert Persons's 'opinion concerning the oath in the late made statute which he utterly disallowed any Catholic to take'. The 'others were also of a traitorous nature, tending to the abuse and corrupting of poor simple souls and stealing all duty and allegiance from them'. But although Drury was arrested in possession of these documents which, one assumes, were to be used to dissuade Catholics from taking the 1606 oath, it emerged that this former appellant may himself have been a good deal less certain about how uncompromisingly he should reject the new oath.[97]

After the jury had given in its verdict, in response to a petition from the priest for 'some private speech with him', 'upon Monday morning', 23 February, the recorder of London, Sir Henry Montagu, 'sent for Drury down unto the sessions house garden' and offered him a reprieve in return for taking the oath. Drury offered to take it, 'and humbly required that the like grace might be afforded to his brother William Davies'. Montagu thought this was absolutely capital and he 'was in his mind persuaded that, if he had put' Drury 'to the oath presently, without any refusal', the priest 'would have taken it'. But Montagu 'as an upright justice... very wisely considered' that Drury's 'fact' was 'openly known'. The 'people' were 'acquainted with his dangerous practices'. Thus 'his public submission and taking the oath would the better witness his obedience and submission and prove

---

[96] ARSJ, Anglia 37, fo. 102ᵛ. Drury had in the 1590s been associated with John Gerard; he was entertained in the house run for Gerard by Anne Line: Caraman, JG, p. 86; AWCBC, p. 1696. For Drury's signing of the appeal of 17 November 1600, drawn up at Wisbech Castle, and his subsequent suspension by Blackwell, see AWCBC, pp. 1696–7; TD, III, pp. cxxxiii–cxliv; Inner Temple, Petyt MS 538/47, fo. 263ʳ. For Drury's subscribing of the protestation of allegiance of 31 January 1603, see AWCBC, pp. 1697, 1704; TD, III, pp. clxxxviii–cxci. He had in 1603 been named by William Watson as 'privy' to the Bye Plot, even without knowing the 'principal matter' of it: AWCBC, p. 1697 (TD, IV, pp. xlii; PRO, SP 14/3/16, fo. 28ᵛ). One of Christopher Grene's sources says that 'ante mortem voluit reconciliari Societati quam offenderat teste P. Gerardi in epistola 2ª ad Calcedonensem'—this implies that John Gerard had intervened in Richard Smith's attempt in and after 1626 to compile a martyrology and had protested that Drury had been determined to reconcile himself to the Society of Jesus, i.e. contrary to some secular clergymen's claims that he had remained at enmity with the Jesuits: ABSJ, Collectanea N/i, p. 56ª.

[97] A True Report of the Araignment...of a Popish Priest, named Robert Drewrie...(1607), sig. Bᵛ. Two letters taken with him were read out in court, 'the one from certain priests, prisoners sometimes in the Clink, to the archpriest Master Blackwell, requiring his judgment in matters when they laboured and hoped for toleration in religion. The other was Master Blackwell's answer thereto': ibid. One rendering of an interrogation of Blackwell at Lambeth, dated 3 July 1607, has the archpriest wish that he might have spoken with Drury before his execution, 'in that he understands his life had been preserved if he would have taken that oath': Mʳ George Blackwel...his Answeres...(1607); A Large Examination taken at Lambeth...(1607), p. 13.

TOLERANCE AND INTOLERANCE IN ENGLAND   357

much more pleasing than anything done in private'. So Montagu deferred putting the oath to him.[98]

Here, however, was the difficulty. Many Catholics believed that, potentially, they could swear the oath, but it was difficult for them to do this publicly because the oath described certain ideas and beliefs as heretical which many Catholics would not regard as such. On 25 February, when Drury was summoned once again to the bar of the court, he seemed a lot less cooperative. He was asked 'why judgment of death should not be pronounced against him' and he 'replied, as he had done before, that he took himself not to be convicted of treason but only for his priesthood'. His 'voluntary offer to take' the 'oath on the Monday before was rehearsed to him'. It was 'further told him that now it was apparently perceived how colourably he cloaked his private and pernicious dealing, answering by equivocation, and setting down one thing under his own hand, then afterwards speaking directly against the same'. In the court the relevant parts of Drury's letter to 'a person of great honour' (perhaps Montagu or, possibly, a privy councillor and, maybe, even Bancroft) were read out. From this 'it appeared that he had been required to set down his censure and opinion according as himself did best gather and conceive thereof concerning' the new oath of allegiance. Drury's opinion was that 'every honest and good Catholic' could 'lawfully and safely' take it. But, when he had 'the book delivered into his own hands' and was told to say what, if anything, in the oath he rejected, he refused. Just to make sure that everyone knew what was at stake, the oath was read out in full in open court. The hostile pamphleteer who narrated this case could conclude that Drury had said 'one thing' and done 'the contrary in making an outward show of duty and obedience under' his 'handwriting and reserving a traitorous intention in' his 'close bosom'. Thus 'religion' was 'the cloak cast over intended treason'. When Drury said that 'a French priest or a Spanish priest' would be similarly guilty, 'all the bystanders were even ready to hiss him'.[99]

Exactly how much was at stake here, and precisely how complex were the available positions and responses concerning the oath, became clear in the answers offered by Drury's co-accused, the priest William Davies. He was more circumspect and said that he was 'a poor simple ignorant man' and he did not have sufficient judgment or wit to determine of such matters or, at least, not without consulting the 'many learned priests whose' opinions 'he would first know, and then perhaps he might be otherwise altered'. Our pamphleteer took this as a sign

---

[98] *A True Report*, sigs B4ᵛ–Cʳ. For Thomas Preston's account of Drury's approval in principle of the oath, see Thomas Preston, *A Theologicall Disputation*...(1613), pp. 250–1, stating that Drury, 'as soon as the oath was published, did even to the last gasp openly maintain the same'. This 'he did publicly protest at his arraignment before the judge', but he 'nevertheless...being desirous to die for that cause, for which he was condemned by the judge, did himself refuse to take the oath'; he had concluded that because of the 'diversity' of opinion over the oath 'neither he, nor any other priest' was bound to take it.

[99] *A True Report*, sigs Cᵛ–Dʳ.

358   CATHOLICS AND TREASON

that Davies was just as duplicitous as Drury. The two clergymen were lectured on the 'many and extraordinary great graces of the king's Majesty towards men of their condition'. He had merely ratified Elizabeth's statutes against Catholics and, indeed, had been content to remit the penalties specified by those laws and was 'loath to meddle with their blood that were enemies to his life, and desirous to win them by mercy if they were not too monstrous'. Nor had he 'sentenced any priest' to 'death since his coming to the crown but such as were men of most dangerous quality and had their hands over deep in most barbarous and inhuman treasons'. But in the face of their 'treacherous devices, mercy (of necessity) must give way to justice'. Both were sentenced to death, but evidently the authorities did not view their spoken responses in the same way.[100]

According to the printed account, Drury had made any other outcome in his case impossible when, in the courtroom, he had publicly absolved a murderer, Humphrey Floyd. Whether Floyd had really been criminally guilty of the offence with which he had been charged (he alleged self-defence), he was a known Catholic who was believed to have been on the fringes of both the Bye Plot and the Gunpowder Plot.[101] Floyd 'forthwith openly confessed' that he was 'a Catholic, so he had been always and so he would die, as if that very name should give fame to his foul fact and, where he died a murderer, his own idle supposition of popish absolution should make him now to die in the case of a martyr, and for his conscience'.[102]

The Drury case was, therefore, the subject of a several-ways contest. The regime was compelled to portray Drury as a hypocrite even though he came, arguably, from the moderate core of the appellant movement. But some Catholic commentators were determined to show that he had been completely consistent. Richard Holtby on 28 February, two days after the execution, maintained that, although Drury had been offered the oath, 'he absolutely refused it because, as he said unto his friends, he would do nothing that should hinder his martyrdom; and yet he wrote' to Bancroft 'that he had been of opinion that it might be taken by a layman, not knowing that there was any breve to the contrary'. He had asked for time to think about it and 'in the meantime' he was 'informed by some Catholics that there was a breve against it' and so remained 'resolute'.[103] Richard Blount wrote on 4 March 1607 that Drury's hesitation had occurred merely because he 'had not had sufficient notice' of the breve of 12/22 September 1606 which condemned the oath. This was why he was 'once in mind, and gave some hope to' Bancroft that he might actually take it, 'though, when he understood from others the unlawfulness

---

[100] Ibid., sig. D^r-2^v. Drury himself penned on the night of 25 February a narrative of his tribulations. It came to the hands of the archducal ambassador, Conrad Schetz, baron de Hoboken, who translated it; there is added a narrative of the execution: AWCBC, pp. 1748–58 (Brussels, Archives Générales du Royaume, Papiers d'Etat et de l'Audience, MS 365, fos 185^r–7^v, cited in Anstr., I, p. 105 and in Redworth, The She-Apostle, p. 253).

[101] A True Report, sig. B2^r–3^v.   [102] Ibid., sig. B4^r.

[103] ARSJ, Anglia 37, fo. 109^r; see also CSPV 1603–7, pp. 479, 480–1.

TOLERANCE AND INTOLERANCE IN ENGLAND 359

of it, he resolved not to take it'.[104] Drury's supporters at the Spanish embassy had provided him with 'a cassock and a biretta' so that there could be, in their view and that of the spectators who gathered to watch the proceedings at Tyburn, no misunderstanding as to the reason for his suffering, even though the ambassador Zúñiga had, said Luisa de Carvajal, also 'been skilfully conducting secret negotiations which gave great cause to hope that his life would be saved'. She spent the 'previous afternoon' with him, evidently to bolster his determination, and to make sure that he did not buckle under 'the massive pressure they were bringing to bear on him' to take the oath. Carvajal drew some comfort from the recent death of the bishop of London, Richard Vaughan, who now would be spending 'Easter in Hell'.[105]

Zúñiga wrote on 5/15 March that he had indeed made an 'earnest endeavour...to prevent the executions'. Catherine Howard, countess of Suffolk, relayed a message from the earl of Salisbury that he would halt the proceedings. Then the French ambassador, Antoine le Fèvre de la Boderie, intervened on the two clerics' behalf. This provoked an outburst from James that Henry IV was ruled by the Jesuit order. This was a dig at the French king's rehabilitation of the Society in France. Boderie riposted that Zúñiga sent 'soutanes to these clerics' and urged them not to take the oath.[106] Of course, James had other reasons to be vexed with the French king—that is, over the French intervention in the recent Venetian interdict controversy. It is possible also that Drury's arrest and prosecution may have become linked in the public mind with the prospect of a peace deal between the Dutch and the Spaniards. The Flanders administration was determined by now to secure a cessation of arms. Some Hispanophile English Catholics may well have regarded that prospect with horror. Luisa de Carvajal certainly did.[107]

---

[104] ABSJ, Collectanea M, p. 101ª; *AWCBC*, p. 1740; for Drury's views about the oath, see also AAW, A XV, no. 51, p. 135.

[105] Redworth, *LLC*, I, p. 246; G. Redworth, *The She-Apostle*, pp. 139–43; *A True Report*, sig. C2ʳ; ARSJ, Anglia 37, fo. 107ᵛ. It was reported that Drury appeared at Tyburn 'after the manner of the Benedictine friars beyond the seas': Anstr., I, p. 105; *A True Report*, sig. D3ʳ; *AWCBC*, p. 1716. The Jesuits, reported John Mush in May 1607, claimed that Drury had been admitted to the Society, though Mush said that Drury's confessor for 'the greater part of the night before his passion' was the secular priest Anthony Hebburn: Anstr., I, p. 105, citing ASV, Nunziatura d'Inghilterra, 19, fo. 24ʳ. It has been argued that Drury may have been an oblate of the Benedictine order and that the 'Benedictine faculty under seals' taken with him at his arrest may have been a document which permitted him to admit others to the same status: *AWCBC*, p. 1716.

[106] Loomie, *SJC*, I, p. 96. Holtby's confrère Blount said that the French ambassador 'spoke very earnestly in their behalf'. This irritated the king. The 'Spanish ambassador spoke not himself, for he saw it bootless, but yet offered to any one English or Scot that would beg their lives 2,000 crowns...but nothing would prevail': ABSJ, Collectanea M, p. 99ᵇ. Zúñiga denied that he had dispatched soutanes to Drury and Davies but Richard Blount confirmed on 27 March that the Spanish ambassador 'was charged by the council to have sent to Mr Drury before his execution a new cassock of black cloth, a square cap and to have sent his barber to have cut his hair of his head and to shave his beard for so did he go to execution': Loomie, *SJC*, I, p. 96; ARSJ, Anglia 37, fo. 107ᵛ. See also E. Nelson, *The Jesuits and the Monarchy: Catholic Reform and Political Authority in France (1590–1615)* (Aldershot, 2005).

[107] In mid-1607, Carvajal noted that 'there is a lot of talk in this miserable Babylon about a peace treaty'. She feared the peace would be overly favourable to the Dutch: 'if we take our eye off Flanders even for a moment, Antwerp will end up lost'. The war had been basically a good thing. Her opinion was that, 'if the peace were broken to the greater glory of God, His faith and His Church, our princes would find themselves much better off with war': Redworth, *LLC*, I, p. 251.

360 CATHOLICS AND TREASON

(As early as 20 February/2 March 1607, she had heard Mass said by Davies in his prison.)[108] Carvajal wrote also that Drury had told her that 'he would, both from the gallows and from Heaven, bless Spain and our king', Philip III.[109] In other words, Drury's doom may have been used by some Catholics in London to articulate by proxy their anger at the sight of the House of Austria apparently selling out in Flanders and allowing northern European Christendom to go to Hell in a handcart.

In the end, although Drury was left to his fate, Davies was reprieved. The Venetian ambassador said it was because Davies had taken the new oath, though this is uncertain. Zúñiga said he definitely had not.[110] James personally explained to Boderie why he would let one priest die and yet reprieve the other. Drury had been taken, said the king, 'saisi de beaucoup de lettres venant de Rome, et d'autres papiers qui le rendoient criminel de lèse-Majesté', that is, the ones mentioned in the court during the trial. It was the letter from Persons warning Catholics against the oath which sealed Drury's fate, for James would not tolerate 'la désobéissance au dit serment, sous lequel il croit sa vie et son autorité plus assurés'.[111] Zúñiga claimed, however, that James 'wanted this one', Drury, 'to hang in order to satisfy parliament' in response to anger expressed there at the proceedings in mid-February 1607 against Sir Christopher Pigott for his outburst against the Scots.[112]

Whatever the exact cause for the carrying out of the sentence, at Tyburn, Drury proclaimed simply that he had come to this end only because he had been ordained as a Roman Catholic priest.[113] Our hostile pamphleteer said that the priest seemed still to be expecting a reprieve and, allegedly, caught hold of the rope when he was hanged.[114] Floyd was among the twenty-five felons who were executed at the same time. He made no secret of his Catholicism.[115] The crowd at

---

[108] Redworth, *LLC*, I., p. 225.

[109] Redworth, *LLC*, I, p. 297.

[110] *CSPV 1603–7*, p. 480; Loomie, *SJC*, I, pp. 96, 99–100. Davies's pardon was procured, alleged Zorzi Giustiniani, by French lobbying (by Charles de Lorraine, prince of Joinville, presumably in addition to the efforts of Boderie): *CSPV 1607–10*, p. 5; Loomie, *SJC*, I, p. 102; Redworth, *LLC*, I, pp. 260, 298; for Joinville's diplomatic visit, see Boderie, *AMLB*, II, *passim*.

[111] Boderie, *AMLB*, II, pp. 102–4.

[112] Loomie, *SJC*, I, pp. 97, 98; *HC 1604–29*, V, p. 709.

[113] ABSJ, Collectanea M, p. 99[b].

[114] *A True Report*, sig. D3[v]–4[r].

[115] The renegade priest John Scudamore, who had become a client of Archbishop Bancroft, had tried to persuade Floyd to conform: ABSJ, Collectanea M, p. 100[a]; M. Questier(ed.), 'The Limits of Conformity in Late Elizabethan England: A Plea for a Priest', in P. Clarke and M. Questier (eds), *Papal Authority and the Limits of the Law in Tudor England* (*Camden Miscellany*, 36, Camden Society, 5th series, 48, Cambridge, 2015), pp. 113–14. In a report sent to Rome in March 1607, it was stated that Scudamore had also been sent to argue with both Drury and Davies: ASV, Borghese MS III, 43, d–e, fos 88[r]–9[v] (transcript at ABSJ; PRO, PRO 31/9/115, fo. 133[r]). On the way to the gallows, said the *True Report*, faced with one 'Master Dove' (just possibly John Dove, though he was a doctor of divinity, who had written, *inter alia*, *A Perswasion to the English Recusants...*(1603)), preaching in front of 'Saint Sepulchre's Church', Floyd 'stopped his ears, not willing to hear anything but, if any Roman Catholics were near, he desired such to pray for him': *A True Report*, sig. B4[r–v].

TOLERANCE AND INTOLERANCE IN ENGLAND   361

Tyburn, or some of it, may have been unconvinced about Drury's guilt. Richard Blount recounted that, once Drury was dead and dismembered, an unnamed 'minister told the people they should now hear his horrible treason for which besides his refusing the oath of allegiance...he was worthily executed' and he pulled 'out his papers to read'. But then, cryptically, he said there really was not time, 'others being to suffer', 'neither would it be greatly material because they should see very shortly in print the whole discourse of all his treasons'. The minister then 'put up his papers again into his pocket, whereat the people' guffawed at him and one spectator said it was 'one of the foolishest speeches that...ever was made at Tyburn'.[116] Blount said on 9 April 1607 that the queen, Anne of Denmark, had berated the crypto-Catholic privy councillor Henry Howard, earl of Northampton, as 'an apostate from his religion' and as 'one of no conscience' because he 'might have saved the life of Drury the priest' and yet refused. 'She marvelled' that 'the State would put him to death having no matter of treason against him, saving his function and religion. She held him a very honest man and, seeing she had gotten his chalice that he said Mass withal, she would keep it as long as she lived'.[117]

About two months after Drury was hanged at Tyburn, Blount described how King James had gone through the modern Marble Arch area on his way to Newmarket. He had ridden past, guided his horse round, and 'returned back to the gibbet', and then rode right under the Tyburn gallows. He 'looked upon it and struck it with his rod, saying scoffingly, all you...Jesuits and priests that have been hanged here, pray for me'.[118]

It does seem that, whatever his queen and, presumably, other court Catholics thought, the king was determined to crush, if he could, Catholic articulations of resistance theory. This determination to tear down the barriers of Catholic mental independence over constructions of royal authority led to the arrest of the archpriest George Blackwell on 24 June 1607.[119] Blackwell had never fully subscribed to Rome's censure of the new oath of allegiance. The ambassador Boderie wrote on 4/14 July 1607 that 'quant à l'archiprêtre, il semble que ledit roi', James, 'n'ait pas été trop aise de sa prise, comme le tenant pour homme assez paisible'.[120] But whether or not the king actually wanted Blackwell roughed up, this did not prevent the regime's interrogators going at him really hard. Under intense pressure Blackwell caved in and reversed his previous condemnation of the oath. On 7 July 1607 he penned a declaration in which he explained why he had now taken the

---

[116] ABSJ, Collectanea M, p. 100a; Brussels, Archives Générales du Royaume, Papiers d'Etat et de l'Audience, MS 365, fo. 187r (*AWCBC*, p. 1755).

[117] ABSJ, Collectanea M, p. 101a; see also A. J. Loomie, 'King James I's Catholic Consort', *Huntingdon Library Quarterly* 34 (1971), pp. 303–16.

[118] ARSJ, Anglia 37, fo. 107v.

[119] See Anstr., I, p. 40; Usher, *REC*, II, pp. 182–3; Boderie, *AMLB*, II, pp. 313–14.

[120] Boderie, *AMLB*, II, p. 327.

362 CATHOLICS AND TREASON

oath, though it could be argued that his affirmation of it was no more than a public expression of what had been his private opinion ever since the oath was promulgated.[121] Blackwell's examinations were then put into print by the regime. Even if with much hesitation, Blackwell could now be taken to have endorsed James's own reading of the relationship between spiritual and temporal authority.[122] The Jesuits at Brussels, as Edmondes reported there on 2 September 1607, remarked that, 'as long as' the martyr and saint Henry Garnet 'lived, he [had] kept' Blackwell 'from these weaknesses into the which he is now fallen.'[123]

At the same time, in c. July 1607, James threw the earl of Tyrone to the wolves in the Irish administration, led by Sir Arthur Chichester, who had been gunning for him for so long. James appeared to credit the claims that Tyrone was fomenting rebellion. The earl was, in effect, forced into exile.[124] This was undoubtedly meant to reassure those such as William James, bishop of Durham, who believed, as he said on 14 December 1607, that 'it was his Majesty's clemency to banish' Catholics 'whom he might have justly executed'. It was only 'his Majesty's late most worthy proclamation against the Irish earls, wherein the priests and Jesuits...are notably deciphered', that had 'comforted and encouraged' good Protestant subjects.[125]

James's ideological aggression towards aspects of contemporary Catholicism which he regarded as monarchomach did not mean that he would tolerate those same tendencies, as he saw them, among Calvinists. The ambassador Boderie commented on 26 January/5 February 1608 that James was hostile 'tous les jours envers les puritains' and that he hated them 'plus que les Catholiques'. The king met with the judges on 15 February 1608. Although he demanded the use of the oath, he allowed for 'a mild inclination towards' those Catholics that were not 'apostates since his time, nor practisers'. James 'commended to favour such priests as would take' the oath. The privy council's subsequent briefing to the judges, in the king's absence, further restricted the judges' scope for action. 'No priest' was

---

[121] Anstr., I, pp. 40–1; Usher, REC, II, p. 183; PRO, SP 14/28/5.

[122] Usher, REC, II, p. 183; Mr George Blackwel...his Answeres. For the translation into Latin of A Large Examination, perhaps at the direction of Archbishop Bancroft, see In Georgium Blacvellum...(1609); CSPV 1607–10, p. 421; see also AAW, A VIII, nos 36–40. Among those who challenged Blackwell in his prison accommodation over his apparent moral and casuistical collapse was Luisa de Carvajal (in September 1607): Redworth, LLC, I, p. 278. By contrast, Boderie thought that Blackwell had behaved appropriately: Boderie, AMLB, II, pp. 350–1. Salisbury insisted to Giustiniani that the king's book in favour of the oath (his Triplici Nodo, Triplex Cuneus; or an Apologie for the Oath of Allegiance...(1607)) did no more than defend 'the freedom and sovereignty of princes in matters temporal' and did not 'touch the question of religion, nor of ecclesiastical jurisdiction at all': CSPV 1607–10, p. 97.

[123] PRO, SP 77/8/ii, fo. 125^r.

[124] J. McCavitt, Sir Arthur Chichester: Lord Deputy of Ireland 1605–1616 (Belfast, 1998), p. 135 and ch. 8 passim.

[125] HMCS, XIX, p. 378.

TOLERANCE AND INTOLERANCE IN ENGLAND   363

'to be executed that would take the oath of allegiance' or would even show himself willing to argue about it and, 'even of them, sparingly'.[126]

This had not, of course, saved Robert Drury, and it did not take much to provoke the king to something very different from tolerance. On 17/27 February 1608, wrote Zúñiga, James erupted after Richard Neile had passed him 'some verses which were printed in Seville under a picture of Father Garnet's straw'. Sir Lewis Lewkenor, the ultra-loyalist but (crypto-) Catholic man about court was dispatched to make a formal protest to Zúñiga. The Spaniard tried to laugh it off, saying that, in Spain, 'simple people' made 'up fables such as this'. But during a fraught four-hour meeting of the privy council, James 'said that there were some among them who favoured Catholics' and declared that he would 'give orders' to the judges for the widespread tendering of the oath to Catholics, both to imprisoned clergy and more generally. If such people, meaning presumably the clergy, 'refused', there would be many more martyrs, for the non-jurors 'would hang'.[127]

It got worse when news of Rome's deposition and dismissal of the archpriest Blackwell reached London. The breve of deposition was dated 22 January/1 February 1608. The senior secular priest George Birkhead was appointed in his place.[128] Zorzi Giustiniani remarked on 24 March/3 April that 'this bull has not yet come to the king's notice, for the pope has addressed fresh letters to the man he has appointed to succeed the late archpriest, instructing him to suspend publication for some days'. But it was 'likely to breed great wrath in the mind of the king and council'. In fact, according to the Spaniards, on the same day that Giustiniani wrote, the news was definitely out that Blackwell had been censured by the Roman curia. Boderie commented subsequently that the king had been enraged at the arrival of the breve, as much as anything because the breve not only deposed Blackwell but also excommunicated all those who took the oath.[129] George Gervase, who was rumoured in early 1606, when he was arrested at Berwick, to have been on the periphery of the Gunpowder conspiracy, was executed on 11 April 1608. This was a direct royal response, said the Venetians, to Rome's cashiering of Blackwell.[130] Asked by Sir Henry Montagu, in court, whether

---

[126] Boderie, *AMLB*, III, p. 79; Usher, *REC*, II, p. 186.

[127] Loomie, *SJC*, I, pp. 110–11. Zúñiga reported on this same day that the earl of Northampton believed that a dynastic marriage with Spain 'was the medicine to cure this ulcer' of 'persecution': Loomie, *SJC*, I, p. 111.

[128] Usher, *REC*, II, p. 192; TD, IV, pp. clvii–ix; Questier, *C&C*, p. 344; PRO, SP 14/31/11.

[129] *CSPV 1607–10*, p. 115; Loomie, *SJC*, I, p. 115; Boderie, *AMLB*, III, p. 226.

[130] Challoner, *MMP*, pp. 294–6; *CSPV 1607–10*, pp. 124–5, 126; see also Loomie, *SJC*, II, pp. 118, 119; T. McCann, 'Some Notes on the Family of George Gervase of Bosham, Martyr', *Sussex Archaeological Collections* 113 (1975), pp. 152–6; Anstr., II, p. 129; Questier, *C&C*, pp. 203, 283, 284. Boderie remarked that on 11 April, 'au même temps que l'on éxécutoit ce pauvre prêtre' Gervase, 'on menoit un ministre prisonnier pour avoir prêché Dimanche', i.e. the day before, 'qu'une des malédictions dont Dieu menaçait anciennement son peuple, était de leur donner des rois étrangers', and that evidently included kings from Scotland: Boderie, *AMLB*, III, p. 228.

364 CATHOLICS AND TREASON

he would take the new oath, Gervase's response was loudly to denounce the oath as heretical and, after some hesitation, to affirm the papal deposing power. Sentence was pronounced against him. A number of Protestant divines arrived at the prison to dispute with Gervase, one of whom was Thomas Morton; but to no avail.[131]

Here, once again, the deployment of the treason law's penalties, in retaliation for refusal to take the oath, was used to send an unmistakable message to the watching public. Gervase's obstinacy over the oath (he even repudiated it from the scaffold) may have been why he was not allowed to hang until he was dead. When he was 'laid on the block, by chance he caught hold of the executioner's knife, as he intended to have ripped up his belly'. By mistake, the executioner sliced into 'his own hand'. As Luisa de Carvajal narrated it, 'when they came to open his chest, they swear for certain' that Gervase 'raised an arm and grabbed hold of the knife they were cutting him open with and yanked so hard on it that he cut off part of the executioner's finger, crying "let me alone"'.[132]

Gervase was immediately acclaimed abroad for his principled stand against the oath which the papacy had condemned. On 4 May 1608 Sir Thomas Edmondes noted that there had 'been a great exclamation' in Brussels at the news of Gervase's death. Edmondes understood 'that the Jesuits are dealing with some of the Benedictines to set out his picture for a martyr to justify that which they did in the like manner for Garnet'.[133] On 22 June 1608 Edmondes recorded that 'the picture of Gervase' had been 'set forth' by the Benedictines 'with the inscription...interfectus ab haereticis qui noluit juramentum Regis Angliae contra sedis Apostolicae authoritatem admittere'.[134] Boderie commented that there were in the London prisons 'quatre ou cinq qui s'offrent au même traitement'.[135]

---

[131] Pollen, AEM, pp. 293–5 (AAW, A VIII, no. 52, pp. 287–9; this manuscript has a postscript in a different hand, endorsed to the effect that it was taken from a letter from London, written in April 1608 and signed by (or attributed to) 'Ro. Cha. pr', presumably Robert Charnock); Redworth, LLC, I, pp. 301–2. See also D. Lunn, The English Benedictines 1540–1688: From Reformation to Revolution (1981), p. 80; Jeaffreson, MCR, II, pp. 202–3 (for the trial proceedings on 9 April 1608). For William James's suspicions in March 1606 that Gervase had been involved in the Gunpowder Plot, see PRO, SP 14/19/2, fo. 2ʳ. Gervase's brother Henry was, or had been, in the service of the king of Spain in Flanders: PRO, SP 94/10, fo. 36ʳ; PRO, SP 77/7, fo. 331ʳ; see also Loomie, Guy Fawkes in Spain, p. 20. One informant had claimed in late July 1604 that the word was going round that the cautionary towns in Flanders would do King James no good, for 'we should shortly see all their throats cut', and that Captain Gervase had written a 'letter to that effect': PRO, SP 94/10, fo. 83ᵛ.

[132] Pollen, AEM, pp. 295–7; Loomie, SJC, I, p. 118; Redworth, LLC, I, p. 302. See also AAW, A VIII, no. 53, p. 291 (a Latin account of Gervase's martyrdom penned by Richard Smith, presumably in the 1620s); ARSJ, Anglia 37, fo. 130ʳ.

[133] PRO, SP 77/9, fo. 71ʳ.

[134] PRO, SP 77/9, fo. 88ᵛ (HMCS, XX, p. 203). For Catholic attempts to appropriate Gervase's martyrdom, see J. E. Kelly, 'The Contested Appropriation of George Gervase's Martyrdom: European Religious Patronage and the Controversy over the Oath of Allegiance', JBS 57 (2018), pp. 253–74, esp. at p. 260; pp. 376–7 n.3 below; L. Hicks (ed.), Letters of Thomas Fitzherbert 1608–1610 (CRS 41, 1948), pp. 25–6, 47, 55–6.

[135] Boderie, AMLB, III, p. 227. For the publication at Rome during 1608 of portraits of Jesuit martyrs, with Henry Garnet and Edward Oldcorne among them, see Effigies et Nomina quorundam e Societate Jesu qui pro Fide vel Pietate sunt Interfecti ab anno 1549 ad annum 1607 (Rome, 1608).

TOLERANCE AND INTOLERANCE IN ENGLAND   365

Though there was no obvious connection with the treason trials in London, a priest, one Matthew Flathers, had been executed at York on 21 March 1608, again with considerable brutality. At the direction of the lord president, Lord Sheffield, this priest had been arrested by Sir Stephen Procter and Sir Timothy Whittingham at Upsall Castle, a Constable family property, in South Kilvington in August 1607 with an unnamed female patron. Taken with Flathers was William Mush (the martyrologist and appellant priest John Mush's brother), who, Procter subsequently claimed, was regarded as 'a supposed confederate in the...powder treason'. Lord Sheffield had written to Salisbury on 24 August 1607 that he should tell the king himself about the recent arrest of 'two priests in one house' while a third escaped. This should alert the king as 'to what store there are of them'. Sir Henry Constable protested that he was a 'Protestant' but his household officers were all recusants and were the principal harbourers 'of priests in this country'. Sheffield demanded to know what the king wanted done with the prisoners. If he meant to pardon them, opined Sheffield, it would be better not to arrest such clergymen at all since they went straight back to their gentry patrons and all the wrong people took 'great encouragement' to continue in their 'obstinacy'.[136]

Flathers and Mush, with their benefactor, were sentenced to death at the Lent assizes in the following year. The latter two were reprieved at the last minute.[137] But the treatment of Flathers was by all accounts fairly horrific. Holtby reported to Persons on 13 April 1608 that 'upon Easter Monday at York was Mr Matthew Flathers executed most barbarously; for, being cut down alive, two persons got hold of him while he was yet amazed in the fall and upon his feet'. He 'shook

---

[136] HHCP 119/97 (HMCS, XVIII, p. 247; the year should be 1607, not 1606); ARSJ, Anglia 37, fo. 102^r (Richard Blount's attribution of the arrest to Archbishop Matthew). The searchers believed that the escaped priest was the Jesuit John Gerard and said that the individual in question 'did suddenly in the night at a backdoor of the said castle break out, giving the watchman there present a sudden blow': PRO, STAC 8/18/1, fo. 118^r; AWCBC, p. 1807. But in fact it was, as John Mush wrote to Anthony Champney on 18 January 1608, Cuthbert Trollop, the former appellant: AWCBC, p. 1790 (citing PRO, PRO 31/9/116, fos 1^r–2^r). In the course of a star chamber action in 1609, Sir Richard Cholmley was accused by Sir Thomas Hoby of favouring recusants and 'popish players'; but Cholmley declared in a deposition dated 22 May that he himself had served as the foreman of the jury which had convicted Matthew Flathers and William Mush as well as their patron: AWCBC, p. 1793 (PRO, STAC 8/12/11); HC 1604–29, III, p. 517.

[137] Challoner, MMP, p. 294; E. H. Burton and T. L. Williams (eds), The Douay College Diaries... (2 vols, CRS 10–11, 1911), I, pp. 92, 352 (William Mush absconded from imprisonment—the college diarist at Douai first recorded Mush's martyrdom and then corrected the diary entry with a note of his escape); Anstr., I, p. 242 (citing PRO, STAC 8/19/10, pt I, fo. 22^r), II, p. 111; PRO, STAC 8/18/1, fo. 118^r; AWCBC, p. 1786; C. Howard, Sir John Yorke of Nidderdale 1565–1634 (1939), p. 15; AAW, B 24, no. 27 (John Mush to Pope Paul V, 27 April 1608); Kn., II, pp. 33–5 (John Knaresborough commented that Flathers's 'crimes were of no deeper guilt (for anything [that] appears to the contrary) than those of his fellow priests' and it was 'very strange that this poor man should be singled out'); ARSJ, Anglia 37, fo. 130^v; Boderie, AMLB, III, p. 227. The patron who sheltered these three priests may have been Lady Margaret Constable, whose husband, Sir Henry, died on 15 December 1607 (AWCBC, pp. 1793, 1800), though it is odd that no source explicitly mentions this and, in particular, not Lord Sheffield's letter of 24 August 1607 to the earl of Salisbury. Dodd wrote that Flathers had been arraigned, convicted, and exiled, presumably in summer 1606: Dodd, CH, II, p. 377; Challoner, MMP, p. 294.

366 CATHOLICS AND TREASON

[them] off, whereupon one with a halberd stroke him upon the head and cut off a piece'. Then 'another, with a sword, cut him overthwart the face and the third with a hatchet cut off his head and so threw him upon the block and quartered him'.[138] The Jesuit James Sharp wrote in 1610 that the spectacle had been so appalling and the public reaction so negative that 'one of the council of York told me that, if it lay in his power, there should be no more blood shed for religion'.[139]

The public impact of these treason trials of clergy may have been amplified by the minor rebellion in Ireland in April 1608 of Sir Cahir O'Doherty.[140] The rumbling on of revolt in the wake of Tyrone's flight in 1607, the earl's apparently ecstatic papal welcome at Rome, and the papacy's hard line on the oath could all be taken to have been in some sense connected.[141] There was a fear in the upper reaches of government that the approaching truce between the Dutch and the Spaniards in Flanders would allow the Spaniards to interfere in a clearly still very unsettled Ireland, though, in fact, Madrid was keen to preserve the peace.[142]

One imagines that, if the authorities had put their minds to it, scores of priests could have been hauled off to Tyburn in the same way as Drury and Gervase, just as many others might have been forced to grovel and submit in the way that Blackwell had done. But another treason trial of a Catholic priest in London, the Jesuit Thomas Garnet (Henry Garnet's nephew), suggested that the authorities were being selective in their use of the law of treason. The authorities had been in receipt of information that Thomas Garnet, with the Benedictine John Roberts, had been with some of the plotters before the Gunpowder conspiracy broke and that he (Garnet) had made some astonishingly suspicious comments (before 'it be long we shall have either a merry or a sorrowful day, either win all or lose all').[143] Like the others, Garnet Jnr was put under massive pressure to offer some mode of compliance.[144] Interrogations of him started as early as 25 October 1607.[145] On 17 November 1607 he made noncommittal replies about the papal deposing power. For the good of the Church the papacy might exercise it, but he could see no circumstances in which it would be used against King James and simply said 'dato uno absurdo mille sequuntur'. However, on 7 April 1608 in front of Bishop

---

[138] ARSJ, Anglia 37, fo. 130ʳ.   [139] Morris, *TCF*, III, p. 455 (ABSJ, Anglia III, no. 100).

[140] Sawyer, *WM*, II, p. 405; McCavitt, *Sir Arthur Chichester*, ch. 8, esp. at pp. 140f.

[141] See, e.g., *CSPV 1607–10*, pp. 126, 137.   [142] *CSPV 1607–10*, p. 137.

[143] AAW, A VIII, no. 85, pp. 432–3 (this section of this document, signed by William Atkinson, is in the hand of Richard Bancroft (AAW catalogue note)).

[144] Thomas Garnet had been, at one time, a page to the Howard family: Pollen, *UD*, p. 259. He had first been arrested after the Gunpowder Plot broke; he was using the name of Thomas Rookwood and was associated with the Rookwood family at Coldham Hall in Suffolk: Foley, *RSJ*, II, p. 483. Interrogated under threat of torture, he was released in 1606, i.e. into exile in the large-scale deportation of clergy in that year, and went to the Jesuit novitiate at Louvain; see ABSJ, Anglia III, nos 74, 82; Foley, *RSJ*, II, pp. 479, 482; McCoog, *SJISE*, II, pp. 541–2. He returned and was, eventually, taken by the pursuivant Humphrey Cross, betrayed by the renegade priest Anthony Rouse: Foley, *RSJ*, II, pp. 482–3, 496; see also Redworth, *LLC*, I, p. 278; ARSJ, Anglia 37, fo. 108ʳ.

[145] For the examination of 25 October 1607, see AAW, A VIII, no. 44, pp. 253–4. This was the same day that legal proceedings were initiated against Thomas Garnet: Jeaffreson, *MCR*, II, pp. 200–1.

TOLERANCE AND INTOLERANCE IN ENGLAND   367

Thomas Ravis, he categorically refused to take the oath of allegiance; and he specifically said that he could not swear the clause which declared the deposing power to be heretical.[146] He also took this opportunity to have a dig at the failing attempt at the union of the crowns. He said he was 'not able to judge of right unto the crown...if, which God forbid, there should grow a question betwixt some challenger in England and some other out of Scotland'. But he then temporarily altered his stance on the oath. By 13/23 April 1608, a disgusted Luisa de Carvajal understood that, under huge pressure from Bishop Ravis, and 'in spite of the efforts of his friends and fellow fathers in prison to support him...and instruct him in the truth of the matter', Garnet 'caved in and took the oath during these same sessions' at which George Gervase was tried. He did this 'in front of everyone, and without showing the slightest sign of difficulty or scruple'. Carvajal claimed that Sir Henry Montagu had told Garnet that his taking of the oath was still not enough to exculpate him from his treason (technically this was true) and he must make further concessions. Faced with Blackwell's and Charnock's rejection of the papal censure of the oath, Garnet had become racked with doubt and was in mental torment. Carvajal heard that Garnet had been 'put together with Father Blackwell'. There they had 'set up a school for faint hearts, lacking in spirit and virtue'. According to Carvajal, when Blackwell 'heard a Catholic say that the glorious martyr', presumably Gervase, 'had died with great constancy', Blackwell confronted this unnamed Catholic and exclaimed, 'Glorious martyr, you call him? Instead he deserves to be called a simple fellow who died for matters not declared by the Church'.[147]

A further interrogation by Bishop Ravis and Sir William Waad on 5 June 1608 tried to establish whether Thomas Garnet had ever been a letter carrier between his uncle Henry Garnet and John Gerard. He was offered yet more time to confer about the oath with Blackwell, though he refused.[148] He then wrote to Richard Holtby to seek permission to use an alternative form of oath.[149] Four days after Ravis's and Waad's interrogation of him, he was summoned to the Old Bailey sessions. Michael Walpole's report of 24 June 1608, sent to Robert Persons in Rome, said that they 'had exceeding little matter against' Garnet 'but would willingly have falsified his examination, at which he took exception in the sessions house, especially about the point of murdering' kings.[150] Garnet now tried to make a protestation based on his alternative form of allegiance oath. He drew out the draft

[146] For the subsequent interrogations, see Foley, *RSJ*, II, pp. 483–5 (AAW, OB III/ii, nos 176, 177, manuscripts which, like AAW, A VIII, no. 44, one assumes, were obtained, by English secular clergy, from Lambeth Palace in the l640s).

[147] Foley, *RSJ*, II, p. 486; Redworth, *LLC*, I, pp. 304, 307–8. Luisa de Carvajal in June 1608 had confronted crowds in Cheapside and Lothbury Street and, in her bad-tempered banter with the people in the street, had defended the recently executed George Gervase as a martyr whereas the London official, in front of whom she was subsequently hauled, said that Gervase was 'a madman': Redworth, *LLC*, II, pp. 2–4, 25; Redworth, *The She-Apostle*, pp. 169–71, 175–7; Foley, *RSJ*, II, p. 502.

[148] Foley, *RSJ*, II, pp. 488–9; cf. AVCAU, Scr. 11/8.   [149] Foley, *RSJ*, II, p. 490.

[150] Foley, *RSJ*, II, pp. 491, 501 (ABSJ, Anglia III, no. 86); Jeaffreson, *MCR*, II, pp. 203–4.

368   CATHOLICS AND TREASON

which he had compiled and had sent to his confrère Holtby, but 'he was stopped and the paper' was 'taken away from him by force and torn'.[151] Francis Burton, the author of the *Fierie Tryall*, narrated the course of Garnet's 'arraignment at the sessions house without Newgate in London', where Garnet was asked by Ravis about the practical political implications of a papal excommunication of the king.[152]

Just how significant Thomas Garnet's resolute stand was can be guessed from the public interest in his case, though of course more quotidian and secular cases of crime and punishment, especially in the metropolis, regularly caught the public's attention. Garnet's execution on 23 June certainly drew a large crowd. There 'was a great concourse of people', allegedly over a thousand, 'and many of the nobility and the gentry' were 'at the place of execution'. Among them was Thomas Cecil, earl of Exeter (Salisbury's brother). He, allegedly for the best part of half an hour, 'endeavoured to persuade the confessor to save his life' by taking the statute oath. He told Garnet that 'several priests had taken it, and that many more looked upon it as a disputable matter, in which faith was not concerned'. Garnet declared that it was not possible to swear 'if the case be so doubtful and disputable'. Moments before death, Garnet said again that he had been willing to swear his alternative form of allegiance oath, 'but this new oath' in the statute, he declared, 'is so worded as to contain things quite foreign to allegiance to which, in my opinion, no Catholic can with a safe conscience swear'. One account of the execution has Garnet say that he had 'an oath of allegiance in his pocket which he would have willingly produced in the sessions house if he had any opportunity'. This account adds that Garnet said that 'no rebellion nor cutting of the throats of English men in Ireland' occurred 'before the murdering of the priest at York', a reference presumably to Matthew Flathers; and Garnet added that the earl of Exeter knew it 'well enough'. Garnet carried on speaking and blurted out that 'the same day that Mr Gervase...', but here he was 'interrupted' and 'broke off abruptly'. The narrator was sure that he would have mentioned that 'Bury in Suffolk, where he [Gervase] was brought up, was burnt', that is, on 11 April when fire broke out there in Eastgate Street, the same day that Gervase was executed in London. Garnet added that he hoped that the guilt of his blood would not fall on the king and the land. But Exeter, who had had in the North, as we saw, a reputation as a tough enforcer of the statutes against Catholics, 'would not permit the rope to be cut' until Garnet 'was quite dead'.[153] After Garnet had expired,

---

[151] Foley, *RSJ*, II, pp. 491–2. For a copy (with some differences) of the oath which Foley says that Garnet sent to Holtby, see ARSJ, Anglia 38/i, fo. 284ʳ; Foley, *RSJ*, II, p. 490.

[152] Francis Burton, *The Fierie Tryall of Gods Saints...As a Counter-poyze to I.W. Priest his English Martyrologe...* (1612), 'A Post-Script to the Well Affected Reader', p. 7. Burton dated the arraignment to 'Thursday the 16 of June 1608'.

[153] Challoner, *MMP*, pp. 297–8; Foley, *RSJ*, II, p. 494–7; ABSJ, Anglia III, no. 83; the account printed in Foley is ABSJ, Anglia III, no. 84 (written by the chaplain of Newgate; for a copy, see AAW, A VIII, no. 65, pp. 339–41); M. Statham, *The Book of Bury St Edmunds* (Buckingham, 1988), pp. 12–13. On 26 July 1608 Michael Walpole wrote to Robert Persons that Exeter's presence at Tyburn could be explained by the need to prevent Garnet declaring that Exeter's brother, the earl of Salisbury, had tried to manufacture

TOLERANCE AND INTOLERANCE IN ENGLAND   369

there was a delay when it emerged there was no one willing to cut him down and dismember him.[154]

The ideological complexity of Garnet's case can be gathered from Michael Walpole's claim that George Blackwell, of all people, 'says that Mr Garnet is a glorious man'. It looks as if Blackwell may have been trying to assert that, despite the dreadful outcome of the trial, Garnet's position on the oath was close to his own.[155] Equally, it is possible that Garnet's carefully judged performance of limited (but insufficient) compliance persuaded the regime that it had misjudged the moment when it indicted and killed him and, probably, Gervase as well. Zúñiga wrote on 29 June/9 July 1608 that 'they have sent a courier after the justices who were travelling about the country bearing letters from the king' forbidding the judges to use the treason penalties against any Catholic and, also, allowing Catholic separatists to compound for recusancy debts, even at low rates.[156] The resentment that these executions may have caused among London's Catholics can perhaps be picked up from Zúñiga's comment in August 1608 that he had recently had to enlarge his chapel for the purpose of accommodating the numbers of Catholics who came to the embassy to hear Mass.[157] On 24 October 1608 the privy council went so far as to order George Lloyd, bishop of Chester, to restrain his proceedings against recusants in his diocese, 'saving when notorious occasion of public scandal or audacity of some obstinate persons shall require it'.[158] The Venetian diplomat Marc'Antonio Corraro believed on 24 November/4 December 1608 that the king loathed puritans 'more than he does the Catholics'. Corraro understood from an informed source that James was galvanizing his bishops into anti-puritan initiatives and, 'a few days' before, Bishop Lancelot Andrewes, 'in the presence of the king', had 'said some very severe things on this subject'.[159]

The Experience of Persecution and the Catholic Demand for Episcopal Regulation of their Community

All these events and the controversies which they generated were crucial to the future shape of the Catholic community in England. As we saw, one of the insistent calls of the appellants had been that the papacy should institute an episcopal

---

yet more libels against his uncle Henry Garnet: Foley, *RSJ*, II, p. 503. Walpole had been a servant of John Gerard (Caraman, *JG*, p. 73) and in James's reign became a principal point of contact in London for Luisa de Carvajal: Redworth, *LLC*, I, II, *passim*; ARCR, I, no. 1619.

[154] Foley, *RSJ*, II, p. 501.

[155] Foley, *RSJ*, II, p. 502. It was reported in late 1608 that the 'figure of Garnet', presumably meaning Thomas rather than Henry, had been 'set up for a saint in the English College [i.e. residence for English priests] at Lisbon': PRO, SP 89/3, fo. 109ʳ.

[156] Loomie, *SJC*, I, p. 120; cf. *CSPV 1607–10*, p. 148.

[157] Loomie, *SJC*, I, p. 123.

[158] PRO, SP 14/37/28, fo. 52ᵛ; Usher, *REC*, II, p. 188.

[159] *CSPV 1607–10*, p. 195; see also *CSPV 1607–10*, p. 243.

370 CATHOLICS AND TREASON

hierarchy among their co-religionists in the English nation. The demand was renewed very soon after the Gunpowder Plot.[160] The discovery of the barrels of explosive and the alleged link to those whom the regime, and some Catholics, had been saying for years were seditious and intolerable presented a heaven-sent opportunity for former appellants to renew their lobbying in the Roman curia. But their lobbying was bound to meet strong opposition there. For those Catholics who did not want Rome to set up episcopal government in England (and the resistance from some in the religious orders and their patrons was very strong), the clinching counterargument to the alleged necessity of episcopacy was that the true Catholic Church in England was still labouring under the cross of persecution. In their suffering, the faithful would derive grace from the blood of the martyrs. But the enmity of the State would make it nearly impossible for a bishop to function as he should; and in addition the appointment of a bishop or bishops would stir up the State's hostility even more. It would be likely to do more harm than good.[161] It was possible, indeed very likely, that a bishop who had been appointed by Rome but was subsequently arrested might be subjected to the kind of relentless interrogation and badgering that had been inflicted on Blackwell. If that person was chosen, as he almost certainly would be, by Rome from among the ranks of the appellants and their friends—they, after all, were the ones who were lobbying hardest for such an appointment—then there was a good chance that such a person would cut some kind of deal with the regime of the day and might even go so far as to take the allegiance oath, as Blackwell had done. That would potentially create a schismatic Church within a Church as the renegade bishop called on Catholics to follow his example.

So said the Catholic opponents of the institution of an episcopal hierarchy in James I's English and Scottish realms. But the new archpriest George Birkhead and his friends begged to differ. They were in no doubt that Catholics were being persecuted. They took care to record in detail the heroic struggles of their co-religionists and to send reports of their sufferings to Rome.[162] But, for Birkhead and his associates, this was no argument against Rome's appointment of a bishop or bishops to rule directly over English Catholics. According to Birkhead (and this may well have been the majority Catholic view), the day-to-day harassment of Catholics was an evil that was directly traceable to the malice of, among others, individual churchmen inside the national Church. It was not, despite James's recent public verbal hostility towards Catholics, the fault of the king.[163] It was necessary, as the appellants had argued, to make the case that the institution in the king's dominions of a Catholic hierarchy would be completely compatible with monarchical government. Episcopacy was, after all, a natural support and mainstay of the monarchical State. A good Catholic bishop, installed in James's

---

[160] Questier, *C&C*, ch. 11. [161] *NAGB*, pp. 4–5 and *passim*. [162] See Chapter 12 below.
[163] See, e.g., AAW, A VIII, no. 188, p. 705.

TOLERANCE AND INTOLERANCE IN ENGLAND   371

English realm, would purge the Catholic community of its bad humours (if there were any), just as bishops in the established Church were supposed to deal with puritanism and its errors. The good and moderating effects of Catholic episcopal governance would one day facilitate a toleration of Catholics which would itself, in turn, enhance royal authority.

Thus it was that on 21 June 1608 George Birkhead had written directly to the pope, Paul V, himself. He described the recent deaths of Drury, Gervase, and Flathers (Thomas Garnet would not be executed for another two days). Birkhead took the opportunity to express the desire of the clergy and many of the laity to have bishops to govern them.[164] Shortly he would send his associates, the priests Richard Smith and Thomas More, to Rome as his agents (displacing Thomas Fitzherbert, who was known to be a friend of the Society) to submit this and other suits for the papacy's consideration. Presumably in connection with this project, More started to draw up a draft martyrology.[165]

Smith and More travelled to Rome in early 1609 using privy council passports. These were signed by, among others, Archbishop Bancroft, who clearly knew what they were doing and in some sense was sponsoring their project. We can detect the outlines of the opposition to it from within the Catholic community in a number of places. For example, one document, which Thomas McCoog has identified and dated to early 1609, lists and describes individual 'churches', based on groups of aristocracy and upper gentry and presided over by Jesuit priests. It was presented in Rome by Sir Oliver Manners (brother of the fifth earl of Rutland) and Thomas Fitzherbert. Manners was a courtier and had sat for Grantham in the 1601 parliament. His name had come up in the investigation of the Gunpowder Plot. He had been converted to Rome by John Gerard. The documentary material that he brought with him was in fact a petition to Rome over the question of episcopal government in England, and requested the papacy, should it decide to set up bishops in England, to take certain factors into account. One extant copy of the list of individual 'churches' is accompanied by petitions, signed by the Jesuit clergy named on that list. They urged Rome not to appoint clergymen who were

---

[164] AAW, A VIII, no. 64, pp. 337–8.

[165] See principally AAW, B 28, no. 5, pp. 165–8 (usually referred to as More I). See also AAW, B 28, no. 1, pp. 1–39 (usually referred to as More II; cf. Stonyhurst MS A VI, no. 37, with a note by J. H. Pollen describing it as 'More's autograph'). See also AAW, B 28, no. 2, pp. 45–66 (usually referred to as More III); for these catalogues, see *AWCBC*, pp. 2507–8. AAW, B 28, no. 1 (intended it seems, as with B 28 no. 2, which is incomplete, to accompany a series of portraits) is introduced with a short address to Cardinal Scipione Borghese (p. 1) and provides a list of the authorities on which this catalogue of martyrs is based (p. 3). In another hand, the list, which originally ended with Robert Drury in 1607, is brought up to date with a further ten martyrs, i.e. up to Thomas Tunstall in 1616 (p. 36), and the piece ends with a statistical analysis of the types of English clergy who had suffered martyrdom (pp. 37–9; by contrast, Stonyhurst MS A VI, no. 37, ends with the name of Matthew Flathers in 1608). AAW, B 28, no. 2 (More III) is dated to 1610 (*AWCBC*, p. 2508), incorporates laymen (and Mary Stuart), and has a brief summary of the facts of each case but extends only up to 1588. See Pollen, *UD*, pp. 4–5; pp. 377–8 below.

372 CATHOLICS AND TREASON

factious or defended the taking of the oath of allegiance or of attending Protestant churches. This might also be taken as a reminder of the way that the Catholic Church in England could in fact function perfectly well in the absence of a local episcopate.[166]

The Jesuit mode of describing recent martyrdoms inevitably overlapped with the narratives written by the Society's critics, but it was, on balance, more insistent about the State's intolerance. This was certainly the case in the letters of the Jesuit clergy's friend Luisa de Carvajal.[167] In March 1609 she gave her opinions about the progress of what she took to be a cruel and continuing persecution: 'I do not know how anyone can say that the persecution is waning, unless it appears so because they do not take priests to the scaffold every month'. If they had, for the time being, 'stopped doing this', it was 'merely for their own infernal ends, seeing how much their deaths set the devotion, zeal and resolution of the Catholics alight, and how much this confuses many heretics'. As other newsletter writers reported at this time, she noted that renegade Catholic clergy were leading searches of Catholic residences. She concluded that, 'what with this and so many blasphemous sermons, so many lay people and priests arrested just for their faith' and 'so many estates confiscated or carved up', this persecution was 'as bad as ever'.[168] 'In less than four years, six or seven most virtuous priests at least have been hanged, and four of them were members of religious orders. We still see the parts of their bodies and their heads in the streets, on spikes on the turrets of the gates that close off the streets and that are locked at night. Some are dried and others are fresher, with birds on top picking at them. With every step we hear endless abuse and curses in the streets, living out the words of the Gospels about lambs among wolves. There is no justice for them in their affairs.' When Catholics partially escaped the penalties of the law, it was 'only because of schismatic friends pulling strings on their behalf in countless different ways, mainly in exchange for money. There are countless similar things, such as their having to move from house to house constantly because they are not welcome in the parishes, and

---

[166] *NAGB*, p. 7; T. M. McCoog, 'The Society of Jesus in England, 1623–1688: An Institutional Study' (PhD, Warwick, 1984), pp. 194–5; *HC 1558–1603*, III, p. 8; Birch, *CTJI*, I, pp. 49–50; *HMCS*, XVII, p. 499; PRO, SP 14/216/1, fos 161^r, 169^r; ARSJ, Anglia 36/ii, fo. 317^r [new foliation], annotated on fo. 316^v as 'Interpretatio Scedularum, 17 January 1609'; a copy of this document (located at fo. 268^r [new foliation] in ARSJ, Anglia 36/ii) was presented to Pope Paul V by Manners and Fitzherbert in Holy Week 1609. Manners was ordained in 1611 by Cardinal Bellarmine: Caraman, *JG*, pp. 185–7; Anstr., II, pp. 209–10. The copy at fo. 268^r is the one which is followed by the affidavits written by Jesuit clergymen: ARSJ, Anglia 36/ii, fos 269^r–77^r. I am very grateful to Dr McCoog for drawing my attention to the second version of this document and for discussing it with me. Arguably, John Gerard's autobiography of his missionary endeavours in England, written in *c.* mid- to late 1609, might be taken to have made the same case; see Caraman, *JG*.

[167] See K. Marshalek, 'Gender, Politics, Sanctity: the Career of Luisa de Carvajal in Anglo-Spanish Contexts' (forthcoming in *Renaissance Quarterly*).

[168] Redworth, *LLC*, II, p. 61; for other reports of renegade clergy being involved in searches of Catholics' houses, see *NAGB, passim*; AAW, A VIII, no. 110, p. 507, no. 130, p. 555, no. 168, p. 661, no. 187, p. 703; AAW, A IX, no. 78, pp. 265–6; AAW, A X, no. 16, p. 37, no. 40, p. 99.

TOLERANCE AND INTOLERANCE IN ENGLAND   373

going out to get married and give birth in remote places where people might not know them on account of the penalties they have imposed on baptisms and Catholic weddings. Is this not persecution?' Joseph Creswell, to whom she wrote, had evidently heard differently from others. Carvajal was pleased to put the record straight: 'if only it were as you say they describe it, sir', she remarked.[169] The reality was 'that the poor Catholics suffer' and 'everything is brimming with malice' and 'licentiousness'.[170]

It was gratifying that recent Spanish diplomatic protests about the arrest of English Catholics at the door of the embassy meant that the authorities had 'not dared' to 'repeat this' particular outrage; but all that this signified was that the stubbornness of hardliners such as herself and the good ambassador Zúñiga had served to rein in the worst excesses of the persecutory State. She added that since Zúñiga's residence was on 'the outskirts of the city . . . the people of the area are not as malicious as others are' and in effect the embassy functioned 'like a proper little parish'. There was even an ageing priest from 'the days of Queen Mary'. He frequented the embassy chapel and heard confessions.[171]

Whether by accident or design, Carvajal was here making essentially the same case as Manners and Fitzherbert were urging at more or less exactly this point to the Roman curia. There was a uniquely evil persecutory cruelty raging in the British Isles, but it was not necessarily the same everywhere. It was more often witnessed in the maelstrom of metropolitan politics where members of a kind of Calvinist nasty party plied their brand of sadism for their own Machiavellian purposes. Outside these centres of cruelty and horror, if nurtured and protected in the right way, that is, in the private houses of the great and the good, Catholicism in its purest form might be practised if not with impunity then certainly with relative safety.[172] Carvajal thus drew a picture of an urban anti-popery which was not necessarily representative of attitudes elsewhere. But that, of course, did not diminish the savagery of what heresy did to good Catholics. That was, again, something which could be identified as all of a piece with the programme of those Machiavels who were trying to broker a ceasefire in Flanders. In the same letter she referred to the 'truce with Holland', 'a worry for all those who love what is good for the Holy Church and for the salvation of souls'.[173]

Others, however, thought that the direction of travel was away from the worst kind of ideological coercion and physical cruelty. The French ambassador Boderie commented on 4/14 March 1609 that the observably moderate Lancelot Andrewes was scribbling away at the king's direction on the topic of the oath of allegiance and, although James kept telling him to go back and do it again, the fact was that

---

[169] Redworth, *LLC*, II, p. 61.   [170] Redworth, *LLC*, II, p. 64.
[171] Redworth, *LLC*, II, p. 62.
[172] John Marshall makes a similar point about London anti-popery during the Popish Plot years 1679–81: J. Marshall, 'The Trial and Execution of Oliver Plunket' (forthcoming).
[173] Redworth, *LLC*, II, p. 62.

374 CATHOLICS AND TREASON

'les Catholiques sont moins persecutés' than at any time since Boderie had arrived in England. He believed that orders had gone out 'à ceux qu'on envoie tous les ans par les provinces pour les recherches, de s'y porter plus modèrement que jamais'. There was a rumour also that Pope Paul V had responded charitably to French lobbying on James's behalf so as to prevent a papal censure of him. Despite the publication of the new and more overtly anti-papal edition of James's defence of the oath of allegiance, in 1609 there were, as Challoner's *Memoirs* grudgingly concedes, no fatal treason proceedings against Catholics at all.[174]

Carvajal would not have seen this as the onset of genuine tolerance. Indeed, the stream of newsletters from the secular clergy at this time insisted that Catholics were subject to endless sequestrations of their property and petty personal harassments.[175] In France, former leaguers and fiery preachers, notably Père Gontier, denounced the British king for persecuting the Catholic faith.[176] Furthermore, the mid-Jacobean period saw what Simon Adams has called the revival of confessional politics, displacing the more politique Salisburian approach, in particular to foreign policy.[177] In the middle years of the reign, after Henry IV's assassination, King James was forced to consider the Protestant option in European politics. But, as is well known, he had his doubts about how far he should pose as a fully paid-up member of the European Protestant princes' club or of the so-called pan-European Protestant cause.

Of all these things, contemporary English Catholics were fully aware. Despite the cataclysm of the Gunpowder conspiracy, and the king's own determination to use the violent and unsettled state of post-accession politics to set a range of interest groups against each other, the records of the early Jacobean prosecutions

---

[174] Boderie, *AMLB*, IV, pp. 271–2; cf. Redworth, *LLC*, II, p. 62 (Carvajal's story that James had consulted Bishop Andrewes about proving the pope to be the Antichrist and that Andrewes had 'begged the king not to do it'); Challoner, *MMP*, p. 299; Lancelot Andrewes, *Tortura Torti: sive, ad Matthaei Torti Librum Responsio...* (1609). The appearance of James's new edition of his defence of the oath was, indeed, a problem. Boderie thought that 'ce livre est le plus fou...et le plus pernicieux qui se foit jamais fait sur tel sujet', since it referred to Rome as Babylon and the pope as Antichrist: Boderie, *AMLB*, IV, pp. 291, 302; James I, *An Apologie for the Oath of Allegiance...together with a Premonition...* (1609). Sir George Carew in Paris reported on 15 June 1609 that it was very galling to be lectured by Henry IV about how best to implement toleration; the French king said that James should have refrained from going into print on the subject of the oath of allegiance and Henry also spoke 'of the persecutions now used' in James's 'dominions': PRO, SP 78/55, fo. 106^{r-v}.

[175] In October 1609, Thomas More, briefly back in England, described how the 'the whole course is for the impoverishing of poor Catholics to take what can be gotten, and not so much to care for the imprisoning or putting to death of priests, thinking that, they increasing without means to maintain them, we shall be fain to eat one another'. More's own brother's 'house was searched for me a little before my arrival where they took away his church stuff and I know not what else', though they also claimed that one of his servants 'was a priest and would have him bound over to appear before the bishop of London': AAW, A VIII, no. 164, p. 649. Another letter from More written in this same month recorded the panic of prominent Catholics as one after another was arrested at this time, including, for example, Richard Cholmeley and his two chaplains: *NAGB*, p. 67 (AAW, A IX, no. 78, p. 265); Richard Cholmeley, 'The Memorandum Book of Richard Cholmeley of Brandsby, 1602–1623', *North Yorkshire County Record Office Publications* 44 (1988), p. 29.

[176] PRO, SP 78/55, fo. 10^r.   [177] Adams, *PC*, chs 6–8.

of Catholics suggest that the realignments inside the Catholic community during the so-called Archpriest Dispute could not be reversed. The set-to between Catholics themselves as much as between their community and its enemies would be rehearsed and re-rehearsed during the middle years of James's reign, all in the context of the king's own priorities and realignments in his dealings with continental European States. The scattering of prosecutions and even executions of Catholics after 1610, mainly of clergymen, although on nothing like the scale of the later 1580s and early 1590s, provided a vehicle for a public discussion of how far Catholic separatists might one day be allowed some form of toleration.

12

Mid-Jacobean Confessional Politics and Anti-Popery

In 1608 the priest John Wilson had published a pamphlet entitled *The English Martyrologe*.[1] It was an uncomfortable reminder that a section of the Catholic community saw James as a persecutor. What was really inflammatory was not just the printing, at the end of the calendar of the post-1530s saints and martyrs, of the names of those Catholics who had been executed since James's accession but also the inclusion in that list of some of those who had been caught up in and suffered on account of the gunpowder business—Henry Garnet, Edward Oldcorne, and Ralph Ashley.[2] In 1608 also, Thomas Worthington, the pro-Jesuit president of the English college at Douai, who had, as we saw, intervened in the Archpriest Dispute with his *Relation of Sixtene Martyrs*, published *A Catalogue of Martyrs in England*. Worthington similarly included Henry Garnet and his friends and insisted that 'the form of his face appears in his blood remaining upon an ear of corn'.[3]

---

[1] John Wilson, *The English Martyrologe conteyning a Summary of the Liues of the…Saintes of the three Kingdoms, England, Scotland, and Ireland.…Whereunto is annexed in the End a Catalogue of Those, who have suffered Death in England for Defence of the Catholicke Cause, since King Henry the 8. his Breach with the Sea Apostolicke, unto this Day.…*(n.p. [St Omer], 1608). The prefatory epistle to English Catholics is dated 1 October 1608. Wilson appears to have served as Robert Persons's secretary in the English College in Rome and, at Persons's direction, he became the supervisor of the St Omer college press: Anstr., II, p. 358; Edwards, *EJ*, p. 308. William Udall reported on 2 November 1608 that copies of Wilson's work were going to be brought to England from Dunkirk and Calais: ARCR, II, no. 806. Richard Smith filed a complaint at Rome in 1626 concerning Wilson's martyrology; see pp. 460–1 n.42 below.

[2] Wilson, *English Martyrologe*, sig. Aa8^{r-v}. The republication of Wilson's work in 1640 and 1672 saw the removal of the Jacobean martyrs from the list: ARCR, II, no. 807; T. H. Clancy (ed.), *English Catholic Books 1641–1700: A Bibliography* (Chicago, 1974), no. 1100.

[3] Thomas Worthington, *A Catalogue of Martyrs in England: for Profession of the Catholique Faith, since the Yeare of our Lord, 1535…unto this Yeare 1608* (n.p. [Douai], n.d. [1608]), quotation at p. 23; ARCR, II, no. 846; reprinted by Joseph Gillow in *Downside Review* 16 (1897), pp. 241–57; see also Burton, *LT*, I, p. 165; Pollen, *UD*, pp. 3–4 (for the relationship between Wilson's and Worthington's martyr lists). The published version, in 1609, of a Paul's Cross sermon delivered by Richard Stock on 2 November 1606 attacked Worthington's recently published edition of Richard Bristow's 'motives' (Richard Bristow, *Richardi Bristoi…Motiva…*(2 vols, Arras, 1608; ARCR, I, no. 117)) for claiming that there was still a persecution in England but that the kingdom would return to the faith: Richard Stock, *A Sermon Preached at Paules Crosse, the second of November. 1606…*(1609), sig. *5^{r-v}. In 1610, Worthington published *Catalogus Martyrum pro Religione Catolica in Anglia Occisorum, ab Anno Domino 1570, Regni Elizabethae Duodecimo, ab Anno 1610. Qui est Regni Jacobi Octavus. De aliis vero Martyribus sub Henrico Octavo summatim Scripsit Insignis Doctor Nicolaus Sanderus lib. 7 de Visibili Monarchis Ecclesiae* (n.p., 1610); ARCR, I, no. 1416. Subsequently Worthington produced a much

MID-JACOBEAN CONFESSIONAL POLITICS AND ANTI-POPERY   377

Francis Burton's *The Fierie Tryall of Gods Saints*, a version of which was penned as early as 1609, replied to Wilson's work. *The Fierie Tryall* was, as the author said, based squarely on John Foxe. The manuscript found its way into the earl of Salisbury's papers. Presumably Burton sent it to him. For some reason it did not appear in print until 1611, with another edition shortly after in 1612.[4] This work insisted that Catholics should desist from accusing James of being an oppressor, 'whose heart bleeds that he is forced to draw blood from others for their intolerable demerits'.[5] The author mocked Wilson by saying that he (Burton) had 'added two' to his roll of dis/honour, namely William Watson and William Clarke, 'both priests executed at Winchester' on 'November 29, 1603', 'I know not how by the pseudomartyrologist omitted, for he might as well have enrolled them as those which he has done, being all alike traitors to their prince and country'.[6]

This, however, was not the only reply to Wilson. It seems likely that the martyr catalogue which, as we saw in the previous chapter, Thomas More compiled in early 1609 (that is, at the time that he went to Rome with Richard Smith to serve there as an agent for the English secular clergy), was, although it replicated a lot of Wilson's list, a rebuttal of Jesuit-inflected versions of the recent Catholic experience of martyrdom. As Monsignor Daniel Shanahan accurately comments, 'the very composition of the catalogues' of martyrs, retained in the papers of the secular clergy's agent, 'betrays their purpose'. They 'list the secular priests who were martyred', 123 in all from the reigns of Elizabeth and of James up to that point; 'they include the lay people who were martyred and then add the Jesuits, Franciscans and Benedictines as a footnote'. The dedicatory epistle to Cardinal Scipione Borghese talks about the 'abundance of seminary priests' who were stationed in England, some of whom had been martyred there. Very few

---

enlarged version of this work: *Catalogus Martyrum pro Religione Catolica ....Cui Praemittitur Narratio de Origine Seminariorum Anglorum, & de Missione Sacerdotum, etiam Variorum Ordinum in Angliam* (n.p., 1614); ARCR, I, no. 1417. For Worthington's hostile account of George Gervase's joining the Order of St Benedict, and his attempt to appropriate Gervase's martyrdom (in the context of the struggles between the English College and the Benedictine foundation in Douai in and after 1607), see J. E. Kelly, 'The Contested Appropriation of George Gervase's Martyrdom: European Religious Patronage and the Controversy over the Oath of Allegiance', *JBS* 57 (2018), pp. 253–74, at p. 265, citing esp. D. Lunn, *The English Benedictines 1540–1688: From Reformation to Revolution* (1981), pp. 72–3, 77, 79–81. John Knaresborough noted that Worthington 'maintains the justice of that rising' of 1569, that is, the rebellion of the northern earls, and 'says that' the rebels were 'to be commended for taking up arms in defence of the Catholic religion against Queen Elizabeth for that she had been declared excommunicate by Pius V' and 'to such of them as lost their lives in the cause he gives the title of martyrs' (even though Worthington is, in fact, more circumspect and says that he will, having mentioned the seventh earl of Northumberland and others, 'only recite the names of such as, neither taking arms nor intending to take, nor attempting to procure or promulgate any excommunication or other ecclesiastical censure against any prince, have spent their blood...solely and directly for religion'): Kn., VII, unpaginated section; Worthington, *A Catalogue*, pp. 10–11.

[4] Francis Burton, *The Fierie Tryall of Gods Saints...As a Counter-poyze to I.W. Priest his English Martyrologe...* (1612), p. 6; HHCP 254/2. The manuscript version at Hatfield is dated in the calendar, evidently in error, to 25 March 1608 (I assume that 1609 is the correct date): *HMCS*, XX, p. 113.

[5] Burton, *Fierie Tryall*, p. 5.

[6] Ibid., p. 7, and 'A Postscript to the Well-Affected Reader', p. 10.

378   CATHOLICS AND TREASON

members of the religious orders had met a similar fate. The claim here was that 'the majority of priests wanted ordinary ecclesiastical jurisdiction restored' instead of an archpresbyterate. Thomas Garnet is included in the visibly brief list of religious but, unsurprisingly, Henry Garnet is not. Francis Page SJ has been transferred from his place in the main list to the list of Jesuit martyrs.[7] In Rome, the enemies of the new archpriest, George Birkhead, or, rather, of the fraction of the Catholic community which had been at the very least in sympathy with the appellant programme, retaliated by denouncing Richard Smith to the Holy Inquisition for what they said was his past refusal adequately to affirm the papal deposing power.[8]

The perpetually angry former appellant Christopher Bagshaw articulated with characteristic venom what, undoubtedly, many had always thought—that the Society of Jesus and its friends were stoking the fires of political conflict and reaping the media splash caused by the regime's retaliation against good priests and yet, all the while, the Jesuits planned to tack and accommodate, to cut and run, and do a deal with the State—they would not be martyrs. As Bagshaw said on 4 August 1609, it was possible that Robert Persons would be made a bishop, 'the pope in his conscience thinking him able, whereof others doubt'. The result would be that Persons would 'go into England from whence he ran away' back in 1581 'and there defend that oath whereof he talks and writes being out of gunshot', leaving others to get the blame.[9] In early 1610, Birkhead knew that the Jesuit Michael Walpole had refused the oath in front of Archbishop Bancroft and yet seemed to suffer no ill consequences.[10] There were all sorts of rumours flying backwards and forwards that individual clergy of all kinds were doing private deals with the authorities—in which context Birkhead, who was the pope's representative in England, and also those who had shed their blood in effect for their refusal to take the oath, risked looking ridiculous and out of touch, making meaningless sacrifices to no purpose at all.[11]

---

[7] D. Shanahan, 'Thomas More IV and his Catalogue of Martyrs 1609', *Essex Recusant* 16 (1974), pp. 59–66, at pp. 60, 65; AAW, B 28, no. 2. Perhaps in order to give extra impetus to More's work, George Birkhead wrote to Richard Smith in Rome on 30 July 1609 that 'the preachers cry out for blood, and in their books and pulpits cry out to the king to draw out his sword against us', so that 'many do think the persecution will be far more grievous than it is': AAW, A VIII, no. 133, p. 562. For the string of letters written by Birkhead in late 1609 and early 1610 which claimed that Catholics were suffering harassment, see also AAW, A VIII, nos 134, 144, 158, 159, 166, 168, 187, 188, 191; AAW, A IX, nos 1, 2, 7. In September 1610 More wrote back home that 'I wish we' in Rome 'might hear of every one that is apprehended, condemned or exiled, or otherwise troubled [so] that particular information may be given of every one. It would make a deeper impression in men than hitherto they seem to have, and herein our friends have been over negligent for, of such as be banished, we hear of none but of the religious. The names of the others', i.e. secular priests, 'are not once here remembered': AAW, A IX, no. 67, p. 229.

[8] *NAGB*, pp. 7, 8, 46, 85.   [9] *NAGB*, p. 49.

[10] *NAGB*, p. 78 n. 234.   [11] *NAGB*, pp. 77–8.

The 1610 Parliament and the Assassination of Henry IV

For the time being, though, all Catholics had reasons to worry, faced as they were by the imminent assembly of parliament. As Birkhead wrote to his agent Smith on 5 January 1610, 'the 9 of February begins our parliament'. He hoped that God would 'direct the king and lords to have compassion of our misery', but 'never was our fear greater than now it is', even though the 'puritans' and their polemics against episcopacy were surely more offensive to the king than Catholics were.[12]

The Stuart court had initially decided not to prepare the ground for the 1610 assembly by explicitly pandering to popular enthusiasm for military intervention in mainland Europe over the Jülich-Cleves succession crisis.[13] James did his rhetorical best to posture as a friend of parliaments by affirming his rejection of the quasi-absolutist arguments put forward by John Cowell. In addition, while dwelling on the need to relieve the burden of crown debt, he called for the better execution of the statutes against Catholic separatists.[14] On 18 March 1610 the priest John Lockwood was sentenced to death, though he was immediately reprieved.[15] On 21 March, James delivered a long speech in favour of prerogative taxation and agreed, in principle, that the laws against Catholic separatists should be enforced.[16] As Birkhead recorded it on 3 April 1610, the king 'protested he would have no more blood, but yet that he meant the oath of allegiance should still be severely exacted. So, although he takes no more blood, he will handle us as evilly in our purses.'[17]

For those who regarded popery as an ever-present danger, the assassination of Henry IV on 4/14 May 1610 served as a grim reminder of that threat. The French State had been on the verge of war against the Habsburgs over the Jülich-Cleves problem. This had dismayed a section of French Catholic opinion; and evidently none more so than the knife-wielding zealot François Ravaillac.[18] He claimed to have been inspired by the Jesuits Mariana, Coton, and Gontier.[19] His exploit was a

---

[12] AAW, A IX, no. 1, p. 1, and see also no. 7, p. 19 (Birkhead to Smith, 18 January 1610); see also S. Babbage, *Puritanism and Richard Bancroft* (1962), pp. 253–6.

[13] Adams, PC, p. 222. As Conrad Russell points out, however, at the start of the 1610 session the threat of war posed by the Jülich-Cleves business meant that the regime would probably need to appeal for revenue: C. Russell, eds R. Cust and A. Thrush, *King James VI and I and his English Parliaments* (Oxford, 2011), p. 76.

[14] HMCD, II, p. 267; T. Rabb, *Jacobean Gentleman: Sir Edwin Sandys 1561–1629* (Princeton, 1998), p. 146; E. R. Foster (ed.), *Proceedings in Parliament 1610* (2 vols, New Haven, 1966), II, pp. 59–63; Sawyer, WM, III, pp. 125, 129, 131, 136, 137; Larkin and Hughes, SRP, I, no. 110.

[15] Anstr., I, p. 212; Jeaffreson, MCR, II, pp. 203–4; AAW, A IX, no. 31, p. 79.

[16] James I, *The Kings Maiesties Speech... on Wednesday the xxi of March...* (1610), esp. sigs G3ᵛ–H2ʳ; Sawyer, WM, III, pp. 136, 141–2.

[17] AAW, A IX, no. 31, p. 79. For another account by Birkhead of James's speech of 21 March 1610, see NAGB, pp. 83–4.

[18] For the Jülich-Cleves issue, see R. Bonney, *The European Dynastic States, 1494–1660* (Oxford, 1991), pp. 184–5.

[19] Sawyer, WM, III, p. 174.

380 CATHOLICS AND TREASON

sign, apparently, that Catholic leaguer sentiment was not dead but merely sleeping. The earl of Salisbury moved to exploit the assassination and urged the parliament to vote supply. But Henry's fate drew predictable anti-popish speeches from MPs. Among those who had some of the best I-told-you-so lines on this topic were Sir William Bulstrode and Sir Francis Hastings. A string of petitions followed—against Catholic recusancy as well as about the scandal of silenced puritan ministers.[20] On 18 May a committee was appointed to consider the allegation made by Bulstrode that, owing to the corruption of paid officials, life in the London prisons was a lot easier for Catholic clergy than it ought to be. They had 'usual access one to the other' and 'divers ladies and other persons of note do resort to them and ordinarily hear Mass in the prisons'.[21] On 21 May, James made a pitch for increasing royal revenues by reference to the threat from Catholics. There was 'more need to relieve my estate now than when parliament was first called' and the king asked, 'if a new sort of leaguers should rise to oppress them of the religion [in France], what security can we have?'[22] An informer, Thomas Felton, pitched in (via a petition brought to the attention of the Commons by Sir Francis Hastings) on 6 June to denounce the royal exchequer official Henry Spiller for, as Felton alleged, corruptly allowing convicted recusants to escape the full force of the penalties levied on them.[23] But there were those who took umbrage at being urged to grant supply on this basis. Thomas Wentworth opined on 14 June 1610 that it was an 'error' to use the French king's fate as an argument for more taxation because Henry 'died not from lack of money' but, rather, because he had 'submitted his soul to Rome'. King James should 'be more careful' both to 'banish prelatry' and 'to punish the Jesuits and priests'.[24]

For Catholic clergy such as Birkhead, the assassination was a catastrophe because the new allegiance oath would now almost certainly be exacted from large classes of people, courtiers, office-holders, and the like; and, while some Catholics would refuse it, many would not—'because the king says he demands nothing else but allegiance'. This would leave the archpriest and his friends looking more out of step than ever.[25]

---

[20] *CSPV 1607–10*, p. 486; PRO, SP 14/53/123; PRO, SP 14/54/29, 78; Usher, *REC*, II, pp. 251–2. On 8 May 1610 the Newgate gaol-keeper was ordered to deliver four Catholic clergymen, including John Lockwood, apparently so that they should be deported: Anstr., I, p. 212.

[21] Foster, *Proceedings*, II, pp. 375–6; *HC 1604–29*, III, p. 360. Sir Francis Hastings cooperated with Bulstrode in this initiative: *HC 1604–29*, III, p. 360.

[22] Foster, *Proceedings*, II, p. 106. For the recommendations made on 25 May 1610 for the restraint of Catholic liberties and execution of the existing laws, see Foster, *Proceedings*, II, pp. 118–19. For Birkhead's note of 4 May 1610 that some said the king wanted to have 'all the penal laws against us in his own hands', *NAGB*, p. 80.

[23] Foster, *Proceedings*, II, pp. 128–31, 377–8.

[24] Adams, PC, p. 223, citing S. R. Gardiner (ed.), *Parliamentary Debates in 1610* (Camden Society, 81, 1862), p. 57; see also, for Wentworth's speech of 22 May 1610, Foster, *Proceedings*, II, p. 108; *HC 1604–29*, III, p. 697. Jean Beaulieu said that Henry's demise was 'the fruit and reward of his favour and trustfulness in the Jesuits': Sawyer, *WM*, III, p. 159.

[25] AAW, A IX, no. 43, p. 117.

Figure 12.1 Alabaster monument of Bishop Robert Bennett, in Hereford Cathedral.

There were some highly placed crown servants and officials who, though they might not always say it publicly, still thought that the law against Catholic separatism was not being enforced with sufficient thoroughness. One of those people was Robert Bennett, bishop of Hereford, who had kicked up such a fuss over the Whitsun disturbances back in 1605. (See Figure 12.1.) On 8 April 1610 (Easter Sunday), Bishop Bennett had secured the arrest of the priest Roger Cadwallader, and this was surely no accident, that is, with parliament's members about to reassemble. Bennett declared that Cadwallader was 'a dangerous and pernicious instrument and seducer of many of his Majesty's subjects' and had been 'the author or agent in that seditious riot made near Hereford' back in summer 1605. He should 'receive his trial here for the terror of others who have been seduced by him'. In order to burnish his own credentials, however, Bennett had also arrested 'one Thomas Baillies, a Brownist'.[26]

There was a new statute against Catholics in early June and a proclamation also.[27] There were rumours that the Gunpowder Plot suspects William Baldwin

---

[26] PRO, SP 14/53/98, fo. 146ʳ; AAW, A IX, no. 62 ('A Brief Discourse of the Proceedings…,' pp. 193–6; copy at ABP, pp. 451–64), p. 193; AWCBC, p. 1892. Cadwallader said that Bennett 'seemed exceeding joyful' on 9 April 'that I was fallen into his hands, as I gathered by his countenance': AAW, A IX, no. 62, p. 193.

[27] CSPV 1607–10, pp. 504–5; SR, IV, pp. 1162–4 ('An Act for administering the Oath of Allegiance, and Reformation of Married Women Recusants', 7&8 James I, c. 6); Larkin and Hughes, SRP, I, no. 111 (2 June 1610); Usher, REC, II, p. 252; Loomie, SJC, I, p. 155; AAW, A IX, no. 51, p. 141.

382 CATHOLICS AND TREASON

and John Gerard were coming back to England to murder the king.[28] On 18 June 1610 the still appalled archpriest Birkhead wrote that 'this impious murder of the French king has incensed all our country against us', and 'every calumniation invented by our enemies is most assuredly believed'. The oath was 'more exacted than ever', though, confusingly, some people were saying that it would be 'qualified'.[29] On 2 July 1610 Birkhead said that leading Jesuits such as Robert Jones were saying that 'the gravest and most learned of the [secular] clergy' were inclined to allow the taking of the oath. Birkhead believed that in reality it was those who looked for guidance to the Jesuit clergy who were doing this.[30] A virtually apoplectic Luisa de Carvajal had written on 25 May/4 June 1610 that there were some Catholics who, to ingratiate themselves, were remembering Elizabeth's reign as a golden age or, at least, not one of persecution, all in order to justify themselves to the present regime. She told these Catholics what she thought of them, and they told her what they thought of her. The fact was that 'criticizing Spain and praising' the ghastly Elizabeth Tudor 'go hand in hand'.[31] Leading Catholics were indeed swearing the 1606 oath of allegiance. Lord William Howard was 'a great Catholic' but he 'took the oath yesterday', she recorded in fury on 24 June/4 July 1610. He announced 'that in his understanding he was taking it according to what the king declares in his book and only out of loyalty'. A very depressed George Birkhead who, as Rome's man in England, was trying to stop a general collapse of morale on this issue, wrote to his agent Richard Smith in August that 'you will not believe what tricks are used to make' Catholics 'think that both myself and divers' secular priests 'do suppose it may be taken'. Birkhead had learned that there were 'some impiously disposed counterfeit letters in my and their names to that end'. These documents were hawked 'about the country' and shown 'to the weaker sort, which has been the cause that many have adventured to take' the godless oath. For all the attempts of Catholics to offer compliance, the oath was 'now most hotly exacted as it lies', that is, exactly as it was worded in the statute. Good but desperate Catholics were busily inventing 'modifications', since they hoped to 'draw the king thereunto'. But the word was that 'none will be admitted'.[32]

As Carvajal saw it, this kind of lapse was destroying the Catholic community far more than overt physical and public acts of punishment and tyranny, bad as they were.[33] If 'everybody stood firm', all would be well, 'but the weak and the

[28] *HMCD*, II, pp. 302–3.
[29] AAW, A IX, no. 42, p. 115. On 3 October 1610 the Jesuit Robert Abercromby reported to Acquaviva that, when he had arrived in Scotland in the previous June, i.e. just after the assassination of the French king, he found a rigorous persecution in progress there: W. Forbes-Leith (ed.), *Narratives of Scottish Catholics under Mary Stuart and James VI* (1889), pp. 290–1.
[30] AAW, A IX, no. 49, p. 131.   [31] Redworth, *LLC*, II, pp. 104–5.
[32] Redworth, *LLC*, II, p. 113; AAW, A IX, no. 58, pp. 163, 164; see also *NAGB*, p. 117.
[33] There is a more or less complete agreement between Carvajal and the secular clergy newsletter writers in London as to the extent of the regime's hostility to Catholics; see *NAGB*, *passim*, and esp., during 1610, even while parliament was not sitting: AAW, A IX, nos 38, 39, 42, 49, 53, 58, 66, 78, 85.

MID-JACOBEAN CONFESSIONAL POLITICS AND ANTI-POPERY   383

timid, who are hurling their souls into mortal danger, bring pain and untold suffering to the bodies of those who are strong and constant in faith'. She noted that 'among the Catholics they say that a great number of them . . . are almost at the point of taking the oath, and that there are clerics whose opinion it is that this can be done'. The new Spanish ambassador, Alonso de Velasco, was, in Carvajal's opinion, not as tough as his predecessor, Zúñiga. English friends of Spain were sacrificing principle to pragmatism. There were a number of go-betweens for Velasco and the king and council. Among them were the former ambassador Sir Charles Cornwallis, Sir Thomas Monson, and Sir Lewis Lewkenor, 'a fine bunch of schismatics' who were taking care 'not to pass on' anything from Velasco that might cause conflict between Madrid and London.[34]

Nevertheless, there were Commons members who were becoming suspicious that, in spite of the new measures, there was not going to be the kind of royal smackdown of Catholic separatism that the situation required. They probably knew what they were talking about. No one was more aware than the king that he had a loyalist and occasional conformist Catholic constituency—one which he did not want to lose. James had, in the end, said the Venetian diplomat Marc'Antonio Corraro, refused any real statutory novelties here.[35]

The Treason Trials of 1610

There was, then, no sense that the king and council collectively wanted to see a cascade of treason prosecutions and Catholics' dismembered bodies all over London and the provinces, although James was, of course, prepared, under certain circumstances, to countenance the executions of Catholic clergy. But, as we have already remarked, there were Protestants who definitely did want didactic and visible harshness inflicted on such people. Between August and December 1610, four prominent English Catholic clerics went to the gallows.[36] We know a good deal about them partly because of Luisa de Carvajal's newsletters to her correspondence network and also because of the survival of the leading secular clergy's correspondence, which was dispatched to Rome for the use of the archpriest's agent there. Of these four martyrs, Roger Cadwallader and the Benedictine John Roberts were, in some sense, obvious candidates. Both were tinged with a reputation for political activism—Cadwallader because of his alleged involvement in the

---

[34] Redworth, *LLC*, II, p. 114.
[35] *CSPV 1607–10*, p. 510; for George Birkhead's report on the new legislation against recusancy, see AAW, A IX, no. 53, p. 148. Corraro had to admit, on 27 June/7 July, that in response to the proclamation the Catholics were 'clearing out of the city': *CSPV 1610–13*, p. 4. (Even the earl of Northampton had had to dismiss Catholic servants in his household: *CSPV 1607–10*, p. 517.) For James's refusal to tighten any further the statute law against separatism, see Babbage, *Puritanism and Richard Bancroft*, pp. 256–7.
[36] Challoner, *MMP*, pp. 299–323.

384 CATHOLICS AND TREASON

rioting of summer 1605 and Roberts because it was suspected that he had known some of the Gunpowder plotters.[37] On the other hand, Cadwallader and Roberts were also believed by some people to be loyalists. Cadwallader had signed the protestation of allegiance in early 1603. Roberts was a noted opponent of Robert Persons. The Benedictine Thomas Preston claimed later that Roberts refrained from teaching that the oath of allegiance was 'lawful', because of the papacy's censure, yet he did not think there was anything in the oath 'contrary to faith or salvation'.[38]

Roger Cadwallader

As for Roger Cadwallader, his enemies were now prepared to force through a treason indictment against him, although some sort of propaganda victory without the full penalties of the law might have been just as acceptable to them. Cadwallader's case is an unusual one, not least because there are so many surviving manuscripts concerning him. It is worth rehearsing the proceedings against him in some detail so as to capture the contingencies and uncertainties created by the prosecution and by the attempts to force concessions out of him. When he was brought on 9 April in front of Bishop Bennett and others, he engaged in a series of theological and ecclesiological disputations, principally over which of them—the bishop or himself—could be more accurately said to be a priest. Among those present was Bennett's chancellor, John Hoskins, younger brother of the man who famously contributed to the collapse of the Addled Parliament in 1614.[39] Predictably, Cadwallader refused to take the 1606 oath of allegiance but,

---

[37] For Roberts's alleged association with the Gunpowder plotters (John and Christopher Wright), see AAW, A VIII, no. 85, pp. 432–3. For Cadwallader's ministry among the people and particularly the 'poorer sort' in Herefordshire and the border region of Wales, see W. Brogden, 'Catholicism, Community and Identity in Late Tudor and Early Stuart Welsh Borderlands' (PhD, Birmingham, 2018), ch. 3, esp. at pp. 148–9.

[38] Lunn, *English Benedictines*, pp. 49, 63; D. Lunn, 'English Benedictines and the Oath of Allegiance, 1606–1647', *RH* 10 (1969), pp. 146–63, at p. 149 and n. 25; Thomas Preston, *A Theologicall Disputation...* (1613), p. 251.

[39] Challoner, *MMP*, pp. 300–1 (relying on, *inter alia*, ABP, pp. 451–56, 468); HC 1604–29, IV, pp. 784–96; *ODNB*, *sub* Hoskins, John the younger (1581–1631), within John Hoskins (1566–1638), (article by W. Prest). Cadwallader's own account of his being interrogated on two occasions by Robert Bennett is contained in AAW, A IX, no. 62, p. 193, which may have been elicited from him by Robert Jones SJ: Foley, *RSJ*, IV, p. 390. A copy of this manuscript is retained in Alban Butler's papers (ABP, pp. 451–6). It was delivered to and apparently then extended by another writer: AAW, A IX, no. 62, pp. 194–6; ABP, pp. 456–64. *AWCBC*, p. 1830, very plausibly suggests that 'the second and third parts' of this document 'were probably written or at least procured from eyewitnesses by' the priest John Stevens. This was Butler's view as well: ABP, p. 477. The copy in AAW appears to be in the hand of Richard Broughton, or at least in the hand in which Broughton's newsletters from this period are generally written, so it may be that it was Broughton to whom the material about Cadwallader in AAW was sent. AAW, A IX, no. 64, pp. 205–10 ('A True Relation...') covers the same ground as the material in Broughton's compilation (no. 62), but one leaf of it is missing, i.e. between the pages numbered 206 and 207: *AWCBC*, pp. 1845, 1855; ABP, pp. 467–77, noting at p. 470 the missing leaf. Butler took this

MID-JACOBEAN CONFESSIONAL POLITICS AND ANTI-POPERY   385

for all his reputation for stroppiness, he did not immediately condemn the oath outright. In words which were discreetly omitted by Richard Challoner, he replied that 'for the present I was not so resolved' and, 'being demanded what was my opinion of it, I answered that I would not impugn it nor allow it'.[40]

The local stakes were, nevertheless, very high. There was a concerted effort to trash Cadwallader's reputation. It was given out that his sister-in-law who visited him in the prison was in fact his 'concubine'.[41] Although he was already extremely ill with some sort of fever, he was summoned to dispute again with Bishop Bennett 'and his doctors, who were prepared for him with a cart-load of books'. Aware of how much all this mattered, Cadwallader tried to get out into the public domain his side of the story, as it were, and thus to preserve the ideological integrity of the Catholic community in that region. Challoner noted that Cadwallader 'wrote several letters in prison', one of which was to the archpriest Birkhead and another to 'Mr John Stevens, a neighbouring missioner, recommending to them the care of his flock'.[42] Cadwallader insisted that 'when they asked me divers questions of dangerous consequence, as of the times and places of being [at] and saying Masses, to that I would answer nothing'. He said also that 'they charged me with a most grievous sin of swearing for that once in heat of contention I said "in good faith" or "of my truth"'.[43] He also described how his enemies had tried to kill his 'body and credit at once'. In case a treason charge did not work against him, 'they laboured to attaint me with other crimes', though 'when these devices succeeded not, they fell to other complots'. They also suborned 'certain renegade poor brethren of ours' to give evidence against him—the implication is that the managers of his trial were trying to turn the local Catholic community against itself. Moreover, Bennett's 'chaplain' 'was sent to make an invective sermon (as the manner is) before the judges against me and my fellows here in prison and abroad'.[44]

Cadwallader was finally executed on 27 August—strung up in a stage-managed, though botched, execution at Leominster.[45] He professed equanimity in the face of death, citing Bishop John Fisher's words 'in the like case'.[46] When he was told

---

piece to have been written by John Stevens: ABP, p. 477. The document AAW, A IX, no. 65, pp. 211–12, ('Of Mr Roger Cadwallader, Priest and Martyr...') is endorsed 'Pleraque ex relatione Joan. Stevens presb. Reliqua ex Joanne Pitzeo [John Pitts, author of *Relationum Historicarum de Rebus Anglicis*...(Paris, 1619)] et aliis'.

[40] AAW, A IX, no. 62, p. 193; ABP, p. 455.

[41] AAW, A IX, no. 62, p. 194; ABP, p. 457 (Challoner, *MMP*, p. 302).

[42] AAW, A IX, no. 62, p. 194; ABP, p. 457; Challoner, *MMP*, p. 302. Cadwallader had demanded books in order to dispute with the bishop about the nature of true priesthood: ABP, p. 468. For five surviving letters from Cadwallader, see AAW, A IX, no. 60, pp. 169–74. The fourth letter (pp. 172–4) survives also in a copy kept by Butler—at ABP, pp. 465–6. For English versions of the two letters at AAW, A IX, no. 60, pp. 169–71, see ABPFC, fo. 38ʳ; *AWCBC*, pp. 1858–62. The originals of these letters apparently are lost: *AWCBC*, p. 1856.

[43] AAW, A IX, no. 61, p. 193; ABP, pp. 454, 455.   [44] ABP, p. 465.

[45] For the date of the execution, see *AWCBC*, p. 1866; Challoner, *MMP*, p. 306; ABP, p. 461; cf. Anstr., I, pp. 61–2; AAW, A IX, no. 86, p. 287.

[46] AAW, A IX, no. 62, p. 194; ABP, p. 460.

386 CATHOLICS AND TREASON

that 'Mr [Robert] Drury suffered the like for the like refusal', that is, of the oath, 'by one that was an eyewitness of his martyrdom, he seemed to joy much thereat, saying that, as Mr Drury and he were true loving friends here on earth', so he had no doubt they would meet in heaven.[47] He remained unperturbed even when the undersheriff turned up at the prison 'accompanied, among others, by the executioners, who were a couple of masons, clad in long garments, all in black, and their faces covered with the same, which made them seem ugly and dreadful'. Once again he was offered the 1606 oath. The 'undersheriff...stepped upon the hurdle with the statute book in his hands and asked him if he would take the oath of allegiance'. If he did, the execution would be stopped 'till the king's pleasure were further known'; but Cadwallader refused.[48] At the place of execution, he was 'taken off the hurdle and brought within sight of the gallows and the block whereon he was to be quartered'. He was made to look at 'these and [the] other instruments of death'. There were also 'two great fires' blazing away, 'the one prepared to burn his heart and bowels, the other to boil his head and quarters'. He was made to walk between them, and he was asked again: would he take the oath? But no, he would not.[49] 'Mr Thomas Coningsby and Mr Humfrey Cornwall and Richardson the preacher' continued to persuade 'him with many fair promises that, if he would take the oath, he might not only do God and his country good service but would cause others to do the like'. This Cadwallader would not do, but 'in public' he 'protested before all the people that he did acknowledge his Majesty to be true and lawful king of England, Scotland and Ireland and withal was willing to swear his true allegiance as far forth as the laws of God and conscience did command all subjects to be true unto their prince'. Cadwallader had, after all, been one of the signatories of the 1603 protestation of allegiance, as had Robert Drury. At this 'Mr Coningsby and Mr Cornwall with others wished him to proceed, saying that he had begun well'. But Cadwallader replied that 'there was some secret poison in the sequel', that is, in the words of the allegiance oath. This was a reference presumably to the main problem clause of the oath, which implied that those who advanced a high view of papal authority, and of the deposing power, must be heretics.[50] From the ladder, Cadwallader delivered a conventional enough speech about the distinction between religion and politics, conscience and allegiance. But he made it clear that he blamed, as well he might, Bishop Bennett for this pass to which he, Cadwallader, had been brought. Bennett's 'finger' had been 'deepest in his blood'.[51]

The execution was horrifically bungled. In brief, Cadwallader swung and strangled slowly because of the 'unskilfulness of the headsman', who had positioned the knot wrongly. This left Cadwallader 'in great pain' still trying to make the sign

---

[47] AAW, A IX, no. 62, p. 194; ABP, p. 460.   [48] AAW, A IX, no. 62, p. 195; ABP, p. 461.
[49] Challoner, MMP, p. 304.   [50] AAW, A IX, no. 62, p. 195; ABP, p. 462.
[51] ABP, p. 474.

MID-JACOBEAN CONFESSIONAL POLITICS AND ANTI-POPERY 387

of the cross. At this point, Mr Coningsby decided that he had really had enough and 'departed (as it seemed) much afflicted in mind'.[52] Then, after 'the vulgar' tried to lift Cadwallader 'upwards by the legs twice or thrice, letting him fall again', the officials mistakenly thought he had expired and he 'was brought to the block to be quartered'. But, 'before the bloody butcher could pull off his doublet, he revived and began to breathe' and the rest was frankly worse. Even 'the multitude, perceiving' it, 'began to murmur'. This 'made the undersheriff cry out to the executioner to hasten'. But 'before they had stripped' Cadwallader 'naked, he was come to a very perfect breathing'. 'It was long after they had opened him before they could find his heart which, notwithstanding, panted in their hands when it was pulled out.' As soon as Cadwallader's head was cut off, one of the sheriff's men lifted it up on the point of a halberd, 'expecting the applause of the people', but there was no loyal acclamation at all. The conclusion of the crowd was that Cadwallader's example 'would give great confirmation to all the papists of Herefordshire'.[53]

So far, so appalling. But Cadwallader's carefully judged manoeuvring between a formal loyalism but, ultimately, non-compliance meant that a number of interest groups had every incentive to appropriate his memory and witness. He had, once upon a time, been on the appellant wing of the secular clergy.[54] But it may well be that he had in some sense cut his ties with those of that persuasion who wanted to drive hard for a deal with the regime and were prepared to make real ideological concessions in order to get it. This would help to explain why the local State was so keen to make an example of him and, particularly, to see if he could be forced by the terrors of the law into some sort of concession over the oath. But equally, for those Catholics around the archpriest who were fed up with being accused of laxity and feebleness in the face of royal authority, Cadwallader had been, as George Birkhead wrote to Thomas More, 'an exceeding stout and resolute man and a most zealous priest'. Birkhead understood that Cadwallader not only had told Bennett 'that he was an usurper and no true bishop' but had been 'eight times brought from the place of execution and...offered the oath but he, always refusing it, became at the length a glorious martyr'.[55]

The argument about what Cadwallader's death proved was, inevitably, linked to rumours about who had stuck to and supported him to the bitter end. The word was going round that Cadwallader had been deserted by the secular clergy. Birkhead was exasperated that Cadwallader 'had been, before his arraignment, visited by divers of our brethren', secular priests, 'as I can prove by a letter of his handwriting', but then, 'a little before his death, none of them (as I have been told

---

[52] ABP, p. 464.   [53] Challoner, *MMP*, pp. 305–6; ABP, p. 464.
[54] Cadwallader had not only signed the 1603 protestation of allegiance but had also put his name to the appeal of 17 November 1600: *AWCBC*, p. 1819.
[55] AAW, A IX, no. 86, p. 287.

388 CATHOLICS AND TREASON

by a father of the Society [of Jesus]) could be gotten to go to him'. The only person who was prepared to perform this charitable act was 'one of the said Society who in that extremity gave him much comfort'. The 'coldness of my brethren has been objected to me and I was sorry to hear it'. The 'charity of the fathers', the Jesuits, had also been 'much urged'. Of course, it was good that Cadwallader, who had previously been known as a critic of the Society, had 'died in charity with them'. But it was definitely not good that those people were trying to bask in the glory of his martyrdom.[56] Nor was it good if Cadwallader made the supreme sacrifice and then the Catholic flock by and large ignored it. As Birkhead put it, 'most of the laity' would 'not be persuaded but that' the oath 'may be taken with a protestation of swearing nothing contained' in it 'but that which appertains to their temporal obedience and allegiance' to the king. At the same time, 'the present loss' of 'goods and liberty' made a number of Catholics 'shrink' and provoked them to fury against Birkhead himself for insisting on this aspect of the authority of the papacy.[57]

The Society had indeed tried to appropriate or, at least, invest in Cadwallader's martyrdom. The Welsh Jesuit Robert Jones had penned an account of Cadwallader's imprisonment, trial, and execution.[58] Jones claimed that Cadwallader had made his last confession to a Jesuit personally.[59] In the past, Cadwallader had held the Jesuit order 'in...little esteem'. But his opinions were so completely changed that he now recommended himself 'with all humility' to the Jesuit's prayers 'in the conflict' that 'he was about to undergo'. He asked 'that, whatever he or any of his brethren might have said or done against the fathers' of the Society, it 'should be buried in oblivion with all religious charity'. Moreover, 'in proof of his gratitude, he made a present of his library to the Society, which was all he possessed in this world'. The Jesuit 'stayed a long time with him, animating him to face with courage

[56] AAW, A IX, no. 86, p. 287.   [57] AAW, A IX, no. 86, p. 287.

[58] For Jones's narrating of Cadwallader's death, see *AWCBC*, pp. 1865–6. Jones sent two letters to Rome at this time, one of 10/20 September and one of 14/24 September 1610, which are in ARSJ, Anglia 37, fos 126^r–7^v. The document AAW, A IX, no. 74, pp. 249–50 is an Italian translation of part of the letter of 10/20 September ('Martyrio del Sacerd. Rogero Cadwallador scritto dal P. Roberto Jones superiore della Compagn. di Giesu in Inghilterra alli 20 di 7bre 1610', for a copy of which see *AWCBC*, p. 1865 (citing Biblioteca Vallicelliana, Rome, N 23, fos 281^r–2^v)). Jones's narrative (part translated and printed in Foley, *RSJ*, IV, pp. 389–91) insists that Cadwallader had been visited in prison by a Jesuit before his death and that no secular priest was prepared to visit him there. Jones made explicit the purpose of the narrative—it was something which could be included in the Society's annual letters: here one could 'see God's special favour and providence towards' Jesuits 'in ministering so fit an occasion of reconciliation with others', even those with whom they had issues: *AWCBC*, p. 1870. Jones had earlier in the year had an acrimonious correspondence with Birkhead. On 31 July 1610 Birkhead waspishly demanded 'to know what Catholics they be' who accused the secular clergy of 'so great a crime as the allowing of the oath is'. Jones insisted that, if he himself had made such charges, he had not done so against secular clergymen alone: AAW, B 47, no. 126. Indeed, he had admonished the Jesuit John Evison for 'seeming to defend the oath upon very idle and frivolous grounds': *AWCBC*, p. 1866. Jones's letter of 14/24 September to Evison pointed to Cadwallader as an appropriate role model in this respect: *AWCBC*, pp. 1870–1.

[59] The Jesuit in question may have been John Salisbury: *AWCBC*, pp. 1871, 1881–2; Anstr., I, p. 298.

MID-JACOBEAN CONFESSIONAL POLITICS AND ANTI-POPERY   389

and constancy the torments and death he was about to endure'. Jones claimed also
that 'on the day on which he received sentence of death...by means of a friend I
managed to visit him', in fact just hours before the judges condemned him.
Sentence was respited for a month to persuade Cadwallader to conform, but he
bravely refused. Jones then described the execution and, in particular, the repeated
offers of the oath of allegiance, which Cadwallader rejected. Those who had been
paid to put an end to him were so cack-handed that 'the whole multitude cried
out shame upon such barbarity'.[60]

The, by all accounts, hot-tempered Welshman Jones subsequently sent a long
and fairly sharp letter to Birkhead. He pointedly reminded him that 'it is not
unknown unto you' that Cadwallader, 'the late worthy martyr', following his
arrest, 'altered his conceits of us' and as for 'what...he received at our hands, both
temporal and spiritual, his letters...and others can testify'. Jones insisted that
other seculars had not been prepared to risk visiting Cadwallader even though he
'much desired' it; and so it was from the Society that he had had 'the last benefit of
sacraments in this world'. This he 'took...in the highest degree of kindness
and...of charity and gratitude on his side'. It was for this reason that 'he assigned
some books...abroad for our use'; and he made it known that 'the worst might
not be made of any speeches that had' passed 'between priests and priests' who
were, after all, 'fellow labourers'. All discord should now be 'buried in perfect
charity'. Referring clearly enough to the archpriest's current campaign to assert
his own authority within the Catholic community, Jones remarked that, 'by this,
you may see whether we desire...union, love and friendship with you and yours'.
This was a sign from heaven almost that all should be 'satisfied by the present
silence and surcease of invectives'. It appears from Jones's letter that the archpriest
had wanted to summon 'an assembly and meeting of many together on both sides
in these most dangerous and troublesome times'. This, said Jones, was madness.
Such 'an extraordinary meeting would make both our friends and foes at home to
be more jealous of us, and perhaps increase our afflictions and persecutions'.

---

[60] Foley, *RSJ*, IV, pp. 389–90; *AWCBC*, pp. 1867–9; Anstr., I, p. 61. As for the claim concerning
Cadwallader's donation of his books to the Society, John Gennings OFM (brother of the Elizabethan
martyr Edmund Gennings), who worked in both Sussex and Wales, said that Cadwallader had often
complained to him of the Jesuits' 'unkindness', and that Cadwallader had sold his books for £10 when
he was arrested, on condition they should be returned if he were released: *NAGB*, p. 108; A. F. Allison,
'Franciscan Books in English, 1559–1640', *Biographical Studies* 3 (1955), pp. 16–65, at p. 16; *AWCBC*,
pp. 1873–5 (AAW, A IX, no. 84, pp. 281–2). William Bishop said that Cadwallader had given his
books to an unnamed priest who was not a member of the Society: *NAGB*, p. 109 (AAW, A X, no.
45, p. 111). Edward Bennett believed that, as for the books which the Jesuits had said were 'given
them by him, it was only a restitution of a couple which he had of them': AAW, A X, no. 139, p. 395.
For an explanation (reconciling the claims of Jones and Gennings) of how Cadwallader may have
disposed of his library, see *AWCBC*, p. 1875. In 1612 there appeared in print a work which had
been translated by Cadwallader: *The Ecclesiasticall History of Theodoret Bishop of Cyrus*...(n.p.
[St Omer], 1612); ARCR, II, no. 114.

390   CATHOLICS AND TREASON

Jones was implying rather strongly that Birkhead's programme for a general reform of the English Catholic community was far from helpful.[61]

On 26 June 1611, a searing missive was penned by Cadwallader's fellow Welshman the secular priest Edward Bennett. Bennett evidently knew of Jones's letter to Birkhead and admitted that Jones had 'written much of the charity of a brother of his to Mr Cadwallader the martyr and that none of us would come at him' and even 'withal that he submitted himself to the Jesuits'. This was plainly rubbish, said Bennett. Cadwallader had simply asked for all past quarrels 'to be forgotten, and that we should all agree and go on like brethren in the harvest'. In addition, 'in the very assizes week, two or three of our brethren', secular clergy-men, 'attended about the prison to have come to him but could not'. But it was the one wretched Jesuit who 'by chance got in and... heard his confessions', and now just look 'how they brag'! If one wanted to know the truth, one needed only to read the letter written by Cadwallader to Edward Bennett's own brother, John (another determined opponent of the Society), whom he thanked profusely 'for his charity'. So, said Edward Bennett, 'I marvel at' the Jesuit, Jones, 'if it be true he has charged us with carelessness to help the holy martyr'.[62] Bennett commented to his friend Thomas More: 'there has been much ado to get Mr Cadwallader's head who most constantly died only because he refused the oath'. Bennett wished that the pope, Paul V, could actually hold the thing 'in his hand'.[63] Then he would understand what was going on in England.

A letter received in Rome by More in February 1612, written by, it seems, the priest John Stevens, alleged that he (Stevens) had received Cadwallader's effusive thanks 'for our brotherly love towards him'. If this letter by Cadwallader was

[61]   AAW, OB I/i, no. 23, fo. 49ʳ⁻ᵛ (this letter is not dated).

[62]   *NAGB*, p. 114. Birkhead had informed his agent in Rome in January 1611 that in fact Cadwallader had been visited in prison by one Vaughan alias Grissold, either George or Roger Grissold (Warwickshire secular priests, relatives presumably of the martyr Robert Grissold) or, perhaps, the priest Lewis Vaughan. Birkhead insisted that Cadwallader 'remained the same man at his death as he was before, as may appear' by this same letter which Cadwallader had addressed to Edward Bennett's brother John, a letter which Birkhead now forwarded to the priest John Jackson and which he expected Jackson would pass on to More in Rome: AAW, A X, no. 3, pp. 7–8 (*NAGB*, pp. 108, 114). Jackson had translated this letter into Latin 'out of the copy which he [Cadwallader] wrote with his own hand': AAW, A IX, no. 125, p. 396. For William Bishop's letter to Thomas More which denied aspects of Jones's account of Cadwallader, see AAW, A X, no. 46, pp. 113–14; Foley, *RSJ*, IV, p. 391; *AWCBC*, pp. 1883–6. Edward Bennett insisted to More that 'here has been great negligence hitherto in the setting forth of the acts of our martyrs. The religious be *prudentiores in generatione sua*; they have not only set forth their own but hindered us also from doing anything which might tend to the honour of our soul and credit of our body. This with many things more we must amend': AAW, A X, no. 139, p. 395.

[63]   *NAGB*, p. 112. In June 1611 Birkhead wrote to More that 'the draft which Father Jones has made of Cadwallader's doings fails in many things as I trust you know by this. I will send it into the country to be scanned. Our brethren are so zealous to honour him that I have much ado to keep them from wrangling about the keeping of his head': AAW, B 47, no. 32. See also, concerning the heads of Cadwallader and Napper, Birkhead's letters to More of 6 October 1611 and 20 May 1612: AAW, A IX, no. 81, p. 273; AAW, A XI, no. 83, p. 237; *NAGB*, p. 112. For the claim made in the nineteenth century that Cadwallader's skull had been located and recovered, see N. C. Reeves, *The Parish of Saint Ethelbert, Leominster* (Leominster, 1974), p. 10; ABSJ, CP (drafts of beatification papers: W. O'Connor to Philip Caraman, 16 February 1964).

MID-JACOBEAN CONFESSIONAL POLITICS AND ANTI-POPERY   391

wanted, said Stevens, it would be easy to send it, or a copy of it. It proved that Cadwallader was 'assisted' by Stevens 'and others', even though Stevens had not personally been able to see him. Another secular priest had 'promised...to go unto him which' he 'did not according to his promise'.[64] Indeed, said a second letter, enclosing Stevens's missive and received by More on the same day (perhaps written by the priest Martin Nelson), three secular clergymen had 'offered to visit' Cadwallader, 'but he refused to have us adventure ourselves without necessity'. Still, if the Jesuit in question 'had not happened to come to him...others would have performed that office'. In other words, the reports of the naysayers and critics of the seculars were 'both vain and untrue, as Mr Stevens in his letter hereinclosed does also testify'.[65]

This was hardly the first time that what appeared to be an instance of true martyrdom had been up for appropriation by those who recognized it as precisely that but who were far from in agreement on other matters. At certain points in the period that was almost par for the course. But in Cadwallader's case, because of the accident of manuscript survival, and with very considerable evidence about the contemporary circulation of the relevant manuscripts and with a plethora of rumour and stories concerning him, we can see how all this worked in unusual detail, and how the rhetoric of martyrology could be tied, at times publicly, into arguments about problems which concerned the Catholic community, particularly ones connected with Church government.

George Napper

Although less well documented, something rather similar occurred in late 1610 in Oxford, where the priest George Napper was put under arrest. The principal

---

[64] AAW, A XI, no. 22, p. 55 (a copy of the original). For the attribution of this letter to Stevens, see *AWCBC*, pp. 1880–1.

[65] AAW, A XI, no. 23, p. 57 (a copy of the original). For Martin Nelson, see pp. 297 n.33 above. Stevens had written to Birkhead at some point after February 1611 acknowledging Birkhead's request for 'some discourse of our glorious martyr Mr Cadwallader, wherein I have done my best to accomplish your desire but cannot as yet send you the copies at large as I promised you in my last letter'. However, in the 'meantime I send you hereinclosed copies of some comfortable letters he sent to me and some other friends. The discourse of all his proceedings (for the most part) in his late troubles—I myself procured it'. Stevens had loaned the same to 'one of the Society', presumably Robert Jones himself, who irritatingly, despite many reminders, had not returned what Stevens had sent him. There were still 'speeches given out that Mr Cadwallader was forsaken of his brethren'. Stevens sent Birkhead 'a copy of some of his letters to myself and some others to the greater shame and overthrow of such false calumniators and calumniations'. 'Now, since his death', added Stevens, 'I have spoken unto some of my good friends to get his quarters and have in my custody more of his flesh than anyone I think in our country so all his quarters are taken away by our friends and I have bidden well to procure his head so I am in good hope that I or one of my brethren will have it' before 'long if it may be had: if you please to have some of his flesh I will send it unto Thomas Davis' in Martin's Court in London's Chick Lane 'after the receipt of your next letter': AAW, B 24, no. 39. Stevens confirmed, however, that the issue for which Cadwallader might be taken to have died—the 1606 oath of allegiance—was not rejected with the same fervency by all Catholics in his region: AAW, B 24, no. 39.

392 CATHOLICS AND TREASON

narrative of Napper's detention and trial, retained in John Knaresborough's manuscripts and written by someone who was in the same prison as Napper, insists that the whole thing was the result of a random quarrel in Oxford within the family of one of the Church of England clergymen there.[66] Whatever the circumstances of the bringing of Napper to the attention of the authorities, the JP responsible for making the arrest was the godly Sir Francis Eure, who had also, from 1609, been on the council of the marches in Wales and so would have been familiar enough with what had happened to Cadwallader.[67] Napper was indicted at the Oxford summer assizes in July 1610.[68] At trial the presiding judge, Sir John Croke, directed the jury to convict. A temporary stay of execution was obtained, but a more formal reprieve was blocked by the vice-chancellor John King, a thoroughgoing Calvinist. The thing that tipped the scales was, allegedly, the ministrations of Napper to a convicted felon called Falkner who, after Napper's own trial and conviction, declared himself a Catholic at his death on the gallows in Oxford.[69] The high sheriff, Benedict Winchcombe, and the vice-chancellor, King, made it clear that this should be enough to cancel the amnesty which Napper currently enjoyed.[70] He was then confronted with the allegiance oath, which he refused to swear. The officials' next gambit was to produce the former archpriest George Blackwell's account in print of why the oath might be taken. Napper delayed for some days but then indicated that he would not comply.[71] Croke returned to Oxford and ordered the execution to go ahead. Another reprieve was secured from London, until 9 November, with the condition that Napper should enter into debate with 'learned divines' on the subject of the oath.[72] From this it seemed that Napper was regarded, by some, as a loyalist, loyal enough to merit permanent

---

[66] The original version of this document is Bodl., Rawlinson MS D 399, fo. 213ʳ *et seq.* (material which was used by Challoner), cited by Davidson, RC, p. 463; Kn., II, pp. 79f ('ex MSS D. Norris', a source which is now unknown: *AWCBC*, p. 1893); see also the copy in Butler's papers, ABPFC, fos 31ʳ–6ʳ, which adds the story (fo. 36ʳ) that, 'since his death, he appeared to one who saluted him…', and also the story of the miracle at Christ Church (see pp. 393–4 below). As Davidson notes, in AAW there are three narratives of the martyrdom: AAW, A IX, nos 89, 90, 91. The document AAW, A IX, no. 90, in Italian, is by Richard Banks; AAW, A IX, no. 91 is a copy of the letter in the Rawlinson MSS; see Davidson, RC, p. 463. The document AAW, A IX, no. 89 ('De felicite obitu Georgii Napperi martyrio coronati', 9 November 1610) was written by John Luttrell and was sent directly to More in Rome; see also AAW, A IX, nos 85 and 88.

[67] In 1604 and 1605 Sir Francis Eure had been involved with the passage of recusancy legislation in parliament; see *HC 1604–29*, IV, pp. 206–7. His father, Lord Eure, had, as vice-president in York in 1586, overseen the proceedings against Margaret Clitherow.

[68] Davidson, RC, p. 469; Challoner, *MMP*, p. 309.

[69] Challoner, *MMP*, pp. 309–10; ARSJ, Anglia 37, fo. 110ᵛ; Kn., II, pp. 90–5. For Sir John Croke, see *HC 1558–1603*, I, pp. 677–8; Davidson, RC, pp. 469–70; see also Redworth, *LLC*, II, pp. 125, 129–30.

[70] Challoner, *MMP*, pp. 310–11; for Winchcombe, see Davidson, RC, pp. 324, 471. For Edward Coffin SJ's account of Napper's attempts in prison to evangelize students from the university, see ABSJ, Anglia III, no. 103 (Edward Coffin to [Robert Persons?], 18/28 May 1611; translation in ABSJ, CP (George Napper); see also Foley, *RSJ*, IV, p. 4).

[71] Challoner, *MMP*, p. 311; Kn., II, pp. 95–6.

[72] Challoner, *MMP*, p. 311; for those who lobbied for the reprieve, see Davidson, RC, p. 472. For the Venetian embassy's attempt to prevent the execution, see Anstr., I, p. 243.

MID-JACOBEAN CONFESSIONAL POLITICS AND ANTI-POPERY 393

suspension of sentence. But John King himself returned from London, where the parliament was in session, and made it clear that he had no time for compromise. He certainly would not tolerate any kind of alternative wording in a substitute allegiance oath of the sort which Napper, imitating Thomas Garnet, had now written out. This had turned into a test case, with neither side prepared to back down. The execution went ahead on 9 November 1610.[73] 'True it is', wrote the Jesuit Richard Banks, 'that on Monday following they granted' to the ambassador Velasco a pardon for Napper, 'though, on [the] Friday before, they had hanged and quartered him'.[74]

It had proved impossible to save the unfortunate Napper, but his secular clergy friends were not going to let his witness be appropriated by the wrong people— not after the utter injustice of what had happened with the memory of their con-frère Cadwallader.[75] (Napper was usefully related by marriage to the circle of clergy around the new archpriest, George Birkhead.)[76] Benjamin Norton in Sussex wrote on 22 November 1610 to Thomas More in Rome that 'it is generally said abroad that there is scarce a priest but takes or allows of the oath, whereas in my last letters I acquainted you' with 'Mr Cadwallader's death for the refusal thereof, and in these letters I acquaint you that Mr George Napper is lately exe-cuted at Oxford for the same'. What clearer proof could there be that secular priests were maintaining Rome's authority? Norton added that, 'because you shall give credit unto' his sacrifice, 'I have sent you a little piece of a cloth which was dipped in his blood'. The good priest had 'died most resolutely, and so I hope we all will do before we will take so abominable an oath'.[77]

The secular clergy friends of Napper also made sure to circulate the stories about miraculous occurrences after his death. As Birkhead later reported to More (on 3 March 1611), 'a quarter' of Napper's body 'was set upon an old arch in Oxford' next to Christ Church and, with 'his hand hanging *perpendiculariter* down to the ground', immediately underneath it there arose 'a spring of most excellent fair water, where never any was before'. One of the 'most impious fellows in all the town had great help to his eyes by means thereof'. Then Dr King came back from London. He 'stopped up the spring' and ordered the decomposing

---

[73] Challoner, *MMP*, pp. 311–12, 314–16; Kn., II, pp. 98–102; cf., for a different rendering of Napper's gallows speech, ABSJ, Anglia III, no. 103.

[74] ARSJ, Anglia 37, fo. 110ᵛ (Grene's summary of letter of 'William Banks alias Bartlet'); see G. Redworth, *The She-Apostle: The Extraordinary Life and Death of Luisa de Carvajal* (2008), p. 198.

[75] Richard Banks SJ wrote an encomium (18 November 1610) for Napper: ARSJ, Anglia 37, fo. 112ʳ, 112ᵛ.

[76] Davidson, RC, pp. 202–8, 444, 473. Joan Napper, George's sister, was the wife of Thomas Greenwood; their son Thomas married Grace More, who was the sister of the secular clergy's agent in Rome, i.e. Thomas More: Davidson, RC, p. 200; Questier, *C&C*, p. 370.

[77] *NAGB*, p. 96; see also AAW, A X, no. 29, p. 67. In early January 1611, Birkhead sent More (for presentation to the cardinal protector of the English nation, Odoardo Farnese) 'a piece of Mr Napper's shirt dipped in his blood' as well as 'a straw moistened with the blood of' the more recent martyrs, John Roberts and Thomas Somers (for whom, see pp. 394–400 below): *NAGB*, p. 96.

394 CATHOLICS AND TREASON

section of Napper's mangled corpse to be 'removed...to another place'.[78] Norton recounted that a Benedictine monk had confirmed the story of 'Napper's Well', in which 'many washed their eyes and drank of the water and got good thereby' and also that Dr King had 'caused' the healing spring 'to be rammed up' and 'flung the quarter of that saint into the Thames'.[79] Within a month yet another version of these facts was reported by Richard Broughton: 'about the time [that] one of' Napper's 'quarters was hanged on an old wall by Christ Church, there broke forth many little springs under a wall hard by and one even under the hand where it did hang, whereof the children made a little well but, after the quarter was taken away by Catholics, that spring did dry up'.[80]

One reason that these signs and wonders were so important was because, as Birkhead wrote to More, 'the day before' Napper 'died, he sent me his voice for bishops under his own hand and nominated those whom he thought fit for such a dignity'.[81] Here a suffering servant of Christ was pegging his imminent death to an affirmation of the crying need for an episcopal hierarchy to regulate the Catholic community in England.

John Roberts and Thomas Somers

These brutalities inflicted on Catholic clergy were, apparently, not enough to persuade some Protestants that there was a sufficient lock on Catholic separatism.[82] The Benedictine monk John Roberts and the secular priest Thomas Somers were executed at Tyburn on 10 December 1610. Both of them had recently attempted to abscond from Newgate.[83] Roberts's and Somers's convictions came at the point

---

[78] *NAGB*, p. 99.   [79] *NAGB*, p. 99.

[80] *NAGB*, p. 99. The Jesuit Edward Coffin was compelled to acknowledge that the story of the healing spring had arrived in St Omer but not directly from the Jesuits' friends in England. Rather, it had come from Rome and, admitted Coffin, had been dispatched by Birkhead to the pope himself and had then been passed back to Flanders by the Society's friend at the papal court, Cardinal Lorenzo Bianchetti: ABSJ, Anglia III, no. 103.

[81] *NAGB*, p. 99 (AAW, A IX, no. 88, p. 293).

[82] This was also the point that saw the 1610 parliament's attempts to reform royal revenue collapse completely in the unravelling of the ill-fated 'great contract': Sawyer, *WM*, III, pp. 235–6.

[83] Challoner, *MMP*, pp. 317–23; AAW, A IX, no. 106, pp. 345–6; AAW, A IX, no. 107, pp. 346–7. The document AAW, A IX, no. 108, is almost identical to no. 106. See also *Discours et Traicté Veritable du Martire Enduré à Londres en Angleterre. Par le R. Pere Iean de Meruinia, autrement dit Roberts...Executé le 20 de Decembre l'An 1610* (Douai, 1611), copied in Ralph Weldon, 'Memorials', Douai Abbey, Woolhampton, Berkshire, deposit IA (6 volumes), I, pp. 26f; for a series of narratives not used by Challoner for his account of Roberts, see Douai Abbey, Woolhampton, Berkshire, martyr papers, deposit IA. c; S. Marron, 'Martyrs' Papers at Woolhampton', *Douai Magazine* 3 (1925), pp. 196–204. The first section of *Discours et Traicté Veritable*, describing the trial, was written by Roberts himself; the narrative of the execution was penned by Robert Haydock OSB (ARCR, I, no. 939), who, it was said, had been present and was responsible for organizing the recovery of Roberts's remains: Weldon, 'Memorials', I, p. 26. There was a German translation printed in Augsburg in the same year: ARCR, I, no. 940. Roberts was known for ministering to plague victims, just as Somers ministered to the poor: Kn., II, pp. 138, 126; Lunn, *The English Benedictines*, p. 63. For Roberts's arrest

MID-JACOBEAN CONFESSIONAL POLITICS AND ANTI-POPERY   395

when London Catholics were being indicted in some numbers for their separatism, and when some of them were being convicted also for refusal of the oath.[84] The trial, on 5 December—the day before parliament was prorogued—saw a sharp verbal confrontation between Roberts and the new bishop of London, George Abbot. Roberts and Somers were offered the oath of allegiance by Abbot, but both refused to take it, at least not in the form that it stood on the statute book. According to one narrative of the court proceedings, retained in Jesuit archives, Abbot insisted repeatedly on the parliamentary origins of the oath to trump Roberts's assertion that he would take an oath of allegiance to the king but not the 1606 oath. Abbot replied to Roberts that it was 'not seemly to discuss further what has been legally decreed and established by both houses of parliament, nor is it in my power to give such a leave, seeing that the houses have ordained it, and that it cannot be altered'.[85] One imagines that this was an entirely different gloss from the one which the king would have put on the oath. For James, it was, even if incorporated into statute, an expression of his own understanding of the nature and extent of royal authority—it was not primarily about the authority of representative bodies. But, as Peter Lake emphasizes, for Abbot, it was parliament which stood as the nation's principal defence against the threat of popery.[86]

What Abbot wanted here was a public backing down by a high-profile London priest, allegedly known as the 'parish priest' of the city. What Abbot did not want was some kind of compromise over the oath, which is what previous and recent victims of the regime, notably Robert Drury and Thomas Garnet, had offered. Nor, one imagines, did Abbot want to see large numbers of Catholics publicly taking, on their own terms, a loyalty oath at all. In Abbot's view, for the 1606 oath to remain serviceable, it had to keep all of its belligerent aspects and overtones. There was indeed a possibility that the widespread tendering of the oath would dilute its effectiveness as a weapon against Catholic separatists. It might even have its darkly funny side. Edward Bennett wryly noted at one stage that 'it is reported in Worcestershire and Staffordshire' that a crowd of as many as '200 [people], being to take the oath of allegiance, viz. cobblers, carpenters, smiths and of mechanic trades', went 'from their houses, tippled drink and swore all the way they went'. When 'some zealous brethren rebuked' them for effing and blinding in

---

in Fleet Street by Humphrey Cross and for his interrogation on 21 December 1607 by Bishop Thomas Ravis and others, see AAW, OB III/ii, no. 178 (a document which was obtained, in all likelihood, from Lambeth Palace in the 1640s). A recusant, William Jenison, was indicted in February 1611 for having been, in September 1606, reconciled to Rome by Roberts; Jenison's interrogation was cited by Abbot at Roberts's trial in late 1610: H. Bowler (ed.), *London Sessions Records 1605–1685* (CRS 34, 1934), pp. 59, 383; Pollen, *AEM*, pp. 151, 154 (ABSJ, Anglia III, no. 102).

[84] Bowler, *London Sessions Records*, pp. 46–90 *passim*; Jeaffreson, *MCR*, II, pp. 214–17.
[85] Pollen, *AEM*, p. 147.
[86] P. Lake, 'Anti-Popery: the Structure of a Prejudice', in R. Cust and A. Hughes (eds), *Conflict in Early Stuart England* (1989), pp. 72–106, esp. at pp. 89–90.

396   CATHOLICS AND TREASON

the face of the king's authority, they answered that, 'seeing they were summoned to swear, they would swear also without summons'.[87]

The Roberts–Somers trial was probably also, in some sense, a job talk for Abbot. Archbishop Bancroft had died only thirty-three days before the date of the proceedings. Abbot was rather publicly brandishing his credentials as a potential successor, though he was not formally nominated to Canterbury until 4 March 1611.[88] To establish his affinity with Bancroft, and to give the impression of continuity, Abbot read out a 'mandate' from Bancroft which had ordered Roberts to be brought to him for interrogation. But those who were watching and following the trial must have known that Roberts in April 1603 had publicly associated himself with those clergy, notably Thomas Bluet and Thomas Wright, who were overtly opposed to the allegedly corrupting influence of the Jesuit clergy, and who had looked to obtain an at-arm's-length form of patronage from Bancroft himself.[89]

It is possible, then, that Abbot was deliberately striking against a known associate of those among the secular clergy whose programme for, among other things, an episcopal hierarchy was completely unacceptable (to Abbot). Also, if it is true that Roberts had been arrested and released as many times over the previous few years as Luisa de Carvajal claimed, this may have been a kind of protest from inside the regime, led by Abbot, against what some people perceived as a de facto toleration for some Roman Catholic clergy in the capital.[90]

For his part, Roberts reiterated that he would not refuse 'to take any oath of allegiance offered me, which shall in truth be only such; but this oath', he said, contained 'other matter besides allegiance'. Roberts might well have rejected the likes of the Jesuit Robert Persons. But he could never make his peace with Calvinists such as Abbot.[91] Roberts's refusal simply triggered the penalties of the

---

[87] AAW, A XI, no. 76, p. 218.

[88] Abbot's nomination shocked George Birkhead, who wrote, on the previous day, 3 March 1611, that Abbot was 'the sorest enemy that ever we had' and the chances were that he would 'have more blood'. Birkhead, like many others, had hoped that Thomas Bilson or Lancelot Andrewes would have been nominated to succeed Bancroft: *NAGB*, pp. 98–9; K. Fincham, 'Prelacy and Politics: Archbishop Abbot's Defence of Protestant Orthodoxy', *Bulletin of the Institute of Historical Research* 61 (1988), pp. 36–64, at pp. 40–1; AAW, A IX, no. 88, p. 293; AAW, A X, no. 9, p. 21; cf. Loomie, *SJC*, I, p. 171. The Calvinist divine John King, who, as we saw, was George Napper's nemesis, succeeded Abbot as bishop of London: *HMCR*, I, pp. 428, 429.

[89] Pollen, *AEM*, p. 150; Lunn, *The English Benedictines*, pp. 62–4, 79. Roberts had, said one informant in May 1604, had 'conference with the bishop of London and others and' would 'deal wholly against the Jesuits': PRO, SP 94/10, fo. 8ʳ.

[90] Redworth, *LLC*, II, p. 134.

[91] Pollen, *AEM*, pp. 146–7. This report says that the recorder, Sir Henry Montagu, also laboured to make Roberts take the oath: Pollen, *AEM*, p. 147. The judge Sir John Croke who had sat in judgment on George Napper was also present at the trials of Roberts and Somers: Pollen, *AEM*, p. 151. Birkhead heard, as he wrote on 5 January 1611, that 'in the arraignment of Mr Somers and Mr Roberts at Newgate, they had been saved if it had not been for the malice of' Abbot 'who urged the recorder to do justice and to proceed against them'. The recorder had been 'willing to put them off' and 'gave them three days' to consider whether they would take the oath but, on their refusal, Abbot demanded their conviction: AAW, A X, no. 2, p. 5.

MID-JACOBEAN CONFESSIONAL POLITICS AND ANTI-POPERY 397

1585 statute, although the allegation was that Roberts was not just technically guilty under that statute but also a dangerous agitator. Abbot declared, for example, though it seems impossible independently to verify this, that Roberts had been 'found on the very day of the powder treason in the house of the wife of its author and contriver'. This was, said Abbot to the court, proof of 'what sort of man this is, and from all these circumstances you can infer how dangerous he is to the king and country', though Roberts simply replied that he had 'established' his 'innocence at the time before the lords of his Majesty's privy council'; and, he added, 'I teach obedience to princes as a matter of conscience against the false doctrine of Luther and his companions' and 'a priest...in regard to his office as priest, which is sacred and holy, cannot be a traitor'.[92]

According to Carvajal, Roberts refused to break prison, although, 'when they' took both him and Somers 'off to be sentenced', Roberts was 'trembling so much that he could barely tie his shoelaces or button the sleeves of his jacket'. Carvajal was attending on him by this stage. One senses that the macabre kind of party that she threw in the prison on the night before the execution was both a celebration of Roberts's defiance and perhaps a way of stopping anyone approaching him at the last minute in an effort to get him to change his mind.[93] Carvajal recorded about six months later (on 6/16 April 1611) that, after sentence was pronounced against Roberts and Somers, they arrived back at the gaol 'at a chamber rather like a church, full of Catholics held prisoner for their religion. I prostrated myself before their joyous feet and kissed them, telling them that...I was full of envy for their happy fate'.[94] As Carvajal told the marquis of Caracena, Roberts's and Somers's final hours had been turned into a massive demonstration of the Catholic faith. The 'devout...had come for their final farewell, women mostly' and 'as many as could fit at the table sat down to dine...as many as twenty or more confessors of our holy faith'. Luisa presided, with 'the two martyrs on either side'.[95] Luisa's report was confirmed by the later admissions of Simon Houghton, the keeper of Newgate. He said that Luisa had come to the prison the night before the execution. 'One Margaret Ash and another younger woman who were laundresses to the priests in Newgate did wash the feet of the said Roberts and presently thereupon', the priest George Fisher 'with other priests and recusant papists' knelt down 'and kissed the feet of the said Roberts, saying certain words in Latin'.[96]

---

[92] Pollen, *AEM*, pp. 149, 153, 156.
[93] Lunn, *The English Benedictines*, p. 64; Pollen, *AEM*, pp. 169–70; Redworth, *LLC*, II, p. 134; cf. *HMCD*, II, p. 407.
[94] Redworth, *LLC*, II, pp. 151–2.
[95] Redworth, *LLC*, II, pp. 156–7. King James got to hear of Carvajal's publicly going to the prison and dining with the two martyrs-to-be. He took it to be a 'foul disorder' and demanded sanctions against those responsible: PRO, SP 14/61/88, fo. 133[r–v].
[96] PRO, SP 14/61/91, fo. 137[r] (18 February 1611); see also PRO, SP 14/61/91, fo. 137[v] (Abraham Reynolds's account of Roberts's leaving Newgate for Tyburn), SP 14/61/92, fo. 139[r], SP 14/61/98, fo. 178[r], SP 14/61/99, fo. 180[r].

398   CATHOLICS AND TREASON

At Tyburn, surrounded by sixteen condemned thieves, Roberts, apparelled in a cassock, exhorted the condemned malefactors to convert, even at that moment, from wickedness to the life of faith. 'No sooner had he climbed' into the cart than he turned 'himself to the criminals and, stretching out his hand to bless them, he spoke as follows: "Here we are all going to die, nor have we any hope of escape"'. But if they should die in the 'religion now professed and established in this country', they would certainly be damned. They should, instead, repent and die with him in the true faith. He urged them to say, after him, 'the following words: I believe in the Holy Catholic Church, and I desire to die a member of that Church. I repent and am sorry for having led so...wicked a life, and that I have so grievously offended my sweet and merciful Saviour'. If they did this 'truly', he would absolve them. At least one of the felons there wept copiously and indicated that he would die as a Roman Catholic.[97]

Whoever the Protestant chaplain in attendance was, he (at least according to the narrator of this account) initially 'stood aside and, so far from opposing himself to anything Father Roberts said, seemed to yield to the dignity of the holy man and to the doctrine he taught', though Roberts was subsequently interrupted by this same Protestant clergyman and by 'some of the criminals behind him', who sang 'hymns made up from the Psalms according to the fashion of Geneva'. The sheriff interjected that 'as long as nothing was said against the king or the State...he saw no reason why' Roberts 'should not say as he wished'. A 'churlish' official objected to the sheriff's decision to let Roberts speak.[98] But Roberts responded with an explicitly loyalist statement: 'I have never said, nor will I ever say, any evil against the king. On the contrary, I pray God to bless him and the queen and their children, and those of his council, also those of the bench that condemned me, and...all you who are here present, and all the other subjects of the king. It is not the king who is the cause of my death' but 'heresy'; 'heresy desires my death, and is the cause of it'. This was a final and fairly explicit attack on George Abbot's brand of Calvinism. Roberts could not take the new oath of allegiance for it was 'so mixed with matters of religion that it is expressly forbidden' by the pope.[99] Thomas Somers, when he got the chance, made a similarly loyal address and, likewise, said that he refused the oath not in 'respect of allegiance...but in regard it is mixed with matter of religion', and so was prohibited by the pope, 'whom all are bound to obey which are Christ's sheep in points of religion'; and, as Roberts had done, he declaimed that, out of the true Church, 'there is no salvation'.[100]

---

[97] Pollen, *AEM*, pp. 161–2; Challoner, *MMP*, pp. 318–19.
[98] Pollen, *AEM*, pp. 163, 165; Challoner, *MMP*, p. 319.
[99] Pollen, *AEM*, pp. 165–6; Challoner, *MMP*, pp. 320–1.
[100] AAW, A IX, no. 109, p. 351; Pollen, *AEM*, pp. 165, 167.

MID-JACOBEAN CONFESSIONAL POLITICS AND ANTI-POPERY 399

The narrator of the hanging that then took place, with the attendant cruelty of the treason penalties for the two priests, insisted that the crowd refused to shout 'Long live the king' when the executioner proclaimed 'this is the heart of a traitor'.[101] Approximately 'one hundred paces from the gibbet on the high road a large trench was dug, into which the quarters of the two martyrs were cast', though not the heads—which went off to London Bridge for display. On top of 'them were thrown the bodies of the sixteen criminals'. Unnamed London Catholics then exhumed the two priests by night. It appears that this took place by arrangement with Luisa de Carvajal. She had been asked to perform this service by William Scot, Roberts's Benedictine confrère.[102] In the attempt of the 'pious thieves' to make their escape from the London watch, parts of the carcasses were dropped. They were taken and put in front of George Abbot. Abbot ordered a burial 'in the Church of St Saviour' in Southwark, attached to Montague House. This may have been meant as a warning to the Catholics there, including Viscount Montague, who, however, the next year came out explicitly against the new oath.[103]

The rest of the martyrs' remains arrived at Carvajal's residence. She had 'provided an English coach'. This, she wrote, 'was how they brought Father Roberts', or most of him 'and half the other saint's body' back from the gallows. They 'put one of the arms with its half of the back and chest on the floor and then did the same with the other one. What an extraordinary spectacle and inspiration to prayer it was to see such frail weapons with which they fought, yet without any frailty at all and with such spirit! They flew up to heaven, increasing the number of intercessors there'.[104]

This display of Catholic devotion to reputed martyrs is really, to a modern mind, very difficult to accept, though Carvajal was hardly unique in what she did. But it suggests how far one section of the Catholic community in London was going in order to face down the authorities and, also, other Catholics who were perhaps less enthusiastic about celebrating martyrdom. Some of her coreligionists in London thought it was insanely provocative to do as she had done. 'Some priests who found out about it, but not from me', remarked Carvajal, 'tried to scare me with the council, and I almost lost my temper with them over this'.[105] It may be that these clergy did not want to goad officialdom in London any fur-

---

[101] Pollen, *AEM*, p. 168. A similar claim was made by Edward Coffin: ABSJ, Anglia III, no. 103.

[102] Redworth, *The She-Apostle*, p. 195; ABSJ, Anglia III, no. 103. For the retrieval of Roberts's and Somers's remains, see also Challoner, *MMP*, p. 321; *HMCD*, II, p. 407.

[103] Challoner, *MMP*, p. 321; *NAGB*, pp. 19, 109, 113, 116–17, 133; Questier, *C&C*, pp. 342, 355, 358–66; Lewis Owen, *The Running Register...* (1626), p. 94; Biblioteca Vallicelliana, Rome, N 23, fo. 203ʳ. Lucy Underwood has pointed out to me that, equally, this could be taken as a kind of concession, in the sense that those convicted and executed thus were not entitled to any church burial at all.

[104] Redworth, *LLC*, II, p. 157. In April 1611, Carvajal sent some of Roberts's remains to Joseph Creswell in Spain, and then more in October: Redworth, *LLC*, II., pp. 145–6, and see p. 402 below; see also Pollen, *AEM*, p. 169.

[105] Redworth, *LLC*, II, p. 157.

400 CATHOLICS AND TREASON

ther or that they sensed and resented the appropriation of the recent martyrdom by those with whom Carvajal was associated—an act of appropriation which was all the more pointed in the context of Roberts's previous alignment with those who were no friends of the likes of Carvajal. Robert Jones SJ, for one, celebrated Roberts's martyrdom. He said that Roberts had, 'going to the hurdle, embraced a friend of ours that was prisoner and sent me most kind commendations' and sent 'diverse tokens' as well. (Thomas Somers, who died with Roberts, was allegedly also well disposed to the Society of Jesus.)[106]

Unsurprisingly, the Spanish embassy reacted very badly to the proceedings against Roberts and Somers. On 21/31 December 1610, Alonso de Velasco described how he had lodged a formal protest at these executions and told Salisbury that he, Velasco, 'stood aghast at their reaching such a heartless decision' and how stupid it was when the Spanish embassy in London (worried, in fact, about the possibility of an Anglo-French marriage alliance) was doing its best to push forward the dynastic marriage which was being suggested between Princess Elizabeth and Savoy. Salisbury replied that 'out of regard for parliament it had not been possible to avoid the deed but that he would give me his word that there would not be a similar case of punishment again', and indeed, while Salisbury lived, there was not.[107]

Mid-Jacobean Dynastic Policy and the English Catholic Community: the Consequences of the King's Protestant Turn

No source explicitly says that these trials were staged at the end of the 1610 parliament in order to bring pressure to bear on, or to embarrass, the court. It was not until early 1611 that the decision was taken to dissolve the parliament. But informed observers may well have concluded that there was at least a chance that the political landscape might change. Thomas Screven observed in early January 1611 that, with the dissolution of parliament imminent, 'the king dined abroad and with him the Spanish ambassador'.[108] Conrad Russell notes that it was at this

---

[106] ARSJ, Anglia 37, fo. 109ᵛ.

[107] Loomie, *SJC*, I, pp. 163–4. On 24 February 1611, George Birkhead believed that, although 'it is thought' that 'two more' priests 'shall die' (indeed, some said that the king 'puts priests to death by one and one, but others' would follow who would extirpate them completely), it would not be 'yet, for the sessions at Newgate are now past' (William Jenison, whose arrest and interrogation had been crucial to Abbot's case against Roberts, had been acquitted and discharged ten days previously). Also, 'some...are of hope that our affliction will be reduced to some pecuniary tribute': AAW, A X, no. 16, p. 37; Bowler, *London Sessions Records*, p. 384. Sir Dudley Carleton made strongly worded representations to the authorities in Venice when news of Roberts's and Somers's executions caused, as John Chamberlain wrote, an 'ill impression' there: McClure, *LJC*, I, p. 302. Carleton remarked to William Trumbull that 'we that know their demeanour may rather marvel why so many escape than why these were executed': Sawyer, *WM*, III, p. 260.

[108] *HMCR*, I, p. 426.

MID-JACOBEAN CONFESSIONAL POLITICS AND ANTI-POPERY   401

time that 'the argument for "new counsels"...was beginning to be heard as faint whispers, proposing that the king should give up relying for taxation on a consent which was never likely to be forthcoming'.[109] Of course, separatist Catholicism was not really an integral part of these political equations but, even at this stage, there were murmurs that compromises over the sequestrations imposed on Catholics under the recusancy statutes might form part of a non-parliamentary platform for upping the tax take—dealing both with royal indebtedness and also the king's relationship with the Catholic community. According to the ambassador Corraro on 13/23 December 1610, unnamed Catholics had offered 'the king 250,000 ducats to remain unmolested' and 'they use his indignation against parliament, to which they attribute their persecution, to assist their aim'.[110] Catholic newsletter writers certainly pointed to the public anti-puritanism of the clerical followers of Bishop Richard Neile.[111]

But the king's own political inclinations and irritations, when faced by the intransigence of the recent parliament, could not, on their own, be allowed to dictate the course of the court's foreign and dynastic policy. The fact was that the assassination of Henry IV had made it very likely that there would be a Protestant turn in the Stuart court's dealings with its European neighbours. During the second half of 1612, it sought a dynastic marriage alliance with Frederick V, the young elector palatine of the Rhine.[112] Although there were no more treason trials during 1611, Catholic commentators insisted that things were not getting any easier for them. The oath was being enforced more widely. There was another proclamation, on 31 May 1611, ordering the oath to be tendered.[113] Clergymen in the London gaols were breaking this way and that over the oath.[114] Those in the Clink prison were largely in favour of the oath, while those in Newgate openly repudiated it. Two priests had been arrested in Wiltshire, namely Henry Mayhew

---

[109] Russell, *James VI*, p. 90.   [110] *CSPV 1610–13*, p. 100.

[111] On Ian Atherton's, David Como's, and Kenneth Fincham's highly persuasive account, Abbot's agenda in the first half of 1611 (against the avant-garde conformist priorities of Bishop Neile and his friends) looked set to be derailed by Neile's anti-puritan campaign, which included the proceedings against the heretic Edward Wightman, though Abbot retaliated by using the affair of Conrad Vorstius at Leiden: I. Atherton and D. Como, 'The Burning of Edward Wightman: Puritanism, Prelacy and the Politics of Heresy in Early Modern England', *English Historical Review* 120 (2005), pp. 1215–50, at pp. 1241–5; K. Fincham, *Prelate as Pastor: The Episcopate of James I* (Oxford 1990), pp. 46–7; the details of the Wightman case were reported to Thomas More in Rome by Edward Bennett: *NAGB*, pp. 34, 153–4; Questier, *DP*, p. 333.

[112] *CSPV 1610–13*, pp. 73–4, 119–20.   [113] Hughes and Larkin, *SRP*, I, no. 118.

[114] Among those who conceded much, if not all of, the regime's case over the oath, there was the Benedictine Thomas Preston and the secular priests William Warmington and Richard Sheldon, and Birkhead's own former secretary John Copley, who, like Sheldon, rejected Rome altogether: *NAGB*, passim; AAW, A XI, no. 67, p. 194; Richard Sheldon, *The Motives of...Richard Sheldon Pr. for his Iust, Voluntary, and Free Renouncing of Communion with the Bishop of Rome...*(1612); William Warmington, *A Moderate Defence of the Oath of Allegiance...*(n.p. [London], 1612). Preston did not, however, say simply that all Catholics should take the oath and, in early 1612, he counselled the imprisoned Lord Vaux to refuse the oath. This goaded George Abbot into making public Preston's use of the pseudonym of 'Roger Widdrington' in his pamphlets on the topic of the oath: *NAGB*, p. 147.

402   CATHOLICS AND TREASON

and Edward Kenion. Mayhew had 'denied the oath directly' and said that 'it was absurd and that no Christian could take it'. George Abbot ranted and swore that 'he deserved to be hanged'. Mayhew was imprisoned in Newgate. But when Kenion answered, in Abbot's opinion, 'more moderately', he 'was sent to the Clink'.[115] The former appellant William Bishop was arrested in London and refused the oath. But he did so in such a way as to mean there was no likelihood of anything worse than being kept in gaol and then deported, which he was. Abbot said, though probably with a considerable degree of sarcasm, that Bishop's reasons for refusing the oath were 'the best he had heard for the denial thereof'.[116] On 1 June, Edward Bennett said that Bishop's opinion 'carries more weight with it than what proceeds from other of our brethren, who be younger'. It was rumoured that the king wanted to speak with him personally. This was evidently all to the good, for 'here has been some speech lately that one or two of our priests should be executed out of Newgate, but I think it will not prove so'.[117] But outright and stubborn non-compliance carried real consequences, as Lord Montague found out when he was hit with a massive fine for refusal of the oath.[118] Secular priests such as Bennett sent reports to Rome that the oath was being offered very widely now that the assize judges had set out on their circuits. Sir Edward Coke had 'made such a cruel speech against all kind of Catholics that he amazed the...heretics' themselves, though Coke seemed more animated against the Jesuit clergy than against others.[119]

Carvajal's letters confirm the reports of clerics such as Bennett. She wrote to her friend Rodrigo Calderón on 25 July/4 August 1611 that 'I see that this king is seeking friendly relations with Catholic princes and, at the moment, more than ever'. But 'Catholics have never been so oppressed since he became king'. 'No door can be locked be it day or night, and nor can any trunk, chest, box, paper or letter be kept from those' who regularly barged into Catholic houses.[120] On 5/15 October 1611 she explained to Joseph Creswell (enclosed in her letter were more 'pieces of the flesh of the holy father John Roberts') what she took to be the immediate context for all this. It was 'being bandied about that an exchange of marriages' had 'been arranged', as indeed it had, 'between Spain and France'. King James was 'taking it very badly', as well he might.[121]

---

[115]   AAW, A X, no. 51, p. 125 (*NAGB*, p. 111).

[116]   AAW, A X, no. 51, pp. 125–6 (*NAGB*, p. 111). William Bishop had written a polemical tract in reply to Archbishop Abbot's brother Robert; see William Bishop, *A Reproofe of M. Doct. Abbots Defence, of the Catholike Deformed by M.W. Perkins* ....(n.p. [printed secretly in England], 1608).

[117]   AAW, A X, no. 58, pp. 159, 160. For what appears, nevertheless, to have been a regime-led attempt to round up prominent clergy at this time, see AAW, A X, no. 61, pp. 165–6.

[118]   AAW, A X, no. 80, p. 209.

[119]   AAW, A X, no. 85, p. 235. For subsequent letters written to Thomas More concerning the tendering of the oath, see e.g. AAW, A X, nos 97, 108, 115, 136, 141, 150.

[120]   Redworth, *LLC*, II, pp. 162–3.   [121]   Redworth, *LLC*, II, p. 179.

MID-JACOBEAN CONFESSIONAL POLITICS AND ANTI-POPERY   403

The Habsburg–Bourbon marriage compact (the regency government in France had little choice while Louis XIII was in his minority) meant that the Stuart court would actively have to look for Protestant friends on the Continent.[122] This Protestant turn in British foreign policy may, as Carvajal implied, have been interpreted by some people as a green light to intensify the pressure on Catholic separatism. In response, it appears, to a rumour that John Gerard was back in the country, there was a search of the Vaux household on 31 October 1611, the eve of All Saints. But this was definitely not trick or treat. Gilbert Pickering 'with fifty horsemen in warlike manner appointed, besides halberds, pikes, scaling ladders', crowbars, 'picklocks and black lanterns, about 12 o'clock at night, with a warrant from the council, suddenly entered while all were asleep'. They arrested the two resident Jesuit chaplains, John Percy and Nicholas Hart. Elizabeth, Lady Vaux, was gaoled in London in the Fleet, while her two chaplains were sent to the Gatehouse.[123] There was, said John Chamberlain, 'some resistance in the taking of them'.[124] Thomas Heath reported that Pickering's son had 'near...lost his life therein, being run through the thigh and into the head'. The two chaplains, 'it is for certain reported...shall be put to death' at 'the end of this Michaelmas term'.[125] Lady Vaux declared, wrote Carvajal, that 'such was the fury of the heretics...that they smashed and destroyed the walls, floors and ceilings of the house, just as they usually do. The most outrageous thing was that they went into her garden and orchard and pulled up the plants, trees and fruit trees by the roots and scattered them in the fields. They even pulled down all the shaded places and ingenious awnings which she had created.' (Glyn Redworth suggests they may have been looking for the body parts of the recent martyrs Roberts and Somers.)[126]

Elizabeth Vaux refused to take the oath. Lord Vaux was arrested the moment he returned from Flanders.[127] Carvajal narrated the subsequent set-to between Lord Vaux and the earl of Salisbury. Vaux had been given five weeks to decide whether to take the oath. Carvajal recounted also that 'the false bishop of Canterbury went to the king...and, they say, he wept in front of him' and protested 'that the Catholics were growing rapidly in number, boldness and liberty'.[128]

---

[122] PRO, SP 94/18, fos 96ᵛ, 137ʳ, 138ʳ, 144ʳ–6ᵛ. The news of the Franco-Spanish dynastic alliance came out in July/August 1611. For the complexities of mid-Jacobean dynastic policy, see A. Thrush, 'The French Marriage and the Origins of the 1614 Parliament', in S. Clucas and R. Davies (eds), *The Crisis of 1614 and the Addled Parliament: Literary and Historical Perspectives* (Aldershot, 2003), pp. 25–35.

[123] ARSJ, Anglia 37, fo. 106ᵛ; *NAGB*, pp. 130–1; McClure, *LJC*, I, p. 313; Caraman, *JG*, p. 252. Richard Smith confirmed that the search was for John Gerard, who was suspected of having returned from abroad: AAW, A XI, no. 20, p. 51.

[124] McClure, *LJC*, I, p. 313; *NAGB*, p. 131; *HMCD*, III, p. 180; AAW, A X, no. 150, p. 421.

[125] AAW, A X, no. 150, p. 421.

[126] Redworth, *LLC*, II, pp. 189–90; G. Redworth, *The She-Apostle*, p. 200.

[127] *NAGB*, p. 138. For William Trumbull's reports in November and December 1611 about Vaux travelling in disguise in Flanders and visiting the Jesuit college in Brussels, which in Trumbull's view gave cause for 'suspicion', see PRO, SP 77/10, fos 148ʳ, 152ᵛ–3ʳ.

[128] Redworth, *LLC*, II, pp. 190, 191; *NAGB*, p. 143.

404   CATHOLICS AND TREASON

All through 1611, in fact, we find Catholic newsletter writers claiming that the regime was hammering into the structures of their community. Even in London there was a sense that the private police force of pursuivants and other officials was nastier than ever. Anthony Champney wrote on 21/31 January 1612 that there was a 'new commission given to the pursuivants' which 'extends to the seizing of all money and goods which by probable conjecture are ordained to the maintenance of priests'.[129] Some Catholics took direct action when faced with such officials. On 22 December 1611 a group of Catholics in Milford Lane had seen George Gage being frogmarched off to be interrogated by George Abbot. Gage was being escorted by the usual-suspect group of high-commission bully boys, including John Wragge and John Griffin, accompanied by the renegade seminary priest Anthony Rouse. One man demanded to know where Gage was being taken; in fact, Gage's escort party had no constable and so was technically acting outside the law. Provoked by a volley of oaths from Griffin, a fracas began. Griffin lost part of his nose; Wragge, who in the course of the struggle killed an innocent bystander who tried to break it up, was wounded in the eye, and Rouse was chucked into the nearby River Thames.[130] It seems that Gage had, some weeks earlier in Holborn, injured Wragge, though evidently not badly enough, when he 'challenged him or his' servant 'for...a priest'.[131]

Anyway, even while the Spaniards were still asking whether, in principle, James would agree to a marriage for Prince Henry with King Philip III's younger daughter, James now opted for a real investment in Protestant-cause politics and, at the end of March 1612, Sir Ralph Winwood concluded an alliance with the so-called German evangelical union. In these circumstances, the casual violence, described above, in Milford Lane makes sense, as does the escalating hostility over Catholic attendance at the Spanish embassy chapel in London. As James's ambassador in Spain, Sir John Digby, reported from Madrid on 4 March 1612, in the previous week a dispatch had arrived from the ambassador Velasco in London and, as a result, 'the rumour of the strict proceeding against Catholics in England was much increased'.[132] The Venetian ambassador, Antonio Foscarini, noted on 28 February/9 March that James had complained about 'the conduct of the Spanish ambassador who caused more than one Mass to be said daily and invited attendance by ringing of bells'. This was a 'scandal that could not be endured'. The French embassy, by contrast, was 'more modest and circumspect'.[133]

---

[129]   AAW, A XI, no. 11, p. 25 (*NAGB*, p. 43). Even at this point, though, several of the secular clergy were speculating that some Catholics might secure composition arrangements for their liabilities under the penal statutes: *NAGB*, p. 142.

[130]   *NAGB*, p. 43; AAW, A X, no. 166, p. 458.

[131]   *NAGB*, p. 43; AAW, A XI, no. 11, p. 25; *HMCD*, III, p. 181. The date of the latter incident involving Gage (22 December 1611) is not, in fact, entirely certain, nor is it known what was the outcome of the earlier reported confrontation.

[132]   *HMCS*, XXI, pp. 333–4.

[133]   *CSPV 1610–13*, p. 303.

MID-JACOBEAN CONFESSIONAL POLITICS AND ANTI-POPERY   405

What the Stuart regime was confronting was the expectation not just that the Franco-Spanish double match would allow a Habsburg tsunami to engulf the Dutch but also that there would be an onslaught against the Huguenots in France. As Carvajal perceived from 'a letter that fell into' her 'hands', written by 'one English heretic to another', once the Huguenots were wiped out, 'the Catholics' would 'thereafter turn their attention to England'. The only defence against this, said the unnamed letter writer, was to provoke a breach of the Truce of Antwerp 'so as to give' Prince Maurice 'more authority there'; and the Huguenots should be spurred into rebellion against the regency government in France.[134]

Historically, the danger from Spain was almost always connected with a threat to Ireland. On 1 February 1612 at Dublin the Franciscan bishop of Down and Connor, Conor O'Devany, who was a known supporter of the earl of Tyrone, met his death. O'Devany was hanged with another Franciscan, Patrick O'Lochran, formerly one of Tyrone's chaplains.[135] At this time, the regime was preparing for a parliament in Dublin, one which finally met in 1613 and which saw an attempt to create a Protestant ascendancy. O'Devany had considerable popular support in Dublin.[136] The majesty of royal justice was presumably not enhanced by the sight of the ageing bishop's head being carried away from the site of the gallows. What should have been really worrying for the authorities was the spectacle of Anglo-Irish Catholics thronging around the scaffold along with Catholics of Gaelic extraction.[137] Some of the stories about O'Devany's martyrdom were retailed for an English audience by supposedly loyal Anglo-Irishmen, such as Lord

---

[134] Redworth, *LLC*, II, pp. 192–3.

[135] John Finet ascribed O'Devany's condemnation to the fact that 'he was titular bishop of Down during Tyrone's rebellion' and was 'guilty of his treasons'; he had 'received a conditional pardon that he should take the oath of allegiance', which he had subsequently refused; and he was 'found [to be] otherwise machinating': *HMCD*, III, p. 285.

[136] *NAGB*, pp. 21, 146; P. J. Corish, 'A Contemporary Account of the Martyrdom of Conor O'Devany, O.F.M., Bishop of Down and Connor, and Patrick O'Loughran', *Collectanea Hibernica* 24 (1984), pp. 13–19; J. McCavitt, *Sir Arthur Chichester: Lord Deputy of Ireland 1605–1616* (Belfast, 1998), p. 175; J. McCavitt, 'The Execution of Bishop O'Devanna, 1612', *Seanchas Dhroim Mór* (1992–3), pp. 66–9; C. Tait, 'Riots, Rescues and "Grene Bowes": Catholic Popular Protest in Ireland, 1570–1640', in R. Armstrong and T. Ó hAnnracháin (eds), *Insular Christianity: Alternative Models of the Church in Britain and Ireland c. 1570–c. 1700* (Manchester, 2013), pp. 67–83; M. Curran (ed.), 'The Indictments of Cornelius O'Devany, O.S.F., Bishop of Down and Connor, and of John Bourke of Brittas, co. Limerick', *Archivum Hibernicum* 6 (1917), pp. 75–82, at pp. 77–80; A. Ford, 'Martyrdom, History and Memory in Early Modern Ireland', in I. McBride (ed.), *History and Memory in Modern Ireland* (Cambridge, 2001), pp. 43–66, esp. at pp. 61–2; *HMCS*, IV, pp. 564–5. English Catholics cited the execution of O'Devany as evidence of the true witness to the faith which might be expected also of an English bishop, should Rome decide to appoint one for England: *NAGB*, p. 21; see also A. Forrestal, 'A Catholic Model of Martyrdom in the Post-Reformation Era: The Bishop in Seventeenth-Century France', *The Seventeenth Century* 20 (2005), pp. 254–80, esp. at p. 256. For O'Devany's arrest, as part of a drive in and after mid-1611 by Lord Deputy Chichester for the 'reformation of religion' in accord with the king's directions, see J. S. Brewer and W. Bullen (eds), *Calendar of the Carew Manuscripts preserved in the Archiepiscopal Library at Lambeth 1515–1624* (6 vols, 1867–73), VI, p. 128; *CSPI 1611–14*, pp. 142, 143. For the preparations made, and draft proposals formulated, at this point for an Irish parliament, see *CSPI 1611–1*, pp. xxxviii–xli and *passim*.

[137] McCavitt, *Sir Arthur Chichester*, pp. 176–7.

406 CATHOLICS AND TREASON

Delvin.[138] John McCavitt's lucid account suggests that these executions were the culmination of a systematic jacking up of the pains and penalties for the expression in Ireland of a certain sort of Catholicism, all on the basis of claims that clergy such as O'Devany were agents for a renewed bout of Tyronian insurrection.[139]

Even though the Stuart court was now opting for something resembling a Protestant foreign policy, the king still did not want to become the prisoner of a rampantly assertive style and expression of anti-popery. According to Edward Kenion on 2 March, when Archbishop Abbot 'moved the king for the trial of' Elizabeth Vaux 'and the two Jesuits which were taken in her house', presumably anticipating that at the very least the two clerics would be executed, James 'replied that he had already been too forward to take blood and would' take 'no more'.[140] From Spain, Sir John Digby wrote back to London on 9/19 March 1612 that, during an audience with the duke of Lerma, the duke 'grew very testy and violent' and spoke 'with bitterness against the new persecutions, as he termed them, and the putting to death of so many martyrs'. With some awkwardness, Digby

---

[138] Benjamin Norton thought that the indictment was based on 'suspicion of powder treason'. He informed Thomas More in a letter of 26 February 1612 that O'Devany had shown great courage in refusing a reprieve (offered in return for conformity). Furthermore, 'a cripple was cured being at his death', the news of which had come to Norton via Lord Delvin who had been 'at the execution'; the 'people [also] took away' O'Devany's 'quarters': *NAGB*, pp. 146–7. Edward Bennett wrote to More on 1 March 1612 that at the execution, which took place in darkness, the Protestant cleric who trooped along to the gallows, intending 'to have perverted' the condemned men, was struck dead the moment that he saw them hanged. Bennett also reported the miracle of healing and said that it happened to 'one whose arm was lame, going out with others to cut off some part of them for devotion'; this man 'returned back with his arm whole': *NAGB*, p. 147. For Delvin's loyalism and his family's resistance to Tyrone's rebels, see *CSPI 1596–7*, p. 72, despite the periodic claims that his loyalty was doubtful; see, e.g., *CSPI 1600–1*, pp. 117–18; *CSPI 1606–8*, pp. 320–1, and *passim*; cf. *CSPI 1608–10*, p. 103; McCavitt, *Sir Arthur Chichester*, p. 133. Delvin was a relative of the Browne family (Viscounts Montague), and this might explain how these stories got into the newsletters of the English secular clergy to whom the second Viscount Montague was a patron: *NAGB*, p. 146. See also Francis Fay, *Martyrium Rmi. D.F. Cornelii Douenii, Dunensis et Connerensis Episcopi . . . et R. D. Patritii Luchrani . . .* (Cologne, 1614); B. Millett, 'Who wrote the *Martyrium . . . . Cornelii Dovenii*, Cologne, 1614?', *RH* 17 (1985), pp. 358–61.

[139] McCavitt, *Sir Arthur Chichester*, pp. 174–7. Tyrone's former supporter, Archbishop Peter Lombard, concluded that O'Devany's fate was the result of the appointment of the controversial Eugene Matthews to the see of Dublin and that overtly loyalist clergy were not treated by the authorities in the same way: A. Clarke with R. Dudley Edwards, 'Pacification, Plantation and the Catholic Question, 1603–23', in T. W. Moody, F. X. Martin, and F. J. Byrne (eds), *A New History of Ireland III: Early Modern Ireland 1534–1691* (Oxford, 1976), p. 210.

[140] *NAGB*, p. 138. John Percy's and Nicholas Hart's subsequent deportation provoked Edward Bennett to comment sarcastically to More, 'you see how sore they [the Jesuits] be persecuted': AAW, A XI, no. 192, p. 555. For his part, Percy on 2 June 1612 reported that Hart had prayed 'that he might come to the like happy death' suffered by William Scot and Richard Newport (for whose executions, see pp. 408–12 below), while Percy himself hoped that 'voluntas Dei . . . fiat in me, per me, de me': ARSJ, Anglia 37, fo. 117ʳ. On 1 March 1612, Bennett had reported that the priest Henry Mayler was put on trial at the Newgate sessions (with Elizabeth Vaux and Richard Kirkham) for refusal of the oath of allegiance; during the proceedings the prosecution was unable to prove, though it suspected, the fact of Mayler's ordination: AAW, A XI, no. 30, p. 77; Anstr., I, p. 223; Anstruther, *Vaux*, p. 398.

MID-JACOBEAN CONFESSIONAL POLITICS AND ANTI-POPERY   407

defended King James's right to do as he did. Lerma declared that people in Spain 'were very sensible of those strict courses taken with the Catholics'.[141]

Whatever the Spaniards thought (and they, of course, had time only for a certain sort of English Catholic), James knew quite well how to distinguish between some Catholics and others. Thus, on Salisbury's recommendation and against Abbot's advice, the king authorized the relatively lenient option of deportation of imprisoned Catholic clergy, among whose number was the former appellant William Bishop. Bishop's freedom had been demanded by the French ambassador 'at the instance of the Sorbonne doctors'—Bishop was himself a doctor of the Sorbonne—and the king was determined to grant it.[142] Bishop himself narrated his confrontation with Abbot before he went off into exile. It was a real shouting match. Abbot accused him of being a traitor and evidently thought that, in the best of all possible worlds, Bishop should end his days at Tyburn, or at least should not publicly appear to be the recipient of what looked like royal favour.[143] In reply, Bishop protested his loyalty to the king and insisted that the secular clergy 'did not desire bishops that should disquiet their estate any more than priests' since 'they would not...come to demand bishoprics here nor to meddle with their matters, but only to see good order kept amongst Catholics'.[144]

James undoubtedly wanted to use clergy such as Bishop in order to keep the channels of communication open with the right sort of French Catholic and also with his moderate Huguenot clients who would be protected by the Calvinist dynastic alliance which was soon in train for James's daughter Elizabeth—that is, with the elector palatine. The moderate Huguenot Henri de la Tour, duke of Bouillon, served as the agent and go-between for the Anglo-Palatine marriage. The support, or at least not open opposition, of a certain sort of 'moderate' Catholic—such as William Bishop—was highly desirable, not least because Bouillon was also going to propose an Anglo-French match—for Prince Henry.[145] This would help to face down the inevitable Catholic opposition to the palatine marriage which, John Thorys remarked on 21 May 1612, was known now to be provisionally concluded.[146]

Hence also the significance, for example, of the patronage that, among others, King James was prepared to offer to the Huguenot Isaac Casaubon, despite the very real irritation that this caused to some Catholics. In fury, the Catholic Thomas Heath wrote in July 1612 that Casaubon 'so much excuses our State to the Christian world abroad' as to say that 'none are punished for Catholic religion' but 'he could not' have 'picked out a time more to the purpose to have discredited

---

[141] PRO, SP 94/19, fo. 45^r. For Lerma's association with Luisa de Carvajal, see Redworth, *The She-Apostle*, p. 197.

[142] *NAGB*, pp. 138, 149; Anstr., I, p. 37. In May 1611 Abbot had blocked an initiative to release William Bishop: *NAGB*, p. 138.

[143] *NAGB*, p. 149.   [144] *NAGB*, pp. 149–50.   [145] *CSPV 1610–13*, p. 364.

[146] *HMCD*, III, p. 297.

408 CATHOLICS AND TREASON

himself than this present' one. Had he not noticed? 'Great men of honour and wealth' were being ruined. This was a 'punishment much exceeding many deaths that many, thus disenabled, live to bear their own and see the miseries of their wife, children' and 'family'. The word was that 'now are they in hand...that all men whose wives go not to Church' would have to 'pay for them 10^l a month' or their wives would be gaoled. Perhaps 'Monsieur Casaubon' would like to consider 'if this be no persecution'?[147]

More to the point, there had already been another two fatal prosecutions of Catholic clergy. Richard Newport and William Scot had sentence pronounced against them on the afternoon of Friday 29 May and were executed the next morning at Tyburn.[148] It may well have been their known Hispanophile opinions which brought them to the gallows. Newport seems also to have been quite aggressive in conducting his own defence at trial. As Bishop Challoner relates it, in the courtroom, Newport said that 'Protestants and puritans were the men that plotted' against the king, for they 'sought to rob him of his life whilst he was yet in his mother's womb'. This was a reference to the occasion of the murder of Mary Stuart's secretary David Rizzio when, allegedly, a pistol was held to her abdomen.[149] In addition, in the intelligence sweeps after the Gunpowder Plot, Newport was marked out as one of those who had visited Lord Mordaunt in the period before the conspiracy.[150]

Velasco ascribed all this simply to the malice of Archbishop Abbot, who had gone to the king to demand blood, not least to demonstrate that the recent death, on 24 May 1612, of the earl of Salisbury would not lead to a toleration. Scot and Newport had both returned from exile without licence—more than once, in fact, in Newport's case. This was the formal grounds for proceeding against them. Velasco's lobbying for a reprieve was unsuccessful. The executions were carried out at five o'clock in the morning rather than at the more usual time of eight o'clock. Thomas Howard, earl of Arundel, 'showed his courage and devotion for, without fear of worldly reprisal, he accompanied them on horseback from the

[147] *ODNB, sub* Casaubon, Isaac (article by J. Considine); AAW, A XI, no. 115, p. 315; *NAGB*, p. 34.

[148] Challoner, *MMP*, pp. 323–9; ABSJ, CP (Richard Newport); Jeaffreson, *MCR*, II, pp. 207–8 (for the proceedings against Scot); J. G. O'Leary, 'The Privy Council and Recusants 1559–1598', *Essex Recusant* 7 (1965), pp. 101–4, at p. 102.

[149] Challoner, *MMP*, p. 327; G. Donaldson, *Scotland: James V to James VII* (1965), p. 121. The story about Newport's trial came from Richard Broughton on 20 June 1612 (AAW, A XI, no. 103, p. 289) and via a letter of Edward Bennett on the same date. Bennett said that the lord chief justice had berated Newport about the 'first treason against the king plotted by secular priests', presumably a reference to the Bye Plot. This had provoked Newport's reply that the 'puritans and Protestants had set on a fellow with a pistol to have killed him and her [Mary Stuart], but that miraculously the powder would take no fire'. Bennett added that 'they threaten that [at] the next sessions there shall be three more called to their trial, but they got so little by the execution of the last that I think they will not be too forward in haste to bring forth any more': AAW, A XI, no. 105, p. 293; Questier, *C&C*, p. 284.

[150] *HMCS*, XVII, p. 626; for Lord Mordaunt and the Gunpowder Plot, see Questier, *C&C*, p. 285. For Newport's imprisonment and the proceedings against him, see Bowler, *London Sessions Records 1605–1685*, pp. 73, 74, 76, 79.

MID-JACOBEAN CONFESSIONAL POLITICS AND ANTI-POPERY   409

moment they emerged from prison until the moment they expired and he uttered threats at the executioner lest he cut the ropes before they were fully dead so as to cut out the entrails and heart while half alive'. Actually, another source (Richard Broughton's letter of 20 June 1612) said that only Scot had been allowed to hang until he expired. Newport, by contrast, 'suffered last and was…quartered half alive', either because of his defiance at trial or because 'he had not' the 'money to fee the hangman and give away as the other [Scot] did, who was not cut down until he was fully dead'. According to Carvajal, though, it was Scot who was eviscerated while he was still alive. Scot spoke 'of his debt to Spain both for the salvation of his soul and the crown of martyrdom which he expected to enjoy shortly and he promised to pray for the destruction' of Philip III's 'enemies and the increase of the glory' of his 'States so that the holy Catholic faith might be exalted and defended'. For his part, Newport declared that 'it was twenty-two years ago in the same place', Tyburn, that he received the 'light as he witnessed the martyrdom of two religious'.[151] By 23 June/3 July, Anthony Champney had seen a letter written to a friend in Paris by a Frenchman who witnessed the executions. It added that Arundel, who had been 'present at their execution…afterwards spoke thereof to the king with admiration both of their constancy and innocence'. James simply retorted that they should have stayed abroad.[152]

Carvajal saw this as all of a piece with the recent persecution of the Vaux family and she was certain that it was attributable to the spite 'they feel at the marriages of our princes', that is, the recent agreement concluded for the Franco-Spanish double dynastic match. Carvajal took the opportunity to vent her own dislike of Princess Elizabeth—she was 'an out-and-out heretic and badly brought up at that, with something of a reputation for being frivolous'. What was more, her features

---

[151] Loomie, SJC, I, pp. 194–6; Anstr., I, p. 249; AAW, A XI, no. 103, p. 289, no. 105, p. 293 (a slightly different account by Edward Bennett: at Tyburn, 'Mr Newport told them that being a heretic in opinion, and coming to that place to see the execution of a seminary priest, [he] was so moved therewith that presently [he] resolved to become [a] Catholic and [a] priest'); Redworth, LLC, II, p. 207. For the version in Challoner (derived in part from Weldon's 'Memorials'), see Challoner, MMP, pp. 324–8. It is not exactly clear which previous executions Newport meant since Tyburn did not see the execution of two priests together in 1590. He may have meant the hanging of Edward Jones in Fleet Street and Anthony Middleton at Clerkenwell on 6 May 1590. Viscount Montague was also present on 30 May 1612 at Tyburn, but he does not seem to have intervened in the way that Arundel did: McClure, LJC, I, p. 355; Questier, C&C, pp. 284, 371. For another report of the trials of Newport and Scot, see ch. 18 of 'Chaos Anglicanum, et Lumen Veritatis Tenebris Mendaciorum Oppositum…', rough draft in BL, Royal Appendix MS 81; there are brief extracts of other chapters in AAW, A XII, no. 254, pp. 589–96; J. Raymond, 'Les Libelles Internationaux à la Période Moderne: Etude Préliminaire', Etudes Epistémè 26 (2014).

[152] AAW, A XI, no. 113, p. 311. Within a few weeks, on 21/31 July 1612, Champney was writing directly to Pope Paul V in order to rebut the accusation that he favoured the 1606 oath and to claim that he was of the same opinion as the martyrs Drury and Cadwallader: AWCBC, pp. 1767–8, citing ASV, Barb. Lat., 8620, fo. 7ʳ. On 18/28 August, Champney noted that Thomas More had written to ask for longer narratives of Catholics' hardships. Champney promised More that he would send him the Frenchman's letter, though Champney believed that 'it is already in Rome [and] turned into Italian': AAW, A XI, no. 141, p. 391.

410   CATHOLICS AND TREASON

were 'growing coarser despite her not yet being twenty'.[153] Carvajal described in horrific and absolutely stomach-churning detail the recovery of the remains of Newport and Scot.[154] One of the embassy servants found the decomposing remnants of an executed felon spattered all over him as he tried to pull aside the body.[155] Carvajal concluded her letter on 11/21 June 1612 by saying that 'at 11 o'clock last night I went in a coach belonging to' the ambassador himself, Alonso Velasco, 'with the two holy bodies' of the martyrs 'and two of my companions to take them somewhere more secure' than the embassy. In the embassy, however, they had been received in the 'entrance hall...in procession with a cross and burning candles and many garlands and flowers', which, Carvajal said, 'we had scattered all the way to the chapel...where there were also many candles and flowers'. This was done 'with such secrecy that no one in the embassy knew, except for the coachman and the porter'.[156]

As some English commentators interpreted it, these proceedings against Scot and Newport signalled the start of yet another major thrust into the body of Catholic opinion, though perhaps, as much as anything, they were calculated to reassure the king's Calvinist friends in Europe that he could be relied upon to make the forthcoming Palatine marriage treaty work. Richard Broughton had written on 20 June 1612 that, shortly before the execution of the two priests, and now that the earl of Salisbury was dead, Abbot was 'on his knees before the king' in order to demand that 'all cruel laws might be executed with...severity upon Catholics'. Lord Vaux, who stood condemned in praemunire and was gaoled in the king's bench prison, had offered to take the oath 'according to the king's interpretation in his books...concerning only temporal allegiance', but this was 'not...admitted'. Leading gentry were being summoned to London and imprisoned.[157] On 5 July 1612 Broughton said that clergy in Newgate were being badly treated (it appeared also that someone had tried to poison them) and Abbot had 'been...[on] his knees' yet again before James in order to demand more executions.[158] On 7/17 July 1612 Champney in Paris reported that 'Mr Widdrington', that is, the Benedictine monk Thomas Preston, 'says that the king' himself 'was

---

[153] Redworth, *LLC*, II, pp. 204–5. The Franco-Spanish match was solemnized in April 1612, and the marriage contract was signed in August: *HMCD*, III, pp. 352, 357.

[154] Redworth, *LLC*, II, pp. 206–7.   [155] Redworth, *The She-Apostle*, p. 211.

[156] Redworth, *LLC*, II, pp. 206–7. For Carvajal's collection of relics, from these two martyrs, for Rodrigo Calderón, see Redworth, *LLC*, II, pp. 212, 219. In her letter of 9/19 October to the marchioness of Caracena, she described the recovery of the remains of the martyrs ('ten or twelve helped to dig up the bodies'), and how they were brought to the embassy. Then 'devoutly, with a mixture of joy and pain, we...put' the martyrs' body parts 'on the carpet before the altar, where they were covered with a large new crimson cloth...with many fragrant flowers sprinkled on top and, kneeling down, we prayed there a while'. The remains were cleaned, 'anointed...with strong aromatic spices and buried...in thick lead caskets': Redworth, *LLC*, II, p. 248.

[157] AAW, A XI, no. 103, p. 289; but for the restitution in April 1613 to Lord Vaux of his forfeited estates, see G. Anstruther, *Vaux of Harrowden: A Recusant Family* (Newport, 1953), p. 419.

[158] AAW, A XI, no. 104, p. 291; see also *NAGB*, p. 174 (Benjamin Norton to Thomas More, 9 July 1612: AAW, A XI, no. 118, p. 323).

MID-JACOBEAN CONFESSIONAL POLITICS AND ANTI-POPERY   411

displeased at the execution of the two priests when he heard how they died with so great affection to his service in all dutiful allegiance', even though they would not take the actual oath of allegiance.[159] James would have been just as disturbed by the reaction abroad. From Flanders his ambassador, William Trumbull, had sent word at the beginning of July that the recent executions had caused the 'Jesuits and malicious fugitives' there to 'calumniate' royal justice and to affirm 'publicly in their profane pulpits and elsewhere that those malefactors were condemned and put to death only for their religion and not for any offence against the State', a claim which Trumbull had done his best to refute.[160] In Louvain, on 30 June/10 July, George Russell had recorded that there had arrived 'many relations...of the martyrdom of the two priests, whereof public sermons have been made in the parish churches and university to excite the people's devotion to resolution and the like'.[161] Russell further reported on 21/31 July that news of the alleged poisoning attempt had arrived at Louvain and that there 'grew, upon this', the belief 'that the archbishop of Canterbury did solicit the king to rid the land of as many' clergy as were in prison.[162]

The stories generated by the recent harshness against Catholics kept on coming. Benjamin Norton wrote on 9 July 1612 to Thomas More, and undoubtedly to others as well, that 'in the western seas' there had been 'a stream of blood which many have seen and dipped their hands in it'; a 'lord of the council and a knight of my acquaintance' had said that the tale was true. There had, said Norton, also been a number of Catholics who could not be regarded as a threat to anyone but who were being hunted from pillar to post—including one unfortunate woman who had tried, 'under a tub', to hide herself and her child from the justices when she was summoned to take the oath and, 'what with cold and fear and I know not what else', she perished.[163] Eight days later, Edward Bennett had his own version of the story about the stream of blood observed in the sea. 'The very day that Mr Newport and Mr Scot were executed...in the west part about Plymouth for three miles the sea appeared as red as blood, whereat, the people wondering, they took of the water in tubs, wherein standing but a while it congealed like putrefied blood and did cast such a stench that no man could abide the smell.'[164]

As with other recent victims of the regime, the memory of these two martyrs was contested among Catholics in London and elsewhere. Carvajal had no doubt that Scot and Newport belonged metaphorically, as indeed after the event they did physically, to her and her Jesuit, Spanish, and Hispanophile friends. The Jesuit Robert Jones wrote on 10 June 1612 that he had been an eyewitness at the executions of Scot and Newport and that Scot 'always was addicted unto us and loved

---

[159] AAW, A XI, no. 121, p. 329.   [160] PRO, SP 77/10, fo. 195ʳ.   [161] HMCD, III, p. 328.
[162] HMCD, III, p. 341.   [163] NAGB, pp. 172, 174.   [164] NAGB, p. 177.

412 CATHOLICS AND TREASON

us very dearly and, a little before his arraignment, he wrote a letter unto all the Society here, highly commending our labours in God's Church'.[165]

For his part, the archpriest George Birkhead was still complaining that, by sticking to the letter of the papal breves against the oath, he and his friends were taking the rap and, moreover, were suffering reputational damage because of the seeming divisions among the Catholic clergy. As he wrote to More on 3 August 1612, 'the enemy has set us one against another, and laughs us to scorn, and cries out in pulpits and everywhere against our want of charity'. In other words, without unity in the face of the godless oath, everything would unravel. Of course, if there had been a grant of episcopal authority to one of the secular clergy, 'this great disorder might have been easily prevented, which now will not be compassed but with abundance of martyrs' blood'. The 'religious are reputed to be as backward as mine, but yet can conceal it better. Some of them' had previously been 'most earnest against the oath' but were 'now exceeding cold'. This raised the suspicion that they had 'some secret direction' from Rome 'to bear with men's frailties for saving of their goods. If this shift had been used in the primitive Church, never had there been so many martyrs'.[166]

Catholic observers were now presented with a rather baffling spectacle. Laid end to end, the tendering of the godless oath, the harassment of people such as the Vaux matriarch, the arrest and imprisonment and, here and there, the executions of priests, did look like a persecution.[167] But, even as the Spanish diplomat Zúñiga arrived in July 1612 with the offer of a Spanish match for Princess Elizabeth, there were those in the regime who wanted to stop, if there was one, a

---

[165] ARSJ, Anglia 37, fo. 114ᵛ; see also ARSJ, Anglia 31/ii, fos 456ʳ–8ʳ. For transcripts of two letters written by Scot, one to his Benedictine confrères, and the second (dated 27 May 1612) to the members of the Society, see ABSJ, Collectanea M, pp. 206ª–7ª. This second letter was 'directed chiefly' to the Jesuits Nicholas Hart and John Percy in the Gatehouse—they were the two household chaplains who had been arrested in late 1611 along with Elizabeth Vaux. Scot had trained for ordination in Spain; he was not one of the Cassinese, some of whom, like Thomas Preston, were overtly loyalist. Scot's two letters were sent out to Rome, it seems, by Richard Blount SJ: ABSJ, Collectanea M, p. 207ª. But, since Scot was a Benedictine and Newport was a secular, it was also possible to take this double martyrdom as a sign that, despite all the trouble in the past between secular priests and other sorts of clergy, there was the potential for unity between them. Thus the monk John Bradshaw commented on 1 July 1612 (in a letter to Thomas More in Rome) that 'their great resolution and constancy has edified all the world'. It was 'now a usual thing for a monk and a secular priest to be hanged together. They were drawn to Tyburn both on one hurdle. Father Maurus [Scot] was carried first unto the cart who took Mr Newport by the hand to take him up. They embraced' one another 'saying *haec est vera fraternitas*.... God who has unified that clergy [i.e. the seculars] and us in this work of the conversion of our country and also in martyrdom will have us to unite in heart and affection here that in heaven we may be never separated': AAW, A XI, no. 109, p. 301. For the narratives of the executions of Scot and Newport retained in the secular clergy agent's papers, see AAW, A XI, nos 88–91, 97; see also AVCAU, Liber 1577 (Anstruther Martyrs File): Biblioteca Vallicelliana, Rome, N 23, fos 167ʳ, 194ʳ, 198ʳ.

[166] AAW, A XI, no. 131, pp. 351, 352.

[167] Edward Bennett commented on 5 September 1612 that 'continually they take priests' and 'there be now in Newgate some twenty-four, and ten or a dozen in the Gatehouse besides them that be in the Clink': AAW, A XI, no. 144, p. 397.

MID-JACOBEAN CONFESSIONAL POLITICS AND ANTI-POPERY   413

surge of oppression of Catholics.[168] Henry Howard, earl of Northampton, may have had no sympathy for Catholic separatists, but he cannot have wanted to see anything that looked like a victory for his puritan enemies. When in July/August 1612 there was a bout of aggressive tendering of the oath in the provinces, particularly in Oxfordshire, Northampton remarked to Viscount Rochester that the 'late sharp proceedings had brought many to church'.[169] But on 13/23 October, Anthony Champney in Paris understood that, although 'many ladies and other gentlewomen' had 'been taken and committed', most of them had been freed now that Northampton had, as it seemed, succeeded to the earl of Salisbury's authority.[170]

None of this meant, however, that James would step back from concluding the Anglo-Palatine marriage for the young Princess Elizabeth. The word was also that Prince Henry would insist on an explicitly Protestant marriage for himself, quite contrary to James's wishes.[171] The Venetian embassy in London had, during August 1612, picked up news of a Catholic assassination conspiracy against the king. There were, according to the Venetian diplomat Foscarini, searches for arms and armour in Lincolnshire and Lancashire.[172] One silver lining for those of a Catholic persuasion was provided by the sight in London of Mary Stuart's honourable reinterment in Westminster Abbey.[173] The reburial evoked a euphoric reaction from Carvajal on 29 October/8 November 1612—James 'had done an excellent thing', perhaps 'for the first time in his life'.[174] Northampton was similarly enthusiastic. It reminded him of the former 'bedlam courses of those times' as they were pursued by the vile Sir Robert Cecil and Lord Burghley 'in inflaming the queen's ears', though they covered themselves by 'the passions of Walsingham'. They—the nasty little hypocrites (very 'little' in Robert Cecil's case)—had changed their tune about the House of Stuart somewhat late in the day.[175] Robert Pett

---

[168] For Zúñiga's embassy's purposes, including trade issues and the offer of Philip III as a husband for Princess Elizabeth—as some thought, to prevent the palatine marriage, see *CSPV 1610–13*, pp. 329–30, 398, 402, 403, 405–6, 408, 427–8; *HMCD*, III, p. 374. Zúñiga's request for the release of the Jesuit William Baldwin (and other clergy) was refused in October 1612: *CSPV 1610–13*, p. 440. Baldwin had been detained in the Rhineland Palatinate in mid-1610 and, at Sir Ralph Winwood's direction, had been brought to imprisonment in England: Sawyer, *WM*, III, pp. 210, 211, 212; PRO, SP 78/56, fo. 196^r; Loomie, *SJC*, I, p. 161; *CSPV 1610–13*, pp. 6, 13–14, 15–16, 24, 50, 58; PRO, SP 14/57/46, 64; PRO, SP 14/58/2; *HMCB*, I, pp. 104, 111; *HMCD*, II, pp. 314, 358, 376.

[169] *NAGB*, pp. 189–90; PRO, SP 14/70/54, fo. 108^r.   [170] AAW, A XI, no. 187, p. 543.

[171] Adams, PC, p. 214.

[172] *CSPV 1610–13*, pp. 409, 419; see also *HMCD*, III, pp. 383–4. On 25 September 1612 Sir Thomas Edmondes claimed that 'sundry priests and Jesuits' were coming across from the Continent, and there were 'some newly gone from Rheims... and, as it is suspected, upon some lewd and dangerous practice': PRO, SP 78/60, fo. 109^r.

[173] For a major study of the ideological significance of the reinterment, see P. Sherlock, 'The Monuments of Elizabeth Tudor and Mary Stuart: King James and the Manipulation of Memory', *JBS* 46 (2007), pp. 263–89.

[174] Redworth, *LLC*, II, p. 265, 272–3.   [175] *CSPD 1611–18*, p. 152; PRO, SP 14/71/16, fo. 24^v.

414   CATHOLICS AND TREASON

remembered how the bells had rung 'all night for joy at the cutting off of' Mary Stuart's 'head'. There had, it seemed, now been a 'change of' the 'times'.[176]

The Execution of John Almond and the Uncertainties of Mid-Jacobean Politics

Yet the black cloud of the Anglo-Palatine match would not go away. Luisa de Carvajal's newsletter to Joseph Creswell of 27 November/7 December 1612 conveyed her feelings of intense nausea at the Protestant Mexican-wave reaction to the elector palatine's visit and forthcoming marriage to Princess Elizabeth, despite the untimely recent death of Prince Henry. What made it even worse was that, on 5 December, a priest called John Almond was then executed at Tyburn. Carvajal had reported that 'seven or eight of the twenty priests held in Newgate' had recently 'escaped...by means of false keys'. Others, however, including Almond, had refused to flee.[177] The Newgate keeper had been made to look ridiculous and negligent.[178] He soon got his revenge by informing against Almond. The word was that Almond's 'enemy Mr Price, the keeper of Newgate', had 'deposed against him that he heard him say that he had power to absolve [some]one [even] though he should kill the king; but Mr Almond upon his oath denied this and said that he only had said' that 'through true penance Ravaillac' might be 'saved'.[179]

Almond had been arraigned on 3 December 1612.[180] Bishop John King, who had been the prime mover in the slaughtering of George Napper, subjected Almond to the same kind of close interrogation over the oath that George Abbot had used with John Roberts. Like Roberts, Almond said he would take any oath as long as it contained no more than mere allegiance. Almond himself pointed to what he

---

[176]   AAW, A XI, no. 226, p. 654.

[177]   Redworth, *LLC*, II, p. 281. For Almond's arrest earlier in the year (and for his refusal to take the oath), see *NAGB*, pp. 148–9, 152. Almond had absconded from gaol back in late 1608, along with John Roberts: Redworth, *LLC*, II, p. 51.

[178]   Redworth, *LLC*, II, p. 281. Challoner's account of Almond is derived from Knaresborough's manuscripts, based in part, it appears, on Almond's own report of his trial (Challoner, *MMP*, pp. 329–38; Kn., II, pp. 161–74), and on the account of the execution set out in Kn., II, pp. 175–99, 'copied from an old MS from Paris, ex collect. D. Norris', for which see also the version in Butler's papers: ABP, pp. 497–505.

[179]   ABSJ, Anglia III, no. 118 (Richard Banks [William Bartlet] to 'Signore Luka [Thomas Owen?] 5 December 1612). Others claimed that it was the prison keeper's wife who asked Almond the fatal question and it was George Abbot who procured his death: ABSJ, Anglia III, no. 119. Richard Sheldon said that another cleric, a Jesuit called Michael Freeman, had also defended 'Ravaillac that in such a kind of repentance he might have true and Christian contrition': Sheldon, *The Motives*, sig. Dd^r. Almond was probably known to be favourable to the Society of Jesus; see his letter of 16 April 1604 to Robert Persons: Pollen, *AEM*, pp. 173–5 (ABSJ, Anglia III, no. 43; ABSJ, Collectanea N/ii, pp. 58–9). For Freeman's remark, reported back in May 1610—just after the murder of Henry IV—that he hoped to see Mass said in St Paul's, see BL, Lansdowne MS 154, fo. 143^r; *HMCS*, XXI, p. 221.

[180]   ABSJ, Anglia III, no. 117; cf. AAW, A XI, no. 220, p. 625. The date of the arraignment is not completely certain.

MID-JACOBEAN CONFESSIONAL POLITICS AND ANTI-POPERY 415

took to be the offending clause of the 1606 oath and said that the bishop had perjured himself in taking it, specifically via the words, 'And I do further swear that I do from my heart abhor, detest, and abjure as impious and heretical, this damnable doctrine and position, that princes excommunicated and deprived by the pope may be deposed'. For 'if in taking it you abjure that position as heretical which is not heretical, then is it perjury and falsehood to take it', even though Almond himself said that the deposing power was not essential to the pope's authority.[181]

Carvajal's account of the trial admitted that the courtroom proceedings were marked by a good deal of vituperation on both sides. Almond had taunted Bishop King, whom Carvajal described as 'swollen and purple with rage, like an aubergine': 'you in the white sleeves, my friend, wearing a surplice. What business have you standing there, passing judgment on unjust cases which have nothing to do with you on either a human or a spiritual level? You are neither a priest not a bishop, let alone a judge.'[182] In these circumstances, it was not surprising that John King's ideological ally, Archbishop Abbot, should then have exploited Almond's controversial views about regicide. As Almond's confrère Anthony Champney related it to Thomas More, Abbot had asked Almond 'what he would do to one who should confess unto him that he had killed a king, whether he would absolve him or no', and Almond had answered in the affirmative, that is, if the king-killer was 'penitent'; and 'this', said Champney, was 'thought to have been the occasion of his death'.[183]

Almond was hanged at Tyburn only twenty-two days before the betrothal of the elector palatine to Princess Elizabeth. (See Figure 12.2.) It was not hard for people to make the connection. Champney later remarked with bitterness that, whatever the formal basis for the prosecution and the evidence presented in the court, Almond had been put to death merely to please the elector palatine, that is, as part of the cynical process of public diplomacy and spin necessary to give credibility to the Anglo-Palatine marriage.[184] Carvajal urged Calderón that there was still time to stop the marriage. She also said that 'they had let it be known' that Almond's execution would be delayed. As she interpreted it, the 'heretics were fearful that his death might inspire the people'. In the end, Almond 'was taken out

[181] Pollen, *AEM*, pp. 176–7, 179; Challoner, *MMP*, pp. 331–2 (out of Kn., II, pp. 162–73; for the transcript in Alban Butler's papers, see ABPFC, fo. 37ʳ⁻ᵛ); ABSJ, Anglia III, no. 117.

[182] Redworth, *LLC*, II, pp. 292–3. Isaac Wake jotted down on 17 December 1612 that Almond's 'impudence at the time of his arraignment was sufficient to condemn him, if he had not been guilty of treason': PRO, SP 99/11, fo. 179ʳ. There are several accounts of Almond's trial and/or martyrdom retained among the manuscripts formerly at Stonyhurst: ABSJ, Anglia III, nos 115–17, 118, 120–1; see also ARSJ, Anglia 31/i, fos 1ʳ–6ʳ, 387ʳ–8ʳ. For the narratives of Almond kept by the secular clergy, see AAW, A XI, nos 219, 221, 223, 225, 227, 228; and especially AAW, A XIV, no. 61, pp. 213–14. For the consensus among Catholics that the crown had offered no evidence that Almond had been ordained, see AAW, A XI, no. 228, p. 658; Redworth, *LLC*, II, p. 292.

[183] AAW, A XII, no. 9, p. 21.

[184] AAW, A XII, no. 34, p. 76.

Figure 12.2 Newsletter concerning John Almond's trial and execution, d.1612 (reproduced with the permission of the British province of the Society of Jesus).

so early that day that it was still not light'. But news spread quickly and, 'when the martyr reached' Tyburn, 'he found over 2,000 people waiting for him'. He 'was very well known in London and had touched the souls of many of the young people who worked in shops, as well as people high and low, of every estate'.[185] Edward Bennett told a similar story 'out of a letter a gentleman wrote unto his friend'. Here it was claimed that 'it was given forth' that Almond 'should not die till Tuesday following, being the 8th', but, 'on Saturday morning…before six, he was drawn forth and' was 'executed all alone'. At the Tyburn gallows he showed extraordinary 'stoutness and invincible courage', challenging the hangman to 'cut me in piecemeal and use me as St Lawrence was, for my cause is so good that if I had a thousand lives I would give them all for my Saviour'. He also, in no uncertain terms, denounced the Protestant clergy there. He 'asked the ministers why they went not abroad amongst the gentiles to urge their faith' and told them that their 'faith was no better than' that of 'the Turks'.[186]

According to Jesuit sources, Almond declared the limitations on the king's power to make laws which contradicted the law of God.[187] He repeated his opinion about regicide, repentance, and the oath. When barracked by 'one of the preachers' (there were, said Carvajal, three of them at Tyburn on that morning)

---

[185] Redworth, *LLC*, II, pp. 295, 292. John Thorpe recorded that, 'to avoid the concourse of people, it was reported that' Almond 'would not be executed until Monday': ABSJ, A V, no. 8 (unfoliated).

[186] AAW, A XI, no. 225, p. 650; see also AAW, A XI, no. 228, p. 658.

[187] Pollen, *AEM*, pp. 186–7. The narrative in Pollen, *AEM*, pp. 184–93, is taken from ABSJ, Anglia III, no. 120.

MID-JACOBEAN CONFESSIONAL POLITICS AND ANTI-POPERY   417

that he 'held it no sin to kill the king', he shouted back that this was indeed a 'wicked and abominable' sin. When heckled further that 'if a man should determine to kill the king, the pope would forgive him that sin', Almond absolutely denied it, though he reiterated his view that, even for the crime of killing a king, 'hearty repentance, contrition and satisfaction' were all possible. Here the unnamed Protestant minister was forced to agree in principle but said, as far as regicide was concerned, 'although it were true doctrine, yet it was an ill instance, and dangerous to speak before a community'.[188]

In one account, written or copied by Richard Broughton, it is asserted that Almond 'protested his loyalty to King James and lamented the death' of the prince of Wales, 'wishing that the king might have many more heirs male to inherit these kingdoms and countries'.[189] A Jesuit narrative of the execution insisted, conventionally but perhaps accurately, that Almond's courage made an impression even on 'Protestants themselves in so much that they spoke exceedingly well of him and blamed the bench for condemning him'. Some who were formerly 'so stout in their' Protestant 'religion' now began 'to stagger'.[190] Allegedly one Protestant spectator went straight from Tyburn to the Gatehouse prison and 'desired to speak with a priest' and was instructed in the Roman Catholic faith by the recently imprisoned Jesuit John Blackfan, who had been attached to the Spanish embassy. This became public knowledge and Archbishop Abbot reacted with predictable fury.[191]

Isaac Wake said that, at Almond's 'execution, though it was early in the morning to avoid concourse of people, there were observed so many papists present as

[188] Pollen, *AEM*, pp. 189–90; Redworth, *LLC*, II, p. 292; Challoner, *MMP*, p. 336; Kn., II, p. 183. For a narrative of the execution by John Jackson which emphasizes Almond's loyalism, see *NAGB*, pp. 206–8. Knaresborough's and Broughton's sources agree that one of the ministers who was present was called Walker (perhaps George Walker, ordained in June 1612, who was known for his clashes with other Protestant clergy over doctrines of justification): Kn., II, p. 190; AAW, A XIV, no. 61, p. 214; *ODNB, sub* Walker, George (article by D. Como). One of those who had disputed with Almond in Newgate before the execution was James Ussher: Pollen, *AEM*, p. 193.

[189] AAW, A XIV, no. 61, p. 214. This story is, however, recited also in ABSJ, Anglia III, no. 116.

[190] ABSJ, Anglia III, no. 117; AVCAU, Scr. 36/12/2a–b. Almond's witness was contested as much as that of other recent martyrs. Carvajal had sent a servant with linen sheets in the hope of mopping up Almond's blood. There was almost a confrontation between her agents and other Catholics who wanted to appropriate his remains; see Redworth, *LLC*, II, p. 293; G. Redworth, *The She Apostle*, p. 210. A relic of Almond was taken to the family chapel of the count of Gondomar in Spain: J. A. Graffius, ' "Bullworks against the Furie of Heresie": Relics, Material Culture and the Spiritual and Cultural Formation of the Sodality of St Omers English Jesuit College 1593–1650' (PhD, Aberdeen, 2018), p. 272, citing B. Camm, *Forgotten Shrines* . . . (1910), p. 367. It was said that Almond's heart had leapt from the fire and came into the possession of Richard Blount SJ, who kept it 'with the reverence due to so precious a relic': ABSJ, Anglia III, no. 117 (Foley, *RSJ*, VII/2, p. 1381); AVCAU, Scr. 36/12/2a–b. But Almond also gave his voice for the appointment of a bishop or bishops in England: AAW, A XI, nos 217 and 218, pp. 619–20. Thomas More, in Rome, was subsequently urged by John Jackson to deny the story concerning Almond's heart: AAW, A XIII, no. 131, p. 331. In January 1613, George Birkhead predicted that the usual suspects would talk down Almond's 'extraordinary zeal and courage': AAW, A XII, no. 4, p. 9; see also AAW, A XII, no. 61, p. 129.

[191] Pollen, *AEM*, p. 193. For Blackfan's enthusiasm for Luisa de Carvajal's evangelical fervour, see ARSJ, Anglia 37, fo. 111[r–v].

418   CATHOLICS AND TREASON

that one of them had the boldness to speak aloud—"let us rescue him for we are strong enough". It is possible, if what Wake said was true, that Tyburn witnessed on that day a kind of Catholic-centred London demonstration against the palatine marriage. Wake thought that the privy council, faced with 'this and other such like audaciousness', had ordered the dispersal of 'some multitudes that' had begun 'to assemble dangerously in many places of this land, particularly in Lancashire, in Wales by Milford Haven, and on the sea coast of Dorset and Hampshire'.[192]

One can see, therefore, how Almond's execution might well have been intended to send an unmistakable signal about the limits of royal tolerance. But court Calvinists were not having everything their own way. Notoriously, Prince Henry's chaplain, Lewis Baily, had preached an inflammatory sermon at St Martin-in-the-Fields on 15 November 1612—shortly after the prince's death (rumoured to have been by poison, administered, some believed, by Northampton) and only twenty days before Almond's execution.[193] Baily, like others, would have been aware that many Catholics were not grief-stricken at the prince's passing. Baily claimed that Henry had, about a month before he died, told him in confidence that 'religion lay a-bleeding'. This was no surprise, said Baily, when 'divers councillors hear Mass in the morning and then go to a court sermon and so to the council, and then tell their wives what passes, and they carry it to their Jesuits and confessors'.[194] As one Catholic newsletter described it, Baily said that these clergy then wrote what they knew directly to the pope. This newsletter added that Baily 'spoke other words aiming at my lord of Northampton, for which he was called before the council and committed'. Baily was told to recant his words, which he did rather unenthusiastically. 'Then was it the common speech that' George Abbot 'had set' Baily and other preachers 'a-work' and that there was a 'public enmity between' Abbot and Northampton although, on the 'Sunday following', Abbot backtracked in council and professed his love and respect for Northampton. Presumably no one believed him, though he went through the same rigmarole again in star chamber on the following Tuesday.[195]

---

[192]   PRO, SP 99/11, fo. 179ʳ.

[193]   McClure, *LJC*, I, p. 392; Adams, PC, p. 229; A. Bellany and T. Cogswell, *The Murder of King James I* (2015), pp. 181–3.

[194]   McClure, *LJC*, I, p. 392; ABSJ, Anglia III, no. 119; Adams, PC, p. 229; A. J. Loomie, 'A Jacobean Crypto-Catholic: Lord Wotton', *Catholic Historical Review* 53 (1967), pp. 328–45, at p. 328.

[195]   ABSJ, Anglia III, no. 119. The earl of Northampton had already struck back hard in November 1612 with a star chamber libel action against selected detractors, notably Sir Richard Cox. Cox had said that, during Northampton's lord wardenry of the Cinque Ports, more priests had passed through the ports than before, and that Northampton had written to Cardinal Bellarmine to ask him to ignore his denunciation of Henry Garnet SJ at the Jesuit's trial in 1606: L. Peck, *Northampton: Patronage and Policy at the Court of James I* (1982), pp. 81–3, 235; McClure, *LJC*, I, p. 394; ABSJ, Anglia III, no. 118. As John Chamberlain had phrased it on 26 November, shortly before Almond was arraigned, the privy council had been busy 'all this week in examining certain persons' about the rumours of the quarrels between Northampton and Abbot. Chamberlain noted in this newsletter that 'on Sunday night seven seminary priests broke out of Newgate', though, as we saw, they left Almond behind. George Birkhead also described, on 5 December, the gaol break and the attack on Northampton 'as a favourer of papists',

MID-JACOBEAN CONFESSIONAL POLITICS AND ANTI-POPERY 419

But another newsletter said that Baily had 'railed both at the king and the State in the pulpit' and asserted not just that there were crypto-Catholic councillors but also that 'there were 6,000 Catholics' in London who were 'in hand with a more dangerous plot than the powder treason'.[196] It got worse when, as John Chamberlain related on 17 December 1612, Baily was ordered to 'explain' his accusation at the same place, St Martin's, where he preached the original sermon, but, 'in a very great audience, he made the matter much more plain, relating the whole matter as it passed at the council table, with justifying and offering to make proof or bring his authors for what he had said'.[197]

The Stuart court, of course, could not afford to present a disunited front. The official line was that the threat to civil peace still came from Catholics. At this time, on the surface, the court's big beasts were following team orders.[198] Rumours of civil disturbances resulted in the issuing of directives that Catholics should have their arms and armour taken away from them.[199] This was highly controversial in places such as Northamptonshire, where Sir Thomas Brudenell protested his personal loyalty to the king, whatever his own family's proclivities in religion.[200] George Birkhead remarked on 2 February 1613 that the 'Catholics are falsely thought to be enemies' to the Anglo-Palatine marriage; but the 'common people' were entirely 'persuaded that the Spaniards and [the] Turk join together to hinder it'. This was why the 'justices in every shire' were seizing Catholics' weaponry.[201]

The immediate upshot of this royal instruction concerning Catholic arms and armour was a buzz that Catholics were going to be massacred and, in effect, that there would be hundreds if not thousands of martyrs. The rumour 'held so violent for three days that nothing else was expected amongst the common people'.[202]

---

but said that 'the contrivers were thought to be priests and Jesuits which was much exaggerated by the lords and yet the accusers were all puritans'. Birkhead believed that both Almond and George Fisher were 'like to go to the pot', though he was unaware that Almond was being hanged on the very morning that he wrote this letter: McClure, *LJC*, I, p. 394; AAW, A XI, no. 220, p. 625.

[196] ABSJ, Anglia III, no. 114.

[197] McClure, *LJC*, I, p. 396.

[198] Richard Banks claimed that, 'if there were any disgusts between' Northampton and Abbot or between the earl of Pembroke and Viscount Rochester, 'they are all appeased, so that with united forces they may join to the depression of papistry': ABSJ, Anglia III, no. 118.

[199] See e.g. ABSJ, Anglia III, no. 119; McClure, *LJC*, I, p. 410.

[200] ABSJ, Anglia III, no. 119; *HMCS*, XXI, p. 221; *HMCD*, IV, pp. 23, 28, 31; *HMCB*, I, p. 240; *HMCB*, III, pp. 152, 156–7, 158–60; Sawyer, *WM*, III, p. 429; PRO, SP 99/12, fo. 64ʳ (*CSPD 1611–18*, p. 168); *CSPD 1611–18*, p. 176 (Sir Thomas Edmondes to Sir Thomas Lake, 16 March 1613). For the council's orders that Catholics should be disarmed, see also *NAGB*, pp. 211–12; AAW, A XI, no. 27 (28 February 1613), incorporating a letter to the same effect of 10 January 1613 (printed in TD, IV, pp. clxxxviii–ix); for the response in Northamptonshire, see also *HMCB*, III, pp. 148–51, 153, 161. For Foscarini's analysis of which Catholics were being targeted for disarming, see *CSPV 1610–13*, p. 491; see also AAW, A XII, no. 112, p. 245. For official clarifications of who exactly was to have their weapons taken from them, see BL, Additional MS 39245, fo. 10ʳ⁻ᵛ; AAW, A XI, no. 28, p. 71 (29 February 1613); *HMCB*, I, p. 244; see also B. W. Quintrell, 'The Practice and Problems of Recusant Disarming, 1585–1641', *RH* 17 (1985), pp. 208–22, at pp. 208, 210–11.

[201] *NAGB*, p. 211 (AAW, A XII, no. 29, p. 68).

[202] ABSJ, Anglia III, no. 119.

420   CATHOLICS AND TREASON

William Trumbull had been informed from London by James Carre, via a letter of 20 January 1613, that there had been a 'great terror' among the Catholics 'from a report that the king was determined, in one night, to cut all the papists' throats in England'. Nine days later Carre said that 'the rumour of a pretended massacre of the Catholics' was growing and made 'a murmur among Protestants' who had 'Catholic friends'.[203] On 31 January, down in Sussex, Benjamin Norton narrated how the JPs there had been depriving recusant Catholics of their 'armour and weapons which made many to think that they intended a massacre'. Norton believed that this exercise was also intended to make the world believe that 'something might be attempted by recusants against the State when they are in their chiefest jollity... at the marriage' of Elizabeth and Frederick, for the wedding celebrations were shortly to go ahead. This would be a reprise in other words, although with the confessional labels reversed, of what had happened in Paris on St Bartholomew's Day in 1572.[204] On 11 February, John Chamberlain repeated the stories about some 'intended treachery'. He mentioned that the city of London had raised 500 musketeers as a guard for the court.[205]

Seven days after the marriage took place, presided over by Archbishop Abbot, Norton was still panicking about the rumours along the south coast that Catholics would go into rebellion and that a Spanish fleet, carrying the earl of Tyrone, was on its way to Ireland.[206] At this point (23 February), Chamberlain was saying of the marriage that 'the Roman Catholics malign it as much' as the 'well-affected' were contented by it. The Catholics did what they could 'to disgrace it' because it was 'the ruin of their hopes'.[207] There was a 'flying report', wrote Chamberlain on 25 March, of a 'bull come from Rome against the king and clapped upon the court gate' (a repeat, after a fashion, of John Felton's exploit in 1570), and that 'the pope prepares forces both in Italy and Spain for Ireland'.[208] Even in late April 1613, Norton was still lamenting that the JPs in Sussex had 'taken all armour and weapons from recusants and put the armour in the custody of the puritans so that they may cut our throats if they list, and the Protestants' throats too'.[209] But contemporary commentators might also have been aware that, for example, Arthur Hildersham, the prominent Midlands puritan, who had been summoned by high commission only three days after John Almond was hanged, was on 22 April 1613 forbidden to preach or carry out any ministerial duty.[210]

---

[203] *HMCD*, IV, pp. 20, 28.   [204] *NAGB*, pp. 211–12 (AAW, A XII, no. 40, p. 85).
[205] McClure, *LJC*, I, p. 421.   [206] *CSPV 1610–13*, pp. 498, 499; *NAGB*, p. 211.
[207] McClure, *LJC*, I, p. 427. Even the dreadful weather of January 1613 was taken by some Catholics as a judgment on the Anglo-Palatine marriage: ABSJ, Anglia III, no. 119; *NAGB*, pp. 211–12; see also *HMCD*, IV, pp. 8, 19.
[208] McClure, *LJC*, I, p. 440. For rumours of an imminent Spanish armada, see, e.g., ABSJ, Anglia III, no. 119; Redworth, *LLC*, II, p. 300.
[209] *NAGB*, p. 222.
[210] L. A. Rowe, 'The Worlds of Arthur Hildersham (1563–1632)' (PhD, Warwick, 2009), p. 18, citing Samuel Clarke, *The Lives of Two and Twenty English Divines...* (1660), p. 148.

MID-JACOBEAN CONFESSIONAL POLITICS AND ANTI-POPERY   421

Some English Catholics, and indeed some of their enemies, probably did conclude at this point that there had been a reversion to the harshness of the Elizabethan persecution or, as many Protestants would have viewed it, godly enforcement of the law. The British king was not at war with any European Catholic State, but recent European political events had meant that the Stuart court was forced to turn to a Protestant dynastic alliance and, in order to force it through, to appeal to a domestic and overtly Protestant constituency. The enforcement, particularly in London, of the penal statutes against Catholics may have made a certain sort of Protestant think that victory was in sight, but that turned out not quite to be the case.

13

The Protestant Turn Turns Sour

Royal Authority, Catholicism, and (Anti-)Calvinism

Despite the recent Protestant turn in public politics represented by the Anglo-Palatine dynastic marriage agreement, what there was not was either a St Bartholomew's moment or even a wholesale resort to the Elizabethan treason laws. Those who had campaigned so hard for this Calvinist dynastic treaty had arguably pushed the envelope too far. Here the rhythms of Catholics' rhetoric about the malice and malignity of those who hounded them fed into the whisperings that the regime had taken a wrong dynastic turn under the influence of evil counsel. There was no worse counsellor than the thoroughly nasty George Abbot. One Jesuit newsletter which recorded John Almond's martyrdom said that, shortly afterwards, 'certain petitions' were 'preferred' to Abbot. In one of them his 'nativity was cast—how from a poor scholar he should be a fellow, doctor, chancellor of the university, a bishop and then archbishop of Canterbury and afterwards he should be hanged'. Everything had come true except the last part. Unsurprisingly, this 'much troubled' Abbot. The framer of the prophecy could not be located, 'but one Wainman...saying that his nativity was cast long before when' Abbot 'was accused in Oxford for abusing of boys...was brought in question for it'. Mr Wainman had known Abbot in Oxford and was asked by him why he should 'so wrong him about those boys'. Wainman retorted that Abbot 'well knew that it was proved against him long ago and, besides', one of the boys in question, 'who is a knight now, had told it unto' him, that is, Wainman, who further pointed out that Abbot currently had 'three...of the finest boys of England' in his 'chamber'. Abbot, in 'great fury', demanded to know the source of the rumours. Wainman would only say that 'one of your own coat told it' to 'me'.[1]

It appears that anti-Calvinist opinion was starting to repeat gossip which had been going round Oxford for ages that Abbot was a danger to children. Who the source was is also uncertain, but Abbot's fiercest Oxford critic, John Howson, had notoriously been in competition with Abbot for a fellowship at Balliol back in the

---

[1] ABSJ, Anglia III, no. 119. I am inclined to identify 'Wainman' as the Thomas Wenman cited in a letter of the Spaniard, Francisco Ruiz de Castro, written from Rome in March 1614, noting that Wenman (who had been at Trinity and Balliol between 1583 and 1587) was the public orator of the university, a post he held from 1594 to 1597: Loomie, *SJC*, II, p. 28. He was, subsequently, tutor to George Gage, the friend of Sir Tobias Matthew: J. P. Feil, 'Sir Tobie Matthew and his *Collection of Letters*' (PhD, Chicago, 1962), pp. 32, 52.

Catholics and Treason: Martyrology, Memory, and Politics in the Post-Reformation. Michael Questier, Oxford University Press. © Michael Questier 2022. DOI: 10.1093/oso/9780192847027.003.0013

THE PROTESTANT TURN TURNS SOUR 423

1580s and, then as now, that kind of common-room bitchiness does not dissipate for decades, if ever.[2] Even at this point, Howson was being mentioned in Catholic newsletters as the right sort of Church of England man.[3]

Moreover, the word was being spread that the king was looking askance at this recent burst of anti-popery in London. One newsletter which set down Almond's death declared that George Abbot had badgered James to agree to Almond's execution. Abbot had done this by 'promising' the king 'that it would be very profitable to their cause, for that the priest was both timorous and unlearned'. It turned out that Almond was neither of these things; and, 'when the king heard' it 'to be otherwise, he raged exceedingly and said he would execute no more'.[4]

It is, of course, not easy to measure the popularity, or otherwise, of the Anglo-Palatine match. But James had no intention that the future of his dynasty and of the British State should be defined in a narrow confessional manner.[5] While James might be compelled to look for friendship from European Calvinists, precisely what he did not want to sign up to, in any active sense, was the cause of pan-European Protestantism, in spite of his, from time to time, conventional statements about the threat from popery. The king was a master of gesture politics, positively Blairite actually, in his capacity for rhetorical obfuscation. When it came to the pan-European Protestant cause, he generally drew a clear line between gesture and action. What he did not want was, in ironically a rather un-Blairite way, to be drawn into and trapped inside an ideologically driven military conflict, especially one based on assumptions about the mutual interests of Europe's Protestants.

In all likelihood, the intimidation and harassment of Catholics at this time were part of a Calvinist campaign to keep the pressure on the king, though some in authority in the provinces never needed much encouragement to go after Catholic separatists. In Paris in early March 1613 Anthony Champney wrote to Thomas More that, if he got back to England he would make a formal record of 'the sufferings of our brethren'.[6] The Jesuit Richard Blount reported to Thomas Owen on 24 April 1613 that 'the state of Catholics continues daily more miserable' and 'many chief houses' were 'overthrown'. Twelve days later he insisted that Catholics were 'daily ruined' and 'priests' were 'daily apprehended' and 'here is nothing' but 'begging' of Catholics' sequestrated estates, 'tendering of the oath, ransacking of houses, imprisoning, excommunicating', and 'impoverishing'.[7] In May 1613 the residence of John Cotton, a Hampshire gentleman, was raided

---

[2] N. Cranfield and K. Fincham (eds), 'John Howson's Answers to Archbishop Abbot's Accusations at his "Trial" before James I at Greenwich, 10 June 1615', *Camden Miscellany* XXIX (Camden Society, 4th series, 1987), pp. 320–41, at p. 341.

[3] *NAGB*, pp. 191–2.   [4] ABSJ, Anglia III, no. 119.   [5] Questier, *DP*, ch. 6 *passim*.

[6] AAW, A XII, no. 61, p. 129. Champney added that he had urged Birkhead to see to the systematic recording of the persecution, and the recently deceased John Mush 'had promised his travail therein': AAW, A XII, no. 61, p. 129.

[7] ARSJ, Anglia 37, fo. 108ᵛ.

424   CATHOLICS AND TREASON

when the regime decided to investigate the scandalous circulating manuscript tract known as 'Balaam's Asse'. This piece, in reply to James's defence of the oath of allegiance, suggested that James, rather than the pope, was the Antichrist. A renegade priest, John Copley, who at one time had been stationed in the Cotton household, was happy to add fuel to the fire by giving circumstantial evidence that Mr Cotton, who had once been a friend of Edmund Campion, was the author of the offensive piece. The searchers came across Cotton's relic collection in a trunk. There were various bones with labels attached to them. Cotton's handwriting was not particularly clear and the tag on one bone could be read either as 'Rigby', that is, the late Elizabethan martyr John Rigby, or, more problematically, 'Digby', that is, Sir Everard Digby, arrested and executed for his part in the Gunpowder Plot.[8]

The more that convinced Calvinists sought to guide the king into what they considered the appropriate paths, the less it appeared that James wanted to follow where some of his Protestant subjects were trying to lead. When an Anglo-Irish delegation came over in order to protest about the elections to the 1613 Irish parliament, to Abbot's horror James decided to strike a tolerant pose. It was said in late September 1613 that, when the Irish deputies complained to the king, he had gone berserk and told his archbishop that 'he had caused him [James] to have the name of a tyrannical and bloody king abroad amongst his neighbour princes which conceit he neither desired to have nor ever would deserve to have'.[9] William Bishop, now in exile in Paris, believed that James had told Abbot that 'by his means...he was accounted cruel and barbarous in Catholic countries contrary to

---

[8] S. C. Lomas (ed.), *Report on the Manuscripts of the Earl of Ancaster, preserved at Grimsthorpe* (1907), pp. 354–81; Anstr., I, pp. 87–8; P. Lake with M. Questier, *The Antichrist's Lewd Hat: Protestants, Papists and Players in Post-Reformation England* (2002), pp. 305–6; James I, *An Apologie for the Oath of Allegiance...together with a Premonition...*(1609). For a definitive reconstruction of the writing of 'Balaam's Asse' (showing that the piece was 'framed explicitly as a refutation' of James's 'Monitory Preface') and of the arrest of the supposed author, John Cotton, and the eventual prosecution and execution of the actual author, John Williams, see E. Jennings, '"Balaam's Asse" Uncovered: New Light on the Politics of Prophetical Exegesis in Mid-Jacobean Britain', *Huntingdon Library Quarterly* 81 (2018), pp. 1–27 (quotation at p. 3). The secular priest Benjamin Norton made clear his distaste for the Jesuit-friendly John Cotton and for his 'bag of bones or, as others say, of relics'—Norton believed that, going by the recorded day of death on the paper tag, the bone in question was labelled 'Digby'. Norton thought that the pope should take order 'that every one particular layman, though Jesuited never so much, may not be a martyr-maker for the scent of the gunpowder is so strong in many men's noses that they will not worship such saints and truly I fear...that our enemies will laugh at it': *NAGB*, pp. 227–8; see also Birch, *CTJI*, I, pp. 248–9, 251; Larkin and Hughes, *SRP*, I, no. 130; *HMCD*, IV, p. 152; Questier, *C&C*, pp. 53, 107; *APC 1613–14*, pp. 22–3 (the order to the bishop of Winchester, of 8 May 1613, to search Cotton's house), 116, 117. Cotton was locked up for five years (in the Tower until March 1618 and thereafter under house arrest) before Williams was found and hanged in May 1619: Birch, *CTJI*, II, pp. 147, 157, 158, 160; *APC 1618–19*, pp. 57, 96, 455; *HMCB*, I, p. 254; Jennings, '"Balaam's Asse" Uncovered', p. 14; see p. 454 n.15 below. For a sequel to 'Balaam's Asse', discovered at Whitehall in November 1613, see Jennings, '"Balaam's Asse" Uncovered', pp. 7–8. It demanded the release of John Cotton and of the Jesuit William Baldwin: ibid., p. 7.

[9] *NAGB*, p. 33; AAW, A XII, no. 179, p. 395; Questier, *DP*, p. 351; cf. Richard Blount's claim on 1 September that the king intended to extirpate Catholicism in England and Ireland: ARSJ, Anglia 37, fo. 134[v].

THE PROTESTANT TURN TURNS SOUR   425

his own disposition'. This, said Bishop, was cause for thinking that 'the king will be easily induced to take a more calm course with his Catholic subjects', both in England and in Ireland.[10]

There was, briefly, a Calvinist public-relations counter-coup after the appearance of the Jesuit Francisco Suárez's controversial publication *Defensio Fidei Catholicae*. The Spanish ambassador Gondomar admitted that Suárez's book had allowed Abbot to retaliate by obtaining royal permission to raid, on 18/28 October, the residence in Spitalfields which Luisa de Carvajal maintained in London.[11] She was arrested, but Gondomar got her released. A procession of carriages followed her back to the Spanish embassy.[12] Still, Chamberlain was able to record with approval that on 21 November 1613, after a kind of disputation at Paul's Cross concerning passages taken out of Suárez, 'a good number of his books' were incinerated there.[13] On 26 December 1613 Blount wrote to Owen that the search of Carvajal's house had been, 'as is supposed', for the Jesuit Michael Walpole. But, out of sheer 'fright', Carvajal's 'gentlewoman died first', and Carvajal soon after. In the margin of Christopher Grene's transcript of Blount's letter it is noted that the gentlewoman and Carvajal were in effect martyrs themselves.[14]

---

[10] AAW, A XII, no. 181, p. 400. John Jackson had in April 1613 retailed the story that a French nobleman had gone from London back to France and, 'at his return, related to' Marie de Médicis, with Louis XIII sitting there, the horrors of the 'execution of priests which he had seen, and other persecutions'. Theatrically the queen regent 'gave order that she should be put in mind thereof when' the English ambassador, Sir Thomas Edmondes had his next audience, at which time Louis XIII 'put his mother in mind of our persecution'. The queen 'thereupon dealt roundly with' Edmondes and ordered a formal diplomatic note to be sent to the Stuart court. When Abbot 'came to solicit to have others executed', James 'reproved him and said that this course made him distasteful to all princes abroad': *NAGB*, p. 219. For Anthony Champney's account (8/18 June 1613) of, presumably, the same confrontation between James and Abbot, derived from John Cecil who heard it from 'a certain Italian merchant come out of England', see AAW, A XII, no. 112, p. 245. Following the deportation of clergy granted in late June at the request of the Savoyard ambassador, according to Champney on 6/16 July 1613, Abbot was 'said to have desired to stay two for sacrifice but the king answered that he would [have] no more blood', although 'the severity against others continues still': AAW, A XII, no. 129, p. 285; *APC 1613–14*, pp. 94–6.

[11] ARSJ, Anglia 37, fos 108ᵛ, 133ʳ⁻ᵛ; Loomie, *SJC*, II, pp. 16–23, 26–7; *HMCD*, IV, pp. 239–40, 242, 260; see G. Redworth, *The She-Apostle: The Extraordinary Life and Death of Luisa de Carvajal* (2008), pp. 217–20; see also K. Fincham, 'Prelacy and Politics: Archbishop Abbot's Defence of Protestant Orthodoxy', *Bulletin of the Institute of Historical Research* 61 (1988), pp. 36–64, at p. 46; K. Marshalek, 'Gender, Politics, Sanctity: the Career of Luisa de Carvajal in Anglo-Spanish Contexts' (forthcoming in *Renaissance Quarterly*).

[12] Redworth, *The She-Apostle*, p. 221; Loomie, *SJC*, II, pp. 16–18, 21–2; *NAGB*, pp. 246, 248. The king used his meeting with the ambassador's secretary to register a formal complaint about Suárez's recent publication: Loomie, *SJC*, II, p. 19.

[13] McClure, *LJC*, I, p. 488; *NAGB*, pp. 254, 261, 263, 265.

[14] ARSJ, Anglia 37, fo. 108ᵛ. Carvajal died on 23 December 1613/2 January 1614. Philip III ordered her interment at Madrid: ARSJ, Anglia 37, fo. 111ʳ; Loomie, *SJC*, II, pp. 26–7; *NAGB*, p. 270. On 16 March 1616, Francis Cottington related that there was a book printed at Valladolid in honour of Carvajal 'relating her miracles and conversions wrought in England, together with the persecutions she suffered'. Cottington had enclosed it so that George Abbot could refute it: PRO, SP 94/22, fo. 22ʳ (the text in question may be Juan de Mendieta de Doyega, *Interrogatio de Preguntas…*(n.p., n.d.); ARCR, I, no. 1618). See also Franciso de Peralta, *Copia de una Carta ….*(n.p. [Seville], n.d. [1614]); ARCR, I, no. 1065), incorporating the funeral sermon preached by Juan de Pineda for Carvajal.

426   CATHOLICS AND TREASON

Some Church of England clergymen may have had doubts about the court's recent Protestant turn, and the way in which it was advertised by resort to the law of treason. It was, obviously, not easy to say this in public. But, for example, the royal chaplain Benjamin Carier threw in the towel in 1613 and announced his conversion to Rome. Among the reasons for his change of heart he listed his certainty that he must have got his status as an ordained clergyman ultimately from Rome: 'I cannot believe that I am a priest at all, unless I be derived from Gregory the Great, from whence all the bishops in England have their being, if they have any being at all'. This was completely incompatible with the 'statute...made by Queen Elizabeth...that it is death for any Englishman to be in England, being made a priest by authority derived, or pretended to be derived, from the bishop of Rome'. Executions for religion under such auspices were intolerable, though, as Kenneth Fincham has shown, Carier had experienced no issues of conscience in hounding to death the Arian heretic Edward Wightman.[15]

Court Calvinists soon found that they had problems—if there was a mid-Jacobean Calvinist supremacy, it did not last very long. Whether for political or for purely physical reasons, James's favourite Viscount Rochester and Frances Howard could not keep their hands off each other. The annulment of her marriage to the earl of Essex proceeded on the basis of her claim that he had become impotent, either because of witchcraft or for some other cause. Rochester (promoted in early November 1613 in the peerage to the earldom of Somerset) wed the now divorced Frances Howard on 26 December 1613.[16] The annulment and new marriage were reckoned to be a victory for those at court who were noted for their hostility to puritans.

Many of the members in the 1614 parliament, one dares say, were none too impressed when they listened to the king's speech at the opening, 'almost two hours long' said Richard Broughton. It was in part an 'invective against Catholics'; but then James 'mitigated it and said he would...have no more laws' against Catholics. The ones already on the statute book were 'sufficient to restrain them and keep them in subjection'. What was more, 'the Devil had his martyrs' and Catholics 'did glory...in their persecution'. Of course, the king would not regard it as persecution as such but, whatever it was, 'it was never seen' that 'it did any good, as they have found by experience'.[17]

---

[15] Benjamin Carier, *A Treatise written by by M ͬ. Doctour Carier*...(Brussels, 1614), pp. 11–12; Fincham, 'Prelacy', p. 54. Sir Dudley Carleton received in February 1614 a report from an informant in Rome, Federico Gotardi, that at the English College in Rome there had been three performances of a five-hour-long Latin play which dealt with the persecution inflicted on Catholics in London: Feil, 'Sir Tobie Matthew', p. 78, citing PRO, SP 84/4, fo. 101ͬ⁻ᵛ; for the play, *Captiva Religio*, see S. Gossett, 'Drama in the English College, Rome, 1591–1660', *English Literary Renaissance* 3 (1973), pp. 60–93, at pp. 64, 65, 66, 67, 81, 83, 84, 86, 89, 91; there are two texts of the play in the English College's archives, in Liber 321 and MS 33.3; see Gossett, 'Drama', p. 66.
[16] Questier, *DP*, p. 352.   [17] AAW, A XII, no. 71, p. 175.

This parliament also saw vituperative attacks on Bishop Richard Neile for his linking together of puritanism, popularity, and opposition to prerogative taxation. The dots all seemed to join up here. The crypto-Catholic exchequer official Henry Spiller, who made it his business to mitigate the penalties levied on recusants, was the target of an astonishing verbal attack by the new secretary of State, Sir Ralph Winwood. The domestic State papers series for this period, particularly after the dissolution of the 1614 parliament, is full of reports about Catholic separatists, almost all garnered by Abbot and Winwood.[18]

The slightly creepy *éminence grise* of the Howard family, the earl of Northampton, died on 16 June 1614.[19] There was still a flow of claims from, for instance, William Trumbull in Flanders that there were conspiracies being fomented at high level both in Brussels and in Madrid, principally to send Spanish troops into Ireland in order to exploit the fuss caused by the maladroit recent attempts to pack the Irish parliament.[20] This may have looked like a response to King James's attempts to mediate in the new Jülich-Cleves succession crisis. In late 1614, Henry Clifford noted that things were tough for English Catholics. The 'miseries of the papists daily increase, which many thought long since could not be greater'. Priests and Jesuits were hunted 'like hares'. It was rumoured that one had been killed attempting to evade arrest. The 'puritans' by contrast were 'very strong' and 'increase[d] daily'.[21] In January 1615 the priest John Ainsworth described how the living conditions of Catholics in Newgate had, by order of the council, been made markedly worse even than they had been before. He gave an

---

[18] *CSPD 1611–18, passim*; Questier, *DP*, pp. 355, 368.

[19] Richard Broughton reported on 3 July 1614 that Northampton had died a Catholic and had regretted that he had not been truer to his faith: AAW, A XIII, no. 141, p. 363.

[20] PRO, SP 77/11, *passim*.

[21] Ghent MSS, I, no. 39, pp. 158, 159 (Henry Clifford to [William Cawley], 10 December 1614); for similar comments from Anthony Champney and John Jackson, see AAW, A XIII, nos 263, 264. For Richard Broughton's description in early July 1614 of the abominable conditions of the clergy imprisoned in Newgate and the Clink (he reported also that Robert Edmunds OSB had died in the Gatehouse), see AAW, A XIII, no. 141, p. 363. Broughton alleged that the gaol-keepers of those two prisons had themselves been imprisoned because they had not been as brutal to their prisoners as the Catholics' 'malicious enemies' wished: AAW, A XIII, no. 141, p. 363. For Broughton's comment on 1 May 1615 that priests who were moved to Wisbech would experience a 'living martyrdom', see AAW, A XIV, no. 89, p. 291. On 19 November 1615, Broughton recorded what he took to be intolerable harshness towards Catholics; in particular, 'three score and more there are in prison at York, eighteen priests in the Clink', and many in other prisons, 'and almost no gaol of any shire where there are not some Catholic prisoners': AAW, A XIV, no. 208, p. 623. For Laurence Worthington's description in October 1616 of the harsh conditions endured in the Gatehouse by Catholic lay prisoners, which he tried to alleviate, see Foley, *RSJ*, II, pp. 96–7. But cf. Francis Kemp OSB's statement reported in April 1616 that priests in Wisbech were 'at as much liberty as they were in Queen Elizabeth's days and that the keeper told them lately that' Lancelot Andrewes, bishop of Ely, had told him to 'show them all favour' as long as they did not abscond: AAW, A XV, no. 65, p. 173. In that month, however, the death of Richard Michall in the king's bench prison was mentioned by Thomas Curtis: 'one Mr Garnet, brother of Father Thomas Garnet the martyr, then prisoner…for debt, perceiving' Michall 'to kneel so long, went towards him and found him stone-dead, with his beads in his hands, lifted up to his face': Stonyhurst MS A V, no. 21, p. 108.

428   CATHOLICS AND TREASON

account of the shocking recent death of the priest George Fairburn in the gaol.[22] On 19/29 January 1615 Trumbull reported that the Spanish and Flemish ambassadors in England had 'advised their friends' in Brussels 'to deal with' the duke of Neuburg, one of the claimants in the Jülich-Cleves crisis, to lobby the papacy and Madrid 'to send Tyrone' and other Irishmen back to Ireland 'for the raising of a war there, and the diverting' of King James from rendering assistance to the margrave of Brandenburg and the princes of the German Protestant evangelical union. The Irish in Brussels were saying that Tyrone was about to set out from Rome. The Habsburg ambassadors in London were demanding that the archduke should not cede the disputed town of Wesel and, to gloss their position here, they 'exclaimed' against James 'for shutting up the priests and awarding certain commissions against the papists of England and taking away their arms, terming it a persecution and tyrannical proceeding'.[23]

One local response, in Scotland, appears to have been the prosecutions of the Scottish Jesuits John Ogilvie and James Moffat.[24] Archbishop John Spottiswoode had engineered the taking of the recently returned Ogilvie, while Archbishop George Gledstanes arrested and prosecuted Moffat.[25] Moffat later reported that the Scottish privy council had cross-questioned him about papal political power as set out in the writings of the Jesuit Suárez.[26] Ogilvie, who seems to have affirmed something very like a full-blown version of the theory of the papal deposing power, was hanged at Glasgow on 28 February 1615, only three hours after sentence was formally pronounced.[27] The king probably did not want Ogilvie to die.[28] Ogilvie's case provoked a pamphlet in his defence published at Douai.[29]

---

[22] AAW, A XIV, no. 60, pp. 209–10; Anstr., II, p. 98.   [23] PRO, SP 77/11, fo. 239ʳ.

[24] The Scottish privy council claimed that the warrant for the trial proceedings came directly from the king as well as from the council itself: D. Masson (ed.), *Register of the Privy Council of Scotland 1613–1616* (Edinburgh, 1891) [hereafter *RPCS 1613–1616*], p. 285.

[25] Ogilvie was arrested on 4 October 1614, interrogated on 5 October, and then again on 12 December in Edinburgh by royal commissioners, and again on 18 January 1615 concerning the relationship between royal and papal authority. He was put on trial on 28 February 1615: *ODNB, sub* Ogilvie, John (article by M. Dilworth); A. S. W. Pearce, 'John Spottiswoode, Jacobean Archbishop and Statesman' (PhD, Stirling, 1998), pp. 171–85; McClure, *LJC*, I, p. 597; ABSJ, A IV, no. 26, p. 9; Forbes-Leith, *Narratives*, pp. 297–9; Loomie, *SJC*, II, pp. 51–2; see also A. Macdonald, *The Jacobean Kirk, 1567–1625* (Aldershot, 1998), pp. 154–5. Spottiswoode wrote *A True Relation of the Proceedings against J. Ogilvie...* (Edinburgh, 1615) to prove that Ogilvie was guilty of treason; see also *RPCS 1613–1616*, pp. 304–7. The arrest of Moffat, according to Calderwood, was made by Gledstanes's son: *RPCS 1613–1616*, p. 284. For the proceedings against Ogilvie's and Moffat's harbourers, see *RPCS 1613–1616*, pp. 283, 336–7, 352, 459–60.

[26] ABSJ, A IV, no. 26, p. 13; see also *RPCS 1613–1616*, pp. 284–6, 288–9, 300, 303–6, 336–7.

[27] W. E. Brown, *John Ogilvie...* (1925), pp. 69, 108, 122–5; *ODNB, sub* Ogilvie, John (article by M. Dilworth). Ogilvie claimed that it was presbyterians who most directly threatened the life of the monarch: Browne, *John Ogilvie*, p. 68.

[28] For the indictment, see *A True Relation*, pp. 17–21. The Jesuit James Gordon in late January 1615 thought that the king would intervene to save Ogilvie: ABSJ, A II, 3, no. 5; ABSJ, A IV, no. 26, p. 9.

[29] *Relatio Incarcerationis et Martyrii P. Ioannis Ogilbei Natione Scoti, e Societati Iesu Presbyteri. Ex Autographo ipsius Martyris, in Carcere Exarato Glasguae in Scotia octiduo ane Mortem...* (Douai, 1615); M. Dilworth, *The Scots in Franconia: A Century of Monastic Life* (1974), pp. 56–9. The *Relatio Incarcerationis...* went into a series of translations in 1616: ARCR, I, nos 848–56. i. Later, on 13/23

THE PROTESTANT TURN TURNS SOUR 429

There may well have been an attempt in England to replicate the show trial of Ogilvie. In May 1615 there were legal proceedings against the recusant John Owen of Godstow. On 25 May 1615 Archbishop Abbot related how Owen had returned from San Lucar and, on arrest, 'uttered execrable words, maintaining the doctrine of killing of kings'. He was 'condemned of high treason to the great contentment of all standers-by' and certainly of Abbot himself, who was presumably rubbing his hands with glee at the prospect of Owen's execution, although it never happened.[30] Anthony Champney had noted on 23 May/2 June 1615 that, 'by occasion of the answers of a Jesuit [Ogilvie] taken in Scotland', similar questions to those put to Owen had also been 'of late proposed to divers priests'.[31] Indeed, earlier in the year, Abbot, Winwood, and others had tried to drag out of prominent Catholic clergymen, imprisoned in London, incriminating statements about the pope's power to excommunicate and depose princes. They were asked, *inter alia*, whether the sentence of excommunication lifted the subject's obligation to obey an excommunicated prince and whether the pope could command the king's subjects or anyone else to kill him. George Fisher (John Almond's close friend) said he needed time to think about it, while John Ainsworth affirmed the pope's power to excommunicate and depose but said that 'princes deposed could in no case be murdered, which was always unlawful'.[32]

Sir John Digby, in Madrid, reported back to the earl of Somerset on 14 July 1615 that 'our English in the seminaries of Seville and Valladolid do commonly once a year, for the moving of greater commiseration towards them from the Spaniard, publish some idle papers of the persecution and their sufferings in England'. Digby enclosed in his letter one such publication. This appears to have been a pamphlet entitled *Algunos Avisos de Inglaterra*.[33] It comprised three letters

---

March 1616, Francis Cottington assured the 'cardinal of Toledo' (presumably Bernardo de Sandoval y Rojas, cardinal priest and archbishop of Toledo, and uncle of the duke of Lerma) that he had seen Spottiswoode's *True Relation* and took care to tell the cardinal 'many particulars of these falsehoods and the truth of the proceeding in Scotland'. The cardinal had 'seemed much satisfied with it' and even wanted a copy of the pamphlet: PRO, SP 94/22, fo. 16[r-v].

[30] McClure, *LJC*, I, p. 597; Loomie, *SJC*, II, p. 48; *HMCD*, V, p. 224; AAW, A XIV, no. 103, p. 327; *CSPD 1611–18*, p. 558.

[31] AAW, A XIV, no. 107, p. 338.

[32] AAW, A XIV, no. 102, p. 325; PRO, SP 14/80/93, fo. 141[r-v] (a list of interrogatories put to Fisher and Ainsworth which is similar to the one in AAW, A XIV, no. 102); Anstr., II, p. 3; TD, IV, pp. cxciii–ccv; PRO, SP 14/82/99. i–ii (fo. 162[r] for Ainsworth's response to the question concerning regicide, though the list of questions in SP 14/82/99. i is a different one from that in AAW, A XIV, no. 102). For a toleration petition to the king, written at around this point by the priests incarcerated in Wisbech, see H. Houston Ball (ed.), 'Three Letters relating to the Treatment of the Catholic Prisoners in Wisbeach [*sic*] Castle, Cambridgeshire, 1615', *Miscellanea III* (CRS 3, 1906), pp. 88–90.

[33] PRO, SP 94/21, fos 139[v]–40[r]; *Algunos Avisos de Inglaterra de la Persecucion grande que Aora de Nuevo ay en aquel Reyno contra los Catolicos* (Seville, 1615); ARCR, I, no. 1067 (PRO, SP 14/80/93); the priest referred to in the first section of the publication is evidently John Ainsworth, who was ordained at Seville. Printed in Spain in the same year was, also, *Relacion del Martirio de Tomas Haso…* (Granada, 1615), an account of Thomas Hackshot's and Nicholas Tichborne's martyrdom in August 1601, 'embiados por un sacerdote del seminario de Sevilla', as the title declared; ARCR, I, no. 624.

430 CATHOLICS AND TREASON

sent to the English college in Seville, two from England and one from Brussels. The first has a narrative of the horrors of Newgate prison and also of the injustice of the recent treatment of Lord Vaux and the salutary example of God's justice in the recent death by drowning of the sons of the lord president of the council in the North, Lord Sheffield. The second letter, from Brussels, celebrated the valiant witness of the priest John Ainsworth (the author, as it seems, of the first letter) and also the tyranny of George Abbot in persuading the king not to release imprisoned Catholic clergy into exile. It also claimed that the council was opposed to an Anglo-Spanish dynastic marriage. The third declared that James had refused to countenance composition arrangements for Catholics who had seen their property sequestrated under the Elizabethan recusancy statutes, even though there had for some time been ad hoc provision for at least some debt-encumbered Catholics to scale down their payments to the royal exchequer. In addition, it described the questioning of the priests Fisher and Ainsworth about the political authority of the papacy. Separately, Ainsworth penned and sent to Rome a long description of his prison ministry and of the conversions he had made. Among his converts was the convicted poisoner John Heydon, who had been a servant of 'the old lord treasurer', that is, the earl of Salisbury and, subsequently, of Salisbury's secretary, John Dackombe. On the last night of his life, Heydon 'defended the Catholic religion to two of the king's chaplains' and, subsequently, 'against two other ministers and, hearing my voice reprehending, though through the door, those professed heretics, he ran to the door...and he, with a humble spirit, said... "I hope I may touch you, howsoever I am a great sinner"'. As he was being taken off to Tyburn, and at the gallows, he 'cried out "All Roman Catholics, pray for me"'.[34]

All in all, this could be taken as a very carefully judged interference in the tentative London–Madrid moves towards a dynastic alliance, the first serious manoeuvres in which project were beginning at this time. This on–off negotiation dictated the course of political events for much of the rest of James's reign. If one wants a sense of how much this might matter to the king and court in terms of reputational damage, one needs only look at the notorious pamphlet entitled *Corona Regia* that seems to have been released in autumn 1615, at around the time of the fall and disgrace of Lord Somerset over the alleged murder of Sir Thomas Overbury in the Tower of London.[35] *Corona Regia* was glossed by some contemporaries as a riposte to the king's recently published attack on Cardinal du

---

[34] PRO, SP 14/80/93; AAW, A XIV, no. 60, pp. 210–11; Jeaffreson, *MCR*, II, p. 218; M. Questier, *Conversion, Politics and Religion in England, 1580–1625* (Cambridge, 1996), p. 194; PRO, SP 14/80/84, fo. 125ʳ, a report which describes Ainsworth as 'a marvellous active priest, full of bitterness'. He had written to the king about the conditions in Newgate gaol and, 'in the same letter, he labours that all the felons that were executed might turn papists and that, going from the prison and at the gallows, they should with a loud voice cry out, "All Catholics, pray for us"'.

[35] W. Schleiner (ed.) and T. Fyotek (trans.), *Corona Regia* (Geneva, 2010); *HMCD*, V, p. 353.

THE PROTESTANT TURN TURNS SOUR   431

Perron.[36] It attacks the corruption of the Jacobean court and says that James was, to all intents and purposes, still a persecutor. His greed led him to mulct Catholics, even if he did not kill them.[37]

European observers might soon have concluded that they were watching the revival of a genuine persecution in the British Isles. During a period of seven days in March 1616, three Catholics (one at York and two at Lancaster) were executed for treason.[38] The priest Thomas Atkinson, who came from the East Riding, was hanged at York on 11 March 1616.[39] John Knaresborough suggests that Atkinson's considerable age made his execution hardly comprehensible to the crowd of thousands that came to watch. This 'poor old man' was cut down immediately and, 'while yet alive, his breast was ripped open' and 'his bowels torn out', all in 'the most cruel, barbarous and butcherly manner that the bloodiest tyrant on earth could devise'.[40] Atkinson's execution may have been unpopular also because of the changing political scene. York had, in the past, witnessed anti-popish crowds yelling abuse at condemned Catholics; but not now, as Anthony Champney in Paris related it on 3/13 June 1616, out of information supplied by his confrère John Jackson. At the point that Atkinson was 'ready to be turned off the ladder', he declared that he had received a miraculous revelation that he would be arrested and 'heard a voice which exhorted him to be constant in the profession of his faith'. This 'moved' the people 'much and [the] officers had difficulty to get a vessel to boil his quarters in. And, in the evening, when the undersheriff and the rest of

---

[36] HMCD, V, p. 377 and passim; Smith, Life, II, pp. 92–3; see also Questier, DP, pp. 364–5, 382; I. Uddin, 'A Jacobean Diplomat at the Court of the Archdukes in Brussels 1605–25' (PhD, Leuven, 2006), ch. 5.

[37] Schleiner and Fyotek, Corona Regia, p. 73.

[38] Challoner, MMP, pp. 339–44; ABP, pp. 601–4.

[39] One description of Atkinson was written by Lady Babthorpe: AAW, A VI, no. 100, p. 367 (saying that he pursued an apostolate directed to the poor, or at least one that was not limited to the houses of gentry patrons); AWCBC, p. 1924. A Latin life of Atkinson was printed at Douai, tacked onto the (re) printed account of Thomas Maxfield (Vita et Martyrium D. Max-fildaei Collegii Anglorum Duaceni Sacerdotis... (Douai, 1616; ARCR, I, no. 313)). It deals in addition with the two martyrs at Lancaster, John Thulis and Roger Warren: Exemplar Literarum... (Douai, 1616); ARCR, I, no. 314, on which John Knaresborough and Richard Challoner relied; see also Francisco de Peralta, Relacion... de los Ingleses de Seuilla... (Seville, 1616); ARCR, I, no. 1070; AWCBC, p. 1913 (explaining the origins of the account of Atkinson, a letter written by an English secular priest, the original of which is lost but, for which, see Foley, RSJ, V, p. 674 (Bibliotheque Royale, Brussels, MS 2158–67, fos 267^r–8^v, photocopy retained at ABSJ, CP (Thomas Atkinson), translated and augmented by a Jesuit priest); ARSJ, Anglia 31/i, fos 25^r–6^r; ARSJ, Anglia 32/i, fo. 21^{r-v}; Biblioteca Vallicelliana, Rome, N 23, fo. 329^v. Other (expanded) editions of the Exemplar Literarum came out in 1617: ARCR, I, nos 315, 316; AWCBC, pp. 1960–3; there were French and Spanish versions also: ARCR, I, nos 317–20. Atkinson, it was claimed, was on good terms with local Jesuits: AWCBC, p. 1903; Foley, RSJ, V, p. 674. A Jesuit priest wrote that Atkinson was a friend to the Society 'and, in testimony of his love, bestowed his books and other things on me and fathers of ours his acquaintance'. This Jesuit 'often visited him in prison and was near him when he died and he seemed glad to see me there'. Atkinson recounted to this priest a vision he had had while in gaol: ARSJ, Anglia 37, fo. 81^r; AWCBC, p. 1909. For another narrative of the double execution, written by Thomas Killingham and reproduced by William Critchley, see ABSJ, Collectanea M, pp. 48^b–9^b; AWCBC, pp. 1974–7.

[40] Kn., II, pp. 220–1.

432 CATHOLICS AND TREASON

his company returned from their butchery, the boys in the street, as they went up Micklegate, cried out against them and cast stones at them, which many wondered at'.[41] William Webster confirmed separately to More on 18/28 June that, 'at the sheriff and his company's return, the boys in the street did' indeed 'shout at them and, following them, threw dirt and stones at them'.[42] On that day Champney sent off another letter to Rome to add that the secular clergy's patron, Thomas Sackville, a younger son of the earl of Dorset, had received a slightly different narrative of the recent legal proceedings against clergy in England, but it confirmed that Atkinson was 'condemned of treason not upon proof but upon mere conjecture, by such things as were found about him, that he was a priest, which made the people murmur'; and when the judges understood this they 'procured a base fellow to come forth and swear that he had seen him say Mass'.[43]

At Lancaster, John Thulis and his harbourer Roger Warren were hanged on 18 March, exactly one week after Atkinson was put to death. They had broken prison and had been rearrested.[44] One source alleged that attempts were made to drag Thulis and Warren into a church.[45] The rope used to hang Warren snapped at the first attempt. The 'Protestant ministers' in attendance tried to make this mishap into a miracle of providence and exhorted Warren to change his mind over the oath. But he would not—'had you but seen what my eyes have just now beheld, you would be as much in haste to be in another world as I am'.[46] The decision to exhibit Thulis's quarters at a variety of places (Lancaster, Preston, Wigan, and Warrington) suggests that this was regarded as an important show trial.[47] The deaths of Thulis and Warren provoked versified accounts of their executions, embedded in a long north-country-dialect collection on a range of topics and, *inter alia*, the relationship between Christ's suffering and the martyrdom of Catholics.[48] These verses alleged also that 'Parson Lee', presumably William Leigh, tried to crack Thulis's resistance and, at the gallows, called on Warren, after the

---

[41] AAW, A XV, no. 92, p. 243; see also AAW, A XV, no. 87, p. 231 (*AWCBC*, pp. 1917–18).

[42] AAW, A XV, no. 97, p. 257.   [43] AAW, A XV, no. 96, p. 254.

[44] Challoner, *MMP*, pp. 342–4; ABP, pp. 604–6; Kn., II, p. 231; AAW, A XV, no. 96, pp. 254–5, no. 98, p. 259; Ghent MSS, II, no. 55, p. 203. The Jesuit Joseph Creswell obtained eyewitness testimonies of the recent trials and executions and translated them into Spanish. They were printed at St Omer and sent to Philip III and others; the aim was to give ammunition to the Spanish ambassador in England with which to negotiate the proposed dynastic marriage alliance: A. F. Allison, 'The Later Life and Writings of Joseph Creswell, S. J. (1556–1623)', *RH* 15 (1979), pp. 79–14, at pp. 119–120, 141; *Relacion de Cinco Martyres en Ynglaterra este Año de 1616* (n.p. [St Omer], 1616); see ARCR, I, no. 320; ARSJ, Anglia 32/i, fos 9ʳ–20ᵛ. Thulis was said to have been arrested at the direction of William Stanley, sixth earl of Derby: Challoner, *MMP*, p. 342; *AWCBC*, p. 1982.

[45] *AWCBC*, pp. 1938, 1946–50 (the document cited is ARSJ, Anglia 32/i, fos 21ᵛ–3ʳ).

[46] Kn., II, pp. 232–3; Challoner, *MMP*, p. 344.

[47] Challoner, *MMP*, p. 344; see also Anstr., I, p. 355, citing ARSJ, Anglia 32/i, fo. 21ᵛ.

[48] Pollen, *AEM*, pp. 194–207 (BL, Additional MS 15225, fos 22ᵛ–7ᵛ), printing two pieces, the first (fos 22ᵛ–5ʳ) headed 'Here follows the song which Mr Thulis writ for himself. To the tune of [ ]' [*sic*] and the second (fos 25ʳ–7ᵛ) headed 'Here follows the song of the death of Mr Thewlis. To the tune of "Dainty come thou to me"'. For the texts, see H. E. Rollins (ed.), *Old English Ballads 1553–1625* (Cambridge, 1920), pp. 79–100.

rope-breaking incident, to take the oath of allegiance.[49] The verse collection then, if briefly, launches into an attack on contemporary puritanism.[50] In the manuscript on which Bishop Challoner relied there is the claim, though Challoner omits it, that 'in the same prison', that is, at Lancaster, there were 'two other priests, Mr Redman and Mr Burske, condemned likewise to die; but upon yielding to take the oath' they were 'as yet misled and of the happy crown of martyrdom deprived'.[51] At the end of the same month, on 29 March, Richard Blount noted that 'forty persons repairing this week to the Gatehouse' in London, 'to hear a sermon, were all stayed and sent to divers prisons'.[52]

The Martyrdom of Thomas Maxfield

It would, of course, be quite easy to argue that all we are seeing here is a largely conventional drive against what some regarded as a separatist Catholic tendency to sedition and disorder. But it does look as if some of the treason cases at this point intersected with debates about the regime's future in a way that had not been the case for some time—perhaps not since the Archpriest Dispute of the late 1590s. The treason trial in 1616 which tells us most about the shifting ideological state of the mid-Jacobean regime—the proceedings against Thomas Maxfield— came at the point when the court was planning the king's progress into James's Scottish kingdom, which took place the following year. Contemporary observers were soon aware that this was going to be a major public-relations exercise. The king would demand new standards of liturgical conformity in the Scots Church, via the articles of Perth.[53]

James naturally had no wish to lose control of the mainstream rhetoric of antipopery and certainly not to see it turned against him. This can be picked up from his star chamber speech to the judges on 20 June 1616 in which he issued his declaration that the Church of England was 'most pure and nearest' to 'the primitive and apostolic Church in doctrine and discipline and is sureliest founded upon the Word of God of any Church in Christendom'. The king reiterated his distinction, made originally in the 'parliament house', between different sorts of Catholics. He condemned what he called 'apostate' and 'polypragmatic' papists. He said that while he was 'loath to hang a priest only for religion's sake and saying Mass', if the priest refused 'the oath of allegiance', then what followed was his own

---

[49] Pollen, *AEM*, pp. 195, 202; *AWCBC*, p. 1973.   [50] BL, Additional MS 15225, fo. 29ʳ⁻ᵛ.
[51] ABP, p. 606; Anstr., II, p. 263. William Redman had been ordained in April 1610. I take it that 'Burske' is Thomas Briscow, who had been arraigned and sentenced at Lancaster back in April 1605 but sentence was not carried out and he was deported, only to return in February 1608: Anstr., I, p. 51; *HMCS*, XVII, p. 144; PRO, SP 14/15/73; TD, IV, p. xcv; see pp. 343, 343 n.51 above.
[52] Ghent MSS, II, no. 55, p. 203.
[53] For the king's purposes in undertaking the Scottish progress, see Questier, *DP*, pp. 372–83 *passim*.

434 CATHOLICS AND TREASON

fault. For, 'let the pope and all the devils in Hell say what they will', the oath was 'merely civil'. Those who decided to 'refuse the oath' were simply 'polypragmatic recusants'. James would happily 'leave them to the law'. This was 'no persecution but good justice'. As for priests who flouted the law by breaking prison, 'such priests as the prison will not hold, it is a plain sign' that 'nothing will hold them but a halter: such are no martyrs that refuse to suffer for their conscience'.[54]

As bad luck would have it, Thomas Maxfield, gaoled in the Gatehouse, had broken prison on 14 June, six days before the king's speech to the judges. James may have been referring to him, though possibly also to Thulis and Warren. On the same day as James's performance in star chamber, Maxfield was arraigned. Ten days afterwards, on 1 July, he was executed at Tyburn.[55]

James presumably intended this as a practical demonstration that he said what he meant and meant what he said, all in order to give some bite to his anti-popish underpinning of his recent statements about the 'apostolic' Church of England. Later in the year, on 22 November, Richard Blount reported to Joseph Creswell that 'the king was' now 'angry with a book printed at Douai in Latin' for, in this pamphlet, James was 'said to have mocked' the ambassador Gondomar 'by appointing him to come to him to know his mind about the execution of Mr Maxfield on Tuesday, and then caused him to be executed the Monday before'. Gondomar denied it and showed the king the 'Spanish relation where no such thing appeared'.[56]

---

[54] James I, *The Workes of the Most High and Mightie Prince, Iames...King of Great Britaine, France and Ireland...* (1616), pp. 554, 565–6.

[55] Anstr., II, p. 215; J. H. Pollen (ed.), 'The Life and Martyrdom of Mr. Maxfield, 1616', *Miscellanea III* (CRS 3, 1906), pp. 30–58 (a translation of the first printed Latin account of the execution of Thomas Maxfield, probably put together for publication at the direction of Matthew Kellison: *Vita et Martyrium D. Max-fildaei Collegii Anglorum Duaceni Sacerdotis...* (Douai, 1616); ARCR, I, no. 313), at pp. 55, 56; *APC 1615–16*, p. 591 (the privy council order for Maxfield to be removed to Newgate); ARSJ, Anglia 37, fo. 134ᵛ; see also ARSJ, Anglia 37, fos 81ʳ⁻ᵛ, 97ᵛ ([Richard Blount] to Joseph Creswell, 6 July 1616). For another narrative of Maxfield's execution retained in Jesuit records, see ARSJ, Anglia 32/i, fo. 27ʳ. For extant copies of the 'Brevis Narratio Martyrii Venerabilis Sacerdotis Thomae Maxfeildii...', see, e.g., AAW, A XV, no. 103; for the version in Edinburgh Advocates Library, Balfour MSS, see J. Maidment (ed.), *Miscellany of the Abbotsford Club*, I (Edinburgh, 1837), item vii; ABPFC, fos 23ʳ–4ʳ. On 27 June 1616 Edward Bennett wrote to Thomas More to say that 'some' (i.e. several) in the Gatehouse might be executed because of Maxfield's attempted escape: AAW, A XV, no. 95, p. 251. See also B. Camm, 'Venerable Thomas Maxfield, Priest and Martyr', *Downside Review* 34: 1 (1915), pp. 30–59 (reprinting and translating, loosely, most but not all of 'Insigne Martyrium Reverendi Viri D. Thomae Maxfeldii Sacerdotis Angli ad Illustrissimi Regis Catholici in Anglia Legatum D. Didacum Sarmiento de Acuna e Carcere Nova Porta Dicto', dated 4 July 1616 and located in the Biblioteca Nacional, Madrid, Gayangos Collection, 18420; it must have been presented, suggests Bede Camm, to Gondomar or to his chaplain, Diego de Lafuente). There is a full transcript, made by Herbert Garland in 1915, of the original text, now in ABSJ, CP (Thomas Maxfield); see also *AWCBC*, pp. 643–4. Camm also incorporates at pp. 53–8 a document entitled 'Copy of the information taken from the archives of the Convent of the Island of St Simon, concerning an English martyr named Thomas Mexphit [Maxfield]'.

[56] Ghent MSS, II, no. 58, p. 212; for Jean-Baptiste van Male's account of the confrontation between James and Gondomar, see Loomie, *SJC*, II, p. 73; Allison, 'Later Life', p. 120; for Knaresborough's rendering of these events, see Kn., II, pp. 260–1, VII, p. 436; see also Challoner, *MMP*, p. 349; AVCAU, Liber 1577 (Anstruther Martyrs File): PRO 31/9/121A (for the statement that Maxfield's brother

THE PROTESTANT TURN TURNS SOUR 435

Challoner's principal source for Maxfield's death insists that the Spanish embassy tried hard to stop the execution and then, when that proved impossible, moved to exploit it for public-relations purposes. Among those who visited Maxfield in prison were 'the better sort of Spaniards that inhabited London' and, among them, were Gondomar's son (presumably his third son, Don Antonio) and his chaplain, the Dominican Diego de Lafuente. 'After these, as the leaders of the company, followed the rest' of the ambassador's 'family and divers others' who paraded 'through the streets unto the prison' to visit the condemned priest. They 'kissed his hands, his chains and the ground that touched his sacred footsteps, desiring his benediction'. The ambassador continued to labour on Maxfield's behalf for a reprieve. In prison, Maxfield asked his visitors 'to pray for him' and also 'to use their good offices with the ambassador, that at his return to Spain' he would commend the college at Douai to Philip III. Lafuente left the prison and 'caused the blessed sacrament to be solemnly exposed in the ambassador's chapel', that is, as dusk approached on 30 June, where the ambassador's 'family and other Catholics spent the night in prayer in behalf of this holy priest, who was in the morning to pour forth his blood in defence of the Catholic religion'.[57] Maxfield sent a message via another priest, 'his last petition', again on behalf of the English College at Douai. It was 'the first seminary of the English nation which' Philip II 'of famous memory embraced with a fatherly affection'. Moreover, there had 'proceeded out of this house more than one hundred priests honoured with the crown of martyrdom, whose blood collected through the maintenance of the Catholic king has been poured out upon the earth for the glory of Christ, whose prayers also in heaven to God...do invocate the divine protection...for the increase of the glory, greatness and majesty of the Spanish monarchy'.[58]

Maxfield had also, in late summer/early autumn 1615, been involved in an exorcism. This itself may explain why the pursuivant John Wragge arrested him on 1 November 1615. Maxfield wrote a letter describing the exorcism and sent it back to the president of Douai, Matthew Kellison. Maxfield said it was a 'wonderful work here lately effected by the great power and goodness of God and by the merits, mediation and relics of his holy saint and martyr' of the college at Douai, that is, Robert Sutton. The exorcism had been carried out by Edward Hands, a Douai priest. After Maxfield was arrested, he had resolutely refused to take the oath of allegiance when he was tendered it by Bishop John King on 3 November

---

similarly sought a reprieve and that the answer was deferred until it was too late). The pamphlet which King James saw was, presumably, the first edition of the *Exemplar Literarum*; ARCR, I, no. 314. William Trumbull wrote on 24 October 1616 to Winwood that he should 'peruse the printed relation of four priests lately executed in England' and 'consider what...great prejudice we reap' from Gondomar's being there: PRO, SP 77/12, fo. 197ᵛ. The 'Spanish relation' mentioned by Gondomar must be *Relacion de Cinco Martyres*.

[57] Pollen, 'Life', pp. 40–1; Challoner, *MMP*, pp. 349–50; Kn., II, pp. 260–1, 264–5; Camm, 'Venerable Thomas Maxfield', p. 37.

[58] Pollen, 'Life', p. 41.

436 CATHOLICS AND TREASON

1615.[59] On 18 May 1616, Maxfield wrote to Kellison again, mentioning once more the exorcism and saying that he hoped that, before 'long, our sorrows will meet in a point of joyful exultation' and that 'matters were never at the height of hopeful expectation as they are now'. Presumably Maxfield was referring to the possibility of an Anglo-Spanish dynastic treaty; according to Maxfield, while 'Catholics are strongly confident, even the pillars of Protestancy shake with fear and, I hope, will shortly ruinate'.[60]

London Catholics, however, were not necessarily so optimistic. They pointed to the horrible case of Margaret Vincent who, presumably affected by some form of depression, had on 9 May murdered two of her children to prevent them being brought up as Protestants; and, failing to kill herself, was tried and executed. What looked to the authorities like a simple felony seemed to Catholic commentators to be evidence of persecution, resulting in a quasi-martyrdom, not least because, said the surviving pamphlet describing her case, she had been badgered into a form of repentance and a rejection of her stubborn Catholicism. William Rayner tacked onto his account of Atkinson, Thulis, and Warren a narrative of the affair. Rayner described how the persecution was worse than ever and that Catholic wives were being harassed; among them was Mrs Vincent. She was hanged at Tyburn on 19 May 1616, the day after Maxfield wrote to Kellison.[61]

Although John Knaresborough recited that 'there was something so very cruel and barbarous in the treatment of Mr Maxfield' that, in the prison, the 'very felons themselves cried out "shame"', the execution went ahead on 1 July.[62] In order 'to prevent the great concourse of people', the 'sergeants and hangmen' called at the prison at five o'clock in the morning. Other Catholic prisoners in Newgate were stopped from seeing the condemned priest. It had, wrote Challoner, following Knaresborough, been 'ordered that a woman should at the same time be burnt in Smithfield, in hopes that this would make considerable diversion, and draw a great part of the people that way'. But these precautions were 'all . . . to no purpose',

[59] Ibid., pp. 52–3; Anstr., II, pp. 214–15; ABP, p. 339; Pollen, 'Life', pp. 34–5; see pp. 182–3 n.17 above. The exorcist, Edward Hands, was subsequently arrested and, on 5 July 1616—four days after Maxfield's execution—was (according to John Gee, writing in the early 1620s) interrogated by, *inter alia*, George Abbot, John King, John Williams, bishop of Lincoln, and the bishops of Rochester (John Buckeridge) and Coventry and Lichfield (John Overall): T. H. B. M. Harmsen (ed.), *John Gee's Foot out of the Snare (1624)* (Nijmegen, 1992), p. 131; for Richard Blount's report of 27 June 1616 that Hands had been 'very busy in exorcizing two maids possessed with devils, wherein it is feared the Devil has foully deluded and deceived him', see ARSJ, Anglia 37, fo. 134[v]. Later in the year Anthony Champney reported that Hands was seriously deluded—'thinking that the blessed Trinity was in him and spoke in him and that the Blessed Virgin and divers saints did also speak in a maid who was thought to have been dispossessed of a devil by him'. John Colleton had ordered him to 'desist from such speeches', but others encouraged him to continue, which he did until he was arrested: AAW, A XV, no. 123, p. 329.

[60] Pollen, 'Life', p. 55. Shortly before his trial, Maxfield wrote again to Kellison in anticipation of his martyrdom: Challoner, *MMP*, pp. 352–3 (for the version in Butler's papers, see ABP, pp. 519–20).

[61] Lake and Questier, *Antichrist's Lewd Hat*, pp. 41, 44, 95–6, 99, 127, 128, 254; *A Pitiless Mother . . .* (1616), sig. B[v]–2[r]; AAW, A XV, no. 98, p. 259; ARSJ, Anglia 32/i, fo. 25[r] (which puts the execution on 18/28 May).

[62] Kn., II, p. 251.

for 'the people poured in from all parts of the town: and streets, windows and balconies were all thronged with unusual numbers to see this holy priest drawn to Tyburn; and great multitudes there were...who accompanied him to the very place of execution, amongst whom were many Catholics of fashion as well foreigners as English'. The 'Spaniards...joined themselves in a body and, though they met with many affronts, forced their way through the crowd to the sledge and accompanied the confessor...frequently exhorting him to constancy and perseverance, and begging for themselves his prayers and blessing, with their heads uncovered and bowed down in the most respectful manner'. The *Vita et Martyrium* which describes Maxfield's ordeal says that 'the Spaniards...mounted upon goodly horses rode two by two in a long train both before and on each side of the martyr', a kind of guard of honour almost to the gates of heaven. Maxfield was attired as a priest with a cassock and a biretta.[63]

The coordinated demonstration of support for Maxfield reached its height at Tyburn itself. 'This gallows, at midnight before, the Catholics had adorned and beset with garlands, flowers and branches round about and had strawed the ground underneath with bays and sweet herbs'. This infuriated 'the public ministers of justice'.[64] Catholics had 'made it their business in the small hours of that morning to decorate the posts of the gallows with green branches, as' if 'it were a bridal chamber or a triumphal chariot'. But the 'halberdiers' stripped 'the decorated gallows, tearing down and cutting off the garlands'.[65] Among those who had turned out in order to face down Maxfield was Samuel Purchas, a thoroughly puritan chaplain of Archbishop Abbot, though Maxfield did not rise to the bait.[66]

This was, then, a massive Catholic demonstration performed in the middle of the capital, in front of a large crowd—4000 according to some Catholic narratives—and sponsored by the Spanish embassy. Maxfield in the middle of the strewn flowers and the branches started to deliver his gallows speech but, once he denied his alleged treason, he was interrupted. Still, he managed to declare that the sole cause of his condemnation was his priesthood. One of the sheriffs said that, in reality, the cause was the Gunpowder Plot and offered the priest a royal reprieve if he would take the oath, but to no avail. Swiftly, the cart was drawn away with one official shouting 'to the executioner to cut the rope and butcher him alive, according to sentence'. But, as so often in the past, waves of disapproval emanated from the watching crowd. 'Loud reproaches' made clear the watchers' 'horror of such a barbarous proposition'. The manuscript account of Maxfield's death which

---

[63] Challoner, *MMP*, pp. 350–1; Kn., II, pp. 266–8, VII, p. 438; Pollen, 'Life', pp. 42–3; AAW, A XV, no. 123, p. 329; Camm, 'Venerable Thomas Maxfield', p. 56. Lords Mordaunt and Compton were present, and it was Gondomar's son, Antonio, who appeared at Tyburn rather than the ambassador himself: Camm, 'Venerable Thomas Maxfield', p. 42.

[64] Pollen, 'Life', p. 43; Anstr., II, p. 215; Lake and Questier, 'Agency', p. 101; Kn., II, pp. 268–9.

[65] Camm, 'Venerable Thomas Maxfield', p. 43.

[66] Pollen, 'Life', pp. 43–4; Camm, 'Venerable Thomas Maxfield', pp. 41, 43, 56; *ODNB*, *sub* Purchas, Samuel (article by D. Armitage).

438   CATHOLICS AND TREASON

is retained in the Biblioteca Nacional in Madrid says that it was the 'noblemen' present who intervened. Faced with this, there was no option but to let Maxfield 'hang till he was dead, at least to all sense of pain, and then he was bowelled and quartered'.[67] Richard Blount, who recorded that early on the Monday he 'went forth to see the execution, and stood under the gallows all the time until he was quartered', 'never saw such a mangling and butchery of a man's body'.[68] One woman cried out 'Gloria in Excelsis Deo – for the conversion of England, for the conversion of England!' There was a scuffle between a spectator who declared that at least Maxfield was now in Hell and another watcher who sharply denied it ('are you the doorkeeper of Hell?').[69]

The Biblioteca Nacional manuscript had no doubts as to the significance of all this. The wretched Benedictine monk Thomas Preston, who had, under his alias of Widdrington, published 'those pestilent books' in justification of the oath of allegiance, had brought on himself the 'guilt not only of this most innocent victim's death but also of all the evils which', via the godless oath, were 'perpetrated throughout Britain'. It might be true that King James could have 'been more severe, yet he is not to be called merciful because he did not put more to death, for he ought not to have slain one of those who were the only faithful friends that his mother had'. But 'against those that will not repent' in the matter of the oath, 'it is right that we should wait on the hand of God, for as the cause is His, so also is the vengeance'.[70] At Douai, Matthew Kellison caused a 'Te Deum and a solemn Mass to be sung in thanksgiving for' Maxfield's 'glorious victory'.[71]

Local officials tried to prevent Maxfield's body becoming a source of holy power. One Catholic letter writer said that there had been 'a proclamation penned very strictly that none should have any of the straw which came near him and great provision that no relic should be had of his' and 'great care was taken that nobody should come near unto him'; but to no avail because 'the French' and 'especially the Spanish ambassador's men pressed unto him and, wrapping relics of him in their handkerchiefs, wept much and complained of the king's cruelty in public'. This letter had, enclosed with it, a 'relic' which was 'part of the same' which Maxfield 'carried in his hand whilst he went to execution'.[72] Among the

---

[67] Challoner, MMP, pp. 350–2; Pollen, 'Life', p. 45; Camm, 'Venerable Thomas Maxfield', p. 56; AAW, A XV, no. 123, p. 329 (Champney's statement that it was understood at Douai that when Maxfield gave 'his blessing upon the gallows, very many put off their hats; but this is not in our letters'). The two sheriffs present were William Gore and John Gore, whose brother Richard had sat in the 1604 parliament: Camm, 'Venerable Thomas Maxfield', pp. 43, 45; HC 1604–29, IV, p. 433. In 1623, Thomas White 'retrieved from England a rib of the recently martyred Thomas Maxfield to serve as a sacred relic at the college' at Douai: ODNB, sub White, Thomas (article by B. Southgate). For the translation of Maxfield's body to Spain and its subsequent disappearance and then, in 1912, its discovery, see Anstr., II, p. 215; Camm, 'Venerable Thomas Maxfield', pp. 53–4.
[68] ARSJ, Anglia 37, fo. 81ᵛ ([Richard Blount] to Joseph Creswell, 6 July 1616).
[69] Pollen, 'Life', p. 46; Camm, 'Venerable Thomas Maxfield', pp. 43, 44.   [70] Ibid., p. 46.
[71] AAW, A XV, no. 123, p. 329.
[72] Pollen, 'Life', p. 58 (the letter (AAW, 16/9/7) is endorsed 'flowers which Mr Maxfield carried in his hand to Tyburn').

THE PROTESTANT TURN TURNS SOUR   439

Figure 13.1 Relic associated with Thomas Maxfield, d.1616 (reproduced with the permission of the cardinal-archbishop of Westminster).

Westminster Cathedral archives' collections on Maxfield there is the calix of a pink, a tiny fragment, which Maxfield allegedly held as he was hanged.[73] (See Figure 13.1.)

The authorities were aware that there would be an attempt to seize Maxfield's remains and so they dug 'a pit of wondrous depth and therein cast the torn and severed body and upon it they' put 'two other putrefied carcasses of two malefactors that had lain stinking in rottenness and which, a month before, they had hanged and buried under ground. Then upon these they piled' the 'thirteen bodies' of those hanged on the same day as Maxfield. They 'covered all with a great heap of earth, supposing by this means [that] none would be so bold, or rather so mad, as they thought, to bestow so great a labour and to feel those stenches in digging out so many carcasses as there were put in, knowing it withal to be forbidden on pain of death'. Mad or not, 'the devotion and boldness of the faithful overcame the counsel of the heretics'. Maxfield's remains were recovered, at the direction of the Spanish embassy, by 'twenty Spaniards and some English

[73] Ibid.; Camm, 'Venerable Thomas Maxfield', p. 49.

440 CATHOLICS AND TREASON

Catholics'. These grave robbers were themselves shielded from discovery, as dawn broke, by a providential and other-worldly 'misty darkness'.[74] For all the alleged oddness of the recently deceased Luisa de Carvajal, her zeal in recovering the butchered remains of martyred priests was evidently shared by Gondomar and his friends.

Gondomar was reported by the Venetian embassy to have said that the gross injustice of Maxfield's execution made an Anglo-Spanish dynastic alliance impossible.[75] Presses in the Spanish Netherlands, principally at Douai, kept the screws on in later 1616 and in 1617 by issuing new editions of the original pamphlet about Maxfield and the other martyrs of 1616.[76] On 13 July 1616, barely two weeks after Maxfield's death, the priest Thomas Tunstall had been executed at Norwich. He, like Maxfield (and Thulis and Warren) had broken prison, though in Tunstall's case it had been a full twelve months previously. It is possible that the authorities in Norwich were copying what they thought was the lead being set elsewhere.[77] Tunstall is said to have been arrested at the insistence of Sir Hamon L'Estrange, a JP, whose wife inadvertently betrayed to him Tunstall's whereabouts and identity.[78] Tunstall may have attempted a modified form of compliance. He 'did earnestly entreat' the judge, Sir James Altham, 'that a conference might be had about religion' with a minister, so 'that truth might appear'. But the judge told him that he was 'a crafty disputant' and a 'cunning sophister'.[79]

The fact that some Catholic clergy were still being dragged to execution did not, it appears, stop other Catholics from trying to exploit the king's distinctions between some Catholics and others, that is, to the extent of offering a modicum of conformity in religion. Thus, on 7 July 1616, six days after Maxfield's death and six days before Tunstall's, George Gordon, marquis of Huntly, the high-profile Scottish Catholic peer, was absolved in London (by none other than Archbishop Abbot) from his excommunication by the Kirk. He received communion as well, thus manipulating the current tensions between the Kirk and the Church of England, and exploiting, one assumes, James's recent statements both about the national Churches of Scotland and England and also about Catholics and loyalty. The Kirk's general assembly had no choice but to acquiesce, though the Scottish

[74] Pollen, 'Life', p. 47; Camm, 'Venerable Thomas Maxfield', pp. 57, 58; Kn., II, pp. 270–6; Challoner, MMP, p. 352; Anstr., II, p. 215.
[75] CSPV 1615–17, pp. 264–5. According to Sir Tobias Mathew on 11/21 November 2016, Lord Roos's embassy to Spain in late 1616, with an informal brief to talk about an Anglo-Spanish match but no formal authority to negotiate it, was also intended 'to justify the execution of these late four priests': PRO, SP 77/12, fo. 208ᵛ; see also CSPV 1615–17, pp. 304, 328, 342, 347, 351, 388, 418.
[76] ARCR, I, nos 314–20.
[77] Challoner, MMP, p. 354; AAW, B 28, no. 10, p. 327; Ghent MSS, II, no. 54, p. 199: letter of Richard Blount, 25 July 1616; TD, V, pp. clxxv–vi; Bibliothèque Royale, Brussels, MS 2158–67, fos 282ᵛ–6ᵛ, photocopy retained at ABSJ, CP (Thomas Tunstall).
[78] Challoner, MMP, p. 354; Kn., II, pp. 281 f., VII, pp. 441 f.; AAW, B 28, no. 10, p. 327. Tunstall appears to have entered the Benedictine order before 1615.
[79] Challoner, MMP, p. 355; Kn., VII, p. 443.

THE PROTESTANT TURN TURNS SOUR   441

bishops made their displeasure very clear. The occasion for Huntly's public conformity was the consecration of the Calvinist Thomas Morton as bishop of Chester. One of Morton's biographers, John Barwick, wrote that many of the English and Scots nobility were present. The 'concurrence of these two great solemnities', the consecration and the absolution, 'occasioned a very great number of communicants'.[80] Huntly was taken back onto the Scottish privy council in February 1617, that is, in time for the king's progress into Scotland in that year.[81]

The earl of Arundel, who had, as we saw, stationed himself so prominently at the executions of Scot and Newport, conformed in the chapel royal at Christmas 1616. He had already been made an English privy councillor in July, the month of Maxfield's and Tunstall's deaths.[82] When Arundel's house at Greenwich caught fire on 3 January 1617, Chamberlain was certain that the 'papists' would 'ascribe and publish it as a punishment for his dissembling or falling from them'.[83] Arundel, remarked Sir Horace Vere on 8 January 1617, 'in his discourses with his Majesty' was 'sharp against the papists', perhaps not surprisingly in view of what some of them may have said about the damage to his Greenwich property the week before; he had also received the 'sacrament with the king, this Christmas'.[84] But this was still a crucial shift of position by a leading English peer, a mimicking of Huntly's example, and one point of reference for James's strategies for constructing a kind of conformist consensus in his three kingdoms. On 17/27 December 1616, in Paris, Anthony Champney had observed that, although 'the persecution was never so great', King James had nevertheless ordered George Abbot 'to charge the ministers that they say nothing against the Spaniard, with whom' the project for a dynastic alliance was now 'so forward' that some ladies about court were taking lessons in the Spanish language.[85]

Indeed, early 1617 saw the British court looking much more determined in its negotiations with the Spanish monarchy for a dynastic marriage treaty. This is another topic entirely, but we get a sense, coinciding as this did with the very controversial royal visit to Scotland, that the culture, as they say, was changing. Richard Blount noted on 14 March 1617 not only that commissioners for the match had been appointed but also that 'the assizes at Lincoln' were 'now past, and nothing' had been 'done against the priests'. Only one man, Christopher Robinson, had been condemned in praemunire.[86]

---

[80] McClure, *LJC*, II, pp. 19–20; BL, Harleian MS 7004, no. 52, fo. 97ʳ; MacDonald, *The Jacobean Kirk*, p. 154; John Barwick, *A Summarie Account of the Holy Life...and Happy Death of...Thomas late Lord Bishop of Durham* (1660), published with John Barwick, *ΙΕΡΟΝΙΚΗΣ, or the Fight, Victory, and Triumph of S. Paul...* (1660), pp. 76–7.

[81] Robertson, *Lordship and Power*, p. 58; D. Masson (ed.), *Register of the Privy Council of Scotland 1616–1619* (Edinburgh, 1894), p. 48; *ODNB, sub* Gordon, George (article by J. R. M. Sizer).

[82] McClure, *LJC*, II, p. 47; *HMCD*, V, pp. 553, 569.   [83] McClure, *LJC*, II, p. 47.

[84] PRO, SP 14/90/11, fo. 14ʳ.

[85] AAW, A XV, no. 188, p. 495.

[86] Ghent MSS, II, no. 59, p. 216. Somebody who had been severely censured (again) by high commission was the puritan Arthur Hildersham in late November 1616: L. A. Rowe, 'The Worlds of

442   CATHOLICS AND TREASON

On 26 May 1617 the godlier members of the privy council back in London (which had, three days before, told the keeper of Newgate to prevent the Catholic clergy there from holding 'correspondence by writing with the colleges of Douai and St Omer') were forced to write to Scotland to admit that there had been 'much speech and rumour here in London of a proclamation published in the county of York' by the high sheriff of Yorkshire, Sir Michael Wharton. Wharton had released this declaration 'against recusants...upon his Majesty's passage that way in his journey towards Scotland', that is, as James was on his expedition northwards. Wharton claimed to have taken 'his warrant from his Majesty's verbal direction'.[87] While he was in York, James had certainly been badgered both by Lord Sheffield and by Wharton himself. They said that Catholics 'cared not to appear after a summons, nor obey orders'. These two officials had concluded that there should be one verbal warning to disobedient papists and then their houses should be demolished—exactly the treatment that, once upon a time, used to be handed out to rebels in Scotland. Allegedly James had (sort of) said that some action ought to be taken against the habitually disobedient.[88] The problem was that, subsequently, those involved in this meeting had different recollections of it. As a result, Wharton was sent to the Fleet prison.[89] On 30 June 1617 the council in London had to record that a letter had come from the court in Scotland setting out what James had actually said to Wharton on his way northwards 'about the proclamation touching recusants according to a declaration' which the king had 'graciously vouchsafed to make' to the councillors attending on him. Wharton refused to back down. The council in London had already written on the previous day to Lord Sheffield to explain 'how his Majesty disavows the sheriff's proceedings'.[90]

To some observers, this was terrifying. James had always talked the language of intolerance rather convincingly, and even during 1616 he had issued macabre gallows-humour one-liners in star chamber, as we saw, about the likely fate of

Arthur Hildersham (1563–1632)' (PhD, Warwick, 2009), pp. 18–19, citing Samuel Clarke, *The Lives of Two and Twenty English Divines*... (1660), p. 150.

[87] *APC 1616–17*, pp. 255–6.

[88] Loomie, *SJC*, II, p. 87.

[89] Loomie, *SJC*, II, p. 88; *APC 1616–17*, p. 273. For Sir Michael Wharton's order concerning recusants (12 April 1617), see PRO, SP 14/91/30; see also PRO, SP 14/92/27, 36, 51. On 23 June 1617 the council in London, responding directly to the king in Scotland, dealt with Wharton, who had 'committed a rash presumption in making a proclamation in sundry places of that county without sufficient warrant, by colour of some verbal direction from his Majesty, utterly mistaken by the sheriff, and strained against law and the justice of the realm': *APC 1616–17*, pp. 269, 281–2. At the same time, the keeper of the Gatehouse gaol was similarly disciplined for ill-treating Catholics imprisoned there. Gondomar attributed these signs of tolerance to Catholics 'to the negotiations now under way about the marriage of this prince [Charles]' with Philip III's daughter: Loomie, *SJC*, II, pp. 88–9; but cf. Ghent MSS, II, no. 65, p. 232, no. 66, pp. 231–2, no. 67, pp. 238–9 (Richard Blount's claims, in July 1617, that the 'persecution' had got worse, including the news that Thomas Sackville was being offered the choice of deportation or being tendered the oath of allegiance).

[90] *APC 1616–17*, pp. 280–2; Aveling, *NC*, p. 210.

THE PROTESTANT TURN TURNS SOUR 443

uncompliant seminary priests. Then, with little warning, James was off humiliating godly officials in the North who by their own lights were just doing their job and holding the line against a tidal wave of popish civil disobedience. On his way back from Scotland through Lancashire, James ran into, in effect, a noisy Catholic public demonstration as the issue of so-called lawful sports and pastimes on the Sabbath was put to the test as a way of attacking local puritans and the godly Calvinist bishop Thomas Morton, whose recent consecration ceremony had been combined with Huntly's public conformity.[91] On 14/24 November 1617, Sir Henry Wotton wrote from Venice that 'all the *gazettanti* here of this week have, in their idle leaves, scattered a report that the king has lately much enlarged the liberties of the papists in England with I know not what hope of farther grants unto them'. These rumours, Wotton established, had originated in Flanders. Wotton sourly remarked that 'the king is besieged', for 'sometimes they preach against his persecutions, sometimes they vaunt of his lenities'.[92] By all accounts, James found this rather vexing. Sir George Villiers, the recently promoted marquis of Buckingham, informed Sir Francis Bacon in February 1618 that the king would not tolerate English Catholics openly celebrating Sir John Digby's commission to negotiate with Spain. It would go harder with them for the time being which, in turn, might make them the more likely to support the proposed match in hope of future leniency.[93]

It became clear that the king was not merely flirting with the Spaniards, though this was not fully apparent until after the slow train wreck of the Bohemian revolt and James's son-in-law Frederick V's acceptance of the Bohemian crown. But it was then almost inevitable that, in the course of negotiating such a treaty, the Spaniards would insist that it should include toleration clauses for James's Catholic subjects. One of the ways in which those who were opposed to the negotiations could demonstrate their dislike of them was by continuing to enforce the statutes against Catholics to the letter of the law.

Here and there we have references to the authorities' attempts to make the statute law mean what it still technically said. On 14 April 1618 someone had sent a letter out of York Castle. It claimed that 'we are all here in very great persecution' and 'all the poor prisoners are in the low gaol in irons and barred of their friends' relief'. The writer said that he had 'got an order the last assizes for their relief' from 'the judges but the gaoler' would 'not obey it'. The writer was himself, for this, about to be gaoled. The impact of official hostility to such Catholics was

---

[91] Barwick, *A Summarie Account*, pp. 79–83; Richard Baddeley, *The Life of Dr Thomas Morton...* (York, 1669), pp. 60–2; Questier, *DP*, p. 383; for cases in Herefordshire in 1618 which may have similarly been informed, *inter alia*, by the book of sports issue, see W. Brogden, 'Catholicism, Community and Identity in Late Tudor and Early Stuart Welsh Borderlands' (PhD, Birmingham, 2018), p. 194.
[92] Smith, *Life*, II, pp. 124–5.
[93] Feil, 'Sir Tobie Matthew', p. 130, citing BL, Harleian MS 7006, fo. 241^r.

444   CATHOLICS AND TREASON

causing some of them to offer compliance. Among the six priests in the prison, one—Thomas Riddle—had been sentenced to death, but he 'was so loath to die the last assizes as, being condemned, before judgment he yielded to take the oath and, as some say, to go to the Church'. He had been set 'at liberty, a silly man God knows, and they insulted upon his want of wit and learning exceedingly'.[94] Worse still, the renegade (or close-to-renegade) priest William Johnson had, it seems, procured the cleric William Southerne's arrest. Johnson was the brother of the Constable family's loyalist chaplain, Cuthbert Johnson. The renegade was in 'great credit with the lord president', Lord Sheffield, presumably because of his betrayal of Southerne. He was also in credit with 'the council and with the pursuivants and' was likewise 'at liberty'. Bizarrely he was insisting that he was still 'a Catholic' and that he did 'no hurt, but he' was 'feared much'.[95] A newsletter from one 'Newburn' in London on 10 May 1618 said that Southerne had been taken 'upon the highway' by Lord Sheffield. Then, 'by a private session', Sheffield 'arraigned him and executed him'. Southerne was, said Blount, offered his life 'twenty times' if he would take the oath.[96] But he refused and on c.30 April 1618 he had been strung up at Newcastle.[97]

Lord Sheffield had reasons at that point to think that he was being undervalued. On 21 April 1618 the privy council had delivered a searing report on his tenure of office and his alleged incompetence and neglect in dealing with 'malefactors'. The letter was signed by a range of councillors, starting with Archbishop Abbot, who was presumably very unenthusiastic about this humiliation of the reliably Calvinist lord president of the council in the North.[98] Southerne was hanged around nine days after the date of this letter. Assuming that Sheffield had received this letter very promptly, the execution looks like a kind of screw-you response to the verbal going-over which he had just received from London—a perfect riposte, but in a thoroughly Hispanophobe register. Another commentator, the Jesuit James Sharp, on 21 May 1618, linked the trial and execution with the progress of the Anglo-Spanish marriage negotiations: 'at the same [time] that Sir John Digby came over, came down the news' of the execution of Southerne at Newcastle. He had been arrested at 'an inn' with 'some gentlewomen' who were 'to come over' to the Continent, presumably so that they might enter religion. Sharp

[94] ABSJ, Anglia IV, no. 51. Riddle was in York Castle awaiting deportation as late as March 1630: Anstr., II, p. 264.
[95] ABSJ, Anglia IV, no. 51; ARSJ, Anglia 32/i, fo. 36^v; Anstr., I, p. 192. For apparently baseless allegations of sedition made against Southerne in July and August 1615, see AWCBC, pp. 1993–4, 2000–6 (PRO, SP 14/81/54. ii, iv; PRO, SP 14/81/58. i).
[96] ABSJ, Anglia IV, no. 52B (Patrick Barry identifies the writer of this letter as Anthony Fletcher SJ: AWCBC, p. 2007); ARSJ, Anglia 37, fo. 135^r (AWCBC, p. 2010).
[97] ARSJ, Anglia 37, fo. 135^{r-v}; Anstr., I, p. 329. For Southerne, see A. M. C. Forster, 'Ven. William Southerne: Another Tyneside Martyr', RH 4 (1957–8), pp. 199–216; AWCBC, pp. 1993–4, 2000–6.
[98] APC 1618–19, p. 111. For Sheffield's difficulties as lord president, see also S. J. Watts, From Border to Middle Shire: Northumberland 1586–1625 (Leicester, 1975), pp. 195–6.

THE PROTESTANT TURN TURNS SOUR   445

said that 'the king laughed at' the news of Southerne's execution when, predictably, Gondomar turned up to complain about what Lord Sheffield had done. The privy council conceded that it was inappropriate but no more.[99]

Sharp declared that there had 'been and' was still 'a greater brunt of persecution' and all, ironically, in order 'to prepare the way for marriage'. The commissions issued to 'pursuivants' were enlarged, allowing for the sequestration of funds suspected to be earmarked for the maintenance of the Catholic clergy. The malice of the JPs was worse than ever, the prisons were full and the poor were mulcted 'even to the clothes off their back for 12^d a Sunday' under the act of uniformity, 'which is extended to wives and servants'. 'This', wrote Sharp sarcastically, was 'all the good we have from...the hopeful marriage'. It was not much consolation to hear the rumour that 'the king frowned' recently on George Abbot.[100] But another Catholic newsletter, of 22 May 1618, which was sent to Rome, asserted that King James had sworn that all this was done without his knowledge and he would punish those who were responsible.[101] The Spaniard Julián Sánchez de Ulloa was sure in late July 1618 that the king had deprived Lord President Sheffield of his post; and, indeed, Lord Scrope, a known crypto-Catholic, eventually took Sheffield's place.[102] On 14/24 September 1618, Ulloa genuinely believed that there had been a step change in political culture, at least as far as the court was concerned. Catholics gave 'infinite thanks to God for the relief and quiet that they now enjoy' and, gratifyingly for this Spanish diplomat, they attributed it 'to the marriage which is being negotiated'. And it got better. Most of the clergy whose release Gondomar had secured in June 1618 on the condition that they went abroad, and never came back, had almost immediately returned. Some of them were 'walking about openly in the streets of London'. Hilariously, when Abbot tried to give James a written memorandum about Catholics, the king, 'without reading it, tore it into pieces'. Now, large numbers of Mass-goers were attending the embassy chapel, sometimes too many for them all to be accommodated.[103]

Not every Catholic was quite this sanguine. In circa late December 1618, Richard Blount was still writing of the ferocity of what he definitely called the 'persecution'. 'Matters go worse than ordinary and yet the expectation is worse, more being promised than is actually put in execution' and 'we hear of troubles

---

[99] ABSJ, Anglia IV, no. 53 (*AWCBC*, p. 2013–14; Sharp uses the alias of John Pollard); ARSJ, Anglia 37, fo. 136[r].

[100] ABSJ, Anglia IV, no. 53.   [101] Anstr., I, p. 326, citing ASV, Borghese MS III, 127, e, fo. 84[r].

[102] Loomie, *SJC*, II, p. 113; Watts, *From Border to Middle Shire*, p. 196. In 1619 Sheffield (who had serious money problems) sold the lord presidency to Scrope, though it seems that he was, in part, coerced into resigning: Adams, PC, p. 435; *ODNB*, *sub* Sheffield, Edmund (article by V. Stater).

[103] Loomie, *SJC*, II, p. 115; *CSPD 1611–18*, pp. 543, 546, 548, 549 (PRO, SP 14/97/95, 113, 114, 129, 135, 136); *CSPV 1617–19*, pp. 241, 244, 341; PRO, SP 77/13, fos 77[v], 79[v]–80[r]; *HMCD*, VI, pp. 455, 467–8; *APC 1618–19*, pp. 175, 196–8, 202–3, 239–40. For the setting free of William Baldwin SJ, see pp. 449–52 below.

446 CATHOLICS AND TREASON

out of all places'. Representatives of the Dutch Republic had arrived in order 'to excuse the insolence of some of their countrymen and to farm, as it is said, the forfeiture of the papists', even if it is not clear that this was true. In fact, it was difficult to know what to make of it all. Two of the clergy who had come back, contrary to the terms of their release, had been arrested. John Chamberlain had heard that 'some three or four of them' were 'taken', and the king had even said that they 'shall truss for it'.[104] The new archpriest, William Harrison, had on 13 December 1618 related to the nuncio in Flanders the scandal of Southerne's treatment and the cruelty exercised by Lord Sheffield. Things were marginally better in the South because of 'the projected match between our prince and the infanta of Spain' but, still, there was a rumour of 'the probable execution of certain priests'. Though this had not happened, Harrison said that 'we live in uncertainty between fear and hope'.[105] Blount wrote on 14/24 March 1619 that, 'upon Palm Sunday', his confrère John Percy was 'apprehended in London'. The 'pursuivants never kept such racket as now, being set on by puritans of purpose to break the match', even though 'his Majesty...seems much affected' to it 'and expects the return of...Gondomar'.[106]

At some level, all of the Jacobean Catholic narratives of martyrdom seem fairly bizarre—with yet more unspeakable savageries being inflicted, although sporadically, on sometimes rather anonymous and inoffensive clergymen—little more than the fag end of the gunpowder business, but written up by some commentators, such as Luisa de Carvajal, in almost apocalyptic terms. At the same time, we have Catholic separatists who were out in the open, particularly in London, watching the execution of their co-religionists, and challenging, from time to time, the mid-Jacobean regime to rethink its approach to the enforcement of conformity. For his part, the king was still playing with the language of tolerance—at one moment almost revelling in the use of treason penalties against Catholic separatists and at other times humiliating and rebuking the likes of the, in any case, thoroughly unpleasant George Abbot for burdening him (James) with the reputation of a persecutor.

---

[104] ABSJ, Anglia IV, no. 55; McClure, *LJC*, II, p. 190. For the visit of the Dutch envoys, see *CSPV 1617–19*, pp. 381f. In late 1618, at the instance of Lord Henry Clifford, there was a particularly active commission of enquiry into recusancy in the Northumberland archdeaconry. Large numbers of Catholic separatists were indicted there in 1619–20 (large certainly when compared with the very low tallies in Bishop Richard Neile's Durham): Watts, *From Border to Middle Shire*, p. 199. The attorney-general, Sir Henry Yelverton, at Michaelmas 1619 laid informations against 131 women in king's bench for their recusancy: S. Healy, 'Persecution and Toleration in Yorkshire: The case of Richard Cholemeley of Brandsby' (forthcoming). See also Feil, 'Sir Tobie Matthew', p. 155, for Sir Tobias Matthew's letter (PRO, SP 77/14, fo. 74^v) to Sir Dudley Carleton of 14/24 April 1620 concerning the enforcement of the recusancy statutes 'with more than ordinary punctuality', despite the negotiations with Spain and the 'appearance of all confidence' between the king and Gondomar.
[105] *Miscellanea III* (CRS 3, 1906), p. 95.   [106] ARSJ, Anglia 37, fo. 135^r.

THE PROTESTANT TURN TURNS SOUR   447

What makes these Jacobean cases so significant, however, is that they are part and parcel of a Catholic agitation for tolerance which also envisaged the creation of structures for Catholic life and worship in England which were normative in other European Christian nations which were in communion with Rome. As we have seen, some Catholic clergy were petitioning Rome to institute a form of episcopacy in England. Others were trying to prevent it; and, in the religious orders, there were attempts to strengthen their own distinctive regulatory structures. In 1619 the Jesuits in England were formed into a vice-province, and a full province four years later. All of these Catholics, however, tended to claim that, despite the regrettable malice towards them of the usual puritan suspects in the upper reaches of the Church of England, the king need have no worries about them. Indeed, they said that the regularization of the methods by which English Catholics were governed, even though technically in separation from the national Church, were compatible with monarchical government and, in fact, were crucial to the king's security. This was because the proper supervision of those in England who regarded themselves as Catholics, even in separation from the national Church, would prevent the use of their religion for seditious purposes.

Towards the end of the 1610s, then, we get a sense of a deeply unstable status quo. Here, the Catholic community was (still) fractured—divided between, on the one hand, those who declared themselves to be loyalists virtually in the terms set out by the State and, on the other, those who were not prepared to endorse royal claims about where the dividing line between conscience and political obedience lay. Yet those who believed they were the victims of persecution also tried to appropriate a loyalist persona, even while they actively celebrated and publicized the tradition of zeal under the cross of persecution in the English Church. Later in the 1620s James Wadsworth reminded his readers that in the Jesuit College at St Omer, where he had been until 1622, the students' devotional exercises still included the reading of 'the Latin Martyrology' and then the 'English' which 'contains the legend of our English martyrs and traitors together, sometimes two in one day'. The 'students hear out the relation' with admiration 'and cap in hand to the memory of Campion, Garnet, Thomas Becket and [Sir Thomas] More'.[107]

Here was an insistent reaffirmation of one of the principal claims that had been made ever since the Elizabethan persecution began (although there was more than one way of making it)—namely that, as long as there was a degree of coherence

---

[107] James Wadsworth, *The English Spanish Pilgrime*... (1629), p. 17; *ODNB, sub* Wadsworth, James (article by A. J. Loomie); J. A. Graffius, '"Bullworks against the Furie of Heresie": Relics, Material Culture and the Spiritual and Cultural Formation of the Sodality of St Omers English Jesuit College 1593–1650' (PhD, Aberdeen, 2018), pp. 46, 297 and *passim*.

448 CATHOLICS AND TREASON

and solidarity inside the Catholic community in the face of the hostility shown to it by malign State officials and certain opinionated Protestants, in the end the complex array of intolerant and increasingly redundant laws that penalized good Catholics would start to disintegrate—all in the context of what seemed like a new royal approach to dealing with Britain's European neighbours.

14

Towards Toleration?

The Change of the Times in Late Jacobean and Caroline Britain

The Release of William Baldwin, European War, and Dynastic Marriage Negotiations

We saw in the previous chapter that during the later 1610s there was real uncertainty as to whether the legal firewall provided by the Elizabethan statutes against a variety of types of Catholic nonconformity was going to last for much longer. For people with worries on this score, their sense of insecurity would definitely have been made worse by what the populace of London was able to witness in June 1618. Only weeks after the long-serving missionary priest William Southerne had been executed at Newcastle, an extraordinary event took place at the Tower of London. Here the Jesuit prisoner William Baldwin was released from his gaol and was greeted by what looked like a degree of public acclaim.

The setting free of Baldwin was about as close to an anti-martyrdom in this period as one could get. If anyone was a candidate for the rope and the disembowelling block in this period, it was probably him. Many contemporaries would have expected this Jesuit already to have been dragged to Tyburn and eviscerated. He had, as we saw, been detained in the Rhineland Palatinate in late 1610 and ended up incarcerated in the Tower. He was believed to have been complicit in the Gunpowder conspiracy and had been suspected also of involvement in the earlier 'Spanish Treason'. In March 1612 King James had professed to think that Baldwin had been part of the 'Main' plot as well.[1] James's diplomats in Brussels had spent a good deal of time haranguing the archducal government about the lack of respect in Flanders for their king because of the harbouring there of his traitors and rebels. But now Baldwin left the Tower in something like triumph. Baldwin was not, of course, the only Catholic clergyman who was let out at this point. Other Catholic priestly prisoners of conscience had already been released

---

[1] Loomie, *SJC*, I, p. 175; Richard Verstegan, *Newes from the Low-Countreyes*...(n.p. [St Omer], 1622), pp. 67–8, where Baldwin's release is cited as proof that the allegations made against Catholics, i.e. that they were seditious conspirators, were nonsense. For Richard Broughton, Baldwin's release proved that 'both priests and Catholics were, upon this pretence [of the Gunpowder Plot], most unjustly persecuted': Richard Broughton, *English Protestants Plea, and Petition, for English Preists and Papists, to the present Court of Parlament*...(n.p. [St Omer], 1621), p. 62.

Catholics and Treason: Martyrology, Memory, and Politics in the Post-Reformation. Michael Questier,
Oxford University Press. © Michael Questier 2022. DOI: 10.1093/oso/9780192847027.003.0014

450   CATHOLICS AND TREASON

in mid-1618.[2] But, as Jean Libigny later complained to William Trumbull on 28 July/7 August 1618, Baldwin and the others had been let out in order to 'add lustre to the triumphal departure from England' of the count of Gondomar.[3]

If asked, royal officials might well have said that all this was in line with rigorous punishment of Catholic separatism and that convicted clergymen were being sent off abroad with dire warnings not to come back; but it may not have looked like that to the general public. Baldwin's emergence from the Tower must, at the very least, have been taken as a serious snub to James's son-in-law Frederick V, the elector palatine of the Rhine in whose territory Baldwin had been arrested. According to Baldwin's own narrative of his 'delivery', Gondomar had gone to the king and had 'demanded my liberty about the 7th or 8th of June'. James displayed 'an exceeding dislike of me' and, allegedly, was still convinced that Baldwin was 'accessory to the powder treason'. But Gondomar put his cards on the table. If James wanted 'a match with Spain', he should 'match first with the Society' because, although he was 'a potent prince, yet' he might 'be assured that' the Jesuit order was 'more potent (as having greater possession of men's hearts) than' James himself or even Philip III. Here, ironically, Gondomar was subscribing to something very similar to a popular anti-popish version of the Jesuits' tentacle-like reach and influence. Apparently James 'laughed at his conceit' and promised that he would think it over, but he said that Catholic clergymen who were freed from prison and deported must not enter the country again. Gondomar said that he could not guarantee it. 'But', riposted James 'what if I hang them upon their return?' Gondomar said that would be a really bad idea. James conceded that they should not perish 'for the first time', that is, for their first offence in that regard. 'Neither', said Gondomar, 'the second nor third', and, when James finally asked how often, Gondomar cited the scriptural precedent of seventy-seven times. In other words, there should be no more martyrs.[4]

Whatever it was that Gondomar actually said to James, Baldwin, like the others, was indeed set free. 'After five days', James sent Lord Buckingham and Sir John Digby to Gondomar with the warrant for Baldwin's freedom. In the interim 'the news' of Sir Walter Raleigh, that is, of his return from his expedition and his subsequent arrest, 'came to the court', which held up matters somewhat. But then the day came and Baldwin was let out. He took the opportunity to declare that he had 'never offended his Majesty'. The earl of Northumberland, incarcerated in the Tower since 1606 for his alleged complicity in the gunpowder treason, was 'walking upon the green' and went up to Baldwin to congratulate him.[5] The 'people

---

[2] For the release of imprisoned clergy in early June 1618, see p. 445 above. For Richard Blount's narrative of Baldwin's liberation, in a letter to Thomas Owen, dated 24 July 1618, see ARSJ, Anglia 32/i, fo. 39r; see also Ghent MSS, II, no. 78, p. 264.

[3] HMCD, VI, p. 461.   [4] ABSJ, Anglia VI, no. 87; Loomie, SJC, II, pp. 109–10.

[5] ABSJ, Anglia VI, no. 87; ODNB, sub, Raleigh, Sir Walter (article by M. Nicholls and P. Williams). The imprisoned Mary Talbot, countess of Shrewsbury, who had 'afforded' Baldwin 'so many favours', sent word that she wanted to speak with him before his departure: ABSJ, Anglia VI, no. 87.

TOWARDS TOLERATION? 451

began to flock about the lieutenant's house upon a bruit raised' of Baldwin's liberty, 'so as at my entrance', said the Jesuit, 'I found many to see and salute me'. One of the officials in charge of the Tower assured Baldwin that he 'was the only prisoner that ever he knew which had given such a universal satisfaction' by his behaviour. As Baldwin prepared to 'go to the coach, the yard wherein it stood was full of people' and he could 'hardly enter' because of the 'press and salutation'. The earl and countess of Somerset were there, to whom Baldwin 'sent a private excuse for not visiting them as they expected'. Baldwin reached the Spanish embassy in Holborn, accompanied by Buckingham. Gondomar described all this on 24 June/4 July in half-humorous mode to Cardinal Bellarmine. He admitted that 'the king had been quite adamant against granting me Father Baldwin' along with the other imprisoned clergy. But in the end Buckingham brought him 'a diamond ring in the shape of a heart in his name' as proof that he (James) would 'stay as firm as this' piece 'had been difficult to carve'; and Baldwin was another jewel which was a 'finer present', especially since James 'knew how puritanical a papist' he (Gondomar) was.[6]

When Baldwin arrived at the embassy, 'there attended a multitude of Catholics', as well as Gondomar's own household. They 'gave such signs of joy' that Baldwin could barely force his way through the throng. With the ambassador were prominent Catholics such as Francis Manners, earl of Rutland, and Thomas, Lord Darcy. They urged Baldwin to 'remain' in his 'habit in that manner which is usual of the Society'. It was known that the principal negotiator with the Spaniards, Sir John Digby, had come 'that morning...from the court and had speech' with Baldwin; and their conversation 'in effect was, after a congratulation', that Baldwin 'was a person which might do the king and realm great service'. Baldwin's response, though he professed himself merely a spiritual man, was naturally that he 'should be ready to perform that which might be required' of him. Baldwin stayed in the ambassador's house for two weeks. He said Mass frequently. On Baldwin's own account, he was besieged by a continuous stream of 'courtiers and ladies' who came to 'visit and salute' him. James, Lord Hay, 'amongst the rest, requested to have correspondence' with him and hoped to visit him in Flanders.[7]

---

[6] ABSJ, Anglia VI, no. 87; Loomie, *SJC*, II, p. 109.

[7] ABSJ, Anglia VI, no. 87; Loomie, *SJC*, II, p. 110. Among those who were rumoured to have visited Baldwin in the Tower was Archbishop Abbot, but the archbishop angrily denied it to Trumbull on 28 December 1618: *HMCD*, VI, p. 624; D. Coast, *News and Rumour in Jacobean England: Information, Court Politics and Diplomacy, 1618–25* (Manchester, 2014), p. 200. In Brussels on 5/15 August 1618 Trumbull had recorded how irritated he was to have recently been called upon by Baldwin and Creswell (while Trumbull was in Ghent). Baldwin had said 'that the grace and favour he had received from his Majesty in England did oblige him' to serve the king's interests, and he had declared how ready he was 'to do' the king 'all humble service': PRO, SP 77/13, fo. 31ʳ. It appears that when Gondomar left the country he took with him some of the physical remains of the priest Robert Sutton, who had been executed at Stafford on 27 July 1588: *AWCBC*, p. 648; see p. 182 above.

452 CATHOLICS AND TREASON

The impact of this reverse martyrdom can be picked up from Thomas Scott's inflammatory pamphlet called *Vox Populi*. The pamphlet makes Gondomar say that he had 'with much difficulty' obtained Baldwin's 'life and liberty'. He then 'solemnly went in person, attended with all my train and divers other well-willers, to fetch him out of the Tower'. Gondomar treated Baldwin with the utmost respect in order to 'provoke the English Catholics to the like devout obedience'. In this fashion 'these Jesuits, whose authority was somewhat weakened since the schism between them and the seculars, and the succeeding powder plot', would be able to serve Spanish interests. For good measure, says this fictive version of the ambassador, 'I have somewhat dashed the authority' of the 'high commission' on the basis of which 'diverse pursuivants' made it their business 'to disturb the Catholics, search their houses for priests, holy vestments, books, beads, crucifixes and the like religious appurtenances'. He had 'caused the execution of their office to be slackened, that so open [a] way' could 'be given to our spiritual instruments for the free exercise of their faculties', even though pursuivants were in fact so easily bribed that 'their malice went off like squibs'.[8]

Many aspects of Scott's lampoon are uncannily accurate. On 26 August/5 September 1618, Trumbull remarked bitterly on the recent 'discharging of the pursuivants from the bishops' and the transferring of them to 'chancery'. It made a 'great noise' in Flanders, where 'our ill-affected countrymen lift up their heads for that and the alliance with Spain as though all were at their command already'. Gondomar had recently met Trumbull in Brussels and, presumably hoping to raise Trumbull's already elevated stress levels, told him 'by way of good counsel and advice...that' Trumbull 'should do well to carry all...with temperance and moderation' because James was 'a prince that would have no wars', while the archducal regime in Flanders had a 'country full of soldiers' and Philip III would back his relatives there to the hilt. While Trumbull was evidently still choking with fury, Gondomar 'shrunk up his shoulders after the Spanish fashion' and said that the British and Spanish kings 'did well understand one another' and were on 'very good terms'. But, said Gondomar, gushing crocodile tears, 'he feared', now that he had left English shores, that '*los mal intencionados* would break up the treaty'. Trumbull subsequently asked Gondomar to lobby in Brussels to secure some of King James's diplomatic goals there, including the punishment of the author of the scandalous *Corona Regia*, but, for various reasons, Gondomar seemed quite unable to help.[9] Trumbull added, at the end of August, that while Gondomar was

---

[8] Thomas Scott, *Vox Populi. Or Newes from Spayne*...(1620), sig. C4ʳ⁻ᵛ. The fury in some quarters at Baldwin's release can be gauged also from Thomas Gainsford's 'Vox Spiritus, or Sir Walter Rawleighs Ghost', which purported to narrate a conference between Gondomar, his chaplain, and Baldwin in the Spanish embassy: S. R. Gardiner (ed.), *The Fortescue Papers; consisting chiefly of Letters relating to State Affairs* (Camden Society, 103, 1871), p. 143; S. Adams, 'Captain Thomas Gainsford, the "Vox Spiritus" and the *Vox Populi*', *Bulletin of the Institute of Historical Research* 49 (1976), pp. 141–4.

[9] PRO, SP 77/13, fos 49ʳ⁻ᵛ, 52ʳ–3ʳ. Matthew Growhoski has reminded me that the archduke, Albert, was sufficiently irritated by John Barclay's *Satyricon* that he felt no need to do anything about *Corona*

in Flanders, 'he was followed by the greatest part of his Majesty's subjects residing in these provinces', including 'the banished priests'. These people were saying that 'the day of their liberty did approach'.[10] Trumbull opined that 'those at home also do with more freedom discover themselves than in former times'; and even the children of the well-to-do were turning up to study at Douai and Louvain. Travellers to Spa for health reasons should be compelled to take the oath of allegiance. They ought to have a licence from the privy council, and a physician's certificate that they were actually ill, so that they did not simply end up going on pilgrimages. Trumbull complained about the corruption among the customs officers in the ports and pointed in particular to one Richard Giles, a client of the countess of Suffolk, who scattered passports like confetti, 'contrary to the statutes'.[11]

Towards the end of 1618, London saw not a Catholic martyr but, arguably, a Protestant one. Sir Walter Raleigh's rather crude attempt, via the Orinoco expedition, to derail the Spanish match resulted in the original sentence passed against him in 1603, as a result of the exposure of the Bye and Main Plots, being carried out on 29 October 1618. Many narratives of his execution insisted that he had died a good death.[12]

Francis Cottington reported from Madrid on 21 June/1 July 1619 that Baldwin, who had now arrived in the Spanish capital, 'speaks well of his Majesty and professes with great oaths much affection to his service' but 'what he has in his heart I cannot tell'. Cottington feared that 'all is feigned, for that' Baldwin 'also speaks much good of my lord's grace of Canterbury', George Abbot, 'whom I think never any of his coat loved'.[13] Cottington had obviously never heard of irony; and the Jesuit martyr manqué Baldwin now made it his business to work for the match.

A detailed memorandum that Baldwin turned out for Gondomar in summer 1619 admitted that James would 'take it badly' if, 'during this marriage negotiation', the Spaniards pressed him for legal guarantees over religion. But Baldwin urged that such a marriage would be impossible without cast-iron pledges of this kind, notably the appointment of Catholics to the privy council. He implied very strongly that the Spaniards would not be able to trust James's promises of tolerance alone. So often in the past it had seemed that a change in the law was imminent and it had then not materialized. On the plus side, James might 'punish' the puritans, 'check their freedom', and procure 'their decline from power and insolence' by 'granting freedom of conscience to Catholics'. Via the marriage it would

---

Regia; see M. Growhoski, 'The Secret History of a "Secret War": John Barclay, his *Satyricon*, and the Politicization of Literary Scholarship in Early Modern Europe, 1582–1621' (PhD, Princeton, 2015), pp. 336–7.

[10] PRO, SP 77/13, fo. 59^{r-v}.   [11] PRO, SP 77/13, fo. 59^{v}.   [12] Questier, *DP*, p. 386.

[13] PRO, SP 94/23, fo. 219^{r-v}. Baldwin travelled from Madrid to Lisbon for a formal audience with Philip III there: PRO, SP 94/23, fo. 219^{v}. On 23 September/3 October 1618 Trumbull had reported that Baldwin and Thomas Fitzherbert were on their way to Rome: PRO, SP 77/13, fo. 76^{v}.

454   CATHOLICS AND TREASON

be possible 'to suppress them by his own and the king of Spain's power', and prevent them from defeating 'him and all his plans'. On the other hand, there was 'great discontent' at Madrid, Rome, and elsewhere that, since 'this marriage' had 'begun to be negotiated, not only' had 'there been as much persecution of the Catholics as in the past but more so because the persecution in Ireland' was 'incomparably greater'. Even in England there had 'been a new enforcement of the law against Catholic wives', although 'their husbands might be of a different faith'.[14]

Some of the promoters of the amity between the Stuart court and Spain certainly wanted to make sure there was no going back on guarantees of tolerance if they were eventually obtained. Diego de Lafuente, the Dominican who had processed to Tyburn with Thomas Maxfield in 1616, had visited Sir John Digby (in London), as Digby described on 4 December 1618. Lafuente said that he was worried that the clergy who had trooped off to Portsmouth when Gondomar left the country in 1618, but then had, as everyone expected, immediately returned, were at risk of being strung up, should they be arrested. There was a danger that they 'would be executed by the ordinary course of law without giving any account thereof unto his Majesty until it was done'. If this were to happen, 'all the blame and dishonour' would 'fall on the count of Gondomar'. Any such event would put a perhaps fatal spoke in the marriage negotiations.[15]

If, for some Protestants, the prospect of an Anglo-Spanish dynastic marriage was not bad enough, the Protestant-cause enthusiasts at James's court were now faced with potential catastrophe in central Europe. James's son-in-law, Frederick, the elector palatine, in September 1619 accepted the offer of the crown of Bohemia following the deposition of the Habsburg Ferdinand of Austria, who subsequently succeeded as emperor. Famously, George Abbot predicted that Frederick would propagate the true gospel of Christ. Catholic sovereigns

[14] Loomie, *SJC*, II, pp. 176–83.
[15] PRO, SP 94/23, fo. 90r–v. In March 1619 the Catholic author of the scurrilous satirical manuscript tract 'Balaam's Asse' (see pp. 423–4, 424 n.8 above), John Williams, was discovered, as if by accident, by a pursuivant who was, allegedly, trying to track down Catholic clergy coming from the house of the Spanish ambassador. Thomas Lorkin, at the same time as he reported the arrest of the Catholic author of this libel, mentioned the rumour (evidently false) that the church in Southwark where the godly Protestant minister Edward Elton was located 'should have been blown up with gunpowder, there being like preparations as for the parliament' of 1605: Birch, *CTJI*, II, pp. 146–8, 157, 158; McClure, *LJC*, II, p. 235; E. Jennings, '"Balaam's Asse" Uncovered: New Light on the Politics of Prophetical Exegesis in Mid-Jacobean Britain', *Huntingdon Library Quarterly* 81 (2018), pp. 1–27, at p. 15. One suspects that the 'Balaam's Asse' trial, producing as it did a quasi-martyrdom (the author, Williams, was hanged at Charing Cross on 5 May 1619 on the basis of charges concerning this and another text, 'Speculum Regali', and he claimed the status of a martyr), was a kind of legal consolation prize in place of the Stuart court's failure to get the archducal government in Brussels to take seriously the libels against James which had come out of Flanders, notably the notorious *Corona Regia*. A copy, it seems, of Williams's libel was sent by Simonds D'Ewes to Joseph Mead in early 1626: BL, Harleian MS 390, fo. 20r. See also D. A. Orr, *Treason and State: Law, Politics, and Ideology in the English Civil War* (Cambridge, 2002), p. 26; T. B. Howell (ed.), *A Complete Collection of State Trials...*, II (1816), pp. 1085–8; Jennings, '"Balaam's Asse" Uncovered', p. 23.

themselves would 'leave the whore' of Babylon 'and make her desolate'.[16] Frederick and James's daughter Elizabeth were, however, soon ejected from Bohemia and then from Frederick's own Palatinate territories. James's nightmare had always been that he might be dragged into a European war of religion between Protestant and Catholic powers. The proposed Anglo-Spanish dynastic alliance became, in effect, a way of trying to resolve this crisis without resort to arms. Had the treaty succeeded, it would have been a dramatic turning point in post-Reformation British political history. The royal rhetoric which was deployed in justification of this policy was saturated with the language of religious tolerance. The 1621 parliament witnessed, in April, an attempt to introduce recusancy legislation, but the king would not countenance it.[17] The pent-up distrust of the court was given vent in May by the case of Edward Floyd, a Catholic prisoner in the Fleet who had expressed his satisfaction at the imperial victory over the elector palatine at the Battle of the White Mountain in 1620. The demands for savage punishment of Floyd made him into a kind of at-one-remove Catholic victim and martyr, even though much of the sentence was remitted. One of Joseph Mead's news sources reported that Floyd, 'at his branding', declared to the crowd that 'he would have given £1000 to be hanged [so] that he might have been a martyr in so good a cause'. He seems to have elicited some sympathy. While he was being publicly shamed by being forced to ride 'from Fleet Bridge to the Standard in Cheapside, his face towards the horsetail', an unnamed gentleman said 'openly' that Floyd 'had injury and his censure was most unjust'. When a constable tried to arrest the gentleman 'for his words', the gentleman stabbed him with a rapier.[18] The draft recusancy bill passed both houses on 15 May but had no chance of receiving the royal assent.[19]

After the dissolution of the hostile 1621 parliament, it became evident that the court would, whatever the political fall-out, try to force through a toleration for Catholics based on the royal prerogative. During 1622 and into 1623 there was a temporary relaxation of the statutes against Catholic nonconformity.[20] This

---

[16] T. Cogswell, *The Blessed Revolution: English Politics and the Coming of War, 1621-1624* (Cambridge, 1989), p. 17.

[17] R. Zaller, *The Parliament of 1621: A Study in Constitutional Conflict* (1971), pp. 130–1; *CSPV 1621-3*, pp. 63, 68, 71. Gondomar had warned that any sort of deal with Madrid or Vienna over the marriage and/or the return of Frederick's palatinate territories would be prevented by the successful passage of the recusancy bill, 'and he himself would feel obliged to leave the court immediately': *CSPV 1621-3*, p. 55.

[18] Birch, *CTJI*, II, pp. 256, 258. For the Floyd case, see Zaller, *The Parliament of 1621*, pp. 104–15; T. Rabb, *Jacobean Gentleman: Sir Edwin Sandys, 1561-1629* (Princeton, 1998), pp. 241–8; McClure, *LJC*, II, pp. 370, 372, 377; *CSPV 1621-3*, pp. 53, 63.

[19] For the bill which passed on 15 May 1621 and for the attempt to formulate a more draconian piece of legislation, see Zaller, *The Parliament of 1621*, p. 132; *CSPV 1621-3*, pp. 54–5; McClure, *LJC*, II, p. 379.

[20] *SDP*, pp. 26–63, 131–217 *passim*.

456   CATHOLICS AND TREASON

provoked a spate of anti-popish sermons and publications, which in turn the court tried to censor and suppress.[21]

The Anglo-Spanish marriage negotiations, of course, were not successful.[22] The high point of the project was the extraordinary and often ridiculed journey of Prince Charles and Buckingham to Madrid in early 1623.[23] The failure of the marriage diplomacy was a 'blessed revolution' as far as many Protestants were concerned. The policy of amity with the Habsburgs was dropped. Some sort of belligerent action in Europe became a virtual certainty. The Stuart court would seek to use military means to restore the king's daughter and son-in-law to their sequestrated territories. But the only way in which this could be achieved was with the cooperation of the French. This was secured in the first instance via an Anglo-French dynastic treaty, one which eventually saw Charles wed Louis XIII's sister Henrietta Maria.

For our purposes what really matters is how far the about-turn in Stuart foreign policy was going to take things back to what Catholics regarded as the bad (and what, for example, Archbishop Abbot looked on as the good) old days. There were, predictably, reports from the provinces that Catholics were on the verge of rebellion. One Yorkshire Catholic had allegedly said that, if the treaty with Spain were to be formally broken off, then there would be a Catholic revolt, with Catholics wearing ribbons in their hats to identify themselves.[24] A Durham lawyer, Henry More, imprisoned at York for persuading people to be reconciled to Rome, was sent up to London to the Fleet prison 'for certain words disgraceful' to the established religion, 'viz. that Queen Mary of Scotland was a martyr and the true heir to this crown; that Queen Elizabeth was a bastard and wrongfully withheld the right from Queen Mary and her issue', and 'lastly that the religion now professed here came out of King Henry VIII's codpiece'. He had also allegedly said that Anne Boleyn was a 'whore'. 'His judgment in the star chamber' before parliament assembled 'was to lose both ears, to stand two days upon the pillory, one in Cheapside, the other at Westminster; to have his nose slit, to ride through London with his face to the horsetail, to pay...ten thousand pounds fine and to be prisoner perpetual'. John Chamberlain commented that More 'laughed all the while' that sentence was being executed in Cheapside in February 1624, in other words displaying the kind of insouciance and insensibility to pain that so many martyrs were said to show.[25]

---

[21] See J. Shami, *John Donne and Conformity in Crisis in the Late Jacobean Pulpit* (Cambridge, 2003).

[22] The best account in print of the politics of the later Jacobean period is still, and looks likely to remain, Thomas Cogswell's *The Blessed Revolution*.

[23] The prospect of the marriage provoked the writing and publication in late 1623 of John Abbot's *Iesus Praefigured*...(n.p. [Antwerp?], 1623). This text mentioned English martyrs, and particularly Margaret Clitherow, John Fisher, and Sir Thomas More; Abbot, *Iesus Praefigured*, pp. 80–1, 96.

[24] See PRO, SP 14/158/44; PRO, SP 14/159/12, 13, 38, 39.

[25] *SDP*, pp. 250–1; McClure, *LJC*, II, p. 545; E. Bourcier (ed.), *The Diary of Sir Simonds D'Ewes (1622–1624)* (Paris, 1974), p. 180. For the proceedings in star chamber against More, see PRO, STAC 8/32/20, a reference for which I am grateful to David Cressy.

It was fairly clear, however, that neither James nor Louis XIII would allow the imminent Anglo-French marriage alliance to be used explicitly to endorse or underpin a European Protestant ideological agenda. The Bourbon court could not possibly sell the match to the French public as a Protestant-cause project. The principal internal threat in France was still reckoned by many to come from the Huguenots. That difficulty would have to be resolved by force before Louis finally trained his guns directly on Spain and the empire. So it was out of the question that French diplomats and negotiators would tolerate real intolerance towards English/British Catholics, the support of whom for the marriage was essential to make it credible in front of a European Catholic audience and, crucially, to get Rome's approval for it.[26]

There was, therefore, still a glaring disjuncture between the British crown's new turn in foreign policy and the world view of the king's many Protestant critics who thirsted for a Catholic–Protestant Armageddon. There was real hostility between the court and some prominent members of the 1624 parliament when it assembled. The parliament had been spun by a cascade of anti-popish polemic, but equally it looks as if there were popular Catholic counterdemonstrations in London. John Gee claimed that on 'this last Good Friday', 26 March 1624, some Catholics went 'before day' in a procession or pilgrimage to Tyburn. Sarcastically, he said that 'it was ancient to visit *memorias martyrum*; and so the sending of disciples to visit Tyburn makes a deep impression in their minds, of the saintship of some that have there paid their debt to our laws. We know, martyr and persecutor are correlatives; and so, in this action of pretended humiliation, there is intended an increase of the Romanists' hatred against the Church and State of England as . . . guilty of the blood of those whom they adore'.[27]

Some might have expected a draconian legislative parliamentary onslaught on Catholic separatism. But none was forthcoming. Towards the end of the parliament, with a bad grace, James consented to a royal proclamation, issued on 6 May, which ordered the Catholic clergy into exile—by mid-June, or else (supposedly).[28] Amid Catholic boasts that they were supporting the proposed Anglo-French dynastic union and that the proclamation would lie in the dust once parliament had dispersed, the authorities in London decided to make a test case out of the octogenarian priest William Davies. He was arrested on 17 June and was dispatched to Newgate. As the former appellant John Colleton reported it on 18 June 1624, initially 'his Majesty refused to confirm any of the laws which the parliament had agreed on against Catholics'. But then he refused to reverse or suspend 'the proclamation for the banishing of priests'. Indeed, 'the day before the

---

[26] *SDP*, introduction.

[27] T. H. B. M. Harmsen (ed.), *John Gee's Foot out of the Snare (1624)* (Nijmegen, 1992), pp. 146–8.

[28] *SDP*, p. 77.

458   CATHOLICS AND TREASON

expiration of the time assigned for priests to depart the land, his Majesty called all the judges before him and...commanded them to execute with rigour all the old laws' against Catholic separatists. This had led to Davies's arrest, though he was 'above fourscore [years] and almost blind'.[29] Colleton took this to be all of a piece with James's worrying readiness to intervene militarily in northern Europe—'the king sends 6,000 men to support the Hollanders'.[30] Shortly after, Davies was dragged on a hurdle to Tyburn. But once he got there, with (it was claimed) over a thousand people waiting to see what would happen, he was reprieved. Anthony Shelley narrated, on 13/23 July 1624, that 'the holy man was exceedingly sorry and wept bitterly' at his reprieve, 'saying that this was the second time they had served him so; for he had been condemned once for the same reason, long before and' was 'delivered'. This was true. He had nearly perished with Robert Drury back in 1607. Davies 'said it was his unworthiness who did not deserve so glorious a crown' and, remarked Shelley, 'with his constancy and good example', he 'did edify the people exceedingly'.[31]

A disgusted Sir Francis Nethersole, who had served as secretary to James's daughter Elizabeth, electress palatine, and as agent to the union of German Protestant princes, lamented on 3 July that all of this had done so much political damage that it would have been better if Davies had not been proceeded against in the first place.[32] On 2 August John Gee himself raised a hue and cry in Holborn, near to the Spanish embassy, to secure the arrest of a priest called Thomas Cole. Cole was brought before the lord mayor and was incarcerated in Newgate. But he was soon released and went off to live in one of the London embassies.[33] At the York assizes, Ursula and Jane Tankard were condemned to death for helping a priest to abscond, but there was practically no chance that sentence would be carried out. They secured a pardon by the end of the year.[34] Not that Catholics immediately concluded that a toleration was at hand. On 4 August 1624, having described the cases of William Davies and the Tankards, John Jackson wrote that Sir Thomas Chamberlain was bullying Catholics in Berkshire. 'Indictments and presentments' were 'never so many'. Recusancy commissions were still being issued. 'Informers' were 'very busy in vexing' Catholics. The 'spite of the people' was 'never so great, no, not in Queen Elizabeth's time. As Catholics go along the streets they cry out, "a papist, a papist"' and hurled 'other reproaches and molestations against them'.[35] English Catholics, of course, had an incentive to remind

---

[29] *SDP*, pp. 96, 271.   [30] *SDP*, p. 272.

[31] *SDP*, p. 277; p. 360 above. Davies's own witness statement (of 21 September 1624) sent to Rome said merely that he had been reprieved on 28 June; see APF (Archivio della S. Congregazione de Propaganda Fide, Rome), SOCG (Scritture Originali Riferite nelle Congregazioni Generali), 347 [transcript, from PRO, Roman Transcripts, at ABSJ, 48/17/5].

[32] *SDP*, pp. 97, 277.   [33] *SDP*, p. 280.   [34] *SDP*, pp. 279–80.

[35] *SDP*, p. 280. Alban Butler provided Challoner with extracts of some of the letters sent around the Catholic network in summer and autumn 1624 which attempted to show that Catholics were still subject to a persecution: ABP, p. 521; *SDP*, p. 297, n. 813.

TOWARDS TOLERATION? 459

the French court that life for them was not a bed of roses. On the other hand, it was necessary also to convince the French that James was himself inclined to tolerance. Richard Smith airily opined in August 1624, though from a safe distance in Paris, that the new proclamation was a dead letter and that Catholic clergy openly walked the streets of London 'as freely as before'.[36]

Once Charles was crowned, following his father's rather unexpected demise, he found out exactly how short a political honeymoon could be. There were a number of serious structural difficulties in the Anglo-French dynastic alliance. Its constituent elements soon started to pull in different directions. Put simply, its architects wanted different things from it and, in the end, British and French expectations of the marriage were simply irreconcilable. Charles and Buckingham therefore had little incentive to honour the, in any case, rather vague guarantees of toleration for Charles's Catholic subjects which had been, in insufficiently specific form, at the centre of the treaty negotiations with the Bourbon court.[37]

Early Caroline Catholicism and the Cult of Martyrdom: Catholics Look Back on their Recent Past

In the face of an avalanche of anti-popery during and after the 1625 parliament, the crown found itself compelled to reimpose many of the standard penalties for recusant nonconformity. This in turn provoked understandable resentment among Catholics. One London recusant, Richard Beak, presented for recusancy on 6 December 1625, allegedly said to the officer summoning him to answer for his offence that 'he "cared not a f*** for the justices and that he had not been at church for ten years, nor would" he "go to church for all the justices could do"; adding further, "let the justices kiss his a***"'.[38] This kind of resentment then fed back into rumours and gossip about popish plotting.[39] The 1626 parliament was preceded by a similar rush of complaints about Catholics, something which Charles's attempt to perform the conventional routines and rhetoric of anti-popery did very little to quell.

At this point, the new regime was unwilling to enforce anything like the full extent of the Elizabethan treason law, even against the large numbers of Catholic clergy in London, let alone anywhere else. But the new bishop of Chalcedon, Richard Smith, was now formally starting the process of petitioning Rome to recognize those Catholics who had been the victims of persecution in England since

---

[36] *SDP*, p. 100.   [37] Questier, *DP*, pp. 420–32; *SDP, passim*.
[38] Jeaffreson, *MCR*, III, p. 6; J. J. LaRocca (ed.), *Jacobean Recusant Rolls for Middlesex: An Abstract in English* (CRS 76, 1997), p. 134.
[39] Questier, *DP*, pp. 420–55 *passim*. In October 1625, prominent Catholic separatists had been, once again, disarmed; see G. Anstruther, *Vaux of Harrowden: A Recusant Family* (Newport, 1953), pp. 448–53; Questier, *C&C*, pp. 428–9.

Figure 14.1 Portrait of Richard Smith, bishop of Chalcedon (reproduced with the permission of the abbot of Douai Abbey, Woolhampton, Berkshire).

the 1530s.[40] (See Figure 14.1.) Smith had succeeded William Bishop (d.1624) in that office just before the arrival of Henrietta Maria from France.[41] In 1626, technically in response to an instruction from the congregation of Propaganda in the Roman curia, Smith ordered his officials to gather information about those English Catholics who could properly be reckoned to have been martyrs. This was a complex process. Many of the alleged martyrs had held opinions about royal authority which were simply unsayable by the 1620s. But Rome's verdict on who could be reckoned to have suffered martyrdom could not be kept separate from the continuing struggles within the Catholic community over how it should be regulated.[42] The claim made in a memorandum which was subsequently sent to

---

[40] In April 1625, the Oratorian priest Thomas Rant had made a formal complaint about the inscription under 'Garnet's picture in the grand Jesus gallery' in the Gesù: *SDP*, p. 361 (AAW, B 25, no. 102).

[41] A. F. Allison, 'Richard Smith, Richelieu and the French Marriage. The Political Context of Smith's Appointment as Bishop for England in 1624', *RH* 7 (1964), pp. 148–211. For William Prynne's interpretation of Smith's election as part of a plot to embed toleration of popery, see Prynne, *PRP*, pp. 59–64.

[42] One full copy of Bishop Smith's catalogue is retained in the Westminster Cathedral archives; see AAW, B 28, no. 3 ('Catalogus Martyrum qui a principio persecutionis per Elizabetham reginam Anglia contra Catholicos excitate [sic] pro fide Catholica in Anglia passi sunt...', in the hand of Thomas White (alias Blacklo)); see also AAW, B 28, no. 4 (imperfect copy of the main section of no. 3 down to the year 1608); C. A. Newdigate, "Quelques Notes sur Les Catalogues des Martyrs Anglais dits de Chalcédoine et de Paris", *Analecta Bollandiana* 66 (1938), pp. 308–33; for the version of the catalogue retained in Rome, see APF, SOCG, 347, fos 590^r–615^r; *AWCBC*, p. 2510. The full version of the

TOWARDS TOLERATION? 461

the secular clergy's agent in Rome was that episcopal governance had conferred extraordinary benefits on English Catholics. Among other things, 'this bishop has gathered together a note and short story of all our English martyrs since persecution began, which also shortly shall be sent up' to Rome, all to prove the secular clergy leadership's contention that it truly represented the spirit, inheritance, and history of the kind of Catholicism which had emerged in England out of the lunatic chaos of the Elizabethan Reformation.[43] It seems that Smith had intended to construct not only, as he did, a basic catalogue of martyrs' names and fates but also a continuation of some of the later sixteenth-century stories of Catholic martyrdom, for instance the *Concertatio Ecclesiae Catholicae*.[44]

The new bishop decided to start this martyrological fact-finding exercise while the English parliament was in session.[45] This was, one assumes, also in some sense a retort to the virulent anti-popery coming out of that assembly. The bulk of the paperwork involved in Smith's martyr project has not survived, that is, other than the relevant catalogues themselves and a few scattered reports from the provinces in response to his demands for information.[46] But, for example, we

catalogue (i.e. AAW, B 28, no. 3) commences with a letter to the cardinals of Propaganda. It deals with the current controversies among the English clergy and it is followed by a preface which explains Smith's working method. The catalogue takes the martyrological record up to 1618 (William Southerne) with a note on Edmund Arrowsmith (d.1628) added in another hand. Smith's 1628 catalogue was compiled directly at the request of the congregation of Propaganda (a formal letter of 4/14 February 1626), though presumably after Propaganda had been lobbied to instruct him to do so: *AWCCBM*, p. 312; *AWCBC*, p. i; Newdigate, 'Quelques Notes', p. 310. Smith wrote to his agent in Rome on 6 August 1626 that the work was proceeding apace. He asked for clarification on exactly how much information Propaganda needed. On 6/16 January 1627, Propaganda urged Smith to persevere and in January 1628 demanded that he hurry up. The catalogue was finally dispatched to Propaganda in Rome on 25 May 1628: ibid., pp. 310–12, citing *inter alia* AAW, A XX, no. 24, p. 91. For Smith's citation to Rome of Wilson's *English Martyrologe*, in part on the grounds that it had been published without Rome's authorization, see AAW, A XIX, no. 103, pp. 355–61; ARCR, II, no. 806; see also the undated Latin objections written in Smith's hand: AAW, A XXXI, no. 32, pp. 105–8. For the congregation of Propaganda's censure of Wilson, see Charles Newdigate's manuscript notes retained at ABSJ, taken from the records of Propaganda: ABSJ, CP (notes on Propaganda; communication to Smith dated 16/26 January 1628). Wilson's printing of George Keynes's translation, *The Roman Martyrologe according to the Reformed Calendar* (n.p. [St Omer], 1627) incorporated (sig. Aa8v), at the end, his own 'Catalogue of those who have Suffered Death in England ... unto this Yeare 1608', with the names of Henry Garnet, Edward Oldcorne, and Ralph Ashley. Propaganda considered Smith's martyrs catalogue, with the pope himself in attendance, on 15/25 September 1628 and issued a decree concerning it on 27 September/7 October, ordering Smith to proceed further. But it appears that progress stalled because of the difficulties in which Smith increasingly found himself in England: Newdigate, 'Quelques Notes', pp. 312–13.

[43] AAW, A XX, no. 102, p. 353 (the memorandum is dated 10 July 1627). For a similar note in a paper, dated 26 April 1627, sent to the clergy agent at Rome, which found its way into the hands of the Society of Jesus, see AAW, A XX, no. 76 ('Instructions for the agent at Rome answerable to the contents of the common letters which were written by the chapter of the English clergy here in England to the pope and cardinals, 26 April 1627'), p. 268; ARSJ, Anglia 32/ii, fo. 401ᵛ.

[44] Newdigate, 'Quelques Notes', p. 312.

[45] Pollen, *UD*, pp. 394–6, 398 (AAW, B 24, no. 101; the date of Benjamin Norton's response to Smith's request for information is 6 May 1626 and Norton says he has already sent Smith a screed of information dated 18 April 1626). The 1626 parliament assembled on 6 February and lasted until 15 June: C. Russell, *Parliaments and English Politics 1621–1629* (Oxford, 1979), p. 269.

[46] As John Pollen observed, a number of the martyrological items retained in the Westminster diocesan archives must have been compiled as a result of Bishop Smith's martyrological fact-finding

462 CATHOLICS AND TREASON

know that Smith's men found details in the York assize records of the indictment of Margaret Clitherow, the original papers concerning which have now been lost.[47] The manuscript responses to Smith in the Westminster Cathedral manuscripts suggest that there may once have been a lot more such material. We have only one complete extant response to Smith's order to gather such information. It was sent to Smith by his friend and official Benjamin Norton from Norton's provincial billet in West Sussex. It was written in reply to a letter from Smith which

project. These documents were used by Challoner: Pollen, *UD*, p. 393 (AAW, B 24, no. 101); AAW, A IV, nos 1–14, 117–32; Pollen, *AEM*, pp. 209–11 (reproducing in print AAW, A II, no. 2, pp. 3f). See also H. Bowler, 'Further Notes on the Venerable John Bretton', *RH* 15 (1979), pp. 1–10, esp. at p. 6, for the compiling of the Paris catalogue, i.e. AAW, B 28, no. 10, which was put together by Richard Smith's secretary, William Harewell, as a preparatory draft for the catalogue which bears Smith's name; see also *AWCBC*, p. xlix. Charles Newdigate demonstrated that the Paris catalogue predated and was a contribution to the principal/Chalcedon catalogue. Newdigate notes that of the 212 individuals who figure in the Paris and Chalcedon catalogues 99 had their names in the county assize registers or the Newgate prison register: Newdigate, 'Quelques Notes', pp. 318 f., esp. at p. 329. The assize records had been combed by Smith's own officials and agents. For information on the Yorkshire martyrs, including Margaret Clitherow, and also Edward Waterson who was executed at Newcastle, see AAW, A IV, no. 22, p. 124; AAW, B 28, no. 10, pp. 301, 302, 303, 305, 309, 315, 317, 324, 326; Newdigate, 'Quelques Notes', pp. 328–9. Richard Broughton was cited as a source for the information gleaned about the martyrs Nicholas Garlick, Robert Ludlam, and Richard Simpson: AAW, A IV, no. 1, p. 6. For information gathered about the martyr John Bretton, see Bowler, 'Further Notes', p. 6; AAW, B 28. no. 10, p. 318. Richard Davies, who had personally known several of the Elizabethan martyrs, deposited affidavits, particularly concerning the priest Richard Dibdale (see p. 161 n.96 above). The priest Joseph Haynes was the source of material on the martyr John Robinson, executed at Ipswich: AAW, A IV, no. 1, p. 10 (ABPFC, fo. 4^{r-v}). Cuthbert Trollop supplied material about John Boste, as did the Jesuit priest Charles Thursby: AAW, A IV, no. 1, p. 11; Anstr., II, p. 320. Trollop also had details on Edward Waterson, the four martyrs of May 1590 (Duke, Holiday, Hill, and Hogg) and the martyrs of August 1600 (Palaser, Talbot, and Norton): AAW, A IV, no. 22, pp. 121, 123, 125. On George Swallowell, information came 'ex relatione D. Jacksoni presbyteri', presumably John Jackson, while John Cornelius's martyrdom, as also that of William Pikes—both in the West Country—were described by the secular priest Thomas Manger, who had become archdeacon of Somerset and Dorset in 1625: AAW, A IV, no. 1, pp. 13, 15; ABP, pp. 409, 420–3; p. 250 n.107 above. Leonard Brakenbury, whose name crops up as a negotiator for Yorkshire recusants with the royal exchequer, was the source for accounts of Marmaduke Bowes (as was a lawyer, one John Ingleby), Thomas Palaser, and Edward Osbaldeston: AAW, A IV, no. 22, pp. 126–7, 128; S. L. Bastow, 'Aspects of the History of the Catholic Gentry of Yorkshire from the Pilgrimage of Grace to the First Civil War' (PhD, Huddersfield, 2002), pp. 346–7; Richard Cholmeley, *The Memorandum Book of Richard Cholmeley of Brandsby 1602–1623* (North Yorkshire County Record Office Publications no. 44, 1988), pp. 24, 66, 115 and *passim*. For James Thompson, the otherwise virtually unknown priest Ralph Fisher served as a source, as also for the martyrs Peter Snow, Ralph Grimston, and Robert Bickerdike: see AAW, A IV, no. 22, pp. 129, 130, 131; ABP, pp. 415–16; p. 279 n.72 above. A widow called Elizabeth Ellison supplied material for Alexander Crow, William Knight, and William Gibson: AAW, A IV, no. 22, pp. 124, 132; *AWCBC*, pp. 448, 449, *AWCBC*, p. 1223; ABP, pp. 412, 416. Harewell compiled a hefty manuscript collection of the lives of British saints, one of which—Robert of Shrewsbury's life of St Winifred—appears to have been translated by the future martyr Edward Morgan, though he was a stern critic of Harewell's master, Richard Smith. The implication of the collection was that post-Reformation Catholic martyrs were part of a long continuum of suffering, in the British Isles, for the true Church; see Yale University Library (Beinecke Rare Book and Manuscript Library), Osborn MS fb 229 (for which reference I am grateful to Kendra Packham and to Samuel Fullerton). It is possible that this manuscript came into the hands of the authorities when Harewell was arrested in autumn 1628; see R. Stanfield (ed.), 'The Archpriest Controversy', part II, 'Papers relating to Doctor Richard Smith...', item I, in *Miscellanea XII* (CRS 22, 1921), p. 173; Anstr., II, p. 145.

[47] K. Longley, *Saint Margaret Clitherow* (Wheathampstead, 1986), pp. 118, 123–4.

TOWARDS TOLERATION?   463

enquired also about the disciplinary action that Norton was taking against recalcitrant Catholic clergymen who did not fully accept Smith's authority. Embedded within this reply we find Norton's research into and memories of local martyrs. Norton said that, from one Mr Cole, presumably the priest Thomas Cole, he had received 'all or most, that was to be known' of the sufferings of Lawrence Humphreys. Norton had also elicited information from Cole about 'Mr F. Thomas and Mr Johnson alias Mr Roger Dickenson, who as I think' was from the same county as Richard Smith himself, and about James Bird, 'sometime a scholar (to my knowledge) at Rheims who was a Winchester man born, and executed at the place of execution called Bardich'. Norton remembered that Bird was apprehended at Jerome Heath's 'house, who was late a citizen of Brussels, in a busy time when they searched that house and many others for my poor self, with whom I had met that night, if he had not been taken'. Of 'Mr F. Thomas', 'condemned at that time after that manner', Norton noted that it had briefly seemed that he might conform: 'they, conceiving that he made a show to recant (which notwithstanding he never did in that manner as they would have wished), deferred his execution until the assizes following, at which time he made a constant and happy end'. Norton said he hoped 'that this report of mine will be confirmed by others with whom I have not spoken, when they shall say what they know thereof'.

Norton remembered also his former teacher, Mr John Bodey, who schooled him 'a year or two before his apprehension at Mr Archdeacon [William] Shelley's father's house, where he was taken and committed by Sir Richard Norton'. Moreover, 'by reason of this former acquaintance, his good mother coming to see her son, came to my mother's house from Wells in Somersetshire'. About the heroic John Slade, Bodey's companion in martyrdom, Norton could say little, although 'I knew the man well', and 'he was reputed to be a Dorsetshire man'. Of other martyrs from the region, Norton had met the high-profile victims of 1586, Robert Anderton and William Marsden, at the college at Rheims. They 'were said to be' from Lancashire. Norton knew that Nicholas Tichborne had been hanged for freeing his brother Thomas from arrest, and he had had written to Archdeacon Shelley to ask for information about the Chichester martyrs Ralph Crockett and Edward James. Norton had also asked Shelley about George Gervase and had talked with one Mr Peacock about Thomas Hemerford and Alexander Rawlins and, 'according to' Bishop Smith's 'direction, I desired him to enquire after Mr Thomas Garnet, Jesuit and priest, a Sussex man', who was the nephew of Henry Garnet, whom the secular clergy thought was no saint, though whether that affected their view of his nephew is unclear. Norton had enquired also about 'my uncle Mr Richard Shelley', meaning presumably Edward Shelley (d.1588), 'who married my aunt and was executed' in London. Norton believed correctly that Thomas Pilchard, executed at Dorchester, was a Sussex man 'and my reason . . . is because I have heard say that he was brother, uncle or kinsman to one Thomas

464   CATHOLICS AND TREASON

Parker his wife, a saddler of Battle'. There were others too (the Kentish martyrs Wilcox, Edwards, Buxton, Widmerpole, Duke, and Filcock) about whom Norton knew little, though he understood that Duke had been hanged at Durham. Norton suggested that Smith should make further enquiries with Humphrey Hyde, the archdeacon of Hampshire. Norton asked whether he ought to 'enquire after Mr Chideock Tichborne, who was one of those which suffered about the business of the queen of Scots, of whom I know no more yet but that he and his father before him were called Tichbornes of Porchester in Hampshire'. Edward Kenion, a leading secular priest, had broken out of prison shortly before his scheduled execution late in Elizabeth's reign, but himself knew nothing of his uncle, the martyr-priest 'Mr Miles Gerard', except that 'he was a Lancashire man'.[48]

This rather lengthy and rambling set of recollections—in its vagueness and imprecision—allows us to glimpse how uncertain the local Catholic martyrological tradition actually was. There had, of course been attempts by William Allen, Robert Persons, John Wilson, Thomas Worthington, Thomas More, and others to collect names and facts about those who had come to grief at the hands of the authorities. But the course of the intra-Catholic quarrels in and after the 1590s had, to put it mildly, caused some confusion as to who the martyrs were. If leading clergy such as Norton and Kenion did not know that much even about their own relatives who had suffered for the faith, Smith clearly had his work cut out.

As we remarked, Smith's attempt to codify what Catholics knew about their martyrs began during the 1626 parliament. How far Smith's martyrdom enquiry was public knowledge in the later 1620s is unclear. But the importance of Smith's research work and of the Catholic community's trials and tribulations may have been publicized when Henrietta Maria, the composition of whose household was already controversial, became embroiled in the difficulties latent in and thrown up by the Anglo-French treaty.[49] Among the attacks on the young queen in summer 1626, there was the claim that she had made a public pilgrimage to the Tyburn gallows.[50] According to the Venetian ambassador in Paris, the king's expulsion of the queen's attendants was directly connected with this alleged political gaffe. Soon after the dissolution of parliament, 'the queen was passing the way where criminals are usually executed in London' and 'someone told her that...a Jesuit named Garnet, who had been involved in a conspiracy against the late King

---

[48] Pollen, *UD*, pp. 394–6, 398 (AAW, B 24, no. 101). For William Shelley, who was the son of Richard Shelley of Warminghurst, see Anstr., II, p. 293.

[49] For the best recent research on this topic, see S. Wolfson, 'Aristocratic Women of the Household and Court of Queen Henrietta Maria, 1625–1659' (PhD, Durham, 2010).

[50] F. Dolan, *Whores of Babylon: Catholicism, Gender and Seventeenth-Century Print Culture* (Ithaca, N.Y., 1999), p. 100. For an excellent analysis of this incident, see K. Britland, 'A Ring of Roses: Henrietta Maria, Pierre de Bérulle and the Plague of 1625–1626', in M.-C. Canova-Green and S. J. Wolfson (eds), *The Wedding Journey of Charles I and Henrietta Maria, 1625: Celebrations and Controversy* (Turnhout, 2020), pp. 85–104, at pp. 98–9.

TOWARDS TOLERATION?   465

James, had suffered cruel torture and death on that spot', that is, Tyburn, although Henry Garnet had actually been executed at the west end of St Paul's churchyard. (It was Thomas Garnet who had been hanged at Tyburn.) Henry Garnet was regarded 'by his fellows' as a 'martyr and saint'. This 'view' was 'impressed upon the queen, who stopped near the spot and prayed there so openly that the people noticed it and were scandalized'. The buzz of it went like a dose of salts through London. Charles supposedly hit the roof and on 1 August 'ordered the dismissal of all the Jesuits [*sic*] and all the French of the queen's household', though the causes of the tension at court which led to the expulsion dated back to June, if not before. This was, in fact, only one version of what had taken place. According to the Venetian ambassador in The Hague, the bishop of Mende and the marquis of Blainville had indeed been meddling, and had 'persuaded the queen to make a pilgrimage outside London'; but when she 'knelt before the place of execution' she 'prayed for the souls of criminals' who had been 'condemned for crimes other than religion'.[51] The former MP and prolific letter writer John Pory believed that Charles was right to do as he had done. Henrietta Maria's clergy's 'insolences' to her 'were not to be endured'. These 'bawdy knaves', in the confessional, would ask her 'how often in a night' she and the king had done you-know-what (though Pory did not say how he had come by this knowledge). And then 'those hypocritical dogs' had, 'on St James's day last [*sic*] ... made the poor queen walk on foot (some add barefoot) from her house at St James's to the gallows at Tyburn, thereby to honour the saint of the day, in visiting that holy place, where so many martyrs forsooth had shed their blood in defence of the Catholic cause'. They had 'made her ... dabble in the dirt, in a foul morning ... her Luciferian confessor riding along by her in his coach'. For Pory, the scandal of all this was, in addition, that if popish infiltrators could control a queen so easily, 'what slavery would they not make us, the people, to undergo?'[52]

The regime's official explanation of what had happened more or less confirmed the popular account, though as Karen Britland notes, the French denied that the alleged incident had ever taken place in the way that was claimed, and there had in any case been a long delay before anything was done about it.[53] In Paris,

---

[51] *CSPV 1625–6*, pp. 517, 531. One source, admittedly difficult to attribute and verify, and dating the incident to 'the Friday next after St Peter's day' (30 June), says that 'the queen having, according to custom and opinion, gained the jubilee in her chapel at St James's, sets forth thence in' a 'coach accompanied with thirty persons, her followers', led by the bishop of Mende and the count of Tillières. Being 'come to the end of the brick walls next and upon the way to Hyde Parke', she 'descended from her coach and went on foot directly through Hyde Park to Tyburn'. When 'one of the company' asked why Henrietta Maria went there, he was told that it was 'to pray to God that he would give her grace with the like constancy to die for her religion that those martyrs had done before in that place': BL, Additional MS 39288, fo. 6[r].

[52] Birch, *CTCI*, I, p. 121. Professor Britland notes that Pory's letter which dates the incident to 25 July is itself misdated: Britland, 'A Ring of Roses', p. 98.

[53] The ambassador Bassompierre claimed that the so-called pilgrimage had not taken place and pointed out that there was a delay of over a month between what was supposed to have happened and

466   CATHOLICS AND TREASON

however, the ambassador Sir Dudley Carleton was instructed to protest that the queen's French courtiers had 'framed a faction like a little republic amongst themselves'. Mende and Blainville had fashioned a party 'of Roman Catholics' in order to break the Anglo-French amity. To cap it all, they had 'so much prevailed' with her 'as under colour of devotion' they persuaded her to visit Tyburn where, with her attendants, 'prayers were made to those whom they falsely called saints and martyrs that have suffered there, who in truth had been executed either for treason or felony against the laws and not for cause of religion'.[54] Carleton was further ordered to say that the meddlesome Catholics who were doing the damage made 'their addresses to Spain'. All 'their forces, power and prayers' were 'for the advancement of that king and his pretended monarchy'. This made an utter nonsense of the current Anglo-French alliance based on the recent marriage. The ridiculous performance at Tyburn was part of a more sinister agitation from inside the British court for a toleration. But, so Carleton was told to repeat in Paris, those executed at Tyburn really were traitors. The offering of prayers there was 'an act of infamy against' Charles's 'predecessors of glorious memory' and argued that they were guilty of tyranny in putting 'to death innocents under false pretexts'. Furthermore, 'nothing could have been done more unhappily to lift up the audacious part of our subjects' who were 'Roman Catholics, nor more to amaze and deject the rest of our subjects'.[55]

Whatever it was that the young queen had or had not done at Tyburn, this was exactly the point at which the Catholic secular clergy leadership was collecting like fury the extant accounts of those who might have been reckoned to have suffered for religion at the State's sites of execution. The claim of those who were assembling this retelling of the death-by-death experience of Catholics in and after the Reformation was that the institution of a Catholic episcopal hierarchy among the English nation was a purely spiritual matter and that Catholics were entirely and commendably loyal to the king. The new Catholic episcopate itself was not a threat to the existing settlement of religion. The only people who had a problem with the bishop's enforcement of his rule, apart from badly intentioned Protestants, were (some) members of the religious orders. (Their attacks on him in the later 1620s are usually referred to as the approbation controversy, that is,

---

the official reaction to it: ibid., p. 99. See also M. Smuts, 'Religion, European Politics and Henrietta Maria's Circle, 1625–41', in E. Griffey (ed.), *Henrietta Maria: Piety, Politics and Patronage* (2008), pp. 13–37, at p. 16 (citing Archive du Ministère des Affaires Etrangères, Paris, Correspondance Politique Angleterre 39, fos 209^v–10^r).

[54] PRO, SP 78/79, fo. 291^{r-v} (copy of PRO, SP 78/79, fo. 123^r); C. Carlton, *Charles I: The Personal Monarch* (2nd edition, 1995), pp. 86, 87; Wolfson, 'Aristocratic Women', pp. 222–3; for Sir Dudley Carleton's embassy, see also PRO, SP 78/79, fos 143^r, 146^r, 147^r.

[55] PRO, SP 78/79, fos 150^v–1^v (23 July 1626). Carleton asked on 27 July 1626 for specific details 'concerning the pilgrimage...to the unholy cross', in other words, 'the day, the hour, the company and the way they took, with the pretended occasion': PRO, SP 78/79, fo. 158^r; see also PRO, SP 78/79, fos 169^r, 214^r, 218^r.

because of their resistance to Bishop Smith's demand that they should seek his licence, or approbation, to hear confessions.) Some of the religious alleged that the institution of episcopacy would provoke further persecution by an angry regime, and that this would damage the fledgling Catholic Church in England. The memorandum of 10 July 1627, cited above, declared that the people who said this were hypocrites, for the reality was that they were afraid of losing 'that monarchy which they, the said regulars, have exercised here for many years together without control, fearing that the splendour of a bishop will obscure them and that his power will crush them and return that oppression upon them which they themselves used upon the secular clergy in the flourishing time of their aforesaid monarchy'.[56] Of course, if these disorders were to be corrected, the religious orders' 'hold and power with the laity' would be 'much impaired'. The monarchical State would then have no reason to persecute good Catholics at all. The attempts of some of the religious to appropriate the martyrological record were highly doubtful. One needed only to remind oneself how 'some regulars do favour the new oath of allegiance, who therefore' also 'fear to undergo the bishops' examination and censure' which would discover their utter hypocrisy in this as in other respects. The truth was that it was secular clergy such as Robert Drury, Roger Cadwallader, George Napper, and William Southerne who, faced with demands that they should swear the godless oath, had sacrificed their lives rather than give way in the face of oppression. (The bishop and his officers were silent, here, about Jesuits such as Thomas Garnet who had done the same; or, perhaps, they would have said that there were very few Jesuits who had really suffered for the faith. If asked about Benedictine martyrs such as Scot and Roberts, they would say that they were of a good mind and at one with their secular-clergy friends.) The blood of the martyrs was undeniably the seed of the Church but, as far as concerned the conversion of England, without this newly instituted episcopal authority, 'the wisest men', who understood 'the case of England truly', believed 'that this great work of the conversion of our country' would 'advance nothing at all, and never be achieved, and that the abuses and inward impediments', which had 'hitherto chiefly hindered the same', would 'rather grow and increase daily', as indeed they did.[57]

Moreover, a fully functioning episcopate would guarantee a measure of unity among English Catholics. The State had often exploited the stresses and incoherences inside the Catholic community so as to divide and rule over Catholics. But if Catholics were to present a united front, persecution of them would be virtually impossible, or so said Bishop Smith and his officials. He insisted that he had sought to create internal harmony in the Catholic community, or, as he called it, 'peace'. He had 'laboured very much... by all means to keep peace and concord

---

[56] AAW, A XX, no. 102, p. 353.   [57] AAW, A XX, no. 102, p. 354.

468 CATHOLICS AND TREASON

between the secular clergy and the regulars here'. He had 'often assured the chief superiors of the said regulars of his good intentions in that kind, both by word of mouth and by writing'. He had 'done no action whereby they' had 'just cause to fear the contrary'. He had appointed excellent and impartial officers, despite what some of the religious said about them. But the religious incensed 'the lay Catholics, their penitents, all they' could 'against the bishop's authority', and had taught them 'to make use of those wicked laws that were made here in derogation of the See Apostolic and in prejudice of Catholic religion'. As if this were not enough, it was 'thought that underhand also they' concurred 'in some sort to incense the heretical State against the bishop and his authority'.[58]

By the later 1620s, accounts and catalogues of English martyrs seem to have been circulating as much as ever around the Continent. The Spanish playwright Pedro Calderón de la Barca put a version of Ribadeneira's great historical and martyrological text on the stage in Madrid—probably in c.1627—playing fast and loose with the political narrative of Henrician politics in order, as it seems, to lay out the possibility that at some stage there might be a radical change in the British State, which itself by rights ought to be a friend of Spain.[59]

The 1628 Parliament and the Case of Edmund Arrowsmith

As with pigs and flight, Bishop Smith's expectations and reality were sadly incompatible. The disputes caused by his attempted enforcement of his authority made his ambitions for peace and consensus unworkable. The immediate question, though, was—what would the Caroline regime actually do in the face of Catholic calls for tolerance? It was, after all, trying to fight a European war with inadequate resources and, in order to plug the funding gap, it was resorting to fiscal expedients which provoked the anger of precisely those who had agitated for an end to appeasement of the Spaniards and had warned against the dangers of popery.

The regime certainly had no incentive to allow itself to be characterized as soft on popery. However, this was exactly what it risked when one of the expedients to which it resorted in the period after the dissolution of the 1626 parliament was a series of compounding schemes for Catholic recusants' debts. In the past, convicted Catholic separatists had frequently negotiated deals with exchequer officers in order to avert the worst consequences of their recusancy.[60] But royal commissions were now used to make this process official. To generate sufficient uptake, guarantees were offered to compounders that they would be protected

[58] AAW, A XX, no. 102, p. 353.
[59] Pedro Calderón de la Barca, ed. A. MacKenzie, transl. by K. Muir and A. MacKenzie, *The Schism in England (La Cisma de Inglaterra)* (Oxford, 1990).
[60] M. Questier, 'Sir Henry Spiller, Recusancy and the Efficiency of the Jacobean Exchequer', *HR* 66 (1993), pp. 251–66.

from further harassment. Public assurances were made that the sums raised by way of composition for recusancy fines and debts would go towards coastal defence for ships engaged in the coal trade between Newcastle and London. Thus would be created a virtuous circle in which separatists purged their offence by contributing to the costs of national security.[61] Some Catholic separatists seem to have paid fairly substantial sums to the royal exchequer under these arrangements. For the martyrologist John Knaresborough, the compounding commissions were another form of persecution for religion.[62] But to the king's critics this looked like a form of de facto tolerance which could just as easily be construed as part of a wider popish plot.

From the case of the priest Edward Bamber, eventually martyred in August 1646, we can get a sense of how the relationship between the regime (or parts of it) and the Catholic community had changed. Bamber had been ordained at Cadiz in July 1626 and then, en route to St Omer and Douai, his ship was forced into Plymouth in early December 1626 and he was arrested and his identity was established. He went so far as to conform and was granted a royal pardon in March 1627. But whereas in the past this would have been a major public-relations coup for a regime which took anti-popery seriously, nothing happened—no public recantation, no sermon, no pamphlet—nothing at all. Bamber was, it seemed, immediately reabsorbed into the Catholic community and served as an active and zealous priest in Lancashire for nearly twenty years.[63]

So, the question was—when, under intense political pressure, Charles summoned parliament again in 1628, what would ensue? A few days before parliament assembled, the secretary of State, Sir John Coke, tried to spin the opening by breaking up the Jesuit novitiate which was located in Clerkenwell. This must have been a welcome development for some Protestant observers and, ironically, for some Catholic ones as well. William Harewell, who served as Richard Smith's secretary, wrote to Thomas White on 28 March 1628 that 'the best learned' of those

---

[61] Larkin, *SRP*, II, nos 62, 71; J. C. H. Aveling, 'Documents Relating to the Northern Commissions for Compounding with Recusants 1627–1642', in Talbot, *MRR*, pp. 291–307. Ralph Thoresby, the antiquarian scholar based in Leeds, wrote to Charles Towneley on 9 March 1708 to say that he had (via Thomas Craven of Ripon) 'met with a curiosity...the original manuscript, thus entitled "Book of Compositions for the lands, goods and arrearages of recusants convicted"'. It was 'the very same that was subscribed either by the gentlemen themselves or such as they sent to compound with the Lord Wentworth'. Thoresby had 'the perusal of it for two days'. He took notes on the entries relating to the Towneley and the Knaresborough families: Kn., VI, unpaginated section; see also Aveling, 'Documents', pp. 307–8, noting that Knaresborough in fact had the composition entry books transcribed for his own purposes, and that this document passed to the library at Ushaw College. Aveling edited it for publication: Aveling, 'Documents', pp. 309–437. As Aveling comments (ibid., p. 308), the significance of this material for Knaresborough was that it could be used to 'refute Rushworth's charges that the' compounding commissioners 'were unduly lenient'. Knaresborough's line was followed by Challoner.

[62] Kn., V, p. 93.

[63] Anstr., II, pp. 13–14; PRO, SP 16/41/19, 20, 20. i–ii; *CSPD 1627–8*, p. 84; ABSJ, CP (Edward Bamber); J. E. Bamber, 'The Venerable Edward Bamber: Some New Facts', *Downside Review* 56: 1 (1938), pp. 31–45; PRO, SP 39/19, no. 38; *AWCBC*, pp. 2324, 2366–79 (PRO, C 66/2382, no. 21).

470 CATHOLICS AND TREASON

that were in the novitiate house, which belonged to George Talbot, earl of Shrewsbury, 'were then actually employed in writing against the bishop of Chalcedon'. This was surely a providential occurrence when they were in the very act of spewing out 'new things against their bishop who (as men say) is too good a man for such subjects'. For Harewell, this was the 'third knock' that 'the Jesuits have had from heaven', the first two being, presumably, the discovery of the Gunpowder conspiracy and the famous collapse of an upper floor in the gatehouse of the French embassy in Hunsdon House, Blackfriars on 26 October 1623 during a Jesuit sermon there. Moreover, and this was crucial said the commentator who compiled this material from Harewell's letter, a 'moderate Protestant' could not but liken Jesuits 'to puritans who cannot' abide 'the name of a bishop'.[64]

Despite the chorus of loud cheers from some of the secular clergy, the regime extracted very little benefit from Coke's public-relations exercise, since it refused to proceed aggressively enough, at least to many MPs' way of thinking, against those who had been detained in Clerkenwell. There were protests against the letters of grace issued to the clerics concerned.[65] A concocted letter did the rounds—it purported to be written by a Jesuit in England to one at Brussels. It had allegedly been discovered in the Clerkenwell novitiate. It recounted and rejoiced, Screwtape-like, in the sheer diabolical cleverness of a Jesuit-directed scheme which, it claimed, was already in train and which would accomplish a *coup d'état* by stealth across the British Isles. The present parliament would be a disaster. The quarrel between the parliament men and the duke of Buckingham was being stirred up by the industry of these Jesuitical meddlers. Furthermore, 'we have planted that sovereign drug Arminianism, which we hope will purge the Protestants from their heresy, and flourish and bear fruit in due season', while 'the materials which build up our other bulwark are the projectors and beggars of all ranks and qualities whatsoever'. These Catholic meddlers were doing their best to 'work upon the duke's jealousy and revenge; and in this we give the honour to such as merit it, which are the church Catholics', in other words, church papists. Equally, puritans had to be discredited so that they did not 'negotiate a reconciliation between the duke and the parliament'. Moreover, 'for the better prevention of the puritans, the Arminians' had 'already blocked up the duke's ears'. The 'Arminians and projectors' could be relied upon, seconded by these Catholic meddlers, to recommend new counsels to the king, arguing that to bring in cash through non-parliamentary means would 'raise a vast revenue' and thus he would 'not be beholding to his subjects'. This could be done 'by way of impositions and excise'. 'Then our church Catholics proceed to show the means how to settle this excise, which must be by a mercenary army of horse and foot.' The cavalry would be comprised of 'foreigners and Germans' who would 'eat up the king's revenues',

[64] Questier, *C&C*, pp. 440–2; AAW, A XXII, no. 42, p. 219.   [65] Questier, *DP*, p. 452.

and, unpaid, would cause havoc in the kingdom. Furthermore, the enforcement of the excise would cause outbreaks of rebellion, and 'if the mercenary army subjugate the country, then the soldiers and projectors shall be paid out of the confiscations'. 'Our superlative design is to work the Protestants as well as the Catholics to welcome in a conqueror', all to benefit 'his Catholic Majesty' of Spain.[66]

This letter was a fairly obvious forgery, but what it claimed was perhaps not a million miles from something like political reality; the king had already thought in terms of prerogative taxation on a large scale—the so-called Forced Loan—and some of those who had been ready to raise it were indeed Catholics.[67] The parliament which met on 17 March 1628 launched a campaign to give proper effect to the statute law against Catholics. A petition on religion was presented to Charles on 31 March. Charles made concessions. A statute against Catholics' children going to foreign educational institutions received the royal assent.[68] But what there was not was the kind of bloodletting purge at Tyburn and other places which many MPs must have thought was really necessary and would themselves have taken as a sign of royal good faith.

However, in summer 1628, the Jesuit Edmund Arrowsmith was arrested and was locked up in Lancaster Castle. (See Figure 14.2.) He was executed on 28 August. It seems that he was something of a local clerical celebrity. Also, he was a practising exorcist. He 'took much pains...with possessed persons; yet seldom or never without the help and assistance of some of his brethren; and so freed many from their troublesome guests'.[69] Arrowsmith may have worked with Ambrose Barlow, himself a martyr in 1641, in exorcism rituals. Arrowsmith came from the heart of the Lancashire Catholic community. His maternal grandfather was Nicholas Gerard, who, 'by order of Sir Thomas Gerard, his own brother', had been 'forcibly carried to the Protestant church' and, despite his physical incapacity (he had gout), had sung 'psalms in Latin with so loud a voice that the parson could

---

[66] T. M. McCoog, 'A Letter from a Jesuit of Liège (1687)?', *RH* 30 (2010), pp. 88–106, at pp. 91–2, 103 (listing some of the manuscript copies of the 1628 letter); J. G. Nichols, 'The Discovery of the Jesuits' College at Clerkenwell', *Camden Miscellany* II (Camden Society, 55, 1853), pp. 33–9.

[67] R. Cust, *The Forced Loan and English Politics 1626–1628* (Oxford, 1987), pp. 121–2, 248–9; Questier, *DP*, p. 436.

[68] Questier, *DP*, p. 442; SR, V, pp. 25–6.

[69] Challoner, *MMP*, p. 364. Among the sources for Edmund Arrowsmith used by Challoner were papers sent to him by Alban Butler from Douai: ABP, pp. 142–3 ('on Mr Arrowsmith, in an old hand, scarce legible, in a separate leaf dated 16 August 1631'), 143–4 ('another MS in an old hand...'). These pieces 'afford many corrections and additions to the story of this gentleman...in Mr Knasb [Knaresborough]': ABP, p. 144. In addition, see ABP, pp. 144–7 ('the English MS account of his arraignment and martyrdom in a fair hand...', taken from AAW, A XXII, no. 129, pp. 573–5); ABP, pp. 523–44 ('Vita Martyrium R.D.D. Edmundi Arrowsmith', which Butler describes (p. 144) as 'the Latin life of Mr Arrowsmith, very full and exact, which must have been collected by some more modern hand'). Among the manuscripts amassed by Butler is also ABPFC, fos 19^v–20^r (a transcript of which is in Foley, *RSJ*, II, pp. 72–4). Our main source for Arrowsmith is, however, Murphy, *TER*; for the sources on which this pamphlet is based, see Murphy, *TER*, p. 3; ARCR, I, no. 31. For Cornelius Murphy, see Foley, *RSJ*, II, pp. 24–5; T. G. Holt, 'Bishop Challoner and the Jesuits', in E. Duffy (ed.), *Challoner and his Church: A Catholic Bishop in Georgian England* (1981), pp. 137–51, at pp. 139–40.

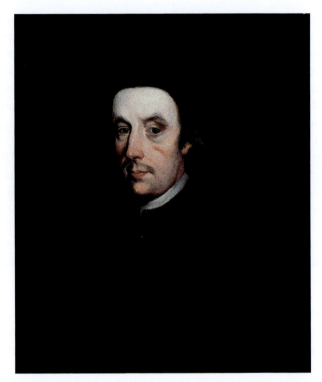

Figure 14.2 Portrait of Edmund Arrowsmith SJ, d.1628 (reproduced with the permission of the governors of Stonyhurst College, Lancashire).

not be heard, and they were obliged to carry him away out of the church'.[70] Robert Arrowsmith (Edmund's father) was imprisoned for nonconformity and then, with his brother, went to serve in the wars in Flanders. When they were ordered to fight against the Spaniards, they refused, at least to the extent that they merely discharged their weapons into the air. They were among those who defected with Sir William Stanley to Philip II, in whose service the uncle, Peter Arrowsmith, was killed.[71]

Edmund Arrowsmith had only recently been admitted to the Jesuit order—at the house of probation of St Ignatius, the Jesuit novitiate in London, at this point located in or close to the French embassy.[72] He had evidently been in sympathy with the Society of Jesus's aims and charism for some time. He had been ordained as far back as 1612. He had entered the Society in London on 21 July 1623, one day after the signing of the draft and, as it turned out, abortive dynastic marriage treaty between the Stuart court and the Habsburg court in Madrid.[73] He was,

---

[70] Foley, *RSJ*, II, p. 26; ABP, p. 523.   [71] Foley, *RSJ*, II, pp. 26, 27.
[72] *ODNB*, sub Arrowsmith, Edmund (article by T. M. McCoog).
[73] T. M. McCoog, *English and Welsh Jesuits 1555–1650* (2 vols, 1994–5), I, p. 125.

TOWARDS TOLERATION? 473

therefore, almost certainly what some secular clergy scornfully referred to as one of the 'votive brethren', that is, those secular priests who secretly pledged themselves to the religious orders while still technically remaining as seculars. From the perspective adopted by Thomas Worthington's martyr pamphlet printed back in 1601, as we saw, this was absolutely fine, that is, when all sorts of clergy laboured merrily together in the common cause and in the same vineyard. Viewed from the perspective of Bishop Richard Smith, however, when the vineyard was out of control because of a lack of order, hierarchy, and discipline, it was definitely not all right. The account of Arrowsmith penned on 16 August 1631 appears to have been written by the secular priest John Melling. But it claims that Arrowsmith tried unsuccessfully to persuade Melling to join the Society. It says also that Arrowsmith 'laboured divers years as one intending on fit occasion to become a Jesuit; and divers times before he was a Jesuit would he ask me about our [secular] clergy affairs, protesting [that] he never would discover anything thereof to the Jesuits for any good and advantage whatsoever; for till such a time as he should enter amongst the Jesuits he would always behave himself as a true member of the secular clergy'. Melling believed that Arrowsmith kept his promise, that is to say, he was unlike some members of the Society who did not have the best interests of the secular clergy at heart. Then, 'some few years before his execution he entered amongst the Jesuits in England, without doing any noviceship, but still in labour amongst us, except for some ten or twelve days once a year for a spiritual recollection at a place where the Jesuits used to meet in Lancashire for that end'.[74]

Perhaps Arrowsmith had been trying to negotiate a path between the Society and the secular clergy. This would certainly help to explain why, as with so many other martyrs, there was a contest over his memory, and why that memory was

---

[74] Foley, *RSJ*, II, pp. 31–2; ABP, pp. 142–3. By contrast, according to Challoner (the evidence for this statement is ABP, p. 527), Arrowsmith had made the spiritual exercises under the direction of a Jesuit priest and had done his novitiate in Essex, i.e. presumably within the network controlled by the Petre family, who were patrons of the Society. 'He did not go abroad to make his noviceship but retired only for two or three months into Essex, which time he employed in a spiritual retreat': Challoner, *MMP*, p. 364. Arrowsmith was listed as a Jesuit novice in the papers (of c.1624–5) which were seized at the Clerkenwell house of the Society in 1628: Foley, *RSJ*, I, p. 132, II, p. 30; PRO, SP 16/99/1 (document P) (*CSPD 1628–9*, p. 55). My identification of John Melling is made on the basis of the narrator's statement that he went to England in 1613 but after 17 June, when Arrowsmith left Douai, and that he was from Lancashire; this narrows it down to Melling (Anstr., II, p. 216), who was in prison at Lancaster in 1626: PRO, SP 16/525/86. Melling had issues with the Society and made it clear he would not become a Jesuit; but another Douai alumnus, Richard Melling (a relative, presumably), admitted there in May 1613, was (briefly) a servant of the pro-Jesuit rector Thomas Worthington: Anstr., II, p. 217. Both Arrowsmith and John Melling were sent away from Douai by the new rector Matthew Kellison in 1613: AAW, A XV, no. 27, p. 77; Challoner, *MMP*, p. 364; for John Melling, see also D. Lunn, 'Benedictine Opposition to Bishop Richard Smith (1625–1629)', *RH* 11 (1971–2), pp. 1–20, at p. 6; D. Lunn, 'Two Other New Benedictine Saints', *Ampleforth Journal* (1970), pp. 390–4, at pp. 392–4. One of Butler's manuscripts stated that, in Arrowsmith's case, his bad health accelerated his ordination and Kellison wanted him to return to England as soon as possible: ABP, p. 144.

474 CATHOLICS AND TREASON

written up and preserved in such detail inside the local Catholic community and then on the Continent. To contemporary Jesuits he was a saint.[75] But another of the narratives of his martyrdom was written by the secular priest William Hargrave, who succeeded the notorious Thomas White alias Blacklo as president of the seminary college at Lisbon. Hargrave addressed his report of Arrowsmith to White himself on 27 December 1628. Hargrave's letter about Arrowsmith refers to the French narrative (*Récit Veritable*) of the martyrdom, evidently with a certain irritation: 'the English Jesuits (as I suppose) have set forth a relation of the business in French, printed at Liège'.[76] There were other accounts of Arrowsmith also compiled and preserved by the secular clergy, notably by Francis Barber.[77] The very considerable narrative material on this one case, in fact two cases, since that of Arrowsmith is inseparable from that of the layman Richard Herst, tells us a good deal about the Catholic community at this point in the early seventeenth century, that is, about its internal contradictions and the way that those fissures intersected with the dysfunctions of the Stuart State immediately after the accession of Charles I.

The circumstances of Arrowsmith's arrest in 1628 were arguably somewhat bizarre. He was already known in his locality as a quite stroppy Catholic priest. When he was detained in the early 1620s and brought before Bishop John Bridgeman of Chester he, it is said, reacted angrily and won a 'glorious victory'.[78] Another manuscript says that Arrowsmith 'was both zealous, witty and fervent and so forward (in disputing with heretics)'—so said the writer—'that I often wished him...to carry salt in his pocket to season his actions, lest too much zeal without discretion might bring him too soon into danger'. Moreover, 'sometimes I have been in his company when meeting with [Protestant] ministers sumptuously mounted and [I] have had much ado to stay him from disputing with those proud dogs, so he was wont to call them, which, if he had done, it would have endangered...both him and his company'.[79]

Arrowsmith's zeal was, therefore, perceived as likely to disrupt what should, in a county such as Lancashire, have been a virtually self-regulating economy of

---

[75] *Récit Veritable de la Cruauté et Tyranie Faicte en Angleterre, a l'Endroit du Pere Edmond Arosmith de la Compagnie de Iesus* (Paris, 1629). Allison and Rogers suggest that this text was 'probably derived from an anonymous English *Relation* of which an edition, dated 1630, is recorded, though no copy is now known'. The 'second, enlarged edition of the English *Relation*' was the one published in London in 1737: ARCR, I, no. 31; Murphy, *TER*; Foley, *RSJ*, II, p. 35. See also Questier, *C&C*, p. 465, following Foley, *RSJ*, I, p. 139, identifying Arrowsmith, perhaps in error, as one of those on whom Bishop Richard Smith relied in Lancashire; Foley (*RSJ*, I, p. 139: PRO, SP 16/99/19, fo. 189ʳ; in Sir John Coke's hand) cites 'Southwerck alias Bradshaw' as Smith's agent, probably John Southworth, but Arrowsmith used the alias of Bradshaw (AAW, A XXII, no. 143, p. 628), whereas Southworth did not.

[76] Anstr., II, p. 146; AAW, A XXII, no. 156, pp. 671–4 (part printed in Foley, *RSJ*, II, pp. 33f); AAW, A XXVII, no. 150, p. 457.

[77] AAW, A XXII, no. 143, p. 627; Foley, *RSJ*, II, p. 34; for Barber, see *AWCBC*, p. 473.

[78] Foley, *RSJ*, II, pp. 32, 33.

[79] ABP, p. 144, cited in Foley, *RSJ*, II, p. 29; Challoner, *MMP*, p. 364.

religion. But Arrowsmith's final conflict with the local State came just as much out of hostility within the local Catholic community, that is, as much as for anything that he had done to annoy local officialdom. Arrowsmith had been, said Melling, 'in labour amongst the rest to reduce a young man to a course of virtue, who was fallen both from God and himself and, having reproved him in particular for an incestuous marriage', was 'so hated by him that, coming once to suspect to what place the priest repaired, he found means to discover' Arrowsmith 'to a justice of peace', one Captain Rawsthorne, 'who dispatched his warrant for him, and so he was apprehended upon the highway'. Arrowsmith 'was committed to the common jail for not taking the oaths and upon vehement suspicion also that he was a priest and Jesuit'.[80]

William Hargrave's version of the story was slightly different. Two individuals 'had married together; the woman was not Catholic' but 'the man was'. His name was Holden; apparently he was Robert Holden of Holden. His bride was Mary Chorley. The pair were first cousins. There was, therefore, 'somewhat in the marriage for which they stood in need of a dispensation'. In fact, they had already been married by a Church of England minister. Arrowsmith 'was employed' in obtaining the dispensation. 'In the meantime the woman became Catholic. When the dispensation came, Mr Arrowsmith would not make use of it before the parties had separated for the space of fourteen days'. This 'incensed them much against him'. When they knew 'the time' at which 'he was to return to' Holden's father's 'house where they lived, they secretly sent word to one Rostern [Rawsthorne], a justice of peace, to come and apprehend a priest'. The 'justice, not willing to bring his neighbour in danger, sent him word that he was to search his house; [so] that, by this means, having intelligence, he might convey away the priest'. The searchers found no one.[81] But approximately a mile from the house, Arrowsmith was detained by Rawsthorne himself who was waiting there. There was a consensus that it was Mrs Holden and her son who had insisted on the arrest, which Mr Holden had no desire to see.[82]

Everything spun further out of control when the case was dealt with by the judge Sir Henry Yelverton. Yelverton had evidently decided to turn what was a local dispute into a test case, not least because 'some before his coming down from London had told him to his face that he durst not hang a priest'.[83] Yelverton's fellow judge was Sir James Whitelock.[84] Sir James had in 1610 emerged as a firm critic of impositions. His son Bulstrode Whitelock was the future

---

[80] Challoner, *MMP*, p. 365; Murphy, *TER*, pp. 5–6.

[81] Foley, *RSJ*, II, pp. 33–4 (AAW, A XXII, no. 156, pp. 671–2).

[82] Foley, *RSJ*, II, p. 34; AAW, A XXII, no. 143, p. 627f. For uncertainty over who made the arrest, see ABP, p. 143; Foley, *RSJ*, II, pp. 32–3.

[83] Foley, *RSJ*, II, p. 35.

[84] Whitelock's brother Edmund had, as we saw, been regarded as a Catholic sympathizer; see pp. 286–7 above.

476   CATHOLICS AND TREASON

parliamentarian. However, among Judge Whitelock's friends were Richard Neile, William Laud, and Richard Montagu, and he himself sided with the anti-puritans in 1628 at Durham over alleged popish innovations there.[85] By contrast, Yelverton was overtly puritan in his attitudes. But neither Yelverton nor Whitelock was a stubborn opponent of royal government. Yelverton had actually come out in 1610 and 1614 in favour of impositions. He had been locked in a bitter dispute with Buckingham about his short-lived appointment in 1617 as attorney-general, terminated in 1620, though Alexander Courtney concludes that Yelverton may have been more to blame for his problems than Buckingham was.[86] By summer 1628 Yelverton was evidently still very angry about something. Either he was reprising his earlier dislike of the favourite or he had thoroughly internalized the link between Arminianism and popery which had been alleged by some of the members of the 1628 parliament.

Yelverton wanted at all costs to secure a conviction in Arrowsmith's case. When Arrowsmith refused to confirm whether he was ordained or not, Yelverton called on the local ministry for evidence and specifically on 'a minister', one Leigh, that is, William Leigh, 'who sat as a justice of peace upon the bench and who, formerly, had had some knowledge of the priest'. Leigh 'went to whisper in the judge's ear; and then, shortly after, began to revile the prisoner aloud, declaring what a seducer he was and that, if some order were not taken with him, he would make half Lancashire papists'.[87] Leigh was the puritan rector of Standish. He and William Harrison had, as we saw, retaliated in print against the Catholic claims about the demise of the godly Katherine Brettergh.[88]

Challoner's rendition of the confrontation between Arrowsmith and Yelverton (there are differences in the extant accounts of the court proceedings[89]) stresses that there was no overt proof of Arrowsmith's ordination. The Holden family was not prepared to appear in court against the Jesuit, whatever the enmity between them and him, though their evidence was used to frame one of the two indictments of him.[90] Instead, a servant of the JP who was responsible for his arrest, with the JP's son, claimed that Arrowsmith had tried to convert them to Rome. As Arrowsmith explained it, he had simply counselled the thuggish servant to 'give over his disorderly life, his drinking, swearing, dissolute talking and all those other things whereby he might offend Almighty God'. He had said to the JP's son

---

[85] *HC 1604–29*, VI, pp. 751–8; *CSPD 1629–31*, p. 31.

[86] A. Courtney, 'Court Politics and the Kingship of James VI & I, c. 1615–c. 1622' (PhD, Cambridge, 2008), pp. 134–45; see also *HC 1604–29*, VI, pp. 894–901. Yelverton emerged in 1629 as a supporter of Peter Smart against John Cosin concerning their confrontation in Durham Cathedral: *HC 1604–29*, VI, p. 901; *CSPD 1629–31*, p. 15, cf. pp. 19, 20. For Smart and for his attack on Cosin, see K. Fincham and N. Tyacke, *Altars Restored: The Changing Face of English Religious Worship, 1547–c. 1700* (Oxford, 2007), pp. 137–9.

[87] Challoner, *MMP*, p. 366.

[88] See pp. 306–7 above; *ODNB*, *sub* Leigh, William (article by S. Wright).

[89] Challoner, *MMP*, pp. 366–7; cf. ABP, p. 145.   [90] Challoner, *MMP*, pp. 368–9; ABP, p. 145.

TOWARDS TOLERATION? 477

no more than that he hoped, 'when he came to riper years, he would look better into himself and become a true Catholic'.[91] Yelverton then cast about for workable indictments against Arrowsmith and made sure that, on 26 August, he was charged and, in short order, sentenced both for his ordination and for persuading.[92]

What Challoner does not mention is that Arrowsmith had, as the diarist Walter Yonge recorded, tried to secure his freedom, after the jury had given its verdict, by dramatically producing a letter of grace written by none other than the duke of Buckingham, who, as it happened, had been assassinated three days before Arrowsmith was arraigned. Whether or not Yelverton was now better disposed to the duke than previously, he told Arrowsmith 'that public affairs were to be preferred before private letters'. Then Arrowsmith brought out 'a kind of pardon from the queen'; but Yelverton answered that he was required 'to take notice of the king's proclamation' of 3 August 1628 'for execution of laws against such persons, which proclamation bore date two days after the pardon'. Arrowsmith also had a letter from the king himself, but Yelverton countered that 'the laws and statutes of the kingdom must be…respected or preferred before letters, and so gave judgment'.[93]

The case allowed Yelverton to make a public statement about what he took to be the supremacy of the law over sporadic appeals to royal prerogative. Arrowsmith evidently used the trial to do something like the reverse. Joseph Mead understood on 20 September 1628 that Arrowsmith had 'at his arraignment' given 'most insolent answers' to the judges, 'saying' that 'they durst not put him to death'. He had also 'asked…Yelverton what he meant' when he wrote 'so injuriously against him to the king'. To prove this, Arrowsmith 'had plucked the copy of Sir Harry's letter out of his pocket'. If this is true, it suggests that Yelverton had tried to prepare the ground by indicating to London what course he would take. Someone had tipped off Arrowsmith, who then sought to embarrass the judge.[94] The other judge, Whitelock, refused to sign the execution warrant, or so Catholic commentators alleged.[95]

Challoner records how far Yelverton went in order to make sure that there was no reprieve. The 'judge would have him die a day before the other condemned persons, a thing unusual at [the] assizes'. Yelverton 'was also pleased to look on out of a window at the execution'. Allegedly most of Lancaster turned out to

[91] Challoner, *MMP*, pp. 366–7; see also Foley, *RSJ*, II, pp. 34–5.
[92] Challoner, *MMP*, p. 368; ABP, p. 145; Foley, *RSJ*, II, p. 60 (Henry Holme's statement that Arrowsmith 'was executed…upon the statute of persuasions').
[93] Questier, *C&C*, p. 465; BL, Additional MS 35331, fo. 24ᵛ (for which reference I am grateful to Thomas Cogswell); Larkin, *SRP*, II, no. 96.
[94] Birch, *CTCI*, I, p. 397. By contrast, the Benedictine William Jones believed on 5 August 1628 that 'the judges had especial order for what they did at Lancaster': AAW, A XXII, no. 131, p. 580.
[95] Foley, *RSJ*, II, p. 46; Murphy, *TER*, p. 19.

478   CATHOLICS AND TREASON

watch.[96] By a prearranged signal, the priest John Southworth gave Arrowsmith absolution as he was 'on his way to the hurdle'.[97] The 'common prisoners in the gaol' strongly disapproved of his condemnation and 'none of the felons would...put him to death'. A local butcher was offered the princely sum of five pounds if his apprentice would do the necessary, but 'the youth, hearing how far his master had yielded', ran 'away and was never heard of since'. Eventually a soldier under sentence for offences against military discipline was hired to do it, though 'the whole town would not lend him an axe'.[98]

William Leigh pressed the point right to the end. Just short of 'gallows, the horse and hurdle were stayed'. Here 'the old limping minister...showed' Arrowsmith 'a huge and terrible fire, with a cauldron boiling, so hot and high that no man was able to stand near it'. He urged Arrowsmith 'to conform' himself and to 'enjoy the mercy of the king'; but the priest refused.[99] Arrowsmith was hanged and disembowelled and his remains were fastened to the castle walls. Yelverton's malice knew no limits. 'He departed' the next day and 'turned his horse and, making him prance in a vainglorious boast of his injustice, he looked towards the martyr's head which he, not thinking [it to be] placed high enough, ordered it to be raised six yards above the pinnacle of the castle'.[100] The officials went to considerable lengths to prevent the spectators acquiring relics. Arrowsmith's apparel, however, was taken by his friend John Southworth. Furthermore, a report dated 3 November 1629, written by Sir John Bridgeman, concerning those who processed to St Winifred's Well at Holywell, including George Talbot, earl of Shrewsbury,

---

[96] Challoner, *MMP*, pp. 369–70; Murphy, *TER*, pp. 19–20.

[97] Challoner, *MMP*, p. 370; Foley, *RSJ*, II, p. 47; Murphy, *TER*, p. 20. As John Knaresborough related it, Ambrose Barlow OSB's 'charity went so far as to put him upon a resolution of being present likewise at the place of execution, in hopes of doing' Arrowsmith 'some further good offices in the last moments of life'; and he would have done so had the execution not been brought forward a day, to Thursday 28 August, i.e. at Yelverton's insistence; 'the news did not reach Mr Barlow till the next morning': Kn., III, pp. 112–14. Knaresborough relied here on a manuscript from one 'Mr Barlow of Barlow' (presumably of the martyr's family—of Barlow Hall, Manchester—now the clubhouse of the Chorlton-cum-Hardy golf club) dated 4 June 1676. It stated that the Benedictine had heard a repeated 'knocking at his chamber door' and finally Arrowsmith, as Barlow believed, entered and 'thanked Mr Barlow for the favour he did in assisting him in prison and withal said: "Mr Barlow I am gone and you will shortly follow me"' and '"three or four others will suffer soon after you and no priest after this shall be put to death at Lancaster for religion"'. Barlow concluded that 'if today had been tomorrow, I should certainly believe that I had seen a spirit': Kn., VI, p. 222; *ODNB*, Barlow, Ambrose (article by T. Cooper, rev. G. Bradley). These events were recalled by Barlow while he was awaiting death at Lancaster (he was executed on 10 September 1641) as he wrote to his brother Rudesind Barlow at Douai on 17 May 1641. Rudesind recited this in his own narrative (1 January 1642) of Ambrose's execution: Challoner, *MMP*, p. 396; Foley, *RSJ*, II, p. 55; Murphy, *TER*, pp. 28–9; Kn., III, p. 114; UCLSC, UC/P1/B2, pp. 18–21 (describing how this narrative of Arrowsmith's apparition to Barlow had descended in Lancashire down to the eighteenth century, i.e. separately from the narrative penned by Rudesind Barlow).

[98] AAW, A XXII, no. 129, p. 573; Foley, *RSJ*, II, p. 45; Murphy, *TER*, pp. 15, 18.

[99] Challoner, *MMP*, pp. 370–1; Murphy, *TER*, pp. 21, 24–5; see also Foley, *RSJ*, II, pp. 50–1.

[100] Challoner, *MMP*, p. 372; Murphy, *TER*, p. 27; ABP, p. 147. William Hargrave insisted that Yelverton had displayed a quite bizarre blood lust. He had, after the execution, insisted on Arrowsmith's dismembered remains being brought to him: Foley, *RSJ*, II, p. 53 (AAW, A XXII, no. 156, p. 673); Richard Carpenter, *Experience, Historie and Divinitie*...(1642), pt II, p. 234; Murphy, *TER*, p. 27.

TOWARDS TOLERATION?   479

Lord William Howard, and Sir Cuthbert Clifton, claimed that Arrowsmith's 'clothes, and the knife that cut him up' were 'at Sir Cuthbert Clifton's house'; or, as another account mentioned, were hanging 'in a chapel within the county for a relic'.[101]

Arrowsmith's execution was followed, the day after, by that of Richard Herst, who had been tried and sentenced for murder. Herst was also a 'recusant convict'. On that basis, warrants had been issued to bring him before the bishop of Chester. An episcopal pursuivant, Christopher Norcross, accompanied by two others, went to arrest him. In the ensuing scuffle one of the pursuivant's men, named Henry Dewhurst, was slightly hurt by Herst's maidservant, and then managed to break his leg as he made his retreat, and from that injury he perished two weeks later. But the man's death was blamed on Herst himself.[102]

According to local Catholic opinion, Herst was the victim of a judicial stitch-up of the worst kind.[103] He was 'certainly clear of the fact' but the 'coroner's inquest' found him 'accessory' and 'he was, besides, obnoxious to the law, on account of his religion'. He then 'began to negotiate his pardon by the best friends he could procure, whom he waited upon in person, but in the most private manner possible'. A pardon passed the king's 'hand, signet and privy seal'. The lord keeper, Sir Thomas Coventry, thought the form of the warrant to be too broad and suspended it 'till the judge's return from the summer assizes, by whom he hoped to be informed how the case stood in the country', and the judge poisoned the lord keeper's mind against Herst. Still, Herst was led to believe that, if he presented himself for trial, he would, even if found guilty, be reprieved and then pardoned; and this was 'signified by the lord keeper to the person who solicited Herst's pardon'. The queen herself had 'been graciously pleased to move his Majesty for the poor man's life'.[104] A *True and Exact Relation* then describes in considerable detail the process whereby the pardon failed to take effect. This source insisted that in the face of the trial jury's inclination to acquit both Herst and his wife, as accessory, the judge 'yielded to the clearing of his wife but insisted vehemently to have it found wilful murder in her husband; and aggravated the

---

[101] Foley, *RSJ*, II, p. 52, citing PRO, SP 16/151/13, fo. 21ʳ; *HMCC*, I, p. 407. The council ordered on 30 September 1628 that Southworth should be transferred to Wisbech Castle. But it seems that he simply ended up back in the London prison system under minimal restraint, whence, with other clergy, it was ordered in April 1630 that he should go into exile—at the request of the queen and 'in regard' of the recent 'peace between the two crowns'; but he probably never left the country: *APC 1628–9*, pp. 178–9; *APC 1629–30*, pp. 127–8, 332, 407; Prynne, *PRP*, pp. 18–20, 24; Anstr., II, p. 306; Kn., V, pp. 178–9. For Arrowsmith's relics, see Foley, *RSJ*, II, pp. 59–60; AAW, A XXII, no. 148, p. 525; ABSJ, CP (note on Arrowsmith—testimony dispatched to Richard Downey, archbishop of Liverpool on 11 October 1942).

[102] Murphy, *TER*, pp. 34–6; Challoner, *MMP*, pp. 373–4.

[103] Murphy, *TER*, pp. 33f. For Herst's own statement declaring his innocence, see Challoner, *MMP*, p. 376.

[104] Murphy, *TER*, pp. 36, 37.

480 CATHOLICS AND TREASON

crime, urging particularly the circumstance of his person, as being a popish recusant'.[105]

If the facts were as related, this was anything other than due process. But one can also see that the authorities, faced with what looked like violent resistance to local authority, could not back down. According to Catholics the jury had consulted with the judge and had been told that 'they must find it murder for example's sake' and 'that Herst should not die' for 'the king had pardoned him'.[106] But Yelverton had returned to London and had given the lord keeper a partial version of events about Herst—a 'barbarous fiction'.[107] This, of course, is the Catholic gloss on this episode. What may have happened was that Yelverton was determined that no reprieve for Herst would be allowed while he remained stubbornly recusant, nor for Arrowsmith while he stayed as aggressively defiant as he was. With Arrowsmith and Herst both claiming to have pardons signed in London, Yelverton could not concede.[108]

Herst's stubbornness held. The day before the execution the high sheriff instructed that he should attend the local church. In fact, all 'the prisoners, according to custom, were to be led to church to hear a sermon'. Herst vigorously refused and he was 'barbarously' dragged 'from the prison to the church, where they took care to place him near to the pulpit. Here the generous soldier of Christ threw himself close to the ground and, with his fingers, stopped his ears' so as 'not to hear any of their doctrine, though the officers from time to time forced them out.'[109] The chances are that this was an attempt on the part of the authorities to score a public-relations victory and possibly to enable a reprieve to be granted. But Herst wanted to make absolutely sure that no one would say that he had conformed.

On the way to 'the place of execution', Herst was confronted by the vicar of Lancaster St Mary, Geoffrey King. He had been one of the translators of the King James Bible and briefly was Regius professor of Hebrew at Cambridge, as well as a royal chaplain. He was, says Adam Nicolson, a 'severe anti-Catholic', although he had been attached to the group of translators around Lancelot Andrewes. He merely challenged Herst as to 'how he thought to be saved', but he did not really press it any further.[110]

There is a long letter of 18 September 1628 from, it appears, the Jesuit Robert Persons's nephew (also called Robert Persons) which describes Arrowsmith's and Herst's case. Persons Jnr forwarded to his correspondent a 'certificate' drawn up by Herst about what had actually happened to him. One Roger Hesketh had pointed out to the coroner that Henrietta Maria had tried to

---

[105] Murphy, *TER*, pp. 38 f.   [106] Murphy, *TER*, pp. 38–9.   [107] Murphy, *TER*, p. 39.
[108] Murphy, *TER*, pp. 44–5, 61.   [109] Murphy, *TER*, pp. 45–6.
[110] Murphy, *TER*, p. 48; CCED, ID 33213; http://kingjamesbibletranslators.org/bios/Geoffrey-King; A. Nicolson, *Power and Glory: Jacobean England and the Making of the King James Bible* (2003), pp. 99, 192, 252.

secure his pardon 'and took it ill to be so crossed'. But the judge forced through the conviction.[111] This letter added that a number of witnesses had perjured themselves. It narrated the tendering of the oath of allegiance to Herst and the hauling of him to the church. Persons encouraged the unnamed recipient of his letter to 'do your best to make the queen', the 'lady of Buckingham' (the duke's widow), the earl of Dorset, and others 'whom you think fit' to understand what had happened. Herst had 'written to the old lady of Buckingham', that is, the countess, Mary Villiers. Persons was 'sorry for her affliction' in the recent 'villainous murdering and dismal death of the duke her son', assassinated by John Felton, though 'whether we have lost a friend or foe it is doubtful'. 'The puritans', for what it was worth, 'thought him to be our chief friend'. It would all make for more difficulty 'about the getting of' Herst's 'lands', but Persons's friend was encouraged to do his best. Persons concluded that, undoubtedly, Herst 'died a martyr'.[112]

The diplomat Amerigo Salvetti construed the trial and execution of Arrowsmith as directly contrary to royal wishes and policy because Charles was at that point trying to negotiate a European peace settlement.[113] Joseph Mead reported on 27 September 1628 that he had heard that 'a certain lord, being an active privy councillor, told Judge Yelverton lately that, by his executing that priest or Jesuit at [the] Lancaster assizes, he had marred all', particularly in the context of the dispatch to Italy of the earl of Carlisle by the king in summer 1628 in order to establish a concord 'between his Majesty, on the one side, and the pope, emperor and king of Spain on the other side'.[114] Rudesind Barlow OSB said that the currently raging

---

[111] ABSJ, CP (Herst, Richard), citing St Mary's College, Oscott, Kirk MSS, I, p. 21 (i.e. a transcript of ABPFC, fos 21ʳ-2ʳ). For the printed version of the 'papers' concerning Herst, including 'Richard Herst's declaration, word for word, as he wrote it a month before his death', and subsequent letters, see Murphy, *TER*, pp. 60-8. For Robert Persons Jnr, see Anstr., II, p. 238; McCoog, *English and Welsh Jesuits*, I, p. 126.

[112] ABPFC, fos 21ᵛ-2ʳ.

[113] H. B. Tomkins (ed.), *The Manuscripts of Henry Duncan Skrine, Esq.: Salvetti Correspondence* (HMC, 11th report, appendix, part I, 1887), p. 165; R. E. Schreiber, *The First Carlisle: Sir James Hay, first Earl of Carlisle as Courtier, Diplomat and Entrepreneur, 1580–1636* (Philadelphia, 1984), pp. 103–14; *CSPV 1628–9*, p. 72 and *passim*.

[114] Birch, *CTCI*, I, p. 400. For a somewhat garbled and inaccurate report on 10/20 October 1628 from Paris by John Roche, bishop of Ferns, speculating that 'Buckingham must have had his part in this execution', see G. D. Burtchaell and J. M. Rigg (eds), *Report on Franciscan Manuscripts Preserved at the Convent, Merchants Quay, Dublin* (HMC, Dublin, 1906), pp. 7–8. For the regime's attempts in later 1628 not to surrender the rhetoric of anti-popery, see, e.g., *APC 1628–9*, pp. 178, 253, 279–80. The Jesuit Henry More was condemned in London in December 1628. Perhaps the proceedings against him were connected with, if not driven by, the temporary stalling of the peace talks with the French: *CSPV 1628–9*, p. 447. For the knock-on effect in Scotland, with the marquis of Huntly (of all people) being ordered to take action against Catholic clergy, see P. Hume Brown (ed.), *The Register of the Privy Council of Scotland 1627–1628* (Edinburgh, 1900), pp. 496–507; B. Robertson, *Lordship and Power in the North of Scotland: The Noble House of Huntly 1603–1690* (Edinburgh, 2011), pp. 64–5. One suspects that the printing of the narrative of the Arrowsmith case in France may have been intended to make an Anglo-French peace more difficult. The same may be true of other late-1620s martyr publications relating to England, notably John Mullan, *Idea Togatae Constantiae...* (Paris, 1629). See also Arnauld Raisse, *Hierogazophylacium Belgicum, sive Thesaurus Sacrarum Reliquiarum Belgii* (Douai, 1628); Arnauld Raisse, *Catalogus Christi Sacerdotum, qui ex Nobili Anglicano Duacenae*

482 CATHOLICS AND TREASON

approbation controversy, as Richard Smith's enemies tried to face him down, was 'so generally known to the Protestants that the parliament men' longed 'to be together to take order with us'. In addition, it had been 'conceived that the king, upon displeasure against the judges who sentenced the martyrs of Lancaster, would have given' Catholics 'some sort of toleration if this foul business', that is, the denunciations of Bishop Smith by his Catholic critics, 'had not brought all' the privy council 'upon' Charles's 'back'.[115] The Catholic community was violently split between the supporters and the opponents of Bishop Richard Smith, but the recent events at Lancaster were a demonstration of the realignments inside the regime as the language of anti-popery became even more overtly oppositional in the face of the crown's alleged resort to 'new counsels'.

The Advent of the Personal Rule

The recall of parliament in early 1629 went spectacularly wrong, even though the regime, via the device of a royal proclamation, publicly denounced Richard Smith.[116] But John Knaresborough undoubtedly captured something of the contemporary Catholic reaction to the dissolution when he opined that 'those men who all along distinguished themselves in the house of Commons for their persecuting spirit against the Catholics were indeed the very men who caused their king so much vexation and trouble'. They were themselves censured by the king after the dissolution of March 1629. Here they were described and condemned as 'ill-affected malevolent disobedient persons, nay vipers, by whose seditious carriage...we and our royal authority have been so highly contemned as our kingly office cannot bear or any former age can parallel'.[117]

There is something of an irony here. Almost all the narratives of the later 1620s take the failure of the early Caroline parliaments as a political morality tale, a dreadful prequel and warning of what was to come in the 1630s. But as yet there has been little attempt to tie in contemporary Catholic reactions to the genesis of the personal rule with the extensive work of Kevin Sharpe on the 1630s—a radical and positive redescription of the post-parliamentary polity— or, even more, to Simon Adams's account of the collapse of British interest and

---

Ciuitatis Collegio Proseminati, Praeclarum fidei Catholicae Testimonium in Britannia Praebuerunt (Douai, 1630), which includes the recent Arrowsmith case: ARCR, I, nos 838, 323, 323. 1; Pollen, *UD*, pp. 5–6.

[115] Stanfield, 'The Archpriest Controversy', part II, p. 173 (the manuscript—a copy of a letter by Rudesind Barlow—is undated, but the letter was, apparently, written shortly after John Felton's assassination of the duke of Buckingham).

[116] Questier, *C&C*, pp. 465–6; *APC 1628–9*, p. 363. For the proclamations put out against Smith, one on 11 December 1628 and then a second on 24 March 1629, see Questier, *C&C*, pp. 464, 466; Larkin, *SRP*, II, nos 104, 109.

[117] Kn., III, pp. 29–30.

TOWARDS TOLERATION? 483

investment in Protestant-cause politics after the death of Prince Maurice in 1625 and, subsequently, the catastrophe of Buckingham's aggressive foreign policy towards France.[118]

The king probably had no deep personal inclination ideologically or intellectually towards the Church of Rome. But the incentives for the regime of the personal rule to follow the logic of post-Reformation anti-popery were virtually non-existent.[119] During that period, it pursued the compounding policy which had been implemented so controversially during the later 1620s so as to deal with Catholic separatism virtually as an administrative category. Equally, the regime now had little reason to avail itself of the treason law against Catholic clergy, even though, in the case of the Irish Dominican Arthur McGeoghan, it was still quite capable of it. He was arraigned on 25 November 1633 for saying, allegedly, at Lisbon on 31 December 1631 that 'I will kill the king if I can...because he is a heretic'. The indictment was drawn under the fourteenth-century Edwardian treason statute. The court used the occasion to state that it was treason alone 'for which all the Jesuits and priests have suffered death within these eighty years and not one of them all for religion; and therefore they do all vainly imagine that they die martyrs for religion'. McGeoghan was dismembered alive at Tyburn on 27 November 1633 with considerable barbarity.[120] However, the chances are that the court's account, in this case, of the link between Catholics and treason would have sounded quite different from the superficially identical claims made on that topic by Lord Burghley in the 1580s and 1590s.

From time to time in the 1630s, life could be hard for Catholics in London. Thomas Holland claimed that, from the point at which he arrived in the metropolis in 1635, the 'search after priests' was still intense and there were periods when he could barely venture outside in the hours of daylight; and at other times he employed a variety of disguises and foreign accents and languages so as to conceal his identity.[121] Notoriously, his confrère Henry Morse, the priest of the plague as he is known, was put on trial in 1637.[122]

The most comprehensive study of the king's secretary, Sir Francis Windebank, has emphasized the extent to which he personally intervened in order to release Catholic clergy who during the 1630s had been put under arrest. Patricia Haskell

---

[118] K. Sharpe, *The Personal Rule of Charles I* (1992); Adams, PC, esp. the conclusion.

[119] The future civil-war martyr Thomas Bullaker returned to England in late 1630 and was arrested at Plymouth, but a prosecution at the Exeter assizes failed and his Catholic friends, by underhand means, secured his freedom: *AWCBC*, pp. 2030, 2085–9; Richard Mason (Angelus of St Francis), *Certamen Seraphicum Provinciae Angliae pro Sancta Dei Ecclesia* (Douai, 1649), section on Bullaker, chs 5, 6.

[120] BL, Harleian MS 738, no. 9, fos 183^r–8^r (quotations at fos 183^r, 186^{r-v}); see also *NCC*, pp. 205, 211; *CSPV 1632–6*, p. 172; Questier, *C&C*, p. 485; T. Flynn, *The Irish Dominicans 1536–1641* (Dublin, 1993), pp. 119–20.

[121] Kn., IV, pp. 81–3.

[122] See pp. 488–9 below. For Morse's ministry to plague victims, see Kn., IV, pp. 310 f.

484 CATHOLICS AND TREASON

suggests that Windebank not only responded to Charles's own inclinations here but also used his initiative to free Catholic prisoners, even those convicted of treason, 'by verbal warrants or warrants under his own hand'.[123] This was compatible with his attempts during the 1630s, once again in accord with Charles's general wishes, to establish a compromise over the oath of allegiance of 1606, for which purpose Windebank had meetings and discussions with the Benedictine Leander Jones in the mid-1630s; and it was a topic that he discussed with Gregorio Panzani, the papal agent dispatched from Rome in 1634 to attend on Henrietta Maria.[124] In addition, while Windebank was prepared, for example, to order the arrest and incarceration of the Jesuit Edward Leedes after Leedes's explicit affirmation, in a manuscript piece, of the papal deposing power, in the case of other clergy who had been gaoled, he provided them with release warrants.[125] As Dr Haskell points out, Catholic clergy had been allowed out of prison before; for example, in April 1630 sixteen Catholics were delivered into the custody of the French ambassador on condition that they left the kingdom.[126] But, although direct orders might come from Charles or his queen to release imprisoned Catholics, 'it became the common practice during the personal rule for Catholic prisoners to be discharged from the London prisons by Windebank's agency'. In December 1640 it was claimed that, during the previous four years alone, sixty-four Catholic clergymen had been let out of the Gatehouse, principally by Windebank.[127] This was not just the outcome of the king's servants, or some of them, believing in tolerance for its own sake. It was, at some level, the inevitable consequence of a recognition that the vast majority of the Catholic community, if that is the right term, did not subscribe to monarchomach political theory, and that a balanced diplomacy with a range of European States, as well as with the papacy, meant that indiscriminate sanctions against Catholics in the capital could not be allowed.[128]

For various reasons, then, the relationship between the Catholic community and the Caroline State was now defined almost entirely by discourses of tolerance and, at the edges, by an insistent rhetoric of anti-puritanism in ways which could bring certain styles of Catholicism quite close to some of the prevailing avant-garde conformist trends inside the national Church. John Southcot wrote in April 1633 that, 'as for that report which the Jesuits' made in Rome 'of persecution' in

---

[123] P. Haskell, 'Sir Francis Windebank and the Personal Rule of Charles I' (PhD, Southampton, 1978), p. 362.

[124] Ibid., ch. 8 *passim.*   [125] Ibid., pp. 371–2.   [126] Ibid., p. 392.

[127] Ibid., pp. 393, 616–28. Windebank also issued numerous warrants to stop proceedings against recusants: ibid., pp. 402–3.

[128] Ibid., p. 399. Dr Haskell notes that the other secretary of State, Sir John Coke, enforced sanctions against Catholic separatism. The king responded by 'encouraging Windebank to arrange for Catholics to escape prosecution or punishment' and thus 'Charles I used the dual secretaryship…to conduct a left-hand, right-hand policy that enabled him to appear to enforce the law, while circumventing it by another route': ibid., p. 402.

TOWARDS TOLERATION? 485

England, it was 'false in all particulars, excepting only compositions', that is, for recusancy fines and sequestrations, 'which, although they' were 'high racked', were 'not so intolerable' as the Jesuits insisted; 'Catholics had rather have them at any rate than lose their lives and liberties'.[129] Charles I was clement and moderate. He allowed 'the execution of the penal laws' only for 'some politic ends'. He was certainly not 'a persecutor'.[130] As for the 1606 allegiance oath—the issue over which, as many Catholics saw it, the Jacobean martyrs had gone to their deaths— it had in effect become a topic over which the Catholic community could negotiate with the crown for tolerance, that is, by describing exactly how loyal they were, even if they could not take the oath exactly as it stood.[131]

At the same point, many Catholic clergymen were commenting on the apparent movement of a certain sort of conformist style and agenda, associated particularly with changes in the style of worship in the national Church, towards positions which were at least compatible with contemporary Catholic understandings of true religion. Some of them were not just commenting; they were positively celebrating it. Those celebrations, however, were more noticeable among the secular clergy, who still thought in terms of the programme of reform in their own community, which was possible only if Rome were to restore direct and local episcopal regulation of Catholics in England.[132]

One can easily see what it was in Laudianism that would have proved attractive to such people. What was crucial here was not just the Laudians' theological reaction to aspects of contemporary Calvinism but also their assertion of divine-right episcopacy and what was arguably, in the English context, a distinctive approach to liturgy and worship. As Jeffrey Collins explains it, Archbishop William Laud 'sought unity in a visible Church hierarchy and in regular administration of the sacraments'. Subscribing as he did to 'the definition of catholicity formulated by the Fathers', he was unable to endorse almost any facet of mainstream anti-popery. Temperamentally he may have had no sympathy for separatist Catholics. Indeed, he had no reasons, personal or political, to see separatist Catholics being publicly tolerated or released from the statutory and practical measures that were supposed to force them to conform. But, equally, they, or some of them, could hardly not have looked favourably on Laud's programme for 'reviving Church courts, renewing sacramentalism and ceremonialism' and 'securing church property' as well as 'promoting the divine right of bishops'.[133] As Peter Lake describes it, 'in Laudianism we are . . . dealing with an attempt to redraw, indeed, to redefine the

---

[129] NCC, p. 168.   [130] NCC, p. 246.   [131] See, e.g., NCC, pp. 247–8.

[132] NCC, passim; Fincham and Tyacke, Altars Restored, chs 4–6.

[133] J. Collins, The Allegiance of Thomas Hobbes (Oxford, 2005), pp. 72–3. For Laud's antipathy to crypto-Catholics on the privy council, notably the earl of Portland and Lord Cottington, and even to his former friend, Sir Francis Windebank, see Haskell, 'Sir Francis Windebank', p. 136. For his opposition to toleration of separatist Catholicism and his disapproval of approaches made by Catholics to the regime in search of a rapprochement between England and Rome, see ibid., pp. 100, 375, 380, 400–1.

486   CATHOLICS AND TREASON

line between the sacred and the profane', something that 'cannot be reduced either to a series of numbered points about predestination nor an assemblage of conventional conformist commonplaces about the need for order, obedience and uniformity'. Laudians focused on 'the importance of the beauty of holiness'; and they did this in the context of their 'vision of the church as the house of God', a vision that was realized in large part through the restoration of altars in the churches and the emphasis on prayer and the sacrament of the eucharist at the expense of preaching. Moreover, 'all the central features of Laudianism…were constructed against a countervailing image of puritan heterodoxy and subversion'.[134]

Catholics could now rewrite some of the narratives of the travails of their community. Persecution had been the work of puritans who bore 'no less (if not more) aversion and malice against' the good 'sort of Protestants' than they did 'against the Catholics'. No Catholic should need, or be allowed, to ask awkward questions about royal authority: 'all manner of writing, as well private as public, by any of the king's subjects concerning the extent of the regal jurisdiction' must 'be strictly forbidden', stated one memorandum sent to Rome by the secular clergy.[135]

It is perhaps worth remarking here that the mid-1630s biographical accounts of Philip Howard, earl of Arundel (d.1595) and his saintly wife, Anne Dacre, who lived until April 1630, had many of the characteristics of contemporary martyrologies—certainly the life of the earl did. But this was not a rant against the Caroline regime—far from it; it was, if anything, a contribution to the arguments which had been aired during the approbation controversy. It was committed to paper by the countess's Jesuit chaplain, none other than Richard Blount, who had witnessed her death at Shifnal manor in Shropshire. But he set it down and completed it in June 1635 right in the middle of Gregorio Panzani's negotiations with the different interest groups among the English clergy and their patrons. This was a negotiation that looked likely to include everyone except the fathers of the Society of Jesus working in England, and might well lead to the reinstatement of Bishop Smith's authority. Blount's lengthy account of the earl and his wife refers back to the sterling work and example of William Weston, Robert Southwell, and John Gerard, as well as to the stunning generosity of the countess of Arundel towards the Jesuit order, and narrates the many conversions to Rome

---

[134] P. Lake, 'The Laudian Style: Order, Uniformity and the Pursuit of the Beauty of Holiness in the 1630s', in K. Fincham (ed.), *The Early Stuart Church, 1603–1642* (1993), pp. 161–86, at pp. 164, 165, 178–9; J. Fielding, 'Arminianism in the Localities: Peterborough Diocese, 1603–1642', in Fincham, *The Early Stuart Church*, pp. 93–113, at pp. 164, 168, 165, 174, 178–9. See also A. Milton, 'The Church of England, Rome and the True Church: The Demise of a Jacobean Consensus', in Fincham, *The Early Stuart Church*, pp. 187–210; A. Milton, *Catholic and Reformed: The Roman and Protestant Churches in English Protestant Thought 1600–1640* (Cambridge, 1995), esp. chs 5, 6. Professor Lake's radical rewriting of Laudian ecclesiology and liturgical culture in the English Church during the personal rule of Charles I will appear in P. Lake, *On Laudianism: Piety, Polemic and Politics during the Personal Rule of Charles I* (forthcoming).
[135] *NCC*, pp. 274–5.

TOWARDS TOLERATION? 487

accomplished by the Society's means and especially through her own spiritual zeal. Nancy Pollard Brown suggests that the work was originally penned in Latin and sent out to Rome—if that is so, it almost certainly was, as well as being a memorial of a great lay Catholic patron of the Society, and of her long-dead husband, a commentary on the debates still raging among the clergy about the best way to sustain and regulate the 'mission' and the Church in England. It mentions, at one point, the life of Magdalen Browne, Viscountess Montague, written by Richard Smith and published in Latin in Rome in 1609 but translated and printed in English in 1627 during the approbation business, now with a dedication to the second Viscount Montague, who was one of Bishop Richard Smith's more vocal aristocratic adherents and advocates. There is a sense in which this manuscript account of Earl Philip and his wife, written by her Jesuit chaplain, is a response to Smith's eulogy of Lady Montague and an oblique refutation of many of the allegations still being levelled at the Jesuit clergy in England and also of the claims to ecclesiastical authority being made by some of the leading secular clergy and their lay supporters.[136]

Anyway, faced with the allegations by some Catholics that persecution was the work and fault simply of puritans, some Protestants predictably reacted by insisting that the existing law should be enforced against all Catholic clergymen, in spite of their protestations that they were carrying out their ministry in a purely pastoral fashion. One of the well-known clerical pastoral double acts of the 1630s comprised the Jesuit Henry Morse (the 'priest of the plague') and John Southworth. They cooperated in providing pastoral care to plague victims in London. Morse himself 'contracted the malady' on more than one occasion.[137] On 6 October 1636, Southworth and Morse released a printed appeal to English Catholics for money to assist plague victims.[138] As William Prynne later related it,

[136] NCC, passim; Richard Smith, The Life of the most Honourable and Vertuous Lady the Lady Magdalen Viscountesse Montague. Written in Latin, and published soone after her death by Richard Smith, Doctour of Divinity, and her Confessour. And now Translated into English, by C. F. (n.p., [St Omer], 1627); The Lives of Philip Howard, Earl of Arundel and of Anne Dacres, his Wife. Edited from the Original MSS by the Duke of Norfolk E. M. (1857). There are two versions of this latter text retained in the archives at Arundel Castle, West Sussex; see also C. A. Newdigate, 'A New Chapter in the Life of B. Robert Southwell' (reprinted from the Month, March 1931), for which reference I am very grateful to Jennifer Binczewski. For this topic, see also P. Lake and M. Questier, Remembering how to be a Catholic in Post-Reformation England: Memory, Piety and Polemic in Post-Reformation England (forthcoming).
[137] Kn., IV, pp. 312, 313; J.F. Merritt, The Social World of Early Modern Westminster: Abbey, Court and Community, 1525–1640 (Manchester, 2005), p. 349.
[138] John Southworth and Henry Morse, To the Catholickes of England (n.p. [London ?], 1636); ARCR, II, no. 726. In late January 1635, Gregorio Panzani had been informed by two Jesuits that there was no need in England for bishops and parish priests, and, in addition, 'si pigliorono sopra di loro ad assistere alli appestati': ABSJ, transcript and translation of Gregorio Panzani's Diary, 1634–7 (ASV, Nunziatura d'Inghilterra 3a), fo. 70ʳ. On 9/19 September 1635 Richard Smith, now in exile in France, wrote that he was 'exceeding glad' that Southworth 'undertakes that heroical work' of tending plague victims. 'He escaped one martyrdom' (in 1628, when he was condemned at Lancaster) 'and now he is in danger of another': AAW, A XXVIII, no. 161, p. 535. Like Morse, Southworth was accused of ministering to plague victims in order to proselytise: Anstr., II, p. 306.

488   CATHOLICS AND TREASON

Southworth was denounced to Archbishop Laud by Robert White, the 'sub-curate of St Margaret's parish in Westminster'. White censured Southworth for proselytizing under cover, as it were, of the plague. Southworth 'was apprehended, indicted', and 'arraigned', and 'the premises' were 'fully proved against him by sundry witnesses'. But, by the intervention of the queen and the secretary of State, Sir Francis Windebank, 'his final trial was put off, to the great discontent of the people'. Southworth was, 'not long after, released, even near the very time' that John Bastwick, Henry Burton, and Prynne himself 'were most grievously censured in the star chamber and most barbarously pilloried, deprived of their ears' and 'stigmatized'.[139]

For his part, Morse recorded how in February 1637 he was arrested by the pursuivants Francis Newton and John Cook. On 5 March, only five days before the date of the star chamber bill of information against Prynne, Burton, and Bastwick, Morse was hauled before the privy council and 'charged with having seduced many from the Protestant religion and reconciled them to the Catholic Church'. (Knaresborough wrote that it was 'incredible what good' Morse 'did at this time' for, 'besides the great numbers of Catholics whom he assisted with the sacraments, he is said to have reconciled above forty Protestants during the time of this plague' in 1636–7.) On 26 March, Morse was remanded to Newgate. On 22 April he was finally brought before the judges at the Old Bailey sessions. Here he was charged both with the fact of his ordination and of having reconciled the king's subjects to the Church of Rome. A series of witnesses testified in detail to both of these allegations. Morse refused either to deny or confirm the accusations. This provoked a verbal attack from one of the judges, apparently Sir John Bramston. Newton claimed that he had been urged by Laud himself to apprehend Morse. Morse admitted that he was a Roman Catholic ('for a Catholic cannot be anything else') but no more. At this point, on Morse's account, 'one of the judges, whose name was Jones', that is, Sir William Jones, 'rising from his seat, said that there was no evidence to convict' him 'under the statute of persuasions, for whatever function of religion' he 'had performed' he had 'not done it with the intent of withdrawing subjects from their allegiance'. To this assertion, 'the whole bench assented'. The jury still found him guilty on the charge framed under the Elizabethan statute of 1585. On 24 April, Morse was summoned back to the Old Bailey where, rather conspicuously, sentence was not pronounced. At the queen's intercession, the king had ordered a stop in the proceedings. After this, the pursuivant Newton was investigated. Henrietta Maria seems to have thought that he should be hanged and, at her insistence, Morse was eventually released on

[139] Prynne, PRP, p. 25; Kn., V, pp. 182–3. For White's petition as cited by Prynne, see PRO, SP 16/330/93, fo. 176ʳ (Foley, RSJ, I, pp. 604–5); see also CSPD Addenda 1625–49, p. 562; Bodl., Clarendon MS 13, fo. 94ʳ; Foley, RSJ, I, p. 579; Southworth's release was procured by the papal agent George Con in April 1637: Anstr., II, pp. 306–7. With John Goodman in late November 1637 Southworth was ordered into custody again: CSPD Apr.–Nov. 1637, p. 572 (PRO, SP 16/372/71, fo. 131ʳ).

TOWARDS TOLERATION? 489

condition that he took himself abroad. Among those who investigated Newton's corrupt practices was the crypto-Catholic Sir Henry Spiller.[140]

Morse's story stands at the centre of two equal-and-opposite readings of the period of the personal rule. For some Catholics, the line was, at least as remembered by the likes of Knaresborough, that after the collapse of the Spanish match negotiations there was still a persecution, even if it did not generally extend to the shedding of blood. Knaresborough wrote, from manuscript 'memoirs' kept at Douai, that 'I find it remarked by an ancient priest who had been a missioner in Queen Elizabeth's days...that, excepting capital punishments...as to all other pains and penalties the penal statutes against recusants were executed at this time with as much rigour and severity as in any part of the former reign'.[141]

Some contemporaries saw it differently. For them, the king had in fact extended tolerance to Catholics. This, as we remarked, was the claim made by clergy such as John Southcot. That claim was endorsed in print in the 1640s by William Prynne. For people such as Prynne, the Spanish match period had seen the start of a conspiracy to tolerate popery. The 'intended popish match' had been the 'original fountain whence' came 'all the...favours and suspensions of our laws against papists, priests' and 'Jesuits, together with the extraordinary increase of them and popery'. After the French marriage, Catholic clergy streamed into the country 'without any restraint or inhibition whatsoever'. While there were 'many private societies and monasteries of Jesuits, monks' and 'nuns secretly erected and maintained in England', there were 'many more openly built, stocked and professedly supported in Ireland'. Worse still, 'there was a new popish hierarchy erected and bishops, archdeacons etc., created by the pope, both in England and Ireland'. Catholics were released from the penalties of the law 'upon pretence of procuring' the 'like favour and liberty of conscience for the Protestants in France and other foreign parts', though look what happened to them—'many thousands of them' were 'massacred' and La Rochelle was 'betrayed'. The confessionally mixed court had opened the way for the insidious effects of the programme of the congregation of Propaganda and the dispatch of papal agents to Henrietta Maria. As part of this conspiracy, 'all informers against priests, Jesuits' and 'papists were discountenanced, menaced and many of them imprisoned by Secretary Windebank their pensioner'. On the other hand, 'most of the painful orthodox Protestant ministers, gentlemen and others throughout the realm were disgraced, persecuted, silenced, fined, imprisoned, banished and thousands of them enforced to flee the realm by

---

[140] Foley, *RSJ*, I, pp. 582–6, 586–9, 606–11; PRO, SP 16/537/40, fo. 59ᵛ; P. Caraman, *Henry Morse: Priest of the Plague* (1957), pp. 129–40; *ODNB*, *sub* Morse, Henry (article by P. Holmes); Kn., IV, pp. 313, 319; Prynne, *PRP*, p. 29; Hibbard, *CI*, p. 66; PRO, SP 16/473/4, fo. 5ʳ (concerning the release warrant of 20 June 1637). Newton, however, was reimbursed by royal warrant in September 1638 to the tune of 200 marks: Foley, *RSJ*, I, p. 611 (PRO, SP 16/398/84, fo. 179ᵛ). Several of Morse's alleged converts claimed that they had always been Catholics: Foley, *RSJ*, I, pp. 605–6, 610–11.

[141] Kn., V, pp. 177–8.

490 CATHOLICS AND TREASON

the tyrannical unjust proceedings against them in the high commission, star chamber, council chamber, bishops consistories and visitation courts', while the 'printing presses were also shut up against all books in refutation of popery and opened to all impressions in defence or propagation thereof'.[142]

During Charles's reign, 'popish doctrines' and 'superstitions' were 'openly maintained' in the universities, cathedrals, and other places, and 'none but such as were popishly affected' were 'advanced to bishoprics, deaneries, ecclesiastical preferments or admitted into the ministry by our bishops'. The king's favourites and those 'in highest authority under him were all either actual papists in profession or well inclined to popery in affection and altogether swayed by popish counsels'—the duke of Buckingham and his relatives (and 'their cabinet council of Jesuits'), Richard Weston, earl of Portland, Sir Tobias Matthew, Sir Basil Brooke—the list went on and on. It extended to Archbishop Laud, Bishop Matthew Wren, Bishop Richard Montagu, and John Cosin, 'with many other prelates and priests' who sought to 'establish their popish doctrines, ceremonies' and 'superstitions in the Church of England', while the earl of Strafford did the same in Ireland, 'where they had absolute toleration, yes, open profession of their religion'. And it was better not even to get Prynne started on the topic of Henrietta Maria 'herself in the king's own bed...their most powerful mediatrix'.[143] Moreover, 'the parliaments during his Majesty's reign till now' had urged 'the execution of old laws against recusants, priests, Jesuits' and had tried to 'make new stricter acts against them'. But they had, 'contrary to the practice of all former ages, been broken up and dissolved in discontent'. The crown had used proclamations to order the Catholic clergy into exile, but to no discernible effect.[144] One wonders what exactly would have satisfied Prynne—presumably the sight of Catholic clergymen's shrunken heads displayed prominently in the city of London?

Scholars still argue whether the emergence in the mid- and late 1630s of yet more strident denunciations of a popish plot was, on the one hand, simply a product of bad public-relations management on the part of an out-of-touch court or, on the other, the result of an intensely high-stakes game being played by the court and by leading churchmen with their opponents, both inside and outside the regime.[145] For contemporaries, the question was: what would happen if the new and more aggressive avant-garde conformist status quo established in the period of the personal rule did not hold, as indeed it did not? Would there be an avalanche of retaliation against Catholics? Would the clock be turned back and the assumptions of the Elizabethan legislators be reinstated in order to deal with the threat, as some saw it, from separatist Catholics and their patrons abroad? Would that mean resorting again to the shedding of blood? The answer to that

---

[142] Prynne, *PRP*, pp. 36 f. (quotations at pp. 44, 54, 55–6); see also Prynne, *PRP*, sig. ¶3r.
[143] Prynne, *PRP*, p. 56.   [144] Prynne, *PRP*, p. 57.
[145] For the latter view, see esp. P. Lake, '1637: Year of Destiny' (forthcoming).

question, as it turned out, was—yes. But in the end there was no apocalyptic massacre of Catholics once the Stuart court's authority collapsed.[146] Nor should we necessarily be surprised by this. The English Catholic community was so multi-layered and complex in its attitudes and allegiances that, just as had been the case before 1640, it found that there were accommodations to be made and deals to be struck with the emergent powers that replaced the monarchy.

[146] See Chapter 15 below.

15

Back to the Future

Catholicism, Persecution, and the Outbreak of the Civil War

Everyone knows that during the 1630s, especially the later 1630s, the language of anti-popery became one of the principal vehicles for expressing critiques of royal authority. The presence of known (crypto-)Catholics at court and on the council made this a relatively easy manoeuvre; and, of course, there was a Catholic queen consort.[1] In many ways, this is so obvious as to be hardly worth discussing—except that Caroline Hibbard wrote an excellent book describing how contemporaries might credibly have come to believe that there was a popish plot inside the regime, one that by rights ought to be resisted.[2] The civil strife in Ireland, Scotland, and eventually England could be construed as the logical outcome of what the court had been doing surreptitiously up to 1640. Just as the court had persecuted the godly during the 1630s, so, now, declared William Prynne's *Popish Royall Favourite* (1643), 'since our late unhappy, civil, bloody wars till this present [time], the best and most zealous Protestants...both in Ireland and England, have been everywhere most cruelly massacred, plundered, tortured, imprisoned' and 'ruined by bloodthirsty popish cavaliers'. This was the end product also of the fact that 'sundry popish recusants and seminary priests' had 'during all' of Charles's reign 'obtained innumerable letters of grace' and 'protection from his Majesty contrary to the law and orders of session in their favour'. The outcome was that, 'since this unhappy civil war, the papists, both in England and Ireland, have been armed against the parliament by his Majesty's special commissions'.[3]

Should there not have been, then, a massive licensed-by-authority retaliatory surge against known Catholic separatists and their clergy? Actually, despite the ubiquity of anti-popery in narratives of the Short and Long Parliaments and then the downward spiral into fighting, actual Catholics are, by and large, absent from most historical studies of the outbreak of war. A glance at Bishop Challoner's lists demonstrates that there was no really large-scale public wave of violence against

---

[1] Malcolm Smuts convincingly argues that the anti-popish critique of the court intensified only when the Caroline regime finally ditched its middle-way approach to dealing with France and Spain: M. Smuts, 'The Puritan Followers of Henrietta Maria in the 1630s', *English Historical Review* 93 (1978), pp. 26–45; M. Smuts, 'Religion, European Politics and Henrietta Maria's Circle, 1625–41', in E. Griffey (ed.), *Henrietta Maria: Piety, Politics and Patronage* (Aldershot, 2008), pp. 13–37.
[2] Hibbard, *CI*.   [3] Prynne, *PRP*, sig. ¶3ᵛ and *passim*.

Catholics and Treason: Martyrology, Memory, and Politics in the Post-Reformation. Michael Questier,
Oxford University Press. © Michael Questier 2022. DOI: 10.1093/oso/9780192847027.003.0015

BACK TO THE FUTURE 493

Catholics along the lines apparently urged by Prynne—at least if one excludes those Catholics who were killed in the fighting after 1642—though some contemporary Catholics did regard them as martyrs.[4] At the same time, even though the fatal proceedings against Catholic clergy that occurred in the 1640s look sporadic enough, a case can be made that, when they did occur, they had just as much political logic about them as such proceedings had had in earlier decades, and so some sort of narrative approach is required to make sense of them. These contemporary accounts of post-1640 Catholicism are potentially much more central to a mainstream narrative of the civil wars and the Interregnum than they have previously been taken to be.

The Fear of Popery

This is not to deny that there were, here and there, some fairly violent manifestations of popular anti-Catholicism. Robin Clifton's work pointed to a widespread 'fear-of-popery' agitation, generated by the spread of rumours about Catholic plotting.[5] The structure of recognizably Catholic interests across the British Isles meant that a change in the circumstances of one of the three kingdoms, starting here with the rebellion in Ireland, would have a ripple effect across the others. This in fact was one of the principal insights of the revisionist three-kingdom account of the causes of the civil war associated principally with the work of Conrad Russell.[6] The single most convincing narrative of the eruption of anti-popery zeal into violence is John Walter's book on the Stour Valley riots. Here we have a real sense of who attacked whom, and why. These expressions of violence and hatred expose local networks of sympathy between, on the one hand, different sorts of Catholics and Arminians and, on the other, their enemies.[7]

So, why did the eventual collapse, in certain parts of the country, of royal authority not lead to a cascade of popish plot trials of Catholics for treason under the Elizabethan statutes? As we have seen all the way through this volume, contemporary Catholicism extended along a broad spectrum. Part of that spectrum

---

[4] AAW, B 28, no. 15, pp. 411–14. For Challoner's list of royalist Catholics killed in the civil war, see Richard Challoner, *Memoirs of Missionary Priests*...(2 vols in 1, Manchester, 1803), II, pp. 176–8, followed by a list of those whose estates were sequestered (pp. 178–9), excluded in Pollen's edition of Challoner in 1924; see also Kn., VI, pp. 181–3; G. Glickman, *The English Catholic Community, 1688–1745: Politics, Culture and Ideology* (Woodbridge, 2009), p. 124; see pp. 540–1 below.

[5] R. Clifton, 'Fear of Popery', in C. Russell (ed.), *The Origins of the English Civil War* (1973), pp. 144–68; R. Clifton, 'The Popular Fear of Catholics during the English Revolution', *Past and Present* 52 (1971), pp. 23–55; R. Clifton, 'The Fear of Catholics in England 1637 to 1645. Principally from Central Sources' (DPhil, Oxford, 1967).

[6] C. Russell, 'The British Background to the Irish Rebellion of 1641', *Historical Research* 61 (1988), pp. 166–82; C. Russell, *The Causes of the English Civil War* (Oxford, 1990), ch. 5, esp. pp. 125–30.

[7] J. Walter, *Understanding Popular Violence in the English Revolution: The Colchester Plunderers* (Cambridge, 1999).

494 CATHOLICS AND TREASON

had tended to define itself via a public scepticism about the extent of Rome's authority, or at least about the claims made on the papacy's behalf by some Catholics. Protestant aversion to Rome/Catholicism, for all its virulence, could not easily lump all contemporary forms of Catholicism into one easily definable target. After 1642, far from all Catholics were active royalists—actually, only a minority were—even if, in certain areas, that minority could bulk fairly large within the royalist officer corps.[8]

As we know, in the face of the covenanter rebellion, an English parliament (the Short Parliament) assembled in April 1640.[9] But the Irish parliament which preceded it, summoned to meet in March 1640, looked as if it was really where the crown's business was going to be done. In other words, it would render to the king the military wherewithal necessary for the suppression of the Scots rebels. In some people's view, Ireland not only might make available the resources for suppression of political dissent but also was a model of good government, in contrast to what had been going on elsewhere in the British Isles. The preamble to the Irish subsidy bill made precisely this case, as did the declaration from both houses in the Irish parliament, which document Thomas Wentworth, earl of Strafford, took with him to England in April 1640. The Irish parliament condemned the Scots covenanter rebels and voted for the recruitment of men for Strafford's expeditionary force.[10]

When the Short Parliament failed to match the loyalism of the Irish, it was dissolved in early May.[11] The reaction to the dissolution was a public anti-popery agitation of exceptional ferocity, one which threatened to overwhelm Archbishop Laud. His attempt to put on his own displays of anti-popish zeal, for example by searching Catholics' houses in London and by refusing to release the Jesuit Henry Morse after he was arrested in June 1640, was too little, too late.[12] The explicitly

[8] See, e.g., K. Lindley, 'The Part Played by Catholics', in B. Manning (ed.), *Politics, Religion and the English Civil War* (1973), pp. 126–76; P. R. Newman, 'Catholic Royalists of Northern England, 1642–5', *Northern History* 15 (1979), pp. 88–95; P. R. Newman, 'Roman Catholic Royalists: Papist Commanders under Charles I and Charles II, 1642–60', *RH* 15 (1981), pp. 396–405; see also Aveling, *NC*, pp. 306–10; A. Hopper, ' "The Popish Army of the North": Anti-Catholicism and Parliamentarian Allegiance in Civil War Yorkshire, 1642–46', *RH* 25 (2000), pp. 12–28. Some people insisted that the king's forces were stuffed with Catholics and the result was that Protestants would be driven from their own churches: Kn., IV, p. 102. For very sensible comments on the neutralism debate, see A. Tompkins, *ECI*, pp. 95–107.

[9] Cust, *CI*, pp. 251 f.; Hibbard, *CI*, pp. 147 f.

[10] I. Gentles, *The English Revolution and the Wars in the Three Kingdoms 1638–1652* (Harlow, 2007), p. 25. For Strafford's recommendation for Irish-based military intervention (including the controversial phrase, 'to reduce this kingdom'), see *HMCC*, II, p. 254. Strafford had opposed the earl of Antrim's very similar scheme (for an Irish force) in 1639; but he took the risk of recruiting his own Irish soldiers to crush the covenanters. Since the plans for this force were in existence before the Short Parliament, there were rumours that it might be used against English critics of the crown as well: Hibbard, *CI*, pp. 155–6; Cust, *CI*, pp. 244–5, 250.

[11] Hibbard, *CI*, p. 150; *HMCP*, III, p. 63. For the grievances expressed in the Short Parliament, see, e.g., *HMCS*, XXII, pp. 310–11.

[12] Hibbard, *CI*, pp. 150–1; P. Caraman, *Henry Morse: Priest of the Plague* (1957), p. 143.

BACK TO THE FUTURE   495

anti-puritan convocation canons passed by the clergy's assembly after the Short Parliament was terminated added fuel to the fire, even though the rhetoric in their preamble about the traditions of the Church of England was deliberately centrist.[13]

The anti-popish reaction became locked into the detection of the so-called Habernfeld conspiracy in August 1640. This was a frankly lunatic yarn, the details of which were sent to London by the king's ambassador in the Netherlands, Sir William Boswell. The claim was that prominent Catholics, coordinated until 1639 by the papal agent George Con, were goading the king into a suicidal conflict against godly Protestants and particularly the Scots.[14] The Scottish general assembly confirmed in mid-August 1640 that episcopacy was abolished, something which was ratified by the Scottish parliament. The failure of the Short Parliament in England encouraged the covenanter military forces to launch on 20 August 1640 a pre-emptive invasion across the northern border, anticipating the second royal strike against them, which slowly started to gather pace after the dissolution of the Short Parliament.[15]

If contemporaries wanted more proof that there was a British popish plot in progress, they could observe that, in this—the so-called Second Bishops' War—a number of Catholics were present, even though, initially, the earl of Northumberland was appointed as the general of the king's forces and, alleging illness, he was replaced by Strafford.[16] The Scots scored their notable victory at Newburn shortly afterwards, on 28 August. The courtier Catholic Endymion Porter's second son was killed there. In the fighting, the Catholic earl of Caernarvon was particularly prominent. He 'fought madly like himself for, being forsaken by his countrymen, he made good the place whilst he had any powder and shot' and, when his powder was spent, 'he threw his pistols at them' and then 'fought manfully' with his sword until a relief force got through to him.[17]

The Irish troops intended for intervention in Scotland were not ready until, in effect, it was too late. The king had lost the last vestiges of his political independence and was forced to call the English parliament again, partly under constraint from concessions made to the Scots covenanters.[18] The proceedings of the Long Parliament in 1640–1 are part of the staple of mid-seventeenth-century political and constitutional history. The collapse of royal authority allowed for the rolling

---

[13] Cust, *CI*, pp. 261–2; *HMCR*, I, p. 522.

[14] For the Habernfeld Plot, see Hibbard, *CI*, pp. 157–62; *A True Relation of the Popish-Plot against King Charles I. and the Protestant Religion* (1679).

[15] Hibbard, *CI*, pp. 152f.

[16] Hibbard, *CI*, p. 165.

[17] Gentles, *The English Revolution*, pp. 28–9; Cust, *CI*, p. 263; *HMCV*, II, pp. 256–7; *HMCC*, II, pp. 259–60.

[18] A. Clarke, 'The Breakdown of Authority, 1640–41', in T. W. Moody, F. X. Martin and F. J. Byrne (eds), *A New History of Ireland III: Early Modern Ireland 1534–1691* (Oxford, 1976), p. 278; Cust, *CI*, pp. 265–6; *HMCR*, I, p. 523; Hibbard, *CI*, p. 166; *HMCS*, XXII, pp. 323–4, 325.

496   CATHOLICS AND TREASON

back of key aspects of the personal rule and also of Laud's government of the Church.[19]

Whatever Charles's expectations of a new parliament (Conrad Russell has argued that Charles thought it would support a revitalized war effort[20]), it would almost certainly open the floodgates against those who were popularly identified as evil counsellors at court and against crypto-Catholics inside the regime.[21] Sir Benjamin Rudyerd declared in the Commons on 7 November 1640 that the recent government of the Church was not just popish in itself but had been defended by actual Catholics. The irenic Franciscan priest Christopher Davenport's name stood out here. So 'let them not say that these are the perverse, suspicious, malicious interpretations of some few factious spirits amongst us when a Romanist has bragged and congratulated in print that the face of our Church begins to alter'.[22] Surely the time had come to purge the kingdom of its evil humours? As Rudyerd put it, 'we are now upon that vertical turning point and therefore it is no time to palliate, to foment our undoing'. First and foremost, that meant disposing of evil advisers, and Rudyerd said a lot on this topic. But, since so much of the evil came through diversity of religion, what about staging salutary trials and executions of Catholics, especially of clergy?[23] On 11 November, the Commons summoned two pursuivants before them as part of an investigation into Sir Francis Windebank's warrants for the release of Catholic clergy from gaol. On subsequent days, despite the hue and cry after Strafford, the Commons returned repeatedly to the issue of Windebank's apparent determination to flout the extant statutes against Romish clergy.[24]

However, the fear of popery, that is to say, of all Catholics indiscriminately, seems to have degenerated into the occasional prosecution of Catholic clergy for reasons that were driven primarily by the day-to-day politics of the confrontation between the king and his critics. This may have been because, at this stage, it was not obvious that Catholics as a bloc had any incentive to declare for the crown. Only a sweeping royal guarantee of tolerance would persuade them to do that. Charles's increasingly subtle, though, in the end, far from successful, manoeuvring between different parties and interest groups seemed to make that unlikely.[25]

---

[19] Cust, *CI*, pp. 268 f., 271 f.; K. Fincham and N. Tyacke, *Altars Restored: The Changing Face of English Religious Worship, 1547–c. 1700* (Oxford, 2007), pp. 275f.

[20] C. Russell, 'Why did Charles I Call the Long Parliament?', in C. Russell, *Unrevolutionary England, 1603–1642* (1990), pp. 253–61, esp. at pp. 254–8.

[21] Hibbard, *CI*, pp. 166–7, 168.

[22] *HMCS*, XXII, pp. 330–1; *ODNB, sub* Rudyerd, Sir Benjamin (article by D. L. Smith); A. Davenport, *Suspicious Moderate: The Life and Writings of Francis à Sancta Clara (1598–1680)* (Notre Dame, Ind., 2017), p. 258.

[23] *HMCS*, XXII, p. 332; for John Pym's speech (also) of 7 November, see Hibbard, *CI*, pp. 170–1.

[24] P. Haskell, 'Sir Francis Windebank and the Personal Rule of Charles I' (PhD, Southampton, 1978), pp. 500–8.

[25] In response to the Long Parliament's agitation, Charles made many concessions over the issue of Catholics at court and in the army: Clifton, 'Fear of Catholics', pp. 162 f. The court attempted to

BACK TO THE FUTURE   497

The other cause that would push Catholics uniformly into overt royalism was if they were all likely to be the targets of popular violence; and that was the case only for a short space of time in certain regions, as John Walter's splendid monograph shows. Henrietta Maria may have tried to summon French support for the House of Stuart, but the French court was delighted to see the annihilation of the friends of Spain in the British Isles and had little reason to intervene, and indeed had been suspected of urging on the covenanters in Scotland.[26] In response, a few Catholics seem to have resorted to violence.[27] Others, notably Sir Francis Windebank, concluded that it was better to up sticks and go abroad.[28]

The Failure of Royal Authority and the Case of John Goodman

But some prominent Catholics at this point simply ramped up their own royalist and loyalist rhetoric—which was not difficult in the sense that they were not the ones who were obviously the king's enemies. On 5 December, Lord Brudenell and the earl of Castlehaven spoke in parliament against the doctrine of regicide.[29] Into this narrative one can fit the first near-martyrdom of the reign of Charles since 1628, that is, when the priest John Goodman was put on trial. He was a first cousin of the bishop, Godfrey Goodman, who had been defended by William Laud as far back as 1626 against the accusations of William Prynne, though subsequently they (Bishop Goodman and Laud) fell out over patronage issues— principally Laud's interference in the appointment made to the see of Hereford in 1633–4. In the 1630s, John Goodman was known to be a friend of Christopher Davenport and the papal agent George Con. He had been a chaplain to the marquis of La Vieuville.[30] He had been released on a warrant issued by Windebank on 17 September 1639. He was then rearrested in 1640, with Henry Morse. After formally admitting to the high commission court on 18 June 1640 their identity as Roman Catholic priests, they were sent to Newgate.[31] On 15 January 1641, at a

reassert control over the rhetoric of anti-popery, e.g. via a proclamation which, as George Pigot observed on 17 November 1640, stated that 'the papists are…restrained ten miles from the king's, queen's and prince's courts, and confined to abide within five miles of their homes' and that their weapons were to be seized: W. J. Hardy (ed.), *The Manuscripts of Lord Kenyon* (HMC, 14th report, appendix, part IV, 1894), p. 59; cf. Walter, *Understanding Popular Violence*, pp. 302, 324.

[26] Hibbard, *CI*, pp. 77–8, 177–9.

[27] *HMCV*, II, p. 260; *HMCB*, III, p. 393; Albion, *CI*, p. 346; Hibbard, *CI*, p. 174.

[28] Hibbard, *CI*, p. 175; *HMCC*, II, pp. 263, 266, 267.

[29] *HMCB*, III, pp. 397–8.

[30] *ODNB*, *sub* Goodman, Godfrey (article by N. Cranfield); *ODNB*, *sub* Goodman, John (article by W. Sheils); Hibbard, *CI*, p. 182; Anstr., II, p. 132. For the fullest treatment of the Goodman case, see Tompkins, *ECI*, pp. 41–51.

[31] Hibbard, *CI*, pp. 182–3; PRO, SP 16/434, fo. 236^r [high commission act book, fo. 205^r]; Challoner, *MMP*, p. 379; Caraman, *Henry Morse*, pp. 142, 143; *ODNB*, *sub* Morse, Henry (article by P. Holmes). According to Richard Johnson, both Goodman and Morse were 'discharged' by Windebank on 3 July: PRO, SP 16/473/4, fo. 5^r.

498   CATHOLICS AND TREASON

Middlesex gaol delivery session, Goodman was convicted on the charge that he had been ordained abroad.[32] He was sentenced to death on 21 January 1641.[33]

Goodman's case, during which there was, in effect, a two-sides dispute about the purpose of the treason laws instituted in the later sixteenth century, was the subject of furious back-and-forth argument between the king and parliament. The king immediately reprieved Goodman, though he did this, as it turned out, at the instance of the queen.[34] Both houses protested. One newsletter, retained in the secular clergy agent's papers, said that priests and other Catholics might well be 'stoned to death if they walk the streets and be known, so infinitely are the common people distasted at the reprieve of this condemned priest and the more because he had been formerly a minister'.[35] Goodman's reprieve was 'a thing so infinitely distasting the city [of London] that' on 22 January 'they went to complain to the parliament and to declare' that 'until the priest were executed they would lay down no more money, so by this means the king's army for want of pay is like to dissolve' and then there would be no defence against the Scots.[36]

On 23 January the recorder of London, Sir Thomas Gardiner, who was a known royalist and supporter of episcopacy, was called in to the Commons to explain what was going on. Some people believed that he could be held responsible for soliciting the reprieve from the king. At a Commons–Lords conference on the same day, the lawyer John Glynne demanded a further meeting concerning the necessary 'discovery of such instruments as have dared to intercede for the interruption of the course of justice against priests and Jesuits'. The context was the 'return of an answer from the city of London concerning the advancing of money for his Majesty's service' and the 'general discontent amongst the citizens of London upon the reprieve of a seminary priest, one Goodman, condemned of high treason upon Wednesday last, who had been formerly condemned for the same offence, and banished the kingdom'.[37]

---

[32] Jeaffreson, *MCR*, III, p. 73; François de Marsys, *Histoire de la Persecution Presente de Catholiques en Angleterre, Enrichie de Plusieurs Reflexions Morales, Politiques & Chrestiennes, tant sur ce qui Concerne leur Guerre Civile, que la Religion...* (Paris, 1646), pt III, p. 52. The three volumes of Marsys's work are dedicated, respectively, to Henrietta Maria, to François II de Harlay, archbishop of Rouen, and to the countess of Brienne; Marsys attaches narratives of civil-war martyrdoms to a full-scale attack on the Elizabethan Reformation and the legal penalties to which Catholics were liable; see B. Camm, *A North-Country Martyr (Venerable John Ducket)* (1900), p. 14; Monta, *Martyrdom*, p. 230; R. G. Asch, *Sacral Kingship between Disenchantment and Re-Enchantment* (2014), p. 100; AWCBC, pp. 2069–70; UCLSC, UC/P9/2/2 (Thomas Graves Law to William Walker, 21 October 1876, *inter alia* about a translation of Marsys's account); see also Davenport, *Suspicious Moderate*, p. 276. For the sources on which Marsys drew, as well as his own experience of being in England in the relevant period, see, e.g., Marsys, *Histoire*, pt III, p. 140. For the other principal contemporary printed recounting of the martyrdoms of the early 1640s, see Jean Chifflet, *Palmae Cleri Anglicani...* (Brussels, 1645); AWCBC, p. 2068.

[33] Anstr., II, p. 133; *ODNB*, *sub* Goodman, John (article by W. Sheils).

[34] Anstr., II, p. 133; see also Warwickshire County Record Office, Throckmorton Papers, CR 1998/box 60/folder 2/28–32, 35, 40–1 (references that I owe to the kindness of Alexandra Tompkins).

[35] AAW, A XXX, no. 1, p. 2.

[36] AAW, A XXX, no. 1, p. 1.

[37] W. Notestein (ed.), *The Journal of Sir Simonds D'Ewes from the Beginning of the Long Parliament to the Opening of the Trial of the Earl of Strafford* (New Haven, 1923), pp. 278–9, 287; *Commons'*

BACK TO THE FUTURE 499

Charles responded formally at a meeting on that day, 23 January, with both houses at Whitehall. Here the king made various concessions but stuck rigidly upon the point of episcopacy.[38] This was reported in the Lords on 25 January. The lord privy seal (the earl of Manchester) signified to the House that, in addition, Charles had acquainted himself with Goodman's conviction and understood that he was 'now lately condemned for being in orders of a priest merely, and was acquitted of the charge of perverting the king's people in their belief, and had never been condemned or banished before'. The king was 'tender in matter of blood in cases of this nature, in which Queen Elizabeth and King James have been often merciful'. Therefore Goodman should be deported, and executed if he returned; and Charles was willing to take advice for the expulsion 'of other priests and Jesuits'.[39] The newsletter just cited was rather more blunt. Here the king was reported to have said that Goodman was 'unlawfully condemned' upon 'weak proof' of his priesthood 'after he had been cleared of the statute of persuasion'. If he had been found guilty of that, Charles would not have reprieved him. But the king 'was resolved to follow his father's steps, of happy memory'. King James 'in his latter days resolved not to take blood for point of pure religion or priesthood'. The Upper House was content but the Lower House was not. All through the day on Monday, 25 January, 'there stood thousands of people about Newgate expecting when the popish priest should come out to execution, which expectation being frustrated, they returned far more incensed than before'.[40]

On 26 January Sir Simonds D'Ewes scribbled down that in the Lords, on the day before, the king had claimed that 'this reprieve' of Goodman 'was only granted in an ordinary way' and only 'for being a priest in orders'. Charles was 'still ready to punish him by imprisonment or banishment'. Sir Henry Mildmay demanded that 'the jurors' in the Goodman trial should be consulted, 'for he heard that it was fully proved that' Goodman 'had laboured to seduce two or three persons at the least'. D'Ewes was sure that, if Goodman was not promptly strung up, it was unlikely that 'money would be lent from the city' in order to deal with the Scots. If he were 'banished, we should but return him to his friends his confederates, his pleasures and his vices, where he might plot new wickedness and villainy'. Even the imprisonment of Catholics was no good: 'for here they are not guarded as those good men were in several castles (I mean Dr Bastwick, Mr Prynne and Mr Burton) without pen, ink or paper; but they have their

---

Journals, II, p. 72; Tompkins, ECI, p. 44; *ODNB, sub* Gardiner, Sir Thomas (article by D. Orr); *Lords' Journals*, IV, p. 141. Glynne had launched an attack on Windebank in the Commons on 1 December 1640: Haskell, 'Sir Francis Windebank', p. 501.

[38] *Lords' Journals*, IV, p. 142; P. Lake, 'Puritans, Popularity and Petitions: Local Politics in National Context, Cheshire, 1641', in T. Cogswell, R. Cust, and P. Lake (eds), *Politics, Religion and Popularity in Early Stuart Britain: Essays in Honour of Conrad Russell* (Cambridge, 2002), pp. 259–89, at p. 278, citing BL, Harleian MS 4931, fos 106ʳ–7ʳ.

[39] *Lords' Journals*, IV, pp. 141–3; Tompkins, ECI, p. 44.　　[40] AAW, A XXX, no. 1, p. 2.

500 CATHOLICS AND TREASON

frequent visitors and relievers; they have books and all other means to write seditious and dangerous pamphlets'. When Nicholas Harpsfield was 'in prison here amongst us, whole volumes of dangerous consequence' were produced 'by which many have been since seduced'. The only answer was blanket deportation and, after that, the use of the death penalty. Those people would never stop plotting 'so long as either they have a harbouring place here or their heads have a resting place upon their shoulders'. John Glynne rehearsed again how in recent years more than one Catholic clergyman had benefited from successive pardons. While he was at it, Glynne insisted that the substance and sense of the Elizabethan statute law had been ratified under King James.[41]

D'Ewes admitted that 'divers others spoke severally'. Clearly everyone knew what was at stake. If the king (wrote the anonymous Catholic newsletter writer cited above) successfully reprieved Goodman, this was to 'begin a deep foundation of his prerogative', and who might not subsequently escape—Strafford and Laud, of course, and also 'the judges and other delinquents'? This was a point made also by the papal agent Carlo Rossetti. One MP, a lawyer, pointed out the obvious though uncomfortable fact that the law against Catholic clergy had been passed under Elizabeth, who had a 'papist princess co-rival with her to the crown, the queen of Scots'. Elizabeth had also been excommunicated and declared 'incapable of the crown'. So all Catholics were at that time inevitably suspected of treason. But things had changed a good deal, so much so that 'the papists did now rather too much adhere to the king'. This led to an argument about the sense in which Catholics might be considered to be obedient when they point-blank refused to observe the legal restrictions levied on them, for example the prohibition against them being in London. Yet another MP said sarcastically that Goodman might not have been guilty of 'persuasion' but he could produce a 'list of sixty that one [John] Southworth, a secular priest, had in one summer seduced from their allegiance and made them papists, which man was now actually in the Gatehouse and had formerly been condemned wherefore, if his Majesty would not give content to the city by letting Goodman die, at least he could not refuse to let this man suffer'. It was rumoured that 'all others that are already condemned shall in like manner be executed to appease the city's fury' if the king would not agree to the hanging of Goodman.[42]

On 27 January, Glynne returned to the attack. He explained the logic of the Elizabethan statute law, particularly the 1585 act. As he saw it, there was in effect a de facto toleration already, what with 'the boldness and impudence of priests, friars and Jesuits, besides such as attended the queen's Majesty, walking at noonday'. No sooner were they in prison than they were out again, and 'divers went as

[41] Notestein, *Journal*, pp. 285–6; Hibbard, *CI*, p. 182.
[42] Notestein, *Journal*, p. 286; AAW, A XXX, no. 1, pp. 2–3; Hibbard, *CI*, pp. 182–3; Haskell, 'Sir Francis Windebank', p. 391; *CSPV 1640–2*, pp. 118–19.

ordinarily and frequently to Mass to Denmark House and St James and to the chapels of foreign ambassadors as to any church in London'. These people were death to the security of the kingdom. The sum of £60,000 which had been 'promised to have been lent by the city of London for the payment of the king's army and the relief of the northern counties had been stayed because of the said Goodman's reprieve'. Glynne now introduced the evidence of the attempt by the queen's circle to raise money from Catholics for the use of military force against the Scots and to do so through the authority of 'the superior of the priests or Jesuits of England'. D'Ewes interjected that what really mattered was that the king had 'by his public manifesto...declared that this was neither a cause of religion nor a national war', but here it appeared that Catholics were indeed contributing cash 'to this expedition merely as Catholics, as if it were a Catholic war'.[43] On the basis of the 'heads brought in by Mr Glynne', there was then a request for a Commons–Lords conference at which the Lower House's representatives demanded a joint petition to Charles for enforcement of the law against Catholic clergy. Several Catholic peers (Arundell, Montague, Brudenell, Rivers, and Morley) withdrew on this day, while the two houses debated this case.[44]

The fate of the Catholic clergy, even while most were not immediately in danger, was now a central strand of the developing narrative about royal and parliamentary authority. On 28 January, John Pym made a long statement about the case of the earl of Strafford—he had counselled the king to 'bring in an infinite and arbitrary dominion'.[45] On 29 January yet another remonstrance was read out in the Banqueting House to the king by the lord keeper. Members had been summoned there in order to deal with the Goodman case. It put many of the points made on 27 January. In particular, it insisted that 'it is enacted in the first year of King James' that all the Elizabethan statutes 'against priests and Jesuits' should 'be put in execution'. Moreover, 'the statute of the third year of King James invites men to the discovery of the offenders'.[46] The Goodman case was now serving as a means for demonstrating the need for the priority of statute law over royal prerogative and, by implication, the avoidance of civil strife.[47] When, in the past, Catholic clergy had been reprieved, 'it was in such time and upon such

---

[43] Notestein, *Journal*, pp. 289–91; Hibbard, *CI*, pp. 183–4; John Nalson, *An Impartial Collection of the Great Affairs of State...* (2 vols, 1682), I, pp. 738–9; see also AAW, A XXX, no. 1, pp. 3–4. Glynne was, *inter alia*, part of the team that managed Strafford's impeachment, and in April 1641 assisted in drafting the protestation oath: *ODNB*, *sub* Glynne, John (article by K. Lindley). For the debates on 27 January, see also Tompkins, *ECI*, pp. 47–8, citing M. Jansson (ed.), *Proceedings in the Opening Session of the Long Parliament. 21 December 1640–20 March 1641*, II (Woodbridge, 2000), pp. 279, 282–3.

[44] *HMCB*, III, p. 411; AAW, A XXX, no. 1, p. 3; Notestein, *Journal*, pp. 292–4; *Commons' Journals*, II, p. 74; Nalson, *Impartial Collection*, I, pp. 738–9; Tompkins, *ECI*, p. 49. For this Lords–Commons conference, and the report of it to the Lords, see *Lords' Journals*, IV, p. 146.

[45] Notestein, *Journal*, pp. 297–8.

[46] Nalson, *Impartial Collection*, I, pp. 739–40, cited by Kn., IV, pp. 335f; Notestein, *Journal*, p. 300; Challoner, *MMP*, pp. 379–80.

[47] Nalson, *Impartial Collection*, I, p. 740.

502 CATHOLICS AND TREASON

circumstances as that the same might be extended unto them without dangers, whereas now of late there has been a great apprehension of endeavours by some ill agents to subvert religion'. If anyone needed evidence that Goodman's reprieve imperilled the kingdom, they needed only to consider that the city had refused to advance loans to fund the war against the Scots.[48] On 30 January, the lord privy seal 'delivered to the clerk the particular charge brought up by the Commons' against Strafford, 'he being called to the bar as a delinquent'.[49]

In the face of this reading of the current conjuncture, the king on 3 February, in front of Commons and Lords members at the Banqueting House, declared his absolute opposition to 'popery and superstition'. Offering another proclamation against Catholic clergy (that they should go into exile), Charles contended that Goodman had been reprieved on the basis of good and established precedents; 'neither Queen Elizabeth nor my father did ever avow that any priest in their times was executed merely for religion, which to me seems to be this particular case'. However, said Charles, 'seeing that I am pressed by both Houses to give way to his' execution and, 'because I will avoid the inconveniency of giving so great discontent to my people as I conceive this mercy may produce, therefore I do remit this particular cause to both the Houses'. Still, he urged them, exactly as King James had often done, to think about the 'inconveniency' of this case being regarded by 'other States' as 'a severity'.[50]

On 4 February, however, Charles 'communicated to the House of Lords a petition sent to him by Mr Goodman', in which the priest urged Charles to reverse the reprieve rather 'than to let him live' as 'the subject of so great discontent in your people against your Majesty'. Goodman might be taken to have set a precedent for the earl of Strafford to follow, that is, by urging the king to avoid strife by suspending this use of his prerogative power.[51] Here the language of martyrdom became compatible with defence of royal authority. After this, Goodman was left alone, or rather left to die in prison—in 1645. His usefulness as a pawn in the conflict between Charles and parliament had come to an end.[52]

All of this coincided with the attempt to do a kind of constitutional deal with the king. This may also be why Goodman was simply sent back to gaol. The marquis of Hamilton was working to bring moderate opposition figures into government under the aegis of the earl of Bedford. The younger Sir John Coke had already reported the details on 2 February 1641. Having mentioned that 'his Majesty' had 'taken two or three days longer to consider of the reprieve of the

---

[48] Ibid., pp. 739–41.   [49] *Lords' Journals*, IV, p. 148.

[50] Challoner, *MMP*, pp. 380–1; Nalson, *Impartial Collection*, I, pp. 745–6, cited in Kn., IV, pp. 339–42; M. Jansson (ed.), *Two Diaries of the Long Parliament* (Gloucester and New York, 1984), p. 127; Tompkins, ECI, p. 50; *Lords' Journals*, IV, p. 151.

[51] Challoner, *MMP*, p. 381; Nalson, *Impartial Collection*, I, pp. 745–6, cited by Kn., IV, pp. 343–4; Tompkins, ECI, pp. 50–1. For the copy of Strafford's letter of 4 May 1641 to the king retained among the secular clergy's papers, see AAW, A XXX, no. 9, pp. 27–8.

[52] Anstr., II, p. 133.

BACK TO THE FUTURE 503

priest', and that support for Strafford was growing in the Lords, Coke noted that the earl of Bedford would be lord treasurer, John Pym would be chancellor of the exchequer, and Lord Saye master of the wards. Coke understood 'from the popish party' that Bedford, Pym, and Saye 'do attend the queen in private'. The earl of Bristol was aiming for the lord deputyship of Ireland and, 'if these men come in by the queen's side', their 'preferment' would be compatible with Goodman's reprieve and with Charles's apparent decision to cut Strafford adrift.[53]

Here, however, Catholic loyalist rhetoric was urging the king to call his enemies' bluff and to reassert his own reading of the relationship between different kinds of law. The sense of this was picked up rather well by the royalist writer John Nalson, which, of course, is why so much of Nalson's text found its way into John Knaresborough's work and then into Bishop Challoner's *Memoirs*. Of Goodman, Nalson remarked that even if his guilt 'as a priest and a papist' was beyond question, his 'uncommon petition' that he should 'fall a sacrifice to the justice of the law' simply 'to advance his Majesty's interest and affairs' would 'assuredly one day rise up in judgment against those who, calling themselves the only true Protestants', eventually rebelled against the king, just as Goodman's petition and offer proved that 'King Charles was a prince of incomparable goodness', as did Strafford's similar case.[54] Pretty good, one might think, for a royalist writer who, as Nalson did, claimed 'perfectly' to 'hate and abhor all popery, superstition and innovation in the Church'. But this was a particular deployment of the word 'popery' in order to explain how Nalson could 'no less detest and abhor all other schismatic practices and persuasions, treacherous and disloyal doctrines and actions of commonwealth Protestants'.[55]

Charles got as far as assenting on 16 February 1641 to the Triennial Act. But the scheme failed a few days afterwards when the Scots' commissioners became unsettled at the moves towards an accommodation and demanded that episcopacy be abolished and that Strafford be put on trial.[56] Anti-Scots sentiment and the rise of a defence-of-episcopacy party was enough, eventually, to build a royalist bloc within the Long Parliament, one which used an anti-presbyterian rhetoric which would have been familiar to all those who had spent so long warning against and worrying about puritan tendencies towards 'popularity'.[57] The moderate royalist and promoter of a settlement, the marquis of Hamilton, was relatively swiftly deprived of influence.[58] Charles's enemies in the parliament retaliated with the impeachment of Strafford. Proceedings against the earl, fuelled by repeated

[53] *HMCC*, II, p. 272; Cust, *CI*, p. 277.   [54] Nalson, *Impartial Collection*, I, p. 746.
[55] *ODNB*, *sub* Nalson, John (article by R. C. Richardson), citing John Nalson, *The True Protestants Appeal*... (1681), p. 1.
[56] Cust, *CI*, pp. 277–8; *HMCS*, XXII, 337–42.
[57] Cust, *CI*, pp. 278–80. For the campaign for defence of episcopacy, see Lake, 'Puritans, Popularity and Petitions'.
[58] Cust, *CI*, p. 280.

504   CATHOLICS AND TREASON

claims from Pym and others that Strafford's Irish army had genuinely been meant for England, finally commenced on 22 March 1641.[59] The more compromises, however, that Charles made, over the prerogative courts, Strafford, the Irish army, and recusant Catholics at court, the further his opponents turned against each other. By April 1641, Charles was exploiting divisions among the covenanters and offering to go northwards to finalize the concessions granted via the treaty made with them.[60]

Obviously this is not the point to launch into a detailed narrative of the events of 1641–2. But it does look as if Charles's attempts to divide his critics were what provoked more accusations and rumours of conspiracies, prominent among which was the so-called 'first Army plot' (to free Strafford by force), which could itself be interpreted as a popish intrigue.[61] In response, the parliament-sponsored protestation oath of 3 May 1641 bound the nation to an affirmation of Protestant religion and appealed to a variety of strains of anti-popery entirely contrary to the king's understanding of what loyalty was.[62] The bill of attainder against Strafford was dealt with in the Lords on 4 May; the army plot revelations of 5 May fed into it.[63] Strafford had his head struck off on 12 May.[64] Charles may still have contemplated a *coup d'état*, or so the discovery of the second army plot in mid-June 1641 suggested.[65]

Charles's opponents' response to the second army plot was the Ten Propositions, which demanded, in tried-and-tested fashion, the removal of evil counsellors and the king's agreement to parliamentary appointees to counsel him—all quite unworkable.[66] Charles had agreed, though far too late to save Strafford, that the Irish army should be disbanded; but then, on the pretext that Irish soldiers might be made available to the Spaniards, he kept the Irish force in being and even, via orders in July 1641 to the earl of Antrim and the earl of Ormond, tried to increase it.[67]

New Treason Trials and Executions of Catholic Clergy

It was at this point that the first execution of an English Catholic clergyman since 1628 took place. William Webster was arrested on 15 July 1641 and was hanged,

---

[59] Cust, *CI*, pp. 280–8; Hibbard, *CI*, pp. 188–93.   [60] *HMCC*, II, p. 280; Cust, *CI*, pp. 289–90.

[61] Cust, *CI*, pp. 283–5; *HMCC*, II, pp. 282, 283, 284–5; Hibbard, *CI*, pp. 194, 195, 202; *HMCS*, XXII, pp. 356–60; ABSJ, Anglia V, no. 1.

[62] Hibbard, *CI*, p. 194; D. Cressy, 'The Protestation Protested, 1641 and 1642', *HJ* 45 (2002), pp. 251–79; Walter, *Understanding*, pp. 292–6; Cust, *CI*, pp. 286, 287. The protestation circulated again in and after January 1642: Cressy, 'The Protestation Protested', pp. 266 f., 275 f.

[63] Hibbard, *CI*, p. 195.

[64] Cust, *CI*, pp. 287–8. For the attainder, see *HMCC*, II, pp. 277–80.

[65] Cust, *CI*, p. 290.   [66] Cust, *CI*, p. 296; Hibbard, *CI*, p. 202.   [67] Hibbard, *CI*, p. 211.

BACK TO THE FUTURE   505

eleven days later, on 26 July.[68] Challoner's source, allegedly written by one of Webster's confessants (and used previously by John Knaresborough), said that he was an aggressive evangelist, 'a rigid ghostly father'.[69] By 10 August, when Charles left for Scotland, the king's cause still seemed to be on the up. There he was enthusiastically received, mainly by those covenanters who had signed the 'Cumbernauld Band' in that month. In Scotland, Charles offered extraordinary concessions to the demands made by the Kirk and the Scottish parliament.[70] Sir Henry Vane, at Holyrood, had anticipated as early as 25 August 1641 that the king 'and his people will certainly agree here'. The Scots army, under its general, Alexander Leslie, 'passes the Tweed, and so they are to disband'; it appeared that now there was a 'happy peace and union made between the two nations'.[71] As Allan Macinnes explains, in the English parliamentary ratification of the treaty of London of August 1641, and in the royal assent given to it, Charles was believed to have recognized the 'sovereign and independent power of the Scottish estates as a "free parliament"'.[72]

This was the moment at which the high-profile treason proceedings against the Benedictine Ambrose Barlow (the friend, as we saw, of the martyr Edmund Arrowsmith) took place. Challoner's narrative says that, 'after above four months [of] imprisonment', Barlow was tried, on 7 September, before Sir Robert Heath, who was 'said to have had instructions from the parliament' that, 'if any priests were convicted at Lancaster', he should 'see the law executed... for a terror to the Catholics, who were numerous in that county'. Barlow was hanged at Lancaster on 10 September 1641.[73] (See Figure 15.1.)

The reaction to the king's Scottish strategy was framed by the so-called 'Incident' on 11 October, a project to seize and/or kill Lords Hamilton, Argyll, and Lanark, which is generally taken to have wrecked the king's plans at this time. The second army plot and its alleged popish elements were still being vigorously

---

[68] *A Most True Relation of the Attachment, Life, Death, and Confession of Will. Waller...* (1641); Anstr., II, p. 344. In August 1643, Francis Newton, Thomas Mayo, and James Wadsworth claimed the credit for Webster's prosecution, and for the proceedings in London against other Catholic clergy after this date: House of Lords (Journal Office; Main Papers), HL/PO/JO/10/1/155 (transcript at ABSJ, 48/17/5).

[69] Anstr., II, pp. 344–5; Challoner, *MMP*, pp. 383–6, 389 (Challoner's source is AAW, A XXX, no. 19); Hibbard, *CI*, pp. 204, 211. For Webster's ministry, see Kn., III, pp. 104–6. Cuthbert Clopton was sentenced on the same day as Webster, 23 July 1641, but he was a chaplain at the Venetian embassy, and the ambassador Giovanni Giustiniani was able to secure his reprieve: *CSPV 1640–2*, pp. 189, 190–3, 195, 197, 198, 217–19, 224, 227, 230; Tompkins, *ECI*, pp. 55–6; see also Morris, *TCF*, I, pp. 319 f.

[70] Cust, *CI*, pp. 298, 302–3, 305; Hibbard, *CI*, pp. 211–12.

[71] *HMCP*, III, p. 80; *ODNB, sub* Leslie, Alexander (article by D. Stevenson).

[72] A. Macinnes, 'The Scottish Constitution, 1638–51: The Rise and Fall of Oligarchic Centralism', in J. Morrill (ed.), *The Scottish National Covenant in its British Context 1638–51* (Edinburgh, 1990), pp. 106–33, at p. 118. In effect, Charles constructed a peace with the Scots by making a similar slate of concessions to them as he had, earlier in the year, granted to the Anglo-Irish: Clarke, 'The Breakdown of Authority, 1640–41', pp. 287–8; *HMCC*, II, p. 291.

[73] Challoner, *MMP*, pp. 398–9.

Figure 15.1 Relic of Ambrose Barlow OSB, d.1641 (with acknowledgment to the Revd Nicholas Schofield and reproduced with the permission of the bishop of Salford).

publicized by Pym.[74] Then there occurred the single most significant political event of late 1641 and, for many, the greatest conspiracy of them all—the rebellion in Ireland of 23 October.[75] There is a consensus that the rebellion broke out because the Anglo-Irish and the Gaelic Irish were driven to make common cause and were trying to fend off any kind of pre-emptive strike from presbyterian Scotland.[76]

If this popish conspiracy outdid all the others, it was, in part, because the king himself could be thought to have no immediate interest in seeing the Irish rebels suppressed. There was, some thought, a degree of 'working towards' the monarch in the rebels' declarations that they had royal warrant for what they did. This may have been played up by parliament's spin doctors, but Lords Dillon and Taaffe did join the king at York, and there were claims that Irishmen were assisting in the

---

[74] Hibbard, *CI*, pp. 212–13.
[75] *HMCF*, pp. 108f; Cust, *CI*, pp. 308–9. For Prynne, the Irish rebellion was a seamless extension of the king's policy towards Catholics in England up to that point: Prynne, *PRP*, p. 59.
[76] T.W. Moody, 'Introduction', *New History of Ireland III*, p. xliii; M. Perceval-Maxwell, 'The Ulster Rising of 1641, and the Depositions', *IHS* 21 (1978), pp. 144–67, at p. 163.

BACK TO THE FUTURE   507

execution of the commission of array.[77] On 4 November 1641 Sir Phelim O'Neill, with Rory Maguire, produced a document, a (probably spurious) proclamation which appeared to come from the king and instructed the rebels to fight for his cause.[78] John Dillingham reported in early January 1642 the rumour that the king was considering going in person to Ireland and that the queen, 'being set on by the pope, labours... to save the extirpating of those papists in Ireland'.[79] The news of the rebellion released a torrent of anti-popish pamphlets about the alleged violence against Protestants in Ireland at the hands of Catholics. One fairly typical newsletter referred to 'the ripping up of women, cutting off the members of ministers' and the 'hanging up [of] men' even after they had said 'that they were content to be Roman Catholics' and to 'abjure' Protestantism.[80]

If anything was going to provoke a tit-for-tat retaliation against Catholics in England, this was probably it.[81] But there was still really nothing of the kind, despite the continuing assertions that a cascade of Catholic rebellions in England (especially in Lancashire and North Wales) would link up with the Irish one or, rather, with incoming Irish rebel troops.[82] Part of the explanation may be that the English Catholic community was already fracturing. There may have been a kind of politique reaction from those who did not think in terms of putting religion before nation. The earl of Castlemaine, in his royalist/Catholic martyrology compiled in the 1660s, averred that, as for the Irish insurrection, 'English Catholics abhorred it' and 'several fought against the rebels' and 'we all decried their proceedings'.[83] Some Catholics, such as Hugh Burke, believed that, if the Irish revolt were to succeed, England and Scotland would convert to Roman Catholicism.[84] But Charles had no intention of declaring himself the head of a British Catholic league.[85]

There were still, at this time, very few formal treason trials of Catholics under the Elizabethan statutes, even though the move towards civil strife was interpreted by many observers as the result of Catholic sedition. It was only when the king

---

[77] K. Lindley, 'The Impact of the 1641 Rebellion upon England and Wales, 1641–5', *IHS* 18 (1972), pp. 143–76, at pp. 163–7; J. L. Malcolm, 'All the King's Men: The Impact of the Crown's Irish Soldiers on the English Civil War', *IHS* 22 (1979), pp. 239–64, at p. 242.

[78] P. J. Corish, 'The Rising of 1641 and the Catholic Confederacy, 1641–5', *New History of Ireland III*, pp. 292–3; Lindley, 'The Impact', p. 164.

[79] *HMCM*, p. 150; cf. *His Majesties Message to the House of Peeres, Aprill 22. 1642. Whereunto is Added His Maiesties Answer to both Houses of Parliament. Concerning the Petition and Reasons to Forbeare his Intended Iourney to Ireland...* (1642); see Hibbard, *CI*, p. 213.

[80] *HMCM*, pp. 135–6; Corish, 'The Rising of 1641'; E. Shagan, 'Constructing Discord: Ideology, Propaganda and English Responses to the Irish Rebellion of 1641', *JBS* 36 (1997), pp. 4–34.

[81] On 15 November 1641, the Lords had issued a warrant for the arrest of Catholic clergy in London and Westminster: House of Lords (Journal Office; Main Papers), HL/PO/JO/10/1/155 (copy of order; transcript at ABSJ, 48/17/5). For the context of this order, i.e. the allegations of Thomas Beale in front of the Commons on 15 November that MPs' lives were in danger, see Hibbard, *CI*, p. 217.

[82] *An Alarum to Warre...* (1642), and *A Continuation of the True Diurnall, of all Passages in Parliament, 14 March 1642* (1642), p. 73, both cited in Lindley, 'The Impact', pp. 156–7. See also M. Stoyle, *Soldiers and Strangers: An Ethnic History of the English Civil War* (2005), ch. 3.

[83] Lindley, 'The Impact', p. 158, citing Roger Palmer, *The Catholique Apology...* (3rd edition, 1674, first published in 1667; Clancy, *ECB*, no. 175), p. 52.

[84] *HMCF*, pp. 113–14.   [85] *HMCF*, p. 138.

508 CATHOLICS AND TREASON

allowed himself to be trapped politically that there was an incentive for his critics to resort to the Elizabethan treason law. An instance of that kind of trapping came with the attempt to abolish episcopacy. The news of the Irish rebellion, as is well known, allowed crowds of apprentices in London to mount an agitation, not least by preventing, in December 1641, the bishops from taking their seats in the Lords.[86] This was the point at which some MPs tried to use the fate of seven incarcerated Catholic clerics against the king. The same newsletter that talked about the 'ripping up of women' in Ireland also mentioned the agitation over the root-and-branch petition against episcopacy, and it noted that there was 'a debate about certain priests, seven in number, who' had been found guilty of treason on 8 December. Over their case, the 'Houses were many times divided'.[87]

In the case of these clerics, the French ambassador, Jacques d'Estampes, marquis de la Ferté Imbault, had attempted to intervene, and he secured the king's permission for deportation instead. Charles sent a 'message to both Houses of parliament' on 11 December, as Challoner put it, to 'know their thoughts'.[88] A series of votes took place in which the Commons decided, though only just, that not all should die. Eighty-eight members outvoted seventy-seven others on the question of whether the whole lot should be hanged. The members then voted on each cleric individually. John Jackson, John Abbot, Walter Coleman, and John Whitbread were thought worthy of death. By a majority of eighty-two to sixty-eight, Edmund Canon was looked upon as deserving a reprieve, and Peter Wilford likewise by a majority of only one vote.[89] Another clergyman, Andrew Waferer, seems to have been similarly regarded as worthy of reprieve.[90] Canon and Waferer were known to have argued in favour of the oath of allegiance of 1606, and Canon had actually taken it.[91] John Jackson had certainly not, in the past, been particularly enthusiastic about the authority of the papacy.[92] But that evidently did not recommend him to the members of the Lower House.

The executions of those clergymen who were marked down for death were scheduled for 13 December. The two houses were still conferring about what was to be done with the condemned men.[93] Whether because of the king's attempt to

[86] *HMCM*, pp. 134, 137, 138; see also F. Bickley (ed.) *Report on the Manuscripts of the late Reginald Rawdon Hastings, Esq....* (HMC, 1930), II, p. 83.

[87] *HMCM*, pp. 134–5; Challoner, *MMP*, pp. 400–2; *HMCF*, p. 112. For the arrest of, and proceedings against, the priests in question (one of whom, John Abbot, appears to have been George Abbot's nephew), see Hibbard, *CI*, pp. 219, 302–3.

[88] Challoner, *MMP*, p. 400; Nalson, *Impartial Collection*, II, pp. 731, 732.

[89] Tompkins, *ECI*, pp. 58–60; *Commons' Journals*, II, p. 339; Challoner, *MMP*, p. 400; ABSJ, Anglia V, no. 7; Nalson, *Impartial Collection*, II, pp. 731, 732.

[90] ABSJ, Anglia V, no. 7; Hibbard, *CI*, p. 303.

[91] Anstr., I, p. 62; PRO, SP 14/128/71, 72, 78, 79; PRO, SP 16/38/17; Anstr., II, p. 330.

[92] *NAGB, passim*, esp. at pp. 67, 125, 126, 127, 219–20, 273.

[93] *Commons' Journals*, II, p. 341; Tompkins, *ECI*, pp. 59–60; *A Coppy of the Prisoners Judgment Condemned to Dy from Nugate on Mundaie the 13. of Decemb. 1641* (1641); for a manuscript copy of the pamphlet, see ABSJ, Anglia V, no. 5.

reprieve all, or because of the Commons' determination to suspend sentence on some, there was a popular outcry. On that day, according to one Catholic newsletter, 'there was a great tumult of thousands...at Newgate to have the priests' hanged. The 'felons' themselves 'got muskets and powder and shot to defend themselves against the keepers', evidently because they thought it was unfair that Catholic clergy should be more favourably treated. 'Both Houses' had 'petitioned the king to have the priests executed'. But he replied only that he would 'consider of it'.[94] On this same day, said another observer, 'in the morning the prisoners in Newgate, that were to be hanged, refused to go unless the priests might also go to execution with them, and so mutinied, insomuch that the sheriff was constrained to shoot many of them with muskets'.[95] The king's proclamation of 10 December to the effect that 'divine service should be observed, as formerly it was settled by statutes and parliaments', proved deeply troubling to 'Brownists and puritans'. This had provoked the Commons 'to print the remonstrance against the king'.[96] When the rioters were hanged on 14 December, this provoked a 'great murmuring of the common people' at the fact that the condemned priests had been spared.[97] The threat of the mob panicked the Commons into a change of heart, and they, conferring yet again with the Lords, called for the immediate execution of all of the seven gaoled Catholic clergy.[98] Their altered stance undoubtedly had a lot to do with the news from Ireland, which in the Lords was considered at the same time on 14 December as the lord keeper reported the recent meeting with the Commons about the reprieved clergy.[99] But there for the time being the matter stuck, as the king delayed his response.[100]

These events were probably integral to the way in which, over a number of issues, the political barometer may have been starting to move now that the king's opponents were, more than ever, as some saw it, beginning to resemble the tyrannical puritan conspiracy against which a range of Catholics and conformists had always warned. John Dillingham commented on 30 December 1641 that 'there is now among the multitude a general crying down [of] the Brownists, and they say that all that go to Westminster in this tumultuous way are such'.[101]

Then the king mounted his attempt at a *coup d'état* by seeking to arrest the five (in fact, six) members in January 1642. This was itself partly prompted by

[94] ABSJ, Anglia V, no. 7 (17 December 1641). John Goodman was, it seems, still locked up in Newgate, but he appears not to have been involved in this stand-off between the king and his parliamentary critics: Anstr., II, p. 133.

[95] *HMCM*, p. 135.

[96] ABSJ, Anglia V, no. 7; Tompkins, ECI, p. 60.

[97] Tompkins, ECI, p. 60; *CSPD 1641–3*, p. 201.

[98] *Commons' Journals*, II, pp. 342–3; *Lords' Journals*, IV, p. 475; Tompkins, ECI, p. 61; *CSPV 1640–2*, p. 265.

[99] *Lords' Journals*, IV, p. 475; ABSJ, Anglia V, no. 7.

[100] Tompkins, ECI, p. 61; *CSPV 1640–2*, p. 265; *The Prisoners of New-Gates Condemnation*...(1642), sig. A2^v–3^r.

[101] *HMCM*, p. 139.

510 CATHOLICS AND TREASON

suspicion that the king's opponents were going to seize the prince of Wales.[102] It may have been, as Richard Cust terms it, one of a number of 'grotesque misjudgments' on the part of the king. But it was entirely logical in the face of the rioting of the previous days (27–29 December) in and around Westminster, the accusations against the earl of Bristol and Lord Digby, and the decision to use treason indictments against the bishops, and also the recent (21 December) city elections.[103]

Perhaps it was no accident that soon after this came the killing of the secular priest Thomas Green alias Richard Reynolds and the Benedictine Alban Roe. Green had been indicted and sentenced in 1628 but was reprieved at Henrietta Maria's intercession. He had been in and out of prison in the 1630s. William Prynne named him as the recipient of a royal warrant of protection in 1635. He and Roe were executed at Tyburn on 21 January 1642. Green was of a considerable age.[104] It was, said the narrative ('a manuscript relation by Father [John] Floyd') used by Challoner, 'almost incredible how much both Protestants and Catholics were moved to tears'. At Tyburn, Green spoke for half an hour and was scarcely interrupted. The sheriff seemed entirely sympathetic to Green and was, apparently, overcome with emotion. When Roe bitterly condemned the laws which proscribed Catholic clergy as 'unjust and tyrannical', the sheriff felt compelled to intervene but did so very politely—'I must not suffer you to vilify the law'. He then silenced a heckler, 'zealous in the lord', who tried to prevent the priests speaking with two suspected Catholics; and 'when the fellow began to murmur and to stir up the people to discontent, the sheriff bade him be quiet or else he would take order with him'.[105]

Virtually every Catholic martyr narrative up to this point had claimed that a proportion of the spectators at these executions showed sympathy for the victims. That might well have been true, and for a range of reasons; but, in these circumstances, when nothing was as it had been, these expressions of sympathy might have had a new political significance. It is possible, for example, that the crowd's behaviour at this execution was part of a royalist reaction in London, even two

---

[102] Hibbard, *CI*, p. 222.   [103] Cust, *CI*, pp. 317, 318, 319, 322, 324–5.

[104] Challoner, *MMP*, pp. 402–11, relying in part on AAW, A XXX, no. 37, pp. 123–6 (narrative assigned to John Floyd SJ; transcript at ABSJ, CP (Thomas Reynolds [*sic*])); *A Warning to all Priests and Jesuites, by the Example of Two Masse-Priests, which for Seducing and Stealing away the Hearts of the Kings Loyall Subjects were Hangd* [*sic*]...*the 21 Day of January, 1642* (1643). Challoner worked from a transcript supplied by Butler: ABP, pp. 571–4; see also Kn., III, pp. 157–63; Anstr., I, p. 138; William Prynne, *Hidden Workes of Darknes brought to Publike Light*...(1645), p. 124; Prynne, *PRP*, p. 24.

[105] Challoner, *MMP*, pp. 404–5; AAW, A XXX, no. 37, pp. 123–6; ABP, pp. 571–4; Kn., III, pp. 157–61. The identity of the sheriff is uncertain. Neither of the two serving officials in the office at this point, George Garrett and Sir George Clarke, seems to have had royalist let alone Catholic sympathies. But since Clarke helped to secure the election of Sir Richard Gurney, who was a royalist, as lord mayor in 1641, the sheriff in question may have been Clarke; see V. Pearl, *London and the Outbreak of the Puritan Revolution* (Oxford, 1961), pp. 124, 299, 295–6, 302–3.

BACK TO THE FUTURE 511

weeks after the embarrassment of the failed royal coup, though, as ever, this depends on how far one believes the martyrological narratives that have come down to us. According to Challoner's source, 'many' who were 'present dipped their handkerchiefs' in the martyrs' blood; 'others gathered up the bloody straws and what they could get else'. The Catholic spectators 'seemed even beside themselves with fervour and zeal'. Nor, allegedly, was sympathy for the two martyr priests evinced only by Catholics. A 'Protestant said, "it would be long enough before any of our religion will die, as these men do, for their faith"'. Another Protestant who lived in the same household as the Jesuit John Floyd had 'no handkerchief about him' and so 'dipped his glove' in the blood of the martyr. A 'Protestant lord' said that he had been 'unwilling they should be put to death, and that it would be the cause that two thousand more papists would rise for these two priests; and that he did not doubt but, when', on 26 July 1641, the priest William Webster had been 'executed, a thousand were made papists'.[106] The Venetian ambassador more or less agreed, and wrote that the execution 'took place...to the extreme regret of not only the Catholics but the Protestants as well who, unlike the puritans, abhor shedding the blood of such innocent victims'.[107]

But, said Challoner's source, it was unlikely that those priests who were still in gaol would be left in peace; indeed, the writer thought that they would 'shortly also be executed, notwithstanding the king's reprieve; for now the parliament proceeds against priests upon their own authority, without asking the king's leave'.[108] Up to this point Charles had proved relatively adept at turning aspects of the current anti-popery agitation back upon its promoters. In March 1642, wrote John Knaresborough, Charles had issued 'a sharp publication against the papists, strictly commanding the judges and justices of the peace to put the laws in execution against those people without favour or connivance'. Knaresborough commented, referring himself to Edward Hyde, earl of Clarendon, and to the ultra-royalist James Heath's *Chronicle of the Late Intestine War*, that 'the parliament had often played this State-engine upon the king with success and, though the farce was long since grown threadbare, yet they seldom cried out popery but found their account one way or other. Why should not his Majesty try the experiment for once? The act would now appear voluntary and not extorted from him, as formerly, by the hectoring complaints and remonstrances of the Commons. He sets forth his royal proclamation to prosecute the papists, and this he does *motu proprio*. What can a prince do more to satisfy his good Protestant subjects that the frequent complaints of the parliament of his favouring popery are indeed no better than so many groundless slanders?'[109]

[106] Challoner, *MMP*, pp. 406–7; AAW, A XXX, no. 37, pp. 125–6; ABP, p. 573.
[107] *CSPV 1640-2*, p. 285.
[108] Challoner, *MMP*, p. 407; AAW, A XXX, no. 37, p. 126; ABP, p. 573.
[109] Kn., III, pp. 169–70; Edward Hyde, earl of Clarendon, *The History of the Rebellion and Civil Wars*...(3 vols, Oxford, 1705–6), I, pp. 489–90; James Heath, *A Chronicle of the Late Intestine War in the Three Kingdoms*...(1676), p. 32; Larkin, *SRP*, II, no. 332.

512 CATHOLICS AND TREASON

This, said Knaresborough, irked the king's enemies. They ridiculed the proclamation 'as a piece of time-serving policy' by 'reminding the people still of the six condemned priests in Newgate, reprieved by the king's warrant' (one of the seven had died in the interim). The sheriffs of London were summoned in order to explain why 'those clergymen had not been executed'. They cited the king's 'gracious reprieve'. The Commons promptly demanded that the reprieve should be rescinded; and 'the king' was 'now again...on the losing hand' or 'at least no great gainer by his late proclamation against the papists'.[110]

In fact, the gaoled clergy's fate became tacked onto the question of who should have control of the armaments magazine at Hull, that is, when the king's officials were resisted there by Sir John Hotham. As Knaresborough put it, following *inter alia* the account penned by the earl of Clarendon, when the parliament in January 1642 sent Hotham to seize the Hull arsenal, they also felt compelled to 'keep up some decorum in their proceedings, lest the people should boggle at such barefaced treasons'. So, in April, they made 'bold with his Majesty a second time, by a mock petition to him for leave to have the magazine of Hull removed to the Tower of London. And, still to mortify him the more, and lessening him with the people, they put him in mind once again of his reprieving the six priests in Newgate' and demanded that 'he would give orders for their execution'.[111]

Challoner, relying on Knaresborough's manuscript account, recounted how the king, now in York, answered the parliament's 'petition concerning the magazine of Hull'. Having made his displeasure clear about the town's munitions, Charles declared that he had reprieved these condemned priests because 'they were, by some restraint, disabled to take the benefit of our former proclamation'. But the king had sworn 'never to pardon any priest, without' parliament's 'consent who shall be found guilty by law'. Deportation was still the king's preferred option. 'But if you', said the king's note, dripping with mordant sarcasm, 'think the execution of these persons so very necessary to the great and pious work of reformation, we refer it wholly to you, declaring hereby that, upon such your resolution, signified to the ministers of justice, our warrant for their reprieve is determined, and the law [is] to have its course'.[112] The king's deliberately nuanced reply made it less politically advantageous to kill them. Knaresborough, following Clarendon, noted that the parliament was 'highly provoked at this unexpected answer...because the king, by referring the matter to them, removed the scandal from himself and laid it at their doors'.[113]

[110] Kn., III, pp. 170–1.

[111] Kn., III, pp. 173–4; Clarendon, *History*, I, p. 456; Cust, *CI*, pp. 338–42; Tompkins, ECI, p. 62; *Commons' Journals*, II, p. 519. Knaresborough also uses the 1676 edition of James Heath's *Chronicle of the Late Intestine War*.

[112] Challoner, *MMP*, pp. 400–1; Kn., III, pp. 178–9; Clarendon, *History*, I, pp. 489–90; *Lords' Journals*, IV, pp. 722–3; Tompkins, ECI, pp. 62–3.

[113] Kn., III, pp. 179–80; Challoner, *MMP*, p. 401.

BACK TO THE FUTURE   513

Then, while Charles was at York, he was in effect forced to sign warrants for the execution of the priests John Lockwood and Edmund Catterick, who had been convicted at the York assizes several weeks before. As Knaresborough described it, the king had nowhere to run, having promised in the case of those detained at Newgate that he would not use prerogative authority 'to pardon any priest, without the parliament's consent, which had been found guilty by the law'. The 'two priests...in York castle had been tried and found guilty'. Should Charles renege, this would be 'ill interpreted by his enemies'. 'The case was perplexing, and', wrote Knaresborough, 'it is the tradition among the Yorkshire Catholics to this day that the king was sorely troubled in mind about it'. The fairly bizarre circumstances of Lockwood's arrest—the dragging to York of a long-retired and octogenarian cleric ('cultivating his little garden when the bloodhounds rushed in upon him')—suggest that the authorities needed a priest at short notice for a local show trial.[114] Catterick was, allegedly, betrayed by one 'Dodsworth', 'a justice of peace' whose wife was Catterick's 'near relation'.[115] This may have been the John Dodsworth of Thorneton Watlass who had married Frances, the daughter of the puritan Sir Timothy Hutton of Marske (the son of Archbishop Matthew Hutton) in December 1615.[116] Knaresborough says that Catterick had had 'many kind invitations from his near kinswoman, wife to the justice of the peace', that is, Dodsworth. But Dodsworth secured his arrest, and 'it is not less certain that in the opinion of the people of that neighbourhood even to this day, Mr Dodsworth and his family for some years after felt the guilt of Mr Catterick's blood very heavy upon them in a long series of surprising and dire disasters'. Since Dodsworth's wife was buried at Thorneton Watlass on 30 July 1642, Knaresborough may, *inter alia*, have been gesturing at her death.[117] Catterick probably reckoned that he was part of a don'task-don't-tell arrangement in his locality and did not expect his puritan relative by marriage, to whom he had in fact privately admitted the fact of his ordination, to behave thus.

The two priests were hanged on 13 April 1642.[118] Lockwood gave spiritual comfort to the more hesitant Catterick.[119] The local opposition to this apparent perversion of royal justice may explain the weird behaviour of the luckless executioner. When Lockwood and Catterick were dead and 'cut down, in order to be bowelled and quartered, the hangman, it seems, scrupled at the butchery part, and for a time flatly refused it, even threatening to hang himself rather than imbrue his hands in the blood of two innocent men. At length he was prevailed

---

[114] Kn., III, pp. 182–3. For John Lockwood's arrest, see Challoner, *MMP*, p. 412. He came from a prominent Yorkshire gentry family: Aveling, *NC*, pp. 154, 186; Anstr., I, p. 211.

[115] Challoner, *MMP*, p. 415; Kn., III, p. 207.

[116] J. W. Clay (ed.), *Dugdale's Visitations of Yorkshire, with Additions* (3 vols, 1899–1917), III, p. 27.

[117] Kn., III, pp. 206–8; see also Challoner, *MMP*, pp. 415–16; Clay, *Dugdale's Visitations of Yorkshire*, III, p. 27.

[118] Charles had arrived in York on 19 March 1642: Cust, *CI*, p. 337.

[119] Challoner, *MMP*, pp. 413–14.

514   CATHOLICS AND TREASON

with to undergo the drudgery, and to work he fell like a fury, cutting, tearing and mangling Mr Lockwood's body in the most inhumane manner. And to revenge himself upon the people, he tore out the entrails and bowels in a rage and with a savage pleasure in his looks he flung them with violence among the crowd, like a furious madman, to the horror and amazement of the spectators.'[120]

The political significance of the executions was made brutally evident immediately afterwards. The 'heads and quarters' of the two priests were 'disposed on the several gates and posterns of the city'. Lockwood's head was 'fixed upon the north gate, called Bootham bar, being close by the king's palace, at the [King's] manor, where his Majesty then resided'. The 'prospect was so nigh and the view so full and direct that it was not possible for him to come out of the palace gate, or even look out from the east, but old Eleazar's bloody head must have struck his sight with horror' and must have affected 'this merciful and tender-hearted prince with some troublesome remembrances' or, more likely, reminded him not to get snared so easily again in the politics of anti-popery.[121]

Evidence that public opinion in the capital was complex and mixed may be deduced from the London populace's reported response to the hanging of the priest Edward Morgan at Tyburn on 26 April 1642.[122] On that day, allegedly, 'the throng of coaches, horses and people' was 'so great and pressing that the hurdle could by no means pass (as usual) to the gallows'.[123] Not only did Morgan preach quite a long sermon, and was then allowed to hang till he was dead, but 'all the people' cried, 'Lord, receive his soul'. Then, quite contrary to the usually desperate efforts of, say, the Elizabethan authorities to prevent the physical remains of the martyrs getting into the hands of the faithful, here 'the officers, calling for the people's handkerchiefs and gloves to wet in the blood', they did exactly this 'and delivered them again to their owners'. One spectator 'got almost his [Morgan's] whole heart out of the fire'.[124]

---

[120] Kn., III, p. 197; Challoner, *MMP*, pp. 414–15.

[121] Kn., III, pp. 197–8; Challoner, *MMP*, p. 415.

[122] The Venetian ambassador on 29 April/9 May 1642 attributed Morgan's death (and the executions of Lockwood and Catterick at York) to the recent 'news...from Ireland' which 'increases their hatred of the true faith': *CSPV 1642–3*, pp. 51–2. For Challoner's account, based in part on 'a Latin manuscript by an eyewitness of his death, sent me from St Omer' (i.e. ABP, pp. 611–17), see Challoner, *MMP*, pp. 417–21. Morgan had been in the Fleet prison in London for over a decade as the result of a star chamber case brought against him in November 1630 on the basis of his libellous words against two Flintshire JPs and his seditious words concerning the king: Anstr., II, p. 224; ABSJ, CP (Edward Morgan; transcript of indictment, Flint assizes, 28 April 1628; transcript of star chamber decree, 26 November 1630); see also *CSPD Addenda 1625–49*, p. 445; PRO, SP 16/231/65, fo. 114ʳ; PRO, SP 16/232/112, fo. 177ʳ⁻ᵛ; [Edward Morgan], *A Prisoners Letter to the Kings most Excellent Maiesty, and the High Court of Parliament* (1642); *Edward Morgan, a Priest, his Letter to the Kings most excellent Majesty, and High Court of Parliament and to all the Commons of England who was Drawne, Hanged, and Quartered on Tuesday, April 26. 1642...* (1642). I am very grateful to Jordan Downs for advice on this point and for his exceptionally helpful comments on this chapter and the next.

[123] Pollen, *AEM*, p. 347 (Nymphenburg papers).

[124] Pollen, *AEM*, p. 352. Morgan may have suffered periodically from mental illness; he certainly was at enmity with Bishop Richard Smith: PRO, SP 16/141/32, fo. 42ʳ; AAW, A XXII, no. 55, pp. 267–70;

BACK TO THE FUTURE   515

The Catholic narrative of the revolting end of Hugh Green may also be part of, or point to, a reaction in favour of the king against a parliament which seemed to have got into the hands of the wrong people. The long euphemism-free account of Green's execution at Dorchester on 19 August 1642 must have been intended to serve as an indictment of the radical puritan mobocratic scum who behaved thus.[125] Dorchester was, as David Underdown notes, by mid-August 1642 'an armed camp' and 'the centre of parliament's war effort in Dorset'. Nearby Sherborne Castle was already occupied by a band of cavaliers.[126] Green's gallows speech was suffused with loyalist and royalist rhetoric, though he condemned the Elizabethan treason statutes.[127]

Anstr., II, p. 224; PRO, SP 16/99/19, fo. 189[r-v]. George Gage wrote to Richard Smith on 28 April 1642, only two days after the execution, to insist that Morgan had not, even at the end, renounced his former errors, and so there would be real problems in publishing 'any relation of his death'. His 'glorious end' was eclipsed with his very particular reflection and persistence in his former conceits of inspirations from heaven concerning the king and kingdom of England'. Gage suspected that Morgan had never been absolved from Smith's suspension of him from his faculties. But those present at the execution were 'infinitely edified' and Morgan 'died...most courageously'. Someone would have to make a decision about the 'relics', which 'everyone holds in great estimation and strives for exceedingly', nor 'can we without danger of infinite scandal either forbid the devotion of so many as well foreigners as [of] our own nation': AAW, A XXX, no. 39, p. 129. Challoner notes that a priest called Wilks (who used the alias of Tomson but whose existence is known really only from Challoner and Knaresborough) had been arrested in or after April 1642 and died in prison at York (before execution); he was said to be Lord Eure's chaplain: Challoner, *MMP*, pp. 416–17; Kn., IV, p. 469; Anstr., II, p. 318.

[125] Challoner, *MMP*, pp. 421–8 (the marginal notes in Elizabeth Willoughby's manuscript, AAW, OB III/ii, nos 179, 180, which record the interventions of hostile elements in the crowd, are omitted in Challoner); Anstr., II, p. 137; see p. 33 above.

[126] Underdown, *Fire from Heaven*, pp. 197–8, 199. Marsys incorporated into his description of Green's death a letter written on 18 August 1642 in which the priest commended himself to the exiled bishop of Chalcedon: Marsys, *Histoire*, pt III, p. 93. The version of Green's execution which is among Christopher Grene's papers at Rome (AVCAU, Liber 1422 [Grene, Collectanea F], section 11) probably rests there because it records that Green was absolved at the point of death by 'a reverend father of the Society of Jesus'. There are very significant differences between this and the narrative by Elizabeth Willoughby (reproduced in Knaresborough and Challoner) and also the version in ABSJ, Anglia V, no. 10 (which, though based on Willoughby's account, excludes, e.g., the claim that Green received absolution from a Jesuit priest). The Collectanea F version came via another eyewitness; whoever wrote it refers to Elizabeth Willoughby in the third person, mentions her narrative, and says also that Green 'threw down from the ladder a little prayer book' to 'an intimate friend from whom we had the relation of his martyrdom'. A printed pamphlet was issued in the name of one Arthur Browne, allegedly a seminary priest, who was condemned (but recanted) at the same assizes where Green was sentenced: *Arthur Browne a Seminary Priest, his Confession after He was Condemned to be Hanged, at the Assizes Holden at Dorchester the Sixteenth Day of August...* (1642).

[127] Challoner, *MMP*, p. 425; Kn., IV, pp. 7–11; S. Monta, *Martyrdom and Literature in Early Modern England* (Cambridge, 2005), pp. 219–20. The crowd may not have been uniformly hostile to Green. Willoughby's account says that Green 'expected almost half an hour his happy passage by the turning of the ladder, for not any one would put a hand to turn it', and also that 'well did one minister say, who was present at his death, amongst forty more of his coat, that if many such men should die, and be suffered to speak as he did, they [the Protestant clergy] should soon shut up their books': Challoner, *MMP*, pp. 426, 428. The version in Collectanea F includes that last detail and says in addition that 'the people' exclaimed against the 'unskilful' hangman: AVCAU, Liber 1422, section 11. Perhaps there is some connection here with the fact that, as Underdown puts it, Dorchester belied its 'puritan reputation by ignominious surrender' when the earl of Caernarvon's army arrived in early August 1643: Underdown, *Fire from Heaven*, p. 204.

516   CATHOLICS AND TREASON

Equally royalist was the Franciscan Thomas Bullaker, who was arrested by the renegade James Wadsworth on 11 September 1642. Bullaker was put on trial on 5 October and executed at Tyburn one week later. He had been interrogated by, among others, the future regicide Sir William Cawley, who had been at the same school as Bullaker. The Franciscan allegedly said that 'the parliament, which made it treason to be a priest, did also by law establish the government of the Church by bishops, the common prayer and ceremonies, all which in this present parliament you oppose'. In retort, Cawley spluttered, 'why may we not amend what was ill-ordered before?' This allowed Bullaker, rather prophetically, to say, 'assure yourself that a parliament will come, and that [in] the very next parliament that shall sit...the religion which you now pretend to establish (viz. Presbytery) will be rejected and thrown out'. If there were traitors to the king, they were not Catholics.[128] One version of Bullaker's ordeal contained in Christopher Grene's manuscripts says that the jury had not wanted to convict. At Tyburn, the sheriff refused to allow him to be disembowelled alive. A section of the crowd believed that his sentence was unjust.[129] At the same time, as Jordan Downs has pointed out to me, the proceedings against Bullaker coincided with the first military confrontations of the civil war. Indeed, on the day that Bullaker was hanged and disembowelled, the lord mayor, Isaac Penington, was making arrangements for the good order of London's military resources. The battle of Edgehill was fought eleven days later.[130]

The uncertainties in London about the wisdom of plunging headlong into a war may have affected proceedings against Catholic clergy. Despite the willingness even at this point to raise large sums of money for defence of the capital in early December, and the petitioning, with the active support of Isaac Penington, for active 'prosecution of the wars' (this is one of the crucial points of Jordan Downs's recent monograph on London and the early years of the civil war), there was a reaction from those who wanted no such thing. In the first week of December this, in Professor Downs's words, 'spurred otherwise peaceable

---

[128] Challoner, *MMP*, pp. 432–4, based on Richard Mason (Angelus of St Francis), *Certamen Seraphicum Provinciae Angliae pro Sancta Dei Ecclesia* (Douai, 1649), followed in part also by Kn., IV, pp. 54, 58–67; *HC 1604–29*, I, p. 470; *AWCBC*, pp. 2038–41. For Grene's narrative of Bullaker's execution, see ABSJ, Collectanea M, pp. 44ᵃ⁻ᵇ, 45ᵃ; see also Monta, *Martyrdom*, pp. 223–4; T. McCann, 'The Catholic Recusancy of Dr. John Bullaker of Chichester, 1574–1627', *RH* 11 (1971–2), pp. 75–86; T. McCann, 'Some Unpublished Accounts of the Martyrdom of Blessed Thomas Bullaker OSF of Chichester in 1642', *RH* 19 (1988–9), pp. 171–82; *An Exact Relation of the Apprehension, Examination, Execution and Confession of Thomas Bullaker...* (1642). This hostile pamphlet does not incorporate the royalist comments attributed elsewhere to Bullaker, as McCann shows. For the circulation of narratives of Bullaker's death, see *AWCBC*, p. 2046. Francis Bell OFM was present at Bullaker's execution: *AWCBC*, pp. 2035, 2262. Bullaker's harbourer, Margaret Powell, was arrested, condemned, and, at the very last moment, reprieved: *AWCBC*, pp. 2043, 2074–5.

[129] *AWCBC*, pp. 2048–9 (ABSJ, Collectanea M, pp. 44ᵇ–5ᵃ).

[130] PRO, SP 19/144/ii, fo. 18ʳ, a reference which I owe to the kindness of Jordan Downs. Penington had become lord mayor after the removal in August 1642 of the royalist Sir Richard Gurney: *ODNB*, *sub* Penington, Isaac and Gurney, Richard (articles by K. Lindley).

BACK TO THE FUTURE   517

Londoners into a frenzy', and they counter-petitioned for peace. This might help to explain the fate of the Jesuit Thomas Holland, who was executed on 12 December 1642. Penington had sat in judgment on him. Holland had prayed for the king and the royal family as well as the council and the parliament.[131] Challoner's source claimed, however, that the jury's verdict came as a 'surprise' to 'the lord mayor and others in the court'. Another contemporary narrative similarly alleged that Penington himself thought there was insufficient evidence to convict.[132] On the other hand, the militants were faced with vigorous peace petitioning. There had been a series of such petitions presented to Common Council, including one on 11 December; on that day, there was a violent demonstration outside the Guildhall against continued hostilities. One imagines that this execution of a Jesuit on the following day might be taken to have been an effective, if brutal, reply.[133]

The number of Catholic martyrs during the rest of the 1640s remained relatively small. Another Franciscan, Henry Heath, was hanged at Tyburn on 17 April 1643.[134] It is not immediately clear what brought about Heath's fate other than his alleged determination to court martyrdom.[135] But the talks aimed at bringing about a cessation of arms with the king are generally taken to have collapsed by mid-April 1643, that is, virtually at the same time as Heath's execution.[136] In August 1643 a demand for 'recompense' was presented to the House of Lords by the leading priest-takers of the day, Francis Newton, Thomas Mayo, and James Wadsworth; with attached documentation, they recited the names of those they had prosecuted and, in particular, of the ones who had been hanged, notably

---

[131] J. S. Downs, *Civil War London: Mobilizing for Parliament, 1641–5* (Manchester, 2021), pp. 105–6, citing I. Gentles, 'Parliamentary Politics and the Politics of the Street: the London Peace Campaigns of 1642–3', *Parliamentary History* 26 (2007), pp. 139–59, at p. 140; *The Image of the Malignants Peace...* (1642); Challoner, *MMP*, pp. 436, 438.

[132] ABSJ, Anglia V, no. 11 (Foley, *RSJ*, I, p. 552); Tompkins, ECI, p. 67. Challoner's narrative adds that the sheriffs of London and Middlesex (the royalist John Langham and the puritan Thomas Andrews) refused to be present at the execution: Challoner, *MMP*, p. 437.

[133] Downs, *Civil War London*, pp. 105–7.

[134] Challoner, *MMP*, pp. 439–47, following principally Mason, *Certamen Seraphicum*, as does Kn., IV, pp. 116f; the relevant passages in the *Certamen Seraphicum* concerning the events from his arrest up to and including his trial are by Henry Heath himself; see AWCBC, pp. 2183 f. For a life of Heath, printed at Douai in the form of prefatory material attached to a devotional work written by him, see *Soliloquies or the Documents of Christian Perfection...* (Douai, 1674). For the arguments between Heath and unnamed Protestant ministers on the way to Tyburn, see ABSJ, Anglia V, no. 14; pp. 61–2 above. On the morning of the execution, Heath penned a rejection of the oath of allegiance and secured signatures to it from three witnesses: AWCBC, pp. 2137, 2196; ABSJ, Anglia V, no. 13.

[135] For Heath's return from Douai to London, his immediate arrest, interrogation, trial, and execution, see AWCBC, pp. 2126–9.

[136] Downs, *Civil War London*, ch. 2 (typescript draft). However, as Professor Downs has argued to me, Heath's fate might not have attracted much notice in the context of the breakdown of peace negotiations with the king and the attempts to rid London's parishes of 'scandalous' ministers. London was then convulsed in early June by the revelation of the Waller conspiracy: *ODNB*, *sub* Waller, Edmund (article by W. Chernaik).

518 CATHOLICS AND TREASON

Heath.[137] Eight months after Heath, yet another Franciscan, Francis Bell, who had been taken at Stevenage by parliamentary soldiers, was dispatched at Tyburn, on 11 December 1643. (See Figure 15.2.) The procession of witnesses against him included the renegades James Wadsworth and Thomas Gage. Bell had apparently been in communication with the Spanish embassy and, on his own account, was a Hispanophile. But the French ambassador, the count of Harcourt, had tried to secure a reprieve for him. The ambassador's chaplain, Charles Marchant, said that parliament had sent four Protestant clergymen ('les plus fameux') to dispute with Bell in his prison.[138] Marchant took care to stress what esteem Bell reserved for Anne of Austria, the French queen regent. Clearly it was important for one section of the French court to identify with the sacrifice made in England by those who were visibly their co-religionists—the ones who did not do deals with politiques and Calvinists.[139]

At least in Bell's case we have some clue about what provoked the proceedings against him. There had been an attempt to mobilize in Rome in order to secure the papacy's recognition of recent martyrs for the faith in England.[140] In Challoner's words, 'a little before Father Bell's trial and execution' there was arrested 'at Yarmouth in Norfolk' one Walter Windsor who was carrying 'a letter from the archbishop of Cambrai to some priests upon the mission, with a copy of a breve' of Urban VIII 'sent to the said archbishop'. This document directed Bell 'to nominate and empower certain priests, then upon the mission, to make diligent inquiry into the cause and manner of death of several priests, lately executed upon the penal statutes, and to transmit the account thereof to Rome'. Those priests who were appointed for London and the South were George Gage, Thomas Middleton (the Dominican provincial), the Benedictine Benedict Cox, and

[137] House of Lords (Journal Office; Main Papers), HL/PO/JO/10/1/155 (transcript at ABSJ, 48/17/5). The petition got an endorsement on 21 September 1643 from John Glynne, now the recorder of London: ibid.

[138] Challoner, *MMP*, pp. 454–5 (including Bell's extensive gallows speech); Kn., IV, pp. 235–6; *AWCBC*, pp. 2217, 2235, 2237–43, 2253, 2259, 2287; ABSJ, Anglia V, no. 17; Marsys, *Histoire*, pt III, pp. 134–5. For the manuscript on Bell sent to Challoner, see (as I take it to be) ABP, pp. 619–22. Père Marchant (prior of La Madeleine in Paris) had been at Tyburn on the fatal day, had absolved Bell at the moment of death, and had obtained relics of him. Marchant had procured a portrait of Bell and subsequently commissioned the writing of his life by the Franciscan Jacques du Bosc, his *Le Martyre du Rever. Pere Francois Bel, Religieux Cordelier* (Paris, 1644), which was commended by Marsys's *Histoire* and served as the basis for Mason's *Certamen Seraphicum*; see *AWCBC*, pp. 2244–7, 2272, 2273. Marsys also visited Bell in prison and assisted at the Mass which he celebrated on the day of the execution: *AWCBC*, p. 2283.

[139] *AWCBC*, p. 2273. For the distribution of Bell's relics to highly placed members of the French court and religious superiors, and to Henrietta Maria, see *AWCBC*, pp. 2273, 2290.

[140] In late 1642, the English Benedictine Congregation's procurator general (Wilfrid Selby) petitioned Rome that the archbishop of Cambrai and the bishops of St Omer and Ypres should be asked to proceed with the relevant enquiries. The papal breve (*Piis Dilecti Filii*) which authorized an Ordinary process was dated 13/23 February 1643. The archbishop of Cambrai, Francis van der Burch, by a letter of 31 May/10 June 1643, set up a commission of nine English priests who would gather the required evidence: *AWCCBM*, pp. vi–vii; *AWCBC*, p. i; C. A. Newdigate, 'Quelques Notes sur Les Catalogues des Martyres Anglais dits de Chalcédoine et de Paris', *Analecta Bollandiana* 66 (1938), pp. 308–33, at pp. 313–14.

Figure 15.2 Portrait of Francis Bell OFM, d.1643 (reproduced with the permission of the British province of the Society of Jesus).

Francis Bell himself. For York and the North, it was the queen's confessor Robert Philip, George Catterick (presumably the brother of the recent martyr Edmund Catterick), the Benedictine Robert Haydock, and the Franciscan William Anderton. This was a renewal in effect of Richard Smith's initiative in the later 1620s to secure accurate information from 'persons of credit and integrity, who had been acquainted with the said priests and the particulars of their trials and behaviours'. It was the seizure of these papers in the possession of Mr Windsor which, it appeared, had provoked or 'hastened' Bell's execution. Challoner emphasized that the documents 'were published by order of parliament the very day that Father Bell was brought upon his trial', that is, on 7 December 1643. Bell had, said John Knaresborough, been arrested 'but a few weeks before', and it did not 'appear that he had fallen under their displeasure upon any other account'. The printed narrative of Bell's execution on 11 December 1643 had a picture of the recently deceased, but 'worthy, religious and truly wise', John Pym on the back.[141] William Prynne's *Popish Royall Favourite* (1643)

---

[141] Challoner, *MMP*, pp. 455–6; Kn., IV, pp. 220–1, 223, 244; *AWCBC*, p. 2216; *The Confession, Obstinacy, and Ignorance of Father Bell, a Romish Priest. Wherein is declared, the Manner of his Tryall, Condemnation, and Execution, on Munday Decemb. 11. 1643…* (1643), quotation at p. 5. For John

520 CATHOLICS AND TREASON

concluded by citing the recent papal breve which authorized the enquiry into Catholic martyrdom.[142]

The year 1644 saw the deaths in, it seems, late July, of the Benedictines Francis Kemp and William Hanson through 'cruel and outrageous usage' by parliamentary troops.[143] The Jesuit Ralph Corby and the secular priest John Duckett were executed at Tyburn on 7 September.[144] Corby and Duckett had been brought to trial on 4 September 1644. Corby alleged that, since he was a native of Ireland, he could not be guilty under the 1585 statute; but this cut no ice with the court.[145] Under sentence, they were visited by 'most of the ministers of Catholic princes and States then residing in London, as also [by] the duchess of Guise, who passed the whole night in watching and prayer with them; and, having made her confession to Father Corby, [she] received the blessed sacrament at his hands, and purchased the chalice in which he said his last Mass, which she afterwards kept as a precious relic'.[146]

Corby wrote, four days before his execution, that he had baulked at allowing another Catholic prisoner, one Dr Belwood, to communicate at his Mass, because Belwood was 'notoriously known to have taken the condemned oath' of allegiance, 'and to persist in the defence thereof'. In that letter Corby also declared that his desire of martyrdom dated from the time that 'the Scots came in, about four years ago'.[147] When Corby was asked whether he was 'in the king's army', he denied it, but the interrogators 'put it down affirmatively'. In *The Kingdomes*

Knaresborough, the episode was a deliberately manufactured piece of anti-popery—'the fashionable policy of that wicked faction to keep the minds of the populace keen in their resentments against the papists': Kn., IV, pp. 216–20; *The Popes Briefe, or Romes Inquiry after the Death of their Catholiques here in England, during these Times of Warre*...(1643); J. Morris, 'A Parliamentary Paper of the Seventeenth Century', *Month* (April 1870), pp. 478–86.

[142] Prynne, *PRP*, p. 76. The Wing P 4039 copy of this pamphlet is manually dated 11 December on the title page—the day of Bell's execution.

[143] Challoner, *MMP*, p. 456; D. Lunn, *The English Benedictines 1540–1688: From Reformation to Revolution* (1981), p. 127. It was claimed that 'about the year 1644 Mr Brown, priest, a very old man, was killed because he was a priest, by being thrown down a pair of stairs in Euxton, a small town between Wigan and Preston, by Major Robinson's soldiers'. The narrator (Christopher Tootell) had these facts from 'Mary Livesey who at that time [in 1644] was about seven years old'; the same information was confirmed by Edward Booth: UCLSC, UC/P1/B2, p. 2. Brown's identity is, however, uncertain.

[144] For a collection of documents on Duckett and Corby, see ABSJ, Anglia V, no. 18; Marsys, *Histoire*, III, pp. 141–58 (*inter alia* translating and printing (pp. 155–8) two letters written by Duckett—one to the bishop of Chalcedon, written on 6 September 1644, for which see AAW, A XXX, no. 60, p. 189). For a copy of Corby's letter, which described the circumstances of his arrest in Co. Durham on 8 July 1644, i.e. six days after the royalist defeat at Marston Moor, see Foley, *RSJ*, III, pp. 72–3. For Alban Butler's transcripts relating to Duckett, used by Challoner, see ABP, pp. 149–60 (summarizing *inter alia* AAW, A XXX, no. 61, p. 191); Challoner, *MMP*, pp. 457–61.

[145] Challoner, *MMP*, p. 464. For the proposal to exchange Duckett or Corby for a Scottish officer (probably Sir Robert Moray) held prisoner in Germany, see Challoner, *MMP*, p. 463; AAW, A XXX, no. 61, p. 193; AVCAU, Liber 1577 (Anstruther Martyrs File): ASV, Nunziatura d'Inghilterra, 4, fo. 171ʳ; Kn., IV, pp. 272–4; *ODNB*, *sub* Moray, Sir Robert (article by D. Allan); P. Ryan, 'Was Sir Robert Moray Proposed in Exchange for Ven. Ralph Corby S. J.?': ABSJ, CP (Ralph Corby).

[146] Challoner, *MMP*, p. 464; Foley, *RSJ*, III, p. 80.

[147] ABSJ, Anglia V, no. 18 (Foley, *RSJ*, III, pp. 89–91).

BACK TO THE FUTURE   521

Weekly Intelligencer for 16–23 July 1644 it was, says one Jesuit narrative, falsely 'printed... that both he [Corby] and Mr Duckett were taken as they fled from' the defeated 'Prince Rupert's army, where they were priests to the popish party in the northern armies employed by his Majesty's authority for the settling of the Protestant religion'. They were interrogated by the 'committee at Sunderland' and sent to London. But, as this pamphlet also noted, this coincided rather closely with the bringing of Archbishop Laud to 'the bar in the house of peers'; and 'the effect of the matter insisted upon against him' included 'priests and Jesuits released out of prison by him, and some entertained by him'.[148] The Portuguese ambassador, Don Antonio de Sousa, processed with Duckett and Corby to Tyburn.[149] The swarm of ambassadors of different nations around the condemned presumably indicates the political investment of their employers in trying to secure the future friendship of whoever eventually took charge of the British State. In France in particular, the anti-politique potential of all this could be enlisted and exploited.

On 22 January 1645, Henry Morse was put to death at Tyburn on the basis of his conviction back in 1637.[150] One eyewitness account of the execution referred to the 'papers' that Morse 'had written', presumably copies of what he intended to say at Tyburn. But 'the pursuivants got and tore' them 'in pieces'.[151] One imagines that observers in London would have made a connection with the execution of William Laud only twelve days earlier and might well have consulted their copies

[148] ABSJ, Anglia V, no. 18; *The Kingdomes Weekly Intelligencer*, no. 64, pp. 516–17.

[149] Challoner, *MMP*, pp. 460–1; Kn., IV, p. 294. The French resident ambassador, Melchior de Sabran, after the martyrdom of Corby and Duckett, 'procured as good a relation as he could get', as well as attempting to secure some of Corby's cassock: ABSJ, Anglia V, no. 18, fo. 4ʳ ('Some few other particulars...'). According to the source relied upon by Knaresborough, Sabran, with others (including the duchess of Guise, whose confession Duckett, out of humility, refused to hear), visited the prison on the evening of 6 September; see Kn., IV, pp. 275–6, 293–4; ABP, p. 152. The count of Egmont, the future duke of Guelders (an avid relic collector, who sent back to the Continent the remains of eleven martyrs) was, with Sabran and the Portuguese ambassador (who stayed in his coach), present at the execution and took 'one of their hats' and one of Duckett's hands: ABSJ, Anglia V, no. 18, fo. 4ᵛ; Kn., IV, p. 279; for Egmont, see *AWCBC*, p. 2105. A letter dated 24 September 1644 from John Horsley (who had been a prisoner in Newgate for three years) to his first cousin Ambrose Corby SJ, i.e. Ralph Corby's brother (Foley, *RSJ*, III, pp. 94–5; ABSJ, Anglia V, no. 18, fo. 54ᵛ) suggests that Ambrose was the recipient of all these accounts and this was how they ended up in the English Jesuits' papers. Ambrose Corby wrote *Certamen Triplex...*(Antwerp, 1645), describing the deaths of Ralph Corby and of Thomas Holland and Henry Morse: Foley, *RSJ*, III, p. 98. In late July 1650, in Paris, Egmont signed an affidavit concerning the relics he had preserved from his time in England 'in order that the memory of such noble persons might be forever preserved among the faithful': Foley, *RSJ*, I, pp. 564–5; 'De Martyribus Angliae, 1640–1646: Instrumentum Ducis Gueldriae &c 1650', 26 July 1650, Municipal Archives, Lille: transcript at ABSJ, 48/17/5; ABSJ 46/19/1, pp. 132–4 (English translation in *The Rambler*, 2nd series, iii (August, 1857), pp. 119–22).

[150] The date is given by Challoner as 1 February, i.e. new style: Challoner, *MMP*, p. 472.

[151] ABSJ, Anglia V, no. 20; *Narratio Gloriosae Mortis quam pro Religione Catholica P. Henricus Mors è Societate Iesu Sacerdos...*(Ghent, 1645). Members of Sabran's and Egmont's households attended on Morse the night before the execution. Henry Rich, earl of Holland, was with Morse so long that Sabran felt unable to visit him personally: ABSJ, Anglia V, no. 20. The ambassador Sabran was father of the Jesuit Louis de Sabran: Foley, *RSJ*, III, p. 80.

522   CATHOLICS AND TREASON

of Prynne's *Popish Royall Favourite* to see the evidence, in print, of the link between Laud, his former client Secretary Windebank, and this Jesuit.

Morse's confrère Brian Cansfield died in, or shortly after release from, prison in the same year.[152] The Benedictine Philip Powel was executed on 30 June 1646.[153] Powel had a reputation as a proselytizer during his years of ministry in Devon and Cornwall.[154] In the face of the spread of the fighting, he had been forced into a royalist garrison or, rather, into George, Lord Goring's, army in the South-West. Challoner says that, in going there, Powel was merely following his flock. This might be taken as a perfect instance of the subsequent Blackloist claim that Catholic royalism was more about self-protection than ideological zeal for the royalist cause; but, according to Knaresborough, Powel was 'hunted out by the rebel soldiers and their abettors with a remarkable spleen and malice'. When Goring's army disintegrated, Powel concluded that it was time to get swiftly from Cornwall into Wales, but he was arrested on board ship on 22 February 1646 by the parliamentarian naval officer John Crowther. Crowther would not have thought that Powel's having been with Goring was politically insignificant. In addition, some of the ship's crew testified that Powel 'had perverted great numbers of the Protestants, particularly in the towns of' Yarnscombe and Parracombe in Devonshire where, allegedly, almost their entire populations had been proselytized by him in spite, it seems, of those places' reputation for puritanism. After he was sentenced to death, Powel's prayers for the king and queen probably did nothing to help his cause.[155]

At Lancaster there were three more Catholics (Edward Bamber, the Franciscan John Woodcock, and Thomas Whitaker) executed on 7 August 1646.[156] Bamber had been in prison for three years and, when proceeded against, showed nothing of the readiness to conform which he had displayed back in 1626-7.[157] It may

---

[152] Challoner, *MMP*, p. 472; ABSJ, CP (Brian Cansfield); Foley, *RSJ*, I, pp. 593-4. For Knaresborough's lists of Catholics who died in prison in the 1640s, see Kn., IV, pp. 469-79. Two Jesuits, Andrew White and Thomas Copley, who had been forcibly returned from Maryland, were indicted in 1645 under the 1585 statute but the prosecution was unsuccessful; see H. Kilburn, 'Jesuit and Gentleman Planter: Ingle's Rebellion and the Litigation of Thomas Copley SJ', *British Catholic History* 34 (2019), pp. 374-95.

[153] Challoner, *MMP*, pp. 474-81 (derived in part from ABP, pp. 633-42, and from three manuscripts kept by the Benedictines at Douai, for which see also ABPFC, fo. 29ʳ).

[154] Kn., IV, p. 351.

[155] Challoner, *MMP*, pp. 475, 477-8 (ABP, p. 634); Kn., IV, pp. 351-3; B. Camm, *Nine Martyr-Monks* (1931), pp. 327-30; M. Stoyle, *Loyalty and Locality: Popular Allegiance in Devon during the English Civil War* (Exeter, 1994), pp. 190, 191; for Crowther, see B. Capp, *Cromwell's Navy: The Fleet and the English Revolution 1648-1660* (Oxford, 1989), pp. 24, 53, 303. Powel used his legal training to argue in king's bench on 16 June 1646 that the Elizabethan statute should not operate in his case which, allegedly, led to a long dispute between him and the 'judge in [the] presence of many lawyers': Challoner, *MMP*, p. 477.

[156] Challoner, *MMP*, pp. 481-9; Anstr., II, pp. 13-14, 347; ABSJ, Anglia V, no. 25; J. E. Bamber, 'The Venerable Edward Bamber: Some New Facts', *Downside Review* 56: 1 (1938), pp. 31-45. It was believed that Woodcock had brought his own fate on himself by volunteering the evidence that he was a priest, even when the judge indicated that the court had no wish to convict in his case: UCLSC, UC/P1/B2, p. 6; *AWCBC*, pp. 2363-4.

[157] Kn., IV, pp. 408f, VII, p. 259; *AWCBC*, pp. 2343-55, 2360, 2361, 2380-5; Challoner, *MMP*, pp. 481-4; see p. 469 above. One source said that Bamber was an exorcist. The accusation against him

BACK TO THE FUTURE   523

be that the butchery used on Bamber was intended to make the others, but particularly the allegedly faint-hearted Whitaker, offer a degree of conformity.[158] Another document which seems likely to have been compiled in response to Knaresborough's researches said that 'they cut' Bamber 'down being yet alive and he stretched out his arms whilst his bowels were ripped up.'[159]

In Knaresborough's version of the martyrdoms of the mid-1640s, these instances of injustice serve as a commentary on the other flagrant injustices committed by the parliament. For Knaresborough, the only reason that in 1647 and 1648 there were no further executions of Catholics or additional ordinances for the seizure of Catholics' estates was that 'the heads of the faction' were 'so intent upon their hellish design of bringing the king to the scaffold that they appeared forgetful of all other matters except such as had a more immediate tendency towards the completing' of 'their long premeditated murder of his Majesty's person.'[160] The legislative attempts to make life worse for Catholics, notably the ordinances of January and February 1650, resumed after the regicide.[161]

The Rise of the Blackloists, Erastianism, Independency, and the Turn away from 'Persecution'

Despite the brutalities, here and there, inflicted on Catholic clergy, the truth was that the collapse of the king's authority was, for some Catholics, not so much a disaster as an opportunity. In short order, there were approaches made by representatives of the Catholic community to the emergent victors in the parliamentary, or rather, the Army's, ranks. The structural failure of royalism in the mid-1640s left a variety of Catholic interest groups making appeals to the new powers that be for something like tolerance. They were able to repeat some of the Catholic toleration discourse of previous years. Since the case for tolerance of Catholic religion and worship had never been pegged exclusively to the recognition and affirmation of royal authority (though at times, notably in the 1630s, Catholic toleration agitation had made it look as if this was the case), it was relatively easy for Catholics to argue that the new political dispensation need have no quarrel with them.

Knaresborough and Challoner might well want to argue that there was a seamless continuum between the executions of clergy up to 1646 and the cruelty of

had come from the husband of a 'possessed woman' out of whom Bamber had 'cast three devils': AWCBC, pp. 2339–40 (ABSJ, Anglia V, no. 25).

[158] AWCBC, pp. 2348, 2353–4; Kn., IV, pp. 436–7. Whitaker was chaplain to the Plessington family of Garstang: ODNB, sub Plessington, John (article by J. Marmion).

[159] AWCBC, pp. 2362, 2363 (UCLSC, UC/P1/B2, pp. 3–5); pp. 13–14 above.

[160] Kn., IV, p. 467.

[161] Kn., V, pp. 20–2; C. H. Firth and R. S. Rait (eds), Acts and Ordinances of the Interregnum, 1642–1660 (3 vols, 1911), II, pp. 329–35, 349–54.

524 CATHOLICS AND TREASON

sequestrations and other legal penalties in and after the second half of the 1640s. But the fact was that, if one took the king's friends now to include presbyterians and Scots, this pointed to the emergence, potentially, of a national Church which would compel a style of conformity which was equally unacceptable to Catholics and to Independents. The rise of Independency, if one can confidently call it that, implied a national Church with freedoms for those who would not accept presbyterian modes of Church government. There developed a kind of 'my-enemy's-enemy-is-my-friend' relationship between Catholic separatists and Independency. This was the basis for, in some quarters, a Catholic claim that Lord Protector Cromwell (as he became) was more tolerant than the first two Stuart kings of Great Britain had been.[162] This lay behind later allegations that Catholics had been in league with the enemies of the monarchy.[163] Indeed, some contemporaries might have reckoned that the analysis of the closeness of Jesuits and Protestant sectaries which informed Thomas Edwards's *Gangraena*, published in 1646, was all too true.[164]

Jesuit clergy and their friends now framed their own allegiance oath. Lord Brudenell with a number of priests, including Henry More SJ, had approached the new regime to see whether there was sufficient common ground for incorporating the right sort of Catholic into the new political order. The resulting discussions with army officers, among them Oliver Cromwell and Henry Ireton, led to the articulation of a series of conditions or demands, one of which incorporated three propositions which Catholics must agree to abjure.[165] The Jesuit Peter Wright, who was a chaplain of John Paulet, the royalist marquis of Winchester, noted apparently with approval on 12 November 1647 that there had been speeches in parliament in which Independents reacted angrily to presbyterian denunciations of popery. In fact, they said, Charles's sins were worse than those of any Catholic. Wright recorded that, 'upon the powder day', 5 November, 'a presbyterian minister, preaching bitterly against Catholics before the lower House,

---

[162] Lunn, *English Benedictines*, p. 128; cf. Tompkins, ECI, pp. 153–4. For the divisions which opened up between presbyterians and those with an Erastian version of what the national Church should be, see J. Collins, *The Allegiance of Thomas Hobbes* (Oxford, 2005), ch. 3, esp. at pp. 95 f. For Oliver Cromwell's willingness, 'whether for pragmatic reasons or from a deeply held belief', to advocate 'if not complete toleration, then liberty of conscience' for Catholics, see W. Sheils, 'English Catholics at Peace and War', in C. Durston and J. Maltby (eds), *Religion in Revolutionary England* (Manchester, 2006), pp. 137–57, at pp. 148–9.

[163] See, e.g., *The History of Popish-Sham-Plots...* (1682), ch. 2.

[164] I. Thackray, 'Zion Undermined: The Protestant Belief in a Popish Plot during the English Interregnum', *History Workshop* 18 (1984), pp. 28–52, at p. 30; A. Hughes, *Gangraena and the Struggle for the English Revolution* (Oxford, 2004).

[165] T. Clancy, 'The Jesuits and the Independents: 1647', *Archivum Historicum Societatis Iesu* 40 (1971), pp. 67–89; AAW, A XXX, no. 86, pp. 271–2; Bossy, *ECC*, pp. 63–4; Tompkins, ECI, pp. 121–2: P. Gillett, 'Probabilism, Pluralism, and Papalism: Jesuit Allegiance Politics in the British Atlantic and Continental Europe, 1644–50', in J. E. Kelly and H. Thomas (eds), *Jesuit Intellectual and Physical Exchange between England and Mainland Europe, c. 1580–1789* (Leiden, 2018), pp. 235–60, at pp. 239–40. For a simultaneous lay declaration which went further than that of these clergy, see Clancy, 'The Jesuits', pp. 77–8; Tompkins, ECI, p. 122.

BACK TO THE FUTURE   525

caused the old inveterate hate to be revived in them and they to begin to talk in the House to act against us, till [Henry] Marten, a professed enemy of the king, stood up and in a speech said that [neither] that treason of the papists nor any treason he could call to mind were to be paralleled with the king's against the State'.[166]

Since this Jesuit allegiance proposal involved denying crucial aspects of papal authority, Rome intervened to suppress it.[167] The failure of the attempt by Jesuit clergy to secure an agreement with the Army triggered a similar manoeuvre from those who were associated with Thomas White, better known by his alias of Blacklo.[168] The group around White (including Henry Holden, Sir Kenelm Digby, and Peter Biddulph, who had been the secular clergy's agent in Rome in the 1630s) devised an oath of allegiance which Catholics would take in return for toleration. The premise was that English Catholics had exactly the same 'natural rights' as Protestants and should be treated equally. On this basis, as Jeffrey Collins explains, it was possible to infer that 'the corrupt interests of the pope', and the papacy's 'meddling' in the attempted negotiation between the royalists and the Independents, had 'ruined a golden opportunity to restore Charles I and secure toleration for Catholics at one blow'.[169] The draft oath of allegiance (12 September 1647) retained in the secular clergy's papers held it to be 'impious and against the word of God... to maintain that any subject may kill and murder the anointed of God'.[170] But, shortly after the execution of the king, Digby and John Winter were in London and were still trying to secure that elusive arrangement with the Independents.[171]

---

[166] ABSJ, Anglia VII, no. 6 (Foley, *RSJ*, II, p. 563); C. Gillett, 'Catholicism and the Making of Revolutionary Ideologies in the British Atlantic, 1630–1673' (PhD, Brown, 2018), p. 304; S. Barber, *A Revolutionary Rogue: Henry Marten and the English Republic* (2000), p. 16; for Winchester, see *ODNB*, *sub* Paulet, John, fifth marquis of Winchester (article by R. Hutton). The Benedictine Humphrey Peto was convicted of treason in December 1647 but in January 1648 was reprieved. William Prynne alleged that this was at the behest of army officers with whom Peto had been in negotiation in 1647 concerning toleration: Richardson, 'Serial Struggles', p. 15, citing *The Substance of a Speech Made in the House of Commons by Wil. Prynne... the fourth of December, 1648* (1649), p. 111.

[167] Clancy, 'The Jesuits', pp. 79, 84–5; Collins, *Allegiance*, p. 112; Gillett, 'Probabilism'.

[168] J. Miller, *Popery and Politics in England 1660–1688* (Cambridge, 1973), pp. 42–4; Bossy, *ECC*, pp. 62–9; Tompkins, ECI, p. 123, citing AAW, A XXX no. 84. See esp. J. Collins, 'Thomas Hobbes and the Blackloist Conspiracy of 1649', *HJ* 45 (2002), pp. 305–31; S. Tutino, 'The Catholic Church and the English Civil War: the Case of Thomas White', *JEH* 58 (2007), pp. 232–55; B. Southgate, 'Covetous of Truth': The Life and Work of Thomas White, 1593–1676* (1993); B. Southgate, '"That Damned Book": The Grounds of Obedience and Government* (1655), and the Downfall of Thomas White', *RH* 17 (1985), pp. 238–53; S. Tutino, *Thomas White and the Blackloists: Between Politics and Theology during the English Civil War* (Aldershot, 2008). For Blackloist deviation from 'orthodox' readings of Rome's authority, see Tutino, *Thomas White*, pp. 36, 43–4.

[169] Tutino, *Thomas White*, p. 44; Collins, *Allegiance*, pp. 113–14, 136 (citing Robert Pugh (ed.), *Blacklo's Cabal discovered in Severall of their Letters...*(Douai, 1680), pp. 26–8, 41–6, 137). As Tutino stresses, the 'peculiar kind of Catholicism in which Digby had come to believe did not require a distinctive form of political government, but could fit easily into either monarchy or republic': Tutino, *Thomas White*, p. 54.

[170] AAW, A XXX, no. 84, pp. 267.   [171] Collins, *Allegiance*, p. 137.

526 CATHOLICS AND TREASON

The underpinning for this Catholic profession of obedience to the new regime was to be an extensive episcopal structure which would in effect be independent of Rome. Blackloism could be taken as an extrapolation of former appellant ideological norms and assumptions. Some of White's associates were one-time clients of Richard Smith, notably Henry Holden and Peter Biddulph. They had more or less given up with Rome when the papacy failed to support Bishop Smith against his opponents in the 1630s. Here the appellant tendency to scale back aspects of Rome's temporal authority and to insist on the need for a robust episcopal mode of governance of English Catholics was taken to its absolute logical limit. This was a position quite close in some ways to the theses about obligation and allegiance which were being developed by Thomas Hobbes, despite Hobbes's arguments for the abolition of episcopacy and indeed the complete incompatibility of, on the one hand, his views about the sovereign's power over the Church and, on the other, the opinions of virtually any contemporary Catholic, let alone most other Christians.[172]

Controversially, some of the Catholic secular clergy asserted that the episcopal chapter which had been set up in the 1620s without Rome's explicit fiat had the right now to elect another bishop, irrespective of whether Rome consented to it or not.[173] As the Blackloists saw it, restored Catholic episcopacy would, in John Bossy's words, 'block the presbyterians and knock out the Church of England with one devastating blow'.[174] Holden's scheme for an oath-based toleration went much further than what the secular clergy had previously looked for. Instead of just one bishop without a territorial see, Holden posited that parliament would 'let the Catholics have, or rather oblige them to have, six or eight bishops' who would use 'some of the ancient national titles of the kingdom'. Exactly how much spiritual power these bishops, dependent for their existence on parliament and in effect completely independent of Rome, would have was left usefully vague. But the claims which the seculars had made before the civil war about the benefits, for the monarchy, of tolerating Catholics and Catholic episcopacy were now transferred to the republican regime. This new Blackloist 'hierarchy would...bring law and order to the Catholic community'. Those who tried to cite papal authority for their missionary status and work would find that they were compelled to look to the new bishops, and lay Catholics would have to obey them as well. As Bossy says, it was 'not a monstrous aberration', but it was an astonishing demonstration

---

[172] Ibid., p. 26; Bossy, *ECC*, p. 63; A. F. Allison, 'An English Gallican: Henry Holden, (1596/7–1662) part I (to 1648)', *RH* 22 (1995), pp. 319–49. For Hobbes's association with the Blackloists, via the so-called Louvre group among the royalists in exile, see Collins, *Allegiance*, pp. 90 f. For the intellectual links between Thomas Hobbes and Sir Kenelm Digby in the 1630s, see Tutino, *Thomas White*, pp. 15–16. But, for the differences between Hobbes and White, e.g. on the relationship of Church and State, and the place of religion in defining sovereign power, see Collins, *Allegiance*, p. 91; Tutino, *Thomas White*, pp. 78–9. See also, for Biddulph's attempt in 1650 to make his peace with the papacy, Tompkins, ECI, p. 127.

[173] Tutino, *Thomas White*, p. 45.   [174] Bossy, *ECC*, pp. 64–5.

BACK TO THE FUTURE   527

of how fluid some of the secular clergy's programme actually was, even though the Blackloist mindset was heavily anchored to tradition. Here, the institution of episcopacy located in 'ancient sees' clearly trumped concepts of papal authority located in supposedly suspect political theory.[175]

Of course, none of this was necessarily acceptable to those who still saw the world primarily from an anti-popish perspective. As John Miller remarks, 'by the end of 1648, Prynne was convinced that the Army had been infiltrated and taken over by priests and Jesuits'. Pride's Purge was evidence of precisely that. As Prynne put it on 26 December 1648, the Army's recent coup against king and parliament was 'nothing else but the designs and projects of Jesuits, popish priests and recusants, who bear chief sway in their councils, to destroy and subvert our religion, laws, liberties, government, magistracy, ministry, the present and all future parliaments, the king, his posterity and our three kingdoms', and to 'betray' everything to 'foreign and popish enemies'. This would 'give a just occasion' to the prince of Wales and to the duke of York, 'now in the papists' power, to alter their religion, and engage them and all foreign princes and estates to exert all their powers to suppress and extirpate the Protestant religion and possessors of it through all the world, which these unchristian, scandalous, treacherous, rebellious, tyrannical, Jesuitical, disloyal, bloody present counsels and exorbitances of this army of saints, so much pretending to piety and justice, have so deeply wounded, scandalized and rendered detestable to all pious' and 'moral men of all conditions'.[176]

This was a near perfect replication of the conventionally understood popish conspiracy to subvert Church and State. Some of those who had been in arms against Charles Stuart now allegedly constituted a kind of host organism for popish parasites. What else could one deduce from the reprinting of Robert Persons's *Conference about the Next Succession*, a version of which appeared in 1648, a work suffused with republican ideology?[177] The evidence was there in Cromwell's known association with people such as Sir Kenelm Digby, who was central to the Blackloist project, even though rational political calculations meant that

---

[175] Bossy, *ECC*, pp. 65–7; Tutino, 'The Catholic Church', p. 238.

[176] Miller, *Popery and Politics*, p. 85, citing *Mr Prynne's Demand of his Liberty to the Generall* (1648), broadside; see also Thackray, 'Zion Undermined', p. 31.

[177] *Severall Speeches delivered at a Conference concerning the Power of Parliament...* (1648; Wing P573). Prynne noted that on 11 January 1648 there 'came a declaration from Sir Thomas Fairfax and the general council of the army...signifying their resolutions to adhere to the Houses [of parliament] for settling and securing the parliament and the kingdom'. The Lords' refusal to cooperate resulted in soldiers being sent to garrison Whitehall and, 'some few days after', Robert Persons's book 'against King James's title to the crown, and concerning the lawfulness of subjects and parliaments deposing and chastising of their kings for their misgovernment, and the good and prosperous success that God commonly has given to the same...printed out of' Persons's 'own printed copy verbatim except [for] the word "parliament" added to it now and then...was published to the world with this title, *Severall Speeches delivered at a Conference concerning the power of Parliaments to proceed against their king for Misgovernment*', and this 'discourse of a Jesuit' was intended to look like 'speeches made by some members of the Commons house at a conference with the Lords': *Substance of a Speech*, pp. 108–9.

528   CATHOLICS AND TREASON

Cromwell continued, at the appropriate moments, to deploy the mainstream rhetoric of anti-popery.[178]

The treason statutes were rarely deployed against Catholic clergy during the Interregnum. Not that Richard Challoner saw that period as a particularly tolerant one. Working from the pamphlets published by the Blackloist John Austin, Challoner (who took this material virtually word for word from Knaresborough's drafts) chose to interpret Austin's pleas for relief from sequestration as proof that life was just as bad under the republic as it had been before. Challoner cites extensively from Austin, and the implication in Challoner's text is that Catholics were suffering simply because they were royalists, that is, merely loyal to the king, or because they had 'never been in any engagement' but had been 'found only in some garrisons of the king, whither they were driven for refuge'. Quoting Austin, Challoner wrote that, 'besides these extreme and fatal penalties' which lay 'upon the recusants merely for their conscience, there are many other afflictions whereof few take notice which, though of lesser weight, yet being added to the former, quite sink them down to the bottom of sorrow and perplexity'. Austin had proceeded to list them and argued that in some respects these penalties were 'a severity far beyond the most rigid practice of the Scotch Kirk'.[179]

Austin, however, posed in his pamphlets not as a Catholic but as a Church of England man considering the question of freedom of worship for those who tended towards Independency. He concluded that sauce for the goose was, here, sauce for the gander, and that Catholics should be tolerated as well. Further parts of the same publication, with new editions, issued from the press in 1652 and 1653; the fourth edition's sheets were stitched together again in 1659. Austin was a friend, in particular, of Thomas White and John Sergeant—the central figures of the Blackloist group. They thought it was possible, with a clear conscience, to offer allegiance to Cromwell in return for tolerance.[180] As Stefania Tutino comments,

[178] Miller, *Popery and Politics*, pp. 85–6; Thackray, 'Zion Undermined', pp. 35–6.

[179] Challoner, *MMP*, pp. 491–9, quotation at p. 495; Kn., V, pp. 52f; cf. William Birchley [John Austin], *The Christian Moderator. Or Persecution for Religion condemned by the Light of Nature, Law of God, Evidence of our own Principles* (1651), esp. pp. 9–11; Davenport, *Suspicious Moderate*, chs 13–14; Tompkins, *ECI*, p. 179. Challoner omits Knaresborough's transcription of Austin's own printing in 1652 of the recent Catholic petition 'to the supreme authority of this nation, the parliament of the commonwealth of England': Kn., V, pp. 71–4; William Birchley [John Austin], *The Christian Moderator, Second Part. Or Persecution for Religion condemned by the Light of Nature, Law of God, Evidence of our own Principles: But not by the Practice of our Commissioners for Sequestrations* (1652), pp. 3–4.

[180] *ODNB, sub* Austin, John (article by J. Blom and F. Blom); Clancy, *ECB*, nos 50–5; Birchley [Austin], *The Christian Moderator*; Birchley [Austin], *The Christian Moderator, Second Part*; Birchley [Austin], *The Christian Moderator. Third Part. Or the Oath of Abjuration Arraign'd...* (1653); for a reply to this pamphlet, see E. Lee, *Legenda Lignea: with an Answer to Mr Birchleys Moderator. (Pleading for a Toleration of Popery.) And a Character of some Hopefull Saints Revolted to the Church of Rome* (1652); see also Collins, *Allegiance*, chs 4, 5. Austin cited, in the third of his toleration pamphlets, a string of authorities for freedom of conscience who were recognizably from the puritan tradition, including John Foxe; see Birchley [Austin], *The Christian Moderator. Third Part*, pp. 26–30. For John Sergeant, the secretary of the chapter from 1655, who was forced to resign only in 1667, see Bossy, *ECC*, pp. 67–8; D. Krook, *John Sergeant and his Circle: A Study of Three Seventeenth-Century English Aristotelians* (Leiden, 1993).

Austin 'used (and misused) Hobbes's *Leviathan* as an example of a theory arguing for toleration' of 'the English Catholic Church'.[181]

This was not to deny that Catholics were being persecuted. What Austin said was that they were capable of being tolerated in the present circumstances. Austin's character in his *Christian Moderator* claimed to be grateful that 'we have so happily shaken off that intolerable yoke of popish infallibility'.[182] He protested that all nonconformists were in the same boat and should be treated equally. Conformity was simply an engine of persecution. 'It is become to us not only tyrannical but absurd to compel others to a way that ourselves confess may possibly be erroneous. We see one parliament repeals those articles of faith which a former enacted; that form of worship, which the laws of the last age introduced, is now generally exploded; nay, the very last Reformation, settled with so solemn a covenant and carried on with so furious a zeal, is already by better lights discovered to be merely human and therefore deservedly laid aside.' The Westminster Assembly's 'confession of faith, hatched by so many years sitting, is now learnedly examined and indeed for a great part solidly confuted by Mr William Parker and other learned persons in print. How preposterous it is then to constrain a soul, not only to forsake his conscience, which may be truth, but drive him contrary to his own heart to a way that may be error!' For 'force is punishment, and consequently not just, unless the offence be voluntary'. But 'he that believes according to the evidence of his own reason is necessitated to that belief, and to compel him against it were to drive him to renounce the most essential part of man, his reason'. The persecutors should consider 'how dangerously' they did 'expose themselves to the just indignation of God' when, 'by oaths, imprisonments' and 'forfeitures', they drove people thus, and themselves fell, 'into eternal perdition'.[183]

Austin saluted 'the unparalleled Army, in all whose proceedings and declarations ... their motto has been "liberty to all tender and oppressed consciences"'. The Heads of the Proposals of 1 August 1647 had 'prudently' distinguished 'between quiet exercisers of their consciences and active prejudicers of the commonwealth and thereupon offer their earnest desires "that all civil penalties for nonconformity be wholly repealed and some other provisions"' be ' "made against such papists as should disturb the public peace"'. Equally to be celebrated was the Army's 'victory over that rigid and severe Kirk-army of the Scots' in September 1650. Austin rejoiced that, 'in memory of' that 'great salvation from the pride and fury of the presbyterian priesthood, the parliament, as a new covenant of

---

[181] Tutino, *Thomas White*, p. 76; Collins, 'Thomas Hobbes and the Blackloist Conspiracy', pp. 329 f.; Collins, *Allegiance*, pp. 139, 179–80; Birchley [Austin], *The Christian Moderator*, p. 12; Birchley [Austin], *The Christian Moderator. Third Part*, p. 21. For presbyterian attacks on, and Independent defences of, John Austin in 1652, see Collins, *Allegiance*, p. 180.

[182] Birchley [Austin], *The Christian Moderator*, p. 1.

[183] Ibid., pp. 1, 2, 3; William Parker, *The Late Assembly of Divines Confession of Faith Examined* ... (1651).

530 CATHOLICS AND TREASON

thanksgiving for so seasonable a mercy, in the same month enacted an abolishment of divers rigorous and penal statutes, contrived on purpose by the haughty prelates to break the hearts of those whose consciences they could not bend'.[184] Professor Collins emphasizes the crucial political significance of the act of 27 September 1650, 'which repealed the Elizabethan act mandating attendance at a recognized place of worship'. This measure 'sounded the death knell for the...presbyterian Church settlement of 1646'. Thomas Hobbes celebrated it as such. This measure, which followed the crushing military victory at Dunbar, was, notes Collins, 'encouraged by Cromwell's letters from Scotland'.[185] Collins remarks that an amnesty to Catholics might assist with the pacification of Ireland and good relations with France and Spain would seriously undercut the exiled Stuart court's prospects of aid from that quarter.[186]

For the time being, this was as far as it went.[187] Cromwell's departure for Ireland allowed for the expression of 'anti-Catholic sentiment in the Rump parliament'. John Winter was gaoled and Sir Kenelm Digby was forced abroad. Henrietta Maria's chaplains George Leyburn and Walter Montagu arrived in England in order to hinder the Blackloist programme.[188] But the tolerance agenda of the Blackloists was far from dead. In a virtual reprise of what writers such as Anthony Copley had said fifty years before in the circumstances of the Archpriest Dispute, Austin claimed that 'the only true means of winning souls to God' was 'the gospellary way of meekness and persuasion'.[189] Here, however, the separatist impulse was endorsed completely without reference to confessional difference. Somewhat disingenuously, the writer said that a friend of his had told him that 'the measures I had cut out for tender consciences would' also 'fit the papists'. But what was wrong with that? For who lived 'more peaceably with their neighbours', and who dealt 'more justly with all men than they'? They took their religion seriously and were ready to suffer for it.[190] Catholics should certainly not be harassed and bothered with, for example, the oath of abjuration. Here many of the arguments against coercion in the tendering of the 1606 oath of allegiance came back again.

---

[184] Birchley [Austin], *The Christian Moderator*, pp. 4, 5. For this aspect of the Heads of the Proposals, see Collins, *Allegiance*, pp. 111–12; R. S. Spurlock, 'Cromwell and Catholics: Towards a Reassessment of Lay Catholic Experience in Ireland', in M. Williams and S. P. Forrest (eds), *Constructing the Past: Writing Irish History, 1600–1800* (Woodbridge, 2010), pp. 157–80, at p. 174.

[185] Collins, *Allegiance*, pp. 133, 155.

[186] Ibid., p. 138. Even the marquis of Antrim may have promised to assist in the subjugation of Ireland in return for toleration: ibid. For the foreign policy reasons for both France and Spain at this moment needing the English/British State to remain neutral, see ibid., pp. 137–8.

[187] Ryan Burns points out that Cromwellian government in Scotland, in the form of George Monck, shielded Catholics there, at least during the early part of the 1650s, from coercive presbyterian discipline and secured professions of loyalty from them in return; but this de facto tolerance was partially reversed in the later part of the decade: R. Burns, 'Unrepentant Papists: Catholic Responses to Cromwellian Toleration in Interregnum Scotland', *History* 103 (2018), pp. 243–61.

[188] Collins, *Allegiance*, pp. 138–9.   [189] Birchley [Austin], *The Christian Moderator*, p. 7.

[190] Ibid., p. 8; Birchley [Austin], *The Christian Moderator, Second Part*, p. 8.

BACK TO THE FUTURE   531

What use was an oath anyway? In Charles's reign, 'many papists were smartly punished for not taking the oath of allegiance, none for not observing it'; and some Catholics could credibly say that the 'utter ruin which now endangers their whole estates proceeds solely from their performing to the late king that service which he called allegiance'.[191]

Austin volubly protested against the ravages of the commissioners who continued to sequestrate Catholics. In his persona of a moderate churchman, he said that he had attended the sequestration proceedings at Haberdashers' Hall. Here he witnessed with astonishment the otherwise 'civil' commissioners saying, 'in many hard cases, that either their instructions... bind them up from being able to give relief or the obligation to the oath they take will not permit them' to alleviate Catholics' circumstances.[192] Austin then morphed seamlessly into a brief round-up of the actual martyrdoms of the civil war. Through his assumed identity of a Church of England man, Austin said that he had twitted a recusant about the recent instances of 'some papists taking the oath of abjuration' and had declared that this was itself a convincing rebuttal of the old saying 'Sanguis Martyrum est Semen Ecclesiae'. *Au contraire*, said the recusant, this maxim was as true of 'England' as 'ten thousand miles off in Japan, in which two islands' there 'have, of late, been sharper persecutions... for matter of religion than in any other place of the world'. The recusant also said that this was how 'his Church increased and prospered still'. Austin pretended to have entered a kind of competition with the recusant by citing the 'late coming in of some papists to our religion'. The recusant was able to retort that, 'as there have been at least twenty priests put to death in England since the beginning of this parliament merely upon the account of their religion or function, so he could name a far greater number of persons of quality who have in the same space of time reconciled themselves to the Catholic union'. In some ways this was a conventional enough thought, though it was reinforced by Austin's printing of his recusant interlocutor's list of 'the priests executed in several places since the year 1641' and those who had 'died prisoners... in Newgate' as well as another list of recent converts to Rome. The recusant said there were many more such people whose names he did not want to reveal. In other words, here the Blackloist tendency in contemporary Catholicism was definitely not

---

[191] Ibid., p. 7; for Austin's further attack on the oath of abjuration, which he compared with the *ex officio* oath, hated by puritans, see Birchley [Austin], *The Christian Moderator. Third Part*, esp. at pp. 18f.

[192] Birchley [Austin], *The Christian Moderator, Second Part*, pp. 11 f. For the legal structures and rules established by the ordinances of March and August 1643, governing the sequestration of Catholics, see Sheils, 'English Catholics', pp. 142–3; Firth and Rait, *Acts and Ordinances of the Interregnum*, II, pp. 106–17, 254–60; Kn., IV, pp. 205–13. As Professor Sheils points out, all royalists were subject to sequestration, while papists (a vague category, of course), 'whether royalist or not, were to have the existing statutes enforced rigorously against them'; but, in practice, non-combatant Catholics were treated differently from those who fought for the king: Sheils, 'English Catholics', pp. 142–3. I am very grateful to Eilish Gregory for advice on this topic; see E. Gregory, 'Catholics and Sequestration during the English Revolution, 1642–60' (PhD, London, 2017), esp. chs 3, 4.

532 CATHOLICS AND TREASON

cutting itself off from its community's martyrological tradition, although Austin's pamphlet took care to add that 'there was only one of these priests...put to death since this nation was established in the present government', that is, the Jesuit Peter Wright.[193]

Wright was seized in the house of his patron, John Paulet, marquis of Winchester. It is not clear who wanted him arrested and charged. The affair, if we believe the extant narratives of it, turned into a trial of strength in London—in effect over whether the recent statute was going to hold up.[194] The coming forward of former professional informers to give evidence against Wright may have been triggered by a sense of the presbyterian outrage at an emerging settlement which would incorporate Catholics but in effect exclude committed presbyterians. Other clergy were charged with, but acquitted of, treason, in Holy Week 1651. The Spanish and Portuguese embassy chapels were packed out and Catholics in droves visited the prisons where their clergy were incarcerated. During this time there was an attempt, sponsored by the marquis of Winchester, to get Wright freed.[195] In the context of the efforts of Winchester and others back in 1647 to make approaches to the Independents, this all makes perfect sense. He had been one of the Catholic grandees who had lobbied the Army back in 1647.[196]

Evidently somebody wanted to make sure that Wright did not escape. According to Jesuit records, the lord chief justice, Henry Rolle, who was reckoned to have presbyterian sympathies, summoned 'Thomas Gage, an infamous apostate priest'. Gage had previously testified against Thomas Holland and Francis Bell and now he gave evidence against Wright and, also, against the Dominican Thomas Middleton, though Middleton was acquitted when Gage admitted that he (Middleton) 'might be no priest'.[197] The incongruity of proceeding against

---

[193] Birchley [Austin], *The Christian Moderator, Second Part*, pp. 18–21. Knaresborough traced Wright's prosecution directly to the 'rascally ordinance' of 26 February 1650: Kn., V, pp. 26–7.

[194] Lucy Underwood has pointed out to me that the act of 27 September 1650 cannot properly be described as tolerationist, as far as Catholics were concerned, because it did not repeal many of the principal Elizabethan statutory measures against Catholics.

[195] Foley, *RSJ*, II, pp. 513–14, 515, 516, 517, 518, 519. For Knaresborough's description of how the marquis of Winchester tried to prevent Wright's arrest, see Kn., V, pp. 38–9; and for Winchester's requesting Wright as a chaplain, see Kn., VII, p. 452.

[196] Tompkins, ECI, pp. 134 (pointing out that Winchester, like Lord Brudenell, 'did not wish for complete independence from Rome in the same way as the Blackloists'), 142; Clancy, 'The Jesuits', p. 78. The Spanish court at this point, as in the previous few years, was trying to cultivate political Independents, something which some English Catholics could endorse: Tompkins, ECI, pp. 137–8; A. J. Loomie, 'Alonso de Cárdenas and the Long Parliament, 1640–1648', *English Historical Review* 97 (1982), pp. 289–307, at pp. 304–7.

[197] Foley, *RSJ*, II, p. 520; Challoner, *MMP*, p. 501; *ODNB*, sub Rolle, Henry (article by S. Handley); *HC 1604–29*, VI, p. 85; Kn., IV, p. 85. For the former Dominican Thomas Gage (who was a son of John and Margaret Gage of Haling manor, Surrey), see *ODNB*, sub Gage, Thomas (article by A. Boyer); see also Thomas Gage, *A Full Survey of Sion and Babylon...*(1654); Thomas Gage, *A Duell between a Iesuite and a Dominican...*(1651), pp. 6–7. Thomas Middleton was one of the clergy who, under his alias of Dade, had subscribed their assent to a declaration that the three propositions drawn up concerning Catholics as part of a freedom-of-conscience deal with the Army, in summer 1647, could be answered in the negative, i.e. as a guarantee of Catholics' loyalty: Clancy, 'The Jesuits', pp. 77, 84; Tompkins, ECI, p. 122; P. A. Richardson, 'Serial Struggles: English Catholics and their Periodicals,

BACK TO THE FUTURE   533

Wright after the passing of the September 1650 act was the topic of a petition which was drawn up on Wright's behalf, but to no effect.[198] The French ambassador and, allegedly, unnamed Independent MPs tried to stop the execution but did not succeed. Meanwhile, Wright was besieged in his prison accommodation by 'Catholics of every rank and condition' and by quite a few who were not Catholics at all. He 'heard the confessions of many'; and 'to many, and especially to those he knew, he gave pictures with his own signature'. In fact, 'one of his friends alone sent him six hundred of these for signature'.[199]

Wright was hanged on 19 May 1651.[200] Catholic narrators said that there were 20,000 spectators, including 'near 200 coaches and 500 horsemen', at Tyburn on the day of the execution. The Jesuit Edward Leedes recorded that in the carriages lining the streets were 'some of the principal nobility', while 'many persons mounting on the tops or hoods of the coaches nearly crushed them in by their weight'. Whatever was going on here, and one assumes it was something of a struggle or contest by proxy over what the new regime meant by tolerance, the London Catholics were visibly out in the open: 'on whichever side the martyr turned his eyes, his fellow religious had...surrounded the gallows'.[201] Other commentators dwelt only briefly on the events of that day, with the *Perfect Diurnall* recording that Wright was hanged with 'twelve men and three women'. One of the men was 'an Arabian', sentenced for 'buggering a boy'.[202] But the Jesuit account noted that the 'sheriff of London' behaved with a 'humanity wholly unheard of'. If the sheriff in question (one of the two serving at this point) was Robert Tichborne, who was a regicide and an aggressive Independent, this might explain why he conducted himself thus towards a Catholic priest who could be regarded as a victim of presbyterian aggression.[203]

1648–1844' (PhD, Durham, 2003), p. 14. Wright had ministered to the mortally wounded Sir Henry Gage, governor of Oxford (Thomas Gage's brother) in 1644: Foley, *RSJ*, II, p. 520.

[198] Foley, *RSJ*, II, pp. 528–9.   [199] Foley, *RSJ*, II, pp. 530–1, 533.

[200] Challoner, *MMP*, pp. 499–504.

[201] Challoner, *MMP*, pp. 500–4; Kn., V, pp. 33–51; Foley, *RSJ*, II, p. 543. The marquis and 'his family had placed themselves in a balcony' to witness Wright going to Tyburn: Kn., V, p. 46, VII, p. 456. For the preservation of a relic from the execution, 'part of the halter', among the possessions of Anthony Englefield (of White Knights, near Reading; d.1711)—it was probably given to him by the marquis— see ABSJ, CP (Peter Wright): a note concerning this relic attested by Charles Eyston of East Hendred (to whom it was passed by Englefield's son Henry); Eyston, as we saw, was one of John Knaresborough's contacts for the gathering of martyr materials; see pp. 15, 15–16 n.35 above. In and after July 1651, Winchester was one of the Catholic royalists who were hit with sequestrations: Kn., V, pp. 96f, VI, p. 181 (based on Palmer, *The Catholique Apology*, pp. 13–14, and the updated 1674 edition); Firth and Rait, *Acts and Ordinances of the Interregnum*, II, pp. 520–45 ('An Act for the Sale of Several Lands...'); see also Kn., V, pp. 132–73, VI, pp. 181–3, VII, p. 452; Firth and Rait, *Acts and Ordinances of the Interregnum*, II, pp. 623–52 ('An Additional Act for Sale of Several Lands...').

[202] *A Perfect Diurnall or Some Passages and Proceedings of, and in Relation to, the Armies ....From Monday May 19. To Monday May 26. 1651* (1651), p. 1054; *The Weekly Intelligencer of the Common-Wealth ....From Tuesday, May 13. to Tuesday, May 20. 1651* (1651), sig. X4ᵛ; *A Perfect Account of the Daily Intelligence ....From Wednesday May 14. to Wednesday May, the 21. 1651* (1651), p. 150.

[203] Foley, *RSJ*, II, pp. 547–8; *ODNB*, sub Tichborne, Robert (article by K. Lindley). The other London sheriff in 1651, Richard Chiverton, may have been similarly minded.

534 CATHOLICS AND TREASON

For Blackloists the event was absolutely incompatible with what they took to be the prevailing temper of the new regime. John Austin reacted with horror to the 'scurvy news...of one Wright, a Jesuit being drawn to Tyburn as a traitor upon a hurdle for his religion'. This was utterly out of step with the 'moderation of the present authority, as having never spilt one drop of blood for religion'. This 'killing has broken quite in pieces all our principles', that is, if we 'fought all this while' against coercion in religion. The trial itself was disturbing. There was only one witness and he 'in open sessions' exhibited 'a particular pique and quarrel towards' Wright. These were 'ungospellary proceedings'. A 'nimble-witted man' remarked on 'the very day of the priest's execution' that 'we are come to this' bizarre 'pass', that is, that 'we can fight against the covenant for reformation of the Kirk, sequester men for recusants...make a close peace with Spain and openly hang up Jesuits'. The fictional Church of England man in Austin's work concluded that 'if any power disaffected to godliness should gain authority over us...then all the precious saints and dearest servants of the Lord may be hanged, drawn and quartered by law, and yet at the same time our executioners may profess...liberty of conscience'.[204]

If Wright's arrest was forced through by those with presbyterian loyalties, and this, of course, is only speculation, then the identification of a presbyterian plot at exactly this point, in spring 1651, and particularly the execution later, on 22 August, of the presbyterian cleric Christopher Love may have been read by the public in the context of the proceedings against Wright, even if there was no for-mal connection between the two cases. Love was arrested on 2 May, only seven-teen days before Wright was executed. (Wright had been detained on 2 February 1651, before the taking in March of the royalist agent Thomas Coke revealed the extent of the presbyterian plotting which involved Love.)[205]

By July 1653, however, the episcopal chapter of the secular clergy concluded that it was safe enough to convene a general assembly of their priests in London.[206] This is not to say that there was some public protectoral agenda for anything like tolerance. Another ordinance, of 19 January 1654, declared that all the penal laws against adherents of the 'Romish religion' 'should not be repealed, but stand'. But there was still, in practice, no regular mechanism in operation to detect popish recusants.[207] Six months later, Cromwell was unwilling to go along with the exe-cution of the London priest John Southworth despite the exposure of a recent royalist assassination conspiracy.[208] In his *Memoirs*, as he dealt with Southworth's

[204] Birchley [Austin], *The Christian Moderator*, pp. 24–5.
[205] *ODNB, sub* Love, Christopher (article by E. Vernon); *ODNB, sub* Wright, Peter (article by T. Cooper, rev. G. Holt); Foley, *RSJ*, II, pp. 506–64; Collins, *Allegiance*, pp. 133, 155.
[206] Anstr., II, p. 307. This was in spite of a parliamentary ordinance of 5 January 1653 ordering Catholic clergy into exile: Kn., V, pp. 111–15.
[207] Firth and Rait, *Acts and Ordinances of the Interregnum*, II, p. 834. I owe this point to Katherine Lazo.
[208] J. Coffey, *Persecution and Toleration in Protestant England 1558–1689* (2000), pp. 157–8; Thackray, 'Zion Undermined', p. 34. Southworth was arrested by 'Colonel Worsley', i.e. the future major-general Charles Worsley, who had commanded the troops which dispersed the Rump

BACK TO THE FUTURE 535

case, Challoner referred to and quoted from William Penn's *A Letter from a Gentleman in the City to a Gentleman in the Country, about the Odiousness of Persecution*. Penn's work was published in 1687 though it was evidently written before 1678. (Knaresborough had used it as well.) Penn wrote that 'it clearly appeared that those who were' Southworth's 'judges did their utmost to preserve his life and to prevent the execution against him of those laws upon which he stood indicted. For they did, for many hours, suspend the recording of his confession, making it their endeavour to prevail with him to plead "not guilty" to the indictment. They pressed him to this in the public court, assuring him that, if he would so plead, his life should be safe, and that they had no evidence which could prove him to be a priest.' But Southworth would not do this, at least in the formal sense of pleading to the indictment, although he did allege himself to be not guilty of treason. He was hanged on 28 June 1654.[209] (See Figure 15.3.)

The Venetian diplomat Lorenzo Paulucci insisted on 29 June/9 July that it was the so-called Gerard conspiracy which had led to the prosecution. The 'high court of justice' had 'opened its sittings for the trial' of the accused on 3 June. The 'same cause' had 'redoubled the persecution of the Catholics', including commissions to the 'triers' to put the Elizabethan statutes into effect; and thus it was that Southworth had been arrested, tried, sentenced, and executed on 28 June. Cromwell, though professing horror at 'violence in matters of religion' and although he was 'in favour of liberty of conscience for all', refused to intervene.[210] Southworth, as we saw in the previous chapter, was a high-profile London cleric. He was known to have been at one time in the circle of George Con and he had also been a friend of George Leyburn, one of Henrietta Maria's clerical clients.[211] There is no evidence that Southworth had any connections either with the alleged

Parliament in April 1653: Challoner, *MMP*, p. 507; *ODNB*, *sub* Worsley, Charles (article by C. Durston); E. E. Reynolds, *John Southworth: Priest and Martyr* (1962), p. 63.

[209] Challoner, *MMP*, pp. 507–9; William Penn, *A Letter from a Gentleman in the City to a Gentleman in the Country, about the Odiousness of Persecution* (1687), pp. 27–8. Southworth was here indicted again (he had been prosecuted already in the pre-civil-war period): Reynolds, *John Southworth*, pp. 64–7. Challoner incorporates a version of Southworth's speech at Tyburn (for which see AAW, A XXX, no. 182, pp. 639–41; Kn., V, pp. 189–96) which is significantly different from the version at AAW, A XXX, no. 59, pp. 185–7 (see p. 536 below); AAW, A XXX., no. 182, pp. 635–7; AAW, OB III/ii, no. 181; *The Last Speech and Confession of Mr John Southworth...June 28. 1654...* (1679); Challoner, *MMP*, pp. 508–9. E. E. Reynolds counted 'five contemporary manuscript versions' of Southworth's last words: Reynolds, *John Southworth*, pp. 69–70, 72–3. Knaresborough's working papers record that his copy of Southworth's speech was sent to him by one Thomas Worthington, 'taken out of a copy writ in my father Thomas Worthington's hand': Kn., VII, unpaginated section. See also A. Marotti, 'Manuscript Transmission and the Catholic Martyrdom Account', in A. Marotti, *Religious Ideology and Cultural Fantasy: Catholic and Anti-Catholic Discourses in Early Modern England* (Notre Dame, 2005), pp. 92–3.

[210] *CSPV 1653–4*, pp. 233–4; D. Underdown, *Royalist Conspiracy in England 1649–1660* (1960), pp. 100–2.

[211] For the story (not, in the end, used by Challoner) that, before his final arrest, Southworth asked Leyburn that he should be allowed to return to Douai, see Kn., VII, p. 272 (which account Knaresborough had from the priest Augustine Smithson in a letter of 10 August 1706, and he from 'Dr Leyburn's own mouth'); Challoner had the same narrative from Edward Paston, president of Douai College (d.1714): ABPFC, fo. 28[r]; Anstr., II, pp. 307–8; Anstr., III, p. 160.

Figure 15.3 The shrine of John Southworth, d.1654, in Westminster Cathedral (reproduced with the permission of the cardinal-archbishop of Westminster).

conspirators (John Gerard was beheaded on Tower Hill on 10 July) or, as such, with the Blackloist circle. However, in his execution speech, Southworth explicitly said not only that 'I never acted nor thought any hurt against the present protector' but also that 'it has pleased God to take the sword out of the hands of the king and put it in the protector's; let him remember that he is to administer justice indifferently, and without exception of persons; for there is no exception of persons before God, whom he ought to resemble'. Furthermore, 'if any Catholic work against the government now established, let him suffer; but why should those that are guiltless, unless conscience be a guilt, be made partakers in a promiscuous punishment with the greatest malefactors?'[212] In another, and more pointed, version of Southworth's words, he says that 'the lord protector has fought long for the liberty of the subject and, having obtained many victories, the people were made' to 'believe there should be a general liberty of conscience and that no man's life should be taken away for matters of religion'. The extent to which some inside the regime did not want the prosecution can perhaps be gauged from the decision not to hang what was left of Southworth in prominent places in London.[213] All of this took place in the context of the preparations for the first protectorate parliament, which eventually met in September 1654.[214]

---

[212] Challoner, *MMP*, p. 509; Kn., V, pp. 189–95.

[213] AAW, A XXX, no. 59, p. 186; for those executed with Southworth, see AVCAU, Liber 1577 (Anstruther Martyrs File): *CSPV 1653–4*, p. 233. Southworth's remains were taken out of the country to be interred at the English College at Douai; and here, as George Leyburn reported to Cardinal Francesco Barberini on 5/15 September 1655, the people of Douai were already flocking to Southworth's tomb; see AVCAU, Liber 1577 (Anstruther Martyrs File): PRO, PRO 31/9/131, fo. 99^r; AAW, A XXXI, no. 71, pp. 335–6; Reynolds, *John Southworth*, ch. 9; Anstr., II, p. 307.

[214] I. Roots, *The Great Rebellion 1642–1660* (1966), p. 184.

BACK TO THE FUTURE 537

No Catholic martyrologist really had any incentive to say that the 1650s were tolerant in the true sense of the word. Catholics were harassed this way and that.[215] The usual suspects still pointed to popery as a danger to the commonwealth. But when someone such as William Prynne could argue that Quakerism was a vehicle for popish infiltration, many of the earlier certainties about contemporary religious identity had changed.[216]

It is in this context that we can construe the much-delayed attempt in 1656–7, after the protectorate's declaration of war against Spain, to bring in new recusancy legislation and the way that this became entangled with the parliamentary attempt to prosecute the Quaker radical James Nayler.[217] What we have here is the continuation of the almost quotidian claims before the civil war about the equivalences between 'Jesuits' and 'puritans'. The second session of the second protectorate parliament, which met in January 1658, was prefaced with the arrest of Catholic clergy. The Venetian ambassador at Rome noted that the laws against Catholics were now being enforced with 'the utmost severity', but no executions followed.[218]

Of course, Cromwellian government was soon to terminate and the monarchy would return. The expectations of those who still thought in terms of a tolerated Catholic fraction of the national Church would also change. From a reading of the work of John Knaresborough and Richard Challoner, one might still think that the travails of the Catholic community all through the mid-seventeenth century and into the popish plot of the later Restoration period were identical to the persecutions of the 1580s and 1590s. In the later 1670s there was, indeed, again something that looked very like a savage persecution, with corrupt officialdom, judicial bias, revolting physical cruelty, and the victims' pious and dignified gallows speeches. But the circumstances in which these new attacks on the community took place were different even from those of the 1650s.

---

[215] Challoner, *MMP*, pp. 491 f.

[216] William Prynne, *The Quakers Unmasked*...(1655), pp. 2, 5; see also Thackray, 'Zion Undermined', pp. 38–9. For Alexandra Tompkins's brilliant summary of the ebb and flow of the moments in the period 1647–63 when the Catholic community sensed that tolerance/toleration might be a possibility, in particular during 1655 after the demise of Pope Innocent X and Richard Smith and the cementing in October of the Anglo-French treaty, see Tompkins, ECI, p. 264.

[217] I owe this point to Katherine Lazo—it constitutes a major section of her dissertation, ' "Rigour upon Men's Consciences": National Identity, Religion, and English Catholics during the Interregnum' (PhD, Vanderbilt, 2018). See also *ODNB*, *sub* Nayler, James (article by L. Damrosch); Tompkins, ECI, pp. 154–60; Loomie, 'Alonso de Cárdenas', p. 307; A. J. Loomie, 'London's Spanish Chapel before and after the Civil War', *RH* 18 (1987), pp. 402–17, at p. 414.

[218] Tompkins, ECI, p. 162, citing PRO, SP 78/114, fo. 10ᵛ; *CSPV 1657–9*, pp. 144, 160.

16

The Restoration and the Popish Plot

The Historiography of Restoration Catholicism

We now move into the Restoration period.[1] From the return of Charles II until the later 1670s there were no executions of Catholics under the Elizabethan treason statutes. For martyrological purposes most of the Restoration period is therefore something of a blank. But contemporaries speculated with as much vehemence as before about the danger from popery, even while the court, after 1660, tried to establish a working association with Rome, including a consensus on whom Rome might appoint as clerical superiors within the British Isles, but with no intention of allowing a full episcopal hierarchy, at least in England and Scotland.[2] To start with, let me sum up, if I can, the burden of the historiography here, and the broader context for it. The Restoration period has been subjected to its own kind of revisionism. Put simply, the claim has been that the difficulties which had led to the civil war were sorted out at or shortly after the return of Charles II. Restoration popery was a problem only in that it was exacerbated by the periodic folly of the Stuart court. Charles II could keep making blunders but he tended to do that sequentially. His brother, James, duke of York, had a unique talent for multiple follies all at the same time. This, it should be said, is not all that far away from what I remember having to learn when doing A-level history. It is, though phrased with far more sophistication, also the thrust of the work of my former colleague John Miller.[3] John Kenyon's influential account of Restoration

[1] For recent work on Catholicism in the Restoration, see esp. D. Magliocco, 'Samuel Pepys, the Restoration Public and the Politics of Publicity' (PhD, London, 2014); G. Glickman, 'Christian Reunion, the Anglo-French Alliance and the English Catholic Imagination 1660–1672', *English Historical Review* 128 (2013), pp. 263–91; the various publications of Adam Morton, and notably his 'Popery, Politics and Play: Visual Culture in Succession Crisis England', *Seventeenth Century* 31 (2016), pp. 411–49; P. Hinds, *'The Horrid Popish Plot': Sir Roger L'Estrange and the Circulation of Political Discourse in Late Seventeenth-Century London* (2010); Tompkins, ECI.

[2] J. Miller, *Popery and Politics in England 1660–1688* (Cambridge, 1973), pp. 44–8. Bossy describes an anti-Blackloist reaction inside the Catholic community, led and driven on by a coalition of 'the gentry, the monarchy, the papacy and the religious orders': Bossy, *ECC*, p. 68. See also S. Tutino, 'The Catholic Church and the English Civil War: The Case of Thomas White', *JEH* 58 (2007), pp. 232–55, esp. at pp. 248–54; S. Tutino, *Thomas White and the Blackloists: Between Politics and Theology during the English Civil War* (Aldershot, 2008), ch. 6. For the arguments in the Catholic secular clergy chapter, see Tompkins, ECI, pp. 227 f. For the Catholic community's approaches to the Restoration regime, in 1661–2, seeking toleration/toleration, see Tompkins, ECI, p. 237 f.

[3] Miller, *Popery*; M. Knights, *Politics and Opinion in Crisis, 1678–81* (Cambridge, 2004), p. 13. Despite the divergence of some of my views from Professor Miller's, I have the utmost respect for his work and it is not inapposite to remark here as well that one could not possibly have had a better departmental colleague.

Catholics and Treason: Martyrology, Memory, and Politics in the Post-Reformation. Michael Questier, Oxford University Press. © Michael Questier 2022. DOI: 10.1093/oso/9780192847027.003.0016

THE RESTORATION AND THE POPISH PLOT 539

anti-popery and the Popish Plot is fully compatible with Professor Miller's narrative.[4]

Catholics got caught up in the new round of Popish Plot fury because, the line is, the regime had indeed flirted with 'popery' and because of the duke of York's lack of political acumen.[5] Here the conservative but essentially apolitical Catholic community ('centred on the households of the Catholic peers and gentlemen who alone could afford to maintain the priests who kept the old religion alive') was a direct extrapolation from the neutralist version of that community which allegedly decided not to get involved in politics during the civil war, and barely did so during the Restoration, while 'some who did, like the earl of Bristol, probably did the Catholics more harm than good'. Most Catholics knew enough to accept their 'exclusion from national life'. Anything else was 'likely to excite fresh persecution'. Catholics who trespassed beyond the limits of the politically sayable were simply unwise.[6] But the logic of anti-popery ran in two different directions. Some commentators, such as William Prynne and Richard Baxter, still insisted that the civil war had been the outcome of a popish plot. Others, by contrast, were content to point to anti-popery as itself a vehicle for presbyterian conspiracy.[7]

A full-scale reconstruction of the politics of anti-popery leading into the Popish Plot allegations of the later 1670s is something that is quite beyond the scope of this volume. One might, however, offer a few brief reflections on this subject as a context for the final and very substantial section of Bishop Challoner's work, which deals with the Popish Plot agitation and trials from 1678 to 1681.[8] First, the restoration of the monarchy not unpredictably witnessed a set of manoeuvres by, among others, Catholics for tolerance which were similar enough to what had happened in 1603-4. Once again, different Catholic interest groups negotiated with the regime for a degree of freedom from the law. Charles II's declaration of indulgence of 1662, rejected by parliament early in 1663, was in some sense not unlike James I's tentative moves towards tolerance in mid-1603 which, as we saw, had also had to be withdrawn, even though the 1662 declaration was specifically about places of worship.[9] When parliament met in early 1663, there was a Commons bill against the growth of popery and a royal proclamation against Catholic clergy, on which basis it was easier for the bill to vanish in the

---

[4] Kenyon, *PP*, ch. 1.

[5] For the political significance of James's conversion to Rome, see Kenyon, *PP*, p. 37 (pointing out that 'James was never the leader of the Catholic community in England, even after his accession to the throne in 1685'). See also S. Sowerby, *Making Toleration: The Repealers and the Glorious Revolution* (2013); S. Pincus, *1688: The First Modern Revolution* (2009), esp. chs 5-7.

[6] Miller, *Popery*, pp. 1, 8, 12-13, 14, 27 and ch. 1 *passim*. Professor Miller shows that the ad hockery of the enforcement, after the Restoration, of the law which sought to define religious conformity was very similar to the ramshackle implementation of recusancy penalties before 1640: ibid., pp. 58-63.

[7] Ibid., pp. 86-7.   [8] Challoner, *MMP*, pp. 510-83.

[9] See pp. 334-43 above; Tompkins, ECI, pp. 254-5; P.A. Richardson, 'Serial Struggles: English Catholics and their Periodicals, 1648-1844' (PhD, Durham, 2003), pp. 21-2.

540 CATHOLICS AND TREASON

Lords, whereas in 1604, after a proclamation against Catholics, the anti-popery legislation succeeded.[10] The earl of Clarendon in 1663 made exactly the same claim as James I had made in 1604, and at other times, that is to say, that the law as it stood was sufficient.[11] All through the 1660s, and particularly in 1665 and 1668, according to Professor Miller, the regime considered using prerogative authority to release Catholics from the full effects of the law. This provoked a fierce reaction at various points—notably in response to the Great Fire, a reaction which replicated the anti-popery scares in 1640–1 described by Professor Clifton.[12] The fire spawned not just rumours that it was started by the French but also that the duke of York had prevented a full investigation of it. (The memory of the fire was revived in 1679.)[13] The year 1667 saw exactly the kind of equal-and-opposite competing popery/puritanism conspiracy theories which had populated so much of the political discourse of the later sixteenth century and which continued to circulate down to the eighteenth. Hence the regime's efforts to appropriate the anti-popish high ground in the period immediately before parliament met in October 1668, when another anti-popery bill failed.[14]

This period saw restatements of the Catholic boast that royalists and Catholics were out of the same stable—and, moreover, that those who had died fighting for the king in the civil wars were, in effect, martyrs. This was meant to refute, of course, those who said that there had been a diabolical compact between papists and the fanatics who had in the late 1640s destroyed the monarchy. This declaration of Catholic loyalism was made publicly by, *inter alia*, the Catholic Roger Palmer, Lord Castlemaine, in his *Humble Apology*, and in turn was vehemently denied by the future bishop William Lloyd.[15] Castlemaine addressed 'all the royalists that suffered for his Majesty' and denied that Catholics were responsible for the civil strife of the 1640s—'all are to remember who are the prime raisers of the

---

[10] See esp. Miller, *Popery*, ch. 5, pp. 101 f.   [11] Ibid., p. 101.
[12] Ibid., pp. 101–5; Kenyon, *PP*, pp. 13–15; R. Clifton, 'The Fear of Catholics in England 1637 to 1645. Principally from Central Sources' (DPhil, Oxford, 1967).
[13] Miller, *Popery*, pp. 103–5, citing *London's Flames...*(1679); for Titus Oates's claims about Catholic responsibility for the fire, see *The Discovery of the Popish Plot, Being the Several Examinations of Titus Oates...*(1679), p. 42 and *passim*; see also *A Memorial of the Late and Present Popish Plots...*(1680), p. 1. For anti-popery and the 1666 fire more generally, see Hinds, 'The Horrid Popish Plot', ch. 10.
[14] Miller, *Popery*, pp. 105–6; P. Lake, '"The Monarchical Republic of Elizabeth I" Revisited (by its Victims) as a Conspiracy', in B. Coward and J. Swann (eds), *Conspiracies and Conspiracy Theory in Early Modern Europe* (Aldershot, 2004), pp. 87–111, esp. at p. 108.
[15] Miller, *Popery*, p. 124; Roger Palmer, earl of Castlemaine, *To all the Royalists...The Humble Apology of the English Catholicks* (1666; Clancy, *ECB*, no. 181); William Lloyd, *The Late Apology in behalf of the Papists Re-printed and Answered in behalf of the Royalists* (1667). For Castlemaine's response, see Roger Palmer, *A Reply to the Answer of the Catholique Apology...*(n.p. [London?], 1668 [Wing C 1246]). Castlemaine, like other Catholics, attacked Thomas White in 1667 as an enemy of monarchy: B. Southgate, '"That Damned Book": *The Grounds of Obedience and Government* (1655), and the Downfall of Thomas White', *RH* 17 (1985), pp. 238–53, at p. 250; Roger Palmer, *The Catholique Apology...*(3rd edition, 1674; Clancy, *ECB*, no. 175), in the composition of which, as with other works, Castlemaine was probably assisted by the priest Robert Pugh.

THE RESTORATION AND THE POPISH PLOT 541

storm and how, through our sides, they would wound both the king and you; for though their hatred to us ourselves', that is, Catholics, 'is great, yet the enmity out of all measure increases, because we have been yours', royalist in heart, 'and so shall continue, even in the fiery day of trial'. If this argument was not strong enough, 'we must conjure you by the sight of this bloody catalogue, which contains the names of your murdered friends and relations who, in the heat of battle, perchance saved many of your lives, even with the joyful loss of their own'. There followed a list of those, all Catholics of some kind, who had sustained injury or death in the fighting. The list was headed by the earl of Caernarvon, 'slain at Newbury, [at the] first battle'.[16] Castlemaine's work was a conscious imitation of the format of the 1660 broadside pamphlet entitled *The Royal Martyrs*.[17]

In reply, Lloyd reprised the line that the civil wars were the product of popish conspiracy. He also reflected on the execution of the penal law against Catholics. The rebellion had started 'in Scotland where the design of it was first laid by Cardinal Richelieu, his Majesty's irreconcilable enemy'. (This had been the burden of the Habernfeld Plot allegations.) Furthermore, it 'broke out in Ireland where it was blest with his Holiness's letters and assisted by his nuncio'. Finally, in England, Catholics did enough 'to unsettle the people and gave them needless occasions of jealousy, which the vigilant fanatics made use of to bring us all into war and

[16] Palmer, *To all the Royalists*, pp. 9–13; *ODNB*, sub Palmer, Roger (article by R. Beddard). This register of those who lost their lives or were injured was followed by the 'names of such Catholics whose estates (both real and personal) were sold, in pursuance of an act made by the Rump, July 16, 1651, for their pretended delinquency, that is for adhering to their king' and of 'other Catholics whose estates were sold by an additional Rump act made August 4, 1662 [*sic* for 1652]', and by a further act of 18 November 1652; see Palmer, *To all the Royalists*, pp. 13–14; cf. AAW, B 28, no. 15, pp. 411–15 ('A catalogue of the lords, knights and gentlemen (of the Catholic religion) that were slain in the late war, in defence of their king and country. Faithfully transcribed from a Catholic Almanac for 1686', i.e. the names in Thomas Blount, *Kalendarium Catholicum for the Year 1686* (1686), sigs B5ʳ–Cᵛ, a work first published at the end of 1660), a virtually identical list to that which is printed in Palmer, *To all the Royalists*, pp. 9–13; for Blount's publication of his *Catalogue* in 1660, and for other editions of Blount's work, see Clancy, *ECB*, nos 106, 107, 109, 150, 183 and Wing 1321A; T. Bongaerts (ed.), *The Correspondence of Thomas Blount (1618-1679)*...(Amsterdam, 1978), pp. 5–6, 33–4; Richardson, 'Serial Struggles', pp. 19–21; see also G. Glickman, *The English Catholic Community, 1688-1745: Politics, Culture and Ideology* (Woodbridge, 2009), p. 124. Paul Richardson notes that Blount's catalogue was 'first circulated' on 29 May 1660, i.e. the same day that Charles II entered London: Richardson, 'Serial Struggles', p. 19. Perhaps bizarrely, Blount was, it seems, part of the Blackloist circle: ibid., pp. 21, 23. For Knaresborough's lists, evidently based on Blount and/or Palmer, but with some additional names, see Kn., VI, pp. 175–83 and, with variations, pp. 201–10; *ODNB*, sub Blount, Thomas (article by I. Mortimer), noting Blount's ultra-Catholic background.

[17] *The Royal Martyrs: Or, a List of the Lords, Knights, Officers, and Gentlemen, that were Slain (by the Rebels) in the late Wars, in Defence of their King and Country. As also of Those Executed by their High Courts of (In)-justice, or Law Martial*...(1660), p. 1. See also Redmond Caron, *A Vindication of the Roman Catholicks of the English Nation*...(1660); Tompkins, *ECI*, pp. 84–6. On 13 November 1706, the priest Thomas Roydon congratulated Knaresborough on the zeal with which he was pursuing his work and hoped that he would 'include' in his 'historical collections those who have suffered for their loyalty or died in the field for the late king Charles the first and his children. I am told my Lord Clarendon is very short in relating the performances of Catholics.' It would be 'charity to do justice to them who suffered for justice'. It would be 'a very ornamental part of your collections' and would 'answer all reproaches of popish treason with experimental convictions of unchangeable fidelity': Kn., VI, unpaginated section.

542 CATHOLICS AND TREASON

confusion'. Admittedly it was not Catholic separatists who were actually fighting against the king. But 'both in England and Scotland, the' rebels' 'special tools...were borrowed out of your shops', in other words from Catholic ideologues such as Martinus Becanus. In case anyone thought that Catholics in Ireland had been loyal, people should remember that they had 'employed iron and steel' against the king. If it was the 'fanatics' who had actually killed the king, this was 'agreed to in the councils of your clergy'. So no one could confidently identify Catholics with royalism. Some Catholics 'did the king very eminent service', but 'so did the Protestants too'. It was no argument to say that Catholics deserved toleration: it was not 'reasonable that, to requite particular persons for their service, we should abandon those laws which may secure the public against as great a danger'. In this context, Lloyd recalled the distinctly unroyalist rhetoric of John Austin. The protestations of the Blackloists were gold dust for those who wanted to refute the alleged connections made between royalism, Catholicism, and martyrdom. 'In all those weak efforts of gasping loyalty...you complied and flattered and gave sugared words to the rebels then as you do to the royalists now', wrote Lloyd, citing liberally from Austin's published oeuvre, without mentioning that the Blackloists were not necessarily representative of majority Catholic thought. In any case, life was not exactly unbearable for Catholics after 1660. It was 'Jesuitical ingenuity' to 'slight those favours' that Catholics had received and to complain about 'those hardships' that they 'had not'. Of 'the laws you complain hideously'; and 'yet those very laws you complain of, you never knew [them] executed in your life'. They were 'enacted', in any case, for 'this cause, to guard the lives of our princes against your traitorous practices'.[18]

This allowed Lloyd to rehearse the 'politics-and-religion' history of the post-Reformation period. In 'the first ten years' of Elizabeth's reign, 'which was twice as long as Queen Mary's reign, though it was fresh in memory what the papists had done', 'not one' of those papists 'suffered death', that is, not until the Northern Rebellion, which was 'raised against' Elizabeth 'only upon the account of her religion'. It was no excuse to say that 'it was a very hard question whether the right of the crown lay in her or in the queen of Scots, for that many thought Queen Elizabeth illegitimate'. The reality was that 'the whole kingdom received' Elizabeth 'and owned her as queen more generally and freely than ever they did Queen Mary'. The subsequent stop–go Catholic approach to the rights of the House of Stuart in England, liberally documented by Lloyd with references to the works of Robert Persons and the appellants, demonstrated what hypocrites and traitors Catholics had been.[19] How traitorous such people were could be shown by reference to the number who really knew in advance about the Gunpowder Plot, far more than the few who were indicted and executed for it. Also, let none forget

---

[18] Lloyd, *The Late Apology*, pp. 11–14, 22; Tompkins, ECI, pp. 87–8.
[19] Lloyd, *The Late Apology*, pp. 23–30.

THE RESTORATION AND THE POPISH PLOT   543

that 'many of you had a high veneration for some of those wretches that were deeply engaged in it' and 'what a coil here was about the miracle of Father Garnet's straw? And perhaps you have seen his picture, and Gerard's too, among the martyrs of your Society'. In this context, the language of martyrdom and suffering was nonsense, that is, as long as Catholics held to their odious principles—'we can apprehend no assurance of you by your sufferings'.[20] Yes, indeed, back in the early 1640s some Catholics had come to grief, but it was 'the policy of the rebels in the beginning of the late war to harass the papists in all parts of the kingdom'. One motive for this was the desire 'to make his Majesty odious, for the papists being his subjects and having none but him to fly to, it was certain he would do what he could to protect them'. This 'would make many zealous people believe that what the rebels pretended was true, viz. that his Majesty was a friend to popery'. But this still did not mean that Catholics who sacrificed their lives were martyrs. The earl of Caernarvon, declared Lloyd, was 'too negligent of his religion' and, 'even in his extremities, he refused a priest of yours and ordered the chaplain of his regiment to pray with him'. Lloyd had no time for 'this liberty of stealing martyrs'.[21]

The court opted, however, for a crackdown on Protestant dissent. There was a new Conventicles act in 1670. The crisis of 1672 came out of the court's Francophile foreign policy and hostility to the Dutch. That crisis was made worse by the Catholic issue even if, as Professor Miller judges, interpretations of Charles's courses here as a popish and absolutist conspiracy are unfounded—although aspects of the rejigging of the government of Scotland under Lauderdale and of Ireland (with the, admittedly short-term, replacement of the earl of Ormond by Lord Berkeley as lord lieutenant) might well have looked ominous.[22] In the context of the failure of the 1672 declaration of indulgence, the Test Act of 1673 and the difficulties associated with the court's attempt to shadow Louis XIV, the real issue was now the right of succession of the duke of York. The number of convictions of recusant Catholics in the shires rose in 1673–4.[23] The Test Act followed the line of thought set out by Thomas Digges in the mid-Elizabethan period. Here an oath was used in order to exclude those who were suspect and to close down the spaces available for displays even of partial nonconformity. One imagines that Digges would have viewed with satisfaction the driving of the duke of York from public office after 1673.[24]

---

[20] Ibid., pp. 34–5.   [21] Ibid., pp. 44, 45.

[22] Miller, *Popery*, pp. 106–7, 120 and ch. 6 (pp. 108 f.), *passim*; Knights, *Politics*, pp. 17–18. For the argument that James was not a subservient client of Louis XIV, see Miller, *Popery*, p. 120, citing J. R. Jones, *The Revolution of 1688 in England* (1972), pp. 176–87.

[23] Miller, *Popery*, ch. 7. For the anti-popery of the 1670s, see also Bongaerts, *The Correspondence of Thomas Blount*, pp. 11–12.

[24] Miller, *Popery*, pp. 55–6; for Thomas Digges, see *Humble Motives for Association to Maintain Religion Established. Published as an Antidote against the Pestilent Treatises of Secular Priests* (1601); P. Lake and M. Questier, 'Thomas Digges, Robert Parsons, Sir Francis Hastings, and the Politics of Regime Change in Elizabethan England', *HJ* 61 (2018), pp. 1–27. For the public linking of the

544   CATHOLICS AND TREASON

These concerns were partly addressed by Thomas Osborne, earl of Danby's, hard-line centrism during the mid- and later 1670s. Faced with Danby's version of the *via media*, the duke of York started to take seriously the approaches made to him by dissenters. The attempts by Charles to row back on tolerance for Catholics were trumped by the public knowledge of the duke of York's conversion, about which Danby could in the end do little. The pressure on Charles to divorce escalated while James compounded the succession problem by marrying the Catholic Mary of Modena. In 1675, James contemplated a political alliance with his future mortal enemy, Anthony Ashley Cooper, earl of Shaftesbury, or at least there were rumours to this effect—though evidently it came to nothing in the face of Anglican dominance in the 1675 parliamentary session. Danby subsequently introduced a parliamentary bill to govern the prospect of James's accession as an overt Catholic, that is, to prevent James exercising authority in ecclesiastical matters.[25] Professor Kenyon sees the bill of March 1677, which would have removed ecclesiastical patronage from James when he was king, as in effect directly providing for the accession of a Catholic.[26]

This period, however, also saw Danby working with the future exclusionist William Lloyd on publication of the regime's plans to suppress what it took to be popery.[27] James's own personal dynastic strategy could be seen as compatible with, perhaps even as an imitation of, that of his grandfather James I in the mid-1610s. In November 1677 the duke of York's daughter, Mary, in an impeccably Protestant move, married her cousin William of Orange, that is, while Mary of Modena was about to produce an heir, who unfortunately did not survive—though it was this, apparently, which persuaded Louis XIV to make public in late 1678 the extent to which Charles had been financially in the pocket of the French court.[28] In 1677–8 James came round to a much more overtly royalist

republican/exclusion project of the mid-1580s and the attempt to exclude James, duke of York, see, e.g., *The Instrument; or Writing of Association: That the True Protestants of England Entred into, in the Reign of Queen Elizabeth...* (1679); *The Act of Parliament of the 27th. of Queen Elizabeth...* (1680); see also Knights, *Politics*, p. 102 and *passim*.

[25] Miller, *Popery*, pp. 136–7, 139, 141–2, 143–5; for Danby's centrism, see ibid., pp. 134 f. Danby in later 1678 tried to exploit the new eruption of anti-popish rhetoric: Knights, *Politics*, p. 25. In 1680 Lord Stafford offered to reveal details of negotiations in 1675 between the duke and Shaftesbury: Kenyon, *PP*, p. 46. For Shaftesbury, see K. H. D. Haley, *The First Earl of Shaftesbury* (Oxford, 1968), esp. chs 21 f.; Hinds, 'The Horrid Popish Plot', ch. 9.

[26] Kenyon, *PP*, p. 24; Richardson, 'Serial Struggles', p. 25.

[27] Miller, *Popery*, p. 146, citing William Lloyd, *Considerations touching the True Way to Suppress Popery...* (1677).

[28] Kenyon, *PP*, p. 23; J. Scott, 'England's Troubles: Exhuming the Popish Plot', in T. Harris, P. Seaward, and M. Goldie (eds), *The Politics of Religion in Restoration England* (Oxford, 1990), pp. 107–31, at p. 117; cf. T. Harris, 'Introduction: Revising the Restoration', in Harris, Seaward, and Goldie, *Politics of Religion*, pp. 1–28, at p. 4. In December 1678, with French assistance, the former ambassador Ralph Montagu disclosed the dealing between Danby and the French court: Knights, *Politics*, pp. 19, 27; *ODNB*, *sub* Montagu, Ralph (article by E. C. Metzger); Haley, *Shaftesbury*, pp. 487–91, 494–6.

THE RESTORATION AND THE POPISH PLOT   545

interpretation of monarchical authority.[29] It was at this point, ironically, that Danby was himself under attack as an evil counsellor, responsible for bringing in arbitrary government, more identifiable according to Marvell with popery even than James and his, by now, open Catholicism.[30]

How does this inform and help to explain the turmoil of the Popish Plot agitation of the later 1670s? One answer is that, for more contemporary observers than for some modern historians, James's brand of Catholicism may have looked politically credible, calculated, and distinctly threatening. Most people in public life who have an irrepressible public-relations death wish, as James is often alleged to have had, are not usually regarded as a threat to anyone and often survive for a lot longer than those who are in some political sense actually more competent.

It is, however, one of the ironies of Professor Miller's PhD and first full-length publication on Restoration anti-popery (that is, by a scholar who has subsequently been associated with a sustained trashing of the political reputation of the duke of York) that his wonderfully accessible account of anti-popery in that period suggests that, in the mid-1670s, James was in fact one of the most practised and expertly manipulative of contemporary political operators, working out a way to square the circle of dissent in order to protect himself in the line of succession. This was allied to a quasi-Gallican expression of Catholicism and it was combined with a policy of alignment with the French court. Professor Miller does, of course, argue that James's sole purpose 'since his conversion...had been to advance his new religion and to protect the English Catholics'. I am inclined to wonder whether this was, on James's part, a product only of the zeal of a proselyte for his new co-religionists.[31] As we saw, for some time after his conversion to Rome, James had been prepared to contemplate something like a Protestant-centred foreign policy, though the quid pro quo had to be the cessation of active harassment of Catholics. March 1677 saw a Lords bill which would have established a licensed toleration of them, but it was rejected by the Commons.[32]

In other words, for all the consensus that the English Catholic community in the 1670s was much as it had been in, say, the 1570s or the 1630s, that is, that it was composed largely of the excluded and of those who were contented with their lot, though they were dwindling in number and ideologically inert, there were, as there had been so often in the past, claims that at least some Catholics did not see

---

[29] Miller, *Popery*, p. 147.

[30] Ibid., p. 148, citing Andrew Marvell, *An Account of the Growth of Popery and Arbitrary Government in England...* (1677), pp. 88, 100; Knights, *Politics*, pp. 17–19; Richardson, 'Serial Struggles', p. 25; A. Marotti, 'Plots, Atrocities, and Deliverances: The Anti-Catholic Construction of Protestant English History', in A. Marotti, *Religious Ideology and Cultural Fantasy: Catholic and Anti-Catholic Discourses in Early Modern England* (Notre Dame, 2005), pp. 160–9.

[31] Miller, *Popery*, ch. 10 and p. 197.

[32] Kenyon, *PP*, p. 23; Richardson, 'Serial Struggles', p. 25; A. G. Petti (ed.), *Recusant Documents from the Ellesmere Manuscripts* (CRS 60, 1968), pp. 263–76.

546   CATHOLICS AND TREASON

themselves thus. As John Evelyn wrote, 'the Roman Catholics were exceedingly bold and busy everywhere since the duke forbore to go any longer to chapel'.[33]

The Popish Plot 1678–1681

Then came the Popish Plot allegations made by Titus Oates, the seventeenth-century equivalent of the bent undercover investigative journalist, though Shaftesbury had made virtually identical accusations even in early 1674 and the earl of Carlisle had introduced a quasi-exclusion bill at that time.[34] It was easy enough for some contemporaries to state that this was the product merely of a toxic mixture of fear and mania, particularly when the consensus is, also, that the evidence offered against those who were accused was simply manufactured—utter nonsense, composed out of Oates's weird and malicious fictions. This was the line taken by the Jacobite martyrologist John Knaresborough and by Bishop Challoner. Challoner gives the final section of his martyrology the label 'Oates's Plot', and he makes virtually no mention of the duke of York.[35] But the exclusion business could not be kept separate from the prosecutions of Catholic clergy. The draft exclusion bill in the 1679 parliament related that the popish clergy had 'traitorously seduced James, duke of York...to the communion of the Church of Rome...and by his means and procurement have advanced the power and greatness of the French king to the manifest hazard of these kingdoms'. It took only the circulating stories of an assassination conspiracy against Charles in order to make the plot allegations credible.[36]

Faced with the violent contemporary response to Oates's tales, historians have tended either to concentrate on what the episode tells us about popular culture or have argued that it is comprehensible only in the context of international politics. The plot was believable because of the league between the British court and Louis XIV.[37] In the interpretation offered by Jonathan Scott, 'the crisis of 1678–81' had 'its root not in ignorance, or hysteria, but in well-informed public belief'. For

---

[33] Kenyon, *PP*, p. 49.

[34] Miller, *Popery*, pp. 133–4; Knights, *Politics*, esp. ch. 1 and p. 30; for Oates, see esp. Hinds, *'The Horrid Popish Plot'*, ch. 1. For Knights's discussion of the succession crisis and the alternatives to exclusion, see Knights, *Politics*, chs 2, 3. Knights argues that exclusion was just one of a number of expedients which were being considered in response to a much broader political crisis than the problem of the duke of York's religion. For contemporary comparison of the duke of York's case to that of Mary Stuart, see, e.g., *A Brief History of the Life of Mary Queen of Scots, and the Occasions that Brought Her, and Thomas Duke of Norfolk, to their Tragical Ends. Shewing the Hopes the Papists then had of a Popish Successor in England; and their Plots to Accomplish them...*(1681).

[35] Challoner, *MMP*, p. 510.

[36] *An Impartial Account of Divers Remarkable Proceedings the Last Sessions of Parliament relating to the Horrid Popish Plot...*(1679), pp. 20–1, 22; *ODNB*, sub James II and VII (article by W. Speck).

[37] Scott, 'England's Troubles'; Miller, *Popery*, p. 90. The stand-out exceptions here, of course, are Knights, *Politics*, and Hinds, *'The Horrid Popish Plot'*. For a genuinely novel approach to the culture of contemporary politics, see Morton, 'Popery, Politics, and Play'.

THE RESTORATION AND THE POPISH PLOT   547

Scott, the issue was not Oates's fantasies or even the duke of York but, rather, 'the policies of Charles II, in their European context, which left the nation feeling dangerously vulnerable'. Underlying everything was the 'menace' of what Scott calls the 'Counter-Reformation'. The truth was that the crisis of 'popery and arbitrary government' was not just about religion, narrowly defined. The 'domestic anti-Catholic tradition' is not enough to explain what happened. Ultimately it came down to popular fear of and protest against Charles's alliance with the regime of Louis XIV.[38]

This seems entirely credible. In fact, the political troubles of the later 1670s do resemble rather closely the anti-popery of the 1620s and the 1630s. Oates's accusations were a reprise of civil-war conspiracy theory. They were, as Miller says, simply 'transposed into the present'. The allegation was that Catholics had been responsible for that earlier crisis and had been implicated subsequently in the Cromwellian tyranny.[39] As Scott argues, from the late 1670s onwards 'the nation was reliving... its own history', though it had been doing that continuously in different modes since the Reformation of the sixteenth century.[40] With the exception of the issue of a royal standing army in England, the account of an imminent change of the times in one pamphlet published by Richard Greene in 1679 was a rehearsal of the situation as it might have been observed in the late 1630s and early 1640s, not least in the build-up of allegedly hostile military forces in Ireland, Scotland, and France. The location of this strand of the conspiracy, as alleged by Oates and his associate Israel Tonge, in Herefordshire and the Welsh marches identified a region which had long been regarded as stubbornly popish.[41]

---

[38] Scott, 'England's Troubles', pp. 108–15, 118.

[39] Miller, *Popery*, pp. 155–6. On the other side of the tracks, as it were, the radicalism of radical Whigs in the 1670s and 1680s could also be traced back to the Interregnum: G. S. de Krey, 'London Radicals and Revolutionary Politics 1675–1683', in Harris, Seaward and Goldie, *Politics of Religion*, pp. 133–62.

[40] Scott, 'England's Troubles', pp. 126, 124. But for Mark Knights's argument that too much can be made of the similarity between 1679–81 and earlier political crises, see Knights, *Politics*, pp. 10–11.

[41] Richard Greene, *The Popish Massacre, as it was discovered to the Honourable House of Commons in the Month of June 1678* (1679), cited by Kenyon, *PP*, pp. 49–50, 321. For the evidence here and there of local circumstances and antagonisms, hard now to recover in detail, which led to the betrayal and discovery of clergy such as David Lewis, see J. H. Canning, 'The Titus Oates Plot in South Wales and the Marches', *St Peter's Magazine* 3 (1923), pp. 159–68, 189–97, 219–26, at pp. 163–4, and pp. 164 f., reprinting *A Narrative of the Imprisonment and Tryal of Mr David Lewis, Priest of the Society of Jesus, written by himself. At the Assizes held at Monmouth March 28 1679. To which is Annexed his Last Speech at the Place of Execution, August 27, 1679* (1679); Foley, *RSJ*, V, pp. 917–24 (AAW, OB III/ii, no. 183); Challoner, *MMP*, p. 560 (Lewis's gallows speech refers to 'my capital persecutor', John Arnold, and to 'my neighbours that betrayed me'). The prosecution of Lewis was apparently made possible by the hostility of people who were already at enmity with him over entirely local issues, though Lewis said that, up to the point of his arrest, Arnold and one Charles Price had been 'two of my good friends'. Lewis's self-justification referred to the spreading of false rumours about himself 'which quickly overran five or six counties and took flight to London itself'; see *A Narrative of the Imprisonment and Tryal of Mr David Lewis*, pp. 2, 6–7; Foley, *RSJ*, V, pp. 917–18; *The Condemnation of the Cheating Popish Priest... who lately Cheated a Poor Woman of 15¹...on Pretence of Praying her Father's Soul out of Purgatory* (1679); *A Letter from a Gentleman in the Countrie to his Friend in London...*(1679); John Arnold et al., *An Abstract of Several Examinations taken upon Oath, in the Counties of Monmouth and*

548   CATHOLICS AND TREASON

There had already been a wave of republication of earlier pamphlets which warned against popish plotting, notably William Prynne's *Romes Master-Peece*.[42]

However, the still dominant rendering of this episode is Kenyon's, in which Oates and Tonge are part of a mainly metropolitan anti-popish freak show.[43] Oates was, says Kenyon, not only physically repulsive but also an active homosexual. Despite his distinctly queeny bitterness about his Anabaptist heritage, he appears to have found a welcome with a kind of 'homintern', as Kenyon controversially puts it, and that included not just the cabin-boy-infested naval route to Tangier but also the Catholic seminary colleges.[44] Anyway, mad as a lot of it seemed, and without going into detail about the twists and turns of either Oates's incredible tales or the possible quasi-absolutist programme of the court, in possession of a sizeable standing army (especially the force raised in winter 1677–8, technically for war against Louis XIV, but only at the point when it seemed inevitable that peace negotiations would start), one can perhaps argue that the seriousness of the plot trials is still absent from much of the existing literature.[45]

Kenyon's line is that, by mid-1679, 'the plot might have collapsed altogether if it had not...merged with the great political struggle over the exclusion of the duke of York from the succession'. The crisis itself began with the exclusion bill brought into the Commons on 15 May 1679, and it was stirred up by the dissolution on 10 July.[46] But here the claim seems to be that the sheer lunacy of the allegations against Catholic clergy meant that they blew themselves out relatively swiftly.

Hereford...(1680), p. 4; *A Short Narrative of the Discovery of a College of Jesuits, at a Place called the Come, in the County of Hereford...To which is Added a True Relation of the Knavery of Father Lewis, the Pretended Bishop of Landaffe*...(1679), pp. 11–18. See also *England's Second Warning-piece; or Observations on the Barbarous Attempt to Murther Justice Arnold April the 15th 1680*...(1680), for the claim that this failed assassination attempt in London was in revenge for the prosecution of the Jesuit Philip Evans; see also Miller, *Popery*, p. 182; Kenyon, *PP*, pp. 244, 245–6; Knights, *Politics*, p. 265; Hinds, 'The Horrid Popish Plot', pp. 270–6. Evans was executed, with John Lloyd, on 22 July 1679 at Cardiff: Challoner, *MMP*, pp. 544–7.

[42] Prynne's *Romes Master-Peece* of 1643 was republished as *The Grand Designs of the Papists*...(1678). For other republications of earlier anti-Catholic works, see Marotti, 'Plots', pp. 192–6; Knights, *Politics*, p. 190.

[43] For a particularly clear rendering, however, of the claims and counterclaims of Oates and his associates, see Hinds, 'The Horrid Popish Plot', ch. 2.

[44] Kenyon, *PP*, pp. 53–6. For a very different reading of the plot, see, e.g., D. Beaver, 'Conscience and Context: The Popish Plot and the Politics of Ritual 1678–82', *HJ* 34 (1991), pp. 297–327. For the counter-attack on Oates by Thomas Knox and John Lane, accusing him of committing sodomy, see *The Tryal and Conviction of Thomas Knox and John Lane, for a Conspiracy to Defame and Scandalize Dr Oates and Mr Bedloe*...(1680); Kenyon, *PP*, p. 219; for the same allegations against Oates by the pamphleteer Nathaniel Thompson, see Richardson, 'Serial Struggles', pp. 40–1; see also P. Hammond, 'Titus Oates and "Sodomy"', in J. Black (ed.), *Culture and Society in Britain 1660–1800* (Manchester, 1977), pp. 39–62; Hinds, 'The Horrid Popish Plot', p. 47.

[45] For the recruitment of soldiers, see Kenyon, *PP*, pp. 47–8; Knights, *Politics*, p. 19; *An Impartial Account of Divers Remarkable Proceedings*, pp. 7–9 (Danby's impeachment); see also J. Miller, 'The Potential for "Absolutism" in Later Stuart England', *History* 69 (1984), pp. 187–207. For the public's capacity to follow the plot trials' 'minutiae', see Morton, 'Popery, Politics, and Play', p. 415.

[46] Kenyon, *PP*, p. 209.

THE RESTORATION AND THE POPISH PLOT   549

After this, exclusion became the major political issue. Kenyon's narrative of the plot—although the breathless aspects of that narrative sometimes make it quite difficult to follow—is such that it makes one wonder how any contemporary could have credited the testimony of prosecution witnesses at all. Ultimately it was an admittedly rather nasty storm in a teacup. For Professor Miller it was 'not surprising that such panic should quickly die down when no invasion or massacre ensued'. Without the alleged murder of the London magistrate Sir Edmund Berry Godfrey it might not have taken off at all. The spreading of the metropolitan anti-popery fury into the provinces was reminiscent of the circulation of panic and rumour in 1641–2, although the evidence against James's secretary, Edward Coleman, fed directly into Shaftesbury's calls for the barring of the duke of York from the line of succession.[47] According to Kenyon, the trial of Thomas Whitbread, William Ireland, John Fenwick, Thomas Pickering, and John Grove, all arraigned on 17 December 1678, was a direct tit-for-tat consequence of the damage to Oates's credibility during the course of Coleman's trial.[48]

I suppose that what one might take from all this is that, apart from the issue of the perceived threat represented by the ambition of the duke of York, there is really no connection between what the allegedly guilty had been doing and what they were said to have been doing (that is, conspiring against the king).[49] In the absence of the discovery of some new archive which throws light on that topic, there may well not be much else to say about this. My sense is that there really is very little to tell us what was 'actually' going on in these cases, at least compared with earlier prosecutions of Catholic clergy. The not unreasonable line taken by Frances Dolan is that 'it is impossible to distinguish between events and their narrative representations because those narratives...were the event' and 'the discursive reveals itself as the real', that is, whether the 'facts' as alleged were in any objective sense true or not.[50] This means that what was at stake was not the factual accuracy of the witnesses' statements per se but, rather, who most probably

[47] Miller, *Popery*, pp. 159–60, 161; for the fortuitous discovery of Coleman's correspondence, see Haley, *Shaftesbury*, pp. 455–6; see also Knights, *Politics*, p. 265; Hinds, *'The Horrid Popish Plot'*, ch. 6; A. Barclay, 'The Rise of Edward Colman', *HJ* 42 (1999), pp. 109–31.

[48] The proceedings commenced on 13 June 1679: Kenyon, *PP*, pp. 143 f., 180 f.; see also *The Information of William Lewis, Gent. Delivered at the Bar of the House of Commons, the Eighteenth of November, 1680. Together with his further Narrative relating thereto. In all which is Contained a Confirmation of the Popish Plot, and the Justice of the Executions done upon Grove, Pickering and the Jesuites...*(1680). Whitbread had been 'often mentioned in Coleman's trial and letters as a grand instrument of mischief': *Some Account of the Tryals and Condemnation of five Notorious Jesuits...*(1679), p. 2. The five defendants were charged with specific treasons rather than under the 1585 treason statute; see *The Behaviour, Last Words, and Execution of the Five Grand Jesuits and Popish Priests...*(1679), p. 1.

[49] John Aveling suggested that 'in 1678 *some* conspiring certainly was afoot within the Catholic community' and some Catholic peers 'had lately been meeting more frequently and travelling backwards and forwards to France': J. Aveling, *The Handle and the Axe: The Catholic Recusants in England from Reformation to Emancipation* (1976), pp. 207, 208, cited in Marotti, 'Plots', p. 279.

[50] F. Dolan, *Whores of Babylon: Catholicism, Gender and Seventeenth-Century Print Culture* (Ithaca, N.Y., 1999), p. 158.

550   CATHOLICS AND TREASON

might be thought to be telling the truth, and who, by contrast, might be credibly thought to have a motive to spread false rumours.[51] Or, to put it another way, a great deal of the public discussion of the plot was not really about the brain-twisting complexities of the evidence offered at trial but, instead, about the previous history of alleged popish plotting and about the political principles which Protestant commentators associated with those whom they regarded as papists. Here it was simply logical to refer back to the St Bartholomew's Day Massacre, the Gunpowder Plot, and other conspiracies, and to attack, as Thomas Barlow, bishop of Lincoln, did, the assertions that 'the Gunpowder treason was more than suspected to be the contrivance of Cecil, the great politician, to render Catholics odious', and that Henry Garnet was innocent of the intrigue.[52] By extension, the use of the Elizabethan treason law against Catholic clergy could be taken, by those who believed in the veracity of the plot allegations, to be an entirely appropriate return to the enforcement of the law as it stood and as the legislators who drafted it had intended that it should work.[53]

But it was clear that the royal court had learned the lessons of earlier anti-popery treason agitation. It did not try to prevent the proceedings against the accused.[54] Charles II did not allow himself to get sucked into the situation in which his father had found himself when, as we saw in the previous chapter, Catholic clerics were indicted in early 1641. Or, rather, he did not stand out against his councillors' refusal to allow reprieves while parliament was in session. As Kenneth Haley says, it was 'not surprising that Charles was reading the history of 1641' and feared 'a similar course of events in 1679'.[55]

---

[51] See, e.g., *The History of Popish-Sham-Plots...* (1682); *Mr Smyth's Discovery of the Popish Sham-Plot in Ireland...* (1681); *News from Ireland, touching the Damnable Design of the Papists in that Kingdom to Forge a Sham-Plott upon the Presbyterians...* (1682).

[52] Thomas Barlow, *Popery: Or, the Principles & Positions Approved by the Church of Rome...in a Letter to a Person of Honor; by T. Ld Bishop of Lincoln* (1679), pp. 1–3 and *passim*; *A True Relation of the Popish-Plot against King Charles I. and the Protestant Religion* (1679); see also, among many other pamphlets which recycled accounts of previous popish conspiracies, *Popish Cruelties. Wherein may be Seen that Romish Traitors have now the same Murthering and Treasonable Principles and Practices they had in Q. Elizabeth's Reign...* (1680). For the line taken by Catholics who posited a connection between their loyalty to the crown and their essentially Gallican attitudes to papal authority, see, e.g., James Corker, *Roman-Catholick Principles, in Reference to God and the King...* (1680); *ODNB*, *sub* Corker, James (article by G. Scott); D. Lunn, *The English Benedictines 1540–1688: From Reformation to Revolution* (1981), pp. 133–5.

[53] See, e.g., William Cawley, *The Laws of Q. Elizabeth, K. James, and K. Charles the First. Concerning Jesuites, Seminary Priests, Recusants, &c....* (1680), bearing a commendatory preface by the chief justice of the Common Pleas, Sir Francis North.

[54] Miller, *Popery*, pp. 162f. A string of royal proclamations against popery could, just about, be interpreted as a sign that the court was pushing along the investigation into the alleged conspiracy; see, e.g., *By the King. A Proclamation for the Apprehending Certain Offenders...* ([17 November] 1678); *By the King. A Proclamation for the Discovery and Apprehending all Popish Priests and Jesuits* ([20 November] 1678); *By the King. A Proclamation for Disarming and Securing of Popish Recusants* ([20 December] 1678); *By the King. A Proclamation for Incouragement of the further Discovery of the Popish Plot* ([30 October] 1680).

[55] Haley, *Shaftesbury*, pp. 491, 496. For Haley's excellent account of the difference between the position of the crown during exclusion and in the early 1640s, see ibid., pp. 466–7.

THE RESTORATION AND THE POPISH PLOT   551

Challoner declares, predictably, that those who were indicted were under attack because they were good royalists. Thus the Jesuit William Ireland's uncle had been 'killed in the king's service' and 'his relations, the Giffords and Pendrells, were instrumental in saving King Charles II after the defeat at Worcester'. The lay Benedictine Thomas Pickering's father had also died in the royalist cause.[56] John Wall's defence of himself included the claim that his 'family had been sufferers in the time of Cromwell, as other loyal families had been'. Wall's father had been gaoled; he was 'a fellow prisoner of Sir Thomas Allen, one of his Majesty's admirals'. Wall's brother had 'served his Majesty'.[57] Henry Starkey, sentenced to death on 17 January 1680, had been in the king's service and had been wounded by a cannonball.[58] Challoner noted that John Plessington's father had been a royalist.[59] John Gavan's gallows speech was explicit in its denial of regicidal doctrine, associated with the Jesuit Juan de Mariana. Gavan cited 'the wise and victorious King Henry IV of France, the royal grandfather of our present gracious king, in a public oration which he pronounced in defence of the Jesuits, amongst other things, declaring that he was very well satisfied with the Jesuits' doctrine concerning kings'.[60]

Not all Catholics, however, saw things exactly this way. The Jesuit Peter Hamerton's narrative of the arrest in September 1678 of the Society's provincial Thomas Whitbread said that those 'Catholics... who were not well affected to the Society' 'cried... up' the conspiracy as a 'Jesuit plot' and 'were scarcely civil when such persons were in their company'. As for the incriminating but forged letters which Thomas Downes alias Mumford SJ 'intercepted at Windsor', those same ill-affected Catholics believed that they were genuine. As a result, they 'railed against' the Jesuits' 'principles as pernicious to government and leading to

---

[56] Challoner, *MMP*, pp. 519, 522.

[57] 'A Relation of Mr Fr Webb's Trial at Worcester Assizes', ABSJ, CP (John Wall): transcript made in 1925 from the original in OFM archives at Forest Gate; for which see also ABP, pp. 665–84. Wall had been baptized by the martyr Edmund Arrowsmith: ABSJ, CP: *F. Davey, Blessed John Wall: Franciscan Martyr* (Office of the Vice-Postulation, 1962), p. 3. For Wall's gallows speech, see *Mr Johnson's Speech which He Deliver'd to his Friend to be Printed (as he Mention'd at the Place of Execution)* (1679); *A Narrative of the Proceedings and Tryal of Mr Francis Johnson a Franciscan...* (1679); *A True Copy of the Speech of Mr Francis Johnson... August 22, 1679* (1679).

[58] Challoner, *MMP*, p. 565; Anstr., II, p. 310; Kenyon, *PP*, p. 220; *A Brief Account*, p. 3.

[59] Challoner, *MMP*, p. 541. John Plessington had been employed as a chaplain to the Massey family at Puddington Hall, Burton (near Chester), where he was apprehended. (William Massey took part in the 1715 Jacobite rebellion.) See also R. Williams, 'The Old Hall, Puddington', *Deesider* 130 (1975), pp. 12–15, at p. 15; see also *ODNB, sub* Plessington, John (article by J. Marmion); G. Holt, 'Bl. John Plessington', *Stonyhurst Magazine* (April 1955), pp. 108–11; P. Phillips, 'St John Plessington, Priest and Martyr', *RH* 28 (2007), pp. 424–33; P. Morrell, article in *The Tablet*, 23 September 1922. Plessington's nephew, Robert, was attainted for high treason in 1716: ABSJ, CP (John Plessington).

[60] Challoner, *MMP*, p. 534. For one broadside published in justification of Gavan and the others executed on 20 June 1679, see [Nicholas Blundell, i.e. Peter Caryll OSB], *Blundel the Jesuit's Letter of Intelligence...* (1679); for a reply, see *An Answer to Blundell the Jesuit's Letter...* (1679); see also *A Narrative of the Apprehending of the Arch-Jesuite Blundell...* (1680); Marotti, 'Plots', pp. 178–84. The Benedictine James Corker's conversion to Catholicism is attributed to his disgust at his father's 'disloyalty to the monarchy': *ODNB, sub* Corker, James (article by G. Scott).

552 CATHOLICS AND TREASON

sedition'. Hamerton said that 'a lady of quality, my acquaintance, returning from her visits, found me at her house; her countenance was so full of a Jesuit plot, in which she really believed, that she laughed and scoffed at them at a high rate'. 'Now', she said, 'all their old scores would be paid off...all their jugglings and intrigues at court exposed to their public shame', though Hamerton said that he managed to convince her that the notorious letters were indeed forged.[61]

These perceptions may have been reinforced in the press by, for example, the republication of a version of the speech made by John Southworth at Tyburn in June 1654, though he had not been a member of the Society. The pamphlet's producer declared that there had been a 'few...noble and worthy gentlemen of that persuasion who faithfully served our late king', but this could not obliterate the 'wickedness' of 'Jesuits, priests' and other Catholics 'who certainly were the cause of, and stirred up, the late rebellion'. They 'brought to pass the horrid murder of our late king' and they 'endeavoured, and still aim at, the assassination of his royal Majesty'. A toleration petition had, it was known, been presented to the Cromwellian regime by Lord Brudenell. It had been 'signed by the most, if not all, the considerable papists then in England, desiring a toleration and free exercise of their religion', and then, they promised, 'they would root out the family of the Stuarts'. Furthermore, it could not 'be proved that hanging any popish priest...contributed to the conversion of numbers to that Church'. In fact, the execution of Popish Plot traitors had 'opened the eyes of many' to, as the person responsible for printing the pamphlet saw it, the truth.[62]

Whether or not Catholics accepted that there had been collusion between their co-religionists and the protectorate in the 1650s, some of them now publicly turned on each other.[63] In the case of Sir Miles Stapleton, one of the witnesses against him was a recently ordained but now 'apostate' seminary priest, John Portman, alias Smith (formerly chaplain to the Jenison family at Walworth in Durham), who also gave evidence at the trial of Viscount Stafford.[64] In the case of John Plessington, executed on 19 July 1679, one of the witnesses—George Massey—had once been a Catholic and had turned Protestant.[65] According to

---

[61] Foley, *RSJ*, V, p. 21; Hinds, *'The Horrid Popish Plot'*, pp. 77 f. For the attempt to associate Whitbread with (among other positions) Independency, see *A Letter from a Minister of the Church of England, Communicated to the Right Honourable the Lord Mayor: Relating to Thomas White, alias Whitbread...* (1679).

[62] *The Last Speech and Confession of Mr John Southworth...June 28. 1654...* (1679), sig. A^v; A. Marotti, 'Manuscript Transmission and the Catholic Martyrdom Account', in Marotti, *Religious Ideology*, pp. 92–3. E. E. Reynolds, by contrast, noting that the pamphlet was printed for Henry Brome, the associate of Sir Roger L'Estrange, suggests that the piece was in fact a covert attack on the credibility of the plot: E. E. Reynolds, *John Southworth: Priest and Martyr* (1962), pp. 73–4.

[63] Haley, *Shaftesbury*, p. 495.

[64] Anstr., III, p. 173; Kn., VI, unpaginated section on Sir Miles Stapleton (indicating that in court Portman 'spoke only to the plot in general', never having seen Stapleton before); Kenyon, *PP*, pp. 226–7, 229, 231; *The Narrative of Mr John Smith of Walworth...* (1679).

[65] ABSJ, CP (John Plessington): ex. inf. city archivist at Chester (Cheshire Record Office), 10 July 1978 (citing Mayor's File [ZMF] 97/109); Challoner, *MMP*, p. 541; UCLSC, UC/P1/B2, pp. 9–13.

THE RESTORATION AND THE POPISH PLOT   553

Portman, Robert Jenison (brother of the Jesuit Thomas Jenison) and his father both declared that they were willing to believe that the Jesuit William Ireland had conspired to kill the king. Robert Jenison abjured his Catholicism and appeared as a prosecution witness during the trials of Sir George Wakeman and Viscount Stafford.[66] John Sergeant, formerly though briefly a secretary to Thomas Morton, bishop of Durham, was a (not uncritical) follower of Thomas White. Sergeant was a vehement enemy of George Leyburn and other secular priests and, particularly, of the Society of Jesus. Leyburn had, back in 1661, singled out Sergeant as the leader of a Blackloist cell in the English secular clergy's chapter—Sergeant was the chapter's secretary. On 31 October 1679, Sergeant gave evidence in front of the king and the privy council; in particular, he testified against the already executed John Gavan, that is, for his defence of the papal deposing power. Sergeant claimed that one Mary Skipwith had declared to him, in Flanders, that Gavan had said that 'the queen might lawfully kill the king for violating her bed'. Sergeant repeated his testimony to the council on 18 February 1680 and in front of the Commons on 26 March. In this attack on Gavan he was joined by another secular priest, David Morris. Both received a royal pension. For his part, Sergeant protested that he had merely unburdened himself of his thoughts about Jesuits rather than having any specific knowledge of the plot. However, the Jesuit annual letter for 1680 emphasized that Sergeant and Morris 'spread abroad a report that the English province of the Society was at an end' and 'that the martyrs had been justly convicted and executed for high treason, and that the rest were about to be banished'.[67] The Society's annual letter also described how Sergeant made suggestions to the privy council about the status of Catholic clergy in England, presumably about the possibility of allowing overtly loyalist Catholic priests a kind of State-sponsored toleration.[68] The Jesuit John Warner said to Cardinal Howard in

---

'Local tradition', says Kenyon, had it that Plessington was 'arrested at the instance of a Protestant landowner because he had forbidden a match between his son and a Catholic heiress': Kenyon, *PP*, pp. 246–7.

[66] *The Narrative of Mr John Smith of Walworth*, pp. 31–4; Kenyon, *PP*, pp. 193, 231; Haley, *Shaftesbury*, pp. 539, 543; *The Narrative of Robert Jenison...*(1679); *The Informations of Robert Jenison...*(1680). Thomas Jenison died in prison on 27 September 1679: Challoner, *MMP*, p. 537.

[67] Anstr., II, pp. 280–7, 225–6; Tompkins, ECI, pp. 246–7; Kenyon, *PP*, pp. 208, 237, 249, 263, 264, 265, 279; Bossy, *ECC*, p. 69; *ODNB, sub* Sergeant, John (article by B. Southgate); Foley, *RSJ*, V, p. 81; ABSJ, Anglia V, nos 100–2; *The Informations of John Sergeant and David Maurice, Gentlemen; relating to the Popish-Plot...Reported to the House of Commons...upon the 26th Day of March, 1681...*(1681), p. 1 and *passim*. Even Elizabeth Cellier, the principal protagonist in the so-called Meal Tub Plot, declared that she experienced hostility from some (unnamed) Catholics: Dolan, *Whores of Babylon*, p. 165. The only Catholic who publicly defended her was John Warner SJ: Dolan, *Whores of Babylon*, p. 163. John Kemble, who was executed near Hereford on 22 August 1678, had been arrested by John Scudamore of Kentchurch. In the past, that branch of the Scudamore family had been Catholic and it was said that Scudamore's own daughter was cured by touching the rope with which Kemble was hanged: Challoner, *MMP*, pp. 555, 556; ABSJ, CP (John Kemble); for the information sent to Challoner by the Franciscan Matthew Prichard, describing Kemble's case, see Archives of the Archdiocese of Birmingham, C 458; hierarchical number Z5/3/40/1/1 (Matthew Prichard OSF, vicar apostolic of the western district, to Challoner, 27 February 1741).

[68] Foley, *RSJ*, V, pp. 81–2.

554   CATHOLICS AND TREASON

Rome that 'not a Jesuit passes into England that Mr Sergeant can hear of but his name is carried to the' privy council 'and...he has his brethren at or about the sea ports, who give him information of such things'.[69] Here, then, a number of Catholics took the plot as an opportunity to assert their opposition to contemporary resistance theory even while others, in turn, accused them of selling out to the regime of the day, just as such people had always done.[70] Warner, under the name of Robert Pugh, retaliated against the Blackloists in 1680 with the publication of the pamphlet entitled *Blacklo's Cabal*.[71]

By December 1679, twenty-one Catholic clergy and laymen had been hanged for their alleged part in the plot, and others had died in gaol. At this point the privy council set up a committee to consider how the enforcement of the law against Catholics could be made more effective.[72] Richard Langhorne had been hanged at Tyburn on 14 July 1679; but, from the point later in this month when, with three co-defendants, the queen's physician Sir George Wakeman, accused of conspiring to poison the king, was acquitted, to December 1680 (the trial of William Howard, Viscount Stafford) there were no convictions in London. By contrast, in the provinces there were ten deaths in July and August 1679, as the lord chief justice, Sir William Scroggs, tried to redeem his reputation at provincial assize hearings in order to make up for the opprobrium which he had incurred as a result of the acquittal of Wakeman, though, as Kenyon notes, the plot found 'no credence in Scotland'.[73] The major attack on provincial Catholicism came in the

[69]   T. Birrell (ed.), *Robert Pugh: Blacklo's Cabal 1680* (Farnborough, 1970), introduction.

[70]   Kenyon, *PP*, pp. 262–6. For Warner's attack on the veracity of the plot allegations, see T. Birrell (ed.), *The History of the English Persecution of Catholics and the Presbyterian Plot* (CRS 47–8, 1953), and various publications, listed therein, notably *A Vindication of the English Catholicks...* (Antwerp, 1680).

[71]   Anstr., II, pp. 258–9, 353; Bossy, *ECC*, p. 73; Robert Pugh (ed.), *Blacklo's Cabal discovered in Severall of their Letters...* (Douai, 1680). The letters in this publication had been collected by Robert Pugh and had been left at the Jesuit college in Ghent. Pugh had been arrested in December 1678 and sent to Newgate, where he died on 22 January 1679 before he could be put on trial: Anstr., II, p. 258; Birrell, *Blacklo's Cabal*, introduction. For Pugh, see Tompkins, ECI, pp. 225–7.

[72]   Miller, *Popery*, p. 166; Challoner, *MMP*, pp. 510f; Marotti, 'Plots', pp. 277–8; for those clergy who died in prison, see Challoner, *MMP*, pp. 537, 562–4, 566; Foley, *RSJ*, V, pp. 32–4 (the number included Thomas Downes SJ, who had formerly been chaplain to the duke of York), 95–7; Stonyhurst MS A V, no. 21, pp. 120–1; for the death of Humphrey Evans SJ, following the search of Poole Hall on 25 December 1678, see Foley, *RSJ*, V, p. 938; Phillips, 'St John Plessington', p. 428. For others who were arrested but survived, at least for a time, see Challoner, *MMP*, pp. 564–6; Foley, *RSJ*, V, p. 45 (James Corker OSB) and *passim*. For Kenyon's estimate of the damage to Catholic networks caused by the plot, see Kenyon, *PP*, ch. 7.

[73]   Miller, *Popery*, p. 176; Challoner, *MMP*, pp. 538f; Kenyon, *PP*, pp. 202–4, 224; Richardson, 'Serial Struggles', pp. 34–5; Dolan, *Whores of Babylon*, p. 204; Knights, *Politics*, p. 35; Haley, *Shaftesbury*, pp. 542–3; see also *The Speech of Richard Langhorn...* (1679); T. M. McCoog, 'Richard Langhorne and the Popish Plot', *RH* 19 (1989), pp. 499–508; Marotti, 'Plots', pp. 189–91. For the rapid publication of John Plessington's speech at execution (on 19 July 1679), see *The Speech of...Mr William Plessington, who was Executed at Chester...* (1679). Christopher Tootell recorded that, when James II came to Chester on progress, he 'made a halt at the place of execution and said: "here then it was that good Mr Plessington suffered. The villains murdered him. For I procured him a reprieve, which came soon enough to have saved his life; but they concealed it" (till the execution was over). This the king spoke to his attendants then nearest him, as Mr Peter Gooden (then chaplain to the king and present when

THE RESTORATION AND THE POPISH PLOT   555

Welsh Jesuit district (the college of St Francis Xavier) and, it seems, it was directed squarely at the principal Catholic patron in the region, the third marquis of Worcester. Kenyon comments that 'the campaign against the South Wales priesthood was conducted with a vicious obstinacy unique even at this time'.[74]

It is arguable, though, that the Whig exclusionists at least had some idea of what they were talking about. On Kenyon's account, the moment at which the plot morphed into exclusion (subscription to the one implied subscription to the other) was also the one that saw the emergence of the duke of York as the strong man of the court. This coincided with the dismissals from office in and after September/October of the duke of Monmouth and the earl of Shaftesbury and the start of the Tory reaction, underwritten by the emergence of Lord Chief Justice Scroggs as a critic of the court's enemies.[75] One assumes that there must also have been some connection between the prorogation of the first exclusion parliament on 27 May—it was later dissolved—and the batch of trials and then executions on 20 June 1679.[76] As some saw it, if the duke of York ever became king, he would simply emulate Mary Tudor. One pamphlet had cited 'her wicked dissimulation with the men of Suffolk' in order to take the crown. The lesson was clear—one should not trust 'popish successors'. They would 'at first blind us with wheedles, till they have got the...kingdom in possession' and would 'tell us, "that not one tittle of our religion shall be changed"'. But, 'once set in the throne', they would renege on their promises with astonishing speed. All the sickening apparatus of fiery tyranny would be set up again.[77]

A number of the Protestant Popish Plot pamphlets are conscious attempts at countering the thrust of Catholic martyrological writing in general and, in particular, the several circulating defences, in manuscript and print, of those accused and put on trial. Thus the author of *England's Second Warning-piece* wrote that 'not one of their villainous priests shall pass the gallows but he shall have a speech

---

he spoke it) told me [Tootell] soon after it happened'. Tootell had 'seen very lately a relic of Mr Thulis, part of Mr Bamber's skull, Mr Woodcock's neck-bone, Mr Whittaker's shoestring, Mr Plessington's blood, with other martyrs' relics, all of which had been gathered and preserved by Mr Dalton's aunts at Aldcliffe Hall near Lancaster': UCLSC, UC/P1/B2, pp. 12–13, 24. I take it that James II's remarks, noted here, were made on the occasion written up by Scott Sowerby when James visited Chester in August 1687: S. Sowerby, *Making Toleration: The Repealers and the Glorious Revolution* (2013), pp. 41–3; S. Sowerby, 'Of Different Complexions: Religious Diversity and National Identity in James II's Toleration Campaign', *English Historical Review* 124 (2009), pp. 29–52. For Peter Gooden, who was resident after 1680 at Aldcliffe Hall, see *ODNB*, sub Gooden, Peter (article by T. Cooper, rev. M. Whitehead).

[74] H. Thomas, 'The Society of Jesus in Wales c. 1600–1679: Rediscovering the Cwm Jesuit Library at Hereford Cathedral', *Journal of Jesuit Studies* 1 (2014), pp. 572–88, esp. at p. 581; Kenyon, *PP*, pp. 244–5; *A Short Narrative of the Discovery of a College of Jesuits*. For the trial and execution of the Franciscan Charles Meehan at Ruthin on 12 August 1679, see *AWCBC*, pp. 2454–88; J. M. Cronin, 'The Other Irish Martyr of the Titus Oates Plot: Ven. Charles Mahony O.S.F. ...' in *Blessed Oliver Plunket Historical Studies* (Dublin, 1937), pp. 133–53.

[75] Kenyon, *PP*, pp. 210, 212–14; Knights, *Politics*, pp. 58, 230.

[76] Miller, *Popery*, pp. 174–5; Kenyon, *PP*, p. 190; Haley, *Shaftesbury*, pp. 540–1.

[77] *Memoirs of Queen Mary's Days...* (1679), pp. 1, 3.

556 CATHOLICS AND TREASON

forged for him, filled with the best and most taking words that can be invented'. This would inevitably find its way into print and 'proclaim him a saint as well as a martyr, though in truth he lived a cheat and a ruffian, and died a traitor and an atheist'.[78] Here the classic tropes of martyr discourse were turned back on their authors. In this pamphlet's reply to the circulating defence of Philip Evans, in response to the claim that 'he kissed the post of the gallows', the pamphlet asked, 'is not the gibbet...sanctified by this holy martyr's kiss?' In all likelihood it would be 'stolen away shortly and sent to Rome to make relics of'.[79]

Samuel Smith, the so-called ordinary of Newgate, and formerly a nonconformist, wrote his own pamphlet on these executions. In reply to the circulating Catholic assertions that these people had died courageously for their religion, Smith declared that either they had been doubtful about their beliefs or they had, like Coleman, 'had an arrogant opinion' of themselves, 'out of a hope to be canonized for a saint'. Smith said that the lay Benedictine Thomas Pickering had plied himself with 'cordial-spirits' and was thus 'unconcerned at the approach of his own death' and 'neither warned the people to take heed of an ill life nor confessed any sin to God of which himself was guilty'. Challoner and Smith could agree only that Pickering had denied being an ordained priest. In the case of the five executed on 20 June 1679, Challoner concentrates on the uplifting speeches which they made at Tyburn, whereas Smith, who was not present at the majority of these executions, merely records that in Newgate, in response to his offers of spiritual aid, they (or certainly John Fenwick) told him what he could do with his prayers.[80] Smith's pamphlet has sections dealing with the 'false courage and cheerfulness at execution' of these Catholics, so different 'from the hidden manna' and 'comforts' of real martyrs.[81]

The logic and credibility of the supposed plot soon started to break apart. Seven Catholic clergymen were prosecuted under the 1585 statute in king's bench on 17 January 1680. All but one of the defendants were convicted; but they were not executed.[82] Thomas Thwing, who had been arrested at Barnbow Hall, the

---

[78] *England's Second Warning-piece*, p. 6.

[79] Ibid., pp. 5–6. The pamphlet prints (at pp. 5–6) the Catholic defence of Evans and Lloyd (published separately) entitled *Short Memorandum's...* (1679; AAW, A XXXIV, no. 136); it refers to 'lying, seducing papers...printed for, or at least openly sold by Turner the popish bookseller in Holborn'. For Challoner's use of *Short Memorandum's*, see Challoner, *MMP*, pp. 544–7.

[80] Challoner, *MMP*, pp. 529–36; Samuel Smith, *An Account of the Behaviour of the Fourteen Late Popish Malefactors...* (1679), pp. 4, 8–9, 20 and *passim*; ODNB, *sub* Smith, Samuel (article by C. Chapman); Hinds, 'The Horrid Popish Plot', pp. 229–31.

[81] Smith, *An Account*, pp. 25–31, 36–8; see also *An Answer to Mr Langhorn's Speech...* (1679); *A Certain Way to Prevent Popery in England, and Effectually Suppress all Jesuits & Popish Priests, without Giving them the Vain-glory of Pretending to be Martyrs...* (1681).

[82] Kenyon, *PP*, pp. 219–23; *A Brief Account of the Proceedings against the Six Popish Priests...* (1680), p. 2; *The True Narrative of the Procedings at the Sessions-House in the Old-Bayly...* (1679 [1680]). James Corker had previously been acquitted when tried with Wakeman: *The True Narrative*, p. 3; ODNB, *sub* Corker, James (article by G. Scott). Two more priests were indicted in February 1680, with one acquitted and the other not executed: Kenyon, *PP*, pp. 223–4. For failed proceedings against

THE RESTORATION AND THE POPISH PLOT   557

abode of his uncle Sir Thomas Gascoigne, back in July 1679 was arraigned, with others, on 17 March 1680. But challenges to the jury meant that the trial did not take place until July. Of those arraigned, only Thwing, briefly respited on 4 August, was executed—on 23 October 1680. His execution speech circulated in print and manuscript at the same time as the authorities' own attempts in print to make the farce of a trial seem like justice. Knaresborough's copy of the speech, written by Thwing himself, was endorsed by Sir Miles Stapleton that he had 'received this paper from Mr Thwing's own hand the morning he went to execution'.[83] Stapleton's own trial was deferred because of his challenges to the jury, though one jury member, Christopher Tankard, was unsuccessfully 'excepted against by Sir Thomas Stringer as one that disparaged the evidence of the plot and called his dogs by the names' of the revolting informer Oates and the equally repulsive William Bedloe, who had alleged that the magistrate Godfrey had been murdered by two of Catherine of Braganza's chaplains. As Kenyon notes, in the plot trials in Yorkshire 'the local Protestant gentry rallied in force to support their Catholic neighbours'.[84]

On 30 November 1680 Lord Stafford's trial began;[85] and there was, of course, the arraignment of Oliver Plunket, archbishop of Armagh. Kenyon sees this as part of Shaftesbury's despairing attempt to keep the plot alive. Plunket, arrested back in December 1679, was finally tried in England and executed on 1 July

---

leading Catholic laity in 1680 (including the earl of Castlemaine), see Kenyon, *PP*, pp. 226–9. Castlemaine, who was under threat from Oates's accusations and was awaiting trial, though free on bail, published *The Compendium: Or a Short View of the Late Tryals, in Relation to the Present Plot against his Majesty and Government: with the Speeches of those that have been Executed. As also, an Humble Address (at the Close) to all the Worthy Patriots of this once Flourishing and Happy Kingdom* (1679), which, by querying the evidence against the plot suspects, functioned as a kind of martyrology of those who had been accused and killed; *ODNB*, *sub* Palmer, Roger (article by R. Beddard). For Castlemaine's court appearance and his acquittal, see Kenyon, *PP*, pp. 228–9.

[83] Anstr., III, p. 226; Challoner, *MMP*, p. 566; Haley, *Shaftesbury*, p. 539; *The Proceedings at the Assizes Holden at York the 24th Day of July 1680...against Severall Prisoners then Indicted for the Horrid Popish Plot against the Life of the King...: with an Accompt at Large of the Arraignment of Sir M. Stapleton..., and of the Tryal, Condemnation and Execution of Thomas Thwing for the Same Plot* (1681); *The Tryal of Sr. Miles Stapleton Bar. For High Treason...: to which is Added the Tryal and Condemnation of Mr Thomas Thwing...* (1681); *The Last Speech of Thomas Thwing Priest...Saturday the 23. Of October 1680* (1680); Kn., VI, unpaginated section; AAW, A XXXIV, no. 175, pp. 657–8 ('The Last Speech of Thomas Thwing...'); for the assize proceedings against Thwing, see ABSJ, PC (Thwing, Thomas), with photostats of PRO, Assizes 44/28, Assizes 45/12/4, no. 149 [new reference]. See also the pamphlets setting out the information volunteered by the prosecution witnesses: *Animadvertions on the Papists most Wicked and Bloody Oath of Secrecy given to Robert Bolron...for the Murdering of Kings...* (1681); *The Narrative of Robert Bolron...concerning the Late Horrid Popish Plot...together with an Account of the Endeavours that were Used by the Popish Party to Stifle his Evidence* (1680); Robert Bolron, *The Papists Bloody Oath of Secrecy and Letany of Intercession...* (1681); for the pamphlet printed in early 1680 to discredit Bolron, see *An Abstract of the Accusation of Robert Bolron and Lawrence Maybury, servants, against their Late Master, Sir Thomas Gascoigne...with his Tryal and Acquittal...* (1680), emphasizing that those who testified in defence of Gascoigne were Protestants.

[84] *The Proceedings*, p. 32; Kenyon, *PP*, p. 227. For Bedloe, see Kenyon, *PP*, pp. 106 f.; *ODNB*, *sub* Bedloe, William (article by A. Marshall).

[85] Kenyon, *PP*, p. 231.

558 CATHOLICS AND TREASON

1681.[86] The reaction to the conspiracy by the court's defenders, such as Sir Roger L'Estrange, may have been as simple as a thoroughly traditional identification of the dangers of popery on the one side and puritanism/Dissent/presbyterianism on the other—virtually a cliché, as Miller says, but it was evidently effective enough.[87] Challoner was happy to take L'Estrange's word for it that the plot was entirely concocted by Oates. It was 'as villainous and malicious a forgery as ever was set on foot'.[88] But Challoner excludes all sense of a violent part-Catholic reaction, principally in the aftermath of Wakeman's acquittal, which saw the unmasking of an alleged presbyterian conspiracy to seize power, with Shaftesbury at its centre; and then a counter-coup, that is, the Meal Tub affair which appeared to show that there was a Catholic conspiracy to do to presbyterians what Catholics alleged that presbyterians and others were trying to do to them.[89] In the speculation about what would have happened if the conspirators had been successful in killing Charles II, one allegation was that, 'the better to colour the' design, the plotters 'would at first have cast the odium of the murder on the presbyterians [so] that, by dividing and weakening Protestants in particular parties, they might have been better enabled to destroy them all in general'.[90] If the king perished, Catholics would 'give it out that it was the still-king-killing presbyterians that had done the fact, and so they thought they should bring the Protestants into their company, to revenge themselves of the presbyterians'. The Catholics had long prepared this tale and 'with great zeal they reminded us of "forty-one" that we might not dream of "seventy-nine"'.[91] The murkier details of the back-and-forth

[86] Kenyon, *PP*, pp. 225, 233–4; Haley, *Shaftesbury*, p. 575; Richardson, 'Serial Struggles', p. 38, concerning Shaftesbury's attempt to exploit Edward Fitzharris's allegations that the queen (Catherine of Braganza), the duke of York, and the earl of Danby had conspired to murder Godfrey; Fitzharris was executed with Plunket. For Archbishop Plunket, see also J. Marshall, 'The Trial and Execution of Oliver Plunket' (forthcoming); Kn., VI, unpaginated section on Plunket at end of volume. The most serious accusations against Plunket came from other Irish Catholics against whom he had used his episcopal authority. They retaliated against him by alleging that he had conspired to assist a French invasion. For the previous difficult relations between himself and, for example, Archbishop Peter Talbot of Dublin over how far there should be a restoration of 'the socio-political power of Catholicism in Ireland', *ODNB*, *sub* Talbot, Peter (article by T. Clavin). For Plunket's listing and refutation of the principal charges against him, see AAW, A XXXIV, no. 185, pp. 697–700 ('The Last Speech of Mr Oliver Plunket…'). See also *A Full and True Relation of a New Hellish Popish Plot in Ireland, Carried on by the Papists in the Province of Munster…* (1679); *A Narrative of the Irish Popish Plot, for the Betraying that Kingdom into the Hands of the French…as the Same was Successively Carryed on from the Year 1662…* (1680).

[87] Miller, *Popery*, pp. 177–9; *ODNB*, *sub* L'Estrange, Sir Roger (article by H. Love).

[88] Challoner, *MMP*, p. 511.

[89] Kenyon, *PP*, pp. 216–17; Knights, *Politics*, p. 61; Dolan, *Whores of Babylon*, p. 160 and ch. 4 *passim*; R. Weil, '"If I did say so, I lyed": Elizabeth Cellier and the Construction of Credibility in the Popish Plot Crisis', in S. Amussen and M. Kishlansky (eds), *Political Culture and Cultural Politics* (Manchester, 1995), pp. 189–209; *The History of the Damnable Popish Plot…* (1681), chs 23, 24.

[90] *The Behaviour, Last Words, and Execution*, p. 2; *A Memorial of the Late and Present Popish Plots*, p. 4; *A True Relation of the Popish-Plot against King Charles I*, pp. 25–8 ('A Vindication of the Dissenting Protestants, from being Authors of the Rebellion against the late King, and Plotters of Treason against His Majesty now Reigning'), 29–36 ('A Complete History of the last Plot of the Papists, upon the Dissenting Protestants').

[91] Roderick Mansell, *An Exact and True Narrative of the Late Popish Intrigue, to Form a Plot, and then to Cast the Guilt and Odium thereof upon the Protestants…* (1680), sig. b[r–v]; *A Short Account of the*

THE RESTORATION AND THE POPISH PLOT 559

accusations here were not really compatible with the framework of contemporary Catholic martyrology. Challoner makes only the briefest mention of the Rye House Plot.[92] However, once the Tory reaction was in full swing, it was possible to reprint Catholic defences and, in effect, martyrologies of those who had perished.

For all the chaos of the proceedings against the Catholics who were accused of treason in 1678–81, some of the trials, notably Nicholas Postgate's and Lord Stafford's, are still quite shocking in their apparently flagrant injustice. At Stafford's execution, the crowd, or sections of it, around the scaffold shouted that they believed him and not his accusers.[93] The trial of Archbishop Plunket, the last of Challoner's martyrs, does look like an astonishing travesty of justice, even by the abysmally low standards of the day.[94] One might take the events of the later 1670s and the early 1680s as a kind of final vindication of the case made by Challoner. He had, as he saw it, been able to demonstrate and narrate a chain of persecutory sins, all the way from the fate of the first Elizabethan martyr to that of the last Restoration one. In Challoner's work, the Popish Plot trials of 1678–81 are deliberately made to resemble a direct continuation of the same processes which had brought Catholics to their doom ever since the arraignment of Cuthbert Mayne back in 1577. But, notwithstanding the persuasiveness of Challoner's rhetoric and the remarkable research which informs his book, a case could be made that, despite the centrality of anti-popery to Restoration politics, by the 1670s narratives of Catholic martyrdom, or at least the ones that came out of the Restoration Popish Plot crisis, have much less to tell us about contemporary Catholicism and its relationship to the State, although they point to political tensions every bit as visceral as those encountered earlier in the period. Yet, as we have seen in Part I of this book, by the end of the seventeenth century, at the point when the State had already abandoned the use of the Elizabethan treason law as it applied to Catholics, the processes of gathering the records of martyrdom and of writing up an English Catholic historical tradition concerning the Reformation, based on narratives of persecution, were themselves only just beginning.

Late Presbyterian and Shaftburian-Plot... (1681); Knights, *Politics*, pp. 11, 61; and for the circumstances of Thomas Dangerfield's attempts to retaliate against the Whigs by planting fabricated evidence of a Protestant/presbyterian plot against the king, see Kenyon, *PP*, pp. 216–17; *ODNB*, *sub* Dangerfield, Thomas (article by A. Marshall); Haley, *Shaftesbury*, pp. 554–5.

[92] Dolan, *Whores of Babylon*, pp. 161–3; Elizabeth Cellier, *Malice Defeated...* (1680); Kenyon, *PP*, pp. 216 f.; Challoner, *MMP*, p. 582. Elizabeth Cellier, the central figure of the Meal Tub affair, was attacked in print *inter alia* for trying to appropriate the status and identity of a martyr: Dolan, *Whores of Babylon*, pp. 175–83, citing, *inter alia*, *Mr Prance's Answer to Mrs Cellier's Libel...* (1680), sig. E2ᵛ; see also Dolan, *Whores of Babylon*, p. 208.

[93] For Postgate, see *AWCBC*, pp. 2402 f. Gilbert Burnet and several other Protestant clergymen went to Stafford, 'after [his] condemnation', in order to persuade 'him to a free confession of the horrid plot': *The Manner of the Execution of William Howard, Late Earl of Stafford...* (1680), p. 2; *The Speech of William Howard, Late Lord Viscount Stafford...* (1680; AAW, A XXXIV, no. 178).

[94] Challoner, *MMP*, pp. 569–82.

17

Conclusion

The Afterlife of the Early Modern English Martyr Tradition

Although this is something of a generalization, it is probably true to say that Catholic historians of the English Reformation have tended to take on trust their own martyrological tradition and its account of the almost insane intolerance and cruelty of those who persecuted men and women of conscience and faith. But it is equally true that more or less all of the rest of the field of English Reformation history has tended to regard Catholic martyrology as a brand of rhetorical and polemical exaggeration and special pleading which is so bizarre and unrepresentative as to be, if not incomprehensible, then certainly far outside the historical mainstream. Here, the guiding assumption has been that the period saw an essentially tolerant ideological and political status quo in England, at least after the mercifully brief insanity of the real persecutions of the 1550s under the Catholic Mary Tudor. This status quo was disrupted in the end only by the allegedly inflexible monarchy of Charles I, which made civil strife in the mid-seventeenth century inevitable and unleashed a series of antagonisms which extended down to the revolution of 1688, when sanity was finally restored. By this point, despite the public obsession with the danger of popery, Catholicism was largely an irrelevance.

Assuming that we have decided that neither of these two positions is really sustainable, at least not in anything like their entirety, what might we want to take from the foregoing overview of one of the nastier sides of the post-Reformation legal code and its enforcement? Let me first briefly play devil's advocate. I can imagine that some people may want to interject, not unreasonably, that the sort of material we have looked at here is hardly very remarkable, no more than a snapshot of how all martyrology works. Someone, somewhere, is always said to be persecuting someone else. That is something that carries on until political circumstances change and one has to put up, for years, with a po-faced truth-and-reconciliation process instead. It is easy to think of modern instances of clashes between State power and individual conscience where those collisions and the often appalling events that result from them can be written up in very similar terms to the ones used by John Foxe and Richard Challoner.

Catholics and Treason: Martyrology, Memory, and Politics in the Post-Reformation. Michael Questier,
Oxford University Press. © Michael Questier 2022. DOI: 10.1093/oso/9780192847027.003.0017

CONCLUSION 561

Secondly, it is hardly surprising that some commentators have concluded that alleged instances of 'persecution' in the period after 1558 tell us no more than that, principally during the years when the post-Reformation English State found itself at war with Spain, it was inevitable that those English men and women who chose to flaunt their Catholicism would be the object of the State's suspicions and that, regrettably, some of those people would come to grief; but that, when the traumas of the war years slackened off, Catholics would be more likely to be left alone. Indeed, it is arguable that, despite the often seemingly shrill insistence of the Catholic troubles-of-our-forefathers tradition that successive post-Reformation regimes were guilty of sickening cruelty against Catholics (and the overriding assumption of Challoner's work is that there was a continuous procession of injustices down to 1681), there was never an unrelieved continuum of violence against Catholics, even those who were entirely separatist, during the later sixteenth and seventeenth centuries in England.

Not only was the use of the treason law erratic, but the State could be taken to have been reticent even when it was faced by what looked like a serious Catholic-inflected threat. During the early 1580s, when the mid-Elizabethan regime was confronted by Edmund Campion and his friends, its response was relatively muted. Despite the trauma of the years of war through the later 1580s and early 1590s, treason proceedings against Catholics were still comparatively few in number and then started to drop away. The early Stuart period saw, again, relatively few of these cases, despite the cataclysm of the Gunpowder Plot. The 1620s and 1630s came close, at times, to de facto tolerance of Catholics. Even the civil war, which one might have expected to unleash a wave of prosecutions and, in effect, revenge killings of Catholics identified as supporters of a popish king and court, did not lead to a slew of treason trials, at least not on the scale of what was undoubtedly possible. As we have seen, when Charles I's authority had finally gone, in the later 1640s, some Catholics felt able to negotiate for toleration with the emergent new power in the land. In this context, the Popish Plot trials of 1678–81 resemble an aberration, although they were a rehearsal of issues which had long been at the centre of contemporary politics.

For all the Catholic accounts of harassment, informers, betrayals, arrests, interrogation, imprisonment, torture, and so on, the fact is, also, that surveillance, incarceration, and enforcement of compliance are what sovereign States do. Sometimes, for example when this process is denounced by an Orwell or a Solzhenitsyn, people take notice, but at other times they do not, or they tell themselves that real brutality is something that happens mainly in other countries and political systems, not theirs, even in the past. If, by chance, it turns out that this sort of thing did happen 'here' (wherever 'here' is), there is a case to be made that it was a temporary anomaly, a minor blip on the otherwise fairly uniform upward path towards liberty and tolerance and liberal (Western) values.

562   CATHOLICS AND TREASON

One does in fact have to situate the English Catholic martyr narratives of the sixteenth and seventeenth centuries in the context of the quite astonishing, to a modern mind, levels of public violence in other territories which were divided in religion. Here one thinks of war-torn Flanders and, of course, of Ireland, and of France during the Wars of Religion. Compared with the slaughter in such places, often on confessional grounds, the Catholic body count under the penal law in England does look fairly minimal. It is still easy to be taken aback by what looks like flagrant abuse of English legal process during the early modern period. But the techniques of reputational destruction of religious dissenters in early modern times are fairly similar to the regime- and media-directed demonization in modern-day secular culture of those who seem out of step with whatever the current consensus is, except that Western nation states have discarded the device of public executions and also of treason legislation, and have replaced it instead with the paraphernalia of national security and the proliferation of statute law criminalizing so-called hate speech.

It is also not difficult to define what it was that post-Reformation Protestant regimes regarded quite rationally, from time to time, as dangerous about contemporary Catholicism. Almost all those English Catholics who were dealt with as traitors affirmed a particular contemporary definition of the authority of the papacy. That definition was not in itself anything other than orthodox Christian political theory but, under certain circumstances, it could be intensely threatening to a regime at war, one which saw the monster of popular political resentment and opposition merging with an ideologically aggressive reading of the limits of temporal sovereign power, backed up by an appeal to papal authority. In addition, the case can be made that even the Elizabethan State was generally reluctant to make use of the statutory arsenal of legislation rendered available to it by parliament. Even while constructing a legal code *in terrorem*, the State had no wish to alienate a substantial Catholic loyalist impulse which may itself have been, at many points, the majority position within the English Catholic community. These were the people to whom, among others, Lord Burghley's famous *Execution of Justice* was directed.

This is precisely the lesson that Challoner's great text was not supposed to teach its readers. This is not to say that Challoner falsified his evidence. Far from it—in fact he was scrupulously attentive to the sources on which he relied. But his work, like that of other Catholic martyrologists before and after him, represents the construction of a tradition which is intensely controversial. It presents the documents relating to a series of cases which had already been identified as the ones that the Roman curia's legal processes would one day take forward, perhaps as far as eventual canonization, and it intentionally makes it difficult to read them in any other way. Challoner's *Memoirs* is, at one and the same time, a summary of the collective memory of the English Catholic community and, also, an opaque screen through which a great deal is not directly or clearly seen.

CONCLUSION   563

I have argued, however, that exactly the wrong historical response to all this material would be either to discard that Catholic martyrological tradition or to deconstruct it out of existence, nor would it work merely to align it with the cultural forms and norms of a wider European martyr discourse. As we have remarked at various points throughout this volume, the materials that contemporaries gathered together about what they took to be a persecution afflicting their Church recorded things that cannot generally be obtained from other sources. Those materials are primarily event-based historical ones, even if their compilers were not thinking merely historically. Those Catholic accounts have to be put alongside other contemporary narratives and perspectives which came out of the same kinds of political tensions and conflict. By locating them in the midst of other historical records of the aggressive deployment of State power against specific individuals accused of sedition, defined in part by reference to religion, we can see some of the interlocking conflicts within local society which generated separatism. Here we have a means of explaining why certain individuals eventually went right to the wire, refusing to back down in the face of State power. The classic case, here, is that of Margaret Clitherow. Had she not been indicted in a botched attempt at a show trial, she would have been just another local-history statistic, enlisted from time to time to demonstrate, for instance, that some conformist husbands had recusant wives. The legal proceedings against her, the confrontation in court between her and her enemies on the council in the North, the appalling nature of the way in which she was killed, and the survival of her chaplain John Mush's narrative of her life, taken all together, allow us to see below the surface of the stand-offs which on most days characterized the tension and hostility between the mid-Elizabethan State and parts of the 'Catholic community'.

In such cases, we have instances when the sorts of things that people, most of the time, did not want to say, or regarded it as unwise to say, or said only in private, got said in public. The resulting martyr stories also remind us that Catholic understandings of and glosses upon certain political questions remained in plain view as alternatives to aspects of the (frequently very unstable) religious and political post-Reformation status quo in a fashion which, many contemporary Protestant commentators argued, the Reformation should have made impossible. At particular points, those alternatives appeared to be actually imminent, for example during the early and mid-Elizabethan period when Mary Stuart seemed to be only a heartbeat away from the English crown or, in the early 1620s, as the Stuart court struggled to secure a dynastic union for the prince of Wales or, in the 1630s, during Charles I's personal rule when withdrawal from the increasingly problematic pan-European 'Protestant cause' was accompanied and glossed by what appeared to be quite radical changes to the face of English worship—changes which were applauded by Catholics; then, during the civil war when large numbers of Catholics fought for the king against parliament; and during the

564 CATHOLICS AND TREASON

Restoration and particularly during the Popish Plot and exclusion crisis of the later 1670s.

Historiographically, this may be an issue of some moment. Revisionist accounts of the period have argued that the Reformation was less ideologically contested than we once thought, certainly as far as the Catholic fraction of the national Church was concerned. Here, even without much in the way of statistical analysis, the claim is that most of the unreformed members of the national Church merged seamlessly with the conformist culture in that Church at some point during the late sixteenth century. On this basis, the records and traditions harboured and celebrated among separatist Catholics were the preserve and concern of a virtually irrelevant minority.

Actually, in the light of the accumulation of research and publication over the last forty years or so, that claim now seems completely unsustainable. It is perhaps worth stating clearly and unequivocally that, in these stories of confrontation with the authorities, and in the resentments and entrenched ideological positions contained in these vignettes of Catholic suffering which we have reviewed in this volume, we have an indication of not just how contentious post-Reformation Tudor and Stuart politics could be but also how central to contemporary political and religious culture certain kinds of contemporary Catholicism, from time to time, actually were. Here, the quotidian cruelties and petty vindictiveness that the Catholic martyr narratives describe, the judicial stitch-ups, the malicious false evidence given to the authorities, the attempts to cajole or terrify the accused into recanting, the stench of the gaols, the by turns hostile and sympathetic crowds gathering to watch executions of condemned Catholics, the horrors of the gallows and the disembowelling block, the officials' attempts to destroy martyrs' remains, the equally determined efforts to secure physical evidence of the sacrifice which the servants of God made rather than deny their faith, and the miracles that God sometimes chose to grant in recognition of that sacrifice—all of these things, and indeed the subsequent apotheoses of the victims of malign persecutory post-Reformation regimes, become historically comprehensible. Here the often seemingly antiquated and antiquarian formats in which most of those apotheoses, in manuscript and in print, were couched become anything but the stuff of conventional hagiography, even if in the work of Bishop Challoner they seem to be all too suspiciously uniform. Here we have accounts of everything from the bloodier and more violent side of local and, particularly, metropolitan politics all the way up to the political and ideological implications of the State's attempts to secure conformist compliance to whatever version of the national Church's religion was in the ascendant at that moment, and indeed of the resistance to the State's efforts to impose a conformist consensus. By looking at these documents through the prism of what one might perhaps call a 'narrative turn' in early modern studies, we can, at the very least, rescue the subject from its, arguably, marginal status and

CONCLUSION 565

bring it back from the abyss of irrelevance into which a modern-day mode of cultural studies still threatens to dispatch it.[1]

I am well aware that much of what is in this volume will, to some readers, still look like a form of historical relativism, a dumping of matters religious into a box marked 'political'. Such people may baulk at seeing martyr narratives contextualized by reference to essentially secular political issues. They would probably also want to say that true religion can never be in conflict with what is self-evidently essential for the maintenance of the structures of civil society. But at the same time (and this is hardly an original insight—though it does allow me right at the end of this book to play, as it were, devil's advocate to the relativist devil's advocate above), there has, historically, been a consensus among virtually all Christians that, for those who take the profession of Christianity seriously, religion has potentially disruptive social consequences. The recruitment of Christianity as an underprop for the State and for political authority has never been an easy process. Even if the tortuous arguments of the sixteenth and seventeenth centuries about whose theology could best lay claim to doctrinal rectitude do often, to the modern mind, seem essentially pointless, there were some on both sides in the struggles of the Reformation who thought that their version of the truth was worth dying for, if that was what was necessary to preserve it against the malign interference of those in authority.

In the end, perhaps one has to ask how far one can completely historicize those people who were recognized by Catholics as martyrs during the English Reformation. For all one's certainty that one has discovered, here and there, the reasons that certain individuals in the sixteenth and seventeenth centuries were identified as public enemies and then went to their deaths for the sake of 'religion', the principal sources on which one has to rely are, exactly as Anne Dillon argues, constructed rhetorically and polemically. But, at the same time, I do not think (and nor does she) that this kind of 'construction' is simply some sort of myth-making procedure. Without wanting to get into arguments about whether conventional modes of doing 'history' are about 'truth', ultimately one is forced to accept that there is something here that cannot, even taking into account everything we have said about the early modern period's familiarity with violence and brutality, simply be explained historically, at least in any conventional sense. In the end, I suppose, I feel compelled to agree with aspects of Brad Gregory's deeply

---

[1] It is ironic that it was the slow and deliberate judicial processes employed by the Roman curia, when it responded to English and Welsh claims that Catholics of the post-Reformation period had displayed heroic sanctity, which drove the investigative research that eventually brought into view the full range of the martyrological tradition of the post-Reformation Catholic community. Without the years of searching into the records demanded by the Sacred Congregation of Rites, one wonders whether much if any of this material would now be in the public domain at all. See M. Questier, *Memory, Sanctity and Religion in England c. 1850–1987* (forthcoming).

566 CATHOLICS AND TREASON

unfashionable, though essentially non-confessional, diatribe against relativism in matters of early modern religion.[2] I can also fully understand Gerard Kilroy's insistence that historical and literary deconstruction in the end does not really work for martyr texts. I am inclined to sympathize with him (though I know plenty of people who would not) when he compares the scholar-priest Campion with Miguel Pro and Oscar Romero and Jerzy Popiełuszko.[3]

There has, in fact, always been, within mainstream Christianity, a tradition that the power to confront evil cannot rely simply on mere physical force, even though there is an equally powerful tradition that the Church is invested with sufficient power to defend itself against its enemies—the weaponry that by process of logical deduction it must have in order to prevent Christ's promises to his Church not being fulfilled. In the words of Ronald Rolheiser, 'to accept' the martyr's pacific 'response to violence does not...rule out the possibility of morally justified self-defence or the possibility of a just war', but ultimately it is prayer and fasting which cast out the demons of persecution and tyranny.[4] Challoner's great book captures something of this. The martyr texts which Challoner gathered together are, at one level, obfuscatory—they are designed to obscure the extent to which, at certain points in the period, Catholicism supplied a critique of contemporary politics which was anything other than quiescent and pious in some merely conventional sense. But at the same time this does not necessarily mean that martyr texts are simply a code for something else—a mask to disguise the supposedly Machiavellian and calculating secular purposes which Catholics' enemies attributed to them, just as many of those Catholics attributed such purposes to their enemies.

It is arguable that those within the Catholic historical tradition who helped to fashion a starkly confessional account of this topic sometimes had a clearer or at least a more vivid idea of what the later sixteenth- and the seventeenth-century confrontations between Catholicism and the State were actually about—clearer, that is, than some professional historians of the period who have tended to avert their eyes from that topic either out of embarrassment or boredom. At the same time, all of this stands as a lesson to people of all faiths and none that, although

---

[2] B. Gregory, *Salvation at Stake: Christian Martyrdom in Early Modern Europe* (1999).

[3] Kilroy, *EC*, p. 345; see also ABSJ, 45/1/6/2 (James Walsh to Paolo Molinari, 13 November 1960; Molinari to Walsh, 17 November 1960, concerning Canon Scantlebury's draft article drawing a parallel between Edmund Campion and Miguel Pro); Kilroy, *EC*, pp. 245–6, citing Lord Bingham's comments (on the use of torture) in *A v Secretary of State for the Home Department* [2005] UKHL 71; [2005] Weekly Law Reports 1249. For Daniel Finkelstein's endorsement of Bingham's views more generally on repression as argued in his *The Rule of Law* (2010), see *The Times* (20 August 2014), p. 23 ('Human Rights are not a Joke. They are Vital').

[4] Ronald Rolheiser, 'The Ultimate Answer to Violence', *Catholic Herald* (17 August 2012). See also K. Rahner, 'Le Martyre' (trans. G. Daoust), in K. Rahner, *Ecrits Theologiques* (12 vols, Paris, 1959–70), III, pp. 171–203, cited in G. Kilroy, 'Edmund Campion: Martyrdom, Toleration and the Secular State' (forthcoming). I am very grateful to Professor Kilroy for sending me a draft of this paper.

we are entitled to peer back into times past, and, of course, the Tudor and Stuart period still seems to be as popular on the heritage trail and on the digital replacements for celluloid as almost anything else, we should be aware that, for all our enthusiasm about 'doing history' and about revisiting and, apparently, celebrating our past, we might not necessarily like what we find there.

Select Bibliography: Manuscripts

Archives of the Archdiocese of Birmingham

C 458 (hierarchical number Z5/3/40/1/1) (Richard Challoner's correspondence)
R 941 (hierarchical number Z6/11/15) (Alban Butler's papers, compiled for Bishop Challoner's published lives of missionary priests)
R 945 (hierarchical number Z6/11/17) (Alban Butler's further collection of material on the English and Welsh martyrs)

Archives of the Archdiocese of Westminster, London

Bo. 1/51 (correspondence of Cardinal Francis Bourne)
Go. 2/147 (correspondence of Cardinal William Godfrey)
Processus Martyrum (1874)
St Edmund's College, Ware MS 16/9
Series A, volumes I–XXXIV Miscellaneous Manuscripts
Series B, volumes 24–27, 28, 47–48 (formerly Stonyhurst Anglia VIII–IX), 57
Series F, volume 1 (Anthony Champney, 'Annales Elizabethae Reginae…')
Series OB (Old Brotherhood) I–III

Archives Générales du Royaume, Brussels

Papiers d'Etat et de l'Audience, MS 365

Archivio Segreto Vaticano, Vatican City

Borghese MS II, 448, a–b
Borghese MS III, 43, d–e
Borghese MS III, 124, g. 1
Borghese MS III, 127, e
Nunziatura d'Inghilterra 4
Segretario di Stato, Inghilterra, 19

Archivum Britannicum Societatis Jesu, London

A IV, no. 26 (Scottish Jesuits)
A V, no. 6 (William Richmond, 'A Trewe Storie of the Catholicke Prisoners in Yorke Castle…')

570　SELECT BIBLIOGRAPHY: MANUSCRIPTS

A V, no. 8 (John Thorpe SJ's notes)
A VII, no. 49 (examination of Catholics, temp. Elizabeth)
ABSJ, 45/1/6/2 (correspondence of James Walsh SJ)
ABSJ, 46/9/4/12 (transcripts of the newsletters written under the name of Anthony Rivers)
ABSJ, 46/12/1–2 (transcripts and translations of letters and papers of Henry Garnet SJ)
ABSJ, 46/12/3–6 (transcripts and translations of letters and papers of Robert Persons SJ)
ABSJ, 46/24/10 (Penelope Renold: transcripts and photocopies: Ghent State Archives: Ghent Jesuits, archives (K44) and charters (K45), 2 files)
ABSJ, 100/967/4 (transcript and translation, from Biblioteca Apostolica Vaticana, Vatican City, Barb. Lat. 2190)
Anglia I–VII (collected manuscripts, 16th–18th centuries)
Collectanea B, C, M, N, P (Christopher Grene SJ's MSS)
CP (Cause papers) Minutes of Meetings of Diocesan Representatives of the Office of the Vice-Postulation
Transcript and translation of Gregorio Panzani's Diary, 1634–1637 (ASV, Nunziatura d'Inghilterra 3a)

Archivum Romanum Societatis Jesu, Rome

Anglia 30–38 (Anglia Historia I–IX)
FG (Fondo Gesuitico) 651/624

Beinecke Rare Book and Manuscript Library, Yale University Library

Osborn a18 (James M. Osborn manuscripts)

Biblioteca Vallicelliana, Rome

N 23

Bodleian Library, Oxford

Carte MS 82
Clarendon MS 13
MS J. Walker c. 1, c. 2
Rawlinson (letters) 5
Rawlinson MS D 399

Borthwick Institute, York

HCAB 10–12 (High Commission Act Books)

SELECT BIBLIOGRAPHY: MANUSCRIPTS   571

British Library, London

Additional MSS 15225, 21203, 29546, 30262, 35331, 39245, 39288, 48023, 48029, 48035, 48064
Harleian MSS 360, 390, 422, 738, 4931, 6265, 6848, 6992, 6994, 6995, 6996, 6998, 7004, 7006, 7021, 7042
Lansdowne MSS 28, 33, 35, 38, 39, 45, 50, 59, 61, 64, 65, 66, 68, 72, 75, 84, 96, 97, 154
Royal Appendix MS 81

Canterbury Cathedral Archives

Literary MS, C. 2, no. 84

Douai Abbey, Woolhampton, Berkshire

Ralph Weldon, 'Memorials', deposit IA (6 volumes)

English College, Rome

Liber 1422 (Christopher Grene SJ, Collectanea F)
Liber 1577 (Godfrey Anstruther: Martyrs File)
Scr. 11/8 (Thomas Garnet)
Scr. 21/2/1–2 (Alexander Rawlins and Henry Walpole)
Scr. 36/8/1 (Christopher Bales)
Scr. 36/8/3 (Thomas Tichborne)
Scr. 36/12/2a–b (John Almond)

Essex Record Office, Chelmsford

Microfilm of Morant manuscripts T/A 391/6 (D/Y, 2/6)

Exeter University Library

MS 389, box 3, item 116 ('An Account of the Travels, Dangers and Wonderful Deliverances of the English Nuns of the Famous Monastery of Sion. From their first leaving England to their Settlement at Lisbon in the Kingdom of Portugal', Syon Abbey Archive)

Hatfield House, Hertfordshire

CP (Cecil Papers) 32, 53, 55, 61, 63, 77, 81, 85, 119, 181, 203, 254

572 SELECT BIBLIOGRAPHY: MANUSCRIPTS

Hendred House, Berkshire

Eyston MSS ('A Poor Little Monument to all the Old Pious Dissolved Foundations of England: A Short History of Abby's, All Sorts of Monastery's, Colleges...', unfoliated manuscript)

Hull History Centre

U DDEV/67/1 (5 vols: John Knaresborough, 'Sufferings of the Catholicks', Papers of the Constable Maxwell Family)
U DDEV/67/2 (a bound collection of materials for U DDEV/67/1)
U DDEV/67/3 ('Various Collections and Foul Draughts of the Sufferings of Catholicks': a bound collection of materials for U DDEV/67/1)

Inner Temple Library, London

Petyt MS 538/38, 47, 54

Kingston History Centre, Kingston-upon-Thames

Chamberlains Accounts, KD5/1/1 (formerly DIV, b1)

Lambeth Palace Library, London

MSS 2004, 2006, 2014, 3472 (Fairhurst manuscripts)
MSS 3198, 3200 (Talbot papers)

Lancashire Record Office, Bow Lane, Preston

RCFE/2/1/(v) (Letter of Christopher Tootell, 9 June 1723)

National Library of Ireland, Dublin

Marsh MS, Z3.5.21, item 8 ('A short view of a large examination of Cardinal Allen, his traitorous justification of Sir W. Stanley and Yorke, written by Mr. H. Cons[table], and this gathered out of his own draft')

National Library of Wales, Aberystwyth

Denbighshire Gaol Files, Great Sessions 4/5/4/7–10

SELECT BIBLIOGRAPHY: MANUSCRIPTS   573

St Mary's College, Oscott

R03351, formerly MS 45 (Francis Tregian)
R11781, formerly MS 98 (Christopher Grene SJ, Collectanea E)

Stonyhurst College, Lancashire

A V, no. 21 (Collections of Christopher Grene)
A VI, no. 37 (Catalogus Martyrum in Anglia)

The National Archives (Public Record Office), Kew

E 368 (Lord Treasurer's Remembrancer's memoranda rolls)
SP 12 (State Papers, Elizabeth)
SP 14 (State Papers, James I)
SP 15 (State Papers, Addenda)
SP 16 (State Papers, Charles I)
SP 39 (State Papers, Supplementary)
SP 77 (State Papers Foreign, Flanders)
SP 78 (State Papers Foreign, France)
SP 94 (State Papers Foreign, Spain)
SP 99 (State Papers Foreign, Venice)

Ushaw College Library, Special Collections

UC/P1/B2 (Joseph Bamber papers)
UC/P9/2/11 (Thomas G. Law papers)
UC/P25/7/812, 814, 816, 821 (John Lingard papers)
UC/P28/2/100 (Vincent Eyre papers)

Warwickshire County Record Office, Warwick

Throckmorton Papers, CR 1998/box 60/folder 2/28–32, 35, 40–1

West Sussex Record Office, Chichester

W.D. Peckham, typescript, Chichester Institutions

Index

For the benefit of digital users, indexed terms that span two pages (e.g., 52–53) may, on occasion, appear on only one of those pages.

Abbot, George 403–4, 430, 436n.59, 440–1, 444, 451n.7, 453
  allegations against, by Thomas Wenman 422, 422n.1
  and Anglo-Palatine marriage and Frederick V 420, 422, 454–5
  brother of, *see* Abbot, Robert
  chaplain of, *see* Purchas, Samuel
  and Conrad Vorstius 401n.111
  and James I, concerning Catholics, and Spain 403–4, 406–11, 424–5, 425n.10, 441, 445, 447; solicits accounts of Catholic separatism 427; and Anglo-Spanish marriage negotiations' failure/'blessed revolution' 454–6
  and John Almond 414n.179, 415, 417, 422–3
  and John Owen 429
  and John Roberts 395–7, 399, 400n.107, 414–15
  and Lewis Baily and the earl of Northampton 418, 418n.195, 419n.198
  and Luisa de Carvajal 425, 425n.14
  nominated to Canterbury 396, 396n.88
  and William Bishop 402, 407, 407n.142, 424–5
Abbot, Henry 267–72, 268n.36, 270n.43
  execution, with others, 4 July 1597, York 270, 272
Abbot, John 508, 508n.87
  Iesus Praefigured 456n.23
Abbot, Robert 402n.116
  brother of, *see* Abbot, George
Abercromby, Robert, SJ 382n.29
Abington, Edward 180
  and James Taylor 185
Achym, Thomas 305n.64
Acquaviva, Claudio, SJ 54n.35, 67n.95, 97n.105, 104, 154–5, 169, 182, 254n.124
  letters from Henry Garnet: 25 May 1590 205–6; 17 March 1593 223
Acuña, Diego Sarmiento de, count of Gondomar 417n.190, 428, 434n.56

and Anglo-Spanish marriage negotiations, and James I 432n.44, 442n.89, 446n.104, 450, 452–4, 455n.17
clergy's release, secured by 445, 450; and his departure in 1618 450, 454
embassy, and chapel 435, 445, 451, 452n.8
and Luisa de Carvajal 425
and Robert Sutton's remains/relics 451n.7
son of (Don Antonio) 435, 437n.63
and Thomas Maxfield and James I 434–5, 434n.55, 434nn.55–56, 437n.63, 439–40; *Relacion de Cinco Martyres* 434n.56
and Thomas Scott's *Vox Populi* 452
and William Baldwin 449–52; release, demanded by 450–2
and William Southerne and Lord Sheffield 445
and William Trumbull 452–3
Adams, John 130n.48, 165n.111
  Anthony Tyrrell's accusations against 166n.113
  trial and execution, with John Lowe and Richard Dibdale, 8 October 1586, Tyburn 165, 180
  and William Weston 165, 165n.111
Adams, S. 167n.116, 374, 482–3
Agazzari, Alfonso, SJ 136n.79, 140, 145, 154–5, 169
  William Allen sends copy of 1585 treason statute to 154–5
Ahab, King 177
Ailworth, Mr death in prison 34n.43
Ainsworth, John 429–30, 429n.32
  account of persecution, 1615 427–8, 429–30, 429n.33, 430n.34
Alabaster, William, and Thomas Wright 275
Alba, duke of, *see* Toledo y Pimentel, Fernando Álvarez de
Albert, archduke of Austria 354, 428, 452n.9
Aldred, Solomon 170n.133
  and English Catholics in Rome 99, 99n.111
Alfield, Thomas 90, 128n.41, 170n.133, 186n.29
  arrested, 7 April 1582, and released 123

576 INDEX

Alfield, Thomas (*cont.*)
arrested, September 1584, and charged under
1585 treason statute 155–6; and copies of
William Allen's *True, Sincere, and Modest
Defence*, distributed by him 155–6
interrogated concerning the duke of Guise's
intentions 155–6, 156n.69
temporary compliance 123
and Thomas Dodwell 155
trial and execution, with Thomas Webley,
6 July 1585, Tyburn 156–7
A True Reporte, in reply to *An Advertisement
and Defence* 116–17, 117n.201, 204n.115;
attacks Thomas Norton 117; printing of, in
Smithfield 117n.201
Alford, Agnes
husband of, *see* Alford, Francis
prosecution of, halted by Walsingham, on
promise of conformity 123n.24
and William Dean 123n.24
Alford, Francis 123n.24
wife of, *see* Alford, Agnes
Algunos Avisos de Inglaterra 429–30, 429n.33
Alkyngton, Samuel, acquitted of speaking in
favour of papal authority 134n.73
allegiance, oath of, *see* oath of allegiance
Allen, Sir Thomas 551
Allen, William, Cardinal (1587) 8–9, 36, 60, 100,
100n.114, 108, 113n.182, 114n.186, 118,
157, 177, 197, 216, 230, 238n.47, 291, 464
An Admonition 179–80, 190
and Alfonso Agazzari 136n.79, 145, 154–5
An Apologie and True Declaration 109, 216
*A Briefe Historie of the Glorious
Martyrdom* 25, 30, 60, 92, 121–2, 124–8,
145, 160–1, 312
and Charles Slade 98n.107
The Copie of a Letter, concerning Deventer
175–7, 202; replies to: by Gilbert Gifford
177n.166; by Henry Constable 177n.166
and Cuthbert Mayne 88n.62
A Declaration of the Sentence 179–80,
179n.1, 190
and deportations of Catholics 152, 154–5
and George Eliot 106n.146
and Gregory Martin's *Treatise of
Schisme* 135n.78
and Jesuit mission of 1580 (Edmund Campion
and Robert Persons) 97n.105, 100; and
Catholic recusancy 104; ridicules
proceedings against Campion and
others 113–14
and John Paine 121

and Nicholas Sander's *De Origine ac Progressu
Schismatis Anglicani* 161n.92
politique Catholicism, condemned by 124–5,
141–2
as prefect of the English mission 230n.6
and puritanism 125–8
and rebellion in Ireland 99, 101–2
and Richard Verstegan's publications 136,
136n.79
and Robert Persons's *Copie of a Double
Letter* 109n.161
A True, Sincere, and Modest Defence 137,
141–5, 151–3; translation by William
Rainolds 137n.81; and royal proclamation
of 12 October 1584 aimed against 151;
distributed by Thomas Alfield 155–6,
156n.69
and William Tedder 167
Allensmore, *see* Whitsun Riot
Allison, A. F. 23n.2, 474n.75
Almond, John 429
arrest, trial, and execution, 5 December 1612,
Tyburn 414–21 *passim*, 423; Almond's
own narrative 414n.178; other
narratives 415n.182, 417n.188; memory
contested 417n.190; relic 417n.190
oath of allegiance, 1606, and George
Abbot 414–15, 414n.177, 422–3
regicide 414–17
and Society of Jesus and Robert
Persons 414n.179
Altham, Sir James 440
Altman, S. 5n.4
Alvechurch, Worcestershire 263–4
Amias, John
problems in identification of 194n.74
trial and execution, with Robert Dalby,
15 or 16 March 1589, York 56, 194–5
'Ancient Editor's Notebook' 66n.93, 224–5
Anderson, Sir Edmund, and trials of Catholics:
Edmund Gennings and others 216; James
Bird 220, 228; John Sugar and Robert
Grissold 337; William Freeman 264–5
Anderton, Mr 294
Anderton, Robert 463
delivers oration at English College, Rheims,
April 1583 162
execution, with William Marsden, 25 April
1586, Isle of Wight 163; proclamation
concerning 162–3
loyalism of 162–3
and William Warford 163n.101
Anderton, William, OFM 519

INDEX 577

Andover, Hampshire, execution of John Bodey,
2 November 1584 131
Andrewes, Lancelot, bishop of Chichester (1605)
and bishop of Ely (1609) 229n.2, 264,
396n.88, 427n.21, 480
and oath of allegiance, 1606 373–4, 374n.174
and puritanism 369
and William Weston 192
Andrews, Thomas 517n.132
Angus, earl of, see Douglas, William
Anjou, duke of, see François, duke of Alençon
Anlaby, William 270n.43
execution, with others, 4 July 1597, York 270
Anne of Austria, queen regent of France 518
Anne of Denmark
and Catholicism 286
and Robert Drury 361
Anne, Ernestine 194n.74
Anselm, St 16
Anstruther, G., OP 108n.157, 202
Antonio, Don, prior of Crato, claimant to
Portuguese throne 211
Antrim, marquis of, see MacDonnell, Randal
Antwerp, truce of, see truce of Antwerp
approbation controversy 466–70, 472–3,
481–2, 486–7
Aquinas, St Thomas 61
archduke, the, see Albert, archduke of Austria
archpriest, see Birkhead, George; Blackwell,
George; Harrison, William
Archpriest Dispute/appellant controversy 9n.17,
41, 261–2, 281–2, 284–5, 352, 375, 530–1,
542, ch. 10 passim; breve of 25 September/5
October 1602 309n.79; see also protestation
of allegiance, 1603
Arden, Edward 141n.3, 150, 317
Argyll, earl of, see Campbell, Archibald, 7th earl;
Campbell, Archibald, 8th earl
Arians/Arianism, see Kett, Francis
Armada, see Spain, Armada of 1588
Armagh
archbishop of, see Ussher, James
Catholic archbishop of, see Lombard, Peter;
Plunket, Oliver
Arminianism 470–1, 476
Arnold, John 547n.41
Arrigoni, Pompeo, Cardinal 289n.6
Arrowsmith, Edmund, SJ, alias Bradshaw 146,
551n.57
and Ambrose Barlow 471, 478n.97, 505
arrest, trial, and execution, 28 August 1628,
Lancaster 56, 460n.42, 471–82; his memory
contested 473–4; narratives (including

A True and Exact Relation) 471n.69, 474n.75,
479, 481n.114; remains and relics 478–9,
479n.101; and Richard Herst 479–81
converts felon 56
as exorcist 471
father of, see Arrowsmith, Robert
grandfathers of, see Arrowsmith, Thurstan;
Gerard, Nicholas
informer against (Crook), providentially
punished 69
and Society of Jesus 472–3, 473n.74
Arrowsmith, John, refuses full conformity 227
Arrowsmith, Peter 472
brother of, see Arrowsmith, Robert
Arrowsmith, Robert 472
brother of, see Arrowsmith, Peter
son of, see Arrowsmith, Edmund
Arrowsmith, Thurstan 146
grandson of, see Arrowsmith, Edmund
Arthington, Henry 209n.131
Arthington, in Nidderdale 247
Arundel, countess of, see Howard, Anne
Arundel, earl of, see Howard, Philip;
Howard, Thomas
Arundel House, London 73
used by Robert Southwell 73
Arundell, Johanna, husband of,
see Bosgrave, Leonard
Arundell, Lady 250n.107
Arundell, Sir John
anti-piracy commission 88–9; excluded
from 89n.65
nephews of, see Bosgrave, Thomas;
Tregian, Francis
wife of, see Arundell, Lady
Arundell, Thomas, 2nd Baron Arundell of
Wardour 501
Asaph, bishop of, see Goldwell, Thomas
Ash, Margaret 397
Ashley, Ralph, SJ 376, 460n.42
Ashton, Ralph 297n.34
Ashton, Roger 269n.41
executed, 23 June 1592, Tyburn 175n.160
and William Allen's Copie of a Letter 175–7
Askew, Snr and Jnr, providential
punishment of 69
Aston, Robert 66n.93
Aston, Sir Walter 66–7
death of 67n.94
and Mary Stuart, lodged at Tixall 67n.94
Athalia, Queen 176–7
Atherton, I. 401n.111
Atkins, Richard 109–10

578 INDEX

Atkins, Thomas 149n.39
Atkinson, Anthony 241, 241n.65, 268n.35
  and the arrest of Alexander
    Rawlins 256n.134, 270
  and the arrest of John Boste, 10 September
    1593 239–40, 256n.134
  and the earl of Essex 274
  and Matthew Hutton 243
  and Thomas Warcop 270
Atkinson, James
  death of 278n.63
  threatened by Richard Topcliffe and Nicholas
    Jones 277
Atkinson, Mr, a Marian priest
  condemned concerning the royal
    supremacy 340, 340n.36
Atkinson, Thomas 267, 270n.43
  execution, 11 March 1616, York 431–2, 436
  Exemplar Literarum 431n.39
  and Society of Jesus 431n.39
Atkinson, William 324n.139, 366n.143
  Thomas Hill, betrayed by 334, 337n.16
  Thomas Tichborne, betrayed by 321
  and William Watson 321
attorney-general, see Coke, Sir Edward; Popham,
    Sir John; Yelverton, Sir Henry
Audebert, Anne, execution 52
Audley, Martin 183n.18
Augustine, St, of Canterbury 49
Augustine, St, of Hippo 61, 177
Austin, John, alias William Birchley 528–32, 542
  The Christian Moderator, pts I–III 528–32;
    and Richard Challoner's and John
    Knaresborough's use of 528, 528n.179
  and martyrdom 531–2
  and Thomas Hobbes 528–9
  and Thomas White 528–9
Aveling, J. 87, 256n.134, 469n.61, 549n.49
  and John Bossy 42
  The Handle and the Axe 42
  scholarship of 42, 42n.72
Aylmer, John, bishop of London 94–5
  courtroom dispute with Richard Leigh
    189n.49
  and Giles Wigginton 174–5
  and the Marshalsea 133n.72
  and puritanism 92
  and Robert Morton 94
  and Thomas Sherwood 92–3
  and Tower disputations with Edmund
    Campion 111n.169
  and trial of Edmund Gennings and
    others 216
  and William Carter 96, 135
  and William Hartley 133n.72

Ayloff, William
  acquittal of Edward Jones 131n.60
  and John Slade and John Bodey
    131n.60

Babington, Anthony
  conspiracy 164–8, 164n.108, 180, 209, 240,
    270, 317
  execution 164–5
  and Swithin Wells 215n.155
Babington, Sir William, death of, at Oxford
    assizes, 1577 64
Babthorpe, Lady Grace 158, 206n.120, 267n.33,
    280n.76, 431n.39
Bacon, Edward 137–8, 138n.84
Bacon, Nathaniel 137–8, 233
Bacon, Nicholas, alias Southwell, SJ
    50n.12
Bacon, Sir Francis 276, 443
Bacon, Sir Nicholas 96, 127n.36
Bagshaw, Christopher 170, 219, 378
  appeal of 1601–02 308
  arrest and release 170n.133
  cousin of, see Bagshaw, Robert
  enmity towards Robert Persons 170n.133,
    318, 378
  persecution and Jesuits 315, 378
  Sir Francis Walsingham's good opinion
    of 170n.133
  and Thomas Benstead 289–90
  A True Relation of the Faction 315n.102
Bagshaw, Robert
  cousin of, see Bagshaw, Christopher
  and Nicholas Garlick 181n.12
Bailey, George 320n.127
Bailey, Mary 320n.127
Baillies, Thomas 381
Baily, Laurence, trial and execution, August 1604,
    Lancaster 339–41, 340n.30
Baily, Lewis
  and George Abbot 418
  sermon, 15 November 1612 418–19
Baker, George 275
Baker, Sir Richard 15n.35, 17
Baldwin, John, and Henry Foxwell (reconciled to
    Rome by) 186n.26
Baldwin, William SJ 424n.8, 453, 453n.13
  arrested and imprisoned 413n.168, 449–50;
    release requested by Pedro de
    Zúñiga 413n.168; Richard Blount's
    narrative 450n.2
  and Gunpowder Plot and 'Spanish
    Treason' 381–2, 449–50, 449n.1
  and Philip III 453n.13
  release of 445n.103, 449–54 passim

INDEX 579

Bales, Christopher 50n.12
  arrest 48n.2
  harbourer of, *see* Thirkell, Henry
  papal deposing power, defended by 48–9
  reputation, attacked by Richard Topcliffe 202
  tortured in Bridewell 50n.10, 210–11,
    211n.137
  trial and execution, 4 March 1590, Fleet
    Street 48–50, 202, 203–4; speech 48–9
Balgavies Castle, demolition of 245
Ballard, John 167, 247
  and Anthony Babington 165
  and John Boste 247, 247n.93
  and William Weston 165
Balliol College, Oxford 170n.133, 422–3
Bamber, Edward 12–14
  arrested, December 1626 469; conformity and
    pardon 469, 522–3
  execution, with John Woodcock and Thomas
    Whitaker, 7 August 1646, Lancaster 522–3;
    relic 554n.73
  as exorcist 522n.157
  nephew of 13–14
Bamber, Joseph 13–14, 13n.28, 25n.9, 28
Bamford, James 223–4
Bancroft, Richard, bishop of London (1597) and
    archbishop of Canterbury (1604) 50n.10,
    165n.111, 228, 278n.67, 301n.50, 309,
    320n.128, 327, 357, 358–9, 366n.143
  anti-puritanism/conformity 232, 259, 347–8;
    anti-puritan publications (*Survay of the
    Pretended Holy Discipline* and *Daungerous
    Positions*) 233n.18, 237, 237n.45
  and appellant clergy/Archpriest Dispute 296,
    304, 312, 315n.102, 324, 323n.138, 324n.139,
    326n.155
  and Cuthbert Trollop 323n.138
  death of 396; succeeded by George
    Abbot 396
  and George Williams 344n.57, 346–7
  and Henry Garnet and Gunpowder
    Plot 352–3, 353n.86
  and John Roberts 396, 396n.89
  and John Scudamore 347, 353n.86,
    360n.115
  and Michael Walpole 378
  Paul's Cross sermon, 9 February 1589 196
  and protestation of allegiance, 1603 326–7
  and recusancy 342
  and Richard Smith's and Thomas More's
    agency in Rome 371
  and Roger Filcock 303–4
  and Sir Robert Cecil 320n.128, 324
  and Whitsun Riot 344, 346–8
  and William Watson 323–4

Banister, servant of Henry Hastings, 3rd earl of
    Huntingdon 60
Bankin, Annis, execution 48n.2
Banks, Richard, SJ 392n.66, 393, 393n.75, 419n.198
Barber, Francis 216n.158, 474
Barberini, Francesco, Cardinal 536n.213
Barca, Pedro Calderón de 468
Barclay, John, *Satyricon* 452n.9
Barham, Nicholas, death of, at Oxford assizes,
    1577 64n.84
Barkworth, Mark, OSB 305n.64
  and Sir John Stanhope 322n.135
  and Society of Jesus 314n.97
  trial and execution, with Roger Filcock
    and Anne Line, 27 February 1601,
    Tyburn 304–5, 304n.58, 317–18
Barlow, Edward (Ambrose), OSB 12
  arrest, trial, and execution, 10 September 1641,
    Lancaster 478n.97, 505
  brother of, *see* Barlow, Rudesind
  and Edmund Arrowsmith 471, 478n.97, 505
  godson of, *see* Booth, Edward
  relic of, at Wardley Hall 28, 28n.19, 506*f*;
    authentication of 28n.19
Barlow Hall 12, 478n.97
Barlow, Lewis, and Anthony Tyrrell 175n.159
Barlow, Mr 478n.97
Barlow, Thomas, bishop of Lincoln 550
Barlow, William (Rudesind), OSB 478n.97,
    481–2, 482n.115
  brother of, *see* Barlow, Edward (Ambrose)
Barlow, William, bishop of Lincoln 30–1,
    336n.15, 338n.23, 342n.45, 343n.51
Barnaby, Francis
  appeal of 1601–02 308
  and search of the Clink prison 324
Barnbow Hall 556
Barnes, Robert 221
  and George Hethershall 275, 276
  and Henry Garnet 352n.85
  and Mrs Bellamy 277
  and Richard Topcliffe 275–80 *passim*
  and Stannardine Passy 276
  trial and charges against (and John Jones and
    Jane Wiseman) 275–80 *passim*, 352n.85
  and 2nd Viscount Montague 275
  and William Weston's exorcisms 278n.67;
    the 'book of exorcisms' 278, 278n.67
Barnes, Robert, bishop of Durham 66n.93
Barnes, Stephen 216n.158
Barnes, Thomas 351–2
Barnstaple, North Devon 53
Baro, Peter 264n.19
Baronius, Caesar, Cardinal 313n.93
Barret, Mr 353n.86

580 INDEX

Barret, Richard 32, 64–5, 132n.65, 136n.79, 140, 145n.20
Barrett, William 264
  sermon of 29 April 1595 264n.19
Barrow, Henry 234–5
  legal proceedings against 234–6; execution 236
Barry, P. 6n.6, 29n.24, 444n.96
  analysis of Christopher Grene's Collectanea F, item 1 26n.13
Barton, Elizabeth 79
Barwick, John 441
Barwise, John
  allegedly reconciled by Thomas Pormort 219n.168
  recantation 220n.171
Basset, Joshua 15n.34
Bassett, William, JP
  feud with Thomas Fitzherbert 183, 183n.18
  and Richard Topcliffe 233n.20
  uncle of, see Fitzherbert, Sir Thomas
  warns of impending search of house of Sir Thomas Fitzherbert 183n.18
Bassompierre, François de, Marshal 465n.53
Bastwick, John 488, 499–500
Bates, Anthony
  execution, with James Harrison, 22 March 1602, York 320, 320n.124
  and Sir John Yorke 320n.124
  wife of, reprieved 320
Bavant, John, martyr catalogue by (lost) 30n.27
Baxter, Richard 539
Bayly, Thomas 174
Baynes, Roger 242n.70, 258, 261
Beak, Richard 459
Beale, Thomas 507n.81
beatifications
  of 1886 and 1895 78, 82
  of 1987 3n.1
Beaulieu, Jean 380n.24
Beaumaris, execution of William Davies, 27 July 1593 57, 60, 237
Beaumont, count of, see Harlay, Christophe de
Beaumont, Francis
  crypto-Catholicism 256n.132
  and Henry Walpole 256n.132
Becanus, Martinus, SJ 542
Beck, George, bishop of Salford 28n.19
Becket, Thomas, St 447
Bedford, earl of, see Russell, Francis, 2nd earl; Russell, Francis, 4th earl
Bedloe, William 557
  death of 69
Bell, Arthur (Francis), OFM 516n.128, 532
  arrest and execution, 11 December 1643, Tyburn 518–20; relics 518n.139

and breve ordering inquiry into martyrdom in England 518–20
  and Charles Marchant 518
Bell, James 145n.21
  ordination 147n.29
  trial and execution, with John Finch, 20 April 1584, Lancaster 146–7
Bell, Sir Robert, death of, at Oxford assizes, 1577 64, 64n.84
Bell, Thomas
  and Anthony Tyrrell 170
  and churchgoing/occasional conformity 182, 228, 229, 256n.134; Henry Garnet's attacks on 182, 205–6, 228n.206, 238; apostasy 200–1, 227n.201, 238, 242n.66, 252, 312
  evades arrest in York Castle 129n.44
  and John Mush 170
  and royal proclamation of 18 October 1591, and information against Catholics 227n.201, 238n.47, 298n.37, 340n.32
  and William Hardesty 200–1, 252
Bellamy, Anne
  mother of, see Bellamy, Catherine (née Forster)
  and Nicholas Jones 221, 276
  and Richard Topcliffe 221, 276–7
  Robert Barnes, denounced by 276–7
  and Robert Southwell's arrest 221, 221n.175, 276–7
Bellamy, Bartholomew 278
Bellamy, Catherine (née Page) 221
Bellamy, Catherine (wife of Richard; née Forster) 221n.176
  daughter of, see Bellamy, Anne
  husband of, see Bellamy, Richard
  and Richard Topcliffe 277
  and Robert Barnes 277
Bellamy, Richard 120n.6, 186, 221
  wife of, see Bellamy, Catherine (née Forster)
Bellamy, Robert, and William Thompson 162n.98
Bellamy, Robert, Dr, and George Swallowell 248–9
Bellarmine, Robert, Cardinal 62, 200n.92, 372n.166, 418n.195, 451
Belson, Thomas
  arrest, trial, and execution, with others, 5 July 1589, Oxford 197–8
  and Edward Grately 197n.83
  and Francis Ingleby 197n.83
  and George Etheridge 197n.82
  and Robert Tempest 200n.92
  and William Forrest 197n.83

INDEX 581

Benedictines/Order of St Benedict, *see* names of
individual Benedictines in this index
Bennett, Edward 402, 406n.138, 406n.140,
408n.149, 409n.151, 411, 412n.167,
416, 434n.55
brother of, *see* Bennett, John, appellant
and the oath of allegiance, 1606 395–6
and Roger Cadwallader 389n.60, 390, 390n.62
Bennett, John 148n.34, 237n.44
Bennett, John, appellant 314–16, 390, 390n.62
brother of, *see* Bennett, Edward
and martyrdom 318
Bennett, John, Dr 252n.116
Bennett, Robert, master of St Cross Hospital,
Winchester, and bishop of Hereford
(1603) 381*f*
and George Williams 346–8, 346n.62, 347n.67
and John Slade and John Bodey, and advice to
Lord Burghley 132–3
and Robert Marsden and William
Anderton 163
and Roger Cadwallader 381, 384–7 *passim*
and Whitsun Riot (Allensmore riots) 343–51
passim, 381
Bennett, Sir John 355n.94
Benstead, Thomas
arrest 288–90, 290n.7
enmity towards Christopher Bagshaw 289–90
execution, with Thomas Sprott, 1 July 1600,
Lincoln 44n.78, 68, 288–9, 308, 345n.60
letter to Henry Garnet, 28 April 1600 289
Bentham, Thomas, bishop of Coventry and
Lichfield, and the prophesyings 85
Bergen-op-Zoom 181n.11, 269n.41
Berkeley, John, 1st Baron Berkeley 543
Berkshire, Catholics in 458
Berwick 107
treaty of, 1586 164
Beseley, George 274–5, 303n.56
trial and execution, with Montford Scott, 1
July 1591, Fleet Street 203, 207–8, 209,
207n.124
hostility to Elizabeth Tudor 207
interrogation 207n.123; Richard
Topcliffe 207n.123
John Cecil's notes concerning 207
notebook of 216
and Robert Humberson
(Humberstone) 207n.124
tortured 210–11
Bessarion, Basilios, Cardinal 354n.91
Bethel, Sir Hugh 69
Béthune, Philippe de 308, 324n.143
Beza, Theodore 102, 237
Bianchetti, Lorenzo, Cardinal 394n.80

Bickerdike, Robert 461n.46
conviction procured by coercion of
jury 168n.124
execution, 23 July 1586/August 1586,
York 168, 168n.124
and John Boste 168n.124
sister of, *see* Maskew, Bridget
and William Hutton's claims concerning
trial 168n.124
Bickley, Thomas, bishop of Chichester, and
proceedings against Catholic clergy at
Chichester 191–2
Biddulph, Peter, alias Fitton 525–6, 526n.172
Bilney, Thomas 307
Bilson, Thomas, bishop of Winchester
(1597) 396n.88, 424n.8
The True Difference 111n.170, 156
Bingham, Thomas, Baron Bingham 566n.3
Bird, Anthony 220n.172
Bird, James 463
and Benjamin Norton 220, 220n.172
execution, 25 March 1592, Winchester 220,
220n.172
at Rheims seminary 220
Bird, John 321
Bird, Richard 220n.172
Birkhead, George, Archpriest 131, 222n.183,
279, 378, 396n.88, 396n.91, 417n.190,
418n.195, 419, 423n.6
as archpriest, replacing George Blackwell 363
and assassination of Henry IV 380, 382
doubts martyr status of James Leyburn 130
and episcopal government and reform,
lobbying for 370–2, 389–90, 412
and George Napper 393–4, 393n.77, 394n.80
and martyrdom and persecution 378n.7,
400n.107
nephew of, *see* Lambton, Joseph
and oath of allegiance, 1606 378, 379, 412
and parliament in 1610 379, 380n.22
and Robert Barnes 276–7
and Robert Jones 388n.58, 389–90
and Roger Cadwallader 387–90, 390n.62,
390n.63, 391n.65
Birkhead, Martin 129n.45
Bishop, William, bishop of Chalcedon
(1623) 9n.17, 407
arrested at Rye, and convicted of plotting the
death of the queen 152n.52
deported (1585) 152n.52, 407(1611)
and George Abbot 402, 407, 407n.142, 424–5
oath of allegiance, 1606, refused by 402
Richard Smith succeeds 459–60
and Roger Cadwallader 389n.60, 390n.62
Blackall, Christopher, and John Jones 278n.69

582 INDEX

Blackburn, Edward 12n.26
Blackburn, John 12n.26
    and Brian Orrell 12
Blackfan, John, SJ 417
    and Luisa de Carvajal 417n.191
Blackloism, *see* White, Thomas
Blackwall, Nicholas 183n.18
    removal as clerk of the peace 183n.18
Blackwell, George, Archpriest 72n.114, 266, 292,
        302n.53, 305, 320, 349–50
    and Archpriest Dispute 261, 284–5, 290–2,
        299, 315, 325, 356n.96; appeal against
        Blackwell, of 17 November 1600 185,
        355n.94, 356n.96, 387n.54; appeal of
        1601–02 308–9; and Thomas
        Tichborne 321; and Robert Southwell's
        Humble Supplication 322
    arrest, 24 June 1607 361; interrogations
        361–2; deposed 363
    and oath of allegiance, 1606 361–2, 366, 370,
        392; challenged by Luisa de Carvajal
        concerning 362n.122; and George
        Gervase 366–7
    and Pope Paul V's warning concerning
        sedition 349–50; Blackwell's letter of
        admonition, 22 July 1605 350n.76
    and Robert Drury 356n.97
    and Thomas Garnet 369
    and Thomas Sprott 288–9
    and William Watson and William Clarke
        335n.12
Blackwell, Nicholas, and legal proceedings
        against Robert Barnes 276
Blainville, seigneur de, *see* Jean de Varignies
Blake, Alexander, execution, 4 March 1590,
        Gray's Inn Lane 49, 202n.104
Blandford, Dorset 216, 216n.158
Blanks conspiracy 243, 245–6, 247n.89, 261–2
'bloody questions' 122, 122n.18, 125, 182
Blount, Charles, 8th Baron Mountjoy, intervenes
        at execution of Robert Southwell 62, 255
Blount, Sir Christopher 303n.55
    and earl of Essex's rebellion 303
    son-in-law, *see* Devereux, Robert
Blount, Richard, SJ 26, 221, 301n.46, 305,
        305n.65, 317, 336, 365n.136, 412n.165, 423,
        425, 424n.9, 433, 434, 436n.59, 440n.77,
        441–2, 444, 442n.89
    and Anne Line 305, 305n.65
    and Henry Garnet 352–3
    and James Duckett 322n.135
    and John Almond 417n.190
    and John Sugar and Richard Blount 337–9
    and persecution at end of Elizabeth's reign
        319–22 *passim*

and Philip Howard and Anne Howard 486–7
and Robert Drury and William Davies 355–6,
        358–9, 359n.106, 361
and Thomas Maxfield 438
and Thomas Tichborne 321n.133
and Thurstan Hunt and Robert Middleton
        300–1
and William Baldwin 450n.2
Blount, Sir Michael, lieutenant of the Tower 240
Blount, Sir Thomas 263n.13
    daughter of, *see* Heath, Dorothy
Blount, Thomas, *Calendarium/Kalendarium*
        541n.16
Bluet, Thomas 317, 396
    appeal of 1601–02 308–9
    Important Considerations 311n.85, 316–18
    and Richard Bancroft 322
    and Squire Plot 289n.6
Blundell, Richard
    books found in house (including Richard
        Bristow's *A Briefe Treatise*) 204n.115
    death in Lancaster gaol 204n.115
    proceedings ordered against 204
    and Robert Woodruff 204
Blundell, William 297n.34, 298n.37
Blythe, George, death of 66
Blythe, Marian priest 194n.70
Boardman, Andrew, and William
        Freeman 263–6
Boderie, Antoine le Fèvre de la 361, 373–4
    and George Blackwell 362n.122, 363
    and George Gervase 363n.130, 364
    intervenes on behalf of Robert Drury and
        William Davies 359–60, 359n.106,
        360n.110
    and James I's *An Apologie... together with a
        Premonition* 374n.174
    and James I's hostility to puritans 362
Bodey, John 463
    ejected from New College, Oxford 87,
        132n.65
    and puritanism in Hampshire 132–3;
        see also Bennett, Robert; Kingsmill, Sir
        William; Humphrey, Laurence
    trial, with John Slade, and execution, 2
        November 1583, Andover 131–2, 131n.56,
        144, 343–4; legal complexity of
        prosecution 131, 131n.58; popular
        comment concerning 133; *The Severall
        Executions* 132n.65; William Allen's
        comments on authorship 133
Bohemia, revolt in 443
Bold, Richard 166–7
    and bond of association 166
    chaplain of, *see* Dibdale, Richard

INDEX 583

cousin of, *see* Peckham, Sir George
household at Harleyford (Harlesford) 166
interrogation 167n.116
quarrels with earl of Leicester 166–7
and William Weston 166–7, 167n.116
Boleyn, Anne 134, 179, 456
and Thomas, Lord Burgh, her lord
chamberlain 244n.75
Boleyn, George, 2ⁿᵈ Viscount Rochford 179
Bolland, James, recantation of, 22 February
1600 280
Bologna, cardinal of (Gabriele Paleotti, bishop of
Bologna (1567)) 100–1
Bolron, Robert 557n.83
Bolsec, Jerome (Jérôme-Hermès Bolsec), *Life
of Calvin* (*Histoire de la Vie...de Jean
Calvin* (Lyons and Paris, 1577)) 111,
111n.171
Bolton, John 185
signs appellant petition 184–5
bond of association 139, 152, 157, 166
Bonner, Edmund, bishop of London
31, 124n.26
servant of, *see* Hamerton, John
and treason act of 1563 81
Booth, Edward, alias Barlow 12, 520n.143
as chaplain to the Houghton family 12n.25
godfather of, *see* Barlow, Edward
(Ambrose) 12
and John Thulis's execution 12n.26
Borghese, Camillo, Cardinal, *see* Paul V, Pope
Borghese, Scipione, Cardinal 371n.165, 377
Bosgrave, James
arraigned 112n.177
deported 152n.52
reprieved 122n.18
Bosgrave, Leonard 250n.107
wife of, *see* Arundell, Johanna
Bosgrave, Thomas
execution, with others, 3 or 4 July 1594,
Dorchester 250n.107
father of, *see* Bosgrave, Leonard
uncle of, *see* Arundell, Sir John
Bossy, J. 45, 231, 288, 324–6, 324n.143, 326n.157,
328, 526–7, 538n.2
doctoral dissertation 43–4
English Catholic Community 41–4; account of
historiography of the post-Reformation
Catholic community 43–4
and John Aveling 42
and martyrology 41–2
and revisionism 42–3
and Robert Persons 129
the 'triumph of the laity' and the 'revolt of the
clerks' 44–5

Boste, John 228, 240n.55, 240n.60, 245, 257,
268n.35, 269–70, 461n.46
arrest of, 10 September 1593 226, 239,
241n.62, 243
as chaplain to Margaret Neville 239
'Cecil's Commonwealth' tracts 240–1
conformity of, until 1576 87–8
connections with Scotland 171n.137,
239–40, 239n.52
and Henry Duffield 240, 248n.96
interrogation and torture 240n.55, 241,
247n.89; and Anthony Major 241
and James VI 240
and John Ballard 247, 247n.93
and John Hewett 187
and John Thornborough 240n.55
prediction of 'day of triumph' 171
and Robert Bickerdike 168n.124
and Roger Widdrington 14
trial, with John Ingram and George
Swallowell, and execution, 25 July 1594,
Durham 14, 60–1, 247–9, 248n.96,
256n.132, 274; reported by John Cecil and
Christopher Robinson 60–1; prevented
from delivering gallows speech 60
Boste, Lancelot 130n.51
Bosvile, John 322
Boswell, Sir William 495
Bothwell, earl of, *see* Hepburn, James; Stuart, Francis
Bouillon, duke of, *see* Tour d'Auvergne, Henri de la
Bourbon, Louis I de, prince of Condé 81
Bourne, Anthony 88–9, 88n.63
father of, *see* Bourne, Sir John
Bourne, Sir John 88n.63
son of, *see* Bourne, Anthony
Bowes, Marmaduke 461n.46
arrest, trial, and execution, 27 November 1585,
York 157–8
conformist tendency of 158
and Hugh Taylor 157–8, 161
and Martin Harrison 158
speaks against royal supremacy 157n.77
Bowes, Robert 240n.60
Bowes, Sir William 239
Bowler, H. 279n.71
Bowyer, Thomas, and proceedings against
Catholic clergy at Chichester 191–2
Bradbridge, William, bishop of Exeter
and Cuthbert Mayne 88
and recusancy survey of October 1577 88n.63
Bradford, John 197n.82
Bradshaw, John (Augustine), OSB 412n.165
Brakenbury, Leonard 296n.30, 461n.46
Bramley, a felon, execution 56
Bramston, Sir John 488

584 INDEX

Brandenburg, margrave of (John
    Sigismund) 428
Breres, Henry 297, 300n.45
Brettergh, Katherine 306–7, 476
    husband of, *see* Brettergh, William
Brettergh, William 293, 299–300
    retaliation against 293, 296, 297n.33
    wife of, *see* Brettergh, Katherine
Bretton, Frances
    conformity of 279n.71
    husband of, *see* Bretton, John
Bretton, John 279n.70, 461n.46
    and Anthony Champney 279n.71
    charges against him/indictment 279n.71
    execution, 1 April 1598, York 279, 280
    recusancy/separatism of 279n.71
    wife of, *see* Bretton, Frances
Briant, Alexander, SJ
    arrested by Thomas Norton 105, 127–8
    tortured 105, 112n.173, 127–8
    and Tower disputations 112n.173
    trial and execution, with Edmund Campion
        and Ralph Sherwin, 1 December 1581,
        Tyburn 113n.179, 115–17
Bridewell
    prison 50n.10, 73, 109–10, 187–9, 198,
        201n.96, 211n.137
    Robert Persons's lodgings, raided 105
Bridgeman, John, bishop of Chester 474, 479
Bridgeman, Sir John 478–9
Brienne, countess of 498n.32
Brinkley, Stephen 96n.101
Briscow, Thomas, condemned, reprieved, and
    deported 343, 343n.51, 432–3, 433n.51
Brisson, Bernabé 136
Bristol
    bishop of, *see* Thornborough, John
    earl of, *see* Digby, George; Digby, Sir John
Bristow, Richard 216
    A Briefe Treatise 106n.147, 113, 204n.115, 321
    Richardi Bristoi Motiva 376n.3
Britland, K. 464n.50, 465–6, 465n.52
Brogden, W. 344n.57
Brome, Henry 552n.62
Bromley, Sir George 66n.92
    and Lord Burghley 150n.44
    and Richard White 66, 148, 150
Bromley, Sir Thomas, and the treason statute of
    1585 153
Brooke, Sir Basil 490
Brooksby, Edward 104n.132
Brooksby, Eleanor 104n.132
    father of, *see* Vaux, William

Brooksby, Mr 85–6
Broughton, Richard 153, 338n.22, 384n.39, 394,
    417, 417n.188, 426, 427n.19, 449n.1
    accounts of Newgate, the Clink, Wisbech, and
        York Castle gaol 410–11, 427n.21
    narratives compiled (for Richard
        Smith) 181n.12, 222n.183, 461n.46
    and Richard Newport and William
        Scot 408n.149, 410
Brown, Mr 520n.143
Brown, N. P. 487
Brown, Thomas, alias Revel 141n.3
Browne, Anthony, 1st Viscount Montague 100,
    120n.10, 199, 208, 278n.67
    brother of, *see* Browne, Francis
    daughter-in-law, *see* Browne, Mrs
        (Mary Dormer)
    regarded as a loyalist 161, 278n.67
    words, reported by William Gifford,
        concerning Mary Stuart 170n.134
Browne, Anthony Maria, 2nd Viscount
    Montague 120n.10, 240, 275, 406n.138,
    409n.151, 487
    and oath of allegiance, 1606 399, 402
Browne, Arthur 515n.126
Browne, Francis
    brother of, *see* Browne, Anthony, 1st Viscount
        Montague
    and Nicholas Woodfen 161
Browne, Francis, 3rd Viscount Montague 501
Browne, Magdalen (*née* Dacre), Viscountess
    Montague 487
    life of (*The Life of La. Magdalen Viscountesse
        Montague*), by Richard Smith 487
Browne, Mrs (Mary Dormer) 221n.175
    father-in-law, *see* Browne, Anthony,
        1st Viscount Montague
    servant/chaplain of, *see* Fletcher, Anthony
Browne, Robert
    and Robert Persons 131n.61
    texts by 131n.61
    Treatise of Reformation 131n.61
    uncle of, *see* Flower, Francis
Browne, William, execution, September (?) 1605,
    York 342–3, 343n.50, 350
Brownlow, F. 219n.170
Bruce, Robert 245n.83
Brudenell, Sir Thomas, 1st Baron Brudenell
    (1628) 419, 497, 500–1, 524, 532n.196, 552
Buckeridge, John, bishop of Rochester
    (1611) 254n.119, 436n.59
Buckhurst, Baron, *see* Sackville, Thomas
Buckingham, countess of, *see* Villiers, Mary

INDEX   585

Buckingham, duchess of, *see* Villiers. Katherine
(*née* Manners)
Buckingham, earl (1617), marquis (1618) and
duke (1623) of, *see* Villiers, Sir George, 1st
duke of Buckingham
Buckle, Cuthbert 141
Bull, hangman 59, 121
Bullaker, Thomas (John Baptist), OFM
arrest, 1630 483n.119
arrest, trial, and execution, 12 October 1642,
Tyburn 516, 516n.128;
narratives 516n.128
and Margaret Powell 516n.128
Bullock, Peter 322
execution, with James Duckett, 19 or 20 April
1602, Tyburn 320
Bulstrode, Sir William, and parliament in
1610 380, 380n.21
Bunny, Edmund, and William Hart 130; reads
papal bull of excommunication at Hart's
execution 130
Burch, Francis van der, archbishop of
Cambrai 518, 518n.140
Burden, Edward, execution, 29 November 1588,
York 194
Burgess, Hugh, disputations with William
Davies 57
Burgess, John, and earl of Essex 301n.47
Burgh, Thomas, 1st Baron Burgh 277
lord chamberlain to Anne Boleyn 244n.75
Burgh, Thomas, 3rd Baron Burgh 244
Burghley, Baron, *see* Cecil, Sir Thomas; Cecil,
Sir William
Burnet, Gilbert, bishop of Salisbury 16–17,
16nn.35–6, 559n.93
Burns, R. 530n.187
Burton Constable, Yorkshire 17n.38
Burton, Francis, *Fierie Tryall* 31, 368, 368n.152,
377; manuscript version 377n.4
Burton, Henry 488, 499–500
Bury, Suffolk 368; fire in Eastgate Street 368
Butler, Alban 26, 145n.21, 194n.70, 384n.39,
385n.42, 392n.66, 473n.74
as Richard Challoner's research assistant 6,
6n.6, 173n.150, 181n.12, 206n.120,
216n.158, 223n.188, 239n.51, 248n.99,
254n.119, 280n.76, 320n.125, 337n.19,
414n.178, 415n.181, 436n.60, 458n.35,
471n.69, 510n.104, 514n.122, 518n.138,
520n.144, 522n.153
Butler, Charles 6n.6, 29
Butler, James, 12th earl and 1st duke of
Ormond 504, 543

Buxton, Christopher 174, 464
arrest and execution, with others, 1 October
1588, Canterbury 174n.156, 192–3
and Nicholas Garlick 192n.63
Bye and Main conspiracies 335, 358, 408n.149,
449, 453

Cadwallader, Roger 346n.62, 409n.152
arrest, disputations, trial, and execution, 27
August 1610, Leominster 69n.105, 381,
383–93, 467
Ecclesiasticall History (translation by) 389n.60
library of 388, 389n.60
manuscripts associated with 384n.39,
385n.42, 388n.58, 391, 391n.65
memory of Cadwallader, contested between
Jesuits and secular clergy 387–91, 393
and oath of allegiance, 1606 384–9
and protestation of allegiance 384, 387n.54
and Robert Bennett 381, 384–7
and Robert Drury 385–6
sister-in-law 385
Whitsun Riot 344, 344n.57
Caernarvon, 1st earl of, *see* Dormer, Sir Robert
Caietani, Enrico, Cardinal 200n.92
Caius College, Cambridge 87, 87n.57, 87n.58
Calamy, Edmund 10, 10n.20
Calderón, Rodrigo 402, 410n.156, 415
Calderwood, David 428n.25
Calvin, John 36, 111, 163n.101, 237; *see also*
Bolsec, Jerome
Cambrai, archbishop of, *see* Burch,
Francis van der
Cambridge
vice-chancellor, *see* Howland, Richard
colleges; *see* names of colleges in this index
Camden, William 17
Camm, B. 434n.55
Campbell, Archibald, 7th earl of Argyll, and battle
of Glenlivet 246
Campbell, Archibald, 8th earl of Argyll 505
Campbell, John Chrysostom, Capuchin 281n.78
Campion, Edmund, SJ 9, 12n.25, 45, 51, 64,
111–12, 127–8, 138–9, 143, 148, 150,
161n.93, 161n.96, 166, 197n.83, 424, 447,
561, 566n.3
and Alexander Nowell 31, 111–12, 111n.170
and appellant critics 73
Campion's 'brag' 103, 103n.131
disputations in the Tower of London
(31 August–27 September 1581) 111–12,
111nn.169–170
and the duke of Anjou 115

586 INDEX

Campion, Edmund, SJ (*cont.*)
and earl of Leicester and Sir Henry Sidney 97, 106n.147
execution, with Ralph Sherwin and Alexander Briant, 1 December 1581, Tyburn 115–18, 119, 291; speech ('We are made a spectacle') 116; subsequent publicity 119–36 *passim*
and George Eliot 64, 85, 106n.146; arrested by Eliot at Lyford Grange 106, 110; death of Eliot 64
and Gervase Pierrepoint 107
and Henry Walpole 55, 116
L'Histoire de la Mort... 117n.201; Henry III tries to suppress 117n.201; translated, and incorporated into *Concertatio Ecclesiae Catholicae* 117n.201
indictment and trial, with others 112–14; under the 1351 treason legislation 112–13, 142; indictment under 1581 statute considered by regime 112–13; proceedings ridiculed by William Allen 113–14
interrogation 106n.147; 'bloody questions' 122n.18
and the Jesuit mission of 1580 96–118, 316–17; and recusancy 97–8
and John Hamerton 119
and papal deposing power 114n.184
A Particular Declaration 117n.201, 122n.18
patrons investigated by the regime 106–7; conformities among 112
and puritanism 98, 118; moderate puritans line up against 70, 111–12, 139
Rationes Decem 12n.25, 116, 132; printed at Stonor Park 105
reprieve sought 115, 115n.190
rumours spread about him by the regime 106, 110–11
sermon of 29 June 1580 103
sermon of 16 July 1581 114
and synod of Southwark 103
torture of 31n.30, 97, 110, 110n.167
and the Vaux family 104n.132
Canon, Edmund 508–9
canons of 1604 342
Cansfield, Brian, SJ 522
Canterbury
archbishop of, *see* Abbot, George; Bancroft, Richard; Cranmer, Thomas; Grindal, Edmund; Laud, William; Parker, Matthew; Whitgift, John
executions at, *see* Buxton, Christopher; Edwards, Gerard; Widmerpole, Robert; Wilcox, Robert

Caracena, marchioness of, *see* Velasco y Mendoza, Isabel de
Caracena, marquis of (Luis Carrillo de Toledo) 397
Caraman, Philip, SJ 23, 65n.91, 192n.61
Cardiff, executions at, *see* Evans, Philip; Lloyd, John
Carew, Sir George 354n.91, 374n.174
Carey, Henry, 1st Baron Hunsdon, urges Burghley to retaliation against Campion and his associates 107
Carey, John, execution, with others, 3 or 4 July 1594, Dorchester 250n.107
Carey, Sir George, and William Marsden and Robert Anderton 163
Carier, Benjamin 426
Carleton, Sir Dudley 400n.107, 426n.15, 466, 466n.55
Carlisle
bishop of, *see* May, John; Robinson, Henry
earl of, *see* Hay, Sir James; Howard, Charles
execution of Christopher Robinson, March 1597 269, 269n.38
Carr, John, postmaster of Newcastle
arrested, indicted, and reprieved 241
and John Boste 241
Carr, Thomas 223n.186
Carre, William 419–20
Carter, William 95–6, 96n.101, 130
arrested, July 1582, and premises in Hart Street searched by Topcliffe 123–4, 134
books and papers of, relating to Mary Stuart 95–6, 96n.100
and Gregory Martin's *Treatise of Schisme* 135, 135n.78; convicted of printing 135
and John Cawood Snr 95–6, 135
and Nicholas Harpsfield 95–6, 96n.100, 123–4, 135
and Richard Verstegan and Thomas Alfield's *True Reporte* 119n.2
and Thomas Norton's 'Chain of Treasons' 134
torture, trial, and execution, 11 January 1584, Tyburn 124, 135, 137, 142–3; Thomas Norton delivers prosecution speech at trial 135; Bishop Aylmer's and Richard Topcliffe's involvement in prosecution 135
Carthusian martyrs 78
Cartwright, Thomas
and Admonition Controversy 85n.42, 282
and Andrew Boardman 263–4
and Richard Howland 86–7
and Robert Some 121

Sir Francis Walsingham commissions reply to Rheims New Testament from 111n.170; task reassigned to Thomas Bilson 111n.170
Carvajal y Mendoza, Luisa de 39–40, 354, 405, 440, 446
  death of 425, 425n.14; funeral sermon 425n.14
  gentlewoman/attendant of 425; death of 425
  and George Abbot 425, 425n.14
  and George Gervase 364, 367n.147
  and John Blackfan 417n.190
  and John Roberts and Thomas Somers 396–7, 397n.95, 399–400, 399n.104
  and Michael Walpole 368n.153, 425
  persecution, perception of 372–3, 374, 382–3, 382n.29, 402–3
  and Princess Elizabeth 409–10; and Anglo-Palatine marriage 414–16
  and prospect of peace with the Dutch 359–60, 359n.107
  and reinterment of Mary Stuart 413
  and Richard Newport and William Scot 409–12
  and Robert Drury 359–60
  Spitalfields residence, raided 425; imprisoned and released 425
  and Thomas Garnet 367
Casaubon, Isaac 407–8
Cashel, archbishop of, see O'Hurley, Dermot
Cassano, bishop of, see Lewis, Owen
Castabala, bishop of, see Milner, John
Castelnau, Michel de, seigneur de Mauvissière 100n.115, 115n.188
Castlehaven, 3rd earl of, see Touchet, James
Castlemaine, earl of, see Palmer, Roger
Castro y de Sandoval-Rojas, Francisco Ruiz de 422n.1
Catesby, Robert, and Thomas Stevenson 188n.44
Catesby, Sir William, prosecuted in star chamber 113
Catelyn, Malivery, informs against Lawrence Mompesson 218n.166
Catherine of Braganza 557, 558n.86
Catherine Wheel, Oxford 197–8; owner of 198
Catholicism/Catholics
  'Catholic history' 21–2, 23–4, 23n.2
  conformist/loyalist tendency 40–1, 63–4, 84–6, 95, 99–100, 112, 124–5, 137, 139, 158, 170–1, 273–4, 318; attack on that tendency, in 1578, by Gregory Martin (*Treatise of Schisme*) 92–3; attack on that tendency by Sir Francis Hastings 273–4; see also Archpriest Dispute

deportations of Catholics in 1585 151–2
  disarming of 419–20, 419n.200, 428, 459n.39; rumour of massacre 419–20
  episcopal government, alleged necessity of 318–19, 319n.119, 352, 369–75, 407, 412, 417n.190, 447, 459–61, 466–8, 485; challenged by religious orders 466–70; Blackloist models of episcopacy 526–7; and sacrament of confirmation 319, 319n.121
  resistance theory 175–8
  tolerance/toleration rhetoric and demands 118, chs 9–13 *passim*; demands for toleration early in James's reign 334–50, 539–40 esp.
  trials and executions of Catholics *passim*; disrupted and subverted 55–6; diversity of opinions concerning 62–3 and *passim*
  see also recusancy; revisionism; treason penalties; treason statutes
Catterick, Edmund, arrest, trial, and execution, with John Lockwood, 13 April 1642, York 513–14, 514n.122
Catterick, George 519
Cause, the (19th century and 20th century promotion of claims to recognition of English and Welsh martyrs as saints) 20; see also Bamber, Joseph; Caraman, Philip; Walsh, James
Cavalleriis, Giovanni Battista de 136n.79
  Ecclesiae Anglicanae Trophaea 77, 136n.79
Cawley, Sir William, and Thomas Bullaker 516
Cawood, Gabriel 141
Cawood, John, Snr, and William Carter 95–6, 135, 141
Cecil, John 248n.96, 251, 334, 425n.10
  and Archpriest Dispute and the appeal of 1601–02 308, 324–5
  and Catholic loyalism 229–30; and tolerance/toleration 229n.3; as critic of Robert Persons 230, 230n.9
  and George Beseley 207
  journey to Rome, 1606 352; Robert Persons's memorandum 352n.83
  Lord Burghley's protection for 229
  sends account of John Boste's execution to Robert Persons 60
  and Sir Robert Cecil 229–30, 229n.2, 229n.3
  Thomas Pormort, identified by, as unsympathetic to Spain 219
  William Warford tries to persuade him not to reply to William Creighton's defence of James VI 163n.101

588 INDEX

Cecil, Sir Robert, 1st Viscount Cranborne and
    1st earl of Salisbury (1605) 188n.44,
    258n.139, 270, 278, 278n.67, 293, 295,
    297n.33, 301n.48, 301n.50, 305, 309,
    316n.104, 324–5, 326n.151, 327, 336,
    340n.36, 341–2, 343, 342n.44, 345n.59,
    346–7, 353n.87, 354n.91, 359, 362n.122,
    365, 374, 377, 400, 403, 407, 413, 430, 550
  Boulogne peace negotiations 284
  brother of, see Cecil, Sir Thomas
  death of 408, 410
  and John Cecil 229–30
  and Miles Dawson 272
  and parliament in 1610 380
  puritan attacks on 326n.151
  and Richard Bancroft 320n.128, 324
Cecil, Sir Thomas, 2nd Baron Burghley and
    1st earl of Exeter 297n.33
  and Cuthbert Trollop 323n.138, 327
  and James Bolland 280
  and sermons in York Castle gaol, 1599–1600
    280, 280n.76
  and Thomas Garnet 368–9, 368n.153
Cecil, Sir William, 1st Baron Burghley 83, 96,
    111n.170, 127n.36, 140, 180n.6, 187n.36,
    190, 199–200, 232, 240n.60, 242–3, 263, 270,
    272–3, 277–8, 413, 483
  and Anthony Copley 229n.2
  and anti-puritanism 232–8 passim, 232n.13,
    234n.26, 236n.43
  A Copie of a Letter 190, 190n.55; reply to, by
    Richard Verstegan and others (The Copy of
    a Letter) 190n.55
  and Everard Hanse 108n.154, 109n.160
  The Execution of Justice 40–1, 137–8, 143–5,
    190, 311, 562; William Allen's reply (A True,
    Sincere, and Modest Defence) 137, 141–5,
    150; distribution of Execution of Justice on
    the Continent 137n.80; and
    A Declaration of the Favourable
    Dealing 137n.80
  and Henry Barrow and John Greenwood, and
    the anti-sectary legislation of 1593 234–6,
    236n.43
  and John Boste 241
  and John Cecil 229–30
  and legal proceedings against earl of
    Arundel 196n.79
  and Lord Hunsdon 107
  memorandum of December 1583 137n.82
  Richard Verstegan's claims concerning 218
  and Robert Morton's interrogation 94
  and Robert Southwell's condemnation of
    corruption 212–13; court of wards and
    recusancy 213

royal proclamation of 18 October 1591 40;
    Burghley solicits reports from the
    provinces concerning enforcement 227;
    report sent by Matthew Hutton, 13 January
    1593 227n.201; Thomas Bell's information
    used in conjunction with 227n.201
  and Sir Francis Knollys's accusations against
    Archbishop Whitgift 199
  and Sir George Bromley 150n.44
  and treason act of 1563 81
Cecil, William, 16th Baron de Roos
    (Ros) 440n.75
Cellier, Elizabeth
  Meal Tub Plot 553n.67, 559n.92
  pilloried 69
Chaderton, William, bishop of Chester, and John
    Finch 146
Chalcedon, bishop of, see Bishop, William;
    Smith, Richard
Challoner, Richard
  and Alban Butler 6, 6n.6, 206n.120, 223n.188,
    239n.51, 248n.99, 254n.119, 280n.76,
    320n.125, 337n.19, 414n.178, 415n.181,
    458n.35, 471n.69, 510n.104, 514n.122,
    518n.138, 520n.144, 522n.153
  and Anthony Champney's 'Annales', as a
    source 173n.150, 206n.120, 262n.11,
    268n.36, 269n.39, 278n.67,
    302n.52, 303n.56
  and Christopher Bales, Alexander Blake, and
    Nicholas Horner 50
  and Conyers Middleton 6
  and Cuthbert Mayne 4, 9, 559
  and Cuthbert Trollop 202n.105
  and death of the earl of Leicester 67
  and Douai College diary 322n.137
  and Edmund Arrowsmith 476–8
  and Francis Bell 518–19
  and George Swallowell 249, 249n.103
  and Grace Babthorpe 206n.120; narrative by,
    transcribed for Challoner by Alban
    Butler 206n.120
  and Henrician martyrs 9n.16
  and history/historiography 7–8
  and John Austin 528
  and John Gother 12n.26
  and John Knaresborough's manuscripts/
    transcripts 280n.76, 414n.178, 415n.181,
    469n.61, 528n.179
  and John Nalson 503
  and John Southworth 534–5, 535n.209; and
    William Penn 534–5, 535n.211
  and Lord Teynham 18–19
  and Mary Stuart's death as martyrdom 171–2
  and Matthew Prichard 553n.67

Memoirs of Missionary Priests... preface, *passim*, 3–10, 28, 30, 41–2, 46, 52–3, 74, 94, 181n.12, 188, 192n.63, 195, 197n.82, 198, 215, 217, 249, 254n.119, 281–2 and *passim*, 320n.125, 339, 352n.85, 374, 385, 392n.66, 431n.39, 433, 436–7, 461n.46, 492–3, 493n.4, 508, 510, 512, 514n.122, 515n.126, 517–19, 517n.132, 523–4, 537, 539, 546, 556n.79, 558–9, 560–1, 564; John Pollen's edition (1924) 6n.6; Thomas Law's edition (1878) 19–20
and Padley martyrs 181n.13
and Philip Powel 522
Popish Plot trials and executions, 1678–81 546, 551, 553n.67, 556–9
and Ralph Grimston and Peter Snow 279
reputation as a controversialist 6
and Richard Newport and William Scot 408, 409n.151
and Roger Ashton 175n.160
and Roger Cadwallader 385
and Thomas Manger 250n.107
and Thomas Maxfield 435; letter of, concerning Richard Sutton 182n.17
and tolerance/toleration 5, 5n.4
and William Harrington 245
and William Webster 505
Chamberlain, John 327, 327n.163, 342n.47, 400n.107, 403, 418n.195, 419–20, 425, 441, 446, 456
and execution of William Scot and Richard Newport 59
Chamberlain, Sir Thomas 458
Champney, Anthony 334, 334n.5, 365n.136, 404, 409, 410–11, 413, 415, 423, 423n.6, 425n.10, 427n.21, 429, 431–2, 436n.59, 438n.67, 441
'Annales Elizabethae Reginae' 6n.6, 50, 173–4, 173n.150, 194–5, 206n.120, 220n.172, 222n.183, 262n.11, 268n.36, 269n.39, 270n.43, 278n.67, 279n.74, 302n.52, 303n.56, 304n.58, 322n.136
as confessor to Robert Thorpe 206n.120
and John Bretton 279n.71
journey to Rome, 1606 352; Robert Persons's memorandum 352n.83
letter to John Cecil, of 21 April/1 May 1603 334
and oath of allegiance, 1606 409n.152
witnesses execution of John Amias and Robert Dalby 194–5
Chapman, John
arrested, August 1582, and respited 130; goes into exile 130
and John Adams 130n.48

Charke, William 111n.171, 122n.17, 126–7
and Tower disputations 111–12
Charles I, (prince of Wales, and) King 11, 509–10, 523–5, 527–8, 541n.17, 543, 560, 563
Anglo-French marriage negotiations and treaty 457–9, 489; and Anglo-French peace 481n.114, 563–4
Anglo-Spanish marriage negotiations 442n.89, 563; *and see* James I, Anglo-Spanish marriage negotiations
and anti-popery 459, ch. 14 *passim*, ch. 15 *passim*, 550
and the Church and court of Rome 482–91 *passim*
and clergy in Newgate, 1641 507–9
coronation 459
and Edmund Arrowsmith and Richard Herst 477, 480–2
and earl of Strafford 495–6, 500–4, 502n.51
first Army plot and second Army plot 504–6
Forced Loan 471
and Henrietta Maria's 'pilgrimage' to Tyburn 464–5
and Henry Morse 488–9
Irish rebellion 506–7
and John Goodman 498–503 *passim*
and John Lockwood and Edmund Catterick 513–14
journey to Madrid 456
Personal Rule 482–91
Scotland and rebellion/covenanters 494–506 *passim*; Cumbernauld Band 505; 'Incident' 505
Ten Propositions 504
and tolerance/toleration of Catholics 459, 468–82 *passim*, 482–91 *passim*, 550
Charles II, (prince of Wales, and) King 5n.5, 509–10, 527, 538, 541n.16, 543–5, 551
declaration of indulgence, 1662 539
declaration of indulgence, 1672 543
and Popish Plot, 1678–81 546–7, 550, 558
Charnock, Robert 290, 299, 364n.131, 367
Chastel, Jean 254, 254n.121, 311, 354n.91
Cheke, Henry, 129
providential death of 66, 66n.92
Chelmsford, execution of John Paine, 2 April 1582 62, 121, 123
Chester
bishop of, *see* Bridgeman, John; Chaderton, William; Downham, William; Lloyd, George; Morton, Thomas; Vaughan, Richard
chief justice of, *see* Bromley, Sir George
dean of, *see* Nutter, John

590 INDEX

Chester (*cont.*)
execution of John Plessington, 19 July
1679 69n.108, 554n.73
recusants in Chester diocese 369
vice-chamberlain, *see* Warburton, Peter
Cheyney, Richard, bishop of Gloucester, and
recusancy survey of October 1577 86–7;
denounces puritans 86–7
Chichester, bishop of, *see* Andrewes, Lancelot;
Bickley, Thomas; Montagu, Richard
Chichester, John 10n.20
Chichester, Sir Arthur 362
Chichester, trials and executions at, in 1588 191–2
Chideock Castle 250, 250n.107
Childwall parish 293, 293n.19
Chingle Hall, Goosnargh, Lancashire 25n.9
Chiverton, Richard 533n.203
Cholmeley, Richard, of Brandsby 374n.175
Cholmley family, of Whitby 215n.152
Cholmley, Sir Richard 365n.136
Chorley, Mary, and Edmund Arrowsmith 475
Christ Church, Oxford 392n.66, 393–4
Circignani, Nicolò, murals 136n.79
Clarendon, earl of, *see* Hyde, Edward
Clargenet, William 185, 185n.24
Clarke, Samuel 6–8
Clarke, Sir George 510n.105
Clarke, Thomas
as chaplain to the Constable family 254n.119
and Edward Osbaldeston 254n.119
information against Catholic clergy 256n.134
recantation sermons 254n.119
Clarke, William 312, 324n.139
Bye and Main conspiracies 335; trial and
execution 335, 335n.12, 377
and dissensions in Wisbech Castle 72–3
and Jesuits, martyrdom and
toleration 314n.97, 315
and Richard Bancroft 312, 324, 324n.139
and search of the Clink prison 323–4
Claxton, Grace
and Lady Margaret Neville 241–2; arraigned
and sentenced 241–2
petition concerning 242
reprieve 242; and Francis Eglisfield 242n.70;
and Matthew Hutton 242n.70
Claxton, James 186
execution, with Thomas Felton, 28 August
1588, Isleworth 188
Claxton, William 239n.50
Clayton, James
death in prison 195n.77
and John Hambley 195n.77
and Thomas Alfield 195n.77

Cleere, Mary 121n.11
Clement VIII (Ippolito Aldobrandini),
Pope 309n.79, 324–5
Clément, Jacques 354n.91
Clench, John 164, 165*f*, 265, 278, 285
Clifford, Henry 427
Clifford, Lord Henry 446n.104
Clifton, Henry 340n.32
Clifton, R. 493, 540
Clifton, Sir Cuthbert 478–9
Clifton, Thomas 340n.32
Clink prison 317, 321n.130
Catholics arrested in, after search,
1602 284n.87, 323–4, 324n.139
Catholics' deaths in 34n.47
clergy in 34n.47, 401–2, 412n.167; support for
oath of allegiance 401–2
keeper 427n.21
Clitherow, Margaret 158, 197n.83, 228, 247n.89,
265, 297n.33, 303, 311, 456n.23, 461–2,
461n.46
and Ann Foster 89–90
burial (conjectured) at Mount Grace,
Osmotherley 28n.19
Catholic critics of 71
chaplains of, *see* Ingleby, Francis; Mush, John
and Francis Ingleby 160, 164
and John Clench 285
life of, by John Mush 25, 158–9, 164, 261,
311, 563
and Oswald Tesimond 82
recusancy survey of October 1577 86
trial and execution (*peine forte et dure*), 25
March 1586, York 55, 65, 71, 158n.84, 159*f*,
163–4, 278, 563
and William Hart 130
Clopton, Cuthbert, arrest, trial, and reprieve
505n.69
Clughen, L. 27n.17
Cobbett, William 19
Cobham, Sir Henry 109n.161
and Charles Slade 98n.107
instructions to 137n.81
Cobham, Lord (Sir John Oldcastle) 307
Coffin, Edward, SJ
and George Napper 392n.70, 394n.80
newsletter of, concerning execution of John
Roberts and Thomas Somers 63, 63n.80,
399n.101
Coffin, Mrs 33n.41
Cogswell, T. 456n.22, 477n.93
Coke, Sir Edward 26, 233n.20, 340n.30, 402
and Thomas Pounde's trial in star
chamber 340–1

INDEX 591

Coke, Sir John 474n.75, 484n.128
and 1628 parliament 469–70; Clerkenwell
Jesuit novitiate, raid of 469–70, 473n.74
Coke, Sir John, Jnr 502–3
Coke, Thomas 534
Coldham Hall, Suffolk 366n.144
Cole, Thomas 463
John Gee arrests 458; released 458
Coleman, Edward 549, 549nn.47–48, 556
Coleman, Walter 508–9
Collectanea volumes of Christopher, Grene SJ,
see Grene, Christopher, martyrological
collections
College, Stephen, execution 69
Colleton, John 457–8
arrested at Lyford with Edmund
Campion 114
deported 114, 152n.52
and Edward Hands 436n.59
and episcopacy 319n.121
and John Lancaster 114
trial and acquittal 113n.179, 114, 114n.186;
cited in star chamber proceedings against
Thomas Pounde in 1604 114
Collier, Jeremy 16–17, 17n.39
Collins, J. 485, 525, 530
Collinson, P. 36n.57, 42, 128
Combe, William, MP 263–4, 263n.13, 264n.21
elder brother of 263n.13
Como, cardinal of, *see* Galli, Ptolomeo
Como, D. 401n.111
Compton, William, 2nd Baron Compton 437n.63
Con, George 488n.139, 495, 497, 535
Concertatio Ecclesiae Catholicae..., ed. John Fenn
and John Gibbons 8–9, 117n.201, 130,
145n.21, 147, 160–1, 461
Condé, prince of, *see* Bourbon, Louis I de
Coningsby, Thomas 386–7
Connell, James 25n.9
Constable, Cuthbert, and John Knaresborough's
research ('Sufferings of the Catholicks')
10, 10n.19
Constable, Henry, and William Allen's defence of
Sir William Stanley 177n.166
Constable, Joseph 240, 270
compliance and conformity 270–2
indicted for harbouring seminary priest 272
wife of 272; promises conformity 272
Constable, Lady Margaret (*née* Dormer) 16–17
husband of, *see* Constable, Sir Henry
indicted for harbouring Edward
Osbaldeston 254n.119
and Matthew Flathers, William Mush and
Cuthbert Trollop 365n.137

Constable, Sir Henry 17n.38, 240, 254n.119, 365
wife of, *see* Constable, Lady Margaret
(*née* Dormer)
Constable, William, 4th Viscount Dunbar 16–17
Conventicles act, 1670 543
Convocation canons, 1640 494–5
Cook, John 488
Cook, Mr, and verdict against James Bird 220n.172
Cooper, Anthony Ashley, 1st earl of
Shaftesbury 544, 546, 549, 555, 557–8,
558n.86
Cooper, Thomas, bishop of Lincoln and bishop
of Winchester
and recusancy survey of October 1577 86
and trial of William Marsden and Robert
Anderton 162
Copinger, Edmund 209n.131
Copley, Anthony 251, 325, 530
and Catholic martyrdom 251n.111, 325;
denial of Jesuit claims concerning
313, 313n.94
and earl of Essex 302n.51
and Lancelot Andrewes 229n.2
and William Waad 229
and William Watson and William Clarke
335n.12
Copley, John 207n.124
John Cotton, denounced by 424
and oath of allegiance, 1606 401n.114
renounces Rome 401n.114
sister of, *see* Gage, Margaret
Copley, Thomas, SJ 522n.152
Copping, John, executed, June 1583, for denial of
royal supremacy 131n.61
Corbet, Richard, and William Davies 57
Corby, Ambrose, SJ 521n.149
Certamen Triplex 521n.149
Corby, Ralph, SJ
arrest, trial, and execution, with John Duckett,
7 September 1644, Tyburn 520–1,
520nn.144–145; narratives and
documents 520n.144; relics 521n.149
brother of, *see* Corby, Ambrose
and Dr Belwood 520
and Melchior de Sabran 521n.149
Cordell, Sir William 100
Corker, James (Maurus), OSB 551n.60,
554n.72, 556n.82
Cornelius, an Irishman, and John Felton 82n.31
Cornelius, John, SJ 461n.46
arrest, 13/14 April 1594 250
charged with possessing Robert
Persons's *Elizabethae Angliae
Reginae...Philopatrum* 250n.107

592 INDEX

Cornelius, John, SJ (cont.)
execution, with others, 3 or 4 July 1594,
Dorchester 33, 68, 250n.107
profession as Jesuit 250n.107
and William Weston's exorcisms 250n.107
Cornwall, divisions among the gentry 88–9
Cornwall, Humfrey 386
Cornwallis, Sir Charles 383
and Henry Garnet 352n.85, 354–5, 354n.91,
355n.93
Cornwallis, Sir Thomas 100, 187n.36
conformist tendencies of 100n.115
Corona Regia 430–1, 452–3, 452n.9, 454n.15
Corraro, Marc'Antonio 369, 383, 401
Cosin, John 476n.86, 490
Coskaer, Charles, marquis de La Vieuville 497
Cotesmore, Thomas, death in prison 34n.43
Coton, Pierre, SJ 397
Cottam, Thomas, SJ 51, 101
allegations against 113n.182, 122n.17; refuted
by William Allen 113n.182, 122n.17
arrest and incarceration 122n.17;
arraignment 112n.177; and execution, with
others, 30 May 1582, Tyburn 122, 122n.20
and Charles Slade 122n.17
Cottesford, Samuel, *A Treatise against
Traitors* 282n.83
Cottington, Sir Francis (knighted 1623),
1st Baron Cottington (1631) 425n.14,
428n.29, 453, 485n.133
Cotton, John
'Balaam's Asse' 423–4, 424n.8, 454n.15
house raided 423–4; imprisoned 424n.8
Cotton, Richard 354
council in the North 269–70, 269n.41, 272–3
lord president, *see* Hastings, Henry; Cecil,
Sir Thomas; Scrope, Emmanuel; Sheffield,
Edmund
and Margaret Clitherow 55, 158–9, 158n.84,
265, 563
and proceedings, under the 1585 statute,
against seminary clergy 157n.76;
proceedings against Marmaduke Bowes
and Hugh Taylor 157n.77, 158, 163–4
court of wards 213
Courtney, A. 476
Coventry and Lichfield, bishop of, *see* Bentham,
Thomas; Morton, Thomas; Overall, John
Coventry, Sir Thomas, 1st Baron Coventry
(1628) 479
Covington, S. 38
Cowdray, West Sussex 120n.10, 161, 222n.183
and royal progress, Hampshire/West Sussex,
1591 208; performances in front of the
queen 208

Cowell, John 379
Cowling, Ralph 172
death of, in York Castle 293n.21
son of, *see* Cowling, Richard
and William Hart 172n.143
Cowling, Richard, SJ 293, 293n.21, 295
father of, *see* Cowling, Ralph
Cox, Robert (Benedict), OSB 518–19
Cox, Sir Richard 418n.195
Coxhoe, Durham 14
Coyney, Edward 11
father of 11
Crab, William 155–6
arrested at Chichester, with Henry
Webley 156n.73, 186n.29
offer of conformity 156n.73
Craft, Daniel, vicar of Farnham, as target of
puritan attacks 133n.69
Cranborne, Viscount, *see* Cecil, Sir Robert
Cranmer, Thomas, archbishop of
Canterbury 143
Craven, Thomas 469n.61
Crawford, earl of, *see* Lindsay, David
Creighton, William, SJ 247, 253–4, 261–2,
286, 307n.71
defence of James VI 163n.101; reproved by
Robert Persons for 163n.101; William
Warford tries to persuade John Cecil not to
reply to Creighton 163n.101
Crespin, Jean 63
Creswell, Joseph, SJ 50n.11, 200n.92, 355n.93,
373, 399n.104, 402, 414, 434, 451n.7
and trials and executions of 1616 432n.44
Critchley, William 431n.39
Crockett, Ralph 463
trial and execution, with Edward James,
1 October 1588, Chichester 191–2, 191n.57
Croke, Sir John 392, 396n.91
Cromwell, Oliver, lord protector 524, 524n.162,
528, 530, 551
and Blackloists 527–8
and John Southworth 534–6
Cromwell, Sir Thomas (knighted 1536) 34–5, 79
Crook, a farmer 69
Cross, C. 273n.52
Cross, Humphrey 366n.144, 394n.83
Crow, Alexander 461n.46
arrest, trial, and execution, 30 November 1586,
York 58–9, 169, 169n.127
rumoured suicide attempt 58–9, 59n.61,
169n.127
Crowley, Robert
church of St Giles-without-Cripplegate,
manuscript left there, concerning James
Bosgrave and Henry Orton 122n.18

INDEX 593

and Everard Hanse 108–9, 108n.157
and Thomas Pounde 108n.154
Crowther, John 522
Crowther, Thomas, death in prison 34n.43
Cullen, Patrick 250
Curry, John, SJ 202, 204
Curtis, Thomas 427n.21

Dackombe, John 430
Dacre, Francis 240
Dailey, A. 27
Dalby, Robert 194n.74
  suicide attempt 194n.74
  trial and execution, with John Amias, 15 or 16
    March 1589, York 56, 194–5
Dale, Mr Justice 282–3, 284n.87
Dalton, James 193n.67, 201, 234
Dalton, Mr 554n.73
  aunts of 554n.73
Dalton, Mr and Mrs, alleged harbourers of
    George Beseley 207n.124
Danby, earl of, see Osborne, Thomas
Danby, John 12, 69–70, 70n.109
Dangerfield, Thomas 558n.91
Daniell, John 245n.80
Danstin, William, and Lawrence
    Humphreys 207n.122
Darcy, Thomas, servants of, see Browne, William;
    Welbourne, Thomas
Darcy, Thomas, 3rd Baron Darcy of Chiche,
    1st Viscount Colchester and 1st Earl
    Rivers 451, 500–1
Darling, Thomas 327–8
  and John Darrell 327–8
  and John Howson 327–8
Darlington, execution of George Swallowell,
    29 July 1594 247n.89, 248
Darnley, Lord, see Stuart, Henry
Darrell, John 300, 327–8
Daussi, Adrien, execution 52
Davenport, Christopher (Francis),
    OFM 496, 497
Davies, Richard 165n.111, 221n.176
  account of Richard Dibdale 165n.111
  associate of Edmund Campion and Robert
    Persons 161n.96
  his claims about Richard Bancroft 165n.111
  and Lady Tresham 161n.96
  narratives of martyrdom, compiled in
    1620s 161n.96, 165n.111, 461n.46
  and Nicholas Woodfen 161n.96
  and Thomas Holford 188
Davies, William, secular priest (ordained 1585)
  arrest, trial, and execution, 27 July 1593,
    Beaumaris 56–8, 60, 237, 237n.44; death of

constable and hangman 67–8;
  unpopularity of sentence 60
blood-stained cassock 57–8
clandestine printing press 237n.44
four Catholics arrested with him 57
prison ministry and evangelizing of 56–8,
  57n.55; disputations with Protestant
  ministers, including Hugh
  Burgess 57
refusal of conformity in Ludlow
  gaol 57
and Richard Corbet 57
Davies, William, secular priest
  arrest, 1607, with Robert Drury 355, 355n.94;
    Zúñiga and Boderie intervene on behalf
    of 359, 359n.106; reprieve 360
  arrest, 1624, proceedings against, and
    reprieve 457–8, 458n.31
  and oath of allegiance, 1606 356–8
Davis, Thomas 391n.65
Davison, William 92
Dawson, Miles, conformity and pardon of
    272–3, 272n.47
Day, D. 42n.72
Day, William, and Tower disputations 111
Dean, William 123
  arrested 123n.25
  at Caius College, Cambridge, and associate of
    Richard Swale 87
  deported 152n.52
  and Edward Shelley 188n.41, 189
  execution, with Henry Webley, 28 August
    1588, Mile End 188
  and Henry Webley 188
  letters intercepted at Colchester
    188n.41
  ordination 87
  Richard Topcliffe's allegations against 123,
    123n.24
  temporary compliance and subsequent
    deportation (gives evidence against
    Mrs Rogers) 123, 130, 152n.52
death penalty, abolition of 37
Dedham classis 121
Delvin, Baron, see Nugent, Richard
Denbigh Castle 53
Derby, countess of 225
Derby, earl of, see Stanley, Henry;
    Stanley, William
Derby, execution of Nicholas Garlick,
    Robert Ludlam, and Richard Simpson,
    24 July 1588 54, 181; conversion of
    felon 54n.35
Derwentwater, earl of, see Radcliffe, James
Deventer, see Stanley, Sir William

594   INDEX

Devereux, Robert, 2nd earl of Essex 259, 264, 303n.55, 304–6
  alleged puritanism and (puritan or Catholic) conspiracy 298–301, 301n.47
  and Anthony Atkinson 274
  and Catholic support for 281, 286–7, 302n.51, 304–5
  father-in-law, see Blount, Sir Christopher
  rebellion and execution 301–5, 333
  and Thomas Wright, SJ 274
Devereux, Robert, 3rd earl of Essex, marriage annulment 426
Devlin, Christopher, SJ 23, 73, 203, 221, 221n.179
D'Ewes, Sir Simonds (knighted 1626) 454n.15, 499–500
Dewhurst, Henry 479
Dibdale, Richard 161n.96, 165n.111, 461n.46
  Anthony Tyrrell's accusations against 166
  arrest 165n.111
  released from Gatehouse prison 166n.113
  and Richard Bold 166
  Richard Topcliffe's accusations against 166n.113
  trial and execution, with John Lowe and John Adams, 8 October 1586, Tyburn 165, 180, 197–8
  and William Weston's exorcisms 165, 165n.111
Dickenson, Francis 201
  betrayed and arrested 201n.96; declaration concerning papal authority 201
  execution, with Miles Gerard, 13 (or 30) April 1590, Rochester 202
  reputation, attack on, by Topcliffe 202
  tortured by Topcliffe in Bridewell 201n.96, 211n.137
Dickenson, Roger 133n.68, 207–8, 463
  execution, with Ralph Miller, 7 July 1591, Winchester 207–8, 208n.125; reprieve offered 208n.125
Digby, Ambrose
  duel with Sir John Killigrew 89n.65
  recipient, with others, of anti-piracy commission 88–9
Digby, George, 2nd earl of Bristol (1653) 510, 539
Digby, Sir Everard 345, 350, 424, 424n.8
Digby, Sir John, 1st Baron Digby (1618), 1st earl of Bristol (1622) 404, 406–7, 429–30, 503, 510
  Algunos Avisos de Inglaterra 429–30
  and Anglo-Spanish marriage negotiations 444–5
  and Diego de Lafuente 454
  and William Baldwin 450–1

Digby, Sir Kenelm 525, 525n.169, 526n.172, 527–8, 530
Digges, Thomas, Humble Motives 543, 543n.24
Dike, James 297
Dillingham, John 507, 509
Dillon, A. 23–4, 24n.4, 28, 78, 565
Dillon, Thomas, 4th Viscount Dillon 506–7
Dilston, Northumberland 28n.18
Diocletian, Emperor 355
Dodd, Charles, vere Hugh Tootell 12, 29
  Church History 16, 16n.37, 18, 365n.137
  Flores Cleri Anglo-Catholici 18n.44
Dodsworth, John 513
Dodwell, M. 304n.58
Dodwell, Thomas
  on conformist tendency among Catholics 158
  informs against Lady West of Winchester 133n.68
  informs against Thomas Alfield 155
  John Adams, denounced by 165n.111
  report on views of James Fenn, Andrew Fowler, Samuel Conyers, and William Hartley 138n.86
Dolan, F. 549–50
Dolan, Gilbert, OSB 28n.18
Dolman, Alban 95n.92
Dolman family 117n.201
Donne, Henry, and William Harrington 244n.77
Donne, Henry, Babington plotter 185–6
  and Henry Foxwell 185–6
Dorchester
  executions at, see Bosgrave, Thomas; Carey, John; Cornelius, John; Green, Hugh; Pikes (Pike), John; Pilchard, Thomas; Salmon, Patrick
  plague at 33, 68
  population of 33
  puritanism 515n.127
Dormer, Sir Robert, 1st earl of Caernarvon 495, 515n.127
  death of 541, 543
Dorset, earl of, see Sackville, Edward; Sackville, Thomas
Douai 440, 453
  Benedictine foundation at (St Gregory's) 376n.3
  English seminary college at 6, 6n.6, 9n.16, 88, 94, 111, 291, 320, 376, 376n.3, 435, 442; diaries 322n.137, 365n.137; and the French Revolution 25n.9; president of, see Allen, William; Barret, Richard; Kellison, Matthew; Paston, Edward; Worthington, Thomas
  John Southworth's remains taken to 536n.213

INDEX 595

senior members forced to move to Rheims,
March 1578 92
see also Martin, Gregory; Rheims New
Testament
Douglas, George, arrest and execution,
9 September 1587, York 174n.154
Douglas, James, 4th earl of Morton 98,
98n.106, 103
arrest, 1581 104–5
Douglas, Margaret, countess of Lennox
117n.201
Douglas, William, 10th earl of Angus 246
Dove, John 360n.115
Dowdall, James 279n.74
Down and Connor, bishop of, *see* O'Devany,
Conor
Downes, Thomas, alias Mumford 551–2, 554n.72
Downey, Richard, archbishop of Liverpool
479n.101
Downham, William, bishop of Chester 147
Downs, J. 514n.122, 516–17, 517n.136
Downside Abbey 28n.19
Doyley, Sir Robert, death of, at Oxford assizes,
1577 64n.84
Dreux, battle of 81
Drummond, Dr 286
Drury Lane, London 15
Drury, Robert 371n.165, 409n.152, 458
arrest, trial, and execution, with Humphrey
Floyd, 26 February 1607, Tyburn 51, 56,
355–61, 363, 366, 371, 385–6, 466–7; his
narrative 358n.100, 359n.105; and Anne of
Denmark and Henry Howard 361
and Benedictine order 359n.105
converts felon 56
and John Gerard 356n.96
and oath of allegiance, 1606 356–60, 357n.98,
359n.104, 385–6, 395, 467; and Luisa de
Carvajal 359
and protestation of allegiance 385–6
and Roger Cadwallader 385–6
and Society of Jesus and appellants 355–6,
355n.94, 356n.96; and John Gerard and
Anne Line 356n.96; appeal of 17
November 1600 and protestation of
allegiance 355n.94, 356n.96; Bye
Plot 356n.96; and letters to and from
George Blackwell 356n.97
A True Report of the Araignment 356–8,
360n.115
Dryburn, Durham 14, 202
Du Plessis, Armand-Jean, cardinal-duke of
Richelieu 541
Du Plessis de la Mothe-Houdancourt, Daniel,
bishop of Mende 465–6, 465n.51

Dublin
Catholic archbishop of, *see* Matthews, Eugene;
Talbot, Peter
executions at, *see* O'Devany, Conor; O'Hurley,
Dermot; O'Lochran, Patrick
Duckett, James 320n.125, 320n.126, 321–2
execution, with Peter Bullock, 19 or 20 April
1602, Tyburn 320–1, 322n.135
godfather, *see* Leyburn, James
and Richard Bristow's *Briefe
Treatise* 320–1
and Robert Southwell's *Humble
Supplication* 320–2
son of, *see* Duckett, John, Carthusian
wife of 322n.135
Duckett, John, Carthusian 320n.125
father of, *see* Duckett, James
Duckett, John, of Sedbergh, Yorkshire
arrest, trial, and execution, with Ralph Corby,
7 September 1644, Tyburn 520–1,
520n.145; narratives and
documents 520n.144; relics 521n.149
and Melchior de Sabran 521n.149
and Richard Smith 520n.144
Dudley, Anne, countess of Warwick 328
Dudley, John, duke of Northumberland 142
Dudley, Richard 247n.89, 269
Dudley, Robert, earl of Leicester 95, 100, 159–60,
176, 179–80, 263n.13, 303n.55
brother-in-law, *see* Hastings, Henry
and Christopher Goodman 149n.37
death of 67–8, 195, 195n.76, 214n.149;
providential nature of, alleged 65n.91,
66–7; commented on by Robert Southwell,
and by Richard Challoner 67–8
and Edmund Campion 97, 106n.147
and Edmund Grindal, and the
prophesyings 85
enmity towards earl of Sussex 121–2
and Evan Lloyd 150
funeral procession 167n.116
and Jasper Heywood 311
and John Hewett 187
and 'Leicester's Commonwealth' (*The Copie of
a Leter*) 101n.119, 159–60
and Lodowick Greville 101, 101n.119
and Richard Bold 166–7, 167n.116
and Richard White 53–4
and Simon Thelwall 150
and treason act of 1563 81
Duffield, Henry 240n.55
and John Boste 240, 248n.96
Duffy, E. 4n.2, 6, 43n.76
Duke, Edmund 202n.105, 461n.46, 464
betrayer of 67

596   INDEX

Duke, Edmund (*cont.*)
  execution, with others, 27 May 1590, Dryburn,
    Durham 14, 202, 249
Dunbar, battle of 530
Dunbar, Viscount, *see* Constable, William
Durham
  assizes, July 1594 247n.89
  bishop of, *see* Barnes, Robert; Hutton,
    Matthew; James, William; Matthew, Tobias;
    Pilkington, James
  cathedral 476n.86
  dean of, *see* Matthew, Tobias
  executions at, *see* Boste, John; Duke, Edmund;
    Hill, Richard; Hogg, John; Holiday, Richard;
    Norton, John; Palaser, Thomas; Speed, John;
    Talbot, John
  recusancy 446n.104
Dutch Republic, envoys of 446, 446n.104
Dymock, Robert 86

East Hendred, Berkshire 15
Ecclestone, Dorcas 282
  husband of, *see* Martin, Sir Richard
Edgehill, battle of 516
Edinburgh 80-1
  execution of James Wood, 27 April
    1601 307n.71
Edmondes, Sir Thomas 352n.82, 353n.87, 354,
    354n.91, 362, 364, 413n.172, 425n.10
Edmunds, Robert, OSB 427n.21
Edward III, King, treason statute of, *see* treason
    statute of Edward III (25 Edward III, c. 5)
Edward VI, King 78-9
Edwards, David, and Richard White 149
Edwards, Francis, legal proceedings against, at
    Chichester 191-2; and conformity 192
Edwards, Gerard, alias Campion 464
  execution, with others, 1 October 1588,
    Canterbury 192-3
Edwards, Thomas 524
Egerton, Sir Thomas, 1st Baron Ellesmere 235,
    323n.138, 326n.155
  and imprisoned Catholic clergy, in July
    1588 182
  speech in star chamber, 20 June
    1605 346, 346n.63
Egerton, Stephen, and Thomas Wright 275
Eglisfield, Francis 268n.35
  and the arrest of John Boste, 10 September
    1593 226, 239
  and Grace Claxton 242n.70
Egmont, count of 521n.149
  and Henry Morse 521n.151
elector palatine of the Rhine, *see* Frederick V

Eliot, George 113-14
  criminal charges against 120n.10
  death of 64
  and Edmund Campion 64, 85, 106n.146, 114;
    Eliot arrests Campion at Lyford
    Grange 106, 110
  and John Paine 120-1, 120n.10
  and the Petre household at Ingatestone 120-1,
    120n.10
Elizabeth, Princess (daughter of James I) 400,
    409-10, 413n.168, 454-5
  marriage to Frederick V 407, 413-20,
    420n.207, 422-3
  secretary of, *see* Nethersole, Sir Francis
Elizabeth Tudor, Queen 45, 83, 94, 143-5, 160,
    176, 195n.76, 203, 222, 231, 241, 248, 273-4,
    294, 299-300, 302, 302n.53, 305n.64,
    318-20, 323-5, 348-9, 376n.3, 382, 500,
    502, 542
  ambassadors in Paris, *see* Cobham, Sir Henry;
    Stafford, Sir Edward
  and Babington's Plot 164, 164n.108
  bastard 456
  Catholic hostility towards 98n.107, 99-101,
    109, 139 and *passim*
  death of 333; burial 334
  and duke of Anjou 90, 90n.69, 90n.70,
    94-100, 102-3, 103n.126, 106, 106n.144,
    111, 117-18, 121-2, 164
  East Anglian progress, 1578 94; Catholics
    imprisoned during 94
  excommunication (*Regnans in Excelsis*
    1570) 82-3, 91, 99-100, 116, 176-7,
    376n.3, 500
  Hampshire/West Sussex progress, 1591 208;
    Cowdray 208
  interregnum schemes 126-7, 152; *see
    also* bond of association; monarchical
    republicanism
  James VI warns, against killing Mary
    Stuart 171n.139; suspicion
    concerning 171
  and persecution 20, 41, 46, 145, 145n.20,
    257-8, 291; and tolerance 155n.65, 257-8,
    309, 458, 499; at the end of the reign
    319-25 *passim*, 325-9 *passim*
  and proceedings against Mary
    Stuart 171-4
  and prophesyings 84-5; Edmund Grindal,
    ordered by, to suppress 84-5; Grindal
    sequestered by 85; prophesyings
    suppressed 85n.44
  and puritanism 70, 104, 117-18, 125-6,
    128-9

INDEX 597

refuses assent, in parliament in 1571, 1572, and 1576, to anti-Catholic legislative proposals concerning receiving communion 84, 316

and Richard Topcliffe, as royal servant 219n.170, 258

Richard Verstegan identifies, as whore of Babylon 218

rumours concerning, and the earl of Leicester 81

settlement of religion, 1559 and after 44, 80–4, 86–7; deprivation of clergy after 80n.18; act of uniformity 308–9

succession problems 80, 213–14; failure to provide for the succession 144–5

Thomas Pormort's claims about Topcliffe's familiarity with 219–20, 219n.170

and Thomas Woodhouse 83

at Tilbury 190

and the Tower disputations 111n.169

and tyranny 140–51, 179–80

vindicated concerning the use of torture 137n.80 (*A Declaration of the Favourable Dealing*)

Ellis, Edward, bishop of Nottingham 65n.91

Ellison, Elizabeth 268n.36, 461n.46

Elsworth, Richard 197n.82, 199

Elton, Edward 454n.15

Elton, Geoffrey 34–5, 79

Elvish, Nicholas 181n.10

wife of (sister of Thomas Metham) 181n.10

Ely, bishop of, *see* Andrewes, Lancelot; Wren, Matthew

Ely, Humphrey 170n.134

Emerson, Ralph, SJ, arrested 155n.67; and copies of 'Leicester's Commonwealth' 155n.67

England, parliament of, *see* parliament

England's Second Warning-piece 555–6

Englefield, Anthony 533n.201

Englefield family 245n.83

Englefield, Henry 533n.201

Englefield, Lady 225

Englefield, Sir Francis 137–8, 198, 225, 229n.3, 251

and John Ingram 245n.83

English, John 199

brother-in-law, *see* Randall

and Sir Christopher Hatton 199–200

episcopacy/episcopal government, *see* Catholicism/Catholics, episcopal government, alleged necessity of

Epitaphs, the First, upon the Death of … Marie, late Queene of Scots 335n.8

Erastianism 16

Errington, George 267, 268n.35, 269n.41

arrested by Henry Sanderson 269n.41; and absconds 269n.41; arrested again 269n.41

and George Williams 269n.41

and John Boste 269n.41

trial and execution, with William Knight and William Gibson, 29 November 1596, York 267–9

Errol, earl of, *see* Hay, Francis

Essex, countess of, *see* Howard, Frances

Essex, earl of, *see* Devereux, Robert, 2nd earl; Devereux, Robert, 3rd earl

Estampes, Jacques, d', marquis de la Ferté Imbault 508

Etheridge, George, and Thomas Belson 197n.82

Eure, Sir Francis 392, 392n.67

Eure, William, 3rd Baron Eure 392n.67

and arrest of Hugh Taylor 157

niece of, *see* Tempest, Nicholas, wife of (Isabel Lambton)

and trial of Joseph Lambton 222n.183

Eure, William, 4th Baron Eure 514n.124

Euxton, Lancashire 520n.143

Evans, Humphrey, SJ 554n.72

Evans, Philip, SJ 547n.40, 556n.79

execution, with John Lloyd, 22 July 1679, Cardiff 547n.41, 556

Evelyn, John 546

Evison, John, SJ 388n.58

Ewbank, Henry 243n.71

and John Boste 239n.50

exchequer, chief baron of, *see* Bell, Sir Robert

Exclusion crisis, *see* James II, succession and exclusion

Exeter

bishop of, *see* Bradbridge, William

earl of, *see* Cecil, Sir Thomas

exorcisms 162, 164–6, 167n.117, 181n.10, 182n.17, 186–7, 197–8, 250n.107, 256n.134, 278, 278n.67, 300, 435–6, 436n.59, 471, 522n.157, 165nn.110–111

Eyam, Derbyshire 65n.91

Eyre, Thomas, of Holme Hall 181n.13

wife of (daughter of John Fitzherbert) 181n.13

Eyre, Thomas, president of Ushaw 181n.13

Eyre, Vincent 181n.13

Eyston, Charles 17

and Henry Englefield 533n.201

and Henry Preston 15, 15n.35

and Jacobitism 17, 17n.39, 17n.41

and John Knaresborough 15, 15n.35, 533n.201; and relic of Peter Wright 533n.201

and John Stow 17, 17n.42

598 INDEX

Eyston, Charles (*cont.*)
  and Joshua Basset 15n.34
  library 15
  'A Poor Little Monument' 15n.35, 16, 16n.36,
    17n.40
  and Sir Richard Baker 15n.35
  and Sir Roger L'Estrange 17
  and Thomas Hearne 15n.35, 135n.78
Eyston, William
  transcription of Nicholas Harpsfield's
    'A Treatise of Marryage' 15n.35

Fairburn, George, death in Newgate 427–8
Fairfax, Mrs
  and John Knaresborough 11–12
  and Nicholas Postgate 11–12
Falkner, a felon 392
Farm Street, London (Office of the Vice-
    Postulation) 13n.28, 25n.9, 28n.19
Farnese, Odoardo, Cardinal 393n.77
Farnham, vicar of, *see* Craft, Daniel
Fathect, James 13
Favour, John 252n.116
Fawkes, Guy 337n.16
Fawther, John, betrays Robert
    Watkinson 320, 322
Feckenham, John, death in prison 34n.43
felons, conversion of 55–6
Felton, John 9, 83, 150
  arrest and execution, 8 August 1570, St Paul's
    churchyard 83, 83n.32, 119; and Cornelius,
    an Irishman 82n.31
  daughter of, *see* Salisbury, Frances
  indictments of 82n.31
  and Laurence Webb 82n.31
  and papal bull of excommunication (*Regnans
    in Excelsis* 1570) 82–3, 420
  son of, *see* Felton, Thomas, gentleman
  and Thomas Radcliffe, 3rd earl of
    Sussex 83n.32
  wife of (Ellyn Goodwin ?) 83n.32; and
    Elizabeth Tudor 83n.32; and Mary
    Tudor 83n.32
Felton, John, assassin 481, 482n.115
Felton, Thomas, gentleman 186
  conformity refused by 188–9; denies royal
    supremacy 189
  execution, with James Claxton, 28 August
    1588, Isleworth 189
  father of, *see* Felton, John (d. 1570)
  receives tonsure from cardinal of Guise 188
  reconciled to Rome 189n.46
Felton, Thomas, recusancy commissioner 285,
    323n.138
  and parliament in 1610 380

Fenn, James
  arraignment and execution, with others,
    12 February 1584, Tyburn 114n.186,
    137–8
  brother of, *see* Fenn, Robert
Fenn, John 130
Fenn, Robert
  arrested and deported 138n.86
  brother of, *see* Fenn, John
Fenner, Sir Edward (knighted 1603) 275–7
Fenwick, John 556
  trial and execution, with others, 20 June 1679,
    Tyburn 549
Fenwick, William 227
  recusant wife 227
Ferdinand II, archduke and holy Roman
    emperor 454
Ferniehurst 240
Ferns, bishop of, *see* Roche, John
Ferrari, Georgio 136n.79
Ferreira da Gama, Esteban 245
Ferté Imbault, marquis de la, *see* Estampes,
    Jacques d'
Fetherston, Leonard 263–4
Fettiplace, Sir John, providential death of,
    alleged 65n.91
Field, John 104
  and Tower disputations 111
Fiennes, William, 1st Viscount Saye and Sele 503
Filby, William
  arraigned 113n.179
  executed, 30 May 1582, Tyburn 122
Filcock, Roger 463–4
  trial and execution, with Mark Barkworth and
    Anne Line, 27 February 1601, Tyburn
    304–5, 304n.57, 304n.58, 317–18
Finch, Henry 233, 235–6
Finch, John 145n.21
  admiration for James Leyburn and Edmund
    Campion 145–6
  arrest, with George Ostcliff 145–6
  churchgoing and enforced compliance 146;
    suicide allegedly attempted by 146
  imprisonment, trial (with three Marian
    priests, Thomas Williamson, Richard
    Hatton and James Bell) and, with
    James Bell, execution, 20 April 1584,
    Lancaster 146–7
Fincham, K. 401n.111, 426
Finet, John 405n.135
Fingley, John 87n.58
  Frances Webster, reconciled by 168n.123
  and Margaret Clitherow 168
  and Paris catalogue (claiming that Fingley said
    Elizabeth Tudor was a heretic) 168n.123

INDEX 599

and Robert Sayer 87
trial and execution, 8 August 1586, York 168, 168n.123
Finkelstein, Daniel 566n.3
Finnis, J. 324
Fisher, George 397, 418n.195, 429, 429n.32
converts felons 56
Fisher, John, bishop of Rochester 77, 145, 161, 385, 456n.23
Fisher, Ralph 279n.72, 461n.46
Fisher, Robert 269
Fitzgerald, James Fitzmaurice 99–100
Fitzharris, Edward 558n.86
Fitzherbert, Jane 181n.13
father of, see Fitzherbert, John
husband of, see Eyre, Thomas, of Holme Hall
Fitzherbert, John 181, 225
daughter of, see Fitzherbert, Jane
reprieved 181n.10, 181n.13; death in prison 181n.13
Fitzherbert, Richard 183n.18
privy council orders arrest of 183n.18
Fitzherbert, Sir Thomas 124n.26, 183, 225, 255
death in Tower of London 225
nephews of, see Bassett, William; Fitzherbert, Thomas
Norbury residence, orders to search 183n.18
Fitzherbert, Thomas, nephew of Sir Thomas Fitzherbert 183n.18
feud with William Bassett 183
and Richard Topcliffe 221, 255
and Robert Sutton 183
and Sir Thomas Fitzherbert 225
Fitzherbert, Thomas, SJ (1614) 113–14, 114n.183, 283n.84, 317–18
displaced as secular clergy agent in Rome 371
as lobbyist in Rome, with Sir Oliver Manners 371–2, 372n.166
and William Baldwin 453n.13
Fixer, John 219, 229
Flanders
cautionary towns 349n.73, 364n.131
Council of Troubles 35
discourse on 35
nuncio (Lucio Morra) 446
see also Brussels
Flathers, Matthew 371n.165
arrest, trial, and execution, 21 March 1608, York 365–6, 368–9, 371, 365nn.136–7
Fleet prison, London 124n.26, 403, 442, 454–6
Fleet prison, Manchester 146
Fleetwood, William 94–5, 108, 127n.36, 139, 291–2
and imprisoned Catholic clergy, in July 1588 182

and Margaret Ward 189n.50
removal from office 216n.157
Richard Verstegan's printing press seized by 119
and Robert Morton 94
and Thomas Sherwood 92
and trial of Edmund Gennings and others 216
Fleming, Sir Thomas (knighted 1603) 131n.57, 408n.149
client of Sir Francis Walsingham 131n.57
and trial of James Bird 220n.172, 228
Fletcher, Anthony, SJ, alias Newburn (?) 444, 444n.96
at River Park, Sussex 221n.175
Fletcher, John 26n.13
Flower, Francis
nephew of, see Browne, Robert
and Sir Christopher Hatton 203
and trial of Edward Jones 203
Floyd, Edward, proceedings against 455
Floyd, Humphrey
execution, with Robert Drury, 26 February 1607, Tyburn 360–1, 360n.115
and Robert Drury's trial 358
Floyd, John, SJ 511
Foley, Henry, SJ 69n.108, 368n.151
forced loan, 1589 212n.141
Forced Loan, 1626–27 471
Forcer, Eleanor 296n.30
Ford, Thomas
and Cuthbert Mayne 88n.62
trial and execution, with John Shert and Robert Johnson, 28 May 1582, Tyburn 113n.179, 114n.186, 122, 122n.18
Forrest, William, and Thomas Belson 197n.83
Forster, A. 269n.41
Fortescue, Anthony 218n.166
Fortescue, Isabel
father of, see Huddlestone, Sir Edmund
and John Rigby 281–2
Fortescue, Sir John 327
Foscarini, Antonio 404, 413, 419n.200
Foster, Ann 89–90
chaplain of, see Marsh, John
death in prison 89–90, 90n.69; exposure of body 89–90
husband of 89–90
son of, see Foster, Seth
Foster, Isabel (née Langley)
brother-in-law, see Foster, Seth
death in prison 90n.69, 169n.126
father of, see Langley, Richard
Foster, Seth 90n.69
and Bridgettine convent in Rouen 90n.69
and Holy League 90n.69

600 INDEX

Foster, Seth (*cont.*)
　mother of, *see* Foster, Ann
　sister-in-law, *see* Langley (Foster), Isabel
　and Yepes's *Historia Particular* 90n.69
Fotheringhay 170n.134, 171
Foucault, M. 51–2, 70
Fox, Nicholas, dies in Tower of
　London 217n.162
Foxe, John 19–20, 25n.10, 28–31, 36n.57, 104,
　110, 265, 377, 560
　Acts and Monuments preface, *passim*, 31, 52,
　　66n.93, 104, 307; narratives of God's
　　punishment of persecutors 63
　lobbies for reprieve of Campion 115n.188;
　　Tower disputations 111n.170; manuscripts
　　of disputations passed to Foxe after seizure
　　in William Carter's premises 124n.26
　and Nicholas Harpsfield 95–6
　and William Gardiner 110
Foxwell, Henry
　and Henry Donne 185–6
　indicted and reprieved 185–6, 186n.26,
　　189n.49
　reconciled to Rome by John Baldwin 186n.26
France
　Anglo-French marriage negotiations with
　　Stuart court, *see* Charles I, prince of Wales,
　　and King, Anglo-French marriage
　　negotiations and treaty
　embassy in London 404
　Franco-Spanish double marriage alliance 403,
　　403n.122, 405, 409–10, 410n.153
　king of, *see* Henry III, Henry IV; Louis XIII
　wars of religion 34–5; *see also* Holy League
Francesco, Jacomo 253
François, duke of Alençon and subsequently
　(1576) duke of Anjou 90
　and Edmund Campion 115; lobbied for a
　　reprieve for Campion 115n.190
　in Flanders 121–2, 157
　and *Paix Monsieur* 92
　proposed dynastic union with Elizabeth
　　Tudor 90, 90n.69, 90n.70, 95–100, 102–3,
　　103n.126, 106, 106n.144, 111–12, 117,
　　121–2, 164
Frank, John, betrays John Gerard 250n.105
Frederick V, elector palatine of the Rhine 401,
　407, 450
　and crown of Bohemia, and revolt in, end
　　ejection from 443, 454–5
　father-in-law, *see* James I
　marriage to Princess Elizabeth 407, 413–20,
　　420n.207, 423
Freeman, Michael, SJ 414n.179
Freeman, T. 25, 63

Freeman, William, ministry, arrest, trial,
　and execution, 13 August 1595,
　Warwick 262–6, 338n.22
Freke, Edmund, bishop of Norwich 266
　and recusancy survey of October 1577 86–7;
　denounces puritans 86
Frost, a minister, providential death,
　alleged 65, 65n.91
Fulke, William, and Tower disputations 111
Fuller, Nicholas 201
Fullerton, S. 10n.20, 461n.46
Fulthrop, Edward 267–70
　execution, with others, 4 July 1597,
　York 270, 272
　and Lord Lumley 269n.41
　Samuel Wharton informs against 269n.41
　temporary compliance 268
　and Ursula Taylor 269n.41

Gage, George, gentleman 404, 404n.131
Gage, George, secular priest, of Framfield, and
　Thomas Wenman 422n.1
Gage, George, secular priest, of Haling
　514n.124, 518
Gage, Henry, Colonel 14
Gage, John 207n.124, 532n.197
　and George Beseley 207n.124
　wife of, *see* Gage, Margaret
Gage, Margaret (*née* Copley) 207n.124,
　532n.197
　and Anne Line 207n.124, 303n.56
　brother of, *see* Copley, John
　brother-in-law, *see* Gage, Robert
　and George Beseley 207n.124
　husband of, *see* Gage, John
　loss of estates to Lord Howard of
　　Effingham 207n.124, 303n.56
　reprieve 207n.124
Gage, Robert
　Babington conspirator 207n.124
　sister-in-law, *see* Gage, Margaret
Gage, Sir Henry 532n.197
Gage, Thomas, OP, and renegade 517–18, 532,
　532n.197
Gainsford, Thomas, *Vox Spiritus* 452n.8
Galli, Ptolomeo, Cardinal of Como 152
Gallicanism 9n.17, 311, 311n.86, 545, 550n.52
Gardener, John 193
Gardener, John, of Grove Place, and John Hewett,
　alias Weldon 186–7
Gardiner, A. B. 23–4
Gardiner, James 340n.32
　forcibly released from arrest 339–40,
　340n.30, 340n.32
Gardiner, Sir Thomas 498

INDEX 601

Gardiner, Stephen, bishop of
Winchester 78–9
Gardiner, William 110
Garland, H. 434n.55
Garlick, Nicholas 461n.46
and Christopher Buxton 192n.63
cousin of, *see* Miller (Milner), Ralph
execution, with Robert Ludlam and Richard
Simpson, 24 July 1588, Derby 54, 65n.91,
181, 335n.8
and William Weston's exorcisms 181n.10
Garlick, servant of Mr Tunstall of Wycliffe 12
Garnet, Henry, SJ 26n.13, 54n.35, 65n.91, 180–2,
216n.159, 227–8, 238–9, 237n.44, 244,
250–1, 254n.120, 254n.124, 256n.132, 257,
269, 278, 278n.67, 278n.69, 302n.53, 303–4,
304n.57, 313n.93, 321, 321n.130, 327,
337n.19, 341, 362, 364, 364n.135, 367–8,
368n.153, 369n.155, 378, 447, 460n.42,
464–5
and Archpriest Dispute and martyrdom
321–2, 327, ch. 10 *passim*
and earl of Arundel's trial 196n.79
and earl of Essex's rebellion 302
and Gunpowder Plot 350–3, 550; trial
and execution, 3 May 1606, St Paul's
churchyard 351–2, 353n.87, 354–5,
355n.92, 376; miraculous straw and
other occurrences 352–4, 352nn.85–86,
354n.91, 363, 376, 542–3; and earl of
Northampton 418n.195
and Henry Walpole's trial, and comments
about the queen 254n.120, 256–7,
256n.132
and James I (petitioned by Garnet, 28 March
1603) 334–5
and James Duckett 322n.135
and John Glanville's death 68, 68n.101
and John Mush 261
and John Pibush 302, 307–8
and John Thomas 220
letters to Claudio Acquaviva: 25 May
1590 205–6; 17 March 1593 223; 11 March
1601 304n.58, 307–8
letters to Robert Persons: 16 August
1600 68n.101; 5 May 1602 322;
4 October 1605 350; postscript of
21 October 1605 350, 350n.79
and Mark Barkworth, Roger Filcock, and
Anne Line 304–5, 304n.58
nephew of, *see* Garnet, Thomas
persecution narratives sent to Rome
by 228n.206
portrait in the Gesù, Rome 460n.40
and Richard Bold 166

and Robert Middleton 299n.40
and Thomas Bell and occasional
conformity 182, 205–6, 238, 252
and Thomas Sprott and Thomas Benstead 68,
289–90, 289n.5
and Thomas Tichborne 321n.133
and Thomas Woodhouse 83n.36
and true martyrdom 206, 307–8,
316n.104
and William Richardson 327
Garnet, Thomas, SJ, alias
Rookwood 369n.155, 463
brother of 427n.21
interrogations, trial, and execution, 23 June
1608, Tyburn 366–9, 371, 378, 465, 467
and oath of allegiance, 1606 366–9, 467;
alternative form of oath 367–9, 368n.151,
393, 395
uncle of, *see* Garnet, Henry
Garrett, George 510n.105
Garstang parish 297
vicar of 295n.25
Gascoigne, Sir Thomas 556–7, 557n.83
Gatehouse prison 166n.114, 225, 277, 295, 299,
403, 412n.165, 412n.167, 417, 427n.21, 433,
434, 434n.55, 484, 500
keeper 442n.89
Gates, John 206n.120
Gatrell, V. A. C. 37, 37n.60
Gavan, John, SJ 551, 553
execution, with others, 20 June 1679,
Tyburn 551, 551n.59
Gawdy, Sir Francis 121n.11, 283, 285–6
Gee, John 436n.59, 457
Thomas Cole, arrested by 458
Gennings, Edmund 389n.60
and Alexander Rawlins and Hugo
Sewel 215n.152, 256n.134
arrest 215, 215n.152, 256n.134
trial and execution, with Swithin Wells, 10
December 1591, Gray's Inn Fields 55, 60,
215n.154, 216–17, 216n.158
pamphlet concerning (*The Life and Death of
Mr Edmund Geninges*) 216n.158,
217n.160, 334n.6
and Thomas Warcop 256n.134
Gennings, John (Thomas), OFM 60, 216n.158,
217n.160, 389n.60
conversion of 55
Gerard, Alexander 191n.56
brother of, *see* Gerard, Thomas
Gérard, Balthasar
assassination of William I, of Orange 38,
135n.78
execution 38, 38n.63

602 INDEX

Gerard, John, SJ 250, 254n.120, 256, 256n.130,
  314n.97, 349, 365n.136, 367, 371, 372n.166,
  381–2, 486–7, 543
  arrested in Holborn 250
  and Gunpowder Plot 352–3, 381–2
  and Henry Huddlestone 281n.78
  John Frank betrays 250n.105
  and John Rigby 282
  Lord Vaux's house, searched for 335n.9, 403,
    403n.123
  and Manners family 286n.95
  martyr catalogue by 32n.36
  and Michael Walpole 368n.153
  and Richard Young 252n.114; and Young's
    death 65n.91
  and Robert Drury 356n.96
  and Robert Sutton, layman 194n.70; relic of
    Robert Sutton, given to Gerard by Abraham
    Sutton 182n.17, 184f
  and Thomas Pilchard's execution 32, 32n.36, 68
  William Clarke's allegations against 314n.97
  and William Dean 188
  and William Pikes's execution 33
  and William Sutton 182n.17
Gerard, John, Colonel 535–6
Gerard, Miles 201, 464
  betrayed and arrested 201n.96
  declaration concerning papal authority 201
  execution, with Francis Dickenson, 13 (or 30)
    April 1590, Rochester 28, 202
  and George Hethershall 202n.99
  nephew of, see Kenion, Edward
Gerard, Nicholas 471–2
  grandson of, see Arrowsmith, Edmund
Gerard, Thomas 191n.56
  brother of, see Gerard, Alexander
Gerard, Sir Thomas 471–2
Gerard, Sir Thomas, knight marshal 298–300
  brother-in-law, see Molyneux, Sir Richard
German, Peter, preacher, of Farnham
  and Daniel Craft 133n.69
  and John Hardy, concerning John Slade and
    John Bodey 133
German evangelical union 404, 458
Gervase, George, OSB 463
  arrest, trial, and execution, 11 April 1608,
    Tyburn 363–4, 366–9, 367n.147, 371; and
    Sir Henry Montagu and Thomas
    Morton 363–4; Latin narrative by Richard
    Smith 364n.132
  and Benedictine order 336n.14, 364, 376n.3
Gervase, Henry 364n.131
Gibbons, John 130
Gibson, T. E. 19

Gibson, Thomas 131n.61
Gibson, William, 461n.46
  execution, with George Errington and William
    Knight, 29 November 1596, York 268–9
Gifford, Gilbert 170–1
  replies to William Allen's pamphlet on
    Deventer 171n.135, 177n.166
Gifford, Lady Philippa, conformity demanded
  from 227
Gifford, William, and Anthony Browne,
  1st Viscount Montague 170n.134
Gilbert, George 96n.101
Giles, Richard 453
Gilpin, George 38
Giustiniani, Giovanni 505n.69, 511, 514n.122
Giustiniani, Zorzi 360, 360n.110, 362n.122, 363
Glanville, John
  providential death of, 27 July 1600, alleged by
    Henry Garnet 68, 68n.101
  and Thomas Sprott and Thomas Benstead 68
Glasgow
  archbishop of, see Spottiswoode, John
  execution of John Ogilvie, 28 February
    1615 428–9, 428n.25, 428nn.27–28
Gledstanes, George, archbishop of St Andrews
  and James Moffat 428
  son of 428n.25
Glenlivet, battle of 246
Glickman, G. 5n.5, 16
Glorious Revolution 5n.5
Gloucester
  bishop of, see Cheyney, Richard;
    Goodman, Godfrey
  dean of, see Rudd, Anthony
  executions at, see Lampley, William; Rowsham,
    Stephen; Sandys, John
  execution of William Lampley 194n.74
Glynne, John 498, 500–1, 498n.37, 501n.43,
  518n.137
Goad, Roger, and Tower disputations 111
Godfrey, Sir Edmund Berry 549, 557, 558n.86
Godfrey, William, Cardinal 28n.19
Godolphin, Francis 89n.65
Goldwell, Thomas, bishop of St Asaph 100n.114
  assists in procuring Regnans in Excelsis 102n.125
  and Edmund Campion 102
Gondi, Pierre de, bishop of Paris 140
Gondomar, count of, see Acuña, Diego
  Sarmiento de
Gontier, Père, SJ 374, 379
Gonzaga, Louis, duke of Nevers 136n.79
Good, William, SJ 109n.161, 130n.53
  godson of, see Hart, William
Gooden, Peter 554n.73

INDEX 603

Goodman, Christopher
  as client of earl of Leicester 149n.37
  deprived of benefice in Bedfordshire 149
  fury at lack of retribution against Catholic
    persecutors 80–1
  puritan nonconformity of 149n.37
  and puritan reform in Chester diocese 149
Goodman, Gabriel, dean of Westminster 147–8,
  148n.32, 275
Goodman, Godfrey, bishop of Gloucester 497
Goodman, John 488n.139, 509n.94
  arrest and trial 497–503
Goodwin, William 252n.116, 268
Gordon, George, 6th earl and 1st marquis of
    Huntly 245, 481n.114
  absolved from excommunication by George
    Abbot 440–1, 443
  and James VI and I 243, 259, 333, 440–1
  and John Ingram 245
Gordon, James, SJ 247, 428n.28
Gore, John 438n.67
Gore, Richard 438n.67
Gore, William 438n.67
Goring, George, Lord 522
Gotardi, Federico 426n.15
Gother, John 12n.26
Graham, David, laird of Fentry 246
  execution 246, 261–2
Grately, Edward 197n.83
  and Edmund Campion 115n.190
  earl of Arundel, betrayed by 153–4, 269n.41
  loyalism 170–1
  Thomas Belson, betrayed by 197n.83
Graves, M. 41n.70, 127, 134n.75
Gravesend 262
Gray, J. 79
Gray, Lady Katherine (*née* Neville) 243n.71
  father of, *see* Neville, Charles
Gray, Patrick, master of Gray 260
Gray, Ralph 227
  recusant wife 227
Gray, Robert 352n.85
(Great) Yarmouth, Norfolk 53n.29
Green, Adam 342n.46, 343n.51
Green, Hugh
  execution, 19 August 1642, Dorchester 33, 56,
    515, 515nn.126–127; narratives 515n.126;
    converts felons 56
  and the Society of Jesus 515n.126
Green, Mr, chaplain to wife of Lawrence
    Mompesson 218n.166
Green, Thomas, alias Richard Reynolds,
    execution, with Bartholomew (Alban) Roe,
    21 January 1642, Tyburn 510

Greene, Richard 547
Greenstreet House, East Ham 104n.132
Greenwood, John 234–5
  legal proceedings against 234–6;
    execution 236
Greenwood, Thomas 393n.76
  sister of, *see* Napper, Joan
Greenwood, Thomas, Jnr 393n.76
Gregory I (Gregory the Great), Pope 49–50, 426
Gregory XIII (Ugo Boncompagni),
    Pope 99–101, 129n.45, 156, 201
Gregory XIV (Niccolò Sfondrato), Pope 214
Gregory, B. 24, 27, 36, 78, 565–6
Grene, Christopher, SJ
  martyrological collections (Collectanea
    volumes and other MSS) 26, 26n.13, 34,
    34n.43, 50n.12, 66–7, 66n.92, 138n.86,
    163n.101, 173, 173n.150, 187, 188n.38,
    189n.50, 211n.137, 232, 247n.89, 254n.119,
    262, 262n.11, 268n.35, 320n.127, 321,
    350n.78, 356n.96, 393n.74, 425, 515n.126,
    515n.127, 516, 516n.128; list of persecutors
    punished by God 65n.91
  and Norfolk conspiracy 1570 82n.28
Grenville. Sir Richard
  accused of piracy 88–9
  and Cuthbert Mayne's arrest 88–9
Greville, Lodowick, and the earl of Leicester 101
Grey, Henry, 6th earl of Kent, and the treason
    statute of 1585 153
Grey, Lady Jane 177
Grey, Robert 217n.162
Griffin, John 404
Grimston, Ralph 461n.46
  arrest, trial, and execution, with Peter Snow,
    15 June 1598, York 279, 279n.72
Grindal, Edmund, bishop of London (1559),
    archbishop of York (1570) and archbishop
    of Canterbury (1576) 88n.62
  critics of, in Church of England 86–7
  and Dr Thomas Vavasour 84
  and Montford Scott and Dominic
    Vaughan 85
  and papal bull of excommunication (*Regnans
    in Excelsis* 1570) and John Felton 82–3
  refuses Elizabeth's order to suppress
    prophesyings 84–5, 87–8
  sequestration of 85, 88, 128; perhaps triggers
    Catholic response 85–8; case reviewed in
    star chamber 91n.81
  supporters of, resort to national anti-popery
    campaign (recusancy survey of October
    1577) 86, 88
  and treason act of 1563 81

604 INDEX

Grissold, George 390n.62
Grissold, John 337n.19
Grissold, Robert 390n.62
  arrest, with John Sugar, July
    1603 335n.9, 337–8
  trial and execution, with John Sugar, 16 July
    1604, Warwick 337–40, 338nn.21–3,
    339n.28; demonstrators at 339, 339n.28
Grissold, Roger 390n.62
Grosmont priory 256n.134, 279; tenanted by
  John Hodgson 256n.134
Grove, John, trial and execution, with William
  Ireland, 24 January 1679, Tyburn 549
Growhoski, M. 452n.9
Guarás, Antonio de
  comments on John Felton's execution 82–3
  residence searched, 19/20 October
    1577 91n.81
Guise, cardinal of, see Lorraine, Louis I de,
  cardinal of Guise
Guise, duchess of (Henriette Catherine de
  Joyeuse) 520, 521n.149
Guise, duke of, see Lorraine, Francis II de
Guise family 135n.78
  as patrons of the English College at
    Rheims 92
  see also Mary Stuart
Gunpowder Plot 336, 350–5, 355n.94, 358, 363,
    364n.131, 366, 366n.144, 370, 371, 374,
    376, 381, 384, 384n.37, 408, 408n.150, 419,
    424, 424n.8, 437, 446, 449, 449n.1, 450,
    454n.15, 470, 542–3, 550, 561
  origins 336, 350, 350n.79
  see also Baldwin, William; Catesby, Robert;
    Digby, Sir Everard; Garnet, Henry; Gerard,
    John; Oldcorne, Edward
Gunter, William, execution, 28 August 1588,
  Shoreditch 188, 190
Gurney, Sir Richard 510n.105, 516n.130

Haberdashers' Hall 531
Habernfeld conspiracy 495, 541
Hacket, William 209, 209n.131
  execution 209
Hackness, manor of 17
Hackshot, Thomas
  execution, with Nicholas Tichborne,
    24 August 1601, Tyburn 308n.73,
    429n.33
  Relacion del Martirio 429n.33
Haigh, C. 43, 102
Haley, K. 550
Hall, Thomas 186
Halsall, Sir Cuthbert 306, 306n.69
Hambley, John 195n.77

arrest, trial, and execution, March 1587,
  Salisbury 167–8, 168n.121, 181
gesture of conformity 167–8; promise of full
  conformity 167–8; Thomas Pilchard
  persuades, to withdraw his conformity
  173
gives evidence against other Catholic
  clergy 73n.125, 167–8
reconciled to Rome by John Ballard 167
separates from Church of England after
  reading Robert Persons's Brief
  Discours 167n.119
and William Tedder and Richard Norris, in
  Marshalsea 168
and William Warmington 168
Hamerton, John, and Edmund Campion 119
Hamerton, Peter, SJ 551–2
Hamilton, James, 3rd marquis of
  Hamilton 502–3, 505
Hamilton, William, 1st earl of Lanark 505–6
Hammond, John, Dr 127n.36, 197
  and Alexander Briant 127–8
  and John Whitgift's subscription
    campaign 163n.102
  prepares advice for Burghley on
    excommunication of princes 163n.102
  and Robert Marsden and William
    Anderton 163
  uncle of, see Nowell, Alexander
Hammond, Thomas, The Late Commotion of
  Certain Papists 346, 348
Hancock(John) 186, 186n.26
Hands, Edward, alias Johnson
  exorcism of demoniac 182n.17, 435–6,
    436n.59; letters of Thomas Maxfield
    narrating 182n.17, 435–6; alleged
    delusions 436n.59
Hanmer, Meredith 111n.171
Hanse, Everard 119
  arrest 64–5, 107–8; death of arresting
    officer 64–5
  and papal authority 108
  and Robert Crowley 108–9
  trial and execution, 31 July 1581, Tyburn
    64–5, 107–10, 108n.154, 109n.160, 116–17,
    126n.33; pamphlets concerning 108–9;
    see also Munday, Anthony; Persons, Robert,
    Copie of a Double Letter
  William Fleetwood interrogates 108
Hanson, William (Alphonsus), alias or vere
  Hesketh, OSB 520
Harcourt, count of 518
Hardesty, Robert, execution, with William
  Spenser, 24 September 1589, York 200,
  200n.94

INDEX 605

Hardesty, William 200–1, 242n.66, 256n.134
sister of 256n.134; arrested with Alexander
Rawlins 256n.134; refuses to conform
256n.134
and Thomas Bell 200–1, 252
Harding, A. 132n.64
Harding, Thomas 143n.12
Hardy, John, and John Bodey and John
Slade 133; and Peter German 133
Harewell, William 469–70
and Paris catalogue 461n.46
Hargrave, William 474, 475, 478n.100
Harlay, Christophe de, count of Beaumont
325–6, 326n.151, 327n.161
Harlay, François II de, archbishop of Rouen
498n.32
Harpsfield, Nicholas 135, 500
Dialogi Sex 95–6
and John Leslie's *A Treatise concerning the
Defence* 96n.100
life of Sir Thomas More (manuscript in
possession of Thomas More of
Barnborough) seized by Topcliffe 124n.26
manuscripts and books (*Vita Henrici VIII* and
'A Treatise of Marriage'), seized by Topcliffe
in William Carter's premises 123–4,
124n.26
secretary of, *see* Carter, William
'A Treatise of Marriage' 15n.35
Harrington, William 314n.97
arrest 244n.77
execution, 18 February 1594, Tyburn 244–5;
exchange with Topcliffe 244–5
and Friswood Williams 244n.77
Harris, Arthur 339n.29
Harrison, James
arrest and release 191n.56
execution, with Anthony Bates, 22 March
1602, York 191n.56, 320, 320n.124
and Thomas Heath 191n.56, 320n.124
Harrison, John 278n.63
Harrison, John, secular priest, death in
prison 34n.43
Harrison, Martin 158
Harrison, Matthew 279n.74
Harrison, William, Archpriest 446
Harrison, William, preacher 306–7, 476
Harsnett, Samuel 244n.77, 264
*A Declaration of Egregious Popish
Impostures* 278n.67
and William Weston's exorcisms 278n.67
Hart, John
arrested, arraigned and sentenced but
reprieved 113n.179, 114n.187
interrogated 134–5

and John Rainolds 143
sermon against heresy in England 101,
101n.120
Hart, Nicholas, SJ 403, 406, 406n.140, 412n.165
deported 406n.140
Hart, William
'apostle of Yorkshire' 130
churchgoing and compliance 130
evades arrest in York Castle 129n.44; arrested
subsequently 130
'exhortation to papistry' 130n.51
godfather of, *see* Good, William
and John Bodey 131n.56
letters from prison 130, 130n.51
and Margaret Clitherow 130
and Ralph Cowling 172n.143
trial and execution, 15 March 1583, York 130
Hartley, Edward
arrested 141
and Cecily Stonor 141
Hartley, William
and Campion's *Decem Rationes* 105–6, 133
and Cecily Stonor 141n.6
deported 152n.52
executed, 5 October 1588, Shoreditch 194
gaoled in 1581 and prosecuted in 1584 133
Haskell, P. 483–4
Hastings, Henry, 3rd earl of Huntingdon 17, 67,
129, 159, 171, 222, 242n.66, 243, 268
and Alexander Rawlins 256n.134
Banister, servant of 60
brother of, *see* Hastings, Walter
brother-in-law, *see* Dudley, Robert
coordinates searches of 2 February 1593
226–7
death of 68, 268, 274
and Grace Claxton 242
and Edward Waterson 223–4, 223n.188
and George Swallowell 249
and Henry Walpole 252, 256
and John Boste's arrest and trial 241, 241n.62,
247, 249
and John Ingram 245–6
and John Mush 164
measures taken by, against northern
Catholics in mid-1580 103n.127;
in 1581 107n.149
Richard Holtby's attack on 225–7; as 'prince
of puritans' 225
and Thomas Vavasour 84
Hastings, Sir Francis
and earl of Essex 301n.47
and parliament in 1601 308–9
and parliament in 1610 380, 380n.21
A Watch-Word 273–4

606 INDEX

Hastings, Walter 68
Hathersage, Derbyshire, parish priest of 65n.91
Hatton, Richard 146–7
Hatton, Sir Christopher 100, 283–4
 anti-puritanism 232; in 1587 parliament 174;
  anti-puritanism in 1589 parliament 196
 death of 214–15, 218, 220; commented on, by
  Francis Holyoake 214–15
 and Francis Flower 203
 and Jasper Heywood 311
 and John English 199–200
 personal religion, speculation
  concerning 214n.149
 reputed favourer of Catholics 99n.110
 and royal proclamation of 18 October
  1591 214
Hawkesworth, Robert 295
Hay, Francis, 9th earl of Errol 246, 259
Hay, Sir James, 1st Viscount Doncaster and
 1st earl of Carlisle 481
Haydock, George
 arrest (by Charles Slade), arraignment, and
  execution, with others, 12 February 1584,
  Tyburn 32, 137–9, 138n.88, 139n.92
 and London prisons 138n.88
 and papal authority and Elizabeth Tudor
  138–9
Haydock, Robert, OSB 394n.83, 519
Haynes, Joseph 461n.46
Heads of the Proposals 529–30, 530n.184
Healey, John 353n.87
Hearne, Thomas, at Campion's execution 116
Hearne, Thomas, antiquarian
 and Charles Eyston 15n.35, 17, 135n.78
 publishes Latin edition of William Roper's life
  of Sir Thomas More 15n.35
Heath, Dorothy 263n.13, 264n.21
 father of, see Blount, Sir Thomas
 husband of, see Heath, William
 and William Freeman 263
Heath, Henry 339n.25
 execution, 17 April 1643, Tyburn 61–2,
  517–18, 517n.134; disputation at 61–2;
  narratives 61–2, 62n.75, 517n.134; and
  oath of allegiance, 1606 517n.134
Heath, James, Chronicle 511
Heath, Jerome 463
Heath, Mrs 191n.56
 death of 191n.56
Heath, Nicholas, archbishop of York 263n.13
Heath, Sir Robert 505
Heath, Thomas
 and James Harrison 191n.56, 320n.124
 wife of, see Heath, Mrs
Heath, Thomas, newsletter writer 403, 407–8

Heath, William 263n.13
 brother of, see Heath, Nicholas
 wife of, see Heath, Dorothy
Hebburn, Anthony 359n.105
Hemerford, Thomas 463
 arraignment and execution, with others, 12
  February 1584, Tyburn 137–8, 139n.92;
  views expressed at 139
Hendred House, East Hendred 15n.34
Henrietta Maria of France 492, 497, 498n.32,
  500–1, 510, 530, 535
 and Anglo-French marriage alliance 456–60,
  489, 490; problems 464–5
 brother of, see Louis XIII
 and Edmund Arrowsmith and Richard
  Herst 477, 479–81, 479n.101
 and Francis Bell's relics 518n.139
 and Gregorio Panzani 484
 and Henry Morse 488–9
 and Irish rebellion 507
 and John Southworth 488
 'pilgrimage' to Tyburn 464–6, 465n.51
 and William Prynne 490
Henry III, King, of France 92–3, 117n.201, 138,
  155–6, 309
 assassination 201
 fails to intervene on behalf of Mary
  Stuart 172
 and Henry of Navarre 161n.93
 Sir Edward Stafford persuades, to imprison
  distributors of book on Edmund Campion
  and others 161n.93
 and Sir Edward Stafford and Richard
  Verstegan's publications 135–6
Henry IV, King, of France and of Navarre 92–3,
  156, 161, 177, 201, 211, 260, 309–10, 324,
  354n.91, 374n.174, 551
 and appeal to Rome of 1601–02 308, 326
 assassination 374, 379–80, 380n.24, 382n.29,
  401, 414n.179
 and Henry III 161n.93, 172
 and the Holy League 231, 238
Henry VII, King 144
Henry VIII, King 9, 9n.16, 16, 18, 20, 124n.126,
  144–5, 160, 179, 456
 Henrician Reformation, legislation and
  persecution 29, 29n.24, 77–9, 79n.12
Henry Frederick, prince of Wales 404, 407,
  413–14, 418
 chaplain of, see Baily, Lewis
 death of 414
Hepburn, James, 4th earl of Bothwell, and
  marriage to Mary Stuart 81
Herbert, William, 3rd earl of Pembroke
  419n.198

INDEX   607

Hereford, bishop of, *see* Bennett, Robert
Hereford, execution of John Kemble 11, 553n.67
Herle, William 135n.78
Herst, Richard
    arrest, trial, and execution, 29 August 1628,
        Lancaster 479–81; refuses conformity 480;
        pardons denied 479–81; narratives
        481n.111
    maidservant of 479
    and oath of allegiance, 1606 481
    wife of 479–80
Hesketh conspiracy 219n.170, 222
Hesketh, Roger 480–1
Hesketh, Thomas 297n.34, 306n.69
    and Robert Nutter and Edward Thwing
        293–4
Hethershall, George, OSB
    arrested 202n.99
    and *A Conference about the Next Succession*
        274, 275, 276
    and Miles Gerard 202n.99
    and Richard Topcliffe 274, 275, 276
    and Robert Barnes 275–6
Heton, Martin, and interrogation of Thomas
        Belson 198
Hewett, John, alias Weldon
    arrested at Sluys, October 1587 186–7
    charged with treason, March 1587 186–7
    execution, 5 October 1588, Mile End 32–3,
        186–7
    and John Boste 187
    pamphlet concerning (*A True Report... of
        John Weldon*) printed by, inter alia, Robert
        Waldegrave 193–4
    and William Weston's exorcisms 186–7
Heydon, John 430
Heylyn, Peter 17
Heywood, Jasper, SJ
    arraignment 137
    differences with Robert Persons and William
        Allen 312n.89
    and Edward Stransham 161n.97
    limited compliance 137–8, 311, 312n.89, 313
    and Sir Christopher Hatton 311
    synod in Norfolk 311–12, 312n.89
Heywood, John 313
Hibbard, C. 492
Higgens, Isaac 180
high commission 207, 233, 267–8, 267n.33, 404,
        420, 442n.86, 489–90, 497; thwarted,
        allegedly, by the count of Gondomar 452
Hildersham, Arthur 420, 442n.86
Hill, Edmund (Thomas), OSB 334
    arrested 334, 337n.16
    petition to James I 334, 336–7, 337n.16

in star chamber 336–7; subsequently
        sentenced, 30 April 1604 337;
        reprieved 337
Hill, Lawrence 14–15
Hill, Richard 461n.46
    execution, with others, 27 May 1590, Dryburn,
        Durham 14, 202
Hill, Thomas 334, 337n.16
Hilton, George 13
    wife of, *see* Ridley, Grace
Hindlip Hall 351
Hobbes, Thomas 526; and Blackloists 526n.172;
        Leviathan 528–9
Hoboken, baron de, *see* Schetz, Conrad
Hoby, Sir Thomas 365n.136
Hodgkinson, Henry 297n.34
Hodgson, Dorothy 202n.105, 222n.183
Hodgson, Jane 222n.183
Hodgson, John 13, 256n.134
Hodgson, Sydney 215, 216n.158
    employer of, *see* Lacey, Brian
    execution, with others, 10 December 1591,
        Tyburn 216
    temporary compliance, at trial 216n.158
Hogg, John 461n.46
    execution, with others, 27 May 1590, Dryburn,
        Durham 14, 202
Holborn, Catholics arrested near 214–15;
        see also Cole, Thomas
Holden, Henry 525–6
    and episcopacy 526–7
Holden, Robert 475
    and Edmund Arrowsmith 475
Holden, Mrs 475
Holdsworth, a minister 223
Holford, Thomas
    celebration of Mass in Chester Castle, August
        1585 188
    execution, 28 August 1588, Clerkenwell 188
    and Richard Davies 188
    and Scudamore family of Holme Lacy 188
    and Swithin Wells 188
Holiday, Richard 461n.46
    execution, with others, 27 May 1590, Dryburn,
        Durham 14, 202
Holland, earl of, *see* Rich, Henry
Holland, Thomas, SJ 483, 532
    execution, 12 December 1642, Tyburn 517,
        521n.149
Holman, Anastasia 4n.2
Holman family 4n.2, 12n.26
Holman, George 4n.2
Holme, Henry 477n.92
Holmes, Robert 133n.68
    death in prison 34n.43

608 INDEX

Holmes, William, and Northern Rebellion 82
Holt, Denbighshire 54
Holt, William, SJ 156, 174, 245n.83
Holtby, Richard, SJ 69, 87n.57, 222–4, 222n.183,
   241, 242nn.66, 70, 359n.106, 367–8,
   368n.151
  accounts of persecution 206n.120, 224–8,
    238–9, 242n.70, 247, 249, 249n.103,
    254n.119, 256–7, 256n.134, 365–6; and of
    the 1591 proclamation 224n.190; attack on
    earl of Huntingdon 225–7; coordinated
    searches, 2 February 1593 226–7
  and Robert Drury 358
Holy League (French Catholic Holy
   League) 41, 90n.69, 151, 156, 196,
   201, 379–80
  and English College at Rheims 92
  formation of, after the *Paix Monsieur* 92
  and Henry of Navarre 231
  opponents of 230–1, 251, 260
Holy Office (Inquisition), judgment on appeal of
   1601–02 309n.79
Holyoake, Francis 215n.151
  comments on death of Sir Christopher Hatton
    and royal proclamation of 18 October
    1591 214–15
Holywell (St Winifred's Well) 350, 478–9
Hopton, Cicely 127, 127n.37
Hopton, Sir Owen 110–11, 126
  daughter of, *see* Hopton, Cicely
  and Robert Morton's interrogation 94
Horne, Robert, bishop of Winchester
  chancellor of, *see* Kingsmill, John
  and ejection of John Slade and John Bodey
    from New College, Oxford 132n.64
  and treason act of 1563 81
Horner, Nicholas
  cited in Persons's *Elizabethae Angliae
    Reginae...Philopatrum* 202n.104
  execution, 4 March 1590, Smithfield 49–50,
    202n.104
Horner, Richard, execution, 4 September 1598,
   York 28, 279
Horner, William, and Richard Lloyd 186
Horsey, Sir Ralph 250n.107
Horsley, John 521n.149
Horsley, Mr, death in prison in Hull 34
Hoskins, John 384
Hotham, Sir John 512
Houghton family of Park Hall 12n.25, 122n.17;
   Campion finishes *Rationes Decem* at Park
   Hall 122n.17; *see also* Houghton, Richard
Houghton, John 9n.16
  execution, 4 May 1535, Tyburn 53

Houghton, Richard 64, 106, 107n.149
Houghton, Simon 397
Houghton, Sir Richard 296–7, 299, 300n.41
Houlbrooke, R. 36
Howard, Anne (*née* Dacre), countess of
   Arundel 305, 486–7
  husband of, *see* Howard, Philip
  and Society of Jesus 486–7
Howard, Catherine, countess of Suffolk 359,
   453
Howard, Charles, 2nd Baron Howard of
   Effingham and 1st earl of Nottingham
   (1597) 116
  and Margaret Gage 207n.124, 303n.56
Howard, Charles, 1st earl of Carlisle 546
Howard, Frances, countess of Essex and countess
   of Somerset 40, 451
  marriage annulment 426
  and Robert Ker 426
Howard, Henry, Lord, and 1st earl of
   Northampton (1604) 100, 333, 335n.9,
   383n.35, 413
  death of, and reconciliation to Rome 427,
    427n.19
  and John Leslie, bishop of Ross 135
  and John Stubbs's *The Discoverie of a
    Gaping Gulf* 95
  and Lewis Baily and George Abbot 418,
    418n.195, 419n.198
  and libels 418n.195
  and Mary Stuart 134–5; her reinterment 413
  niece of, *see* Neville, Lady Margaret; lobbies
    Matthew Hutton on her behalf 257n.138
  and persecution 363n.127, 413
  and Philip Howard 154n.61
  and Robert Drury and Anne of
    Denmark 361
  and Thomas Norton's 'Chain of
    Treasons' 134–5
Howard, Philip, Cardinal 553–4
Howard, Philip, 1st earl of Arundel 73, 195, 197,
   240n.60, 486
  arrested, May 1585 153–4, 185
  betrayed by Edward Grately 153–4, 269n.41
  legal proceedings against 120, 196–7, 196n.79
  refuses Lord Henry Howard's persuasions to
    conform 154n.61
  sister of, *see* Sackville, lady Margaret
  testified against by Walton 194n.72
  wife of, *see* Howard, Anne (*née* Dacre)
Howard, Thomas, 4th duke of Norfolk 134
  execution 96
  and Gregory Martin 135
  and Mary Stuart 81

INDEX   609

Howard, Thomas, 2nd earl of Arundel
  conformity 441
  Greenwich property 441
  privy councillor 441
  and Richard Newport and William
    Scot 408–9, 409n.151, 441
Howard, William, Lord, of Naworth 478–9
  oath of allegiance, 1606, taken by 382
Howard, William, Viscount Stafford 4n.2,
    544n.25, 552, 554, 557, 559, 559n.93
Howell, Dr 216n.158
Howes, Edmund 17
Howland, Richard, vice-chancellor of Cambridge
  and anti-puritanism of 86–7
  and John Whitgift 86–7
  and recusancy survey of October 1577 86–7
  and Thomas Cartwright 86–7
Howlin, John 147n.30
Howson, John 327, 422–3
Huddlestone, Henry, as patron of John
    Gerard 281n.78
Huddlestone, Sir Edmund 281–2, 283
  daughter of, see Fortescue, Isabel
  son of, see Huddlestone, Henry
Huggard, Miles 51
Hughes, Edward 274
Hughes, Edward, sheriff 148
Hughes, of Winchester 181n.10
Huguenots 309, 405, 407–8, 457
Hull
  arsenal 512
  blockhouses 34
Humberson (Humberstone), Robert 207n.124
  death in the Tower of London 207n.124
Humphrey, Laurence 291–2
  and ceremonial conformity 132n.63
  and Edmund Campion's Rationes Decem 132
  and John Slade and John Bodey 132
Humphreys, Lawrence 463
  employer of, see Danstin, William
  execution, 1591, Winchester 207
  hostility to Elizabeth Tudor 207, 207n.122
Hunne, Richard 307
Hunsdon, Baron, see Carey, Henry
Hunt, Eleanor, as patron of Christopher
    Wharton 317
Hunt, Thurstan 293, 340
  anti-puritan/toleration petition 298–9
  and rioting in May 1600 293, 293n.19; and
    William Brettergh 296, 297n.33
  and, with Robert Middleton, arrest, trial, and
    execution, 3 April 1601, Lancaster
    296–302, 305–7 passim, 317–18
Huntingdon, earl of, see Hastings, Henry

Huntly, earl of, see Gordon, George, 6th earl
    (1st marquis 1599)
Hurlestone, Ralph, providential death of,
    alleged 66
Hutton, Luke 226
  uncle of, see Hutton, Matthew
Hutton, Matthew, bishop of Durham (1589), and
    archbishop of York (1595) 202, 222n.183,
    227n.201, 267, 269–70, 272–3
  and earl of Essex, and puritanism 301n.48
  and Edmund Duke, Richard Hill, John Hogg,
    and Richard Holiday 202
  and Frances Bretton's conformity 279n.71
  and Grace Claxton's reprieve 242n.70
  and James VI 273, 273n.52, 343; sermon
    concerning James's right to succeed
    Elizabeth 273n.52
  and Joseph Constable's conformity 270–2
  Lady Margaret Neville persuaded by, to
    conform 242, 272; Hutton lobbies for her
    reprieve 257–8, 257n.138, 258n.139;
    Hutton, lobbied by Lord Henry Howard, on
    her behalf 257n.138
  and Miles Dawson's conformity and
    pardon 272–3
  nephew of, see Hutton, Luke
  and Nicholas Tempest and his wife 272n.48
  and Richard Stapleton's conformity 271–2,
    272n.46
  and royal proclamation of 18 October
    1591 227n.201
  sermon at Durham assizes, 22 July
    1594 247n.89
  and sermons in York Castle gaol,
    1599–1600 280
  slackness alleged (by Lord North, Tobias
    Matthew, and Archbishop Sandys),
    concerning Catholics 243, 268–9,
    272–3, 272n.48
  son of, see Hutton, Sir Timothy
  and William Hart 130
Hutton, Sir Timothy 513
  father of, see Hutton, Matthew
Hutton, William 247n.89
  and Robert Bickerdike's conviction 168n.124
Huyton parish 293
Hyde, Edward, 1st earl of Clarendon 512, 540
Hyde, Henry 464

Ignatius of Loyola 313
Ingatestone Hall, Essex 27–8, 120–1, 120n.10
Ingleby, David 240, 270
  brother of, see Ingleby, Francis
  father-in-law, see Neville, Charles

610 INDEX

Ingleby, Francis 17, 17n.38, 160
  arrest 164n.106
  brother of, *see* Ingleby, David
  and earl of Leicester 160
  execution, 3 June 1586, York 65, 66n.92, 163–4
  and Margaret Clitherow 160, 164
  and Mr Frost 65, 65n.91
  and Robert Bickerdike 168n.124
  and Thomas Belson 197n.83
Ingleby, John 461n.46
Ingram, John 245n.83, 246n.85, 254n.119
  arrest 245
  as chaplain to Sir Walter Lindsay 245–6
  and earl of Huntingdon 245–6
  epigrams 246–7
  torture 247n.89
  trial, with John Boste and George Swallowell,
    and execution, 26 July 1594,
    Gateshead 247–9, 256n.132, 314
Innocent X (Giovanni Battista Pamphili),
    Pope 537n.216
Interregnum
  acts and ordinances 523, 529–30, 532–3,
    532nn.193, 194, 533n.201, 534n.206
Ipswich, execution of John Robinson, 1 October
    1588 192n.63
Ireland, (religious) violence and rebellion
    in 37, 98–102, 405–6; in 1641 506–8,
    541–2
  episcopacy/Catholic bishops in 319
  experience of martyrdom/persecution
    37n.59, 454
  parliament, 1613–15 405–6, 405n.136, 425,
    427–8; 1640 494
  proclamation of July 1605 350
Ireland, William, SJ 551
  trial and execution, with John Grove, 24
    January 1679, Tyburn 549, 553
Ireton, Henry 524
Isabella Clara Eugenia, daughter of Philip II,
    infanta-archduchess of Austria and ruler of
    the Spanish Netherlands 274
Isle of Wight, execution of Robert Anderton and
    William Marsden 162–3
Ithell, Ralph 180

Jackson, John 248n.99, 390n.62, 417nn.188, 190,
    425n.10, 427n.21, 431–2, 458, 461n.46,
    508–9
Jacobitism 5n.5, 15, 17, 17n.41, 27–8; *see also*
    Eyston, Charles
James, Edward 192n.61, 463
  and Anthony Tyrrell 192n.61
  trial and execution, with Ralph Crockett,
    1 October 1588, Chichester 191–2, 191n.57

James I (James VI and I), King 78, 156, 363, 377,
    383, 397n.95, 401–2, 417, 420, 423–4,
    428–30, 452–3, 457, 466, 544
  accession in England 30, 45, 70–1, 231–2, 260,
    285–8, 333; succession campaign
    preceding 260–2, 273, 285–6, 287
  Anglo-French marriage negotiations and
    treaty 456–8, 489
  and Anglo-Spanish marriage negotiations, and
    toleration issue 430–1, 432n.44, 435–6,
    440–3, 440n.75, 443–8 *passim*, 450, 452–6,
    472, 489
  association scheme and proposed repatriation
    of Mary Stuart 123, 131–2
  Blairite obfuscation 423
  Catholic lobbying of 238, 243, 259, 334–5,
    348–50; meeting with Scots Catholic peers
    at Fala 243; *see also* Tresham, Sir Thomas
  and Church of Rome/papacy 338n.24
  and *A Conference about the Next
    Succession* 231–2, 243–4, 260
  and *Corona Regia* 430–1, 452, 452n.9, 454n.15
  cross-confessional alliances/confessional
    inclusivity 243, 333–43, 383, 441
  death of 459
  and earl of Morton 98
  and George Abbot 406–11, 423–5, 425n.10,
    441, 445–7
  and George Blackwell 361–2
  and Gondomar 434, 434n.56, 446, 446n.104,
    450; and William Southerne 444–5;
    see also Maxfield, Thomas
  and Gunpowder Plot, *see* Gunpowder Plot
  and Henry IV 359
  and Huguenots 407–8; Isaac Casaubon 407–8
  and Irish deputies, 1613 424–5
  and John Boste 240
  and John Sugar and Robert Grissold 338,
    338nn.22–23
  and the judges, at Greenwich, 9 June 1605 345
  and Lancelot Andrewes 373–4, 374n.174
  legitimist turn in favour of 180
  and Lord Sheffield and Sir Michael
    Wharton 442–3, 442n.89, 445
  and Matthew Hutton's support of James's right
    to succeed Elizabeth 273, 273n.52
  and North Berwick witches 286
  and oath of allegiance, 1606 362–3, 373–4,
    374n.174, ch. 11 *passim*, 379; James I,
    *An Apologie...together with a
    Premonition* 374n.174; and 'Balaam's
    Asse' 424n.8, 454n.15
  and Oxford University disputations, 1605 349
  and parliament in 1610 379–80, 379n.13,
    380n.22; speech of 21 March 379, 379n.17;

parliament in 1614 speech of, against persecution 426; parliament in 1621, recusancy legislation rejected by James 454–5, 455n.19

and puritanism 362, 369, 453–4

and Raid of Ruthven 123; freed from Ruthvenite control 131–2, 134

and reinterment of Mary Stuart 413–14

and Richard Newport and William Scot 408–11

and Robert Drury and William Davies 359–61, 359n.106

Robert Persons's distrust of 260, 336, 350n.78

and royal proclamation of 6 May 1624 457

royal progress to Scotland, 1617 433, 441–2, 442n.89; and return, through Lancashire 443

rumour of Catholic sympathies of 174

rumour of Spanish marriage alliance 100

son-in-law, *see* Frederick V

speech, 19 March 1604, to parliament 336

speech, 20 June 1616, in star chamber 433–4, 443

sports and pastimes, and book of sports 443, 443n.91

and Suárez' s *Defensio Fidei Catholicae* 425n.12

Tobias Matthew's suspicions of 238–9

tolerance/toleration and intolerance/ persecution 334–43, 376, 383n.35, and ch. 12 *passim*, ch. 13 *passim* (esp. 426–8, 430, 438, 442–3, 445–7), ch. 14 *passim* (esp. 453–6, 458–9), 500, 502, 539–40; Catholic and puritan lobbying of, concerning 334–43; James's tolerance of Catholics, alleged 358, 406–7

Triplici Nodo, Triplex Cuneus 362n.122

and William Baldwin's arrest and release 449–51, 451n.7, 453–4

and William Bishop 407

and William Creighton's defence of 163n.101

James II, (duke of York, and) King 5n.5, 15n.34, 527, 538–9, 539n.5, 549, 555, 558n.86

chaplain of, *see* Downes, Thomas

conversion to Rome 539n.5, 544–6

and John Plessington 554n.73

popish plot, 1678–81 546–7

and Protestant dissenters 544

succession and exclusion/Exclusion crisis 543–9, 543n.24, 546n.34, 555, 563–4

James III, King (Old Pretender) 27–8

James, William, bishop of Durham (1606) 362, 364n.131

Japan, persecution in 531

Jefferson, Robert 11

Jeffrey, Sir John, and Cuthbert Mayne 91

Jehoiada 177

Jenison family, Walworth, Durham 552–4

Jenison, Robert 552–3
brother of, *see* Jenison, Thomas

Jenison, Thomas, SJ 552–3, 553n.66
brother of, *see* Jenison, Robert

Jenison, William, recusant
acquitted and discharged 400n.107
reconciled to Rome by John Roberts 394n.83

Jenison, William, MP, and Joseph Lambton 223n.186

Jenks, Rowland, at Oxford assizes, 1577 64, 89, 150n.41; pilloried 89

Jennings, E. 424n.8

Jerome, St 61

Jetter, John, death in prison 34n.43

Jewel, John, bishop of Salisbury, *Apologia Ecclesiae Anglicanae* 87

John Paul II (Karol Wojtyła), Pope 37n.59

Johnson, Cuthbert 169n.126, 444
brother of, *see* Johnson, William

Johnson, Lawrence, alias Richardson 116, 291
arraigned 113n.179
executed, 30 May 1582, Tyburn 122
at Park Hall 122n.17; slandered 63–4

Johnson, Richard 497n.31

Johnson, Robert 99
arraigned 112n.177
executed, 28 May 1582, Tyburn 122
travels from Rome with Charles Slade 100–1; arrested by Slade 103

Johnson, William 444
brother of, *see* Johnson, Cuthbert

Jollett, Thomas 303n.56, 304–5, 304nn.57–8

Jones, Edward, acquitted at Hereford assizes 131n.60

Jones, Edward, seminarist 26
disputation, 5 May 1590, in church of St Sepulchre 203
and Francis Flower 203
tortured, by Topcliffe 203, 211
trial and execution, 6 May 1590, Fleet Street 203–6, 409n.151

Jones, John (Godfrey Maurice), OFM 282–3
and Richard Topcliffe 275–6, 278
and Robert Barnes 275–6
and Society of Jesus 275n.59, 314n.97
and Stannardine Passy 276
trial and execution, 12 July 1598, St Thomas-a-Watering 278, 279–80; and Christopher Blackall 278n.69

612 INDEX

Jones, John (Leander), OSB 484
Jones, Nicholas 221n.175, 276–7
  and Anne Bellamy 221, 276
Jones, Robert, SJ 345
  and George Birkhead 388n.58, 389–90,
    390n.63
  and John Roberts 400
  and oath of allegiance, 1606 382
  and Roger Cadwallader 384n.39, 388–90,
    390n.63, 391n.65; narrative of 388n.58
  and William Scot 411–12
Jones, Sir William 488
Jones, William (Benedict), OSB 477n.94
Judith and Holofernes 93, 135, 135n.78
Jülich-Cleves succession crises: in 1609 379,
    379n.13; in 1614 427–8

Kellison, Matthew 473n.74
  and Thomas Maxfield 434n.55, 435–6,
    436n.60, 438
Kelly, C. 197n.83, 200n.92
Kemble, John
  execution, 22 August 1679, Hereford 11,
    553n.67; speech 11
  and John Scudamore 553n.67
Kemp, David 186
Kemp, Francis (Boniface), OSB
    427n.21, 520
Kendal, vicar of, see Tirer, Ralph
Kenilworth 95, 167n.116
Kenion, Edward 401–2, 406, 464
  uncle of, see Gerard, Miles
Kent, earl of, see Grey, Henry
Kenyon, J. 538–9, 544, 548–9, 552n.65, 554–7,
    554n.72
Ker, Robert, 1st Viscount Rochester (1611) and
    1st earl of Somerset (1613) 40, 413,
    419n.198, 430, 451
  and Frances Howard 426
Kett, Francis, execution 38–9
Keynes, George, *The Roman Martyrologe*
    460n.42
Killigrew, Henry, and William Davison and
    Thomas Sherwood 92–3
Killigrew, Sir John, fights duel with Ambrose
    Digby 89n.65
Killingham, Thomas 431n.39
Kilroy, G. 82n.28, 96–7, 101–2, 106, 105n.142,
    106nn.143, 148, 112, 114, 114n.184, 116,
    136n.79, 155n.64, 566
King, Geoffrey 480
King, John, bishop of London (1611) 396n.88,
    436n.59
  and George Napper 392–4, 396n.88, 414–15
  and Henry Walpole 257

and John Almond 414–15
and Thomas Maxfield 435–6
and William Spenser 200
king's bench 344, 347, 347n.67, 446n.104,
    522n.155, 556; *see also* queen's bench
  prison 277, 324, 410, 427n.21
King's Lynn, Norfolk 53n.29
Kingdomes Weekly Intelligencer 520–1
Kingsmill, family of 132n.64
Kingsmill, George 286, 337–8, 338n.21
Kingsmill, Henry 132n.64
Kingsmill, John 132n.64
  and Bishop Horne of Winchester 132n.64
Kingsmill, Richard, and 1566 succession
    debates 132n.64
Kingsmill, Sir William
  at executions of John Slade and John
    Bodey 132
  and the royal supremacy 132
Kingston-upon-Thames
  execution of William Way, 23 September
    1588 193
  and John Udall 193; lectureship at parish
    church 193; and Robert Waldegrave
    193, 193n.67
Kirby, Luke 51, 99n.110, 100
  arraigned 112n.177
  executed, 30 May 1582, Tyburn 122
Kirkham, Richard 340n.32, 406n.140
Kirkman, Richard, arrest, arraignment, and
    execution, with William Lacey, 22 August
    1582, York 129, 129n.45
Kitching, Mr 13
Klause, J. 221–2, 221n.179
Knaresborough, John 337n.19, 431n.39, 469,
    471n.69, 489, 512, 512n.111, 521n.149,
    523–4, 532n.193, 537
  and Brian Orrell 12
  and Charles I 511–13
  and Charles Dodd 18
  and Charles Eyston 15, 15n.35, 533n.201
  and Charles Townley 10
  and Christopher Robinson's narrative of trial
    of John Boste and John Ingram 247n.89
  and Christopher Tootell 12
  and Christopher Watson 34
  compounding commissions and composition
    entry books 469n.61
  and Cuthbert Constable 10, 10n.19
  death of (1722) 18
  and Edmund Arrowsmith and Ambrose
    Barlow 478n.97
  and Edward Bamber 523
  and Edward Coyney and John Kemble 11
  and Elizabeth Tudor 333

INDEX 613

and F. P. (a Jesuit) 12
and Francis Bell 519, 519n.141
and George Napper 391–2
and Henry Morse 488–9
historical writers and sources used by
    (William Camden, John Stow, Edmund
    Howes, Sir Richard Baker, Peter Heylyn,
    Jeremy Collier) 17
and Hugh Green's execution
    narratives 33n.41, 515n.126
and John Almond 417n.188
and John Austin 528, 528n.179
and John Danby 12, 70n.109
and John Lockwood and Edmund
    Catterick 513
and John Nalson 503
and John Southworth 12, 535,
    535nn.209, 211
and John Yaxley 14–15, 55n.41,
    61n.73, 248n.96
and Lady Margaret Constable 16–17
martyrological collections ('Sufferings of the
    Catholicks') 10, 11f, 11–18 and *passim*
and Matthew Flathers 365n.137
and Mr C. Tunstall 16–17, 17n.38
and Mrs Fairfax 12
and Nicholas Postgate 12
and parliament of 1629 482
and Philip Powel 522
Popish Plot, 1678–81 546
prisons, Catholics' deaths in, 1640s 522n.152
and Ralph Thoresby 11n.21
and Robert Jefferson 11
and Robert Nutter and Edward Thwing,
    manuscript account of 294
and sermons in York Castle gaol,
    1599–1600 280n.76
and Sir Miles Stapleton 11n.21
and Sir Richard Baker 15n.35, 17
and Sir Roger L'Estrange 17
and Thomas Atkinson 431
and Thomas Maxfield 436–7
and Thomas Metcalfe 15
and Thomas Roydon 541n.17
and Thomas Thwing 11, 11n.21, 557
and Thomas Worthington 376n.3
and William Webster 504–5
and Worthington family of Blainscow 12
Knaresborough, Peter 256n.134
Knavesmire, York 130, 168
Knight, Edward 215n.151
Knight, William 267, 267n.33, 461n.46
    execution, with George Errington and
    William Gibson, 29 November 1596,
    York 267–9

Knights, M. 546n.34, 547n.40
Knollys, Sir Francis 59, 197n.81, 205, 273
    and Edmund Campion's execution 116
    opposition to ceremonial conformity and to
        Archbishop Whitgift 196–7, 199
    and prosecution of Catholics in Oxford
        (Thomas Belson, Richard Yaxley, George
        Nichols, and Humphrey ap Richard)
        196–200
    and prosecution of earl of Arundel 197n.82
    and treason statute of 1581 105
Knollys, Sir William
    denounces toleration of Catholics 323
    and parliament in 1601 308–9
Knott, J. 24
Knox, Ronald 4n.2
Knox, Thomas 548n.44

La Rochelle 489
La Vieuville, marquis of, *see* Coskaer, Charles
Lacey, Brian 160n.86, 214–15
    brother of, *see* Lacey, Richard
    execution, with others, 10 December 1591,
        Tyburn 215–16, 215n.156
    servant of, *see* Hodgson, Sydney
Lacey, Richard 160, 160n.86, 215n.156
    brother of, *see* Lacey, Brian
    and Sir Edward Suliard 160n.86
Lacey, William
    arrested in York Castle and prosecuted under
        either 1571 or 1581 treason
        legislation 129, 129n.45
    execution, with Richard Kirkman, 22 August
        1582, York 129
Lafuente, Diego de, OP 452n.8
    and Sir John Digby 454
    and Thomas Maxfield 434n.55, 435, 454
Lake, P. 6–8, 9n.16, 45, 62n.76, 85–6, 85n.42, 88,
    152n.54, 160, 164n.108, 190, 231, 264, 395,
    485–6, 486n.134
Lambeth Palace, documents obtained from, by
    secular clergy 367n.146, 394n.83
Lambton, Joseph
    arrest, with Edward Waterson 222
    execution, 31 July 1592, Newcastle 33,
        223, 314
    and Francis Montford 222
    uncle of, *see* Birkhead, George
Lampley, William, execution, 1588, Gloucester
    194n.74
Lanark, earl of, *see* Hamilton, William
Lancashire Daily Post 69
Lancashire
    exorcisms 300
    preachers 300, 300n.42

614 INDEX

Lancashire (*cont.*)
  recusants 300
  Thomas Bell's information concerning
    recusants and clergy in 227n.201,
    238n.47, 340n.32
Lancaster 54, 130, 432, 481–2
  Castle 293–4, 478; gaol 293, 471
  executions at, *see* Arrowsmith, Edmund; Baily,
    Laurence; Bamber, Edward; Barlow, Edward
    (Ambrose); Bell, James; Finch, John; Herst,
    Richard; Hunt, Thurstan; Leyburn, James;
    Middleton, Robert; Nutter, Robert; Thulis,
    John; Thwing, Edward; Warren, Roger;
    Whitaker, Thomas; Woodcock, John
  Lancaster St Mary, vicar of, *see* King
    Geoffrey
  vicar of, *see* Porter, Henry
Lancaster, John, and John Colleton 114
Lane, John 548n.44
Langham, John 517n.132
Langhorne, Richard, execution, 14 July 1679,
    Tyburn 554
Langley, Richard 90n.69
  and Alexander Crow 169
  arrest, trial, and execution, 1 December 1586,
    York 168–9, 168n.124
  daughter of, *see* Foster (*née* Langley), Isabel
  as patron of John Mush 168–9
Laqueur, T. 52, 70
Lassells, Mrs 11–12
Laud, William, archbishop of Canterbury 476,
    485–90, 485n.133, 495–7, 500
  anti-popery 494–5
  Laudianism 485–6, 486n.134
  trial and execution 521–2
Lauderdale, duke of, *see* Maitland, John
Launceston, Cornwall
  assizes 90
  execution of Cuthbert Mayne, 30 November
    1577 53, 91, 95, 101n.120
Law, Thomas Graves 9n.16, 498n.32
  1878 edition of Challoner's *Memoirs of
    Missionary Priests* 19–20
Lazo, K. 537n.217
Leak, Thomas 255n.125
Leedes, Edward, SJ 484, 533
  papal deposing power, affirmed by 483–4
Leicester, earl of, *see* Dudley, Robert
'Leicester's Commonwealth' (*The Copie of a
    Leter*) 159–60, 189, 298
  copies brought from Norwich by Ralph
    Emerson 155n.67
Leigh, Richard 175n.159, 190
  and Anthony Tyrrell at Paul's Cross 175, 189

  courtroom dispute with Bishop
    Aylmer 189n.49
  execution, with others, 30 August 1588,
    Tyburn 189–90
  see also Cecil, Sir William, *A Copie of a Letter*
Leigh, William 306–7, 432–3
  and Edmund Arrowsmith 476, 478
Lennox, countess of, *see* Douglas, Margaret
Lennox, earl of, *see* Stuart, Esmé, sieur
    d'Aubigny
Leo XIII (Vincenzo Gioacchino Raffaele Luigi
    Pecci), Pope 78
Leominster 161n.96
  execution of Roger Cadwallader, 27 August
    1610 69n.105, 385–6
Lerma, duke of, *see* Sandoval y Rojas, Francisco
    Gómez de
Leslie, Alexander 505
Leslie, John, bishop of Ross 152, 155
  L'Innocence 96n.100; and *Treatise of
    Treasons* 96n.100
  and Lord Henry Howard 135
L'Estrange, Sir Hamon 440; wife of (Alice
    Stubbe) 440
L'Estrange, Sir Roger 17, 552n.62, 558
Leveneur, Tanneguy, count of Tillières 465n.51
Lever, Ralph 248–9
Lever, Thomas 248–9
Lewen, Christopher 222n.183
Lewen, Edward
  arrests Joseph Lambton and Edward
    Waterson 222
  and earl of Huntingdon 222
Lewis, David, SJ
  accuser (Trot), providential death of,
    alleged 69
  arrest, trial, and execution, 27 August 1679,
    Usk 58, 547n.41; speech, not delivered
    58, 547n.41
Lewis, Owen, bishop of Cassano
  and Robert Persons 219
  and Thomas Pormort 219
Lewkenor, Sir Lewis (knighted 1603) 251,
    363, 382–3
  Estate of English Fugitives 251n.111
Leyburn, George 530, 535, 535n.211, 536n.213
  and John Sergeant 553
Leyburn, James 95
  execution, 22 March 1583, Lancaster 130,
    320; denies Elizabeth's supremacy 130;
    George Birkhead doubts martyr
    status of 130
  godson, *see* Duckett, James
  and Mary Stuart 141n.3

INDEX 615

Libigny, Jean 450
Lilly, Edmund 198n.85
Lincoln
  assizes 441–2
  bishop of, *see* Barlow, Thomas; Barlow,
    William; Cooper, Thomas; Williams, John
  execution of Thomas Benstead and Thomas
    Sprott 288–9
Lindsay, David, 9th earl of Crawford 245–6
  son of, *see* Lindsay, Sir Walter
Lindsay, Sir Walter 245–6
  father of, *see* Lindsay, David
  and John Ingram 245–6
  militates against conformity 246
  narrative of Scots Catholicism 246
Line, Anne 303
  arrest, trial, and execution, with Mark
    Barkworth and Roger Filcock, 27 February
    1601, Tyburn 303–5, 303n.56, 305n.65, 317;
    narratives of 304n.58
  and Robert Drury 356n.96
  and William (or Richard) Thompson 162
Lingard, John 19
  History of England 19
Lingen, Edward 244n.76
Lion, John 279n.74
Lisbon, residence for English priests at 369n.155
Lister, Thomas, SJ 313, 345
Liverpool, archbishop of, *see* Downey, Richard
Livesey, Mary 520n.143
Lloyd, Evan, and earl of Leicester 150
Lloyd, George, bishop of Chester 369
Lloyd, John 556n.79
  execution, with Philip Evans, 22 July 1679,
    Cardiff 547n.41
Lloyd, Owen 186n.29
  brother of, *see* Lloyd, Richard
Lloyd, Richard (alias Flower)
  brother of, *see* Lloyd, Owen
  condemned for harbouring William
    Horner 186
  execution, with others, 30 August 1588,
    Tyburn 186
Lloyd, William 544
  The Late Apology 540–3, 540n.15
Lockwood, John 380n.20
  arrest, trial, and execution, with Edmund
    Catterick, 13 April 1642, York 513–14,
    514n.122
  sentenced but reprieved, 18 March 1610 379
Lok, Henry 278n.64
Lomax, James, death in prison 34n.43
Lombard, Peter, archbishop of Armagh 147n.30,
  406n.139

London
  All Saints parish, Bread Street 155
  bishop of, *see* Abbot, George, Aylmer, John;
    Bancroft, Richard; Bonner, Edmund;
    Grindal, Edmund; King, John; Ravis,
    Thomas; Ridley, Nicholas; Sandys, Edwin
  Blackfriars 73; French embassy 470
  Bridewell 105; *see also* Bridewell prison
  Charterhouse 53; prior of, *see* Houghton, John
  Cheapside 327–8, 455, 456; puritan
    demonstration in 233; Luisa de Carvajal
    in, and Lothbury Street 367n.147
  Chick Lane 391n.65
  Christ-Church Hospital 73
  Clerkenwell 203–6, 218–19; Jesuit novitiate
    469–70, 473n.74
  Denmark House 500–1
  enforcement of royal proclamation of
    18 October 1591 in 227n.202
  executions in London and environs 73 and
    passim (listed separately in this index); in
    summer 1588 59, 67, 72, 187–90, 214
  Farringdon Ward 73
  Fetter Lane 48
  Fleet Street 48, 161n.96, 203
  Gray's Inn, Gray's Inn Fields, and Gray's Inn
    Lane 49, 114, 216–17
  Great Fire 540
  Greyfriars 73
  Hart Street 123–4; William Carter's premises
    there, searched by Topcliffe 123–4
  Holborn/Holborn Bars 48, 73, 141, 188, 215,
    222, 250, 404, 451, 458
  Holywell Lane, Shoreditch 188
  Hyde Park 465n.51
  Islington Woods, arrest of puritans in
    233–4
  Lincoln's Inn Fields 188
  London Bridge 399
  lord mayor 83
  Mile End, executions at 187, 188, 194n.73
  Milford Lane 404
  prisons 55n.43, 133; *and see* under names of
    prisons: Bridewell; Clink; Fleet; Gatehouse;
    king's bench; Marshalsea; Newgate; Tower
    of London; White Lion, Southwark
  recorder, *see* Fleetwood, William; Gardiner,
    Sir Thomas
  River Thames 103, 166, 262, 394, 404
  Sackville House 73, 203
  St Bride's 203
  St Giles-without-Cripplegate 122n.18
  St James's 465n.51, 500–1
  St Margaret's, Westminster 487–8

616 INDEX

London (*cont.*)
St Paul's churchyard 83n.32, 219–20
St Sepulchre's church 203, 360n.115
sheriffs of 83; *see also* Masham, William;
Spencer, John
Shoe Lane 203
Smithfield 50, 117n.201, 436–7
Southampton House 73–4, 141n.5, 221
Temple Bar 73
Tothill Street 161n.96, 165n.111
treaty of, *see* treaty of London, 1604
Tyburn *passim*
Westminster 456
see also Paul's Cross
London Oratory 6n.6
Loomie, A., SJ 336–7
Lopez, Rodrigo 244–5
execution 250
lord chancellor, *see* Bromley, Sir Thomas;
Egerton, Sir Thomas; Hatton, Sir
Christopher; More, Sir Thomas
lord chief justice 82–3 (Sir Robert Catlyn);
see also Fleming, Sir Thomas; North, Sir
Francis; Rolle, Henry; Scroggs, Sir William;
Wray, Sir Christopher
lord keeper, *see* Bacon, Sir Nicholas; Coventry, Sir
Thomas; Puckering, Sir John
lord privy seal, *see* Montagu, Sir Henry
Lorkin, Thomas 454n.15
Lorraine, Charles de (or Charles de Guise), duke
of Mayenne 136n.79
Lorraine, Charles de, prince of Joinville 360n.110
Lorraine, duke of (Charles III), envoys of 338n.24
Lorraine, Francis II, prince of Joinville, duke of
Guise 136n.79, 155–6
Lorraine, Louis I de, cardinal of Guise
136n.79, 188
Louis XIII, King 403
Anglo-French marriage negotiations and
treaty 456–7
and persecution in England 425n.10
sister of, *see* Henrietta Maria
Louis XIV, King 543, 543n.22, 544–8
Louvain/Leuven 80–1
Love, Christopher 534
Lowe, John 165n.111
father of, *see* Lowe, Simon
trial and execution, with John Adams and
Richard Dibdale, 8 October 1586,
Tyburn 165, 180
and William Weston 164–5, 165n.111
Lowe, Mrs 189n.46
betrayed by William Tedder 189n.46
Lowe, Simon 90
son of, *see* Lowe, John

Lowther, William 267, 268, 271
Lucy, Sir Thomas 265
Ludlam, Robert 461n.46
execution, with Nicholas Garlick and Richard
Simpson, 24 July 1588, Derby 54, 65n.91,
181, 335n.8
Ludlow gaol 57
Lumley, John, 9th Baron Lumley 269n.41
Luther, Martin 163n.101
Lutterworth, Leicestershire, Robert Sutton
beneficed at 182n.17
Luttrell, John 392n.66
Lydney, dean of, *see* Turner, Thomas
Lydney, vicar of, *see* Turner, Thomas

MacCaffrey, W. 97
Macinnes, A. 505
MacCulloch, D. 42
MacDonnell, Randal, 1st marquis of
Antrim 494n.10, 504, 530n.186
Maguire, Rory 507
Maire, Grace 14
husband of, *see* Maire Robert
puritan father of 14
Maire, Robert 14
wife of, *see* Maire, Grace
Maitland, John, 1st duke of Lauderdale 543
Major, Anthony 242n.66, 253, 256n.134
and John Boste 241, 241n.65
Male, Jean-Baptiste van 434n.56
Manaerts, Oliver, SJ 97n.105
Manchester, earl of, *see* Montagu, Sir Henry
Manger, Thomas 220n.172, 461n.46
as source for Challoner's account of John
Cornelius and William Pikes 250n.107
Manners, Anne 273n.49
Manners, Francis, 6th earl of Rutland 451
Manners, Roger 103n.126, 117
Manners, Roger, 5th earl of Rutland 286–7; and
John Gerard 286n.95
brother of, *see* Manners, Sir Oliver
Manners, Sir Oliver
brother of, *see* Manners, Roger, 5th earl
as lobbyist, with Thomas Fitzherbert, in
Rome 371–3, 372n.166
Manners, Sir Thomas 273n.49
daughter of, *see* Manners, Anne
Manningham, John 333
Manwood, Sir Roger (knighted 1578) 131n.60,
164n.109
and legal proceedings against Cuthbert Mayne
and others 90
and legal proceedings against John Slade and
John Bodey 131
and trial of William Lampley 194n.74

INDEX   617

Marchant, Charles, and Francis Bell 518, 518n.138
Maria of Spain, daughter of Philip III 442n.89
Mariana, Juan de, SJ 379, 551
Markland, Alexander 256n.134
Marprelate (Martin Marprelate) agitation 86–7, 193n.68, 196, 200, 233–4, 237n.44
Marsden, William 463
  execution, with Robert Anderton, 25 April 1586, Isle of Wight 162–3; proclamation concerning 162–3
  loyalism of 162–3
  and William Rainolds and William Whitaker 162
Marsh, John 186
  and Ann Foster 90n.69
  arrested and released 186n.28
Marshall, Gilbert, and John Finch 146
Marshall, J. 373n.172
Marshall, P. 24
Marshalsea prison 50n.10, 64–5, 107–8, 124n.26, 167–8, 191n.56
  lax management of, denounced by Bishop Aylmer 133n.72
  Mass celebrated in 133, 133n.72
  raid on, 26 February 1600 281n.78
Marston Moor, battle of 520n.144
Marsys, François de 498n.32, 515n.126, 518n.138
Marten, Henry 524–5
Martin, Gregory
  and John Hart 101n.120
  and Lord Henry Howard 135
  and Thomas Howard, 4th duke of Norfolk 135
  Treatise of Schisme 93, 102, 135; printed by William Carter 135, 135n.78; Richard Topcliffe's annotated copy 135n.78
Martin, Mrs 33n.41
Martin, P. 324
Martin, Richard, as harbourer of Robert Morton 188n.44
Martin, Sir Richard
  dedicatee of Samuel Cottesford's *A Treatise against Traitors* 282n.83
  and John Rigby 282–3
  wife of, *see* Ecclestone, Dorcas
Martin, Roger, chaplain of, *see* Vivian, John
martyrology (Catholic)
  and archives 24–5, 25n.9; (fortuitous) survival of 24–5; loss of 25n.9
  and 'body scholarship' 27–8
  contested by Catholics 72–3 and *passim*

martyr catalogues 30n.27, 371, 371n.165, 377–8; *see also* Smith, Richard, Chalcedon dossier/catalogue; Smith, Richard, Chalcedon dossier/catalogue, Paris catalogue
martyr narratives 45–6, ch. 3 *passim*; common features of 29, 29n.25; emergence of mid-Elizabethan Catholic martyr narrative 88
  perceptions of, as a topic 23–30
  see also, inter alia Allen, William; Blount, Richard; Butler, Alban; Challoner, Richard; Champney, Anthony; Davies, Richard; Garnet, Henry; Gerard, John; Knaresborough, John; More, Thomas, secular clergy agent; Mush, John; Norton, Benjamin; Warford, William; Worthington, Thomas
Marvell, Andrew 545
Mary of Modena 544
Mary, Princess (Mary II) 544
Mary Stuart, queen of Scots 9, 67n.94, 70–1, 80–1, 83, 92, 96, 100, 120, 121n.11, 123n.24, 126–7, 133–4, 140, 141n.3, 145n.17, 152, 155n.65, 156, 157, 159, 170–1, 175, 177n.166, 185, 188n.44, 218n.166, 267, 274, 303n.55, 349, 438, 500, 542, 546n.34, 563
  and Anthony Babington 164–8, 164n.108, 209, 464; *see also* Gifford, Gilbert
  Anthony Browne, 1st Viscount Montague's alleged hostility towards 170n.134
  association scheme and proposed repatriation 122–3, 131–2
  and David Rizzio 240n.56, 408, 408n.149
  deposed in Scotland 81
  and James Hepburn, earl of Bothwell 81–2
  and Lord Henry Howard 134–5
  as martyr for the Catholic faith 32n.36, 171–4, 231, 260, 334–5, 335n.8, 348–9, 371n.165, 413–14, 456; pictures concerning fate of, derived from Richard Verstegan 172
  reinterment 413–14
  secretary of, *see* Nau, Claude
  Thomas Worthington allegedly recognises as queen of England 141n.3
  trial and execution, 8 February 1587, Fotheringhay 171–4, 179–80, 341, 413–14; French court fails to intervene 171; rejoicing in London and York 172; James VI's perceived betrayal of Mary 260
  and William Carter 95–6, 96n.100
Mary Tudor, Queen 19–20, 78–9, 143, 542, 555
  and John Felton's wife, as maid of honour to 83n.32

618   INDEX

Mary Tudor, Queen (*cont.*)
  Marian persecution 30–1, 36–7, 36n.57, 203,
    236, 265, 325, 555, 560; *see also* Foxe, John;
    Massey, Perotine
Masham, William 139n.92
Maskew, Bridget 168n.124, 269–70, 270n.42
  brother of, *see* Bickerdike, Robert
  imprisoned in York Castle 168n.124
Mason, John, execution, with others, 10
  December 1591, Tyburn 216
Massey family, Puddington Hall, Burton 551n.59
Massey, Perotine 31, 143, 143n.12, 307
Massey, William 551n.59
Matthew, Sir Tobias 422n.1, 440n.75,
  446n.104, 490
Matthew, Tobias, dean of Durham (1583) and
  bishop of Durham (1595) 222, 223n.188,
  241–3, 296, 365n.136
  and Francis Stuart, earl of Bothwell 239,
    239n.48
  and Henry Sanderson 222, 295–6
  interrogates Edward Waterson 222
  and John Boste 239n.50
  and Matthew Hutton 272
  suspicions concerning James VI 238–9
Matthews, Eugene, archbishop of Dublin
  406n.139
Maurice, Prince, of Orange-Nassau 405, 482–3
Mauvissière, seigneur de, *see* Castelnau,
  Michel de
Maxfield, Humphrey 141n.3
Maxfield, Thomas
  arrest (by John Wragge), trial, and execution,
    1 July 1616, Tyburn 61, 433–40 *passim*;
    demonstration around the scaffold 61;
    reprieve offered 437; relics 438–9,
    438nn.67, 72, 439*f*; burial with malefactors,
    and retrieval 439–40; translation of body
    to Spain 438n.67
  brother of 434n.56
  and Diego de Lafuente 434n.55, 435, 454
  father of, *see* Maxfield, William
  and Gondomar 434–5, 434n.55, 437n.63,
    439–40
  and Matthew Kellison 434n.55, 435–6,
    436n.60, 438
  and oath of allegiance 435–8
  and Robert Sutton's relics, and cure of
    demoniac 182n.17, 435–6
  Vita et Martyrium 431n.39, 434n.55, 437;
    Exemplar Literarum 431n.39, 434n.56;
    'Brevis Narratio' 434n.55; 'Insigne
    Martyrium' 434n.55
Maxfield, William 84n.39, 182
  son of, *see* Maxfield, Thomas

May, John, bishop of Carlisle 269
Mayenne, duke of, *see* Lorraine, Charles de (or
  Charles de Guise)
Mayhew, Henry 401–2
Mayler, Henry 406n.140
Mayne, Cuthbert 142, 559
  arrest, trial (and of others), and execution, 30
    November 1577, Launceston 4, 9, 53,
    88–93, 90n.71, 91nn.75, 81, 95, 101n.120,
    142, 559; possession of printed jubilee 88,
    91, 91nn.77, 78; Sir John Popham 91n.78;
    death of hangman 64; distribution of
    Mayne's body parts 53
  as chaplain to Francis Tregian 88, 352n.82
  leaves St John's Oxford for Douai and
    ordination 88n.62; warned by Thomas
    Ford to leave country 88n.62
  relic (skull) of 28n.19
  and Sir John Jeffrey 91, 91n.78
  'treatise against the book of common
    prayers' 91
Mayo, Thomas 505n.68, 517–18
McBride, Damian 128, 128n.41
McCavitt, J. 406
McCoog, T., SJ 97n.105, 304n.57, 371–2, 372n.166
McGeoghan, Arthur, OP, trial and execution,
  27 November 1633, Tyburn 483
Mead, Joseph 454n.15, 455, 477, 481
Meal Tub Plot 553n.67, 558, 559n.92
Médicis, Marie de, and persecution in
  England 425n.10
Meehan, Charles, OFM, execution, 12 August
  1679, Ruthin 555n.74
Melling, John 473, 475, 473n.74
Melling, Richard 473n.74
memory
  and history 3–4, 20–1
  and John Knaresborough 10
  and martyrology preface, *passim*
Mende, bishop of, *see* Du Plessis de la
  Mothe-Houdancourt, Daniel
Mendoza, Bernardino de 95, 106, 112, 115n.188,
  117n.201, 196, 196n.79, 240n.56
  and death of the 8th earl of
    Northumberland 154
  secretary of, *see* Serrano, Pedro
Mercurian, Everard, SJ 97n.105
Meredith, Jonas 180, 185
  relationship to Cecil family 185n.23
  in Wisbech Castle, opposes clergy favourable
    towards Jesuits 185n.23
Metcalfe, Thomas, and John Knaresborough 15
Metham, Thomas
  arrested, indicted, and gaoled 94
  sister of (wife of Nicholas Elvish) 181n.10

INDEX 619

Meyer, A. O. 43–4
Michall, Richard, death in king's bench
  prison 427n.21
Middleton, Anthony 26
  arrested by Topcliffe 203
  disputation, 5 May 1590, in church of
    St Sepulchre 203
  execution, 6 May 1590, Clerkenwell 203–4,
    205, 409n.151
Middleton, Conyers, and Richard Challoner 6
Middleton, Robert, SJ
  arrest, 1599 297n.33
  sister of 306
  and Society of Jesus 299, 299n.40
  and, with Thurstan Hunt, arrest, trial, and
    execution, 3 April 1601,
    Lancaster 296–301, 305–7 passim, 317–18
  supporter of archpresbyterate 297n.33
Middleton, Thomas, alias Dade, OP 518–19, 532,
  532n.197
Mildmay, Sir Henry 499
Mildmay, Sir Walter
  accuses Stephen Vallenger of writing Thomas
    Alfield's True Reporte 119
  and 1581 parliament 105
Miller, J. 527, 538–9, 538n.3, 543, 545, 547,
  549, 558
Miller, Ralph 181n.10
Miller (Milner), Ralph 207–8
  execution, with Roger Dickenson, 7 July 1591,
    Winchester 207–8; reprieve offered
    208n.125
Milner, John, bishop of Castabala 29
Milton, John 45
Moffat, James, SJ 428
Molino, Nicolò 360
  early Jacobean measures against Catholics
    338, 342
  Whitsun Riot 344, 345n.59, 347n.68, 348–9
Molyneux, Sir Richard 300, 300n.41, 306n.69
  alleged conspiracy 298–300, 305–6
  brother-in-law, see Gerard, Sir Thomas
Mompesson, Lawrence
  goes into exile, at Brussels 218
  wife of 218n.166
  and William Pattenson 218
monarchical republicanism 126–8, 152n.54
Monchy, Michel de, archdeacon of Rouen
  155, 155n.64
Monck, George 530n.187
Monk Fryston 123n.24
Monmouth, duke of, see Scott, James
Monson, Sir Thomas 383
Monta, S. 24
Montagu, Ralph 544n.28

Montagu, Richard, bishop of Chichester (1627)
  and bishop of Norwich (1638) 475, 490
Montagu, Sir Henry, 1st earl of Manchester
  (1626) 499, 502
  and George Gervase 363–4
  and John Roberts 396n.91
  and Robert Drury 356–7
Montagu, Walter 530
Montague House, Southwark 141, 177n.166, 399
Montague, Viscount, see Browne, Anthony;
  Browne, Anthony Maria; Browne, Francis
Montford, Francis 222
  as agent of earl of Tyrone 222
  brother of, see Montford, Thomas
Montford, Thomas
  brother of, see Montford, Francis
  reprieved 339n.29
Moray, Sir Robert 520n.145
Mordaunt, Henry, 4th Baron Mordaunt 408
Mordaunt, John, 5th Baron Mordaunt 437n.63
More, George 133n.69
More, Grace 393n.76
  brother of, see More, Thomas, secular
    clergy agent
More, Henry, proceedings against 456, 456n.25
More, Henry, SJ 250n.107, 256–7, 313n.94, 524
  proceedings against, 1628 481n.114
More, Hugh 186
  execution, with Robert Morton, 30 August
    1588, Lincoln's Inn Fields 188n.44
  reconciled to Rome by Thomas
    Stevenson 188n.44
More, John 341
More, Sir Thomas 36–7, 161, 447, 456n.23
  circulation of biographies of 77
  and Elizabeth Barton 79
  execution, 6 July 1535, Tower of London
    29, 77, 145
  grandson of, see More, Thomas, of
    Barnborough
  life of, by Nicholas Harpsfield, seized by
    Richard Topcliffe 124n.26
  William Roper's life of 15n.35, 77
More, Thomas, of Barnborough 124n.26
  grandfather of, see More, Sir Thomas
More, Thomas, secular clergy agent
  draft martyrologies/martyr catalogues 371,
    371n.165, 377–8, 378n.7, 464
  on persecution 374n.175, 378n.7
  as secular clergy agent in Rome 371, 378n.7,
    387, 390–1, 390n.62, 392n.66, 393–4,
    393nn.76, 77, 401n.111, 402n.119,
    406nn.138, 140, 409n.152, 411, 415,
    417n.190, 423, 434n.55
  sister of, see More, Grace

620 INDEX

More, William 133n.69
Morgan, Edward 461n.46
  enmity towards Richard Smith 514n.124
  execution, 26 April 1642, Tyburn 514,
    514n.122
Morgan, Thomas 180, 185, 185n.23
Morgan, William, and Whitsun Riot 344,
  344nn.56–57
Morice, James, and high commission 233
Morison, S. 78
Morley and Monteagle, Baron, *see* Parker, Henry
Morrice, Richard, and Nicholas Postgate 69–70
Morris, David 553
Morris, John, SJ 6n.6, 26n.13, 350n.79
Morse, Henry, SJ 489, 489n.140
  arrested by Francis Newton and John Cook,
    1637 488–9; trial and release 483,
    488–9, 521–2
  arrest, 1640 494, 497, 497n.31
  and John Southworth, and care of plague
    victims 487–8
  trial and execution, 22 January 1645,
    Tyburn 521–2, 521n.149
Morton, earl of, *see* Douglas, James
Morton, Nicholas 99n.112, 100n.114, 102n.125
  assists in procuring *Regnans in Excelsis* 94, 188
  nephew of, *see* Morton, Robert
Morton, Robert
  arrest and interrogation (by Aylmer,
    Fleetwood and Hopton), and release, of 94
  and conspiracy to release Mary
    Stuart 188n.44
  execution, with Hugh More, 28 August 1588,
    Lincoln's Inn Fields 188, 188n.44
  harbourer of, *see* Martin, Richard
  uncles of, *see* Morton, Nicholas; Norton,
    Thomas
Morton, Sir George 250n.107
Morton, Thomas, bishop of Chester (1616)
    and of Coventry and Lichfield
    (1619) 355n.94, 364
  as bishop of Chester 441, 443; and sports and
    pastimes 443
  and John Barwick 441
  secretary of, *see* Sergeant, John
Moseley, executioner 182
Mount Grace, Osmotherley, Lady Chapel 28n.19
Mountjoy, Baron, *see* Blount, Charles
Mullan, John, *Idea Togatae Constantiae* 481n.114
Munday, Anthony 113
  A Breefe and True Reporte 282
  A Discoverie of Edmund Campion 117n.202;
    attacked by Thomas Alfield 117n.202
  and George Haydock 138

mockery of Catholic martyrs 51
pamphlet on Everard Hanse 108–9, 108n.157
replies (*A Breefe Aunswer*) to Thomas Alfield's
  True Reporte 117n.201
Munden, John, arraignment and execution, with
  others, 12 February 1584, Tyburn 137–8
Murnnen, James 13
Murphy, Cornelius, SJ 471n.69
Musgrave, Edward, comments on John Boste's
  execution and demeanour 60–1,
  61n.73, 248n.96
Musgrave, Leonard 269n.38
Musgrave, Robert 222n.183, 269n.41
Mush, John 17, 17n.38, 58–9, 164, 256n.134,
  319–20, 359n.105, 365n.136, 423n.6
  arrest, October 1586 169, 169n.126; absconds
    with Cuthbert Johnson and Bernard
    Pattenson 169n.126
  brother of, *see* Mush, William
  and Margaret Clitherow, and biography of
    her 25, 158–9, 164, 563
  and Marmaduke Bowes and Hugh Taylor 157–8
  martyr catalogue by (lost) 30n.27
  and Richard Langley, his patron 168–9
  and Robert Bickerdike 168n.124
  and Society of Jesus and the appeals to
    Rome 261, 308, 311–12, 314
  and Thomas Bell and occasional
    conformity 170, 205–6, 252
  and true martyrdom 314
  and 'Yorkshire Recusant's Relation'
    158n.84, 164
Mush, William
  arrested, with Matthew Flathers 365;
    reprieved 365; absconds 365n.137
  brother of, *see* Mush, John

Nalson, John 503
Napper, George
  arrest, trial, and execution, 9 November 1610,
    Oxford 63n.80, 391–4; relic 390n.63;
    narratives 392nn.66, 70, 466; declaration
    in favour of episcopacy 394
  and John King 392–4, 396n.88, 414–15
  loyalist declaration offered by 185n.25
  and oath of allegiance, 1606 392–3;
    alternative oath 393
Napper, Joan 393n.76
  husband of, *see* Greenwood, Thomas
Nau, Claude 152
Navarre, king of, *see* Henry IV
Nayler, James 537
Nayler, William 194n.70
Neale, John 105, 234

INDEX 621

Nedham, Francis 140
Neile, Richard, bishop of Rochester (1608),
    Coventry and Lichfield (1610), Lincoln
    (1614) and Durham (1617) 363, 401,
    446n.104, 476
  attacked in 1614 parliament 427
  and Edward Wightman 401n.111
Nelson, John
  arrest, trial, and execution, 3 February
    1578, Tyburn 58, 92–3, 95, 101n.120,
    126n.33, 297n.33
  declaration concerning Elizabeth 92
Nelson, Martin 297n.33, 391
  recantation 297n.33
Netherlands, intervention in, 1585 70–1, 129
Nethersole, Sir Francis 458
Neuburg, duke of (Wolfgang William) 428
Nevers, duke of, see Louis Gonzaga
Neville, Charles, 6th earl of Westmorland 81–2,
    140–1
  cousin of, see Stapleton, Richard
  daughters of, see Gray, Lady Katherine;
    Neville, Lady Margaret
  son-in-law, see Ingleby, David
Neville, Lady Margaret 239
  chaplain of, see Boste, John
  father of, see Neville, Charles
  indicted and reprieved 241–2, 242n.70;
    Matthew Hutton persuades her to conform
    242, 272; Hutton lobbies for her reprieve,
    and is approached by Lord Henry
    Howard 257–8, 272–3, 257nn.138–139
Neville, Sir Henry 106
Neville, Sir Henry (knighted 1599) 345–6
New College, Oxford 87, 132n.64
New Salisbury assizes 94n.90
Newburn, battle of 495
Newcastle upon Tyne, chamberlains
  accounts 223
  executions at, see Lambton, Joseph; Southerne,
    William; Waterson, Edward
Newdigate, C., SJ 194nn.73, 74, 217n.160,
    460n.42, 551n.60
Newgate prison 39–40, 56, 175n.159, 194n.70,
    233, 320n.124, 324n.139, 351, 394,
    396n.91, 397, 397n.96, 401–2, 410,
    412n.167, 414, 417n.188, 418n.195,
    427–8, 427n.21, 430, 430n.34, 434n.55,
    436–7, 457, 458, 488, 497, 499, 509n.94,
    521n.149, 531, 554n.71
  Catholics' deaths in 34
  chaplain of 368n.153, 556 (Samuel Smith)
  clergy in, repudiate oath of allegiance 401–2;
    seven clergy in, 1641 509, 512–13
  felons in 39–40, 56, 218–19

  keeper 380n.20, 397; (Mr Price) 414, 427n.21;
    (Simon Houghton) 442
  prison register 461n.46
  see also Smith, Samuel
Newgate sessions 189, 193, 207n.124, 281–2, 368,
    400n.107, 406n.140, 488
Newport, Richard
  conversion 408–9, 409n.151
  trial and execution, with William Scot, 30 May
    1612, Tyburn 59, 69, 406n.140, 408–12,
    412n.165; narratives of 412n.165; and earl
    of Arundel 408–9
Newton, D. 347n.68
Newton, Francis 488, 489n.140, 505n.68, 517–18
Nicholls, D. 37–8, 52, 54, 63
Nicholls, M. 351
Nichols, George
  arrest, trial, and execution, with others, 5 July
    1589, Oxford 197–200
  and Harcourt Taverner 198n.86
  tortured in Bridewell 198
Nicolson, A. 480
Norcross, Christopher 479
Norfolk conspiracy 1570 82n.28
Norfolk, enforcement of royal proclamation of
    18 October 1591 in 227n.202
Norfolk, duke of, see Thomas Howard
Norris, Richard 114n.186
  deported in January 1585 167–8
  and the distribution of Campion's 'brag'
    138n.85, 167–8
  and John Hambley 167–8
  and Mass in the Marshalsea 133n.72
North, Roger, 2nd Baron North, alleges slackness
    on Matthew Hutton's part 268, 272; allows
    petition from recusant gentry 187n.36
North, Sir Francis 550n.53
Northampton, earl of, see Howard, Henry
Northern Rebellion (rebellion of the northern
    earls) 1569 9, 81–2, 96, 113, 150, 316,
    376n.3, 542–3
  and excommunication (Regnans in Excelsis)
    of Elizabeth 81–2, 83
  and martial law 82
  and religion 82n.25
  and treason legislation of 1571 84
  see also Neville, Charles; Percy, Thomas
Northumberland, duke of, see Dudley John
Northumberland, earl of, see Percy, Algernon,
    10th earl; Percy, Henry, 8th earl; Percy,
    Henry, 9th earl; Percy, Thomas
Northumberland, recusancy in 446n.104
Norton, Benjamin 344n.57, 420
  comments unsympathetically on execution of
    convicted felons 40

622 INDEX

Norton, Benjamin (*cont.*)
  gatherer of martyrological information,
    1626 40, 40n.68, 406n.138, 411, 462–4,
    461n.45
  and George Napper 393
  and James Bird 220, 220n.172
  and John Cotton 424n.8
Norton, John 296n.30, 461n.46
  arrest and execution, with Thomas Palaser
    and John Talbot, 8 September 1600,
    Durham 296, 317
Norton, Margaret 296n.31
Norton, Sir Richard 131n.57, 463
Norton, Thomas 41n.70, 65, 109n.160, 127n.36
  and Alexander Briant 105, 127–8
  'Chain of Treasons' 134–5, 134n.75
  death of 65, 66
  A Declaration of the Favourable Dealing
    137n.80
  A Discoverie of Treasons 134, 134n.75
  disgrace and imprisonment 117, 117n.202,
    126–8, 255–6; rehabilitated 134
  and Edmund Campion 106n.147
  and Elizabethan puritanism 128
  father and uncle of, paralysed 64–5
  and George Haydock and the Throckmorton
    Plot 139
  and John Foxe 111n.170
  and Nicholas Harpsfield 96n.100, 124
  and Richard Topcliffe 127n.36
  and Thomas Alfield's *True Reporte* 117
  and Thomas Walmesley's attitude to
    Catholics 205n.117
  wife of (Alice Cranmer) 65, 126
Norton, Thomas, rebel in 1569, nephew of,
  see Morton, Robert
Norwich 36, 53n.29
  bishop of, *see* Freke, Edmund; Montagu,
    Richard
  execution of Francis Kett 38–9
  execution of Thomas Tunstall, 13 July
    1616 371n.165, 440
Nottingham, bishop of, *see* Ellis, Edward
Nottingham, earl of, *see* Howard, Charles
Nowell, Alexander 31
  nephew of, *see* Hammond, John
  and Tower disputations 111–12
Nugent, Richard, 15th Baron Delvin 405–6,
  406n.138
Nuttall, G. 43, 43n.76
Nutter, John, arraignment and execution, with
  others, 12 February 1584, Tyburn 137–8
Nutter, John, dean of Chester, alleged
  conspiracy 298, 298n.37
Nutter, Robert, OP 133n.68, 292n.17

arraignment in 1584 137n.83
arrest in Lancashire 293, 293n.20; retaken
  293–4
breaks prison at Wisbech 292–3
deported 152n.52
disputation with Ralph Tirer and others
  293–4
hostility to Christopher Bagshaw 292n.17
trial and execution, with Edward Thwing, 26
  July 1600, Lancaster 292–5,
  295n.25, 317–18
and William Weston and George Blackwell
  292–3, 296n.29

Oates, Titus 14–15, 540n.13, 546–8, 548n.43,
  556n.82, 557–8
oath of abjuration 530–1, 531n.191
oath of allegiance, 1606 168, 351, 351n.81,
  356–64, 362n.122, 366–74, 374n.174,
  378–99 *passim*, 401–4, 401n.114, 405n.135,
  406n.140, 409n.152, 410–17, 414n.177,
  423–4, 432–8, 442n.89, 444, 453, 467, 475,
  481, 484–5, 508, 517n.134, 520, 530–1; and
  papal breve of 12/22 September 1606
  358–9; statute and proclamation
  concerning, 1610 382; proclamation,
  1611 401
oath of allegiance (draft), 1647 525
oath of royal supremacy 81, 249, 270, 272, 283,
  334, 339n.25, 340, 347, 351, 475
oath of succession 37
O'Devany, Conor, bishop of Down and Connor
  147n.30
  execution, with Patrick O'Lochran, 1 February
    1612, Dublin 405, 405nn.135, 136,
    406n.138; miracle at 406n.138
O'Doherty, Sir Cahir 366
Ogilvie, John, SJ, arrest, interrogation, trial, and
  execution, 28 February 1615,
  Glasgow 428–9, 428nn. 25, 27–28
O'Hurley, Dermot, archbishop of Cashel,
  execution, 20 June 1584, Dublin 147n.30
O'Lochran, Patrick, OFM, execution, with
  Conor O'Devany, 1 February 1612,
  Dublin 405–6
Old Bailey (sessions house) 281, 367–8, 488
Oldcorne, Edward, SJ 345, 364n.135, 460n.42
  converts Calvinist felon 56
  executed for alleged involvement in
    Gunpowder Plot 56, 376; miraculous
    occurrences reported 352n.85
O'Neill, Hugh, 2nd earl of Tyrone 405, 420, 428
  agent of, *see* Montford, Francis
  chaplain of, *see* O'Lochran, Patrick
  forced into exile 362, 366

O'Neill, Sir Phelim 507
Ormond, earl and duke of, *see* Butler, James
O'Rourke, Sir Brian, execution, c. 3 November 1591, Tyburn 210n.134
Orrell, Brian (alias John Martin) 12n.25, 15n.35
 and Henry Preston 15n.35
 and John Blackburn 12
 and John Knaresborough (information supplied to, on Edward (Ambrose) Barlow, Edward Bamber, Thomas Whitaker, and William Thompson) 12
 and Thomas Townley 12
Orton, Henry 99, 122n.18
 arrested by Charles Slade 103; arraigned 112n.177; deported 152n.52
Osbaldeston, Edward 461n.46
 arrested, with Francis Sayer, by Thomas Clarke 254n.119
 execution, 16 November 1594, York 254n.119
 Lady Margaret Constable, indicted for harbouring 254n.119
Osborn, Edward 87
Osborne, Thomas, 1st earl of Danby 544–5, 544nn.25, 28, 558n.86
Oscott, St Mary's College 6n.6
Ostcliff, George 145n.21
 arrested, with John Finch 145–6
Overall, John, bishop of Coventry and Lichfield 436n.59
Overbury, Sir Thomas 430
Owen, John, of Godstow 429
 and regicide 429
Owen, John, secular priest
 proceedings against, at Chichester 191–2; conformity and loyalist declaration 191–2
Owen, Thomas, SJ 423, 425, 450n.2
Oxford
 Black Assizes, July 1577 64, 89; celebrated by Richard White 150n.41
 colleges; *see under* names of colleges in this index
 disputations, 1605 349
 prosecution and execution of Catholics (Thomas Belson, Richard Yaxley, George Nichols and Humphrey ap Richard) 197–200; *Breve Relatione del Martirio* and French versions (*Discours Veritable* and *Sommaire Discours*) 200n.92; (George Napper) 63n.80, 391–4
 vice-chancellor 89; *see also* Heton, Martin; Howson, John; King, John

P., F. (a Jesuit), and John Knaresborough 12
Packham, K. 461n.46
Padley Hall, Derbyshire 181

Page, Anthony
 arrest and execution, 20 April 1593, York 226–7, 237, 237n.44
 and Bellamy family 237n.44
Page, Francis, SJ 378
 arrest 303, 303n.56
 execution, with Thomas Tichborne and Robert Watkinson, 20 April 1602, Tyburn 320, 322, 322nn.136–137, 324n.139
Paget, Charles 180, 185, 253
 denial of regime's case against 8th earl of Northumberland 154n.61
Paget, Lady 225
Paget, Thomas, 3rd Baron Paget 96n.101
Paine, Jerome 121n.12
 brother of, *see* Paine John
Paine, John 85–6
 arrest, 1576, and release 85, 120; arrested in 1581 120
 brother of, *see* Paine, Jerome
 George Eliot's claims concerning (assassination conspiracy) 120–1; Paine's refutation 120n.10
 and George Withers and Robert Some 121
 tortured 120
 trial and execution, 2 April 1582, Chelmsford 62, 121, 123; William Allen's account 121
Palaser, Thomas 295n.26, 317–18, 461n.46
 arrest and imprisonment, March 1597 295; absconds with Francis Tilletson and Robert Hawkesworth 295
 arrest and execution, with John Norton and John Talbot, 8 September 1600, Durham 296, 317
 and George Blackwell 296, 296n.29
 loyalism 295–6
Palmer, Roger, 1st earl of Castlemaine 556n.82
 arraignment and acquittal 556n.82
 The Catholique Apology 16, 507; *Reply to the Apology* 540n.15; *To All the Royalists... The Humble Apology* 540–1, 541n.16; *The Compendium* 556n.82
Panzani, Gregorio 484, 487n.138
 negotiations with English clergy 486
papacy
 papal deposing power 48–9, 114n.184, 366–7
 see also names of individual popes in this index
Paris
 bishop of, *see* Gondi, Pierre de
 catalogue (martyrology; AAW, B 28, no. 10) 164n.107, 168n.124, 461n.46
 parlement 311, 311n.87
 sermons preached in, against Elizabeth Tudor 155

624 INDEX

Park Hall 12n.25, 64, 107n.149, 122n.17
Parker, Henry, 14th Baron Morley and
    Monteagle 501
Parker, Matthew, archbishop of Canterbury 121
    and treason act of 1563 81
Parker, Thomas 463–4
Parker, William 529
parliament
    sessions of 1571, 1572, 1576 84
    1581 105; treason statute (23 Eliz., c. 1)
        105; sedition statute of 1581 (23 Eliz., c. 2)
        105, 279; amendments in passage into
        law 105n.141; puritans indicted
        under 234–6
    1585: *see* treason statute, of 1585 (27 Eliz., c. 2)
    1586/7: *see* bill and book; recusancy
        statute of 1587
    1593 232–8; anti-Catholic and anti-puritan/
        sectary bills 232–8, 249
    1601 308–9; failure of recusancy bill 308–9
    1604–10 *see* oath of allegiance, 1606; 1610
        session 379–83, 394n.82, 395, 400–2
    1614 426–7
    1621 455, 455n.19
    1624 457–8
    1625 459
    1626 459–61, 461n.45, 464–5, 468
    1628 469–71, 476
    1629 482
    1640/Short Parliament 492–5, 494n.10
    1640/Long Parliament 492, 495–6, 496n.25,
        497–503, 511; Triennial Act 503; and seven
        Catholic clergy in Newgate 508–9,
        512–13
    1648/Rump Parliament 527, 530, 541n.16
    1654/first Protectorate parliament 536
    1658/second Protectorate parliament 537
    1663–78/Cavalier parliament ch. 16 *passim*;
        anti-popery bills 539–40; ecclesiastical
        patronage bill 544; toleration bill 545
    1679 exclusion bills 546, 548–9
    treason statutes passed in, *see* treason statutes
Parry Plot 152
Parry, William 152–3, 317
    speech in parliament, 17 December
        1584 152
Pascall, John 99–100
    recants 99n.110
Passy, Stannardine 276
Paston, Edward 535n.211
Pattenson, Bernard 242, 243
    breaks prison 169n.126, 243n.71
    and Lady Katherine Gray 243n.71
Pattenson, William
    converts felons in Newgate 56, 218–19

execution, 22 January 1592, Tyburn 56,
    218–19
    harboured by Lawrence Mompesson in
        Clerkenwell 218
Paul V, Pope (Camillo Borghese; elected
    6/16 May 1605) 289n.6, 349–50, 372n.166,
    374, 390, 420
    deposition of George Blackwell 363
Paul's Cross 143, 175, 189, 196, 198, 254n.119,
    327n.163, 376n.3, 425
Paulet, John, 5th marquis of Winchester 524,
    532n.196
    and Peter Wright 524–5, 532–3, 532n.195,
        533n.201
Paulet, Sir Amias 67n.94
Paulucci, Lorenzo 535
Peacock, Mr 463
Peckham, Edmund
    and William Weston's exorcisms 165n.111
    wife of 165n.111
Peckham, Sir George
    cousin of, *see* Bold, Richard
    and William Weston's exorcisms 167n.117
peine forte et dure 55
Pembroke, earl of, *see* Herbert, William, 3rd earl
Penington, Isaac 516–17, 516n.130
Penketh, John, SJ 13, 13n.28
Penkevell, Mark 50n.10
Penkevell, Peter 50, 50n.10, 166n.113, 189n.46,
    195, 195n.76, 207n.124
Penn, William, *A Letter from a*
    Gentleman 534–5
Penry, John 193n.68, 233–4, 236
    execution 236, 236n.40
Percy, Algernon, 10th earl of
    Northumberland 495
Percy, Henry, 8th earl of
    Northumberland 100, 317
    death in Tower of London, June 1585 154;
    case against him, denied by Charles
        Paget 154n.61
    and Robert Widmerpole 192n.63
    secretary of, *see* Wicliffe, William
    and William Shelley 154
Percy, Henry, 9th earl of Northumberland 450
Percy, John, SJ 406n.140, 412n.165, 446
    Lord Vaux's house, searched for 335n.9, 403,
        406; gaoled in Gatehouse 403;
        deported 406n.140
Percy, Thomas, 7th earl of Northumberland
    Ann Foster buried with remains of 90
    beatification 82
    execution, 22 August 1572, York 82
    and Northern Rebellion 9, 81–2, 376n.3;
        reluctance to rebel 82n.25

INDEX 625

Pere, William, recantation 186n.27
Perfect Diurnall 533
Perron, Jacques Davy du, Cardinal 430–1
persecution, modern attitudes to 35–6; as a
    questionable category/topic 34–41
persecutors, God's revenge on, perception
    of 63–70
Persons, Robert, SJ, Jnr
  and Edmund Arrowsmith and Richard
    Herst 480–1
  uncle of, *see* Persons, Robert, SJ
Persons, Robert, SJ 26n.13, 31n.30, 32, 89, 97–8,
    99n.110, 125, 128–9, 138–9, 155, 161n.96,
    170, 195–6, 198n.88, 200n.92, 208, 232,
    237–8, 248n.96, 251–3, 254n.120, 255n.125,
    266, 269, 287n.96, 301, 301n.46, 319,
    321n.130, 324n.139, 333n.1, 336n.15,
    342n.49, 343n.51, 352n.83, 365–6, 368n.153,
    396, 464, 542
  An Appendix to the Apologie 289–90
  and Archpriest Dispute 261–2, 303–4,
    304n.57, 309–13, 313n.93, 314n.97, 316–18,
    317n.111, 321n.130, 464
  A Briefe Apologie 289
  A Briefe Censure 111n.171
  A Brief Discours 104, 149; printed at
    Greenstreet House, East Ham 104n.132;
    and John Hambley 167n.119
  A Conference about the Next Succession
    231–2, 243–4, 260, 261–2, 262n.9, 274, 275;
    authorship 244n.74, 260; reprinted in 1648
    (*Severall Speeches*) 527, 527n.177
  The Copie of a Double Letter (concerning
    Richard Atkins) 109–10, 109n.161
  and Edmund Campion and the Jesuit mission
    of 1580 96–118, 316–17; and recusancy
    97–8, 161n.96
  and Edward Grately 80n.19
  Elizabethae Angliae Reginae...Philopatrum
    202n.104, 250n.107, 252
  enmity towards Christopher Bagshaw
    170n.133, 318, 378
  and episcopal government 319
  Epistle of the Persecution 52–3, 89n.67, 110,
    122–3, 136n.79; *De Persecutione
    Anglicana* 136n.79; Georgio Ferrari
    136n.79
  Henry Garnet's letters to: 16 August
    1600 68n.101; 5 May 1602 322; 4 October
    1605 350; postscript of 21 October
    1605 350, 350n.79
  and James VI, distrust of, before and after
    accession in 1603 243–4, 260, 336, 350n.78
  and James Younger's account of executions of
    10 December 1591 216, 217n.160

  and Jasper Heywood 161n.97, 311–12, 312n.89
  and John Almond 414n.179
  and John Cecil 60, 229n.3, 230, 230n.9
  and John Roberts 384, 396
  and John Wilson 376n.1
  nephew of, *see* Persons, Robert, SJ, Jnr
  and Nicholas Sander's *De Origine ac Progressu
    Schismatis Anglicani* 161n.92
  and oath of allegiance, 1606 356
  and Owen Lewis 219
  Relacion de Algunos Martyrios, incorporating
    Relacion de Quatro Martyrios 190n.52,
    200n.92
  and Robert Browne 131n.61
  and Robert Drury 356, 360
  and Robert Southwell's *Humble
    Supplication* 317–18
  and Seth Foster 90n.69
  and synod of Southwark 103
  and Thomas Benstead and Thomas
    Sprott 289–90
  and William Warford 163n.101
  and Yepes's *Historia Particular* 90n.69
Peryam, Sir William (knighted 1592), concerns
    about verdicts on John Slade and John
    Bodey 133
Peterhouse, Cambridge 128n.41
Petit, John 285–6
Peto, Humphrey (Placid), OSB 525n.166
  and toleration 525n.166
Petre, family of 28n.18, 120–1, 120n.10, 473n.74
Petre, Sir John 121
Pett, Robert 413–14
Petti, A. G. 136n.79, 237n.44
Phelippes, Thomas 180, 235, 301n.48, 303,
    325
Phelips, Sir Edward 340n.36, 342n.44
Philip II, King 44, 83n.35, 97–100, 135n.78,
    138n.86, 155–7, 176–7, 179, 185n.25, 196,
    206, 210, 214, 230, 249, 435, 472
  visit to English College (St Alban's),
    Valladolid 207n.124
Philip III, King 360, 404, 409, 413n.168, 432n.44,
    435, 450, 452, 453–4
  daughter of, *see* Maria of Spain
  and Luisa de Carvajal 425n.14
  and William Baldwin 453n.13
Philip IV, King 466, 471, 481
Philip, Robert 519
Phillips, John, alias Elston 14–15
Pibush, John 314n.97
  arrest, trial, and execution, 18 February 1601,
    St Thomas-a-Watering 302–3, 302n.52,
    317–18
  and Henry Garnet 308

626 INDEX

Pickering, Gilbert 403
  son of (John Pickering) 403
Pickering, Thomas, OSB 11, 551
  trial and execution, 9 May 1679,
    Tyburn 549, 556
Pierrepoint, Elizabeth 267
  husband of, *see* Stapleton, Richard
Pierrepoint, Gervase, and Edmund
    Campion 107
Piers, John, bishop of Salisbury (1577) and
    archbishop of York (1589) 268–9
  and John Hambley's conformity 167
Pigot, George 496n.25
Pigott, Sir Christopher 360
Pilgrimage of Grace 81
Pikes (Pike), William 33, 208n.125, 461n.46
Pilchard, Thomas 133n.68, 463–4
  execution, 21 March 1587, outside
    Dorchester 32, 54, 62, 68, 173
  John Hambley, persuaded by, to withdraw his
    conformity 173
  and William Pikes (Pike) 208n.125
Pilkington, James, bishop of Durham
    132n.64
Pineda, Juan de 425n.14
piracy, commissions against 88–9, 89n.65
Pitts, John 384n.39
Pius V (Antonio/Michele Ghislieri), Pope 201
  Regnans in Excelsis 1570 9, 82, 91, 94, 99–101,
    102n.125, 108n.154, 113, 116, 130, 144, 150,
    188, 194, 294, 376n.3, 495; renewal reported
    in 1580 100
Plasden, Polydore 314n.97
  trial and execution, with others, 10 December
    1591, Tyburn 216–17; and Sir Walter
    Raleigh 217, 228
Plessington family, Garstang 523n.158
Plessington, John 551, 551n.57, 552n.65
  accusers of (Robert Wood, George
    Massey) 69n.108, 552–3
  execution, 19 July 1679, Chester 69n.108,
    554n.73; speech 69n.108, 554n.73;
    relic 554n.73
  nephew of, *see* Plessington, Robert
Plessington, Robert 551n.59
  uncle of, *see* Plessington, John
Plowden, Charles, SJ 25n.9
Plumtree, Thomas 9
Plunket, Oliver, archbishop of Armagh
    17n.39, 37n.59
  trial and execution, 1 July 1681, Tyburn 5n.5,
    557–8, 559, 558n.86
Plymouth, sea turns red 69
Pole, Edward, death in prison 34n.43
Pole, Reginald, Cardinal 78

politiques/politique tendencies 36, 98, 124–5,
    142, 157, 214, 238–9, 243–4, 260, 298, 349,
    374, 507, 518
Pollen, John, SJ 6n.6, 43–4, 149, 262n.11,
    278n.64, 352n.85, 493n.4
  and Richard Smith's gathering of martyr
    material 461n.46
Pollini, Girolamo, OP, *Historia Ecclesiastica*
    83n.35, 124n.26, 135n.78
the pope, *see* Clement VIII, Gregory I;
    Gregory XIII; Gregory XIV; Innocent X;
    John Paul II; Leo XIII; Pius V; Urban VIII
Pope Joan 162
Popham, Sir John 236, 275–6, 283, 302,
    302nn.52, 53, 304n.57, 322n.134, 323–4,
    326, 326nn.154, 155, 334
  and Anne Line 303n.56
  Cuthbert Mayne, prosecuted by 91n.78
  denounces toleration of Catholics 323,
    323n.138
  and James Duckett 320n.126
  and recusancy 301n.46, 323; and Thomas
    Felton 285, 323n.138
  and search of Clink prison 324n.139
  and Thomas Tichborne 321n.133
  and trial of Edmund Gennings and
    others 216
  and William Freeman 264
  William Lacey, Richard Kirkman, and James
    Thompson, prosecuted by 129
  and William Richardson 327, 327n.161
  and William Watson 323–4
Popiełuszko, Jerzy 566
Popish Plot (1678–81) 30, 69–70, 114, 537,
    538–40 545–59, 563–4
  pamphlets 14–15
Pormort, Thomas, alias Whitgift 275
  and Hesketh conspiracy 219n.170
  and John Barwise 219n.168; recantation of
    Barwise 220n.171
  and Owen Lewis 219
  and Richard Topcliffe's alleged comments
    about the queen 219–20, 219n.170; and
    about Archbishop Whitgift 232
  and Robert Persons 219
  and Robert Southwell 219n.169
  trial and execution, 21 February 1592,
    St Paul's churchyard 219–20, 314
  unsympathetic, allegedly, to Spain 219; and to
    Society of Jesus 314n.97
Porter, Endymion 495
Porter, Henry 294
Portland, earl of, *see* Weston, Sir Richard
Portman, John, alias Smith 552–3, 552n.64
Pory, John 465

INDEX 627

Postgate, Nicholas 11–12, 559
  accused by Richard Morrice 69–70
  arrested by John Reeves 70n.109
  and Mrs Fairfax 11–12
Pounde, Thomas, SJ
  and Campion's 'brag' 103
  Mary Stuart's death, recalled by 172, 341
  and Robert Crowley and Henry Tripp
    108n.154
  in star chamber, 1604 114, 340–2
Powel, Roger (Philip), OSB
  arrest, trial, and execution, 30 June 1646,
    Tyburn 522, 522n.155; narratives
    522n.153
  in Lord Goring's army 522
Powell, Margaret, arrest, condemnation and
  reprieve 516n.128
Prague 97, 101
Preston, Henry, and Charles Eyston 15, 15n.35
Preston, Lancashire 54, 141n.3, 293, 297,
  297n.34, 432–3, 520n.143; mayor of,
  see Hodgkinson, Henry
Preston, Mr 294
Preston, Roland (Thomas), OSB
  and John Roberts 384
  and oath of allegiance, 1606, and
    loyalism 401n.114, 412n.165, 438; and
    Lord Vaux 401n.114
  pseudonym (Roger Widdrington) 401n.114,
    410–11, 438
  and Richard Newport and William Scot
    410–11
  and Robert Drury 357n.98
Price, Charles 547n.41
Price, John, SJ 68n.101
Price, Mr 414
  wife of 414n.179
Price, Robert 153
Prichard, Matthew, OFM 553n.67
Pride's Purge 527
Prince, John 10n.20
prisons
  Catholics' deaths in 34, 34n.43, 140n.1,
    185n.25
  clergy in prison, as a visible sign of the Church
    under the cross 72
  conversion of felons in, and at execution 47,
    55–6, 198n.86, 218–19, 306, 392, 398,
    430n.34; particular investment in, by
    Jesuit clergy 71–2; contested by other
    clergy 71–3
  see also individual prisons, by name, in
    this index
privy council 48, 102, 112, 116, 120, 122, 134,
  138n.85, 146, 162–3, 168n.122, 177n.166,

182, 191n.56, 193n.67, 201, 212, 219n.170,
  222n.183, 256n.130, 272, 277–8, 280, 291,
  293n.20, 302n.53, 305, 314, 321–2, 323,
  323n.138, 326n.155, 328, 338n.21, 344,
  347n.67, 363, 369, 397, 418n.195, 428,
  434n.55, 482, 488, 492, 553–4
  act books 84n.39
  and Anjou marriage proposal 94–9
  censures Lord Sheffield 444–5
  and northern Catholicism 103n.127, 129;
    issues execution warrants for Lacey,
    Kirkman, and Thompson 129
  orders arrest of Catholics in Oxford 197n.82
  orders Cuthbert Mayne's execution 91, 91n.78
  orders deprivation of nonconformists,
    1604 342
  orders disarming of Catholics 419n.200
  orders proceedings against Catholic clergy in
    London prisons, 1588 184
  orders Richard Blundell's and Robert
    Woodruff's executions 204
  orders Richard Fitzherbert's arrest 183n.18
  orders search for Montford Scott 160n.86
  orders search of Lord Vaux's house 335n.9
  passports, for Richard Smith and Thomas
    More 371
  protestation of allegiance, rejected by 326–7
  and Sir Michael Wharton 442, 442n.89
  and Thurstan Hunt and Robert Middleton
    296, 299–300
Pro, Miguel, SJ 565–6, 566n.3
Procter, Sir Stephen 281n.77, 320n.124, 365
Propaganda, Congregation/cardinals of 10, 460,
  460n.42, 489
prophesyings 84–5
  suppressed 85n.44
protestation of allegiance, 1603 326–7, 326n.157,
  344, 355–6, 356n.96, 384, 386, 387n.54
protestation oath, 1641 501n.43, 504, 504n.62
Prynne, William 487–9, 492–3, 497, 499–500,
  506n.75, 527n.177, 537, 539
  and Richard Smith 460n.41
  and the toleration of popery 489–90, 492, 510,
    525n.166, 527; *Popish Royall Favourite* 492,
    519–20, 521–2, 520n.142; *Rome's
    Master-Peece* 548, 548n.42
Puckering, Sir John (knighted 1592) 120, 235–6,
  247n.93, 263, 278n.67
  notes on Catholic clergy, 1588 185–7,
    186n.26, 188n.44, 191, 192
Pugh, Robert 540n.15, 554, 554n.71
  death in Newgate 554n.71
Pugh, Roger 540n.15
Purchas, Samuel 437
Purfrey, Humphrey 241

628 INDEX

puritanism/puritans 6–8, 14, 44–5, 55–6,
58–9, 70–1, 85, 92, 95, 97–8, 104,
105n.141, 121, 125–34, 133n.69,
137–8, 143–4, 147–9, 160, 189,
193–200 *passim*, 225–6, 244, 248–9,
260, 265, 268, 275, 277, 278n.64, 283,
293–4, 298–303, 306–7, 310, 328,
334–43 *passim*, 350, 355n.94, 362,
370–1, 380, 413, 418n.195, 420, 427,
433, 437, 442n.86, 443, 446–7, 453–4,
470, 476, 481, 487–8, 513, 522,
528n.180, 537, 540, 558
and Archpriest Dispute ch. 10 *passim*
bill and book, in parliament, 1587 174
conformist/anti-puritan, and latterly
'Arminian' and 'Laudian', pushback
against 70–1, 174–5, 196–7, 204–5, 214–15,
228, 231–8 *passim*, 259, 263–4, 266, 308–9,
342, 347–8, 369–71, 401, 401n.111, 426–7,
484–8, 494–5; *see also* Aylmer, John;
Bancroft, Richard; Grindal, Edmund;
Hatton, Sir Christopher; Howland, Richard;
Howson, John; Knollys, Sir Francis; Laud,
William; Montagu, Richard; Neile, Richard;
Sutcliffe, Matthew; Swale, Richard;
Walmesley, Thomas; Whitgift, John
disputations in Tower, with Edmund
Campion 111–12
and earl of Essex 298–303
ex officio oath 531n.191
moderate puritans 70, 85, 87, 111–12, 118,
130, 139, 193n.67, 347
and persecution/toleration at end of
Elizabeth's reign 318, 321–2, 324–6
and prosecutions of John Slade and John
Bodey 132–3
puritan radicalism and potential rebellion,
perceived by Catholics and others 41, 70–1,
84–6, 97n.105, 160, 164, 209, 209n.131, 220,
231–8 *passim*, 298–303, 408, 408n.149,
503–4, 509, 511, 515; Thomas Gibson,
Elias Thacker, John Copping, and Robert
Browne 131n.61, 203; *see also* Arthington,
Henry; Barrow, Henry; Copinger, Edmund;
Darrell, John; Greenwood, John; Hacket,
William; Penry, John; Rippon, Roger;
Waldegrave, Robert; Wightman, Edward
toleration campaign, 1603/1604 334–43
passim; Royston petition 341; regime
response 342
see also Bacon, Edward; Bacon, Nathaniel;
Bennett, Robert; Bunny, Edmund;
Cartwright, Thomas; Clarke, Samuel;

Dalton, James; Egerton, Stephen; Finch,
Henry; Goodman, Christopher; Harrison,
William; Hastings, Henry; Hastings, Sir
Francis; Hildersham, Arthur; Humphrey,
Laurence; Hutton, Matthew; Hutton, Sir
Timothy; Kingsmill, George; Kingsmill,
Henry; Kingsmill, John; Kingsmill, Richard;
Kingsmill, Sir William; Knollys, Sir Francis;
Knollys, Sir William; 'Leicester's
Commonwealth'; Leigh, William; Lucy, Sir
Thomas; Morice, James; Norton, Thomas;
Peryam, Sir William; Porter, Henry;
Purchas, Samuel; Rainolds, John; Rogers,
Richard; Some, Robert; Smart, Peter;
Stubbs, John; Throckmorton, Job; Whitaker,
William; Yelverton, Sir Henry
pursuivants 212, 262–3, 280, 404, 435, 444–6,
452, 454n.15, 479, 488–9, 496, 521; *see
also* Cook, John; Cross, Humphrey;
Newton, Francis; Mayo, Thomas; Norcross,
Christopher; Wadsworth, James, Jnr;
Wragge, John
Pym, John 496n.23, 501, 503–4, 505–6, 519

queen's bench 92, 94n.90, 112n.177, 275;
see also king's bench
The Queen's College, Oxford 87–8, 239n.50,
269n.38

Radcliffe, Francis 227
recusant wife 227
Radcliffe, James, 3rd earl of Derwentwater
execution, 24 February 1716, Tower
Hill 27–8, 28n.18
Radcliffe, Thomas, 3rd earl of Sussex 83n.32
advocate of Anjou marriage proposal 90,
90n.70; advice to queen concerning 90n.69
enmity towards earl of Leicester 121–2
and Francis Tregian 90
as patron of Petre family 121
Ragazzoni, Girolamo, papal nuncio, lodges
protest with Henry III on behalf of Richard
Verstegan 136
Raid of Ruthven 123, 131
Rainolds, Edmund
brothers of, *see* Rainolds, John;
Rainolds, William
and Thomas Alfield 156n.69
Rainolds, John 163n.101
and Anthony Tyrrell's Paul's Cross recantation,
early 1588 175
brothers of, *see* Rainolds, Edmund; Rainolds,
William

INDEX 629

and John Hart 143
and the Rheims New Testament 111n.170
Rainolds, William
  A Refutation of Sundry Reprehensions 162n.100
  brothers of, *see* Rainolds, Edmund;
    Rainolds, John
  De Iusta Reip. Christianae 162n.100
  William Allen's *True, Sincere, and Modest
    Defence*, translated by 137n.81
  and William Marsden 162
Rains, Mrs 16, 17n.38
Raisse, Arnauld
  Catalogus Christi Sacerdotum 337n.19,
    481n.114
  Hierogazophylacium Belgicum 481n.114
Raleigh, Sir Walter 250n.107
  execution 453
  Orinoco/2nd Guiana expedition 450, 453
  and Polydore Plasden 217, 228
Randall, a recusant 199
  brother-in-law, *see* English, John
Rant, Thomas
  and Henry Garnet 460n.40
  as secular clergy agent in Rome 460n.42,
    461n.43
Ravaillac, François 379–80, 414, 414n.179
Ravis, Thomas, bishop of London 366–7,
    394n.83
Rawlins, Alexander 215n.152, 256n.134, 463
  and Edmund Gennings and Hugo
    Sewel 215n.152
  execution, with Henry Walpole, 7 April 1595,
    York 256–7, 256n.134, 257n.135
  interrogations and trial 256n.134
  and Thomas Warcop 270
  and William Weston's exorcisms 256n.134
Rawlinson, Thomas 15n.35
Rawson, Mr, proceedings against 339–40, 341,
    340n.30
Rawsthorne, Captain
  and Edmund Arrowsmith 475, 476–7
  servant of 476–7
Rayner, William 436
recusancy/recusants 109n.161, 132–3, 145–6,
    147n.31, 151, 153, 158, 182, 183n.18,
    186n.28, 187n.36, 198, 199–200, 204–5, 208,
    215, 217, 220, 220n.172, 228, 227n.201,
    228n.206, 249, 254, 263, 267–73 *passim*, 275,
    279n.71, 280–1, 293, 293n.19, 296n.30, 300,
    341–50 *passim*, 342n.49, 365, 365n.136, 380,
    394n.83, 397, 429, 434, 442, 442n.89,
    446n.104, 459, 461n.46, 479–80, 490, 492,
    504, 527, 531, 534, 539n.6, 543

Catholic attacks on occasional conformity/
  church attendance (as schism) 97–8, 104
  (Persons's *Brief Discours*), 135; *see also*
  Garnet, Henry; Martin, Gregory;
  Mush, John
commissions 217–18, 227, 344, 350, 458
composition/compounding schemes, for
  debts 369, 400–1, 404n.129, 430, 468–9,
  469n.61, 483
fines and sequestrations 148, 213, 268n.37,
  280, 301n.46, 308, 323, 349–50, 400, 420,
  427, 430, 459, 484–5, 489, 528, 531,
  531n.192, 533n.201, 534, 539n.6, 543;
  ordinances of March and August
  1643 531n.192; corruptly
  appropriated 213, 226n.199, 285, 323n.138,
  380; relief from 484–5; *see also* Felton,
  Thomas, recusancy commissioner; Spiller,
  Sir Henry; Windebank, Sir Francis
and Jesuit mission of 1580 97–8, 103
and parliament in 1581 148
and parliament in 1587 174, 174n.157
and parliament in 1593 224, 227, 232–8
  passim
and parliament in 1604 and 1605 336,
  392n.67
and parliament in 1610 381–2, 381n.27,
  383n.35; *see also* Felton, Thomas, recusancy
  commissioner; Spiller, Sir Henry
and parliament in 1621 455, 455n.17,
  455n.19
and parliament in 1628 471
and parliament in 1656–7 537
statutes and legislation against 45, 70–1, 208,
  537, *and see under* individual parliaments;
  Spanish translation of recusancy
  statutes 354
survey of (October 1577) 86–7, 88n.63, 89, 95
temporary suspension, and reimposition,
  of recusancy penalties, 1603 336; in
  1622–3 455–6
women's/wives' recusancy 31, 226–7, 243, 273,
  336n.15, 381n.27, 408, 446n.104, 454
Redhead, Robert 281
Redman, William 433, 433n.51
Redworth, G. 403
Reeves, John, providential punishment of 70n.109
Regnans in Excelsis, 1570 9, 81–2, 82n.25, 83, 94,
  100, 116, 130, 150, 188, 201
A Reply with the Occasion thereof 93–4, 94n.89
revisionism/revisionist accounts of the English
  Reformation 42–3, 328, 564
Reynolds, E. E. 552n.62

630 INDEX

Rheims, seminary at (transferred from Douai) 122, 162, 166n.114, 168, 197
New Testament, reply to, commissioned by Walsingham from Thomas Cartwright 111n.170; reassigned to Thomas Bilson 111n.170
rector, *see* Allen, William; Barret, Richard
visited in 1584 by the cardinal of Guise and the dukes of Guise, Mayenne, and Nevers 136n.79
Rhodes, Francis
and Margaret Clitherow 158n.84
and Marmaduke Bowes 158n.84
and Robert Bickerdike 168n.124
Ribadeneira, Pedro de, SJ 18–19, 50, 190n.52, 195n.76, 198n.88, 200n.92, 203–4, 468
and Mary Stuart's death as martyrdom 172
and William Hacket 209n.131
Rich, Henry, 1st earl of Holland, and Henry Morse 521n.151
Richard III, King 142, 177
Richard, Humphrey ap, arrest, trial, and execution, with others, 5 July 1589, Oxford 197–8
Richardson, Mr 386
Richardson, W. 218, 233n.18, 234n.23, 236nn.39, 43
Richardson, William
and the appellant clergy and Jesuits 327
arrest, trial, and execution, 16 or 17 February 1603, Tyburn 327, 327n.161, 333
and Sir John Popham's malice 327; denounced by Richardson 327
Richelieu, cardinal-duke of, *see* Du Plessis, Armand-Jean
Riddle, Thomas 444
conformity 444
Ridley, Grace 13
husband of, *see* Hilton, George
Ridley, Nicholas, bishop of London 143
Ridley, Richard 13
Ridolfi, Roberto 83
and papal bull of excommunication (*Regnans in Excelsis* 1570) 82–3
Rigby, Alice 282n.79
Rigby, John 424
arrest, charges against, trial, and execution, 21 June 1600, Southwark 33, 281–7, 288, 290, 308; *see* Worthington, Thomas, *A Relation of Sixtene Martyrs*
conformity of 281–2
and John Jones 282
oath of royal supremacy refused by 283
and Sir Richard Martin 283
Rippon, Roger 233
death in Newgate 233

Rishton, Edward
arraigned 112n.177
and Nicholas Sander's *De Origine ac Progressu Schismatis Anglicani* 160–1, 160n.90
Rites, Congregation of 565n.1
Rivers, Earl, *see* Darcy, Thomas
Rizzio, David 240n.56, 408
Robert of Shrewsbury 461n.46
Roberts, John (Augustine), OSB
arrest 394n.83
and George Abbot 395–7, 399, 400n.107, 414–15
and Gunpowder Plot 366, 384n.37, 397
and John Almond 414.177
loyalism and oath of allegiance 383–4, 394–400, 467
and Luisa de Carvajal 396–7, 397n.95, 399–400, 402
and Richard Bancroft 396n.89
and Robert Jones 400
and Robert Persons 384, 396
trial and execution, with Thomas Somers, 10 December 1610, Tyburn 59, 63, 383, 394–400, 403, 467; reported by Edward Coffin 62–3, 63n.80; narratives concerning 394n.83; speech 56; relics 393n.77, 399–400, 403
Robinson, Christopher 247n.93
arrest, trial, and execution, March 1597, Carlisle 269, 269n.38
reports John Boste's (and John Ingram's) trial and execution 60–1, 247, 247n.89, 269
Robinson, Christopher (recusant) 441
Robinson, Henry, bishop of Carlisle (1598) 269n.38
Robinson, John
execution, 1 October 1588, Ipswich 192n.63, 461n.46
relic of 192n.63
Robinson, Major 520n.143
Robinson, Thomas 342n.49
Roche, John
execution, with others, 30 August 1588, Tyburn 189
and William Watson 189n.51
Roche, John, bishop of Ferns 481n.114
Rochester, bishop of, *see* Buckeridge, John; Fisher, John; Neile, Richard
Rochester, executions at, *see* Dickenson, Francis; Gerard, Miles
Rochester, Viscount, *see* Ker, Robert
Rochford, Viscount, *see* Boleyn, George

INDEX 631

Roe, Bartholomew (Alban), OSB
  execution, with Thomas Green, 21 January 1642,
    Tyburn 56, 510–11; converts felons 56
Rogers, D. M. 23n.2, 474n.75
Rogers, Mrs 123n.24
Rogers, Richard 355n.94
Rogers, Thomas (alias Nicholas
    Berden) 175n.159, 180, 239n.52
  and betrayal of Edward Stransham 161n.97
Rolheiser, Ronald 566
Rolle, Henry 532
Rolson (Rolston), Francis 224–5
Rome
  English College 26n.13, 38, 188n.44,
    202n.105, 219, 273n.49, 376n.1;
    archives 26n.13, 164n.109, 426n.15;
    murals 136n.79; William Allen's oration at,
    concerning the Irish rebellion 99; troubles
    at 185, 288n.2, 303–4, 313n.93, 321;
    theatrical performances at (including
    Captiva Religio) 426n.15; see also Agazzari,
    Alfonso; Persons, Robert
  French ambassador in, see Béthune,
    Philippe de
  Judaizers burnt in, February 1583 38
Romero, Oscar (Óscar Arnulfo Romero y
    Galdámez), archbishop of San Salvador 566
Rookwood, Thomas 240n.60
Roos (Ros), Baron de, see Cecil, William
Roper, Henry, 11th Baron Teynham 18
Roper, Sir William 354
Roper, William, biography of Sir Thomas
    More 15n.35, 77
Roscarrock, Nicholas, and Ralph Sherwin
    115n.189
Ross, bishop of, see Leslie, John
Rossetti, Carlo 500
Rouen, archbishop of, see Harlay, François II de
Rouse, Anthony 366n.144, 404
Rowsham, Stephen
  execution, c. March 1587, Gloucester 62–3,
    173n.147; pelted by apprentices 63, 63n.79
The Royal Martyrs 541
royal proclamations
  27 September 1579 99
  10 January 1581 104
  1 April 1582 121, 152, 153n.56
  12 October 1584 151
  c. 6 May 1586 163, 163n.103
  1 July 1588 179–80
  18 October 1591 40, 202n.104, 208, 210,
    214–17, 215n.154, 220, 229, 236, 246,
    250n.107, 320, 322; enforcement of
    210n.134, 217–18, 224, 224n.190, 227,
    232, 246, 263

  5 November 1602 325–7, 326n.154,
    326nn.150–151
  24 March 1603 333
  22 February 1604 336, 539–40
  July/October 1605, concerning Ireland 350
  15 November 1607 362
  2 June 1610 381–2, 383n.35
  31 May 1611 401
  6 May 1624 457–8
  3 August 1628 477
  11 December 1628 482
  24 March 1629 482
  11 November 1640 496n.25
  8 March 1641, offered on 3 February 502
  10 December 1641 509, 511–12
  17 November 1678 550n.54
  20 November 1678 550n.54
  20 December 1678 550n.54
  30 October 1680 550n.54
royal supremacy 36, 48–9, 77, 84–5;
  oath of, see oath of royal supremacy
Roydon, Thomas 14n.32, 541n.17
  and Christopher Tootell 12n.26
  and John Knaresborough 541n.17
Rudd, Anthony, dean of Gloucester, intervenes at
    execution of Stephen Rowsham 63
Rudyerd, Sir Benjamin 496
Rupert, Prince 521
Rushworth, John 469n.61
Russell, C. 349n.73, 379n.13, 400–1, 493, 496
Russell, Francis, 2nd earl of Bedford 100
Russell, Francis, 4th earl of Bedford 502–3
Russell, George 411
Ruthin, Denbighshire 53–4
  execution of Charles Meehan at, 12 August
    1679 555n.74
Rutland, earl of, see Manners, Francis; Manners,
    Roger
Rydell, Francis 95n.92
Rye House Plot 559

Sabran, Louis, de, SJ 521n.151
Sabran, Melchior de 521n.149
  and Henry Morse 521n.151
  and John Duckett and Ralph Corby 521n.149
Sackville, Edward, 4th earl of Dorset 481
Sackville, Lady Margaret 73
  brother of, see Howard, Philip
  as patron of Robert Southwell 73
Sackville, Thomas, 1st Baron Buckhurst and
    1st earl of Dorset 16–17, 327
  cousin of, see Alford, Francis
  and trials of Catholic clergy at Chichester,
    1588 191n.57
Sackville, Thomas, Jnr 432, 442n.89

632 INDEX

St Andrews, archbishop of, *see* Gledstanes, George
St Bartholomew's Day Massacre 35, 420, 550
St John, Lady 16
St John's College, Oxford 198
St Omer
  bishop of 518n.140
  college and printing press 376n.1, 432n.44, 442, 447
Salford, bishop of, *see* Beck, George
Salisbury, bishop of, *see* Burnet, Gilbert; Jewel, John; Piers, John
Salisbury, earl of, *see* Cecil, Sir Robert
Salisbury, execution at, *see* Hambley, John
Salisbury, Frances 82n.31
  father of, *see* Felton, John
Salisbury, John, SJ 388n.59
Salmon, Patrick, execution, with others, 3 or 4 July 1594, Dorchester 250n.107
Salusbury, John, and Richard White 147–8
Salvetti, Amerigo 481
Sander, Nicholas 18–19, 101, 113, 124n.26, 216
  and claims, in mid-1561, about persecution in England 81
  De Monarchia Ecclesia 106n.147
  De Origine ac Progressu Schismatis Anglicani (1585 and 1586 versions) 30n.26, 77, 160–1; and Edward Rishton 160n.90; attacks earl of Leicester 161; and William Allen's *True, Sincere and Modest Defence* 161n.91; additional material contributed by Robert Persons and William Allen 161n.92
  De Visibili Monarchia 82, 82n.28, 316
  and Northern Rebellion 82, 316
  and rebellion in Ireland 99, 101, 150, 317
Sanderson, Henry 222, 222n.183
  and earl of Huntingdon 226–7
  and George Errington 269n.41
  and Thomas Palaser's arrest 295–6
  and Tobias Matthew, dean of Durham 222, 295–6
  and William Jenison 223n.186
Sandoval y Rojas, Bernardo de, cardinal priest and archbishop of Toledo 428n.29
Sandoval y Rojas, Francisco Gómez de, duke of Lerma 428n.29
  protests against persecution in England 406–7
Sandys, Edwin, bishop of London (1570) and archbishop of York (1577)
  and George Withers 121
  and Matthew Hutton 272n.48

Sandys, John
  arrest, as the product of local antagonism 164n.109
  execution, 11 August 1586, Gloucester 62–3, 164n.109, 173n.147
Sandys, Miles 234
Savoy, ambassador of 425n.10
Saye and Sele, Viscount, *see* Fiennes, William
Sayer, Francis 254n.119
Sayer, Richard
  arrest 296
  conformity 296n.31
Sayer, Robert (Gregory), OSB
  at Caius College Cambridge 87; and John Fingley 87
  refutes aspects of John Jewel's *Apologia Ecclesiae Anglicanae* 87
Scantlebury, Canon 566n.3
Schetz, Conrad (de Grobbendonck), baron de Hoboken, and Robert Drury's narrative 358n.100
Scotland
  covenanter rebellion 492–506 *passim*, 494n.10
  general assembly 495
  Kirk 440–1, 505, 528
  parliament 495
  privy council 428, 428n.24, 441
  rumours of tolerance of Catholics in 174
Scot, William (Maurus), OSB 399
  letters of 412n.165
  trial and execution, with Richard Newport, 30 May 1612, Tyburn 59, 69, 406n.140, 408–12, 412n.165, 467; narratives of 412n.165; and earl of Arundel 408–9
Scott, J. 546–7
Scott, James, 1st duke of Monmouth 555
Scott, Montford 95, 95n.97, 160n.86, 207n.124, 215n.156
  arrest, December 1576, and return to Douai 85
  execution, with George Beseley, 1 July 1591, Fleet Street 203, 207–8, 209
  ordination 85
  words of, reported by Robert Lacey 160
Scott, Thomas, *Vox Populi*, and Gondomar 452
Screven, Thomas 400
Scroggs, Sir William 554–5
Scrope, Emmanuel, 11th Baron Scrope 445, 445n.102
Scrope, Lady (Margaret Howard, 2nd wife of Henry Scrope, 9th Baron Scrope) 297n.33
Scudamore, John, of Holme Lacy
  and Richard Bancroft 347, 353n.86, 360n.115
  and Robert Drury and William Davies 360n.115

INDEX 633

Scudamore, John, of Kentchurch 553n.67
  and John Kemble 553n.67
Second Bishops' War 495
Selby, Richard (Wilfrid), OSB 518n.140
Sergeant, John 528, 553–4
  and George Leyburn 553
  and John Gavan 553
  and Thomas Morton 553
Sergeant, Richard
  trial and execution, with William Thompson,
    20 April 1586, Tyburn 162, 162n.98
Serrano, Pedro, and Edmund Campion
    117n.201
Seville, English college 429–30
Sewel, Hugo, and Alexander Rawlins and
    Edmund Gennings 215n.152
Shaftesbury, earl of, see Cooper,
    Anthony Ashley
Shagan, E. 21, 41n.70
Shakespeare, William
  The Comedy of Errors 194n.71
  Titus Andronicus 221–2
Shanahan, D. 377–8
Sharp, James, SJ, and persecution 366, 444–5
Sharpe, J. 51–2, 70
Sharpe, K. 482–3
Shaw, Francis, and Richard Williams
    219n.169
Sheffield, Edmund, 3rd Baron Sheffield 17n.38,
    343, 344, 429–30
  and Matthew Flathers 365
  and Matthew Hutton and James I 343
  privy council censures 444–5; replaced, as
    lord president 445, 445n.102
  and recusants 442
  Sir Robert Cecil, warned by, against Thomas
    Walmesley 340n.36
  sons of 430
  and Thomas Pounde 343
  and Thomas Welbourne and William
    Browne 342–3, 342n.49
  and William Southerne 444–5
Sheils, W. 531n.192
Sheldon, Jane 263
Sheldon, Ralph 262
Sheldon, Richard 414n.179
  and oath of allegiance, 1606 401n.114;
    renounces Rome 401n.114
Shell, A. 21n.53, 27–8, 27n.17
Shelley, Anthony 458
Shelley, Edward 463
  brother of, see Shelley, Richard
  execution, with others, 30 August 1588,
    Tyburn 189
  and 'Leicester's Commonwealth' 189

letters intercepted at Colchester 188n.41
  and William Dean 188n.41, 189
Shelley, Jane 225
  husband of, see Shelley, William
Shelley, Richard
  brother of, see Shelley, Edward
  imprisoned in the Marshalsea 50n.10, 153
  toleration petition of March 1585 153, 189
Shelley, William
  and 8th earl of Northumberland 154
  trial, February 1586 154n.61
  wife of, see Shelley, Jane
Shelley, William, archdeacon 463
  father of, see Shelley, Richard
Sherborne Castle, Dorset 515
Sherburn Hospital 248
Sherson, Martin, death in prison 34n.43
Shert, John 51
  arraigned 113n.179
  executed, 28 May 1582, Tyburn 122
Sherwin, Ralph 51, 106n.147
  arrested 115n.189
  and Nicholas Roscarrock 115n.189
  trial and execution, with Edmund Campion
    and Alexander Briant, 1 December 1581,
    Tyburn 112n.177, 115–16, 127
Sherwood, John 165n.111, 250n.107
  brother of, see Sherwood, Richard
Sherwood, Richard 165n.111
  brother of, see Sherwood, John
Sherwood, Thomas 165n.111
  declaration concerning the papal sentence
    against Elizabeth 92
  torture, trial and execution, 7 February 1578,
    Tyburn 92–3, 95
  uncle of, see Tregian, Francis
  William Fleetwood interrogates 92
Shifnal manor, Shropshire 486
Shrewbury, countess of, see Talbot, Elizabeth (née
    Hardwick); Talbot, Mary
Shrewsbury, earl of, see Talbot, George, 6th earl;
    Talbot, George, 9th earl
Sicklemore, Humphrey, denounced by John
    Healey 353n.87
Sidney, Sir Henry, and Edmund Campion 97
Sidney Sussex College, Cambridge 15n.34
Simpson, Richard, historian 43
Simpson, Richard, secular priest 181n.11,
    461n.46
  execution, with Nicholas Garlick and Robert
    Ludlam, 24 July 1588, Derby 54, 181–2,
    335n.8
  offer of compliance 181; withdrawal of, and
    verses concerning 181, 181n.13
Simpson, Thomas 180

634 INDEX

Singleton, Hugh 94n.89
Sixtus V (Felice Peretti di Montalto), Pope 201
Skinner, William
and Job Throckmorton 134
opinions concerning Elizabeth Tudor, Anne
Boleyn, and Henry VIII 133–4; acquitted
at Warwick assizes 134
Skipwith, Mary 553
Slade, Charles 113
arrests George Haydock and gives evidence
against him and others 138n.88
arrests Henry Orton and Robert Johnson 103
information laid against English Catholics
98–102
Slade, John 463
ejected from New College, Oxford 132n.64
and puritanism in Hampshire 132–3;
see also Bennett, Robert; Kingsmill,
Sir William; Laurence Humphrey
trial, with John Bodey, and execution, 30
October 1583, Winchester 131–2, 144, 343;
legal complexity of prosecution 131,
131n.58; popular comment concerning 133;
The Severall Executions 132n.65; William
Allen's comments on authorship 133
Slater, Henry 181n.11
Slyvell, Ralph 303n.56
Smart, Peter 476n.86
Smith, James 340n.32
Smith, Richard, bishop of Chalcedon
(1624) 6n.6, 8, 181n.10, 378n.7, 403n.123,
468, 474n.75, 515n.126, 526, 537n.216
approbation controversy, and disputes with
religious orders 466–8, 470, 472–3, 481–2,
486–7, 526
Chalcedon dossier/catalogue of 1628 6n.6, 9,
269n.39, 279, 460n.42; Paris
catalogue 30n.27, 164n.107, 168n.123,
169n.127, 175n.160, 279n.71, 461n.46
collection of martyr records in and after
1626 9–10, 29n.23, 161n.96, 181n.12, 249,
279, 279n.71, 335n.8, 356n.96, 364n.132,
459–67, 518–20
denounced to the Inquisition 378
and Edward Morgan 514n.124
and John Duckett 520n.144
and John Southworth 487n.138
John Wilson's English Martyrologe, censured
by 376n.1, 460n.42
life of Lady Magdalen Browne (The Life of La.
Magdalen Viscountesse Montague) 487
reconciles Edward Waterson to Rome 222n.183
royal proclamations (11 December 1628 and
24 March 1629) against 482

secretary of, see Harewell, William
as secular clergy agent in Rome 371, 377–8,
379, 382
and tolerance 459
Smith, Samuel 556
Smith, Thomas 180
Smith, William, of Edlington 345n.60
Smith, William, of Esh, and Northern
Rebellion 82
Smith, William, seminarist, arraignment 137n.83
Smithson, Augustine 535n.211
Smuts, M. 492n.1
Snow, Peter 461n.46
execution, with Ralph Grimston, 15 June 1598,
York 279, 279n.72
Society of Jesus/Jesuits 221n.175, 450, 486–7
allegations concerning Jesuit conspiracy 72–3
and Anne Howard 486–7
in Brussels 354, 362, 403n.127
Clerkenwell novitiate 469–70, 473n.74
College of St Francis Xavier 554–5
in France 359, 380n.24
and Henry IV 359
Jesuit mission of 1580 96–118
and martyrdom and resistance 312–13,
313n.94; and appellants 313–14;
understandings of true martyrdom
313–14, 372–3
novitiate at Louvain 366n.144
prison ministry and evangelism 72
suppression of 25n.9, 26n.13
vice-province and province in England 447
see also approbation controversy; Archpriest
Dispute; see names of individual Jesuits in
this index
Some, Robert 121
Somers, Thomas 393n.77, 400
execution, with John Roberts, 10 December
1610, Tyburn 62–3, 63n.80, 394–400
passim, 403; relic 393n.77
Somerset, countess of, see Howard, Frances
Somerset, earl of, see Ker, Robert
Somerset, Edward, 4th earl of Worcester 301
secretary of, see Sterrell, William
and Whitsun Riot 347–8, 347n.68
Somerset, Henry, 3rd marquis of Worcester
554–5
Somerville, John 141n.3, 150, 317
Sorbonne 407
disputation at 92–3
Sousa, Antonio de, and John Duckett and Ralph
Corby 521, 521n.149
Southampton, countess of, see Wriothesley, Mary
Southampton, earl of, see Wriothesley, Henry

INDEX   635

Southampton House 73–4, 141n.5, 221
Southcot, John 121n.11
Southcot, John, secular priest 484–5, 489
Southerne, William
    arrest, trial, and execution, c. 30 April 1618,
        Newcastle 444–5, 444n.95, 446, 467, 449,
        460n.42, 467
    refusal of oath of allegiance, 1606 444, 466–7
Southwell, Robert, SJ 38–9, 180–1, 189n.49,
        221n.176, 227–8, 244, 252, 252n.114,
        254n.120, 254n.123, 313, 322, 486
    account of Christopher Bales 49–50, 50n.10, 51
    and Anthony Babington's conspiracy 208–9,
        209n.130, 317
    aristocratic patrons 73, 203, 221–2, 221n.179;
        Sackville House 73, 203
    arrest, and Anne Bellamy 221, 276–7
    arrival from Continent in 1586 169
    Christopher Devlin's study of 73
    and death of earl of Leicester and Sir Francis
        Walsingham 67, 67n.95, 214
    and death of 8th earl of Northumberland 154
    Epistle of Comfort 73, 221–2; chapter entitled
        'A Warning to the Persecutors' 66
    equivocation 221, 221n.175, 254–5, 289, 294
    and Gilbert Gifford's reply to William Allen's
        defence of Sir William Stanley 177n.166
    and Giles Wigginton 174–5
    Humble Supplication 67, 215, 215n.154,
        221–2, 317, 320–1; cited and distributed by
        appellants 317n.111, 322; justified by
        Robert Persons 317–18
    and Margaret Ward 189
    and Mary Stuart's death as martyrdom
        172, 335n.8
    and persecution, in late 1586 169–70;
        in 1588 180, 188, 189, 195; witnesses
        executions of 28 and 30 August 1588 190;
        persecution, in late 1591, account of, sent to
        Richard Verstegan 208–15, 227–8
    and Richard Bold 166
    and Richard Topcliffe 210–11, 222; Topcliffe
        arrests Southwell at Uxendon 221
    and royal proclamation of 18 October
        1591 210, 214
    and Thomas Bell 238
    and Thomas Pormort 219n.169
    tortured 222
    trial and execution, 21 February 1595,
        Tyburn 62, 228, 254–6; Lord Mountjoy
        intervenes 62
Southworth, John 474n.75, 479n.101,
        488n.139, 500
    arrested and released, 1637 487–8

and Edmund Arrowsmith 477–9
and Henry Morse, and care of plague
    victims 487–8, 487n.138
trial and execution, 28 June 1654, Tyburn
    534–6; speech 12, 535–6, 535n.209;
    reprinted 552
Sowerby, S. 555
Spain
    ambassador of, in London, see Acuña, Diego
        Sarmiento de; Mendoza, Bernardino de;
        Spes, Guerau de; Velasco, Alonso de;
        Zúñiga, Pedro de
    Armada of 1588 53–4, 179–96 passim, 198,
        201, 204, 206, 210; Catholic peers and
        gentry offer to serve against 187, 187n.36;
        see also Allen, William, An Admonition;
        Allen, William, A Declaration of the Sentence
    Franco-Spanish double marriage alliance 403,
        403n.122, 405, 409, 410n.153
    infanta of: see Isabella Clara Eugenia; Maria
        of Spain
    king of, see Philip II; Philip III, Philip IV
    see also Spanish match/Anglo-Spanish
        marriage negotiations
Spanish match/Anglo-Spanish marriage
    negotiations, see James VI and I, and
    Anglo-Spanish marriage negotiations
Speed, John 241–2
    execution, 4 February 1594, Durham
        242, 242n.70
Speed, John, cartographer 141
Spence, John 226
Spencer, John 138, 139n.92, 141
Spenser, William 163n.101, 200n.94
    execution, with Robert Hardesty, 24
        September 1589, York 200
Spes, Guerau de, chaplain of, and papal bull of
        excommunication (Regnans in Excelsis
        1570) 82
Spiller, Sir Henry (knighted 1618) 380, 489
    attacked by Winwood 427
spiritual exercises 202n.105
Spottiswoode, John, archbishop of Glasgow, and
        John Ogilvie 428; True Relation 428nn.25, 29
Sprott, Thomas
    arrest 288–90, 290n.7
    breaks prison at Wisbech 289, 289n.5
    execution, with Thomas Benstead, 1 July 1600,
        Lincoln 68, 288–9, 308, 345n.60
    as supporter of George Blackwell 288–9;
        and of the Society of Jesus 308
Squire Plot 289
Stafford, execution of Robert Sutton, 27 July
        1588 66–7, 182–3, 183n.18

636 INDEX

Stafford, Sir Edward 137n.81, 176n.162
   complex loyalties 136n.79
   persuades Henry III to imprison distributors
      of book on Campion and others 161n.93
   tries to suppress Richard Verstegan's
      publications 135–6
Stafford, Viscount, see Howard, William
Staffordshire, recusancy in 84n.39
Stansby, John 355n.94
Standish, Lancashire 306–7, 476
Standish, James 287n.96
   statements about Thomas Pormort 219n.169
Stanhope, Sir Edward (knighted 1603) 267–8,
     268n.35, 270n.42, 273, 355n.94
   brother of, see Stanhope, Sir John
   and Joseph Constable's conformity 273
Stanhope, Sir John 322
   brother of, see Stanhope, Sir Edward
   and Mark Barkworth 322n.135
Stanihurst, Richard, De Vita S. Patricii 147n.30
Stanley, family of 219n.170
Stanley, Henry, 4th earl of Derby 145
Stanley, Sir William 251
   and the surrender of Deventer, justified by
      William Allen (Copie of a Letter) 175–6,
      181n.11, 202, 244n.76, 247, 472
Stanley, William, 6th earl of Derby 432n.44
Stanney, Thomas, SJ, narrative written by, 2
     November 1609 65n.91, 207n.122
Stapleton, Richard 267, 271–2
   conformity of 271–2, 272n.46
   cousin of, see Neville, Charles
   wife of, see Pierrepoint, Elizabeth
Stapleton, Sir Miles 552, 552n.64, 557
   and Thomas Thwing 11n.21, 557
Stapleton, Thomas, Tres Thomae 77
Stapper, Henry 226
star chamber 91n.81, 113, 114, 119, 327, 337,
     340, 341–2, 346, 346n.63, 365n.136, 418,
     418n.195, 433–4, 443, 456, 456n.25, 488,
     490, 514n.122
Starkey, Henry 551
Sterrell, William 301, 301n.48, 337n.16, 339–41,
     340nn.30, 36
   and John Sugar and Robert Grissold 338–9
   persecution at end of Elizabeth's reign 320–4,
     320n.126, 322n.134, 323n.138,
     324n.139, 326–8
Stevens, John, and Roger Cadwallader 384n.39,
     385, 390–1, 391n.65
Stevenson, Thomas, SJ
   arraignment 137n.83
   reconciles Hugh More to Rome 188n.44
Stock, Richard, A Sermon 376n.3
Stoker, George 189n.50

Stonor, Lady Cecily 105, 106–7
   and Edward Hartley 141
Stonor Park
   Robert Persons's printing press and Campion's
     Rationes Decem 105–7; sequestrated, and
     the printers arrested 107n.149; see also
     Stonor, Lady Cecily
Stonyhurst, Lancashire 26n.13, 115f
Story, John 83, 150
   execution, 1 June 1571, Tyburn 9, 58, 82n.28,
     83n.35, 119; Richard Topcliffe, spectator
     at 83n.35
   and Marian Protestants 83n.35
   and treason statute of 1571 (13 Eliz., c. 1)
     83n.35
Stoughton, Laurence 133n.69
Stour Valley riots 493
Stourton, Charles, 8th Baron Stourton 250n.107
Stow, John 17, 17n.42, 50, 245
Strafford, earl of, see Wentworth, Sir Thomas
Stransham, Edward 161
   associate of Jasper Heywood 161n.97
   betrayal by Thomas Rogers 161n.97
   and Cardinal Toledo 161n.97
   execution, with Nicholas Woodfen, 21 January
     1586, Tyburn 161
   and Francis Throckmorton 161n.97
Strickland, Mr 114n.183
Stringer, Sir Thomas 557
Stuart, Esmé, sieur d'Aubigny, 1st earl and
     1st duke of Lennox 123
Stuart, Francis, 5th earl of Bothwell 239
   and North Berwick witches 286
Stuart, Henry, Lord Darnley
   and Mary Stuart 81
   murder of 81
Stuart, Mary, see Mary Stuart
Stuart, William, Colonel 174
Stubbs, John 102, 158–60
   Discoverie of a Gaping Gulf 94n.89, 95, 125–6;
     royal proclamation against 99; prosecution
     of Stubbs 100; see also Howard, Henry;
     Singleton, Hugh
Stukely, Thomas 317
Suárez, Francisco, SJ 428
   Defensio Fidei Catholicae 425, 425n.12; burnt
     at Paul's Cross 425
succession, oath of, see oath of succession
Suffolk, countess of, see Howard, Catherine
Sugar, John
   arrest, July 1603 335n.9, 337–8
   trial and execution, with Robert Grissold,
     16 July 1604, Warwick 337–40,
     338nn.21–23, 339n.25; demonstrators
     at 339, 339n.28

INDEX   637

Sussex, earl of, *see* Radcliffe, Thomas
Sutcliffe, Matthew
  An Answere to a Certaine Libel
    Supplicatorie 234n.22
  attacks Richard Verstegan 234n.22
Sutton, Abraham, and relic of Robert Sutton,
  given to John Gerard 182n.17
  brothers of, *see* Sutton, Robert, secular priest;
    Sutton, William
Sutton, Robert, layman 194n.70
  denies royal supremacy 193–4
  execution, 5 October 1588, Clerkenwell
    193–4, 194n.70
  pamphlet concerning (*A True Report...of*
    John Weldon) 193–4
Sutton, Robert, secular priest
  arrested with, *inter alia*, Erasmus Wolseley and
    William Maxfield 182
  brothers of, *see* Sutton, Abraham;
    Sutton, William
  execution, 27 July 1588, Stafford 66–7, 182–3,
    183n.18
  and Gondomar 451n.7
  relics of 184f, 451n.7; recovered by
    wife of Erasmus Wolseley 183n.19;
    relic cures demoniac 182n.17,
    435–6
  and Sir Walter Aston 66–7
Sutton, William 182n.17
  brothers of, *see* Sutton, Abraham; Sutton,
    Robert, secular priest
  and John Gerard SJ 182n.17
Swale, Richard
  anti-puritanism of 87
  and Edward Osborn 87
  and William Dean 87
Swallowell, George 461n.46
  and Dr Robert Bellamy 248–9
  royal supremacy, rejected by 248–9
  trial, with John Boste and John Ingram, and
    execution, 29 July 1594, Darlington
    247n.89, 248–9
Swarbrick, Robert 13
Sykes, Edmund 173n.151
  deported in September 1585 173; temporary
    compliance 173
  execution, 23 March 1587 or 23 March 1588,
    York 173, 173n.150, 180n.6
  synod of Southwark 103

Taaffe, Theobald, 2nd Viscount
  Taaffe 506–7
Talbot, Elizabeth (*née* Hardwick), countess of
  Shrewsbury 225, 267
  husband of, *see* Talbot, George, 6th earl

Talbot, George, 6th earl of Shrewsbury 108n.154,
  129n.45, 181, 204n.114
  reports conformity in Derbyshire, following
    arrest of John Fitzherbert 184
  wife of, *see* Talbot, Elizabeth
Talbot, George, 9th earl of Shrewsbury
  469–70, 478–9
Talbot, John 461n.46
  arrest and execution, with John Norton and
    Thomas Palaser, 8 September 1600,
    Durham 296, 317
  recusancy 296n.30
Talbot, Mary (*née* Cavendish), countess of
  Shrewsbury 450n.5
Talbot, Peter, archbishop of Dublin 558n.86
Talmud 38
Tankard, Christopher 557; his dogs 557
Tankard, Jane 458
Tankard, Ursula 458
Tarazona, bishop of, *see* Yepes, Diego de
Taverner, Harcourt 198n.86
Taverner, Richard 198n.86
Taylor, Hugh
  arrest, trial, and execution, 26 November
    1585, York 157–8, 161
  and Marmaduke Bowes 157–8, 161
Taylor, James 180
  and Edward Abington 185
  sent to Wisbech 185
  signs appellant petitions 185
Taylor, Ursula
  and Edward Fulthrop 269n.41
  and George Errington 269n.41
Tedder, William
  deported 152n.52
  and John Hambley 167
  Mrs Lowe, betrayed by 189n.46
  recantation, 1588 167
Tempest, Nicholas 272, 272n.48
  wife of (Isabel Lambton) 272, 272n.48; uncle
    of, *see* Eure, William
Tempest, Robert 200n.92
Tesh, Anne 269–70, 270n.42
Tesimond, Oswald
  and Margaret Clitherow 82
  reveres Thomas Percy, 7th earl of
    Northumberland 82
Test Act, 1673 543
Teynham, Baron, *see* Roper, Henry
Thacker, Elias, execution 131n.61
Thackwell (a printer), and William Davies
  237n.44
Thelwall, Simon 150
  and earl of Leicester 150
  and Richard White 150

638 INDEX

Thimbleby, Gabriel 31n.29
  death in prison 34n.43
Thirkeld, Richard, arrest, trial, and execution,
  29 May 1583, York 130–1
Thirkell, Henry, and Christopher Bales 202n.104
Thirkell, Mr 274
Thomas, D. A. 148–9
Thomas, John 463 ('F. Thomas')
  execution, August 1593, Hampshire 59, 220,
    220n.173
  temporary conformity and reprieve 220
Thompson, James 461n.46
  converts felons 55–6
  arrest, trial, and execution, 28 November
    1582, York 55–6, 129
Thompson, Nathaniel 548n.44
Thompson, William 12
  and Anne Line 162
  and Richard Bellamy 162n.98
  trial and execution, with Richard Sergeant, 20
    April 1586, Tyburn 162, 162n.98
  and William Weston's exorcisms 162
Thomson, arrests Henry Stapper, Marian
  priest 226
Thoresby, Ralph 11n.21, 469n.61
Thornborough, John, bishop of Bristol
  and John Boste 240n.55
  and Thomas Hill 334
Thorndon Hall, Essex 28n.18
Thorne/Thornes (Nicholas), associate of Richard
  Topcliffe 66n.93
Thornton Woods 256n.134
Thorpe, John, SJ 130n.53, 164n.109, 416n.185
Thorpe, Robert
  and Anthony Champney 206n.120
  execution, with Thomas Watkinson, 31 May
    1591, York 206–7, 208
  and papal authority 206–7
Thorys, John 407
Throckmorton, Francis 138, 139, 150, 156, 317
  and Edward Stransham 161n.97
  execution, 10 July 1584 147
  and Thomas Norton's 'Chain of Treasons', and
    Discoverie of Treasons 134–5
  see also Throckmorton Plot
Throckmorton, Job, arrests William Skinner
  133–4
Throckmorton Plot 127n.37, 133, 134, 134n.75,
  138, 139, 140, 317
Thulis, John 222n.182
  execution, with Roger Warren, 18 March
    1616, Lancaster 12n.26, 54, 222n.182,
    431n.39, 432–3, 434, 436, 440; verses
    on 432n.48; distribution of body parts 54,
    432; relic 554n.73

Thursby, Charles, SJ 239n.50, 241n.62,
  248n.96, 461n.46
Thwing, Edward 237n.44
  arrest 293, 293n.20
  disputation with Ralph Tirer and others 294
  execution, with Robert Nutter, 26 July 1600,
    Lancaster 292–4, 295n.25, 317–18; defends
    equivocation and papal deposing
    power 294
  supporter of the archpriest Blackwell 292–3,
    296n.29
Thwing, Thomas 11
  arrest, trial, and execution, 23 October 1680,
    York 557; execution speech 11n.21, 556–7;
    Knaresborough's copy 557; and Sir Miles
    Stapleton 11n.21, 557
  and Mary Ward 11
  and Mrs Lassells 11n.21
Thwing, William 237n.44
Tichborne, Chideock 464
Tichborne, Nicholas 464
  brother of, see Tichborne, Thomas
  execution, with Thomas Hackshot, 24 August
    1601, Tyburn 308n.73, 429n.33; Relacion
    del Martirio 429n.33
Tichborne, Robert 533
Tichborne, Thomas, alias Bartholomew Audley
  308n.73, 320n.127, 321n.130, 463
  betrayed by William Atkinson 321
  brother of, see Tichborne, Nicholas
  execution, with Robert Watkinson and
    Francis Page, 20 April 1602, Tyburn 320
  and George Bailey and Mary Bailey 320n.127
  Sir John Popham's accusations against
    321n.133
  and Society of Jesus, appellants, and George
    Blackwell, Henry Garnet, and Richard
    Blount 321, 321n.133
Tierney, Mark 29, 350n.79
Tilletson, Francis 295
Tillières, count of, see Leveneur, Tanneguy
Tinoco, Manuel Luis 245
Tippet, seminarian 94–5
Tirer, Ralph, vicar of Kendal 294
Tixall, Staffordshire, see Aston, Sir Walter
Toledo, Francisco de, SJ, Cardinal 161n.97
Toledo y Pimentel, Fernando Álvarez de, 3rd
  duke of Alba 83n.35
tolerance/toleration (and intolerance) 24, 30,
  35–7, 43–6, 94–5, 106, 118, 174
  and Archpriest Dispute chs 9–10 passim
  Catholic rhetoric of toleration in and after the
    1580s 117–18, 211–12, 221–2, 229–31,
    chs 9–10 passim, esp. at 309–11; toleration
    petition of 1585 153, 189

INDEX 639

and Charles I ch.14 *passim*
and civil war and Interregnum ch. 15 *passim*;
   see also Austin, John; Blackloism;
   White, Thomas
and earl of Essex 281
and James VI 45, 70–1, 238, 258, chs 9–14
   passim; Catholic and puritan toleration
   campaigns in 1603–04 334–43; *see also*
   Whitsun Riot; Bennett, Robert
John Cecil and loyalism/tolerance 229–30
and the Restoration ch. 16 *passim*
Richard Challoner and tolerance 5,
   5n.4, 20–1
secular power, use of, to regulate religious
   dissent 35–7
Tompkins, A. 5n.4, 537n.216
Tonge, Israel 547–8
   providential death of, in house of Stephen
   College 69
Tootell, Christopher 12, 13n.27, 293–4
   account of Lancashire executions 12n.26,
   13–14, 13n.28
   and John Plessington 554n.73
   and Mary Livesey 520n.143
   nephew of, *see* Dodd, Charles
   and Thomas Roydon 12n.26
Topcliffe, Charles 256n.130
Topcliffe, Richard 59, 73–4, 127n.36, 140–1,
   163n.101, 183n.18, 184–5, 189n.51, 199,
   204n.114, 205, 207n.123, 210–11, 215, 241,
   258, 258n.140, 266, 269n.41, 272, 295,
   316n.104
   and Anne Bellamy 221, 276
   and Catherine Bellamy 277
   Christopher Bales, tortured by, in
   Bridewell 50n.10, 202, 210–11
   'A Consolatory Letter' 120n.6
   coordination of London raids: of 27 August
   1584 141; of 15 March 1594 250
   and Edmund Campion 116; Tower
   disputation manuscripts 124n.26
   and Edmund Gennings, Swithin Wells, and
   others, trial and execution of 215–17
   and Edward Jones and Anthony
   Middleton 203; Jones tortured by 203, 211
   and Elizabeth Tudor 219, 219n.170, 232, 257
   Eustace White, tortured by 216
   and Francis Dickenson 202; tortured by
   Topcliffe, in Bridewell 201n.96, 211n.137
   and George Hethershall and *A Conference
   about the Next Succession* 273, 274, 275, 276
   and Gregory Martin's *Treatise of
   Schisme* 135, 135n.78
   and Henry Walpole 245, 252, 257;
   discrediting of Topcliffe 254–6, 256n.130

imprisoned 255–6, 256n.130, 257; and
   rehabilitation 258, 258n.140
and James Atkinson 277, 278n.63
and John Barwise's recantation 220n.171
and John Boste 240, 247n.93
and John Frank 250n.105
and John Harrison 278n.63
and John Ingram 247n.89
and John Jones 275–6, 278
and John Story 83n.35
and Lord Burgh 244, 244n.75, 277
and Miles Dawson's pardon, allegedly
   hindered by 272
and Montford Scott 207n.124
and Nicholas Harpsfield 124n.26
and Nicholas Jones 276–7
and Richard Dibdale 166n.113
and Richard Leigh 189n.49
and Robert Barnes and Jane Wiseman
   275–80 *passim*, 352n.85; 'book of
   exorcisms' 278, 278n.67
and Robert Morton 188n.44
and Robert Southwell 210–11; arrest at
   Uxendon 221–2, 276; tortured by
   Topcliffe 221–2; and trial 254–5
and Robert Thorpe and Thomas
   Watkinson 206–7
searches William Carter's premises in Hart
   Street, and seizes manuscripts of Nicholas
   Harpsfield and Stephen Vallenger 123–4,
   124n.26; and Thomas Norton's account of
   the seized papers 123–4; papers
   concerning Tower disputations passed to
   John Foxe 124n.26
as spectator at executions 83n.35, 116,
   122n.17, 166n.113, 189n.49, 203, 206–7,
   219–20, 244–5, 278
and Stannardine Passy 276
and surveillance of Catholics 140–1
and Swithin Wells 73–4, 215, 216–17
and Thomas Fitzherbert, Robert Sutton, and
   Sir Thomas Fitzherbert 183n.18, 221,
   225, 255
and Thomas Norton 127n.36
and Thomas Pormort's allegations, about
   Topcliffe and the queen 219–20, 219n.170,
   232; and about Archbishop Whitgift 232
and Thomas Woodhouse 83n.36
and Thomas Worthington 141n.3, 176n.161
and Thomas Wright 275; summons Stephen
   Egerton to dispute with 275
and Thorne/Thornes 66n.93
and William Bassett 233n.20
William Carter's trial 135
and William Dean 123, 123n.24

640 INDEX

Topcliffe, Richard (*cont.*)
  and William Harrington 244–5
Touchet, James, 3rd earl of Castlehaven 497
Tour d'Auvergne, Henri de la, duke of
  Bouillon 407
Tower of London 31, 65, 112, 112n.173, 115f,
  117–18, 120–1, 124, 126, 127, 128, 128n.41,
  138, 141n.3, 154, 161n.97, 166, 190,
  191n.56, 194, 198, 207n.124, 211, 217n.162,
  225, 231, 238, 240, 251, 269n.41, 289, 301,
  311, 320n.124, 335, 424n.8, 430–1, 449–52,
  451n.7, 512
  disputations (31 August–27 September 1581)
    111–12, 117–18, 119, 124n.26; fifth
    disputation cancelled 111n.169, 111n.170,
    112n.173
  lieutenant, *see* Blount, Sir Michael; Hopton,
    Sir Owen
Towneley, Charles 469n.61
  and John Knaresborough 10
Towneley, Richard, library of 280n.76
Towneley, Thomas 12
  and Brian Orrell 12
Tracy, Paul, and execution of John Sandys 62,
  164n.109
Traves, Gervase 296–7, 297n.34
treason penalties 31–3, 40, 53–4 and *passim*
  Robert Persons's account of, in *Epistle of the
    Persecution* 52–3
  ritual 51–4; subversion of 54–9; official
    retaliation against 58–9; carnivaleque
    inversion of the State's purposes 52
treason statute of Edward III (25 Edward III,
  c. 5) 83n.35, 112–13, 113n.178, 142,
  186n.26
treason statutes post-1558, against
  Catholics 5n.5, 59, 70, 78–9, 284, 500–2
  of 1563 (5 Eliz., c. 1 [An Act for the
    Assurance…]) 81, 81n.24, 90–1, 94,
    94n.90, 131, 131n.56; *see also* Bodey, John;
    Slade, John
  of 1571 (13 Eliz., c. 1 [An Act whereby Certain
    Offences be Made Treason] and 13 Eliz.,
    c. 2 [An Act against the Bringing in and
    Putting in Execution of Bulls…]) 90–1,
    108, 129n.45, 316, 83nn.35–36
  of 1581 (23 Eliz., c. 1 [An Act to Retain the
    Queen's Majesty's Subjects…]) 105,
    105n.140, 107–8, 112–13, 113n.178,
    129–31, 129n.45, 133n.72, 145, 146–7,
    150n.42, 186n.26; introduced into
    Commons by Sir Francis Knollys 105; *see
    also* Rigby, John; sedition statute of 1581
    (23 Eliz., c. 2)

  of 1585 (27 Eliz., c. 1 [An Act for
    Provision…]) 171n.136; (27 Eliz., c. 2
    [An Act against Jesuits…]) 26, 49, 55n.43,
    71, 152–3, 153n.56, 155–6, 162, 163n.103,
    163n.105, 167, 169, 222–3, 229, 247,
    256n.132, 269n.38, 276, 278, 337, 396–7,
    426, 488, 500, 520, 522n.152, 549n.48,
    556; felony penalties created by 71;
    extrapolated from royal proclamation of
    1 April 1582 152–3
A Treatise of Treasons 96n.100, 127, 145n.17
treaty of London, 1604 339
Tregian, Francis 88–9, 92
  chaplain of, *see* Cuthbert Mayne
  legal proceedings against, and others 90–1,
    90n.71, 91n.81, 143–4, 352n.82
  nephew of, *see* Sherwood, Thomas
  recipient, with others, of anti-piracy
    commission 88–9; excluded from 89n.65
  search of his house, by Sir Richard Grenville,
    and arrest of Cuthbert Mayne 88–9
  summoned by privy council 90; earl of Sussex
    tries to persuade Tregian to conform 90
  uncle of, *see* Arundell, Sir John
Tresham, Francis 304
Tresham, Lady 161n.96
Tresham, Sir Thomas 229–30, 337
  [John Lacey], *A Petition Apologeticall* 334–5
  and Thomas Pounde and Marian priest,
    Atkinson 340–1
  prosecuted in star chamber 113
Trevor-Roper, H. 23
Trimble, W. 328
Trinity College, Oxford 200, 292, 422n.1
Tripp, Henry, and Thomas Pounde 108n.154
Trollop, Cuthbert 202n.105, 223, 239, 296n.30,
  327, 334, 365n.136, 461n.46
  and Richard Bancroft 323n.138, 327
Trollop, Thomas 242, 243, 243n.71
  and Bernard Pattenson 242, 243, 243n.71
  reprieve 243n.71
Trot (a dwarf), accuser of David Lewis 69
truce of Antwerp (Twelve Years truce) 366, 405
Trumbull, William 400n.107, 403n.127, 411,
  420, 427, 428, 434n.56, 450, 451n.7,
  452–3, 453n.13
  and Gondomar 452–3
Tunstall, C., 17n.38
Tunstall, Mr, of Wycliffe 12, 16–17
Tunstall, Thomas, OSB 371n.165, 440n.78
  execution, 13 July 1616, Norwich 371n.165,
  440, 441
Turner, Catholic bookseller 556n.79
Turner, Edward 345n.60

Turner, Thomas 164n.109
Tutino, S. 528–9
Tyburn 39–40, 39f, 55, 58, 138–9, 437and
  passim; Catholic procession to, 26 March
  1624 457
Tyrone, earl of, see O'Neill, Hugh
Tyrrell, Anthony 170n.132, 192
  evades arrest in York Castle 129n.44
  and John Cornelius 250n.107
  and Lewis Barlow 175n.159
  recantations, at Paul's Cross, 1588 175,
    175n.159, 189, 198
  and Richard Dibdale, John Lowe, and John
    Adams 166, 166n.113
  Richard Yaxley identified by 198
  temporary rejection in late 1586/early 1587 of
    loyalty to Elizabeth 192n.61; Edward
    James's involvement 192n.61
  and Thomas Bell 170
  and William Weston's exorcisms 166; Weston
    and others, accused by Tyrrell, of
    involvement in Babington's Plot 166, 170

Udall, John
  death in prison 236n.40
  and Kingston-upon-Thames 193
  and Robert Waldegrave 193
Udall, William 376n.1
Ulloa, Julián Sánchez de 445
Underdown, D. 515, 515n.127
Underwood, L. 209n.130, 328, 399n.103,
  532n.194
Upsall Castle, South Kilvington, Yorkshire 16, 365
Urban VIII (Maffeo Barberini), Pope 518
  breve (Piis Dilecti Filii) ordering inquiry into
    martyrdom in England 518, 520, 518n.140
Ushaw College (St Cuthbert's) 469n.61
  Vincent Eyre collection 181n.13
Usk, execution of David Lewis 58, 547n.41
Ussher, James, archbishop of Armagh 417n.188
Uxendon 120n.6, 221, 276

Valentine, John, recantation and reprieve
  186, 186n.27
Valladolid, English College (St Alban's) 207n.124,
  230, 230n.9
Vallenger, Stephen
  dies in prison 119
  manuscripts of the Campion disputations,
    seized by Topcliffe 123–4
  prosecuted in star chamber 119
  Sir Walter Mildmay accuses, of having
    written Thomas Alfield's True
    Reporte 119

Vane, Sir Henry 505
Varignies, Jean de, seigneur de Blainville 465–6
Vaughan, Dominic 85
Vaughan, Lewis 390n.62
Vaughan, Richard, bishop of Chester (1597)
    and bishop of London (1604) 296,
    300, 355n.94
  alleged conspiracy 298, 299–300
  chaplain of, see Morton, Thomas
  death of 359
  and Robert Nutter and Edward Thwing
    293, 293n.20, 294–5
  and William Brettergh 296, 297n.33, 300
Vaux, Anne 256n.132
Vaux, Edward, 4th Baron Vaux 335n.9, 401n.114,
    403, 403n.127, 410, 430
  search of house, 31 October 1611 403;
    arrested 403; and oath of allegiance, 1606,
    refused by 410; restitution of forfeited
    estates 410n.157
Vaux, Lady Elizabeth (née Roper; daughter of
    John Roper, 1st Baron Teynham)
  arrested and gaoled in Fleet 403, 406, 409,
    412, 412n.165
  chaplains of, see Percy, John; Hart, Nicholas
  oath of allegiance, 1606, refused by 401n.114,
    403, 406n.140
  trial 406n.140
Vaux, Lawrence, death in prison 34n.43
Vaux, William, 3rd Baron
    Vaux 104n.132, 229–30
  daughter of, see Brooksby, Eleanor
  offers to serve against Spaniards 187n.36
  prosecuted in star chamber 113
Vavasour, Dorothy 84n.38
  husband of, see Vavasour, Thomas
Vavasour, Henry 273n.49
Vavasour, Thomas, Dr 84n.38
  imprisoned at Hull 84
  wife of, see Vavasour, Dorothy
Vavasour, Sir William 273n.49
Vavasour, William, of Hazlewood
  conformity of 273
  son of, see Vavasour, Henry
  wife of, see Manners, Anne
Velasco, Alonso de 383, 393, 400, 404,
    408, 410
  embassy, and chapel 404, 410
Velasco y Mendoza, Isabel de 410n.156
Venice
  impression made in, by executions of John
    Roberts and Thomas Somers 400n.107
  interdict controversy 359
Vere, Sir Horace 441

642 INDEX

Verstegan, Richard 55, 211, 217n.162, 221–2,
222n.182, 227, 228, 237–8, 237n.44,
242n.70, 250n.107, 255, 256, 257–8
Advertisement Written to a Secretarie 218
and *A Conference about the Next Succession* 261
The Copy of a Letter 190n.55
A Declaration of the True Causes 214n.149
Descriptiones and *Briefue Description* 135–6,
136n.79, 155n.64; engravings by Giovanni
Battista Cavalleriis 136n.79
and Henry Walpole 256, 257
and James VI, Verstegan's low opinion
of 239n.49; and James's approaches to
Catholics 243; and James, Lord Burgh and
Scots presbyterians 244
Lord Burghley, allegations against,
made by 218
Matthew Sutcliffe's *Matthaei Sutlivii de
Catholica* 234n.22
and Nicholas Fox 217n.162
and persecution of late 1591/early 1592 (letter
of 5 March 1592) 217–19, 227, 228
*Praesentis Ecclesiae Anglicanae
Typus* 119, 136n.79
printing press sequestrated by William
Fleetwood 119
and proceedings against puritans (Barrow,
Greenwood, and others) 233–6,
234n.22, 236n.40
and Richard Bancroft's *Survay of the Pretended
Holy Discipline* 237
and Richard Topcliffe 211, 221–2, 255, 257
Robert Southwell's account of persecution,
late 1591 sent to 208–14
and Roger Rippon 233
and royal proclamation of 18 October
1591 214, 217, 227n.204
and Sir Edward Stafford 135–6; Verstegan,
detained, January 1584, but then released
135–6
Theatrum Crudelitatum Haereticorum 77,
172, 234n.22; illustration of execution of
Margaret Clitherow in 55, 172, 172n.145
and Thomas Alfield's *True Reporte* 117n.201,
119, 119n.2
and William Pattenson 218–19
Villiers, Katherine (*née* Manners), duchess of
Buckingham 481
Villiers, Mary, countess of Buckingham 481
Villiers, Sir George, 1st earl, 1st marquis and
1st duke of Buckingham 443, 459, 470,
483, 490
assassination 477, 481, 482n.115
and Edmund Arrowsmith 477, 481n.114
journey to Madrid 456

and Sir Henry Yelverton 476
and William Baldwin 450–1
Vincent, Margaret, execution 436
Vivian, John 186
arrested and released 186n.28
as chaplain to Roger Martin of Long
Melford 186n.28
Vorstius, Conrad 401n.111

Waad, Sir William (knighted 1603)
219n.170, 367
and Anthony Copley 229, 229n.2
and Thomas Palaser 295
and Thomas Tichborne 321
Wadsworth, James, Jnr 447, 505n.68, 516, 517–18
Wadsworth, James, Snr, *Las Leyes* 355n.92
Waferer, Andrew 508–9
Wainewright, J. B. 114n.186
Wainman/Wenman, Mr, death of, at Oxford
assizes, 1577 64
Wainman, Mr (*see* Wenman, Thomas)
Wake, Isaac 415n.182, 417–18
Wakeman, Roger, death in Newgate
prison 34, 34n.43
Wakeman, Sir George 553–4, 556n.82, 558
Waldegrave, Robert
and John Hewett 193; pamphlet concerning
(*A True Report...of John Weldon*) 193
and John Penry 193n.68
and John Udall 193
Wales, council in the marches 149n.39, 392
Waller, Edmund 517n.136
Walker, George (d. 1747) 417n.188
Walker, John 10, 10n.20
Walker, John (d. 1588), and Tower
disputations 111
Walker, William 9n.16, 498n.32
Wall, John (Joachim), OFM 551, 551n.57
execution, and speech, 22 August 1679,
Worcester 551n.57
Walmesley, Thomas 205, 250n.107
alleged crypto-Catholicism 340n.36
attitude to Catholic separatists 205n.117;
noted by Thomas Norton 205n.117
Walpole, Christopher, SJ 338n.24
Walpole, Henry, SJ 49, 228, 245n.80, 254n.119,
254n.120, 254n.123
arrest 244, 244n.76
conversion of (at Edmund Campion's
execution) 55, 116
and Edward Shelley 189
interrogation, confessions, and
disputations 245, 251–4, 256; and Persons's
Elizabethae Angliae Reginae...Philopatrum
252; statement of 17 June 1594 253

INDEX   643

and Mr Strickland 114n.183
trial and execution, with Alexander Rawlins,
    7 April 1595, York 68, 255–7, 256n.132,
    256n.134
Walpole, Michael, SJ 338, 338n.24, 367, 369,
    368n.153
    and Luisa de Carvajal 368n.153, 425
    oath of allegiance, 1606, refused by 378
Walpole, Thomas 244n.76, 245n.83, 246n.86
Walsh, James, SJ 28n.19
Walsingham conspiracy 53n.29
Walsingham, Sir Francis 95, 100, 155, 161n.97,
    175n.159, 181n.10, 190, 197, 197n.81, 199,
    240n.60, 317, 413
    and Christopher Bagshaw 170n.133
    commissions Thomas Cartwright to write
        against Rheims New Testament 111n.170;
        task reassigned to Thomas Bilson 111n.170
    death of, commented on by Robert
        Southwell 214
    and Edward Grately 197
    John Hardy's words, reported to 133n.69
    and John Hart 114n.187
    and John Rainolds 111n.170
    and Malivery Catelyn's information against
        Lawrence Mompesson 218n.166
    providential death of, alleged 65n.91; by
        Robert Southwell 67, 214
    and Richard Dibdale's arrest 165n.111
    and Thomas Fleming 131n.57
    and William Dean and Mrs Alford 123n.24;
        William Dean's and Edward Shelley's letters
        intercepted by 188n.41
Walter, J. 493, 497
Walton, testifies against William Hartley 194,
    194n.72
Warburton, Peter, vice-chamberlain of
    Chester 299
Warcop, Ralph 106
Warcop, Thomas 256n.134
    execution, with others, 4 July 1597,
        York 256n.134, 270
Ward, L. J. 55n.43, 72n.118, 79, 83n.35, 83n.36,
    90–1, 90n.71, 94n.90, 102, 108, 112–13,
    113n.178, 131, 131n.56, 131n.58, 133,
    133n.72, 138, 145, 152, 153n.56, 156n.71,
    157n.76, 163n.103, 163n.105, 165n.111,
    168n.122
Ward, Margaret
    execution, with others, 30 August 1588,
        Tyburn 189
    felony offence, under 14 Eliz., c. 2 189n.50
    and William Watson 189, 189n.51
Ward, Mary 11
Wardley Hall, Worsley, near Manchester 28

Warford, William, SJ 32n.36, 132n.64, 163n.101
    martyrology (AAW, A IV, no. 12) 163n.101;
        elicited from him by Robert Persons 163n.101
    narrative of trial of Marsden and
        Anderton 162–3
    tries to persuade John Cecil not to reply
        to William Creighton's defence of
        James VI 163n.101
Warkworth manor, Northamptonshire
    4n.2, 12n.26
Warmington, William
    deported 152n.52
    and John Hambley 168
    and oath of allegiance, 1606 401n.114
Warner, John, SJ 553–4, 553n.67
    Blacklo's Cabal [under the name of Robert
        Pugh] 554
Warren, R. 10, 10n.20
Warren, Roger, execution, with John Thulis, 18
    March 1616, Lancaster 222n.182, 431n.39,
    432–3, 434, 436, 440
Warrington, Lancashire 54, 432
Warwick 167n.116
    executions at, see Freeman, William; Grissold,
        Robert; Sugar, John; Warwick, countess of,
        see Dudley, Anne
Warwickshire
    enforcement of royal proclamation of
        18 October 1591 in 227, 227n.202, 263
    puritans 338
Waterhouses, Durham 239, 239n.50, 268n.35
Waterson, Edward 461n.46
    arrest, with Joseph Lambton 222
    execution, 8 January 1593, Newcastle 223–4
    interrogation 222–3
    reconciled to Catholic faith by Richard
        Smith 222n.183
    temporary compliance 223
    temporary reprieve 223, 223n.188
Watkinson, Robert
    execution, with Thomas Tichborne and
        Francis Page, 20 April 1602, Tyburn 320,
        322, 322n.137
    and John Fawther 320, 320n.128, 322
Watkinson, Thomas, of Menthorpe 206–7
    compliance over churchgoing 206–7
    execution, with Robert Thorpe, 31 May 1591,
        York 206–7, 208
Watson, Christopher, death in York Castle 34
Watson, William
    appellant pamphleteering (Decacordon of Ten
        Quodlibeticall Questions), and Jesuits,
        martyrdom, persecution and toleration
        309–11, 311n.85, 313–15, 313n.93, 314n.97,
        319, 321

644   INDEX

Watson, William (*cont.*)
  arrested in search of Clink prison,
    1602 323–4, 324n.139
  assisted to abscond, by Margaret Ward and
    John Roche 189, 189n.51
  Bye and Main conspiracies 335, 356n.96; trial
    and execution, Winchester 335,
    335n.12, 377
  conformity in Bridewell 189
  and George Williams 347
  and James I, and tolerance 334
  and William Atkinson and Thomas
    Tichborne 321
Way, William, execution, 23 September 1588,
  Kingston-upon-Thames 193
Webb, Laurence, and John Felton 82n.31
Webley, Henry 156n.73, 186, 186n.29
  execution, with William Dean, 28 August
    1588, Mile End 188
Webley, Thomas 155, 156–7, 186n.29
Webster, Frances
  imprisonment and death in York Castle
    168n.123
  reconciled by John Fingley 168n.123
Webster, William, alias Ward 432
  arrest and execution, 26 July 1641, Tyburn
    504–5, 505nn.68–69, 511
Welbourne, Thomas
  charges against 342, 342n.49
  execution, 1 August 1605, York 342–3, 350
Wells, Gilbert 141
  arrested at Southampton House 141n.5
Wells, John, alleged harbourer of George
  Beseley 207n.124
Wells, Swithin 188
  and Anthony Babington 215n.155
  and Nicholas Woodfen 161
  residence, near to Southampton House 73–4;
    raided 215
  and Richard Topcliffe 73–4, 215, 216–17
  trial and execution, with Edmund Gennings,
    10 December 1591, Gray's In Fields
    215–17
  and Wriothesley family 73
Wenman, Thomas
  allegations against George Abbot 422
  and George Gage 422n.1
  at Trinity and Balliol, Oxford 422n.1
Wentworth, Sir Thomas, 1st Viscount Wentworth
  (1628), 1st earl of Strafford (1640) 490, 495,
  496, 500
  impeachment, attainder, and execution
    501–4, 501n.43, 502n.51
  Irish parliament, 1640 494, 494n.10
  recusancy and compounding 469n.61

Wentworth, Thomas, and parliament in
  1610 380, 380n.24
Wernham, R. B. 211–12
Wesel, town of 428
West, Lady, of Winchester 133n.68, 220n.172
Westminster, dean of, *see* Goodman, Gabriel
Westminster Hall 196n.79, 256n.130, 341
Westminster, archbishop of, *see* Godfrey, William
Westmorland, earl of, *see* Neville, Charles
Weston, Sir Richard, 1st earl of
  Portland 485n.133, 490
Weston, William, SJ 141, 180, 254n.123,
  292–3, 486
  and Anthony Babington 164–6, 167n.118
  conference and disputation with Lancelot
    Andrewes 192, 192n.61
  exorcisms 162, 164–7, 165nn.110–111,
    167n.117, 181n.10, 186–7, 197–8, 250n.107,
    256n.134, 278, 278n.67, 165nn.110–111
  and John Ballard 165
  and Richard Bold 166–7, 167n.116
  and William Clargenet 185, 185n.24
West Tarring, Sussex 50n.10
Wharton, Christopher
  arrest, by Sir Stephen Procter 281n.77
  and Eleanor Hunt 317
  execution, 28 March 1600, York 280–1,
    290, 317
  relic (skull) of 28n.19
  and the Society of Jesus and George
    Blackwell 292
Wharton, Sir Michael 442
  declaration against recusants 442, 442n.89;
    imprisoned 442
  and James I 442, 442n.89
Wharton, Samuel 269n.41
Whatmore, Leonard 6n.6
Whitaker, Thomas 12, 12n.26
  execution, with Edward Bamber and John
    Woodcock, 7 August 1646, Lancaster
    522–3; relic 554n.73
  and Plessington family 523n.158
Whitaker, William 163n.101
  and predestination and universal
    grace 264, 264n.19
  and Tower disputations 111, 111n.170
  and William Rainolds 156n.69, 162
Whitbread, John 508–9
Whitbread, Thomas, SJ 549n.48, 551, 552n.61
  arrest, trial, and execution, with others,
    20 June 1679, Tyburn 549, 551
White, Andrew, SJ 522n.152
White, Eustace
  execution, with others, 10 December 1591,
    Tyburn 216

report concerning, written by Stephen Barnes for Francis Barber 216n.158
tortured 216, 216n.159
White (Gwyn), Richard
arrest (on several occasions), prosecution, and execution, 17 October 1584, Wrexham 31–2, 53–4, 68, 95, 147–51; Simon Thelwall's prosecution speech 150; distribution of body parts 53–4; God's punishment of his persecutors 65
and Black Assizes, Oxford, 1577 150n.41
and *Concertatio Ecclesiae Catholicae* 147, 147n.31, 149
conformity of, until 1576, and rejection of compliance 87, 147–8, 147n.31
contemporary accounts of White 147, 149n.37
and David Edwards 149
and papal authority/supremacy 150
Protestant and puritan enemies of 148–51
reputation, attempts to destroy 148
and Robert Persons's *Brief Discours* 149
and Sir George Bromley 66, 148, 150
verses (alleged) against married clergy/ministers 150
verses in praise of assassin (Balthasar Gérard) of William the Silent 149–50; link with further prosecution of White 150
at Wrexham assizes 149
White, Robert 487–8
White, Thomas, alias Blacklo 438n.67, 469–70, 523–37 *passim*, 540n.15
Blackloism, toleration, and episcopacy 523–37 *passim*
Blackloist claims about Catholic neutralism 522, 528
and John Austin 528–9, 542
and John Sergeant 553–4
and Thomas Blount 541n.16
Whitelock, Bulstrode 475–6
father of, *see* Whitelock, Sir James
Whitelock, Edmund, Captain 286–7, 475n.84
Whitelock, Sir James 475–6
and Edmund Arrowsmith 475–6, 477
son of, *see* Whitelock, Bulstrode
White Mountain, battle of 455
Whitgift, John, bishop of Worcester (1577) and archbishop of Canterbury (1583) 263, 272, 272n.48, 283, 327
and Admonition Controversy 85n.42, 282
and Edward Knight 215n.151
and John Greenwood, Henry Barrow, and John Penry 234, 235, 236n.43
and John Hammond 163n.102
nominated to Canterbury 131
and recusancy survey of October 1577 86–7

Richard Topcliffe's words concerning, reported by Thomas Pormort 232
and royal proclamation of 18 October 1591 214
subscription and conformity 121, 137, 138n.84, 149n.37, 163n.102, 237–8; and anti-puritanism 214, 232, 234n.23, 237–8; Sir Francis Knollys's accusations 197, 199; Whitgift's response 197n.81
and William Barrett 264
and William Freeman 263–4
and William Watson 323–4
White Lion prison, Southwark 172
Whitsun Riot (Allensmore riots) 343–51
Whittingham, Sir Timothy 365
Whittington manor, near Holme Hall 181n.13
Wicliffe, William, released from the Tower of London 138
Widdrington, Roger
and John Boste's execution 14, 55, 248n.96
Widmerpole, Robert
execution, with others, 1 October 1588, Canterbury 192n.63, 464
and Henry Percy, 8th earl of Northumberland 192n.63
Wigan, Lancashire 54, 432
Wigginton, Giles 174–5
Wiggs, William 90–1, 180
Wightman, Edward 401n.111, 426
Wilcox, Robert 464
execution, with others, 1 October 1588, Canterbury 192–3
Wilford, Peter 508–9
Wilkes, Sir Thomas (knighted 1591) 151n.50, 254n.120
Wilks, Mr 514n.124
William I, of Orange ('the Silent') 34, 142, 157
assassination 38, 135n.78, 154; *see* Gérard, Balthasar
William II, King 16
William III, of Orange (King William III) 544
Williams, Friswood 244n.77
Williams, George, alias Rice Griffith
and George Errington 269n.41
and Richard Bancroft 344n.57, 346–8
and Robert Bennett 346–8, 346n.62, 347n.67
and William Morgan 344n.57
and William Watson 347
Williams, John
'Balaam's Asse' and 'Speculum Regali' 454n.15
execution 424n.8, 454n.15
Williams, John, bishop of Lincoln 436n.59
Williams, Richard, Marian priest
execution, April 1592, Tyburn 219n.169
and Francis Shaw 219n.169

646 INDEX

Williams, Sara 198
Williamson, Thomas 146
Willie, John 248
Willis, Francis, interrogation of Thomas
  Belson 198
Willoughby, Elizabeth
  eyewitness account of the execution of Hugh
    Green 33, 515nn.125–127; versions
    of 33n.41, 515n.126; circulation of
    33n.41
Wilson, John 78, 464
  The English Martyrologe 376, 376n.1, 376n.3;
    and Francis Burton's *Fierie Tryall* 377;
    Richard Smith's censure 376n.1, 460n.42;
    Propaganda's censure 460n.42;
    republication in 1640 and 1672 376n.2
  and George Keynes's *Roman Martyrologe*
    460n.42
  and Robert Persons 376n.1
Winchcombe, Benedict 392
Winchester 131
  bishop of, *see* Bilson, Thomas; Cooper,
    Thomas; Gardiner, Stephen; Horne, Robert
  Catholic houses in, raided 133; Lady West's
    house, searched, 6 December 1583
    133n.68, 220n.172
  executions at, *see* Bird, James; Clarke, William;
    Dickenson, Roger; Humphrey, Lawrence;
    Miller (Milner), Ralph; Slade, John;
    Watson, William
  dean of, *see* Humphrey, Laurence
  diocese 107n.151
  prison searched for Catholic printed texts,
    11 January 1583 131n.57
  St Cross Hospital 132; *see* Bennett, Robert
Windebank, Sir Francis 485n.133, 498n.37
  tolerance towards Catholics 483–4,
    484nn.127–128, 488, 489, 496–8, 497n.31,
    521–2, 484nn.127–128
Windsor, Walter 518
Winifred, St 461n.46
Winter, John 525, 530
Winter, Sir William, and John Sandys 164n.109
Winterborne St Martin 130n.48
Winwood, Sir Ralph (knighted 1607) 301n.48,
    341, 404, 413n.168, 429, 434n.56
  attacks Henry Spiller 427
  solicits accounts of Catholic separatism 427
Wisbech Castle 72–3, 72n.118, 94, 185, 185n.23,
    195, 204n.115, 240n.55, 289, 289n.5, 292–3,
    292n.17, 294n.24, 302n.52, 356n.96,
    427n.21, 429n.32, 479n.101
  keeper 427n.21
Wiseman household and family 250n.105, 275–6
Wiseman, Jane 275–80, 278n.64

Withers, George 121
  suspended by Archbishop Matthew Parker 121
Wolley, Sir John 241
Wolseley, Erasmus 182
  pardon of 183n.19
  wife of, recovers relics of Robert Sutton 183n.19
Wood, Anthony 198n.86
Wood, James, laird of Boniton, execution,
    27 April 1601, Edinburgh 307n.71
Wood, Robert, and John Plessington 69n.108
Woodcock, John 13–14
  nephew of, *see* Woodcock, Seth
  trial and execution, with Edward Bamber and
    Thomas Whitaker, 7 August 1646,
    Lancaster 522–3, 522n.156; relic 554n.73
Woodcock, Seth 14
  father of 14
  uncle of, *see* Woodcock, John
Woodfen, Nicholas 160–1
  and Browne family of Cowdray 161
  execution, with Edward Stransham,
    21 January 1586, Tyburn 161
  and Swithin Wells 161
  and Thomas Alfield 161
Woodhouse, Thomas, SJ 9
  refuses to denounce *Regnans in
    Excelsis* 1570 83
  and Richard Topcliffe 83n.36
  trial and execution, 19 June 1573, Tyburn 58,
    83n.36; Henry Garnet's account, sent to
    Rome 83n.36
Woodruff, Robert
  proceedings ordered against 204; and against
    Richard Blundell 204
  in Wisbech Castle 204n.115
Woodward, Philip 335
Worcester 352n.85
  bishop of, *see* Whitgift, John
  earl of, *see* Somerset, Edward
  execution of John Wall, 22 August 1679 551n.57
  marquis of, *see* Somerset, Henry
Worsley, Charles, Colonel 534n.208
Worswick, Thomas, and Robert Sutton 182
Worthington, Edward 282n.79
Worthington family of Blainscow, and John
    Knaresborough 12
Worthington, Laurence 427n.21
Worthington, Thomas, secular priest 78,
    337n.19, 464, 473n.74
  arrest and imprisonment 141n.3
  A Catalogue of Martyrs in England 78n.6,
    376, 376n.3
  Catalogus Martyrum 1610 376n.3; *Catalogus
    Martyrum* 1614 279n.71, 376n.3
  and George Gervase 376n.3

INDEX   647

and James Leyburn 141n.3
and John Bretton 279n.71
and John Rigby 281–7; relationship to 282n.79
and Marmaduke Bowes 157n.77
A Relation of Sixtene Martyrs 281–7 *passim*,
   288n.3, 312–13, 473; as a contribution to the
   Archpriest Dispute 283–4, 290–2, 312–13, 376
and Sir William Stanley's surrender of
   Deventer, and the publication of William
   Allen's *Copie of a Letter* 176n.161
and Thomas Percy, earl of Northumberland
   and Northern Rebellion 376n.3
Worthington, Thomas, son of (also Thomas
   Worthington), and Southworth's execution
   speech 535n.209
Wotton, Sir Henry 345n.59, 350n.78, 443
Wragge, John 404, 435
Wray, Sir Christopher 138
   and Edmund Campion's trial 114
   and Jasper Heywood's compliance 137
   and trial of Edmund Gennings and
      others 216
   and trial of William Marsden and Robert
      Anderton 162
Wren, Matthew, bishop of Ely 490
Wrexham, execution of Richard White,
   17 October 1584 31, 53–4, 150
Wright, Christopher 384n.37
Wright, John 384n.37
Wright, Peter, SJ
   arrest, trial, and execution, 19 May 1651,
      Tyburn 68, 532–4; relic 533n.201
   and Henry Marten 524–5
   and the marquis of Winchester 524–5, 532,
      532n.195
Wright, Thomas(formerly) SJ 396
   and the earl of Essex 274
   and Richard Topcliffe and Stephen
      Egerton 275
   and William Alabaster 275
Wrightington, John 296
Wriothesley, Henry, 3rd earl of Southampton
   221n.179
Wriothesley, Mary, countess of Southampton,
   harbours clergy at Southampton House 73
Wyatt, Sir Thomas 143, 250

Yaxley, Edward
   killed at Basing House 14
   nephew of, *see* Yaxley, John
Yaxley, John 14n.32, 202n.105
   his family's tribulations in the civil war 14–15
   father of, *see* Yaxley, Richard
   and John Knaresborough (information from
      Yaxley, on Richard Holiday, John Hogg,

Richard Hill, Edmund Duke, Robert Maire,
   Grace Maire, and John Boste) 14, 55n.41,
   60–1, 61n.73, 248n.96
   uncle of, *see* Yaxley, Edward
Yaxley, Richard 14
Yaxley, Richard, secular priest 14n.32
   Anthony Tyrrell identifies 198
   arrest, trial, and execution, with others, 5 July
      1589, Oxford 197–200
   and Richard Dibdale and William Weston's
      exorcisms 197–8; attempts to secure Sara
      William's release 197–8
   tortured in Bridewell 198
Yelverton, Sir Henry 446n.104
   and Edmund Arrowsmith and Richard Herst
      475–82 *passim*; bloodlust 478, 478n.97
   and Peter Smart 476n.86
   and Sir George Villiers 476
Yepes, Diego de, bishop of Tarazona 50
   Historia Particular 50, 50n.11, 57–8, 59n.61,
      169–70, 189nn.50–51, 200n.92; reprinting
      of 90n.69, 278n.67; preface supplied by
      Robert Persons out of material supplied by
      Seth Foster 90n.69
Yonge, Walter 477
York
   archbishop of, *see* Grindal, Edmund; Heath,
      Nicholas; Hutton, Matthew; Piers, John;
      Sandys, Edwin
   Castle (gaol) 34, 168n.123, 168n.124,
      200n.94, 246, 252, 254n.119, 267, 267n.33,
      293n.21, 342, 427n.21, 444n.94, 513;
      Catholic clergy arrested in, 1582 129;
      sermons in, 1599–1600 280–1, 280n.76;
      William Richmond's manuscript account
      of 280n.76; conditions in (1618) 443–4
   executions at, *see* Abbot, Henry; Amias, John;
      Anlaby, William; Atkinson, Thomas; Bates,
      Anthony; Bickerdike, Robert; Bowes,
      Marmaduke; Bretton, John; Browne,
      William; Burden, Edward; Catterick,
      Edmund; Clitherow, Margaret; Crow,
      Alexander; Dalby, Robert; Douglas, George;
      Errington, George; Fingley, John; Flathers,
      Matthew; Fulthrop, Edward; Gibson,
      William; Grimston, Ralph; Hardesty,
      Robert; Harrison, James; Hart, William;
      Horner, Richard; Ingleby, Francis; Kirkman,
      Richard; Knavesmire, York; Knight,
      William; Lacey, William; Langley, Richard;
      Lockwood, John; Osbaldeston, Edward;
      Page, Anthony; Percy, Thomas; Rawlins,
      Alexander; Snow, Peter; Spenser, William;
      Sykes, Edward; Taylor, Hugh; Thirkeld,
      Richard; Thompson, James; Thorpe, Robert;

648 INDEX

York (*cont.*)
    Thwing, Thomas; Walpole, Henry; Warcop, Thomas; Watkinson, Thomas; Welbourne, Thomas; Wharton, Christopher
  King's Manor 514
  minster 272
Yorke, Edmund 247
Yorke, Rowland 177n.166, 247
Yorke, Sir John 320n.124
Yorkshire prisons 34; *see also* Hull blockhouses; York, Castle (gaol)
Young, an apostate 66
Young, Richard 232, 252n.114
  arrest of Catholics near Holborn 215
  coordination of London raids of 27 August 1584 141
  providential death of, alleged 65n.91
  and Roger Rippon 233

Younger, James 56n.46, 216, 215n.152, 232
  arrest and confessions 232n.14
  and raid on house of Lawrence Mompesson 219
  writes account for Robert Persons of executions of 10 December 1591 216, 217n.160
Younger, N. 214n.150
Ypres, bishop of 518n.140

Zouch, Edward, 11th Baron Zouch 347n.68
Zúñiga, Pedro de 355, 363, 363n.127, 369, 373, 382, 412–13, 413n.168
  embassy, and chapel of 369, 373
  requests release of William Baldwin and other clergy 413n.168
  and Robert Drury and William Davies 359, 359n.106, 360